Archimedes in the Middle Ages

VOLUME FIVE

Memoirs of the
AMERICAN PHILOSOPHICAL SOCIETY
held at Philadelphia
for Promoting Useful Knowledge
Volume 157   Part A

ARCHIMEDES

in the Middle Ages

VOLUME FIVE

Quasi-Archimedean Geometry in the Thirteenth Century. A Supplementary Volume Comprising the *Liber de Motu* of Gerard of Brussels, the *Liber philotegni* of Jordanus de Nemore together with its longer Version known as the *Liber de triangulis Iordani,* and an Appended Text of John Dee's *Inventa circa illam coni recti atque rectanguli sectionem quae ab antiquis mathematicis Parabola appellabatur.*

Parts I–III.   Texts and Analysis.
Part IV.   Appendixes.

MARSHALL CLAGETT

THE AMERICAN PHILOSOPHICAL SOCIETY
Independence Square
Philadelphia
1984

Publication of this and other volumes has been made possible
by a generous grant from The Institute for Advanced Study,
Princeton, New Jersey.

Library of Congress Catalog Card No. 62-7218
International Standard Book Number: 0-87169-157-4
US ISSN: 0065-9738

PREFACE

In this second supplemental volume I have presented the texts, English translations, and analyses of three of the most interesting geometrical works of the thirteenth century: the *Liber de motu* of Gerard of Brussels, the *Liber philotegni* of Jordanus de Nemore, and the expanded and altered version of Jordanus' work completed by an unknown author under the title of *Liber de triangulis Iordani*. These texts will allow the student of medieval geometry to see how Latin mathematicians responded to the wave of translations from Greek and Arabic which appeared in the preceding century and particularly how these mathematicians utilized certain Archimedean and quasi-Archimedean techniques. The works which were translated in the twelfth century and proved particularly important for the authors of the works that I have edited here included the *De mensura circuli* of Archimedes, the Archimedean-type text *Liber de curvis superficiebus Archimenidis* (put together or translated by Johannes de Tinemue), and the *Verba filiorum* of the Banū Mūsā, another Archimedean-like work. These three Archimedean works I edited in Volume One of my study. The translations of the twelfth century also included various versions of the *Elements* of Euclid and a translation by Gerard of Cremona of a now lost version of the *Liber divisionum* [*figurarum*] of Euclid, an anonymous *Liber de ysoperimetris* based ultimately on a work of Zenodorus, and the *Liber de similibus arcubus* of Aḥmad ibn Yūsūf, together with numerous fragments translated from the Arabic that concerned triangles and other polygons and the theory of proportions.

I should explain why I picked these three works to edit. The *Liber de motu* I first edited in a preliminary fashion in 1956. Since that time I have found another manuscript of it and altered my interpretation and understanding of the text, particularly as to the way in which it fits into medieval geometry. Hence I have thoroughly revised the text, extended the variant readings, provided an English translation, and given a lengthy analysis of the mathematical contents of the text. It obviously belongs with works under the rubric of "Quasi-Archimedean Geometry" since it borrowed and widely used the particular form of the method of exhaustion that appeared in the *Liber de curvis superficiebus*. Furthermore, the author developed a method not unlike that used by Archimedes to compare areas of figures and their motions by comparing the corresponding line elements of these figures. This was a brilliant *tour de force* that singles out this author as one of the most original mathematicians of the Middle Ages. The second of the works, the *Liber philotegni* of Jordanus, the separate existence of which has never before been recognized, is here edited for the first time. It is clearly a masterpiece, which treats of the areas and perimeters of triangles (and other polygons), of their divisions, of their comparisons one to the other when inscribed and/or circumscribed in circles and when possessing equal perimeters. Only two manuscripts contained the last and most interesting of the propositions of this work (Propositions 47–63), and one of these manuscripts has no diagrams while the other is wanting a number of crucial diagrams. I mention these deficiencies only to inform the reader that the reconstruction of texts and diagrams of the last part of this treatise was often a difficult task. Still it seems to me that my reconstruction makes both mathematical and linguistic sense and I trust that the reader will agree. I have put it forward as a quasi-Archimedean work primarily because it adopts a kind of geometrical trigonometry that was familiar to Aristarchus and Archimedes (as well as to other later Greek geometers including especially the author of the *Liber de ysoperimetris*). It will be evident to the reader that Jordanus takes his basic Proposition 5, which he learned from the *Liber de ysoperimetris,* and from it develops many nice theorems in a way that appears to be original with him. I further believe that the main objective of the treatise, in seeking out theorems concerning inscribed and circumscribed polygons, probably arose because of the Archimedean concern with such polygons found in the *Liber de curvis superficiebus* and perhaps the *De mensura circuli.* Finally I chose the *Liber de triangulis Iordani* (a work till now assigned to Jordanus) to edit not only because it was poorly edited by Curtze on the basis of a single manuscript and thus deserves a new edition but also because of its relationship to the *Liber philotegni* upon which it is based and which it vastly alters and because it contains a good many extra propositions translated from the Arabic that concern some of the basic problems of Greek geometry often associated with the name of Archimedes. For example it includes the trisection of an angle (associated with Archimedes' name in the pseudo-Archimedean *Lemmata,* a work which reduces the trisection to a *neusis* that can be easily related to the *neusis* that the author of Proposition IV.20 drew from the *Verba filiorum* of the Banū Mūsā, a *neusis* not unlike those found in the *On Spiral Lines* of Archimedes), the inserting of two mean proportionals between two given magnitudes so that all four magnitudes are in continued proportion (a problem whose Greek solutions are summarized by Eutocius in his *Commentary on the Sphere and the Cylinder of Archimedes*), and the construction of a regular heptagon (a problem of which an Archimedean solution is extant in an Arabic work attributed to Archimedes). It is my hope, then, that this new edition with its accompanying English translation and its extended analysis will make clear the relationship the *Liber de triangulis* has to the *Liber philotegni* and its contributions to medieval geometry. So much then for the texts that make up the main subject of this volume. The reader will also note that I have edited for the first time the *Inventa* of John Dee on the parabola in Appendix II. This work belongs more properly to my Volume Four, but during the preparation of that Volume I was unfamiliar with the contents of Dee's work. Then, on reading it, I realized that it was a work that joined the medieval traditions of works on the parabola with Archimedean propositions developed in Archimedes' *On the Quadrature of the Parabola.* Hence its inclusion as an appendix to my new volume.

Readers familiar with my earlier volumes will see that I have adopted the same format and organization here. Diagrams, along with the Bibliography and the Indexes, are included in a separate fascicle, and thus are easily related to references to them in the texts. I have attempted to give quite complete information on the nature of the variant forms of the diagrams from manuscript to manuscript, and this information is encapsulated in the legends attached to the diagrams. In general, analysis of the three texts is included in the chapters preceding them, though particular points are often raised in footnotes to the English translations of the texts. I have been especially generous in giving variant readings because so often we find variant forms of the proofs in the margins or texts of the manuscripts. Occasionally I have translated such variant forms of the proofs and given them in the footnotes to the English translations of the texts.

Once more I am pleased to acknowledge the assistance I have received from librarians and scholars abroad, and I have attempted to single out each instance of that help in the body of the text or in the notes. Here at The Institute for Advanced Study I was particularly fortunate to have the help of two stalwart friends: Dr. Herman Goldstine and Professor Harold Cherniss. How often and with what patience did Dr. Goldstine listen to my efforts to reconstruct some badly preserved proof of Jordanus, and if I have been successful in these reconstructions not a little credit belongs to him. Only Professor Cherniss will know how important to me his linguistic guidance has been. I must also acknowledge the expert help of my assistant Mr. Mark Darby and my secretary Mrs. Ann Tobias. Mr. Darby has constantly read proof, checked references, and prepared the indexes, while Mrs. Tobias has, as usual with these volumes, typed the manuscript more than once, read the proofs, and prepared the final diagrams in exemplary fashion. Also helpful have been the library and administrative staffs of the Institute. They have combined to make the Institute the ideal place for scholarly work. Furthermore I would surely be remiss if I did not thank the Institute and its Director, Harry Woolf, for the financial aid given to the publication of this volume. Last, I thank my colleagues at the American Philosophical Society for publishing these difficult and costly volumes and the editorial staff of the Society for "putting the book into light," as Renaissance authors were wont to say.

Marshall Clagett

Contents

PART I

The *Liber de motu* of Gerard of Brussels

CHAPTER 1

Gerard of Brussels and the Composition of the *Liber de motu*

In Volume One of this work I briefly mentioned the use that a little-known geometer Gerard of Brussels made of Archimedes' *On the Measurement of the Circle* and the *Book on the Curved Surfaces of Archimedes* attributed to Johannes de Tinemue.[1] I did not at that time examine Gerard's work, the *Liber de motu,* in detail since I had already published an edition of it in 1956 and had discussed its role in the development of medieval kinematics, both in the edition and in my *The Science of Mechanics in the Middle Ages.*[2] In the twenty-eight years since the appearance of the first edition certain questions of the proper interpretation of the *Liber de motu* have arisen,[3] and furthermore another manuscript of it has been located (see MS *E* among the *sigla* of Chapter Three below). Because of the importance of the text to geometrical studies such as those I have treated in the first four volumes of my *Archimedes in the Middle Ages,* I have decided to publish a corrected version of the text with a fuller presentation of the variant readings, an accompanying English translation, and a detailed analysis of the text. It is hoped that the new text and translation will lead to a closer consideration of the work than has hitherto been possible.

In the twentieth century attention was first called to a short fragment of the *De motu* that appears in a manuscript of the Bibliothèque Nationale (BN

---

[1] M. Clagett, *Archimedes in the Middle Ages,* Vol. 1 (Madison, Wisc., 1964), pp. 9–10.

[2] For the first edition of the *Liber de motu,* see M. Clagett, "The *Liber de motu* of Gerard of Brussels and the Origins of Kinematics in the West," *Osiris,* Vol. 12 (1956), pp. 73–175. Cf. my *The Science of Mechanics in the Middle Ages* (Madison, 1958; 3rd reprint, 1979), Chap. 3.

[3] V. Zubov, "Ob 'Arkhimedovsky traditsii' v srednie veka (Traktat Gerarda Bryusselskogo 'Odvizhenii')," *Istoriko-matematicheskie issledovaniya,* Vol. 16 (1965), pp. 235–72. I must thank Prof. Michael Mahoney of Princeton University for sending me a draft of his English translation of this article, which has been of great help to me in going through Zubov's article. While Zubov's article proved of considerable assistance to me in my analysis of the content of the treatise in Chapter Two below, let me say that I have found some cases in which I disagree with Zubov and some in which he has overlooked difficulties in the text. I believe that the new analysis solves all of the principal difficulties that appear in Gerard's work.

3

lat. 8680A, 4r–5r; siglum *P* below) by Pierre Duhem.[4] Duhem knew nothing of the author of this work, nor its original title since the fragment he discovered was without indication of author or title. Furthermore, that fragment included only the initial postulates of Book I (which I have numbered 1–8) and Proposition I.1. Thus the remaining twelve propositions were missing. But fragmentary as this piece was, Duhem sensed its significance for the study of medieval kinematics. He suggested in fact that the composition of the work inaugurated kinematic studies in the West. He correctly saw that the object of this preliminary material was to prove that the motion of a rotating line or radius was made uniform by the speed of its middle point. That is, if the speed of the middle point is given to all points of an equal line segment moving in translation always parallel to itself, that motion of translation in the same time produces a rectangular area equal to the curvilinear area produced by the rotating segment. In Gerard's terminology the rotating segment is said "to be moved equally as its middle point" (see my discussion of the intentions of Gerard's treatment in Chapter Two below). Furthermore Duhem discovered that Thomas Bradwardine, whom we can call the founder of the school of kinematics at Merton College, Oxford, cited the *De motu* in his *Tractatus de proportionibus* of 1328, giving our treatise the title *De proportionalitate motuum et magnitudinum*.[5] Though refuting the conclusion of Gerard's initial proposition, Bradwardine nevertheless made the earlier tract one of his points of departure, as we shall see in Chapter Two below. With only the Parisian fragment at hand, Duhem was able to say little that was precise concerning the author or the tract's date of composition. In fact he was able only to establish the year 1328 as a *terminus ante quem* for the composition of the tract. But Duhem also noticed in a somewhat later fourteenth-century treatise entitled *De sex inconvenientibus* that a view concerning the motion of rotation similar to that expressed in the Parisian fragment was assigned to a Ricardus de Versellys (according to one manuscript of the *De sex inconvenientibus*) or Ricardus de Uselis (according to another manuscript of it).[6] But Duhem admitted that it was impossible for him to say whether Ricardus composed the tract on motion or merely repeated views he found expressed in the tract written by someone else. However, progress was made

---

[4] P. Duhem, *Études sur Léonard de Vinci,* Vol. 3 (Paris, 1913), pp. 292–94, where Duhem, apparently starting his numbering with the first of two unnumbered folios, gives the pagination of the fragment as folios 6r–7r.

[5] *Ibid.;* cf. the edition of H. Lamar Crosby, *Thomas of Bradwardine. His Tractatus de Proportionibus. Its Significance for the Development of Mathematical Physics* (Madison, 1955; 2nd pr. 1961), p. 128. Notice that Themon Judei in a question on the motion of the moon, which he determined at Erfurt in 1349, cites the *De motu* under the titles *De proportionibus motuum et motorum* and *De proportione motuum et motorum.* See H. Hugonnard-Roche, *L'Oeuvre astronomique de Thémon Juif maître parisien du XIVe siècle* (Paris, 1973), pp. 337, 345, 353–55. He writes with the context of Bradwardine in mind.

[6] Duhem, *Études,* Vol. 3, p. 295. Duhem cites Paris, BN lat. 6559, 34r, 36r, and BN lat. 7368, 162r and 164r. Cf. MS Venice, Bibl. Naz. Marc. Lat. VIII, 19, 129r and my *Science of Mechanics,* p. 262, n. 8.

when in 1921 G. Eneström published a short article in which he correctly identified Duhem's fragment as a part of a longer work by one Master Gerard of Brussels.[7] He made this identification on the basis of three manuscripts: those of Berlin, Oxford, and Naples (see the manuscripts *B, O,* and *N* described in Chapter Three below), though in actuality he saw only the first page of the tract in the Berlin manuscript and nothing from the other manuscripts, his knowledge of manuscripts *O* and *N* coming orally from A. A. Björnbo. Eneström spoke of the treatise as containing three "chapters" with four, five, and four propositions respectively. In fact the "chapters" are specified as "books" in manuscripts *B* and *N* and remain undesignated in the other manuscripts (see the variant readings for the beginning of each book in the text below). Since Eneström had in hand a photograph of only the first page of the Berlin copy, he confined himself (like Duhem) to publishing the postulates and the enunciation of Proposition I.1, designating both the postulates and the enunciation as "propositions." In regard to the author he suggested that because two of the manuscripts (in fact, as we now know, three of them: *O, B,* and *N*) have the Flemish form "de Brussel" rather than the common Latin form "de Bruxella," the author might have been Flemish. However, the recently discovered manuscript *E* contains in its colophon the reading "de bruxella" (see the variant reading for the colophon), which makes that suggestion somewhat more doubtful. Eneström further suggested that Ricardus de Uselis may be identical with Gerardus de Brussel, the praenomen being a slip of the pen and the "Uselis" arising from "Uccle," a town near Brussels, while I suggested in my first edition of the *De motu* that the author of the *De sex inconvenientibus* might have seen a manuscript in which the author's name was mutilated and read ". . . russelis," on the basis of which he read the "r" as "Ricardus" and the remainder as "Uselis," having missed a scribal reading for double "s."[8] This is a suggestion I would not press strongly.

In fact modern references to Gerard of Brussels' *Liber de motu* go back much further than the accounts of Duhem and Eneström. In the sale catalogue of Libri manuscripts, we find a description of the manuscript that later passed to Berlin.[9] The authors of this catalogue describe this codex (with the catalogue no. 665) as of the twelfth century, though Eneström in two different places would date the manuscript as of the fourteenth century,[10] and I would prefer a date in the thirteenth century (see Chapter Three, *Sigla,* MS *B*). The Libri

---

[7] G. Eneström, "Sur l'auteur d'un traité 'De motu' auquel Bradwardin a fait allusion en 1328," *Archivio di storia della scienza,* Vol. 2 (1921–22), pp. 133–36.

[8] Clagett, "Gerard of Brussels," p. 103.

[9] *Catalogue of the Extraordinary Collection of Splendid Manuscripts, Chiefly Upon Vellum, in Various Languages of Europe and the East, Formed by M. Guglielmo Libri. . . . Which Will be Sold by Auction by Messrs. S. Leigh Sotheby and John Wilkinson,* (London, 1859), pp. 145–48. Note that in publishing the comment made by Gregory that is quoted below in the text the authors of the catalogue omitted "Gerardi" from the title given in the first line of the comment, as my inspection of Gregory's comments attached to MS *B* reveals.

[10] Eneström, *op. cit.* in n. 7, p. 135, and his "Das Bruchrechnen des Jordanus Nemorarius," *Bibliotheca mathematica,* 3. Folge, Vol. 14 (1913–14), p. 42.

catalogue (*op. cit.* in note 9, p. 147) quotes from the first part of the manuscript a comment by the celebrated David Gregory (who prepared a kind of analytical index of the manuscript):

> The next is *Liber Magistri* [*Gerardi*] *de Brussel de Motu.* It contains three books in seven leaves. In the first, there are four propositions; in the second, five; in the third, four. This was never printed that I know. It does not handle motion in the present acceptance of the word, it only shows, that in the rotation of Lines and Plain (*!*) Figures about an immovable Axis whereby surfaces and solids are generated, there is sometimes equal motion in different generations, and sometimes more in one than in another. There are some initial small instances of the proposition: Tantum movetur Figura quantum ejus centrum gravitatis.

As we shall see in Chapter Two, this is by no means an accurate description of the treatise, but it shows at least a fleeting acquaintance with the tract in the seventeenth century.

What may we say about the author and the date of the tract? It is clear that all but one of the extant manuscripts listed below in Chapter Three date from the thirteenth century. More explicitly we know that MS *E* was once a part of the collection of manuscripts described by Richard of Fournival in his *Biblionomia*,[11] a catalogue composed when he was chancellor of the church at Amiens.[12] We know that he was already chancellor in 1246 at the time of the death of his brother Arnoul, and we also know that Richard was no longer living in 1260.[13] Hence his *Biblionomia* must have been written before that year. Birkenmajer in his fine study of the work suggests "vers 1250" and surely this would not be far off the true date.[14] The item in the *Biblionomia* reads:[15]

> 43. Jordani de Nemore liber philothegny CCCCXVII [*!* LXIIII] propositiones continens. Item ejusdem liber de ratione ponderum, et alius de ponderum proportione. Item cujusdam ad papam de quadratura circuli. Item Gerardi de Bruxella subtilitas de motu. In uno volumine cujus signum est littera D.

As I pointed out in my edition of the *Liber de motu* this also constitutes the earliest datable reference to Jordanus' longer treatise on weights, the *Liber de ratione ponderum,* as well as to his *Liber philotegni* which I edit in Part II below. In fact, as I note under the rubric *Sigla* in Chapter Three, Gerard's

---

[11] N. R. Ker, *Medieval Manuscripts in British Libraries,* Vol. 2 (Oxford, 1977), p. 547 (concerning Cr. 1.27, our MS *E*).

[12] L. Delisle, *Le Cabinet des manuscrits de la Bibliothèque Nationale,* Vol. 2 (Paris, 1874), p. 521.

[13] *Histoire littéraire de la France,* Vol. 23 (Paris, 1856), p. 717.

[14] A. Birkenmajer, *Études d'histoire des sciences et de la philosophie du moyen age* (Wrocław, etc., 1970), p. 119. Cf. R. H. Rouse, "Manuscripts belonging to Richard de Fournival," *Revue d'histoire des textes,* Vol. 3 (1973), pp. 253–69 (whole article), and particularly pp. 255, 260. Rouse believes that this is one of the manuscripts prepared for Fournival. He notes earlier (p. 254) that the commissioned books were "contemporary with his [i.e. Fournival's] mature years, ca. 1225–1260."

[15] Delisle, *Le Cabinet,* Vol. 2, p. 526; Cf. Birkenmajer, *Études,* p. 166.

work often appears with the works of Jordanus de Nemore, with the *Liber de curvis superficiebus Archimenidis* of Johannes de Tinemue, with the *On the Measurement of the Circle* of Archimedes, and with the *Elements* of Euclid. This suggests, as my analysis of the contents of the *Liber de motu* in the next chapter tends to confirm, that these various works were integral parts of a lively geometrical activity at the end of the twelfth century and the beginning of the thirteenth.[16] While remarking on the possible close ties of Gerard's work with the mathematical activity of Jordanus de Nemore, I hasten to admit that there is no definite evidence of which author precedes the other.[17] But, as I note in my analysis of Proposition I.4 in the next chapter, several propositions of Jordanus' *Liber philotegni* also deal with the relationships existing, mutually and separately, between inscribed and circumscribed regular polygons, and indeed they are probably the source of Gerard's knowledge of such relationships.

As for Gerard's citations of the other geometrical works mentioned above, we should note first that he cites Archimedes' *On the Measurement of the Circle* under the title *De quadratura circuli* (e.g., see Prop. I.1, line 32, and var. to line 180 in Tradition I; and Prop. II.1, line 112). In doing so, he is no doubt referring to the second tradition of Gerard of Cremona's translation of that work rather than to the first tradition which bore the title *De mensura circuli.*[18] Incidentally Archimedes' name does not appear in the citations given in the *Liber de motu.* Nor does an author's name appear in the citations to the *De curvis superficiebus.* Gerard of Brussels in the text and the scribe of MS *O* in the margins always cite this work under the title of *De piramidibus* (see Prop. I.1, Trad. I, var. to lines 77–78; I.2, var. to lines 7–9, text line 11; II.2, lines 6 and 17; II.3, lines 103–04). When preparing my edition of the *Liber de curvis superficiebus,* I was unable to find any extant manuscript in which the work bore the title *De piramidibus,* which is ordinarily reserved for a fragment of Apollonius' *Conics* translated from the Arabic by Gerard of Cremona.[19] However it is possible that a manuscript briefly described in Fournival's *Biblionomia* contains the *De curvis superficiebus* under that title:[20]

> 42. Dicti Theodosii liber de speris, ex commentario Adelardi. Item Archimenidis Arsamithis liber de quadratura circuli. Liber de piramidibus. Liber de ysoperimetris. Item libri de speculis, de visu et de ymagine speculi. In uno volumine cujus signum est littera D.

I suggest that the title *De piramidibus* used here refers to the *De curvis superficiebus* since it is given immediately after Archimedes' *De quadratura circuli,* and the *De curvis superficiebus* is often found in close proximity to

---

[16] Clagett, *Archimedes,* Vol. 1, *passim,* Vol. 3, pp. 212–13.

[17] See my remarks on Jordanus' career in Part II, Chap. 1 below.

[18] Clagett, *Archimedes,* Vol. 1, p. 31.

[19] *Ibid.,* Vol. 4, p. 3. Notice that Zubov, *op. cit.* in note 2, p. 243, misidentifies the *De piramidibus* with Jordanus' *De triangulis* when in fact it was the *Liber de curvis superficiebus.*

[20] Delisle, *Le Cabinet,* Vol. 2, p. 526; Cf. Birkenmajer, *Études,* p. 166.

Archimedes' work in extant manuscripts.[21] How does one explain the use by Gerard of Brussels of *De piramidibus* for a title of the *De curvis superficiebus*? I suppose that the most sensible answer is that Gerard read a manuscript of the *De curvis superficiebus* in which the work was without title and so he decided, on the basis of the prominent position given to cones in that work (cf. Propositions I, IV, V, VII, and IX of the *De curvis superficiebus* in my text in Volume One), to call it *De piramidibus*. Not only does Gerard depend specifically on Propositions I and IV of the *De curvis superficiebus*, but, even more fundamentally, he uses a form of the exhaustion procedure in several propositions that is like the form used in the *De curvis superficiebus*, a form which the Renaissance mathematician Francesco Maurolico called the "easier way" and which was ultimately based on Proposition XII.18 of Euclid's *Elements*.[22] Speaking of Euclid's *Elements*, we should add that Gerard of Brussels' *Liber de motu* displays a thorough knowledge of the *Elements*. But unlike most medieval geometers he did not cite the work. The only specific references to the *Elements* are found in additions made by the scribe of MS *O* (see the variant to Prop. I.1, Trad. I, line 63, citing Prop. I.16 of the *Elements*, and the variant to Prop. II.1, line 120, citing Props. VI.17 and VI.1 of the *Elements*) and citations added to the text by the compositor of Tradition II of Prop. I.1 (see line 46, citing VI.4; line 60, citing V.15; line 81, citing I.29; line 85, citing I.26; and line 93, citing I.34). Thus the knowledge of Euclid shown by Gerard is never specific enough for us to determine which version he used of the several translations of Euclid that might have been available to him in the late twelfth or early thirteenth century.[23] Perhaps his readers' knowledge of the *Elements* was so taken for granted by him that he felt no need to give exact citations. At any rate, it is clear that Gerard's proofs show proper knowledge of Euclidian propositions concerning similar triangles, the relationships of cylinders and cones, the Euclidian theory of proportions, and other areas of Euclidian geometry.

In addition to the geometrical tracts that he knew and used (like the *De quadratura circuli*, the *De curvis superficiebus*, and the *Elements*) and the geometrical tract of Jordanus *Liber philotegni* that he may have known, there are certain other treatises with kinematic rules that may have influenced his treatment of motion. These include the following texts: (1) *On the Moved Sphere* of Autolycus, translated by Gerard of Cremona, with its definition of "equal [i.e. uniform] motion" and its statement of the fundamental kinematic proportion for two uniform but unequal motions:

---

[21] See the MSS listed in Clagett, *Archimedes*, Vol. 1, pp. xix–xxvi (where MS *B* is mistakenly written "Q.150" instead of "Q.510"—see p. xxiv).

[22] For a description and discussion of the "easier way" see M. Clagett, *Archimedes in the Middle Ages*, Vol. 3 (Philadelphia, 1978), pp. 798–808.

[23] Clagett, "The Medieval Latin Translations from the Arabic of the *Elements* of Euclid, with Special Emphasis on the Versions of Adelard of Bath," *Isis*, Vol. 44 (1953), pp. 16–42; cf. J. Murdoch, "Euclid: Transmission of the Elements," *Dictionary of Scientific Biography*, Vol. 4 (New York, 1971), pp. 437–59.

$S_1 / S_2 = T_1 / T_2$;[24] (2) the *Physics* of Aristotle, available in several translations, with its demonstration (given in quasi-geometric form) of the three cases of "quicker," "slower" and "equal" motions;[25] (3) the *Elementatio physica* of Proclus, available in a twelfth-century translation from the Greek, with its repetition of the Aristotelian rules cast in strictly geometrical form;[26] and (4) the *Mechanica* attributed to Aristotle, which was perhaps (though not surely) translated into Latin in the twelfth century, and which contained the statement from which Gerard's tract begins: "but of two points that which is farther from the fixed center is the quicker."[27] Having examined the possible influ-

[24] Clagett, *Science of Mechanics,* pp. 166–68.

[25] *Ibid.,* pp. 175–83.

[26] H. Boese, *Die mittelalterliche Übersetzung der Στοιχείωσις Φυσική des Proclus. Procli Diadochi Lycii Elementatio physica* (Berlin, 1958), p. 34:

"8. Inequali celeritate motorum celerius in equali tempore maius movetur.

Esto enim inequaliter motorum celerius A, tardius autem B, et moveatur A ab G super D in ZI tempore. Quoniam ergo tardius est B, in ZI tempore non veniet ab G super D. Celerius enim est prius in finem veniens, tardius autem posterius. Moveatur ergo in ZI tempore in E veniens. In eodem igitur tempore A quantitatem GD pertransit, B vero quantitatem GE; maior autem GD quam GE. Celerius ergo in eodem tempore maiorem quantitatem pertransit.

9. Si fuerint mota inequalis celeritatis, sumentur quedam tempora, plus quidem tardioris, minus vero celerioris, in quibus celerius quidem maiorem movetur quantitatem, tardius autem minorem.

Sint enim inequalis celeritatis A, B, et A quidem celerius, B vero tardius. Quoniam ergo celerius in eodem tempore maiorem pertransit quantitatem, in ZI tempore A quidem GD pertranseat et B, GE. Et quoniam A in toto ZI tempore pertransit GD quantitatem, ergo GT in minori pertransiet quam sit ZI. Sumatur ergo illud tempus minus et sit ZK. Quoniam ergo A quidem in ZK pertransit GT, B vero in ZI pertransit GE, maior autem GT quam GE maiusque tempus ZI quam ZK, sumpta ergo sunt tempora quedam, maius quidem ZI eius quod est B, minus vero ZK eius quod est A, in quibus A quidem progreditur maiorem GT, at vero B minorem GE.

10. Inequaliter motorum celerius in minori tempore equalem pertransit quantitatem.

Sint enim inequaliter mota sitque celerius A quam B moveaturque A in ZI tempore quantitatem GD, at vero B in eodem minorem, scilicet GE. Quoniam ergo A in toto ZI quantitatem GD progreditur, minorem GE in minori progredietur; progrediatur ergo in ZK. At vero B quantitatem GE in ZI progrediebatur, plus vero ZI tempus quam ZK. Equalem ergo quantitatem, scilicet GE, A quidem in minori tempore progreditur, B vero in maiori.

Aliter: Esto A quam B celerius et moveatur B quantitatem GE in ZI tempore; A ergo in eodem tempore movetur GE vel in maiori vel in minori. Sed si in eodem, erunt equalis celeritatis; si autem in maiori, erit tardius, positum est autem celerius. In minori ergo tempore progredietur A quantitatem GE."

I have made slight changes in punctuation in Prop. 9, writing "A, B," instead of "A B" and "B, GE" instead of "B GE." Like the editor I have not given any diagrams, but the magnitudes specified are so obvious that no diagrams are needed to follow the text.

[27] Clagett, *Science of Mechanics,* pp. 182–83, and see pp. 5, 71. In the last reference (p. 71) I give the one passage that may indicate the existence of a medieval translation of the Pseudo-Aristotelian *Mechanica.* It is found in the *De arte venandi cum avibus* of Frederick II: "Portiones circuli quas faciunt singule penne sunt de circumferentiis equidistantibus, et illa que facit portionem maioris ambitus et magis distat a corpore avis iuvat magis sublevari aut impelli et deportari, quod dicit Aristotiles (!) in libro de ingeniis levandi pondera dicens quod magis facit levari pondus maior circulus." Still one could argue that, even if there was no medieval translation of the *Mechanica,* the basic approach to statics found in the works of Jordanus and in the *Liber*

ences of the first two and the fourth of these works on Gerard in great detail in my earlier publications, I shall refrain from saying anything more about them at this point. As for the third work, the inclusion here of the actual text in footnote 26 and the observation that it contained Aristotle's rules on velocity which I discussed in my earlier works should make any further discussion unnecessary.

Though the reader will now have some sense of the works that influenced Gerard's composition of the *Liber de motu,* he will still have no precise information about the life of the author and where he studied and taught. In four of the MSS (see the variants for the title of the treatise in MSS *O, B,* and *N,* and for the colophon in *E*) Gerard is spoken of as *Magister Gerardus.* It seems possible that this is an indication of some university connection for Gerard. But with which university I do not know. At this early stage of university history, Paris seems the most likely, just as it does for Jordanus, whose works appear so often in the same codices as Gerard's *De motu.* Though the *Liber de motu* is the only extant work ascribed to Gerard of Brussels, Gerard himself seems to mention another of his works in Proposition II.3 of the *Liber de motu* when he tells us that he has proved elsewhere that the ratio of the curved surfaces of similar polygonal bodies is equal to the square of the ratios of their sides (see the translation below, Prop. II.3, note 1). There is the intriguing possibility that our Gerardus is identical with another mathematician of about the same period, *Magister Gernardus,* who composed an *Algorismus demonstratus* (entitled in its two parts *Algorismus de integris* and *Algorismus de minutiis*), which bears a close relationship to the mathematical works of Jordanus.[28] But, though one manuscript of the *Algorismus* seems to have *Gernandus* instead of *Gernardus,* I conclude from Eneström's list of its manuscripts that no manuscript has *Gerardus,* at least in the hand of an original scribe.[29] So, in fact, the person of Gerard of Brussels remains as elusive as that of his more illustrious contemporary Jordanus (see Part II below) or as that of Johannes de Tinemue, who played some role in the preparation or translation of the *De curvis superficiebus.* In regard to the latter, we can note the existence of a canonist,

---

karastonis of Thābit ibn Qurra (translated by Gerard of Cremona) assumes (no doubt ultimately from the *Mechanica*) that a weight that is on an arm that is farther from the center of the balance moves faster than one at a position closer to the center, and it is precisely this idea assumed for points that Gerard of Brussels uses at the beginning of his treatise. Hence, one can perhaps say that this basic idea is so well-known from the statical traditions circulating in the thirteenth century that it is unnecessary to assume a translation of the *Mechanica.*

[28] G. Sarton, *Introduction to the History of Science,* Vol. 2 (Baltimore, 1931), p. 616. See the edition of G. Eneström, "Der 'Algorismus de integris' des Meisters Gernardus," *Bibliotheca mathematica,* 3. Folge, Vol. 13 (1912–13), pp. 289–332, and "Der 'Algorismus de minutiis' des Meisters Gernardus," *ibid.,* Vol. 14 (1913–14), pp. 99–149.

[29] *Ed. cit.* of *Algorismus de integris* in note 28, p. 290. The aberrant form "Gernandus" appears in MS Oxford, Bodl. Libr., Digby 161, 1r. Eneström says that this manuscript was formerly attributed to Gerard of Cremona (and indeed in a later hand on the title page we find "Gerhardus"); cf. R. B. Thomson, "Jordanus de Nemore: Opera," *Mediaeval Studies,* Vol. 38 (1976), p. 112.

John de Tynemuth, who, among other positions, held that of archdeacon at Oxford from 1215.[30] But I have found nothing to connect him with the writing of mathematical works.

The fortune of Gerard of Brussel's work has been alluded to in the beginning of this chapter. The *Liber de motu* certainly exerted some influence on the kinematic concepts found in the *Tractatus de proportionibus* of Thomas Bradwardine and in the works of his successors at Merton College, Oxford, and at the University of Paris (e.g. on Themon Judei). Because this kinematic material of the fourteenth century has received wide consideration since Pierre Duhem first drew attention to it, I shall not go over it again, except to note a few specific citations in my discussion of the content of the *Liber de motu* in the next chapter. I know of no description of this work after the fourteenth century until David Gregory's brief estimate of it in the seventeenth century, although it seems possible that the French scholar Charles de Bouelles (*or* Bovelles) read Gerard's work in the early sixteenth century, and perhaps Nicholas of Cusa had seen it a half century earlier.[31] Furthermore, John Dee, the well-known mathematician and magician of the sixteenth century, singles out its presence in MS *O* (Oxford, Bodleian Library, MS Auct. F.5.28, 116v–125r), which he had borrowed from Ricardus Bruarnus.[32]

[30] A. B. Emden, *A Biographical Register of the University of Oxford to A.D. 1500,* Vol. 3 (Oxford, 1959), p. 1923.

[31] Clagett, *Archimedes,* Vol. 3, pp. 1180, 1182 n. 4, 1187, 1192 n. 19, 1196.

[32] M. R. James, *Lists of Manuscripts Formerly Owned by Dr. John Dee* (Oxford, 1921), p. 13, item 43.: "I borowed one volume of master bruern (!) written in parchment in 4to two ynches thik in which are many and good bokes and Jordan de datis numeris and Gerardus Brussellensis de motu which I never saw elsewhere and mr bruarun's name is written on the back." This is identical with MS. C.13 (see p. 16). I have identified the manuscript with *O* by the reference to Bruarnus (see F. Maddan, H. H. E. Craster, and N. Denholm-Young, *A Summary Catalogue of Western Manuscripts in the Bodleian Library at Oxford,* Vol. 2, Part 2 (Oxford, 1937), p. 708. It had been tentatively and wrongly identified by James with the Libri MS 665 (my MS *B;* see the *Sigla* in Chapter Three below). A. G. Watson has kindly informed me that he and R. J. Roberts have also made the identification with *O* in their edition of *John Dee's Library Catalogue* (London, The Bibliographical Society, forthcoming), which includes further comments on MS *O.*

CHAPTER 2

An Analysis of the Mathematical Content of the *Liber de motu*

In my earlier discussions of the *Liber de motu* of Gerard of Brussels I emphasized the importance of the treatise for the development of kinematics as a part of mechanics.[1] Now in this account, I shall stress somewhat more the geometrical aspects of the treatise, for it is clear that it is primarily a geometrical work that fits well with the geometrical texts that were becoming increasingly popular in the early thirteenth century. As I said earlier, the *Liber de motu* is divided into three short books containing respectively four, five and four propositions. The first book is concerned with the assignment of uniform-making punctual speeds to lines in rotation or revolution and the relations one to another of such speeds, the second with finding uniform-making punctual speeds for surfaces in rotation and the relations of these speeds, and the third with discovering the relations between the uniform-making punctual speeds of solids in rotation. Thus it is evident that the whole tract involves motions of rotation (or revolution) and their reduction to uniformity. Nowhere in the tract is the author interested in angular velocity, but only in curvilinear or rectilinear speed. Hence it seems likely that, despite the occasional use of astronomical terms like *circulus equinoctialis* and *circulus colurus,* and the interest in rotating spheres in Book III, the focus in the tract is entirely on geometry rather than on astronomy. The knowledge he displays of geometrical formulae like those for rectilinear and curved figures are the ones he found in Euclid's *Elements,* Archimedes' *On the Measurement of the Circle,* or Johannes de Tinemue's *De curvis superficiebus.* The same may be said of the mathematical techniques he employs. They are all either Euclidian or Archimedean.

---

[1] See the citations in Chap. 1, n. 2. To these add my "Gerard of Brussels," *Dictionary of Scientific Biography,* Vol. 5 (New York, 1972), p. 360. Note that my analysis in this chapter completely supersedes my earlier treatments so far as the mathematical content of the *Liber de motu* is concerned. However my earlier discussion of the significance of the treatise for the development of kinematics in the fourteenth century is, I believe, still substantially correct.

Before initiating a close analysis of the tract, proposition by proposition, it may prove enlightening to the reader to present a few of the basic concepts and techniques that will be revealed in more detail in the subsequent analysis.

(1) The *Liber de motu* represents what we may call a generative approach to geometry. In this approach figures are not considered as loci but as the results of the motions of magnitudes. Hence we find in the tract the following generations: a line (whether curved or straight) by the motion of a point, a circle by the rotation of a radius or a circular band by the revolution of a segment of a radius, a rectangle by the translation of a straight line, a right cone by the rotation of a right triangle and hence a conical surface by the motion of the hypotenuse of such a triangle, a truncated cone by the rotation of a segment of such a triangle cut out by two lines parallel to the base and hence the surface of such a truncated cone by the revolution of a segment of the hypotenuse, a polyhedral figure by the rotation of a regular polygon [of 4n sides] about one of its diagonals and hence the composite conical surface of such a polyhedron by the rotation of the perimeter of the polygon, a cylinder by the rotation of a rectangle about one of its sides, a rectangular parallelepiped by the translation of a rectangle, a sphere by the rotation of a circle about its diameter, and other figures that arise from the motions of segments of the generating figures.[2]

(2) As I have suggested above, a central objective of the *Liber de motu* is to find and relate by ratios punctual speeds that reduce the variable speeds of the points of rotating magnitudes to uniformity. A brief word of explanation will be useful. When magnitudes are rotated to produce the various figures mentioned above, those points asymmetrically situated with respect to the center or axis of motion have distinct and different curvilinear speeds. This variation in speed makes difficult the comparison of the movements of these rotating figures. Hence the author of this tract proposes to find a single uniform rectilinear speed which may be said to reduce the variation in speed to uniformity. This uniform punctual speed is the speed which when given to each point of the magnitude causes the magnitude to move in translation always parallel to itself and so produce in the same time as that of the rotation or revolution of the magnitude a space (be it a line, surface, or volume) equal to the space traversed by the magnitude when it is rotated or revolved. Hence Gerard has presented a concept of average speed, and throughout I have identified the average speed by the abbreviation *Vm* (which I shall pluralize by *Vms*).

(3) Gerard's effort to find in each case a uniform rectilinear speed has interesting geometrical consequences. It brings to the fore the rectangular measure of "curved" figures and in doing so it shows the influence of the

---

[2] See the closely similar generative geometry of Charles de Bouelles (or Bovelles) in his *Liber de circuli quadratura* and *Liber cubicationis sphere,* which were published with Jacques Le Fèvre's *Introductio in libros arithmeticos divi Severini Boetii* (Paris, 1503). I have presented the pertinent propositions with English translations in my *Archimedes in the Middle Ages,* Vol. 3 (Philadelphia, 1978), pp. 1180–96, and have noted there the similarities of the generative geometry of de Bouelles' tracts with that of the *Liber de motu* of Gerard of Brussels.

Liber de curvis superficiebus where some of the circular measures of such figures were converted to rectangular measures.[3] In this connection, it is of interest to note that in the one genuine tract of Archimedes read by Gerard, the *On the Measurement of the Circle,* Archimedes gives the measure of the circle in terms of a rectilinear figure, i.e., a right triangle whose sides about the right angle are equal respectively to the radius and the circumference of the circle. And this proposition stands as a model for the development of rectangular measures for curved figures. It is not surprising that an acute mathematician like Francesco Maurolico, who produced in the sixteenth century a version of Archimedes' *On the Sphere and the Cylinder* which was little more than an elaboration of the medieval *De curvis superficiebus,* saw the necessity of adding corollaries that convert the rectangular measures of the curved surfaces of a cone, a cylinder, a truncated cone, a solid of rotation and segments of these figures to the circular measures which were the object of the Archimedean demonstrations (see Volume Three, p. 806). The reader will also see that Gerard has concerned himself with the motions of just those figures whose areas and volumes were treated in the *Liber de curvis super-ficiebus:* circles, cones, regular polygons inscribed in and circumscribed about circles, the solids produced by the rotation of such regular polygons, and spheres.

(4) In proving his various propositions concerning the motions of the rotating magnitudes, Gerard frequently uses proofs *per impossibile,* i.e. indirect proofs in which the contrary of the enunciation leads to contradiction. These proofs contain examples of a form of exhaustion proofs like that often used in the *Liber de curvis superficiebus* rather than that evident in Archimedes' *On the Sphere and the Cylinder.* This form of the exhaustion proof assumes that to any figure in a plane surface there exists some equal conical, cylindrical, or spherical surface; and with two surface figures given there is a surface figure similar to one of the given surface figures and equal to the other. Furthermore, with two solids given, there exists some solid similar to one of the given solids and equal to the other. These assumptions are coupled with the principle that an "included figure" cannot be greater than an "including figure." The including figure must always surround the included and in no way touch it (cf. Euclid, *Elements,* Proposition XII.16). For confirmation the reader may examine the proofs given in Corollary II of Proposition II.3, Propositions II.5, III.2, and III.4 and my analysis of these various proofs in this chapter below. As I have shown in Volume Three (pp. 799–805, 1005–

---

[3] See my *Archimedes in the Middle Ages,* Vol. 1 (Madison, 1964), pp. 439–520. Note the following examples of rectilinear measures of curved surfaces: p. 451 "I. The lateral surface of any [right circular] cone is equal to a right triangle, one of whose two sides containing the right angle is equal to the slant height of the cone, while the other [is equal] to the circumference of the base." p. 461: "II. The lateral surface of any [right] cylinder is equal to the rectangle contained by lines equal [respectively] to the axis of the cylinder and the circumference of the base." p. 479: "VI. The surface of any sphere is equal to the rectangle contained by lines equal to the diameter of the sphere and the circumference of the greatest circle [of the sphere]." See also Proposition IV (p. 467) and Proposition V (pp. 469–71) for other rectilinear measures, where the measures are presented as the products of lines.

1022) this form of proof seems to have had its ultimate origin in Proposition XII.18 (with its attendant Proposition XII.17) of the *Elements* of Euclid.

(5) One further technique skillfully used by Gerard in his proofs was the probable application of Proposition V.12 (=V.13 in the Adelard II and Campanus versions) of the *Elements* of Euclid, though he does not actually cite the proposition. That proposition asserts that "If any number of magnitudes be proportional, as one of the antecedents is to one of the consequences, so will all the antecedents be to all the consequences."[4] That is, if $A \,/\, a = B \,/\, b = C \,/\, c = D \,/\, d = \cdots$, then $(A + B + C + D + \cdots) \,/\, (a + b + c + d + \cdots) = A \,/\, a$. Its restricted use to finite sets of magnitudes seems to be present, for example, in Gerard's Proposition II.3 and its first corollary (see my remark below concerning steps [8] and [9] in my summary of the proof of that proposition). But a much more interesting application appears to have been made in Proposition II.1 where the sets of antecedents and consequents are infinite or, better, indefinitely large. There we find two areas, one "curved" and the other rectilinear, and any element of the one area (Gerard simply calls the elements "lines") is equal and equally moved as the corresponding element in the other area (Gerard speaks of the corresponding elements as "lines taken in the same ratio"); then the one whole surface is equal and equally moved with the other whole surface. Gerard's line by line comparison of the two surfaces reminds us of a rather similar technique used by Archimedes in his *On the Method.* But Gerard's route to his use of corresponding infinitesimal elements was no doubt by way of Euclid rather than by way of Archimedes, since Archimedes' treatise was not known in the West until 1906 when Heiberg discovered it in a codex in Constantinople. The reader should also realize that the application of the Euclidian proposition to infinite sets of magnitudes like that I have assumed to be in the *Liber de motu* is also evident in the proof of the mean speed theorem at Merton College and in late scholastic efforts to sum infinite series.[5]

Book I

Postulates

Since Gerard is concerned with motions of rotation, it is not surprising that he presents as his first postulate the well-known idea that the curvilinear

---

[4] T. L. Heath, *Euclid. The Elements,* Vol. 2 (Annapolis, 1947), p. 159, Prop. 12. For the equivalent proposition (=V.13) in Adelard II's version of the *Elements,* see MS Oxford, Bodl. Library, Auct. F.5.28, xii r: "XIII. Si fuerint (!) quotlibet quantitatum ad totidem alias proportio una, [quo]que erit proportio unius ad unam eadem proportio omnium harum pariter acceptarum ad omnes illas pariter acceptas." For the closely similar enunciation in Campanus' version, see Euclid, *Elementorum geometricorum libri XV* (Basel, 1546), p. 123. Cf. the remarks of Zubov, "Ob 'Arkhimedovsky traditsii'," p. 236 (see full title in Chap. 1 above, n. 3).

[5] M. Clagett, *The Science of Mechanics in the Middle Ages* (Madison, 1959; 3rd pr. 1979), p. 300 (lines 60–63 for the presentation of the Euclidian proposition but without reference to Euclid). See also M. Clagett, *Nicole Oresme and the Medieval Geometry of Qualities and Motions* (Madison, 1968), p. 507.

speed of points or parts of the rotating figures increases as we proceed from the center of rotation. I have already noted in Chapter One (note 27) that this view was explicitly stated in the *Mechanica* attributed to Aristotle and also underlay the approach to statics found in the statical works attributed to Jordanus de Nemore and in the *Liber karastonis* of Thābit ibn Qurra. In connection with this first and the succeeding postulates and propositions, it should be observed that Gerard very often used the phrase "magis moventur (*or* movetur)." It surely has the meaning "velocius moventur (*or* movetur)," as Bradwardine was later to point out in his *De proportionibus,* when he said that the author of the *De proportionalitate motuum et magnitudinum* (i.e. Gerard of Brussels in his *Liber de motu*) points out that in the case of two straight lines moved in equal time that which traverses the greater space to greater termini is moved more quickly.[6] Needless to say, the phrases "moventur minus" and "moventur equaliter" mean to "be moved less quickly" and to "be moved equally fast."

In Postulate 2 Gerard assumes that when a line "is moved equally, uniformly, and equidistantly [i.e. uniformly parallel to itself], it is moved equally in all of its parts and points." This postulate concerns a line moving in translation and always parallel to itself. It will be seen that such a motion of translation is compared with a motion of rotation in Proposition I.1. The concept of the uniform motion of translation of a straight line is a commonplace in antiquity and goes back at least to the fifth century B.C. when Hippias of Elis is said to have invented the quadratrix for trisecting an angle and squaring a circle.[7] By Gerard's time such a motion of translation had become the common property of geometry.

Postulate 3 indicates that when the halves of a line are moved equally and uniformly with respect to each other, the whole line is moved equally as its halves. The purpose of this postulate may have been to provide a stepping-stone from a comparison of the motions of lines to the comparison of the motions of points found in Postulate 8, with perhaps the implication of a further proportional division toward infinity of the moving line according to the ratio of 2 to 1 (a favorite technique of the kinematicists at Merton College in the fourteenth century in their treatment of infinitesimals, as evident in the passages cited in note 5 above). But be that as it may, it is in fact already implied in both Postulates 2 and 3 that a line is an aggregate of points, just as later in Books II and III he will conceive of a surface as an aggregate of lines and a solid as an aggregate of surfaces. And so Postulate

---

[6] Thomas of Bradwardine, *His Tractatus de Proportionibus. Its Significance for the Development of Mathematical Physics,* Ed. and tr. by H. L. Crosby, Madison, 1955; 2nd pr. 1961), p. 128: "Auctor vero *De proportionalitate motuum et magnitudinum,* subtilior istis multum, ponit quod linearum rectarum aequalium temporibus aequalibus motarum, quae pertransit maius spatium superficiale et ad maiores terminos moveri velocius, et quae minus et ad minores terminos tardius, et quae aequale et ad aequales terminos aequevelociter moveri supponit. Et intendit, per terminos maiores, terminos ad quos a terminis a quibus magis distantes."

[7] Clagett, *The Science of Mechanics in the Middle Ages,* p. 169.

3 may be expressed in punctual speeds as follows: if the uniform-making punctual speed (or *Vm*) of one half a line is equal to the *Vm* of the other half (and they are both moving in translation), then the *Vm* of the whole line is equal to the *Vm* of each half. Postulates 4–7 give positive and negative statements concerning the comparison of the motions of lines. In the case of lines moved in the same time, that which traverses greater space is moved more and that which traverses less space is moved less, and that which does not traverse more space is not moved more and that which does not traverse less space is not moved less. The reason for Gerard's negative statements will be immediately clear when the reader examines Proposition I.1 and realizes the crucial importance there of indirect proofs. Equality of motions in that proposition (and in most of the succeeding ones) is demonstrated by showing that one motion is neither more nor less than another. In the course of stating Postulates 4–7 Gerard uses two phrases that are somewhat ambiguous: "ad maiores terminos" and "ad minores terminos." Thus Gerard says that lines that are moved more traverse greater space "to greater termini," and those that are moved less traverse less space "to lesser termini." Presumably these phrases mean "to more distant termini" and "to less distant termini." At any rate, this is the interpretation that Bradwardine gives to them: "By 'greater termini' he [i.e. the author of the *De proportionalitate motuum et magnitudinum,* who, as I have said, was Gerard of Brussels] means *termini toward which* [the motion takes place] that are farther removed from the *termini from which* [it proceeds]."[8] This certainly seems a proper interpretation when we are comparing the motions of straight lines that are moving in translation. But one wonders what the phrase means when one line is moving in translation and the other is rotating. Thus in Proposition I.1 (Tradition I, lines 128–33) we have precisely such a case where *SL* is moving in translation and segment *CF* of the radius is revolving about the center *O*. In the indirect statement given there they are said to move equally and to equal termini because *SL* does not describe greater space "to greater termini" than *CF*; nor does it describe less space "to lesser termini." The perplexity arises in considering the termini of all the points of the rotating segment where obviously the termini vary from a maximum distance at the outer circumference to a minimum distance at the inner circumference. And in the case where it is the whole radius that is rotating, the distances of the termini vary from a maximum at the outer circumference to zero at the center of the circle. It is this case that particularly puzzled Bradwardine.[9] I suspect that Gerard merely meant that in sum the distances of the termini of the points on the rotating line were neither more nor less than the distances of the points on the line moving in translation, the latter distances also being

---

[8] See the last sentence of note 6 above.

[9] Bradwardine, *His Tractatus de proportionibus,* ed. cit. in note 6, p. 128: "Non enim pertransit aliquod spatium ad aliquos terminos, sed ad terminum unicum (quoniam unum extremum semidiametri non movetur)."

taken in sum. We could put it a more modern way by saying that the average distances of the termini of the two lines (one rotating and one moving in translation) are the same. It could well be that the ambiguities involved in the use of the concept of distances to the termini of the motions of points on a revolving segment, and especially of the termini of the motions of points on a rotating radius (where one point does not move with any curvilinear speed), are partially responsible for the considerable use of proofs *per impossibile*.[10] It is also possible that the phrases "to greater termini" and "to lesser termini" were added to eliminate the possibility of comparing motions where discontinuity was present, as, for example, motions of oscillation. Thus the added phrases would assure that the motions compared are continuous and always in the same direction whether they be along arcs or straight lines.

Postulate 8 declares that the ratio of punctual motions is as the ratio of lines described in the same time. And it is quite clear that the lines described may be either arcs or straight lines, and further that such lines are comparable one to another. A similar statement is found in Autolycus' *De spera mota,* as I pointed out in Chapter One above note 24, which in the translation of Gerard of Cremona could have easily been available to Gerard of Brussels. This eighth postulate was one of two principal axioms expressed by Bradwardine, though it reflects Bradwardine's rather different view of the measure of rotating bodies.[11] One important point should be made here. In this postulate Gerard does not define speed in the modern manner, namely as the ratio of the unlike magnitudes of distance and time, since he would hold the Euclidian view that ratios are between like magnitudes. Still Gerard does seem to imply that the speed of motion can be assigned some number or quantity not simply identical with either the quantity of distance or that of time. For when he says that the ratio of motions is that of the distances traversed in the same time, he appears to mean that some magnitude V_1 representing one motion is to another magnitude V_2 representing a second motion as some distance S_1 is to another distance S_2. Otherwise it would make no sense for him to use the language of proportions which implies number or magnitude. However, it should be obvious to the reader that throughout the treatise the comparison is always between motions that take place in the same time and hence the ratio of motions is always said to be as that of the distances traversed in the course of those motions.

---

[10] Zubov, "Ob 'Archimedovsky traditsii'," p. 243, makes the further, important point that Gerard uses proofs *per impossibile* to substantiate any transition from the speed of the motion along a straight line to the speed of the motion along an arc. Gerard perhaps had in mind the necessity of setting aside the Aristotelian refusal to equate curvilinear and rectilinear speeds because the paths were of differing species (see my *The Science of Mechanics*, p. 182).

[11] *Ed. cit.*, p. 130: "Quorumlibet duorum motuum localium, velocitates et maximae lineae a duobus punctis duorum mobilium eodem tempore descriptae, eodem ordine proportionales existunt." The use of the term "maximae" reflects Bradwardine's view (against Gerard) that the speed of a rotating body is measured by the speed of its fastest moving point.

Proposition I.1

Enunciation of Prop. I.1 (lines 23–27). This proposition has two parts. In the first part we are told that any segment of a rotating radius that is not terminated at the center is moved equally as its middle point. By which he means that the motion of the segment of the radius is made uniform by the punctual speed of the middle point of the segment. Part two of the proposition extends the conclusion to the whole radius, namely that the radius is moved equally as its middle point. Then is added a corollary, namely that the ratio of the radii is that of their motions (i.e. *Vms*). We should note once more that when Gerard uses the expression "is moved equally as" here and in the succeeding propositions he means "is made uniform in motion by." Hence what is clearly meant in this proposition is that if we allow the segment of the radius or the whole radius to move in translation uniformly with the punctual speed of the middle point of the segment or .of the radius equal spaces would be traversed in the same time. Thus Gerard is not comparing the motion of a line with the motion of a point as the literal statement seems to say but rather is simply finding the mean speed of all of the curvilinear punctual speeds that would allow the line if it were to move uniformly in translation to describe the same space as it traversed when it moved in revolution (the segment) or rotation (the whole radius). The sense of "uniformly moved" that is implied in the expression "equally moved" is also contained in Autolycus' *De spera mota* (again see Chapter One, note 24).

Preliminary Lemma to Prop. I.1 (Tradition I, lines 28–79; Tradition II, lines 28–123). See Figs. I.1a(A) and I.1b. This lemma holds that

circle *OF* − circle *OC*
  = (radius *OF* − radius *OC*) · (½ circum. of *OF* + ½ circum. of *OC*).

I summarize here the proof as given in Tradition I, though that of Tradition II is essentially the same.

(1) Let line *RL* = line *OF* and let line *LN* = circum. of circle *OF*.

(2) Hence circle *OF* = triangle *RLN*, by Archimedes, *On the Measurement of the Circle,* Prop. 1.

(3) Let line *SL* = line *CF* [and let line *SQ* be parallel to *LN*]. Bisect *QN* so that *ON* = *OQ*, and draw *MP* [through *O*] to be parallel to *SL*.

(4) Therefore, since triangle *RLN* is similar to triangle *RSQ*, hence *LR* / *SR* = *LN* / *SQ*.

(5) But *LR* / *SR* = radius *OF* / radius *OC* = circum. of *OF* / circum. of *OC*.

(6) Hence, from (4) and (5), together with (1), *SQ* will be equal to the circumference of *OC*, and so triangle *RSQ* = circle *OC*.

(7) Therefore, surface *SLNQ* = circle *OF* − circle *OC*.

(8) But triangle *OMN* is congruent to triangle *OPQ*, from (3).

(9) Therefore, surface *SLNQ* = surface *SLMP*.

(10) Since *LN* + *SQ* = circum. *OF* + circum. *OC* = *LM* + *SP*, and [since *LM* = *SP*, so *LM* = ½ (circum. *OF* + circum. *OC*). And *SL* = *CF*, from

(3)]. Thus surface $SLMP = CF \cdot \frac{1}{2}$ (circum. OF + circum. OC) = circle OF − circle OC. Q.E.D.

This lemma is like Proposition IV of the *Liber de curvis superficiebus,* which concerns the difference between the curved surfaces of two unequal but similar cones, and perhaps Gerard was influenced by the earlier tract. It is of interest that in connection with Gerard's statement that "This same thing (i.e. the lemma) could be proved in another way" (see Tradition I, lines 77–78), the scribe of MS *O* adds in the margin "as is evident in the end of the comment [i.e. proof] on the fourth [proposition] of the *On Cones* [i.e. the *Liber de curvis superficiebus*]" (see variant to lines 77–78). The reference is to lines 30–37 of Proposition IV of the *Liber de curvis superficiebus* (see Volume One, p. 468).

Proof of the first part of Proposition I.1 (Tradition I, lines 124–80; Tradition II, lines 124–80). He is now prepared to prove that the segment *CF* is moved equally as its middle point. My summary follows the text in Tradition I closely, but there is no substantial difference in the proof given in Tradition II.

(1) *SL* moves through surface *SLMP* in the same time that *CF* moves through the difference between circles *OF* and *OC*. Hence *SL* and *CF* are moved equally since they traverse equal spaces, by the preceding lemma. This is confirmed *per impossibile.*

(2) If *SL* does not move equally as *CF*, it is moved either more or less than *CF*.

(3) But it can be shown that it is not moved more than *CF*. For if so, and if we assume a segment equal to *CF* but taken so much farther out from the center that it would move equally as *SL*, then because it is farther removed from the center it would describe more space than *SL* in the same time and so in fact it would be moved more than *SL* and not equally as *SL* as was hypothesized.

(4) A similar contradiction ensues if we hypothesize that it is moved less than *SL* and take a segment equal to *CF* that is closer to the center.

(5) And so it is clear that *SL* and *CF* are moved equally.

(6) But *SL*, moving uniformly in translation, is moved equally as any point of it (that is to say, each point of *SL* is moved with the same punctual speed). Hence *SL* is moved equally as its middle point, i.e., it has a *Vm* equal to the speed of its middle point.

(7) But the middle point of *SL* is moved equally as the middle point of *CF*, for these points described equal lines in equal times. This can be proved in the same way that it was proved in the proof of the lemma that *SQ* is equal to the circumference of circle *OC*.

(8) But the lines *SL* and *CF* are moved equally, from (5).

(9) And so *CF* is moved equally as its middle point, i.e., its *Vm* is equal to the speed of its middle point. Q.E.D.

Gerard then remarks that the same demonstration applies to any other segment of the radius that is not terminated at the center.

Proof of the second part of Proposition I.1 in Tradition I (lines 181–246 and Figs. I.1a[A] and I.1b). Gerard then proceeds to the proof of the second part of the proposition, which holds that the whole radius is moved equally as its middle point.

(1) *RL* is moved equally as *OF*. For, if not, it is moved more or less.

(2) If *RL* is moved more than *OF*, let us assume a line *DF* not terminated at the center that it is moved equally as *RL*, and we assume a line *XL* (on *RL*) that is equal to *DF*.

(3) Now *RL* and *XL* are equally moved because all points of *RL* (including those of *XL*) are moved at the same punctual speed.

(4) But it can be shown that *DF* is moved more than *XL* since it would traverse more space in describing the difference between the circles *OF* and *OD*. Hence *DF* is also moved more than *RL* and not equally as it, as was hypothesized. The detailed proof of this is confusing and prolix.

But Gerard was perhaps somewhat dissatisfied with this part of the proof, for he suggested (without detailing) another proof. Let me make his suggestion more specific. If we say that *RL* is moved more than *OF* rather than equally as *OF*, let us assume as in the proof of the first part of the proposition, and on the authority of Postulate 1, that *RL* is moved equally as a segment equal to *OF* or *RL* that is not terminated at the center, say segment *DE*, farther from the center. The first part of the proposition, already proved, would then be pertinent and it would be evident that in fact that segment *DE* would traverse more space than *RL* and so would not be moved equally as *RL*, as was hypothesized.

(5) A similar refutation follows if we assume that *RL* is moved less than *OF*.

(6) Therefore, lines *RL* and *OF* are equally moved.

(7) But *RL* is moved equally as its middle point, i.e. its *Vm* is equal to the speed of any point of it and hence of its middle point.

(8) And point *C*, the midpoint of *OF*, is moved equally as the middle point of *RL*, for they traverse equal lines (that is, the circumference at *C* is equal to line *SZ*, which can be proved as in the first part of the proposition).

(9) But from (6) lines *OF* and *RL* are equally moved.

(10) Hence, *OF* is moved equally as its middle point, i.e., its *Vm* is equal to the speed of its middle point. Q.E.D.

First proof of the second part of Proposition I.1 in Tradition II (lines 181–276 and Figs. I.1a [C and D]). It was perhaps because of the confusion present in the proof given in Tradition I that the author of Tradition II decided to give a rather different indirect proof.

(1) Radius *OF* is either moved equally as its middle point or it is moved more or less. If it is more, let it be hypothesized that it is moved equally as some other point of the radius. But by the first postulate that other point will be a point farther from the center than the middle point *C*. We are able to assume this because of the continually increasing speeds of points of the

radius as we move towards the circumference. Let the point beyond C that satisfies the equality be point E'.

(2) Since $OC = CF$, then $OE' > E'F$. And $OE' = E'F + 2\ CE'$, since $CF - CE' = OC - CE' = E'F$.

(3) Then, if we start from the center, let OE' be cut so that a segment equal to $2\ CE'$ remains toward the center and a line equal to $E'F$ is coterminal with it. Let the first cut (equal to $2\ CE'$) be OA and the second cut (equal to $E'F$) be AE'.

(4) Hence $AE' = E'F$, and so E' is the middle point of AF, and so, by the first part of the proposition already proved, segment AF is moved equally [i.e., is made uniform by] the speed of point E'.

(5) But OF has been hypothesized to be moved equally as point E'.

(6) Therefore AF and OF are equally moved, which contradicts the first postulate, or so the author of Tradition II believes.

(7) Hence OF is not moved equally as a point farther from the center than the middle point C.

(8) A similar refutation is presented if it is hypothesized that OF is moved equally as a slower point nearer the center than point C, say point D' (see Fig. I.1a[D]). I need not detail the rather confused argument here, except to note that it results in showing that radius OF and segment BG would each be moved equally as point D', which is again contrary to the first postulate according to the author's belief.

(9) And so we conclude that radius OF is moved equally as its middle point C, i.e., the speed of point C is the Vm of radius OF. Q.E.D.

The second proof of the second part of Proposition I.1 in Tradition II (lines 277–300 and Fig. I.1a[D]). In addition to the indirect proof already outlined, the author of Tradition II presents a direct proof that the radius is moved equally as its middle point.

(1) With straight lines FH and OL each equal to the circumference of circle OF, and with these lines bisected respectively at K and N, it is evident [from Archimedes' *On the Measurement of the Circle*, Prop. 1] that circle OF is equal to rectangle $ONKF$.

(2) When NK is moved in translation and OF is moved in rotation, they traverse equal spaces, and so are equally moved, which, the author adds, can be proved *per impossibile,* as before.

(3) But NK is moved equally as its middle point (since all of its points are moved with the same punctual speed) and that middle point is moved equally as point C, the middle point of radius OF.

(4) Therefore, from (2), OF is moved equally as its middle point C. Q.E.D.

The similarity of this proof to the proof of the first part of the proposition is evident.

The Corollary to Proposition I.1 (Tradition I, lines 301–19 and Fig. I.1a[A]; Tradition II, lines 301–28 and Fig. I.1a[D]). We are to prove that Vm of radius OF / Vm of radius OC = radius OF / radius OC. This is easily proved by proportions. The circumferences are proportional to the radii and the *Vms* are proportional to the circumferences. Hence the radii are as the *Vms*.

Before leaving Proposition I.1 I should remind the reader that it was mentioned by Bradwardine, only to be refuted.[12] Bradwardine would rather measure the rotating line by the speed of its most rapidly moving point. Clearly he had a different objective than did Gerard. Bradwardine was not really seeking a uniform-making speed, as was Gerard. Nor was he interested in comparing motions of translation with those of rotation. Rather he had in mind the astronomical problem of rotating spheres and for this reason was only interested in arcal motions on the surfaces of the spheres. Still, though Bradwardine rejects Gerard's first conclusion, it is evident, as I have said before, that his discussion of kinematics was much influenced by Gerard's earlier treatment. Hence it is not surprising to find that Themon Judei, whose work was quite dependent on that of Bradwardine and the works of other schoolmen of Merton College, notes in his discussion of Bradwardine's conclusion the contrary view of the author of the *De proportione motuum et motorum (! magnitudinum)*,[13] which, as we have repeatedly said, was in fact the *Liber de motu* of Gerard of Brussels.

Finally, in connection with Proposition I.1 of the *Liber de motu,* I once more remark that this proposition may have been influential in the formation of the Merton College Rule of uniform acceleration, i.e. $Vm = \frac{1}{2}(V_f - V_0)$, where V_f is the final speed and V_0 is the initial speed. For the fourteenth-century kinematicists were wont to hold that motion (i.e. speed) could vary either according to space (that in the parts of the magnitude in motion) or according to time. Gerard's proposition gave those later kinematicists a rule for finding the mean speed when the curvilinear speeds were continually and uniformly varying in space. It would not be surprising if the later authors then saw that a similar rule held if the speed were continuously and uniformly varying according to time. I shall not pursue this analogy further, but merely cite my earlier account of the development of the Merton Rule.[14]

---

[12] *Ibid.,* p. 128: "Ista autem positio videtur in aliquo contraria rationi. Nam secundum eam quaelibet pars semidiametri circuli circumducti non terminata ad centrum, et etiam tota semidiametri, moverentur (! movetur) aequaliter suo medio puncto (ut primi huius conclusio prima dicit) et, per consequens, tardius suo puncto extremo." Bradwardine virtually repeats Gerard's Corollary to Proposition I.1, merely expanding it to include that the speeds of rotating radii are proportional to the diameters as well as radii (*ibid.,* p. 130): "Omnium duorum diametrorum seu semidiametrorum eodem tempore uniformiter circulos describentium, proportio velocitatum est tanquam proportio diametrorum seu semidiametrorum illorum." Of course, the speed or *Vm* of the rotating radius for Bradwardine was the speed of the fastest moving point, namely the speed of the point farthest from the center instead of the speed of the middle point as Gerard had held.

[13] H. Hugonnard-Roche, *L'Oeuvre astronomique de Thémon Juif maître parisien du XIVe siècle* (Paris, 1973), p. 353: "Sed tamen contra istam instantiam iam factam faciliter se iuvarent adversarii capto modo loquendi autoris in *De proportione motuum et motorum,* conclusione sua prima."

[14] Clagett, *The Science of Mechanics in the Middle Ages,* pp. 186, 216, 221–22, 261–62.

Proposition I.2

Enunciation of Proposition I.2 (lines 1–5). The first part holds that any segment of a generator that describes the [lateral] surface of a [right circular] cone is moved equally as its middle point, i.e., the segment is moved uniformly by the speed of its middle point, or in the terminology I have adopted, its *Vm* is the speed of its middle point. The expression for generator used by Gerard is the common medieval one employed by the author of the *Liber de curvis superficiebus,* i.e. hypotenuse, and I shall follow Gerard throughout by calling it the "hypotenuse." It is easy to see how it arose when we realize that the cone is one that is generated by a right triangle. Thus it is the hypotenuse of the triangle that generates the surface and so becomes the hypotenuse of the cone. Similarly, I shall follow Gerard throughout in calling the lateral surface of the cone, its "curved surface." The second part of the proposition holds that the whole hypotenuse is moved equally as its middle point, i.e., the *Vm* of the hypotenuse is the speed of its middle point. The structure of enunciation and proof is like that of Proposition I.1.

Note that just as in the first proposition a preliminary lemma is proved: the difference between the curved surfaces of right cones is equal to the product of the difference between their hypotenuses and one half the sum of the circumferences of their bases, a lemma equivalent to Proposition IV of the *Liber de curvis superficiebus* (see Volume One, p. 466).

Proof of the Lemma for Proposition I.2 (lines 6–25) and Figs. I.1a and I.2).

(1) Construct a right triangle *RLN* such that *RL* = *BH* and *LN* = circum. of the base of cone *OBH*.

(2) Hence triangle *RLN* = surf. of cone *OBH*, by Prop. I of the *De piramidibus* (i.e. the *Liber de curvis superficiebus*).

(3) Let *RS* = *KH*. Then tri. *RSQ* = surf. of cone *IKH* because *SQ* is equal to the circumference of the base of cone *IKH*, which Gerard shows easily by similar triangles.

(4) Therefore surf. *SLNQ* = surf. of cone *OBH* − surf. of cone *IKH*.

(5) But, as in the first proposition, surf. *SLNQ* = surf. *SLMP*, and *SLMP* = *SL* · *LM*, where *SL* = hyp. *BH* − hyp. *KH* and where *LM* = ½ (circum. of base of cone *OBH* + circum. of base of cone *IKH*).

(6) Therefore, by (4) and (5), surf. cone *OBH* − surf. cone *IKH* = (hyp. *BH* − hyp. *KH*)· ½ (circum. base of cone *OBH* + circum. base of cone *IKH*). Q.E.D.

Proof of Proposition I.2 (lines 26–52 and the same figures).

(1) *SL*, moving in translation through surface *SLMP*, is moved equally as segment *BK*, moving in revolution about its axis, for these lines describe equal spaces.

(2) This may be confirmed by indirect reasoning like that employed in the proof of the first part of Proposition I.1. That is, *SL* is either moved equally as *BK* or it is moved more or less. If it is moved more, let there be

taken a segment equal to *BK* of the hypotenuse of a cone whose base circle is just so much greater than circle *OB* that the new segment equal to *BK* will be moved equally as *SL*. But this is impossible to effect, for the base circles of the truncated cone whose surface is described by the new segment are greater than the circles of the truncated cone whose surface is described by *BK*. Hence the product of the new segment and one half its circumferences is greater than the product of *BK* and one half of its circumferences. Hence, in fact, *SL* will not be moved more than *BK*. A similar refutation follows if we assume that *SL* is moved less than *BK*. Hence the two lines are equally moved.

(3) Since *SL* is moved equally as any of its points, it is moved equally as its middle point, i.e. its *Vm* is the speed of its middle point.

(4) But the middle point of *BK* is moved equally as the middle point of *SL*, for those points traverse equal lines.

(5) Since, by (2), *SL* and *BK* are equally moved, hence *SL* is moved equally as its middle point, i.e., its *Vm* is the speed of its middle point. Q.E.D.

Gerard then concludes the proposition by saying that the second part of the proposition, which holds that the whole hypotenuse *BH* is moved equally as its middle point, can be demonstrated by a double proof similar to the double proof used to prove that the whole radius is moved equally as its middle point in Proposition I.1.

An imaginative device that would show the equivalence of the first two propositions may be proposed, though Gerard does not propose it. Suppose we imagine that the altitude of the right cone shrinks until it disappears and its vertex becomes the center of the base. In this case the hypotenuse has now become the radius of the base. Then we could immediately apply the first proposition since we have reduced the revolving hypotenuse to the case of the rotating radius.

Corollary to Proposition I.2 (lines 53–75 and Fig. I.2). The corollary holds that all hypotenuses of right cones with equal bases are moved equally, i.e., the *Vm* of each of such hypotenuses is the same. The corollary is simply proved in two different ways by similar triangles. Thus the proofs demonstrate that if we take any two cones *OBH* and *OBF*, the speed of point *K*, which makes uniform the motion of hypotenuse *BH*, is equal to the speed of point *G*, which makes uniform the motion of hypotenuse *BF*.

Proposition I.3

Enunciation of Proposition I.3 (lines 1–5). Gerard now extends his technique to the perimeter of a regular polygon [of 4n sides] that rotates about a diagonal to describe a polygonal body. The objective of this proposition is to find the *Vm* of the rotating perimeter, that is, the speed that would allow a straight line equal to the perimeter to move in translation and describe the same space as the perimeter in rotation.

The corollary notes that if the polygon is inscribed and has more sides [than another regularly inscribed polygon], it (the polygon of more sides) is moved more. But if the polygon is circumscribed and has more sides, it is moved less.

Before analyzing the proof, I should note in passing that the regular polygon employed in Gerard's proofs (though not so specified in the enunciations) is always a polygon of 4n sides, while the polygons employed by Euclid in Propositions XII.16–XII.18 of the *Elements* are simply called polygons with an even number of sides. The same is true of the polygons used in Propositions I.21 and I.22 of Archimedes' *On the Sphere and the Cylinder*. But in Propositions I.23–I.34 of that work Archimedes specifies polygons of 4n sides. Similarly in the *Liber de curvis superficiebus* the polygon most often used was the polygon of 4n sides, though in Proposition V a special proof is given for the case where the number of sides in the semipolygon is an odd number (see Volume One, p. 476 and see also Proposition VII [*ibid.*, pp. 495, 547–77]).

I am sure that the reason Gerard limited himself to the polygon of 4n sides was that in the case of each proposition where the polygon played a role, Gerard could confine himself to studying in detail the conditions in a single quarter and then noting that the treatment for the other quarters was the same. Furthermore, in the case of polygons of 4n sides the combined surface of the polygonal body would be composed entirely out of the surfaces of cones (whether truncated or full), and similarly the body would be composed of truncated and complete cones. If the semipolygons were of an odd number of sides, one would have to consider that one of the surfaces comprising the surface of the polygonal body would be the surface of a cylinder and an additional argument would have to be made, as was noted in Proposition V of the *Liber de curvis superficiebus*. It was simply more economical for Gerard to confine his cases to polygons of 4n sides.

Proof of Proposition I.3 (lines 6–55 and Fig. I.3a).

(1) *CG* and *M'G* are sides of a square rotating about diagonal *CM'*.

(2) The *Vm* of *CG* is the speed of its middle point *R*, by Proposition I.2; and similarly the *Vm* of side *M'G* is that of its middle point *Y*.

(3) The speeds of *R* and *Y* are equal to each other, and thus the two sides taken together are moved equally as either *R* or *Y*, i.e., the *Vm* of *CG* + *M'G* is that of *R* or *Y*.

(4) Similarly the other two sides together are moved equally as *R* or *Y*.

(5) Therefore the whole perimeter is moved equally as *R* or *Y*, i.e., the *Vm* of the whole perimeter is that of *R* (or *Y*). [This simply means that a straight line equal to the perimeter of the square traverses in translation a space equal to the space traversed by the perimeter in rotation, and since each of the points of the straight line has the punctual speed of point *R* (or point *Y*), the *Vm* of the perimeter is equal to the speed of *R* (or *Y*).]

(6) Proceed to the case of the octagon of sides *CE*, *EG*, etc. rotating about *CM'*. Let straight lines be drawn from point *O* to points *E* and *G*, and let

perpendiculars be drawn from point O to each of the sides, perpendiculars that meet those sides in points I and Q. Then it can be shown that points H and S, the intersections of OI and OQ with CG, are together moved equally as middle point R of the straight line connecting H and S (that R is indeed the middle point of line HS is demonstrated in lines 40–55). [When Gerard says that points H and S together are moved equally as point R, he means that if instead of moving with their present speeds, which are different, they are each moved with the speed equal to that of R, then together they would traverse as much space as they now do.]

(7) Similarly points I and Q together can be considered as being moved equally by the middle point P of the line connecting them.

(8) But the sides of the octagon CE and EG are moved equally as their middle points I and Q, by Proposition I.2.

(9) Therefore, by (7) and (8), the sides of CE and EG together are moved equally as point P. [This means that a straight line equal to $CE + EG$ which is moved uniformly in translation, i.e., every point of it being moved with the speed of P, traverses the same space as do the two sides moving in rotation about CM'.]

(10) Similarly it can be shown that the other two sides of half of the octagon when taken together are moved uniformly by the speed of point Z, equal to the speed of point P, and further that all four sides of half of the octagon when taken together are moved equally by the speed of U, equal to the speed of P.

(11) The same holds for the other four sides of the octagon in rotation. Thus we may conclude that the whole perimeter of the octagon is moved equally as U (or P). [That is, a straight line equal to the perimeter and moving in translation uniformly with each point moving with the speed of U (or its equal, that of P) will traverse the same space as the perimeter moving in rotation about axis CM'. Thus the speed of point U (or P) is the desired Vm of the perimeter of the octagon.]

(12) By a similar procedure it is shown that the punctual speed of M (or of its equal, that of X) is the desired punctual speed or Vm that produces uniformity for a rotating polygon of sixteen sides, which, adopting the Latin terminology, we may call a sedecagon.

From these three examples of square, octagon, and sedecagon, we can, although Gerard does not, state his general procedure for finding the punctual speed that makes uniform the motion of rotation of any regular polygon of 4n sides. In any given quadrant of the circle in which the regular polygon is inscribed, connect the midpoints of each pair of adjacent sides. [In the case of the square there is only one side in the quadrant and hence its midpoint is the point whose speed makes uniform the motion of the perimeter of the square, i.e., whose speed is the Vm of the square.] Then, if possible, connect the midpoints of each pair of adjacent lines which themselves connect the midpoints of each pair of adjacent sides. [In the octagon there will be only one line connecting the midpoints of the pair of adjacent lines that will themselves connect the midpoints of the two sides of the octagon in the quadrant. And thus the midpoint of that single line is the desired point whose speed makes uniform the motion of the perimeter of the octagon, i.e. whose speed is the *Vm* of the octagon.] Proceed thus until there is one final connecting line in the quadrant [for example, line *LN* in the sedecagon], and the speed of its midpoint is the desired *Vm* of the perimeter of the regular polygon under investigation. [In the sedecagon the desired point was point *M*, the midpoint of line *LN*.]

First part of the Corollary to Proposition I.3 (lines 56–71 and Fig. I.3a). We are to prove first that the greater the number of sides of the inscribed regular polygon, the greater is the *Vm* of its perimeter. The proof details only the comparison of the *Vms* of the perimeters of octagon and square.

(1) Speed of point *P* / speed of point *R* = *OP* / *OR*, since speed of *P* / speed of *R* = *DP* / *RB*, by the corollary to Proposition I.1, and *DP* / *RB* = *OP* / *OR*, by similar triangles.

(2) But the speed of *R* = speed of *V*, since *VR* is parallel to the axis *CM'* and hence all points on *VR* have the same speed.

(3) But the speed of *P* > speed of *V* [by the first postulate].

(4) Therefore, speed of *P* > speed of *R*, by (2) and (3).

(5) But the speed of *P* is the *Vm* of the octagon and the speed of *R* is the *Vm* of the square, as proved in the main part of Proposition I.3. And so, *Vm* of octagon > *Vm* of square, and the one is greater than the other by the ratio of *OP* to *OR*.

(6) "By a similar demonstration it will be demonstrated that the perimeter of the sedecagon is moved more than the perimeter of the octagon in the ratio of line *OM* to line *OP*. And thus is evident the first part of the corollary. But (*!* for) the diligent reader should realize that he knows how suitably to adapt this kind of demonstration to other kinds of [regular] polygons."

Second part of the Corollary to Proposition I.3 (lines 72–87 and Fig. I.3b).

Now we are to prove that the fewer the number of sides of the circumscribed polygon, the greater is its *Vm*. Again the proof is detailed only in the case of a circumscribed square compared to a circumscribed octagon.

(1) The *Vm* of the circumscribed square is the speed of point *N* and the *Vm* of the circumscribed octagon is the speed of point *Q*, which are proved as in the main part of the proposition.

(2) But speed of point *N* / speed of point *Q* = *ON* / *OQ*, as in the first part of the corollary.

(3) But *ON* is greater than *OQ*, and so the speed of point *N* is greater than the speed of point *Q* by the ratio of *ON* to *OQ*. Hence, the *Vm* of the perimeter of the square is greater than the *Vm* of the perimeter of the octagon by the ratio of *ON* to *OQ*. And, Gerard concludes, "you will find the same thing in regard to other [regular] polygons."

Proposition I.4

Enunciation of Proposition I.4 (lines 1–5). If we put this proposition in a symbolic form, we can express it as follows:

$$(Vm \text{ of } Piq - Vm \text{ of } Pir) = (Vm \text{ of } Pcr - Vm \text{ of } Piq),$$

where *Piq* is an inscribed regular polygon of 8n sides, *Pir* is an inscribed regular polygon of 4n sides, and *Pcr* is a circumscribed regular polygon of 4n sides, the polygons being inscribed in or circumscribed about the same circle and all rotating about the same axis.

Proof of Proposition I.4 (lines 6–32 and Fig. I.4). The reader will notice that the proof embraces only the case where the polygons are an inscribed octagon, an inscribed square, and a circumscribed square.

(1) the *Vm* of the perimeter of a circumscribed square with sides *AB* and *BC* is the speed of point *G* (or its equal, that of point *V*), by Proposition I.3.

(2) The *Vm* of the inscribed square with side *DH* is the speed of point *P* (or its equal, that of point *N*), again by Proposition I.3.

(3) The *Vm* of the inscribed octagon with sides *DG*, *GH*, *HV*, etc. is the speed of point *L* (or its equal, that of point *R*), once more by Proposition I.3.

(4) Line *OG* bisects lines *AB*, *DH*, and *EF* [at points *G*, *P*, and *L*].

(5) Triangle *PGH* is similar to triangle *LGF*, for angles *P* and *L* are right angles and angle *G* is common.

(6) Hence *GH* / *GF* = *GP* / *GL*.

(7) But *GH* = 2 *GF*, since *GH* has been bisected at *F*; and so, from (6), *GP* = 2 *GL*; and accordingly *GL* = *LP*.

(8) Also, tri. *PGK* is similar to tri. *LGI*, for angles *K* and *I* are right angles and angle *G* is common.

(9) Hence *GP* / *GL* = *GK* / *GI*.

(10) But, from (7), *GP* = 2 *GL*; and so *GK* = 2 *GI*; and accordingly *GI* = *IK*.

(11) Hence, speed of point *G* − speed of point *I* = speed of point *I* − speed of point *K*.

(12) But the speeds of points *G*, and *I*, and *K* are respectively equal to the speeds of points *G*, *L*, and *P*, for the lines of which they are points are moved equally in all their parts and points.

(13) Therefore, speed of point *G* − speed of point *L* = speed of point *L* − speed of point *P*.

(14) But, by steps (1)–(3) the speeds of points *G*, *L*, and *P* are the desired *Vms* of the polygons. Hence the proposition follows for this case.

I have already mentioned in Chapter One above that Jordanus de Nemore was also interested in the relationships between inscribed and circumscribed polygons, though of course in the relationships of their sides and areas rather than of their motions (see Part II below, Props. 44, 45 and 46, and Part III, Props. IV.8, IV.9, IV.11, and IV.15).

Book II

Postulates

Postulates 1–6 (lines 1–13). In the first book Gerard was concerned with the finding of punctual speeds by which the varying motions of lines in rotation could be made uniform. Now in the second he turns to finding such speeds that would make uniform the motions of surfaces in rotation. Again it is evident that the desired punctual speed or *Vm* of a rotating surface is a speed which when applied to all points of the surface so that the surface moves uniformly in translation would allow it to traverse the same space as when it was rotated.

The first four postulates relate the motions of squares to the motions of their sides: the square whose sides are moved more or less is moved more or less, while the square whose sides are not moved more or less is not moved more or less. The fifth and sixth postulates hold that if surfaces are equal and all their line elements taken in the same ratio are equal, the one none of whose lines so taken is moved more is not moved more; the one none of whose lines so taken is moved less is not moved less. The "lines" that Gerard refers to are line elements, the aggregate of which comprises the surface in question, whether they are the circular line elements aggregating the circle or rectilinear elements aggregating a rectilinear figure. The comparison of the magnitudes and motions of such elements reminds us of Archimedes' technique in *On the Method*. But, as I have said earlier, Gerard could not have had access to that rare tract, and his route to the comparison of elements appears to have been through an extension of Proposition V.12 of the *Elements* to infinite sets (see the text above note 5 of this chapter). Note that the postulates of Book II are similar to those of Book I, except that they refer to surfaces in motion while the earlier ones referred to lines in motion. Again note the negative form of Postulates 5 and 6. Such a form is necessary for the proof *per impossibile* of the equality of the motions of surfaces, just as the similar form of Postulates 6 and 7 of Book I were necessary for the proof *per impossibile* of the equality of the motions of lines.

Proposition II.1

Enunciation of Proposition II.1 (lines 15–18). This proposition holds that an equinoctial circle is moved in 4/3 ratio to its diameter, i.e., the uniform-making speed or *Vm* of an equinoctial circle that is rotating on itself (*in se*, as Bradwardine was later to say; see note 21 below) about its center is to the uniform-making speed or *Vm* of the diameter rotating about the center as 4 is to 3. The key to the proof given by Gerard is his ingenious conception that the motion of the equinoctial circle rotating about its center is equivalent to the motion of a right triangle equal to the circle and rotating about an external axis drawn parallel to the altitude of the triangle and passing through the end point of the base of the triangle (in Fig. II.1b the triangle *BDF* rotating about line *BG*). This conception has not been properly understood either by me in the first edition of the *Liber de motu* or by Zubov in his perceptive analysis of the treatise, and I shall discuss it at length later.[15] The corollary to this proposition asserts that the ratio of equinoctial circles is the square of the ratio of their motions, i.e., their *Vms*.

[15] See note 16 below.

Proof of Proposition II.1 (lines 19–136 and Figs. II.1a and II.1b).

(1) Square *BDFH* when it revolves about an external axis *AI* will sweep out a volume equal to that swept out by an equal square *OLMN* when it moves uniformly in translation so that all the lines of square *OLMN* are moved equally as line *CG* and hence so that all the points of the square are moving with the punctual speed of point *C* (when *BDFH* is revolving). Thus the speed of point *C* is the *Vm* of square *BDFH*. This is confirmed by an indirect proof that develops contradictions with the postulates. While it is not necessary to repeat the whole proof here, we should observe that Gerard believed not only that lines *BD* and *FH* are moved equally as corresponding lines *OL* and *MN* (for each of the four lines has a *Vm* equal to the speed of point *C* by Proposition I.1) but also that in the case of any pair of horizontal lines symmetrically placed with respect to line *CG* (e.g., lines *DF* and *BH*) the sum of their motions will be equal to the sum of the motions of the corresponding lines (*LM* and *ON*) in the square moving in translation. What is true for the comparison of any pairs is true for comparison of all pairs of line elements aggregating the squares. Hence the squares are equally moved.

(2) Furthermore, if square *BDFH* is rotated about one of its sides (say *BH*) instead of about an external axis, the squares are still equally moved and the *Vm* of *BDFH* is the speed of point *C*. This move from a square revolving about an external axis to one rotating about one of its sides is similar to the move in Proposition I.1 from a segment of a rotating radius not terminated at the center to the full radius, and also to the move in Proposition I.2 from the segment of the hypotenuse of a cone to the whole hypotenuse.

(3) Since the *Vm* of square *CDEK* is the motion of point *P* and the *Vm* of square *KEFG* is also the motion of *P*, then the *Vm* of the rectangle *CDFG* is still the motion of point *P*. Similarly the *Vm* of the rectangle *BCGH* is the motion of the midpoint of line *BC*. These statements can be proved *per impossibile* in the manner of the proofs given for (1) and (2).

(4) Hence the *Vm* of *BDFH* = 2 *Vm* of *BCGH*.

(5) But since rectangle *CDFG* is moved equally as point *P* and point *P* is moved in 3/2 ratio to point *C*, therefore *Vm* of *CDFG* / *Vm* of *BCGH* = $(2/1) \cdot (3/2) = 3/1$. This is easily confirmed by comparing the cylindrical spaces described by *CDFG* and *BCGH*, which are shown to be in a ratio of 3/1.

(6) Now let us consider triangles *BDF* and *BFH*. The volumes they describe in rotation about *BH* are shown to be as 2 is to 1, since the upper triangle describes ⅔ of the whole cylinder described by *BDFH* and the lower triangle describes ⅓ of that cylinder. And this also is the ratio of the *Vm*s of these triangles.

(7) Since the total space described by rectangles *CDFG* and *BCGH* together is equal to the total space described by the triangles *BDF* and *BFH* together, and rectangle *CDFG* describes ¾ of that space, triangle *BDF* describes ⅔ of it, rectangle *BCGH* describes ¼ of it, and triangle *BFH* describes ⅓ of it, so

Vm of *CDFG* / *Vm* of *BDF* = (3/4) / (2/3) = 9/8, and *Vm* of *BFH* / *Vm* of *BCGH* = (1/3) / (1/4) = 4/3.

(8) Now from Proposition I.1 the radius *BD* is moved equally as point *C*, its midpoint. So *Vm* of *CDFG* / *Vm* of *BD* = 3/2, while, from (7), *Vm* of *CDFG* / *Vm* of *BDF* = 9/8.

(9) Therefore *Vm* of *BDF* / *Vm* of *BD* = (3/2) / (9/8) = 4/3.

(10) Turning to Fig. II.1b, Gerard shows that for any triangle *BDF* whose base is the rotating radius *BD* no matter what is the length of side *BF* the proportion in (9) holds: *Vm* of *BDF* / *Vm* of *BD* = 4/3. This is because the same ratios between the motions of the upper and lower rectangles and triangles hold as before and the rectangles together equal the triangles together.

(11) Then Gerard constructs a triangle *BDF* such that *BD* is equal to the radius of the equinoctial circle and whose side *DF* is equal to and is equally moved as the circumference of the circle (see Fig. II.1b). Similarly any line parallel to *DF* will be equal to and equally moved as the corresponding circular element of the equinoctial circle. Hence, he concludes, "the circle and the triangle are equal and are equally moved." That is to say, the *Vm* of triangle *BDF* is equal to the *Vm* of the equinoctial circle.

(12) But, since, from (9), *Vm* of triangle *BDF* / *Vm* of radius *BD* = 4/3, therefore *Vm* of equinoct. circle / *Vm* of radius *BD* = 4/3. But the *Vm* of the radius equals the *Vm* of the diameter, and so the proposition follows.

The point that requires some elaboration is point (11) that holds that the equinoctial circle is moved equally as the triangle. Now if it is mistakenly assumed, as I did in my first edition and as Zubov also did in his critique of my view, that the equinoctial circle was rotating about its diameter rather than rotating on itself about its center, then there is no way in which the triangle *BDF* and the equinoctial circle of radius *BD* can be said to be equally moved.[16] A moment's reflection will show that the motion of the triangle is not line for line equal to the motion of the circle when the circle is rotating about its diameter, for the circle would sweep out a sphere equal to $\frac{4}{3} \pi r^3$, while the triangle sweeps out a volume equal to $\frac{2}{3}$ of the cylinder with πr^2 as the base and $2\pi r$ as the altitude, i.e. a volume equal to $\frac{4}{3} \pi^2 r^3$, as I said in my first edition (see note 16 again). But it is clear that Gerard did not

----

[16] This mistaken assumption that Gerard in this proposition conceives of the equinoctial circle as rotating about its diameter vitiates my discussion in the first edition of the *Liber de motu* (pp. 163–64) and in *The Science of Mechanics in the Middle Ages*, pp. 195–97. Zubov, "Ob 'Archimedovsky traditsii' " p. 254, declares that I have misunderstood the essence of the proposition, and that judgment is certainly correct. But, in fact, so has Zubov, for earlier (p. 249) he also makes the mistake of assuming that a great circle (and here he is talking about the equinoctial circle of Proposition II.1) is rotating about its diameter, and he goes on to say that the speed of that circle is 4/3 times the speed of the rotating radius, which is true for a circle rotating about its center but not for the circle rotating about its diameter. Hence Zubov's detailed criticisms of my position are themselves mistaken. I believe that it is only when we consider Gerard's imaginative device for equating the motion of the rotation of the equinoctial circle about its center with the rotation of the equivalent triangle (*BDF*) about axis *BG* that we may correctly understand his proof.

consider the equinoctial circle as rotating about its diameter but rather about its center. Thus each point on the circumference of the circle that rotates about its center traverses a line equal to the circumference, i.e., equal to $2\pi r$. Hence there are $2\pi r$ circumferences traversed on the circumferential line by all points of the circumference. These $2\pi r$ circumferences would be superimposed on the same line, and if we could somehow disengage them from the circumference on which they are all transcribed we would have a total space described by all the points of the circumference that would be equal to $4\pi^2 r^2$. The same thing would be true of all of the points on all the other circular elements of the equinoctial circle, so that if we could disengage all transcriptions of all of the points of all of the elements we would produce a volume equal to $\frac{4}{3} \pi^2 r^3$. But Gerard's rotating triangle BDF produces just such disengagements. Line DF in its revolution about BG accomplishes the transformation of the superimposed circumferences to produce a surface equal to $4\pi^2 r^2$ (where $BD = r$) and the summation of the surfaces produced by all the lines parallel to DF produces a solid equal to $\frac{4}{3} \pi^2 r^3$ rather than a surface consisting of the totality of circumferential elements assumed in the rotation of the circle on itself. With Gerard's view properly interpreted point (11) is confirmed, and the proposition follows in the proof.

That Gerard conceived of the equinoctial circle as rotating about its center instead of its diameter, the consequences of which I have outlined in the preceding paragraph, is confirmed by Proposition II.2, which, we shall see, makes use of Proposition II.1, and conceives of a cone rotating on itself about its axis as consisting of circular elements rotating about their centers lying on the axis. Furthermore we shall see that the curved surface of the cone when rotating on itself is essentially similar to a circle rotating about its center. If any further confirmation is needed, it comes from Corollary IV to Proposition II.5 where the rotation of an equinoctial circle about its center is distinguished from the rotation of a colure about its diameter (see my discussion of that corollary below).

One further comment concerning the proof of Proposition II.1 is in order before passing on to its corollary. This concerns Gerard's summation technique when he passes from the fact that any corresponding elements of the equinoctial circle and triangle BDF are equal and equally moved to the conclusion that the whole circle and the whole triangle are equal and equally moved. As I have said at the beginning of the chapter, in making these summations he appears to have extended Proposition V.12 of the *Elements* of Euclid to indefinitely large or infinite sets of line elements. Recall that Proposition V.12 holds that if $A / a = B / b = C / c = D / d \cdots$, then $(A + B + C + D + \cdots) / (a + b + c + d + \cdots) = A / a$. Thus if we say that the lines of the triangle (or their motions) are $A, B, C, D, \cdots$ *ad infinitum* and that the lines of the circle (or their motions) are $a, b, c, d, \cdots$ *ad infinitum,* then the summation of the lines of the triangle (or their motions), namely, $A + B + C + D + \cdots$, is related to the summation of the lines of the circle (or their motions), namely, $a + b + c + d + \cdots$, as A is related to a. But $A = a$. and so the summations are equal.

Corollary to Proposition II.1 (lines 137–52 and Fig. II.1b). This corollary asserts that circle / circle = $(Vm$ of circle / Vm of circle$)^2$.

(1) Assume point I whose speed is $\frac{4}{3}$ the speed of point C.

(2) Hence speed of $I = Vm$ of circle of radius BD, by the main part of Proposition II.1.

(3) Assume point L whose speed is $\frac{4}{3}$ the speed of point M.

(4) Hence speed of $L = Vm$ of circle of radius BC, by Proposition II.1.

(5) Speed of I / speed of $L = BI$ / BL.

(6) But BI / $BL = BC$ / BM, for BI / $BC = BL$ / BM.

(7) Vm of circle of radius BD / Vm of circle of radius $BC = BC$ / BM = radius BD / radius BC = diameter / diameter.

(8) But circle / circle = (diameter / diameter)^2.

(9) Therefore, circle / circle = $(Vm$ of circle / Vm of circle$)^2$. Q.E.D.

Gerard briefly notes that the same thing holds for squares, i.e., square / square = $(Vm$ of square / Vm of square$)^2$, and for [similar right] triangles, i.e., triangle / triangle = $(Vm$ of triangle / Vm of triangle$)^2$.

We may observe that Proposition II.1 and its corollary were cited by Bradwardine[17] and its corollary by Themon Judei.[18] Whether de Bouelles in his faulty formulation for the volume of a sphere was somehow influenced by Gerard's treatment of the rotation of the equinoctial circle cannot be determined.[19]

Proposition II.2

Enunciation of Proposition II.2 (lines 1–4). This proposition asserts that every curved surface of a [right] cone is moved [when rotating on itself] about its own axis in 4/3 ratio to its hypotenuse, i.e., its Vm is $\frac{4}{3}$ the Vm of its hypotenuse. The corollary adds that all the curved surfaces of [right] cones that have the same base are moved equally, i.e., the Vm of the curved surface of each such cone is the same.

Proof of Proposition II.2 (lines 5–42 and Fig. II.2). This proof is related to the proof of Proposition II.1 as the proof of Proposition I.2 is to the proof of Proposition I.1.

[17] *Ed. cit.,* p. 128: "Et tunc circulus aequinoctialis moveretur in sesquitertia proportione velocius suo diametero (et prima conclusio vult secundi) . . ." and p. 132: "Quorumlibet duorum circulorum eodem tempore uniformiter circumductorum, sive in seipsis motorum, sive spheras describentium, sive unius hoc modo et alterius reliquo, proportio est velocitatum in motibus proportio duplata."

[18] Hugonnard-Roche, *L'Oeuvre astronomique de Thémon Juif,* p. 345: "Hec enim satis videtur contraria conclusioni autoris in *De proportione motuum et motorum,* antiqui mathematici, ubi dicit: *proportio circulorum est proportio motuum duplicata,* que sic intelligitur quod proportio circulorum uniformiter circumductorum in eodem tempore est proportio motuum eorumdem circulorum duplicata que est ibi demonstrata." Unlike Bradwardine, Thémon does not specify that this corollary holds both for circles rotating on themselves and for circles rotating about their diameters, but presumably he meant this to be understood.

[19] Though there seems to be some general influence of Gerard's generative geometry on Charles de Bouelles, the latter's faulty treatment of the cubature of the sphere seems to have been uninfluenced by Gerard's specific propositions (see M. Clagett, *Archimedes in the Middle Ages,* Vol. 3 [Philadelphia, 1978], pp. 1180–96).

(1) Using the formulation of Proposition I of the *De piramidibus* (i.e. the *Liber de curvis superficiebus*), construct triangle *LNP* equal to the curved surface of cone *OAE*, i.e., by assuming *LN* = *AE* and *NP* = circum. of base of cone *OAE*.

(2) Then all of the lines of the triangle are equal to all the circular lines of the curved surface "taken in the same ratio" (i.e. all of the corresponding straight and circular lines of the two figures are equal).

(3) Let the curved surface of cone *OAE* move on itself as the cone rotates about its axis, and let line *NP* revolving about axis *LQ* be moved equally as hypotenuse *AE* rotating about axis *OE*, so that the speed of point *M* is equal to the speed of point *T*.

(4) Therefore triangle *LNP* is moved equally as the curved surface of cone *OAE*, "for the surfaces are equal and the lines taken in the same ratio are equal and are equally moved." This latter is true because "just as line *NP* is moved equally as the circumference of radius *OA* so line *MR* is moved equally as the circumference of radius *TV*. . . . And so the lines are moved equally as the circumferences and are equal to them. It is thus for [all the lines and circumferences] taken in the same ratio." It should be clear to the reader that the comparison of movements and the summation procedure used here is precisely like that used in Proposition II.1. For in that proposition we had a triangle (*BDF*) whose line elements corresponded to the circumferential elements of the equinoctial circle, while here we have the triangle *LNP* whose line elements correspond to the circumferential elements of the curved surface. In both cases the triangles are moving about similar axes and the circumferential elements are rotating about centers. The equality of the motions of triangle *LNP* and the curved surface of cone *OAE* is then confirmed by a simple proof *per impossibile*.

(5) But the *Vm* of triangle *LNP* / *Vm* of radius *LN* = 4/3, by Proposition II.1.

(6) Since the motion of triangle *LNP* is equal to the motion of the curved surface of cone *OAE* by (4) and, since the *Vm* of *LN* = the *Vm* of *AE* (because of the equality of the speeds of points *M* and *T*, which are the *Vm* of *LN* and the *Vm* of *AE* respectively), therefore the *Vm* of curved surface *OAE* / *Vm* of hypotenuse *AE* = 4/3. Q.E.D.

An imaginative device like the one I employed in discussing Proposition I.2 may also be used here to stress the similarity between Propositions II.2 and II.1. Suppose, as in Proposition I.2, we let the altitude of cone *OAE* decrease to zero so that the vertex of the cone coincides with the center of the base circle. Then in this case the curved surface of the cone becomes itself a circle and the hypotenuse becomes the radius of the circle. That circle would then be rotated about its center and would be a case of the equinoctial circle of Proposition II.1 and so the *Vm* of that circle (which was the curved surface) would be related to the *Vm* of the radius (which was the hypotenuse of the cone) as 4 is to 3.

Corollary to Proposition II.2 (lines 43–50 and Fig. II.2).

(1) Consider cone *OAC* on the same base as *OAE*. As in the preceding proof, *Vm* of curv. surf. cone *OAC* / *Vm* of hyp. *AC* = 4/3.

(2) But *Vm* of hyp. *AC* = *Vm* of hyp. *AE*, by the corollary to Proposition I.2.

(3) Therefore the *Vm* of curved surf. cone *OAC* = *Vm* of curv. surf. cone *OAE*, and the present corollary follows.

The corollary is also evident by an alternative reasoning:

(1) *Vm* of curv. surf. cone *OAE* / *Vm* of hyp. *AE* = 4/3, by the main part of Proposition II.2.

(2) *Vm* of hyp. *AE* = *Vm* of radius *OA*, by Propositions I.1 and I.2 together.

(3) *Vm* of circle of radius *OA* / *Vm* of radius *OA* = 4/3, by Proposition II.1.

(4) Therefore, *Vm* of curv. surf. cone *OAE* = *Vm* of circle of radius *OA*.

(5) Thus the *Vm* of the surface of any [right] cone is equal to the *Vm* of its base circle, [and so the *Vm* of the curved surface of each cone constructed on the same circle is the same].

Proposition II.3

Enunciation of Proposition II.3 (lines 1–5). Here Gerard tells us that the ratio [of the areas] of similar rotating polygons [of 4n sides] that describe polygonal bodies is equal to the square of the ratio of their motions, i.e. their *Vms*. In the corollary we are told that the ratio of the [composite] curved surfaces of the solids described by those polygons is equal to the square of the ratio of the *Vms* of those surfaces.

Proof of Proposition II.3 (lines 6–38 and Fig. II.3a).

(1) Since triangles *OCE* and *ONQ* are similar because of the equality of angles *O* and *O* and the equality of angles *C* and *N*, hence *Vm* of tri. *OCE* / *Vm* of tri. *ONQ* = *OC* / *ON* = *Vm* of *OC* / *Vm* of *ON*, by Proposition II.1. The last ratio in the equality, *Vm* of *OC* / *Vm* of *ON*, is superfluous for the proof.

(2) Now triangles *FDE* and *RPQ* are similar because of the equality of the exterior (and hence interior) angles at *F* and *R* and the equality of the angles at *D* and *P*.

(3) Therefore, *Vm* of tri. *FDE* / *Vm* of tr. *RPQ* = *FD* / *PR*, by a proof based on similar triangles and Proposition II.1 that I need not detail here.

(4) But *DF* / *PR* = *OC* / *ON*, again by similar triangles.

(5) Then, by (2) and (4), *Vm* of tri. *OCE* / *Vm* of tri. *ONQ* = *DF* / *PR*.

(6) Therefore, by (2) and (5), and the subtraction of ratios, *Vm* of surf. *OCDF* / *Vm* of *ONPR* = *DF* / *PR*, since surf. *OCDF* = tri. *OCE* − tri. *FDE*, and surf. *ONPR* = tri. *ONQ* − tri. *RPQ*.

(7) By a demonstration similar to that of steps (1)–(6), *Vm* of surf. *OABC* / *Vm* of surf. *OLMN* = *AB* / *LM* = *DF* / *PR*.

(8) Therefore, [by V.12 of the *Elements* of Euclid], *Vm* of semipolygon *OABCDF* / *Vm* of semipolygon *OLMNPR* = *DF* / *PR*.

(9) Therefore, [by the same proposition of Euclid], Vm of whole polygon / Vm of whole polygon = DF / PR = side of polygon / side of polygon.

(10) But area of polygon / area of polygon = (side / side)^2.

(11) Therefore, area of polygon / area of polygon = (Vm of polygon / Vm of polygon)^2. Q.E.D.

As I said earlier, Gerard appears in steps (8) and (9) of this proof to have applied Proposition V.12 of the *Elements* of Euclid, but this time to finite sets of magnitudes rather than to the indefinitely large sets present in the proof of Proposition II.1.

Corollary I to Proposition II.3 (lines 39–67 and Fig. II.3a). Gerard proves that the ratio of composite curved surfaces of bodies described by similar polygons [*of* 4n sides] is equal to the square of the ratio of the motions or *Vms* of those surfaces.

(1) Vm of curv. surf. cone OCE / Vm of curv. surf. cone GDE = OC / DG, by the corollary to Proposition II.2 [and the corollary to Proposition I.1].

(2) Vm of curv. surf. cone OCE / Vm of curv. surf. cone ONQ = OC / ON, by the same reasoning.

(3) Vm of curv. surf. cone GDE / Vm of curv. surf. cone SPQ = GD / SP, by the same reasoning.

(4) Curv. surf. cone GDE = curv. surf. cone FDE, and curv. surf. cone SPQ = curv. surf. cone RPQ, for in each case the conic figures differ only in their bases. Gerard calls the solids generated by the rotations of triangles FDE and RPQ cones, though their bases are not circles but rather the surfaces of conic caps. We can better call them conic figures. At any rate, it is obvious that their lateral surfaces are equal to the lateral surfaces of cones GDE and SPQ.

(5) Vm of curv. surf. cone FDE / Vm of curv. surf. cone RPQ = GD / SP = DF / PR.

(6) Vm of curv. surf. cone OCE / Vm of curv. surf. cone ONQ = DF / PR, by (2) and the fact that OC / ON = DF / PR.

(7) Therefore, by the subtraction of ratios, Vm of curv. surf. described by DC / Vm of curv. surf. described by NP = DF / PR.

(8) Also, Vm of curv. surf. cone GDF / Vm of curv. surf. cone SPR = DF / PR, by (3) and the fact that GD / SP = DF / PR from the similarity of the polygons.

(9) Hence, as in step (7), Vm of curv. surf. described by DF / Vm of curv. surf. described by PR = DF / PR.

(10) Therefore, [by Proposition V.12 of the *Elements*], Vm of the sum of the curv. surfs. described by DC and DF / Vm of the sum of the curv. surfs. described by NP and PR = DF / PR.

(11) Therefore, [by the same proposition of Euclid,] Vm of curv. surf. described by semipolygon / Vm of curv. surf. described by semipolygon = DF / PR.

(12) Similarly, Vm of curv. surf. described by whole polygon / Vm of curv. surf. described by whole polygon = DF / PR = side / side.

(13) But curv. surf. polyg. body / curved surf. polyg. body = (side / side)^2.

(14) Therefore, curv. surf. polyg. body / curv. surf. polyg. body = (Vm of curv. surf. polyg. body / Vm of curv. surf. polyg. body)^2. Q.E.D.

It is of some interest that Gerard mentions in connection with step (13): "Hoc alibi probavimus." From which we may infer that he composed another treatise, perhaps in the tradition of the *Liber de curvis superficiebus*. I say that perhaps it was in the tradition of the *Liber de curvis superficiebus* because Proposition *V* of that work (see Volume One, page 474) proves that the composite curved surface of such a polygonal body is equal to the product of (1) a side of the polygon describing the body and (2) the sum of the circumferences described by the angles of the polygon. Hence if S_1 and S_2 are the surfaces of two such similar polygonal bodies described by regular polygons P_1 and P_2, then S_1 / S_2 = (side of P_1 · circums. of P_1) / (side of P_2 · circums. of P_2). But it can be shown that circums. of P_1 / circums. of P_2 = side of P_1 / side of P_2. Hence it would follow that S_1 / S_2 = (side of P_1 / side of P_2)^2, as step (13) asserts.

Corollary II to Proposition II.3 (lines 68–89 and Fig. II.3b). This and the succeeding corollary were not expressed with the enunciation of the proposition. This corollary states that the ratio of circles describing spheres is equal to the square of the ratio of the motions or Vms of the circles. The proof follows upon the proof of a lemma: the ratio of the motions or Vms of similar inscribed [regular] polygons [of 4n sides] is equal to the ratio of the motions or Vms of the circles in which they are inscribed. The lemma is proved by a form of the exhaustion procedure that appears in the *Liber de curvis superficiebus*, which, as I have already said, may have originated with Proposition XII.18 of the *Elements* of Euclid. It is the first of several such proofs. In all of the remaining cases of Gerard's use of this type of proof, Gerard's procedure is correct. But here something went wrong with the text, either as the result of a lapse on the part of the author or, which is more likely, the result of some errors on the part of a scribe who produced the text prior to the production of Tradition I of our extant text. I say that the latter is "more likely" simply because, as I have said, elsewhere in the tract this form of proof is presented correctly. At any rate, whoever is responsible, the proof is confused in all of the extant copies. The confusion starts after the statement in lines 72–73 that the motion (i.e. Vm) of circle OV is to the motion (i.e. Vm) of circle ON as the motion (Vm) of the polygon [inscribed in circle OV] is to the motion (Vm) of the polygon [inscribed in circle ON], or the one ratio is greater or less than the other. This statement leads us to expect when he assumes that the one ratio is greater than the other in order to refute it, that it will be the ratio of the Vms of the circles that is greater than the ratio of the Vms of the inscribed polygons. But in fact the author goes on to say in lines 74–77 "let it be as the motion of circle

OV to the motion of circle *OR*" where circle *OR* is a smaller circle inscribed in *ON* of such a magnitude that the *Vm* of circle *OV* / *Vm* of circle *OR* = *Vm* of the polygon inscribed in circle *OV* / *Vm* of the polygon inscribed in circle *ON*. Now this statement could be made compatible with the statement of lines 72–73 if the latter were altered to read: "Motus ergo poligonii ad [motum] poligonii est tanquam motus circuli *OV* ad [motum] *ON* circuli, aut maior aut minor." The first part of this corrected statement ("Motus . . . *ON* circuli") would then be a restatement in specific terms of the general statement of lines 71–72 ("motuum . . . circulorum."). The lapse represented by the extant version of lines 72–73 would have been trivial were it not that the proof which follows, after a promising start, ends up not with a contradiction but rather with the position he has hypothesized in lines 74–77, namely that the *Vm* of circle *OV* / *Vm* of circle *ON* < *Vm* of polygon in circle *OV* / *Vm* of polygon in circle *ON*. So let us now see how to correct this proof, retaining as much of the text as possible.

(1) *Vm* of polygon / *Vm* of polygon = *Vm* of circle *OV* / *Vm* of circle *ON*, or the one ratio is greater or less than the other.

(2) If greater, let circle *OR* be so drawn that *Vm* of polygon *OV* / *Vm* of polygon *ON* = *Vm* of circle *OV* / *Vm* of circle *OR*, a regular polygon similar to the specific polygon inscribed in *ON* being inscribed in circle *OV*. [It is perhaps needless to add that Gerard understands the following proposition: the specific polygon inscribed in circle *OV* / specific polygon inscribed in circle *ON* = any other regular polygon inscribed in *OV* / a similar regular polygon inscribed in *ON*.]

(3) But *Vm* of polygon *ON* > *Vm* of circle *OR*, since polygon *ON* was inscribed so as not to touch circle *OR*.

(4) And so *Vm* of polygon *OV* / *Vm* of circle *OR* > *Vm* of polygon *OV* / *Vm* of polygon *ON*.

(5) But the *Vm* of circle *OV* > *Vm* of polygon *OV*.

(6) Hence, *multo fortius, Vm* of circle *OV* / *Vm* of circle *OR* > *Vm* of polygon *OV* / *Vm* of polygon *ON*.

(7) But conclusion (6) does not stand with assumption (2).

(8) Therefore the ratio of the *Vms* of the polygons is not greater than the ratio of the *Vms* of the circles in which the polygons are inscribed.

[Steps (1)–(4) are in the extant text and so lines 74–80 appear to be sound. But lines 80–84 ("et . . . poligonii") appear to be off the track and ought to be replaced by a text that would contain steps (5)–(8). I would suggest the following text to replace lines 80–84: "et *OV* circulus magis movetur poligonio inscripto *OV* circulo. Ergo multo fortius maior est proportio motus circuli *OV* ad motum circuli *OR* quam motus poligonii inscripti *OV* circulo ad motum poligonii inscripti *ON* circulo. Sed secundum adversarium motus circuli *OV* ad motum circuli *OR* sicut motus poligonii ad motum poligonii. Non igitur maior est proportio motus poligonii ad motum poligonii quam motus circuli ad motum circuli."]

(9) Gerard then says that if the ratio of the *Vms* of polygons inscribed in circles *OV* and *ON* is hypothesized to be less than the ratio of the *Vms* of circles *OV* and *ON*, a similar refutation follows.

(10) Therefore the ratio of the motions of the *Vms* of the polygons is the same as the ratio of the *Vms* of the circles.

(11) But *Vm* of polygon / *Vm* of polygon = radius *OV* / radius *ON*.

(12) Therefore, *Vm* of circle / *Vm* of circle = radius *OV* / radius *ON*.

(13) But circle / circle = (radius / radius)^2.

(14) Therefore, circle / circle = (*Vm* of circle / *Vm* of circle)^2. Q.E.D.

Corollary III to Proposition II.3 (lines 89–105). This corollary shows that surf. of sphere / surface of sphere = (*Vm* of surf. of sphere / *Vm* of surf. of sphere)^2.

(1) It has already been proved that (*Vm* of curv. surf. of polyg. body inscribed in sphere / *Vm* of curv. surf. polyg. body inscribed in sphere)^2 = surf. of sphere / surf. of sphere.

(2) *Vm* of curv. surf. polyg. body inscribed in sphere / *Vm* of curv. surf. polyg. body inscribed in sphere = *Vm* of surf. sphere / *Vm* of surf. sphere. "And this [is proved] *per impossibile* completely in the same way we have proved [the similar enunciation] concerning circles and inscribed polygons."

(3) But it was already proved that *Vm* of curv. surf. polyg. body / *Vm* of curv. surf. polyg. body = radius / radius.

(4) Therefore *Vm* of surf. sphere / *Vm* of surf. sphere = radius / radius.

(5) But (radius / radius)^2 = surf. sphere / surf. sphere.

Gerard says that this was proved in the *De piramidibus* (i.e. the *Liber de curvis superficiebus*). This is essentially correct since from the corollary to Proposition VI in the *Liber de curvis superficiebus* (see Volume One, p. 480) we know that the surface of a sphere is quadruple a great circle of the sphere, and hence we would immediately conclude that the surfaces of two spheres are as the squares of their radii.

(6) Therefore, surf. of sphere / surf. of sphere = (*Vm* of surf. sphere / *Vm* of surf. sphere)^2. Q.E.D.

Note that Corollaries II and III to Proposition II.3 were given later by Bradwardine.[20]

Proposition II.4

Enunciation of Proposition II.4 (lines 1–6). This proposition tells us that the *Vm* of a right triangle [rotating about one of its sides including the right angle] is to the *Vm* of a regular polygon [of 4n sides rotating about one of its diagonals] as the *Vm* of the hypotenuse of the triangle is to the *Vm* of

---

[20] For Bradwardine's citation of Corollary II, see note 17 above. On the same page (*ed. cit.*, p. 132) we see also his citation of Corollary III: "Quarumlibet duarum superficierum sphericarum eodem tempore uniformiter super suos axes immobiles circumientium, proportio est velocitatum in motibus proportio geminata."

the perimeter of the polygon. At this point he adds a double-barreled corollary which I have later in my summary designated as Corollary II. As Gerard puts it here, the corollary holds that the more sides an inscribed [regular] polygon has, the more it is moved, i.e., the greater is its Vm; but in the case of circumscribed [regular] polygons, the fewer the number of sides, the more it is moved, i.e., the greater is its Vm. We shall see in the summary below that there is another corollary interposed between the main part of the proposition and the corollary posed here. Accordingly, in my account below this additional corollary is specified as Corollary I.

Proof of Proposition II.4 (lines 7–76 and Fig. II.4).

(1) Construct right triangle *LMR* and inscribe [regular] polygon [of 4n sides] *DEFGHIKLM* . . . in circle *OH*. Extend side *HI* to *Y*. Then either triangle *OHY* is similar to triangle *LMR* or it is not.

(2) If the triangles are similar, then the proof follows directly from them [in steps similar to those which follow but with the letter changes made that are necessitated by imagining *R* to be in the place of *Q* in the figure on the right hand]. If they are not similar, let triangle *LMQ* be constructed similar to triangle *OHY* and draw *NV* parallel to *LM* so that *LMNV* / *LMQ* = *OHIQ* / *OHY*.

(3) Vm of tri. *LMQ* / Vm of tri. *OHY* = Vm of *MQ* / Vm of *HY*. [This can be easily proved. In the proof of Proposition II.1, step (5), the Vm of triangle *BFH* (see Fig. II.1a), moving as the triangles here, was, in effect, shown to be ⅓ of the Vm of its side *FH*. Hence Vm of tri. *LMQ* / Vm of tri. *OHY* = Vm of *LM* / Vm of *OH*. But from Propositions I.2 and I.1, Vm of *MQ* / Vm of *HY* = Vm of *LM* / Vm of *OH*. Thus the conclusion of this step immediately follows.]

(4) Vm of tri. *VNQ* / Vm of *QIY* = Vm of *NQ* / Vm of *IY* = Vm of *MQ* / Vm of *HY*.

(5) Therefore, by the subtraction of ratios, Vm of surf. *LMNV* / Vm of surf. *OHIQ* = Vm of *MQ* / Vm of *HY*, since surf. *LMNV* = tri. *LMQ* − tri. *VNQ*, and surf. *OHIQ* = tri. *OHY* − tri. *QIY*.

(6) But Vm of *MQ* / Vm of *HY* = Vm of *NQ* / Vm of *IY* = Vm of *MN* / Vm of *HI*.

(7) Therefore, from (5) and (6), Vm of *LMNV* / Vm of *OHIQ* = Vm of *MN* / Vm of *HI*.

(8) Since tri. *QIS* is not similar to tri. *VNQ*, take tri. *QIY* which is similar to tri. *VNQ* because tri. *OHY* is similar to tri. *LMQ*.

(9) But Vm of tri. *QIY* = Vm of tri. *QIS* because they have the same base *QI* and the Vms of their hypotenuses *IY* and *IS* are the same by Proposition I.2.

(10) Therefore, Vm of tri. *VNQ* / Vm of tri. *QIS* = Vm of *NQ* / Vm of *IS*.

(11) Then let *ZT* = *KP* [and let the lines be parallel].

(12) Therefore, Vm of tri. *PKS* = Vm of tri. *TZY*, since their bases are equal.

(13) So, with (9) and (12), and the subtraction of the magnitudes made, the *Vms* of the remainders will be equal, i.e. *Vm* of *QIKP* = *Vm* of *QIZT*.

(14) Then draw *TO* parallel to *NV* so that tri. *VNQ* / tri. *TOQ* = tri. *QIY* / tri. *TZY*.

(15) Therefore, *Vm* of tri. *TOQ* / *Vm* of tri. *TZY* = *Vm* of *OQ* / *Vm* of *ZY* = *Vm* of *NQ* / *Vm* of *IY* = *Vm* of tri. *VNQ* / *Vm* of tri. *QIY*.

(16) Therefore, *Vm* of *VNOT* / *Vm* of *QIZT* = *Vm* of *NQ* / *Vm* of *IY* = *Vm* of *NO* / *Vm* of *IZ* (as was proved before for lines *MN* and *HI*).

(17) Therefore, from (13) and (16), *Vm* of *VNOT* / *Vm* of *QIKP* = *Vm* of *NO* / *Vm* of *IK*.

(18) In a similar way it can be shown that *Vm* of *TOPS* / *Vm* of *PKLN* = *Vm* of *OP* / *Vm* of *KL*.

(19) Also, it is proved in an easy manner, that *Vm* of tri. *SPQ* / *Vm* of tri. *NLM* = *Vm* of *PQ* / *Vm* of *LM*.

(20) Summing up the movements of all the parts, *Vm* of tri. *LMQ* / *Vm* of quarter polygon *OHIKLM* = *Vm* of $(MN + NO + OP + PQ)$ / *Vm* of $(HI + IK + KL + LM)$.

(21) Since the relationships established in step (2) hold not only for the first quarter but as well for the remaining quarters, so they hold for the semipolygon and indeed for the whole polygon. Thus *Vm* of tri. *LMQ* / *Vm* of whole polygon *DHMD* = *Vm* of *MQ* / *Vm* of perimeter of polygon *DHMD*. [This can be easily proved by Proposition V.12 of the *Elements* of Euclid. Suppose that A_1p, A_2p, A_3p, and A_4p are successively the *Vms* of the summations of the sides in the quarter polygons and A_1, A_2, A_3, and A_4 are the *Vms* of the four quarter polygons, and similarly suppose that *Bh* is the *Vm* of the hypotenuse *MQ* of triangle *LMQ*, and that *B* is the *Vm* of triangle *LMQ*, then from step (20) we know that $A_1p / A_1 = Bh / B$, $A_2p / A_2 = Bh / B$, $A_3p / A_3 = Bh / B$, and $A_4p / A_4 = Bh / B$. Therefore $(A_1p + A_2p + A_3p + A_4p) / (A_1 + A_2 + A_3 + A_4) = Bh / B$, or $B / (A_1 + A_2 + A_3 + A_4) = Bh / (A_1p + A_2p + A_3p + A_4p)$.]

(22) To this point we have proved the proposition for triangle *LMQ*, which is similar to tri. *OHY*. But to make the proof of the proposition complete, the proportion of step (21) has to be proved for triangle *LMR*. But this is simple, since *Vm* of tri. *LMQ* = *Vm* of tri. *LMR* because they have the same base, and the *Vm* of *LQ* = *Vm* of *LR* by the corollary to Proposition I.2. Therefore, from (21), *Vm* of tri. *LMR* / *Vm* of polygon *DHMD* = *Vm* of hyp. *MR* / *Vm* of perimeter of polygon *DHMD*. Q.E.D. The proof of this last step follows Corollary I in the text (see lines 87–91).

Corollary I to Proposition II.4 (lines 77–91 and Fig. II.4). This corollary, which was not given with the enunciation, holds that the *Vm* of the curved surface of a right cone [moving in rotation upon itself around its axis] is to the *Vm* of the curved surface of a polygonal body described by the rotation of a [regular] polygon [of 4n sides] as the *Vm* of the cone's hypotenuse is to the *Vm* of the perimeter of the polygon. The proof is placed before step (22) above since the specific proof is in terms of cone *LMQ* and hence follows out of the prior considerations concerning triangle *LMQ*. The proof starts like the proof for the triangle and polygon, but is quickly cut off after three steps.

(1) *Vm* of curv. surf. of cone *LMQ* / *Vm* of curv. surf. of cone *OHY* = *Vm* of hyp. *MQ* / *Vm* of hyp. *HY*.

(2) *Vm* of curv. surf. of cone *VNQ* / *Vm* of curv. surf. of cone *QIY* = *Vm* of *NQ* / *Vm* of *IY*.

(3) Therefore, *Vm* of curv. surf. described by *LMNV* / *Vm* of curv. surf. described by *OHIQ* = *Vm* of *MQ* / *Vm* of *HY* = *Vm* of *MN* / *Vm* of *HI*. "And so," Gerard tells us, "by proceeding in the same way as before in regard to the triangle and polygon, you will prove what has been proposed." This proof then is for cone *VNQ*.

(4) But step (22) above applies equally to the corollary, and so the corollary is also proved for cone *LMR* (again see lines 87–91). Q.E.D.

Corollary II to Proposition II.4 (lines 92–105). The first part (steps 1–5) shows that in the case of [regular] polygons [of 4n sides] inscribed in circles and rotating about diameters, the polygon which has more sides is moved more (i.e., its *Vm* is greater). But in the second part (steps 6–9) it is proved that in the case of polygons which are circumscribed, the polygon which has fewer sides is moved more (i.e., its *Vm* is greater).

(1) *Vm* of inscribed polygon / *Vm* of triangle = *Vm* of perimeter of inscrib. polygon / *Vm* of hypotenuse of triangle (by inverting the proportion demonstrated in the main part of Proposition II.4).

(2) If the inscribed polygon has more sides, the *Vm* of its perimeter is greater, by Proposition I.4.

(3) Therefore, *Vm* of perim. of inscribed polygon of more sides / *Vm* of hyp. of triangle > *Vm* of perim. of an inscribed polygon of fewer sides / *Vm* of the hyp. of the same triangle.

(4) Therefore, *Vm* of inscribed polygon of more sides / *Vm* of triangle > *Vm* of inscribed polygon of fewer sides / *Vm* of triangle.

(5) Therefore, *Vm* of inscribed polygon of more sides > *Vm* of inscribed polygon of fewer sides. Hence the first part of the corollary is proved.

(6) *Vm* of perim. of circumscribed polygon of fewer sides > *Vm* of perim. of circumscribed polygon of more sides [by Proposition I.4].

(7) But *Vm* of perim. of circum. polygon / *Vm* of hyp. of triangle = *Vm* of circum. polygon / *Vm* of triangle [cf. step (1)].

(8) Therefore, *Vm* of polygon of fewer sides / *Vm* of triangle > *Vm* of polygon of more sides / *Vm* of triangle.

(9) Therefore, *Vm* of polygon of fewer sides > *Vm* of polygon of more sides. Q.E.D.

Proposition II.5

Enunciation of Proposition II.5 (lines 1–6). This holds that the *Vm* of a [right] triangle [rotating about one of the sides including the right angle] is to the *Vm* of a circle describing a sphere as the *Vm* of the hypotenuse of the triangle is to the *Vm* of the circumference of the circle. At this point Gerard adds only two corollaries of the six he later gives, namely Corollaries I and IV. The first states that the ratio of the *Vm*s of the curved surfaces of the cone and sphere described respectively by the right triangle and circle is that of the ratio of the *Vm*s respectively of the hypotenuse and the circumference. The second corollary affirms that the *Vm* of an equinoctial circle [rotating on itself about its center] is to the *Vm* of a colure [rotating about a diameter to describe a sphere] as the *Vm* of the circumference of the one is to the *Vm* of the circumference of the other.

Proof of Proposition II.5 (lines 7–30 and Fig. II.5).

(1) *Vm* of tri. *LMN* / *Vm* of circle *OC* = *Vm* of hyp. *LM* / *Vm* of circum. of circle *OC*, or the one ratio is greater or less than the other.

(2) If the one is greater than the other, then let *Vm* of tri. *LMN* / *Vm* of circle *OC* = *Vm* of *LM* / *Vm* of circum. of smaller circle *OF*, circle *OF* being constructed so much smaller that the proportion holds. And inscribe in circle *OC* a [regular] polygon [of 4n sides] *ABCDEA* which does not touch circle *OF*.

(3) Then *Vm* of tri. *LMN* / *Vm* of polygon *ABCDEA* = *Vm* of *LM* / *Vm* of perim. of polygon *ABCDEA*, by Proposition II.4.

[(4) *Vm* of perim. *ABCDEA* > *Vm* of circum. of circle *OF*, as the result of the construction.]

(5) And so *Vm* of tri. *LMN* / *Vm* of polygon *ABCDEA* < *Vm* of *LM* / *Vm* of circum. of circle *OF*.

(6) Furthermore, since *Vm* of polygon *ABCDEA* < *Vm* of circle *OC*, then *multo fortius Vm* of tri. *LMN* / *Vm* of circle *OC* < *Vm* of *LM* / *Vm* of circum. of circle *OF*.

(7) But (6) cannot stand with (2). Hence *Vm* of tri. *LMN* / *Vm* of circle *OC* ≯ *Vm* of hyp. *LM* / *Vm* of circum. of circle *OC*.

(8) By similar steps it is shown that *Vm* of tri. *LMN* / *Vm* of circle *OC* ≮ *Vm* of hyp. *LM* / *Vm* of circum. of circle *OC*, and so the proposition is proved.

Corollaries to Proposition II.5 (lines 31–92 and Fig. II.5). There are six corollaries, the first and the fourth of which were given with the enunciation of the proposition (and here in the proofs of the corollaries Gerard labels Corollary IV as "the second part of the corollary").

Corollary I (lines 31–51). This corollary shows that *Vm* of curv. surf. of a [right] cone / *Vm* of the surf. of a sphere = *Vm* of the hypotenuse of the cone / *Vm* of the circum. of the sphere. Its proof needs no further detailing here, since it is clear in the translation below.

Corollary II (lines 52–57). *Vm* of circle describing a sphere / *Vm* of a [regular] polygon [of 4n sides] = *Vm* of the circum. of the circle / *Vm* of the perimeter of the polygon. This is demonstrated by simple proportions.

Corollary III (lines 57–63). *Vm* of surf. of sphere / *Vm* of surf. of polyg.

body = Vm of circum. of sphere / Vm of the perim. of polygon describing polyg. body.

Corollary IV (lines 64–76). Vm of equinoctial circle / Vm of colure = Vm of circum. of equinoct. circle / Vm of circum. of colure. The equinoctial circle (as in Proposition II.1) rotates on itself about its center, while the colure rotates about its diameter to describe a sphere.[21] The proof is an interesting one and in view of its relation to Proposition II.1 I summarize it here.

(1) Following Proposition II.1 and its Fig. II.1b, note that Vm of equinoctial circle = 2 Vm of tri. *BFH*, since Vm of equinoctial circle = Vm of tri. *BDF* and Vm of tri. *BDF* = 2 Vm of tri. *BFH*.

(2) Vm of circum. of equinoct. circle = 2 Vm of hypotenuse *BF*, since Vm of *DF* = Vm of circum. of equinoct. circle and Vm of *DF* = 2 Vm of *BF*.

(3) Therefore, Vm of equinoct. circle / Vm of tri. *BFH* = Vm of circum. of equinoct. circle / Vm of *BF*.

(4) From the main part of Proposition II.5, Vm of colure / Vm of tri. *OCE* = Vm of circum. of colure / Vm of hyp. *CE*, points *C* and *E* having been connected in Fig. II.5.

(5) Rearranging the terms of (4), Vm of tri. *OCE* / Vm of hyp. *CE* = Vm of colure / Vm of circum. of colure.

(6) But triangle *BFH* is a right triangle rotating about its axis like the triangle constructed in Prop. II.5, and a triangle similar to *BFH* may be constructed on the base of triangle *OCE*, whose Vm is consequently the same as that of triangle *OCE*.

(7) Hence Vm of tri. *BFH* / Vm of *BF* = Vm of tr. *OCE* / Vm of *CE*.

(8) Thus by (3), (4), and (7), Vm of equinoct. circle / Vm of colure = Vm of circum. of equinoct. circle / Vm of circum. of colure. Q.E.D.

Corollary V (lines 77–89). (Vm of circle describing a sphere / Vm of circle describing a sphere)^2 = circle / circle. Proved by simple proportions, Gerard notes that it can also be proved *per impossibile*.

Corollary VI (lines 89–92). Surface of sphere / surface of sphere = (Vm of surf. of sphere / Vm of surf. of sphere)^2. "And this can be proved directly by the motion of the curved surface of a cone or indirectly by the motion of similar inscribed polygonal bodies."

---

[21] I had originally misinterpreted this to apply to concentric circles (see my first edition of the *Liber de motu*, p. 171; cf. Zubov's correct interpretation, *op. cit.*, p. 263). I have thought it useful to summarize the whole proof of this corollary because neither I nor Zubov did more than state the corollary before, and because the proof throws interesting light back on Proposition II.1. Bradwardine does not quite give this corollary but he does distinguish the motions of the circumferences of the two circles nicely (*ed. cit.*, pp. 130–32): "Omnes duas circumferentias circulorum in eodem tempore uniformiter circumductas, sive in seipsis sive superficies spherarum describentes sive unam in se et aliam per totam superficiem spherae, suis velocitatibus proportionales ostendes. Circumferentia enim circuli quaedam movetur in se, ut circumferentia aequinoctialis, et quaedam describit totam superficiem spherae, ut circumferentia telluris (*!* coluri)."

Book III

Postulates and Proposition III.1

Postulates to Book III (lines 2–6). Before presenting the propositions of Book III, which concern solids in rotation, Gerard tells us in the first postulate that if equal, similar cylinders are moved in the same time and no circle of one is moved more [than any circle of the other], neither is the one cylinder moved more than the other. The second postulate states that if no circle of the one is moved less than any circle of the other, neither is the one cylinder moved less than the other.

Enunciation of Proposition III.1 (lines 8–9). Polygonal body / polygonal body = (*Vm* of polygonal body / *Vm* of polygonal body)^3. The polygonal bodies are similar, regular bodies described by similar, regular polygons of 4n sides.

Proof of Proposition III.1 (lines 10–78 and Fig. III.1).

(1) Two equal and similar cylinders are posited to be moved in the same time. The first is moved in rotation to describe itself. The second is moved continually in a straight line so that any circle of it is moved equally to the corresponding circle of the first cylinder. And so these two cylinders are moved equally. This may be proved *per impossibile* by reference to the postulates. As I pointed out in Proposition II.1 the circular elements of the cylinder which rotates are equivalent to equinoctial circles rotated on themselves about centers lying on the axis.

(2) If there are two unequal but similar cylinders "and each of them is moved by describing itself," then *Vm* of cylinder / *Vm* of cylinder = *Vm* of base circle / *Vm* of base circle = *Vm* of radius of base / *Vm* of radius of base. But volume of cylinder / volume of cylinder = (*Vm* of radius of base / *Vm* of radius of base)^3, for the same ratio exists between the radii and the *Vms* of those radii and the ratio of the volumes of similar cylinders is the same as the cube of the ratio of the radii [see Euclid, *Elements,* Proposition XII.12]. Therefore cylinder / cylinder = (*Vm* of cylinder / *Vm* of cylinder)^3.

(3) By similar reason it can be shown that the ratio of similar right cones that describe themselves is the same as the cube of the ratio of their *Vms*.

(4) Now we proceed to the similar polygonal bodies of the enunciation of the proposition and use a procedure like that of Proposition II.3.

(5) So cone *OAC* / cone *OLN* = (*OA* / *OL*)^3 = (*Vm* of *OA* / *Vm* of *OL*)^3, and cone *FBC* / cone *QMN* = (*FB* / *QM*)^3 = (*OA* / *OL*)^3 = (*Vm* of *OA* / *Vm* of *OL*)^3, since *FB* / *QM* = *OA* / *OL*.

(6) Subtracting ratios, truncated cone *OABF* / trunc. cone *OLMQ* = (*Vm* of *OA* / *Vm* of *OL*)^3.

(7) Now, cone *FBD* / cone *QMP* = (*Vm* of *OA* / *Vm* of *OL*)^3.

(8) Hence, from (6) and (7), polygonal body described by *OABD* / polygonal body described by *OLMP* = (*Vm* of *OA* / *Vm* of *OL*)^3.

(9) The same steps used on the first quarter will apply to the bodies described by *GIAO* and *TSLO*.

(10) Hence by a summation procedure similar to that of Proposition II.3, whole polyg. body described by *GIABD* / whole polyg. body described by $TSLMP = (OA \ / \ OL)^3 = (Vm$ of body / Vm of body$)^3$, since Vm of body / Vm of body $= OA \ / \ OL$. Q.E.D.

Proposition III.2

Enunciation of Proposition III.2 (lines 1–2). Sphere / sphere $= (Vm$ of sphere / Vm of sphere$)^3$. This is, of course, similar to the classical proposition of Proposition XII.18 of the *Elements* of Euclid, with the Vms of the spheres replacing the radii.

Proof of Proposition III.2 (lines 3–43 and Fig. III.2).

(1) If we have similar polygonal bodies inscribed in spheres *OL* and *OB*, then Vm of polyg. body / Vm of polyg. body $= Vm$ of sphere *OL* / Vm of sphere *OB*, or the one ratio is greater or less than the other. [Note: the similar polygonal bodies here are called by Gerard "the first polygonal bodies" and are distinguished from polygonal bodies *QLPQ* and *GBFG* later inscribed in the spheres.]

(2) If the one ratio is greater than the other, let Vm of sphere *OL* / Vm of sphere $OB < Vm$ of polyg. body / Vm of polyg. body. And so construct a sphere *OA* less than sphere *OB* such that the Vm of sphere *OL* / Vm of sphere $OA = Vm$ of polyg. body / Vm of polyg. body. Inscribe in sphere *OB* a polygonal body *GBFG* that does not touch sphere *OA*. Inscribe a similar regular body *QLPQ* in sphere *OL*.

(3) By Proposition III.1, Vm of polyg. body *QLPQ* / Vm of polyg. body $GBFG = OL \ / \ OB$, and this is also true of the first polygonal bodies, since Vm of polyg. body / Vm of polyg. body $= Vm$ of polyg. body *QLPQ* / Vm of polyg. body *GBFG*.

(4) Following the assumption of (2), Vm of sphere *OL* / Vm of sphere $OA = Vm$ of polyg. body *QLPQ* / Vm of polyg. body *GBFG*.

(5) But this is impossible, for Vm of polyg. body *QLPQ* / Vm of sphere $OA > Vm$ of polyg. body *QLPQ* / Vm of polyg. body *GBFG* because the Vm of polygonal body *GBFG* is greater than the Vm of sphere *OA*, by construction.

(6) Therefore, *multo fortius, Vm* of sphere *OL* / Vm of sphere $OA > Vm$ of polyg. body *QLPQ* / Vm of polyg. body *GBFG*.

(7) But the conclusion of (6) does not stand with the deduction of (4). Hence the assumption from which (4) follows is false, and so Vm of polyg. body / Vm of polyg. body $\not> Vm$ of sphere *OL* / Vm of sphere *OB*.

(8) A similar refutation follows if we assume that Vm of polyg. body / Vm of polyg. body $< Vm$ of sphere / Vm of sphere.

(9) Hence Vm of polyg. body / Vm of polyg. body $= Vm$ of sphere / Vm of sphere.

(10) But *Vm* of polyg. body / *Vm* of polyg. body = radius *OL* / radius *OB*.

(11) Therefore, *Vm* of sphere / *Vm* of sphere = radius *OL* / radius *OB*.

(12) But sphere / sphere = (radius / radius)^3.

(13) Therefore, sphere / sphere = (*Vm* of sphere / *Vm* of sphere)^3.

This proposition was cited later by both Bradwardine and Themon Judei.[22]

Proposition III.3

Enunciation of Proposition III.3 (lines 1–4). This proposition holds that the *Vm* of a right cone [rotating on itself about its axis] is to the *Vm* of a polygonal body described by a regular polygon [of 4n sides and rotating on itself about a diagonal of the polygon] as the *Vm* of the hypotenuse of the cone is to the *Vm* of the perimeter of the polygon. This proposition should be compared with Proposition II.4 and its first corollary. It occupies a similar position in the progression of propositions concerning solids in motion that the earlier proposition and its corollary occupied in the progression of propositions concerning areas and surfaces in motion. Similarly the corollary to this proposition (unexpressed here with the enunciation) is similar to Corollary II of Proposition II.4.

Proof of Proposition III.3 (lines 5–54 and Fig. III.3).

(1) A preliminary lemma used in the proof is demonstrated first, namely, that all [right] cones of the same base are equally moved, i.e., have equal *Vms*. This is proved by showing that cones *LMP* and *LMQ* are the same aliquot parts of cylinders *LMTP* and *LMVQ*, which are themselves equally moved. He then proceeds to prove that *Vm* of cone *LMQ* / *Vm* of polyg. body inscribed in sphere *OA* = *Vm* of hypotenuse *MQ* / *Vm* of the perimeter of the polygon describing the polyg. body.

(2) Let side *AB* of the polygon be extended until it intersects the continuation of *OG* at point *D*.

(3) Triangle *OAD* is either similar to triangle *LMQ* or is dissimilar to it. If similar, the proof follows directly from steps like those of (4)–(14) without the necessity of steps (15) and (16).

(4) If dissimilar, let tri. *LMP* be similar to tri. *OAD*. And so cone *LMP* is similar to cone *OAD*.

(5) Hence *Vm* of cone *LMP* / *Vm* of cone *OAD* = *Vm* of radius *LM* / *Vm* of radius *OA* = *Vm* of hyp. *MP* / *Vm* of hyp. *AD*.

(6) Then let *BI* be parallel to *OA* and *NS* parallel to *LM* in such a way

---

[22] Bradwardine, *His Tractatus de proportionibus, ed. cit.*, p. 132: "Omnium duarum spherarum eodem tempore uniformiter super suos polos immobiles revolutarum, proportio est velocitatum in motibus proportio triplicata." Cf. Hugonnard-Roche, *L'Oeuvre astronomique de Thémon Juif,* p. 354: "3° supponitur quod proportio sperarum est proportio motuum earumdem triplicata. Hec patet per unam conclusionem autoris in *De proportione motuum et motorum* quam etiam Bracwerdin in ultimo suo capitulo allegavit."

that *NS* divides tri. *LMP* into the same aliquot parts in which *BI* divides tri. *OAD*.

(7) *Vm* of cone *SNP* / *Vm* of cone *IBD* = *Vm* of *SN* / *Vm* of *IB* as before.

(8) But *Vm* of *SN* / *Vm* of *IB* = *Vm* of *LM* / *Vm* of *OA*, by similar triangles and similar aliquot parts.

(9) Hence *Vm* of cone *SNP* / *Vm* of cone *IBD* = *Vm* of hyp. *MP* / *Vm* of hyp. *AD* = *Vm* of hyp. *NP* / *Vm* of hyp. *BD*.

(10) Hence by subtraction, *Vm* of (cone *LMP* − cone *SNP*) / *Vm* of (cone *OAD* − cone *IBD*) = *Vm* of *MN* / *Vm* of *AB*. Or, to put it another way, *Vm* of truncated cone described by *LMNS* / *Vm* of truncated cone described by *OABI* = *Vm* of *MN* / *Vm* of *AB*.

(11) By similar steps Gerard shows that *Vm* of trunc. cone descr. by *SNOR* / *Vm* of trunc. cone descr. by *IBKH* = *Vm* of *NO* / *Vm* of *BK*.[23]

(12) He also proves in a similar way that *Vm* of cone *ROP* / *Vm* of cone *HKG* = *Vm* of *OP* / *Vm* of *KG*.

(13) The same relationships may be proved for the parts of the polygonal body described by *NO'PAO*.

(14) Hence, by the summation of ratios, *Vm* of cone *LMP* / *Vm* of polygonal body = *Vm* of *MP* / *Vm* of the perimeter of the polygon.

(15) Then, by the lemma of step (1), *Vm* of cone *LMQ* = *Vm* of cone *LMP*, and *Vm* of *MQ* = *Vm* of *MP*.

(16) Therefore, *Vm* of cone *LMQ* / *Vm* of polygonal body = *Vm* of hyp. *MQ* / *Vm* of perimeter of polygon. Q.E.D.

Corollary to Proposition III.3 (lines 55–65). A two-part corollary follows that was not given with the enunciation of the proposition. The first part holds that the more "sides" a polygonal body inscribed in a sphere has, the more it is moved, i.e., the greater is its *Vm*. By "sides" he means the more conical segments there are that comprise its composite surface. The second part concludes that the fewer "sides" a polygonal body circumscribed about a sphere has, the more it is moved, i.e., the greater is its *Vm*. The brief proof follows:

(1) *Vm* of inscribed polyg. body of more sides / *Vm* of cone = *Vm* of perim. of polygon / *Vm* of hyp. of cone, by the inversion of the proportion proved in the main part of Proposition III.3.

(2) *Vm* of perim. of inscribed polygon of more sides > *Vm* of perim. of inscribed polygon of fewer sides, by Proposition I.4.

(3) Therefore *Vm* of inscr. polyg. body of more sides / *Vm* of cone > *Vm* of inscr. polyg. body of fewer sides / *Vm* of the same cone.

---

[23] If one follows the details of the proof, it will be evident that here and later line *CF* does double duty, for the author not only assumes that *F* is the point of intersection of the extension of line *BK* with the extension of line *OG* but he also assumes that line *CF* = *KH*. In order to fulfill this latter condition the line would have to be in the new position marked in the diagram by *C'F'*. But this error does not affect the cogency of the proof. For if we assume a new line *C'F'* which is equal to *KH* and we connect *B* and *F'*, cones *IBF* and *IBF'* would be equally moved because they have the same base. The same would be true for cones *HKF* and *HKF'*.

(4) Therefore, *Vm* of inscr. polyg. body of more sides > *Vm* of inscr. polyg. body of fewer sides.

(5) In a similar way it can be proved that *Vm* of circum. polyg. body of fewer sides > *Vm* of circum. polyg. body of more sides. And hence both parts of the corollary are proved.

Proposition III.4

Enunciation of Proposition III.4 (lines 1–3). *Vm* of a right cone [moving as before] / *Vm* of a rotating sphere = *Vm* of hyp. of cone / *Vm* of circum. of sphere. This is obviously an extension of Proposition III.3 from an inscribed polygonal body to its circumscribing sphere. The proof is again by the form of the method of exhaustion found in the *Liber de curvis superficiebus*.

Proof of Proposition III.4 (lines 4–32 and Fig. III.4).

(1) *Vm* of cone *OPQ* / *Vm* of sphere *OA* = *Vm* of hyp. of cone *OPQ* / *Vm* of circum. of sphere *OA*, or the one ratio is greater or less than the other.

(2) If greater, then let *Vm* of cone *OPQ* / *Vm* of sphere *OB* = *Vm* of *PQ* / *Vm* of circum. of *OA* (sphere *OB* having been so constructed as to produce the equation).

(3) Let a polygonal body (i.e. one described by polygon *HLBEH*) be inscribed in sphere *OB* without touching sphere *OA*.

(4) Therefore, by Proposition III.3, *Vm* of cone *OPQ* / *Vm* of polyg. body *HLBEH* = *Vm* of *PQ* / *Vm* of the perim. of polygon *HLBEH*.

(5) But the *Vm* of sphere *OB* > *Vm* of polyg. body *HLBEH*.

(6) Hence *Vm* of cone *OPQ* / *Vm* of sphere *OB* < *Vm* of *PQ* / *Vm* of the perim. of polygon *HLBEH*.

(7) But *Vm* of *PQ* / *Vm* of circum. of *OA* > *Vm* of *PQ* / *Vm* of perim. of polygon *HLBEH*, since polygon *HLBEH* does not touch circumference of *OA*.

(8) Therefore, *multo fortius, Vm* of cone *OPQ* / *Vm* of sphere *OB* < *Vm* of *PQ* / *Vm* of circum. of *OA*.

(9) But (8) cannot stand with (2), and so the one ratio cannot be greater than the other, as was assumed in (2). An alternative proof to that of steps (4) to (9) is introduced with the words: "vel sic melius":

(a) *Vm* of cone *OPQ* / *Vm* of polyg. body = *Vm* of hyp. *PQ* / *Vm* of perim. of polygon, from Proposition III.3.

(b) *Vm* of cone *OPQ* / *Vm* of sphere *OB* = *Vm* of hyp. *PQ* / *Vm* of circum. of *OA*, as stated in step (2).

(c) But *Vm* of cone *OPQ* / *Vm* of sphere *OB* < *Vm* of cone *OPQ* / *Vm* of polyg. body.

(d) Therefore, *Vm* of hyp. *PQ* / *Vm* of circum. of *OA* < *Vm* of hyp. / *Vm* of perim. of polygon, which is impossible, since the ratio is greater inasmuch as the polygonal body was inscribed so that it did not touch sphere *OA*. Therefore the assumptions in step (2) and substep (b) are false.

(10) A similar refutation is given when it is assumed that Vm of cone / Vm of sphere $< Vm$ of hyp. of cone / Vm of circum. of sphere.

(11) Hence if the one ratio is neither greater nor less than the other, it is equal to it. Q.E.D.

So ends Gerard's treatise. On the whole, my analysis of the content of the *Liber de motu* has shown that not only was the tract influential in the development of kinematics by Bradwardine and his successors in the fourteenth century but that it was also significant mathematically in its conscious use and adaptation of the results and techniques of the *Liber de curvis superficiebus* of Johannes de Tinemue and the *On the Measurement of the Circle* of Archimedes and in its interesting and completely original technique of finding uniform average punctual speeds with which to convert the varying speeds present in the motions of rotations of magnitudes, be they lines, surfaces, or solids. Needless to say, a fair number of errors survive in the extant text. Whether they are errors of the author or of some early copyist cannot be easily determined. I have alerted the reader to these errors in the course of the text, the translation, or my summary of the contents in this chapter. But we may list here the principal errors or types of errors:

(1) The very frequent omission of the word "motion" in the statement of proportions where the word is necessary to make the proportion correct. In every case I have supplied the word in brackets in my English translation. In one important case the text omits a crucial *proportio motuum* (see Prop. II.3, line 29). We can also point to an instance when *motus* was added to the text when it should not have been (see the variant reading to line 39 of Prop. II.3). Similarly in Prop. III.4, line 22, *corporis* appears in all the manuscripts but it certainly should have been omitted. On the other hand *corporis* was often omitted in Prop. III.2 when the text required it (see my translation of that proposition, where I have added "[body]" in a number of instances).

(2) The confusion in the exhaustion proof of Corollary II of Proposition II.3 (see my analysis and correction of this proof in my summary above in this chapter). In another case of the use of the exhaustion proof *maior* appears where *minor* is required (see Prop. III.4, lines 18–19).

(3) The ambivalent double use of the line CF in the proof of Prop. III.4 (see above, footnote 23 of this chapter).

(4) Occasional transpositions, omissions, or alterations in the letters marking magnitudes (e.g., Prop. I.1, Trad. II, vars. to lines 82, 89, 91; Prop. II.1, line 37; and vars. to lines 43 and 44; Prop. II.3, line 45; Prop. II.4, var. to line 72; Prop. II.5, line 7; Prop. III.1, line 60; Prop. III.3, vars. to lines 19 and 47).

(5) Confusion in the numbers in Prop. II.1, line 98.

(6) Occasional slips, such as the writings of *angulos* when *triangulos* was needed in Prop. II.4, line 61.

(7) An occasional use of "circle" when "circumference of circle" was meant (e.g., Prop. I.1, Trad. II, lines 56–57; Prop. II.5, line 18).

CHAPTER 3

The Text of the *Liber de motu*

Two principal traditions of the *Liber de motu* are represented in the six extant manuscripts listed below under the rubric *Sigla*. However it is only in the text of Proposition I.1 that the divergencies between the traditions are serious enough to warrant the presentation of two distinct texts. In the case of that proposition I have published the two texts in parallel columns. Tradition I is primarily represented by MSS *O*, *B*, and *N*, and Tradition II by MSS *P* and *V*. The sixth MS, *E*, while adhering generally to Tradition I (in fact, enough so that I list it under Tradition I in the *Sigla* below), may also have been corrupted by Tradition II, though it is possible that it preserves a part of Tradition I that has dropped out of the text presented by MSS *O*, *B*, and *N*. But at this point let us put aside MS *E* and describe the divergencies of the two traditions on the basis of the other five manuscripts, returning to the consideration of MS *E* later. If we do this, we see that the proof of the first part of Proposition I.1 (which concerns the motion of a line segment) is presented in much the same way in both traditions, but that even so two distinct texts are evident (see Tradition I, lines 34–180, and Tradition II, lines 34–180). In the case of the second part of Proposition I.1 (which concerns the motion of the whole radius), Tradition II gives two proofs (see Tradition II, lines 181–300) that differ markedly from the single proof given in Tradition I (see Tradition I, lines 181–246). Finally we should note that the corollary to Proposition I.1 is presented somewhat differently in the two traditions (see lines 301–28).

In regard to the two proofs of the second part of Proposition I.1 in Tradition II, it should be realized that there is some evidence that the original text, which none of the manuscripts gives with complete faithfulness, included both proofs. Without considering MS *E* yet, the evidence is twofold: (1) Fig. I.1a in Tradition I contains a rectangle as well as a circle, a rectangle that is not used in any of the proofs of Tradition I. Further, that rectangle bears the letters *O*, *F*, *G*, *H*, *I*, and *K*, the last four of which are not found in the proofs of Tradition I. Now Tradition II also contains the rectangle but with letters *O*, *F*, *K*, *H*, *L*, and *N*, and in Tradition II the rectangle is used for the second or direct proof of the second part of Proposition I.1. Hence one would judge that Tradition I also had such a proof but that it dropped out of Tradition I as represented by MSS *O*, *B*, and *N*. (2) There is a statement in Proposition I.2 (included in both traditions) to the effect that the motion of the whole radius has earlier received a double proof (*duplici probatione*), for which statement see Proposition I.2 lines 50–51. But, as I have already said, the second part of Proposition I.1 in Tradition I as based on MSS *O*, *B*, and *N* contains only a single proof. The inference is clear: a second proof has dropped out of Tradition I.

It is at this point that we must consider MS *E*. As I have said, that manuscript follows Tradition I for the most part (albeit quite carelessly), but suddenly, immediately following the single proof of the second part of Proposition I.1 as given in Tradition I, the scribe of MS *E* adds a confused fragment of the first proof of Tradition II and follows that fragment with Tradition II's second or direct proof, couched in terms very much like those given in the proof in Tradition II (see Tradition I, variant reading for line 180). The only important difference in MS *E*'s text of that second proof is that there the letters on the rectangle in Fig. I.1a in Tradition I are used rather than the letters given on that diagram in Tradition II. For example, the proof in MS *E* speaks of surface *OFGK* where Tradition II speaks of surface *ONFK* (see Tradition II, line 287). Similarly, MS *E* says that lines *FG* and *OK* together equal the circumference, while MS *V* of Tradition II (MS *P* has already broken off before this point) says that lines *FK* and *ON* equal that circumference (see composite Fig. I.1a and Tradition II, lines 285–86). In view, then, of the fact that MS *E* contains the letters on the rectangle that are given in the diagram of Tradition I, the reader might well say that MS *E* goes back to the lost, original text rather than that MS *E* merely conflates the two traditions which were consulted in different manuscripts. However, I seriously doubt that this is a proper inference, for MS *E* ends up with the whole or parts of *three* proofs of the second part of Proposition I.1: the single proof of Tradition I, a fragment of the first proof of Tradition II, and the second or direct proof of Tradition II. But the phrase quoted above from Proposition I.2 speaks only of a "double proof" for the motion of the radius. Hence, I believe that we can tentatively conclude that the scribe of MS *E* consulted both traditions and thus that both traditions had already had some independent development by the time of the preparation of MS *E* (that is, before 1260, the *terminus ante quem* of that manuscript, as noted below under the *Sigla*).

Let us now say something about the temporal and paleographical relationships of the manuscripts, first about those of Tradition I and then about those of Tradition II. MS *O*, which on the whole strikes me as the best of the manuscripts in terms of its completeness, its cogency, and the accuracy of its drawings, was written sometime before the middle of the thirteenth century (see the *Sigla* below). It stands, I believe, at the head of Tradition I. Thus I consider it to be the oldest of the manuscripts of that tradition. MS *B*, which would appear on paleographical grounds to be of about the same date as MS *O*, was perhaps copied from MS *O*, or possibly from a close copy of *O*. There is certainly no question that the two manuscripts are very closely related throughout the text. Notice that even erroneous scribal repetitions found in MS *O* are also present in MS *B*. A good example may be seen by consulting the variant reading to lines 59–64 in Proposition I.2. Further, see the marginal note that appears in both MSS *O* and *B* and is given below in the variant reading to lines 29–52 of Proposition I.2, a note that was probably not in the original text. I say this because the note tells us to omit those lines, though in fact they are useful for a proof that is similar to but not identical with the proof found in Proposition I.1, and furthermore the lines are also in MSS *E* and *V*. Only MS *N* has taken the advice of this note and omitted the lines, an indication, I believe, that MS *N*, also of the thirteenth century, was prepared after *O* and *B* and was dependent in some direct or indirect way on one or the other of them, while at times it includes readings found only in MS *E* of Tradition I. A rather strong indication that MS *O* was prepared before both MSS *B* and *E* is evident in Proposition I.1, where the scribe of MS *O* copied various passages in the wrong order, and then, in an effort to indicate the proper order to the reader, placed in the margins opposite these passages the letters C, A, B, and D. Let me outline the details and consequences, of this disorder in MS *O*. After "minus" in my line 129 of Tradition I MS *O* includes my lines 166–80 of Tradition I, and letter C is placed in the margin at the beginning of the passage. Then follows in MS *O* my lines 137–49 of Tradition I, identified in the margin by the letter A. Immediately following this passage MS *O* has my lines 150–61 and the passage is identified in the margin as B. Then follows in MS *O* the corollary (i.e., lines 301–19 of Tradition I), with the designation D in the margin. Now these marginal letters do not completely straighten out the disorder, for after the passage marked D there is a sharp break or lacuna in the text in MS *O* that is followed by my lines 129–36 of Tradition I. This passage is unmarked in the margin and is, as my reconstructed text shows, wildly out of place since it should precede all of the passages marked with marginal letters in MS *O*. After this unmarked passage MS *O* finally concludes the proposition, in a second unmarked passage, with my lines 181–246 of Tradition I. In summary, we should note that if the scribe of MS *O* had marked the first unmarked passage before all of the passages marked with letters by a letter in the margin prior to A (for convenience let us say A′), and had marked the text after that first unmarked passage (i.e. after our suggested A′) with a letter between C and D (say D′), then all of the disorder would have been corrected. Now it is clear that the scribe of MS *B* has put to right the disorder of MS *O* except that he has left the unmarked passages (A′ and D′ as we have called them) in their erroneous position after the corollary. From this fact I would conclude that the scribe of MS *B* had MS *O* (or a close copy of it) before him and that he carried out the rearrangement suggested by the marginal letters of MS *O*. MS *E* shows the same basic rearrangement as MS *B*, and thus also has the unmarked passages out of order. Thus it would seem that MSS *B* and *E* were written after MS *O*, since their scribes made the changes of order suggested by the marginal letters of

MS *O* but did not make those necessary changes that the scribe of MS *O* failed to indicate. Finally, we come to MS *N*, the only manuscript of Tradition I to put the unmarked passages A' and D' in their proper place. From this we would be tempted to believe that it preceded MSS *O*, *B*, and *E*, except that the scribe of MS *N* did not include the passages marked B and C, both of which are necessary for the proof. Hence I would conclude that he too was attempting to rearrange the text in accordance with the suggestions of the scribe of MS *O* (either directly or indirectly by means of MS *B*'s rearrangement) but that in doing so he inadvertently skipped passages A and B. This conclusion is reinforced by the fact I noted above, that MS *N* follows the advice of the marginal note to Proposition I.2 in MSS *O* and *B* and omits lines 29–52 of the proposition. I should add that despite the fact that MS *N* appears to follow after MSS *O*, *B*, and *E*, its scribe is the most keenly conscious of the geometrical context of any of the scribes and there are fewer mathematical blunders in MS *N* than in the other manuscripts. All of this argument is, I believe, a plausible account of how Tradition I might have developed out of MS *O*. To complete this we would have only to remark once more that in the course of MS *E*'s rearrangement the scribe of that manuscript added after line 180 of Tradition I the pieces of Tradition II that I have discussed above.

As plausible as this general account is, it still leaves many problems of detail unsolved, problems that no doubt arise because we must depend on so few manuscripts. One would suppose that there were intermediate manuscripts long since lost. Let me mention two cases of these problems of detail. If our general account is correct, we must account for the fact that MSS *OB* have omitted one phrase that is present in MSS *EN* and which is necessary for the proof (see Proposition I.3, variant to lines 31–33). We could perhaps lay that omission to carelessness on the part of the scribe of MS *O*, a carelessness in which he was followed by the scribe of MS *B*. To explain the presence of the necessary phrase in MSS *E* and *N*, we could say that perhaps the scribe of *E*, in addition to having MS *O* or MS *B* before him, had still another manuscript which included the phrase and that the scribe of MS *N* then picked up the phrase from MS *E* (I have already noted the close affinity between the readings of MS *E* and MS *N*). Or we could say that the scribe of MS *E* saw the mathematical necessity of the addition and so produced it himself. Similarly, we must also explain how another phrase equally necessary to the text (see Proposition II.1, variant to lines 48–49) was omitted from MS *O* but appeared in MSS *BENV*. Do we say that the scribe of *B* realized the mathematical necessity of adding such a phrase, and that he was followed in that addition (either directly or indirectly) by the scribes of *E*, *N*, and *V*? Or did the scribe of MS *B* have access to a manuscript very close to *O* but more complete than MS *O* in regard to this added phrase? With the paucity of extant manuscripts we simply cannot be sure of the true explanation of such conundrums of detail.

I have to this point emphasized the divergencies that exist in the manuscripts of Tradition I and in doing so have perhaps obscured the large elements of agreement, particularly among manuscripts *O*, *B*, and *N*. They are all written in the same kind of incipient Gothic hand, and at least MSS *O* and *B* seem to have been written in England (see *Sigla* below). There is no great discrepancy among the diagrams of these three manuscripts. Further, they bear the same title and form of the author's name (see the variant readings for the title). They all assume a threefold division into books, though MS *O* omits the designations of "First Book," "Second Book," and "Third Book". (But that MS *O* assumes such a division is clear from the fact that the propositions of the three books are separately numbered in that manuscript). Further, we should note that MSS *O*, *B*, *E*, and *N* contain an internal reference in Proposition III.3, line 59, to "ultimam prime particule" (i.e. to Proposition I.4).[1] Hence, if the reader peruses the variant readings I think he will be struck by the general agreement of these three manuscripts, while recognizing that the fourth manuscript of that tradition (*E*) has many careless readings that diverge from MSS *O*, *B*, and *N*.

I have little to say about Tradition II as represented by MSS *P* and *V*. MS *P*, a manuscript of the thirteenth century (see *Sigla* below), contains only the postulates of Book I and Proposition I.1 through line 242 of my text. I have already mentioned in Chapter One above that this fragment in MS *P* includes neither the title nor the author's name. For the most part I have adopted its readings where they differ from those of MS *V*. MS *V*, a manuscript of the fifteenth and sixteenth centuries, like MS *P*, diverges widely from the text of Tradition I in Proposition I.1. But after that proposition it converges, to a significant extent, with MSS *O*, *B*, *E*, and *N* until it terminates at the end of Proposition II.4. Thus MS *V* omits Proposition II.5, the postulates of Book III, and Propositions III.1–III.4. On the whole, MS *V* was rather carelessly copied, particularly in regard to the letters used to mark the magnitudes. Hence considerable confusion is left in the text presented in MS *V*. Nevertheless I have thought it useful to include the variant readings of MS *V* since it remains the only copy we have of a tradition that is divergent in much of the text of the *Liber de motu*. Note finally in connection with MS *V* that it contains a completely distinct title (without author's name): *De motu ambitus et poligonii* (see the variants to the title).

A word is necessary about orthography. There is considerable divergence in the spelling of geometrical terms among the manuscripts. Most often I have adopted the readings of MS *O*. However I have used *circumferentia* instead of the much more common *circumferencia* of MS *O* and most of

---

[1] In Proposition II.5, line 68, MS *N* has a reference to Proposition II.1: "per primam huius libri" while the other MSS omit "libri", though of course all of the MSS imply by the phrase a division into books. Cf. the similar reference: "per ultimam primi" in Proposition II.4, line 94 (all MSS).

the other manuscripts. The same thing is true of *proportio,* which I have employed instead of *proporcio.* On the other hand I have written *spacium* (which is everywhere in the manuscripts) instead of *spatium.* The reader will notice that I have used (largely from MS *O*) the following forms: *equidistans* (though often the form *equedistans* is found, even in manuscripts that generally have *equidistans*), *oportet* instead of *opportet, duplicata* instead of *dupplicata, piramis* instead of *pyramis, ypotenusa* instead of a wide variety of other spellings (see Proposition I.2, variants to lines 1 and 3). I have adopted *voluimus* (sometimes found in *E* and always present in MS *N*) instead of *volumus* (found everywhere in MSS *O* and *B*), for surely the author intended the conventional concluding phrase of a geometrical proof: *quod voluimus demonstrare.* The manuscripts are often divided on whether the phrase *per precedentem* should appear or whether *per presentem* is to be preferred. I have tried to determine in each case which is the more appropriate. Needless to say the division of the manuscripts on this particular reading are completely reported in the variant readings. Note also that I have followed MS *O* in writing the genitive *octogoni* instead of *octogonii* and *sedecagoni* instead of *sedecagonii.* I have preferred *orthogonaliter* everywhere, although *ortogonaliter* is used with some frequency, even in manuscripts that employ the former spelling. I have used *columpna,* which appears in all of the manuscripts except MS *V,* instead of MS *V*'s *columna.* I have also written the medieval *sexquialtera* instead of MS *V*'s *sesquialtera,* the medieval *spera* instead of MS *V*'s *sphaera* (in fact I have always used the medieval "e", though in reporting the variant readings from MS *V* I always give MS *V*'s "ę" as "ae"). I have also written *poligonium* from the medieval MSS rather than MS *V*'s *polygonium.* One rather interesting case of a divergent spelling is MS *B*'s *soffista* instead of the *sophista* which is in the other manuscripts and which I have used. It is of interest because one might suppose that this odd spelling was produced by an Italian, though, as I have said, MS *B* was probably written in England.

Further observations concerning my Latin text and English translation are now in order. As usual in the texts of these volumes, I have punctuated and capitalized at will. Furthermore I have followed my usual practice of using majuscules for the postulates and enunciations as an indication that these are written in a larger hand in the manuscripts. Similarly I have capitalized (and italicized) the letters marking magnitudes, though they usually appear as minuscules in the manuscripts, and, needless to say, it is I who have added the prime sign to one of a pair of identical letters that appear on the same diagram. I have occasionally added words in brackets for the convenience of the reader (e.g., "[Petitiones]", "[Propositiones]", "[Traditio I]", "[Traditio II]", "[Corollarium]" and so on). I have also added in brackets numbers for the postulates in all three books. On occasion I have singled out errors in the text by a succeeding "(*!*)", and when a correction appears helpful to the reader I have added it in parentheses; for example, I write "*CBGH* (*! BCGH*)." In reporting the variant readings below the text I follow my usual procedures. The only point worth making in this regard is that italic type always indicates something that arises from the editor and so the letters marking magnitudes (which are in italics in the text) are given in roman type in the variant readings. Note in particular that in both the text and variant readings I have ignored the ambiguous punctuation and spacing of letters that mark magnitudes. Thus I write *SLMP* when the letters stand for a rectangle and *SL*, *MP* when they mark the two lines *SL* and *MP*, regardless of whether the manuscript has *SLMP* or *SL.MP* or *S.LMP* or any other odd spacing. One incidental difficulty I encountered concerned the distinguishing of "i" and "1" when used for letters marking the magnitudes. It was often impossible to distinguish between these letters, particularly in the texts of MSS *O* and *B*. But since they were rather clearly distinguishable on the diagrams, and were usually given correctly at the beginning of a proof only to be changed in the course of the proof, I have simply read the ambiguous letters as the diagrams and mathematical cogency of the text demanded without making any comment in the variant readings. A similar difficulty is found with the letters "u" and "v" as reported in the manuscripts. Again I have sought consistency between the diagrams and the texts without making any effort to record in the variant readings all of the ambiguities connected with these two letters.

The marginal folio numbers in my text are those of manuscript *O*.

In preparing the diagrams I have ordinarily followed those in MS *O*. I have noted all the significant divergencies in the legends below the diagrams. I have given additional diagrams when I thought they would be useful to the reader: namely the simplified drawings which I have added to Fig. I.1a and the additional diagram I have given in Fig. III.2. Finally notice that MS *E* omits the diagrams entirely and that MS *V* omits Figs. I.1b, I.2, I.3, I.4, II.1a, II.1b, II.2, II.3a, II.3b, and II.4 (and of course all the remaining figures, since the text in MS *V* stops at the end of Proposition II.4).

In my English translation I have followed the procedures of the preceding volumes. Thus I ordinarily use a quasi-modern notation in translating proportions without implying that Gerard held a modern view of rational numbers. So "Que est enim proportio *MQ* ad *NQ* ea est *HY* ad *IY*" becomes in translation "For *MQ* / *NQ* = *HY* / *IY*." Sometimes when the statement of the proportion is a lengthy one and contains subsidiary verbal elements which I do not want to ignore, I translate the proportion literally. I also rather freely translate "proportio . . . duplicata (*or* triplicata)" by "the square (*or* the cube) of the ratio". I have been free with bracketed additions that might aid the reader. The most common addition is "[motion]," for again and again the scribes have omitted that term when stating a proportion.

Sigla

Tradition I

O = Oxford, Bodleian Library, MS Auct. F.5.28, 116v–125r. 13c. This codex is made up of two manuscripts, both written by English hands in the thirteenth century. I am only interested here in the first Manuscript (marked A in the *Summary Catalogue*). In the *Summary Catalogue* (see title below, p. 706) this part of the codex is dated "middle 13th cent." If my argument that MS *O* stands at the head of Tradition I is correct and if we observe that MS *E* must be dated before 1260 (and, I suspect, considerably before that date), then *a fortiori* MS *O* must have been written before 1260. MS *O* contains many geometrical works that seem to have been part of the geometrical activity of the early thirteenth century. Note that it contains all of the works that we know for sure that Gerard of Brussels used in the composition of his *Liber de motu:* the *Elements* of Euclid (in the Adelard II version)[2] on folios ii recto–xli verso, 1r–15r, Archimedes' *De quadratura circuli* (in the second tradition of Gerard of Cremona's translation of that work)[3] on folios 101v–102v, and Johannes de Tinemue's *De curvis superficiebus* (in the first tradition of that work)[4] on folios 111r–116r. The codex also contains several works of Jordanus de Nemore, which Gerard of Brussels may or may not have known.[5] The best description of that manuscript (though now out-of-date in identifying the various tracts included therein) is F. Madan, H. H. E. Craster, and N. Denholm-Young, *A Summary Catalogue of the Western Manuscripts in the Bodleian Library at Oxford,* Vol. 2, Part 2 (Oxford, 1937), pp. 706–08. See the comments on this manuscript by A. G. Watson and R. J. Roberts, *John Dee's Library Catalogue* (London, The Bibliographical Society, forthcoming).

B = Berlin, Staatsbibliothek, Preussischer Kulturbesitz, Lat. Q.510, 81v–88v, 13c. I have already noted in Chapter One above (text over n. 10) that Eneström dates this as from the fourteenth century. I already had become convinced of its earlier date in the first edition of my text of the *Liber de motu.*[6] It was also so dated by H. L. L. Busard,[7] D. Lindberg,[8] and R. B. Thomson.[9] From the appearance of English names in the codex, we may deduce that it was written in England (see the Libri catalogue, given below, p. 146). Like MS *O* it contains the geometrical tracts that were used by Gerard of Brussels: the *Elements* of Euclid (again in the Adelard II version) on folios 1r–59v, Archimedes' *De quadratura circuli* (in the second tradition of Gerard of Cremona's translation) on folios 89r–90r, and Johannes de Ti-

---

[2] See M. Clagett, "The Medieval Latin Translations from the Arabic of the *Elements* of Euclid, with Special Emphasis on the Versions of Adelard of Bath," *Isis,* Vol. 44 (1953), p. 22.

[3] M. Clagett, *Archimedes in the Middle Ages,* Vol. 1 (Madison, 1964), p. 37.

[4] *Ibid.,* pp. 446–47.

[5] R. B. Thomson, "Jordanus de Nemore: Opera," *Mediaeval Studies,* Vol. 38 (1976), p. 141.

[6] M. Clagett, "The *Liber de motu* of Gerard of Brussels and the Origin of Kinematics in the West," *Osiris,* Vol. 12 (1956), p. 111.

[7] H. L. L. Busard, "Die Traktate *De proportionibus* von Jordanus Nemorarius und Campanus," *Centaurus,* Vol. 15 (1971), p. 197.

[8] D. C. Lindberg, *A Catalogue of Medieval and Renaissance Optical Manuscripts* (Toronto, 1975), pp. 47, 50.

[9] Thomson, "Jordanus de Nemore: Opera," p. 136.

nemue's *De curvis superficiebus* (in its first tradition) on folios 90r–94v. Furthermore it has two works of Jordanus.[10] The most detailed description of that codex is still that found in *Catalogue of the Extraordinary Collection of Splendid Manuscripts, Chiefly Upon Vellum, in Various Languages of Europe and the East, Formed by M. Guglielmo Libri . . . Which Will be Sold by Auction by Messrs. S. Leigh Sotheby and John Wilkinson* (London, 1859), pp. 145–48, which though detailed is out-of-date.[11] It appears that that description was prepared by Libri himself. The codex was sold to the Phillipps Library, and an abbreviated description of it (taken from the Libri Catalogue) appears in the Phillipps Catalogue. See the reprinted edition entitled *The Phillipps Manuscripts, Catalogus librorum manuscriptorum in Bibliotheca D. Thomae Phillipps, Bt* (London, 1968), p. 316, MS. no. 16345. The manuscript was acquired by the Königliche Bibliothek in Berlin in 1896.

N = Naples, Bibl. Naz., Latin MS VIII.C.22, 60v–65v, 13c. The first part of the manuscript (the mathematical part) contains the following works: the *Elements* of Euclid, in the Adelard II Version, folios 1r–44v; a part of Jordanus' *Liber de ratione ponderis* (through Proposition R2.09, here designated as Prop. "18ᵃ"), ff. 44v–45v; *Euclidis de speculis,* folios 47r–48v; *Demonstratio Jordani de algorismo,* folios 51r–53r; *Demonstratio Jordani de minutiis,* folios 53r–55r; *Ysoperimetra,* folios 55v–56v, with "56" written over "55" on 56r: *Liber de curvis superficiebus,* folios 57r–60r, with "57" written over "56" on 57r; Gerard of Brussels, *Liber de motu,* folios 60v–65v; *Archymenides de circuli quadratura,* folios 65v–66v. In the other part of the manuscript two items are of interest to historians of science: "Investigantibus chilindri compositionem quod dicitur orologium . . ." (=Thorndike-Kibre, c. 776), folios 67r–68v; and *Alfragani liber differentiarum,* folios 71r–90v. See my brief descriptions in *Archimedes in the Middle Ages,* Vol. 1 (Madison, 1964), pp. xix, 80–81, 449.

E = Edinburgh, Crawford Library of the Royal Observatory, MS Cr. I.27, 42r–52v, middle 13c. I have already noted its early description by Richard de Fournival in his *Biblionomia* (see Chapter One, over notes 11–14), which allows us to date this manuscript before 1260. It contains two of the works of Jordanus: the *Liber philotegni* (the shorter version of the *De triangulis*)

---

[11] In the Libri Catalogue it bears the number 665. Because the description in the Libri Catalogue does not specify the folio numbers and is somewhat out-of-date in other respects, I note here briefly the tracts included in the codex: 1r–59v: Euclid, *Elements* (in the Adelard II version); 59v–63v: Euclid, *De speculis;* 63v–72v: Euclid, *De visu;* 72v–77r: Jordanus, *Demonstratio de algorismo;* 77r–81v: Jordanus, *De minutiis;* 81v–88v: Gerard of Brussels, *Liber de motu;* 89r–90r: Archimedes, *De quadratura circuli;* 90r–94v: Johannes de Tinemue, *De curvis superficiebus;* 94v: Anonymous (Simplicius), *Quadratura circuli per lunulas;* 94v–112v: Theodosius, *De speris;* 113r–v: blank; 114r–175v: Ptolemy-Geber, *Almagesti minoris libri vi;* 175v–178v: Thābit ibn Qurra or Jordanus de Nemore, *De proportionibus;* 178v–91r: Euclid, *Data;* 191v: Anonymous, very brief astrological tract; 192r–v, 193r–v, leaves missing or numbers were skipped; 194r–209r: Alfraganus, *Rudimenta astronomie (Liber differentiarum);* 209v–211v: rough diagrams.

on folios 1r–13v and the *De ratione ponderum* on folios 14r–21v.[12] See the excellent description of this manuscript in N. R. Ker, *Medieval Manuscripts in British Libraries,* Vol. 2 (Oxford, 1977), pp. 546–47. Note once more that, though the text of the *Liber de motu* in this codex is largely from Tradition I, it has a section in Proposition I.1 (see the variant reading to line 180 of Tradition I) that perhaps came from Tradition II.

Tradition II

P = Paris, Bibl. Nationale, MS lat. 8680A, 4r–5r, 13c. (except for last item from 14c). Heiberg dates this manuscript as from the fourteenth century in his text of Alhazen's *De speculis comburentibus,*[13] as does the cataloguer in *Catalogus codicum manuscriptorum Bibliothecae Regiae,* Vol. 4 (Paris, 1744), p. 534, which contains an inadequate description of the codex. I used this codex for my new text of the *De ponderibus Archimenidis* in *Archimedes in the Middle Ages,* Vol. 3 (Philadelphia, 1978), pp. 1286–1311 (and particularly, p. 1297), where I dated it as from the thirteenth century. The codex contains several works of Jordanus and also the *Algorismus demonstratus* of Gernardus.[14]

V = Vienna, Nationalbibliothek, MS lat. 5303, 1r–10v, 15–16c. It also contains Johannes de Tinemue's *De curvis superficiebus* (in its first tradition) on folios 11r–21v[15] and the *De numeris datis* of Jordanus on folios 87r–98r.[16] For a description of this codex, see *Tabulae codicum manu scriptorum praeter Graecos et orientales in Bibliotheca Palatina Vindobonensi asservatorum,* Vol. 4 (Vienna, 1870), pp. 93–94.

---

[12] Thomson, "Jordanus de Nemore: Opera," p. 140.

[13] J. L. Heiberg and E. Wiedemann, "Ibn al Haiṭams Schrift über parabolische Hohlspiegel," *Bibliotheca mathematica,* 3. Folge, Vol. 10 (1909–10), p. 232.

[14] Thomson, "Jordanus de Nemore: Opera," p. 135. Since there is no up-to-date description of this manuscript, I venture here a brief description of its contents from a microfilm copy in my possession: 1r–4r: Thābit ibn Qurra, *Liber karastonis;* 4r–5r: fragment of Gerard of Brussels, *Liber de motu;* 5r–9v: Jordanus de Nemore, *Liber de ratione ponderum;* 10r–11r: Anonymous, *De ponderibus Archimenidis;* 11r–21r: Jordanus de Nemore, *De numeris datis;* 21v–22r: anonymous astronomical diagrams; 23r–28v: Anonymous, *De angulis,* Inc. "Aliqui duo anguli . . . ;" 28v–50v: Gernardus, *Algorismus demonstratus;* 50v–52r: Anonymous, *Practica geometrie,* Inc. "Geometrie due sunt partes principales . . . ;" 52r–53v: fragment of *De ysoperimetris;* 53v: Pseudo-Euclid, *De ponderoso et levi;* 53v–55r: Anonymous, *De canonio;* 55r–v: Jordanus de Nemore, *Elementa de ponderibus;* 55v–59r: Jordanus de Nemore: *De plana spera* (Version II); 59r–62r: Alhazen, *De speculis comburentibus;* 62r–63r: fragmentary translation by Gerard of Cremona from the beginning of Apollonius' *Conics;* 63v–64v: beginning of a comment on Peter Lombard's *Sentences* in a hand of the 14c. Regarding this manuscript Madame Denise Bloch, Conservateur des manuscrits, writes me: "le manuscrit 8680A porte au f. de garde Aᵛ une ancienne cote 293 qui correspond au numéro d'ordre du volume dans l'inventaire après décès du mathématicien Claude Hardy, contenu dans le manuscrit latin 9363, f. 137 sq.; cf. f. 142; le manuscrit a été acheté à cette succession par Baluze pour la Bibliothèque de Colbert; cf. *ibid.,* f. 146. Au f. de garde A ancienne cote 4948 et indication du contenu du manscrit à la mine de plomb (XVIIᵉ s.) (Colbert 2440; Regius 54595)."

[15] Clagett, *Archimedes in the Middle Ages,* Vol. 1, p. 448.

[16] Thomson, "Jordanus de Nemore: Opera," p. 134.

THE BOOK ON MOTION OF GERARD
OF BRUSSELS
THE LATIN TEXT AND ENGLISH
TRANSLATION

/ Incipit Liber Magistri Gerardi de Brussel de Motu

Liber Primus

[Petitiones]

[1.] QUE MAGIS RECEDUNT A CENTRO, VEL AXE IMMOBILI,
5 MAGIS MOVENTUR: QUE MINUS, MINUS.

[2.] QUANDO LINEA EQUALITER ET UNIFORMITER ET EQUI-
DISTANTER MOVETUR, IN OMNIBUS PARTIBUS ET PUNCTIS SUIS,
IPSIS EQUALITER MOVETUR.

[3.] QUANDO MEDIETATES EQUALITER ET UNIFORMITER
10 MOVENTUR AD SE INVICEM, TOTUM EQUALITER MOVETUR SUE
MEDIETATI.

[4.] INTER LINEAS RECTAS EQUALES EQUALIBUS TEMPORIBUS
MOTAS, QUE MAIUS SPACIUM PERTRANSIT, ET AD MAIORES
TERMINOS, MAGIS MOVETUR;

15 [5.] ET MINUS, ET AD MINORES TERMINOS, MINUS MOVETUR.

Title, Pet., Prop. I.1

 Tit. 1 Incipit . . . Motu *OBN om. EP* De motu ambitus et poligonii *V / post* Motu *m. rec.
  add. O* Gerardus de motu / *mg. sup. f. 117r hab. O* de motu Liber / *mg. sin. f. 81v
  hab. B* de motu *et mg. 82r* INCIPIT MAGISTRI GERARDI DE BRUSSEL LIBER
  PRIMUS / Brusseł *N*
  2 Liber Primus *B* (*cf. var. prec.*) *N om. OEPV*
  3 [Petitiones] *addidi*
Pet. & Prop. I.1
  4 [1] *addidi, et etiam numeros sequentium petitionum* / recedunt *OBEN* removentur
  V renoventur *P* / vel axe immobili *om. PV* / axe: ab axe *E*
  5 que: et *N* et que *PV*
  7 movetur *om. N* / punctis: in punctis *PV* / suis *tr. PV post* partibus
  8 equaliter *bis E*
 9–11 Quando . . . medietati *mg. N*
  9 Quando: Quando vero *V*
  10 moventur *tr. N ante* equaliter / ad: a *P* / equaliter movetur *tr. N*
  12 Inter *om. E* / lineas *bis E* / equales *bis P* equalis *V*
  13 maius: magis *P* / pertransit *OBN* transit *EPV*
  14 magis: in magis *V* in (?) magis *P*
  15 Et[1]: et que *PV* / et[2] *supra scr. B om. E* / terminos *om. E* / minus[2]: in minus *P*

63

Sp

Sp

[6.] QUE NEC MAIUS SPACIUM, NEC AD MAIORES TERMINOS, MAGIS NON MOVETUR;

[7.] QUE NEC MINUS SPACIUM, NEC AD MINORES TERMINOS, MINUS NON MOVETUR.

20   [8.] PROPORTIO MOTUUM PUNCTORUM EST TANQUAM LI-NEARUM IN EODEM TEMPORE DESCRIPTARUM.

[Propositiones]

1ª. QUANTALIBET PARS SEMIDIAMETRI CIRCULUM DESCRI-BENTIS AD CENTRUM NON TERMINATA EQUALITER MOVETUR

25   SUO MEDIO PUNCTO. UNDE ET SEMIDIAMETER SUO MEDIO. EX QUO MANIFESTUM QUOD, SEMIDIAMETRORUM ET MOTUUM, UNA EST PROPORTIO.

Age ergo. Dico quod *CF* movetur equaliter suo medio puncto [Fig. I.1a(A)], prius probato quod differentia circulorum fit ex ductu differentie semidi-

30   ametrorum in medietates circumferentiarum.

Sint enim linee *OF*, *RL* equales [Figs. I.1a(A) et I.1b]. Et linea *LN* equetur circumferentie *OF* circuli. Patet per primam de quadratura circuli quod circulus *OF* et triangulus *RLN* sunt equales.

[Traditio I]	[Traditio II]
35 Item sint linee *SL*, *CF* equales, et	35 Item sint linee *CF*, *SL* equales, et
linee *ON*, *OQ* equales, et linee *SL*,	item linee *MO*, *OP* equales, et *SL*

16–19 Que. . . . movetur *mg. N*
16 nec[1] . . . spacium: nec ad maius spacium nec ad maius spacium *E* / maiores: minores *E*
17 moventur *N*
18 nec[1]: nec ad *E* / ad *om. V* / minores: maiores *P*
19 moventur *N*
20 proportio: porcio *E* / punctorum *om. N*
21 eodem: eorum *P*
22 [Propositiones] *addidi*
23 1ª *N om. VEP* I *O* Iª *B* / semidyametri *P*
25 medio puncto *tr. E* / Unde . . . medio *om. V* / semidiameter *O* (semi- *supra scr. O*), *EN* diameter *B*
26 manifestum *OB* manifestum est *ENPV*
27 una est *tr. V* / *post* proportio *scr. et del. V* Duo itaque primi. Dat orbibus nomina, et comparat eos inter se et cum tota solis sphaera
28 ergo *OB om E* / igitur *NPV* / Dico: proba *PV* / CF: C (?) *P* / medio *om. E*
31 Sint: sicut *P* / RL: KL *PV* NL (?) *O* / equetur: equalis *PV*
32 OF circuli *tr. PV* / primam: predicta *E*
33 RLN: KLN *PV*
34 [Traditio I] *et* [Traditio II] *addidi*
35 Item: vel *E* / CF: OF (?) *E*
35–36 et . . . equales: et dividatur NQ in duo equalia in puncto *O* per lineam MP, linee OP (*!* ON), OQ equales *E*
36 OQ: OP *B* / equales *om. N*   36 item *V* I.F *P*

MP equidistantes. Oportet ergo quod triangulus *RSQ* equetur circulo *OC*, et linea *SQ* circumferentie
40 *OC* circuli, quia cum trianguli *RLN*, *RSQ* sint similes, que est proportio *LR* ad *SR* ea est *LN* ad *SQ*. Sed que est *LR* ad *SR* ea est *OF* ad *OC*; et que est *OF* ad *OC*
45 ea est circumferentie *OF* circuli ad circumferentiam *OC* circuli, quia que est diametrorum ea est et circumferentiarum. Cum ergo et circumferentia *OF* circuli equetur li-
50 nee *LN*, et *SQ* equabitur circumferentie *OC* circuli, et superficies *SLNQ*, que est differentia triangulorum, equabitur differentie circulorum *OF*, *OC*. Superficies autem
55 *SLNQ* equatur quadrangulo (*!*) superficiei *SLMP*. Hoc sic probatur: Trianguli *OMN*, *OPQ* sunt equales

linea equidistet linee *MP*. Patet quod trianguli *KLN* et *KSQ* sunt similes, uterque enim angulus *S* et *L* rectus est et cum *KN* cadit super
40 *SP*, *LN* equidistantes, facit angulum *N* intrinsecum angulo *Q* extrinseco equalem, et item angulus *K* communis est utrique; quare omnes angulos habent equales. Ergo per
45 quartam sexti elementorum latera equos angulos respicientia sunt proportionalia; que est ergo proportio *LK* ad *SK* eadem est *LN* ad
50 *SQ*. Sed eadem proportio est *FO* ad *CO* que *LK* ad *SK*. Ergo eadem est proportio *LN* ad *SQ* que *FO* minoris ad *CO*. Sed que proportio est *FO* semidiametri maioris circuli
55 ad *CO* semidiametrum *CO* circuli minoris eadem est maioris circuli ad minorem. Que ergo est proportio

37 Oportet *ON* opportet *BE*
38 RSQ: LSQ *E*
40 quia: et *E*
41 RLN, RSQ: LNRSQ *E*
42 LR: LK (*?*) *E*
44 *post* OC² *scr. et del. N* et que est OF ad OC
47, 48 et *om. E*
53–54 circulorum *om. E*
55 *post* equatur *add. injuste E* quadratura
57 OPQ: OP que *E*

37 aequedistet *V*
39 *ante* angulus *scr. et del. P* a
40 cadit *P* cadat *V*
41 equidistantes *hic et quasi ubique V*
42 extrinseco *P* intrinseco *V*
44 quare *V* quia *P*
45 *post* per *mg. scr. V* Ex hac prima sequitur: Si in quolibet triangulo rectangulo item moveatur quodlibet duorum laterum rectum angulum contentium supra reliquum uniformiter illud non excedendo et semper rectum angulum faciendo cum eadem quando (*?*) ex suo ultimo puncto et medio reliqui lateris supra quod movetur (*et supra scr.* moveatur?) fiet punctus unus ex medio (*? supra scr.*) eiusdem (*in textu et supra*) moti et medio basis puncto fiet punctus unus, ex quo manifestum est quod quando unum duorum laterum facientium rectum angulum motum suum (*? sive* secundum) reliquum supra suum extremum punctum intersecabit basim equaliter in (*?*) aequa quoque (*sive* quosque) ab ea intersecabitur
50 proportio *tr V post* SK
57 Que ergo *tr. V*

et similes quia *M, P* anguli sunt recti, cum linea *MP* sit equidistans *SL* linee; et *O* utrobique est equalis; ergo *N* angulus equatur *Q* angulo. Ergo latera sunt proportionalia. / Sed *ON* equatur *OQ*, ut sit divisa *NQ* in duo equalia in puncto *O*. Ergo *OM, OP* sunt equales, et *MN, PQ*. Ergo trianguli sunt equales. Sic ergo superficies *SLNQ, SLMP* sunt equales. Sed linee *LN, SQ* equantur lineis *LM, SP* quia linee *MN, PQ* sunt equales. Sed linee *LN, SQ* equantur circumferentiis circulorum *OF, OC*. Ergo linee *LM, SP* equantur illis circumferentiis. Sic ergo superficies *SLMP* fit ex ductu differentie semidiametrorum in medietates circumferentiarum, et equatur differentie circulorum. Hoc idem alio modo probari posset. Sed hec probatio sufficiat ad presens.

FO circuli ad *CO* circulum eadem *LN* linee ad *SQ* lineam. Ergo permutatim per 15[am] quinti elementorum que est proportio circumferentie *OF* circuli ad *LN* lineam eadem est circumferentie *OC* circuli ad *SQ* lineam. Sed circumferentia *OF* circuli est equalis *LN* linee ex ypotesi. Ergo et circumferentia *OC* equalis est linee *SQ*. Sed *SK* equalis posita est semidiametro circuli *OC* et angulus *S* rectus. Ergo *KSQ* triangulus equalis circulo *OC*. Sed triangulus *KLN* equalis erat circulo *OF*. Quantum ergo habundatur triangulus *KLN* a triangulo *KSQ* tantum circulus *OF* a circulo *OC*. Ergo spacium *LNQS* equale est differentie circulorum *OF, OC*. Trianguli autem *MNO, OPQ* sunt equales, quoniam *M* angulus equalis *P* angulo, uterque rectus. Item angulus *N* angulo *Q* equatur per 29[am] primi elementorum, et latus *OP* respiciens *Q* angulum equalis est per positionem lateri *OM* respicienti *N* angulum. Ergo per 26[am] primi elementorum triangulus *MNO* equalis est triangulo

[margin left:] 117r

[margin right:] Sp.

---

58 quia . . . anguli: et anguli M, P *E*
59–60 MP . . . linee: scilicet eadem linea SL *E*
60 equalis: equaliter *E*
62 sunt *om. E*
63 *ante* Sed *mg. scr. O* vel ex XVI primi euclidis argumentum elice / ut: cum *N*
65 et MN *O* (et *supra scr. O*) MN *BE* NM *N*
68, 71, 73 equatur *E*
69 quia: OP *E*
74 SLMP: NMP *E*
77–78 *de* Hoc . . . posset *mg. scr. O* sicut patet in fine commenti super IIII[am] de piramidibus
78 probari posset *tr. N*
79 sufficat *E* spectat *OBN*

60 15[am] *supra scr. V lac. et* IIII[am] *P*
62 LN *V L P*
63 circumferentie *P om. V*
66 ypotesi *P* hypotesi *V*
72 habundatur *P* abundat (?) *V*
77 Trianguli *V et corr.* (?) *P ex* triangulus / OPQ *P* OQP *V*
80 angulus . . . Q *P* N angulus Q angulo *V*
82 OP *correxi ex* CP *in PV*

OQP. Ergo, trapetia *LM[O]QS* addita, est quadrangulus *LMPS* equalis spacio *LNQS*; quare et differentie predictorum circulorum. Item linea *MN* equalis est linee *PQ* per predicta et linea *SQ* linee *LR'* per 34[am] primi elementorum. Ergo *SQ* est medietas *SQ, LR'* simul iunctarum; deficit autem a medietate *LN, SQ* simul iunctarum, in medietate huius cum (?) quo predicte *LN, SQ* maiores sunt quam *LM* (!*LR'*), *SQ*, hoc est, in medietate *R'N.* Medietas autem *R'N* est *R'M, R'M* enim equalis est *PQ* per 34[am] primi elementorum. Sed *QP* equalis est *MN,* ut probatum est antea. Ergo *R'M* equalis est *MN.* Ergo *QP* equalis est medietati *R'N.* Si ergo *QP* addatur *SQ,* tota *SP* equalis erit medietati *LN, SQ* simul iunctarum. Sed circumferentie *OF* et *OC* circulorum simul iuncte equales erant *LN, SQ* simul iunctis. Ergo medietates medietatibus. Ergo linea *SP* equalis est medietati circumferentiarum *OF, OC; SL,* differentie semidiametrorum. Sed spacium *LSPM* fit ex ductu *SL* in *SP* que sunt differentie (!) semidiametrorum, etiam medietas circumferentiarum. Equalis autem erat predictus quadrangulus differ-

87 trapetia *V, lac. P* / -[O]- *addidi*
89 LNQS *corr. V ex* LMNQS
91 MN *correxi ex* MO in PV / *post* est
   scr. et del. V linea per
95–96 deficit . . . iunctarum *bis P*
  97 cum *sive* in *P* in *V*
 101 PQ *P* QP *V*
 103 probatum est *V* probatur *P*
 108 Sed *V* hec (?) *P*
 110 erant *P* sunt *V*
 112 *post* est *scr. V et delevi* medietati arc
   (?)
 117 etiam *P* et *V*

120 entie circulorum. Ergo differentia circulorum fit ex ductu differentie semidiametrorum in medietatem circumferentiarum.

Moveatur ergo *SL* per superficiem *SLMP*, et *CF* linea per differentiam
125 circulorum *OF, OC.* Dico igitur quod *SL, CF* linee equaliter moventur, pertranseunt enim equalia spacia et ad equales terminos, ut iam ex dictis constat.

Movetur ergo equaliter *SL, CF,* vel magis vel minus. Non magis,
130 quia nec maius spacium describit nec ad maiores terminos. Item non minus, quia nec minus spacium describit nec ad minores terminos. Cum ergo nec magis nec minus, nec
135 aliquis sit excessus motus ad motum, equaliter movetur.

Si movetur magis, sumatur differentia semidiametrorum in maiori circulo equaliter *CF,* et
140 moveatur equaliter *SL* describendo differentiam illorum circulorum. Patet ergo quod maius spacium describit quam *SL* in equali tempore, et ad maiores terminos, quia
145 si diameter maior, et circumferentia

Aut ergo equaliter moventur aut alterum altero magis, et tunc aut
130 *SL* magis movetur quam *CF* aut minus. Si equaliter, habeo propositum.

135

Si autem dicat adversarius quod *SL* magis movetur, sumatur differentia semidiametrorum que est *CF* vel
140 linea sibi equalis in maiori circulo quam sit *OF* in tantum maiori, ut augmentetur motus ipsius *CF* sed supra motum quem habebat primo, donec sit equalis secundum adver-
145 sarium motui *SL.* Moveatur ergo

---

124 superficiem *Trad. I, et corr. V ex* sum / SLMP *Trad. I* SLPM *P* et LMP *V* / et *Trad. I* Item moveatur *PV* / CF: EF *E et corr. V ex* OF

125 OF, OC *Trad. I* (*sed* OF et OC *in E*) CF, OF *P* OC, OF *V* / igitur *om. PV* / SL, CF *Trad. I* hee 2 *P* hae duae *V*

126 equalia: equa *E* / ut: non *E* / iam ex *OBE tr. NPV*

128 equaliter SL *tr. E*

129–319 *de* Non. . . . OC *est magna turbatio in textu MS O (cum litteris in mg. O indicantibus ordinem correctum); vide meum commentum longum in cap. 3° supra*

131 Item: vel *E*

132 nec: neque *E*

134 nec magis *om. E*

136 moventur *N*

137–62 Si. . . . movetur *om. N*

137 movetur *om. E*

139 et: quia *E*

143 SL: sub *E*

131 habeo *V* habet *P*

143 supra *V lac. P* / quem (?) *P* quam *V*

maior et circulus maior. Sic ergo patet per ultimam petitionem illa movetur magis *SL*; non ergo equaliter.

150 Si *SL* movetur minus *CF*, sumatur differentia semidiametrorum in minori circulo equaliter *CF*, que moveatur equaliter *SL* describendo differentiam illorum circulorum.

155 Patet ergo quod illa describit minus spacium in equali tempore et ad minores terminos quam *SL*. Ergo minus movetur per eandem petitionem. Non ergo equaliter. Cum

160 ergo *SL* nec minus nec magis movetur quam *CF*, equaliter ei movetur.

165

describendo differentiam illorum circulorm. Patet ergo quod maius spacium quam *SL* describit in equali tempore et ad maiores terminos, quia maioris circuli maior est circumferentia et maiori simul iuncte circumferentie quam minori. Sed circulus *OE* maior est quam *OC* (*! OF*) atque circulus *OG* maior quam *OF* (*! OC*); quare et cetera. Sic ergo per ultimum principium plus movetur *CF*, si sumatur in maiori circulo, quam *SL*.

Eodem modo si dicatur *SL* minus moveri quam *CF*, accipiatur equalis *CF* in minori circulo, et patebit quoniam quantumcumque moveretur motus eius minor erit quam motus *SL*. *SL* igitur equaliter movetur *CF*.

Sed *SL* movetur equaliter cuilibet suo puncto per secundam petitionem, quia equaliter movetur et uniformiter in omnibus suis partibus et punctis. Ergo movetur equaliter suo medio puncto. Sed medius punctus *SL* movetur equaliter medio puncto *CF*, quia illa puncta equales lineas describunt in

170 equalibus temporibus. Quod autem ille linee sunt equales, eodem modo probabis sicut probatum est quod

equalibus temporibus. Quia probari potest sicut probatum est lineam *SQ* equalem esse circumferentie

147 ultimam: penultimam *in numeris quos addidi; sed probabiliter auctor petitiones 4–5 esse unam petitionem considerat*
150 CF *O* OF *BE*
153 *ante* equaliter *del. B* s
160 nec[1] . . . magis: nec magis nec minus *E*
166 SL movetur: si moventur *N* / movetur equaliter *tr. EV* / cuilibet *om. V* / secundam petitionem: secundum principium *PV*
167–68 quia. . . . puncto: ergo et medius *P* ergo et medio *V*
167 movetur *tr. E post* uniformiter / in *om. E* / suis partibus *tr. N*
168 movetur equaliter *tr. E* / *post* suo *scr.* (*et forte del.*) *O* predicto *quod delevi quia non est in BENPV* / SL *Trad. I, et corr. V ex* GL
168–69 movetur equaliter *tr. EPV*
169 illa puncta *Trad. I.* in movendo *PV* / describunt: transcribunt *P*
171 linee *om. N*
172 probabis *OBN* probatur *E*

147 maius *V* magis *P*
148 SL descripit *P* sit GB describit *V*
151 maiori *P* maiorum *V*
152 minori *P* minorum *V*
154 OG (?) *V* AG *P*
156 Sic *P* Si *V* / per *P* secundum *V*
161 CF (?) *V* C *P*
163 moveretur *P* minore *V*

170 Quia *P* Quod *V*
172 equalem esse *P tr. V*

linea *SQ* equatur circumferentie
OC circuli. Sic ergo *SL* movetur
175   equaliter medio puncto *CF.* Sed *SL*
movetur equaliter *CF,* ut probatum
est. Ergo *CF* movetur equaliter suo
medio puncto. Eadem est demonstratio de quantalibet parte *OF*
180   semidiametri non terminata ad *O.*

circuli *CO. SL* ergo movetur equaliter medio puncto *CF.* Sed *CF*
175   equaliter movetur linee *SL.* Ergo
CF equaliter movetur suo medio
puncto, et eadem est demonstratio
de quantalibet parte *OF* semidiametri ad centrum *O* non termi-
180   nata.

175   medio: suo medio *E* / CF: OF *N*
180   *post* O *add. E* (*Cf. Trad. II, lin.
181–300*) Dico ergo quod OF mov-
etur equaliter suo medio puncto.
_____ (*?* Si enim non) ergo moveatur equaliter, aut magis aut minus. Si magis (*et scr. et del.* ergo)
moveatur (*correxi ex* morantur?*)
igitur equaliter D puncto, et sic BD
equaliter DF. Cum ergo BF movetur equaliter D puncto per precedentem (*!* presentem?*) propositionem et CF movetur (*sive moveatur*) equaliter idem puncto OF
movebitur equaliter BF, quod est
contra primum principium. Sic ergo
D punctus movetur magis F (*!* OF
sive et *?*) linea; non ergo equaliter.
Si minus, sit quod movetur equaliter E puncto et sit CA equalis
EC et AE equalis ED. Sic ergo
AD movetur equaliter E puncto
per precedentem (*!* presentem?*)
propositionem. Ergo AD movetur equaliter OF. Contra, magis
excedit EF motu suo ED quam
AE excedit motu suo OC. Hoc
per se patet. Cum ergo ille linee
sint similes medietates totalium linearum, manifestum est quod totalis motus OF collectus ex motibus
OC, CF maior est motu AD collecto
ex motibus OC, CF, maior est motu
AD (collecto . . . AD delendum?*)
collecto ex motibus AE, ED. Sic
ergo OF magis movetur EC (*!*)
puncto; non ergo equaliter. Sic ergo
OF movetur equaliter *C.* Idem potest probari directo hoc modo. Sit
quod linea GK mota sit per superficiem OFGK et OF mota sit per
circulum. Et sit linea FH equalis
circumferentie. Patet ergo per

173   CO *P* OC *V*
173–174   movetur equaliter *P tr. V*
177   et *P om. V*

Dico ergo quod *OF* movetur equaliter suo medio puncto, quia movetur equaliter linee *RL* describenti superficiem *RLTV*. Sit *LT* medietas *LN*. Aut ergo *RL* movetur equaliter *OF*, aut magis, aut minus. Si magis, sumatur linea supra centrum non terminata que equaliter moveatur *RL*, quelibet enim talis moveatur equaliter suo medio puncto, ut iam probavimus, et ita linee equidistanter et equaliter in omnibus partibus et punctis mote. Sit illa *DF*. Ergo *DF* movetur equaliter *RL*. Equetur ergo *DF*, *XL*. Ergo *DF*, *XL* moventur equaliter. Quare *RL*, *XL* moventur

equaliter, quia *RL* equaliter movetur in omnibus partibus et punctis. Contra, *DF* maius spacium describit quam *XL*, et ad maiores terminos. Hoc sic constet. Proportio

Rursus probare volo quod semidiameter suo medio. Si enim non equaliter, tunc aut magis aut minus. Si magis, moveatur igitur equaliter alicui puncto, qui magis moveatur quam *C* medius punctus eius. Ille ergo punctus magis distabit a centro quam *C* per primum principium. Sic igitur est ut apparet in secunda figuratione huius [Fig. I.1a(C)]. Cum ergo *OC* sit equalis *CF*, *OE'* erit maior quam *E'F* et maior quam [illa] secundum duplum *CE'*, quia cum *OC* equalis sit linee *CF*, tunc *CE'* ablata ex *CF* et equali *CE'* ablata ex *OC*, residua erunt equalia; ablata ergo quorum *CE'* est unum sunt equalia. Utrumque autem est cum linea que erat equalis *E'F* et hec est linea *OE'*. Ergo linea *OE'* continet quantum *EF* et insuper duplum *CE'*. Ex parte igitur centri resecetur *OE'* ita ut dupla portio ad *CE'* relinquatur versus

---

prima[m] de quadratura quod superficies OFGK equatur circulo et patet quod linee FG, OK equantur circumferentie. Dico quod GK equaliter mota est OF, quod potest probari per impossibile, sicut ex predictis patet. Sed GK movetur equaliter suo medio puncto et medius punctus GK movetur equaliter C puncto. Hoc est quod probare volumus.

183 RL: LR (*sive* LX?) *E*
183–184 describenti *N* describente *OBE*
184 RLTV: CLTU (?) *E*
187 supra: super *E*
188 non *mg. O om. BEN*
190 movetur *BN*
197–200 Quare . . . equaliter[1] *om. N*
197 Quare *O* quia *BE*
200 equaliter[2] *om. E*
200–01 movetur *om. N*
202 spacium: spera *O*
203 XL: RL *E*

182 Si enim *corr. V ex* sic min
185 qui *V* que *P* / movetur *V*
189 est *P* C (?) *V*
191 ergo *P* igitur *V* / OE' *P* OC *V*
197 ergo *P* etiam *V*
199 est: e (?) *V*
200 OE' *P* OC *V*
201–03 Ergo. . . . OE' *bis P*
201 Ergo . . . OE' *om. V*
203 OE' *P, et corr. V ex* OC / ut *P* quod *V*
203–04 dupla *P* duplex *V*
204 portio *V* proportio *P*

205 superficiei *RLTV* ad superficiem
RXYV est tanquam *RL* ad *RX*, cum
sint inter lineas equidistantes. Sed
proportio *OF* circuli ad *OD* circulum est proportio *OF* semidi-
210 ametri ad *OD* semidiametrum duplicata, quia proportio circulorum
est semidiametrorum duplicata, hoc
est, proportio *RL* ad *RX* duplicata.
117v / Ergo maior est proportio circuli
215 *OF* ad circulum *OD* quam superficiei *RLTV* ad superficiem *RXYV*.
Sed circulus *OF* et superficies
RLTV sunt equales, quia quadrangula superficies que dupla est circuli
220 est dupla *RLTV*. Sic ergo maior est
proportio circuli *OF* ad circulum
OD quam ad superficiem *RXYV*.
Ergo *OD* circulus minor est *RXYV*.
Ergo differentia *OF, OD* circulorum
225 maior est differentia *RLTV, RXYV*
superficierum. Ergo *DF* maius spacium describit quam *XL* et ad maiores terminos, quia circumferentia
OF circuli equatur lineis *LT, XY*.
230 Ergo addita circumferentia *OD* circuli maius efficitur. Cum ergo

205 centrum et equalis *E'F* relinquatur
conterminabilis eidem. Et sit prima
portio *OA*, secunda *AE'*. Age igitur
AE' equalis est *E'F*. Ergo *E'* medius
punctus est *AF*. Quare per prece-
210 dentem probationem *AF* movetur
equaliter *E'* puncto, et *OF* secundum adversarium eidem. Ergo *AF*
et *OF* equaliter moventur, quod est
contra primum principium. Non
215 ergo *OF* equaliter movetur alicui
puncto magis remoto a centro
quam sit medius eius. Quare nec
magis quam medius eius punctus
movebitur.
   Si autem dicat quod minus movetur [Fig. I.1a(D)], sumatur ergo
punctus qui minus movetur quam
C medius *OF*, quem oportebit per
primum principium minus remo-
veri a centro quam *C*. Sumatur ergo
et sit *D'* punctus. Linea ergo *OD'*
minor quam *D'F* in duplo *D'C*. Hoc
probatur similiter primo. Abscindatur item ex *OD', BD'* ita quod
BD' non terminetur ad centrum.
Linea igitur *OD'* minor erit quam

205 superficiei *om. E super et lac. in B
     hic et alibi* / RLTV: LRTV *N*
206 RXYV: RXYN (?) *E hic et saepe*
     / est *N om.* OBE
207 sint: fiant *N* / equidistantes: equales
     E
208–09 circulum *om. E*
210–11 dupplicata *EN*
212, 213 dupplicata *E hic et saepe*
219–20 circuli . . . dupla *om. E*
220–21 est proportio *tr. E*
222 quam *om. E*
223 OD circulus: circulus AD *E*
225 RLRV (?) *O*
226–27 spacium: spera *O*
227 XL *BN* RL *OE*
228 circumferentia: differentia *E*
229 XY *N* RY *OBE*
231 maius: magis *E*

206 conterminabilis *P* conterminalis *V*
207 portio *V* proportio *P* / OA *V, et corr.*
     P ex AO
208 AE' *P, et corr. V ex* AG / est *P. om.*
     V / E' *P om. V*
209 est *tr. V post* Ergo *in lin. 208*
210 movetur *P* movebitur *V*
217 quam *P, et corr. V ex* qualis
220 quod *P* quis quod *V*
221 ergo *P om. V*
226 OD' *V* CD *P*
228 probatur *P* probabitur *V* / primo *P*
     Item primo *V*
229 item *om. V hic* / OD' *P* CD *V*

maius spacium describit et ad maiores terminos, magis movetur. Sic
ergo *DF* magis movetur *RL*: non
235 ergo equaliter. Si autem velit su-
mere lineam supra centrum
equalem *RL*, ut *DE*, eadem inprobatio. Sic ergo *RL* non movetur
magis *OF*. Simili demonstratione
240 probabis quod non minus; ergo
equaliter. Sed *RL* movetur equaliter
suo medio puncto. Et punctus *C*
movetur equaliter medio *RL*, quia
circumferentia *C* equatur *SZ*. Ergo
245 *OF* semidiameter movetur equaliter
suo medio puncto.

250

255

260

D'F in duplo *D'C* et linea *BD'* minor est quam *OD* secundum quantitatem *OB*. Ergo linea *BD'* minor
235 est quam linea *D'F* secundum duplum *D'C* et secundum quantitatem *OB*. Abscindatur ergo ex *D'F*
portio conterminalis *BD'*, equalis
eidem linee, scilicet, *BD'*. Et sit *D'G*.
240 Residuum igitur, quod est *GF*,
equale est duplo *CD'* et linee *OB*,
in tantum enim habundat *D'F* a
BD'. Linea igitur *BG* per primam
probationem movetur equaliter *D'*
245 puncto, et *OF* secundum adversarium eidem. Ergo *OF* movetur
equaliter *BG*, quod iterum est contra primum principium. Nam *CF*
magis removetur a centro plusquam
250 *CG* quam *BC* plusquam *OC*.
Etenim *CF* secundum quantitatem
OB et duplum *CD'* plus elongatur
a centro quam *CG*. Sed *BC* plus
removetur quam *OC* secundum
255 quantitatem *OB* solum. Ergo *CF*
magis removetur a centro respectu
CG plusquam *BC* respectu *OC* secundum duplum *CD'*. Quare *CF*
magis removetur quam *CG* plus-
260 quam *BC* magis removetur quam
OC secundum quantitatem motus
dupli *CD'*. Ergo totalis motus col-

232 spacium *EN* spera *OB* / describat
   N
236 centrum *N* circulum *OBE*
237 ut: et *E*
237–38 inprobatio *ON* improbatio *E* ῑpro-
   batio *B*
238 RL: R (?) *E*
239 Simili *N* sine *OBE*
240 probabis *EN* probabit *OB* / quod:
   quia *E*
241 Sed *N* ergo *OBE*
243 movetur equaliter *tr. E* / medio:
   medio puncto *N*
244 SZ: ST (*sive* SC) *N* / Ergo *om. E*

238 portio *V* proportio *P*
239 *post* linee *scr. et del. P* b
242 habundat *V* ha *P et hic desinit P*
250 plus- *corr. V ex* ut
252 et *corr. V ex* etiam / CD' *corr. V ex*
   et D
253 *ante* CG *scr. et del. V* G (?)
257–58 secundum *supra scr. V*
260 *supra* removetur *scr. V* movebitur

265

270

275

280

285

290

295

300

265 lectus ex motu *OC, CF* maior est totali motu collecto ex *BD', GD',* [cuius] medius punctus est *D'. OF* igitur magis [movetur] quam *D'* punctus vel quam quicunque plus accedens ad centrum quam accedat medius punctus eius. Quare plus

270 movetur quam punctus minus mo-tus medio puncto. Si enim minus movetur, minus removetur a cen-tro. Ergo non minus movetur quam medius punctus eius. Sed nec magis

275 eam moveri monstratum est. Ergo eidem equaliter movetur.

   Idem potest probari directe hoc modo [Fig. I.a(D)]. Sit quod linea *NK* mota sit per superficiem *OFNK*

280 et *OF* mota sit per circulum. Et sit linea *FH* equalis circumferentie, que sit divisa in duo equalia in puncto *K*, et linea *OL* equalis etiam circumferentie sit divisa in puncto

285 *N* in duo equa. Patetque quod linee *FK, ON* equantur circumferentie, et superficies *ONFK* equatur cir-culo. Dico igitur quod *OF* mota est equaliter *NK*, et probari potest per

290 impossibile sicut ex predictis patet. Sed *NK* movetur equaliter suo me-dio puncto, et medius punctus *NK* movetur equaliter medio puncto *OF*, et cum hoc totum pateat ex

295 predictis. *NK* ergo movetur equal-iter *C* puncto. Sed *OF* equaliter movetur linee *NK*. Ergo *OF* linea equaliter movetur *C* suo medio puncto. Et hoc est quod probare

300 proposui.

270–71 motus *bis V*

272 re- *supra scr. V*

283 OL *correxi ex* OB *in V*

293 *ante* movetur *scr. et del. V* et

[reverte ad fol.

117r] / Corollarium sic pateat. Dico quod proportio *OF* ad *OC* est tanquam motuum *OF*, *OC*, quia proportio *OF* ad *OC* est tanquam circumfe-
305 rentie *F* ad circumferentiam *C*. Sed circumferentie *F* ad circumferentiam *C* est tanquam circumferentie *C* ad circumferentiam *B*. Sit *B* medius punctus *OC*. Sed circumfe-
310 rentie *C* ad circumferentiam *B* est tanquam proportio motus *C* puncti ad motum *B* puncti. Ergo a primo proportio *OF* ad *OC* est tanquam proportio motus *C* puncti ad mo-
315 tum *B* puncti. Sed motus *C* puncti est motus *OF* linee et motus *B* puncti est motus *OC* linee. Ergo *OF* ad *OC* proportio est tanquam proportio motus *OF* ad motum *OC*.
320

325

Corollarium sic pateat. Dico quod proportio *OF* semidiametri maioris circuli ad *OC* semidiametrum minoris est tanquam propor-
305 tio motus *OF* semidiametri maioris circuli ad motum *OC* semidiametri minoris. Proportio enim *OF* semidiametri ad *OC* semidiametrum est sicut circumferentie *OF* maioris circuli ad circumferentiam minoris
310 vel *OC* circuli. Sit item *P* medius punctus *OC* linee. Eadem est proportio *OC* circumferentie ad *OP* circumferentiam, que est *OF* circumferentie ad *OC* circumferen-
315 tiam. Ergo a primo eadem est proportio *OF* semidiametri ad *OC* semidiametrum, que est *OC* circumferentie ad *OP* circumferen-
320 tiam. Sed proportio *OC* circumferentie ad *OP* circumferentiam est tanquam motus *C* puncti ad motum *P* puncti. Sed motus *C* est motus semidiametri *OF* et motus *P*
325 motus est semidiametri *OC*. Ergo que est proportio *OF* semidiametri ad *OC* semidiametrum, eadem est motus unius ad motum alterius.

301–19 *in re* Corollarium. . . . *OC scr. O mg. f. 117r* Si supponetur quod C est medius punctus; eodem autem modo concludetur probatio, sumpto quolibet alio puncto pro medio, scilicit (?) per ultimam petitionem
302 OC: EC *E*
303 quia proportio *bis E*
305 F *supra scr. E*
308–09 medius *om. E*
310 C *ON om. BE*
311 motus *OBE om. N*
318 proportio *O hic, sed tr. BEN ante* OF *in lin. 317*

303 *post* ad *scr. et del. V* circunferentiam
306 motum *scr. et injuste del. V*
308 OC *correxi ex* DC

[procede iterum ad fol.

117v]   / 2ª. QUANTALIBET PARS YPOTENUSE CURVAM SUPERFICIEM
ROTUNDE PIRAMIDIS DESCRIBENTIS CITRA CONUM TERMINATA
MOVETUR EQUALITER SUO MEDIO PUNCTO; UNDE YPOTENUSA
SUO MEDIO. EX QUO MANIFESTUM EST QUOD OMNES YPOTE-
5   NUSE EQUALIUM BASIUM EQUALITER MOVENTUR.

Age igitur. Probabis quod *BK* movetur equaliter suo medio puncto, prius
probato quod differentia curvarum superficierum rotundarum piramidum
fit ex ductu differentie ypotenusarum in medietates circumferentiarum ipsarum basium. Verbi gratia, sit linea *RL* equalis ypotenuse *BH*, et linea *LN*
10   equalis circumferentie basis rotunde piramidis *OBH* [see Figs. I.1b and I.2].
Patet ergo, per primam de piramidibus, quod triangulus *RLN* equatur curve
superficiei piramidis *OBH*. Item sit linea *RS* equalis *KH*. Patet quod triangulus
RSQ equatur curve superficiei piramidis *IKH*, quia *SQ* equatur circumferentie
basis. Quod sic probatur.

15   Quia proportio *LR* ad *SR* ea est *LN* ad *SQ*, quia similes sunt trianguli.
Item que est *BH* ad *KH* ea est *OB* ad *IK*, quia similes sunt trianguli. Sed
que est *OB* ad *IK* ea est circumferentie *OB* semidiametri ad circumferentiam
IK semidiametri. Ergo que est *BH* ad *KH* ea est circumferentie ad circumferentiam. Ergo que est *LN* ad *SQ* ea est circumferentie ad circumferentiam.

Prop. I.2

    1 2ª *N* II *OB om. EV* / ypotenuse *O* hypothenuse *B* ypoteneuse *E* ypothenuse *N*
       hypotenusae *V*

    2 pyramidis *V hic et ubique* (*post hoc lectiones huiusmodi non laudabo*)

    3 ypotenusa *O* hypothenusa *B* ypotheneusa *E* ypothenusa *N* hypotenusa *V* (*post hoc
       lectiones huiusmodi non laudabo*)

    4 est *OBV om. EN*

  7–9 *de* differentia . . . basium *scr. mg. O* Istud idem probat quarta de piramidibus sed
       modo alio

    8 fit *ON om. BE* / ducte *B* / differentie *om. V* / medietatem *V*

  11 triangulus *om. N* / *ante* curve *scr. et del. V* circumferentiae

  12 Patet: dico *V*

  13 IKH: K *in ras. V*

  15 Quia[1] . . . trianguli: quia enim similes sunt trianguli quae est proportio LR ad SR
      eadem est LN ad SQ. Item quae est LR ad SR eadem est BH ad KH, LR enim linea
      aequalis est BH lineae et SR (*corr. V ex* GR) KH. Ergo quae proportio LN ad SQ
      eadem est BH ad KH *V* / proportio: que proportio *N*

  16 ea: eadem *V* / quia . . . trianguli: Ista enim latera in similibus triangulis BHO, KHI
      aequales angulos respiciunt *V*

 17–19 ea. . . . circumferentiam[1]: eadem est circumferentiae basis pyramidis BHO ad cir-
      cumferentiam basis pyramidis KIH. Ergo quae proportio LN ad SQ eadem est cir-
      cumferentiae BO semidiametri ad circumferentiam KI semidiametri. Permutatim
      ergo quae est proportio LN ad circumferentiam BO semidiametri eadem est SQ ad
      circumferentiam KI semidiametri *V*

 18–19 *post* circumferentiam *add. EN* Sed que est BH ad KH ea est RL ad RS quia equales
      sunt ad se (*om. E*) invicem. Ergo que est RL ad RS ea est circumferentie ad circum-
      ferentiam

20   Sed *LN* equatur circumferentie *OB* semidiametri. Ergo *SQ* equatur relique
circumferentie. Sic ergo *RSQ* triangulus equatur curve superficiei *IKH* piramidis. Ergo superficies *SLNQ* est differentia curvarum superficierum que
equatur superficiei *SLMP*. Sit *NQ* divisa in duo equalia in *O* puncto, quod
probatur eodem modo penitus quo prius probatum est de differentia cir-
25   culorum.

Moveatur ergo *SL* per superficiem *SLMP*, et *BK* per differentiam curvarum
superficierum. Dico igitur quod *SL* movetur equaliter *BK*, quia equalia spacia
describunt, et ad equales terminos, ut iam patet ex dictis.

Aut ergo *SL* movetur equaliter *BK*, aut magis, aut minus. Si magis, pro-
30   ponatur curva superficies cuius basis sit maior *OB* circulo. Et sumatur pars
ypotenuse equalis *BK* que equaliter moveatur *LS*. Dico quod illa movetur
magis *SL*, quia maiorem superficiem describit, et ad maiores terminos, ambe
enim circumferentie maiores sunt. Et ideo quod fit ex ductu illius linee in
medietates circumferentiarum maius est; et ita linea illa movetur magis *SL*.
35   Non ergo equaliter.

118r   Si *SL* movetur minus *BK*, sumatur curva superficies piramidis / cuius
basis sit minor circulo *OB*. Et sumatur pars ypotenuse equalis *BK*, que equaliter
moveatur *SL*. Dico quod *SL* magis movetur illa, quia maius spacium describit,
et ad maiores terminos. Ille enim circumferentie sunt minores lineis *LM*,
40   *SP*, quia circulis *OB*, *IK* semidiametri. Et ideo superficies *SLMP* maior
superficie quam describit illa linea. Sic ergo *SL* magis movetur illa linea.

20   equatur[1]: æqualis posita fuit *V* / OB: BO *V* / semidiametri *om. V* / equatur[2]: aequalis
est *V*
20–21 relique circumferentie: circumferentiae KI *V*
21   Sic: sicut *V* / RSQ: SQR *V* / curve *om. N*
21–22 IKH piramidis *tr. V*
22   SLNQ *corr. V ex* ILNQ / que: et *V*
23   superficiei: quadrangulo *V* / *ante* NQ *scr. et del.* B ite / NQ *corr. V ex* enim Q / O
puncto *tr. V*
24   quo: sicut *V*
27   igitur *om. V*
29   BK: B- *supra scr.* OB K *E*
29–52 Si. . . . demonstrare *OBEV*; *et mg. scr.* OB hoc omitte usque corollarium et age
eodem modo penitus ut in prima *et totum lin. 29–52 om. N et in suo loco scr.* et age
eodem modo penitus ut prius
30   sit *om. V*
30–32 Et. . . . describit: quousque secundum adversarium quod BK aequaliter movetur
SL. Moveatur in maiori circulo portio hypotenusae aequalis BK. Et patet quod maius
spacium describet *V*
33   sunt *om. V* / quod: id quod *B* illud quod *V*
34   et . . . illa: spacio per quod movetur SL et ita illa linea *V*
36   movetur minus: dicatur minus moveri quam *V* / *ante* BK *scr. et del.* B KB
37   circulo OB *tr. V* / *post* que *add. V* secundum falsigraphum
37–38 equaliter moveatur *tr. V*
38   illa: quam illa *V*
39–40 LM, SP: SP, LM *V*
40   quia . . . semidiametri *om. V* / semidiametri *corr. (?) OB ex* semidiametro *et hab.*
E semidiametrorum / SLMP: LMSQ *V* / maior: maior est *V*
41   illa linea[1]: BH *V* / Sic . . . linea[2] *om. V*

Sic ergo cum *SL* nec magis nec minus movetur *BK*, movebitur ei equaliter. Eodem modo probabis de qualibet parte ypotenuse *BH*. Cum ergo *SL* moveatur equaliter suo medio puncto et medius punctus *SL* moveatur equaliter

45   medio puncto *BK* (medius enim punctus *BK* movetur per circumferentiam que equatur linee per quam movetur medius punctus *SL* linee; hoc probabitur per similes triangulos, sicut prius), sic ergo *SL* movetur equaliter medio puncto *BK*. Sed *BK* movetur equaliter *SL*. Ergo *BK* movetur equaliter suo medio puncto.

50   Postea probabis duplici probatione, sicut prius probatum est de semidiametro, quod *BH* ypotenusa movetur equaliter suo medio puncto; et hoc est quod voluimus demonstrare.

Corollarium sic pateat. Dico quod *BH*, *BF* ypotenuse equaliter moventur. Sit *K* medius punctus *BH* et *G* medius punctus *BF*. Ut iam ergo probavimus

55   *BH* movetur equaliter *K* puncto, et *BF* movetur equaliter *G* puncto. Sed *K* movetur equaliter *G*. Hoc sic probatur.

I, *C* anguli sunt recti [cum] sit *IC* equidistans *OB*; et *K* utrobique equalis. Ergo *B*, *H* anguli sunt equales. Ergo trianguli *KBC*, *KIH* sunt similes. Ergo latera proportionalia. Sed *BK* est equalis *KH*. Ergo *IK* est equalis *KC*. Simili

60   modo probabis quod *GBD*, *GFH* trianguli sunt similes, quia *D*, *H* anguli sunt recti, cum *DH* linea sit equidistans *OB*; et *G* angulus utrobique equalis. Ergo *B*, *F* anguli equales. Cum ergo linea *BG* sit equalis *GF*, et linea *DG* est equalis *GH*. Cum ergo linee *IC*, *HD* sint equales, et medietates earum equales.

42   nec[1] *V* non *OBE* / BK, movebitur: BK mota in propria superficie movetur *V*
43   SL: SH *V*
44–45 medius . . . BK[2]: BK aequaliter movetur SL, BK aequaliter movetur suo medio SL. Sed medius punctus BK aequaliter movetur medio puncto SL quia *V*
46   linee[2] *om. V* / probabitur *OB* probatur *EV*
47–48 sic. . . . SL: medius ergo punctus (*hic scr. et del. V* KL) BK movetur aequaliter medio puncto SL. Sed BK aequaliter movebatur eidem *V*
48   movetur equaliter[2] *tr. V*
50   prius *tr. V post* est
51   movetur equaliter *tr. V*
52   voluimus *E* volumus *OB* volui *V*
53   patebit *V*
54   ergo *om. V*
55   movetur equaliter[1] *OBN om. V (sed habet V unam litteram quam non legere possum)*
57   I: R(?) *V* / [cum] *addidi (cf. lin. 61)* Nam *V* / sit *om. V* / OB: est OB *V*
58   Ergo[2] . . . similes: Triangulus igitur BCK similis est triangulo KIH (*corr. V ex* KLH) *V*
59   latera: latera sunt *V* / IK *OBEN, et corr. V ex* LK
59–64 KC. . . . equalis *bis OB, et de priore mg. scr. OB* vacat
60   GBD, GFH trianguli: trianguli BGD, GFH *V* / GBD: BGD *in repet. B*
61   aequedistans *V hic et quasi semper; postea lectiones ulteriores non laudabo*
62   Ergo *mg. V* / equales: sunt equales *NV* / ergo *om. V* / GF: BF *N*
63   ergo *om. V* / HD: BD *N* / sint *OBV* sunt *EN*
63–75 et. . . . demonstrare: moveantur per spacium BO, EF earum media puncta aequales lineas describent. Ergo aequaliter moventur media puncta et lineae igitur K punctus aequaliter movetur G puncto. Sed BH aequaliter movebatur K puncto. Ergo BH (*hic ante* B- *juste del. V* R *sed injuste supra scr.* L) aequaliter movebatur G puncto. Sed BF aequaliter movetur eidem. Ergo BF, BH aequaliter moventur, et hoc voluimus ostendere *V*

Ergo *IK* est equalis *HG*. Ergo *K, G* puncta describunt equales circumferentias.
65 Ergo moventur equaliter. Sed *BH, BF* moventur equaliter *K, G* punctis. Ergo *BH, BF* moventur equaliter.

Hoc idem sic probari potest. Trianguli *OBH, IKH* sunt similes, quia *IK* est equidistans *OB*. Ergo latera sunt proportionalia. Sed *BH* dupla est *KH*. Ergo *OB* est dupla *IK*. Ergo *OA* est equalis *IK*. Sit *A* medius punctus *OB*.
70 Ergo *K* movetur equaliter *A*. Ergo *OB* movetur equaliter *BH*, quia *OB* movetur equaliter *A* et *BH* movetur equaliter *K*. Eodem modo probabis quod *BF* movetur equaliter *OB* per similes triangulos *OBF, HGF*. Sicut ergo *BF* dupla est *GF*, ita *OB* dupla est *HG*, et ita *A* punctus movetur equaliter *G* puncto, ergo *BF* linee. Ergo *BF* linea movetur equaliter *BH* linee. Et hoc voluimus
75 demonstrare.

3ª. PUNCTUM ASSIGNARE CUI AMBITUS POLIGONII EQUILATERI ET EQUIANGULI CORPUS POLIGONIUM DESCRIBENTIS MOVETUR EQUALITER. UNDE MANIFESTUM QUOD AMBITUS POLIGONII IN-SCRIPTI CIRCULO, SI FUERIT PLURIUM LATERUM, MAGIS MO-
5 VETUR. IN CIRCUMSCRIPTIS VERO ECONTRARIO.

In hunc modum procede [Fig. I.3a]: *CG* latus quadrati movetur equaliter *R* puncto. Sit *R* medius punctus *CG*. Et hoc per precedentem. Similiter *M'G* movetur equaliter *Y* puncto. Ergo illa duo latera moventur equaliter illis duobus punctis. Et totalis ambitus quadrati movetur equaliter illis duobus lateribus. Ergo totalis / ambitus movetur equaliter illis duobus punctis. Ergo
11 alteri illorum cum illi equaliter moveantur. Postea probandum quod *H, S* puncta moventur equaliter *R*, medio puncto *HS* linee. *KG'* linea est equidistans *BA* linee. Ergo *K, G'* anguli sunt recti; et *R* angulus utrobique equalis. Ergo *S, H* anguli sunt equales. Ergo trianguli *HKR, RG'S* sunt similes. Ergo latera
15 sunt proportionalia. Sed *RS* equatur *RH*. Hoc postea probabitur. Ergo *G'S* equatur *HK*. Quanto ergo excessu magis movetur *S* punctus *G'* puncto, tanto

118v (margin, left of line 10)

64 K, G *ON* (*et corr. O ex* K, H?) K, H *B* H, K *E*
65–66 K, G. . . . equaliter *BEN, mg. O*
67 probari potest *tr. N*
69 est² *om. N* / *ante* OB² *scr. et del. B* BH, HF
72 OBF *EN et corr. B ex* ABF *et hab. O* ABF
73 *ante* G *scr. et del. B* g. p / *post* puncto *add. EN et ita* OB movetur equaliter G puncto
74 voluimus *N* volumus *OBE*

Prop. I.3
1 3ª *N om. EV* III *OB*
5 *ante* circumscriptis *scr. et. del. V* 1 / vero *om. V*
6 hunc: hunc ergo *V* / modum: modum ergo *N*
7 precedentem *NV* presentem *OB, E* (?) / M'G: MC *V*
8 equaliter¹ *NV om. OBE* / puncto: puncto suo medio *V*
9–10 de Et . . . lateribus *mg. scr. N* quia debet intelligi tanquam OM' esset axis immobilis
11 illorum: eorum *V* / illi *om. V*
12–16 KG'. . . . HK: Age igitur KL, GA sunt aequedistantium per positionem et K angulus rectus, ergo G angulus rectus erit, ergo extrinsecus eidem, et R angulus (*correxi ex* angulo) utrobique est aequalis. Quare S, H reliqui anguli duorum triangulorum KHR, RGS erunt aequales. Ergo trianguli sunt similes; quare latera sunt proportionalia. Sed HR aequatur RS, ut postea patebit. Ergo KR, RG erunt aequalia *V*
14 RG'S: RSG *N*
16 *ante* excessu *scr. et del. O* mag / puncto *om. V*

magis movetur *K* punctus *H* puncto. Ergo *G'*, *K* insimul equaliter moventur *H*, *S* insimul. Sed *K*, *G'* moventur equaliter *R*, quia omnes partes et omnia puncta *KG'* linee equaliter et uniformiter moventur. Ergo *H*, *S* puncta mo-

20 ventur equaliter *R* puncto. Eadem probatione *I*, *Q* puncta equaliter moventur *P* medio puncto. Similiter *L*, *N* puncta equaliter moventur *M* medio puncto. Quod sint media puncta postea constabit. Latera ergo *CE*, *EG*, que sunt latera octogoni, moventur equaliter suis mediis punctis, scilicet, *I*, *Q*: et *I*, *Q* moventur equaliter *P* puncto. Ergo illa latera moventur equaliter *P* puncto.

25 Eadem ratione opposita duo latera moventur equaliter *I'*, *B'* punctis, ergo *Z* puncto. Ergo illa IIII latera octogoni moventur equaliter *P*, *Z* punctis; ergo *U* puncto, quia *PZ* linea equaliter et uniformiter movetur in omnibus partibus et punctis suis. Sed IIII latera moventur equaliter totali ambitui octogoni. Ergo totalis ambitus movetur equaliter *U* puncto.

30 Eodem modo duo latera *EF*, *FG* moventur equaliter suis mediis punctis, et ita medio puncto linee dividentis illa latera in duo equalia. Similiter duo latera *CD*, *DE* moventur equaliter medio puncto linee dividentis illa in duo equalia. Ergo illa IIII latera moventur equaliter *L*, *N* punctis. Sed *L*, *N* puncta moventur equaliter *M* puncto. Ergo illa IIII latera moventur equaliter *M*

35 puncto. Similiter alia IIII latera moventur equaliter *Z'* puncto. Ergo illa VIII

17 K²: H *V*
18 H, S: S, H *V* / moventur: movetur *V* / R: R suo medio puncto *V*
18–19 et . . . linee: GK *V*
19 puncta² *om. N*
19–20 moventur *bis O*
20 puncto: medio SH lineae puncto *V* / puncta *om. V*
21 medio: suo medio *V* / puncta . . . moventur *OBV* puncta moventur equalia *E* moventur equaliter *N* / moventur aequaliter *V* / M medio: in medio *B* R (?) *V* / M *supra scr. O*
22 sint: sit *B*
22–24 *de* Latera . . . puncto¹ *mg. scr. O* per precendentem propositionem
23 octogoni *ON* octogonii *BEV* (*post hoc lectiones huiusmodi non laudabo*) / *ante* suis *scr. et del. B* p- (?) / I¹: R *V*
24 *ante* P¹ *scr. et del. B* I, B punctis / Ergo . . . puncto *om. V*
25 Eadem: e. *N* / I', B' *text. OBEN, om. fig. O* C, B *V* E, B *fig. B*
26 Z¹ *corr. V ex* ER
27 linea . . . uniformiter: uniformiter et aequaliter *V* / linea: linea movetur *N*
29 ambitus: ambitus octogoni *N* ambitus octogonii *V*
30–33 EF. . . . equalia: CD, DE sedecagonii moventur aequaliter suis mediis punctis et ita medio puncto lineae dividentis illa duo latera in duo latera in duo aequalia, scilicet L (*supra scr. V*) puncto. Similiter CF (*! EF*), FG latera eiusdem sedecagonii moventur aequaliter suis mediis punctis; quare movebuntur aequaliter medio puncto lineae dividentis ea in duo aequalia, scilicet N puncto *V*
31 latera *N mg. O* duo latera *EV et scr. et del. B*
31–33 Similiter . . . equalia *EN om. OB*
33 IIII latera: 4 puncta sedecagonii *V*
34 M¹ *subscr. in lac. O* in *B* / M²: in *B*
35 alia . . . latera: atque eodem modo reliqua 4 latera eiusdem sedecagoni (*!*) *V* / Z' *V* (*cf. leg. Fig. I.3a*) Z *OB* q; *N* CE *E*

latera sedecagoni moventur equaliter *M, Z'* punctis; ergo *X* puncto, quia linea *MZ'* movetur equaliter in omnibus partibus et punctis. Sed totalis ambitus sedecagoni movetur equaliter medietati. Ergo totalis ambitus movetur equaliter *X* puncto.

40 Nunc probandum quod polliciti sumus. *OE* linea protracta est per medium *CG* linee. Ergo orthogonaliter dividit illam. Similiter *OQ* protracta est per medium *EG* linee, et *OI* per medium *CE* linee. Et *CE, EG* sunt equales, quia latera octogoni. Ergo *OQ, OI* sunt equales, latera enim *OE, EQ; OE, EI* sunt equalia; et angulus angulo; ergo basis basi; ergo *OQ, OI* sunt equales.

45 Quod autem anguli sint equales sic probatur. Latera *RE, RC; RE, RG* sunt equalia; et angulus angulo, quia uterque rectus; ergo basis basi, et cetera. Cum ergo *RC, RG* sint equales, oppositi anguli sunt equales, *SOP, POH* sunt equales, et anguli contenti sunt equales. Ergo latera *OQ, OP; OI, OP* sunt equalia, et angulus angulo; ergo basis basi, et cetera. Ergo *PQ, PI* sunt

50 equales, et *P* angulus utrobique rectus. Similiter *R* angulus utrobique rectus. Ergo *QI, SH* sunt equidistantes. Per similes ergo triangulos, probabis quod que est proportio *OI* ad *OH* ea est *OP* ad *OR* et *OQ* ad *OS*. Sed *OI, OQ* sunt equales. Ergo *OH, OS* sunt equales. Ergo latera *OH, OR; OS, OR* sunt equalia, et angulus angulo, et cetera. Ergo *HR, RS* sunt equales. Similis est

55 probatio quod *LM, NM* sunt equales.

---

36 sedecagoni *OBNV* sedecagonii *E et post hoc lectiones V huiusmodi non laudabo* / *Z'*
    V q; *OBN* CE *E* / *post* quia *scr. et del. B* q

37 MZ' *V* Mq; *OBN* MCE *E* / in *om. V* / punctis: punctis suis *V*

38 medietati *om. V*

40 polliciti *ENV* policiti *OB*

41 orthogonaliter *ENV* ortogonaliter *OB* / illam: eam *V*

42 CE[1]: GE *V*

43 *de* latera octogoni *mg scr. O aliquid quod non legere possum* / OI *supra scr. O* M
    (?) B

43–44 latera[2]. . . . equales *om. V*

  44 OI: M (?) B

45–46 RE[1] . . . uterque: RC, RG sunt aequalia et IE (! RE) commune et uterque angulus
    I (! R) *V*

  45 RE[2] *N. mg. O om. BE*

47–50 Cum. . . . rectus[1]: Item *EQ, EI* sunt aequalia et CP (!) et (?) C (! E?) angulus utrobique
    aequalis, ut probatum est; ergo basis basi et cetera. PQ, PL (! PI) ergo sunt aequales,
    et N angulus P (*? corr. V ex* quam) extrinsecus aequalis alteri, ergo uterque
    rectus *V*

  47 sunt *O* erunt *BEN* / *post* equales[2] *add. mg. O vel* IO, QO

47–48 SOP, POH . . . equales[1] *om. N*

  47 SOP, POH *O (et supra scr. O* POH) SOQM *B* he OZ OI *E*

  48 Ergo latera *bis N* / OQ: ON *B*

  50 R angulus *tr. V*

  51 QI, SH: CG, QI *V* / QI : QI et *N* / *post* equidistantes *add. V* postea probabis quod
    4 anguli supra centrum sunt equales / Per . . . ergo: Deinde per similes *V* / triangulos
    om. N

  52 que: eadem *V* / OI[1]: OC *V* / ea est: quae *V* / OQ[1]: AQ *V*

52–55 Sed. . . . equales: ergo per premissam (*scr. et del. V*) permutatim eadem erit proportio
    OB (!) ad OQ et OH, OS (*corr. V ex* OI). Sed OI, OQ aequales, ergo OH, OS erunt

[Corollarium.] Ex dictis ergo patet quod proportio OQ ad OS est tanquam OI ad OH et tanquam OP ad OR. Sed OP ad OR proportio est tanquam motus P puncti ad R punctum. Quod sic probabitur. Trianguli OPD', ROB sunt similes, quia D' angulus rectus; similiter B angulus rectus, quia BR equidistat PD', O angulus communis. Proportio ergo OP ad OR tanquam $D'P$ ad RB. Sed $D'P$ ad RB tanquam motus P puncti ad motum R puncti. Hoc patet per corollarium prime. Ergo motus P puncti ad motum R puncti tanquam OP ad OR. Sed R movetur equaliter V. Ergo motus P puncti ad motum V puncti tanquam OP ad OR. Sed P movetur magis V. Ergo P movetur magis R. Sed R movetur equaliter ambitui quadrati. Et P movetur equaliter ambitui octogoni, ut prius demonstratum est. Ergo ambitus octogoni movetur magis ambitu / quadrati in proportione OP ad OR. Simili demonstratione demonstrabitur quod ambitus sedecagoni magis movetur ambitu octogoni in proportione OM linee ad OP lineam. Et ita patet prima pars

60 (marginal, line 60)

65 (marginal, line 65)

119r (marginal)

aequales. Postea distingue 2 triangulos qui sunt OSR, ORH, quorum duo latera, scilicet OS, OH, sunt aequalia et OR commune, angulusque angulo de hiis qui sunt supra centrum, ergo basis RX (!) basi RH. Postea protraha vel ne confundis figuras intellige protractam lineam EN, EL probeoque (!) triangulum ONE, aequalem esse triangulo OEL; EN igitur aequalis est EL, et E angulus utrobique aequalis. Ergo ENM, EML triangulorum basis NM basi ML adaequatur. Sic ergo patet lineas HS, IQ, LN divisas esse per medium, quod probandum remanserat V

56   OS est: OF V

57   OH: OA BN / OP ad OR^2: OB ad DR V

58   motus om. V / P puncti O (et supra scr. O P) NE om. B (et om. B P) puncti P V / Quod: Hoc V / probatur V

58–71   Trianguli. . . . adaptare: Trianguli ORH, OHB (!) aequales sunt, quoniam anguli supra centrum sunt aequales, et angulus uterque tum R quam B (et supra scr V L) rectus, ergo reliqui sibi invicem aequales, scilicet uterque angulus H et cum OH sit commune latus utriusque reliquae latera aequalia erunt, latus ergo OI aequale est lateri OB' et sic aequidistet a centro, ergo aequaliter moventur. Protrahatur igitur linea RB (?). Deinde supra latus OC protrahatur linea abscindens OM aequalem OP. Ergo OP, OB (?) aequaliter move[n]tur. Item OR, OB aequaliter. Proportio igitur motus RO, BO sicut PO, RO. Sed motus OR ad puncti (!) ad B punctum, sed P aequaliter movetur V et R punctus B puncto. Ergo proportio OP ad OR est sicut motus P puncti ad motum R puncti. Sed OP maior est OR; ergo motus P maior est motu R in proportione OP ad OR. Sed ambitus quadrati movetur aequaliter R puncto, ut prius probatum est; et ambitus octogonii P puncto; ergo motus octogonii maior est motu quadrati secundum proportionem OP ad OR. Et sic patet pars prima corrolarii, nam sicut est in hiis similiter et in aliis idem evenit V

58   ROB OB RPB EN

59   D': A (?) B, N / BR correxi ex BGR in O et BG in BEN

60   PD', O correxi ex AD, O in O et AD, P in BEN

61   RB^{1,2} O DB BEN / R O B BEN

62   corolarium O hic et saepe / R O B BE B (sive V) N

63   V correxi ex B (sed saepe scr. O B et V in simili modo) / P corr. O ex B et hab. BEN B

64   V^1 correxi ex R in BEN et B sive V in O (corr. O ex R) / V^2 correxi ex B sive V in O et R in BEN

67   movetur magis tr. N

70 corollarii. Sed consideret diligens lector ut sciat hoc genus demonstrationis
ad alia genera poligoniorum convenienter adaptare.

Secunda pars corollarii sic pateat [Fig. I.3b]. Ex presenti probatione patet
quod ambitus quadrati circumscripti movetur equaliter *N, P* punctis. Dividat
NP linea duo latera quadrati in duo equalia. Item duo latera octogoni cir-
75 cumscripti, *DE, EF,* moventur equaliter *I, K* punctis. Dividat *IK* illa duo
latera in duo equalia; ergo *Q* puncto. Dividit enim *OE* linea latus *AB* in duo
equalia, et angulum *E* in duo equalia, et *IK* lineam in duo equalia. Ergo *I,*
K puncta moventur equaliter *Q* puncto. Simili probatione opposita duo latera
moventur equaliter *L, M* punctis. Dividat *LM* linea opposita latera in duo
80 equalia. Et *L, M* puncta moventur equaliter *R* puncto. Et *Q, R* moventur
equaliter [et] similiter *N, P* moventur equaliter, quia ille linee moventur
equaliter in omnibus partibus suis et punctis. Que est ergo proportio motus
N puncti ad motum *Q* puncti ea est proportio motus ambitus quadrati ad
motum ambitus octogoni. Sed *N* punctus magis movetur *Q* puncto in pro-
85 portione *ON* ad *OQ,* per presentem probationem. Ergo ambitus quadrati
magis movetur ambitu octogoni in proportione *ON* ad *OQ.* Idem in aliis
poligoniis invenies.

4ª. EX HOC ETIAM MANIFESTUM QUOD QUANTUM AMBITUS
POLIGONII INSCRIPTI CIRCULO MOTU SUO EXSUPERAT MOTUM

72 pars . . . pateat: sic patebit *V*
72–75 Ex. . . . EF: Ambitus quadrati ABCS circumscripti circulo O aequaliter movetur N,
 P punctis ex praecedenti probatione quia NP linea dividit illa duo latera in duo
 aequalia. Item duo latera DE, EF octogonii circumscripti eidem circulo *V*
72 presenti *OB* precedenti *EN*
73 punctis *om. N*
75 moventur: movetur *ex corr. V ex* moventur / puncti *B* / IK: autem linea IK *V*
76 in duo¹ *corr. V ex* per
76–77 ergo. . . . equalia³ Linea autem OC (! OE) dividit latus quadrati AB in duo aequalia,
 quare latus octogonii dividet etiam in aequas partes, ergo et lineam subtensam illi
 angulo, scilicet IKQ. Ergo punctus est medius IK (*corr. V ex* IKH) lineae *V*
77–78 I, K . . . moventur: IK movetur *V*
78 Simili probatione: Similiter *V*
79 L: et *B* I *N* / LM: IM *N* / opposita: illa *V* / *ante* latera *scr. et del. V* puncta
80 L, M . . . moventur¹: LM linea movetur *V* / L: I *N* / puncta *om. N*
80–84 Et². . . . octogoni: ergo 4 latera octogonii moventur aequaliter R, Q punctis. Sed R,
 Q aequaliter moventur (*injuste del. V* -n-), quoniam RQ linea aequaliter et uniformiter
 movetur in omnibus partibus suis et punctis, ergo totalis ambitus octogonii aequaliter
 movetur Q puncto. Eodem modo totalis ambitus quadrati N puncto movetur aequaliter.
 Eadem est ergo proportio motus ambitus quadrati ad motum octogonii quae est
 motus N puncti ad Q punctum *V*
81 [et] *addidi* / similiter . . . equaliter² *om. N*
85 per . . . probationem *om. V* / presentem *OB* precedentem *EN* / ambitus quadrati:
 quadratum *V*
86 ambitu octogoni: octogonio *V*
Prop. I.4
1 4ª *om. ENV* IIII *OB* / quod: est quod *V*
2 exuperat *V hic et ubique*

AMBITUS POLIGONII DUPLO PAUCIORUM LATERUM INSCRIPTI
EIDEM CIRCULO, TANTUM EXSUPERATUR A MOTU CIRCUM-
5   SCRIPTI.

Ex dictis patet quod ambitus exterioris quadrati movetur equaliter punctis
G, V [Fig. I.4]. Linea enim GV dividit illa duo latera in duo equalia. Et
ambitus interioris quadrati movetur equaliter punctis P, N, quia PN linea
dividit illa duo latera in duo equalia. Et ambitus inscripti octogoni movetur
10   equaliter punctis L, R. Oportet autem quod linea OG, que dividit AB latus
in duo equalia, dividit etiam DH in duo equalia et EF in duo equalia. Hoc
totum patet ex dictis. Quantum ergo exsuperat motus G puncti motum L
puncti, tantum exsuperat motus ambitus exterioris quadrati motum ambitus
inscripti octogoni. Et quantum exsuperat motus L puncti motum P puncti,
15   tantum exsuperat motus ambitus octogoni motum ambitus inscripti quadrati.
Postea sic procede.

Trianguli PGH, LGF sunt similes, quia P, L anguli sunt recti, et G angulus
communis. Ergo F, H anguli sunt equales. Ergo latera sunt proportionalia.
Que est ergo proportio GH ad GF ea est GP ad GL. Sed GH dupla est GF,
20   est enim divisa in duo equalia per lineam EF. Ergo GP dupla est GL. Ergo
GL est equalis LP. Item trianguli PGK, LGI sunt similes. Anguli enim K, I
sunt recti, eo quod GM linea equidistat OH linee, et G angulus communis.
Ergo reliqui anguli equales. Que est ergo proportio GP ad GL ea est GK ad
GI. Sed GP dupla est GL. Ergo GK dupla est GI. Ergo GI equalis est KI.
25   Quantum ergo exsuperat motus puncti G motum puncti I, tantum exsuperat

3 pauciorum *ENV* paucorum *OB* / inscripti *tr. V post* circulo
4 exuperatur *V hic et ubique*
4–5 motu circumscripti: circumscripto ambitus motu *V*
6 dictis *corr. V ex* ipsis
6–7 punctis G, V *tr. V et corr. V* G, V *ex* GIR
7 Linea enim: cum enim *corr. V ex* et IR / dividit *O (hic -di- simile est -a-) BN* dividat
   ENV et cf. lin. 9 et 10-11 / illa: ista *V* / duo equalia: partes equales *V*
8–9 quia . . . ambitus *om. V*
9 dividit *O (-di- simile est -a-) BEN* dividat *V*
10 Opportet *B* / autem: autem ex praedictis *V* / OG, que: OY *V*
10–11 dividit . . . EF: dividat AB, EF, DH quodlibet *V*
11–12 Hoc . . . dictis *om. V*
14 puncti[1] *om. V*
15 octogoni: inscripti octogonii *V* / inscripti: interioris *V*
18 F, H anguli: H, F *V*
19 Que . . . GL *om. V* / duplum *V* / est[3]: est ad *V*
20 est[1] . . . EF *om. V* / dupla est: ad *V*
20–21 Ergo[2] . . . LP: Respiciunt enim aequales angulos, ergo GL, LP sunt aequales *V*
21 est *EN om. OB* / LP ras. ON GP BE / PGK *ENV* BGK *OB* / Anguli enim: quia *V*
22 GM linea: R M *V* / equedistat *N* / OH linee: OK *V* / communis: est communis *NV*
23 reliqui: P, L, *V* / equales *OBE* sunt equales *NV*
23–24 GP . . . GI[1]: GP, LP respicientium eadem est GI, IK respiciunt P, L angulos
   aequales *V*
24 duplum[1,2] *V* / GK: GH *N* / est GI: est ad GI *V* / equalis est *tr. N*
25 *supra* I *scr. V* Y

motus puncti *I* motum puncti *K*. Sed ista tria puncta moventur equaliter punctis *G*, *L*, *P*. Linee enim quarum sunt puncta moventur equaliter in omnibus partibus suis et punctis. Ergo quantum exsuperat motus *G* puncti motum *L* puncti, et motus *L* puncti motum *P* puncti. Ergo quantum exsuperat motus ambitus circumscripti quadrati motum / ambitus octogoni inscripti, tantum motus ambitus octogoni motum ambitus quadrati inscripti. Et hoc voluimus demonstrare.

119v
31

Liber Secundus

[Petitiones]

[1.] QUADRATORUM EQUALIUM MAGIS DICITUR MOVERI CUIUS LATERA MAGIS MOVENTUR.

5 [2.] CUIUS MINUS, MINUS.

[3.] CUIUS LATERA MAGIS NON MOVENTUR, NEC IPSUM MAGIS MOVERI.

[4.] CUIUS NON MINUS, NEC IPSUM MINUS.

[5.] SI SUPERFICIES FUERINT EQUALES ET OMNES LINEE
10 EARUM IN EADEM PROPORTIONE SUMPTE EQUALES, CUIUS NULLE LINEE SIC SUMPTE MAGIS MOVENTUR, IPSA NON MAGIS MOVETUR.

[6.] CUIUS NULLE MINUS, NEC IPSA MINUS.

[Propositiones]

15 1ª. CIRCULUS EQUINOCTIALIS IN SEXQUITERTIA PROPORTIONE MOVETUR AD SUAM DIAMETRUM. UNDE MANIFESTUM QUOD PROPORTIO CIRCULORUM EST PROPORTIO MOTUUM GEMI-NATA.

---

27 punctis . . . equaliter *ENV om. OB* / *post* equaliter *add. V* et uniformiter

29 L¹ *corr. V ex* I / et . . . puncti²: tantum exuperat motus puncti L *V* / *P N G BE, et O del.* G *et scr.* P

31 tantum: tantum exuperat *V* / *post* octogoni *scr. et del. O* motum ambitus octogoni

32 voluimus *N* volumus *OBE* volo *V* / demonstrare *OBEV* probare *N*

Pet. et Prop. II.1

1 Liber secundus *mg. sin. et mg. super. N; om. OEV; et mg. sup. ff. 83v–84r scr. B* Explicit primus. Incipit secundus de motu

2 [Petitiones] *addidi*

5 cuius: et *V* / *ante* minus² *scr. et del. V* cuius

6 magis non *tr. V*

7 moveri *OB om. ENV*

12 moventur *V*

13 nulle: nullae lineae *V*

14 [Propositiones] *addidi*

15 1ª: I *OB om. ENV* (*sed habet E* ipsa [*vel forte* prima] probatio) / sesquitertia *V et post hoc lectiones huiusmodi non laudabo*

16 suam *NV* suum *OBE* / quod: est quod *V*

Sint quadrata *BDFH, OLMN* equalia [Fig. II.1a]. Et moveatur superficies
20   *ADFI* describendo columpnam super axem *AI*; et moveatur quadratum
OLMN uniformiter et equaliter in omnibus partibus suis et punctis recte
procedendo ita quod latus eius moveatur equaliter *C* puncto *CG* linee dividentis *BDFH* quadratum in duo equalia. Patet ergo quod quadratum *LMNO*
movetur equaliter *CG* linee, eo quod *CG* linea movetur equaliter in omnibus
25   partibus et punctis suis et *LMNO* similiter. Dico igitur quod quadrata *BDFH,*
LMNO equaliter moventur; aut enim equaliter aut alterum magis. Si *BDFH*
magis movetur, contra latera eius non moventur magis lateribus *OLMN,*
quia *BD, FH* moventur equaliter *OL, MN* et *DF, BH* moventur equaliter
LM, NO, et sic deinceps. Ergo hoc quadratum non movetur magis illo.
30   Eadem ratione nec minus. Ergo equaliter.

Proponatur aliud quadratum equale quod dicatur *Z*; et moveatur tantum
magis *OLMN* quantum *BDFH* movetur magis *OLMN*; et directe procedat
sicut *OLMN.* Cum ergo *Z* equaliter moveatur in omnibus partibus et terminis
suis, patet quod latus eius movetur magis *C* puncto et ita magis movetur
35   *BD* latere, quia *BD* movetur equaliter *C* puncto, et ita magis movetur *FH*
latere, similiter aliis intermediis inter *BD, HF.* Sic ergo per datam descriptionem *Z* quadratum magis movetur *BDFH* quadrato; non ergo equaliter.

Si autem sophista opponat quod *DF* latus magis movetur latere *Z*, dicimus
quod *DF, BH* latera simul iuncta equaliter moventur *BD, FH* lateribus simul
40   iunctis. Quanto enim motu suo exsuperat *DF* motum *DB*, tantum exsuperat
motus *DB* motum *BH*; et ita *DF, BH* latera simul iuncta minus moventur
lateribus *Z*. Patet ergo quod *BDFH* non movetur magis *LMNO*. Si minus,
eodem modo inprobabitur, proposito quadrato equali quod minus moveatur
LMNO et quod respondens dat equaliter moveri *BDFH*. Patet ergo quod

19 OLMN *BEN* OLNM *V* OLMR *O* / moveantur *V*
20 columnam *V hic et ubique* (*post hoc lectiones huiusmodi non laubado*)
22 C puncto: puncto C qui est punctus *V* / line *B*
24 CG[1]: G *in ras. B*
25 simile *V* / igitur *OB om. V* ergo *EN* / quadrata: latera *V*
26 equaliter moventur *tr. V*
27 OLMN *OBE* LMNO *NV*
28 moventur equaliter[1] *N* moventur *OBE* movetur *V* / OL, MN . . . equaliter[2] *om. V*
29 deinceps: de aliis *N*
30 Eadem ratione *OV* er. *BE* e. r. *N* / *post* equaliter *add. N* vel sic
32 magis[2] *om. BV*
33 O- *in ras. B* (?)
34 movetur[2] *om. V*
35 *ante* quia *scr. V et delendum* quia BD latere / *post* BD[2] *scr. et del. V* latere
37 Z *N* et (?) *OEBV* / magis *injuste del. V* / BDFH: BDHF *V* / non: et non *V* / ergo
    om. V
38 sophista *OENV* soffista *B* / opponat *corr. O ex* opppnat (?)
39 *ante* latera *scr. et del. B* sunt / lateribus *om. V*
41 motus *NV* motu *OBE* / DF *ON* BF *BEV* / latera *om. N*
42 BDFH *V et ex corr. O* (*ex* DEFH) DBFH *EN* DEFH *B*
43 inprobabitur *B* improbabitur *NV* īprobabitur *OE* / minus moveatur *tr. V*
44 respondens: hiis *V*

45 *BDFH* movetur equaliter *LMNO*. Sed *LMNO* movetur equaliter cuilibet suo
120r lateri; ergo movetur / equaliter *BD*; ergo movetur equaliter *C* puncto. Ergo
BDFH movetur equaliter *C* puncto. Eadem probatione penitus probabitur
quod *CDEK* quadratum movetur equaliter *P* puncto, et *KEFG* similiter *P*
puncto, et ita quadrangulus *CDFG* movetur equaliter *P* puncto, et *BCGH*
50 quadrangulus medio puncto *CB*. Similis est demonstratio de aliis quadrangulis rectangulis. Per impossibile ergo probabis, sicut probatum est de
semidiametro, quod quadratum *BDFH* movetur equaliter *C* puncto, si moveatur super axem *BH* immobilem describendo columpnam. Sic ergo moveatur. Cum ergo moveatur equaliter *C* puncto, et quadrangulus *BCGH* mo-
55 vetur equaliter medio puncto *BC*, quadratum *BDFH* duplo movetur ad quadrangulum *BCGH*. Sed quadrangulus *CDFG* movetur equaliter *P* puncto,
et *P* punctus in sexquialtera proportione ad *C* punctum. Ergo quadrangulus
CDFG movetur ad quadrangulum *CBGH* (*! BCGH*) in proportione ducta
ex dupla et sexquialtera, hoc est, in tripla; et in eadem proportione se habet
60 descriptum a *CDFG* quadrangulo ad descriptum a *BCGH* quadrangulo. Columpna enim descripta a *BDFH* quadrangulo ad columpnam descriptam a
BCGH quadrangulo se habet in proportione basis ad basem, cum sint inter
lineas equidistantes. Sed basis ad basem quadrupla, quia semidiameter *BD*
ad semidiametrum *BC* duplus (*!*). Ergo circulus ad circulum quadruplus. Sic
65 columpna ad columpnam quadrupla. Ergo residuum maioris columpne quod
relinquitur, subtracta minore, triplum est ad minorem. Et illud describitur
a quadrangulo *CDFG*. Que est ergo proportio descripti a *CDFG* ad descriptum
a *BCGH* ea est motus ad motum.

Ex hoc patet quod que est proportio descripti a triangulo *BDF* ad descriptum
70 a triangulo *BFH* ea est proportio motus ad motum. Excessus enim motus
CDFG ad motum *BDF* est excessus motus *KFG* ad motum *BCK*. Motus

45 BDFH: DBFH *B* (*corr. ex* DFH)
46 BD *ex corr. B* B *OENV*
48–49 et . . . puncto[2] *BENV om. O*
49 CDFG: DFG *V*
53 BH *N et ex corr. B* BF *OFV* / movetur *V*
55 BDFH: BDRH *O ante corr.*
57 ad C punctum: ad P punctum *V et tr. V ante* in
58 in proportione ducta *N* in producta *OEV* inpro ducta *B*
59 sesquialtera *V et post hoc lectiones huiusmodi non laudabo*
60 ad descriptum: ad columnam descriptam *V* / a BCGH *ON* a DCGH *BV* ad
CGH *E*
61 BDFH: BDFG *V*
62 BCGH quadrangulo: BCDH *N* / se habet *N om. OBEV* / basem: basim *V*
62–79 cum. . . . quadranguli *hab. V hic et repet. post* constabit *in lin. 80*
64 Sic: sic ergo *N*
66 tripla *V hic sed* triplex *in repet.*
67 Que . . . proportio *om. V hic sed. hab. in repet.*
68 ea: eadem *V*
69 que: et quae *in repet. V* / proportio: proportio motus *V hic, sed in repet. hab. tantum*
proportio
70 ea: eadem *in repet. V*

enim *CDFK* communis est utrique. Et excessus motus *BFH* ad motum *BCGH* est excessus motus *FGK* ad motum *BCK*. Motus enim *BKGH* est communis utrique. Idem ergo est excessus motus superioris quadranguli ad motum
75   superioris trianguli qui est excessus motus inferioris trianguli ad motum inferioris quadranguli. Sic ergo motus quadrangulorum et triangulorum sunt equales. Preterea quantum descriptum a superioris quadranguli motu exsuperat descriptum a superiori triangulo, tantum descriptum a motu inferioris trianguli exsuperat descriptum a motu inferioris quadranguli. Hoc postea
80   constabit. Sic ergo idem est excessus motuum et idem est excessus descriptorum et totales motus sunt equales et totalia descripta sunt equalia. Sed que est descripti a superiori quadrangulo ad descriptum ab inferiori ea est motus superioris ad motum inferioris. Ergo que est descripti a superiori triangulo ad descriptum ab inferiori ea est motus ad motum. Sed descriptum a superiori
85   triangulo ad descriptum ab inferiori duplum, quia piramis rotunda tertia pars est columpne rotunde. Ergo residuum duplum est ad piramidem, quod [residuum] describitur a superiori triangulo. Ergo motus superioris ad motum inferioris duplus. Cum ergo motus quadrangulorum equentur motibus triangulorum et motus superioris quadranguli triplus est ad motum inferioris, et
90   motus superioris trianguli duplus sit ad motum inferioris, illi motus ad se invicem se habent sicut 9 et 3, et 8 et 4. Ergo superior quadrangulus movetur ad superiorem triangulum sicut se habent 9 ad 8, hoc est, in sexquioctava proportione. Et inferior triangulus movetur ad inferiorem quadrangulum sicut se habent 4 ad 3, hoc est, in sexquitertia proportione. Cum ergo superior

72–73 CDFK. . . . enim *om. V hic sed hab. in repet.*
   72 *CDFK*: DCFK *in repet. V* / Et *om. V in repet.* / BFH: BFK *in repet. V* / BCGH *EN* BGCH *OB* BCFG *in repet. V*
   73 FGK: FGHK *in repet. V*
   74 est *om. V* / *post* ad *scr. et del. B* s
   75 est *om. V in repet.*
75–76 motum . . . quadranguli *NV* inferioris quadranguli motum *OEB*
   76 quadrangulorum et triangulorum *OBE* triangulorum et quadrangulorum *NV*
   77 superioris *ENV* superiori *OB* / motu *tr. V post* a
77–78 exsuperat *OB* exuperat *EV; lac. et* superat *N*
   80 est[2] *om. V*
   81 totales: columnae *V* / et[2]: ergo *N* / totalia: talia *V* / Sed: sicut *V*
   82 est[1]: est proportio *V* / ab inferiori *om. V* / ea: eadem *V*
   84 ea: eadem *V*
   85 duplum, quia: duplum est quod *V*
   86 quod: quae *V*
   87 [residuum] *addidi*
   88 aequatur *V*
89–90 et[2] . . . inferioris *om. V*
   90 se *om. V*
   91 9 et 3, et 8 et 4 *EV* ix et tria et viii et iiii *OB* 9 et 3[ia], 8 et 4 *N*
   92 9 ad 8 *ENV* ix ad viii *OB* / sesquioctava *V hic et ubique*
   93 Et *om. V* / *ante* inferiorem *scr. et del. OB* superiorem / inferiorem quadrangulum: superiorem triangulum *V*
   94 4 ad 3 *ENV* iiii ad tria *OB*

95 quadrangulus moveatur in sexquialtera proportione ad *BD* et moveatur ad
superiorem triangulum in sexquioctava, superior triangulus movebitur ad
BD in sexquitertia; subtracta enim a sexquialtera sexquioctava, remanet sexquitertia, ut patet in 9, 8, 6 (! 9, 8, 3, 2, ?). Item cum descriptum a superiori
quadrangulo sit triplum ad descriptum ab inferiori, et descriptum a superiori

100 triangulo sit duplum ad descriptum inferioris, et equalia sint totalia descripta,
idem erit excessus particularium descriptorum, ut patet in 9, 3, 8, 4.

120v / Nunc respice ad proximam figuram [Fig. II.1b]. Probabo quod trianguli
BDE, BDF equaliter moventur. Quadranguli enim *BDEH, BDFG* equaliter
moventur, per presentem probationem; et in qua proportione movetur *BDEH*

105 ad suum superiorem triangulum, in eadem proportione movetur *BDFG* ad
suum superiorem triangulum. Et hoc patet ex proxima probatione, scilicet
in subsexquitertia proportione. Ergo cum illi quadranguli equaliter moveantur,
quadrangulus *BDEH* in subsexquitertia proportione movetur ad utrumque
triangulum. Ergo illi trianguli moventur equaliter; eodem modo et inferiores

110 trianguli.
Sit ergo linea *DF* equalis circumferentie circuli cuius semidiameter est *BD*.
Patet ergo per primam de quadratura circuli quod triangulus *BDF* equatur
circulo semidiametri *BD*. Appelletur ille circulus *C*. Linee ergo trianguli et
circuli *C* in simili proportione accepte sunt equales; linea enim *DF* equatur

115 circumferentie circuli *C*. Sed que est proportio semidiametri *BD* ad semidiametrum *BC* ea est circumferentie ad circumferentiam. Et que est proportio
BD ad *BC* ea est *DF* ad *CK*; similes enim sunt trianguli, quia *CK* equidistat
DF. Sed *DF* est equalis maiori circumferentie. Ergo *CK* minori. Et ita linee
sumpte in eadem proportione, quia sicut proportio *BD* ad *BC* duplicata est

$9-8=1$

$4-3=1$

95 movetur[1,2] *V* / BD: DB *V*
96 sexquioctava *corr. O ex* sexquioctatva / movetur *V*
97 *ante* BD *injuste supra scr. V* L
98 9, 8, 6 *ENV* ix, viii, vi *OB*
99 *post* ad *scr. et del. N* quadrangulum
100 sint *OBN* sunt E / sint totalia: sicut columna *V*
101 idem: idē *B* / 9, 3, 8, 4 *E* ix, iii, viii, iiii *OB* 9, iii, 8, 4 *N* 9, 8, 6 *V*
103 BDFG: BDEG *V*
104 presentem *OB* precedentem *EN,* (?)*V* / proportione movetur *tr. V*
105 suum: suam *V* / BDFG *B* BCFG *OEN* BCFG scilicet *V*
107 subsesquitertia *V hic et ubique* / equaliter *supra scr. OBN om. EV* / moventur *V*
108 quadrangulus *om. V* / sesquitertia *V*
109 triangulum: angulum *V* / Ergo: ergo et *V* / eodem: et eodem *N* / eodem modo:
ergo *V*
110 trianguli: anguli *V*
112 circuli *N om. OBEV*
113 Appelletur *BEN* applicetur *OV* / ille: iste *V* / trianguli: anguli *V*
114 sint *V* / enim: n *V*
116 ea: eadem *V*
117 est *om. V* / CK² *ONV* EK *B* OK (?) *E*
118 maiori circumferentie *tr. N*
119 sumpte: sunt sumpte *NV* / -C *supra scr. O* / dupplicata *N*

120 proportio circuli ad circulum. Ita proportio *BD* ad *BC* duplicata est proportio
maioris trianguli ad minorem. Sicut ergo maior circulus et maior triangulus
sunt equales, ita minor circulus et minor triangulus. Sic ergo omnes linee in
eadem proportione accepte sunt equales et equaliter moventur, quia sicut
DF equaliter movetur maiori circumferentie, ita *CK* minori. Idem est in
125 omnibus. Dico ergo quod circulus et triangulus moventur equaliter, quod
probabitur per impossibile, non enim magis vel minus movetur per ultimam
descriptionem. Si enim circulus moveatur magis triangulo, sumatur triangulus
equalis *BDF* qui magis moveatur *BDF*; et sit similis *BDF* et moveatur equaliter
circulo. Ex dictis ergo patet quod omnes linee in eadem proportione sumpte
130 moventur magis similibus lineis in *BDF*, cum ille triangulus moveatur magis
BDF. Si ergo linee illius trianguli equales lineis illius circuli et in eadem
proportione acceptis, magis moventur. Sic ergo ille triangulus magis movetur
circulo, cum sit ei equalis. Sic ergo circulus ille non magis movetur triangulo
BDF. Simili ratione nec minus; ergo equaliter. Sed triangulus in sexquitertia
135 proportione movetur ad *BD*. Ergo circulus in sexquitertia proportione movetur
ad *BD*; ergo ad diametrum.

Corollarium sic pateat [Fig. II.1b]. Sit punctus *I* qui in sexquitertia proportione moveatur ad punctum *C*. Ergo *I* movetur equaliter circulo. Eodem
modo sit punctus *L* qui in sexquitertia proportione moveatur ad punctum
140 *M*, qui est medius punctus *BC*. Ergo minor circulus movetur equaliter *L*
puncto. Sed motus *I* ad motum *L* tanquam *BI* linea ad *BL* lineam. Sed *BI*
linea ad *BL* lineam tanquam *BC* ad *BM*, quia *BI* ad *BC* tanquam *BL* ad
BM. Ergo a primo motus circuli maioris ad motum circuli minoris tanquam
proportio *BC* linee ad *BM* lineam; ergo tanquam *BD* linee ad *BC* lineam;
145 ergo tanquam diametri ad diametrum. Sed proportio circuli ad circulum est
proportio diametri ad diametrum duplicata. Ergo proportio circuli ad circulum
est proportio motus ad motum duplicata.

---

120 circuli. . . . proportio[2] *om. V* / *ante* Ita *mg. add. O* per XVII sexti euclidis vel
_____ erit per primam et ___ iterum (*?*) primam sexti euclidis triangulus BDK (*?*)
medio loco proportionalis inter triangulos BDF et BCK. Unde ex deffinitione (*?*)
proportionis duplicis argumentum elice.
122 *post* triangulus *add. V* sunt aequales
126 probatur *V* / impossibilia *V* / non enim *N* nam D *OBV* non D *E*
128 moveatur[1]: movetur *V*
129 eadem *tr. N post* sumpte
130 in BDF *ENV* MBDF *OB* / moveatur: movetur *V*
131 Si: sic *N* / illius[2] *om. N*
132 ergo ille: iste *V*
133 ei: illi *V*
135–36 Ergo . . . BD *om. V*
137 I *om. V*
138 moveatur: movetur *V*
139 L: I *V* / movetur *V*
140 L: I (*?*) *V*
141 I *om. O, supra scr. B* / *post* L *scr. N* est / linea: lineae *V*
142 BL[1] *corr. V ex* BPL / tanquam[1]: est tanquam *V* / BC[1] *ex corr. B* BM *O*, B (*ante
corr.*) *NV* LM *sive* IM *E*

Idem satis probatum est de quadratis simili modo motis, eo quod quadrata moventur equaliter costis; que est proportio coste ad costam ea est motus quadrati ad motum quadrati. Sed proportio quadrati ad quadratum est proportio coste ad costam duplicata. Ergo proportio quadrati ad quadratum est proportio motus ad motum duplicata. Idem contingit in triangulis.

2ª. OMNIS CURVA SUPERFICIES ROTUNDE PIRAMIDIS IN SEXQUITERTIA PROPORTIONE MOVETUR AD YPOTENUSAM. UNDE / MANIFESTUM QUOD OMNES CURVE SUPERFICIES ROTUNDARUM PIRAMIDUM EIUSDEM BASIS EQUALITER MOVENTUR.

Age igitur. Sit linea *LN* equalis ypotenuse *AE* et linea *NP* equalis circumferentie basis [Fig. II.2]. Patet ergo per primam de piramidibus quod triangulus *LNP* equatur curve superficiei rotunde piramidis *OAE*. Patet etiam quod omnes linee trianguli et curve superficiei in eadem proportione sumpte sunt equales. Que enim est proportio *OA* ad *TV* ea est circumferentie ad circumferentiam, et que est *OA* ad *TV* ea est *AE* ad *TE*, propter similes triangulos. Sed que est *AE* ad *TE* ea est *LN* ad *LM*; sunt enim linee divise in duo equalia. Sed que est *LN* ad *LM* ea est *NP* ad *MR*, propter similes triangulos; est enim *MR* equidistans *NP*. Ergo que est proportio *NP* ad *MR* ea est circumferentie *OA* semidiametri ad circumferentiam *TV* semidiametri. Sed prima equatur *NP*; ergo secunda equatur *MR*. Item sicut proportio *OAE* curve superficiei ad *VTE* curvam superficiem ea est proportio *AE* ad *TE* duplicata. Hoc patet ex prima de piramidibus. Ita proportio *LNP* trianguli ad *LMR* triangulum ea est proportio *LN* ad *LM* duplicata. Sicut ergo quadruplus est maior triangulus ad minorem, ita maior curva superficies quadrupla est ad minorem. Moveatur ergo curva superficies *OAE* piramidis circumvolvendo cum piramide. Et moveatur triangulus *LNP* ita quod *LN* moveatur

148 satis *ENV* superius *OB* / de . . . modo: simili modo in quadratis *N*
149 est¹: est enim *V* / motus: proportio motus *V*
Prop. II.2
 1 2ª: II *OB om. ENV* (*et in fine propositionis E hab.* sexta propositio)
 2 ad: ad suam *V*
 3 quod: est quod *V*
 5 LN *om. V* / et: etiam et *B*
 6 primam *ENV* premissam *OB*
 7 LNP: MP *V* / etiam: et *B*
 8 curve *om. N*
 9 enim est *tr. N* / OA: CA *V* / TV: M *V* / ea: eadem *V*
 10 OA: CA *V* / TV: TB (*sive* TV?) *B* M vel CV *V* / TE: CE (?) *V*
 11 LM: M *V*
 12 LN ad LM: LM ad LN *V* / est² *om. N*
 13 equedistans *N* / est³: etiam est *V*
 14 circumferentie . . . ad: OA ad semidiameter (!) *V* / OA *mg. B* / semidiametri ad *tr. OB* / TV: CV *V*
 15 OAE: CAE *V*
 16 ea *om. N* / TE: TELM *V*
 18 ea *om. N*
18–19 *ante* quadruplus *scr. et del.* (?) *O* quadrangulus
 20 piramidis: super pyramidem *V*

equaliter *AE*, hoc est, quod *M* punctus moveatur equaliter *T* puncto. Dico igitur quod triangulus *LNP* movetur equaliter curve superficiei *OAE* piramidis. Sunt enim equales superficies et linee in eadem proportione sumpte sunt
25   equales et moventur equaliter. Sicut enim linea *NP* movetur equaliter circumferentie *OA* semidiametri, ita *MR* linea movetur equaliter circumferentie *TV* semidiametri; circumferentie enim moventur equaliter *A*, *T* punctis et linee *N*, *M* punctis; et ita linee moventur equaliter circumferentiis et sunt eis equales. Ita est de omnibus in eadem proportione sumptis. Ergo triangulus
30   movetur equaliter curve superficiei piramidis *OAE*.

Si enim curva superficies movetur magis triangulo, sumatur alius triangulus similis et equalis triangulo *LNP* et moveatur equaliter curve superficiei *OAE* piramidis. Movebitur ergo magis triangulo *LNP*, et linee moventur magis lineis in eadem proportione sumptis. Sic ergo ille triangulus movetur magis
35   curva superficie, quia cum sit equalis et omnes linee in eadem proportione sumpte equales et magis moveantur, triangulus magis movetur. Sic ergo curva superficies non movetur magis triangulo *LNP*. Eadem est inprobatio, dicto quod minus. Ergo movetur equaliter. Sed *LNP* triangulus movetur in sexquitertia proportione ad *LN* latus. Hoc patet ex precedente probatione.
40   Et *LN* movetur equaliter *AE*. Ergo *LNP* triangulus movetur in sexquitertia proportione ad *AE*. Ergo curva superficies *OAE* piramidis movetur in sexquitertia proportione ad *AE*.

Eadem probatione curva superficies *OAC* piramidis movetur in sexquitertia proportione ad *AC* ypotenusam. Et *AC*, *AE* moventur equaliter per secundam.
45   Ergo curve superficies *OAE*, *OAC* piramidum moventur equaliter. Preterea curva superficies *OAE* piramidis movetur in sexquitertia proportione ad *AE* ypotenusam, et *AE* ypotenusa movetur equaliter *OA* semidiametro, et circulus

22 M: NR *V* (*et supra scr. V* TN) / aequaliter *tr. V post* puncto
23 igitur: ergo N / OAE: OCA *V*
24–25 sunt equales *om. V*
25 enim *corr. V ex* n / NP *corr.* O *ex* MP (?) *et hab.* B VP (?) *in ras.*
27 TV: TN *V* / movetur *V* / A, T: A, C (?) *V* / et *corr. V ex* oc
28 N *OBE* L *NV* / *post* punctis *add.* OBEN *et* M, T *sed juste om. V*
30 OAE: OCA *V*
31 *post* triangulo *textu scr.* N *et mg. scr.* B hic age sicut prius *et mg. scr. V* age ut prius
32 similis: qui similis *V* / triangulo *om.* O / equaliter: equales O
32–33 et^2 . . . LNP *om. V*
33 moventur: moveantur *V*
36 *ante* sumpte *scr. et del. V* aequales
37 movetur magis *tr.* N / inprobatio *OBN* probatio E improbatio *V*
39–41 LN. . . . ad *om. V*
43–44 Eadem . . . AC^1 *om.* N
43 OAC *correxi ex* OAE *in OBEV*
44–47 AC^1. . . . AE *om.* E
44 AC^1 *correxi ex* AE *in OBV*
45 OAC *om. V* / piramidum moventur: pyramidis movetur *V*

OA semidiametri movetur in sexquitertia proportione ad *OA*. Ergo curva superficies *OAE* movetur equaliter circulo; et ita omnis curva superficies
50 rotunde piramidis circumvolvendo movetur equaliter basi.

3ª. SIMILIUM POLIGONIORUM POLIGONIA CORPORA DESCRI-BENTIUM PROPORTIO EST PROPORTIO MOTUS AD MOTUM DU-PLICATA. UNDE MANIFESTUM QUOD CURVARUM SUPERFICI-
121v ERUM IPSORUM CORPORUM EST / PROPORTIO MOTUUM SU-
5 PERFICIERUM DUPLICATA.

Age ergo. Dico quod poligonium inscriptum *OC* circulo ad poligonium inscriptum *ON* circulo in proportione motus ad motum duplicata [Fig. II.3a]. Trianguli enim *OCE, ONQ* sunt similes quia anguli *O, O* sunt equales, eo quod recti, et angulus *C* equalis angulo *N*, quia similia sunt poligonia; ergo
10 anguli *E, Q* sunt equales. Patet ergo per antepenultimam quod motus *OCE* trianguli ad motum *ONQ* trianguli est in proportione *OC* ad *ON*. Sed proportio *OC* ad *ON* tanquam motus ad motum; ergo motus trianguli ad motum trianguli tanquam motus *OC* ad *ON*. Item *FDE, RPQ* sunt similes, quia *F, R* anguli intrinsecus sunt equales; ergo extrinsecus. Similiter *D, P* intrinsecus
15 sunt equales; ergo extrinsecus. Cum ergo similes sint trianguli, motus ad motum tanquam *DF* ad *PR*. Sed ne aliquod dubium a tergo relinquamus, sit *DG* equidistans *OC* et *PS* equidistans *ON*. Patet ergo quod *GDE, SPQ* trianguli sunt similes, quia *G, S* anguli sunt recti et *E, Q* equales; ergo reliqui equales. De istis ergo triangulis patet per antepenultimam quod motus ad

48 *post* proportione *scr. et. del.* (?) *O et hab. B* movetur / OA: AE, OA *V*
48–49 curva superficies *om. N*
49 *ante* circulo *scr. et del.* (?) *V* basi
50 *post* basi *add. E* sexta propositio
Prop. II.3
1 3ª: III *OB om. ENV*
2 proportio est *om. V*
2–3 duplicata *NV* dupplicata *OEB et post hoc lectiones huiusmodi non laudabo*
4 *post* motuum *scr. et del. V* corporum
6 ergo *OB* igitur *ENV*
7 ON: ON est *N*
8 O, O *N et ex corr. O* O, C *E* O, I *OB* O, R *V*
9 quia: non quia *V*
10 E, Q *om. V*
11 est *NV om. OBE*
11–13 est (*om. E*) . . . trianguli *EN om. OB* / Sed . . . ON *om. V*
13 Item FDE, RPQ *BNV* Item FD, OR, QP *O vel* FD et PQ *E*
14 intrinsecus[1]: extrinsecus *V* / D, P: PD *V*
15 sint: sunt *NV*
17 PS *alii MSS et corr. V ex* PF / GDE: DE *V* / SPQ *ENV et ex corr. O* (*ex* SPN) SPN *B*
18 similes: aequales *V* / E, Q *ONE* DEQ *B* EN *V*
18–19 ergo . . . equales *om. V*
19–21 De. . . . equales *om. N*
19 ergo: igitur *V*

20 motum in proportione *GD* ad *SP*. Item *GDF*, *SPR* trianguli sunt similes,
quia *G, S* anguli recti et *F, R* intrinsecus equales; ergo reliqui equales. Constat
ergo quod motus *GDF* ad motum *SPR* in proportione *GD* ad *SP* et motus
totalium triangulorum in proportione *GD* ad *SP*. Ergo motus residuorum
triangulorum similium in proportione *GD* ad *SP*. Sed *GD* ad *SP* in proportione

25 *DF* ad *PR* propter similes triangulos; ergo proportio motus *FDE* ad motum
RPQ in proportione *DF* ad *PR*. Sed proportio *DF* ad *PR* est proportio *OC*
ad *ON*, quia proportio *GD, SP* et *OC, ON* una propter similes triangulos.
Et proportio *DG, SP* et *DF, PR* una; ergo proportio *OC, ON*; *DF, PR* una.
Sic ergo [proportio motuum] *OCE, ONQ* triangulorum in proportione *DF*

30 ad *PR*, et proportio motuum *FDE, RPQ* triangulorum est proportio *DF* ad
PR. Ergo residuarum superficierum, scilicet *OCDF, ONPR*, motus in eadem
proportione, hoc est, in proportione *DF* ad *PR*. Eadem demonstratione probabis quod motus *OABC* ad motum *OLMN* in proportione *AB* ad *LM*, hoc
est, in proportione *DF* ad *PR*. Ergo motus medietatis poligonii ad motum

35 medietatis alterius poligonii in proportione *DF* ad *PR*. Ergo motus totalis
poligonii ad motum totalis in proportione lateris ad latus. Sed proportio
poligonii ad poligonium est proportio lateris ad latus duplicata. Ergo proportio
poligonii ad poligonium est proportio motus ad motum duplicata.

Corollarium sic pateat. Dico quod curve superficies poligoniorum de-
40 scriptorum se habent in proportione motuum duplicata. Motus enim curve
superficiei rotunde piramidis *OCE* ad motum curve superficiei *GDE* in proportione *OC* ad *GD*. Hoc patet per precedentem, cum similes sint superficies.
Eadem ratione motus curve superficiei *OCE* piramidis ad motum curve
superficiei *ONQ* piramidis in proportione *OC* ad *ON* et motus curve superficiei

45 *GDE* piramidis ad motum curve superficiei *SPR* (*! SPQ*) piramidis in pro-

21 S: L *V* / recti: sunt recti *V* / F: E *V*
22 *ante* SP *scr. et del. B* anguli recti et F, R intrinsecus equales
23 tottalium *B*
24 GD^1: BD *V*
25 PR: PZ *V*
26 PR^1 *alii MSS et corr. V ex* PZ
27 quia: quare (?) *O* / GD *ENV et corr. O ex* GA (?) *et hab. B* GA / una: una est *V*
28 DG: GD *V* / ON: NC *N*
29 Sic: sicut *V* / [proportio motuum] *addidi* / OCE: OCR *V*
32 PR *alii MSS et corr. V ex* PZ
34, 35 PR: PZ *V*
34–35 Ergo . . . PR *om. N*
35 totalis (*et corr. O ex* medietatis): medietatis *B*
36 motum: motus *V*
39 patebit *V* / curve superficies *correxi ex* motus curvarum superficierum *in OBEN et ex* motus superficierum curvarum *in V*
41 rotunde piramidis *tr. V* / curve superficiei *tr. V*
42 precedentem *EN* presentem *OB* precedentem (?) probationem *V* / superficies: superiores *N*
43 curve^2 *om. V*
45 SPR: P̈S̈R *N*

portione *GD* ad *SP*. Et curva superficies *GDE* piramidis est curva superficies *FDE* piramidis, differunt enim tantum in basi. Similiter curva superficies *SPQ* piramidis est curva superficies *RPQ* piramidis. Ergo motus curve superficiei *FDE* piramidis ad motum curve superficiei *RPQ* piramidis in pro-

50 portione *GD* ad *SP*, hoc est, in proportione *DF* ad *PR*. Sed proportio motus curve superficiei *OCE* piramidis ad motum curve superficiei *ONQ* piramidis in proportione *OC* ad *ON*, hoc est, in proportione *DF* ad *PR*. Ergo proportio motus residue curve superficiei quam describit *CD* linea ad motum residue curve superficiei quam describit *NP* linea in proportione *DF* ad *PR*. Item

55 motus curve superficiei *GDF* piramidis ad motum curve superficiei *SPR* piramidis in proportione *GD* ad *SP*, cum similes sint superficies, hoc est, in proportione *DF* ad *PR*. Ergo motus totalis curve superficiei que describitur

122r a *CD*, *DF* ad motum totalis / curve superficiei que describitur ab *NP*, *PR* in proportione *DF* ad *PR*. Eadem ratione motus totalis curve superficiei que

60 describitur ab *AB*, *BC* ad motum totalis curve superficiei que describitur ab *LM*, *MN* in proportione *AB* ad *LM*, hoc est, in proportione *DF* ad *PR*. Ergo motus medietatis curve superficiei totalis poligonii corporis ad motum medietatis curve superficiei alterius poligonii corporis in proportione *DF* ad *PR*. Ergo motus totalis curve superficiei ad motum totalis in proportione *DF* ad

65 *PR*. Sed proportio curve superficiei ad curvam est proportio lateris ad latus duplicata. Hoc alibi probavimus. Ergo proportio curve superficiei ad curvam est proportio motus ad motum duplicata.

Ex hoc etiam manifestum quod proportio circulorum speras describentium est proportio motuum duplicata. Verbi gratia, dico quod proportio circuli

70 *ON* ad circulum *OV* in proportione motus ad motum duplicata [Fig. II.3b], prius probato quod motuum poligoniorum inscriptorum proportio est tan-

---

46 *ante* SP *scr. et del.* V DS / SP: SPF *B* / Et *OBV* Sed *N* G *E*
47 in *om.* V
48–49 motus . . . superficiei[1]: superficiei curve motus *V*
48 curve *supra scr.* N
50 GD ad SP: DGE, ASP *V* / DF ad PR: DEF, APZ *V*
51 superficiei[2] *EV om. OBN* / ONQ piramidis *tr. V*
52 DF: DEF *V*
53 CD: FD (*del. V*) SEDE *V*
54 in: est in *V*
57 PR: PR *sive* PZ *in V* / curve *supra scr. V* / curve superficiei *tr. N* / *post* superficiei *add. V* SPR piramidis in proportione GD ad SP (*et del. V* in . . . SP)
60 ab . . . describitur *mg. V* / AB *om. V* / BC: RC *V*
61 AB *super scr.* O, *om.* B / PR: PF *V*
65 *post* curvam *add.* E superficiem *et om. omnes alii MSS*
67 *post* duplicata *add.* OBEV, *om.* N, *et delevi* Probatio (probo *E*, proportio *V*) que (quod *E*) sequitur (super *E*) est (*tr. V post* omittenda) omittenda (obmittenda *E*) et querenda est (*V, om.* OBE) in corollario (col̄a *E*) prime (prius *sive post V*) tertie (*om. E*) particule
68 manifestum *om. V* / *post* proportio *add. V* maiorum / sphaeras *V hic et ubique*
70 circulum *om.* N
71 prius *om. V*

quam motuum circulorum. Motus ergo *OV* circuli ad *ON* circulum est tanquam motus poligonii ad poligonium, aut maior aut minor.

Si maior, sit tanquam motus *OV* circuli ad motum *OR* circuli. Inscribatur
75   ergo *ON* circulo poligonium minime contingens *OR* circulum. Et simile
inscribatur *OV* circulo. Motus ergo *OV* circuli ad *OR* circulum est tanquam
motus poligonii ad motum poligonii. Contra, poligonium inscriptum *ON*
circulo magis movetur *OR* circulo. Ergo maior est proportio motus poligonii
inscripti *OV* circulo ad motum *OR* circuli quam ad motum poligonii inscripti
80   *ON* circulo, et *ON* circulus magis movetur poligonio inscripto et circulo *OR*.
Ergo minor est proportio motus circuli *OV* ad circulum *ON* quam ad circulum
OR. Sed motus circuli *OV* ad motum circuli *OR* sicut motus poligonii ad
motum poligonii. Ergo minor est proportio motus *OV* circuli ad motum *ON*
circuli quam motus poligonii ad motum poligonii. Non igitur maior.

85   Simili modo inprobabitur, dicto quod minor. Sic ergo proportio motuum
poligoniorum et motuum circulorum est eadem. Sed motuum poligoniorum
et semidiametrorum *OV*, *ON* una est proportio. Ergo motuum circulorum
et semidiametrorum una est proportio. Sed proportio circulorum est proportio
semidiametrorum duplicata, ergo et motuum duplicata. Simili ratione pro-
90   babis quod curvarum superficierum sperarum proportio est proportio motuum
duplicata. Et hoc probabis per motus curvarum superficierum similium poligoniorum corporum inscriptorum, ut enim probatum est per precedentem,
motus curve superficiei poligonii corporis ad motum curve superficiei poligonii
corporis duplicata est proportio superficiei ad superficiem. Postea probabis
95   quod motuum curvarum superficierum poligoniorum corporum speris inscriptorum et motuum curvarum superficierum sperarum una est proportio.
Et hoc per impossibile, eodem modo penitus quo iam probavimus de circulis

72   OV: ON *NV* / ON: OV *NV*
73   poligonii: polygoniorum *V*
74   OV: ON *V* / circuli[1] *supra scr. N om. V* / OR: OI *V*
76   OV[1,2]: ON *V* / OR: OI *V*
77–78   ON circulo *tr. V*
78   *ante* motus *scr. et del. V* OR
79   OV: ON *V* / circulo *om. V* / OR *alii MSS et corr. V ex* OI
80   et[1]: ad circulum *V*
81, 82   OV: ON *V*
83   motus OV: ON motus *V et post* motus *scr. et del. V* polygonii
84   igitur: ergo *N*
85   inprobabitur *B* probabitur *O* ĩprobabitur *E* improbabitur *N et corr. V ex* improbat
     / Sic ergo: sit *V* / motuum: motus *V*
86   motuum[1,2]: motus *V* / est: ergo est *V*
87   OV, ON: ON, OM *V*
89–90   probabis: pro *V, et supra scr. V* probabitur
90   *post* quod *add. MSS* motuum *quod delevi* / proportio[1] *V om. alii MSS*
91   motus *EV* motum *OBN*
92   precedentem *EN,* (?) *V* presentem *OB* (*et corr. B ex* precedentem)
93   corporis . . . poligonii[2] *om. V*
95   *ante* quod *scr. et del. B* motum
97   quo: sicut *NV*

et poligoniis inscriptis. Sed motus curve superficiei poligonii corporis ad motum curve superficiei poligonii corporis est proportio semidiametri ad
100 semidiametrum, ut iam ante probavimus. Ergo proportio motus superficiei spere ad motum superficiei spere est tanquam semidiametri ad semidiametrum. Sed proportio semidiametri ad semidiametrum duplicata est proportio superficiei spere ad superficiem spere, ut alibi probatum est per librum de piramidibus. Ergo proportio superficiei ad superficiem spere est proportio
105 motus ad motum duplicata, et hoc voluimus demonstrare.

4ª. MOTUS TRIANGULI RECTANGULI AD MOTUM POLIGONII EQUILATERI ET EQUIANGULI TANQUAM MOTUS YPOTENUSE AD MOTUM AMBITUS POLIGONII. EX HOC MANIFESTUM QUOD QUANTO POLIGONIUM INSCRIPTUM CIRCULO PLURIUM FUERIT
122v LATERUM, / TANTO MAGIS MOVETUR; IN CIRCUMSCRIPTO VERO
6 ECONTRARIO.

Sit triangulus propositus *LMR* et poligonium propositum inscriptum *OH* circulo [Fig. II.4]. Protrahatur ergo latus *HI* quousque concurrat cum linea *YM* puncto *Y*. Quod concurret manifestum est, quia *O* angulus est rectus;
10 ergo *H* angulus minor recto. Si ergo *OHY, LMR* trianguli sunt similes, procedatur ex eis. Si sint dissimiles, sit *LMQ* similis *OHY*; et quota pars trianguli *OHY* est superficies *OHIQ*, tota superficies sit *LMNV* trianguli *LMQ*. Motus igitur trianguli *LMQ* ad motum trianguli *OHY* tanquam motus ypotenuse ad ypotenusam, et motus trianguli *VNQ* ad motum trianguli *QIY*
15 tanquam motus ypotenuse ad ypotenusam. Sed motus *NQ* ypotenuse ad *IY* ypotenusam tanquam motus *MQ* ypotenuse ad *HY* ypotenusam, quia *NQ, IY* similes sunt aliquote illarum ypotenusarum. Que est enim proportio *MQ* ad *NQ* ea est *HY* ad *IY*, et ita que est *MQ* ad *HY* ea est *NQ* ad *IY*. Constat

98–99 ad . . . corporis *om. V*
100–102 ut. . . . semidiametrum[1] *om. N*
101 est: semper est *V*
102 *ante* Sed *scr. et del. V* dup
104 *ante* ad *add. B* spere *sed om. alii MSS*
105 motum: motus *V* / voluimus *N* volumus *OBEV*
Prop. II.4
1 4ª: IIII *OB om. ENV*
2 tanquam: est tanquam *V* / motus *om. V*
4 circulo *om. N* / plurium *om. V*
5 circumscripto *alii MSS et corr. V ex* inscripto
7 LMR *alii MSS et corr. V ex* BNR / propositum *om. N* / OH: OB *V*
9 YM *OV* Y in *BE* OY in *N* / est rectus *BENV tr. O*
10 minor: est minor *N* / OHY . . . trianguli: anguli *V* / trianguli (*et supra scr. O* tri-): anguli *BE*
12 tota . . . sit: toto (*!*) pars sit superficies *N* / sit LMNV: erit LMNR *V*
13 igitur *OB* ergo *ENV* / LMQ[2] *om. V*
14 motus: motum *V* / QIY: QRY *V*
15–16 Sed . . . ypotenusam[2]: Sed motus IY ypothenuse ad HY ypothenusam tanquam motus NQ ypothenuse ad IY ypothenusam *N*
15 IY: RY *V*
18 IY[2]: LY *V*

ergo per precedentia quod eadem est proportio motuum illarum ypotenu-
20   sarum. Sic ergo proportio motus *LMQ* trianguli ad motum *QIY* trianguli
est tanquam motus *MQ* ad motum *IY*; et motuum totalium triangulorum
eadem est proportio. Ergo motuum residuarum partium eadem. Ergo motus
LMNV ad motum *OHIQ* tanquam [motus] *MQ* ad motum *HY*. Sed motus
MQ ad motum *HY* tanquam motus *NQ* ad motum *IY*. Ergo motuum re-
25   siduarum partium eadem est proportio. Ergo motus *MN* ad motum *HI* tanquam motus *MQ* ad motum *HY*. Sic ergo motus *LMNV* ad motum *OHIQ*
tanquam motus *MN* ad motum *HI*. Item quia triangulus *QIS* non est similis
triangulo *VNQ*, assumamus triangulum *QIY* qui est ei similis. Sicut enim
trianguli *LMQ*, *VNQ* sunt similes eo quod *LM*, *VN* sunt equidistantes, ita
30   *OHY*, *QIY* trianguli sunt similes eo quod *OH*, *QI* sunt equidistantes; et
omnes linee ducte ad *QI*, *VN* sunt equidistantes, quod non indiget probatione.
Motus ergo trianguli *VNQ* ad motum trianguli *QIY* tanquam motus ypotenuse
NQ ad motum ypotenuse *IY*. Sed trianguli *QIY*, *QIS* equaliter moventur,
quia habeant eandem basem, scilicet, *QI*; et ypotenuse eorum equaliter mo-
35   ventur *IY*, *IS*. Ergo motus *VNQ* trianguli ad motum *QIS* trianguli tanquam
motus *NQ* ypotenuse ad motum *IS* ypotenuse. Sit ergo linea *ZT* equalis linee
KP. Patet ergo quod trianguli *PKS*, *TZY* equaliter moventur cum sint equalium basium. Et trianguli *QIS*, *QIY* moventur equaliter. Ergo residue partes
equaliter moventur. Ergo motus *QIKP*, *QIZT* sunt equales, et similiter motus
40   *IK*, *IZ* sunt equales, per similes. Ergo [in] aliquotas dividatur triangulus *VNQ*

19 precedentia *ENV* presentia *O* presentiam *sive* presentia *B* / quod: et *B* / motuum
om. *V*
20 *ante* motus *scr. et del. V* illarum hypothenusarum / LMQ: IMQ *B* (*cf. var. lin. 24
inferius*) VNQ *V*
21 IY *N* HY *OBE* HI *V* / totalium triangulorum *tr. N*
22 partium: portionum *V* / motus *om. N*
23 OHIQ: OHQ *V* / [motus] *addidi*
24 MQ: MLQ *V* / IY: LY *V hic et saepe postea in MSS* (*cf. mea commenta in cap. 3*);
et post hoc lectionem "l" *pro* "i" *sive vice versa non laudabo*
26 MQ *ON et corr. B ex* MK *et hab. V* MK / ad motum[2] *om. N*
27 MN *alii* MS *et corr. B ex* MK / *ante* HI *scr. et del. B* HX
28 est ei *OB tr. NV* est *E*
29 VN: NV *V* / ita: ita quod *V*
30–31 QIY . . . VN: diametrum a circumferentia *V* / et . . . equidistantes *om. N*
31 QI: DI *OB* / *post* equidistantes *scr. et del. B* ita OHY, QLY trianguli sunt similes eo
quod OH, QL
32 Motus ergo: Igitur motus *V* / *ante* QIY *scr. et del. B* 1 / QIY: QNY *V*
33 NQ *EN et corr. B* NV *OV et ante corr. B* / IY: HY *V*
34–35 quia . . . moventur *mg. V*
34 basim *NV* / QI: IQL *V* / eorum *correxi ex* earum *in MSS*
35 motus *om. V*
36 NQ ypotenuse *tr. N* / IS ypotenuse *tr. N* / Sit: Sic *B* / ZT: ZTE *V*
37 KP *corr. B ex* KB / PKS: PKZ (?) *V* / TZY: CKY *corr. V ex* CLY
38 QIS: Q̦KIS *O* K̦QIS *B* (*et corr. E ex* KLS *et hab. NV* KIS) / QIY: K̦QIY *OB* KIN
EN KLY *V*
40 IK, IZ: LKA *V* (*corr. V. ex* LHA) / [in] *addidi*

per lineam *TO*, ut triangulus *QIY* divisus est per lineam *TZ*. Motus ergo trianguli *TOQ* ad triangulum *TZY* tanquam motus *OQ* ad motum *ZY*, ergo tanquam motus *NQ* ad motum *IY*. Et motus totalium triangulorum *VNQ*, *QIY* in eadem proportione se habent. Ergo motus residuarum partium in
45 eadem proportione se habent cum sint similes aliquote. Ergo motus *VNOT* ad motum *QIZT* tanquam motus *NQ* ad motum *IY*; ergo tanquam motus *NO* ad motum *IZ*, sicut prius probatum est in aliis lineis. Sed *QIZT*, *QIKP* moventur equaliter, et *IZ*, *IK* moventur equaliter. Ergo motus *VNOT* ad motum *QIKP* tanquam motus *NO* ad motum *IK*. Item cum triangulus *PKR*
50 non sit similis triangulo *TOQ*, sit triangulus *PKX* similis illi, ita quod *K* angulus sit equalis *O* angulo. Motus ergo *TOQ* trianguli ad motum *PKX* trianguli tanquam motus *OQ* ad motum *KX*. Sit ergo linea *Vq* equalis linee *NL*. Sic ergo trianguli *PKX*, *PKR* equaliter moventur cum sint in eadem basi, et trianguli *VqX*, *NLR* equaliter moventur cum bases sint equales. Ergo
55 superficies *PKqV*, *PKLN* equaliter moventur, sicut prius, et *Kq* equaliter *KL*. Distinguat ergo *PS* linea triangulum *TOQ* per similes aliquotas sicut *Vq* distinguit triangulum *PKX*. Eodem ergo modo procedendo sicut prius probabis quod motus *TOPS* ad motum *PKqV* / tanquam motus *OP* ad motum *Kq*. Sed *PKLN*, *PKqV* equaliter moventur et similiter *Kq*, *KL* equaliter moventur.
60 Ergo motus *TOPS* ad motum *PKLN* tanquam motus *OP* ad motum *KL*. Ventum ergo est ad externos [tri]angulos *SPQ*, *NLM*. Sed quoniam non sunt similes, constituatur super basem *SP* similis triangulo *NLM*. Motus ergo illius trianguli ad motum trianguli *NLM* tanquam motus ypotenuse ad motum ypotenuse trianguli *NLM*. Sed ille triangulus movetur equaliter *SPQ* triangulo

123r (left margin, line 57)

41 QIY: QLY *V* (*corr. V ex* QLS) / TZ: CZ *V* (*corr. V ex* CQ)
42 TZY: TOS *V* / OQ *om. V et corr. B ex* AQ / ZY: TY *V*
44 QIY: QLY *V* (*corr. V ex* QLR)
46 IY: HI *B* HY *V*
47 IZ: IV *V* / QIZT, QIKP: LQZC, QLKP *V*
48 VNOT: RONT *V*
49 motum[1] ENV *om.* OB / IK: LH *V*
50 TOQ: POQ *V* / sit: sicut *V* / PKX: PKY *V* / illi: est illi *V*
51 TOQ trianguli *tr. V* / PKX: PKY *V*
52 OQ *corr. O ex* VQ / KX: KY *V* / -q: q; *MSS* (*V excepto hic et quasi ubique*) Z *V*
     (*et post hoc lectiones huiusmodi non laudabo*)
53 PKR: PHKR *V*
53–54 cum . . . moventur BENV (*sed. om. E* sint *in lin. 53 et hab. E* super eandem basim
     pro in . . . basi *in lin. 53–54*) *om.* O
54 VqX *B* NqX *E* VOX *N* NZ *V*
55 PKqV: PKZN *V*
56 TOQ *correxi ex* TQV *in OBN et* TQN *in E et* TQB *in V* / sicut *bis B* / Vq: Nq *V*
58 PKqV *BEN* QKqV *O* PKZV *V*
59 Sed *bis B* / PKLN: KPLN *V* / PKqV *correxi ex* TKqV *in OBEN et* CKqN *in V* /
     et *om. V*
61 Ventum: Unde tum *V* / ergo est *tr. N* / externas *B* / [tri]- *addidi*
62 constituatur *EN* constituantur *OBV*
64 SPQ *N* SP *OBEV*

65 cum sint eiusdem basis, et ypotenusa movetur equaliter *PQ*. Ergo motus
SPQ trianguli ad motum *NLM* tanquam *PQ* ad *LM*. Ergo motus omnium
predictarum partium *LMQ* trianguli ad motum omnium predictarum partium
superficiei *OHM* tanquam motus predictarum partium ypotenuse *MQ* ad
motum laterum *OHM* superficiei. Ergo motus totalis trianguli *LMQ* ad motum
70 totalis superficiei *OHM* tanquam motus ypotenuse ad motum ambitus *OHM*.
Eadem ratione motus trianguli *LMQ* ad motum superficiei *OHD* tanquam
motus *MQ* ad motum *HD*. Et ita motus trianguli *LMQ* ad motum *MHD*
superficiei tanquam motus *MQ* ad motum *MHD* ambitus. Ergo motus *LMQ*
trianguli ad motum semipoligonii tanquam motus ypotenuse ad motum
75 semiambitus, et ita motus trianguli ad motum totalis poligonii tanquam
motus ypotenuse ad motum ambitus.

Ex hoc etiam manifestum est quod motus curve superficiei piramidis *LMQ*
ad motum curve superficiei poligonii corporis quod describitur a poligonia
superficie tanquam motus ypotenuse ad motum ambitus. Motus enim curve
80 superficiei *LMQ* piramidis ad motum curve superficiei *OHY* piramidis tanquam motus ypotenuse ad ypotenusam. Hoc constat ex dictis. Eodem modo
motus curve superficiei *VNQ* piramidis ad motum curve superficiei *QIY*
piramidis tanquam motus ypotenuse ad ypotenusam, hoc est, tanquam *NQ*
ad motum *IY*. Ergo motus curve superficiei *LMNV* superficiei ad motum
85 curve superficiei *OHIQ* tanquam motus *MQ* ad motum *HY*; ergo tanquam
MN ad motum *HI*. Et ita eodem modo procedendo sicut prius de triangulo
et poligonio probabis propositum. Sed *LMQ* triangulus movetur equaliter
dato triangulo, scilicet *LMR*, cum sint in eadem basi, et eadem ratione
ypotenusa ypotenuse et curva superficies curve. Ergo motus *LMR* trianguli
90 dati ad motum poligonii tanquam motus ypotenuse ad motum ambitus
poligonii, et motus curve superficiei ad motum curve in eadem.

65 PQ: PA *V*
66 SPQ: SPA *V* / omnium *om. N*
68 superficiei *corr. V ex* spez
69 motum[1]: motus *V* / *post* motum[2] *scr. et del. B* OHD superficiei tanquam motus
70 OHM[1]: OHL *O*
72–73 HD. . . . motum *om. V*
72 MHD *correxi ex* OHD *in MSS*
74 semipoligonii: semidiametri *V*
76 motum: motus *V*
77 etiam *om. V*
78 poligonici *N* / a: qr (?) *V* / poligonica N
81 motus *ENV om. OB*
81–83 Hoc. . . . ypotenusam *om. V*
82–83 QIY piramidis *tr. N*
83 NQ: motus NQ *V*
84 superficiei[2] *om. N*
85 OHIQ: OHM *V*
86 MN: NM *V*
87 et . . . propositum *om. V* / probabis *OEN* probabit *B* / movetur equaliter *tr. V*
90 *post* dati *add. V* polygonii / motum poligonii: polygonium motum est *V* / *ante* motus
scr. B n / ambitus *om. V*

Corollarium sic pateat. Motus poligonii ad triangulum tanquam motus ambitus ad ypotenusam. Sed si poligonium inscriptum fuerit plurium laterum, ambitus eius magis movetur, per ultimam primi. Ergo motus ambitus poligonii
95 plurium laterum inscripti ad motum ypotenuse maior est proportio quam motus ambitus poligonii pauciorum laterum. Ergo motus poligonii plurium laterum inscripti ad motum trianguli maior est proportio quam motus poligonii pauciorum laterum ad eundem triangulum. Ergo magis movetur poligonium plurium laterum inscriptum quam poligonium pauciorum laterum.
100 Item motus ambitus poligonii pauciorum laterum circumscripti maior est motu ambitus poligonii plurium laterum circumscripti. Sed que est proportio motus ambitus ad ypotenuse motum ea est motus poligonii ad motum trianguli. Ergo maior est proportio motus poligonii pauciorum laterum circumscripti ad triangulum quam motus poligonii plurium laterum. Ergo maior
105 est motus. Habemus ergo propositum.

5ª. MOTUS TRIANGULI AD MOTUM CIRCULI SPERAM DESCRIBENTIS TANQUAM MOTUS YPOTENUSE AD MOTUM CIRCUM-
123v FERENTIE. / UNDE MANIFESTUM QUOD MOTUUM CURVARUM SUPERFICIERUM EADEM EST PROPORTIO ET QUOD MOTUS
5 EQUINOCTIALIS CIRCULI AD MOTUM COLURI TANQUAM MOTUS CIRCUMFERENTIE AD MOTUM CIRCUMFERENTIE.

Age igitur. Dico quod motus trianguli *LMN* ad motum circuli *OF* (*! OC*) tanquam motus *LNM* ypotenuse ad motum circumferentie, aut maior aut minor [Fig. II.5].
10 Si maior, sit motus *LMN* trianguli ad motum *OC* circuli tanquam motus ypotenuse ad motum circumferentie *OF* circuli. Inscribatur poligonium *OC* circulo minime contingens *OF* circulum. Motus ergo *LNM* trianguli ad poligonium tanquam motus ypotenuse ad motum ambitus. Ergo minor est proportio motus ypotenuse ad motum ambitus poligonii quam ad motum
15 circumferentie *OF* circuli. Ergo minor est proportio motus *LMN* trianguli ad motum poligonii quam motus ypotenuse ad motum circumferentie *OF* circuli. Ergo multo fortius minor est proportio motus *LMN* trianguli ad motum *OC* circuli quam motus ypotenuse ad motum [circumferentie] *OF* circuli. Non ergo tanta.

93 ambitus *alii MSS et corr. V ex* ad ambitum
98 eundem *alii MSS et corr. V ex* eiusdem
101 *post* laterum *scr. et del. V* curvae superficiei
102 ypotenuse motum *tr. NV*
105 propositum: *hic desinit V*
Prop. II.5
1 5ª: V *OB om. EN*
8 LMN *OB* MN *EN*
10 Si *ON* sit *BE*
11 OF: AF *B*
14–16 quam. . . . poligonii *N om. OBE*
17 multofortius *O hic et ubique et post hoc lectiones huiusmodi non laudabo*

20   Si minor est proportio motus trianguli ad circulum quam motus ypotenuse
ad motum circumferentie, sit motus *LMN* trianguli ad motum *OF* circuli
tanquam motus ypotenuse ad motum circumferentie *OC* circuli. Minor ergo
est proportio motus ypotenuse ad motum ambitus poligonii quam ad motum
circumferentie *OC* circuli. Sed motus ypotenuse ad motum ambitus poligonii
25   tanquam motus trianguli ad motum poligonii. Ergo maior est proportio
motus trianguli ad motum poligonii quam motus ypotenuse ad motum circumferentie *OC* circuli. Ergo multo fortius maior est proportio motus *LMN*
trianguli ad motum *OF* circuli quam motus ypotenuse ad motum circumferentie *OC* circuli. Non ergo eadem. Sic ergo constat quod motus trianguli
30   ad motum circuli tanquam motus ypotenuse ad motum circumferentie.

Dico ergo quod motus curve superficiei *LMN* piramidis ad motum superficiei *OF* spere tanquam motus ypotenuse ad motum circumferentie, aut
maior aut minor.

Si maior, sit motus curve superficiei piramidis ad motum curve superficiei
35   *OC* spere tanquam motus ypotenuse ad motum circumferentie *OF* circuli.
Sed motus curve superficiei piramidis ad motum curve superficiei poligonii
corporis inscripti *OC* spere tanquam motus ypotenuse ad motum ambitus.
Ergo maior est proportio motus ypotenuse ad motum circumferentie *OF*
circuli quam motus ypotenuse ad motum ambitus. Ergo maior est proportio
40   motus ypotenuse ad motum circumferentie *OF* circuli quam motus curve
superficiei piramidis ad motum curve superficiei poligonii corporis. Ergo
multo fortius maior est proportio motus ypotenuse ad motum circumferentie
OF circuli quam motus curve superficiei piramidis ad motum superficiei *OC*
spere. Non ergo eadem.

45   Si minor est proportio motus curve superficiei piramidis ad motum superficiei spere quam motus ypotenuse ad motum circumferentie spere, sit
motus curve superficiei piramidis *LMN* ad motum superficiei *OF* spere tanquam motus ypotenuse ad motum circumferentie *OC* spere. Procedendo
ergo eodem modo sicut prius probabis quod minor est proportio motus
50   ypotenuse piramidis *LMN* ad motum circumferentie *OC* circuli quam motus
curve superficiei piramidis ad motum superficiei *OF* spere.

20 *ante* ypotenuse *scr. et del. B* ibate (*!*)
22 *ante* circuli *scr. et del.* (?) *B* quam
23 est proportio *tr. N*
28 ad[1] *supra scr. B, et del. B* quam
29 ergo[1] *N om. OBE*
32 *post* tanquam *scr. et del. O* piramidis
35–36 OC. . . . superficiei[2] *om. N*
43 *post* motum *scr. et del. N* curve
43–44 OC spere *N* spere OC spere *OBE*
45 *ante* piramidis *add. E* motus
45–47 ad . . . piramidis *NE* (*sed add. E* motus *ante* piramidis *in linea 45*) *om. OB*
47–50 ad . . . LMN *om. E*
47 *post* motum *scr. et del. O* LMN ergo *et scr. B sed non del.* LMN ad motum
49 prius probabis *N* probavimus prius *OB*

Ex presenti probatione patet quod motus circuli ad motum poligonii est tanquam motus circumferentie ad motum ambitus, quia cum motus circuli ad motum trianguli est tanquam motus circumferentie ad motum ypotenuse, et motus trianguli ad motum poligonii est tanquam motus / ypotenuse ad motum ambitus, ergo motus circuli ad motum poligonii tanquam motus circumferentie ad motum ambitus. Item cum motus superficiei spere ad motum superficiei rotunde piramidis tanquam motus circumferentie ad motum ypotenuse, et motus superficiei rotunde piramidis ad motum corporis poligonii superficiei tanquam motus ypotenuse ad motum ambitus, ergo motus superficiei spere ad motum superficiei poligonii corporis tanquam motus circumferentie ad motum ambitus poligonie superficiei poligonium corpus describentis.

Secunda pars corollarii sic pateat. Inscribatur triangulus coluro, cuius duo latera rectum angulum continentia sint medietates duorum (!) diametrorum. Motus illius trianguli ad motum coluri tanquam motus ypotenuse ad motum circumferentie. Hoc est iam probatum. Item motus trianguli ad motum equinoctialis subduplus. Hoc probatum est per primam huius libri. Et motus ypotenuse ad motum circumferentie equinoctialis subduplus. Eadem est ergo proportio motus trianguli ad motum equinoctialis que est motus ypotenuse ad motum circumferentie. Sed motus huius trianguli ad motum dati trianguli tanquam motus ypotenuse ad motum ypotenuse. Hoc patet si constituatur triangulus similis dato super eandem basim. Sed motus trianguli ad motum coluri tanquam motus ypotenuse ad motum circumferentie coluri. Ergo motus equinoctialis circuli ad motum coluri tanquam motus circumferentie ad motum circumferentie.

Item ex predictis patet quod motuum circulorum speras describentium proportio duplicata est proportio circulorum. Propositis enim duobus circulis motus primi circuli ad motum trianguli tanquam motus circumferentie ad motum ypotenuse. Et motus trianguli ad motum secundi circuli tanquam motus ypotenuse ad motum circumferentie. Ergo motus primi circuli ad motum secundi tanquam motus circumferentie ad motum circumferentie, hoc est, in proportione circumferentie ad circumferentiam, hoc est, in proportione diametri ad diametrum. Sed proportio diametri ad diametrum duplicata est proportio circuli ad circulum. Ergo proportio motus ad motum duplicata est proportio circuli ad circulum. Idem potest probari per impos-

52 presenti *OB* precedenti E precedenti etiam *N*
58 rotunde piramidis *tr. N*
59 superficiei: circumferentie *N*
59–60 corporis . . . superficiei: superficie poligonii corporis *N*
62 poligonie: pili^e *B*
68 libri *N om. OBE*
73 dato *N* dati (?) *OB* daī *E* / basim *OE* basem *BN*
77 circulorum *EN* circulo *OB* / describentium *N* circumscribentium *OBE*
81 *post* motum *scr. et del. O* circuli
85–86 Ergo . . . circulum *om. N*

sibile, dicto quod maior aut minor. Sit proportio motus circuli ad motum circuli, que motus circumferentie ad motum circumferentie. Et hoc per inscriptionem poligoniorum similium. Ex hoc etiam manifestum quod proportio
90   curvarum superficierum sperarum est proportio motuum ipsarum duplicata. Et hoc potest probari directe per motum curve superficiei rotunde piramidis vel indirecte per motum similium poligoniorum corporum inscriptorum.

Liber Tertius

[Petitiones]

[1.] INTER COLUMPNAS EQUALES ET SIMILES EODEM TEMPORE MOTAS, CUIUS NULLUS CIRCULORUM MAGIS MOVETUR, NEC
5   IPSA MAGIS.
[2.] CUIUS NULLUS CIRCULORUM MINUS, NEC IPSA MINUS.

[Propositiones]

1^a. POLIGONIORUM CORPORUM SIMILIUM PROPORTIO EST PROPORTIO MOTUS AD MOTUM TRIPLICATA.
10   Age ergo. Prima columpna moveatur describendo se ipsam. Secunda columpna equalis et similis moveatur in continuum et directum, ita quod quilibet circulus eius equalis circulo prime moveatur equaliter cuilibet circulo prime. Et ita iste due columpne moventur equaliter. Hoc patet per impossibile.

124v   Quia si prima non movetur equaliter / secunde, vel magis vel minus mo-
15   vetur. Si magis, contra, [quia] nullus eius circulus magis movetur. Cum ergo columpne sint equales et similes et eodem tempore mote et nullus circulus prime movetur magis aliquo circulo secunde, ergo prima non movetur magis secunda. Eadem ratione probabitur quod prima non movetur minus secunda. Ergo equaliter.
20   Sint ergo due columpne inequales et similes et utraque se ipsam describendo moveatur. Patet ergo per presentem probationem quod motus columpne ad

87 maior *OBE* aut maior *N*
88 que *O* quam *BEN*
90 motuum: mutuum *B*
Pet. and Prop. III.1
    1 Liber Tertius *mg. sin. et mg. sup. N; om. OEV; et mg. sup. scr. B* EXPLICIT SE-
       CUNDUS INCIPIT TERTIUS DE MOTU *et mg. inferius add. B aliquid quod non
       legere possum*
    2 [Petitiones] *addidi*
    7 [Propositiones] *addidi*
    8 1^a: I *OB om. EN*
    10 ergo *OB* igitur *EN* / se *EN om. OB sed cf. lin. 20, 23, 24, 27, 37*
    13 iste *OBE* ille *N*
    15 [quia] *addidi*
    17 prime *om. N* / movetur magis *EN* movetur movetur *OB* / aliquo *N* alicui *E* accidentali
        (?) *O* ac^{li} *B*
    21 presentem *OB* precedentem *EN*

columpnam est tanquam motus basis ad basem, quia ut iam probatum est
columpna que describit se ipsam movetur equaliter sue basi, quia movetur
equaliter illi que equaliter movetur basi. Sic ergo omnis columpna que se
25   ipsam describit equaliter movetur sue basi. Sic ergo proportio motuum columpnarum similium est tanquam proportio motuum basium sive circulorum
quando columpne motu suo se ipsas describunt. Si ergo proponantur due
columpne similes se ipsas motu suo describentes, proportio motuum columpnarum est tanquam proportio motuum basium. Sed proportio motuum
30   basium est tanquam proportio motuum semidiametrorum ipsarum basium.
Sed proportio columpne ad columpnam est proportio motus semidiametri
basis ad motum semidiametri triplicata, quia semidiametrorum et motuum
una est proportio. Sed proportio semidiametrorum basium columpnarum
similium triplicata est proportio columpnarum, cum semidiametrorum et
35   diametrorum una sit proportio. Ergo proportio columpnarum similium est
proportio motuum triplicata.

Eadem ratione similium piramidum se ipsas describentium proportio est
proportio motuum triplicata.

Age igitur. Trianguli *OAC, OLN* sunt similes, quia *O, O* anguli sunt recti
40   et *A, L* anguli sunt equales ex dato, quia similia sunt poligonia similia corpora
describentia [Fig. III.1]. Ergo *C, N* anguli sunt equales. Sic ergo piramides
illorum triangulorum sunt similes. Motus ergo piramidis *OAC* ad motum
piramidis *OLN* tanquam motus *OA* ad *OL*, hoc est, in proportione *OA* ad
OL. Sed piramis ad piramidem in proportione *OA* ad *OL* triplicata. Ergo
45   piramis ad piramidem in proportione motus ad motum triplicata.

Eadem ratione piramis *FBC* ad piramidem *QMN* in proportione motus
FB ad motum *QM* triplicata, quia in proportione *FB* ad *QM* triplicata. Sed
proportio *FB* ad *QM* est tanquam proportio *OA* ad *OL*. Similes enim trianguli,
est enim protracta *FB* equidistans *OA* et *QM* equidistans *OL*. Sic ergo pro-
50   portio *FB* ad *QM* est tanquam proportio *OA* ad *OL*. Ergo proportio *FBC*
piramidis ad *QMN* piramidem est proportio *AO* ad *OL* triplicata. Ergo proportio *FBC* piramidis ad *QMN* piramidem est proportio motus *OA* ad motum
OL triplicata. Et motus totalis piramidis *OAC* ad motum totalis piramidis
OLN est tanquam proportio *OA* ad *OL* et proportio totalis piramidis ad
55   totalem est proportio *OA* ad *OL* triplicata. Ergo motus differentie *OAC, FBC*
piramidum ad motum differentie *OLN, QMN* piramidum in proportione
OA ad *OL* et ipsarum differentiarum proportio est proportio *OA* ad *OL*

25–26 columpnarum . . . motuum *N. om. OBE*
    27 proponantur *EN* proportionantur *OB*
    29 *post* motuum[1] *scr. et del. N* columpnarum
    34 triplicata: est proportio triplicata *N*
    39 OLN: CLN *B*
    42 ad *EN om. OB*
    43 OA[1] *EN* GA *OB* / est *om. N*
    44 piramis *N* piramidis *OBE*
    48 enim *O* enim sunt *BEN*
    52 FBC *om. B*

triplicata. Ergo proportio ipsarum differentiarum est proportio motus ad motum triplicata.

60   Preterea trianguli *FBD, QMP* sunt similes, quia *Q, F* (*! F, Q*) anguli sunt recti. Ille enim linee protracte sunt equidistantes *OA, OL* lineis et *D, P* anguli sunt equales, quia poligonia sunt similia. Ergo *B, M* anguli sunt equales. Ergo trianguli sunt similes et piramides illorum triangulorum similes. Ergo proportio piramidis ad piramidem est proportio motus ad motum triplicata,

65   hoc est, proportio *FB* ad *QM* triplicata, hoc est, proportio *OA* ad *OL* triplicata, hoc est, proportio motus *OA* ad motum *OL* triplicata. Sed proportio differentie *OABF* ad differentiam *OLMQ* est proportio *OA* ad *OL* triplicata et proportio motus differentie ad motum differentie est tanquam proportio *OA* ad *OL*. Ergo proportio totalis corporis constantis ex piramide et differentia ad totale

70   constans ex piramide et differentia est proportio *OA* ad *OL* triplicata. Et
125'r   proportio motus ad motum est tanquam / proportio *OA* ad *OL*.

Eadem demonstratione probabis quod proportio residue quarte totalis corporis ad residuam quartam totalis est proportio *OA* ad *OL* triplicata, et motus ad motum tanquam *OA* ad *OL*, et ita medietas totalis corporis ad medietatem

75   totalis in proportione *OA* ad *OL* triplicata. Et motus ad motum in proportione *OA* ad *OL*. Ergo totale corpus ad totale in proportione *OA* ad *OL* triplicata, et motus ad motum in proportione *OA* ad *OL*. Ergo proportio corporum est proportio motuum triplicata.

2ª. EX HOC MANIFESTUM QUOD SPERARUM PROPORTIO EST MOTUUM PROPORTIO TRIPLICATA.

Dico igitur quod motus *OL* spere ad motum *OB* spere est tanquam *OL* semidiametri ad *OB* semidiametrum [Fig. III.2]. Inscribantur enim illis speris

5   poligonia similia. Dico quod motus poligonii corporis ad motum poligonii corporis tanquam motus spere ad motum spere; aut enim eadem est proportio, aut maior aut minor.

Si maior, ergo minor est motus spere ad motum spere quam motus poligonii corporis ad motum poligonii corporis. Sit ergo motus *OL* spere ad motum

10   *OA* spere tanquam motus poligonii ad motum poligonii. Inscribatur ergo *OB* spere poligonium equilaterum et equiangulum, non contingens *OA* speram. Et inscribatur simile *OL* spere et sint illa poligonia corpora *OGHIKBCDEF, OQRSTLMNOP*. Proportio ergo motuum istorum poligoniorum corporum est tanquam proportio *OL* linee ad *OB* lineam per dictam pro-

15   bationem. Et motuum poligoniorum primorum est tanquam proportio *OL* linee ad *OB* lineam per eandem probationem. Ergo eadem est proportio motuum istorum poligoniorum corporum et motuum primorum. Ergo motus istius poligonii ad motum sui consimilis est tanquam proportio motus *OL*

60 trianguli *om. N*
61 protracte *tr. N ante* OA / D, P *tr. N*
69 totale: totalem *B*

Prop. III.2

1 2ª: II *OB om. EN* / quod: est quod *N*
3 igitur *OB* ergo *EN* / est *O om. BEN*

spere ad motum *OA* spere, quod manifeste est impossibile. Maior enim est
20 proportio motus poligonii iam inscripti *OL* spere ad motum *OA* spere quam
ad motum consimilis poligonii inscripti *OB* spere, quia illud poligonium
magis movetur *OA* spera. Ergo multo fortius maior est proportio motus *OL*
spere ad motum *OA* spere quam motus poligonii ad motum poligonii. Ergo
maior est proportio motus *OL* spere ad motum *OA* spere quam motuum
25 poligoniorum corporum.

Si minor est proportio motus poligonii ad motum poligonii quam motus
spere ad motum spere, ergo maior est motus spere ad motum spere. Circumscribatur ergo spera *OB* ab alia spera; et sit motus *OL* spere ad motum
illius spere tanquam motus poligonii corporis ad motum poligonii. Inscribatur
30 ergo poligonium illi spere minime contingens *OB* speram et circumscribatur
OL spere simile poligonium, similiter non contingens [*OL* speram]. Motuum
ergo istorum poligoniorum proportio est tanquam proportio motuum primorum poligoniorum, quia semidiametrorum eadem est proportio. Procedendo ergo sicut prius probabis quod motuum istorum poligoniorum multo
35 maior est proportio quam sit proportio motus *OL* spere ad motum spere
circumscripte *OB* spere. Ergo motuum primorum poligoniorum maior est
proportio quam motuum istarum sperarum. Sic ergo cum nec maior nec
minor sit proportio, eadem erit proportio. Sed proportio motus poligonii ad
motum poligonii est tanquam proportio *OL* semidiametri ad *OB* semidi-
40 ametrum. Ergo motus spere ad motum spere tanquam *OL* semidiametri ad
OB semidiametrum. Sed proportio sperarum est proportio semidiametrorum
triplicata, quia diametrorum. Ergo proportio sperarum est proportio motuum
triplicata.

3ª. MOTUS PIRAMIDIS RECTANGULE AD MOTUM POLIGONII
CORPORIS A POLIGONIO EQUILATERO ET EQUIANGULO DE-
125′v SCRIPTI TANQUAM MOTUS YPOTENUSE AD MOTUM LA/TERUM
POLIGONII.
5 Primo monstrandum quod omnes piramides eiusdem basis equaliter moventur. Dico enim quod *LMP*, *LMQ* piramides descripte a triangulis *LMP*,
LMQ equaliter moventur [Fig. III.3]. Columpne enim *LMTP*, *LMVQ* moventur equaliter; ergo et piramides illarum, cum sint similes aliquote, totarum

19–20 quod . . . spere² *EN om.* OB
21 OB *EN* AB *OB*
22 movetur magis *N* (et *supra scr.* N magis)
25 poligoniorum *bis B*
26 Si: sed *B*
28 spera OB ab *correxi ex* spera ab *in N et* spere OB *in OBE*
29 illius *correxi ex* Vi *in OB et* M *in E et lacuna in N*
31 [OL speram] *addidi*
32 proportio¹ *om. N*
32–33 primorum poligoniorum *N* poligoniorum *O* poligoniorum poligoniorum *BE*
Prop. III.3
1 3ª: III OB *om. EN*
8 totarum *N* totorum *OB* tantorum *E*

enim et similium aliquotarum eadem est proportio. Ergo ille piramides mo-
10 ventur equaliter. Dico ergo quod motus piramidis *LMQ* ad motum poligonii
corporis inscripti *OA* spere tanquam motus ypotenuse ad motum laterum.

Protrahatur enim latus *AB* quousque concurrat cum linea *OD* in puncto
D. Trianguli ergo *OAD*, *LMQ* aut sunt similes aut dissimiles. Si similes, ex
eis procedatur.

15 Si dissimiles, sit *LMP* similis *OAD*. Sic ergo piramides *LMP*, *OAD* sunt
similes. Ergo motus *LMP* piramidis ad motum *OAD* piramidis tanquam
motus basis ad basem; ergo tanquam motus *LM* semidiametri basis ad motum
OA semidiametri basis; ergo tanquam motus *MP* ypotenuse ad motum ypotenuse *AD*. Sit ergo *BI* equidistans *OA* et *NS* equidistans *LM* per similes
20 aliquotas dividens *LMP* triangulum sicut *IB* dividit *OAD* triangulum. Sic
ergo motus piramidis *SNP* ad motum piramidis *IBD* tanquam motus *SN* ad
motum *IB* eadem ratione qua prius. Sed motus *SN* ad motum *IB* tanquam
motus *LM* ad motum *OA*. Hoc patet per similes triangulos et per similes
aliquotas divisas. Sic ergo motus piramidis *SNP* ad motum piramidis *IBD*
25 tanquam motus ypotenuse *MP* ad motum ypotenuse *AD* et tanquam motus
ypotenuse *NP* ad motum ypotenuse *BD*. Ergo motus differentie piramidum
ad motum differentie piramidum in eadem proportione et in proportione
motus *MN* ad motum *AB* que eadem est.

Item *IBD*, *IBF* piramides moventur equaliter et ypotenuse earum. Sit ergo
30 *HK* equalis *FC*. Sic ergo *HKF*, *FCD* piramides moventur equaliter, ypotenuse
earum moventur equaliter. Cum ergo totales piramides moveantur equaliter,
scilicet *IBD*, *IBF*, et residua movebuntur equaliter, sic ergo *IBKH*, *IBCF*,
que sunt differentie maiorum et minorum piramidum, moventur equaliter
et *BC*, *BK* linee moventur equaliter. Cum ergo *SNP*, *IBD* piramides sunt
35 similes et trianguli similes, motus *SNP* ad motum *IBD* tanquam motus basis
ad motum basis et tanquam motus *SN* semidiametri ad motum *IB* semidiametri et tanquam motus *NP* ad motum *BD*.

Item simili modo dividat *RO* triangulum *SNP* ut *FC* triangulum *IBD*. Sic
ergo motus *ROP* piramidis ad motum *FCD* piramidis tanquam motus *RO*
40 ad motum *FC* et tanquam motus *OP* ad motum *CD*. Sed motus *OP* ad
motum *CD* tanquam motus *NP* ad motum *BD*. Sic ergo cum motuum

9 aliquotarum *EN* aliquorum *OB*

12 AB *om. N*

19 BI *correxi ex* BL *in MSS (alibi hab.* N I *et hab.* OBE L; *ex figuris praefero* I *et post
hoc lectiones huiusmodi non laudabo)*

20 sicut *N* sumatur *OBE* / dividit *N* dividens *O* divid. *BE*

21 SN: LN *B*

25–26 AD . . . ypotenuse[2] *bis N*

30 HK: BK (?) *B* / HKF, FCD: HK, SF, CD *B* / *ante* ypotenuse *add. N* et

33–34 et . . . equaliter *OBE om. N*

34, 35 SNP: LNP *sive* LUP *B*

35 IBD: SBD *B*

36 SN: LN B

37 NP: VP *B*

38 SNP *N* (*et corr. O ex* SVP) SVP *BE* / ut FC *N* MFC *BE* et FC *corr. O ex* MFC

38–41 Sic. . . . BD *om. N*

41 motuum: motus *N*

totalium piramidum et similium partium una sit proportio, et motuum residuarum partium eadem erit proportio et tanquam motus *NO* ad motum
BC, que sunt differentie ypotenusarum. Sed *IBD*, *IBF* piramides equaliter
45 moventur et ypotenuse earum; et *HKF*, *FCD* similiter et ypotenuse et differentie. Sic ergo motus *SNOR* differentie piramidum ad motum *IBKH* differentie piramidum tanquam motus *NO* ad motum *BK*. Item cum trianguli
ROP, *HKG* sint dissimiles, sit *HKE* similis *ROP*. Sic ergo motus piramidis
ROP ad motum piramidis *HKE* tanquam motus ypotenuse ad motum ypo-
50 tenuse. Sed *HKE*, *HKG* moventur equaliter et ypotenuse earum. Ergo motus
ROP ad motum *HKG* tanquam motus *OP* ad motum *KG*. Idem invenis in
alia parte poligonii corporis. Sic ergo ex partibus conclude quod motus piramidis *LMP* ad motum poligonii corporis tanquam motus ypotenuse ad
motum laterum simul sumptorum.
55   Ex hoc manifestum quod quantum poligonium corpus inscriptum spere
125r fuerit plurium laterum tanto magis movetur, / in circumscriptis vero econtrario. Cum enim motus poligonii corporis plurium laterum inscripti spere
ad motum piramidis tanquam motus laterum ad motum ypotenuse, sed si
plurium fuerit laterum, latera magis moventur per ultimam prime particule,
60 ergo maior est proportio motus poligonii corporis plurium laterum inscripti
ad motum piramidis quam motus poligonii corporis pauciorum laterum.
Ergo corpus plurium laterum magis movetur. In circumscriptis econtrario
contingit quia latera corporis plurium laterum minus moventur. Ergo maior
est proportio motus corporis pauciorum laterum ad motum piramidis quam
65 corporis plurium laterum. Ergo corpus pauciorum laterum magis movetur.
    4ª. MOTUS PIRAMIDIS RECTANGULE AD MOTUM SPERE TAN-
QUAM MOTUS YPOTENUSE AD MOTUM CIRCUMFERENTIE
COLURI.
    Dico igitur quod motus *OPQ* piramidis ad motum *OA* spere est tanquam
5 motus ypotenuse ad circumferentiam coluri, scilicet circuli speram describentis, aut maior aut minor [Fig. III.4].
    Si maior, sit motus *OPQ* ad speram *OB* tanquam motus ypotenuse ad
circumferentiam *OA* spere. Inscribatur ergo *OB* spere corpus poligonium

   44 IBD *N* IBC (*sive* LBC) *OBE*
   45 et HKF *EN* IBF *OB*
   46 SNOR *N* suorum *OB* SNO, RI (*?*) *E* / IBKH *EN* CBKH (*?*) *OB*
   47 BK *correxi ex* FG *in OBE et* IB *in N*
 48, 49 HKE *N* BKE *OBE*
   49 ROP *EN* MP *OB*
   50 Sed: FED (*?*) *B*
   51 Idem invenis *N lac. in OBE*
   56 in *BEN om. O*
   59 latera *OBE om. N* / moventur *OB* movetur *EN*
61, 64, 65 pauciorum *E* (*?*), *N* paucorum *OB*
   62 circum- *mg. add. O*
Prop. III.4
     1 4ª: IIII *O om. BEN*
    4 est *O om. BEN*
    7 tanquam *OBE* quam *N*

minime contingens *OA*. Motus ergo *OPQ* piramidis ad motum poligonii
10 tanquam motus ypotenuse ad motum laterum poligonii corporis per precedentem. Ergo minor est proportio motus piramidis ad motum *OB* spere
quam motus ypotenuse ad motum laterum poligonii.

Si maior est proportio motus ypotenuse ad motum circumferentie *A* quam
motus ypotenuse ad motum laterum, ergo multo fortius minor est proportio
15 motus piramidis ad motum *OB* spere quam motus ypotenuse ad motum
circumferentie *A*. Vel sic melius: Motus piramidis ad motum poligonii corporis
tanquam motus ypotenuse ad motum laterum, et motus piramidis ad motum
OB spere tanquam motus ypotenuse ad motum *A* circumferentie. Sed maior
(*!* minor) est proportio motus piramidis ad motum *OB* spere quam motus
20 piramidis ad motum poligonii corporis. Ergo minor est proportio motus
ypotenuse ad motum circumferentie *A* quam motus ypotenuse ad motum
laterum poligonii corporis (*!*, *del.*) quod est impossibile, quia maior est.

Si minor est proportio motus piramidis ad motum *OB* spere quam motus
ypotenuse ad motum circumferentie *B*, sit motus piramidis ad motum *OA*
25 spere tanquam motus ypotenuse ad motum circumferentie *B*. Sic ergo maior
est proportio motus piramidis ad motum *OA* quam motus piramidis ad
motum poligonii corporis. Sed maior est proportio motus ypotenuse ad motum
B quam motus ypotenuse ad motum laterum. Ergo minor est proportio
motus ypotenuse ad motum *B* quam motus piramidis ad motum poligonii
30 corporis. Sic ergo minor est proportio motus piramidis ad motum *OA* quam
motus piramidis ad motum poligonii corporis. Non ergo maior.

Sic ergo neque maior neque minor. Ergo equalis.

Explicit liber Gerardi de motu.

10 corporis *om. N*
10–11 precedentem *EN* presentem *OB*
13 Si *OBE* sed *N* / A *BE* (*et cf. lin. 16, 18, 21*) OA *ON*
16 A *OBE* OA *N* / melius: et melius *N*
18 Sed: et *N*
22 corporis *OBEN, sed delendum*
23 OB: OB^a *B*
25 motum circumferentie *N tr.* OB circumferentie *E*
26 est *OBE om. N*
32 Ergo equalis *N om. OBE*
33 Explicit . . . motu *mg. sin. N* (*forte in manu. rec.*) *et om. O* Explicit liber de motu
   text. N (*forte in manu rec.*) EXPLICIT DE MOTU *mg. sup. B* Explicit Subtilitas
   magistri Gerardi de bruxella de motu *E*

Here Begins the Book of Master Gerard
of Brussels on Motion

Book I

[Postulates]

[1.] THOSE WHICH ARE FARTHER FROM THE CENTER OR IM-
MOBILE AXIS ARE MOVED MORE: THOSE WHICH ARE LESS [FAR]
ARE MOVED LESS.

[2.] WHEN A LINE IS MOVED EQUALLY, UNIFORMLY, AND
EQUIDISTANTLY [i.e. UNIFORMLY PARALLEL TO ITSELF], IT IS
MOVED EQUALLY IN ALL OF ITS PARTS AND POINTS.

[3.] WHEN THE HALVES [OF A LINE] ARE MOVED EQUALLY
AND UNIFORMLY WITH RESPECT TO EACH OTHER, THE WHOLE
IS MOVED EQUALLY AS ITS HALF.

[4.] OF EQUAL STRAIGHT LINES MOVED IN EQUAL TIMES, THAT
WHICH TRAVERSES GREATER SPACE AND TO MORE [DISTANT]
TERMINI IS MOVED MORE.

[5.] AND [THAT WHICH TRAVERSES] LESS [SPACE] AND TO LESS
[DISTANT] TERMINI IS MOVED LESS.

[6.] THAT WHICH [DOES] NOT [TRAVERSE] MORE SPACE, NOR
TO MORE [DISTANT] TERMINI IS NOT MOVED MORE.

[7.] THAT WHICH [DOES] NOT [TRAVERSE] LESS [SPACE], NOR
TO LESS [DISTANT] TERMINI, IS NOT MOVED LESS.

[8.] THE RATIO OF THE MOTIONS OF POINTS IS AS THAT OF
THE LINES DESCRIBED IN THE SAME TIME.

[Propositions]

1. ANY PART AS LARGE AS ONE WISHES OF A RADIUS DE-
SCRIBING A CIRCLE, [WHICH PART IS] NOT TERMINATED AT THE
CENTER, IS MOVED EQUALLY AS ITS MIDDLE POINT. HENCE THE
RADIUS [IS ALSO MOVED EQUALLY] AS ITS MIDDLE POINT. FROM
THIS IT IS CLEAR THAT THE RADII AND THE MOTIONS HAVE
THE SAME RATIO.

Proceed therefore: I say that *CF* [see Fig. I.1a (A)] is moved equally as its
middle point, it having been previously proved that the [annular] difference
between [concentric] circles is equal to the product of the difference of the
radii and half [the sum of] the circumferences.

For let lines *OF* and *RL* be equal [see Figs. I.1a (A) and I.1b], and let *LN*
be equal to the circumference of circle *OF*. It is evident by the first [proposition]

of *On the Quadrature of the Circle* [of Archimedes][1] that circle *OF* and triangle *RLN* are equal.

[Tradition I]

Also let lines *SL* and *CF* be equal, and let lines *ON* and *OQ* be equal, and lines *SL* and *MP* be parallel. It is necessary, therefore, that triangle *RSQ* be equal to circle *OC* and line *SQ* be equal to the circumference of circle *OC*. For since triangles *RLN* and *RSQ* are similar, then *LR / SR = LN / SQ*. But *LR / SR = OF / OC* and *OF / OC* = circum. of circle *OF* / circum. of circle *OC* because the ratio of the diameters is the same as the ratio of the circumferences. Hence since the circumference of circle *OF* is equal to line *LN, SQ* will also be equal to the circumference of circle *OC*, and surface *SLNQ*, which is the difference between the triangles, will be equal to the difference between circles *OF* and *OC*. But the surface *SLNQ* is equal to the quadrangular surface *SLMP*. This is proved as follows. Triangles *OMN* and *OPQ* are equal and similar because angles *M* and *P* are right angles since line *MP* is parallel to line *SL*, and the angles at *O* on both sides are equal. Therefore angle *N* = angle *Q*. Therefore the sides are proportional. But *ON = OQ*, so that *NQ* is bisected in point *O*. Therefore, *OM = OP* and *MN = PQ*. Therefore the triangles are equal. Thus, therefore, surface *SLNQ* = surface *SLMP*. But line *LN* + line *SQ* = line *LM* + line *SP*, because line *MN* = line *PQ*. But line *LN* + line *SQ* = circum. circle *OF* + circum. circle *OC*. Therefore lines *LM* and *SP* are [in sum] equal to those circum-

[Tradition II]

Also let lines *CF* and *SL* be equal, and also let *MO* and *OP* be equal, and let line *SL* be parallel to line *MP*. It is evident that triangles *KLN* and *KSQ* are similar, for the angle at *S* and the angle at *L* are right angles and since *KN* falls upon the parallel lines *SP* and *LN* it makes intrinsic angle *N* equal to extrinsic angle *Q* [and hence to intrinsic angle *Q*] and also angle *K* is common to both [triangles]. Hence, they have all of their angles equal. Therefore, by VI.4 of the *Elements*,[2] the sides opposite the equal angles are proportional. Therefore, *LK / SK = LN / SQ*. But *FO / CO = LK / SK*. Therefore, *LN / SQ = FO / CO*. But *FO / CO* = [circum.] greater circle / [circum.] lesser circle, *FO* being the radius of the greater circle and *CO* the radius of the lesser circle. Hence, [circum.] circle *FO* / [circum.] circle *CO* = line *LN* / line *SQ*. Therefore, permutatively, by V.15 of the *Elements*, circum. *OF* circle / line *LN* = circum. *OC* circle / line *SQ*. But, by hypothesis, circum. *OF* circle = line *LN*. Therefore the circum. of *OC* [circle] = line *SQ*. But *SK* has been posited equal to the radius of circle *OC* and angle *S* is a right angle. Therefore triangle *KSQ* = circle *OC*. But triangle *KLN* = circle *OF*. Therefore triangle *KLN* exceeds triangle *KSQ* by the same amount that circle *OF* exceeds circle *OC*. Therefore space *LNQS* is equal to the difference between circles *OF* and *OC*. But triangle *MNO* = triangle *OPQ*, since angle *M*

---

[1] See Clagett, *Archimedes in the Middle Ages*, Vol. 1, p. 40.

[2] As I have noted in Chapter One, the *Elements* of Euclid are specifically cited only in Tradition II of Proposition I.1 and elsewhere in the margins by the scribe of MS *O*, though, of course, a knowledge of the *Elements* is everywhere reflected in the text. The numbers of the Euclidian propositions that are cited are those that originated with the Adelard II version of the *Elements* and appear in the various editions of Campanus' version of the *Elements*. I have used the edition *Elementorum geometricorum libri xv* (Basel, 1546), which contains both the Campanus and Zamberti versions.

ferences [in sum]. Thus, therefore, surface *SLMP* is equal to the product of the difference between the radii and half [the sum of] the circumferences, and it is equal to the difference between the circles. This same thing could be proved in another way.[3] But let this proof suffice for the present.

= angle *P* (each being a right angle), and angle *N* = angle *Q* by I.29 of the *Elements,* and side *OP* opposite angle *Q* is, by supposition, equal to side *OM* opposite angle *N.* Therefore triangle *MNO* = triangle *OQP* by I.26 of the *Elements.* Therefore, with trapezium *LMQS* (!*LMOQS*) added [to triangle *OQP*], rectangle *LMPS* = space *LNQS*, and hence [rectangle *LMPS*] is also equal to the difference between the aforesaid circles. Also line *MN* = line *PQ* by what has been said before, and line *SQ* = line *LR'* by I.34 of the *Elements.* Therefore *SQ* = ½ (*SQ* + *LR'*). But ½ (*LN* + *SQ*) − ½ (*SQ* + *LR'*) = ½ [(*LN* + *SQ*) − (*LR'* + *SQ*)] = ½ (*LN* − *LR'*) = ½ *R'N.* But ½ *R'N* = *R'M*, for *R'M* = *PQ* by I.34 of the *Elements.* But *QP* = *MN*, as was proved before. Therefore *R'M* = *MN.* Therefore *QP* = ½ *R'N.* Therefore, if *QP* is added to *SQ*, the whole *SP* = ½ (*LN* + *SQ*). But circum. circle *OF* + circum. circle *OC* = *LN* + *SQ.* Therefore the halves are equal to the halves. Therefore *SP* = ½ (circum. *OF* + circum. *OC*) and *SL* = radius *OF* − radius *OC.* But space *LSPM* = *SL · SP*, *SL* being the difference between the radii and *SP* half [the sum of] the circumferences. But the aforesaid rectangle was equal to the difference between the circles. Therefore the difference between the circles is equal to the product of the difference between the radii and half [the sum of] the circumferences.

Therefore let *SL* be moved through surface *SLMP* and line *CF* through the difference between circles *OF* and *OC.* I say, therefore, that lines *SL* and *CF* are equally moved, for they traverse equal spaces and to equal termini, as is clear from the things already said.

Therefore *SL* is moved equally as *CF* or more or less.[4] Not more, because it neither

Either, therefore, they are moved equally or one is moved more than the other, and

[3] This is no doubt a reference to the *Liber de curvis superficiebus,* as the scribe of MS *O* suggests (see the variant to lines 77–78), though he refers to the work under the title used by Gerard, namely, *De piramidibus.* See my remarks at the end of my discussion of the lemma in Chapter Two above.

[4] From this point to the end of the proposition, the manuscripts of Tradition I are in considerable disorder. I have discussed this disorder in detail in Chapter Three above.

describes more space nor [is moved] to more [distant] termini. Also, not less, because it neither describes less space nor [is moved] to less [distant] termini. Since, therefore, it is moved neither more nor less, and there is no excess of motion to motion, it is moved equally.

If it is moved more, let the difference between the radii equal to *CF* be taken in a circle greater [than *OF*], and let it be moved equally as *SL* in describing the difference between the circles. It is evident, therefore, that it will describe more space than *SL* in equal time and to more [distant] termini, because if the diameter is greater, so also is the circumference greater, and also the circle is greater. Therefore it is evident by the last postulate that it (i.e. the equal to *CF*) is moved more than *SL* and so not equally [as *SL*].

If *SL* is moved less than *CF*, let the difference of radii equal to *CF* be taken in a circle smaller [than *OF*] such that it be moved equally as *SL* as it describes the difference between those circles. [But] it is evident, therefore, that it describes less space in equal time and to less [distant] termini than does *SL*. Therefore, by the same postulate, it is moved less and hence not equally [as was assumed]. Since, therefore, *SL* is not moved more or less than *CF*, it is moved equally as it.

then *SL* is either moved more or less than *CF*. If [they are moved] equally, then I have the proposition.

But if the adversary would say that *SL* is moved more [see Figs. I.1a(B) and I.1b], let the difference between the radii, which is *CF* or a line equal to it (i.e. *GE*), be taken in a circle greater than *OF* i.e., one so much greater that the motion of this *CF* (i.e. *GE*) be increased beyond that motion which it had at first until, according to the adversary, it is equal to the motion of *SL*. Hence let it be moved to describe the difference between those circles. It is evident, therefore, that it describes more space than does *SL* in equal time and to more [distant] termini, for greater is the circumference of a greater circle, and the sum of the circumferences in the greater circle is greater than that of those in the lesser circle. But circle *OE* is greater than circle *OF* and circle *OG* is greater than [circle] *OC*; therefore, etc. So, by the last postulate, *CF*, if it is taken in a larger circle, is moved more than *SL*.

In the same way, if it is said that *SL* is moved less than *CF*, let a line equal to *CF* be taken in a lesser circle. Then it will be evident [by the postulates, that so long as *CF* is taken in a lesser circle] however much it would be moved its motion will be less than the motion of *SL* [and so not equally. Hence the assumption that *SL* is moved less than *CF* is false.] Therefore, [since *SL* is moved neither more nor less than *CF*,] *SL* is moved equally as *CF*.

But, by the second postulate, *SL* is moved equally as any one of its points because it is moved equally and uniformly in all its parts and points. Therefore, it is moved equally as its middle point. But the middle point of *SL* is moved equally as the middle point of *CF* because those points describe equal lines

in equal times. But that those lines are equal you will prove in the same way it was proved that line *SQ* is equal to the circumference of circle *OC*. So, therefore,

in equal times. For it can be proved as it was proved that *SQ* is equal to the circumference of circle *OC*. Therefore *SL* is moved equally as the middle point of *CF*.

SL is moved equally as the middle point of CF. But SL is moved equally as CF, as was proved. Therefore CF is moved equally as its middle point. The demonstration is the same for any part however great of radius OF, i.e., any part not terminated at O.

I say, therefore, that OF is moved equally as its middle point because it is moved equally as line RL describing surface RLTV [see Fig. I.1a(A) and I.1b]. Let LT = ½ LN. Therefore RL is moved equally as OF, or more or less. If more, let a line be taken that is not terminated at the center which would be equally moved as RL, for any such line would be moved equally as its middle point, as we have already proved, and so as a line moved [always] parallel [to itself] and equally in all parts and points. Let that line be DF. Therefore DF is moved equally as RL. Hence let DF be equal [in length] to XL. Therefore DF and XL are equally moved. Wherefore RL and XL are equally moved, because RL is moved equally in all parts and points. But, in refutation, DF describes more space than XL and to more [distant] termini. This should be clear as follows. Surface RLTV / surface RXYV = RL / RX, since they are between parallel lines. But circle OF / circle OD = (radius OF / radius OD)², for the ratio of circles is the square of the ratio of their radii, i.e., (RL / RX)². Therefore circle OF / circle OD > surface RLTV / surface RXYV. But circle OF = surface RLTV, for the rectangle that is double the circle is double RLTV. So, therefore, circle OF / circle OD > circle OF / surface RXYV. Therefore circle OD < RXYV. Therefore circle OF − circle OD > surface RLTV − surface RXYV. Therefore DF describes more space than XL and to more [distant] termini, for the circumference of circle OF is equal to [the sum of] lines LT and XY. Therefore, with the circumference of circle OD added, more is produced. Since, therefore, it describes more space and to more [distant] termini, it is

But CF is moved equally as line SL. Therefore CF is moved equally as its middle point. And the demonstration is the same for any part however great of radius OF, i.e. any part not terminated at the center O.

Further, I wish to prove that a radius [is moved equally] as its middle point. For, if [it is] not [moved] equally, then [it is moved] either more or less. If more, let it be moved equally as some point which would be moved more than its middle point C. Therefore that point is more distant from the center than is C, by the first postulate. That it is so appears in the second figure of this [proposition, Fig. 1.1a(C)]. Since, therefore, OC = CF, so OE' > E'F and OE' = E'F + 2 CE'. For, since OC = CF, then CF − CE' = OC − CE' = E'F. Therefore, the subtrahends, of which one is CE', are equal. Now 2CE' + E'F = OE'. Therefore line OE' contains the quantity E'F and in addition twice CE'. Therefore, starting from the center, let OE' be cut so that 2 CE' remains toward the center and the line equal to E'F remains coterminal with it. Let the first segment be OA and the second AE', proceeding so that AE' = E'F. Therefore E' is the middle point of AF. Hence, by the preceding proof, AF is moved equally as point E', and also OF is so moved according to the adversary. Therefore AF and OF are equally moved, which is against the first postulate. Therefore OF is not moved equally as some point that is farther removed from the center than is its middle point. Hence it will not be moved more than its middle point.

But if one should say that it (the radius) is moved less [see Fig. I.1a(D)], therefore let a point be taken which is less moved than C, the middle point of OF, which, by the first postulate, must be less far removed from the center than is C. Let it be taken, therefore, and let it be point D'. Therefore, OD' = D'F − 2 D'C. This is proved in the same way as the first case.

moved more. So, therefore, DF is moved more than RL and so not equally. Now if one should wish to take above the center a line equal to RL, as [for example] DE, the same refutation [follows]. So, therefore, RL is not moved more than OF. By a similar demonstration you will prove [that it is] not [moved] less; therefore, it is moved equally. But RL is moved equally as its middle point. And point C is moved equally as the middle [point] of RL because the circumference [described by] C is equal to SZ. Therefore the radius OF is moved equally as its middle point.

Also let BD' be cut from OD' so that BD' is not terminated at the center. Therefore line $OD' = D'F - 2\,D'C$, and line $BD' = OD' - OB$. Therefore line $BD' = D'F - 2\,D'C - OB$. Let there be cut from $D'F$ a coterminal segment equal to BD', and let it be $D'G$. Then the remainder $GF = 2\,CD' + OB$ [since $BD' = D'G$ and so by substitution $GF = D'F - D'F + 2\,CD' + OB$.] But this is also the amount by which $D'F$ exceeds BD'. Therefore, by the first proof, line BG is moved equally as point D', and so moved also is line OF according to the adversary. Therefore OF is moved equally as BG, which again is against the first postulate. For the amount by which CF is farther removed from the center than CG is greater than the amount by which BC is farther removed from the center than OC. For CF is farther from the center than CG by the quantity $OB + 2\,CD'$, while BC is farther removed than OC by the quantity OB alone. Therefore CF is farther removed from the center with respect to CG than is BC with respect to OC by an amount equal to $2\,CD'$. Wherefore CF is farther removed [from the center] than CG by an amount greater than is BC farther removed than OC according to the quantity of the motion of twice CD'. Therefore the total motion of $OC + OF >$ the total motion of $BD' + GD'$, of whose [sum] the middle point is D'. Therefore OF is moved more than D' or [in fact] more than any point that is closer to the center than is its middle point. Wherefore, it is moved more than any point that is moved less than [its] middle point. For if it is moved less, it is less removed from the center. Therefore it is not moved less than its middle point. But it has [already] been demonstrated that neither is it moved more [than its middle point]. Therefore it is moved equally as that same [middle point].

The same thing can be proved directly in this way. Let it be that line NK [see Fig. I.1a(D)] is moved through the surface $OFNK$ ($!OFKN$) and OF is moved [in rotation] through the circle. And let line *FH* be equal to the circumference, which line is bisected in point *K*, and line *OL*, also equal to the circumference, is bisected in point *N*. And it is evident that line *FK* + line *ON* is equal to the circumference and [that] surface *ONFK* (!*ONKF*) is equal to the circle [by Archimedes, *On the Measurement of the Circle*, Prop. 1]. I say, therefore, that *OF* is moved equally as *NK*, and it can be proved *per impossible*, as is evident from the things said before. But *NK* is moved equally as its middle point, and the middle point of *NK* is moved equally as the middle point of *OF*, and, with this, the whole should be evident from the things said before. Therefore *NK* is moved equally as point *C*. But *OF* is moved equally as line *NK*. Therefore line *OF* is moved equally as its middle point *C*. And this is what I proposed to prove.

The corollary should be evident as follows [see Fig. I.1a(A)]. I say that *OF* / *OC* = motion of *OF* / motion of *OC* because *OF* / *OC* = circum. of *F* / circum. of *C*. But circum. of *F* / circum. of *C* = circum. of *C* / circum. of *B*. Let *B* be the middle point of *OC*. But circum. of *C* / circum. of *B* = motion of point *C* / motion of point *B*. Therefore, immediately *OF* / *OC* = motion of point *C* / motion of point *B*. But the motion of point *C* is the motion of line *OF* and the motion of point *B* is the motion of line *OC*. Therefore *OF* / *OC* = motion of *OF* / motion of *OC*.

The corollary should be evident as follows [see Fig. I.1a(D)]. I say that radius *OF* of the greater circle / radius *OC* of the lesser circle = motion of radius *OF* of the greater circle / motion of radius *OC* of the lesser circle. For radius *OF* / radius *OC* = circum. of the greater circle *OF* / circum. of the lesser circle *OC*. Also let *P* be the middle point of line *OC*. Circum. *OC* / circum. *OP* = circum. *OF* / circum. *OC*. Therefore, by the first, radius *OF* / radius *OC* = circum. *OC* / circum. *OP*. But circum. *OC* / circum. *OP* = motion of point *C* / motion of point *P*. But the motion of *C* is the motion of radius *OF* and the motion of *P* is the motion of radius *OC*. Therefore radius *OF* / radius *OC* = motion of radius *OF* / motion of radius *OC*.

2. ANY PART HOWEVER LARGE OF A HYPOTENUSE[1] DESCRIBING THE CURVED SURFACE OF A CONE, A PART TERMINATED

Proposition I.2

[1] I have everywhere translated *ypotenusa, curva superficies,* and *motus* by the terms "hypotenuse," "curved surface," and "motion," instead of by the modern terms "generator," "lateral surface," and "speed." See my general remarks on "magis movetur" in my discussion of the postulates of Book I in Chapter Two above, and my remarks on "hypotenuse" and "curved surface" in the same chapter at the beginning of my summary of Proposition I.2.

WITHIN THE CONE, IS MOVED EQUALLY AS ITS MIDDLE POINT. HENCE THE HYPOTENUSE [IS MOVED EQUALLY] AS ITS MIDDLE POINT. FROM THIS IT IS CLEAR THAT ALL HYPOTENUSES OF EQUAL BASES ARE EQUALLY MOVED.

Proceed therefore. You will prove that BK is moved equally as its middle point after it has been previously proved that the difference between the curved surfaces of cones is equal to the product of the difference between [their] hypotenuses and half [the sum of] the circumferences of their bases.[2] For example, let RL be equal to hypotenuse BH, and line LN be equal to the circumference of the base of cone OBH [see Figs. I.1b and I.2]. Therefore it is evident, by the first [proposition] of *On Cones* [i.e. *The Book on the Curved Surfaces*][3] that triangle RLN is equal to the curved surface of cone OBH. Also let line RS be equal to KH. It is evident that triangle RSQ is equal to the curved surface of cone $IKH,$ because SQ is equal to the circumference of the base. This is proved as follows.

For $LR / SR = LN / SQ$, since the triangles are similar. Also $BH / KH = OB / IK$, since the triangles are similar. But $OB / IK =$ circum. of radius OB / circum. of radius IK. Therefore $BH / KH =$ circum. / circum. Therefore $LN / SQ =$ circum. / circum. But LN is equal to the circumference of radius OB. Therefore SQ is equal to the remaining circumference. So, therefore, triangle RSQ is equal to the curved surface of cone IKH. Therefore surface $SLNQ$ is equal to the difference between the curved surfaces, which is equal to surface $SLMP$. Let NQ be bisected in point O, which is thoroughly proved in the same way as it was proved before concerning the difference between circles.

Therefore let SL be moved through surface $SLMP$, and BK through the difference between the curved surfaces. I say, therefore, that SL is moved equally as BK, for they describe equal spaces and to equal termini, as is already evident from the things said.

Therefore either SL is moved equally as BK, or more or less. If more, let there be proposed a curved surface whose base is greater than circle OB. And let there be taken a part of the hypotenuse equal to BK such that it (the part) is moved equally as LS. I say that it [in fact] is moved more than SL because it describes a greater surface and to more [distant] termini, for both circumferences are greater. Therefore the product of that line and half [the sum of] the circumferences is greater, and so that line is moved more than SL. Therefore it is not moved equally [as was proposed].

If SL is moved less than BK, let there be taken a curved surface of a cone whose base is less than circle OB. And let there be taken a part of the hypotenuse equal to BK such that it (the part) is moved equally as SL. I say

---

[2] Note that the scribe of MS O says (variant to Prop. I.2, lines 7–9) that this is proved by the fourth proposition of the *De piramidibus* (i.e. *Liber de curvis superficiebus;* see my Volume 1, p. 466).

[3] This is Proposition I of the *Liber de curvis superficiebus.* See my Volume 1, p. 450.

that [in fact] *SL* is moved more than that [part] because it describes more space and to more [distant] termini, for those circumferences are [together] less than lines *LM* and *SP* [together] because they are less than [the circumferences of] circles with radii *OB* and *IK*. And therefore surface *SLMP* is greater than the surface which that line [taken from the hypotenuse] describes. So, therefore, *SL* is moved more than that line [and hence not equally as was proposed].

So, therefore, since *SL* is neither moved more nor less than *BK*, it will be moved equally as it. You will prove [this] in the same way concerning any part of hypotenuse *BH*. Since, therefore, *SL* is moved equally as its middle point and the middle point of *SL* is moved equally as the middle point of *BK* (for the middle point of *BK* is moved through a circumference which is equal to the [straight] line through which the middle point of *SL* is moved, which will be proved by similar triangles as before), so, therefore, *SL* is moved equally as the middle point of *BK*. But *BK* is moved equally as *SL*. Therefore *BK* is moved equally as its middle point.

Afterwards you will prove by a double proof, as was proved before concerning the radius, that hypotenuse *BH* is moved equally as its middle point, and this is what we wished to demonstrate.[4]

The corollary should be evident as follows. I say that hypotenuses *BH* and *BF* are equally moved. Let *K* be the middle point of *BH* and *G* the middle point of *BF*. Therefore just as we have already proved that *BH* is moved equally as its middle point *K*, so [we may prove] also [that] *BF* is moved equally as point *G*. But *K* is moved equally as *G*. This is proved as follows.

Angles *I* and *C* are right angles [since] *IC* is parallel to *OB*; and angle *K* is equal on both sides [i.e., the opposite angles at *K* are equal]. Therefore angles *B* and *H* are equal. Therefore triangles *KBC* and *KIH* are similar. Therefore the sides are proportional. But *BK* = *KH*. Therefore *IK* = *KC*. In a similar way you will prove that triangles *GBD* and *GFH* are similar, because angles *D* and *H* are right angles, since *DH* is parallel to *OB;* and angle *G* is equal on both sides. Therefore angles *B* and *F* are equal. Since, therefore, line *BG* = *GF*, so also line *DG* = *GH*. Therefore since lines *IC* and *HD* are equal, their halves are also equal. Therefore *IK* = *HG*. Therefore points *K* and *G* describe equal circumferences. Therefore they are equally moved. But *BH* and *BF* are moved equally as points *K* and *G* (respectively). Therefore *BH* and *BF* are equally moved.

The same thing can be proved as follows. Triangles *OBH* and *IKH* are similar because *IK* is parallel to *OB*. Therefore the sides are proportional. But *BH* = 2 *KH*. Therefore *OB* = 2 *IK*. Therefore *OA* = *IK*. Let *A* be the middle point of *OB*. Therefore *K* is moved equally as *A*. Therefore *OB* is moved equally as *BH* because *OB* is moved equally as *A* and *BH* is moved equally as *K*. In the same way you will prove that *BF* is moved equally as

---

[4] The significance of this statement for the original form of Proposition I.1 has been discussed in Chapter Three above.

OB by means of similar triangles *OBF* and *HGF*. Therefore just as *BF* = 2 *GF*, so *OB* = 2 *HG*, and so point *A* is moved equally as point *G* and therefore as line *BF*. Therefore line *BF* is moved equally as line *BH*. And this we wished to demonstrate.

3. TO ASSIGN A POINT BY WHICH THE PERIMETER OF A REG-ULAR POLYGON IS EQUALLY MOVED WHEN DESCRIBING A PO-LYGONAL BODY.[1] HENCE IT IS CLEAR THAT IN THE CASE OF THE PERIMETER OF A [REGULAR] POLYGON INSCRIBED IN A CIRCLE, IF IT HAS MORE SIDES, IT IS MOVED MORE. BUT IN THE CASE OF CIRCUMSCRIBED [POLYGONS] THE CONTRARY [IS TRUE].

Proceed in this way [see Fig. I.3a]: *CG*, the side of a square, is moved equally as point *R* when *R* is the middle point of *CG*, by the preceding [proposition]. Similarly *M'G* is moved equally as point *Y*. Therefore these two sides are moved equally as these two points. And the total perimeter of the square is moved equally as those two sides. Therefore the total perimeter is moved equally as those two points; therefore as either one of them since they are moved equally. It has to be proved afterwards that points *H* and *S* are moved equally as *R*, the middle point of line *HS*. Line *KG'* is parallel to line *BA*. Therefore angles *K* and *G'* are right angles and angle *R* is equal on both sides. Therefore angles *S* and *H* are equal. Therefore triangles *HKR* and *RG'S* are similar. Therefore the sides are proportional. But *RS* = *RH* (which will be proved later). Therefore *G'S* = *HK*. Therefore point *S* is moved more than point *G'* by the same amount that point *K* is moved more than point *H*. Therefore *G'* and *K* together are moved equally as *H* and *S* together. But *K* and *G'* are moved equally as *R*, for all the parts and points of line *KG'* are moved equally and uniformly. Therefore points *H* and *S* [together] are moved equally as point *R*. By the same proof, points *I* and *Q* [together] are moved equally as the middle point *P*. Similarly points *L* and *N* [together] are moved equally as middle point *M*. That those [points *P* and *M*] are middle points will be clear later. Therefore sides *CE* and *EG*, which are sides of a [regular] octagon, are moved equally as their middle points *I* and *Q*, and *I* and *Q* are moved equally as point *P*. Therefore those sides are moved equally as point *P*. By the same reasoning the two opposite sides are moved equally as points *I'* and *B'*, and, therefore, as point *Z*. Therefore those four sides of the octagon are moved equally as points *P* and *Z*, and, therefore, as point *U*, because line *PZ* is moved equally and uniformly in all its parts and points. But those four sides are moved equally as the total perimeter of the octagon. Therefore the whole perimeter is moved equally as point *U*.

In the same way, the two sides *EF* and *FG* are moved equally as their middle points, and so as the middle point of the line bisecting those two

---

Proposition I.3

[1] By this expression Gerard always understands a polyhedron described by the rotation of a regular polygon of 4n sides about a diagonal. See my remarks on the use of regular polygons in my discussion of the enunciation of Proposition I.3 in Chapter Two above.

sides. Similarly the two sides *CD* and *DE* are moved equally as the middle point of the line bisecting those [sides]. Therefore those four sides are moved equally as points *L* and *N*. But points *L* and *N* are moved equally as point *M*. Therefore those four sides are moved equally as point *M*. Similarly the other four [opposite] sides are moved equally as point *Z'*. Therefore those eight sides of the sedecagon[2] are moved equally as points *M* and *Z'*, therefore as point *X*, because the line *MZ'* is moved equally in all its parts and points. But the whole perimeter of the sedecagon is moved equally as its half. Therefore the whole perimeter is moved equally as point *X*.

Now we must prove what we promised. Line *OE* has been protracted through the middle of line *CG*. Therefore it cuts it at right angles. Similarly *OQ* has been protracted through the middle of line *EG* and *OI* through the middle of line *CE*, and *CE* = *EG* because they are sides of a [regular] octagon. Therefore *OQ* = *OI*, for sides *OE* and *EQ* are [respectively] equal to sides *OE* and *EI*, and the angle to the angle; therefore the base to the base; and therefore *OQ* = *OI*. But that the angles are equal is proved as follows. Sides *RE* and *RC* are equal to sides *RE* and *RG* [respectively], and the angle to the angle (because each is a right angle); therefore the base to the base, etc. Therefore, since *RC* = *RG*, the opposite angles *SOP* and *POH* are equal, and the angles contained are equal. Therefore side *OQ* = side *OI*, and side *OP* = side *OP*, and the angle to the angle; therefore the base to the base, etc. Therefore *PQ* = *PI*, and angle *P* is a right angle on both sides. Similarly angle *R* is a right angle on both sides. Therefore *QI* is parallel to *SH*. Therefore, by similar triangles, you will prove that *OI* / *OH* = *OP* / *OR* = *OQ* / *OS*. But *OI* = *OQ*. Therefore *OH* = *OS*. Therefore side *OH* = side *OS* and side *OR* = side *OR*, and the angle to the angle, etc. Therefore *HR* = *RS*. Similar is the proof that *LM* = *NM*.

[Corollary] Therefore, from the things said, it is evident that *OQ* / *OS* = *OI* / *OH* = *OP* / *OR*. But *OP* / *OR* = motion of point *P* / [motion of] point *R*, which is proved as follows. Triangles *OPD'* and *ROB* are similar because angle *D'* (and similarly angle *B*) is a right angle (for *BR* is parallel to *PD'* and angle *O* is common). Therefore *OP* / *OR* = *D'P* / *RB*. But *D'P* / *RB* = motion of point *P* / motion of point *R*. This is evident by the corollary of the first [proposition]. Therefore the motion of point *P* / motion of point *R* = *OP* / *OR*. But *R* is moved equally as *V*. Therefore the motion of point *P* / motion of point *V* = *OP* / *OR*. But *P* is moved more than *V*. Therefore *P* is moved more than *R*. But *R* is moved equally as the perimeter of the square. And *P* is moved equally as the perimeter of the octagon, as was demonstrated. Therefore the perimeter of the octagon is moved more than the perimeter of the square in the ratio of *OP* to *OR*. By a similar demonstration it will be demonstrated that the perimeter of the sedecagon is moved more than the perimeter of the octagon in the ratio of line *OM* to line *OP*.

---

[2] There is no conventional term in English for a sixteen-sided polygon, and so I Anglicize the Latin term in my translation.

And thus is evident the first part of the corollary. But the diligent reader should realize that he knows how suitably to adapt this kind of demonstration to other kinds of [regular] polygons.

The second part of the corollary should be evident as follows [see Fig. I.3b]. From the proof at hand it is evident that the perimeter of the circumscribed square is moved equally as points N and P. Let line NP bisect two sides of the square. Also two sides of a circumscribed octagon, sides DE and EF, are moved equally as points I and K. Let IK bisect those two sides. Therefore [IK moves equally] as point Q. For line OE bisects side AB, bisects angle E, and bisects line IK. Therefore points I and K [together] are moved equally as point Q. By a similar proof the two opposite sides are moved equally as points L and M, [for] line LM should bisect the opposite sides. And points L and M are moved equally as point R. And Q and R are moved equally, and similarly points N and P are moved equally, for [each of] those lines [connecting the two pairs of points] is moved equally in all its parts and points. Therefore motion of point N / motion of point Q = motion of perim. of square / motion of perim. of octagon. But point N is moved more than point Q in the ratio of ON to OQ, by the proof at hand. Therefore the perimeter of the square is moved more than the perimeter of the octagon in the ratio of ON to OQ. You will find the same thing in regard to other [regular] polygons.

4. FROM THIS IT IS ALSO CLEAR THAT THE PERIMETER OF A [REGULAR] POLYGON INSCRIBED IN A CIRCLE EXCEEDS IN ITS MOTION THE MOTION OF THE PERIMETER OF A POLYGON OF HALF AS MANY[1] SIDES INSCRIBED IN THE SAME CIRCLE BY THE SAME AMOUNT [THAT ITS MOTION] IS EXCEEDED BY THE MOTION OF A CIRCUMSCRIBED [POLYGON OF HALF AS MANY SIDES].

From the things said it is evident that the perimeter of an exterior [circumscribed] square is moved equally as points G and V [see Fig. I.4]. For line GV bisects the two sides. And the perimeter of the interior [inscribed] square is moved equally as points P and N because line PN bisects its two sides. And the perimeter of the inscribed octagon is moved equally as points L and R. But it is necessary that line OG, which bisects side AB, also bisects DH and EF. All of this is evident from the things said. Therefore the motion of point G exceeds the motion of point L by the same amount that the motion of the perimeter of the exterior square exceeds the motion of the perimeter of the inscribed octagon. And the motion of point L exceeds the motion of point P by the same amount that the motion of the perimeter of the inscribed octagon exceeds the motion of the perimeter of the inscribed square. Proceed as follows.

Triangles PGH and LGF are similar because angles P and L are right angles and angle G is common. Therefore angle F = angle H. Therefore the

Proposition I.4

[1] In the Latin text I have used *pauciorum* from MSS *ENV* in place of *paucorum* in MSS *OB* since the comparative form is demanded with *in duplo*. See note 2 to Proposition III.3.

sides are proportional. Therefore *GH / GF = GP / GL*. But *GH = 2 GF*, for it (*GH*) has been bisected by line *EF*. Therefore *GP = 2 GL*. Therefore *GL = LP*. Also triangles *PGK* and *LGI* are similar, for angles *K* and *I* are right angles (because line *GM* is parallel to line *OH*) and angle *G* is common. Therefore the remaining angles are equal. Therefore *GP / GL = GK / GI*. But *GP = 2 GL*. Therefore *GK = 2 GI*. Therefore *GI = KI*. Therefore the motion of point *G* exceeds the motion of point *I* by the same amount that the motion of point *I* exceeds the motion of point *K*. But these three points [*G*, *I*, and *K*] are moved equally as points *G*, *L*, and *P*, for the lines of which they are points are [each] moved equally in all their parts and points. Therefore the motion of point *G* exceeds the motion of point *L* by the same amount that the motion of point *L* exceeds the motion of point *P*. Therefore the motion of the perimeter of the circumscribed square exceeds the motion of the perimeter of the inscribed octagon by the same amount that the motion of the perimeter of the octagon exceeds the motion of the perimeter of the inscribed square. And this we wished to demonstrate.

Book II

[Postulates]

[1.] OF EQUAL SQUARES, THE ONE IS SAID TO BE MOVED MORE WHOSE SIDES ARE MOVED MORE.

[2.] THE ONE [WHOSE SIDES ARE MOVED] LESS IS SAID TO BE MOVED LESS.

[3.] THE ONE WHOSE SIDES ARE NOT MOVED MORE IS NOT MOVED MORE.

[4.] THE ONE [WHOSE SIDES ARE NOT MOVED] LESS IS NOT [MOVED] LESS.

[5.] IF SURFACES ARE EQUAL AND ALL LINES OF THEM TAKEN IN THE SAME RATIO ARE EQUAL, THE ONE NONE OF WHOSE LINES SO TAKEN IS MOVED MORE IS NOT MOVED MORE.

[6.] THE ONE [NONE OF WHOSE LINES SO TAKEN IS MOVED] LESS IS NOT MOVED LESS.

[Propositions]

1. AN EQUINOCTIAL CIRCLE IS MOVED IN 4/3 RATIO TO ITS DIAMETER. HENCE IT IS CLEAR THAT THE RATIO OF [EQUI-NOCTIAL] CIRCLES IS AS THE SQUARE OF THE RATIO OF [THEIR] MOTIONS.

Let squares *BDFH* and *OLMN* be equal [see Fig. II.1a]. And let surface *ADFI* be moved to describe a cylinder on axis *AI*, and let square *OLMN* be moved uniformly and equally in all its parts and points by proceeding directly [i.e. in a direction perpendicular to itself] so that a side of it would be moved equally as point *C* of line *CG* which bisects square *BDFH*. It is evident, therefore, that square *LMNO* is moved equally as line *CG* because line *CG* is moved equally in all its parts and points, as also is *LMNO* in the same way. I say, therefore, that squares *BDFH* and *LMNO* are equally moved, for they are either moved equally or one more [than the other]. If *BDFH* is moved more, [we say] in refutation [that] its sides are not moved more than the sides of [square] *OLMN* because *BD* and *FH* are moved equally as *OL* and *MN*, and *DF* and *BH* are moved equally as *LM* and *NO*, and so on. Therefore this square is not moved more than that one. By the same reasoning neither [is it moved] less. Therefore [it is moved] equally.

Let another equal square be proposed which we let be designated *Z*; and let it be moved more than *OLMN* by the amount that *BDFH* [is supposed] to be moved more than *OLMN*; and let it (*Z*) proceed directly in the manner of *OLMN*. Since, therefore, *Z* is moved equally in all its parts and termini (i.e. lines), it is evident that a side of it is moved more than point *C* and so is moved more than side *BD*, for *BD* is moved equally as point *C*; and so it is moved more than side *FD* and similarly [more] than the other lines intermediate between *BD* and *HF*. So, therefore, by the given description, square *Z* is moved more than square *BDFH* and therefore not equally [as was proposed].

But if the sophist objects that side *DF* is moved more than the side of *Z*, we answer that sides *DF* and *BH* joined together are moved equally as sides *BD* and *FH* joined together. For *DF* in its motion exceeds the motion of *DB* by the same amount that the motion of *DB* exceeds the motion of *BH*; and so sides *DF* and *BH* joined together are moved less than the sides of *Z*. It is evident, therefore, that *BDFH* is not moved more than *LMNO*. If [it is said to be moved] less, this is refuted in the same way, an equal square having been proposed which is moved less than *LMNO* but which the respondent supposes to be moved equally as *BDFH*. It is evident, therefore, that *BDFH* is moved equally as *LMNO*. But *LMNO* is moved equally as any side of it; therefore it is moved equally as *BD*; therefore it is moved equally as point *C*. Therefore *BDFH* is moved equally as point *C*. By the same proof it will be completely proved that square *CDEK* is moved equally as point *P*, and similarly *KEFG* as point *P*, and so rectangle *CDFG* is moved equally as point *P*, and rectangle *BCGH* as the middle point of *CB*. Similar is the demonstration for other rectangles. Therefore you will prove *per impossibile* (as has been proved for the radius) that square *BDFH* is moved equally as point *C* if it is moved on immobile axis *BH* to describe a cylinder. Therefore let it be so moved. Therefore, since it is moved equally as point *C* and rectangle *BCGH* is moved equally as the middle point of *BC*, square *BDFH* is moved twice as much as rectangle *BCGH*. But rectangle *CDFG* is moved equally as point *P*, and point *P* is moved in 3/2 ratio to point *C*. Therefore the rectangle *CDFG* is moved with respect to rectangle *BCGH* in the ratio composed of 2/1 and 3/2, i.e. in triple ratio; and in the same ratio is related that which is described by rectangle *CDFG* to that which is described by rectangle *BCGH*. For the cylinder described by rectangle *BDFH* is to the cylinder described by rectangle *BCGH* as is the ratio of base to base since the rectangles are between parallel lines. But the base to the base is a quadruple ratio, for radius *BD* is twice radius *BC*. Therefore one circle is quadruple the other. Thus one cylinder is quadruple the other. Therefore what remains of the greater cylinder after the lesser cylinder has been subtracted is triple the lesser cylinder. And that remainder is what is described by rectangle *CDFG*. Therefore the ratio of that which has been described by *CDFG* to that which has been described by *BCGH* is the ratio of motion to motion.

From this it is evident that the ratio of that which is described by triangle *BDF* to that which is described by triangle *BFH* is the ratio of motion to motion. For the excess of the motion of *CDFG* over the motion of *BDF* is the excess of the motion of *KFG* over the motion of *BCK*. For the motion of *CDFK* is common to both. And the excess of the motion of *BFH* over the motion of *BCGH* is the excess of the motion of *FGK* over the motion of *BCK*. For the motion of *BKGH* is common to both. Therefore the excess of the motion of the superior rectangle over the motion of the superior triangle is the same as the excess of the motion of the inferior triangle over the motion of the inferior rectangle. So, therefore, the motions of the rectangles and the triangles are equal. Moreover the [space] described by the motion of the superior rectangle exceeds the [space] described by the [motion of the] superior triangle by the same amount that the [space] described by the motion of the inferior triangle exceeds the [space] described by the motion of the inferior rectangle. This will be clear later. So, therefore, the excess of the motions is the same and the excess of the [spaces] described is the same, and the total motions are equal and the total [spaces] described are equal. But [the ratio of] the [space] described by the superior rectangle to the [space] described by the inferior [rectangle] is as that of the motion of the superior [rectangle] to the motion of the inferior [rectangle]. Therefore [the ratio of] the [space] described by the superior triangle to the [space] described by the inferior [triangle] is that of motion to motion. But the [space] described by the superior triangle is to the [space] described by the inferior [triangle] as two is to one, because the cone is a third part of the cylinder. Hence the remainder [of the cylinder] is double the cone because the remainder is described by the superior triangle. Therefore the motion of the superior [triangle] is double the motion of the inferior [triangle]. Since, therefore, the motions of the rectangles [together] equal the motions of the triangles [together] and the motion of the superior rectangle is triple the motion of the inferior [rectangle] and the motion of the superior triangle is double the motion of the inferior [triangle], those motions are related as 9/3 and 8/4. Therefore the superior rectangle is moved with respect to the superior triangle as 9 to 8, i.e. in 9/8 ratio. And the inferior triangle is moved with respect to the inferior rectangle as 4 to 3, i.e. in 4/3 ratio. Therefore, since the superior rectangle is moved in 3/2 ratio to *BD* and is moved in 9/8 ratio to the superior triangle, the superior triangle will be moved in 4/3 ratio to *BD*; for if a 3/2 ratio is divided by a 9/8 ratio, a 4/3 ratio remains, as is evident in the [numbers] 9, 8, 3, 2. Also since the [space] described by the superior rectangle is triple that described by the inferior [rectangle] and the [space] described by the superior triangle is double that described by the inferior [triangle], and the total [spaces] described are equal, then the excess of the particular [spaces] described will be the same, as is evident in the [numbers] 9, 3, 8, 4.

Now look at the next figure [Fig. II.1b]. I shall prove that triangles *BDE* and *BDF* are equally moved. For rectangles *BDEH* and *BDFG* are equally moved, by the proof at hand, and in which ratio *BDEH* is moved with respect to its superior triangle, in that same ratio is *BDFG* moved with respect to its superior triangle. And this is evident in the immediately preceding proof, [and that ratio is] a 3/4 ratio. Therefore, since those rectangles are moved equally, rectangle *BDEH* is moved with respect to each triangle in a 3/4 ratio. Therefore those triangles are moved equally; and in the same way the inferior triangles [are moved equally].

Therefore let line *DF* be equal to the circumference of the circle whose radius is *BD*. Therefore it is evident by the first [proposition] of *On the Quadrature of the Circle*[1] that triangle *BDF* is equal to the circle of radius *BD*. Let that circle be called *C*. Therefore the lines of the triangle and circle *C*, taken in equal ratio, are equal, for line *DF* = circum. of circle *C*. But radius *BD* / radius *BC* = circum. [of radius *BD*] / circum. [of radius *BC*]. And *BD* / *BC* = *DF* / *CK*, for the triangles are similar because *CK* is parallel to *DF*. But *DF* is equal to the greater circumference; therefore *CK* [is equal] to the lesser [circumference]. And so the lines are taken in the same ratio because $(BD / BC)^2$ = circle / circle. So $(BD / BC)^2$ = greater triangle / lesser triangle. Therefore just as the greater circle and the greater triangle are equal, so also are the lesser circle and the lesser triangle. So, therefore, all the lines taken in the same ratio are equal and are equally moved, for just as *DF* is moved equally as the greater circumference, so *CK* [is moved equally] as the lesser [circumference]. It is the same in regard to all [lines and circumferences]. I say, therefore, that the circle and the triangle are moved equally, which will be proved *per impossibile,* for neither is moved more or less, by the last postulate. For if the circle is moved more than the triangle, let there be assumed a triangle equal to *BDF* but which is moved more than *BDF*; and let it be similar to *BDF* and let it be moved equally as the circle. Therefore, from the things said, it is evident that all lines taken in the same ratio are moved more than the corresponding lines in *BDF* since that triangle is moved more than *BDF*. If, therefore, the lines of that triangle are equal to the lines of that circle and are taken in the same ratio, they are moved more. So, therefore, the triangle is moved more than the circle when [at the same time] it is equal to it. So therefore, that circle is not moved more than triangle *BDF* [as was assumed]. By a similar reasoning, it is not moved less;

[1] See Volume 1, p. 40.

therefore [it is moved] equally. But the triangle is moved in 4/3 ratio to *BD*. Therefore the circle is moved in 4/3 ratio to *BD*; therefore [it is so moved] with respect to the diameter.

The corollary should be evident as follows [see Fig. II.1b]. Let there be a point *I* which is moved in 4/3 ratio to point *C*. Therefore *I* is moved equally as the circle. In the same way let there be a point *L* which is moved in 4/3 ratio to point *M*, which is the middle point of *BC*. Therefore the lesser circle is moved equally as point *L*. But motion *I* / motion *L* = line *BI* / line *BL*. But line *BI* / line *BL* = *BC* / *BM*, for *BI* / *BC* = *BL* / *BM*. Therefore, from the first statement, the ratio of the motion of the greater circle to the motion of the lesser circle equals the ratio of line *BC* to line *BM*, and therefore [equals the ratio of] line *BD* to line *BC*, and therefore [equals the ratio of] diameter to diameter. But circle / circle = (diameter / diameter)^2. Therefore circle / circle = (motion / motion)^2.

The same thing is sufficiently proved for squares moved in a similar way, because squares are moved equally as [their] sides. So side / side = motion of square / motion of square. But square / square = (side / side)^2. Therefore square / square = (motion / motion)^2. The same thing appertains to triangles.

2. EVERY CURVED SURFACE OF A CONE IS MOVED IN 4/3 RATIO TO [ITS] HYPOTENUSE. HENCE IT IS CLEAR THAT ALL CURVED SURFACES OF CONES OF THE SAME BASE ARE EQUALLY MOVED.

Proceed therefore. Let line *LN* be equal to hypotenuse *AE* and line *NP* equal to the circumference of the base [see Fig. II.2]. It is evident, therefore, by the first [proposition] of *On Cones,* that triangle *LNP* is equal to the curved surface of cone *OAE*.[1] It is also evident that all the lines of the triangle and of the curved surface taken in the same ratio are equal. For *OA* / *TV* = circum. / circum., and *OA* / *TV* = *AE* / *TE*, on account of similar triangles. But *AE* / *TE* = *LN* / *LM*, for the lines are bisected. But *LN* /*LM* = *NP* / *MR*, on account of similar triangles, *MR* being parallel to *NP*. Therefore *NP* / *MR* = circum. of radius *OA* / circum. of radius *TV*. But the first [circumference] is equal to *NP*; therefore the second is equal to *MR*. Also curved surf. *OAE* / curved surf. *VTE* = (*AE* / *TE*)^2. This is evident from the first [proposition] of *On Cones.*[2] So triangle *LNP* / triangle *LMR* = (*LN* / *LM*)^2. Therefore, just as the greater triangle is quadruple the lesser so the greater curved surface is quadruple the lesser. Therefore let the curved surface of cone *OAE* be moved by rotating with the cone. Let triangle *LNP* be moved so that *LN* is moved equally as *AE*, i.e., so that point *M* is moved equally as point *T*. I say, therefore, that triangle *LNP* is moved equally as the curved surface of cone *OAE*, for the surfaces are equal and the lines taken in the same ratio are equal and are equally moved. For just as line *NP* is moved equally as the circumference of radius *OA* so line *MR* is moved equally as

Proposition II.2
[1] See Volume 1, p. 450.
[2] *Ibid.*

the circumference of radius *TV*, for the circumferences are moved equally as points *A* and *T* and the lines as points *N* and *M*. And so the lines are moved equally as the circumferences and are equal to them. It is thus for all [the lines and circumferences] taken in the same ratio. Therefore, the triangle is moved equally as the curved surface of cone *OAE*.

For if the curved surface is moved more than the triangle, let there be assumed another triangle similar and equal to triangle *LNP* but which is moved equally as the curved surface of cone *OAE*. Therefore it will be moved more than triangle *LNP*, and the lines [of it] will be moved more than the lines taken in the same ratio. So, therefore, that [assumed] triangle is moved more than the curved surface, for, since it is equal and all the lines taken in the same ratio are equal but are moved more, the triangle is moved more. So, therefore, the curved surface is not moved more than triangle *LNP*. The refutation is the same when it is said [that it is moved] less. Therefore it is moved equally. But triangle *LNP* is moved in 4/3 ratio to side *LN*. This is evident from the preceding proof. And *LN* is moved equally as *AE*. Therefore triangle *LNP* is moved in 4/3 ratio to *AE*. Therefore the curved surface of cone *OAE* is moved in 4/3 ratio to *AE*.

By the same proof [it is shown that] the curved surface of cone *OAC* is moved in 4/3 ratio to hypotenuse *AC*. And *AC* and *AE* are moved equally by the [corollary of the] second [proposition of Book I of this work]. Therefore the curved surfaces of cones *OAE* and *OAC* are equally moved. Moreover the curved surface of cone *OAE* is moved in 4/3 ratio to hypotenuse *AE*, and hypotenuse *AE* is moved equally as radius *OA*, and the circle of radius *OA* is moved in 4/3 ratio to *OA* [by Prop. II.1]. Therefore the curved surface of *OAE* is moved equally as the circle; and so every curved surface of a cone when rotating is moved equally as the base [and so all the curved surfaces of cones on the same base are moved equally].

3. THE RATIO OF SIMILAR [REGULAR] POLYGONS DESCRIBING POLYGONAL BODIES IS THE SQUARE OF THE RATIO OF MOTION TO MOTION. HENCE IT IS CLEAR THAT THE RATIO OF THE CURVED SURFACES OF THESE BODIES IS THE SQUARE OF THE RATIO OF THE MOTIONS OF [THESE] SURFACES.

Proceed therefore. I say that a [regular] polygon inscribed in circle *OC* is to a [similar] polygon inscribed in circle *ON* as the square of the ratio of motion to motion [see Fig. II. 3a]. For triangles *OCE* and *ONQ* are similar because angles *O* and *O* are equal (being right angles) and angle *C* = angle *N* (because the polygons are similar); therefore angle *E* = angle *Q*. It is evident by the antepenultimate [proposition, i.e. Prop. II.1] that the motion of triangle *OCE* is to the motion of triangle *ONQ* as is the ratio of *OC* to *ON*. But *OC* / *ON* = motion / motion. Therefore motion of triangle / motion of triangle = motion of *OC* / [motion of] *ON*. Also *FDE* and *RPQ* are similar, because angles *F* and *R* on the inside are equal [and] therefore [also] on the outside. Similarly *D* and *P* on the inside are equal [and] therefore [also] on the outside. Therefore, since the triangles are similar, motion / motion = *DF* / *PR*. But in order that we may not leave behind any doubt, let *DG* be parallel to *OC* and *PS* parallel to *ON*. It is evident, therefore, that triangles *GDE* and *SPQ* are similar, because angles *G* and *S* are right angles, and angles *E* and *Q* are equal, [and] therefore the remaining [angles] are equal. From these triangles, therefore, it is evident by the antepenultimate [proposition, II.1] that motion / motion = *GD* / *SP*. Also triangles *GDF* and *SPR* are similar, because angles *G* and *S* are right angles, and angles *F* and *R* on the inside are equal, [and] therefore the remaining [angles] are equal. It is clear, therefore, that motion of *GDF* / motion of *SPR* = *GD* / *SP*, and also that the motions of the total triangles [*GDE* and *SPQ*] are in the ratio of *GD* to *SP*. Therefore the motions of the remaining similar triangles [*FDE* and *RPQ*] are in the ratio of *GD* to *SP*. But *GD* / *SP* = *DF* / *PR*, on account of similar triangles. Therefore motion of *FDE* / motion of *RPQ* = *DF* / *PR*. But *DF* / *PR* = *OC* / *ON*, because *GD* / *SP* = *OC* / *ON*, on account of similar triangles. And *DG* / *SP* = *DF* / *PR*; therefore *OC* / *ON* = *DF* / *PR*. So, therefore, [motion of] triangle *OCE* / [motion of] triangle *ONQ* = *DF* / *PR*, and motion of triangle *FDE* / motion of triangle *RPQ* = *DF* / *PR*. Therefore the motions of the remaining surfaces, namely *OCDF* and *ONPR*, are in the same ratio, that is, in the ratio of *DF* to *PR*. By the same demonstration you will prove that motion of *OABC* / motion of *OLMN* = *AB* / *LM* = *DF* / *PR*. Therefore the motion of half of [one] polygon to the motion of half of the other polygon is as the ratio of *DF* to *PR*. Therefore the motion of the whole polygon is to the motion of the whole [polygon] as the ratio of side to side. But polygon / polygon = (side / side)^2. Therefore polygon / polygon = (motion / motion)^2.

The corollary should be evident as follows. I say that the curved surfaces described by the polygons are related in the square of the ratio of [their] motions. For motion curv. surf. cone *OCE* / motion curv. surf. cone *GDE* = *OC* / *GD*. This is evident by the preceding [proposition] since the surfaces are similar. By the same reasoning motion curv. surf. cone *OCE* / motion curv. surf. cone *ONQ* = *OC* / *ON*, and motion curv. surf. cone *GDE* / motion curv. surf. cone *SPQ* = *GD* / *SP*. And the curved surface of cone *GDE* is the curved surface of cone *FDE*, for they differ only in the base. Similarly the curved surface of cone *SPQ* is the curved surface of cone *RPQ*. Therefore motion curv. surf. cone *FDE* / motion curv. surf. cone *RPQ* = *GD* / *SP* = *DF* / *PR*. But motion curv. surf. cone *OCE* / motion curv. surf. cone *ONQ* = *OC* / *ON* = *DF* / *PR*. Therefore the ratio of the motion of the remainder of the curved surface which line *CD* describes to the motion of the remainder of the curved surface which line *NP* describes is the ratio of *DF* to *PR*. Also motion curv. surf. cone *GDF* / motion curv. surf. cone *SPR* = *GD* / *SP* = *DF* / *PR*, for the surfaces are similar. Therefore the motion of the total curved surface which is described by *CD* and *DF* is to the motion of the total curved surface which is described by *NP* and *PR* as *DF* is to *PR*. By the same reasoning the motion of the total curved surface which is described by *AB* and *BC* is to the motion of the total curved surface which is described by *LM* and *MN* as *AB* is to *LM*, that is, as *DF* to *PR*. Therefore the motion of the total curved surface of half of the [one] polygonal body is to the motion of the total curved surface of half the other polygonal body as *DF* is to *PR*. Therefore the motion of the total curved surface [of the one whole polygonal body] is to the motion of the total [curved surface of the other] as *DF* is to *PR*. But curved surface / curved [surface] = (side / side)^2. We have proved this elsewhere.[1] Therefore curved surface / curved [surface] = (motion / motion)^2.

From this it is also clear that the ratio of circles describing spheres is the ratio of [their] motions squared. For example, I say that circle *ON* / circle *OV* = (motion / motion)^2 [see Fig. II.3b], it having been previously proved that the ratio of the motions of the inscribed polygons is as that of the motions of the circles. Therefore the motion of circle *OV* is to [the motion of] circle *ON* as the motion of the polygon is to [the motion of the] polygon, or it is more or less.

If more, let it be as the motion of circle *OV* to the motion of circle *OR*.[2] Therefore let a [regular] polygon be inscribed in circle *ON* that does not at all touch circle *OR*. And let a similar [polygon] be inscribed in circle *OV*. Therefore motion of circle *OV* / [motion of] circle *OR* = motion of polygon / motion of polygon. Now in refutation, the polygon inscribed in circle *ON* is moved more than circle *OR*. Therefore motion of inscr. polyg. in circle *OV* / motion of circle *OR* > motion of inscr. polyg. in circle *OV* / motion of inscr. polyg. in circle *ON*, and circle *ON* is moved more than [its] inscribed polygon and more than circle *OR*. Therefore motion of circle *OV* / [motion of] circle *ON* < motion of circle *OV* / [motion of] circle *OR*. But motion of circle *OV* / motion of circle *OR* = motion of polygon / motion of polygon. Therefore motion of circle *OV* / motion of circle *ON* < motion of polygon / motion of polygon. Therefore not more.

It is refuted in a similar way when it is said that it is less. So, therefore, the ratio of the motions of the polygons is the same as that of the motions of the circles. But the ratio of the motions of the polygons is the same as that of the radii *OV* and *ON*. Therefore the ratio of the motions of the circles is the same as that of the radii. But the ratio of the circles is as the square of the ratio of the radii, and therefore also as the square of the ratio of the motions. By similar reasoning you will prove that the ratio of the curved surfaces of spheres is the square of the ratio of [their] motions. And this you will prove by the motions of the curved surfaces of similar inscribed polygonal bodies. For, as has been proved by the preceding [demonstration], (motion of curv. surf. of polyg. body / motion of curv. surf. of polyg. body)^2 = surface / surface. Afterwards you will prove that the ratio of the motions of the curved surfaces of polygonal bodies inscribed in spheres is the same as the

---

[1] So far as I know, the work in which Gerard proved this is not extant.

[2] The confusion evident in the succeeding use of the exhaustion procedure has been discussed and corrected in my summary of Corollary II to Proposition II.3 in Chapter Two above.

ratio of the motions of the curved surfaces of the spheres. And this [is proved] *per impossibile* completely in the same way we have proved [the similar enunciation] concerning circles and inscribed polygons. But the motion of curv. surf. of polyg. body / motion of curv. surf. of polyg. body = radius / radius, as we have already proved before. Therefore motion of surf. of sphere / motion of surf. of sphere = radius / radius. But (radius / radius)² = surf. of sphere / surf. of sphere, as has been proved elsewhere by *The Book on Cones.*[3] Therefore surf. [of sphere] / surf. of sphere = (motion / motion)², and this we wished to demonstrate.

4. THE MOTION OF A RIGHT TRIANGLE IS TO THE MOTION OF A REGULAR POLYGON AS THE MOTION OF THE HYPOTENUSE TO THE MOTION OF THE PERIMETER. FROM THIS IT IS CLEAR THAT THE MORE SIDES A [REGULAR] POLYGON INSCRIBED IN A CIRCLE HAS, THE MORE IT IS MOVED. IN A CIRCUMSCRIBED [REGULAR POLYGON] THE CONTRARY [IS TRUE].

Let the proposed triangle be *LMR* and the proposed polygon be inscribed in circle *OH* [see Fig. II.4]. Let side *HI* be extended until it meets with line *YM* in point *Y*. That it will meet [*YM*] is clear because angle *O* is a right angle and angle *H* is less than a right angle. If, therefore, triangles *OHY* and *LMR* are similar, it [the proposition] should proceed [directly] from them. If they are dissimilar, let *LMQ* be similar to *OHY* and let surface *OHIQ* be just as great a part of triangle *OHY* as surface *LMNV* is of triangle *LMQ*. Therefore motion of triangle *LMQ* / motion of triangle *OHY* = motion of hypotenuse / [motion of] hypotenuse, and motion of triangle *VNQ* / motion of triangle *QIY* = motion of hypotenuse / [motion] of hypotenuse. But motion of hyp. *NQ* / [motion of] hyp. *IY* = motion of hyp. *MQ* / motion of hyp. *HY*, for *NQ* and *IY* are similar aliquot parts of those hypotenuses. For *MQ* / *NQ* = *HY* / *IY*, and so *MQ* / *HY* = *NQ* / *IY*. Therefore it is clear from the preceding things that the ratio of the motions of those hypotenuses is the same. So, therefore, motion of triangle *LMQ* / motion of triangle *QIY* = motion of *MQ* / motion of *IY*, and the ratio of the motions of the whole triangles is the same. Therefore [the ratio of] the motions of the remaining parts is the same. Therefore motion of *LMNV* / motion of *OHIQ* = [motion of] *MQ* / motion of *HY*. But motion of *MQ* / motion of *HY* = motion of *NQ* / motion of *IY*. Therefore the ratio of the remaining parts is the same. Therefore motion of *MN* / motion of *HI* = motion of *MQ* / motion of *HY*. So, therefore, motion of *LMNV* / motion of *OHIQ* = motion of *MN* / motion of *HI*. Also, because triangle *QIS* is not similar to triangle *VNQ*, let us assume triangle *QIY* which is similar to it. For just as triangles *LMQ* and *VNQ* are similar because *LM* is parallel to *VN*, so triangles *OHY* and *QIY* are similar because *OH* is parallel to *QI*; and all the lines drawn to *QI* and *VN* are parallel, which does not demand proof. Therefore motion of triangle *VNQ*

---

[3] See the comment at the end of my discussion of Corollary III to Proposition II.3 in Chapter Two above.

/ motion of triangle *QIY* = motion of hyp. *NQ* / motion of hyp. *IY*. But triangles *QIY* and *QIS* are equally moved because they have the same base, namely *QI*, and their hypotenuses *IY* and *IS* are equally moved. Therefore motion of triangle *VNQ* / motion of triangle *QIS* = motion of hyp. *NQ* / motion of hyp. *IS*. Therefore let line *ZT* be equal to line *KP*. It is evident, therefore, that triangles *PKS* and *TZY* are equally moved since they are of equal bases. And triangles *QIS* and *QIY* are equally moved. Therefore the remaining parts are equally moved. Therefore the motions of *QIKP* and *QIZT* are equal and similarly the motions of *IK* and *IZ* are equal by similar [reasons]. Therefore let triangle *VNQ* be divided into the [same] aliquot parts by line *TO* that the triangle *QIY* has been divided into by line *TZ*. Therefore the motion of triangle *TOQ* / motion of triangle *TZY* = motion of *OQ* / motion of *ZY* = motion of *NQ* / motion of *IY*. And the motions of whole triangles *VNQ* and *QIY* are related in the same ratio. Therefore the motions of the remaining parts are related in the same ratio since they are similar aliquot parts. Therefore motion of *VNOT* / motion of *QIZT* = motion of *NQ* / motion of *IY* = motion of *NO* / motion of *IZ*, as has been proved before for the other lines. But *QIZT* and *QIKP* are moved equally, and *IZ* and *IK* are moved equally. Therefore motion of *VNOT* / motion of *QIKP* = motion of *NO* / motion of *IK*. Also, since triangle *PKR* is not similar to triangle *TOQ*, let triangle *PKX* be similar to it, so that angle *K* = angle *O*. Therefore motion of triangle *TOQ* / motion of triangle *PKX* = motion of *OQ* / motion of *KX*. Therefore let line *Vq* be equal to line *NL*. So, therefore, triangles *PKX* and *PKR* are equally moved since they are on the same base, and triangles *VqX* and *NLR* are equally moved since [their] bases are equal. Therefore surfaces *PKqV* and *PKLN* are equally moved, as before, and *Kq* [is moved] equally as *KL*. Therefore let line *PS* divide triangle *TOQ* into aliquot parts similar to those into which *Vq* divides triangle *PKX*. Therefore, by proceeding in the same way as before, you will prove that motion of *TOPS* / motion *PKqV* = motion of *OP* / motion of *Kq*. But *PKLN* and *PKqV* are equally moved, and similarly *Kq* and *KL* are equally moved. Therefore motion of *TOPS* / motion of *PKLN* = motion of *OP* / motion of *KL*. Therefore we have come to the exterior triangles *SPQ* and *NLM*. But since they are not similar, let there be constructed on base *SP* a triangle similar to triangle *NLM*. Therefore the motion of that triangle is to the motion of triangle *NLM* as the motion of [its] hypotenuse is to the motion of the hypotenuse of triangle *NLM*. But that triangle is moved equally as triangle *SPQ* since they are on the same base, and [its] hypotenuse is moved equally as *PQ*. Therefore motion of triangle *SPQ* / motion of [triangle] *NLM* = [motion of] *PQ* / [motion of] *LM*. Therefore the motion of all the aforesaid parts of triangle *LMQ* is to the motion of all the aforesaid parts of surface *OHM* as the motion of all the aforesaid parts of hypotenuse *MQ* is to the motion of the sides of surface *OHM*. Therefore the motion of the whole triangle *LMQ* is to the motion of the whole surface *OHM* as the motion of the hypotenuse [of triangle *LMQ*] is to the motion of the perimeter of [surface]

OHM. By the same reasoning, motion of triangle *LMQ* / motion of surface *OHD* = motion of *MQ* / motion of *H*[*GFE*]*D*. And so motion of triangle *LMQ* / motion of surface *MHD* = motion of *MQ* / motion of perimeter *MHD*. Therefore the motion of triangle *LMQ* is to the motion of the semi-polygon as the motion of the hypotenuse is to the motion of the semiperimeter, and so the motion of the triangle is to the motion of the whole polygon as the motion of the hypotenuse is to the motion of the perimeter.

From this it is also evident that the motion of the curved surface of cone *LMQ* is to the motion of the curved surface of a polygonal body which is described by a polygonal surface as the motion of the hypotenuse is to the motion of the perimeter. For motion of curv. surf. cone *LMQ* / motion of curv. surf. cone *OHY* = hypotenuse / hypotenuse. This is clear from the things said. In the same way, motion of curv. surf. cone *VNQ* / motion of curv. surf. cone *QIY* / = motion of hypotenuse / [motion of] hypotenuse = [motion of] *NQ* / motion of *IY*. Therefore motion of curv. surf. of surf. *LMNV* / motion of curv. surf. of *OHIQ* = motion of *MQ* / motion of *HY* = [motion of] *MN* / motion of *HI*. And so by proceeding in the same way as before in regard to the triangle and polygon, you will prove what has been proposed. But triangle *LMQ* is moved equally as the given triangle, namely *LMR*, since they are on the same base; and, by the same reasoning, hypotenuse / hypotenuse = curved surface / [curved] surface. Therefore the motion of the given triangle *LMR* is to the motion of the polygon as the motion of the hypotenuse [of the triangle] is to the motion of the perimeter of the polygon, and the motion of the curved surface to the motion of the curved [surface] is in the same [ratio].

The corollary should be evident as follows. The motion of the polygon to the [motion of the] triangle is as the motion of the perimeter to [the motion of] the hypotenuse. But if the inscribed [regular] polygon has more sides, its perimeter is moved more, by the last [proposition] of the first [book]. Therefore the ratio of the motion of the perimeter of an inscribed polygon of more sides to the motion of the hypotenuse is greater than the ratio of the motion of the perimeter of the polygon of fewer sides [to the motion of the same hypotenuse]. Therefore the ratio of the motion of an inscribed polygon of more sides to the motion of the triangle is greater than the ratio of the motion of an [inscribed] polygon of fewer sides to the [motion of the] same triangle. Therefore the inscribed polygon of more sides is moved more than the [inscribed] polygon of fewer sides. Also the motion of the perimeter of a circumscribed polygon of fewer sides is more than the motion of the perimeter of a circumscribed polygon of more sides. But motion of perimeter / motion of hypotenuse = motion of polygon / motion of triangle. Therefore the ratio of the motion of the circumscribed polygon of fewer sides to [the motion of] the triangle is greater than is [the ratio of] the motion of the polygon of more sides [to the motion of the same triangle]. Therefore the motion [of the circumscribed polygon of fewer sides] is greater [than that of the circumscribed polygon of more sides]. Therefore we have what has been proposed.

5. THE MOTION OF A TRIANGLE IS TO THE MOTION OF A CIR-
CLE DESCRIBING A SPHERE AS THE MOTION OF THE HYPOTEN-
USE [OF THE TRIANGLE] IS TO THE MOTION OF THE CIRCUM-
FERENCE [OF THE CIRCLE]. HENCE IT IS CLEAR THAT THE RATIO
OF THE CURVED SURFACES [DESCRIBED BY THE TRIANGLE AND
CIRCLE] IS THE SAME, AND THAT THE MOTION OF AN EQUI-
NOCTIAL CIRCLE IS TO THE MOTION OF A COLURE AS THE MO-
TION OF [ONE] CIRCUMFERENCE IS TO THE MOTION OF THE
[OTHER] CIRCUMFERENCE.

Proceed therefore. I say that the motion of triangle *LMN* is to the motion
of circle *OC* as the motion of the hypotenuse of *LMN* is to the motion of
the circumference, or [is] greater or less [see Fig. II.5].

If greater, let the motion of triangle *LMN* be to the motion of circle *OC*
as the motion of the hypotenuse to the motion of the circumference of circle
OF. Let a [regular] polygon be inscribed in circle *OC* that does not at all
touch circle *OF*. Therefore motion of triangle *LMN* / [motion of] polygon
= motion of hypotenuse / motion of perimeter. Therefore the ratio of the
motion of the hypotenuse to the motion of the perimeter of the polygon is
less than [the ratio of the motion of the hypotenuse] to the motion of the
circumference of circle *OF*. Therefore motion of triangle *LMN* / motion of
polygon < motion of hypotenuse [*LM*] / motion of circum. circle *OF*. Therefore *multo fortius* motion of triangle *LMN* / motion of circle *OC* < motion
of hyp. [*LM*] / motion of [the circumference of] circle *OF*. Therefore [the
one ratio is] not as much [as the other, as was assumed].

If the ratio of the motion of the triangle to [the motion of] the circle is
less than the ratio of the motion of the hypotenuse to the motion of the
circumference, let motion of triangle *LMN* / motion of circle *OF* = motion
of hypotenuse / motion of circum. circle *OC*. Therefore the ratio of the
motion of the hypotenuse to the motion of the perimeter of the polygon is
less than [the ratio of the motion of the hypotenuse] to the motion of the
circumference of circle *OC*. But motion of hypotenuse / motion of perim.
polygon = motion of triangle / motion of polygon. Therefore the ratio of
the motion of the triangle to the motion of the polygon is greater than [the
ratio of] the motion of the hypotenuse to the motion of the circumference
of circle *OC*. Therefore *multo fortius* motion of triangle *LMN* / motion of
circle *OF* > motion of hyp. / motion of circum. circle *OC*. Therefore [the
one ratio is] not the same [as the other, as was assumed]. So, therefore, it is
clear that the motion of the triangle is to the motion of the circle as the
motion of the hypotenuse is to the motion of the circumference.

I say, therefore, that the motion of the curved surface of cone *LMN* is to
the motion of the surface of sphere *OF* as the motion of the hypotenuse is
to the motion of the circumference, or [the one ratio is] greater or less [than
the other].

If greater, let the motion of the curved surface of the cone be to the motion
of the curved surface of sphere *OC* as the motion of the hypotenuse is to

the motion of the circumference of circle *OF*. But the motion of the curved surface of the cone is to the motion of the curved surface of a polygonal body inscribed in sphere *OC* as the motion of the hypotenuse is to the motion of the perimeter. Therefore motion of hypotenuse / motion of circum. circle *OF* > motion of hyp. / motion of perim. Therefore motion of hyp. / motion of circum. circle *OF* > motion of curv. surf. cone / motion of curv. surf. polyg. body. Therefore *multo fortius* motion of hyp. / motion of circum. circle *OF* > motion of curv. surf. cone / motion of surf. sphere *OC*. Therefore [the one ratio is] not the same [as the other, as was assumed].

If the ratio of the motion of the curved surface of the cone to the motion of the surface of the sphere is less than the motion of the hypotenuse to the motion of the circumference of the sphere, let the motion of the curved surface of cone *LMN* be to the motion of the surface of sphere *OF* as the motion of the hypotenuse is to the motion of the circumference of sphere *OC*. Therefore, by proceeding in the same way as before, you will prove that motion of hyp. cone *LMN* / motion of circum. circle *OC* < motion of curv. surf. cone / motion of surf. sphere *OF*.

From the proof at hand it is evident that the motion of the circle is to the motion of the polygon as the motion of the circumference is to the motion of the perimeter, for, since motion of circle / motion of triangle = motion of circumference / motion of hypotenuse, and motion of triangle / motion of polygon = motion of hypotenuse / motion of perimeter, therefore motion of circle / motion of polygon = motion of circumference / motion of perimeter. Also, since motion of surf. sphere / motion of surf. cone = motion of circum. / motion of hyp., and motion of surf. cone / motion of surf. polyg. body = motion of hyp. / motion of perim., therefore motion of surf. sphere / motion of surf. polyg. body = motion of circum. / motion of perim. polyg. surf. describing polyg. body.

The second part of the corollary should be evident as follows. Let a triangle be inscribed in a colure so that its two sides containing the right angle are halves of the two diameters. The motion of that triangle is to the motion of the colure as the motion of the hypotenuse is to the motion of the circumference. This has already been proved. Also the motion of [another given] triangle is one half the motion of the equinoctial [circle] [cf. triangle *BFH* in Fig. II.1b]. This has been proved by the first [proposition] of this book. And the motion of the hypotenuse [*BF* in that figure] is one half the motion of the circumference of the equinoctial [circle]. Therefore motion of the triangle / motion of equinoc. [circle] = motion of hyp. / motion of circum. But the motion of this triangle [*OCE*][1] to the motion of the given triangle is as the motion of the hypotenuse to the motion of the hypotenuse. This is evident if a triangle similar to the given [triangle] is constructed on the same base. But motion of triangle / motion of colure = motion of hyp. / motion

---

[1] One must suppose that a line has been drawn to complete tri. *OCE* in Fig. II.5.

of circum. of colure. Therefore motion of equinoc. circle / motion of colure = motion of circum. / motion of circum.

Also it is evident from the things said before that the square of the ratio of the motions of circles describing spheres is equal to the ratio of the circles. For, with two circles proposed, motion of first circle / motion of triangle = motion of circum. / motion of hyp. And motion of triangle / motion of second circle = motion of hyp. / motion of circum. Therefore motion of first circle / motion of second circle = motion of circum. / motion of circum. = circum. / circum. = diameter / diameter. But (diameter / diameter)^2 = circle / circle. Therefore (motion / motion)^2 = circle / circle. The same thing can be proved *per impossibile* after it has been said that one is greater or less [than the other]. Let motion of circle / motion of circle = motion of circum. / motion of circum. And this [is proved] by the inscription of similar polygons. From this it is also clear that the ratio of the curved surfaces of spheres is as the square of the ratio of their motions. And this can be proved directly by the motion of the curved surface of a cone or indirectly by the motion of similar inscribed polygonal bodies.

Book III

[Postulates]

[1.] AMONG EQUAL AND SIMILAR CYLINDERS MOVED IN THE SAME TIME, THAT ONE NONE OF WHOSE CIRCLES IS MOVED MORE IS NOT [MOVED] MORE.

[2.] THAT ONE NONE OF WHOSE CIRCLES [IS MOVED] LESS IS NOT [MOVED] LESS.

[Propositions]

1. THE RATIO OF SIMILAR POLYGONAL BODIES IS THE CUBE OF THE RATIO OF THEIR MOTIONS.

Proceed therefore. Let the first cylinder be moved by describing itself. Let the second cylinder, equal and similar [to the first], be moved continuously in a straight line so that any circle of it equal to a circle of the first [cylinder] is moved equally as any circle of the first [cylinder]. And so these two cylinders are moved equally. This is evident *per impossibile*.

For if the first is not moved equally as the second, it is moved more or less. If more, this is refuted because no circle of it is moved more. Since, therefore, the cylinders are equal and similar, and are moved in equal time, and no circle of the first is moved more than some circle of the second, therefore the first is not moved more than the second. By the same reasoning it will be proved that the first is not moved less than the second. Therefore [it is moved] equally [as it].

Therefore let there be two cylinders which are unequal but similar, and each of them is moved by describing itself. It is evident, therefore, by the proof at hand that motion of cylinder / [motion of] cylinder = motion of base / [motion of] base. For it has already been proved that a cylinder which describes itself is moved equally as its base because it is moved equally as that which is moved equally as the base. So, therefore, every cylinder which describes itself is moved equally as its base. So, therefore, the ratio of the motions of similar cylinders is equal to the ratio of the bases (i.e. circles) when both cylinders by their motion describe themselves. Therefore, if two similar cylinders are proposed which by their motion describe themselves, the ratio of the motions of the cylinders is equal to the ratio of the motions of the bases. But the ratio of the motions of the bases is equal to the ratio of the motions of the radii of these bases. But cylinder / cylinder = (motion of radius of base / motion of radius of base)³, for the same ratio exists between the radii as between the motions. But [by Euclid's *Elements,* Prop. XII.12] the cube of the ratio of the radii of the bases of similar cylinders is equal to the ratio of the cylinders since the same ratio exists between the radii as between the diameters. Therefore the ratio of similar cylinders is equal to the cube of the ratio of their motions.

By the same reasoning the ratio of similar cones that describe themselves is equal to the cube of the ratio of their motions.

Proceed therefore. Triangles *OAC* and *OLN* are similar because angle *O* = angle *O* and angle *A* is given equal to angle *L* (for the polygons describing similar bodies are similar); and therefore angle *C* = angle *N* [see Fig. III.1]. So, therefore, the cones [described by] those triangles are similar. Therefore motion of cone *OAC* / motion of cone *OLN* = motion of *OA* / [motion of] *OL* = *OA* / *OL*. But cone / cone = (*OA* / *OL*)³. Therefore cone / cone = (motion / motion)³.

By the same reasoning cone *FBC* / cone *QMN* = (motion of *FB* / motion of *QM*)³, for cone / cone = (*FB* / *QM*)³. But *FB* / *QM* = *OA* / *OL*, for the triangles are similar. They are similar because *FB* is drawn parallel to *OA* and *QM* parallel to *OL*. So, therefore, *FB* / *QM* = *OA* / *OL*. Therefore cone *FBC* / cone *QMN* = (*AO* / *OL*)³. Therefore cone *FBC* / cone *QMN* = (motion of *OA* / motion of *OL*)³. And motion of whole cone *OAC* / motion of whole cone *OLN* = *OA* / *OL*, and whole cone / whole [cone] = (*OA* / *OL*)³. Therefore the motion of the difference between cones *OAC* and *FBC* is to the motion of the difference between cones *OLN* and *QMN* as *OA* is to *OL*, and the ratio of these differences is equal to the cube of the ratio of *OA* to *OL*. Therefore, the ratio of these differences is equal to the cube of the ratio of motion to motion.

Furthermore triangles *FBD* and *QMP* are similar because angles *F* and *Q* are right angles (for the protracted lines [*FB* and *QM*] are parallel [respectively] to lines *OA* and *OL* and angle *D* = angle *P* because the polygons are similar). Therefore angle *B* = angle *M*. Therefore the triangles are similar and the cones [described by] those triangles are similar. Therefore cone / cone = (motion / motion)³ = (*FB* / *QM*)³ = (*OA* / *OL*)³ = (motion of *OA* / motion of *OL*)³. But [corporeal] difference [described by] *OABF* / [corporeal] difference [described by] $OLMQ = (OA / OL)^3$, and motion of difference / motion of difference = OA / OL. Therefore the ratio of the [one] whole body consisting of the cone and the difference to the [other] whole [body] consisting of the cone and the difference is equal to the cube of the ratio of OA to OL. And motion / motion = OA / OL.

By the same demonstration you will prove that the ratio of the remaining quarter of the [one] whole body to the remaining quarter of the [other] whole body is equal to the cube of the ratio of OA to OL, and motion / motion = OA / OL, and so half the [one] whole body / half the [other] whole body = $(OA / OL)^3$. And motion / motion = OA / OL. Therefore whole body / whole body = $(OA / OL)^3$, and motion / motion = OA / OL. Therefore the ratio of the bodies is equal to the cube of the ratio of [their] motions.

2. FROM THIS IT IS CLEAR THAT THE RATIO OF SPHERES IS EQUAL TO THE RATIO OF [THEIR] MOTIONS CUBED.

I say, therefore, that motion of sphere OL / motion of sphere OB = radius OL / radius OB [see Fig. III.2]. For let there be inscribed in those spheres similar polygonal [bodies]. I say that motion of polyg. body / motion of polyg. body = motion of sphere / motion of sphere. For either the ratio is the same or is greater or less.

If greater, therefore motion of sphere / motion of sphere < motion of polyg. body / motion of polyg. body. Therefore let motion of sphere OL / motion of sphere OA = motion of polyg. [body][1] / motion of polyg. [body]. Therefore let a regular polygonal [body] be inscribed in sphere OB that does not touch sphere OA. And let a similar [polygonal body] be inscribed in sphere OL, and let these polygonal bodies be $OGHIKBCDEF$ and $OQRSTLMNOP$. Therefore the ratio of the motions of these polygonal bodies is equal to the ratio of line OL to line OB by the said proof. And [the ratio] of the motions of the first polygonal [bodies] is equal to the ratio of line OL to line OB by the same proof. Therefore the ratio of the motions of these polygonal bodies is equal to the ratio of the motions of the first [polygonal bodies]. Therefore the motion of this polygonal [body] is to the motion of one similar to it as is the ratio of the motion of sphere OL to the motion of sphere OA, which is manifestly impossible. For the ratio of the motion of the polygonal [body] inscribed in sphere OL to the motion of sphere OA is greater than [the motion of the polygonal body inscribed in sphere OL] to the motion of a similar polygonal [body] inscribed in sphere OB, for that [latter] polygonal [body] is moved more than sphere OA. Therefore *multo fortius* the motion of sphere OL / motion of sphere OA > motion of polyg. [body] / motion of polyg. [body]. Therefore the ratio of the motion of sphere

Proposition III.2

[1] In this whole proof (and particularly in the second half of it) either Gerard or an early copyist has continually used "polygon" where "polygonal body" is required, thus making the proof as it stands incomplete. I have accordingly added "[body]" in my translation to make the proof coherent. Other instances of the omission of crucial terms like "motion" or "circumference" have been noted in my summary of errors at the end of Chapter Two.

OL to the motion of sphere *OA* is greater than the ratio of the motions of the polygonal bodies [and not equal to it as was supposed].

If the ratio of the motion of [one] polygonal [body] to the motion of the [other] polygonal [body] is less than [the ratio] of the motion of [one] sphere to the motion of the [other] sphere, therefore [the ratio of] the motion of [one] sphere to the motion of the [other] sphere is the greater [ratio]. Therefore let sphere *OB* be circumscribed by another sphere and let the motion of sphere *OL* be to the motion of that [circumscribed] sphere as the motion of [one original] polygonal body is to the motion of the [other original] polygonal [body]. Therefore let [still another] polygonal [body] be inscribed in that [circumscribed] sphere that does not at all touch sphere *OB* and let there be circumscribed a similar polygonal [body] about sphere *OL* that does not touch [sphere *OL*]. Therefore the ratio of the motions of these polygonal [bodies] is equal to the ratio of the first polygonal [bodies], for the ratio of their radii is the same. Therefore, by proceeding as before, you will prove that the ratio of these polygonal [bodies] is even greater than the ratio of the motion of sphere *OL* to the motion of the sphere circumscribed about sphere *OB*. Therefore the ratio of the first polygonal [bodies] is greater than the ratio of the motions of these spheres [and therefore not less, as was assumed]. So, therefore, since the ratio is neither greater nor less, it will be the same. But the motion of polyg. [body] / motion of polyg. [body] = radius *OL* / radius *OB*. Therefore motion of sphere / motion of sphere = radius *OL* / radius *OB*. But the ratio of the spheres is equal to the cube of the ratio of [their] radii, because [it is equal to the cube of the ratio] of the diameters. Therefore the ratio of the spheres is equal to the cube of the ratio of [their] motions.

3. THE MOTION OF A RIGHT CONE IS TO THE MOTION OF A POLYGONAL BODY DESCRIBED BY A REGULAR POLYGON AS THE MOTION OF THE HYPOTENUSE IS TO THE MOTION OF THE SIDES OF THE POLYGON.

In the first place, it is to be demonstrated that all cones on the same base are moved equally. For I say that cones *LMP* and *LMQ* described by triangles *LMP* and *LMQ* are equally moved [see Fig. III.3]. For cylinders *LMTP* and *LMVQ* are equally moved, and also, therefore, the cones [are equally moved] since they are similar aliquot parts, for the same ratio exists between the wholes and between the aliquot parts. Therefore those cones are equally moved. I say, therefore, that the motion of cone *LMQ* is to the motion of the polygonal body inscribed in sphere *OA* as is the motion of the hypotenuse to the motion of the sides.

For let side *AB* be protracted until it meets with line *OD* in point *D*. Therefore triangles *OAD* and *LMQ* are either similar or dissimilar. If they are similar, the proposition proceeds [directly] from them.

If they are dissimilar, let *LMP* be similar to *OAD*. So, therefore, cones *LMP* and *OAD* are similar. Therefore motion of cone *LMP* / motion of cone *OAD* = motion of base / [motion of] base = motion of radius *LM* of the base / motion of radius *OA* of the base = motion of hyp. *MP* / motion of hyp. *AD*. Therefore let *BI* be parallel to *OA* and *NS* parallel to *LM*, *NS* dividing triangle *LMP* into aliquot parts similar to those in which *IB* divides triangle *OAD*. So, therefore, motion of cone *SNP* / motion of cone *IBD* = motion of *SN* / motion of *IB*, by the same reasoning as before. But motion of *SN* / motion of *IB* = motion of *LM* / motion of *OA*. This is evident by similar triangles and by the similar aliquot parts into which they are divided. So, therefore, motion of cone *SNP*/ motion of cone *IBD* = motion of hyp. *MP* / motion of hyp. *AD* = motion of hyp. *NP* / motion of hyp. *BD*. Therefore the ratio of the motion of the difference of the cones [described by *LMNS*] to the motion of the difference of cones [described by *OABI*] is equal to the ratio of the motion of *MN* to the motion of *AB*.

Also cones *IBD* and *IBF* are equally moved, as are their hypotenuses. Therefore let *HK* be equal to *FC*.[1] Therefore cones *HKF* and *FCD* are moved equally, for their hypotenuses are moved equally. Since the whole cones *IBD* and *IBF* are moved equally, therefore their remainders will be moved equally [and] so, therefore, *IBKH* and *IBCF*, which are the differences of the larger and of the smaller cones, are moved equally and lines *BC* and *BK* are moved equally. Therefore, since cones *SNP* and *IBD* are similar and the triangles are similar, [so] motion of *SNP* / motion of *IBD* = motion of base / motion of base = motion of radius *SN* / motion of radius *IB* = motion of *NP* / motion of *BD*.

Also, in the same way, let *RO* divide triangle *SNP* as *FC* [divides] triangle *IBD*. So, therefore, motion of cone *ROP* / motion of cone *FCD* = motion of *RO* / motion of *FC* = motion of *OP* / motion of *CD*. But motion of *OP* / motion of *CD* = motion of *NP* / motion of *BD*. So, therefore, since the ratio is the same between the motions of the whole cones and between [the motions of] the similar parts, so also the ratio between the sections of the remaining parts will be the same as the ratio of the motion of *NO* to the motion of *BC*, *NO* and *BC* being the differences between the [two sets of] hypotenuses. But cones *IBD* and *IBF* are equally moved, as are their hypotenuses; and similarly [equally moved] are *HKF* and *FCD*, as are their hypotenuses [*KF* and *CD*] and the differences. So, therefore, the motion of *SNOR* (the difference between the [one set of] cones) is to the motion of *IBKH* (the difference between [the other set of] cones) as the motion of *NO* is to the motion of *BK*. Also, since triangles *ROP* and *HKG* are dissimilar, let *HKE* be similar to *ROP*. So, therefore, motion of cone *ROP* / motion of cone *HKE* = motion of hyp. / motion of hyp. But *HKE* and *HKG* are equally moved, as are their hypotenuses. Therefore motion of *ROP* / motion of *HKG* = motion of *OP* / motion of *KG*. You find the same thing in the other part of the polygonal body. So, therefore, from the parts conclude that the motion

---

[1] See my comment on the double use of *FC* in note 23 of Chapter Two above.

of cone *LMP* is to the motion of the polygonal body as the motion of the hypotenuse is to the motion of the sides taken together.

From this it is clear that the more sides the polygonal body inscribed in the sphere has, the more it is moved, while the contrary is true in the case of circumscribed [bodies]. For, since the motion of the polygonal body of more sides inscribed in the sphere is to the motion of the cone as the motion of the sides is to the motion of the hypotenuse—and if there are more sides the sides are moved more by the last [proposition] of Book I—therefore the ratio of the motion of the inscribed polygonal body of more sides to the motion of the cone is greater than the ratio of the motion of the polygonal body of fewer[2] sides [to the motion of the same cone]. Therefore the body of more sides is moved more. Contrariwise in the case of circumscribed bodies it happens that the sides of the body of more sides are moved less. Therefore the ratio of the motion of the body of fewer sides to the motion of the cone is greater than [the ratio of] the motion of the body of more sides [to the motion of the same cone]. Therefore the body of fewer sides is moved more.

4. THE MOTION OF A RIGHT CONE IS TO THE MOTION OF A SPHERE AS THE MOTION OF THE HYPOTENUSE IS TO THE MOTION OF THE CIRCUMFERENCE OF A COLURE.

I say, therefore, that the motion of cone *OPQ* is to the motion of sphere *OA* as the motion of the hypotenuse is to [the motion of] the circumference of the colure (i.e. the circle describing the sphere), or [the one ratio is] greater or less [than the other]. [See Fig. III.4].

If greater, let the motion of [cone] *OPQ* be to [the motion of] sphere *OB* as the motion of the hypotenuse is to [the motion of] the circumference of sphere *OA*. Therefore let there be inscribed in sphere *OB* a polygonal body that does not at all touch [sphere] *OA*. Therefore the motion of cone *OPQ* is to the motion of the polygonal [body] as the motion of the hypotenuse is to the motion of the sides of the polygonal body, by the preceding [proposition]. Therefore the ratio of the motion of the cone to the motion of sphere *OB* is less than [the ratio of] the motion of the hypotenuse to the motion of the sides of the polygonal [body].

If the ratio of the motion of the hypotenuse to the motion of circumference *A* is greater than [the ratio of] the motion of the hypotenuse to the motion of the sides, therefore *multo fortius* is the ratio of the motion of the cone to the motion of sphere *OB* less than [the ratio of] the motion of the hypotenuse to the motion of circumference *A*. Or [reason] better as follows. Motion of cone / motion of polyg. body = motion of hyp. / motion of sides, and motion of cone / motion of sphere *OB* = motion of hyp. / motion of circum. *A*. But motion of cone / motion of sphere *OB* < motion of cone / motion of

---

[2] In these last sentences I have adopted the reading of *pauciorum* as found in MS *N* (and perhaps *E*) rather than the *paucorum* of MSS *OB* because the comparative form is necessary to contrast with *plurium*. Furthermore in a similar context of Proposition II.4 (cf. lines 96 *et seq.*) all of the manuscripts have *pauciorum*. See also note 1 to Proposition I.4.

polyg. body. Therefore motion of hyp. / motion of circum. A < motion of hyp. / motion of sides of the polygon, which is impossible, for it is greater.

If the ratio of the motion of the cone to the motion of sphere OB is less than [the ratio of] the motion of the hypotenuse to the motion of circumference B, let the motion of the cone be to the motion of sphere OA as the motion of the hypotenuse is to the motion of circumference B. Therefore let motion of cone / motion of sphere OA > motion of cone / motion of polyg. body. But motion of hyp. / motion of [circum.] B > motion of hyp. / motion of sides. Therefore motion of hyp. / motion of [circum.] B < motion of cone / motion of polyg. body. So, therefore, motion of cone / motion of [sphere] OA < motion of cone / motion of polyg. body. Therefore [the first ratio is not greater] than the second [as was hypothesized above][1].

So therefore [the ratio of the motion of the cone to the motion of the sphere is] neither more nor less [than the ratio of the hypotenuse to the motion of the circumference.]. It is therefore equal [to it].

So ends the Book of Gerard on Motion.

---

[1] That is, in the second sentence of this paragraph it was hypothesized that "motion of cone / motion of sphere OA > motion of cone / motion of polyg. body."

PART II

The *Liber philotegni* of Jordanus de Nemore

CHAPTER 1

Jordanus and the *Liber philotegni*

In the first part of this volume I mentioned how often the *Liber de motu* of Gerard of Brussels appeared in manuscripts with the works of Jordanus de Nemore and I noted that several propositions of Jordanus' *Liber philotegni* concerning relationships between inscribed and circumscribed regular polygons found resonance in the *Liber de motu.*[1] I also said that there is no conclusive evidence as to which author preceded the other, though I should at least suppose that the *Liber philotegni* preceded the *Liber de motu.* The most sensible conclusion in the face of the scanty evidence that now exists is that both authors lived about the same time in the early thirteenth century. If we reject the identification of Jordanus de Nemore with Jordanus of Saxony, the second general of the Dominican Order, as I still feel we should,[2] then

---

[1] See Part I, Chapter 1, text above n. 17.

[2] I shall not repeat here the evidence for and against this identification. Considerations of Jordanus' identity and date can be found in the following works: M. Curtze, ed., *Jordani Nemorarii Geometria vel de triangulis libri iv* (Thorn, 1887), p. iv (and especially n. 4); E. A. Moody and M. Clagett, *The Medieval Science of Weights* (Madison, Wisc., 1952, 2nd pr. 1960), pp. 121–23; M. Clagett, *The Science of Mechanics in the Middle Ages* (Madison, 1959, 3rd pr. 1979), pp. 72–73; E. Grant, "Jordanus de Nemore," *Dictionary of Scientific Biography,* Vol. 7 (New York, 1973), pp. 171–79; R. B. Thomson, "Jordanus de Nemore and the University of Toulouse," *The British Journal for the History of Science,* Vol. 7 (1974), pp. 163–65; B. B. Hughes, O.F.M., "Biographical Information on Jordanus de Nemore To Date," *Janus,* Vol. 62 (1975), pp. 151–56; G. Molland, "Ancestors of Physics," *History of Science,* Vol. 14 (1976), pp. 64–67 (whole article, pp. 54–75); R. B. Thomson, *Jordanus de Nemore and the Mathematics of Astrolabes: De plana spera* (Toronto, 1978), pp. 1–17; and B. B. Hughes, O.F.M., ed., *Jordanus de Nemore: De numeris datis* (Berkeley, Los Angeles, London, 1981), pp. 1–4. The only really new information bearing on Jordanus' life in the recent works is that provided by Thomson, who showed in his article of 1974 that Jordanus can no longer be said to have taught at Toulouse, as Curtze asserted and one might reasonably (but—alas—falsely) conclude from the catalogue description of folios 177r–185v of MS Dresden C.80 (repeated in Thomson, "Jordanus de Nemore and the University of Toulouse," p. 164): "Bl. 177–185′. Jordanus (13. Jahr.), de minuciis libri duo . . . Bl. 181. et ad instructionem tholose studentium sufficiat hec dixisse. Bl. 185′. Explicit 2us liber de M^{ys} Jordani." Thomson indicates that, though indeed folio 185r has the quoted colophon, the tract on algorism contained in folios 177r–81r is quite distinct from the tracts on that subject attributed to Jordanus, and hence it is unlikely that the colophon was written by Jordanus. I still stick to my belief that Jordanus de Nemore and Jordanus of Saxony are not identical because the name "de Nemore" never appears in any of the Saxon's writings or in any sources pertaining to him,

we are left with only the vaguest sort of evidence of Jordanus' chronology. Certainly, like Gerard, and for the same reasons, he lived before (probably considerably before) 1260, the date before which Richard of Fournival died, for the *Biblionomia* of Fournival contains several references to the works of Jordanus.[3] It is also obvious that Jordanus de Nemore lived and wrote after the translating activities of the twelfth century, more specifically after the translations of the *Elements,* of the *De similibus arcubus,* and of the *Liber de ysoperimetris,* all of which he cited by title as we shall see. Furthermore Jordanus' *Liber philotegni* made specific reference to the *Liber de curvis superficiebus,* which, if attributable to the canonist John of Tinemue, would have to have been composed toward the end of the twelfth or the beginning of the thirteenth century.[4] But this does not move us along toward any hard evidence of Jordanus' career, as we shall see when we examine briefly Jordanus' use of his sources below. Since at least once he is cited in a thirteenth century manuscript as *Magister Iordanus,*[5] it could be that Jordanus was a master of arts at Paris or some other early university.

Whatever the details of his life are, there can be no doubt that Jordanus was a first-rate and greatly influential mathematician, the author of at least six works (most of them extant in more than one version):[6] (1) *Liber philotegni,* with a longer version *Liber de triangulis Iordani* composed by someone else; (2) *Elementa super demonstrationem ponderum* (also known as *Elementa de ponderibus*), a work surely by Jordanus, which spawned many other versions,

---

and vice versa. Further, in none of the writings of Jordanus of Saxony do we find any interest displayed in mathematics. But it seems pointless to go over the same evidence, and hence I refrain from treating the question once more.

[3] A. Birkenmajer, *Études d'histoire des sciences et de la philosophie du moyen âge,* (Wrocław, etc., 1970), pp. 166 (items 43, 45), 167 (items 47, 48), 172–173 (item 59). Cf. the discussion Part I, Chap. 1, above nn. 11–15.

[4] See Part I, Chap. 1, above n. 30.

[5] For example, see G. Eneström, "Über die 'Demonstratio Jordani de algorismo'," *Bibliotheca mathematica,* 3. Folge, Vol. 7 (1906–07), p. 25, quoting MS Berlin, Lat. Q.510 (our MS *B*).

[6] The best listing of the works of Jordanus de Nemore (with manuscripts and editions) is that of R. B. Thomson, "Jordanus de Nemore: Opera," *Mediaeval Studies,* Vol. 38 (1976), pp. 97–144. Editions that have appeared since the publication of that article are Thomson's *Jordanus de Nemore and the Mathematics of the Astrolabe* and Hughes' *Jordanus de Nemore: De numeris datis,* both of which books have been cited in note 2 above. Now with my editions of the *Liber philotegni* and the *Liber de triangulis Iordani* here in this volume, the only works of Jordanus left without modern editions are the *De elementis arismetice artis,* and the *Demonstratio de algorismo* (with *de minutiis*) or its perhaps earlier version, the "Communis et consuetus" (with its accompanying *Tractatus minutiarum*). Of the latter we have only the partial editions given by G. Eneström in "Ueber die 'Demonstratio Jordani de algorismo,' " *Bibliotheca mathematica,* 3. Folge, Vol. 7 (1906–07), pp. 24–37, in "Über ein dem Jordanus Nemorarius zugeschriebene kurze Algorismusschrift," *ibid.,* Vol. 8 (1907–08), pp. 135–53, and in "Das Bruchrechnen des Jordanus Nemorarius," *ibid.,* Vol. 14 (1913–14), pp. 41–54. I am not completely convinced by Eneström's argument that the "Communis et consuetus" and *Tractatus minutiarum* precede the *Demonstratio de algorismo* and the *Demonstratio de minutiis,* and I believe it would be prudent to wait until these works have been edited from all of the manuscripts before deciding upon their relationships.

including the brilliant *Liber de ratione ponderis,* whose authorship by Jordanus I am inclined to accept though this is doubted by Brown;[7] (3) "Communis et consuetus" (followed by a *Tractatus minutiarum*) that may have stimulated a longer but closely similar form known as the *Demonstratio de algorismo* (followed by a *Demonstratio de minutiis*); (4) *De elementis arismetice artis;* (5) *De numeris datis;* and (6) the *Demonstratio de plana spera,* in three versions. A seventh work entitled *Praeexercitamina* was mentioned by Jordanus in his *Elementa de ponderibus* but has not yet been properly identified or located.[8] Still other works appear to have been doubtfully or falsely attributed to Jordanus.[9]

Our concern in this volume is of course with the *Liber philotegni* and its longer version, the *Liber de triangulis Iordani,* because of the overtones of Archimedean geometry that we find in those works. It is my opinion, which I shall argue at length in Part III of this volume, that the longer work was not composed by Jordanus. That the *Liber philotegni* was the earlier, genuine work of Jordanus is certain. It is clearly earlier than the *Liber de triangulis Iordani* since its earliest manuscript is datable before the death of Richard de Fournival, it being mentioned in the latter's *Biblionomia,* as I have said,[10] and no manuscript of the *Liber de triangulis Iordani* is nearly so early. Furthermore, it will be shown in the next part of the volume that the *Liber de triangulis Iordani* is dependent on the *Liber philotegni* and in effect refers to it. All of its five manuscripts bear Jordanus' name.[11] This is by no means a certain piece of evidence, since all but one of the manuscripts of the longer version that include the beginning of the tract also bear the name of Jordanus and it seems not to have been composed by Jordanus. Fortunately we have one piece of quite conclusive evidence of Jordanus' authorship of the *Liber*

---

[7] J. E. Brown, "The Scientia de Ponderibus in the Later Middle Ages," thesis, University of Wisconsin, 1967, pp. 64–66.

[8] See Moody and Clagett, *Medieval Science of Weights,* pp. 132, 379–80.

[9] See Thomson, "Jordanus de Nemore: Opera," pp. 111–12, 124–33. The only one of these spurious attributions that is of interest to my investigations here is the version of the *De ysoperimetris* attributed in Vienna, Nat. Bibl. cod. 5203 to Jordanus, from which I have quoted a passage in Appendix III.A below. H. L. L. Busard, "Der Traktat *De isoperimetris,* der unmittelbar aus dem Griechischen ins Lateinische übersetzt worden ist," *Mediaeval Studies,* Vol. 42 (1980), p. 65, notes that Proposition V.28 of the Campanus Version of the *Elements* (which is not in any version prior to the Campanus Version) is cited in the so-called Jordanian version of the *De ysoperimetris,* and hence he reasoned that this citation made the ascription to Jordanus rather dubious, for Campanus' version of the *Elements* was almost certainly composed after Jordanus had completed his work. In Vol. 3 of *Archimedes in the Middle Ages,* p. 349n, I also had expressed doubt about this ascription to Jordanus. Finally we should note that the text in which the Campanus proposition is cited (see Appendix III.A below) is present in the Vienna manuscript of Regiomontanus alone and in none of the other copies that may be related to it. Hence it seems better to call the text I have edited in Appendix III.A the "Version of Regiomontanus" or at least the "Pseudo-Jordanian Version" rather than the "Version of Jordanus".

[10] See above, Part I, Chap. 1, text over notes 11–15.

[11] See the text of the *Liber philotegni* below, variant readings to lines 1–2 of the Title and Introduction.

philotegni from a citation in Jordanus' *Elementa de ponderibus* to the *Liber philotegni* in the first person: "sicut demonstravimus in *Philotegni*."[12] Incidentally I have adopted the reading *Philotegni* (as opposed to *Phylotegni, Phyloteigni,* or *Philothegni*) because of Jordanus' reference and because of the reference in the colophon of the earliest and most complete manuscript (see the preceding footnote and the text of the colophon below). Needless to add, *Philotegni* is a better transliteration of the Greek word (see below). Another outside reference is made to the *Liber philotegni* in an observation that accompanied some manuscripts of the fragment of Version I of Hero's theorem for the area of a triangle in terms of its sides, a fragment I have already published in Volume 1, Appendix IV: "Haec est pars Phyloteigni et debet ei subiungi."[13] In fact the observation is incorrect, for none of the manuscripts of either the *Liber philotegni* or the longer *Liber de triangulis Iordani* have made this proposition a part of the text. The source of the comment may have been a work called *Liber de triangulis datis,* which in all likelihood consisted in a reworking of Propositions 14, 18–20, 22 and 23 of the *Liber philotegni* together with the fragment of Version I of Hero's theorem that was no doubt translated from the Arabic.[14]

Though I shall examine the mathematical content of the *Liber philotegni* in considerable detail in the next chapter, I shall point here to some of the works which Jordanus used in composing his geometrical work. Certainly it is evident that Jordanus had a good command of the *Elements* of Euclid, which is everywhere understood even when not cited. There are only ten specific citations to Euclid (as compared to dozens in the longer version).

---

[12] Moody and Clagett, *Medieval Science of Weights,* Prop. E.5, pp. 134, 136. Note that Moody on p. 326, gives "declaratum est" as a variant reading for "declaravimus" in MS Oxford, Bodleian Library Auct. F.5.28. Since Moody had used only three manuscripts for his text of the *Elementa* this alternate reading caused me some unease. But I checked the Bodleian manuscript and found that in fact it too had "declaravimus." Indeed I checked the passage in eight other manuscripts of the *Elementa* and I found that the reading was always "declaravimus." The *Liber philotegni* was also cited earlier in Prop. E.2 of the *Elementa* (*ed. cit.,* p. 130) but there the citation is "sicut declaratum est in philotegni," which of course offers no evidence for the determination of Jordanus' authorship of the *Liber philotegni.* Incidentally, it is of interest that on the nineteen occasions of the use of *philotegni* which I examined in the manuscripts that include these citations of the *Liber philotegni* I found the form *philotegni* used thirteen times, *philothegni* twice, and *filotegni* three times, and in one manuscript the title was omitted in the reference in Prop. E.5. (Note that in checking these references I used a tenth manuscript which included Prop. E.2 but not Prop. E.5.)

[13] MS Vat. reg. lat. 1261, 57v; MS. Edinburgh, Crawford Libr. of the Royal Observatory (our MS *E*), Cr. I.27, 24r. Compare MS Utrecht, Bibl. Univ. 725, 107V: "hec sequens conclusio est pars phylotegni et debet ei addi" and on 108r: "Trianguli mensurandi Regula Philotegni Tractatusque de proportionibus mixtorum per pondera finiuntur." And see MS Venice, Bibl. Naz. Marc. VIII, 8, 7r: "Philotegni (?) propositio de trianguli area."

[14] For the first two propositions of the anonymous *Liber de triangulis datis* and their probable relationship with the *Liber philotegni,* see below Appendix III.A. The third proposition is Version I of the theorem of Hero for the area of a triangle in terms of its sides, which I have just mentioned.

All but three of them specify the book and proposition (and two citations of Euclid, Prop. I.4, in Proposition 62 are probably by a commentator rather than by Jordanus). The reader will readily find the Euclidian citations in Propositions 7, 9, 18, 19, 27, 28, 34, and 62, and he will notice that they all lie within the first six books of the *Elements*. The practice of occasionally omitting the proposition numbers (as was done in three of the citations) is somewhat reminiscent of the even more radical practice of Gerard of Brussels in his *Liber de motu,* who, as I said in the first chapter of Part I, though having an extensive understanding of the *Elements* nevertheless failed to cite the *Elements* at all. While not quite so sparing, Jordanus probably also felt that his reader had sufficient knowledge of the *Elements* so that only rarely need reference be made to it. Two of the Euclidian citations, those in Propositions 18 and 28, paraphrase the enunciations but not closely enough for us to decide which of the various twelfth-century versions of the *Elements* was being used, though I lean toward the belief that the second of these paraphrases was made from either the Adelard II or Hermann of Carinthia Versions.[15]

As I also indicate in the next chapter and in Appendix III.A below, Jordanus, somehow or other, had knowledge of several propositions from the *Liber divisionum* of Euclid, perhaps through the now lost translation of Gerard of Cremona or possibly through some fragments of that work translated from the Arabic. Jordanus may also have learned in part from this work how to manipulate the terms of ratios that are related to each other as greater or lesser ratios, as for example the consequence of manipulating the terms by "conjunction" or by "disjunction". Hence it seems likely that this lost version of Gerard's translation of Euclid's *Liber divisionum* may have been quite influential in the development of Jordanus' mathematical competence. It could also be that Jordanus absorbed some of the knowledge of Euclid's *Book of Divisions* from the *Liber embadorum* of Savasorda (Abraham bar Ḥiyya), translated in 1145,[16] though, as the passages given below in Appendix III.A show, Savasorda's treatment of these problems is quite distinct from that of Jordanus.

In addition to his knowledge of the two above-mentioned works of Euclid, we should appreciate that the *Liber de ysoperimetris* played an important role in Jordanus' overall objectives in the *Liber philotegni,* for the citations of it in Propositions 5 and 30 indicate its importance for the development of Jordanus' trigonometric geometry that culminated in the beautiful proof of Proposition 49, as I shall show in the next chapter. Furthermore, the last three propositions (Props. 61–63) are isoperimetric theorems. It has long been known that the *Liber de ysoperimetris* was translated from the Greek.[17]

---

[15] See the translation of the *Liber philotegni* below, Prop. 28, n. 1.

[16] C. H. Haskins, *Studies in the History of Mediaeval Science,* 2nd ed. (Cambridge, Mass., 1927), p. 11.

[17] H. L. L. Busard, "Der Traktat *De isoperimetris,*" pp. 61–88.

Unfortunately neither the name of the translator nor his date is known. Busard sees in it some philological likeness with the anonymous translation of Ptolemy's *Mathematical Syntaxis,* made in Sicily around the year 1160,[18] and he further suggests a "certain similarity" with the *Liber de curvis superficiebus,* a work which, I have reasoned, was translated in the late twelfth or early thirteenth century.[19] But Busard's final opinion is that the *De ysoperimetris* was translated in the last quarter of the twelfth century in Sicily or southern Italy.[20] Unfortunately none of this speculation gives us any conclusive evidence on which to base Jordanus' career.

While I have just indicated that the *Liber de curvis superficiebus,* which Jordanus also specifically cited, is equally uncertain as to date, I should single it out as one of the works which influenced Jordanus, just as it influenced Gerard of Brussels. Not only does Jordanus quote it in the course of the proof of Proposition 29, he also seems to have had his interest in inscribed and circumscribed regular polygons stimulated by it, and it is not accidental that the final propositions of the *Liber philotegni* show Jordanus' concern with such polygons. So we might say that the Archimedean flavor represented by the *Liber philotegni* probably came as much from the *Liber de curvis superficiebus* as it did from the *Liber de ysoperimetris.* But it is true that Jordanus' genuine text appears not to have considered problems of quadrature where use would be made of the geometry of regular polygons that he had established, and so there is no direct citation of the *Liber de mensura circuli.* Still it is not without interest that one of the two manuscripts that contain the whole of the *Liber philotegni,* namely the Bruges manuscript (*Br*), contains the first half of the proof of Proposition 3 of the *Liber de mensura circuli,* which the scribe places after Proposition 46 + 1 before he proceeds to Proposition 47.[21]

Finally we must mention the *Liber de similibus arcubus* of Ametus filius Iosephi (Aḥmad ibn Yūsuf) used by Jordanus in the course of Propositions 29, 32, and 36. Surely this is the work translated by Gerard of Cremona and listed by his associates merely as *De similibus arcubus.*[22] Its propositions certainly became one of the points of departure for Jordanus' treatment of arcs and chords, as we shall see. But once more the fact that Jordanus used this work is not at all useful for fixing the chronology of Jordanus' activity.

As I suggested at the beginning of the chapter and as the succeeding discussion of the works used by Jordanus has tended to confirm, Jordanus's citations are not much help in narrowing the period of composition of the

---

[18] *Ibid.,* p. 63.

[19] Clagett, *Archimedes in the Middle Ages,* Vol. 3, p. 213.

[20] Busard, *op. cit.* in n. 17, p. 64.

[21] See the insertion in the text of the *Liber philotegni* below after Proposition 46.

[22] E. Grant, *A Source Book in Medieval Science* (Cambridge, Mass. 1974), p. 36. The Arabic and Latin texts have been edited in H. L. L. Busard and P. S. van Koningsveld, "Der *Liber de arcubus similibus* des Ahmed ibn Jusuf," *Annals of Science,* Vol. 30 (1973), pp. 381–406. Note that Jordanus always entitles the work as *Liber de similibus arcubus* rather than as *Liber de arcubus similibus.*

Liber philotegni further than "late twelfth through first half of the thirteenth century." One might be tempted to make an argument from silence to help narrow the gap. From the fact that Jordanus seems well acquainted with geometrical works one might expect that he would have known and used Leonardo Fibonacci's *Practica geometrie,* which was composed in 1220.[23] However such does not appear to have been the case. Though the two authors often treat like problems there is no hard evidence that Jordanus knew this work. It is possible, then, that Jordanus did not know or use this work because it had not yet been written. If this is so, it would then mean that the *Liber philotegni* was composed before 1220. But this kind of an argument is treacherous, for we might just as well argue that, because Leonardo does not appear to have employed the *Liber philotegni,* the *Liber philotegni* was not yet written by 1220. So it is best to put little stock in the significance for dating of the apparent diversity between Jordanus' *Liber philotegni* and Leonardo's *Practica geometrie.*

One final topic should be discussed briefly before proceeding to an examination of the mathematical content of the *Liber philotegni.* This concerns the title. The Greek word φιλότεχνος is quite common in the meaning "one attentive to or a lover of some art or arts." Though the Latin term *tegna* for "art" exists in Jordanus' time[24] and though the term *philotechinus* was used by Vitruvius for "technical,"[25] I know of no other medieval usage of *philotegnus.* I would suppose that Jordanus is using the term in the meaning of the Greek word and that the "art" implied by the title "Book of the Lover of the Art" is the art of geometry, though it is not impossible that it simply means "the liberal arts" or even "the technical arts."[26] But without knowledge of Jordanus' source for the term we can say nothing more definite.

---

[23] B. Boncompagni, ed., *Scritti di Leonardo Pisano,* Vol. 2: *Leonardi Pisani Practica geometriae ed opuscoli* (Rome, 1862), p. 1.

[24] R. E. Latham, *Revised Medieval Latin Word-List* (London, 1965), p. 477.

[25] *De re architectura,* Bk. VI, Pref. 4.

[26] In discussing P. Duhem's opinion ("Un ouvrage perdu cité par Jordanus de Nemore: le Philotechnes," *Bibliotheca mathematica,* 3. Folge, Vol. 5 [1904–05], pp. 321–25, and "A propos du φιλότεχνης de Jordanus de Nemore," *Archiv für die Geschichte der Naturwissenschaften und der Technik,* Vol. 1 [1909], pp. 380–84) that the original title of Jordanus' work was a book "Filotegni" or "Philotechnes", G. Eneström ("Über den ursprünglichen Titel der geometrischen Schrift des Jordanus Nemorarius," *Bibliotheca mathematica,* 3. Folge, Vol. 13 [1912–13], pp. 83–84) remarks that against the assumption that "Philotechnes" was Jordanus' original title is the fact that the treatise has very little to do with practical geometry, Eneström thereby assuming that the word "Philotechnes" means the lover of practical geometry. But he gives no evidence from Jordanus' time that the word was to be so interpreted. Incidentally H. Bosmans, "Le 'Philotechnes' de Jordan de Nemore," *Revue des questions scientifiques,* Vol. 83 (Sér. 4, Vol. 3, 1923), p. 54 (full article pp. 52–63), gave the first manuscript evidence to support the view that Jordanus' work was entitled *Liber philotegni* by noting the title and colophon of the Bruges MS (MS *Br* in our *sigla* below). But none of these authors knew certainly that there were two distinct versions of the treatise and that only the first or original version bore the title *Liber philotegni.* Finally, we should note that, though we do not have any precise evidence as to what Jordanus understood by the word *philotegnus,* the author of the longer version *Liber de triangulis Iordani* used the Latin term *ars* by itself with the meaning of "geometric art."

CHAPTER 2

The Mathematical Content of the *Liber philotegni*

According to the title of the oldest manuscript of the *Liber philotegni,* MS *E*, and the colophons of MSS *E* and *Br*, the *Liber philotegni* contains sixty-four propositions. MS *E* in fact has only sixty-three propositions, which are numbered successively. MS *Br* has numbered the propositions through Proposition 46 only. As I note below in a passage given after Proposition 46, that manuscript adds two extra propositions (not in MS *E*) after which follow Propositions 47–63 without proposition numbers. The other three manuscripts (MSS *M*, *Fa*, and *Bu*) contain only Propositions 1–46 of the *Liber philotegni.* The textual significance of these variations in structure and length will be discussed in the next chapter. From the fact that all five of the manuscripts number the propositions successively (at least as far as they go) I deduce that the *Liber philotegni* was not divided into four books, each book with its own proposition numbers, as was surely the case of the longer *Liber de triangulis Iordani,* though the *Liber philotegni* might have been divided into four books with the propositions numbered consecutively throughout the whole work. The contamination of the manuscripts of the *Liber philotegni* by the *Liber de triangulis Iordani* will be examined at some length in the next chapter, but I should like to mention here that one such contamination is found in the opening title of MS *Br: Phylotegni Iordani de triangulis incipit liber primus.* I mention this now simply to point out that the addition of *de triangulis* to the title (presumably taken from the longer version) is not an entirely appropriate designation of either the contents of the *Liber philotegni* or of the *Liber de triangulis Iordani.*[1] The overall objective of the *Liber philotegni* appears to have been the determination and comparison of polygons (regular and irregular): either (1) when inscribed in or circumscribed about

---

[1] This was pointed out by G. Eneström, "Über den ursprünglichen Titel der geometrischen Schrift des Jordanus Nemorarius," *Bibliotheca mathematica,* 3. Folge, Vol. 13 (1912–13), p. 83. Of course Eneström knew only the longer version *Liber de triangulis Iordani,* and it is evident that that work diverges even farther from the subject matter of triangles than does the *Liber philotegni.*

given circles or (2) when inserted in one another, or (3) when possessing equal perimeters. And although there is considerable treatment of triangles in the work, that treatment is, at least in large part, directed to propositions that will serve that objective. I say "at least in large part" because it is evident that some propositions concerning triangles (for example most of those on the division of triangles) are independent of that objective, as my succeeding account will show.

Propositions 1–13 all concern triangles, and primarily their comparison in terms of angles and sides and lines drawn from angles to sides. These propositions thus serve as a basis for a kind of geometric trigonometry of the sort familiar to Archimedes, Zenodorus, Aristarchus, Ptolemy *et al.* Propositions 14–25 concern the division of triangles and in one incidence (Prop. 13) the division of quadrilaterals, and the basic auxiliary propositions necessary for the proof of the propositions concerning divisions. Propositions 26–37 embrace the comparisons of arcal and circular segments cut off by chords, both those within a single circle and those within tangent circles, and extra-circular areas included between tangents and arcs. Finally, Propositions 38–63 concern those theorems and problems which fulfill the overall objective of the treatise in comparing regular and irregular polygons. It should be clear to the reader of the longer *Liber de triangulis Iordani* that, however different the enunciations and proofs of the later tract may be and however eclectic are its additions to Book IV, these four groups are precisely the groups that form the four books of that longer treatise.

Now let us take a more leisurely look at the contents of the tract. The seven definitions (and the commentary on the seventh definition) attempt to characterize as continua the polygonal surfaces that are the objects of this treatise. In the first, continuity is defined as the property of indetermination as to limit with the potentiality of being limited. It is a point that fixes a limit on simple continuity, simple continuity being the continuity possessed by a line. A surface possesses a "double" continuity and a body a "triple" continuity. Continuity may be either "straight" or "curved", which in terms of the kind of planar polygons treated here means that a straight line possessing "straight" continuity has a simple (or one-dimensional) medium between any two points of the straight line but that a curved line (in a plane) possessing "curved" continuity has a medium between any two points in the curve that can only be described in two dimensions. An angle is produced by a discontinuity of two continua that come together in a single limit. Finally a figure (a plane figure is meant) is a form that arises from the quality or character of its limiting lines and from the method of applying these lines (i.e. their angular application). The examples of figures given are largely those of the treatise: those contained by curved lines (in this tract, circles), those by curved and straight lines (here segments of circles), those by straight lines and two or more curved lines, and those by three or more straight lines (i.e. polygons).

The first four propositions are auxiliary theorems concerning triangles. The first tells us that if the line drawn from an angle to its opposite base is equal to half of that base, then the angle from which it is drawn is a right angle. The second declares that in an isosceles triangle a line drawn within the triangle from the angle included by the equal sides to the base is less than either of the equal sides, but if it is drawn to the base extended, that is outside of the triangle, then it will be greater than each of the equal sides. On the other hand, according to the third proposition, if the triangle is not isosceles, the line descending to the base will always be shorter than the larger side but may be equal to, greater than, or less than the shorter side. Finally, the fourth indicates that in a triangle that is not isosceles a line drawn from the angle included by the unequal sides to the middle of the base will form with the longer side the smaller angle. The proofs given by Jordanus are elementary and need no comment.

The fifth proposition is an exceedingly important proposition, since it is one of the main propositions in the basic geometric trigonometry found in Jordanus' work. Jordanus asserts: "If in a right [triangle] a line is drawn from one of the remaining angles to the base, the ratio of the angle farther from the right angle to the angle closer to the right angle is less than the ratio of its base to the base of the other." Jordanus does not give a proof but cites the demonstration in the anonymous *Liber de ysoperimetris*, the work translated from the Greek which I mentioned in the preceding chapter. Indeed the proof of Jordanus' proposition is included in the course of the first proposition of that work (for the Latin text and other details of that work, consult Appendix III.A below):

> But that line *gt* has a greater ratio to *tk* than angle *gzt* has to angle *kzt* [see Fig. Ap.III.A.1] has been demonstrated by Theon in the commentary to the *Small Astronomy*. Nevertheless it will now be demonstrated. With the center at *z* and with radius *zk* let arc *mkn* of a circle be described and let *zt* be extended to *n*. Therefore, since *gk* is to *kt* as triangle *gkz* is to triangle *kzt*, while straight line *gk* has a greater ratio to *kt* than sector *mkz* has to sector *zkn* and conjunctively, and sector is to sector as angle is to angle, therefore *gt* has a greater ratio to *tk* than has angle *gzt* to angle *kzt*.

It is obvious that if the conjunctive operation had not been performed the conclusion would have been the converse of that of Jordanus' Proposition 5: *gk* / *kt* > angle *gzk* / angle *kzt*. The part of the proof that is not immediately evident is the statement that *gk* / *kt* > sector *mkz* / sector *zkn*. But support is supplied by a marginal note in one of the best manuscripts (our MS *O*) of the *Liber de ysoperimetris* (see variant reading to line 6 of the text given in Appendix III.A): "since triangle *gzk* is greater than sector *mzk* and triangle *kzt* is less than sector *kzm*; see V.8 [of Euclid]."

A later version of the *Liber de ysoperimetris*, which bears the name of Jordanus, but which I have labeled the "Pseudo-Jordanian Version", gives the whole proof spelled out in detail (again see Appendix III.A for the Latin text):

> But that *ac* / *fc* > angle *aec* / angle *fec* is obvious as follows [see Fig. Ap.III.A.2]:
> For with the circle made in center *e* according to the quantity of radius *ef*, the

circle will cut *ae*; let it be in *o*. And it will cut *ec* extended, and let that be in *p*. So one sector, namely *oef*, is a part of triangle *aef*. Therefore triangle *aef* / triangle *fec* > sector *oef* / triangle *fec*, by V.8 [of Euclid]. But sector *oef* / triangle *fec* > sector *oef* / sector *fep*, by the second part of V.8. Therefore *a fortiori* triangle *aef* / triangle *fec* > sector *oef* / sector *fep*. Therefore, conjunctively by V.28 [of Euclid], triangle *aec* / triangle *fec* > sector *oep* / sector *fep*. But sector *oep* / sector *fep* = angle *aec* / angle *fec*. Therefore triangle *aec* / triangle *fec* > angle *aec* / angle *fec*. But triangle *aec* / triangle *fec* = *ac* / *fc*, by VI.1 [of Euclid] and the conjunctive procedure. Therefore *ac* / *fc* > angle *aec* / angle *fec*, which was to be proved finally.

As I have noted in Appendix III.A where I give the main Latin texts, essentially the same proof would have been available to Jordanus in the text of the *Optics* of Euclid, either in the translation from the Greek entitled *Liber de visu* or in the translation by Gerard of Cremona from the Arabic entitled *Liber de aspectibus,* and also in Gerard of Cremona's translation of Ptolemy's *Almagest.* Therefore, with so many versions of the proof available, it is not surprising that Jordanus, after noting that the proof was to be found in the *Liber de ysoperimetris,* did not bother to give the proof (in fact, giving only the first step of the proof, namely the drawing of the arc centered in the terminus of one of the sides including the right angle and then following this with a mere repetition in different terms of the enunciation). It is also not surprising that, with so many versions of the proof available, the scribe of manuscript *Fa*, who had a penchant for additions, should add a proof that is essentially like those I have already discussed (see the variant reading to lines 10–11 of the text of Proposition 5 below). We would also expect to see Witelo (writing after 1270) present a proof of such a useful proposition in his *Perspectiva*, where he adopts almost verbatim Jordanus' enunciation and follows it with a version of the proof that goes back to the *Liber de ysoperimetris* (see Appendix III.A for the Latin text of Witelo's proposition). Finally in connection with the proof of Proposition 5, the reader should note that the scribe of manuscript *Bu* substituted an entirely different (but fallacious) proof for Jordanus' lean comments (see footnote one of the English translation of Proposition 5).

Before passing on to Proposition 6, I should remind the reader that Proposition 5, or rather its conjunctive extension that is the object of the proofs in the *Liber de ysoperimetris,* Euclid's *Optics,* and in the *Almagest,* was assumed, without proof, in the general form that we may modernize as tan *a* / tan *b* > *a* / *b*, when *a* is the greater angle and both are less than 90°, by Archimedes in his *Sandreckoner*,[2] and in a special case by Aristarchus in his *On the Sizes and Distances of the Sun and Moon.*[3] Both of those authors

[2] Archimedes, *Opera omnia cum commentariis Eutocii,* 2nd ed., Vol. 2 (Leipzig, 1913), pp. 230, line 26–232, line 3.

[3] T. L. Heath, *Aristarchus of Samos, The Ancient Copernicus* (Oxford, 1913), "Aristarchus on the Sizes and Distances of the Sun and Moon. Text, Translation, and Notes," p. 366, lines 6–8, and also n. 1.

assumed this relationship without proof; but presumably neither felt it necessary to prove it because of the existence of a proof in Euclid's *Optics*. Incidentally the latter work and Aristarchus' tract were part of the collection called *Little Astronomy* that the anonymous author of the *Liber de ysoperimetris* designated (perhaps falsely) as the object of a commentary by Theon [of Alexandria] in which the key proposition we are discussing was proved. Of course neither the work of Archimedes nor that of Aristarchus was available in Latin to Jordanus, or indeed until the Renaissance. Still I mention these early references to the theorem to reinforce what I said earlier, namely that when Jordanus put forth Proposition 5 as fundamental for his trigonometric geometry he was doing the same thing that Archimedes and other Greek mathematicians were doing. We shall see how Jordanus uses this proposition later.

Proposition 6 is clearly a consequence of Proposition 5, and will be useful later in Proposition 36. It tells us that "In a triangle whose two sides are unequal, if from the angle [included by these sides] a perpendicular is drawn, the ratio of the segment of the base cut off between the perpendicular and the longer side to the remaining [segment of the base] will be greater than the ratio of angle to angle," the angles being those opposite the base segments that are formed by the perpendicular and each of the sides of the triangle. The important element of the proof is the extension by conjunction of the ratios of Proposition 5: "Therefore, since $AE / ED >$ angle ABE / angle EBD by the preceding [proposition], and because $ED = CD$ and angle $EBD =$ angle CBD, so by conjunction $AD / CD >$ angle ABD / angle CBD" [see Fig. P.6]. An important methodological point that may be made here is that Jordanus from here onward often uses the conjunctive and disjunctive manipulations of ratios in expressions that indicate "greater-than" or "less-than" relationships between ratios. These procedures are designated by Jordanus as *coniunctim* and *disiunctim,* and appear in other literature as *coniunctim* and *divisim,* or *composite* and *separate,* or *componendo* and *separando,* or *componendo* and *dividendo.* Thus the reader should realize that the "conjunction" of a ratio (or the "composition" of a ratio) is the procedure of going from a / b to $(a + b) / b$, and the "disjunction" or "separation" of a ratio is the procedure of going from a / b to $(a - b) / b$. Thus the procedures being adopted by Jordanus may be represented in modern formulation as follows: when $a / b \gtreqless c / d$, then $(a + b) / b \gtreqless (c + d) / d$ and $(a - b) / b \gtreqless (c - d) / d$. He also silently uses other auxiliary theorems that assert inversive, permutative, and cross-multiplicative manipulations of ratios in "greater-than" and "less-than" expressions. Such manipulations were confined to proportions in the *Elements* of Euclid, but in their expanded usage some of them appear as auxiliary propositions in the *Liber divisionum* of Euclid,[4] and they are often

---

[4] R. C. Archibald, *Euclid's Book on Divisions of Figures* (Cambridge, 1915), pp. 58–60 for Propositions 23–25. See also the historical excursus on the history of these and other auxiliary propositions, pp. 55–57, n. 111. I should note that Campanus added such auxiliary propositions

used by the later Greek geometers, as well as by Jordanus in his *Arithmetica* and Campanus in Book V of his version of the *Elements* of Euclid (again see note 4).

Pursuing further the comparison of angles and sides of triangles, Jordanus in Proposition 7 tells us that if two triangles are constructed on the same base between parallel lines, the one having the longer of the two intersecting sides will have the smaller vertical angle. Or, if we put it in terms of Fig. P.7, Jordanus shows that the superior angle *H* of triangle *EHF* is less than the superior angle *G* of triangle *EGF* if side *HF* is greater than side *EG*. The proof is neat and may be easily followed with the help of my notes to the English translation. Here I limit myself to noting that the most interesting part of the proof is Jordanus' assumption of point *L* such that *FK / KE*

to Book V in his version of the *Elements* (Propositions V.26–V.30, V.33, as given in New York, Columbia University, Plimpton MS 156, 47r–48r, 48v; cf. Euclid, *Elementorum geometricorum libri xv* [Basel, 1546], pp. 134–36): "[26] Si fuerint quatuor quantitates proportio prime ad secundam quam tertie ad quartam, erit conversim e contrario secunde ad primam minor quam quarte ad tertiam. . . . [27] Si fuerint quatuor quantitates maior proportio prime ad secundam quam tertie ad quartam, erit permutatim maior proportio prime ad tertiam quam secunde ad quartam. . . . [28] Si fuerint quatuor quantitates quarum prime ad secundam sit maior proportio quam tertie ad quartam, erit quoque coniunctim maior proportio prime et secunde ad secundam quam tertie et quarte ad quartam. . . . [29] Si fuerint quatuor quantitates quarum prime et secunde ad secundam sit maior proportio quam tertie et quarte ad quartam, erit quoque disiunctim proportio prime ad secundam maior quam tertie ad quartam. . . . [30] Si fuerint quatuor quantitates quarum prime et secunde ad secundam sit maior proportio quam tertie et quarte ad quartam, erit eversim e contrario minor proportio prime et secunde ad primam quam tertie et quarte ad tertiam. . . . [33] Si fuerit proportio totius ad totum maior quam abscisi ad abscisum, erit residui ad residuum maior proportio quam totius ad totum. . . ." Indeed Jordanus had earlier included some of these propositions in his *Arithmetica* (Propositions II.11–II.15 in MS Paris, BN lat. 16644, 10r–11r, cf. *In hoc opere contenta: Arithmetica decem libris demonstrata. . . . Jordani Nemorarii . . . Elementa Arithmetica cum demonstrationibus Jacobi Fabri Stapulensis* etc. (Paris, 1514, a repr. of 1496), sig. [a vi recto-verso]): "XI. Si fuerit proportio primi ad secundum maior quam tertii ad quartum, erit secundi ad primum minor proportio quam quarti ad tertium. . . . XII. Si fuerit proportio primi ad secundum maior quam tertii ad quartum, erit primi ad tertium maior quam secundi ad quartum. . . . XIII. Si fuerit proportio totius ad totum maior quam detracti ad detractum, erit residui ad residuum maior proportio quam totius ad totum. . . . XIV. Si vero detracti ad detractum fuerit maior proportio quam totius ad totum, erit residui ad residuum minor proportio quam totius ad totum. . . . XV. Si primi ad secundum fuerit maior proportio quam tertii ad quartum, erit primi et secundi ad secundum maior proportio quam tertii et quarti ad quartum, ad primum vero minor quam tertii et quarti ad tertium. . . ." See also Prop. II.27 of the *Arithmetica*, fol. 13r: "XXVII. Si proportio primi ad secundum maior quam tertii ad quartum, qui ex primo in quartum producatur maior est secundo producto ex secundo in tertium. Quod si productus maior fuerit, et proportio primi ad secundum maior erit. . . ." (*cf. ed. cit.* sig. [a vii verso]). This proposition is not among Campanus' additions. For convenience we may represent the propositions from the *Arithmetica* in modern form as follows. II.11. If $a / b > c / d$, then $b / a < d / c$. II.12. If $a / b > c / d$, then $a / c > b / d$. II.13. If $a / b > c / d$, with c and d parts of a and b respectively, then $(a - c) / (b - d) > a / b$. II.14. If $c / d > a / b$, with c and d parts of a and b respectively, then $(a - c) / (b - d) < a / b$. II.15. If $a / b > c / d$, then $(a + b) / b > (c + d) / d$, and $(a + b) / a < (c + d) / c$. II.27. If $a / b > c / d$, then $a \cdot d > b \cdot c$; and conversely, if $a \cdot d > b \cdot c$, then $a / b > c / d$.

= *EK* / *KL*. With this assumption and with line *GL* drawn, triangle *LGK* has been made similar to triangle *EHK* so that angle *EHK* = angle *LGK* and hence angle *EHF* is less than angle *EGF*. Proposition 8 follows directly from Proposition 7, and from it we learn that if we have triangles on the same base between parallel lines, the one that is isosceles has the largest superior angle, and, further, the more removed that superior angle is from the superior angle of another triangle the more the superior angle of the isosceles triangle exceeds the superior angle of the other triangle. In short, Jordanus shows [see Fig. P.8] that superior angle *B* of isosceles triangle *ABC* is greater than superior angle *D* of any other triangle *ADC* on the same base whose sides are unequal; and in addition he shows that superior angle *D* of triangle *ADC* whose superior angle is farther removed from angle *B* than is superior angle *E* of triangle *AEC* is less than *E* and so is exceeded more by *B* than *E* is exceeded by *B*.

Proposition 9 is a particularly fine proposition with a very nice proof. It tells us that if we have two triangles that are equal in area and have one equal angle, the triangle that has the longest of the four sides including the equal angles of the two triangles will have the greater perimeter. If we consult Fig. P.9, we see then that Jordanus proves that the perimeter of triangle *ABC* is greater than that of triangle *DEF* when the areas of the two triangles are equal, angle *B* = angle *E*, and side *AB* is longer than each of sides *BC*, *DE*, and *FE*. From Adelard-Euclid VI.14 (=Gr. VI.15) we know that the sides including the equal angles are reciprocally proportional, and since *AB* is greater than *DE* and *EF*, it is evident that *BC* is less than each of those sides. And so Jordanus is able to extend *ED* to *G* so that *EG* = *BA* and is able to cut *EF* at *H* so that *EH* = *BC*. Hence triangle *EHG* has been made congruent to triangle *BCA*. Thus the proposition will easily follow if we can show that *GH* > *DF*, that is, that *AC* > *DF*. This Jordanus does by showing that *GH* / *DF* = *LH* / *LD*. Now if *LH* > *LD*, then *GH* > *DF*, and since by Proposition V.25 of the *Elements* (*AB* + *BC*) > (*DE* + *EF*), the proposition would follow. But *LH* is greater than *LD*, since if it is taken as equal to or less than *LD*, contradictions would ensue. Incidentally, Proposition 7 is used here in developing the second of these contradictions. As we shall see, Proposition 9 will play a key role in the proof of one of Jordanus' final isoperimetric propositions, namely Proposition 61.

Proposition 10 compares the sums of the sides of the triangles on the same base between parallel lines whose vertical angles were compared in Proposition 8. Here we are told that the sum of the sides of the isosceles triangle is less than that of any other such triangle whose sides are unequal, and the closer the vertical angle of such a triangle is to the vertical angle of the isosceles triangle by such an amount less is the excess of the sum of its sides over the sum of the sides of the isosceles triangle. Following Fig. 10a, Jordanus proves that, if triangle *ABC* is isosceles and triangle *ADC* is not but side *AD* > *DC*, then (*AB* + *BC*) < (*AD* + *DC*). With *AB* extended to *G* so that *BG* = *BC*, and *AD* extended to *H* so that *DH* = *DC*, Jordanus shows by a series of angular comparisons that the angle subtended by AH is greater than the angle subtended by AG. From this it follows that AH is greater than AG and thus that $(AB + BC) < (AD + DC)$. Since the triangles are on the same base it also is evident (though this is not stated) that the whole perimeter of triangle ABC is less than the whole perimeter of triangle ADC. Following Fig. 10b, Jordanus proves in the second part that if triangle ABC is not isosceles but its vertical angle is closer to that of the isosceles triangle than is the vertical angle of triangle ADC, then its sum, while still exceeding that of the isosceles triangle by the preceding part of the proposition, exceeds it less than the sum of the sides of triangle ADC whose vertical angle is farther from the isosceles triangle. Though Jordanus states the enunciation as if the ratio of distances of vertical angles from that of the isosceles triangle is the same as that of the excesses of the sums of the sides, all that he really proves is that any one triangle whose vertical angle is farther from that of the isosceles triangle than the vertical angle of another triangle has a sum of sides that is greater than that of the other triangle. Like Proposition 9, Proposition 10 also plays a role in the proof of Proposition 61.

Then follow three propositions concerning the comparison of triangles that we need mention only in passing. Proposition 11 tells us that the ratio of the areas of two triangles on the same base is equal to the ratio of their altitudes, while Proposition 12 holds that in the case of two isosceles triangles whose equal sides are the same, the ratio of that triangle whose base is greater to the other triangle will be less than the ratio of the bases of the triangles. And finally Proposition 13 indicates that in the case of equal triangles their bases are reciprocally proportional to their altitudes. So much then for the first group of propositions concerning triangles.

Moving to the second group of Propositions (Propositions 14–25), the reader will see that Propositions 14–20 are preliminary to or auxiliaries of the propositions on the division of triangles into two and three equal parts and to the division of quadrilaterals into two equal parts (Propositions 21–25). The auxiliary propositions I shall treat briefly, proposition by proposition, referring to the magnitudes that appear in the figures given by Jordanus for each proposition (i.e. Figs. P.14–P.20).

Proposition 14: Given lines AB and BC, to divide AB at H so that AH / $HB = HB$ / BC.

Proposition 15: Given lines AB and BC, to divide AB at E so that $(CB + BE)$ / $BE = BE$ / EA.

Proposition 16: Given lines AB and BC, to divide AB at E so that AE / $EB = EC$ / BC.

Proposition 17: Given lines AB and BC, to divide AB at F so that BC / $AF = (BC + FB)$ / $FB = FC$ / FB.

Proposition 18: Given lines AB and BC such that $BC < \frac{1}{4} AB$, to add to BC (or to its equal BH) a line EH such that EH / $EB = EB$ / AB. The solutions given by Jordanus are of special interest and hence I note their key points. Since BC is given as less than one-fourth AB, Jordanus uses the method of application of areas, referring to Book VI of Euclid (the proposition understood as Adelard-Euclid VI.27 [=Gr. VI.28]), to apply to line AB a rectangle $AEFG$ that is equal to rectangle $ABCD$ but is deficient to a whole rectangle on AB by the square of EB.[5] This then provides him with point E and so allows him to prove the proposition. A second solution commences by joining AB and BC and then drawing a semicircle on AC. Jordanus also draws a semicircle on line AB. At B he erects a perpendicular DB, which is obviously the mean proportional between AB and BC (i.e., $DB^2 = AB \cdot BC$). A perpendicular EG is also erected on the center E of AB. Then line DL is drawn parallel to AB. It will cut semicircumference AGB at point T. Perpendicular TM is dropped on AB and it is obviously the mean proportional between AM and MB (or $TM^2 = AM \cdot MB$). Since $TM = DB$, thus $AB \cdot BC = AM \cdot MB$. But the rectangle $AM \cdot MB$ is equivalent to rectangle $AEFG$ in the first solution,[6] and so Jordanus tells us to proceed as in the first part.

Proposition 19: Given lines AB and BH with AB divided at E so that $EH / EB > EB / AB$, to prove that $BH < \frac{1}{4} AB$.

Proposition 20: Given lines AB and BC with AB cut so that BC is the mean proportional between AE and EB and with a line CD added to line BC so that $CD / BD > BD / AB$, to prove that BD is greater than either AE or BE. Again I note the key point of the proof since it involves application of areas, a technique that Jordanus evidently considered fruitful. By the preceding proposition the assumption that $CD / BD > BD / AB$ guarantees that $BC < \frac{1}{4} AB$. Thus Jordanus may apply to AB rectangle AF equal to rectangle BC and deficient from rectangle AT by square FB. He is then able to show that rectangle $AR >$ rectangle AF. With common area AQ subtracted from each of these rectangles, rectangle $ER >$ rectangle PF. Thus rectangle RT, which is equal to rectangle ER, is greater than rectangle PF. Hence line $RN >$ line PQ. Consequently line $BM >$ line AE; and since $BM = BD$, the proposition follows.

With the preliminary propositions proved, Jordanus now presents three problems (Propositions 21–23) concerned with the bisections of triangles: (1) by a line drawn from any point in any one of the sides, (2) by a line drawn

---

[5] It is of interest to note that the application of area here proposed, namely to apply to AB a rectangle deficient of a rectangle on AB by a square on EB is a special case of the more general application shown in Euclid Gr. VI.28. Jordanus' special case is made an auxiliary proposition in Euclid's *Book of Divisions* (i.e. Proposition 18). See Archibald, *op. cit.* in n. 4, pp. 50–52, and particularly the discussion in note 103. A solution to the application of a rectangle equal to a given area and falling short by a square can be solved without resorting to Euclid Gr. VI.28 by using Euclid II.5 (see T. L. Heath, *Euclid, The Elements*, Vol. 1 [Cambridge, 1926], pp. 383–84). I hardly need point out that the application may not be made if $BC > \frac{1}{4} AB$, though of course it may be made if $BC = \frac{1}{4} AB$, as the author of the longer version points out in Proposition II.5. In both cases where Jordanus uses the application, BC is taken as less than one-fourth AB (see the comments concerning Proposition 20 below).

[6] It is obvious that these rectangles are equivalent, for if BC were greater than one-fourth AB no line TM equal to DB could be dropped from the circumference of the circle to AB, and so no rectangle $AM \cdot BM$ equal to rectangle $AB \cdot BC$ could be found by this method.

from any point outside of the triangle, and (3) by a line drawn from any point inside of the triangle. The solution and its proof for the first case (see Fig. P.21) is exceedingly simple. If the point is in the middle of side *AB* at *E*, then the line drawn to the opposite angle immediately bisects the triangle (by Proposition 13). (This first part of the proof where the given point is assumed to be the midpoint is in fact not put forth as a separate part of the proof by Jordanus, though Jordanus assumes it in the second part of the proof. However, the first part was given separately in the proofs of the proposition found in the works of Savasorda and Leonardo Fibonacci mentioned below and in the *Liber de triangulis Iordani*). If the point is not at the midpoint of *AB* but is at any other point *D* in *AB*, then draw line *DC* and a line *EG* parallel to line *DC*. Draw line *DG*, which intersects *EC* at point *T*. Now tri. *CDE* = tri. *DGC* (since the triangles are on the same base between parallel lines). With the common area subtracted, tri. *ETD* = tri. *GTC*. With each of these equal triangles added to area *ADTC*, then area *ADGC* will equal triangle *AEC*. But tri. *AEC* is one half the given triangle *ABC*, and so line *DG* divides that triangle into two equal parts. As I have shown in Appendix III.A, almost exactly the same proof (but with slightly different lettering) was given by Leonardo Fibonacci, and the enunciation of Jordanus' proposition is essentially that of Proposition 3 of the *Liber divisionum* of Euclid. The source of the proposition could have been the lost translation of Euclid's tract by Gerard of Cremona. I also give in Appendix III.A the proposition with a slightly defective proof that appeared in the *Liber embadorum* of Savasorda.

The solution of the second case, the one presented and proved in Proposition 22 (see Fig. P.22) is more difficult than that of the first case, and Jordanus' proof is ingenious. Let point *D* be outside of the triangle and between the bisectors of the triangle, namely lines *AEF* and *HBL*, for it is evident that if *D* fell on either of these bisectors (or their extensions) then the problem is immediately solved. From *D* draw a line parallel to *AC* and meeting *CB* extended at *G*. Drawing *DC*, we have a triangle *DCG*. (1) Now take a line *MN* such that tri. *DCG* / tri. *AEC* = *CG* / *MN*, tri. *AEC* being half the given triangle *ABC*. (2) By Proposition 14 divide line *CG* at *K* so that *GK* / *KC* = *KC* / *MN*. Then draw *DK* and extend it to meet *AC* in *P*. Triangles *DGK* and *KPC* will be similar, and (3) tri. *DGK* / tri. *KPC* = $(GK / KC)^2$, evidently by Adelard-Euclid VI.17 (=Gr. VI.19), though that proposition is not specifically cited. (4) Then from (2) and (3), it follows that tri. *DGK* / tri. *KPC* = *GK* / *MN*. (5) Then by similar triangles, *GK* / *KC* = *DK* / *KP*. (6) Hence, by (2) and (5), *DK* / *KP* = *KC* / *MN*. (7) But *DK* / *KP* = tri. *DCK* / tri. *CKP*, by disjunction. (8) Therefore, by (6) and (7), *KC* / *MN* = tri. *DCK* / tri. *CKP*. (9) By adding the proportions deduced in (4) and (8), we conclude that (*GK* + *KC*) / *MN* = (tri. *DGK* + tri. *DCK*) / tri. *CKP*, i.e. *CG* / *MN* = tri. *DCG* / tri. *CKP*. (10) Hence, by (1) and (9), tri. *DGC* / tri. *AEC* = tri. *DGC* / tri. *CKP*, i.e. tri. *AEC* = tri. *CKP*. (11) And since triangle *AEC* is one half the given triangle, so also is triangle *CKP*, and the proposition follows. As I have noted in Appendix III.A, the ultimate source of this proposition was no doubt Proposition 26 of the *Liber divisionum* of Euclid, but the proof of the proposition given by Leonardo Fibonacci (and presented in Appendix III.A) is quite distinct from that of Jordanus'. I also note in that appendix that this proposition of Jordanus was apparently closely paraphrased by the unknown compositor of the *Liber de triangulis datis*.

The last case of triangle bisection, namely that given in Proposition 23 (see Fig. P.23), seeks a line drawn from a point within the triangle that bisects the triangle. First let AG and BE be bisectors of the triangle (points G and E being the midpoints of sides BC and CA), between which is included point D. Let FH be drawn through D parallel to AC, and let line BD be drawn. Then let line MN be taken such that BF / MN = tri. BDF / tri. BCE, the latter triangle being half the given triangle ABC. Also let TY be taken such that BF / TY = tri. BFH / tri. BCE. It is clear that $MN > TY$, since tri. FBH / tri. CBE > tri. FBD / tri. CBE, with the consequence that BF / TY > BF / MN. Therefore $BF / BC > BC / MN$. Hence, by Proposition 19, FC < ¼ MN. And by Proposition 18, let line FZ be added to line FC so that $ZF / ZC = ZC / MN$, and so clearly, by Proposition 20, $ZC < CB$, and so Z falls within BC. Now if we draw a line ZD and extend it to K in AB, we have the desired bisector of the triangle.

The proof is quite simple. Since tri. BDF / tri. $DZF = BF / ZF$ (the triangles being on the same base and sides BF and ZF having the same ratio as the altitudes) and since tri. ZFD / tri. $ZCK = ZF / MN$ (as explained in note 3 of the English translation of this proposition), therefore, if we invert the latter proportion and divide the former by it, BF / MN = tri. BDF / tri. ZCK. But by hypothesis BF / MN = tri. BDF / tri. BCE. Therefore tri. ZCK = tri. BCE, the latter being half the given triangle ABC. Hence since ZCK is now proved as half ABC, the solution is demonstrated.

This proposition, as I suggest in Appendix III.A, has its probable origin in Proposition 19 of Euclid's *Liber divisionum*. The proof given by Leonardo Fibonacci, which I include in the appendix, is like the proof of Jordanus in a fundamental way since it too depends on the technique of the application of areas. Still Jordanus' proof has been refined by the prior proof of his Propositions 18–20. Again I direct the reader to the same appendix for the text of Proposition 2 of the anonymous *Liber de triangulis datis*, which was almost surely taken from Jordanus' text of Proposition 23 and includes as subsidiary parts proofs of Jordanus' Propositions 18–20.

In Proposition 24 Jordanus moves to the problem of trisecting a triangle by drawing lines from a point in the triangle to each of the three angles. He simply takes one-third of a side (say DC in Fig. P.24), draws line DE parallel to side AC, bisects that line at G, and finally draws lines from G to each of the three angles. Hence the triangle is trisected. The proof is simple, clear, and needs no comment. As I note below in Appendix III.A, the extant Arabic text of the *Liber divisionum* of Euclid does not contain this proposition. However, the proposition with a somewhat different proof was included in

Savasorda's *Liber embadorum* and Leonardo Fibonacci's *Practica geometrie* (see Appendix III.A for both of these proofs).

The last of the problems concerned with the division of surfaces is Proposition 25 on the bisection of a quadrilateral by a line drawn from one of its angles. Skipping the obvious case of the rectangle, we should mention the general case (see Fig. P.25). The two diagonals of the quadrilateral are *BD* and *AC*, intersecting at *G* so that *GC* > *AG*. From point *C* strike off on *AC* segment *CE* equal to *AG*. Draw *EL* parallel to *BD*. Bisect *LD* at *T* and draw line *BT*, which is the bisector that is sought. If we draw *BL*, this is easily proved as follows. Tri. *DBC* / tri. *LBC* = *DC* / *LC* (since the triangles are on the same base and their sides *DC* and *LC* have the same ratio as their altitudes). Then *DC* / *LC* = *GC* / *CE* = *GC* / *AG*, and *GC* / *AG* = tri. *DBC* / tri. *ABD*. Therefore tri. *DBC* / tri. *LBC* = tri. *DBC* / tri. *ABD*. Therefore tri. *ABD* = tri. *LBC*. But we bisected *LD* at *T* and drew *BT*. Hence if each half of the bisected triangle *DBL* is added to the equal triangles *ABD* and *LBC*, then tri. *CBT* = surf. *TDAB*, and thus we have proved that *BT* is the bisector of the quadrangle. The proof of this proposition given by Leonardo Fibonacci is somewhat different (see the text in Appendix III.A and Fig. Ap. III. A.11), for there the diagonal *bd* is bisected at *z* (and this *z* is also the point of bisection of the segment between *be* and a segment equal to *be*). So we draw a line parallel to *ac* from *z* and it intersects *bc* at *i*. Hence the line drawn from *a* to *i* becomes the bisector of the quadrilateral, which is easily proved. Thus it is obvious that the crucial bisection of the segment takes place on the diagonal in Leonardo's proof while it takes place on a side in Jordanus' proof.

Jordanus at this point begins the group of propositions (Props. 26–37) that are concerned with arcal and circular segments, tangents, segments in circles that are tangent to each other, and areas contained outside of circular arcs by tangents to the arcs. In short we find here a treatment of what we might call the elements of the polygons inscribed in or circumscribed about circles that make up the subject of some of the final group of propositions. Proposition 26 holds that, if there are three parallel chords of decreasing length which cut off equal arcs, the perpendicular distance between the longest and the middle chord is greater than the perpendicular distance between the middle and the shortest chord. It also holds that the longest and the middle chords together cut off a larger circular segment than the middle and shortest chords. The proof is quite simple (see Fig. P.26). It involves the analysis of triangles *ACG* and *CGE* to show that *AG* > *GE* and that angle *CGE* is an obtuse angle. Thus he shows that *ZT* > *ZE*, and the first part of the proposition is proved. No proof is given for the second part. Jordanus says it will be manifest after we have drawn perpendicular *FK*, and thus produced an arrangement on the right side that is symmetrical to the arrangement of the left side. Indeed it is obvious that quadrangles *ACZT* and *BDPK* are greater than triangles *CEZ* and *DPF*, and since the circular segments *AC*, *CE*, *FD*, and *DB* are equal, the total area cut off by lines *AB* and *CD* is greater than the total area cut off by *CD* and *EF*. Proposition 26, it should be realized, was cited by Jordanus in his *Elementa de ponderibus* and played a crucial role in his mistaken idea that in a tilted, equal-arm balance, the weight which is elevated enjoys a theoretical, mechanical advantage that will drive the balance arm to a level position.[7]

From Proposition 27 we learn that if an arc is divided into equal arcs, the sum of the chords subtending the equal arcs is greater than the sum of the chords subtending the arcs of any other division of the original arc. We are further told that if the point of any other division of the arc is closer to the point of equal division, the sum of the chords subtending the arcs produced by the division closer to the equal division is greater than the sum of the chords resulting from any division whose point of division is farther from the point of equal division. This will be clear if we consult Fig. P.27, where *C* is the point of equal division of arc *AB*, and *D* and *E* are the points of other divisions, *E* obviously being farther from *C* than *D*. Triangles *AGC* and *BGD* are similar (since their angles are respectively equal). Further, *AC* > *BD*. Hence *AC* + *GC* > *BD* + *DG*. Then, because of the equality of the ratios of the sides, $(AC + CG) / GA = (BD + DG) / BG$. Hence by the last of the fifth of Euclid, *AC* + *CG* + *GB* > *BD* + *DG* + *GA*, and the first part of the proposition is proved. But the proof of the second part is precisely the same, since *AD* > *BE*. This leads us to the conclusion that *AD* + *BD* > *AE* + *BE*.

To this point we have been concerned with arcs and chords in the same circle. Now we shift to arcs and chords in unequal circles. Proposition 28 asserts that, if equal chords cut arcs from unequal circles, a longer arc will be cut from the smaller circle. The proof is too obvious to pursue. It was this proposition that Jordanus cited in the course of the proof of the fifth proposition of his *Elementa de ponderibus*[8] and a similar proposition is employed in Proposition 11 of the *Speculi almukefi compositio*.[9]

Now in Proposition 29 Jordanus again returns to chords and arcs in a single circle but uses the previous proposition in doing so. Proposition 29 holds that the ratio of arcs cut off by unequal chords in a circle is greater than the ratio of the chords, and the ratio of the segments of the circle cut off by the chords will be greater than the square of the ratio of the chords. Referring to Fig. P.29, we note that the proposition proves first that chord *BC* / chord *DE* < arc *BDC* / arc *DE*, and second that circ. seg. *BCD* / circ. seg. *DE* > $(BC / DE)^2$. The first part is proved as follows. Take line *KL* such that diam. *GH* / line *KL* = chord *BC* / chord *DE*. (1) Describe a circle about *KL* as a diameter, and assume on that circle arc *MN* as similar to arc *BC*,

[7] E. A. Moody and M. Clagett, *The Medieval Science of Weights* (Madison, Wisconsin, 1952; 2nd pr. 1960), p. 130. Cf. M. Clagett, *The Science of Mechanics in the Middle Ages* (Madison, Wisc., 1959; 3rd pr. 1979), pp. 75–77.

[8] Moody and Clagett, *The Medieval Science of Weights,* pp. 134–36.

[9] Clagett, *Archimedes in the Middle Ages,* Vol. 4, p. 157. See also the elaboration of Jordanus' proposition in Francesco Barozzi's *Admirandum problema,* republished in Vol. 4, p. 401.

drawing chord *MN*. By Proposition III of the *Liber de curvis superficiebus*,[10] (2) *GH* / *KL* = circum. / circum. By Proposition 4 of the *De similibus arcubus*,[11] (3) circum. / circum. = arc *BC* / arc *MN*. (4) Then *GH* / *KL* = chord *BC* / chord *MN*, by Proposition 5 of the same work.[12] Now from (4) and (1) together, *DE* = *MN*. Hence by the previous proposition, i.e. Proposition 28, arc *MN* > arc *DE*. By (2), (3), and (4), chord *BC* / chord *MN* = arc *BC* / arc *MN*. Therefore chord *BC* / chord *DE* < arc *BC* / arc *DE*, for arc *BC* / arc *DE* > arc *BC* / arc *MN*. The second part is also easily proved, for circ. seg. *BC* / circ. seg. *MN* = (chord *BC* / chord *MN*)² = (*BC* / *DE*)². But circ. seg. *MN* is greater than seg. *DE*. Therefore circ. seg. *BC* / circ. seg. *DE* > (*BC* / *DE*)², which was to be proved. Perhaps the most important thing for the reader to understand here is that Jordanus has now for the first time specifically had recourse to Archimedean considerations by citing the *Liber de curvis superficiebus*.

Propositions 30, 31, and 32 continue the development of Jordanus' geometric trigonometry. Proposition 30 tells us that if two parallel lines cut a diameter orthogonally, the ratio of the segments of the diameter cut off by these lines will be greater than the ratio of the arcs subtended by the lines. In short, he shows (see Fig. P.30) that *BD* / *GD* > arc *EDC* / arc *HDL*. If we draw lines *EKD* and *EL*, then angle *EDL* is obtuse, since it falls in an arc that is greater than a semicircle. Then Jordanus says that Proposition 5 can be proved for an obtuse angle (as well as for a right angle). Hence if we describe a circle with center *L* on radius *LK*, it can be proved here (as Proposition 5 was proved according to the *Liber de ysoperimetris*) by sectors that *EKD* / *KD* > angle *ELD* / angle *KLD*. Since angle *ELD* / angle *KLD* = arc *ED* / arc *HD*, therefore *ED* / *KD* > arc / arc. But by similar triangles (or as Jordanus says "by parallelity") *ED* / *KD* = *BD* / *GD*. Therefore *BD* / *GD* > arc *ED* / arc *HD*, and so *BD* / *GD* > arc *EDC* / arc *HDL*, the latter arcs being double the former. And so the proposition is proved. It is worth reminding the reader that Proposition 5 provides the key step in the proof, though, to be sure, that proposition has been extended in two ways. First it has been extended to obtuse angles and second it has been extended by the application of conjunctive ratios in the manner that this was done in Proposition 6.

Moving on to Proposition 31, we see that if we have two pairs of equal tangents to a circle, the one pair consisting of tangents that are longer than those of the other, then the ratio of the lengths of the different tangents (as well as that of the areas contained by the respective pairs of tangents and by their arcs) is greater than the ratio of the arcs. Putting this in terms of specified

---

[10] Clagett, *Archimedes in the Middle Ages*, Vol. 1, p. 462: "III. Quorumlibet duorum circulorum circumferentie suis diametris sunt proportionales."

[11] H. L. L. Busard and P. S. van Konigsveld, "Der *Liber de arcubus similibus* des Ahmed ibn Jusuf," *Annals of Science*, Vol. 30 (1973), p. 397: "Proportio arcuum similium ad suos circulos est proportio una."

[12] *Ibid.*, p. 399: "Omnium duorum arcuum similium proportio corde unius ad cordam alterius est sicut proportio dyametri primi circuli ad dyametrum circuli secundi."

magnitudes (see Fig. P.31), we note that the proposition holds (1) that *BC* / *HE* > arc *CD* / arc *EF*, and (2) that extra-circular area *CBD* / extra-circular area *EHF* > arc *CD* / arc *EF*. If we take *GC* = *HE*, then it is clear by Proposition 5 (extended conjunctively) that *BC* / *HE* > angle *BAC* / angle *GAC*. Then it is easily shown that arc *DC* / arc *EF* = angle *BAC* / angle *GAC*, so that the first part of the proposition is proved. It can also be shown that quadrangles *BCAD* and *HEAF* have the same ratio as lines *BC* and *GC*, and similarly that the residual areas *BCD* and *HFE* (between the arcs and the respective pairs of tangents) have the same ratio. Thus the second part of the proposition follows.

In Proposition 32 Jordanus takes two pairs of tangents such that all four lines are equal. One pair he applies to the larger of two circles, the other to the smaller. The proposition asserts that the pair applied to the larger circle includes a longer arc, or, as is evident in Fig. P.32, arc *EG* > arc *CD*. The pair of tangents to the smaller circle consists of *BC* and *BD*, that to the larger circle of *HE* and *HG*. Extend *EH* to *L* so that diam. smaller circ. / diam. larger circ. = *CB* / *EL*. As in the proof of the preceding proposition we can show that (1) *LE* / *HE* = quadrangle *AELM* / quadrangle *AEHG*. And since the quadrangles *AELM* and *TCBD* were constructed to be similar, hence (2) *AELM* / *TCBD* = (*LE* / *BC*)² = (*LE* / *HE*)², *HE* being equal to *BC*. Accordingly (3) *AEHG* is the mean proportional between *AELM* and *TCBD*. Then it is easily shown that arc *CD* is similar to arc *EM*, from the length of *EL* hypothesized. Therefore (4) arc *EM* / arc *CD* = radius / radius = *LE* / *BC* = *LE* / *HE*. And, from (1) and (3), we can conclude (5) that *LE* / *HE* = *AEHG* / *TCBD*. Therefore, from (4) and (5), it is evident (6) that arc *EM* / arc *CD* = *AEHG* / *TCBD*. But from the preceding proposition we know (7) that arc *EM* / arc *EG* < line *EL* / line *EH* and also that arc *EM* / arc *EG* < *AEHG* / *TCBD*. Therefore from (6) and (7) we conclude that arc *EM* / arc *EG* < arc *EM* / arc *CD*. Therefore arc *EG* > arc *CD*, which was proposed. Again I note the importance of Proposition 5, since Proposition 31, based on it, provided the key step to the proof of Proposition 32.

Jordanus now presents a subgroup of four propositions that involve circles that are tangent to each other on the inside and their common sections by chords with the resulting relationships of their intercepted arcs. Proposition 33 is a simple proposition holding that, if a chord is drawn from the point of tangency through both circles, it will cut off similar segments from the circles. The proof is simple and needs no commentary, except to say that, though the proposition is valid for circles that are tangent on the outside as well as on the inside (and indeed the author of the *Liber de triangulis Iordani* later expanded the enunciation to include circles tangent on both inside and outside), Jordanus' proof (as specified and illustrated by Fig. P.33) concerns circles tangent on the inside, and indeed it is for such circles that Proposition 33 is later used in the succeeding propositions.

Proposition 34 is an exceedingly interesting and complex proposition, best described in terms of the specific magnitudes of Fig. P.34. The enunciation has three parts that concern the cutting of two circles tangent on the inside by lines perpendicular to the line containing the diameters of both circles, the perpendicular lines being drawn successively above, through, or below the center of the larger circle. The first part concerns two separate cases. The first (see Fig. P.34a) tells us that perpendicular EG, which is drawn through both circles and point Z, which point is above point M, the center of the larger circle, intercepts less arcal length from the smaller circle than from the larger, i.e., arc EAG > arc BAD. The second subcase (see Fig. P.34b) assures us that if the perpendicular EG passes through the larger circle and is tangent at point C to the smaller circle, which point is above point M, then once more it intercepts less arcal length from the smaller circumference than from the larger, i.e., arc EAG > circum. circ. AC (If I may use the term "intercept" to include the limiting case of the whole circumference). In the second part of the proposition we are told that the perpendicular EG which proceeds through the center M of the larger circle and is tangent to the smaller circle at M intercepts as much from the one circle as from the other, i.e. arc EAG = circum. $ACMD$ (see Fig. P.34c). Finally the third part of the proposition informs us that if the perpendicular EG proceeds through the larger circle and is tangent at point C to the smaller circle, which point is below the center M of the larger circle, then it intercepts more from the smaller circumference than from the larger, i.e., arc EAG < circum. of circ. AC. It will be noticed that I have added to the translation of the third part the condition that the perpendicular is tangent to the smaller circle (as indeed did the author of the *Liber de triangulis Iordani* later), for only in that situation will the intercept from the larger circle always be less than that from the smaller, as the enunciation asserts. Furthermore, at the end of the proof of that case (where the cutting perpendicular is tangent to the smaller circle below the center of the larger circle) Jordanus has the conventional phrase terminating the proof: "et hoc est quod proponitur." If this is truly the end of the proposition, then lines 45–51 represent an addition produced sometime after the completion of the original tract (for the addition see note 2 of the English translation of this proposition below). At any rate, let us at this point confine ourselves to the proofs of the three parts of the enunciation. Looking at Fig. P.34a, we see that Jordanus instructs us to draw line EA (actually missing in the diagrams of the manuscripts and added by me as a broken line). Line EA intersects the smaller circle at K. Then draw line KT parallel to the perpendicular EG, which, it will be recalled, intersects line AC in point Z above center M of the larger circle. From Proposition 33 it is evident that arc EAG / arc KAT = line ZA / line LA. But, by Proposition 30, ZA / LA > arc BAD / arc KAT. Hence arc EAG / arc KAT > arc BAD / arc KAT. Therefore, arc EAG > arc BAD, as the first part of the enunciation declares. Exactly the same kind of proof will show us that arc EAG > circum. circ. AC if line EG cuts the larger circle and is tangent to the smaller circle at C, which latter point is above the center M of the larger circle (see Fig. P.34b). And so the second subcase of the first part is evident.

In the second part of the proposition (see Fig. P.34c), it is immediately evident that, since EG is tangent to the smaller circle at the center M of the larger circle, the semicircumference of the larger circle is equal to the whole circumference of the smaller one, and indeed this is what the second part declares. Finally, in the third part of Proposition 34, we first draw line *BD* through the center *M* of the larger circle (Fig. P.34d). Hence *MF* / *CF* > semicircum. circ. *AF* / arc *EFG* (by Proposition 30, based, as we have said, on the all-important Proposition 5). Therefore *CF* / *AF* < arc *EFG* / circum. circ. *AF*. Therefore disjunctively *CF* / *CA* < arc *EFG* / arc *EAG*. Therefore conjunctively *FA* / *CA* < circum. circ. *FA* / arc *EAG*. But *FA* / *CA* = circum. larger circ. / circum. smaller circ. Thus circum. larger circ. / circum. smaller circ. < circum. circ. *FA* / arc *EAG* (circle *FA* being the larger circle). Therefore circum. smaller circ. > arc *EAG*, and the proposition is now proved in all three of its parts.

Proposition 35 is another ingenious proposition involving circles tangent on the inside. It has three parts (see Fig. P.35). In the first part the interior circumference cuts the diameter of the exterior circle below the center *F* of the exterior circle. Then any line *FDB* proceeding from the center *F* to cut both circumferences anywhere beyond point *A* will intercept a shorter arc from the interior circumference than from the exterior, i.e., arc *AB* > arc *AD*. In the second part the interior circumference cuts the diameter of the exterior circle at the center *F* of the exterior circle. Then any line *FDB* cutting both circumferences beyond point *A* will intercept the same arcal length from the interior and exterior circumferences, i.e., arc *AB* = arc *AD*. Finally in the third part the interior circumference cuts the diameter of the exterior circle above the center *F* of the larger circle. Then any line *FDB* cutting both circumferences beyond point *A* will cut more from the interior circumference than from the exterior, i.e., arc *AB* < arc *AD*.

Proceeding to the proof of the first part (see Fig. P.35a), we first draw line *FDB* as specified, *D* and *B* being its intersections with the two circumferences. Then draw a line from the point of tangency *A* through *D* extending it to point *G* on the larger circumference. Since the interior circumference intersects below *F*, line *AD* > line *GD*. Hence if we draw *FZT* perpendicular to *AG*, then the point of intersection *Z* will fall inside of *AD*. Hence we may apply Proposition 5 and (upon noting that the ratio of arcs is as the ratio of their central angles) the result is that, after conjunction and inversion of the ratios, line *ZG* / line *DG* < arc *TG* / arc *BG*. Doubling these ratios, we see that line *AG* / line *DG* < arc *AG* / arc *BG*. Successively applying disjunction, inversion, and conjunction to these ratios, we conclude that line *AG* / line *DA* > arc *AG* / *AB* (see footnote 2 to the English translation of this proposition). But, by Proposition 33, arc *AG* / arc *AD* = line *AG* / line *AD*. Hence arc *AG* / arc *AD* > arc *AG* / arc *AB*. Hence arc *AB* > arc *AD*, as the first part of the proposition requires.

In the second part of Proposition 35 (see Fig. P.35b), line *FDB* is drawn as the condition demands. Then it is evident that arc *AF* is a semicircumference, that *D* is a right angle, that *AD* = *DG*, and that arc *AB* = arc *BG*. By Proposition 33, arc *AG* / arc *AD* = line *AG* / line *AD*. Hence it is clear that arc *AB* = arc *AD*, as the second part asserts. Finally in the third part, since the interior circumference cuts the diameter of the exterior circle above center F, then $DG > AD$, and the perpendicular FZT will intersect at Z between D and G. Then from Proposition 5 we may conclude that arc TBA / arc $BA >$ line ZA / line AD. Doubling the ratios, we conclude that arc GA / arc $BA >$ line AG / line AD. But arc AG / arc $AD =$ line GA / line AD by Proposition 33. Therefore arc AG / arc $AB >$ arc AG / arc AD. Hence arc $AB <$ arc AD, as the third part intended.

We have now come to the last of the propositions involving circles tangent on the inside. Recall that Proposition 34 assumed that these circles were cut successively by lines perpendicular to the line of the diameters above, through, and below the center of the larger circle. Proposition 35 assumed cutting lines that proceed from the center of the larger circle and cut the circumferences of both circles when the center of the larger circle was successively within the smaller circle, on the circumference of the smaller circle, and outside of the smaller circle. Now Proposition 36 indicates that if the cutting line proceeds from the center of the smaller circle, it will always intercept more from the larger circumference, i.e., that arc $AB >$ arc DA (see Fig. P.36). The proof is simple. Let line EDB be any line proceeding from the center E of the smaller circle and cutting the two circumferences at D and B respectively. Then draw a line from the point of tangency A to B, which line cuts the smaller circumference at C. Draw line EC. Now construct a perpendicular EZ to line AB at Z and let it be extended to T. Hence $AZ = ZC$ and arc $AT =$ arc TC. By Proposition 6, BZ / $ZA >$ angle BEZ / angle AEZ. Since arcs are as their central angles, then BZ / $ZA >$ arc DT / arc TA. Hence, by conjunction, AB / $ZA >$ arc DA / arc AT. But because of the similarity of arcs, arc AB / arc $AC =$ chord AB / chord AC. Taking half of the ratios in the penultimate expression, AB / $AC >$ arc DA / arc AC. And so, putting both of the last expressions together, arc AB / arc $AC >$ arc DA / arc AC. Therefore arc $AB >$ arc DA, as the proposition asserts.

The final proposition among those that concern circles, chords, arcs, and tangents is Proposition 37, which can be readily understood if we consult Fig. P.37. We are told that we have three arcs AB, DB, and BF such that $AB - DB = DB - BF$, the arcs being on the same circumference. There are tangents AC and CB to arc AB, tangents DE and BE to arc DB, and tangents FG and BG to arc BF. The proposition holds (1) that $CE > EG$, these lines being the so-called "distances" between the tangents, and (2) that area $ADEC$ > area $DFGE$, these areas being the respective differences between extracircular areas ACB and DEB on the one hand and areas DEB and FGB on the other. Then from the angles that the three pairs of the tangents make are drawn to the center bisectors of the given arcs, namely lines CHZ, ELZ, and GMZ. Because arc AD is given as equal to arc DF, and because $EZ > EG$, since angle CZG is bisected, so line $CE >$ line EG as the first part of the proposition asserts. The proof of the second is unusual since it involves angles of contingence (i.e. angles composed of an arc and a tangent to the arc). Because arcs AD and DF are equal and it is supposed that tangent DE lies inside of

AC and *FG* inside of *DE*, and because the angles of contingence at *A*, *D*, and *F* are equal, so area *ADEC* > area *DFGE*.

Now Jordanus passes to the last group of Propositions (props. 38–63), propositions which are concerned with polygons that are irregular or regular, inscribed or circumscribed, inserted in one another, isoperimetric or not. Proposition 38 is a simple proposition holding that if one circle is circumscribed about and another inscribed in an irregular polygon, the circles cannot have the same center. The proof is given in terms of a triangle and rests on showing that if we assume that *D*, the center of the interior circle (see Fig. P.38), is also the center of the exterior circle, then the triangle can be shown to have equal sides, which is against the datum of a triangle of unequal sides. Obviously the same proof would be valid for other irregular polygons.

Proposition 39 tells us that of all the triangles described in a circle on the same base, the one whose remaining sides are equal is the maximum in area, and further it asserts that the closer the apex of any other such triangle is to the apex of the isosceles triangle the greater is its area. The proof is quite simple (see Fig. P.39). Since triangles *AHD* and *BCH* are similar and since *BC* > *AD*, therefore triangle *BCH* is greater than triangle *AHD*. Then if we add triangle *AHB* to both of the aforesaid triangles, triangle *ACB* > triangle *ADB*, as the first part of the proposition declares. The second part may be proved in exactly the same way, starting with similar triangles and the one side of the triangle closer to the isosceles triangle being greater than the corresponding side of the triangle that is farther from the isosceles triangle. The reader will see that this proposition is very much like Proposition 27, except that there Jordanus sought the sum of the remaining sides and here he seeks the areas.

Proposition 39 leads us to Proposition 40. It seems obvious that Jordanus took this proposition (but not its proof) from some earlier work (perhaps a fragment translated from the Arabic), for as we shall see the enunciation contains a *ratio* on which the proposition is based, but Jordanus' proof depends on Proposition 39 and does not mention the *ratio*. The proposition asserts that of triangles described in a circle with the radius as a base and one angle at the center of the circle, the one whose angle at the center is a right angle is the maximum of such triangles. Further, in the case of those triangles whose angle at the center is obtuse, by the amount that it is more obtuse—and in the case of those triangles whose angle at the center is acute, by the amount that it is more acute—will the area of the triangle be less. The *ratio* specified as the authority for this proposition declares that every obtuse-angled triangle or similarly every acute-angled triangle of the kinds mentioned has respectively an equal acute-angled or an equal obtuse-angled triangle of which the perpendicular line from the angle at the center to the side opposite of the one triangle is equal to half the side opposite the center angle of the other triangle. For example (see Fig. P.40 *var. Fa*), any obtuse-angle triangle *ABD* with half-side *HB* has an equal acute-angled triangle *ABC* with perpendicular *AB* = half-side *HB*.

The first part of the proposition is easily proved (see Fig. P.40). If *AE* is drawn perpendicularly from right angle *A* to side *BC*, then, by the converse of Proposition 1, *AE* = *EB*. Further, if we draw the perpendicular *AH* to the side of any other triangle, we may draw a single circle through *A*, *H*, *E*, and *B*. Hence, by Proposition 39, triangle *AEB*, as an isosceles triangle, is greater than the other triangle *ABH*. Consequently triangle *ABC*, double *AEB*, is greater than triangle *ABD*, double triangle *AHB*. The second part of the proposition follows immediately from the second part of Proposition 39, and from the *ratio* given in the enunciation, though Jordanus does not bother to indicate this. But it is clear that the second part of Proposition 39 assures us that *ABC* is increasingly greater than any obtuse-angled triangle *ABD* as the obtuse angle increases, while the *ratio* confirms that there will be an acute-angled triangle corresponding and equal to any obtuse-angled triangle. It is obvious that as the obtuse angle increases its corresponding acute angle decreases.

In Proposition 41 Jordanus easily proves that the sum of any two opposite sides of a quadrilateral circumscribed about a circle is equal to the sum of the other two sides. Also easily proved is Proposition 42, which declares that any parallelogram circumscribed about a circle is equilateral. Neither proof requires commentary.

Much more interesting is Proposition 43, which presents the following problem: With a triangle constructed in a circle, to describe a rectangle equal to it in the same circle. Two cases are presented, the first case involving an isosceles triangle, the second a scalene triangle. In the first case concerning isosceles triangle *ABC* (see Fig. P.43a), we extend perpendicular *CE* through *E*, the midpoint of *AB*, to the circumference at *D*. Draw line *AD*, and then draw *EF* parallel to *AD*. Now draw line *FD*. It is then clear that triangle *EFD* = triangle *EFA* (since they are on the same base between parallel lines). Therefore, with triangle *EFC* added to each triangle, triangle *DCF* = triangle *ECA*, and triangle *ECA* is half the given triangle. Then draw *FZ* parallel to *CED*, and draw lines *CZ* and *DZ*. Now the triangle *CZD* just formed is equal to triangle *DCF* (again because they are on the same base between parallel lines), and so triangle *CZD* = triangle *ECA*. Hence triangle *CZD* = ½ triangle *ABC*. But *CD* is a diameter and hence angle *Z* is a right angle. If we construct triangle *CGD* similar and equal to triangle *CZD*, the completed rectangle *CZDG* will be equal to the given triangle *ABC*, as was required in the first case.

The second case concerning the scalene triangle *ABC* (see Fig. P.43b) is somewhat more complicated. First we draw diameter *DZ* perpendicular to *AB* and intersecting the latter at its midpoint *E*. A perpendicular *CH* is dropped to diameter *DEZ* and this is parallel to *AB*. Triangle *AEH* = triangle *AEC* (since they are on the same base between parallel lines). Draw *ZA* and line *HL* parallel to it. Hence triangle *ZLE* = triangle *AEH*, and thus triangle *ZLE* = triangle *AEC*. Draw *DL*, and then *EM* parallel to it, *M* being on line *ZL*. Draw *DM*, and triangle *DMZ* = triangle *ZLE*. Hence triangle *DMZ* = triangle *AEC*. Then with line *MN* drawn parallel to *DZ*, and line *ND* drawn, right triangle *ZDN* is formed, and triangle *ZDN* = triangle *DMZ* = triangle *AEC*, and so triangle *ZDN* is equal to one half of triangle *ABC*. Then rectangle *ZNDY* is completed as in the first case, and that rectangle will equal the scalene triangle *ABC*, as the second case requires.

Proposition 44 is the first proposition to be concerned with inscribed and circumscribed regular polygons in and about a circle and it declares that if we have similar inscribed and circumscribed polygons in and about a given circle, then there exists as a mean proportional between the similar polygons a regular polygon inscribed in the same circle that has twice as many sides. The proof is given in terms of inscribed and circumscribed equilateral triangles, and the mean proportional is found to be an inscribed regular hexagon (see Fig. P.44). If we draw lines *ZD* and *ZHGA* (the latter bisecting side *DF* at *H* and arc *DF* at *G*), then triangle *ZDH* is similar to triangle *ZDA* (since each has a right angle and they share a common angle). Let *D* be connected to *G*, forming triangle *ZDG*. Since *ZA* / *ZD* = *ZD* / *ZH* (because of the similarity of the triangles) *ZA* / *ZG* = *ZG* / *ZH* (*ZG* being equal to *ZD*). Therefore triangle *ZAD* / triangle *ZDG* = triangle *ZDG* / triangle *ZDH* (for all of these triangles having a common altitude *DH* will be related as their bases). If we then draw lines *ZB*, *ZC*, *ZE*, and *ZF*, lines *ZB* and *ZC* will bisect arcs *FE* and *ED*, and if we connect the points of bisection we shall have a regular hexagon inscribed in the circle. Then it is obvious that that hexagon is equal to the six triangles each equal to triangle *ZDG*, that the exterior triangle is equal to the six triangles each equal to *ZAD*, and finally that the interior triangle is equal to the six triangles each equal to *ZDH*. Hence it is evident that if we multiply the terms of the proportion established above for triangles *ZAD*, *ZDG*, and *ZDH* by six, the hexagon will be the mean proportional between the exterior and the interior triangles (and of course the hexagon has twice as many sides as each of the similar triangles). A similar proof can be constructed for any other regular polygon if we divide the polygon into triangles.

Next follow two propositions concerning the inscription and circumscription of regular polygons in and about equal circles (Propositions 45 and 46). Proposition 45 asserts that if regular polygons are inscribed in equal circles, that which has the more sides will be the greater. Further, the ratio of the area of the polygon with the greater number of sides to the area of the other polygon will be greater than the ratio of their perimeters. The proof is developed for a square *ABCD* and an equilateral triangle *EFG* (see Fig. P.45), and would apply to any other regular polygons after they are resolved into partial triangles. In this square we draw four lines from the center *O* to the angles, thus resolving it into four equal partial triangles. In the triangle we draw three such lines, resolving it into three equal partial triangles. Since one side of a partial triangle of the triangle is greater than one side of a partial triangle of the square (that is *EF* > *AB*), then by Proposition 29 (not specifically mentioned by Jordanus) the ratio of the arcs subtending those sides will be greater than the ratio of the sides (i.e. arc *EF* / arc *AB* > side *EF* / side *AB*). Hence angle *ETF* / angle *AOB* > side *EF* / side *AB*. Hence 3 side *EF* / 4 side *AB* < 3 angle *ETF* / 4 angle *AOB*. But 3 angle *ETF* = 4 angle *AOB*. Hence 3 *EF* is less than 4 *AB*, and so the perimeter of the square is greater than the perimeter of the equilateral triangle. Furthermore the area of this square is greater than the area of the equilateral triangle, since not only is its perimeter greater but the common altitude of its partial triangles is greater than the common altitude of the partial triangles of the equilateral triangle. The second part of the proposition is also evident, though not spelled out by Jordanus. By Proposition 12, partial triangle *ETF* / partial triangle *AOB* < side *EF* / side *AB*. Hence 3 triangle *ETF* / 4 triangle *AOB* < 3 side *EF* / 4 side *AB*. Hence equilateral triangle *EFG* / square *ABCD* < perimeter of triangle / perimeter of square. Inverting the proportion, the second part of the proposition follows, namely that square / triangle > perim. of square / perim. of triangle.

Proposition 46 moves on to circumscribed regular polygons and tells us that if such polygons are circumscribed about equal circles, the one that has the fewer sides is the greater, and that the ratio of their areas is as the ratio of their perimeters. Again Jordanus proves the proposition for an equilateral triangle and a square (see Fig. P.46), assuming of course that the proof would be the same for any regular polygons since such polygons are resolvable into equal partial triangles. First, since angle *BHC* > angle *DLE*, side *BC* > side *DE*. Now by Proposition 5 (not mentioned by Jordanus but obviously used in the proof added in MS *Fa* and translated in note 1 of the English translation of this proposition), side *BC* / side *DE* > angle *BHC* / angle *DLE*, that is, side *BC* / side *DE* > arc of angle *BHC* / arc of angle *DLE*. But 3 arc of angle *BHC* = 4 arc of angle *DLE*, each sum being equal to the circumference. Hence perimeter of equilateral triangle *ABC* > perimeter of square *DEFG*. Since the common altitudes of all the partial triangles of both the equilateral triangle and the square are the same (being radii of the equal circles), the area of the equilateral triangle is greater than the area of the square. The second part of the proposition is also obvious because the altitudes of all the partial triangles are the same.

With this proposition completed, the shortened version of the *Liber philotegni* ends. This is the version contained by MSS *M*, *Fa*, and *Bu* (except that MSS *Fa* and *Bu*, as well as *Br*, add a Proposition 46+1 which has a proof that differs from the proof given of this same proposition when it later became Proposition IV.4 of the longer *Liber de triangulis Iordani*). And it is this shortened version that became the point of departure for the *Liber de triangulis Iordani*, as we shall see. I have already stated at the beginning of this chapter that MSS *E* and *Br* contained seventeen more propositions (Propositions 47–63) that appear to be an integral part of the original *Liber philotegni*. Though I suppose it is not impossible (as I once believed before studying these texts in detail)[13] that the original text of Jordanus was simply

---

[13] This view I communicated to R. B. Thomson and he mentions it in his "Jordanus de Nemore: Opera," *Mediaeval Studies,* Vol. 38 (1976), p. 118. I now reject this view because the only two manuscripts (*E* and *Br*) that bear the title *Liber philotegni* also contain all 63 propositions. Further, the number of propositions is indicated in the title and colophon of MS *E*, and in the colophon in MS *Br*.

the one of forty-six propositions (or perhaps 47) reflected in MSS *M, Fa,* and *Bu.* I think my earlier view is extremely unlikely since MSS *E* and *Br,* the only two manuscripts which have the title *Liber philotegni,* are also the only two manuscripts that contain Propositions 47–63. Now before adding these extra propositions, MS *Br* includes Proposition 46+1 and a truncated and unique version of Proposition III of the *Liber de mensura circuli* of Archimedes, a version that I have described in Volume One of this work (see pp. 96–97n). One can readily see why the scribe of *Br* made this latter addition, for Propositions 45 and 46 can be regarded as guaranteeing the use of inscribed and circumscribed regular polygons that is found in Archimedes' proposition. And so at least the scribe of *Br* joins the *Liber philotegni* solidly to the Archimedean tradition.

Beginning with Proposition 47, Jordanus gives a series of propositions that compare irregular, partially regular, and regular inscribed and circumscribed polygons. In Proposition 47 we are told that if two polygons of the same number of sides are constructed on equal bases in equal circles, the one whose remaining sides are equal will be greater. These polygons are *ABCD* (of equal remaining sides) and *HLMN* (of some or all unequal remaining sides), as indicated in Fig. P.47. Since the sides of the latter are unequal at least one of the sides, say *ML*, will be greater than one of the equal sides, say *AD*. Then let us draw line *HM* and construct on line *HM* by Proposition 39 triangle *HOM* that is greater than triangle *HNM* (if that is possible, and of course it will be possible unless *HN = NM* when triangle *HMN* would be the largest possible triangle on *HM* and then the argument will be even simpler, as we shall see). Needless to say with *HOM* constructed as greater than *HNM,* surface *HLMO > HLMN.* Then we insert lines *EG* and *ZT* equal respectively to *MO* and *OH* (which we let be equal to each other, thus producing the greatest possible area for *HLMO*), *EG* and *ZT* being drawn parallel to *AD* and *DC* in the left circle. We also let *PR* (equal to *AD*) be inserted as a parallel to *LM* in the right circle. Further insert *XY* parallel to *PR* and *LM* so that it bisects arcs *LP* and *MR,* the half arcs being equal to arcs *DG* and *DZ* and to arcs *AE* and *CT* opposite them. Therefore surface *LPRM* > surface *ADGE* + surface *DCTZ.* Therefore circular segments *LM* + *MO* + *OH* > circular segments *AD* + *DC* + *CB.* Therefore quadrangle *ABCD* > quadrangle *HLMO.* But we noted that *HLMO* was constructed to be greater than *HLMN* if that were possible, and so *ABCD > HLMN.* Of course, if *HN = NM,* then *HLMN = HLMO* and the proposition would immediately follow. As Jordanus points out, a similar argument would be valid for all such polygons.

In Proposition 48 Jordanus takes the final step toward comparing a regular polygon with an irregular polygon of the same number of sides, both inscribed in equal circles. This proposition asserts that the regular polygon is greater in area. The proof is very much the same as that of Proposition 47. We construct a regular polygon *ABCDE* and an irregular one *FGHKL* in equal circles (see Fig. P.48). One side of the latter must be greater than one of the equal sides of the regular polygon. Let that longer side be *GH.* Upon *GH* we now construct a third polygon *GHMNO* whose remaining sides are equal.

Then by Proposition 47 it is clear that *GHMNO* > *FGHKL*. Following the procedure of the preceding proposition, we insert beyond four sides of *ABCDE* lines parallel to the four sides and each equal to one of the four equal sides of *GHMNO*. We also insert beyond side *HG* line *A'B'* parallel to it and equal to *AB*. Then we divide arcs *HA'* and *GB'* into four equal parts by the parallel lines *PR*, *TS*, and *YX*. Hence, as in the preceding proposition, we see that the exterior circular segments beyond polygon *GHMNO* are greater than the exterior circular segments beyond polygon *ABCDE* (for surf. *HA'B'G* > surf. *CH'M'D* + surf. *DM"N'E* + surf. *EN"O'A* + surf. *AO"G'B* and so circ. segments *GH* + *HM* + *MN* + *NO* + *OG* > circ. segments *AB* + *BC* + *CD* + *DE* + *EA*). Therefore polygon *ABCDE* > polygon *GHMNO*, and *GHMNO* was constructed greater than *FGHKL*. Therefore polygon *ABCDE* > polygon *FGHKL*, as the proposition asserts. Finally Jordanus assures us that the same kind of demonstration is valid for all other such polygons that have the same number of sides.

Proposition 49 is complementary to Proposition 48. Here Jordanus shifts to regular and irregular polygons having the same number of sides and circumscribing equal circles. It asserts that the regular polygon will be the one less in area. Let the regular polygon be *ABCDE* and the irregular one *FGHKL* (see Fig. P.49). Jordanus simplifies the proof by taking one side of the irregular polygon as equal to any side of the regular polygon (i.e., *KH* = *AB*). The proof follows. In taking *KH* = *AB*, we have made two sets of equal triangles comprising surface *E'KHSV* in the irregular polygon equal to the two sets of equal triangles comprising surface *H'BAH"O* in the regular polygon. There thus remains to prove that the remaining parts of the irregular polygon (namely, the three surfaces *LE'VM*, *FMVN*, and *GNVS*) are greater than the corresponding surfaces that comprise surface *H'CDEH"O* in the regular polygon. The text of the proof is quite corrupt in both manuscripts (*E* and *Br*), and also the diagram, which appears only in MS *E*, is imperfect and must be corrected in the manner which I have indicated in the legend to Fig. P.49. But in spite of these imperfections, I believe that my corrections and additions now make an understandable text. Jordanus draws *OP* and *OQ* in the regular polygon so that each half-side of the irregular polygon that is less than the half-side *AZ* of the regular polygon is indicated on the regular polygon (i.e. *PZ* = *QZ* = *FM* = *FN*). Similarly he marks off on the half-sides of the irregular polygon that are longer than the half-sides of the regular polygon lines equal to the half-sides of the regular polygon (i.e. *RM* = *AZ* = *BZ* = *NT*). Jordanus then indicates the equalities that exist amidst the various triangles: *LVM* / *RVM* = *LVM* / *AOZ*, *NVG* / *NVT* = *NVG* / *ZOB* [=*NVG* / *AOZ*], *LVR* / *RVM* = *LVR* / *AOZ*, *TVG* / *NVT* = *TVG* / *ZOB* [=*TVG* / *AOZ*], *FVM* / *RVM* = *FVN* / *NVT* = *POZ* / *AOZ* [=*FVM* / *AOZ*], and *FVY* = *AOP* = *BOQ*. Then the proof is indicated in a very general way: Since all of these equalities exist, "the ratio of the triangles at the center [in sum] is greater than the ratio of the [central] angles of those [triangles] because the ratio of the individual triangles [each] is greater [than the ratio of the angles of the individual triangles considered singly]. Therefore the three surfaces [*LE'VM, FMVN,* and *GNVS*] are [in sum] greater than [the sum of] the three surfaces of the regular polygon each [equal to *BZOH'* and thus] double triangle *AOZ,* since the former [three surfaces] are double the triangles *LVM, FVM,* and *GVN.* Since the two remaining surfaces of the latter are upon [i.e. are equal to] the [two] remaining surfaces of the former, therefore the one [i.e. irregular polygon] is greater than the equilateral [polygon]." Since the proof is mentioned in such a general fashion, it needs expansion, which I now give.

Let us concentrate first on the central angles, and simplify the designations. We take r to be a central angle subtended by a half-side of the regular polygon (i.e. *AZ*). It is also the central angle for lines *RM* and *NT* each equal to *AZ.* Then let x_1 be the angle subtended by *LR,* x_2 the angle subtended by *TG,* y the angle subtended by *FY* and by lines *RY'* and *TY''* each equal to *FY.* Now it is evident that the sum of the central angles of the partial surface *E'LFGSV* must equal the sum of the central angles of the partial surface *H'CDEH''O,* since the central angles of those partial surfaces of both polygons that were assumed to be equal are equal and since the sum of all central angles of each polygon is 360°. Therefore applying our letters to the central angles we conclude that $2(x_1 + r + r - y + r + x_2) = 2(3r)$. Hence $x_1 + x_2 = y$. Now *LR* / *RY'* > x_1 / y, and *TG* / *TY''* > x_2 / y, by Proposition 5 applied to an obtuse-angled triangle (as Jordanus already noted it may be so applied in Proposition 30). Then since *RY'* = *TY''* = *FY,* so (*LR* + *TG*) / *FY* > $(x_1 + x_2)$ / y. But since we have shown that $x_1 + x_2 = y$, we conclude that *LR* + *TG* > *FY,* or *LR* + *TG* > *RM* − *FM* (since *FY* = *RM* − *FM*). Now if we add to each side of this expression the sum 2*RM* + *FM,* we find that *LR* + *TG* + 2*RM* + *FM* > 3*RM.* The sum on the left side of the expression is equal to half the perimeter of the surface *E'LFGSV,* and 3*RM* is half the perimeter of the corresponding surface in the regular polygon. Multiplying these expressions by two and adding to them the equal partial perimeters of the initially assumed equal partial surfaces of the two polygons we can conclude that perimeter of polygon *FGHKL* > perimeter of polygon *ABCDE.* Then if we multiply each of these perimeters by the common radius, we have the proposition, namely that the area of polygon *FGHKL* > area of polygon *ABCDE.*

The same kind of proof may be used if all of the sides of the irregular polygon are unequal. All we have to realize is that the sum of all of the surplus angles marked with x's (i.e. x_1, x_2, etc.) will be equal to the sum of all the deficient angles marked with y's while the sum of the line segments subtending the x's will be greater than the sum of the line segments subtending the y's, which may be proved by applying Proposition 5 as many times as necessary. We should also realize that the same proof may be used for any other pairs of polygons having the same number of sides.

Proposition 50 is a very neat proposition that in a sense supplements Proposition 46. The latter proposition, it will be recalled, asserted that if we

had two regular polygons circumscribed about equal circles, the one with
the fewer sides would be the greater. The original expression for regular
polygons in the enunciation of that proposition was undoubtedly simply
figure equalium laterum, which certainly meant in common parlance "regular
polygons." Presumably Jordanus took the enunciation from some earlier
work where it had the simple expression, but then he correctly understood
it as if it were written *figure equalium laterum et equalium angulorum* (as
indeed I have so emended it). At any rate in Proposition 50, he now takes
the expression in its literal meaning and he tells us that it is possible to have
equilateral polygons circumscribed about equal circles such that the one with
the greater number of sides is [equal to or] larger in area. Turning to Fig.
P.50, we may follow this very fine proof of Jordanus, where he shows that
it is possible to have an equilateral hexagon which is greater than a square
even though they are both circumscribed about equal circles. We first circumscribe a square about circle A (and call it square A) and then a regular
hexagon $BCDEFG$ about an equal circle. Then we extend three sides of the
hexagon until they meet and form a circumscribed equilateral triangle KLM.
The points of tangency of that triangle with the circle are N, O, and P. Let
$Q = \frac{1}{3}$ (triangle KLM − square A). Then we draw lines NR, OS, and PT
from points N, O, and P so that each of the equal triangles NKR, OLS, and
PMT is equal to or less than Q. Then we draw from points R, S, and T so
established lines RH, SX, and TY so that they are tangent to the circle and
meet the regular hexagon at points H, X, and Y. With these last lines drawn,
we now have a hexagon that it is equilateral but not equiangular and which
is circumscribed about the circle, namely hexagon $HRXSYT$. That it is equilateral is evident because KR, LS, and MT are equal. Now it is immediately
clear that this hexagon is [equal to or] greater than square A, since the three
triangles HRK, XSL, and YTM that constitute the excess of triangle KLM
over that hexagon are [equal to or] less than $3Q$, which is the excess of
triangle KLM over square A. Hence hexagon $HRXSYT \geqslant$ square A, which
was proposed.

Note that the bracketed phrases added to my translation and to the preceding
summary of Proposition 50 allow for the apparent assumption by Jordanus
in line 14 that the triangles NKR, OLS, and PMT are [each] made equal to
or less than Q (*equales vel minores Q*). But if the original text assumed only
that the triangles should each be less than Q, then the bracketed phrases are
not needed and the final sentence above ought to read: "Hence hexagon
$HRXSYT >$ square A, which was proposed."

So much for polygons that are inscribed in or circumscribed about equal
circles. Now Jordanus moves to a series of propositions that concern the
construction of polygons in one another. These are Propositions 51–60. Proposition 51 requires the construction of a square on a given side of a given
triangle that touches the remaining sides, when the angles on the given side
are either one acute and one right angle or are both acute angles. The proof
is simple and may be outlined as follows (see Fig. P.51): (1) With AB the

given side of given triangle *ABC*, we take a line *E* of such length that (*AB* + *CD*) / *CD* = *AB* / line *E*. Line *E* is placed within triangle *ABC* parallel to line *AB* and is there designated *FH*. (2) (*AB* + *CD*) / *CD* = *AB* / *E* = *AB* / *FH* = *AB* / *ML*. (3) *AB* / *CD* = (*AB* − *E*) / *E* = (*AM* + *BL*) / *ML*. (4) But *AM* / *FM* = *AD* / *CD* and *BL* / *LH* = *BD* / *CD*. (5) Therefore, (*AM* + *BL*) / *FM* = (*AD* + *BD*) / *CD* = *AB* / *CD*. (6) Hence, from (3) and (5), we conclude that (*AM* + *BL*) / *ML* = (*AM* + *BL*) / *FM*. (7) Therefore, *ML* = *FM*, and *FMLH* is a square, as the proposition required.

Proposition 52 is another imaginative proposition that compares squares constructed respectively on the hypotenuse and on other sides of a given right triangle. The proposition tells us that the square constructed on the hypotenuse (and touching the remaining sides) is less than the square constructed on the remaining sides (that is, possessing a right angle in common with the triangle) and touching the hypotenuse. First, by the preceding proposition we construct square *DEFG* on the hypotenuse of right triangle *ABC* and square *H* on the other sides of right triangle *H* (equal to triangle *ABC*) as shown in Fig. P.52. If we extend side *EF* of the square *DEFG* until it meets at point *M* the extension of side *AC*, we shall have formed a triangle *AEM* similar to triangle *ABC* (and to its equivalent, triangle *H*). But we have also formed two small triangles *FCM* and *FEB*, which are similar. Now side *FG* > *FC* (since *FG* is the hypotenuse of triangle *FCG*). Hence *FE* > *FC*, and *a fortiori FB*, as the hypotenuse of triangle *FEB*, is greater than *FC*. Therefore triangle *AEM* is less than triangle *ABC*. Therefore it will be less than triangle *H*. Accordingly the square placed in *H* in the same fashion as square *DEFG* was placed in the smaller triangle *AEM* will be greater than square *DEFG*, as the proposition asserts.

Proposition 53 shifts from the right triangle of the preceding proposition to an acute-angled triangle and tells us that the square constructed on the longest side (and touching the other sides) is less than the square constructed on either of the other sides, as illustrated in Fig. P.53. I remind the reader that MS *E*, the only one to give a figure, gives one that is hopelessly erroneous, and I have therefore had to redraw that figure. First we construct *DEFG* on the longest side *AB* of the given acute-angled triangle *ABC* and we also construct *H* on one of the other sides of triangle *H* (congruent to triangle *ABC*). Then we apply an angle *L* equal to angle *B* beyond *C* on the extension of *AC* so that the side *LM* of the angle passes through point *F*. With such a line drawn we have formed similar triangles *FMB* and *CLF*. Then if we draw *FN* perpendicular to *AC*, we shall have formed a triangle *FNC* similar to triangle *FEM* (since both triangles have a right angle and angle *C* in *FNC* is equal to angle *M* in *FEM*). Then we proceed as in the preceding proposition. *FG* > *FN* (because *FG* is the hypotenuse of triangle *FNG*). Therefore *FE* (equal to *FG*) is greater than *FN*. So *FM* > *FC*. Consequently triangle *ABC* > triangle *ALM*. And so it is obvious that square *H*, inserted in triangle *H* in the same fashion as square *DEFG* was inserted in the smaller triangle *ALM*, will be greater than square *DEFG*, as the proposition holds.

Proposition 54 concerns the construction of a rectangle on the side of the triangle by applying its upper angles to the midpoints of the remaining sides of the triangle. It holds (1) that the rectangle so constructed is half the triangle, and (2) that the rectangle is the maximum of all rectangles described on the same side with upper angles applied to the remaining sides. The proof is so simple that it requires no commentary. The same is true for the next two propositions. Proposition 55 declares that if we join the midpoints of the adjacent sides of any quadrangle, a parallelogram will be formed inside the quadrangle. Proposition 56 holds that if we construct a parallelogram within a parallelogram by applying the sides of the latter to the midpoints of the adjacent sides of the former, and if we construct a third parallelogram within the second in the same way by applying its sides to the midpoints of the adjacent sides of the second parallelogram, that third parallelogram will be similar to the first.

Let us move from these easily proved propositions to a more interesting one. Proposition 57 requires that we construct an equilateral polygon within a rectangle so that it touches the rectangle at a given point on either of the shorter sides. We suppose the rectangle to be $ABCD$ and the given point X (see Fig. P.57). It is obvious that if point X were at the midpoint of a shorter side, we would merely have to join it and the midpoints of the other three sides by lines connecting each pair of adjacent sides and the problem would be immediately solved. In fact this case is so obvious that Jordanus does not even mention it. He assumes rather that $AX > XB$. Then he takes a line YT such that $AX^2 - XB^2 = YT^2$ and a line Z such that $BC \cdot Z = YT^2$. Then he cuts BC at T so that $BT > TC$ (and thus so that $BC \cdot BT > BC \cdot TC$). Hence he has assigned point T and a given line Z so that $BC \cdot BT - BC \cdot TC = BC \cdot Z = YT^2$, for $BC (BT - TC) = BC \cdot Z$ and thus $BT - TC = Z$. Now $BT^2 - CT^2 = (BT + CT) \cdot (BT - CT) = BC \cdot Z = YT^2$. Then let $AM = CT$ and $CN = AX$. Draw the quadrilateral $XTNM$. This is the required equilateral because $BT^2 - AM^2 = AX^2 - XB^2$, and $AX^2 + AM^2 = XM^2$ (by the Pythagorean theorem). Also $BX^2 + BT^2 = XT^2$ by the same theorem. Therefore $XM^2 = XT^2$, or $XM = XT$, and thus it is evident that $XTNM$ is an equilateral drawn within the rectangle so that it touches at any point X in a shorter side of the rectangle.

Proposition 58 is another clever proposition. Once more I note that the text was quite poor in both manuscripts and that the diagram was missing and had to be constructed after the text was corrected. The proposition requires the description of a square in a regular pentagon. Let the pentagon be $ABCDE$ (see Fig. P.58). Draw line EB (which will be parallel to DC) and CFG and DHL perpendicular to EB and intersecting it at points F and H. Then these lines are obviously greater than BC and DE. Now $FH = CD$. To line CG let there be added to each end lines equal to BF and HE so that there results a line $MCFGN$, which is greater than BE (since $GC > HF$, and the additions to lines GC and HF are equal). Let BE be cut at O and P in the same proportion that MN is cut at G and C, and it is obvious that BP

< *GN*, that is, that *BP* < *BF* and *EO* < *EH*. From points *O* and *P* let perpendiculars *RPX* and *TOY* be drawn and let their intersections with the four sides of the pentagon be connected so that a quadrangle *RTYX* is formed. It is this quadrangle that is the required square. The proof of this I paraphrase as follows. Because we divided *BE* at *O* and *P* in the same proportion that line *MN* was cut at *C* and *G*, so (1) $(2GN + GC) / GC = (2BP + OP) / OP$. From this it follows that $GN / GC = BP / OP$, or $GN \cdot OP = BP \cdot GC$. (2) $GN / YX = FB / OP$, since $GN = FB$ and $YX = OP$. (3) $FB / BP = GC / RX$ (by similar triangles). (4) From (2) and (3), $(GN \cdot OP) / YX = (GC \cdot PB) / RX$. (5) Therefore, from (1) and (4), $YX = RX$, and hence *RTYX* is indeed a square.

Having shown how to describe a square in a pentagon in Proposition 58, Jordanus now tells us in the next proposition how to describe a square in a regular hexagon. The diagram was missing from the manuscripts, but I have constructed it on the basis of the text (see Fig. P.59). The given hexagon is circumscribed by a circle. Then the arcs subtended by the sides of this hexagon are bisected. With the adjacent points of bisection connected, a second regular hexagon is formed. The sides of the two hexagons intersect at points *A*, *B*, *C*, *D*, *E*, *F*, *G*, *H*, *K*, *L*, *M*, and *N*. Jordanus then tells us to connect points *A* and *D*, *A* and *L*, *D* and *G*, and *L* and *G*, thus forming a quadrilateral. We also connect *A* and *G*, and *D* and *L*. Then it can be easily shown by an examination of the partial triangles that would be drawn on the chords connecting the half-arcs and of the remaining triangles that the opposite sides of the quadrilateral *ADGL* are equal, that the adjacent sides are also equal, and that its angles are right angles. Consequently quadrilateral *ADGL* is the desired square. It is further obvious that, since *A*, *D*, *G*, and *L* are points of intersection of the sides of the two hexagons, the square *ADGL* is accordingly described in both hexagons and hence in the given hexagon.

The last of the propositions requiring the construction of one regular polygon in another is Proposition 60: "To place an equilateral triangle in a square or a regular pentagon." In fact the instructions given by Jordanus specifically concern the construction of the equilateral triangle in a regular pentagon, but it should be evident to the reader that the instructions would apply equally well to a square. The instructions are quite general and hence I have added Fig. P.60 to give them specificity. First Jordanus tells us that there are two methods of placing an equilateral triangle in a regular polygon, first starting from an angle of the polygon and second starting from the midpoint of a side of the polygon. We begin the first method by circumscribing a circle about a regular polygon *ABCDE*. Then within the circle we construct equilateral triangle *DFG* (i.e. starting from angle *D* of the pentagon). Sides *DF* and *DG* of the triangle intersect sides *AE* and *BC* of the pentagon at points *H* and *K*. Connecting *H* and *K*, we form a triangle *DHK*, which is also an equilateral triangle since it is similar to triangle *DFG*, and so *DHK* is the required equilateral triangle to be placed within a regular pentagon. Now if we start from the midpoint of a side of the polygon, say from point

L, we first inscribe a circle within the pentagon. In that circle we construct equilateral triangle LMN. Then we extend the sides LM and LN of that triangle to points O and P on sides ED and CD of the pentagon. We have now formed triangle LOP, which is equilateral because it is similar to triangle LMN, and thus we have placed an equilateral triangle in a regular polygon in the second way.

The treatise is completed by three isoperimetric propositions. Proposition 61 declares that if an equilateral triangle and any other triangle are of equal perimeters, the equilateral triangle will be the greater in area. Let us spell out the proof in somewhat more detail than does Jordanus, referring to Fig. P.61, which was missing from the manuscripts and which I had to construct from the text. Let the equilateral triangle be A and the other triangle BCD, the triangles being isoperimetric. Since some side of triangle BCD must be greater than a side of A, let the greater side be BC. Further let EC be equal to a side of A. Now let ED be extended to F so that $BC / EC = FE / DE$. Let a line parallel to BC be drawn through F. Hence by the converse of Proposition 13, triangle BCD = triangle FCE. Jordanus then asserts that the perimeter of triangle BCD is greater than the perimeter of triangle FCE, it having been assumed properly that BD is less than CE. Jordanus does not go on to prove that the perimeter of triangle BCD is greater but we may do so easily using his earlier propositions. Let us extend CD to K and draw KE. Then, since CD is assumed to be less than CE and since $BC / EC = KC / DC$ (for $KC / DC = FE / DE$), therefore BC is the longest of the four sides KC, DC, BC, and EC that include equal angles. Therefore by Proposition 9, the perimeter of triangle BCD > perimeter of triangle ECK. Then by the second part of Proposition 10, the perimeter of triangle ECK is greater than the perimeter of triangle EFC. Therefore, perimeter of triangle BCD > perimeter of triangle EFC. Now assume point G on the line through F parallel to BC such that triangle EGC = triangle EFC and $EG = CG$. By Proposition 10 once more, $EG + GC < EF + FC$. Therefore EG and GC are less than two sides of triangle A, since the perimeter of A is equal to the perimeter of BDC, the perimeter of ECG is less than the perimeter of EFC and hence less than the perimeter of BDC, and EC is equal to a side of A. Therefore if we place an equilateral triangle ECH (equal to triangle A) upon line EC, its sides EH and HC (equal to each other) will respectively be greater than sides EG and CG (equal to each other) and therefore triangle EHC is greater than triangle EGC, since it includes it. Hence triangle A > triangle EGC. But triangle EGC = triangle BDC. Therefore triangle A > triangle BDC, though their perimeters are equal, and this is what was proposed.

Proposition 62 is similar to the preceding proposition except that this proposition concerns isoperimetric quadrilaterals instead of triangles and says: "Every square is greater than any other quadrilateral having a perimeter equal to its [perimeter]." Once more I have had to construct the diagram from the text since it was missing from the manuscripts (see Fig. P.62). Let A be the square and $BCDE$ the other quadrilateral. Draw diagonal BD and construct in opposite directions triangles *BFD* and *BGD* equal respectively to triangles *BCD* and *BED*, with *BF* = *FD* and *BG* = *GD*. Therefore, by Proposition 10, *BF* + *FD* < *BC* + *CD* and *BG* + *GD* < *BE* + *ED*. Hence we have so far shown that *BFDG*, a quadrilateral with equal adjacent sides, is equal in area to *BCDE* but has a lesser perimeter. Then we draw a diagonal *FG* and in the same fashion as before construct an equilateral parallelogram *FHGM* that is equal in area to *BFDG* but which has a perimeter that is less than that of *BFDG*. Hence it is also clear that equilateral parallelogram *FHGM* is equal in area to *BCDE* and has a perimeter that is less than that of *BCDE*. Now *FHGM* is either rectangular or it is not rectangular. If it is rectangular, it is a square. But since its perimeter is less than that of *BCDE* and hence than that of square *A* it is obvious that its area will be less than that of square *A* (see Fig. 62a, top). Then if *FHGM* is not rectangular, its area will always be less than if it were a square, as is evident from the comment added to the proof and illustrated by the remaining two diagrams in Fig. 62a. It may be easily proved by a proposition like Proposition IV.18 added later to the *Liber de triangulis Iordani* (see below). Hence in all circumstances *FHGM* will be less in area than square *A*. But *FHGM* is equal in area to *BCDE*. Thus *BCDE* is less in area than square *A* though it has the same perimeter, as the proposition asserted. Though this proposition and the preceding one lead to one of the major objectives of the *Liber de ysoperimetris*, a work which, as we have seen, Jordanus knew and cited in Propositions 5 and 30, Jordanus' enunciations and proofs are quite distinct from what is found in the *Liber de ysoperimetris* and depend rather on his own previously proved propositions.[14]

---

[14] See the remarks in the *Liber de ysoperimetris*, ed. of H. L. L. Busard, "Der Traktat *De isoperimetris* der unmittelbar aus dem Griechischen ins Lateinische übersetzt worden ist," *Mediaeval Studies*, Vol. 42 (1980), p. 71: "In his demonstrandum quoniam ysoperimetrorum et eque multa latera habentium rectilineorum maius est quod equilaterum et equiangulum." Then after some lemmata (numbered by Busard 2–4), the following proposition appears (pp. 79–80): "[5] HIIS DEMONSTRATIS PROPONATUR DEMONSTRARE QUOD PRIUS DICTUM EST, QUONIAM YSOPERIMETRORUM ET EQUE MULTITUDINIS LATERUM RECTILINEORUM MAIUS EST QUOD EQUILATERUM ET EQUIANGULIUM EST.

Esto enim exagonum *abdmeg* et subiaceat maius existens omnibus ysoperimetris ipsi et eque multitudinis laterum figuris (Fig. P.62b, left figure). Dico autem quoniam est et equilaterum et equiangulum.

Esto enim prius, si possibile est, non equilaterum sitque maior *ba* quam *ag* et copuletur *bg* et trigono existente anisocheli *bag* super *bg* constituatur trigonus ysocheles ysoperimeter ei qui est *abg* sitque *btg* (qualiter enim oportet facere, demonstratum est in primo presumptorum); maius ergo *gtb* quam *gab* (et hoc enim in eodem demonstratum est). Commune adiaceat *bdmeg* penthagonum, totum ergo *tbdmeg* maius est quam *abdmeg* et est ipsi ysoperimetrum, quod est impossibile. Subiaceat enim omnibus maius. non ergo anisopleuron est. /

Dico autem quoniam neque anisogonium est.

Si enim possibile, sit angulus *abd* maior angulo *age* et copulentur *ad*, *ae* (Fig. P.62b, right figure). Quoniam ergo due *ag*, *ge* duabus *ab*, *bd* equales, angulus vero angulo maior, maior et *da* basis basi *ae*. Duobus ergo dissimilibus existentibus trigonis ysochelibus duum equalium laterum *abd* et *age* super *ad* et *ae* constituantur similia trigona ysochela ysoperimetra ipsis sintque

Finally the tract ends with Proposition 63, which holds that: "If two regular polygons are bounded by the same perimeter, that which has more sides will be greater." The proof is constructed in terms of a square and a pentagon, but it could be as easily used for any other regular polygons. Once more the diagram was missing from the manuscripts and needed construction from the text (see Fig. P.63). Let A be the square and B the regular pentagon having the same perimeter as the square. Let a circle be inscribed in the square and then let another regular pentagon (pentagon A) be circumscribed about the circle. I shall now summarize the proof briefly. (1) square A / pent. A = perim. of square A / perim. of pent. A (by the second part of Proposition 46). (2) pent. B / pent. A = (perim. of pent. B / perim. of pent. $A)^2$, by VI.18 (=Gr. VI.20). (3) Hence pent. B / pent. A = (square A / pent. $A)^2$, from steps (1), (2), and the given datum that perimeter of square A is equal to the perimeter of pentagon B. Or, pent. B / pent. A > square A / pent. A, with square A > pent. A, from Proposition 46. Therefore pent. B > square A, as the proposition requires. Jordanus also notes that square A is the mean proportional between the two pentagons, i.e., pent. B / square A = square A / pent. A, as is clear in the first formulation of step (3). And it is once more obvious that since square A is greater than pentagon A by Proposition 46, pentagon B must be greater than square A. As in the case of the two preceding propositions, Proposition 63, though no doubt originally inspired by the *Liber de ysoperimetris,* is quite distinct from the corresponding proposition in the Greek work, both as to enunciation and proof, and depends primarily on Jordanus' own Proposition 46.[15]

aid, aze (qualiter enim oporteat facere dictum est); maiora ergo *aid* et *aez* quam *abd* et *age.* Commune adiaceat *adme* quadrilaterum; totum ergo *aidmez* exagonum maius quam *abdmeg* ysoperimetron ipsi existens, quod est inconveniens. Non ergo anisogonium est. Ysogonium ergo ostensum est et ysopleurum, maximum ergo ysoperimetrorum eque multorum laterum equilaterum est et equiangulum, quare et econverso."

[15] *Ibid.,* pp. 69–71: "[1] PRELIBANDUM VERO PRIMUM QUONIAM YSOPERIME-TRORUM YSOPLEURORUM RECTILINEORUM ET CIRCULIS CONTENTORUM QUOD PLURIUM EST ANGULORUM MAIUS EST.

Adiaceant enim duo rectilinea ysopleura et ysoperimetra *ab, gd* et sint circulis circumscripta pluresque habeat angulos *ab* quam *gd* (Fig. P.63a). Dico quoniam maius est *ab* quam *gd.*

Sumantur enim eorum que circa ipsa centra circulorum *e* et *z* et copulentur *ea, eb, gz, zd* et protrahantur ab *e* et *z* in *ab* et *gd* catheti *ei* et *zt.* Manifestum vero quoniam maior *gd* quam *ba.* Idem enim in minus multitudine divisum (velut nunc pentagoni divisio minor existens multitudine / exagoni divisione) in maius magnitudine dividitur. Est autem ea propter ysoperimetra dari esse ambo. Et *gt* ergo quam *ai* maior est. Iaceat ei que est *ai* equalis *tk* et copulentur *zk.* Quoniam ergo equilaterum est *gd,* pars est *gd* totius perimetri, eadem pars est que secundum *gd* portio eius qui circa *gdoz* circuli ad totum circulum, hoc est *gzd* ad quattuor rectos. Equalis vero eius quod est *gdo* perimetros ei que eius quod est *abp.* Et sicut ergo *gd* ad *abp* perimetron ita *gzd* ad 4 rectos, sed sicut *abp* perimetros ad *ab* ita 4 recti ad *aeb,* et per equale ergo sicut *gd* ad *ab* ita *gzd* ad *aeb* et dimidia ergo sicut *gt* ad *ai,* hoc est ad *tk,* sic *gzt* ad *aei.* Maiorem vero proportionem habet *gt* ad *tk* quam *gzt* ad *kzt* angulum, sicut ostendetur, et angulus ergo *gzt* ad angulum *aei* maiorem proportionem habet quam ad angulum *kzt.* Ad quod vero maiorem habet proportionem illud minus est, minor ergo *aei* angulus angulo *kzt,* equalis vero qui ad *i* ei qui ad *t,* rectus enim uterque. Reliquus ergo *eai* maior quam *zkt.* Constituatur autem ad *k* angulo

This rather lengthy account of the contents of the *Liber philotegni* will, I hope, convince the reader of Jordanus' originality as a geometer. Regardless of how often Jordanus borrowed some proposition from treatises recently translated from the Arabic or the Greek, he put his own stamp on its demonstration, often producing an imaginative or ingenious proof. So many of the Archimedean fragments that we have already examined in other volumes of this work have seemed to be repetitious and halting when reworked, as for example the countless versions of the *Liber de mensura circuli,* which we edited or mentioned in Volume One. It was as if the compositor of the new version feared to stray too far from the original text. But it was otherwise with Jordanus, who seemed to use the conventional theorems he inherited from his predecessors as an excuse for new ways of proving the old theorems or generating new ones. It is not surprising, then, that this work served as a magnet to attract other original and interesting propositions that circulated in translations from the Arabic but were not sufficiently germane to Jordanus' objectives to have been included by him. The result of this attraction was the new version which we have called *Liber de triangulis Iordani* and which we have edited, translated, and analysed in Part III below.

---

eai equalis angulus *lkt* et coniungatur *kl* recte *tz* educte secundum *l*, equiangulum ergo *lkt* ei / quod est *eai* et est sicut *ai* ad *ie* ita *kt* ad *tl* et permutatim. Equalis vero *ai* ei que est *kt*, equalis ergo et *ei* ei que est *tl*, quare maior *ei* quam *zt*. Equalis vero perimetros perimetro, mäius ergo quod sub *ab* perimetro et *ei* eo quod sub perimetro *gd* et *zt*, quare et dimidia; maius ergo *abp* quam *gdo*." The promise to prove that *gt* / *tk* > *gzt* / *kzt*, comparable to Jordanus' Proposition 5, follows after the text I have given above. I give it in Appendix III.A below rather than here because I used a text there that is slightly different from the one established by Busard.

CHAPTER 3

The Text of the *Liber philotegni*

As I indicated in the beginning of the preceding chapter, five manuscripts contain all or parts of the text of the *Liber philotegni*. These manuscripts are identified and described under the rubric *Sigla* below. In my remarks in this chapter I shall identify the manuscripts solely by the *sigla* assigned to them below. The two manuscripts which contain the title *Liber philotegni* (with some variation in the spelling of *philotegni,* as I noted in Part II, Chap. 1, nn. 12 and 26, and the text after n. 12) are manuscripts *E* and *Br.* It is apparent that *E* is the oldest of the manuscripts and is dated sometime before 1260. Similarly the section of *Br* containing the *Liber philotegni* appears to date from the thirteenth century, though I suppose it to be somewhat later than *E.* Although these two manuscripts are the oldest and most complete copies of the text, they are by no means the best in terms of intelligent readings, for they are often poor and unintelligible.[1] Thus it is unfortunate that these two manuscripts are the only ones to contain Propositions 47–63. Furthermore *Br* contains no diagrams at all and *E* omits diagrams for Propositions 58–63. Hence I have had to reconstruct both text and diagram on many occasions in the last propositions, as the reader can plainly see by examining the variant readings and the legends to the figures. Manuscript *M* occasionally gives more reliable readings, i.e. as far as it goes through Proposition 46 (e.g. see Prop. 10, var. lin. 20; Prop. 32, var. lin. 20), but sometimes it too has absurd readings (e.g. see Prop. 9, var. lin. 24, where *M* has the absurd reading of "FAL figura" for the correct reading of "falsigraphus"). Manuscripts *Fa* and *Bu* are the manuscripts that contain considerable elaboration in the margins and even in the text. They are also the manuscripts that show the most influence of the longer *Liber de triangulis Iordani.* The whole question of the influence of the longer work on the copies of the original text must now be treated at length.

The influences are of the following kinds: (1) influence of the later title *Liber de triangulis Iordani;* (2) influence of the book division followed in most of the manuscripts of the longer treatise, a division that went so far as

---

[1] Some of the errors and the misunderstandings found in these manuscripts I have discussed below.

to renumber the propositions in each book; (3) the addition of proofs similar
to proofs in the longer version, additions that are found either in the margins
or in the text itself. Manuscript *E* seems not to have suffered any of these
influences, though there is one case that may imply some kind of book
division (no doubt without change of the proposition numbers) adopted prior
to the division found in the longer version. But I am doubtful of the meaning
of this case. In Proposition 40, we are told in line 14 "Per primam primi
huius. . . ." This implies that the authority quoted is the first proposition
of the first [book] of this work. If Jordanus really wrote this and meant what
is implied by the phrase, then he considered his work divided into books.
One might add that the grouping of the propositions into four rather distinct
categories (as I pointed out in the preceding chapter) is an indication that
Jordanus originally had four books in mind. But against this we note that
there is no other bit of evidence in *E* that reflects such a division. Furthermore,
it is possible that the phrase means rather "by the first [part] of the first
[*propositum*]," for in fact it is the converse of the first part of Proposition 1
that is the proper authority for the step of the proof being given. Of course
it is also possible that this phrase does represent an intrusion after the preparation of the *Liber de triangulis Iordani*. If so, we would then have to
conclude that the longer version was prepared before the middle of the thirteenth century and that the copyist of MS *E* was somehow influenced by
that new version, but influenced in only this one place. Again I must express
my doubt that such was the case. On the whole, we would be more prudent
to accept the conclusion that the copy of the *Liber philotegni* represented
by manuscript *E* was uninfluenced by the longer version and this probably
because the latter was prepared sometime after the middle of the century.

As we turn to Manuscript *Br,* we notice that the title reads *Phylotegni
Iordani de triangulis incipit liber primus.* It seems, then, that the longer
version has influenced the scribe in the title, both in the addition of the
expression *de triangulis* and in the mention of *liber primus.* I believe these
influences must have come from the longer version and were limited to the
title, for the colophon has no reference to *de triangulis* or to the book division
and merely says "*Explicit liber phylotegni Iordani.*" Furthermore there are
no references, marginal or otherwise, to the beginning of any of the remaining
three books, and, as I have said in the previous chapter, the numbering of
the propositions (so far as that numbering goes through Proposition 46) is
continuous. Nor are there any references in the proofs (other than the one
in Proposition 46, which I have already discussed) that link the text in *Br*
to the longer version *Liber de triangulis Iordani.* Scanty also are the links
of MS *M* with the longer version. These links all are primarily with the title
of the longer version and its division into books. The references to the title
are all marginal ones: 7v mg. sup. "L. I"; 8r mg. sup. "DE TRIANGULIS";
8v mg. sup. "L. I"; 9r mg. sup. "L.II DE TRI." and mg. sin. "l' 2us"; 9v mg.
sup. "L. II"; 10r mg. sup. "DE TRI."; 11r mg. sup. "L. III" and mg. sup.
"[L.] III"; 11r mg. sup."DE TRI."; 11v mg. sup. "L. III"; 12r mg. sup. "DE

TRI."; 12v mg. sup. "L. IIII DE TRI." and mg. sin. "l. 4ᵘˢ"; 13r mg. sup. "IIII DE TRI."; 13v mg. sup. "L. IIII DE TRI." The marginal proposition numbers show no influence of the longer version, all forty-six propositions contained therein bearing successive numbers. The colophon, however, shows the influence of the longer version (13v): "*Explicit liber Iordani de triangulis.*"

The last two manuscripts reflect considerably more influence from the longer version than do the manuscripts we have already discussed. Let us first examine MS *Fa* of the late thirteenth century. The title in *Fa* was, I believe, taken directly from the longer version: *Incipit liber Iordani de triangulis* (see below, variant readings for the title). This title is repeated on the superior margin of folio 124v: *Liber iordani de triangulis de almania,* the *de almania* having been added in a later hand. This addition, because of its lateness, has no significance for the question of whether Jordanus was Jordanus Saxo, a question I raised above in Chapter One of this part of the volume (see footnote 2). Another influence of the longer version on the copy of the *Liber philotegni* in MS *Fa* appears in the confusion in its proposition numbers. *Fa* has the correct numbers of the propositions through Proposition 22. Then suddenly *Fa* designates the next eleven propositions with the numbers 30–40. These are the same numbers that MSS *PbEs* of the *Liber de triangulis Iordani* have, these manuscripts being two of the three manuscripts of the longer version that tend to number all of the propositions consecutively (see Chapter Two of Part III below for a discussion of the proposition numbers of the longer version). After this switch in MS *Fa* to the numbers of MSS *PbEs,* the scribe returns to the correct number for Propositions 34–36, and thereafter abandons numbers for the remaining propositions (Propositions 37–46).

The scribe of *Fa* also shows influence of the longer version on his copy of the *Liber philotegni* by additions in the text of references to the numbering of propositions by books apparent in the *Liber de triangulis Iordani* (e.g., see Prop. 22, var. lin. 12; Prop. 30, var. lin. 8–16; Prop. 31, var. lin. 9; Prop. 32, var. lin 8–20; Prop. 35, var. lin. 10–16; Prop. 36, var. lin. 7–8; Prop. 45, var. lin. 10, 18–19). Finally, the influence of the longer version on the copy in *Fa* is evident in many of the latter's additions to the text that were taken from the longer version or based upon passages in or notes to the longer version (for example, see the following variant readings: Prop. 1, lines 9, 11; Prop. 5, line 3; Prop. 15, line 3; Prop. 37, lines 10–12, 14–15; Prop. 45, lines 14–18, 18–19). Not only were the foregoing passages (and many others not derived from the longer version) added by the scribe of *Fa,* but further he added (1) Proposition 46+1 in the position it occupied in the *Liber de triangulis Iordani* as Proposition IV.4, that is between Propositions 40 and 41 of the *Liber philotegni* (though, to be sure, *Fa*'s proof of this proposition was that found in MSS *Br* and *Bu* rather than that present in the *Liber de triangulis Iordani*), and (2) Propositions IV.12–IV.13 and IV.10 (in that order) from the *Liber de triangulis Iordani.* Also, the copyist of *Fa* added many specific citations of Euclid's *Elements* that were present in the longer version but were absent either in whole or part from the *Liber philotegni* (for example, see the variant readings for Prop. 5, lines 10–11; Prop. 7, lines 8, 9, 11; Prop. 9, lines 6, 9, 12, 19, 22–26; and so on for many other propositions, as an examination of the variants recorded for *Fa* and their comparison with the texts of the *Liber philotegni* and the *Liber de triangulis Iordani* will reveal). But the reader ought to realize that the scribe of *Fa* added many other citations of Euclid that were not in either text. Indeed it ought to be quite clear to the reader who studies the variant readings of *Fa* that this copy was by far the most complete and extensive treatment of the propositions of the *Liber philotegni* as far as it goes through Proposition 46.

   Finally we may note the influence of the longer version on the preparation of the text of the *Liber philotegni* found in manuscript *Bu* of the middle fourteenth century. First evidence of influence is in its title: *Iordanus de triangulis,* and in the confusion of its proposition numbers, a confusion rather like that found in MS *Fa. Bu* has the correct proposition numbers for the propositions through Proposition 18. After this, the numbers for Propositions 19–22 are missing in *Bu.* Then Propositions 23–37 are marked with numbers 30–44, i.e. with the numbers found in MSS *PbEs* of the *Liber de triangulis Iordani.* The final propositions are without numbers. There are some references to the book division added by the scribe of *Bu* (e.g. see Prop. 22, var. lin. 12; Prop. 45, var. lin. 10). Three further points are worth making concerning the influence of the longer version on the copy of the *Liber philotegni* in *Bu.* (1) The scribe of *Bu* added in the margins Propositions II.9–II.12 and II.14–II.16 of the longer version, propositions that the author of the *Liber de triangulis Iordani* had felt were necessary for the development of the propositions concerning the divisions of triangles. (2) Like MS *Fa,* MS *Bu* contains Proposition 46+1 in the position that it occupies in the longer version as Proposition IV.4, that is between Propositions P.40 and P.41 (recall that in *Br* this proposition was added after Proposition 46). (3) After Proposition 46, *Bu* adds Propositions IV.10 and IV.12–IV.28 from the longer version, thus making *Bu* a hybrid copy of both texts.[2] I note finally that the scribe

---

[2] Note that MS *Bu* has added three extra propositions and part of a fourth, the first being on the superior margin of folio 149r and the others on the inferior margin of the same folio. The first three, which concern triangles, are somewhat similar to propositions in the *Liber philotegni* and I give their enunciations below. The fourth, which is cut off by the bottom of the page, is of less concern since it treats of the addition of unequal quantities to equal quantities, and I omit its enunciation. Here are the first three propositions: "[1] Omnium triangulorum in eodem circulo super eandem basim ex eadem parte consistentium proportio trianguli cuius reliqua latera vicem sunt ad equalitatem acta (?) ad quemlibet alium maior est quam eius omnium laterum ad omnia latera alterius proportio duplicata. . . . [2] Omnium triangulorum intra eundem circulum descriptorum maximus est triangulus equilaterus et omnia latera pariter aggregata sunt longiora et illius proportio ad quemlibet alium maior est quam eius omnium laterum ad omnia alterius latera quando acers'vata (*!* acervata) proportio duplicata. . . . [3] Omnium duorum triangulorum super bases equales constitutorum angulus unius super basim existens angulo alterius similiter super basim existenti fuerit equalis cuius latus cum basi angulum equalem continens furit minus illius anguli basim respiciens. . . ." In the course of the proof of the first

of MS *Bu* tends to give a somewhat abbreviated version of the texts and that occasionally he acts independently of both of them, as for example in his entirely distinct version of Proposition 5 (see the English translation of Proposition 5, note 2, for a summary of *Bu*'s proof, and of course the variant readings to the text of Proposition 5 for *Bu's* version of that proposition).

A few words are now in order concerning the orthographic variations found in the manuscripts. In all of the manuscripts we find both *equidistans* and *equedistans.* The former is the one more widely used in this text, though in the beginning *equedistans* was also used frequently (e.g. see Prop. 4, var. lin. 6; Prop. 12, var. lin. 11). I have adopted *equidistans* in my text. There are also multiple spellings for the term for parallelogram. I have adopted *parallelogrammum,* though I cannot find a sure case of this spelling. Probably the most popular form in the manuscripts is *paralellogramum,* but we also find *parallelogramum* and other more divergent forms (e.g., see Prop. 42, var. lin. 1, 4; Prop. 55, var. lin. 3). *Ortogonius* is preferred in the manuscripts to *orthogonius,* though both are used (e.g., see Prop. 40, var. lin. 2, 10; Prop. 43, var. lin. 12; cf. Prop. 30, var. lin. 2, 6) and so I use *ortogonius* in my text. Similarly *ysoperimeter* is preferred to *isoperimeter,* but the latter does occur in MS *M* (see Prop. 5, var. lin. 5). Both *duplicata* and *dupplicata* are found (e.g. Prop. 29, var. lin. 19, 20, 22; Prop. 32, var. lin. 12; Prop. 45, var. lin. 18–19). I have used the former form. Note that a very common error arises from the wide misuse of the abbreviation *eq'd'* or *equid'* for *equidistans* when it ordinarily stands for *equidem.* The result is that we occasionally find the abbreviation falsely expanded to *equidem* (e.g. see Prop. 7, var. lin. 4). There is also a common usage in several of the manuscripts of *reliqū* for *reliquum.* The result is that occasionally it is written as *reliqum* (cf. Prop. 5, var. lin. 9; Prop. 14, var. lin. 2). Similarly *eqū* is expanded to *equm* instead of *equum* (see Prop. 43, var. lin. 1; cf. Prop. 9, var. lin. 14). We also find both *ypotesis* and *ypothesis* (e.g., see Prop. 18, var. lin. 11; Prop. 20, var. lin. 12; Prop. 26, var. lin. 14; Prop. 29, var. lin. 13; Prop. 38, var. lin. 10; Prop. 42, var. lin. 4), and I have used the latter in my text. These then are but a few of the more common variations in spelling that appear in the five manuscripts.

There are still other errors of writing that result rather from a lack of understanding of the tenor of the text by the scribes and we can mention a few of them for each of the three principal manuscripts (*E, Br* and *M*). In addition to misusing *equidem* for *equidistans,* MS *E* also has written *rerum* for *termini* (Intro., var. lin. 3), and *equalis* for *equidistans* (see Prop. 12, var. lin. 11). Furthermore the scribe of *E* has replaced *Age AF* by *AGAF* (Prop. 18, var. lin. 13), *quantitatem* by *equalitatem* (Prop. 28, var. lin. 13), *oxi-*

---

proposition the author refers to the long version ("per xi primi Iordani"). I cannot guarantee the correctness of my transcription of the third enunciation, for as it stands it does not appear to make sense, and it may be that the enunciation continues on to the next line the beginning of which I cannot read.

goniorum by *ortogonorum* (Prop. 40, var. lin. 3), *oxigonius* by *exigonius* (Prop. 40, var. lin. 5), *perpendicularis* by *particularis* (e.g. Prop. 11, var. lin. 7, 8–9; Prop. 12, var. lin. 7, 8; Prop. 13, var. lin. 4) and by *propinquioris* (Prop. 40, var. lin. 7), *G erit* by *girum* (Prop. 44, var. lin. 9), *triangulos* by *angulos* (Prop. 45, var. lin. 9), *minor* by *maior* (Prop. 19, var. lin. 4), and others that can be found by a perusal of the variant readings. I should also note that the rubricator of the text in MS *E* made a number of careless errors (e.g. *Non* for *Cum, Cunctus* for *Punctus, Sineis* for *Lineis,* and *Quobus* for *Duobus*).

Although not directly copied from MS *E* (or at least not exclusively copied from MS *E*), MS *Br* appears to come from the same general tradition as *E* since they share exclusively the title of *Liber philotegni,* are the only manuscripts to include all sixty-three propositions, and share a number of unique readings, a few of which I shall list here: *exteriorum* for *ex terminorum* (Intro., var. lin. 12, 14), the omission of *extrinsecus* (Prop. 2, var. lin. 8), *dicat* for *dicatur* (Prop. 9, var. lin. 13), *sed* for *et* (Prop. 14, var. lin. 13), *EB* for *BE* (Prop. 15, var. lin. 8), the transposition of *quadrato totali* (Prop. 19, var. lin. 11), *Ducaturque* for *Ducatur itaque* (Prop. 25, var. lin. 9), the spelling *dupplicata* (Prop. 29, var. lin. 20, 22), the inclusion of the word *propositum* (Prop. 29, var. lin. 22), *corde* for *cordis* (Prop. 44, var. lin. 14). But despite the common origin of the two manuscripts, MS *Br* has many distinct spellings and readings: *dyameter* (e.g. Prop. 17, var. lin. 6; Prop. 28, var. lin. 11; Prop. 29, var. lin. 6, 19; Prop. 46+1, var. lin. 5; Prop. 62, var. lin. 5), *circonferentie* (Prop. 29, var. lin. 8–9), *circonscribo* (Prop. 49, var. lin. 3; Prop. 57, var. lin. 3; Prop. 63, var. lin. 6); *optusus* (Prop. 8, var. lin. 8; Prop. 26, var. lin. 15; Prop. 30, var. lin. 8); *orthogonaliter* (Prop. 30, var. lin. 6; cf. the passages cited for *ortogonius* and *orthogonius* above), *queconque* (Prop. 34, var. lin. 2–3), *proportionatur* for *proponatur* (Prop. 5, var. lin. 6), *sectoris ad sectorem* for *sectionis ad sectionem* (Prop. 5, var. lin. 10), *FBG* for *FKG* (Prop. 7, var. lin. 7), *arcus* for *acutus* (Prop. 8, var. lin. 7), *mutekefia* for *mutue* (Prop. 13, var. lin. 2), *in propria* for *improba* (Prop. 9, var. lin. 22), *triangula* for *rectangula* (Prop. 13, var. lin. 5), *Sed assignata* for *Falsigraphus* (Prop. 18, var. lin. 8), *patientem* for *partiatur* (Prop. 22, var. lin. 3), *ypostasi* for *ypothesi* (Prop. 22, var. lin. 22), *proportionis* for *probationis* (Prop. 32, var. lin. 10), *vel aliter* for *ultimum* (Prop. 33, var. lin. 8), *supra* for *infra* (Prop. 34, var. lin. 4), *ABES* for *AB eis* (Prop. 40, lin. 11), *equaliter* for *equilaterum* (Prop. 48, var. lin. 3), *principaliter* for *perpendiculariter* (Prop. 58, var. lin. 4), *sequens* for *secans* (Prop. 59, var. lin. 5), *equalium* for *equiangulum* (Prop. 62, var. lin. 16), and *partialis* for *parallelogrammum* (Prop. 62, var. lin. 24).

In addition to the readings given by *M* in the passages already cited above, we can note several more distinctive readings or spellings present in MS *M:* *contiguitas* for *continuitas* (Intro., var. lin. 3) *quidem* for *autem* (Intro., var. lin. 16), *BA* for *AB* (Prop. 3, var. lin. 8), *EBD* for *EDB* (Prop. 4, var. lin. 9); *EB* for *AB* (Prop. 9, var. lin. 8), *cum prima* for *composita* (Prop. 17, var. lin. 2), *comunis* for *communis* (Prop. 18, var. lin. 25), *RK* for *RN* (Prop. 20, var. lin. 29), the omission of *ratione* (Prop. 27, var. lin. 10), *sint* for *sicut* (Prop. 29, var. lin. 10), *contacttum* (Prop. 34, var. lin. 6), *equa* for *equales* (Prop. 35, var. lin. 19), the omission of *equalis* (Prop. 43, lin. 7), *ad scilicet* for *AB* [*sed*] (Prop. 43, var. lin. 15). There are of course other singularities in MS *M* that may be culled from the variant readings, such as the transposition of letters in magnitudes or the transmission of words or the rendering of *E* by *C* or vice versa, *T* by *C* or vice versa, and the reader of the variant readings will also see which readings in *M* concur with or diverge from those in MSS *E* and *Br*. The peculiarities of spelling or expression that occur so often in MSS *Fa* and *Bu* I refrain from listing. They are far too numerous and many result from the great number of additions to or changes from the text as given in MSS *E*, *Br*, and *M*. Suffice it to say, I have included all of those changes and additions in my variant readings so far as I could make them out, and I have discussed and translated a number of them in the notes to my English translation. I have one further comment to make concerning the peculiarities of the readings and content in the various manuscripts: though the text is best served by MSS *E*, *Br*, and *M,* it cannot be established on the basis of them alone and hence I have included the complete readings from all five manuscripts.

There are some peculiarities to the text as a whole that I ought to allude to here, e.g. the frequent use of *infra* where *intra* is preferable (see Propositions 23, 24, 34, 35, 36, 44, and 45). It would seem that Jordanus understood "inside" as one of the possible meanings of *infra*. We also find, as in the case of the *Liber de motu* of Gerard of Brussels, that Jordanus uses *circulus* and *semicirculus* when *circumferentia* and *semicircumferentia* give the meaning more precisely (e.g., see Proposition 34). But this kind of looseness is not very important and continues on down to modern times. We should also note that Jordanus (again like Gerard of Brussels) often merely identifies by name the first term in a ratio or a proportion or a similar expression relating ratios, the second or rest of the terms being identified solely by their letters. For example, we read in lines 11–12 of Proposition 36: "maior est proportio *AB* arcus ad *ATC* quam *AD* ad *AC*," where not only the first but all the terms are arcs. Most of the time it is clear enough as to what is the nature of the magnitudes that are not identified, but sometimes it is confusing and it would have been useful if Jordanus had completed the identifications, and indeed I have often included the identifications in brackets in my English translation. Incidentally, this practice of limited identification is present with other magnitudes like *corda, recta, triangulus, superficies,* etc. Of course if we are concerned only with a ratio, we know that the second term must be the same kind as the first, for Jordanus follows Euclidian proportionality theory in understanding ratios as existing only between magnitudes of the same kind.

I have used the same techniques of capitalization in the text here that I have used in the *Liber de motu* and indeed everywhere in these volumes. Hence I capitalize the enunciations of the propositions and definitions, thereby indicating that these appear in larger hands in the manuscripts (the only exception being the definitions given in MS *Fa*). Diagrams appear in all manuscripts but MS *Br*, where there are no figures. The diagrams vary widely from manuscript to manuscript and hence I have included long legends to many of the figures to indicate the variations. I remind the reader once more that there are no diagrams for Propositions 58–63 in the manuscripts and I have had to construct them on the basis of the text. No comments on my English translation of the *Liber philotegni* need be made beyond those I already made in the translation of the *Liber de motu*. Finally, I give brief descriptions of the manuscripts and assign the following sigla to the manuscripts in the succeeding table, the marginal references in the text being to MS *E*.

Sigla

E = Edinburgh, Crawford Library of the Royal Observatory, MS Cr. I.27, 1r–13v, middle 13c. Contains Props. 1–63. For a description of this manuscript, see *sigla* in Part I, Chap. 3.

Br = Bruges, Bibliothèque Publique, MS 530, 1r–8v, 13c (rest of the manuscript, folios 9–55, 14c). Contains Props. 1–63, and Prop. 46+1 (=Prop. IV.4 of the longer version but with a different proof). Folio 1r–v contains a fragment translated by Gerard of Cremona which was the source of Prop. IV.23 of the longer version. See App. III.B. A description of the manuscript is given in A. de Poorter, *Catalogue des manuscrits de la Bibliothèque Publique de la ville de Bruges* (Gembloux, Paris, 1934), pp. 627–28. This is Vol. 2 of the *Catalogue général des manuscrits des bibliothèques de Belgique*.

M = Milan, Biblioteca Ambrosiana, MS A 183 Inf., 7v–13v, 14c. It contains Props. 1–46 only. The manuscript is described by A. L. Gabriel, *A Summary Catalogue of Microfilms of One Thousand Scientific Manuscripts in the Ambrosiana Library, Milan* (Notre Dame, Ind., 1968), pp. 44–45. The codex contains many astronomical and mathematical works.

Fa = Florence, Biblioteca Nazionale, MS Conv. soppr. J.I.32(=Codex S. Marci Fiorent. 206), 124r–135v, end of 13c. Contains Props. 1–46, plus Prop. 46+1 (with the proof of MS *Br*) and Props. IV.12, IV.13 and IV.10 (in that order) taken from the longer version, *q.v.* On folio 124v (upper margin) we read "liber iordani de triangulis de almania," with the *de almania* written in a later hand. The codex is described by A. A. Björnbo, "Die mathematischen S. Marcohandschriften in Florenz," *Bibliotheca mathematica*, 3. Folge, Vol. 12 (1911–12) pp. 206–11 (see also the new edition of Björnbo's articles on this collection, *Die mathematischen S. Marcohandschriften in Florenz*, ed. of G. C. Garfagnini, Pisa, 1976, pp. 75–81). This codex contains many astronomical, mathematical, optical and physical works, and several works of Jordanus (see R. Thomson, "Jordanus de Nemore: Opera," *Mediaeval Studies*, Vol. 38, 1976, p. 137). Note finally that this manuscript contains on folios 18r–v a *Liber de triangulis datis* (the title written in a later hand) which consists of three main propositions. The first is equivalent to Proposition 22 of the *Liber philotegni* and appears to have been taken therefrom. But because Proposition 22 depends fundamentally on Proposition 14 of the Jordanian work, that latter proposition is first proved before the proof of the main proposition. Again the source was the *Liber philotegni*. The second main proposition in this patchwork is equivalent to Proposition 23 of the *Liber philotegni,* which is probably its source. Again note that Proposition 23 depends on Propositions 18, 19, and 20 of the *Liber philotegni* and hence those subsidiary propositions are given (in a loose fashion) and proved before the proof of the main proposition. Finally, the third main proposition of the *Liber de triangulis datis* is Version I of Hero's theorem for the area of a triangle in terms of its sides which I have published in Appendix IV of Volume 1 of *Archimedes in the Middle Ages.* For the first two propositions, see below, Appendix III.A, where the text is based on this manuscript and on Paris, BN lat. 16647, 92v–95r, 13c.

Bu = Basel, Oeffentliche Bibliothek der Universität, MS F.II.33, 146r–48v (Props. 1–46 of the *Liber philotegni*), 14c. Contains in addition Prop. 46+1 (with the proof of MSS *BrFa*), and on folios 148v–150v Props. IV.10, IV.12–IV.28 of the longer version, *q.v.* It also contains in the margins Props. II.9–II.12 and II.14–II.16 added to the longer version. This then is a hybrid composition of both versions. By far the best description of this manuscript is the unpublished work of B. B. Hughes, *Medieval Mathematical Latin Writings in the University Library, Basel* (1972). Until this work is published consult the inadequate (though still best published) description of A. A. Björnbo and S. Vogl, "Alkindi, Tideus and Pseudo-Euklid," *Abhandlungen zur Geschichte der mathematischen Wissenschaften,* 26_3. Heft (1912), pp. 124–29, 171–72. The manuscript is very rich in mathematical and astronomical works and contains several works of Jordanus (cf. Thomson, "Jordanus de Nemore: Opera," p. 139) and most of the geometrical works used by Jordanus and the author of the longer version.

Pf = Paris, Bibliotheque Nationale, MS lat. 16647, 92v–95r, 13c. These folios contain a copy of the anonymous *Liber de triangulis datis* mentioned above in my description of MS *Fa.* See Appendix III.A below for the text of the first two propositions that relate to the text of the *Liber philotegni.* This manuscript was in the Fournival collection and was discussed by A. Birkenmajer, *Études d'histoire des sciences et de la philosophie du moyen âge* (Wrocław, etc., 1970), pp. 162–65.

THE BOOK OF THE PHILOTECHNIST
OF JORDANUS DE NEMORE
(THE SHORTER VERSION OF THE BOOK
ON TRIANGLES)
THE LATIN TEXT AND ENGLISH
TRANSLATION

/ Incipit liber philotegni Iordani de Nemore
lxiiii (*!*) propositiones continens

[1.] CONTINUITAS EST INDISCRETIO TERMINI CUM TERMI-
NANDI POTENTIA.
5   [2.] PUNCTUS EST FIXIO SIMPLICIS CONTINUITATIS.
[3.] SIMPLEX AUTEM IN LINEA EST, DUPLEX IN SUPERFICIE,
TRIPLEX IN CORPORE.
[4.] CONTINUITAS ALIA RECTA, ALIA CURVA.
[5.] RECTUM EST QUOD NON OMITTIT SIMPLEX MEDIUM.
10   [6.] ANGULUS AUTEM EST CONTINUORUM INCONTINUITAS
TERMINO CONVENIENTIUM.

Title and Introduction

1–2 Incipit . . . continens *E* Phylotegni Iordani de triangulis incipit liber primus *Br*
Iordanus de triangulis *Bu* / Incipit . . . continens *om. M hic sed mg. sup. fol. 8r et
aliis fol. hab. M* DE TRIANGULIS / Incipit . . . continens *om. Fa hic sed ante
Prop. 1 hab. Fa* Incipit liber Iordani de triangulis *et mg. sup. fol. 124v hab. Fa* Liber
Iordani de triangulis de almania (*!*)

1 philotegni *correxi ex* phyloteigni *in E et ex* Phylotegni *in Br; vide Par. II, cap. 1, n.
12 et vide coloph. inferius*

3 [1] *addidi et etiam numeros petitorum sequentium* / Continuitas: contiguitas *M* /
termini: rerum *E*

5 Punctus: Cunctus *E* / est *Fa om. MEBrBu* / *supra* fixio *scr. Bu* simplex / continuiatis
(*!*) *E*

6 *post* autem *add. Br* continuitas / in¹ *om. E* / est *Br om. ME et tr. Fa post* autem /
est duplex *tr. Bu* / duplex: duplex autem *E*

7 triplex: triplex autem *E*

8 alia²: et alia *Bu*

9 est *om. E* / non *om. E* / omittitur *Br*

10 continuorum in- *tr. E*

11 termino convenientium: *lac. Fa*

[7.] FIGURA VERO EST EX TERMINORUM QUALITATE ET AP-
PLICANDI MODO FORMA PROVENIENS.

Superficiei igitur figura accidit "ex terminorum qualitate," quia alia curvis,
15 alia curvis et rectis, alia tantum rectis terminis continetur. Et curvis quidem
uno vel pluribus, rectis autem et curvis duobus vel pluribus, rectis vero tribus
vel amplioribus. Ex "applicandi modo," quoniam ex eo provenit diversitas
angulorum. Quidam enim rectis equales, et quidam minores, et quidam
maiores efficiuntur.

1. IN OMNI TRIANGULO, SI AB OPPOSITO ANGULO AD MEDIUM
BASIS DUCTA LINEA DIMIDIO EIUSDEM EQUALIS FUERIT, ERIT
ILLE ANGULUS RECTUS; QUOD SI MAIOR, ACUTUS; SI VERO MI-
NOR, OBTUSUS.

5 Sit triangulus *ABC,* et ad medium *AC* ab angulo *B* ducatur linea *BD.* Si
ergo *BD* equalis fuerit *DC* [Fig. P.1a], et angulus *B* partialis erit equalis angulo
C, et eadem ratione angulus partialis *B* erit equalis angulo *A,* et sic duo anguli
supra basim, scilicet *A* et *C,* erunt equales reliquo, scilicet *B* angulo totali,
sic quod idem erit rectus. Si vero *BD* erit maior [Fig. P.1b], erunt anguli
10 supra basim reliquo maiores; ille ergo est acutus. Si minor econtrario [Fig.
P.1c], ille idem reliquis maior erit, sequiturque eum inde obtusum esse.

12 vero *MBrBu om. EFa* / ex terminorum: exteriorum *EBr* / qualitate *om. E*
12–13 amplicandi *Fa*
13 modo *om. Fa*
14 ex terminorum: exteriorum *EBr* / alia: a *Fa*
15 tantum *om. Fa* hic sed add. post continetur / terminis continetur *tr. E* / Et *om. Bu*
16 rectis[1] . . . pluribus *om. Fa* / autem *BrBu om. E* quidem *M*
17 amplioribus: pluribus amplioribus *Br* / applicandi modo: amplicandi *Fa* / provenit
      diversitas *tr. Bu* / provenit: procedit *Fa*
18 quidam[1,2,3]: quidem *Br,* ? *E* / enim *om. Bu* ex *E* / equalis *Fa* / et[2] *om. Bu*

Prop. 1

1 1 *mg. sin EBu, mg. dex. Br* 1[a] *Fa* p[um] *mg. dex. M* / omini (?) *Fa* / ab *om. Fa*
2 dimidio eiusdem *om. E* / erit *om. Br*
5 triangulus: angulus *Bu* / ad medium AC *BuBr om. MEFa* / B: BB *Bu*
6 equalis fuerit *tr. E* / B partialis *MFa* partialis *E* DBC *BrBu*
6–7 angulo C *M tr. EBr* C *Fa* angulo DCB *Bu*
7 partialis B *MEBrFa* DBA *Bu* / erit *om. Bu* / angulo A *MBr* A angulo *E* A *Fa* DAB
      Bu
8 supra: super *Bu* / scilicet[1] . . . erunt *om. Bu* / et *om. E* / reliquorum *E* / scilicet[2]
      . . . totali *om. Bu* / scilicet[2] *om. Fa* / B *om. Br*
9 sic quod: sicque *Br* sic *E* / erit rectus *tr. Br* / rectus: sunt *Fa* et add. *Fa* (*cf. var. vers.
      long. Prop. I.1, lin.* 5–6) quoniam anguli super basim equipollent angulo extrinseco
      ad B / *post* vero *scr.* (*et del.?*) *Br* m / erit *E om. MBrBuFa*
10 supra: superiora (?) *Br* super *Bu* / *ante* reliquo *scr. E* alteri *et Fa* ex / reliquo: tertia
      Br / maiores *Bu* maius *MBrFa* maior *E* / ergo: igitur *Br* / est acutus: ductus est *E*
11 idem . . . erit: tertio maius *Br* / reliquus *Fa* / maior: minor *E* / eum inde *MBrFa*
      eum *E* inde eum *Bu* / obtusum esse *tr. E* et supra scr. inde / *post* esse add. *Fa* (*cf.
      var. vers. long. Prop. I.1, lin.* 6–9) Hec probatio manifestum est si circulus circum-
      scribatur quia angulus in primo modo consistet in semicirculo, secundo modo in
      maiori portione, tertio modo in portione minori semicirculo

2. INFRA (*!* INTRA) TRIANGULUM CUIUS DUO LATERA
EQUALIA SINT LINEA AB ANGULO AD BASIM DUCTA QUOLIBET
EORUM MINOR ERIT, EXTRA VERO MAIOR.

Sint in triangulo *ABC* duo latera *BA*, *BC* equalia [Fig. P.2a], et ab angulo

1v   *B* ad basim infra (*!* intra) triangulum / linea ducta sit *BD*. Quia igitur angulus

6   *D* maior angulo *C* cum sit intrinsecus, erit et maior angulo *A*, quia est equalis
angulo *C*. Et sic *AB* maior *BD*. Sit item *BD* cadens extra triangulum applicans
basi producte in *D* [Fig. P.2b]. Et quia *A* angulus extrinsecus (*!* intrinsecus)
maior angulo *D*, erit et angulus *C* maior eodem; et ita *BD* maior *BC*, quod

10   intendimus.

3. SI TRIANGULUS DUO HABUERIT LATERA INEQUALIA, ET AB
ANGULO QUEM CONTINENT INFRA (*!* INTRA) TRIANGULUM LI-
NEA FUERIT AD BASIM DUCTA, LONGIORE BREVIOR ERIT, BRE-
VIORI VERO EQUALEM SIVE MAIOREM SIVE MINOREM ESSE

5   CONTINGIT.

Esto triangulus *ABC*, cuius latus *AB* sit maius *BC* [Fig. P.3], atque ut prius
infra (*!* intra) triangulum ducatur ad basim linea *BD*, quam minorem esse
linea *AB* constat, quoniam angulus *D* extrinsecus maior est angulo *C*, quare

Prop. 2

  1   2 *mg. dex. Br mg. sin. Bu om. E* 2ᵃ *Fa* 2ᵘᵐ *mg. dex. M*

  2   equalia sint *tr. Fa* / sint *EFaBr om. Bu* sunt *M* / ab angulo *supra scr. Bu* / quodlibet
Fa

  3   *ante* eorum *supra scr. Bu* laterum / minor erit *tr. Fa*

4–5   Sint . . . infra tri- *scr. M ante* Infra *in lin. 1* (*et post hoc lectiones huiusmodi non
laudabo*)

  4   duo . . . BC *om. E* / ab angulo: a ergo (?) *Fa*

  5   ad basim *tr. Bu post* triangulum / Quia: et *Bu*

  6   D: ADB E (*sive* est) *Bu* / angulo C *M* C anguli *E* est C angulo *Br* C *Fa* angulo DCB
Bu / cum . . . intrinsecus *om. Bu* / intrinsecus *ME* extrinsecus *BrFa* / et *om. E* /
angulo² *om. Fa* / angulo A: A anguli *E* angulo DAB *Bu*

6–7   quia . . . C *om. Bu*

  6   quia *ME* qui *Br* quia A scilicet *Fa*

  7   angulo C: C anguli *E* / AB: AB est *Bu* / maior a° *Br* / item: inter (?) *E* ei[us?] *Br* /
cadens: candens (!) *E* / ampplicans *Fa*

  8   basim *E* / Et quia: eritque *M* / A . . . extrinsecus: angulus CAB *Bu* / extrinsecus
om. EBr

  9   maior¹: maior est *Bu* / angulo D *M tr. Br* DM *E* D *Fa* angulo ADB *Bu* / angulus
C *M tr. EBr* C *Fa* angulus BCD *Bu* / maior eodem *tr. Bu* maior *Fa* / ita: ita erit *Bu*

9–10   quod intendimus *om. Br.* secundum quod intendimus *Bu*

Prop. 3

  1   3 *mg. sin. MEBu mg. dex. Br* 3ᵃ *Fa* / duo habuerit: hubuereit (!) duo *Fa* / et *om.
Bu* / ab: ab C *E*

  2   quam *Bu*

  3   fuerit: fuerint *Fa* / fuerit *supra scr. Bu* / ducta *tr. E ante* fuerit

  5   contingit: convenit *Br*

  6   Esto: Esto exemplum *E* / BC: AB *E*

  7   esse *om. E*

  8   AB: BA *M* / constat quoniam: probatur igitur *Bu* / D extrinsecus *MEFa* D *Br* BDA
Bu / angulo C *M tr. Br.* C *EFa* angulo BCA *Bu* / quare: sic *Bu*

et maior angulo *A*. Item contingit etiam *BD* equalem esse *CB* si angulus *C*
10 est acutus quoniam tunc reliqui anguli, scilicet *B* totalis et *A*, eo maiores
erunt, et sic ut *ABD* angulus sit secundum quem *C* sit maior *A*, erit itaque
D angulus intrinsecus equalis angulo *C*, et sic latera sunt equalia, et omnis
infra (*!* intra) ducta linea ea minor, et omnis extra maior.

4. IN OMNI TRIANGULO CUIUS DUO LATERA INEQUALIA SUNT,
LINEA AB ANGULO AB IPSIS CONTENTO DUCTA AD MEDIUM BA-
SIS CUM MAIORE IPSORUM MINOREM ANGULUM CONTINEBIT.

Sit triangulus *ABC*, sitque *AB* maius *BC* [Fig. P.4], et protrahatur linea
5 *BD* dividens basim per equalia; dico ergo quod angulus *B* versus *A* minor
B reliquo. Designetur enim linea *DE* equidistans linee *CB*. Quia igitur linea
DE est dimidium linee *BC*, erit et *DE* minor dimidio *AB*, quod est *EB*. Ergo
angulus *BDE* maior est angulo *ABD*. Ergo angulus *DBC* maior est eodem
quia est equalis angulo *EDB*, et hoc est propositum.

5. SI IN ORTOGONIO AB UNO RELIQUORUM ANGULORUM AD

9 A: DAB *Bu* / Item *om. Bu* laterum (*?*) *Fa* / etiam: autem *Bu* / equalem esse *tr.*
Fa / CB: B *Br* / angulus C *M tr. EBr* C *Fa* BCA angulus *Bu*
10 acututus (*!*) *Fa* / quoniam: quia *Br*
10–12 reliqui . . . equalia: reliquo maior erit angulo CBD, quare CDB ei erit equalis *Bu*
10–11 scilicet . . . sic: et sic ut secundum CDB scilicet B et A eo maius erunt CE sit *Br*
10 maiores *E* maius *MFa*
11 ABD . . . sit[1]: BDE sunt *E* / ABD *Br* CBD *MFa* / angulus . . . A *om. Fa* / erit:
erunt (*?*) *Fa* / ita *E*
12 D *om. Fa* / equalis: maior equalis *E* / angulo C *M tr. EBr* CA (*?*) vero *Fa* / latera
sunt: sint latera *Fa*
13 linea *tr. E ante* infra / ea: EA *Br* / omnis *om. Bu* omnis erit ducta *Fa* / extra *supra*
scr. Fa / *post* maior *add. Fa* per primam

Prop. 4

1 4 *mg. sin. EBu mg. dex. Br* 4ᵃ *Fa* (*et om. M qui hab. mg. sup.* L.I *et in fol. 8r* DE
TRIANGULIS) / inequalia sunt *tr. Fa* / sunt *om. Bu*
2 ab[2]: sub *Bu* / ducta *tr. Bu post* basis / medium: me dum (*!*) *Fa*
3 ipsorum: eorum *Fa* / minorem . . . continebit: continebit angulum minorem *Fa*
4 sitque: sunt que *E* sit *Bu* / maius: minus *Fa*
5 ergo: itaque *Bu* / quod que (*?*) *Br*
5–6 B . . . reliquo: DBC maior est angulo DBA *Bu*
5 B . . . minor: verus A est maior *Fa* / AC (*?*) *Fa* / minor *correxi ex* maior *in M et*
maior est *in EBr et* est maior *in Fa*
6 B: K (*?*) *Br* / enim *om. E* / DE: recta *E* / equidistans *Fa* equedistans *MBr*(*?*)*Bu* (*et*
post hoc lectiones huiusmodi non laudabo et vide com. meum in Cap. 3) equid' *E*
7 linee *om. Fa* / BC: CB *Bu* / minor: maior *Fa* / *post* AB *add. Bu* dimidium / Ergo:
et ideo *Bu*
8 BDE *BrBu* BD *ME* EBD (*?*) *Fa* / maior . . . ABD: est maior BDE *Fa* / est[1] *om.*
Bu / ABD *correxi ex* ABC *in M et* ABE *in EBr et* EBD *in Bu* / Ergo: quare et *Bu*
/ angulus *om. Fa* / DBC: DBE *EBr*
8–9 maior[2] . . . propositum: qui est illis equalis eodem maior erit *Bu* / eodem . . . EDB:
DBC *Fa*
9 EDB: EBD *M* / et . . . propositum: Item equidem hoc est *Br* / propositum *E om.*
MBrFaBu

Prop. 5

1 5 *mg. sin. M* (*?*), *EBrBu* 5ᵃ *Fa* / angulorum *bis E*

BASIM LINEA DUCATUR, ERIT REMOTIORIS ANGULI AD PROPIN-
QUIOREM RECTO MINOR PROPORTIO QUAM BASIS SUE AD BASIM
ALTERIUS.

5   Huius autem probatio requirenda est que in libro ysoperimetrorum. Nam
si triangulus ortogonius proponatur et describatur circulus secundum exigentiam linee que subtenditur recto angulo, fixo scilicet centro in termino
linee continentis rectum angulum, deinde linea ab eodem angulo supra centrum protrahatur ad reliquum latus continens rectum angulum, erit maior
10   proportio sectionis ad sectionem quam anguli supra centrum ad alium angulum supra centrum [cf. Figs. P.5].

2r   / 6. IN TRIANGULO CUIUS DUO LATERA INEQUALIA SUNT, SI
AB ANGULO PERPENDICULARIS DUCATUR, PORTIONIS BASIS

2 basem *Bu* / remorioris (*?*) *E* / anguli *om. E*
3 recto *om. E* / minor proportio *tr. Br* / *post* basis *add. Fa* (*cf. enunt. vers. long. Prop.
I.5+ et var. lin. 1–19*) et anguli recto propinquioris super latus rectum constituti ad
angulum remotiorem minor est proportio quam lateris secti ad eius partem recto
angulo propinquiorem / basem *Bu*
5–11 Huius. . . . centrum: Statuatur triangulus ABC, et sit A angulus rectus et producatur
linea BE, dividatur linea AE per medium et medietas per medium et ita donec
proveniat ad dimidium minus et que sit ED cui sit equalis EF, ducta linea BF, et
quia angulus FBE est minor angulo EBD, sit differentia EBG; posito G ex parte A,
dividatur angulus EBD per medium et medietas per medium donec occurrat minus
angulo EBG qui sit H et similis potest linee ED, sit ER cuius angulo (*!* angulus) ADB
(*!* EBR) erit minor H. Detrahatur igitur ER ab EC, faciens post ita ut relinquatur
CL ei equalis vel minor cuius angulus B (*et lac.*) erit minor H quia minor angulo
ER (*!* EBR). Cum igitur angulus EBF cum angulo CL (*!* FBL) ——— (*verbum hic
del.*) sit minus angulo EBD, non erit idem cum illo, totus multiplex H quotus multiplex
est linea EF, ER. Sed cum linea LF sit multiplex ER, non erit totus multiplex angulus
LBF angulo H, quia nec angulo EBR. Addit igitur CE super multiplicem ER cum
non addat angulus CBE super totum multiplicem H. Cum sit ergo CE ad ER maior
proportio quam anguli CBE ad H, atque H tota pars anguli ABE quota ER linee
EA, est CE ad EA maior proportio quam CBE ad EBA. Inde est quod sequitur *Bu*
5 autem *ME om.* BRF*a* / probatio: proportio *Br* / requirenda est *tr. E* / que *M om.
Fa* quo (*?*) *E* / in *om.* MB*r* / isoperimetrorum *M*
6 ortogonio *E* / proponatur: proportionatur *Br* / *post* circulus *add. E* et
7 scilicet centro in: centro scilicet *Br*
9 protrahatur: procuratur *Fa* / reliquum (*!*) *M*
9–11 erit . . . angulum *om. E*
10 sectionis ad sectionem: sectoris ad sectorem *Br*
10–11 angulum *om. Br*
11 *post* centrum *add. Fa* (*cf. Fig. P. 5 var. Fa*) Sit ortogonus FAD et ab F descendat
FC. Dico quod minor est proportio DFC anguli ad CFA (-A *supra*) angulum quam
DC ad CA. Super centrum F describatur circulus secundum quantitatem FC qui
secabit DF in E et pertranssibit FA que producatur ad B. Age ex prima parte octave
(*?*) quinti Euclidis maior est proportio FDC ad FCA quam FCE ad FCB. Ergo a
primo maior est proportio FDC ad FCA quam CF$\overset{E}{A}$ ad CFB. Ergo ex prima et ultima
quinti Euclidis maior est proportio DC ad CA quam anguli CFE ad CFA angulum,
quod est propositum

Prop. 6

1 6 *mg. sin.* MBrBu v[i^a] *mg. dex. E* 6^a *Fa* / sunt *om. Bu*
2 *post* angulo *add. Bu* ad basem

QUE INTER IPSAM ET MAIUS LATUS DEPREHENDITUR MAIOR
ERIT AD RELIQUAM PROPORTIO QUAM ANGULI AD ANGULUM.

5   Sit triangulus *ABC* [Fig. P.6] longiusque latus *AB* et perpendicularis *BD*
et *AD* est maior *DC*, non enim *CD* est equalis *DA*, sic enim *CB* est equalis
BA; item nec *CD* est maior *DA*; quia, si hoc, secetur equalis ei que est *DA*,
DG. Ducta *BG* hinc sequitur quod *CB* sit maior *AB*, quia *BG*. Quia igitur
AD est maior *DC*, sic ut *DE* sit ei equalis, et protrahatur linea *BE*. Cum
10   igitur *AE* ad *ED* sit maior proportio quam anguli *ABE* ad angulum *EBD*
per proximam; et coniunctim et quia *ED* ut *CD* et angulus *EBD* ut angulus
CBD, erit proportio *AD* ad *CD* maior quam anguli *ABD* ad angu-
lum *CBD*.

7. SI SUPER EANDEM BASIM INTER LINEAS EQUIDISTANTES
DUO TRIANGULI STATUANTUR, CUIUS LATUS LATERUM SE SE-
CANTIUM MAIUS FUERIT EIUS ANGULUS SUPERIOR MINOR ERIT.

Sint linee equidistantes *AB*, *CD*, inter quas super basim *EF* consistant
5   trianguli *EGF* et *EHF*, lateraque eorum *EG* et *FH* se super *K* secantia [Fig.
P.7]. Si ergo ponatur *FH* maior *EG*, erit angulus *EGF* maior angulo *FHE*
hac ratione. Quia enim *FKG* triangulus triangulo *EKH* est equalis, erit linea
FK ad *EK* sicut *KH* ad *KG* per sextum Euclidis. Quare tota ad totam sicut

3 ipsam: ipsa *ME* / deprehendimus *E*

5 Sit: Sit ut solet *Bu* / BD: est DB *Br*

6 et: et quidem (?) *Fa* quia igitur *Bu* / est[1] *om. E*

6-9 non . . . DC *om. Bu*

6 est equalis[1,2] *tr. E* / CB: DB *E* / est[3]: erit *Fa*

7 BA . . . maior *om. E* / secetur: sequetetur (!) *E* sc se t (?) *Fa*

8 DG: FDG *Fa* / BG[1] *EBrFa* DG *M* / quia BG *E* quia DG *MBr* et D maior est G
   Fa / igitur AD: GAD *Br*

9 AD: maior AD *E* / DC: DE *E* / DE: D *Fa* / sit: sunt *E* / linea: ei linea *Br*

9-10 Cum igitur: igitur *Fa* et *Bu*

10 sit: est *Bu*

11 per . . . coniunctim: et probatur coniunctum ut AD ad ED sit maior proportio quam
   anguli ABD ad angulum EBD *Bu* / proximam: premissam *Br* / post coniunctim *add.*
   Fa verbum quod non legere possum / post quia *scr. et del. Bu* angulus / ut[1]: est ut
   FaBu / EBD . . . angulus *om. E* / ut[2]: est ut *Fa*

12 CBD: EBD *Br* / AD: AB *E* / ad[1,2] *om. Fa*

Prop. 7

1 7 *mg. sin. MBrBu* vi[i[a]] *mg. dex. E* 7[a] *Fa* / eamdem *E* / basem *BrBu* / equidistantes:
   equidem *E*

2 trianguli *EBu* anguli *MBrFa*

3 maius: maior *E*

4 equidistantes: equidem *E* / basem *M* / consistant (?) *Fa*

5 trianguli: anguli *Fa* / EGF: EFG *E* / et EHF *om. Fa* / FH: FG *E* / se . . . secantia:
   sint se secantia super K *Fa* / K: R *Bu* (*et paene ubique in ista propositione hab. Bu*
   R *pro* K *sed in figura hab.* K)

6 angulo *om. E*

7 Quia enim *om. Fa* / FKG: FBG *Br* / EKH: KH *Fa* / *post* equalis *add. Fa* quia EGF
   triangulus et EHF sunt equales per xxx.7 [i.e. 37] primi ergo dempto communi /
   erit: igitur *Fa*

8 per . . . Euclidis *om. Bu* / sextum Euclidis: 14[am] (?) 6[i] eius precedente 16[a] (?) 5[ti]
   eiusdem *Fa* / tota: tota HF *Fa* / totam: totam GE *Fa*

FK ad *KE*. Maior ergo *FK* quam *EK*. Sicut igitur *FK* ad *KE* ita sit *EK* ad
10 *KL*, que minor est *KF*. Ducta igitur linea *GL*, sequitur angulum *LGK* equalem
esse angulo *EHK*, nam illi trianguli sunt similes, et ita totus angulus *FGE*
maior erit angulo *EHF*, et hoc est quod proponitur.

8. SI INTER LINEAS EQUIDISTANTES SUPER EANDEM BASIM
TRIANGULI CONSISTANT, EIUS SUPERIOR ANGULUS MAXIMUS
ERIT CUIUS RELIQUA LATERA SUNT EQUALIA, ET QUANTO EI
PROPINQUIORES, TANTO REMOTIORIBUS AMPLIORES.
5 Sit triangulus cuius latera equalia *ABC*, et alter *ADC* [Fig. P.8]. Est igitur
angulus *CBD* obtusus. Nam latera *AB*, *BC* sunt equalia, et sic angulus *C* est
acutus; sed angulus *C* et *B* totalis sunt equales duobus rectis, et sic *B* totalis
est obtusus. Ergo *CD* est maior *AB* quia *BC* suo equali. Ergo per proximam
angulus *B* maior est angulo *D*. Item statuatur triangulus *AEC* cuius angulus
10 *E* inter *B* et *D* cadat, eritque *CE* minor *CD* per tertiam huius. Sed *CE* est
maior *AE*, quod patet quia angulus *EAC* est maior *C* partiali quia est maior
C totali cum *C* sit equalis *A* partiali. Erit itaque *DC* maior *AE*. Deinde ut
prius [poteris] argumentare.

9 *post* KE¹ *add. Fa* per 13ᵃᵐ [5ᵗⁱ] Euclidis / igitur: igitur est *Bu* / sit: sicut (*sive* sunt)
E
10 KL *lac. Bu* / est: erit *Bu* / KF: DEF *E* / Ductaque *E* / GL: LG *Br*
11–12 nam . . . EHF *om. E*
11 nam . . . similes *om. Bu* / illi: isti *Fa* / *post* similes *add. Fa* ex viᵃ 4ⁱ 6 (!) Euclidis
et diffinitione similium superficierum (?)
12 et . . . proponitur *M* et hoc proponitur *E* et hoc est propositum *BrFa* secundum
quod proponitur *Bu*

Prop. 8

1 8 *mg. sin. BrBu mg. dex. M* viiiᵃ *mg. sin. E* 8ᵃ *Fa* / Si *om. E et om. Fa* hic sed add.
post basim / supra *Fa* / eamdem *E* / basem *M*
2 conssistant (?) *Fa* / maximus: maior *E*
3 cuius . . . equalia *tr. Bu ante* eius *in lin. 2 et om. Bu* sunt / et: in *Fa*
5 ADC: ADE *Bu* / Est: quia *Bu*
6 CBD: CDB *E*
6–9 Nam. . . . D: est, erit linea CD maior linea AB et per premissam argumentum est
Bu
6 Nam: na (!) *Fa*
6–7 angulus² . . . sed *om. E*
7 acutus: arcus *Br* / et¹: vel *Fa* / totales¹ *Br* / B²: L *Br*
8 optusus *Br* / Ergo² . . . proximam: proxima *E* / *post* proximam *hab. Fa aliquid quod
non legere possum*
9 Item statuatur *tr. Bu*
10 eruntque *Fa* / CE¹ ME *om. Br* linea CE *Bu* C *Fa* / minor: minorum (!) *Fa* / Sed
CE: Set (?) C *Fa*
10–13 Sed . . . argumentare: et cum ipsa maior sit quam AE, ut prius poteris arguere *Bu*
11 maior¹: minor *Br* / C . . . maior³ *om. E*
12 *ante* C¹ *scr. Br aliquid quod non legere possum* / C² *om. EFa* / itaque: ita *M* igitur
Fa
13 [poteris] *addidi sed cf. var. lin. 10–13* / argumentare *MFa* argueⁱˢ *E* argʳᵉ *Br*

2v   / 9. SI DUO TRIANGULI QUORUM DUO ANGULI EQUALES SUNT
FUERINT EQUALES, CUIUS LATUS EQUOS ANGULOS AMBIEN-
TIUM ILLORUM MAXIMUM FUERIT, EIUS OMNIA LATERA PARI-
TER ACCEPTA MAIORA ERUNT.

5   Sint trianguli equales *ABC* et *DEF* et anguli *B* et *E* equales [Fig. P.9],
sitque linea *AB* maior *DE* et *EF*, eritque ob hoc *BC* minor utraque earum,
nam latera sunt mutekefia. Protrahatur igitur *DE* usque ad *G* ut sit tota *EDG*
equalis *AB*. Sed et de *FE* resecetur *EH* ad equalitatem *CB*, et subtendatur
linea *GH*, que erit equalis *AC*, et triangulus *ABC* erit equalis *GHE*. Dico

10   igitur lineam *GH* maiorem esse *DF*. Sit enim sectio earum *L*; et quia trianguli
FED et *HEG* sunt equales, erunt *FHL* et *LGD* equales. Sed et angulus angulo
est equalis. Erit ergo sicut *GL* ad *LF* ita *LH* ad *LD*, et tota *GH* ad *DF*
tanquam *LH* ad *LD*. Si ergo *LH* est maior *LD*, et tota maior tota. Si autem
dicatur quod sit equalis, ducta linea *DH* erit angulus *LDH* equalis angulo

15   *LHD*. Et quia angulus *HDE* est minor angulo *DHE* quia *C*, *GHE* anguli
sunt equales et *C* est maior *FDE*, si enim equalis esset *ABC* similis *FDE*. Si
minor, simile inconveniens remanebit: angulus *FDG* maior angulo *GHF*. Si

Prop. 9

       1 9 *mg. sin. EBrBu mg. dex. M* 9ᵃ *Fa* / anguli *corr. Fa ex* angulo / sunt *om. Bu*
  2-3 ambeuncium *E*
       3 illorum *BrFa om. Bu* (*et tr. E post* fuerit) illorum 4 *M* / latera *om. E*
       4 accepta . . . erunt *om. Br*
       5 *post* equales[1] *add. Bu* proponuntur / equales[1] *om. E* / DEF *EBu* DFE *MFaBr*
       6 sitque: sit itaque *Br* / *post* hoc *add. Fa* per 14ᵃᵐ 6ᵗⁱ Euclidis / minor: maior *M* /
           utrumque *Fa*
       7 nam . . . mutekefia *om. FaBu* / protrehatur (?) *Fa* / ut: et *Bu* / sit: sunt *E* / *post*
           tota *scr. et del. Bu* EG / EDG: DG *E*
       8 equalis: equaliter *E* / AB: EB *M* / Sed *om. Bu* / et[1] *om. E* / secetur (?) *Fa* / EH: CH
           Br
       9 *post* AC *add. Fa* per 4ᵃᵐ primi Euclidis / et . . . GHE *om. FaBu*
     10 igitur: ergo *Br* / linea *Fa* / maiorem esse *tr. E* / earum L: illarum *E*
 10-12 quia . . . equalis: trianguli id G et angulus angulo quod patet quia totus EFD toti
           EH GH (! EHG) est equalis. Dempto ergo communi et cetera *Fa*
 10-11 trianguli . . . Sed: triangulus LFH est equalis triangulo LGD *Bu*
     11 LGD: LDE *E* LDG *Br*
     12 est equalis *om. Bu* / est *om. E* / ergo *om. Bu* / LF: FL *E* / *post* LD *add. Fa* ex prima
           parte 1ᵉ g (? 14ᵉ) 6ⁱ (?) Euclidis et ita 6ᵃ (? 13ᵃ) quinti / et tota: tota ad *E*
 12-15 GH. . . . DHE *om. Br hic sed add. post* inconveniens *in lin.* 17 (*et hab.* igitur *ante*
           GH)
     13 tanquam *E* / LD[1]: LF *Br* id itaque (?) el (?) *Fa* / *ante* Si[1] *scr. E* Si ergo LH et ad
           LD / ergo: igitur *Br* (*et post* hoc *lectiones huiusmodi non laudabo*)
     14 dicatur quod sit *om. Bu* / dicat *EBr* / sit equalis: sunt equales *E* / *post* equalis[1,2] *add.*
           FaBu vel minor / equalis[2]: equs (!) *E*
     15 quia[1] *om. Br*
 15-17 quia[2] . . . inconveniens *om. FaBu*
     15 C: C et *Br* / GHE: G *E* / anguli *MEBr om. FaBu*
     16 essent *Br* / ABC: ABE *E*
     17 angulus: cuius *Fa* / FDG: DFG *E et corr. Br ex* FGG (?)

itaque fiat angulus *LDT* equalis angulo *LHF*, quoniam trianguli similes sunt,
erit *TL* equalis *LF* et ideo *GL* maior eadem, et sic tota *GH* maior *FD*,
20   similiterque *AC* maior *FD*, atque *AB* et *BC* pariter sumpte maius sunt *DE*
et *EF* per ultimam quinti Euclidis, quare et tria tribus maius erunt.

Si autem *HL* sit minor *LD*, improba: isti trianguli *HDG* et *FHD* sunt
equales et super eandem basim, ergo inter lineas equidistantes, et *FD* est
maior *GH*, ut ponit falsigraphus. Ergo angulus *F* est minor angulo *G* per
25   ante proximam. Sed *C* est maior *G*, ergo est maior *F*, quod est falsum, et
deinde ut prius.

10. SI SUPER EANDEM BASIM INTER LINEAS EQUIDISTANTES
TRIANGULI STATUANTUR, CUIUS RELIQUA LATERA EQUALIA
FUERINT EADEM PARITER ACCEPTA MINORA ERUNT, ET
QUANTO EIS PROPINQUIORA, TANTO REMOTIORIBUS BREVIORA.
5   Sint inter lineas equidistantes duo trianguli *ABC* et *ADC* [Fig. P.10a], et
sint *AB*, *BC* equales; a *B* protrahatur linea ad equalitatem *BC* et sit tota linea

18 LDT: LDE (?) *Fa* / similes sunt *tr. E*
19 TL *om. E* CL *M* / equalis: maior vel equalis *Bu* / GL: GF *E* / eadem . . . maior
  om. E / ante FD *scr. et del. Bu* FG / post FD *add. Fa* resumpta 14ª 6ti et 13ª 5ti ut
  superius
20 similiterque: similiter quia *EFa* sitque *Br* / AC: AD *E* / atqui *Fa* / sumpte . . . sunt:
  sunt maius *Fa* / sumpte *E om. MBrBu*
21 *post* EF *add. Fa* simul acceptis / per . . . Euclidis *om. FaBu* / ultima (?) *E* / Euclidis:
  eī eumdem *E*
22–26 Si. . . . prius *om. Bu* Aliter, ut authorus indicat (*sive* iudicat), est idem de maiore.
  Sit triangulus HDF; est equalis triangulo HDG. Ergo per XXX.9ªm primi Euclidis
  HD et FG sunt equidistantes. Dico ergo quod GH maior est FD. Si enim equalis,
  igitur sectiones earum apud vel (! L) equales, quod patet ex 14ª 6ti et 13ª quinti
  Euclidis consideratis LFH, LDG triangulis (?) equalibus et angulis (?) ad L contra se
  positis ——— (?) equalibus, ergo per 4ªm primi Euclidis erit HF equalis DG et sicut
  HF ad DG sic AC ad ED propter equidistantem et 16ªm (?) 5[ti] Euclidis. Quare est
  equalis ED, et erat minor propter suam equalem BC. Si det adversarius FD maiorem
  esse GH, ex hoc et prehabitis concludo oppositum. Sic angulus F totalis maior est
  angulo G totali quia sic se habent H et D sui equales propter equidistantes. Sed HFD
  est minor HDG per septimam huius. Ergo residus (!) F maior residuo G. Igitur LH
  linea maior LF. Sed sicut LG ad LF sic tota HG ad FD, quod satis patet, ergo et
  cetera *Fa*
22 sit: minor st (?) minus *E* / improba: in propria *Br* / isti: ibi *E* / HDG: BDG *M* HGD
  E / FHD: FAD *E*
23 eamdem *E* / equidistantes: equales *E* / FD: FA *M*
24 falsigraphus *E* FAL figura *M* falsigraficus *Br* / minor: maior *E*
25 *ante* Sed *scr. Br* vel (?) / C: D *Br* / *post* G *add. Br* Sed et est maior D / est falsum
  M tr. EBr
26 ut: est *M*
Prop. 10
    1 10 *mg. sin. E mg. dex. MBrBu* 10ª *Fa* / Si *om. Fa* / eamdem *E*
    3 fuerunt *E*
    5 equidistantes: equidem *E*
  5–6 ABC . . . equales: et ABC triangulus cuius latera AB, BC sunt equalia et alio modo
    ADC *Bu*
    5 et ADC *om. Fa*
    6 equales: equalia *M* equalia et *Fa* / a B *om. Br et tr. Bu post* linea¹ / ad equalitatem
    EBu AD equalis *M* BG equalis BC *BrFa* / tota: una *Fa* / linea² *om. Bu*

ABG. Sed et *AD*, quod sit longius latus, producatur ad equalitatem *CD* usque ad notam *H*, appliceturque *G* cum *H* et cum *D*. Et quia angulus *CBD* equalis est angulo *DBG* propter equidistantes lineas quia *B* extrinsecus est equalis

10 *A*, et *A*, *C* sunt equales propter *AB*, *BC* equales, et *C*, *B* equales coalterni *BD*, *AC*, et linea *BG* equalis linee *BC*, et *BD* communis, erit basis *GD* equalis *DC*, et ideo equalis *DH*. Cum sit ergo angulus *DGH* equalis angulo *DHG*, erit totus angulus *AGH* maior angulo *AHG*, et ideo linea *AH* maior linea *AG*. Ex quo constat propositum.

15 Secunde parti deserviat figura eadem [cf. Fig. P.10b], et sit *BA* maior *BC*. Et quia *CAB* angulus minor est angulo *ACB*, erit angulus *DBG* minor angulo *CBD* ratione equidistantie. Et quia *BG* equatur *BC*, erit basis *DG* minor *DC*

3r et ideo minor *DH*. / Quare cum sit angulus *GHD* minor angulo *DGH*, erit minor toto *AGH*, et sic linea *AG* minor linea *AH*, secundum quod exigit

20 propositio.

11. OMNIUM DUORUM TRIANGULORUM QUORUM BASES EQUALES ERIT PROPORTIO UNIUS AD ALTERUM TANQUAM ALTITUDINIS UNIUS AD ALTITUDINEM ALTERIUS.

7 Set *Fa* / et *om. Bu* / sit *MEBrFa* sicut *Bu* / equalitatem: qualitatem *Bu*

8 appliceturque *MBr* amplicetur *E* ampliceturque *Fa* applicetque (?) *Br* / G cum H *om. E* / cum D: C *Bu*

9–11 propter . . . AC *om. Bu*

10 A¹: A intrinseco *Fa* / C¹: et C *Fa*

10–11 BC . . . BD¹: C equalis coalterius D *Br*

10 equales²: latera equalia *Fa* / C, B: BC *E* / equales coalterni *correxi ex* equa coalterni *in M* equale CE alterni *in E* coalterni sunt equales *in Fa*

11 BD, AC *om. Fa* / linee *om. Fa* / et² *om. Bu* qua propter *Fa* / BD²: LD *E* / communis *Br* communiter *M* communi *EBu* facta communi *Fa*

12 *ante* DC *scr. et del. Bu* B

12–13 equalis¹ . . . ideo *om. E*

12 Cum . . . ergo: quare *Fa*

13 AHG: DHG *Br* ABG *Fa*

13–15 linea² . . . maior: quam *M*

14 AG: G *E* / quo *om. E*

15 Secunde . . . BC: De secunda parte reiteremus figuram flem̄ (*! eandem*) *Bu* / deservit *Fa* / BA maior: BA maior quam *Fa* basis maior angulus A quam *Br* / BC: quam DC *E* / *post* BC *add. Fa* et hanc suppositionem cum facilitate ostende per hoc quod AB, BC prioris trianguli sunt latera equalia et anguli super basim equales er̤it (*!*) erunt secundum hoc CAB angulus partialis minor ACB partiali quarum (?) et ACB (?) totali et sic AB (?) secundi trigoni maior (?) BC eiusdem

16 CAB angulus *tr. Bu* ACB angulus *Br* / est *om. E* / angulo ACB *M* AEB angulo *Br* angulo AEB *E* ACB *Fa* / erit: erit et *Bu* in (?) erit *scr. et del.* (?) *Fa*

17 ratione equidistantie *om. Bu* / DG: BG *Fa* / *post* DC *add. Fa* per 2 (?) 4ᵗⁱ Euclidis

18 Quare: quia *Br* / *ante* GHD *scr. et del. Bu* DHG / GHD: BHD *Br* / *post* erit *add. Bu* et

19 *post* toto *add. Bu* scilicet / et: quod *Br* / sic *om. Bu*

20 propositio *M* proportio *EBr* propō̄ *Fa* propō *Bu*

Prop. 11

1 11 *mg. sin.* ME *mg. dex.* BrBu 11ᵃ *Fa* / duorum *om. E*

2 tamquam ME (*et hab. M ubique et E saepe; post hoc lectiones huiusmodi non laudabo*)

3 unius: ipsius *FaBu* / ad altitudinem: ab altitudine *M*

Sint trianguli *ABC* et *DEF* quorum bases *AC* et *DF* equales [Fig. P.11],
5 eriganturque perpendiculares a terminis predictarum basium, ductisque equidistantibus ipsis basibus per *B* et *E* et concludantur rectangula *ACGH* et
DFLM. Quia igitur rectangulum ad rectangulum sicut perpendicularis ad
perpendicularem, et quia trianguli dimidia sunt rectangulorum, et quia item
perpendiculares altitudines triangulorum determinant, erit trianguli ad trian-
10 gulum tanquam altitudinis sue ad altitudinem alterius.

12. OMNIUM DUORUM TRIANGULORUM QUORUM UNIUS DUO
LATERA EQUALIA DUOBUS EQUALIBUS ALTERIUS LATERIBUS
EQUA FUERINT, CUIUS BASIS MAIOR FUERIT IPSIUS AD ALTERUM
MINOR ERIT PROPORTIO QUAM BASIS EIUS AD BASIM ALTERIUS.
5 Designentur itaque trianguli *ABC* et *DEG* [Fig. P.12], et *AC* maior *DG*,
lateraque *AB* et *BC* equalia et equa sunt *DE* et *EG* equalibus. Divisis itaque
basibus per equa ducantur linee *BF* et *EH* que erunt perpendiculares, et ob
hoc perpendicularis *BF* erit minor *EH*. Nam quadrata *DH* et *EH* sunt equalia
quadratis *AF*, *FB*; sed quadratum *AF* est maius quadrato *DH*, nam basis
10 maior basi; ergo quadratum *EH* est maius quadrato *BF*; ergo *EH* est maius
BF. Signetur itaque linea *KLM* in triangulo *ABC* equidistans *AC* et equalis

4 *post* Sint *add. E* duo / et² *supra scr. Bu*
5 erigaturque *Fa* / a terminis: alterius *Br* / a: in *M* / -que² *MBu om. EBrFa*
5–6 equistantibus (!) *E*
6 ipsius *Fa*
7 DFLM: DFEM *Br* / rectangulum¹: triangulum (?) *E* / ad rectangulum *om. Fa* /
   perpendicularis: particularis *E*
8 perpendicularem: particularem *E* / *post* perpendicularem *add. Fa* quod patet per
   proximam et coniunctis superficiebus ad bases equales / *post* trianguli *add. E* ductudia
   (?) / *pro* dimidia *hab. E* verbum quod non legere possum / *post* rectangulorum *add.*
   Fa per xl (! xli ?) primi
8–9 item perpendiculares: recte particulares *E*
8 item: ratione (?) *M* cetere *Br*
9 determinantur (?) *Fa* / trianguli: triangulus *Br*

Prop. 12
1 12 *mg. sin. ME mg. dex. BrBu* x[ii²] *mg. dex. E* 12ª *Fa* / duo *om. Fa*
2 equalibus *ME*, bis *Fa*, *om. BrBu* / lateribus *om. Fa*
3 fuerint: fuerit *Fa* / basis *om. Bu* / ad: at *Fa*
4 minor . . . proportio: terminorum perit (?) proportio *E* (*et corr. E* perit *in* erit) /
   eius: ipsius *Br* / basim: basem *E*
5 et² . . . DG *om. FaBu*
6 -que¹ *om. E* / *ante* BC *scr. et del. Bu* AC / et² *om. Bu* / equa: equales *E* / sunt *MBrFa*
   sint *EBu* / EG: CG *Br* / equalibus *om. FaBu*
7 linee: BE *Fa* / EH: EB *Br* HEH *Fa* / perpendiculares: particulares *E*
8 perpendicularis: perpendiculares *Bu* particulares *E* / BF erit: EF erunt *E* / erit minor
   tr. Bu
8–11 EH¹ . . . BF: cum sit AC maior DG *Bu*
8 DH: DA *E*
9 FB *MEBr* BF *Fa* et BF *Bu* / nam (?) *Fa*
10 est¹ *om. MFa*
11 singnetur *Fa* / KLM: K LMI *Fa* / equidistans *MFa* equedistans *Bu* equalis *E* equid'
   Br / AC . . . equalis *om. Bu*

DG, sitque *AC* ad *KLM* sicut *KLM* ad *PT*. Quia ergo *BL* ad *BF* sicut *KM* ad *AC*, erit *PT* ad *KM* sicut *BL* ad *BF*. Ergo maior est proportio *PT* ad *KM* quam *BL* ad *EH*. Sed que est proportio *BL* ad *EH* eadem est *KBM* trianguli

15 ad triangulum *DEG* per proximam. Ergo maior est proportio *PT* ad *KM* quam *KBM* ad *DEG*. Sed que est proportio *AC* ad *PT* ea est trianguli *ABC* ad *KBM* quia sunt similes. Ergo maior est proportio *AC* ad *KM* sive ad *DG* quam trianguli *ABC* ad triangulum *DEG*.

13. SI FUERINT DUO TRIANGULI EQUALES, ERUNT EORUM BASES IPSORUM ALTITUDINIBUS MUTUE.

Statuantur trianguli ut solet *ABC* et *DEG* [Fig. P.13], et perpendiculares altitudines determinent, extrahanturque perpendiculares a terminis basium,

5 et basibus equidistantes per *B* et *E* transeant donec rectangula concludantur *ACFH* et *DGKL*; et quia trianguli equales sunt, et rectangula quia ipsis dupla.

---

12 DG: basi DG *Bu* / sitque: suntque (*sive* sicutque) *E* sit quia *Fa* / KLM^{1,2}: KM *Bu* / sicut KLM: N *E* / PT: PC *BrFa*

12–13 BL . . . AC: BF ad BL sicut AC ad KM *Bu*

13 *post* AC *add. Fa* quia KL ad AF sicut BL ad BF, sit LM ad FC et per xi^{am} quinti Euclidis KL ad AF ut LM ad FC, et per 11^{am} 5^{ti} LK ad AF ut KM (?) ad AC. Quare per cxi^{am} (? 11^{am}) 5^{ti} BLA, DBF (! BL ad BF) sicut KM ad AC, et sicut KM ad AC sit PT ad KM / erit: ideo *Fa* / PT^{1,2}: PC *Br* / KM^{1,2}: RM *Bu* / BL ad BF: BLA, DBF (! BL ad BF) et BLA, BF (! BL ad BF) maior quam BL ad EH per xiii^{am} 5^{ti} Euclidis per secundum partem quinti Euclidis *Fa* / Ergo maior est: maior igitur *Bu* / est *om. E*

14 EH^{1}: H *E*

14–17 Sed. . . . similes: Sed trianguli ABC ad triangulum KBM sicut AC ad PT. Quare est (?) trianguli KBM ad triangulum DEG tanquam BL ad EH *Bu*

14 Sed . . . EH *om. M* / Sed . . . proportio: Set *Fa* / eadem est *E* ea est *MBr* sicut *Fa* / KBM *M* (*et corr. Br ex* KEM) KLM *E* HBM (?) *Fa*

14–16 trianguli . . . KBM *om. E*

15 *post* proximam *add. Br* DEG / PT: PC *Br*

16 DEG: DEF (?) *Fa* / PT: PC *Br*

16–18 ea. . . . DEG: eadem est trianguli ABC ad triangulum DEG ordinemur ———— (?) quod ex ipsa et 7^a (?) et hinc ex una parte post hoc (?) AC (?) ———— (?) PT ———— (?) KM ———— (?) trianguli ex alia parte presentis (?) AB ———— (?) vel KB triangulus (*sive* in 3us) DEG quoniam ergo AC ad PM sicut ABC triangulus ad KBM triangulum, et PT ad KM maior quam KBM trianguli ad DEG triangulum. Ergo linee (?) AC ad lineam KM maior quam ABC trianguli ad triangulum DEG et habet istud argumentum certitudinem iuxta 1 iiii^a (! in xiiii^a ?) quinti *Fa*

17 KBM: KLM *E* / Ergo . . . proportio: maior proportio erit *Bu* / sive: et *Bu*

Prop. 13

1 13 *mg. sin.* ME *mg. dex.* BrBu 13^a *Fa* / erunt eorum *tr. M*

2 *post* bases *scr. et del. Bu* equales / ipsorum *MBrBu* eorum *E* eorumdem *Fa* / altitudini *E* / mutue: mutekefia *Br*

3 DEG: DG *E* / et^2: et quia *Fa*

4 determinant *FaBu* / extrahanturque *MEBr* extrahantur *Bu* extrantur (!) *Fa* / perpendiculares: particulares *E*

5 basilibus (!) *Fa* / equidistantes: equidem *Br* / rectangula: triangula *Br*

6 ACFH *FaBu* ACHF *MEBr* / sunt *om. Br* / *post* dupla *add. Fa* per 41^{am} primi

Et ideo sicut AC ad DG ita KG ad CF, nam sunt mutekefia, et hoc est quod proponitur.

14. LINEIS DATIS ITA QUAMBILET ILLARUM DIVIDERE UT SI-
3v CUT UNUM / DIVIDENTIUM AD RELIQUUM ITA IDEM RELIQUUM AD ALTERAM PROPOSITARUM.

Sint linee date et coniuncte AB, BC [Fig. P.14], et supra compositam
5 designemus semicirculum ADC, erigentes perpendicularem BD, qua posita diametro circumducamus circulum BDF circa centrum G, et producamus lineam $AFGE$, continuantes cum B lineam BE, equidistantem ei ducamus FH. Quia ergo quod ex AE in AF equatur quadrato AB contingentis, erit AE ad AB sicut AB ad AF. Itemque propter lineas equidistantes erit EF ad
10 FA sicut BH ad HA, et permutatim AF ad AH sicut EF ad BH. Quare tota AE ad AB sicut FA ad AH. Et quia EA ad AB sicut AB ad AF, erit AB ad AF sicut AF ad AH. Erit ergo AB ad FA sicut FE ad BH. Itaque permutatim

---

7 *post* ideo *add.* Fa per primam partem 13me 6^{ti} / DG: GD *Fa* / KG: GK *FaBu* / CF *Fa* EF *MEBrBu* / nam . . . mutekefia *om.* FaBu / mẹtekefia *E*

7–8 et . . . proponitur *om.* Br quod proponitur *M* propositum *EFa* secundum quod proponitur *Bu*

Prop. 14

1 *ante* 14 *scr. mg. sin.* M liber secundus *et mg. super.* L.II DE TRI. / 14 *mg. sin.* ME *mg. dex.* BrBu xi[iii^a] *mg. dex.* E 14^a *Fa* / Lineis: Sineis (*!*) *E* / *post* Lineis *add. mg. sin.* Bu duabus / ita *tr.* FaBu *ante* dividere / itaque *E* / illarum *MFa om.* E istarum *Br* earum *Bu*

1–2 ut sicut: et secundum *E*

2 ad: atque *E* / reliquum[1] *correxi ex* reliqum *in* EBr reliqũ *in* Fa et reliqũ *in* MBu / idem *om.* E / reliquum[2] *E* reliqum *MFa* reli^m *Bu* reliqũ *Br*

4 linee date *tr.* FaBu / et coniuncte *om.* E / coniuncte *MBu* cōnĩcte *Br* coniucte *Fa* / BC: et BC *Bu*

5 semicirculum: circulum *Br* / ADC *BrFaBu* AB (*sive* a B) *M* AD (*sive* a D *sive* ad) *E* / qua posita *Br* qua posito *EBu* quo (*sive* qua) posito *M* quam posita *Fa*

6 dyametro *BrBu* / circumdamus *Fa* / BDF: BẸDF *Fa* / circa: contra *E* / et producamus *MEBr* producamusque *Fa* prodicamus *Bu*

7 AFGE *FaBu* AFG et *MEBr* / continuantes: et continentes *Fa* / cum: E cum *FaBu* / lineam *E* liã *MBr* lia *Fa* li^a *Bu* / equidistantem: equidem *Br* / equidistantem ei: ei quẹ (*del.*) equidistantem *Bu* / cumducamus *Br*

8 ergo . . . ex: ex quo *E* / equantur *E* / AB contingentis: contingentis scilicet AB per 3$^{[am]}$ 5^{ti} libri (*?*) *Fa* contingentis scilicet AB *Bu*

9 AB[2]: AE *E* / AF: AF per 16^{am} 6^{ti} *Fa* / Itemque propter: Item per *Br* / equidistantes: equidem *Br* equidemtantes (*!*) *Fa* / erunt *Fa*

10 FA: FH *Br* / BH[1]: BA *Br* ḌBH *Fa* / *post* HA *add.* Fa per aliam (*sive* tertiadecimam) sexti / ad AH *om.* E / AH: HA *Br* / BH[2]: DH *Fa* (*et post* DH *add.* Fa per 16^{am})

11 AE: EA *Br* / AH: AB (*?*) *M* HA *Br* / *post* AH *add.* Fa per 13^{am} 5^{ti} / EA: AE *Br*

11–12 erit . . . AF[1] *om.* E

12 *post* AH *add.* Fa proxima 5^{ti} / Erit ergo *tr.* Fa / FA: AF *Br* / FE: EF *FaBu* / *post* BH *add.* Fa proxima (*sive* per xi^{am}) / Itaque permutatim: permutatim iterumque (*?*) *Fa*

FE ad *BA* sicut *BH* ad *FA*, et *BD* equatur *EF*, et *BC* ad *BD* sicut *BD* ad *AB*, et sicut tandem *BC* ad *EF* sicut *BH* ad *AF*. Sed *EF* ad *BH* sicut *AF* ad

15   *AH*. In equalitate ergo proportionis *CB* ad *BH* sicut *BH* ad *AH*, et convertitur sicut *AH* ad *HB* sicut *HB* ad *BC*, quod propositum fuit.

15. DUABUS LINEIS PROPOSITIS ALTERAM ITA DIVIDERE QUOD SICUT RELIQUA CUM MAIORE DIVIDENTIUM SE HABET AD EANDEM ITA EADEM SE HABEAT AD MINOREM.

Date linee ut prius sint *AB*, *BC* [Fig. P.15], quibus coniunctis super totam

5   designetur semicirculus *ADC*, et super terminum linee *AB* in communi puncto *B* statuatur angulus medietas recti ducta linea *BD*, et a *D* demittatur perpendicularis super *ABC*, que sit *DE*. Quia ergo angulus *BED* rectus est, erit angulus *BDE* medietas recti. Linea ergo *DE* equalis *BE*. Cum itaque sit linea *DE* inter lineas *CE*, *EA* proportionaliter constituta, erit *CB* cum *BE* ad *BE*

10   sicut *BE* ad *EA*.

13 FE: EF *FaBu* / BA: HA *E* / sicut[1]: si *Bu*
13–14 et[1] . . . AF[1]: et quia EF equatur ED (*!*) atque CB ad BD sicut BD ad BA per primam partem correllarii octave (*?*) 6[ti] erit CB ad EF sicut BH ad AF per interpositum huius proportionis CB ad EF sicut EF ad AB (*?*) et EF ad AB sicut BH ad ad (*?*) AF et tandem per xi[am] 5[ti] *Fa*
13 et[1] *MBu* sed *EBr* / BD[1]: EF *Bu* / EF: BD *Bu* / et[2]: atque *Bu* / BC: CB *Bu*
14 AB: BA *Bu* / et . . . tandem: erit *Bu* / sicut[1]: sic *Br* / BC: CB *Bu* / EF *corr. Br ex* BF / sicut[2]: sic *E* / Sed: set *Fa*
15 AH[1]: AB *Br* / BH[2]: AF *Fa* / AH[2]: HA *Bu* / et convertitur: in equalitate a lineis sicut ad invicem ordinantis (*?*) ut ex una parte sit CB prima termina (*?*), EF secunda, BH tertia, ex alia parte BH prima, AF secunda, HA tertia inconvertitur *Fa*
16 sicut[2]: ita *FaBu* / quod . . . fuit *MBr* quod proponitur *E* tunc (*? quod?*) propositum fuit facere *Fa* quod propositum fuit facere *Bu* / post fuit *hab. Br aliquid quod non legere possum*

Prop. 15
1 15 *mg. sin. MEBr mg. dex. Bu* 15[a] *Fa* / Duabus: Quabus (*?*) *E*
2 sicut: sic *E* / habet *MBrFaBu* habeat *E*
3 *post* minorem *add. Fa* (*et cf. var. vers. long.*) cui (*?*): Intentio propositionis est hec, quod conposita et ex indivisa et maiori portione alterius linee (*?*) divise se habeat ad maiorem portionem sicut maior portio ad minorem
4 AB: AD *Fa* / BC: et BC *FaBu* / coniunctim *Bu*
5 designetur: de singnetur *Fa* / terminum linee *tr. E* / AB: AD *Fa* / comuni *E* / punctum *Fa*
6 medietas: metas (*!*) *E* / a D *om. Fa* / demittatur *MBr*, (*?*)*Fa* dimittatur *E* deducatur *Bu*
7 que: quam *Fa* / BED: HED (*?*) *Fa* / rectus est *tr. Br* / est *om. FaBu* / erit: erit et *FaBu*
8 BDE *om. E* / DE equalis: D est qualis *Fa* DE est equalis *Bu* / BE: EB *EBr* linee BE per quintam primi Euclidis *Fa* linee BE *Bu* / itaque: ita *Br*
9 lineas *MEBr*, (*?*)*Fa* lineam *Bu* / EA: et EA *FaBu* / proportionabiliter *Bu* / *post* constituta *add. Fa* per primam partem 8[ve] 6[ti] / erit: quia (*sive* que) *Br* / *post* erit *add. FaBu* ut proponitur / BE[1]: HE *E* / ad: ab *E*
10 *post* EA *add. Fa* et est BE maior (*corr. ex* minor *?*) proportio (*!* portio), EA minor secundum propositionis exigentiam

16. LINEAM DATAM ITA SECARE UT QUE UNIUS PORTIONIS AD RELIQUAM EA SIT ILLIUS RELIQUE CUM QUALIBET DATA LINEA AD EANDEM PROPORTIO.

Sint ut prius linee *AB, BC* [Fig. P.16], et sit *BC* data linea, et semicirculus
5   super eas *ADC*, et linea perpendicularis *BD*, et continuetur linea *CD*, et posito centro in *C* circuetur portio circuli que sit *ED*. Quia igitur sicut *AC* ad *DC* ita *DC* ad *BC*, et quia *DC* equatur *EC*, erit ut que *AC* ad *EC* ea sit *EC* ad *BC*. Ergo divisim que *AE* ad *EC* ea est *EB* ad *BC*. Ergo permutatim que *AE* ad *EB* ita *EC* ad *BC*, et hoc est quod proponitur.

17. DUABUS LINEIS DATIS ALTERAM SIC SECARE UT SICUT SE
4r   / HABET ALTERA AD UNUM DIVIDENTIUM ITA COMPOSITA EX EADEM ET RELIQUO DIVIDENTIUM SE HABEAT AD IDEM.

Sint linee *AB, BC* [Fig. P.17], et continuate, et illis etiam directe applicemus
5   equalem *BC*, que sit *EC*, et super lineam *AE* fiat circulus *ADEG*, continuemus lineam *DG* que sit equalis *AC*, et inscribatur in circulo ita quod diameter *AE* secet in *F* et sit *FD* equalis *AB* et sit *GF* equalis *BC*. Quia igitur *EF* ad *DF* sicut *FG* ad *FA*, erit et *FE* ad *AB* sicut *BC* ad *AF*. Quare permutatim

Prop. 16

  1-9 *mg. sin. totam propositionem hab. Fa*
   1 16 *mg. sin. EBr mg. dex. MBu* 16ᵃ *Fa, et ante Prop.* 17 *hab. Fa* 16ᵃ *et* 17ᵃ / *ita: sic E*
  2-3 *data linea tr. Br*
   3 *eamdem E*
   4 *post* linee *add. Fa* coniuncte / BC¹: et BC *Bu* / et¹ . . . linea *om. FaBu* / BC² (?) *E*
   6 *ante* C *scr. et del. Bu* cir- / circuetur (?) *Br* / portio: proportio *Fa* / sit: sunt *E* / igitur *om. E* / *ante* AC *scr. E* ad (*sive* AD)
   7 DC¹: DE *E* / DC²ʼ³: DT (?) *Br* / *post* BC *add. Fa* per secundam partem 8ᵛᵉ 6ᵗⁱ / *post* EC¹ *add. E* et quia DCᴱ / que: que est *FaBu* / sit: sicut *E* / *post* sit *scr. et del. Fa* AC ad
   8 Ergo divisim: erit ergo *Bu* / Ergo . . . AE: erit ergo quo AC *Fa* / AE: AG (?) *E*
  8-9 est . . . proponitur: AE ad EB per 19ᵃᵐ 5ᵗⁱ et ideo AE ad EB proportio que est EC ad BC per xiᵃᵐ eiusdem et hoc est propositum *Fa* / est . . . que: AE ad EB et ideo *Bu*
   9 ita: ea *E* proportio que est *Bu* / et hoc est: secundum *Bu* / est quod *om. E* / quod proponitur: propositum *Br*

Prop. 17

   1 17 *mg. sin. BrE* (*et hab. E etiam* xviiᵃ) *mg. dex. M, om. Bu* 16ᵃ et 17ᵃ *Fa*
   2 altera: alteram *Fa* / composita *EBrBu* conposita *Fa* cum prima *M*
   3 *post* idem *mg. scr. Bu* reliqū
   4 Sint . . . continuate: Si eadem (*! Fa,* Sed *Bu*) linee ut solet continuate sunt (*Fa,* sint *Bu*) AB et (*Bu om. Fa*) BC *FaBu* / et¹ *tr. Br ante* BC / applicemus *tr. Fa post* BC *in lin.* 5 / applicavimus *E*
   5 sit: sunt *E* / EC: CE *FaBu* / fiat circulus: statuamus semicirculum *FaBu*
  5-7 continuemus . . . equalis²: continuet que (? quam?) sub statuata DEFG cuius portio DF sit equalis AB et FG equaliter *Fa*
   6 lineam DG *tr. E* / DG: DFG *Bu* / sit: sunt *E*
  6-7 que . . . GF: cuius portio DE sit AB et FG *Bu et add. et del. Bu* equales
   6 in *om. E* / dyameter *Br*
   7 in F: MF *Br* / equalis²: equatur *Bu* / Quia: quare *E*
   8 DF: FD *Fa* / sicut¹: sic *Bu* / FG: perpendicularis *E* GF *Br* / *post* FA *add. M* per penultimam tertii *et add. E* perpendicularem *et add. Fa* per ʒᵃᵐ X (*!* xxxivᵃᵐ) 3ᵗⁱ et secundam partem 15ⁱᵐᵉ (?) HG (*!* libri 6ᵗⁱ)

sicut *FE* ad *BC* ita *AB* ad *AF*. Et quoniam *BC* equatur *CE*, ergo disiunctim
10 erit *FC* ad *CB* sicut *FB* ad *FA*; ita permutatim sicut *FC* ad *FB* ita *BC* ad
AF, quod est propositum.

18. PROPOSITIS DUABUS LINEIS QUARUM UNA SIT MINOR
QUARTA ALTERIUS MINORI TALEM ADIUNGERE UT QUE
ADIECTE AD COMPOSITAM EA SIT COMPOSITE AD RELIQUAM
PROPOSITARUM PROPORTIO.

5 Sint date linee *AB*, *BC* rectum continentes angulum, concluso rectangulo
ABCD [Fig. P.18a]. Deinde super lineam *AB* statuamus rectangulum equale
rectangulo *ABCD* cui desit ad complementum totius linee quadratum per
6^m librum Euclidis, sitque illud *AEFG*, linea *EF* equalis *EB*. Falsigraphus:
AE est equalis *EB*. Dissolutio: rectangulum *AF* est equale *DB* et angulus
10 angulo. Ergo que est proportio *AB* ad *AE* ea est *EF* sive *EB* ad *BC*, et sic
BC est quarta *AB*, quod est contra ypothesim. Item nec *AE* est minor medietate

9–10 FE . . . sicut *om. M*
   9 AF: FA *FaBu* / Et *om. FaBu* / equatur (?) *Fa* / ergo disiunctim *tr. FaBu ante* quoniam
   10 FC¹: FO (*sive* FC?) *E* / ad CB: ad C ad CB *E* / sicut¹: sic *Bu* / *post* FA *add. Fa per*
        18^am 5^ti / ita permutatim: itaque permutatim *E* permutatim itaque *FaBu* / FC² *Fa*
        FE *BrBu* / FB²: BF *FaBu*
   11 AF: FA *FaBu* (*et post* FA *add. Fa* quare econverso BC ad FA sicut FC ad BF) /
        quod est propositum *MBr* quod proponitur *E* et hoc est propositum *Fa* et ut propositum
        erat *Bu*

Prop. 18
   1 18 *mg. sin.* EBr *mg. dex.* MBu 18^a *Fa* / Propositis: positis *M* Prepositis *E*
   2 minori: minorem *MBu*
   3 adiecte: adiuncte *E* / compositam ea *MBrBu* compositum ea *E* conpositam eam
        Fa / composite: proposite *M* conposite *Fa*
   4 propositarum: positarum *Br*
6–7 equale . . . ABCD: rectangulos (?) recti angulo equalem *Bu*
   6 equale: equalem *Br* / equale *tr. Fa post* ABCD
   7 cui desit: cum d e sit *E* / quadrate *E*
7–8 per . . . Euclidis *om. FaBu*
   8 librum: lib' *Br* / illud *MFaBu om. Br* istud *E* / AEFG: AFEG *E*
8–19 linea. . . . intuenti: per xx 7^am 6^ti Euclidis cum sit rectangulum ABCD equm (!)
        trigonum constituere sitque ergo linea EF equalis linee CB, erit igitur AB ad AE sicut
        EF sive EB ad BC per primam partem xime (! xiiime) 6^ti Euclidis, ergo permutatim
        per 16^am 5^ti AB ad BE sicut AE ad BC, utrumque igitur tam AE quam EB maior
        CB, quod palam est ex proportione, igitur ab altera illarum dematur (?) BE et si
        placet de BE cui equalis sit BH quia igitur AB ad BE sicut AE ad BH, erit AB (*supra
        scr.*) ad BE sicut BE ad EH per 19^am 5^ti sitque hoc est propositum; si fiat conversio
        (?), EH ad EB sicut EB ad AB *Fa*
   8 EB: BE *M* / Falsigraphus: Sed assignata *Br*
8–10 Falsigraphus . . . angulo *om. Bu*
   9 rectanguli *Br*
   10 Ergo . . . proportio: erit igitur *Bu* / que: qui (?) *Br* / ea est: sicut *Bu* / ad² *bis E* /
        BC: BE *Br*
10–19 et. . . . intuenti: ubicumque (?) igitur tam AE quam EB erit maior CB, de altera
        ergo earum demetur BC et si placet de BE cui (?) equalis sit BH. Quia igitur AB ad
        BE sicut AE ad BH, erit AB ad BE sicut BE ad EH. Sicque huius propositum si fiat
        conversio *Bu* (*et cf. var. lin. 8–19 in Fa*)
   10 sic: sicut *E*
   11 ypotesim *E* / Item: idem *Br*

AB. Nam secundum hoc, que est proportio *AB* ad *AE* ea est minor quam *AB* ad *BC*; sic itaque *EB* est minor medietate *AB*. Age. *AF* est equalis *DB*. Ergo que est *AB* ad *AE* ea est *EB* ad *BC*, et sic *BC* est minor *AE*, et etiam

15 *EB*; dematur ei equalis ab *EB*, et sit illud *HB*; itaque que est *AB* ad *EA* ea est *BE* ad *HB*. Ergo permutatim que est *AB* ad *EB* ea est *AE* ad *HB*. Ergo que est *AB* ad *BE* ea est *BE* ad *EH* iuxta illam quinti Euclidis: si linea ad lineam ut pars ad partem, ergo ut residuum ad residuum. Ergo econverso que est *EH* ad *EB* ea est *EB* ad *AB*, et hoc est propositum diligenter intuenti.

20 Aliter. Sit una linea ex *AB*, *BC* [Fig. P.18b], supra quam describatur semicirculus *ADC*, et producatur perpendicularis *DB*, que erit minor dimidio *AB*, nam *BD* est medio proportionalis inter *AB*, *BC*. Et deinde ut supra divisa sit igitur *AB* per equalia ad *E*; et circumscripto semicirculo *AGB* extrahatur *EG*, que cum sit maior *BD* eidem equalis sit *EL*; et ducta linea *DL* sit

25 communis sectio ipsius et circumferentie *T*, a quo demittatur perpendicularis super *AB*, et sit *TM*, que etiam est equalis *DB*. Sed quadratum *DB* est equale quadrangulo quod est ex *AB* in *BC*, et quadratum *TM* fit ex *AM* in *MB*.

4v Ergo quadrangulum / *AB* in *BC* equatur quadrangulo *AM* in *MB*, et abhinc sicut superius procedendum est.

12 secundum hoc: FH *E* / AE: AC (?) *Br*
13 AB[1]: EB *E* / sic: sicut *E* / minor *bis E* medietatis *Br* / Age AF: AGAF *E* / equalis (?) *M* equale *EBr*
14 que: qui (?) *Br* / BC[1]: HC *E* / sic: sicut *E* / etiam *om. Br*
15 equalis *M* equale *EBr* / sit illud *tr. Br* / EA *M* AE *EBr*
16 AE *om. E*
17 BE[1]: DE *E* / *post* est[2] *add. E* ad / si linea: similia *E*
19 est[3] *om. E*
20 Sit: sunt *E* / BC: et BC *Bu*
21 ADC: ADB *EBu* / DB: BD *EFaBu*
22 nam . . . inter: nam BD est medio AB nam BD est medio portionalis (!) inest *E* / nam . . . supra *om. FaBu* / medio: medio loco *Br*
23 sit *ME om. BrFaBu* / ad E: ADE (?) *Br*
24 EG: EGT *Br* perpendicularis EG *FaBu* / que: et *Bu* / cum (?) *E* / BD: DB *Br* / eadem *Fa* / EL: ei et ducta linea EL *E*
25 communis: comunis *M* sectionis *Bu* / et *MBr om. EFaBu* / T: punctus T *Fa* punctus C *Bu* / dimittatur *E*
26 et: que *FaBu* / etiam *om. Br* / DB[1]: AB *Bu*
26–28 Sed. . . . MB: est enim MTDB est superficies equidistantium laterum, quod patet quoniam per xxxiii[am] primi Euclidis LT (?) de (?) et ———— tur (?) equales et equidistantes, liquet ergo per xxx.4[a]m (?) primi Euclidis, igitur ———— (?) in mediante, quadrangulum AB in BC equabitur quadrangulo AM in MB per primam partem corelarii octave sexti et per 16[am] eiusdem *Fa* / Sed. . . . Ergo: et ea mediante *Bu*
27 fit: sit *Br*
28 AB *om. E* / BC: BE *Br* / equabitur *Bu* / abhinc: hinc *M*
29 est: erit *FaBu et add. Fa* dicit commentator, procedatur ergo sic et probatio patet per secundam partem 16[e] 6[ti]: quod proportio AB ad AM, sicut BM maior est, BC secetur a[d] equalitatem et sit BH (!) equalis BC, erit ergo AB ad AM velut MB ad BH. Quare permutatim AB ad MB sicut AM ad BH, et per 10[am] (? 19[am]?) 5[ti] AC (?) ad BM (*sive* LM ?) sicut MB ad MH. Quare econverso MB ad ML (!) ut (?) MB ad DB (?) et hoc est propositum

19. CUM SIT LINEE BREVIORI ADIECTE MAIOR PROPORTIO AD
COMPOSITAM QUAM COMPOSITE AD LONGIOREM, BREVIOREM
QUARTA LONGIORIS MINOREM ESSE NECESSE EST.

Ut si *EH* ad *EB* maior sit proportio quam *EB* ad *AB*, *BH* minor erit
5   quarta *AB* [Fig. P.19]. Erit enim ob hoc *AB* ad *EB* maior proportio quam
EB ad *EH*. Et ideo rectangulum ab *AB* et *EH* maius erit quadrato *EB*. Nam
si eadem esset proportio *AB* ad *EB* que est *EB* ad *EH*, esset rectangulum
equale quadrato. Ergo si maior est proportio, maius est rectangulum. Signetur
ergo quadratum super *EB*, quod sit *EBGD*, et rectangulum super *AB* cuius
10   alterum latus *BL* equale *EH*, producaturque linea *HKM*; *EHK* et *KLG* sunt
quadrata quia similia sunt quadrato totali. Sed supplementa *HL*, *DK* inter
illa sunt proportionalia. Ergo supplementa vel quadratis sunt equalia vel

Prop. 19

1 19 *mg. sin. EBr mg. dex. M om. Bu* 19ᵃ *Fa* / Cum: Non *E* / brevioris *Bu* / adiecte:
    adiuncte *E*
2 conpositam *Fa* / conposite *Fa*
4 *ante* Ut *add. E sed om. omnes alii MSS hic (revocat enim Prop. 18; cf. Prop. 18, lin.*
    8–19, 10–19) Que est proportio AB ad AE ea est EB ad BC. Ergo si AB est maius
    EB, AE est maius BC per ix⁽ᵃᵐ⁾. Item que est proportio AB ad AE ea est EB ad BC.
    Ergo permutatim que est AB ad EB ea est AE ad BC. Ergo si AB est maior AE, EB
    est maior BC (?). Ergo tam AE quam EB est maior BC; de utralibet dematur equalis
    BC et primo de EB que sit HB / sit ME *om. FaBu* est *Br* / EB ad AB: AB ad EB
    Br / minor: maior *E*
6 *post* EH¹ *add. Fa* quoniam propter dictam proportionem erit proportio EH ad EB
    sicut EB ad aliquam minorem AB, si enim ad maiorem sit illa BH (*sive* BK). Quoniam
    ergo EH ad EB sicut EB ad BK (*sive* BH) et EB ad BH (*sive* BK) minor quam EB
    ad AB, etiam suppositum erat quod maior, sic ergo EH ad EB sicut EB ad aliquam
    maiorem; quare sit BZ (?) ad EB ut EB ad EH et quoniam AE ad EB maior quam
    ZB (?) ad EH per primam partem octave 5ᵗⁱ erit AB ad EB [maior] quam EB (?) ad
    EH iuxta 11ᵃᵐ 5ᵗⁱ / Et ideo: erit ergo *Fa et om. Fa* erit *post* maius / rectangulum ab:
    quod sub *Bu, sed add. Bu* rectangulum *post* EH / ab *EFaBu om. MBr* / et *om. E*
6–8 Nam. . . . rectangulum *om. Bu* ———— (?) explanationem prioris argumenti, quare
    (?) quadratum EB erit equale rectangulo quod fit ex ZB (?) in EH *Fa*
7 est *om. Br* / EB²: EH (?) *M*
8 *post* proportio *add. M* et / maius: et maius *E* / Signetur: significetur *E* sicnetur
    (!) *Bu*
10 alterum: altitudo *Br* / producaturque: producatur *Br* et producatur *Fa* / HKM:
    BKM *Br*
10–17 EHK. . . . propositum: dico quod suplementum HBL est medio loco proportionale
    inter duo quadrata AEK (! EHK) et KLG per primam 6ᵗⁱ Euclidis bis sumptam;
    quare duplum erit, non erit illis maius per ultimam 5ᵗⁱ Euclidis, cumque sit ipsum
    alteri supelemento (!) equale non erit ipsum maius quarta quadrati EB ut ideo non
    erit quarta rectanguli BAL, in (! non) ergo BH tanquam quarta AB sed minus *Fa*
10 KLG: KLM *Br* KLD *Bu* / sunt: super *Br*
10–11 sunt quadrata: sint quadrata *Bu et tr. Bu ante* EHK *in lin.* 10
11–17 quia. . . . propositum: erit supplementum BHL proportionale. Quare duplum eius
    non erit illis maius; cumque sit ipsum alteri supplemento equale non erit ipsum
    maius quarta quadrati, et ideo non erit quarta rectanguli BAL, neque ergo BH tanquam
    quarta AB sed minus *Bu (et cf. var. lin. 10–17 in Fa)*
11 quadrato totali *tr. EBr* / supplementa: suppleta (!) *E*
11–12 HL. . . . supplementa *om. Br*

minora per ultimam quinti Euclidis. Sed supplementa inter se sunt equalia.
Ergo supplementum *HL* vel est quarta quadrati *EG* vel minor. Sed rectan-
15 gulum *AL* est maius quadrato *EG*. Ergo *HL* minus est quarta *AL*. Ergo quod
fit ex *AB* in *HK* est plus quam quadruplum ad id quod fit ex *HB* in *KH*.
Ergo linea *HB* minor est quarta *AB*, et hoc est propositum.

20. SI FUERIT MINOR INTER DIVIDENTIA MAIORIS PROPOR-
TIONALIS, ADIECTE AD MINOREM SIT AD COMPOSITAM MAIOR
PROPORTIO QUAM COMPOSITE AD MAIOREM, EANDEM COM-
POSITAM ALTERO DIVIDENTIUM MAIORIS NECESSE EST ESSE
5 MAIOREM.

Sit composita *BCD* et rectangulum *AEF* equale rectangulo *ABC* et desit
ad complementum superficies quadrata *FB* [Fig. P.20], et sit *AB* divisa in
E, et ab *AB* resecetur equalis *BCD*, que sit *BM*. Itaque *BM* est equalis *EB*
vel maior vel minor. Si maior, propositum habeo. Nam tunc composita, cum
10 sit equalis *BM*, est maior altero dividentium *AB*. Item si est equalis *EB*, non
potest esse quod *AE* sit equalis *EB*. Nam, si hoc, cum *BC* sit medio loco
proportionalis inter *AE*, *EB* ex ypothesi, quadratum *BC* est equale quadrato
MB sive *BD*, et sic *BC* est equalis *BD*, pars toti, quod est impossibile. Item
nec potest esse quod *BD* sit equalis *EB* et etiam *AE* sit maior *EB* sive *MB*.
15 Nam, cum *BC* sit medium inter *AE*, *EB*, quadratum *BC* est equale quadrangulo ex *AE* in *EB*, et sic quadratum *BC* est equale ei quod fit ex maiore

14 quarta: quadrata vel *E*
15 minus est *tr. Br* / quarta: quadrato *M*
15–16 Ergo² . . . KH *om. Br*
16 id *om. E*
17 minor est *tr. Br* / et . . . propositum *om. Br* / propositum *om. M*
Prop. 20
1 20 *mg. sin. MEBr om. Bu* 20ª *Fa* / fuerit minor *tr. Fa* / inter: inter duo *Br* / dividentia:
proportionalia *M*
2 adiecte: ad recteque (?) *Fa* / ad¹: aut ad *Br* / sit *om. Bu* / sit ad compositam: ad
conpositam sit *Fa* / *post* compositam *add. Bu* si
3 quam *om. M* / conposite *Fa* / eamdem *E*
3–4 conpositam *Fa*
4 est *om. Bu*
6 conposite *Fa* (*et post hoc lectiones huiusmodi non laudabo*) / et²: cuius *Fa*
6–8 et² . . . E *om. Bu*
6 desit: DE sit (?) *E*
7 conplementum *Fa* / FB: FH *M* scilicet FB *Fa* / sit: sic *E*
7–8 in E: inest (?) *Fa*
8 et: quia *Fa* / ab *bis E* / resecetur: secetur (*sive* recetur ?) *Fa* / BCD: BED *Br*
8–18 Itaque. . . . EB *om. Bu*
8 EB: et *Fa*
9 vel maior *om. E*
10 alteram *Fa* / *post* dividentium *add. E* omnium
11 potest: potum (?) *Fa* / AE sit *tr. M* / *post* hoc *add. M* est / cum *om. M*
12 EB: et EB *Fa* / ypothesi *MBr* ypotesim *E* ypotesi *Fa* / equale: equalis (?) *E*
13 MB *MFa*, (?)*Br* LB *E* / BC: BE *Br* / BD²: per D *Fa* / pars: sicut pars *Br*
14 esse: est *Fa* / BD: BM *Fa* / etiam *MBrFa om. E* / sive *EBr* si non *M* / MB *om. Fa*
15 BC¹: BE *Br*
15–16 quadrangulo: rectangulo *Fa*
16 AE: AC (?) *Br* / maiore: maiorem ipso *Fa*

5r in maius, quod est impossibile, nam / tam *AE* quam *EB* est maior *BC*. Cadat
igitur *BM* citra *E*, et sit minor *EB*. Fiat itaque super *AB* rectangulum ad
latitudinem *MB*, quod sit *BNQPA*; erecta linea *MR*, quia ergo linea *BM*
20 minor est linea *EB* et linea *EF* est maior *BN*, concurrant ergo *GF* et *BN*
super *T*; producta linea *MR* usque ad *Z*, erit itaque rectangulum *AMR* maius
AEF. Proba: Maior est proportio *CD* ad *BD* quam *BD* ad *AB*. Ergo econverso
maior est *AB* ad *BD* quam *BD* ad *CD*. Ergo quod fit ex *AB* in *CD* maius
est quadrato *BD*, hoc est *MB*. Sed superficies ex *AB* in *CD* est *DB* (*! CD′*).
25 Sed impletur superficies [*AN*] et quadratum *MB* est *MN*. Ergo *DB* (*! CD′*)
est maius *MN*. Sed superficies *ABCD* [i.e. *AB* in *BD*] est equalis *AN*, ergo

17 quod: eo quod *Fa*
18 igitur *BrFa* ergo *E*, (*?*)*M* / minor: maior *Fa* / EB *BrFa* BE *E* AB *M* / Fiat itaque:
Fiatque *Bu*
19 MB *MEBr* BM *FaBu* / erecta (*?*) *Br* / quia: si *Bu* / ergo: igitur *Br* / linea² *om. Bu*
20 est¹ . . . EB: fuerit BE *Bu* / et linea: erit *Bu* / est² *om. Br* / post BN¹ *add. Br* equalis
BM et ex ypothesi quod ad complementum rectanguli a EF, DC est superficies
quadrata FB / post BN¹ *add. Fa* quoniam posita est BN erat (*?*) BM et ex ypotesi
quod ad conplementum rectanguli AEFD (*!*) est superficies quadrata FB / ergo *ME*
itaque *BrFaBu*
21 linea *om. FaBu* / ad *om. FaBu* / erit itaque: et quia *FaBu* / maius: est maius rectangulo
FaBu
22 AEF, Proba: AEF rectangulo quod sic probatur *Br* quod sic probatur *Fa*
22–29 Proba. . . . PF: quoniam cum sit proportio AB ad BM maior proportione (*?*) BM
ad MH erit proportio AM ad BH maior proportione AE ad BM, quod ergo continetur
sub AM et MB, quod est rectangulum AMR, erit maius eo quod continetur sub AB
et BC sed ei est equale rectangulum AEFG et ob hoc minus (*?*) est ipsum rectangulo
AMR, et cum hoc sit, communi dempto erit supplementum ER maius residuo quod
est GFQP. Quare et supplementum RT est eodem maius *Bu*
23 BD¹: DB *M*
23–30 Ergo. . . . reliqua: hoc argumentum patet incomento (*? in commento*) precedentis
propositionis quia ergo MB est (*sive* eidem) EBD (*! CBD*) et MB sicut CD erit maior
proportio AB ad BM quam ad MH (*!*) et ob hoc AM ad BH maior quam AB ad
BM. Probatio: quia proportio MH ad BM maior est proportione MB ad [BH (*?*)],
erit MH ad MB sicut MB ad minorem AB, ut ostensum est superius. Sic igitur MH
ad BM velud MB ad BK (*?*). Dico ergo quod AB ad BM sicut BM ad minorem MH,
quia si possibile est sic a[d] maiorem, scilicet ad MZ (*?*), quoniam ergo AB ad BM
sicut BM ad MZ et BM ad MZ minor quam BM ad MH, erit AB ad DM minor
(*? maior?*) BM ad MH. Set HM ad MH sicut KB ad BM. Quare AB ad BM minor
HB ad BM, quod est contra primam partem octave (*?*) 5ᵗⁱ Euclidis. Sic ergo AB ad
BM sicut BM ad minorem MH que sit gᵐ (*?*). Quare AB ad BM sicut AM ad BG
per 19ᵃᵐ 5ᵗⁱ. Quare AB ad BM minor AM ad BH per secundam partem 8ᵛᵉ 5ᵗⁱ. Quare
(*?*) quare AB ad BM minor AM ad BH. Igitur que (*? quod*) ex ductu AB in BH
minus est eo quod ex AM in BM quia quod ex AM in BM est rectangulum ABC,
quod est equale AEFG. Quare rectangulum AMR maius est rectangulo AEF. Ergo
contradictio: erit suplementum ER maius residuo alterius quod est GFQP (*?*) quarum
(*?*) et suplementum RT erit eodem maius, sicque RN maius erit PQ per ipsam sexti
et BM maior AE sic conposita ABCD maior erit altero dividentium AB, et hoc est
propositum *Fa*
23 CD²: ED *M*
24 est MB: et BM *E* / AB: AD (*?*) *E* / DB *EBr* BD *M*
25 Sed impletur *correxi ex* Si (*?*) impletur *in EBr et* supplentur (*!*) *in M* / [AN]
addidi / MB: in B *E* / DB *EBr* BD *M*
26 [i.e. AB in BD] *addidi* / equalis *M* equale *EBr*

AE (*! AR*) est maior *AC*. Ergo *AF*, equalis [*AC*], est minor eadem [*AR*]. Ergo dempto communi *ER* est maius *PF*. Ergo *RT* equale supplementum est maius *PF*. Ergo linea *RN* est maius *PQ*. Ergo et *BM* est maior *AE*; et sic, si
30 sit minor una dividentium, est maior reliqua.

21. IN QUOLIBET LATERUM TRIANGULI PUNCTO SIGNATO AB EO LINEAM EXTRAHERE QUE TRIANGULUM PER DUO EQUA PARTIATUR.

Sit triangulus *ABC* [Fig. P.21] et punctus *D* in latere *AB* datus, ad medium
5 cuius lateris ab angulo *C* ducatur linea que sit *CE* continuetur etiam linea *CD*. Deinde ab *E* ducatur equidistans linee *DC*, que sit *EG*; appliceturque *G* cum *D*, que secet *EC* apud *T*. Quia ergo triangulus *CDE* est equalis triangulo *DGC*, communi dempto erit triangulus *ETD* equalis triangulo *GTC*. Equalibus ergo additis erit superficies quam abscindit linea *DTG* equalis
10 triangulo *EAC*, qui est dimidium totius trianguli, nam *EC* dividit triangulum in equa, et hoc est propositum.

22. TRIANGULO DATO ET PUNCTO EXTRA SIGNATO LINEAM PER PUNCTUM TRANSEUNTEM DESIGNARE QUE TRIANGULUM PER EQUA PARTIATUR.

Sit triangulus *ABC* [Fig. P.22], et punctus *D* extra triangulum exceptum
5 inter lineas *AEF* et *HBL*, que dividant latera trianguli per equalia atque

27 maior: minor (?) *E* / AC (?) *E* / [AC] *addidi* / [AR] *addidi*
28 ER *Bu* (*cf. var. lin. 22–29*) ei *M* N *EBr* / RT: FT et *Br*
29 PF: PH *E* / Ergo[1]: sicque *Bu* / RN *EBrBu et Fa* (*cf. var. lin. 23–30*) RK *M* / est[1]
    om. E / est maius: maius est PB̥ (*del.*) *Bu* / Ergo[2] *om. Bu* / et BM *Bu* RNB *M* RNP
    E et NP *Br*
29–30 sic . . . reliqua: ita si sit una minor, erit reliqua maior et sic altera *Bu*
Prop. 21
1 21 *mg. sin. M*, (?)*E mg. dex. Br om. Bu* x[xi^a] *etiam mg. dex. E* 21^a *Fa* / latere *Br*
5 cuius: eius *EBr* / sit (?) *Fa* / continuetur: continetur *E* (?)*Fa* / etiam: et *Br*
6 E *om. E* / equidistans linee DC: eq^s linea EDC (?) *E* / equidistans: eqd' *Br et corr.*
    Fa ex equidistantia / linee: linea linee *Fa* / DC: CD *BrFa* / appliceturque *Br* am-
    pliceturque *Fa* applicetque *MEBu*
7 cum: cum per *Fa* / *post* D *add. Fa* lineam GD *et Bu* linea GD / EC: et *Fa* / aput
    Bu / T: Z *Br* / CDE: CD *Fa* DCE *Br* / est equalis *tr. Bu*
8 DGC *M* GDC *E* DGT *Br* CGD per 3 5^{ti} (?) 7^{am} (!) primi Euclidis *Fa* CGD *Bu* /
    communi: comuni *ME et hab. alii MSS abbreviationes*
8–11 dempto . . . propositum: addito, scilicet ad (!) triangulo, erit ADGC superficies
    equalis triangulo EAC, qui est dimidium totius trianguli *Fa*
8 ETD *E* ECD *M* EDT *Br* / GTC *Bu* TGE *ME*
9 abscindat *Br*
10 trianguli: anguli *Br*
10–11 nam . . . propositum *om. Bu*
10 EC *om. Br, correxi ex* E *in* M *et ex* C *in* E
11 propositum *om. M*
Prop. 22
1 22 *mg. sin. ME mg. dex. Br. om. Bu* xx[ii^a] *mg. dex. E* 22^a *Fa*
2 transeuntem *om. M* / que *om. Br*
3 partiatur: patientem *Br*
4 Sit: sicut *Fa*
5 HBL *FaBu* BGL *M* BG *E* BGD *Br* / dividatur *Br* / atque: atque similiter *M*

ipsum triangulum, et extra quantumlibet. Si enim in aliqua illarum incideret finem sumeret intentio. Puncto ergo infra (*!* intra) illas posito ab ipso ducamus equidistantem linee *AC* donec cum *CB* concurrat quantum necessarium fuerit protracta, signumque concursus sit *G*, et concludat triangulum linea

10   *DC* qui sic se habet ad triangulum *AEC*, qui est dimidium dati trianguli, ita se habeat linea *CG* ad aliquam; illa sit *MN*. Dividatur item *GC* secundum rationem 14ᵉ [huius] in *GK* et *KC* ita quod *GK* ad *KC* sicut *KC* ad *MN*, et continuetur linea *DK* in puncto *P* linea *AC* offendens, eruntque trianguli *DGK* et *KPC* similes, et proportio trianguli *DGK* ad triangulum *KPC* sicut

15   linea *GK* ad *KC* duplicata, hoc est sicut *GK* ad *MN*. Item que est *GK* ad *KC* ea est *DK* ad *KP*, quia trianguli sunt similes, et que est *GK* ad *KC* ea est *KC* ad *MN*. Ergo que est *DK* ad *KP* ea est *KC* ad *MN*. Sed que est *DK* ad *KP*

6 ipsum: supra ipsum *Br* / quantumlibet: quantumbilibus (*!*) *Fa et add. Fa* protractum / *post* quantumlibet *add. Bu* protractas / aliqua *BrFaBu* alia *M* aliquam (*?*) *E* / illarum: earum *FaBu* / incidit *Br*

7 finem: et finem *Br* finem ş *M* / intentio: *lac. Bu* / ducamus *EFaBu* ducimus *MBr*

8 equidistantem: equideṁpitatem (*!*) *E* equid' *Br* / CB: BC *Br* / concurat *Fa* / necessarium: n *Bu*

9 -que *om. E* / concurrsus *M* / concludat *EFaBu* concludit *MBr* / linea *om. Fa*

10 qui¹ *MBrFa* que *EBu* / sic *EBrBu* sicut *MFa* / est dimidium *tr. E* / dati trianguli *tr. Fa*

11 habeat *MBr* habent (*?*) *E* habet *Fa* habeant (*?*) *Bu* / CG: EG *E* / aliquam: aliam *Br* / illa: que *FaBu* / Dividatur item: Dividaturque *Fa* / item GC: CGF *E* / GC: GE *M* GT (*?*) *Br*

11–12 secundum rationem: ratione *E*

12 14ᵉ: prime [secundi] *Bu* primi (*!*) *Fa* primi *huius* secundi *Fa* / [huius] *addidi* (*sed cf. var. preced.*) / KC¹: BC *Bu* / ita *om. FaBu* / KC²: KE *M* KC sit *FaBu* / KC³: KG *Br*

13 continuetur: continetur (*?*) *E* / DK: D DK *Fa* / puncto *bis Bu* / linea²: lineam *Fa* / offendens: oñs *M* ostendens *E* / eritque (*?*) *E*

14 *post* DGK¹ *scr. et del. Bu* GK / *post* similes *add. Fa* propter AC et DG equidistantes et angulos coalternos equales et per 4ᵃᵐ 6ᵗⁱ Euclidis inductio (*?*) inde (*?*) super (*?*) lineam (*?*) superficiei / triangulum: trianguli *E*

15 GK¹: GH *Br*

15–23 KC¹. . . . proponitur: lineam MN 17ᵐᵉ 6ᵗⁱ correlario (*?*) et quia triangulus CDG ad triangulum DGK sicut basis CG ad basem KG per primam 6ᵗⁱ erit inproportio (*?*) covali[di]tate equalitatis triangulus CDG ad triangulum KPC sicut linea CG ad lineam MN per 11ᵃᵐ 5ᵗⁱ Euclidis. Set erat linea CG ad lineam MN sicut triangulus CDG ad dimidium trianguli ABC, constat 11ᵃ KPC esse dimidium dati trianguli. Linea DKP que a dato progreditur puncto eundem (*?*) dividentem (*!*) ut proponebatur quod omnino G erat non sit alibi quam inter B et C (*! E ?*), quia si alibi accidet maius equale fore minori quia idem est processus ad hoc et ad principale. Item quod DK protracta secet AC super punctum inter H et A patet quia si alibi accidet minus dimidio fore dimidium iuxta modum probandi principaliter intentum (*?*); etiam (*?*) hic bene notentur medietates ABC trianguli quas ş ig (*del.*) significant linee AEF et HBL *Fa* lineam MN. Sed erat linea CP ad lineam MN sicut triangulus CDG ad dimidium trianguli ABC, constat itaque KPC esse dimidium dati trianguli, [et] linea (*?*) DKP que a dato progreditur puncto omnino dividente sicut proponebatur *Bu*

15 KC¹: lineam KC *E* / dupplicata *E* dupl' *Br* / est sicut *om. E*

16 est³ *om. Br*

17 DK² *M* DQ *E* KC *Br*

ea est trianguli *DCK* ad triangulum *CKP.* Ergo que est *KC* ad *MN* ea est trianguli *CKD* ad triangulum *CKP.* Sed prius probatum est quod que est proportio *GK* ad *MN* / ea est trianguli *DGK* ad triangulum *CKP.* Ergo que est proportio totius linee *CG* ad *MN* ea est trianguli *DCG* ad triangulum *CKP.* Sed ex ypothesi eadem est *DGC* ad *CEA*, dimidium dati trianguli. Ergo *CKP* est dimidium dati trianguli. Et hoc est quod proponitur.

23. PUNCTO INFRA (*!* INTRA) TRIGONUM PROPOSITUM DATO LINEAM PER IPSUM DEDUCERE QUE TRIANGULUM SECET PER EQUALIA.

Statuatur trigonus descriptus notis *A, B, C* [Fig. P.23], punctumque infra (*!* intra) ipsum comprehensum *D* ex parte *B* inter lineas *AG, BE* dividentes opposita latera per equa sed et triangulum. Ducaturque linea per *D* equidistans linee *AC*, que sit *FDH*, continueturque linea *DB*, sitque linea *BF* ad aliquam que sit *MN* sicut triangulus *BDF* ad triangulum *BCE*, qui est dimidium dati trigoni. Sit item *BF* ad *TY* lineam sicut *BFH* triangulus ad *BCE* triangulum. Sed maior est proportio *FBH* ad *CBE* quam *FBD* ad eundem. Ergo maior est proportio *BF* ad *TY* quam ad *MN*. Ergo *MN* est maior *TY*. Est autem *BF* ad *BC* sicut *BC* ad *TY* quia triangulus *BFH* est similis triangulo *BEC*.

5v

21

5

10

18 trianguli DCK: DKC trianguli *Br* / CKP: KCP *E* / Ergo: igitur *Br* / est² *om. E*
18–20 ea². . . . MN *MBr om. E*
19 CKD: KCD *Br* / Sed: Et *Br*
20 ea est *tr. Br* / DGK: GDK *Br*
21–23 ad¹. . . . proponitur *MBr om. E*
21 DCG: DGC (*sive* DGT) *Br*
22 ypothesi *M* ypostasi *Br* / est DGC *M om. Br*

Prop. 23

1 23 *mg. sin. E mg. dex. MBr om. Bu* [xxii]i[a] *etiam in mg. sin. E* 23ᵃ *Fa* (*et hab. fig. in FaBu* 30ᵃ) / Puncto: Cuncto (*!*) *E* / trigonum propositum *E tr. BrBu* propositum *M* positum trigonum *Fa*
2 ducere *Br* / quo *Fa*
4 trigonus: triangulus *M* / *post* infra *scr. et del. Bu* M
5 D *om. Br et tr. FaBu post* punctumque *in lin.* 4 / lineas *FaBu* lineam *MEBr* / AG, BE: AB, BE *E*
6 opposita: composita *E* / sed: set *Fa* / -que: quia *Fa* / equidistans: eq̇ᶦ *E* equid' *Br*
7 linee *om. Br* line (*!*) *Fa* / AC: AE *Br* / sit: sunt *Fa* / continetur *Fa* / -que¹ linea: quia linea per D equedistans line (*!*) AC que sint *Fa* / DB: per DB *Br* / -que²: quia *Fa* / BF *supra scr. Bu et corr. M ex* DF (*?*) / aliquam: aliam *Br* quod (*?*) quam *Bu*
8 sit . . . sicut: sunt in N sic *E* / triangulus: angulus *Fa* / BCE *M* BCD (*corr. ex* DCD) *E* BCM̃ *Br* B et *Fa* BEC *Bu* / qui: que *Br*
9 item: inter *E* / TY: ER *Bu* / lineam *BrFaBu* linea *ME* / triangulus: triangulo (*?*) *Br* / BCE: BC *E*
9–11 triangulum. . . . est²: et quia triangulus BFH est maior triangulo BFD erit MN *FaBu*
10 FBD: sit BD *E* / eumdem *E*
11 BF: FB *Br* / TY²: TR (*?*) *Bu* / *post* TY² *add. Fa* per primam partem 8ᵉ 5ᵗⁱ et priorem (*?*) partem eiusdem
12 TY: TR (*?*) *Bu* / *post* TY *add. Fa* per 17ᵃᵐ 6ᵗⁱ / BFH: BHF *FaBu* / *post* BEC *add. Fa* propter FDH et AC equidistantes

Quare proportio *BF* ad *BC* est maior proportione *BC* ad *MN*. Minor igitur est *FC* quarta *MN* per 19[am] huius. Addatur igitur linee *FC* linea que sit *FZ*

15 ita quod *ZF* ad *ZC* sicut *ZC* ad *MN* per 18[am] huius, eritque *ZC* minor *BC*, si quis subtiliter ad memoriam revocet prius hic concessa et etiam probationem superius positam in 18[a] huius; transeatque linea per *Z* et *D*, que sit *ZDK*. Quia igitur triangulus *BDF* ad triangulum *ZDF* sicut linea *BF* ad lineam *ZF*, itemque triangulus *ZFD* ad triangulum *ZCK* sicut *ZF* ad *MN* quoniam

20 trianguli sunt similes, in equa igitur proportione sicut *BF* ad *MN* ita triangulus *BFD* ad triangulum *ZKC*. Fuit autem linea *BF* ad *MN* sicut idem triangulus ad dimidium dati trigoni. Quare et triangulus *ZKC* eiusdem est dimidium, linea per *D* transeunte per equa dividente, et hoc est propositum.

13 *post* MN *add. Fa* quia BC ad TY maior BC ad MN
13–14 igitur est *tr. E*
14 per . . . huius *om. Bu* / huius *om. Fa* / linee *om. FaBu*
15 quod: quam *Br* / per . . . huius: ita TY (?) quod ZE sit minor BC ratione premissorum *Fa* / per . . . ZC: ita cum ut ZC sit *Bu* / eritque: erit igitur que *Br* / ZC³: ZT (?) *Br*
16–17 si . . . huius: ratione premissorum *Bu*
16 siquis *M*
16–17 probationem . . . positam: superius positis probatio est *E*
16 probationem: p̄om̄ (?) *Br*
17 18[a] (?) *M* / transeatque: et transeat *FaBu* / *post* ZDK *scr. et del. Bu* K
18 ZDF: et DF *E* / BF: BF est *Fa*
19 *post* ZF¹ *add. Fa* per primam vi[ti] Euclidis / itemque *MBu* item *EBrFa* / triangulus: angulus *Fa* / ZCK: ZC et (?) *Fa* ZEK *Bu* / *post* MN *add. Fa* per corolarum (!) 17[e] 6[ti]
20 sunt similes *tr. Bu* / *post* similes *add. FaBu* et ZF ad ZC erat sicut ZC ad MN / triangulus: trianguli *Fa*
21 *post* ZKC *add. Fa* per 11[am] 5[ti] / autem: quidem *Br*
22 triangulus . . . est: triangulis (!) erit eius *Fa* / est dimidium *tr. E* dimidium *Bu*
23 *ante* per *add. Bu* eum *et Fa* cum (*sive* eum) / D *corr. E ex* A (?) / et . . . propositum: et hoc est *M* ad hoc est propositum *E* secundum quod propositum fuerat *Fa* secundum quod propositum est *Bu* / *post* propositum *add. Fa* quod dicitur ratione premissorum;

sic explicemus: sunt (?) sint MN, FC angulum coniuncte, concluso rectangulo f̄[m] (?) et super MN statuatur hoc equale triangulum MKPZ, cui desit quadratum PN, erit igitur tam MZ quam ZM (!) maior FC ut patuit in conmento (!) 18[e]. Si ergo ex ZN secetur FC, posito C iuxta N, erit MN ad ZC sic ZC ad ZF, ut ibidem probatum est. Quare ergo sic ZE aut est equalis BC proportio MN ad BC quam ad BF quia econverso aut minor a (! aut) maior; quod non sit equalis patet, erat n (! enim) maior proportio MN ad BC quam BC ad BF quia econverso si minor habeo propositum; si maior habeo propositum secetur ZC ad equalitatem apud (?) B erecta BK usque ad que et quia ZCE (?) maior est BC et ut eadem maior erit, sic ergo HC protracta HFGD equidistanter MN angulo sit maior est proportione MN ad BC quam BC ad BF, ergo maior est MB ad FC quam MN ad BC, hinc (*sive* huic) argumenta simile probatum (?) est in commento 18[e] quod ex ductu MB in BC, scilicet rectangulo MV (!), maius est eo quod ex ductu MN in FC; quare suo equali, scilicet (?) PZ, hoc idem patuit in suo simili; igitur dempto communi MDGZ erit ZBCG (?) maius GOKP (?); quare simili (?) equale maius eodem. Sed KC (*sive* ut?) et KZ (?) sunt suplementa equalia per (? quam?) 4[am] 3[ti]. Si igitur FC maius est PDQF linea HR (?) maior GD; quare BC maior maior (!) MZ, igitur ex MZ (?) secetur equalis FC, posito C iuxta M;

24. INFRA (! INTRA) DATUM TRIGONUM A PUNCTO UNO TRES LINEAS AD ANGULOS TRES QUE TRIANGULUM PER TRIA EQUALIA DIVIDANT PROTRAHERE.

Esto triangulus ABC [Fig. P.24], et ab uno laterum, BC, abscindatur tertia
5 pars, que sit CD, et protrahatur linea DE equidistans AC in cuius medio
ponatur G, et producantur linee AD, AG, CG. Et quia trianguli AGC et ADC
sunt equales, cum sit triangulus ADC tertia pars dati trianguli quia basis eius
tertia pars totius, erit AGC tertia pars eiusdem. Ducta itaque linea GB fiet
triangulus GEB equalis triangulo GDB quoniam bases equales. Itemque
10 trianguli GEA et GDC equales quia inter equidistantes. Quare triangulus
AGB equalis triangulo CGB, et ob hoc quisque eorum tertia totius, sicque
a puncto G prodeunt tres linee ad angulos dividentes triangulum per tria
equalia, et hoc est [propositum].

25. AB ANGULO QUADRANGULI ASSIGNATI LINEAM EDUCERE
6r / QUE TOTAM IPSIUS SUPERFICIEM PER DUO EQUALIA PARTIATUR.

quoniam ergo MN ad MZ sicut ZC ad FC ex prima parte 13me (?) 6^{ti}, erit per 19^{am}
5^{ti} MN ad MZ sive ZC velut ———— (*duo verba del.*) ZC ad CF; quare econverso;
sic ergo habemus propositum quoniam ZC minor est BC quod ZD protracta super
AC dividat AC et non pertranseat AC super aliud punctum quam super ad (?) quod
est inter duo puncta A et E, nec et super AB decendat (!) patet quoniam accideret
maius vel minus dividendo ABC trigoni equale esse sue medietati, in nullo diversificato
modo procedendi ad hoc et ad principale, habita etiam consideratione ad dimidia
trianguli ABC per EBC, per EB et AG significata.

Prop. 24

1 24 *mg. sin.* EBr *mg. dex.* M *om.* Bu [xxi]iii^a *etiam mg. sin.* E 24^a Fa (*sed hab. fig.
in FaBu* 31^a (!)) / trigonum: triangulum Fa / uno: dato E

2 qui EBr / tria *om.* E

3 equa E

4 BC: Verbi gratia ab (a Bu) BC FaBu / tertia *om.* Bu

5 pars: pras (!) Fa / equidistans FaBu equid' M equidist' E equidem Br

6 linee (?) Fa / AD Bu *om.* MEBrFa / CG: EG Br / AGC: ACE Br / et^3 *om.* E / ADC:
ACD Br ADE (?) Bu

7 *post* equales *add.* Fa per 3^{am} 7^{am} (! 37^{am}) primi Euclidis / tertia . . . trianguli: trianguli
dati pars tertia FaBu *et add.* Fa per primam 6^{ti} / dati trianguli: trianguli BAC Br /
quia: quoniam FaBu / eius: eius est Fa

8 pars^1 *om.* Bu / *ante* totius *add.* Fa basis / erit: erit et Fa / tertia^2 . . . eiusdem:
similiter eiusdem tertia Fa / tertia^2 *tr.* Bu *post* eiusdem / itaque linea *tr.* E / itaque:
igitur FaBu / fiat Br

9 *post* equales *add.* Fa per 3^{am} 8^{am} (! 38^{am}) primi Euclidis / Itemque: Item EFa

10 trianguli: triangulus EBr / GDC: GEC E GDE (?) Br / quia: quoniam Bu / quia . . .
equidistantes: per eandem quoniam super bases EG et DE equales et inter equidistantes
(?) Fa / inter (?) Bu / equidistantes: equidem Br

11 CGB: CBG Br / *post* CGB *add.* Fa per secundam conceptionem primi Euclidis / et
ob hoc: igitur Fa / totius: pars totius trianguli Fa / sicque: sicutque E

12 prodeunt: producte sunt Br prodeant Bu / triangulum *tr.* Br. *post* equalia

13 et . . . est ME *om.* BrFaBu / [propositum] *addidi*

Prop. 25

1 25 *mg. sin.* EBr *mg. dex.* M *om.* Bu [xx]v^a *etiam mg. sin.* E 25^a Fa (*sed. hab. fig.
in FaBu* 32^a (!))

2 equa E

Propositum quadrangulum designetur notis *A, B, C, D*, [Fig. P.25], et per
5 oppositos angulos transeant linee que sint *AGC, BGD*. Si igitur *AG* fuerit
equalis *GC*, erit trangulus *BCD* equalis triangulo *BDA* quoniam que est *AG*
ad *GC* ita triangulus *ADB* ad reliquum, quod per partiales triangulos poterit
constare. Si autem altera sit maior, ponatur ut *GC*, de qua resecetur linea
equalis *AG*, que sit *CE*. Ducatur itaque *EL* equidistans *BG*, fixo *L* in linea
10 *DC*, et continuetur *B* cum *L*. Et quia triangulus *DBC* ad triangulum *LBC*
sicut *DC* ad *LC*, atque *DC* ad *LC* sicut *GC* ad *CE*, et sicut ad *CE* ut ad *AG*,
et ut *GC* ad *AG* ita *CBD* ad *ADB* per partiales triangulos, erit triangulus
DBC ad triangulum *LBC* sicut ad triangulum *ADB*. Trianguli ergo *ADB* et
LBC equales. Divisa ergo linea *LD* per medium apud *T*, et protracta linea
15 *BT*, quoniam triangulus *DBT* equalis est triangulo *TBL*, erit et triangulus
TBC equalis superficiei *TDAB*, et sic linea *BT* ducta ab angulo dividet quadrangulum per equalia, et hoc est propositum.

26. SI TRES LINEE IN CIRCULO EQUIDISTANTES EQUALES IN-
TER SE ARCUS COMPREHENDANT, MAXIME AD MEDIAM MAIOR

4 signetur *Br*
5 que sint *om. Fa* que sunt *Br*
6 BCD *MBr* BDE *E* BDC *FaBu*
6-8 que . . . constare: triangulus AGB ad GBC sicut AGD ad GDC medios (*!*) AG, GC
   et per 13^am (*?*) 5^ti coassumpto quod sicut AG ad GC sic AGB triangulus ad GBC
   triangulum *Fa*
6 que est: sicut *Bu*
7 *ante* GC *scr. et del. Bu* BC / reliquum quod: regulam (*? reqam !*) que *E* reilqū qui
   Br (*et post hoc lectiones huiusmodi non laudabo*) / per *om. Br* / poterit: ponunt *Br*
8 GC: GE *Br*
9 Ducatur itaque: Ducaturque *EBr* / equidistans: equidem *EBr* equidem communi
   Fa / BG: BC *Bu* / L: LM *E et supra scr. E in* (*?*) / in: ita *M*
10 B cum L: BCA (*!*) *Fa* / DBC: BDC *Br*
11-13 sicut^1 . . . LBC *hic om. E sed cf. var. lin. 14*
11 *post* LC^1 *add. Fa* per primam 6^ti / LC^2: CL *Bu* / sicut^2: ut *Fa* / CE^1: EC *Fa*
11-12 et . . . triangulos *om. BrBu* / sicut^3 . . . ADB: GC^A ad EC sicut GC ad AG et GC
   ad AG ut CDB ad ADB, quod patet ut prius *Fa*
12 *ante* erit *add. Fa* ergo a primo
13 DBC: ABC *Fa* / *post* sicut *add. Fa* idem DBC / ADB^2: ADG *Br* / et *corr. Bu ex* ad
14 *post* LBC *add. Fa* sunt / *post* equales *add. Fa* per 9^am 5^ti / medium: mod' *Br* / T:
   TC (*sive* TE) *Fa* / *post* T *add. E hic* ad AG ita CBD ad ABC propter partiales
   triangulos AC (*sive* AT) quia DC ad LC sicut GE ad CE erit triangulus DBC ad
   triangulum LBC sicut ad triangulum ADB, trianguli ADB et LBC sunt equales, divisa
   ergo linea LD per medium apud T
15 BT: BC *E* DT *Fa* / triangulus^1: trianguli (*?*) *Fa* / DBT *BrBu om. ME* TBD *Fa* /
   equalis est *tr. EBr* / et: etiam (*?*) *Br*
16 TBC: CBD *E* / equalis: equali equali *E* / *ante* superficiei *scr. et del. Bu* superis (*?*)
   / TDAB: TB.AB *Br* / *post* TDAB *add. Fa* per secundam conceptionem primi
   Euclidis / BT: BC *E*
17 equalia: equa *Br* / et . . . propositum *E om. MBrFaBu*
Prop. 26
   1 *mg. hab. M* l. 3us (liber tertius) *et mg. sup. fol. 10v hab. M* L. III *et mg. sup. fol. 11r*
      De Tri. / 26 *mg. sin.* EBr *mg. dex. M* xxv[i]^a *mg. dex. E* 26^a *Fa* 33^a *mg. dex. Bu et*
      fig. in FaBu / Si: Ai (*!*) *E* / ëquidistantes ïn circulo (*i.e.* in circulo equidistantes) *E*
   2 archus (*!*) *Fa* / conprehendant *Fa*
2-3 maior erit *tr. Br*

ERIT DISTANTIA ET MAIOREM CUM EA CIRCULI PORTIONEM
COMPREHENDET.

5   Sint in circulo linee *AB*, *CD*, *EF* equidistantes [Fig. P.26], et sit *AB* longior
EF et media sit *CD* ita ut arcus *AC* sit equalis arcui *CE*. Et ideo, quia anguli
coalterni sunt equales, si linee intelligantur quasi protracte ab *A* in *D* et a *D*
in *E*, erunt arcus in quos cadent illi anguli equales, et sic *BD* et *DF* et inter
se et ad alios sunt equales. Continuentur ergo linee *AC*, *CE*, *AE*. Et quia *AC*
10   est equalis linee *CE* ratione arcuum, et angulus *ACD* maior est angulo *DCE*
quia eadem in arcum maiorem, erit *AG* maior *GE*, posito *G* in sectione *CD*
et *AE*. A centro igitur transducta perpendiculari donec conveniat cum *EF*
in *H*, et *AB* lineam tangat in *L*, erit *LA* maior *EH* quoniam sunt dimidia
totorum et *AB* est maior *EF* ex ypothesi. Quia *A*, *E* anguli sunt equales et
15   *ACG* maior est *GCE*, ergo *CGE* obtusus. Ergo perpendicularis [ab *E*] cadet
inter *A* et *L*. Ducta autem perpendiculari *EZT* erit *ZT* maior *EZ*, nam que
est proportio *AG* ad *GE* ea est *TZ* ad *ZE* ratione equidistantie. Et sic constat

3   ea *FaBu* eo *MEBr*
5   linee *tr. Fa post* EF / EF: et EF *FaBu* / equidistantes *om. E* equid' *Br*
6   sit[1] *om. E* / arcus AC *tr. Fa* / AC: CA *Br* / sit equalis *bis E* / CE: esse *Fa*
7   coalterta (*!*) *Fa*
7–8 si . . . E: productis lineis AD et DE *Fa* productis lineis AD et DE erit arcus erunt
     arcus *Bu*
7   et *om. E*
8   in[2] . . . sic *om. FaBu* / caderent *Br* / sic: sicut *E* / inter: ad *FaBu*
9   ad *om. EBr* / alios: aliis *Br* / sunt equales *tr. E* equales *Bu* equales esse ad invicem
     et 5ª 3[i] Euclidis *Fa* / Continentur *Fa* / ergo linee EF*aBu tr. M* linee *Br* / CE: CD
     Bu / AE: AE.S (*?*) *Br*
10 CE: C per xx.8^{am} 3^{ii} *Fa* / ratione arcuum *om. FaBu* / est[2] (*?*) *Br om.* MEF*aBu* /
     DCE: CDE *M*
11 quia . . . maiorem: per ultimam 6[ti] (*?*) quia arcus AB maior arcu EF per ultimam
     partem 27me 3[ii] Euclidis, ergo additis, scilicet BD, DF arcubus, erit AD maior CD
     per secundam conceptionem primi *Fa* / quia . . . arcum: quare arcus *Bu* / maiorem:
     maior est (*?*) *E* / *post* GE *add. Fa* per xx^{[am]} 4^{am} primi / sectionem (*?*) *M*
12 *post* AE *add Fa* linearum / perpendiculare (*?*) *M* perpendicularis *Br* / donec *om.*
     Fa / EF: FE *Fa* DE *Bu*
13 AB lineam *tr. FaBu* AB linea *E* / in[2]: et *Fa* / erit: EF enim linea una propter
     equidistantiam AB et EF, quare linea *Fa* / dimidium *E*
14 totarum *M* / et[1]: per tertiam 3[ii] et quoniam *Fa*
14–16 et[1]. . . . L *om. Bu*
14 est *om. Fa* / ypothesi *MBr* ypotesi EF*a* / Quia: et quia *Fa* / A . . . equales: anguli
     ad A et E equales sunt propter equalitatem AC, CE laterum *Fa* / anguli *tr. M ante*
     A *in lin. 14*
15 maior est *tr. Br* / est *om. Fa* / ergo[1]: erit *Fa* / CGE: GCE *E* / optusus *Br* / Ergo:
     Ergo et *E* et igitur *Fa*
15–17 Ergo . . . ZE *non bene legere possum in Br*
15–16 perpendicularis . . . L: et G cadet inter A et B *M*
15 [ab *E*] *addidi*
16 Ducta . . . erit: a puncto et sic ergo EZC (*?*) erit igitur *Fa* / autem *om. Bu* / EZ: ZE
     per primam 6[ti] Euclidis *Fa*
16–17 nam . . . equidistantie *om. Fa* propter equidistantes *Bu*
17 sic: sicut *E* ita *Bu*

prima pars. Reliqua vero constat ducta perpendiculari per *EF* ad reliqua latera. Et hoc est propositum.

27. SI IDEM ARCUS IN PLURES DIVISIONES SEPARETUR, QUE EQUALIBUS IPSIUS PORTIONIBUS SUBTENDUNTUR CORDE CON-IUNCTE MAIORES ERUNT, ET QUANTO EIS PROPINQUIORES, 6v / TANTO REMOTIORIBUS LONGIORES.

5   Sit arcus *AB*, cuius equalis divisio sit in *C*, et alie due sint: propinquior in *D* et remotior in *E* [Fig. P.27], et subtendantur corde *AC, AGD, AHE, BGC, BHD, BE*. Quia trianguli *AGC, BGD* sunt similes et linea *AC* maior linea *BD*, erunt *AC, GC* maius quam *BD, DG*. Cum igitur sint *AC, CG* ad *GA* sicut *BD, DG* ad *BG*, erit igitur *AC, CG, GB* maius quam *BD, DG, GA* 10 per ultimam quinti Euclidis. Unde constat prima pars. Consimili ratione argues *AD, DB* maiores esse *AHE, BE* secundum quod proponitur.

18 prima pars *tr. Bu* / pars *om. E, et post* pars *add. Fa* propositi / constat *om. Bu* constabit *Fa* / *post* perpendiculari *add. Br* D / per: super *Bu*

18–19 reliqua². . . . propositum: FK, protractis etiam KD, ET lineis erit eundem (*? sed del. Fa?*) ABDC portio maior DFEC portione. Probatio, que est proportio (*et lac.*) TZ ad ZE ea est rectanguli TKPZ ad rectangulum ZPFE. Set TZ maior est EZ. Igitur rectangulum maius rectangulo. Tunc TZ ad ZE sicut se habet sicut (*!*) triangulus TZC ad triangulum ZCE. Triangulus ergo TZC maior est triangulo ZCE. Multo fortius quadrangulum TACZ maius est triangulo Z[C]E. Ergo equalibus additis, scilicet AC, CE portionibus, erit rectangulum (*! quadrangulum*) cum portione cui adiuncta maius triangulo cum portione addita. Simili modo ex altera parte ostenso quod rectangulum (*! quadrangulum*) KBDP cum portione B[D] maius est triangulo PAF (*? PDF*) facilis (*?*) cum portione FD est pertractio ad propositum *Fa* reliqua per equalia *Br*

19 Et . . . propositum: facile patere poterit *Bu* / propositum *om. M*

Prop. 27

Vide sigla in cap. 3 de qualitate MS Br hic

1 27 *mg. sin. MEBr* xxv[ii]ª *mg. dex. E* 27ª *Fa* 34ª *mg. dex. Bu et hab. fig. in FaBu*

1–2 que equalibus *tr. E post* portionibus

2 portionibus: proportionibus *Br*

2–3 coniucte (*!*) *Fa*

3 eis: ei *Br*

4 remotioribus longiores *tr. E*

5 cuius: eius *E* / equalis divisio *tr. Fa* / C: E (*?*) *Br* / sint: sunt *Fa*

7 BGC: BGE *Fa* / Quia: Quia igitur *Fa* / *post* similes *add. Fa* per 4[am] 6[ti] Euclidis quia anguli ad G contra se positi sunt equales et residui per xx.3[am] / maior *om. Fa*

8 *post* BD¹ *add. Fa* iuxta xx.7[am] tertii / erunt: erunt erit *Fa* / AC¹, GC: ACGBG (*?*) *E* / GC: BC (*?*) *Br* et GE *Fa* / quam *E om. MFa* / quam . . . DG: BD et G *Bu* / DG: et GD et quia AC ad AG sicut BD ad BG propter similitudinem (*?*) triangulorum et permutatim proportioni *Fa*

8–9 Cum . . . DG² *om. E* / Cum . . . GA¹: itemque GC ad AG sicut GD ad GB p (*!*) quare per xx.4[am] 5[ti] Euclidis erunt AGC et GC ad AG *Fa* / CG . . . BG: et GC ad AG sicut BD et (*corr. Bu ex* ad) GD ad GB *Bu*

9 *post* BG *add. Fa* igitur per ultimam 5[ti] / erit: erunt *Fa* / igitur *om. Fa* ut *Bu* / CG: GC *Bu* / *post* GB *add. Fa* similis (*! simul*) iuncta / maius quam: maiora *Fa* maius sint quam *Bu* / BD²: DB *BrBu* / *post* GA² *add. Fa* similis (*! simul*) iunctis

10 per . . . Euclidis *om. FaBu* / constat . . . pars: pars prima constat / Consimili: cum simili *E* consimili etiam *FaBu* / ratione *om. M*

11 argue *Br* / DB: BD *Br* et DHB (*!*) lineas *Fa* et DHB *Bu* / esse: lineis *FaBu* / BE: et BE *FaBu*

28. SI LINEE EQUALES IN CIRCULIS INEQUALIBUS ARCUS RE-
SECENT, DE MAIORI MINOREM ET DE MINORI MAIOREM RESE-
CABUNT.

Circuli designati sint: maior *A*, minor *B* [Fig. P.28], positis *A* et *B* in centris
5   ipsorum, et in *A* designetur linea *CD* et ei equalis in *B*, que sit *EF*. Ducantur
etiam a centris linee eis perpendiculares que sint *AGT*, *BHK*; et protractis
lineis *BE*, *AC*, quoniam *EH* est equalis *CG*, erit *BH* minor *AG*, nam quadrata
AG, *GC* maiora sunt quadratis *BH*, *HE* ratione quadratorum *AC*, *BE* eis
equalium. Sit itaque *GL* equalis *BH*; ductaque *LC* erit et ipsa equalis *BE*.
10   Sed et linea protracta *DL* erit equalis *LC*. Et utraque maior *LT* iuxta illud
Euclidis in 3°: si a puncto in diametro preter centrum assignato etc. Descripto
itaque circulo circa centrum *L* secundum quantitatem *LC* et protracta *LT*
ad eius quantitatem usque ad *M* transibit circulus per *C*, *M*, *D* equalis circulo
B, et arcus *CMD* equalis arcui *EKF*, atque arcus *CMD* maior arcu *CTD*,
15   quoniam circumdat, erit et *EKF* maior arcu *CTD*, et hoc est propositum.

29. SI LINEE INEQUALES IN EODEM CIRCULO ARCUS RESECENT,
ERIT ARCUUM PROPORTIO MAIOR QUAM CORDARUM; POR-
TIONUM VERO CIRCULORUM MAIOR QUAM CORDARUM DU-
PLICATA.

5   In circulo cuius centrum *A* designentur linee: maior *BC* et minor *DE*, et
diameter eius *GAH* [Fig. P.29]. Sit igitur *GAH* ad lineam que sit *KL* sicut
BC ad *DE*, cuius sit circulus *KMNL*, posito arcu *MN* simili arcui *BC*, et

Prop. 28

     1 28 *mg. sin. MEBr* [xxv]iii^a *mg. sin. E* 28^a *Fa* 35^a *mg. dex. Bu et hab. fig. in Fa*
   1-2 recessent *Fa*
     2 minori *corr. M ex* minore
   4-5 Circuli . . . designetur *non bene legere possum in Br*
     4 sint *om. E* / minor: et minor *Fa* / A et B: et A, B *E*
     5 desingnentur *Fa* / ei equalis *tr. E* / ei: est *Fa*
     6 sunt *Fa* / pertractis *E*
   7-9 nam. . . . BH: per dulk [*i.e.* per penultimam primi Euclidis] AC non sit equalis GL
        ei equalis *Fa* / nam . . . equalium *om. Bu*
     8 maiora sunt *tr. E* / BH: GH *Br*
     9 equalis BH: ei equalis *Bu* / LC: LE *M* / et *om. Br et forte ras. E* / ipsa: inp^a (*!*) *Fa*
   10 Sed: Set *F si E* / pertracta *E* / protracta DL *tr. Fa* LD protracta *Bu* (*et scr. et del.*
       Bu prod- *ante* protracta) / erit *om. FaBu* / erit equalis *tr. E*
 10-11 iuxta . . . etc. *om. Bu per* vii^am 3^ti *Fa*
   11 dyametro *Br* / preter: punctum (?) *Br* / assignato *om. E*
   12 et protracta: protractaque *E* / LT: LC *E* linea LT *Br*
   13 quantitatem: equalitatem *E* / C: E *E*
 13-14 circulo . . . equalis *om. E*
   14 CMD^1: TMD (?) *Fa* / EKF: CKF *E* / atque *BrBu* at enim (*sive* erit) *M* atqui *E* adqui
      Fa / arcus^2: arcucus (!) *Fa* / CMD^2: EMD (?) *E* / arcu: arcui *Fa*
   15 quoniam: quem *E* / erit: enim *Br* / EKF: EPF *E* / et^2 . . . propositum *EBr om.*
      FaBu et hoc est *M*

Prop. 29

     1 29 *Fa mg. sin. ME dex. Br* [xxi]x^a *mg. sin. E* 36^a *mg. dex. Bu et hab. fig. in Fa*
   2-3 portionum: proportionum *E*
     5 In: n (?) *E* / designetur *Fa* / BC: BE *E* B *Br*
     6 dyameter *Br* / GAH^1: GHA *E* HAG *Br*
     7 sit circulus *tr. FaBu* / KMNL: KLMNL *Fa*

subtendatur corda *MN*. Age. Que est proportio *GAH* ad *KL* ea est circumferentie ad circumferentiam ut est in libro de curvis superficiebus, et que
10 circumferentie ad circumferentiam ea est arcuum similium, sicut etiam
suarum cordarum, ut habetur in libro de similibus arcubus. Ergo que est
proportio *GH* ad *KL* ea est *BC* ad *MN*. Ergo permutatim que *GH* ad *BC* ea
est *KL* ad *MN*. Sed ex ypothesi que est *GH* ad *BC* ea est *KL* ad *DE*. Ergo
DE et *MN* sunt equales. Et quia arcus *MN* maior est arcu *DE* per proximam,
15 et quia linee *BC* ad *MN* sicut arcus ad arcum, erit *BC* ad *DE* minor proportio
quam arcus *BDC* ad *DE* arcum, nam maior est proportio arcus *BDC* ad
arcum *DE* quam eiusdem ad arcum *MN*, et sic constat prima pars.

Item quia similium portionum est proportio que circulorum, atque circulorum que diametrorum duplicata, et ideo que cordarum duplicata, erit
20 portionis *BDC* ad portionem *MN* tanquam *BC* ad *MN* sive *DE* duplicata.
Et quia portio *MN* maior portione *DE*, erit portionis *BCD* ad portionem
DE maior quam linee *BC* ad *DE* proportio duplicata, et hoc est propositum.

7r / 30. SI DUAS LINEAS IN EODEM SEMICIRCULO EQUIDISTANTES
DIAMETER ORTOGONALITER SECUERIT, PORTIONUM QUAS DE

8 Age. . . . proportio: et quia *FaBu* / GAH: GHA *E* GH *Br*
8–14 KL. . . . equales: BC sicut KL ad MN atque sicut KL ad DE, erit DE equalis
MN *Bu*
8 ea est: sicut *Fa*
8–9 circonferentie *Br* (*hic et saepe*)
9 est: ostensum est *Fa* / curvis superficiebus *tr. E*
10 ad: AD ad (*sive* ad *bis*) *Br* / est *om. Fa* / similium: similitudinum (*sive* similitudinem)
E / sicut: sed *Br* sint *M* et *Fa* / etiam: et *E*
12 ea[1]: eadem *Br* / ea[2] *om. E*
13 KL[1]: L *Fa* / Sed: set *Fa* / ex *om. Fa* / ypothesi *MBr* ypotesi *EFa* / GH *forte corr.*
Br ex BH / *post* ad[2] *add. Fa* KL ea est BC ad DE et permutatim GH ad / ea est: ut
Fa / Ergo: quare *Fa*
14 *post* equales *add. Fa* per secundam partem ix[me] quinti / Et: ergo *Bu* / maior est *tr.*
E maior *Bu* / DE: D *Fa* / per proximam *om. Bu* / proximam: proximum commentum
Fa
15 *post* et *scr. et del. M* i / linea *EBu*
16 BDC[1]: BDE (?) *Br* / DE arcum *MBr, tr. EFaBu*
16–17 nam . . . pars *om. Bu*
16 arcus BDC *tr. E*
17 prima pars *tr. E*
18 Item: et item *Bu* / portionum: proportionum *E* / atque: atque que *E*
19 dyametrorum *Br* / dupplicata[1,2] *E* / duplicata[1] *om. Bu* / et ideo: quod patet per
secundam 11[i] (*!* 12[i]) Euclidis et ob hoc similium portionum *Fa* / duplicata[2]: proportio
duplicata *Bu*
19–20 erit . . . BDC: quare erit proportio BDC portionis *Fa*
20 portionis: proportionis *E* / tamquam *ME* / MN[2]: lineam MN *Bu* / sive: sicut *ME* /
DE *om. Br* / dupplicata *EBr*
21 maior: minor (?) *E*
22 dupplicata *EBr* / et . . . propositum *EBr om. Bu* et hoc est *MFa*
Prop. 30
1 30 *mg. sin. E mg. dex. MBr* xxx[a] *mg. dex. E* 30[a] *Fa* 37[a] *mg. dex. Bu et hab. fig. in*
Fa / duas lineas: due linee *Fa*
2 *ante* diameter *add. E* se / dyameter *Br* diametrum *Fa* / ortogonaliter secuerit: secuerit
orthogonaliter *Br* / secuerit: secerint (*!*) *E* secuerint *Fa*

DIAMETRO RESECANT MAIOR ERIT PROPORTIO QUAM ARCUUM
QUI AB EIS SUBTENDUNTUR.

5   Circuli diameter sit *ABGD* [Fig. P.30], linee vero equidistantes quas per
medium secat et ortogonaliter *CBE, HGL*. Aio ergo quod proportio *BGD*
ad *GD* maior est quam arcus *CDE* ad arcum *HDL*, continuetur enim linea
EKD et linea *EL*. Rationis causa *EDL* est obtusus quia cadit in arcum
maiorem semicirculo. Ergo sicut quinta huius probata est sicut in ysoperimetris
10   itaque hic probari potest per sectores circuli descripti secundum *LK* lineam
quod erit proportio *EKD* ad *KD* maior quam anguli *ELD* ad angulum *KLD*.
Itemque que est anguli *ELD* ad angulum *KLD* ea est arcus *ED* ad arcum
HD. Ergo maior est proportio *ED* ad *KD* quam arcus ad arcum. Sed que
est linee *ED* ad *KD* ea est *BD* ad *GD* ratione equedistantie. Ergo maior est
15   *BD* ad *GD* quam arcus *ED* ad arcum *HD*, ergo quam arcus *CDE* ad arcum
HDL quoniam sunt dupli priorum, et hoc est propositum.

31. DUABUS LINEIS AB EODEM PUNCTO CIRCULUM CONTIN-
GENTIBUS SI MINORES ILLIS EUNDEM CIRCULUM CONTINGANT,

3 dyametro *Br*
4 qui . . . eis: quibus *E* / subtenditur *Fa*
5 Circulus *E* / dyameter *Br* (*et post hoc lectiones huiusmodi non laudabo*) / equidistantes:
   equalis (?) *E* eqd' *Br* (*et post hoc lectiones huiusmodi non laudabo*)
6 secat *om. E* / orthogonaliter *Br* / CBE: EBC *M* / aio *M* ait *EFaBu* dico *Br* / quod
   om. E
7 maior est *tr. FaBu* / HDL: HDB *E* / enim: xx *Fa*
8 linea EL: linee CL et DL *Bu* linea EL et DL *Fa*
8–16 Rationis. . . . propositum: quia igitur proportio EHD (? EKD) ad KD que BGD ad
   GD propter equidistantiam linearum CB (*sive* EB) et HG et quia proportio EKD ad
   KD maior quam anguli ELD ad angulum KLD quoniam angulus EDL est obtusus
   et quod nunc diximus patet per demonstrationem 5te propositionis primi huius,
   itemque anguli ad angulum sicut arcus ED ad arcum KD, erit BD ad GD maior
   proportio quam arcus ED ad arcum HD. Patet ergo quod maior est quam archus
   (!) CDE ad arcum HDL quoniam sunt dupli aliorum *Fa*
8–11 Rationis. . . . erit: quia igitur proportio CKD (? EKD) ad KD que BGD ad GD
   propter equidistantiam linearum CB (! EB) et HG et quia *Bu*
8 optusus *Br* / cadit: eadem (?) *Br*
9 maiorem: minorem *E* / sicut[1]: sic *E* / est *om. E*
10 itaque: ita et *EBr* / secundum . . . lineam: pro (?) LK linea *E*
11 proportio: maior proportio *Br* / ad KD *om. E* / ELD: CLD (?) *Bu* / *post* KLD *add.*
   Bu quoniam angulus EDL est obtusus et hac ratione premissa inde (?) a triangulo (?)
12 Itemque . . . KLD *om. E* / Itemque: Item que que *Br* / que est *om. Bu* / ELD *om.*
   Bu / KLD *om. Bu* / ea est: sicut *Bu* / ED *om. E* CD *Bu*
13–15 Ergo. . . . GD: erit BD ad GD maior erit proportio *Bu*
14 equistantie (!) *E*
15 ad GD: AGD *M* ad AGD *E* / ergo: patet ergo quod maior etiam *Bu*
16 quoniam: quam (?) *E* / sunt: sit *E* / priorum: aliorum *Bu* / et . . . propositum *E*
   om. FaBu et hoc est *M* et hoc est quod fuit propositum *Br*

Prop. 31

1 31 *Fa mg. sin. E mg. dex. MBr* x[xxi[a]] *mg. dex. E* 38[a] *mg. dex. Bu et hab. fig. in*
   Fa / *ante* Duabus *add. Fa* Si
2 eumdem *E om. Br* / contingunt *E*

MAIOR ERIT LINEARUM SIVE AB IPSIS ET ARCUBUS CONTEN-
TARUM SUPERFICIERUM PROPORTIO QUAM ARCUUM.

5   Centrum circuli sit *A* [Fig. P.31], lineeque maiores contingentes circulum
BC, *BD*, minores vero sint *HE*, *HF*. A centro igitur ad contactus linee ducantur: *AC*, *AD*, *AE*, *AF*, itemque *AB*, *AH*. Separentur autem a *BC* et *BD*
equales *HE*, *HF*, que sunt *GC*, *LD*. Ductis lineis *AG*, *AL* et quia *BC* ad *GC*
maior quam anguli *BAC* ad angulum *GAC* per quintam huius, anguli autem
10   ad angulum sicut arcus ad arcum, erit trianguli *BAC* ad triangulum *GAC*
maior quam arcus ad arcum. Item cum triangulus *AGC* sit equalis triangulo
LAD, et uterque sit equalis dimidio quadranguli *AFHE*, et arcus arcui, erit
quadranguli *ACBD* ad quadrangulum *AEHF* maior proportio quam arcus
CD ad arcum *EF*. Sed sectoris *ADC* ad sectorem *AEF* sicut arcus ad arcum.
15   Ergo residuum, scilicet superficies *CBD*, ad superficiem *EHF* similiter est
maior, et hoc est propositum.

32. SI DUE LINEE AB EODEM PUNCTO CIRCULUM CONTIN-
GANT, SI EISDEM EQUALES MAIOREM CIRCULUM CONTINGANT,
MAIOREM DE IPSO ARCUM COMPREHENDENT.

       Maioris centrum sit *A* et minoris *T* [Fig. P.32], linee contingentes minorem
5   sint *BC*, *BD*; equales eis contingant maiorem que sint *HE*, *HG*. Sicut autem
7v   diameter minoris se habet ad diametrum / maioris ita sit *CB* ad *EL*, protracta
EH ad *L*. Et ab *L* ducatur linea contingens que sit linea *LM*. A centris etiam

3 sive: sive et *Br* / et: et ab *Br*

6 *ante* BC *add.* Fa sunt / BC, BD: HB, CD *E* / sint *MBu om. Br* sunt *EFa* / HE *EBr*
HE et *FaBu* BE *M* / *ante* HF *scr. et del. Bu* HF / igitur: vero *E* / ad *om. Bu*

7 itemque AB: item est AB et *Fa* / AH: et AH *Bu* / a *om. Br* ab *Fa*

8 equales HE, HF: reliquis scilicet HE et HF equales *Fa* reliquis equales *Bu* / HE: BE
(?) *M* / sint *Fa* / GC, LD: LD, GC *FaBu* GC, HD *E* / lineis AG: angulis *E* / *post*
AL *scr. et del. M* eq. *et add. FaBu* quia (*Fa,* erit *Bu*) igitur proportio trianguli BCA
ad triangulum GCA sicut linea BC ad GC

9 angulum: triangulum *Fa* / per . . . huius *om. Bu* / huius: primi huius *Fa*

10 BAC: ABC *E*

11 Item cum: cumque *Fa* et cum *Bu* / triangulo: triangulus *Fa*

12 LAD: ALD *FaBu* / sit *om. FaBu*

13 ACBD *FaBu* ABCD *EM,* (?) *Br* / *ante* arcus *scr. et del. Bu* AC

14 Sed: set *Fa* / sectoris *EBr* sector *MFaBu* / ADC: ADE *E*

15 superficies: superficiei *EM* / ad *bis Fa* / EHF: CHF *Br,* (?) *E* / est *om. FaBu*

16 et . . . propositum *E om. FaBu* et hoc est *MBr*

Prop. 32

1 32 *Fa mg. sin. E mg. dex. MBr* xx[xii^a] *mg. dex. E* 39 *mg. dex. Bu* 39^a *fig. in Fa*

2 eisdem *MFaBu* eiusdem *EBr* / circulum *BrFa om. MEBu* / contingat *Br*

3 ipso: proposito (?) *E* / arcu *E* / comprehendunt *E* conprehent (!) *Fa*

4 T: sit T (*sive* C) *Fa* / lineeque *Br*

5 sint¹: sicut *Fa* / BD: et D *E* / eis: eas *M* / contingant *corr. Br ex* contingentem /
maiorem: minorem *Fa* / sint² *FaBu* sint (*sive* sicut) *M* sunt *EBr* / HE: HE et *FaBu*

6 diameter: diametri *Fa* / se habet *om. FaBu*

7 EH: CH *Br* / Et ab L *om. E* / linea¹: linea recta *E* alia linea *Fa* / linea LM: BM
Fa / linea² *om. Bu* / etiam: igitur *Br*

ducantur linee *CT, TD, AE, AG, AM*. Que est proportio *LE* ad *HE* ea est quadranguli *AELM* ad quadrangulum *AEHG*, quod haberi potest ex parte
10   probationis in proxima probatione. Sed cum quadranguli *AELM* et *TCBD* sunt similes ex ypothesi, erit proportio *AELM* ad *TCBD* tanquam *LE* ad *BC*, hoc est ad *HE* sibi equalem, duplicata. Erit ergo quadrangulum *AEHG* proportionale inter quadrangulum *AELM* et *TCBD*; item *CD* arcus est similis arcui *EM*, nam *AELM* est simile *TCBD* et angulus *T* est equalis angulo *A*
15   totali. Itaque *TC* vel *TD* sit minor *AE* sive *AM*; erunt *AE* (*! TD*) et *AM* quasi secantes arcus *CD, EM*, et erit arcus *CD* quasi inclusus ab *EM*. Ergo per librum de similibus arcubus *EM, CD* sunt arcus similes. Ergo que est *EM* arcus ad *CD* arcum ea est semidiametri ad semidiametrum, ea est etiam *LE* ad *BC*, hoc est *HE*. Sed que est *LE* ad *HE* ea est *AEHG* ad *TCBD*. Ergo

8   ducantur: elimatur (*!*) *Fa* / CT, TD: ZC (*?*), DT *E* TC, TD *FaBu*
8–20   Que. . . . TCBD: quia igitur quadrangulum AELM simile est quadrangulo TCBD quia ex ypotesi CB ad EL sicut diametri ad diametrum et diametri a[d] diametrum sicut semidiametri ad semidyametrum. Quare latera quadrangulorum erunt proportionalia et anguli unius angulis alterius equales, quod patet per 6[ti] (*!*) 6[ti] Euclidem (*!*), AL et TB lineis intellectualiter protraṇctis erit igitur proportio quadranguli ad quadrangulum (*corr. Fa ex* quadralium triangulum) LE ad BC, sive ad HE, duplicata; et quia quadrangulum AELM ad quadrangulum AEHG sicut LE ad ME, erit quadrangulum AEHG inter illas (*!*), scilicet AELM et TCBD, proportionale; ideoque arcus EM ad arcum CD tanquam quadrangulum AEHG ad TCBD quoniam ut dictum est supra in 4[ta] huius 3[i] circumferentiarum et similium arcuum et diametrorum eadem est proportio, et ex ypotesi diametri ad diametrum sicut CB ad LE, et quod arcus EM et CD sunt (*?*) similes patet consideratis quadrangulis ZCKD (*! ZCBD*), KMLE, angulis, scilicet A totali et T, equalibus et duplis ad B et K per xix[am] 3[i] Euclidem (*!*) et cum his assumpta 11[a] (*?*) 5[ti] erunt anguli K et Z equales; quare ex descriptione similium portionum et similium arcuum erunt arcus EM et CD similes *Fa*
8–11   Que . . . TCBD: quia igitur quadrangulum AELM simile est quadrangulo TCBD, eorum proportio erit *Bu*
8   LE (*?*) *E*
9   quadranguli: quadrangula *E* / quadrangulum: quadratum *M*
9–10   ad . . . AELM *om. E*
10   probationis: proportionis *Br* / probatione: proportione (*sive* propositione) *Br* / TCBD: TEBD *E*
11   ypothesim *E* / TCBD: TEBD *E* / tamquam *E*
12   hoc est: sive *Bu* / sibi equalem *om. Bu* / dupplicata *EBr*
12–20   Erit . . . est[2]: et quia quadrangulum AELM ad quadrangulum AEHG sicut LE ad HE, erit quadrangulum AEHG sicut inter illa, scilicet AELM et TCBD, proportionale. Ideoque arcus EM ad arcum CD tanquam quadrangulum *Bu*
12   AEHG: AE, BG (*?*) *M*
13   inter: item *E* / TCBD: TEBD *E*
14   est equalis *tr. Br*
14–15   angulo A totali: totali A (*?*) *Br*
15   TC: TE (*?*) *Br*
15–16   erunt . . . EM[2] *om. E*
16   EM[1]: et EM *Br*
17   EM[1] *EBr* AM *M* / CD: ED *Br*
18   semidiametri: semidiameter *E* / est[2] *om. E* / etiam: et *Br*
19   AEHG: EAHG *Br* / TCBD: TEBD *E* CBD *Br* / *ante* Ergo *injuste scr. E hic* Sed ut habetur per proximam arcus EM *sed delendum est quia juste iteravit post* TCBD *in lin. 20*

20 que est arcus *EM* ad arcum *CD* ea est *AEHG* ad *TCBD*. Sed ut habetur per proximam arcus *EM* ad *EG* minor est proportio quam linee *EL* ad *HE* sive *AEHG* ad *TCBD*. Ergo *EM* ad *EG* minor est proportio quam *EM* ad *CD*. Ergo maior est *EG* quam *CD*, et hoc est quod proponitur.

33. DUOBUS CIRCULIS SE TANGENTIBUS SI A TACTU PER-TRANSIENS UTRUMQUE LINEA DUCATUR, SIMILES DE ILLIS PORTIONES ABSCINDET.

   Circuli contingentes sint *ABG* et *ACF* [Fig. P.33], continueturque linea
5 *ABC* secans eos, ducaturque linea *AGF* que transeat per centra eorum. Et quia angulus *GAC* in utroque consistit, erit arcus *BG* similis arcui *CF*. Residui ergo de semicirculis similes erunt, scilicet *AB* et *AC*, et ob hoc etiam portiones circulorum; ultimum ductis lineis *BG*, *CF*. Nam si linee *BG*, *CF* protrahantur,

  20 CD *M* ED *EBr* / Set *Fa*

20-21 per proximam *om. Bu*

  21 EM: eundem *Fa* / quam *om. E*

21-22 linee . . . AEHG: quadranguli AEH.D *Fa*

  21 EL: EI *Br*

21-22 sive . . . TCBD *om. Bu*

  22 ad TCBD: igitur ad CEBD *Br* ad TCHD *Fa* / EG: ES (?) *Fa*

22-23 EG. . . . est[1]: DC maior proportio EM ad EG, maior igitur *Bu*

  22 CD *corr. Br ex* CG / *post* CD *add. E* Ergo AE ad EG minor est proportio quam EM ad C (!)

  23 est[1] *supra scr. Fa om. E* / et . . . proponitur *om. Bu* / proponitur: dictum est; nunc per proximam et quos supra, scilicet quod AELM et AEHG sicut LE ad HE, totum patet per figuram sic signatam et eiusdem dispositionis cuius figure precedentis propositionis (?) *Fa*

Prop. 33

   1 33 *Fa mg. sin. EBr mg. dex. M* xxx[iii[a]] *mg. sin. E* 40 *mg. dex. Bu* 40[a] *fig. in Fa* / Duobus: Quobus (!) *E* / se *om. E* sese *Br* / tangentibus: contingentibus *Br* / a: de *E* / tactu: contactu *Fa*

 1-2 pertransiens utrumque *tr. Br*

   3 portiones *tr. E post* similes

   4 ACF: AEF (?) *Fa* / -que: quia *Fa*

   5 -que *om. Bu* etiam *Fa*

   6 GAC: GAT (?) *Fa* / utraque *E* / arcus *om. FaBu* / CF: EF *BrBu*

 6-12 Residui. . . . proponitur: statutis angulis BHG (! BAG), CKF (! CAF) et assu[m]pta 11[a] tertii Euclidis et diffinitione similium arcuum; tunc quia anguli ad B et C recti sunt, erunt linee BG, CF equidistantes et anguli G et F equales propter equidistantiam. Quare statutis angulis ad B et arc (! ad C), erunt AB et AC similes portiones, sic iuvante ut prius 11[a] 3[i] et diffinitione similium portionum et patet propositum quod iam dicitur verum est sive circuli intrinsecus se contingant sive extrinsecus, set alia erunt (?) in parte media quia prius erat angulus A communis. Nunc autem sunt anguli contra se positi ad A et ob hoc equales; item (*sive* tunc) anguli B et C recti, modo sunt anguli coalterni prius aliter se ♭ (*del.*) habentes; quod autem sit una linea que transit per centrum et per contactum in utraque dispositione per xx[am] tertii Euclidis est confirmandum *Fa*

   7 sçimiles *M* / et AC *om. M* / *post* et[2] *scr. et del. Br* l

   8 *post* circulorum *add. Bu* similes / ultimum: vel aliter *Br* / CF[1] *correxi ex* EF *in Br* (*et om. ME*)

 8-11 Nam. . . . CF *om. Bu*

   8 CF[2] *correxi ex* EF *in MEBr*

erit angulus *B* et similiter *C* rectus, et sic linee *BG, CF* erunt equidistantes.
10 Ergo angulus *G* erit equalis angulo *F*. Ergo arcus in quos cadunt erunt similes,
nam supra quos cadunt erunt similes [*BG* et] *CF* equidistantibus. Et hoc est
quod proponitur.

34. SI CIRCULUS ALIUM INFRA (*!* INTRA) CONTINGAT ET A
CONTACTU LINEA PER CENTRA EORUM TRANSEAT, QUE-
CUMQUE LINEA EI PERPENDICULARIS CONSISTIT HINC INDE PER
UTRUMQUE CIRCULORUM TRANSIENS SI INFRA (*!* INTRA) CEN-
5 TRUM MAIORIS DUCATUR, SIVE ALIUM SECET SIVE CONTIN-
GAT, DE MINORI VERSUS CONTACTUM MINUS CONCLUDET;
QUOD SI PER MAIORIS CENTRUM ET CONTINGAT MINOREM,
8r TANTUMDEM SI[C] SECET UTRIUS; QUOD SI EXTRA / ECONTRA-
RIO SEMPER MAIUS.

10 Sint circuli contingentes *ABCD, AEFG,* et protrahatur *ACF* transiens per
centra eorum, que sint *M* et *N,* et inter *M,* quod sit centrum maioris, et *A*
transeat perpendiculariter linea *EBDG* minorem secans circulum *BC* [Fig.
P.34a], et equidistans ducatur linea *KLT* ita ut si linea esset protracta ab *E*
ad *A* transiret per *K,* et sit *KLT* in minori circulo arcum secans *KAT.* Erit
15 itaque proportio arcus *EAG* ad arcum *KAT* que est linee *ZA* ad *LA,* quod

9 sic: sicut *E* / CF *correxi ex* EF *in EBr,* (?)*M*

11 [BG et] *addidi* / CF: EF *Br*

11–12 Et . . . proponitur *EBr om. Bu* Et hoc est *M*

Prop. 34

1 34 *mg. sin. MEBr* [xx]xiiiiª *mg. sin. E* 34ª *Fa* 41ª *mg. sin. Bu* / alium: circulum *E*

2–3 quecumque *MEFa* queconque *Br* quodcumque *Bu*

3 perpendiculariter *FaBu* / consistit: insistit *FaBu*

4 infra: supra *Br*

4–5 *supra* centrum maioris *scr. M* versus contactum (*cf. Prop. III.3 vers. long.*)

5 maioris: maiores *Fa* / ducantur (?) *Fa* / sive¹: sit due (?) *Br* / sive²: a sive alium *Br*

6 contacttum (*!*) *M* / minus (?) *Br* mius (*!*) *Fa* / minus concludet *tr. E* miniss (*!*) concludo *Br*

7 per *Br* super *M* sit *E* supra *FaBu* / maioris *om. FaBu* / minorem *om. FaBu*

8 si[c]: si similis *Br* / secet: ceset (*!*) *Fa* / utrius *correxi ex* minus *in MEBu,* (?)*Br, et
ex* unius *in Fa*

10 protratur (*!*) *Fa* / ACF: AEF *E* linea ACF *FaBu*

11 centra: centrum *Fa*

12 *ante* linea *scr. et del. Bu* E *et post* linea *scr. et del Bu* EBGD / linea *om. Fa* / minorem
secans: secando minorem *Fa* / BC: huic *Br* huic (*sive* B *in* C) *Fa* huic (*sive* hinc) *Bu*

13 equidistanter *Fa*

13–14 ita . . . KLT *om. Bu*

13 ut: quod *Br*

14 A: D *E* / resecans *FaBu* / KAT: EAG *Bu* / *post* KAT *add. Fa* et patet per proximam
arcus KAT et EAG similes esse

15 itaque: quoque *Bu* / est: et *Bu*

15–16 quod . . . huius *ME om. BrBu* quoniam per librum de similibus arcubus eadem est
proportio arcuum et cordarum. Quare KAT ad EAG sicut linee KT ad EG sicut
EKA linea intellectualiter protracta ad KA et GTA ad TA quia si protraherentur
EKA et GTA fierent duo trianguli EAG et KAT similes ob hoc etiam EKA ad KA
ut ZA ad LA. Quare manifestus (*!*) quod eadem est proportio arcus EAG at (*!* ad)
arcum KAT que est linea ZA ad LA *Fa*

constat per secundam sexti Euclidis et per proximam huius. Sed linee ZA ad LA maior est proportio quam arcus BAD ad arcum KAT per quartam ab ista [i.e. per 30^{am} huius]. Ergo maior est proportio arcus EAG ad arcum KAT quam arcus BAD ad arcum KAT. Ergo EAG est maior BAD.

20   Item sit perpendicularis transiens inter M et A et sit contingens minorem circulum [Fig. P.34b]. Erit ergo EAG minor semicirculo. Sumatur autem similis arcus de minori circulo et sic ille erit minor semicirculo. Sit autem ille arcus dictus KAT, et centrum minoris circuli ut supra sit N. Maior itaque est proportio NA ad LA quam semicirculi ad arcum KAT. Ergo dupli NA,

25   quod est CA, maior est proportio ad LA quam totius circumferentie ad arcum KAT. Sed que est proportio CA ad LA ea est EAG ad arcum KAT. Sic itaque maior est arcus EAG totali circumferentia.

Amplius sit EMG transiens super centrum maioris et contingens minorem [Fig. P.34c]. Erit ergo semicirculus maioris equalis minori. Nam que est

16   *post* secundam *est lac. in M* / sexti: v^{ti} E / Set Fa F E / linee *om. BrFa*

17   *post* proportio *add. Fa* arcus EAG ad arcum KAT / quam *om. Bu* / *post* arcus *scr. et del. Bu* B / ad arcum KAT *om. Fa*

17–19   per . . . KAT *om. Br*

17–18   per . . . ista: quod probatum est si Z et L cadant in semicirculo versus A. Quando autem cum sit L ex parte A si Z sit ex parte M quoniam NC ad ZC maior proportio quam arcus semicirculi ad arcum BCD erit linee ZA ad NA maior proportio quam arcus BAD ad arcum alterius semicirculi et item NA ad LA maior proportio quam arcus semicirculi ad arcum KAT. Sic ergo linee ZA ad LA maior proportio quam arcus BAD ad arcum KAT *Bu*

18   Ergo . . . est: maior ergo *Bu* / arcum *om. Bu*

19   arcum KAT: eundem *Bu* / KAT: BAT *Fa* / Ergo . . . est: et ideo EAG *Bu* / EAG: arcus EAG E / BAD^2: LAD E

20–53   Item. . . . proba: Si item transeat perpendicularis linea EAG inter M et A, erit tota circumferentia minor arcu BAD, sit enim ut prius arcus KAT similis arcui EAG; quia igitur L cadet inter N et A erit tota circumferentia minor arcu BAD (*del. Bu*) NA ad LA maior proportio quam arcus semicirculi ad arcum KAT. Dupli ergo NA, quod est linea CA, ad LA est maior proportio quam totius circumferentie ad KAT, maior itaque EAG ad KAT quam circumferentie ad eundem et sic EAG maior circumferentia. Simili ratione sicut sit apud M et transeat linea ECG, erit arcus EAG equalis circumferentie. Similiter si KL (?), EB, et DG extra M transeat sive (?) linea ECG econtrario continget, erit enim quod de interiori circulo CBA (?) assumitur maius arcu exterioris *Bu*

20   A: L *Fa*

21   EAG: EAS (?) *Fa* / Sumantur *Fa*

22   sic: sicut E

23   dictus: ductus E / N: cum E enim N *Br* / itaque: ita quod (?) *Br*

24   ad^1: ab *Fa* / *post* KAT *add. Fa* per quartam ab ista

24–26   Ergo . . . KAT^1 *om. E*

24   duplicis *Br*

25   quod: que *Br* / CA: EA *Br*

26   Sed . . . KAT *om. Fa* / CA: EA *Br* / arcum *om. E* / Sic: sicut E

27   *post* circumferentia *add. Fa* quoniam CA ad LA sicut EAG ad KAT

28   EMG: EMS (?) *Fa*

29   semicirculus: semicircumferentia *Fa* / minori: circumferrentie (!) minoris *Fa*

30 proportio diametri *AF* ad diametrum *AM* ea est circumferentie ad circumferentiam. Sed diameter est duplex ad diametrum. Ergo circumferentia est dupla ad circumferentiam. Ergo medietas est equalis circumferentie minoris, et sic *EAG* est equalis circumferentie *ACMD*.

Rursus sit *ECG* extra centrum secans maiorem [Fig. P.34d], et sit contingens
35 intrinsecum circulum. Dico quod circulus interior maior est arcu cuius est corda *ECG* versus contactum. Protrahatur ergo per centrum *M* linea *BMD* secans utrumque circulum. Maior est proportio *MF* ad *CF* quam semicirculi ad arcum *EFG*. Ergo minor est *CF* ad *AF* quam arcus *EFG* ad circumferentiam totam. Ergo divisim minor est proportio *CF* ad *CA* quam arcus *EFG* ad
40 arcum *EAG*. Ergo coniunctim minor est proportio *FA* ad *CA* quam totius circumferentie ad arcum *EAG*. Sed que est proportio *FA* ad *CA* ea est circumferentie maioris ad minorem. Ergo minor est proportio maioris ad minorem quam eiusdem ad arcum *EAG*. Ergo circumferentia minor est maior arcu *EAG*, et hoc est quod proponitur.

45 Preterea sit *BMD* transiens per centrum maioris et secans minorem [Fig. P.34e]; arcus minoris erit minor semicirculo maioris. Hoc autem manifestum est si fiat circulus secundum medietatem diametri *AF*, hoc est *AM*. Nam tunc ille circulus erit equalis semicirculo maioris, ut probatum est in tertia parte huius propositionis. Sed arcus *BAD* esset minor illo, ut probatum est
50 in proxima parte huius propositionis. Ergo arcus *BAD* est minor semicirculo maioris.

30 AF: ADF *E* / circumferrentie (*!*) *Fa*
30–31 *post* circumferentiam *add. Fa* ut ostensum est in libro de curvis superficiebus
31 est[1] . . . diametrum: ad diametrum est duplum *Fa* / duplex: duplum *M*
31–32 est dupla *tr. E, et tr. Fa post* circumferrentiam (*!*)
33 EAG: ea igitur *Fa* / circumferentie ACMD: AKCT (*!*) *Fa*
34–36 extra . . . ECG *om. Br*
34 extra *Fa* infra *ME*
35 intrinsecus *Fa*
36 M: N *E*
37 MF: in F *E* / CF: EF *Br hic et in lin. seq.*
38 *post* EFG[1] *add. Fa* quare econverso / est *om. Fa* / circumferrentiam (*!*) *Fa*
39 est *om. E* / CF: EF *E* / CA: EA *Br* / *post* EFG *add. Fa* Hoc argumentum manifestabitur ratione (*?*) totius commenti
40 CA: EA *Br*
41 Set *Fa* / CA M AC *EBrFa* / est[2] *om. E*
42–43 Ergo . . . minorem *mg. M sed hab. M* Quare *pro* Ergo
42 est *om. E* / maioris[2]: circumferentie maioris *BrFa*
43 *post* eiusdem *add. E* A / ad: at (*?*) *Fa* / est maior *tr. Fa* / est (*?*) *supra scr. E*
44 et . . . proponitur *Br om. Fa* et hoc est *ME*
45 *de* BMD *scr. mg. M* ponitur hic BMD pro ECG eo quod M est centrum maioris et C punctus infimus minoris / BMD: BD *Br*
46 *post* maioris *add. Br* aliquid quod non bene legere possum
47 est[1]: erit *E* erunt *Fa* / circulus: circulis (*?*) *Fa*
48 probatum est: brobatur (*!*) *Fa*
49 propositionis: proportionis *E* / Set *Fa*
49–50 esset . . . BAD *om. Fa* / probatum . . . in *om. E*
50 propositionis: proportionis *E*

Ad ultimum dic *A* (*! M*) centrum maioris et transeat sub *M*, id est extra, et persecans *AC* circulum [cf. *EG* in Fig. P.34e], et modo predicto proba.

35. CIRCULO ALIUM INFRA (*!* INTRA) CONTINGENTE LINEA A CENTRO MAIORIS UTRUMQUE PERTRANSIENS ET PRETER CON-
8v TACTUM DUCTA / DE INTERIORE, SI EXTRA CENTRUM DUCA-
TUR, ARCUM MINOREM VERSUS CONTACTUM CONCLUDET; SI
5 SUPRA CENTRUM, EQUALEM; SI VERO INFRA (*!* INTRA), MAIOREM.

Sint circuli ut prius contingentes *ABC* et *ADE* et diameter *AFEC*, posito *F* centro maioris, transeatque linea *FDB* [Fig. P.35]; applicetque *A* cum *D* linea ad *G*, posito *G* in circumferentia maioris circuli, ducta linea *FG*. Si
10 ergo extra *F* ductus est circulus interior [Fig. P.35a], erit *AD* maior *GD*.

52-53 Ad . . . proba: quod supposuimus. Hoc argumentum (*?*). Minor est proportio CF ad AF quam arcus EFG ad circumferentiam totam. Sic potest manifestari, que enim est proportio EFG ad circumferentiam ea sit RS ad XT (*?*). Igitur cum sit proportio CF ad AF sicut sicut (*! del.*) RS (*?*) ad RT (*?*) habeat CF ad CA velut RS (*?*) ad FC (*sive* SC). Probatio. Sicut se habet RS (*?*) ad RT (*?*) sic FC ad minorem FA quoniam FC ad FA maior est proportio quam FC ad maiorem FA, et sic RS ad RT maior quam FC ad maiorem FA. Sit ergo proportio RS ad RT ut CF ad minorem FA; sic igitur que sit FG (*? FC?*). Quare divisum (*?*) per 17 (*?*) quinti erit proportio FC ad EG sicut RS ad FC. Set FC ad CA minor est quam FC ad EG (*?*) per secundam partem 8ᵉ 5ᵗⁱ. Igitur FC ad CA minor est proportio quam RS ad FC et sicut RS ad FC sic FDG (*!*) ad EAG, ergo minor est CF ad CA quam FEC (*?*) ad CDG (-C *supra scr.*), et hoc est quod voluimus ostendere. Quod autem consequenter ergo coniuctum (*!*) minor est proportio FA ad CA quam totius circumferentie ad arcum EAG patet in predictis lineis, sicque si fuerit proportio FC ad minor[em] quam RS ad FC (*sive* FT) erit coniunctim FA ad CA minor quam RS ad FC FA ad (*scr. et del.*), sicut enim RC ad FC (*?*) FA ad CA, et ad maiorem CA et minorem CA. Set non ad CA quia tunc esset divisim et patet inconveniens, nec etiam ad maiorem CA, sit enim RC ad HC (*?*) ut FA ad CP (*?*), quare divisim RS ad FC (*sive* SC) sicut FC ad CP. Set ex ypotesi RS ad FC (*sive* SC) maior quam FC ad CA et FGC ad CA maior quam FC ad CP. Ergo a primo RS ad FC (*?*) maior quam FC ad CP. Relinquitur ergo proportio RC (*?*) ad FC (*?*) sicut FA ad minorem CA, que sit CK (*?*). Sed FA ad CK minor quam FA ad CH (*?*). Ergo FA ad CA minor quam RT (*?*) ad FC (*sive* SC) sicut circumferentia AEFG ad arcum EAG. Ergo FA ad CA minor quam totius circumferentie ad arcum EAG. Sic ergo patefecimus *Fa*

52-53 dic . . . proba *om. M*
52 sub M: sub (*?*) A (*!*) *Br*
53 circulum *correxi ex* circulus *in* E

Prop. 35

1 35 *mg. sin. MEBr* xxx[v]ᵃ *mg. dex.* E 35ᵃ *Fa* 42ᵃ *mg. sin. Bu* / Circulo: Sirculo (*!*) *Bu* / infra contingente *tr.* E / lineam E
3 ducta: de ducta *Fa* / *post* extra *scr. et del. Bu* circulum
5 equale *Fa*
7 ut prius *tr. Fa post* contingentes / et¹: etiam *Br* / AFEC: ACFEC E
8 maior s *Fa* / applicetque: applicet E amplicetque *Fa*
9 G¹ *om. Br* / G²: igitur E / in *om. M*
10 est: sit (*sive* sicut) *Bu*
10-16 AD. . . . AD: ADE semicirculus et angulus ad D totalis rectus et partialis versus [A] acutus et etiam angulus ad A acutus. Quare perpendiculari protracta ab F super AG cadet inter A et D et sit FZT. Dico per 5ᵃᵐ primi huius quod maior est proportio GD ad AZ quam GFD ad angulum DFG (*!*). Probatio huius arti (*! argumenti*) quia

Cadat ergo perpendicularis *FZT* super *AG*. Cumque sit angulorum et arcuum eadem erit proportio, linee *ZDG* ad *DG* minor proportio quam arcus *TG* ad arcum *BG*, et ideo tota linea *ADG* ad *DG* minor quam arcus *AG* ad *BG*, et econverso linee *AG* ad *DA* maior quam arcus *AG* ad *BA*. Sed arcus *ABG*

15 ad arcum *AD* tanquam linea *AG* ad lineam *AD*, cum sint similes. Maior ergo arcus *AB* arcu *AD*.

Si interior supra centrum *F* transeat [Fig. P.35b], erit *AF* semicirculus et *D* rectus et *AD* equalis *DG*, et sicut *ABG* ad *ACD* sic *AG* ad *AD*. Ergo *AB*, *ACD* sunt equales.

20 Si vero infra (*!* intra) centrum, erit *DG* maior *DA* [Fig. P.35c], et perpendicularis *FZT* cadet inter *D* et *G*, eritque proportio arcus *TBA* ad *BA* maior

GD ad DZ sicut GFD ad minorem angulum [quam] DFZ quoniam ad maiorem esset minor. Igitur econverso ZD ad DG sicut minoris anguli angulo ZFD ad angulum DFG. Set ipsius minoris anguli ad FG (*!* DFG) minorem quam ZFD ad DFG. Ergo ZD ad DG minor est quam ZFD ad DFG. Ergo coniunctum ZDH (*!* ZDG) ad DG minor est quam anguli ZFG ad angulum DFG. Set sicut anguli ad angulum sit arcus TG ad arcum BG. Ergo minor est proportio ZDG ad DG quam arcus TG ad arcum BG. Quare tota linea AG ad DG minorem habet proportionem quam arcus AG ad arcum BG quoniam AG linea dupla est ad ZG et AG arcus duplus est ad TG. Quare econverso linee AG ad DA maior quam arcus AG ad arcum BA. Set arcus ABG ad arcum AD, cum sint similes, tanquam linea AG ad lineam AD. Maior igitur est proportio arcus ABG ad arcum BA (*!* DA). Quare maior est arcus AB arcu AD *Fa*

11 FZT: FECT *E* / arcuum et angulorum *E*

12 erit proportio *tr. Bu* / ZDG: et (?) DG *E* / proportio quam *tr. Br* / proportio²: proportione *E* / TG: CG *Br*

13 DG: AG *Br*

15 tanquam . . . AD²: tamquam AG *M sed add. M* (*cf. E*) ad AD *post* similes / tamquam *E* / linea . . . lineam *om. E* / lineam *om. Bu* / lineam AD *tr. Br* / cum . . . similes *om. Bu* / *post* similes *add. E* ad AD (*cf. M*)

17 F *om. Br*

17–19 erit . . . equales: quoniam ADG apud D secabitur per equalia, ab F ad D linea ducta erit ei perpendicularis et sicut fal (*del. Bu*) facile patet proportio *Bu*

17 *post* semicirculus *add. Fa* per 11 tertii Euclidis

18 D: angulus D *Fa* / *post* rectus *add. Fa* per xxx / *post* DG *add. Fa* per secundam partem tertie eiusdem tertii Euclidem (*!*) / *ante* ABG *add. M* ADG ad AD sic AG ad AD et sicut / ABG: ABG arcus *Fa* / ACD: ADAB (*!* ADC) arcum *Fa* / sic: sicut *E* / AG: linea AG *Fa* / *post* AD² *add. Fa* quoniam utrumque est proportio dupli ad subduplum et sicut ABG arcus ad arcum AD sicut linea AG ad lineam AD per librum de similibus arcubus, ergo a primo sicut arcus ABG ad arcum AD sit idem ABG ad arcum AD / Ergo: erunt ergo *Fa*

19 ACD: ABC *E* et AD *Fa* / sunt *om. MBr* / equales: equa *M*

20–23 DG . . . DA²: angulus D versus OD obtusus (*!*) adiuvante xi tertii et etiam xxx et linea AF intellectualiter protracta. Quare angulus D versus G erit acutus (*!*) et ipse angulus G acutus. Est ergo linea ab F super AG ducta perpendiculariter procedet (?) inter D et G, et sic fiet, erit quia proportio arcus TBA ad arcum BA maior proportione ZDA ad DA, hoc patet per predicta intellecta linea GA (?) et totius arcus GBA ad BA maior quam linee GDA ad DA quoniam arcus AG dividitur per equalia ad Z (*!* T) *Fa*

20 DA *Br* GA *M* GDA *E*

21 FZT *Br* AZT *MEBu* / cadet: eadem et *Bu* / D et G: G et D *E*

proportione *ZDA* ad *DA*, et similiter totius arcus *GBA* ad *BA* maior quam
linee *GDA* ad *DA*. Sed arcus *GBA* ad arcum *DA* sicut linea *GA* ad *DA*. Maior
itaque proportio arcus *GA* ad *BA* quam ad *DA*. Minor itaque *BA* quam *DA*
25 secundum quod intendimus.

36. SI CIRCULUS CIRCULUM INFRA (*!* INTRA) CONTINGAT, LI-
NEA A CENTRO MINORIS DUCTA UTRUMQUE SECANS DE MAIORE
EORUM VERSUS CONTACTUM MAIOREM ARCUM RESECABIT.

Sint circuli contingentes *AB*, *AD* [Fig. P.36], et transeat linea *ACB*, posito
5 *C* in circumferentia minoris circuli, et centrum eiusdem sit *E*, ducanturque
linee *EA* et *EDB* et *EZT*, que sit perpendicularis *ACB*, et *EB* maior *EA*. Erit
proportio *BZ* ad *ZA* maior quam anguli *BEZ* ad angulum *AEZ* per sextam
huius, et ideo maior quam *DT* ad *TA*, sic etiam totius linee *BZA* ad *ZA*
maior quam arcus *DTA* ad arcum *TA*. Et quia arcus *AB* est similis arcui *AC*
10 erit eadem proportio *AB* ad *AC* que *ACB* corde ad *AZC* cordam, per librum
de similibus arcubus. Ergo si memineris priorum, maior est proportio *AB*
arcus ad *ATC* quam *AD* ad *AC*. Ergo *AB* arcus est maior arcu *ATD*, et hoc
est quod proposuimus.

23 GDA: GAD *Bu* / Set *Fa* / sicut: sic *Bu* / linea *corr. Fa ex* linee (*?*)
25 secundum quod: quam *Fa*

Prop. 36

1 36 *mg. sin. E mg. dex. MBr* [xxx]vi^a *mg. sin. E* 36^a *Fa* 43^a *mg. sin. Bu*
2 secans *EBu om. Fa* secant *M* semicirculus *Br* / maioris (*?*) *Br*
3 contractum (*!*) *Fa*
4 transea (*!*) *M*
5 in *om. M* / minoris circuli *tr. E* / minoris *corr. Bu ex* maioris / -que *om. Br*
6 EDB: EBD *E* EDEB *Fa* / sit: sicut (*sive* sint) *Br* / ACB: super ACB *Fa* / *post* ACB
    add. Fa quoniam ducta linea et (*?*) fiet angulus ad E acutus, angulus ad A acuto
    (*?*) / et^2: et quia (*?*) *Fa* / Erit: erunt (*?*) *Fa*
7 *post* quam *scr. et del. Bu* arcus
7–8 per sextam huius *M om. BrBu* pro vi^a huius *E* per 6^m primi huius *Fa*
8 et . . . TA: quare maior BZ ad ZA quam arcus DT ad arcum TA *Fa* / DT *M* DC
    E BT *Br* arcus DT *Bu* / sic . . . linee: ergo coniunctim *Fa* / sic: sicut *E*
9 DTA: DCA (*sive* DEA) *Br* / ad . . . TA *om. Fa sed add. Fa* hoc argumentum superius
    ostensum est et quoniam AC linea dupla est ad AZ et arcus AC duplus ad AT, erit
    maior proportio BZA ad AC quam arcus DTA (*?*) ad arcum ATC / TA: CA *M*
9–13 AB . . . proposuimus: CT equalis TA et linea CZ equalis ZA erit linea BCA ad CA
    maior quam arcus DCA ad arcum CA. Sed arcus BA ad arcum CA proportio est
    que linee BA ad CA. Maior ergo proportio arcus BA ad arcum CA quam arcus DA
    ad eundem. Sit itaque arcus BA maior arcu DA *Bu*
9 arcui *om. Br*
10 AC: ATC *E* CE (*sive* TE) *Br* / que: que est *E* / ACB *correxi ex* EAB *in M et* AEB
    in EBr et AB *in Fa* / corde *bis Fa* / AZC *E* AZT *M* ACZ *Br* AC *Fa*
11 si *om. M* / si . . . priorum *om. Fa* / meminis (*?*) *E* / est *om. E* / proportio:
    portio *E*
11–12 AB arcus *tr. EFa*
12 ATC: arcum AC *Fa* / AD *om. E* arcus AD *Fa* / AC: eundem *Fa* / Ergo . . . ATD:
    Quare maior est arcus AB arcu AD *Fa* / arcu ATD *tr. Br*
13 quod proposuimus *ME* quod proponitur *Br* propositum *Fa*

37. SUPERFICIERUM QUE INTER ARCUS EQUALITER SE EX- CEDENTES ET LINEAS CONTINGENTES CONTINENTUR SICUT IP- SARUM CONTINGENTIUM LINEARUM MAIOR QUIDEM MAIOR ERIT DIFFERENTIA.

5   Sit primo maior arcus *AB* [Fig. P.37] et linee contingentes *AC*, *CB*, et
medius *DB* et contingens altera *DE*, et minimus *BF* et altera contingens
9r   / *FG*, et ab angulis ad centrum transeant linee *CHZ*, *ELZ*, *GMZ*, que secabunt
arcus datos per medium. Et ideo quia arcus *AD* et *DF* sunt equales et quia
linea *EZ* maior est quam *GZ*, et linea *CE* erit maior *EF* (! *EG*) quoniam
10   angulus *CZG* est divisus per equa. Patet ergo prima pars, scilicet quod maior

Prop. 37

1 37 *mg. sin.* (?)*E*, *mg. dex. MBr om. Fa* [xxx]vii[a] *mg. sin. E* 44[a] *mg. sin. Bu* /
   superficiem *M* / equaliter *om. Br et corr. M ex* equales
2 continentur: continuantur *Fa* / sicut: sed et *Bu*
3 linearum *om. Fa* / maior[1]: maiorum *Fa* / quidem maior *tr. Fa*
4 erit *om. E*
5 arcus AB *tr. Fa* / AC, CB: AE, EB *Br*
6 DB: BD *MBu* / DE: D *E* / et[2] *BrBu om. E* ç *M de Fa* / minimus *BrFaBu et abbrev.*
   ambig. in ME / BF *om. Fa*
7 FG (?) *Fa* / *post* angulis *add. Fa* F, G, et A, B angulis / CHZ, ELZ: CH et EK *M* /
   ELZ: ESZ (?) *E* / GMZ: et GMZ *Fa*
8 quia[1] *om. BrBu* / et[2] *corr. Bu ex* ad / quia[2]: que *Fa*
9 EZ *MEFa* EZT (?) *Br* CZ *Bu* / est . . . maior *om. Fa*
9–10 quam. . . . est *om. E*
10 est divisus *tr. Fa* / equa: equalia *Fa*
10–12 Patet . . . contingentium: Hoc argumentum patet si secetur CZ ad equalitatem GZ
   et a puncto sectionis ad E linea protracta que sit CE, erit enim angulus ZC (!) equalis
   angulus angulus (!) ZGE, quare reliquis (!) C equalis reliquo G. Set ille reliquus (!) G
   (! Z) maior quam (?) C, G cum sit extrinsecum intrinseco maior. Quare _____ (?)
   equalis a DC maior eodem (!) linea. Ergo et maior est linea CE. Set EC et EG
   opponuntur angulis equalibus ad Z. Quare per 8[vam] primi Euclidis erunt equales
   _____ (?) Z et GZ sunt equales. Relinquitur ergo C[E] maior GE *Fa; et post* GE
   add. Fa (*cf. var. vers. long. Prop. III.12, lin. 18–20*) aliter est idem ostendere cum (?
   etiam?) sic: angulus ZGC ambligonius quoniam idem et eodem modo potest ostendi
   de ambligonio, quod ostenditur illa quinta primi huius de triangulo orthogonio; quare
   maior est proportio CE ad EG quam anguli CZE ad angulum CZE (! GZE). Set
   anguli ad angulum sicut equalis EG ad EG. Ergo maior est CE ad EG quam equalis
   EG ad EG. Ergo per primam partem 8[e] 5[ti] erit DE (! CE) maior EG (*desinit hic var.*
   vers. long.). Quod dictum (?) est consequenter: angulus CZG divisus est per equalia;
   patet quia arcus inter (?) que cadunt SHL et LM sunt excessus medietatum predictorum
   arcuum et arcus predicti equaliter se excedunt ex ypotesi et hoc est quod diximus,
   arcus AD et DF equales erunt. Set si aliqua tertia sic se habet quod illud in quo
   primum excedit secundum est equale ei in quo secundum excedit tertium, erit illud
   in quo medietas primi excedit medietatem secundi equale ei in quo medietas primi
   (! secundi) excedit medietatem tertii manifestum est, hoc _____ (?) patet etiam in
   lineis sic excedat AD, ED, patet ED excedat ca (?) per equalem (?) AC (*sive* at), que
   sit CE, quoniam ergo EB est equalis ED et medietas EB cum medietate AE facit
   medietatem totius AB (!), medietas igitur AB (!) excedit medietatem ED per medie[ta]tem AE, eadem ratione medietas CD (! ED ?) excedit medietatem EF (?) per
   medietatem EC, si EC et AC sunt equales, quare et medietates; igitur si excessus

est differentia vel distantia *AC* ad *DE* quam *DE* ad *FG*, maior est enim *CE* quam *EG*, quas hic dicit distantias contingentium.

Secunda pars constat per suppositionem. Supponatur enim *AD*, *DF* sibi equali, et *DE* super *AC*, et *FG* super *DE*; et cum anguli contingentie sint equales, maior erit *ADEC* quam *DEGF*.

totorum sunt equales et excessus medietatem (*!* medietatum) redeundum est ad hoc quod superius demonstratum est, scilicet quod CE maior est EG, et ex hoc ———— (*?*) concludendum quod maior est differentia vel distantia AC ad DE quam DE ad FG, et hoc est quod dicit autor, contingentium linearum maiorum maior erit differentia, intendit enim (*?*) de habitis (*?*) argumentis cuiusmodi sunt CE et EG, et sic patet prima pars nostre propositionis.

10–15 scilicet. . . . DEGF: secunda (*?*) hac ratione maneat quidem priorum dispositio et sit arcus minimus DF et altera contingens FG, producta linea FG versus Z (*?* G*?*) quod sit in linea AC (*!* BC) et quia superficies ADEC maior superficie ADGZ, erit et maior sua equali, id est FBEG (*!*), ut proponitur *Bu*

11 est¹ *om. Br* / enim: ei *E*

13 per: ex *Br* / Supponatur enim: superponatur *Br*

13–14 AD . . . et¹ *om. Fa*

14 AC: AE *Br* / FG: GF *Br*

14–15 FG . . . DEGF: sit AK et a K procedat contingens ad circulum que continget circulum super punctum inter F et B (*?*) quoniam neque super F neque super B quia tunc accideret lineam ———— (*?*) ductam stare super duas intersecantes se ortogonaliter, quod est inconveniens, quod etiam non contingat ultra F vel ultra B quoniam nec (*?*) ultra F ante contingentiam pertransiret FG et potest (*!* post) contingentiam iterum productis utrumque contingentibus et sic accideret duas rectas lineas includere superficiem; si ultra B idem accidet (*!* accideret) inconveniens quoniam quando con (*!* ante) contingentiam bis pertransiret CB. Sit ergo contingens KSP; dico quod superficies ADEK equalis est superficiei DFGE, et usque iam suppono istud argumentum: extremitates sunt equales extremitatibus, ergo superficies superficiei. Probatio: [per] premissam AK equalis est D[E] ex ypotesi, item DS (*!* DE *?*) linea equalis FG. Probatio: AK, KP contingentes sunt equales DE, EB contingentibus. Ergo arcus AP est equalis aɩcui DB, habent (*?*) consequentiam. Probatio iam et conversam. Quare dempto communi, scilicet DP, erit PB equalis AD, quare suo equali DF. Igitur communi addito, scilicet FP, erit arcus DP equalis arcui FB. Igitur DS, SP contingentes equales sunt FG, GB contingentibus. Quare DS et FG sunt equales. Item, quoniam AK, KP sunt equales, quod patet ductis lineis a centro ad contractus (*!* contactus) et concursum per dulcarnon [i.e. per penultimam primi Euclidis] et AK equalis DE, et DE, EB, erit KP equalis EB. Sit SP equalis GB, igitur residuum SK equale residuo EG, superficies ergo ADSK equalis superficiei DFGE. Set superficies ADEC maior est [DFGE], quod volumus ex principali intentione ostendere. Nunc voluimus rectificare per suppositam per demonstrationem. Ducantur ergo AD, DF arcuum corde et DK, FE linee. Probatio huius argumenti: superficies ADSK, DFGE habent equales extremitates, ergo sunt equales. Triangulus ADK equalis est angulo (*!* triangulo) DFE per 8ᵛᵃᵐ primi Euclidis. Ergo demptis portionibus equalibus erit residuum residuo equale. Item DSK triangulus equalis est FGE triangulus (*!* triangulo) similiter per 8ᵃᵐ. Quare superficies ADSK equalis est superficiei DFGE. Probatio huius consequentie: AK, KP contingentes sunt equales DE, EB contingentibus. Ergo arcus AP equalis arcui DB. Protrahantur linee AZ, KM in PZBZ (*?*) et ———— (*?*) ḌẒ i̱g̱i̱tu̱ṟ (*!* DZG *?*) quoniam AZ, ZK sunt equales KZ, ZP, et basis basi, erit angulus KZA equalis angulo KZP et arcus AM equalis arcui MP; eadem ratione arcus NB est equalis arcui ND. Item KP, PZ sunt equales EB, BZ (*?*) et angulus angulo; ergo angulus KZP est equalis angulo EZB; quare arcus MP et NF equales erunt et etiam

38. CIRCA FIGURAM INEQUALIUM LATERUM DESCRIPTO CIR-
CULO ALIOQUE INFRA (! INTRA) CONSTITUTO EORUM IDEM ESSE
CENTRUM EST IMPOSSIBILE.

Inscribatur *ABG* non equilaterus circulo *A* [Fig. P.38], et circumscribatur
5 circulo *C*, et ubi linea *AB* contingit interiorem circulum sit *C*, centrumque
interioris circuli sit *D*. Ductis ergo lineis *DA*, *DC*, *DB*, si ponatur *D* centrum
exterioris, quoniam *DA* et *DB* equales, erit *BC* equalis *CA*. Sic ergo ductis
lineis ad reliquos contactus et angulos argues omnia latera secta per equalia
apud contactus, sed et ipsas medietates equales quoniam linee ad contactus
10 sunt equales, et sic omnia latera erunt equalia, quod est contra ypothesim.

39. TRIANGULORUM SUPER EANDEM BASIM IN CIRCULIS DE-
SCRIPTORUM MAXIMUS EST CUIUS RELIQUA LATERA SUNT
EQUALIA, QUANTOQUE PROPINQUIORES TANTO REMOTIORIBUS
MAIORES.

5 Sit super basim *AB* in circulo triangulus *ABC* cuius reliqua latera equalia
[Fig. P.39], et triangulus *ABD* cuius latera inequalia, posito *D* inter *A* et *C*,
linea *AC* secante *BD* apud *H*. Patet itaque triangulum *AHD* et [triangulum]

arcus AP, DB quando sunt dupli NB et MP, ut ostensum est. Item sint arcus AD,
DB equales ex suppositione. Erunt ergo contingentes contingentibus equales. Erit
etiam (?) angulus AZP equalis angulo DCB (?). Quare medietas medietati, scilicet
PZ, MB, ZN. Set et angulus P rectus angulo B recto, et linea ZP linee ZB. Ergo per
xxxi^{am} primi Euclidis erit KP equalis ED. Quare habemus propositum *Fa* (*cf. var.
vers. long. Prop. III.12, lin. 21–26*)

    15 erit ADEC: ADET *E*

Prop. 38

    1 *mg. hab. M* l. 4us (liber quartus) *et mg. sup.* L. IIII DE TRI. / 38 *mg. sin. E mg.
dex. MBr om. FaBu* xxxviii^a *mg. dex. E* / latum (!) *Br*
    3 inpossibile *E*
  4–5 Inscribatur . . . C¹: Sint duo anguli proximis (? proximi?) figure A et B *Bu*
    4 Scribatur *M* / A: ABG *Fa*
    5 C¹: D *Fa* AC *E* / interiorem *Fa* (*cf.* interioris *postea*) inferiorem *MEBrBu*
    6 circuli *BrFaBu om. ME* / D¹: A *E* / DB: AB *E* / si *om. Br* / D²: C *Br*
    7 quoniam: erunt linee *Fa* / DB: BD *Fa* / *post* equales *add. Fa* quare anguli super
basim equales anguli ad C recti. Ergo per xxxi^{am} primi Euclidis / erit: erunt (?) *E* /
BC: linea BC *Fa* / ergo *om. E*
    8 angulus *Fa* / omnia: circa *E* / per *FaBu om. MEBr*
    9 *ante* equales *add. Bu* esse / linee: equales quoniam contingentes concurrentes (?) a
concursu *Fa*
   10 *post* latera *add. Fa* ABG / *post* latera *scr. et del. Bu* sunt e / ypothesim *MBrFa*
ypotesim *EBu* / *post* ypothesim *add. Br* Et illud est quod et cetera

Prop. 39

    1 39 *mg. sin. E mg. dex. MBr om. FaBu* xxxix^a *mg. dex. E* / Triangula *E* / eamdem
E / basem *FaBu*
    2 est *om. E*
    3 quanto *E*
    5 Sint *Bu* / AB: BA *Br* / trianguli *Br* / *post* latera *add. EFa* sunt
    6 ABD: ADB *M* ABCD *Bu* / D: DE *Fa*
    7 AC: C *E* AD *Bu* / BD: lineam BD *Bu* / [triangulum] *addidi*

BCH esse similes. Et quia *BC* maior *AD*, que sunt reliqua latera, erit triangulus *BCH* maior triangulo *AHD*. Communi ergo addito erit triangulus *ACB* maior

10 triangulo *ADB*. Pars quoque secunda eadem ratione constabit.

40. TRIANGULORUM QUI IN CIRCULO SUPRA CENTRUM CONSISTUNT MAXIMUS EST ORTOGONIUS. AMBLIGONIORUM AUTEM QUANTO OBTUSUS ANGULUS MAIOR, ET OXIGONIORUM QUANTO ACUTUS MINOR FUERIT, TANTO ET IPSE TRIANGULUS

5 MINOR ERIT HAC RATIONE: OMNIS AMBLIGONIUS ET OXIGONIUS
9v / QUORUM ANGULI SUPRA CENTRUM EIUS CIRCULI CONSISTUNT ET QUORUM ALTERIUS BASI INSISTENS PERPENDICULARIS A CENTRO FUERIT EQUALIS DIMIDIO BASIS ALTERIUS ILLI, INQUAM, SUNT EQUALES.

10 Sit centrum circuli *A* [Fig. P.40], et triangulus ortogonius *ABC* et *ABD* reliquus, linea *AB* eis communis facta a centro. Ergo ad bases trahantur perpendiculares, *AE* super *BC* et *AH* super *BD*. Centro igitur etiam posito in medio *AB* circumducatur circulus per *E*, qui cum sit rectus cadet in semicirculo, qui etiam transibit per *A* et *H* et *B*. Per primam primi huius

---

8 BCH: BTH (?) *Br* BHC *Fa* / esse similes: similes esse quoniam anguli D et C sunt equales per xx tertii Euclidis et anguli ad H contra se positi equales et tertius tertio et per 4^{tam} (?) 6^{ti} et diffinitionem similium superficierum *Fa* / BC: BC est *Br* / que . . . latera *om. Fa* / sunt *om. Bu* / erit: est *Bu*

9 BCH: BHC *Fa* / maior[1]: esse maior *Br* esse maiorem *MBu* / *post* AHD *add. Fa* per 17 6^{ti} Euclidis / comuni *E* / ACB: ABC *Br*

10 quoque (?) *Br* / secunda . . . ratione: secundam rationem *E* / eadem: ē *Fa*

Prop. 40

1 40 *mg. sin. E mg. dex. MBr om. FaBu* xl^a *mg. dex. E* / que *Bu* / super *Br*

1-2 consistunt *om. Br*

2 est *om. E* / orthogonius *BrFa* / ambligoniorum: amblicavit *E* abligoniorum (!) *Br* / autem *om. E*

3 obtusus: obtus *E* / oxigoniorum: ortogonorum *E*

5 abligonius (!) *Br* / et: et omnis *Br* / oxigonius: exigonius *E* otigonius *Fa*

6 angulus *E* / eius: eiusdem *Br*

7 et: de *E* / alterius: alterum *Br* / basis *Br et tunc scr. Br aliquid quod non legere possum* / perpendicularis: propinquioris *E* perpendiculare *Br*

8 basis *om. E*

10 A *om. E* / orthogonius *Br* / ABC: BAC *E*

10-11 ABD reliquus *tr. Bu*

11 reliquus: reliquṣ *M* reliquis *Fa* / AB eis: ABES *Br* / communi *Fa* / facta *om. Br* / trahantur: ducantur *E*

12 AH: AB (?) *Fa* / etiam *om. BrFa*

13 *post* E *add. Fa* et H

13-14 qui . . . semicirculo *om. Bu*

13 qui: quia *Br* / sit rectus: sunt anguli recti *Fa* / cadet (?) *Fa*

13-14 in semicirculo: circumferentia circuli *Br*

14 semicirculo: semicirculum *EFa* / qui: que *Br*

14-17 qui. . . . intendimus: Quoniam igitur angulus BAC rectus est et due linee AB, AC equales, erunt duo anguli super BC semirecti, et quia anguli ad E recti sunt, erunt partiales ad A semirecti. Quare linea AE erit equalis EB. Ergo per premissam triangulus

15 constat quod *AE* et *EB* sunt equales, diviso angulo recto [ad *A*] per equa. Ergo per premissam triangulus *AEB* maior est triangulo *AHB*. Quare duplum duplo maius est, secundum quod intendimus.

41. OMNIS QUADRILATERI CIRCA CIRCULUM DESCRIPTI DUO QUELIBET LATERA OPPOSITA SUNT EQUALIA RELIQUIS PARITER ACCEPTIS.

Sit quadrilaterum *ABDC* contingens circulum in punctis *E, F, G, H* [Fig.
5 P.41], ut sit *E* in linea *AB*, eritque *EB* equalis *BF* et *FD* equalis *DG*. Quare *EB* et *DG* equantur *BD*. Similiter *AE* et *GC* equantur *AC*. Coniuncta ergo *AC* et *BD* sunt equalia *AB* et *DC* coniunctis, secundum quod proponitur.

AEB maior erit triangulo AHB. Quare duplum duplo, scilicet B.ABAD (*!* BAD). Sic patet primum. Secundum patet [Fig. P.40 *var. Fa*] quia quanto obtusus angulus maior et acutus minor tanto perpendiculares (*!* perpendicularis) a centro remotius cadet ab E et in exigoniis (*!* oxigoniis) super (*!* semper) propinquis (*!* propinquius) B et ambligoniis (*?*) semper propinquius D, hoc nato (*!*) quod casus (*?*) perpendiculares super aliquam lineam semper est inter angulos acutos super eandem quod ultimo dixit (*?*) Iurdanus (*!*) hac ratione et cetera. Sic pateat. Sit triangulus anbligonius (*!*) ABC (*!* ABD) et exigonius (*!* oxigonius) ABD (*!* ABC). Ductis ergo perpendicularibus AE et AH sic fuerit perpendicularis unius equalis dimidio basis alterius erunt duo puncta E et H eque distantia a medio puncto arcus AEHB (*!* AHEB). Quare triangulus AEB equalis triangulo AHB per ratione[m] premisse quia si fuerit AE equalis HB erit arcus equalis arcui. Quare medius punctus arcus EH erit medius punctus totius AEHB (*!* AHEB). Similiter si fuerit AH equalis EBC erit arcus equalis arcui. Igitur communi demto erit arcus AE equalis arcui HB. Quare medius punctus EH et cetera, et quia ita est, erit triangulus AEB equalis triangulo AHB quoniam linea HB equalis AE et triangulus ZHB (*!* ZHA) similis triangulo ZAE (*!* ZEB) et sic ZḄHB (*!* ZHA) equalis ZAE (*!* ZEB) per 17ᵃᵐ sexti Euclidis. Quare communi addito, scilicet BZA, aliter est idem concludere, scilicet per 4ᵃᵐ primi Euclidis sive per 8ᵛᵃᵐ eiusdem, quoniam si fuerit AE equalis HB erit AH equalis EB et econverso, quod patet ex predictis si ita evenerit quod triangulus ambligonius fuerit ex una parte linee AB producte sive in uno sem[i]circulo et oxigonius in altero fiat (*?*) uni illorum equalis ex eadem parte ex qua est alter et hoc fiet si fiat angulus equalis super centrum, facto vero super centrum angulo equali et concluso triangulo, per hunc fiat de reliquo demonstratio *Fa*

14 Per: propter *MBu*

15 quod: autem quod *Bu* / [ad A] *addidi* / per equa *om. E*

16 Ergo *tr. Bu post* premissam / per premissam *om. Br* / AEB: ABE *Br* / maior est *Br* maior *MBu* maioris *E* / *post* duplum *scr. et del. Bu* di

17 maius est *om. Br* / est *om. Bu* / secundum *BrBu om. ME*

Prop. 41

1 41 *mg. sin. ME mg. dex. Br om. FaBu* [xl]iᵃ *mg. sin. E* / Oomnis (*!*) *Fa* / equadrilateri (*!*) *E* / circulum: angulum *E*

2–3 reliquis . . . acceptis *om. Fa*

4 Sit: sed *Bu* / ABDC *FaBu* ABDE *MBr* ABCD *E*

5 ut . . . AB *om. Fa* / -que *om. Bu* / EB: BE *E* / BF: FB *corr. Fa ex* RB / FD: DF *E* / *DG:* GD *M*

6 EB: BE *Fa* / equantur¹⸴²: equaliter *Fa* / *post* Similiter *add. Bu* et / AE: et AE *Fa* / GC: EG (*?*) *E* GE *Br* / AC: AE *E*

7 AC: A et C *ME* / DC: DE (*?*) *Br*

42. QUODLIBET PARALLELOGRAMMUM CIRCA CIRCULUM CONSTITUTUM EST EQUILATERUM.

Sit parallelogrammum *ABCD* [Fig. P.42], eritque *AB* et *CD* tanquam *BC* et *AD*. Sed *AB* dimidium duorum *AB* et *CD* quia unum uni equale. Sed
5 etiam *BC* dimidium *BC* et *DA*. Cum sint ergo tota equalia et dimidia, equalis ergo *AB* ei que est *BC*. Singula ergo singulis equalia, et hec est intentio demonstrationis.

43. TRIANGULO IN CIRCULO CONSTITUTO EQUUM EI IN EODEM CIRCULO PARALLELOGRAMMUM RECTANGULUM DESIGNARE.

Sit triangulus in circulo constitutus *ABC* [Fig. P.43a], cuius unum latus,
5 quod sit *AB*, dividatur per equa in puncto *E*, et pertranseat linea perpendiculariter *DEC*, appliceturque *D* cum *A*, et ducatur *EF* equidistans *AD*, [et] constituetur linea *FD*. Erit ergo triangulus *EFD* equalis triangulo *EFA*. Ergo erit triangulus *DCF* equalis triangulo *ECA*, qui est dimidium dati trianguli. Transeat item ab *F* ad circumferentiam *FZ* equidistans *CED*, et protrahantur

Prop. 42

1   42 *mg. sin. MEBr om. FaBu* [xl]ii[a] *mg. sin. E* / parallelogrammum *correxi ex* para-
    lellogramum *in M et* peralellogramum *in E et* parallellogramum *in BrFa et* paralel-
    legramum *in Bu* (*et post hoc lectiones huiusmodi non laudabo*)

3   Sit: Sit itaque *Br* / eritque . . . CD *om. Fa* / tamquam *M* / BC: CB *Fa*

4   et[1]: ad *M* / Sed[1]: Set *Fa* / AB[1]: ad *E* / AB[2]: AB (*sive* AD) *E* / quia: quod *E* quid (*?*)
    Fa / *post* equale *add. Fa* et hoc quia ABCD superficies erat ex ypotesi parallellogramum

5   etiam: et etiam *Br* / Cum . . . dimidia *om. Fa* / dimidia: dimidium *E* / equalis:
    equale *E*

6   ei *tr. E post* est / Singula . . . singulis: singulis singula *E* / equalis *M*

6–7 hec . . . demonstrationis: illud est quod et cetera *Br*

6   hec *M* hoc *EBu* h' *Fa*

Prop. 43

1   43 *mg. sin. MEBr om. FaBu* [x]liii[a] *mg. sin. E* / trianguli *Fa* / equum: equum est
    Fa equm (*!*) est *M* eqū est *Br*

2   rectangulum *om. M*

2–3 designare: assignare *Br*

4   constitutus: conditus (*!*) *Fa* / unum *corr. M ex* unus

5   equa *MBrBu* equalia *E* equales *Fa* / pertranseat: percurrat *Br*

6   DEC: DC *E* DEZ *Fa* (*et tr. Fa post* linea *in lin. 5*) DEZ concurrere cum C *Bu* / *ante*
    appliceturque *add. Fa* et ponatur primo Z concurrere cum C / applicetque *Bu* /
    appliceturque . . . A: ampliceturque DA *Fa* / -que D *om. Br* / ducantur (*?*) *E* / AD:
    AD (*Bu om. Fa*) consignato (*Fa*, signato *Bu*) F in AC *FaBu* / [et] *addidi*

7   constituetur *MBu* continuetur *EBr* continueturque *Fa* / Erit: quia *FaBu* / triangulus
    corr. Fa ex triangulum / EFD: DEF *Br* / equalis *om. M* equalis est *Fa* / triangulo:
    triangulus *Fa*

7–8 EFA. . . . triangulo *om. E*

7   *post* EFA *add. Fa* quia constituti sunt super unam basim inter lineas et equidistantes
    / Ergo *om. Bu* Quare addito EFC (*?*) *Fa*

8   DCF: DEF *Br* DCA *Bu* / ECA: CEA *Br* / trianguli: trigoni *Fa*

9   item: ante (*?*) *Br* / FZ: FCZ (*?*) *Br* linea FZ *Fa*

10   linee *CZ* et *DZ*; et hic triangulus, scilicet *CDZ*, equalis erit dimidio dati
      trianguli mediante *CFD* utrique triangulo equali. Sed et eius angulus *CZD*
      rectus quoniam *DEC* est diameter. Statuto ergo in alia parte ortogonio ei
10r   simili, qui sit *CGD*, ita ut *GD* equidistet *CZ*, erit parallelogrammum / *CZDG*
      rectangulum et equale triangulo *ABC*.

15   Quod si *CE* non sit perpendicularis *AB* [Fig. 43b], [sed] diameter *DZ* [sit
      perpendicularis *AB*], descendat a *C* perpendicularis *CH* super diametrum
      DEZ, eritque *CH* equidistans *AB*, et pertranseat linea *HA*, eritque triangulus
      AEH equalis triangulo *AEC*. Ducta item linea *ZA* et ei equidistante *HL* et
      continuata *ZL*, erit triangulus *ZLE* eidem equalis, quia *ALH*, *ZHL* sunt
20   equales super eandem basem inter equidistantes. Deinde, ut supra, ducatur
      linea *DL* et equidistans *EM*, posito *M* in linea *ZL*, et applicante *D* cum *M*,
      erit et triangulus *DMZ* equalis eidem. Ducta deinde *MN* equidistante diametro
      ZED et protracta *DN* fiet ortogonius *ZDN* et dimidio dati trianguli equalis.
      Perfecto igitur, ut prius, parallelogrammo *ZNDY* constat propositum.

      44. INTER QUASLIBET DUAS FIGURAS POLIGONIAS EQUILA-

      10 CZ: EZ (?) *E* / DZ: DE *Bu* / scilicet *om. Br* / equalis *BrFaBu* (*et tr.* FaBu *post*
         triamguli) *om. ME* / erit (?) *E*
      11 trianguli: EFD *Br* / mediante . . . equali *om. Bu* equalis *E* / CFD . . . equali:
         triangulo DFC *Fa* / CFD: CBD *M* EFD *Br* / triangulo *om. M* / equali *Br* equalis
         ME / eius *om. Fa* / CZD: EZD *Br*
      12 rectus: est rectus *E* / DEC: DCE *E* DC *Fa* / *post* diameter *add. Fa* per corellarium
         prime tertii Euclidis / alia: aliqua *Br* / orthogonio *Br*
      13 simili qui *bis M* / CGD: CDG *Br* ed' D *Fa* CTD *Bu* / ita . . . GD *om. E* / GD: TD
         Fa CD *Bu* / CZ: EZ *Br* CE *Bu* / eritque *E* / CZDG: CZGD *E* CTDZ *Fa* CZDT *Bu*
      14 triangulo *corr. E ex* rectangulo
      15 CE . . . DZ: DEZ perpendiculariter transeundo per AB non transeat per C *Fa* ob-
         liquatur Z a C *Bu*
      15–16 AB . . . perpendicularis² *om. E*
      15 AB . . . [sed]: ad scilicet *M* / [sed] *addidi* / DZ: LDZ *M*
      15–16 [sit . . . AB] *addidi*
      16 a C *om. Br* / dyametrum *Bu*
      17 eritque¹: erit *E* / et: CE *Br* / triangulus *om. E*
      18 *post* AEC *add. Fa* quoniam super unam basim inter quidem (*!* equidistantes) inter
         (*!* lineas) / item *om. Fa* inter *E* tunc *Br* / HL: H et L *E*
      19–22 ZLE . . . . eidem: ZLH equalis triangulo HAL et communi addito HEL erit triangulo
         triangulus ZLH equalis triangulo HAZ (?) et per consequens AEC dimidio dati trian-
         gulus (*!* trianguli). Deinde ducatur linea DL et ei equidem (*!* equidistans) EM (*!* M)
         posito in linea ZL, appliceturque D cum M, erit igitur triangulus DLE equalis triangulo
         DLM. Quare communi dempto QDL triangulus erit QLM equalis triangulo QDE.
         Ergo communi addito QEZ in quadrangulo et (*sive* erit) triangulo DMZ equalis
         triangulus ELZ et per consequens dimidio dati trigoni *Fa*
      19 ZLE: LEZ *Br*
      19–20 quia . . . equidistantes *om. BrBu*
      20 eamdem *E* / inter *super scr. M* / *ante* equidistantes *add. E* lineas / ut: non (?) *Br*
      22 deinde: ergo *Fa* / equidistanter *Fa*
      23 ZED: DEZ *Fa et corr. Br ex* ZDE / orthogonius *Br* / ZDN: DNZ *Fa* / et² *om. Fa*
         etiam *EM* / dimidio . . . equalis: equalis triangulo DMZ et eo mediante dimidio
         dati trigoni *Fa* / equalis *om. Bu*
      24 ZNDY: YDNZ *Fa* CNDY *Bu* / constat: habebimus *Bu*

      Prop. 44
          1 44 *mg. sin. MEBr om.* FaBu xliii[i]ᵃ *mg. dex. E* / qualibet *Fa* / *post* figuras *injuste*
            add. Fa et qui / poligonias *om. Fa*

TERAS ET SIMILES QUARUM UNA CIRCULO INSCRIPTA, ALIA CIR-
CUMSCRIPTA FUERIT, PROPORTIONALIS CONSISTIT QUE DUPLO
PLURIUM LATERUM EXISTENS INFRA (! INTRA) EUNDEM CIR-
5 CULUM DESCRIBITUR.

Sit triangulus *ABC* circulo circumscriptus [Fig. P.44], cuius centrum *Z*,
et triangulus infra (! intra) scriptus *DEF*, applicans angulos suos ad contactus
alterius. Protractis igitur lineis *ZD* et *ZHGA* dividetur linea *DF* per equa
apud *H* et arcus similiter apud *G*. Erit triangulus *ZDH* similis triangulo *ZDA*.
10 Applicetur itaque *D* cum *G* et fiet triangulus *ZDG*. Quia ergo *ZA* ad *ZD*
sicut *ZD* ad *ZH*, erit *ZA* ad *ZG* sicut *ZG* ad *ZH*. Triangulus ergo *ZAD* ad
triangulum *ZDG* sicut triangulus *ZDG* ad triangulum *ZDH*. Ductis etiam
lineis a *Z* ad *B* et *C* et *E* et *F*, quoniam que ad angulos exteriores ducuntur
linee arcus per equa partiuntur singulis medietatibus arcuum cordis extensis
15 fiat exagonus qui est duplo plurium laterum cuius partiales trianguli super
singula latera consistentes inter partiales triangulos datorum triangulorum
proportionales esse ratione predicta argues, sicque totus exagonus inter triangulos proportionalis erit, et sic de ceteris figuris.

45. SI FIGURE POLIGONIE ET EQUILATERE CIRCULIS EQUA-
LIBUS INSCRIBANTUR, QUE PLURIUM LATERUM ERIT MAIOR
ERIT, ET PROPORTIO IPSIUS AD ALIAM MAIOR QUAM OMNIUM
LATERUM SUORUM AD OMNIA LATERA ALTERIUS CONIUNCTA.

  2 *ante* circulo *add. Br* in / inscripta alia *om. E*
 2-3 circōscripta *Br*
  3 que: qui *MBr*
  4 plurimum *E*
  6 circumscriptus: inscriptus *Bu*
  7 DEF: DF *E*
  8 Protractis igitur *tr. Br* / ZD: in (?) D *Fa* / ZHGA: ZHDA *E* / dividetur: dividantur
   Br / linea DF *tr. Bu* / DF: FD *Bu* / equa: equalia *E*
  9 arcus similiter: arcus *Br* (*et tr. Br post* G) / G. Erit: girum (!) *E* / Erit: eritque (?)
   Fa / ZDH: et DH *E* / *post* ZDA *add. Fa* per viii^am^ 6^ti^ Euclidis
 10 applicet *EBu* / itaque *om. Fa* / D: ZD *E* / ergo *om. E*
 11 sicut . . . ZH¹ *om. E* / *post* ZH¹ *add. Fa* per secundam partem correllarii 8^ve^ 6^ti^ et
   ZD equalis ZG / erit: et A erit *E* erit et *Bu*
 12 ZDG^1,2^: ZGD *Br* / ZDH *FaBu* ZAB *MEBr* / *post* ZDH *add. Fa* per primam 6^ti^ /
   etiam *ME* igitur *Br* ergo *Fa* et *Bu*
 13 a: ad *Bu* / ad¹: et *Bu* / B: H *Br* / et E *om. Fa* / et F: ZF *E* / quoniam que *bis Fa* /
   ad² *supra scr. M* et *Br* / ducuntur *MEFa* (*et corr. Fa ex* ducantur) ducentur *Br*
 14 partientur *Br* / singulis *MFa* singuli *EBrBu* / cordis *MFaBu* corde *EBr* / extensis:
   subtensis *Fa*
 15 fiet *FaBu* / qui est *om. Fa* / qui *M* que *EBr* / duplo *tr. M post* laterum / cuius: eius
   Br / partialis *E* / supra *E*
 16 latera *in ras. M* / consistens *BrFa*
 17 sicque: sic quia *E*
 17-18 triangulos: triangulum *Br* datos triangulos *Fa*
  18 *post* erit *add. Fa* adiuvante 13ª 5^ti^ Euclidis / et . . . figuris *om. Fa* / *mg. sin. add.*
   Fa et c^a^ (? cetera)
Prop. 45
  1 45 *mg. sin. EBr mg. dex. M om. FaBu* xlvª *mg. dex. E* / Si *om. Fa*
  3 *ante* ipsius *scr. et del. Bu* ipsis / omnium *tr. E post* suorum
  4 coniuncta: iuncta *Fa*

5   Infra (*! Intra*) unum circulum describatur quadratus *ABCD* [Fig. P.45a], et infra alium circulum et ei equalem triangulus equilaterus *EFG* [Fig. P.45b]. Ducantur autem quatuor linee ab angulis quadrati ad centrum circuli sui, quod sit *O*, et ab angulis trianguli *GEF* ad centrum sui, quod sit *T*, linee tres, divideturque quadratum (*!*) in quatuor triangulos equales et triangulus
10 in tres. Et quia singula latera trianguli singulis quadrati maiora sunt, erit maior proportio trium angulorum trianguli ad tres angulos quadrati quam trium laterum trianguli ad tria latera quadrati. Maior ergo proportio trium angulorum trianguli ad quatuor angulos quadrati quam trium laterum trianguli ad quatuor latera quadrati. Quia tunc minor proportio lateris / trianguli
10v
15 ad latus quadrati quam arcus eius ad arcum alterius, erit et minor proportio

5 quadratus ABCD *tr. E* / ABCD: ABC *Br*

6 equale *Fa*

7 quatuor: 4 *M (hic et ubique)*, (?)*Fa* (*post hoc lectiones huiusmodi non laudabo*) ubique *E* / ad . . . sui *om. Br*

8 O: Z *Fa* / O . . . sit *om. EBu* / et . . . GEF: ad angulum TA (*sive* CA) *Br* / GEF *om. Fa* / sui: circuli sui *BrFa*

9 divideturque *M* dividentur quia *E* dividaturque (?) *Br* dividenturque *Fa* dividetur quia *Bu* / *ante* quadratum *scr. et del. Bu* quadrangulum / in *om. Fa* / triangulos: angulos *E* / triangulus: angulus *Fa*

10 quia *om. E* quod (?) *M* / singula . . . sunt: latus trianguli equilateri maior est latere quadrati *Fa* / maiora: ma maiora *E* / erit: erit per 12^{am} primi huius *Fa* erit per xii^{am} primi *Bu*

11 maior *om. E et correxi ex* minor *in aliis MSS* (*et tr. Br* minor *post* quadrati *in lin. 11*)

11–13 trianguli . . . trianguli *om. E*

12 Maior *correxi ex* minor *in MSS* (*et tr. Br* minor *post* quadrati *in lin. 13*)

13 angulorum: triangulorum *FaBu* / quatuor: am (?) *E* / angulos: triangulos *FaBu*

14 latera: angulos *E* / Quia: quare *Br*

14–18 Quia. . . . equalis: Probatio huius argumenti. Sit linea AB divisa super puncta T et ES (*! S*) sicut tres partiales trianguli EFG trianguli, linea vero KD divisa super puncta E, L, N sit sicut quatuor trianguli quadrati ABCD. Item si linea EF divisa super puncta M, R sicut tria latera trianguli EFG, linea vero PH divisa super punta G, O, V sit sicut quatuor latera quadrati ABCD. Quoniam ergo minor est proportio AB [ad CD quam EF] ad GH, erit AB ad minorem ED (?) sicut EF ad GH, quia ad maiorem CD semper minor esset, quod patet. Sit ergo AB ad GD sicut EF ad HG. Quoniam autem minor est AT ad KE quam EM ad PG, sit AT ad KZ sicut EM ad PG. Quare et tripli AT, scilicet (?) AB, ad KZ sicut circuli (*! tripli*) EM, scilicet EF, ad PG; quare et tripli EM, scilicet EF, ad PG, per penultimam 5^{ti} Euclidis, et iterum per eandem quia AB ad QD sicut EF ad HG, erit AB ad aggregatum ex KZ et QD sicut EF ad PH. Set AB ad KE minor est proportio quam eiusdem ad angulum (*! aggregatum ex KZ et QD*) per secundam partem 8^{eve} (*! 8^{ve}*) 5^{ti}. Ergo minor est proportio AB ad [KD?] quam EF ad PH et sicut patet eas (?) pars positi prima pars patet. Sic minor est proportio lateris trianguli ad latus quadrati quam arcus eius ad arcum alterius. Hoc patebit, iam quare minor erit proportio trium laterum trianguli ad proportio (*! quatuor*) quadrati quam trium arcuum ad quatuor. Set trianguli ad quadratum minor est quam laterum ad latera. Ergo quod arcuum ad arcus sive circumferentie ad circumferentiam, set circumferentie sunt equales *Fa* (*cf. var. vers. long. Prop. IV.9, lin. 6–24 in principio*)

14 tunc: igitur *Bu*

trium laterum trianguli ad quatuor quadrati quam trium arcuum ad quatuor. Minor ergo trianguli ad quadratum quam circumferentie ad circumferentiam. Sed una aliis (! alteri) equalis. Triangulus itaque quadrato minor, ut intendimus.

46. SI CIRCA EQUALES CIRCULOS FIGURE EQUALIUM LA-
TERUM [ET EQUALIUM ANGULORUM] DESIGNENTUR, QUE PAU-
CORUM LATERUM FUERIT MAIOR ERIT, EIUSQUE AD ALIAM
PROPORTIO TANQUAM LATERUM IPSIUS AD LATERA ALTERIUS
5 PARITER ACCEPTA.

Circa equales circulos describantur triangulus equilaterus *ABC* [Fig. P.46a] et quadratus *DEFG* [Fig. P.46b], et a centris circulorum *H* et *L* protrahantur linee ad angulos et ad contactus. Diviso ergo triangulo in tres triangulos, quadrato et in quatuor, omnes erunt eiusdem altitudinis quoniam linee ad
10 contactus equales. Sed et partialium triangulorum trianguli maiores sunt bases quam quadrati quoniam anguli super centrum sunt maiores. Proportio

16 quatuor[1] *om. Bu* / *post* quadrati *add. E* latera
17 *post* ergo *add. E* proportio
18 una . . . equalis: *lac. et* equalis alii *E* / aliis *M* alteri *Bu* alii *EBr* / itaque: ergo *Fa* / minor: minor est *Fa*
18–19 *post* intendimus *add. Fa* (*et cf. var. vers. long. Prop. IV.9, lin. 6–24 in fine*) Aliter (?) patet prima pars per tertiam huius quarti. Probatio, quod minor est proportio lateris triangulum (!) ad latus quadrati quod (! quam) arcus ad arcum. Quoniam arcus ad arcum, EF ad arcum AB sexquitertia est proportio quia eadem est que anguli ad angulum, scilicet ETF ad AZB. Sed AZB rectus est et ETF continet rectum et tertiam recti quia duplus est ad angulum EGF per xix tertii Euclidis. Item proportio linee EF ad lineam AB est subsexquialtera. Proportio laterum dupplicata (!) est proportio quadratorum per 18 sexti, set quadratorum sexquialtera quia quadratum EF triplum est ad quadratum semidiametri per 8^m tertiidecimi libri Euclidis et quadratum AB duplum est ad quadratum eiusdem semidiametri, igitur EF ad AB est proportio subsexquialtera, et arcus ad arcum sexquitertia. Quare minor est EF ad AB quam arcus ad ad (! *del.*) arcum.

Prop. 46

1 46 *mg. sin. EBr mg. dex. M om. FaBu* xlvi^a *mg. sin. E*
2 [et equalium angulorum] *addidi* / desingnetur *Fa*
2–3 paucorum *EFa* pauciorum *MBu*, (?)*Br*
3 fuerit: fiunt *M* / eiusque: eius *M* eiusdem *Br*
4 proportionem *E* / tamquam *ME*
6 describantur *EFa* describatur *MBrBu* / trianguli *E*
7 DEFG: ADFG (?) *E* / a *om. M* / H: Q (?) *Fa* / protrantur (!) *Fa*
8 ad[1] *bis E* / ad[2] *Br om. MEBu* in *Fa* / contactos *Fa* / triangulos: angulos *MEBu* / *post* triangulos *add. Fa* et contractus (!)
9 quadrato et *tr. Br* etiam quadrangulo *Bu* / et: etiam *MFa* / omnis *FaBu* / eiusdem: eius *Bu* / quoniam: quam (?) *E*
10 *post* contactus *add. Fa* scilicet semidiametri sunt / *post* equales *add. Fa* et perpendiculares / triangulorum: tri (!) triangulorum *Fa*
11 quam: ex *Fa* / sunt maiores: maiores sunt quia et hii et illi quatuor rectis sunt equales. Patet ergo quod maiores sunt bases et cetera, cum sit una et eadem triangulorum altitudo *Fa* / *post* sunt *scr. et del.* (?) *Bu* st (=sunt)

ergo omnium triangulorum trianguli ad tres triangulos quadrati, cum sit ea
que omnium laterum eius ad tria latera alterius, erit ipsius ad quadratum
proportio que laterum eius ad latera quadrati. Cum sit autem proportio lateris
15   ipsius ad latus illius maior quam angulorum super centrum, et ob hoc maior
quam arcuum erit, et trium laterum trianguli ad tria latera quadrati maior
quam trium arcuum ad tres; maior ergo omnium laterum ad omnia quam
omnium arcuum ad omnes. Maior ergo trianguli ad quadratum quam arcuum
ad arcus. Sed arcus arcubus equales. Maior ergo triangulus quadrato secundum
20   quod proponitur.

Further Propositions Appearing in MSS *E* and *Br*

[At this point after Proposition P.46, MS *Br* has added two propositions
not in MS *E*. The first (folios 6r–6v), which I label Proposition 46+1, has
the enunciation of Proposition IV.4 of the longer version of the *De triangulis,*
but it has a different proof. This form of proof is also contained in MSS *Bu*
and *Fa*. While MS *Bu* contains all the propositions of the longer version,
the proofs are often, as in this case, dependent on the shorter version. As
for MS *Fa*, though it is generally dependent on the shorter version, it also
shows some contamination from the longer version. But this is not so in this
proposition, where *Fa*'s proof is completely different from that of the longer
version. In both MSS *Fa* and *Bu* this proposition appears after Proposition
P.40 (=Proposition IV.3 of the longer version). The second proposition added
at this place in MS *Br* (folios 6v–7r) is the first half of Proposition 3 of the
De mensura circuli in a unique version described in Volume 1 of my *Ar-*

12   omnium triangulorum *om. E et correxi ex* triangulorum *in Br et* omni triangulorum
in Fa et omnium *in MBu* / trianguli: trianguli M *E* / tres *om. EBr* / triangulos:
angulos *M*
13   tria: omnia *E* / *post* alterius *add. Fa* per primam sexti / erit: erunt *Fa*
14   quadrati *corr. Bu ex* quadratu
15   latus illius: latera alterius *E* / illius: ipsius *scr. et del. Br et tunc add.* illius / *post*
centrum *add. Fa* quod posterius patebit
16   trium *om. Fa*
17, 18   omnium: omni: *Fa*
18   omnes: omnis *Fa*
19   Set *EFa* / triangulus quadrato: quadratus triangulo *E*
19–20   secundum . . . proponitur *BrBu* secundum proponebatur. Explicit liber Iordani de
triangulis *M* secundum quod apponitur *E* Quod maior sit laterum proportio quam
angulorum super centrum, probatio. BC est maior DE, ergo medietas medietate.
Resecetur ergo BK ita quod KL (! KS) sit equalis medietati DZ (! DE), sit KP sicut
altera medietas, et a centro Q procedant linee ad L (! *S*) et P. Quia ergo maior
est (! *del.*) proportio KL (! BS) ad KL (! KS) quam anguli BQL (! BQS) ad angulum
LQK (! SQK) [per 5^{am} huius] erit coniunctum BK ad KL (! KS) quam anguli ad L,
K (*del. Fa?*) maior quam anguli BQK ad angulum LQK (! SQK). Quare sic erit de
duplis, scilicet quod BC ad SP maior erit proportio quam anguli BQC ad angulum
LQP (! SQP). Set angulus LQP (! SQP) rectus est quoniam S (! et) K, Q sunt equales
et ob hoc uterque angulus super basim semirectus cum sit K rectus et eadem ratione
KPQ (! KQP) semirectus est. Quare patet intentum *Fa*

chimedes in the Middle Ages, pp. 96–97n. I have thus not edited it here. Finally note that MS *Fa* contains after Proposition P.46 three propositions taken directly from the longer version: Propositions IV.12, IV.13, and IV.10— in that order, and the text in *Fa* ends with Proposition IV.10. The readings in *Fa* for these additional propositions have been collated with the text of the longer version below.]

[46+1.] OMNE PARALELLOGRAMUM (*!*) IN CIRCULO DESCRIP-TUM EST RECTANGULUM.

Sit paralellogramum (*!*) in circulo descriptum *ABCD* [Fig. P.46+1], cuius, quoniam latera opposita sunt equalia, et arcus similiter. Quare arcus *AC*
5 equalis *CA*. Ducta ergo linea *AC* erit dyameter et ob hoc anguli *B* et *D* recti et ita reliqui. Aliter, *A* et *C* anguli sunt tanquam *B* et *D* quoniam hii et illi tanquam duo recti. Sed *A* equalis *C* et *B* equalis *D*. Quilibet ergo eorum rectus.

47. SI IN EQUALIBUS CIRCULIS CONTRA EQUALES BASES DUO POLIGONIA IN EANDEM PARTEM QUORUM LATERA NUMERO EQUALIA STATUANTUR, QUOD OMNIA RELIQUA LATERA EQUALIA HABUIT MAIUS ERIT.

5 Primo quidem proponimus quod si due figure poligonie quarum latera unius lateribus [alterius] quocumque modo interpositis equalia fuerint circulis [equalibus] inscribantur, ipse etiam equales erunt. Hoc sumpto, describantur in equalibus quadrilatera super equales bases que sint *AB, HL* [Fig. P.47], et sic quadrilaterum cuius reliqua latera equalia *ABCD* et alterum *HLMN*.
10 Unum igitur laterum ipsius maius erit quolibet laterum equalium alterius, maius et sit ipsum *LM*, si enim aliud esset, quod non copularetur basi debet basis (*!* basi) copulari, quoniam ob hoc non permutaretur figure equalitas. Ducta igitur linea *HM*, super ipsas (*!* ipsam) construatur [tri]angulus ad

Prop. 46 + 1
    1 [46 + 1] *addidi*
    1–8 Omne. . . . rectus *BrFaBu om. ME*
    3 *post* ABCD *add. Fa* angulus
    4–5 arcus² . . . CA: AB, EL, CD *Br*
    4 arcus² *om. Bu*
    5 dyameter *Br* diameter *FaBu* / B et D: BC, CD *Br*
    6 ita: recta *Fa* / anguli . . . B *non legere possum in Br* / anguli sunt *om. Bu* / hii: et hii *BrBu*
    7 A *om. Fa* / et: se (?) *Fa* / B: *lac. Bu* / *post* D *add. Fa* per xxxviiiiᵃᵐ primi Euclidis
    8 *post* rectus *add. Fa* est
Prop. 47
    1 47 *mg. sin. E om. Br* xlviiᵃ *mg. sin. E* / in equalibus: inequalibus *E*
    2 eamdem *E*
    3 omnia reliqua *tr. E*
    6 [alterius] *addidi*
    7 [equalibus] *addidi* / describatur (?) *Br*
    8 sint: sunt *E*
    11 si enim: sin *Br*
    13 [tri]- *addidi*

circumferentiam, sitque *HMO*, qui maior erit alio [*HMN*], et latera eius

15   maiora lateris (*! latere*) cum [maiore] singulis *ABCD*. Ducantur igitur linee
EG, *ZT* equidistantes ad [*AD* et] *DC* in circulo suo, et sint equales *HO* et
MO. Sit item *PR* equalis *AD* et equo (*! equidistans*) *LM* in circulo suo.

11r   Transeat etiam linea *XY* equidistans / utrique dividens arcus *LP* et *MR* per
equa; eruntque singule medietatum equales arcubus *DG* et *DZ* et eorum

20   oppositis. Superficies ergo *LPRM* maior est duabus superficiebus *ADGE* et
DTZ (*! DCTZ*). Manifestum igitur plus esse portiones *LM*, *MO* et *OH* quam
AD et *DC* et *CB*. Maius [ergo] quadrangulum *ABCD* quadrangulo *HLMO*.
Maius itaque [quam] [*H*]*LMN*, et sic in omnibus.

48. SI IN EQUALIBUS CIRCULIS DUO POLIGONIA DESCRIBAN-
TUR, ALTERUM EQUILATERUM, ALTERUM AUTEM NON, QUOD
EQUILATERUM FUERIT MAIUS ERIT.

Sit [equilaterum] poligonium in circulo suo statutum *ABCD*[*E*] [Fig. P.48],

5   et istud (*! aliud*) *FGHKLM* (*! FGHKL*); erit itaque aliquod laterum huius
maius quolibet latere alterius, quod sit *GH*, super quod construatur aliud
totidem laterum, sed reliqua latera sunt equalia, ipsumque priore maius erit,
sitque *AGMNO* (*! GHMNO*); itaque quatuor lateribus *ABCD*[*E*] subtendantur
equidistantes linee, etiam equales quatuor equalibus lateribus illius [*GHMNO*,

10   i.e. *HM*, *MN*, *NO*, *OG*], atque *GH* subtendatur linea equalis *AB*. Ut in
premissa habebimus exteriores portiones i.e. circuli *HGMNO* (*! GHMNO*)
maiores portionibus circuli *ABCDE*. Quare poligonium *ABCDE* maius alio
[*GHMNO*]. Maius ergo poligonio *FGHKL*, et erat demonstrandum. Et in
ceteris quoque demonstrabitur similiter.

49. SI IN EQUALIBUS CIRCULIS DUO POLIGONIA QUORUM LA-
TERA NUMERO EQUALIA ET ALTERUM EQUILATERUM ET

14 sitque HMO: QHMO *Br* / qui: sic qui *Br* / [HMN] *addidi*
18 Transeat etiam: et *Br* / utrique *correxi ex* uterque (?) *in EBr*
19 -que *correxi ex* quia *in EBr* / DZ: D est *Br*
21 et OH *correxi ex* et OB *in E et* EC, OB *in Br*
22 et[1]: EC *Br* / CB: DB *Br* / [ergo] *addidi*
23 [quam] *addidi* / [H]- *addidi*

Prop. 48
1 48 *mg. sin E om. Br* xlv[iii][a] *mg. dex. E* / in equalibus: inequalibus *E*
3 equilaterum: equaliter *Br*
4 [equilaterum] *addidi* / -[E] *addidi*
7 erit: exᶦ *Br*
8 sitque: sit quod (?) *Br* / AGMNO: AG in NO *Br* / -[E] *addidi*
9 equalibus *tr. E post* lateribus
9-10 [GHMNO . . . OG] *addidi*
10 AB: AD *E*
13 [GHMNO] *addidi* / FGHKL: FHKL *Br* / erat: exᵃ (?) *Br* / Et: est *Br*
14 ceteris quoque: centris quod *Br*

Prop. 49
1 49 *mg. sin. E om. Br* xlixᵃ *mg. dex. E*

EQUIANGULUM, ALTERUM MINIME, CIRCUMSCRIBANTUR,
QUOD EQUILATERUM EST MINUS ERIT.

5   Conscribatur pentagonus equilaterus *ABCDE* [Fig. P.49], centrumque *D*
(*! O*), unus contactuum [*Z*], et alius pentagonus non equilaterus *FGHKL*,
centrum *V*, duo contactus *M*, *N*, [et latus *KH* equale *AB*], sintque *ME*
(*! LE'*), *ML*, *MGM* (*! GS*) et *GN* maiores *AZ* et quolibet et quolibet (*! del.*)
reliquorum, minores vero eorum sunt relique a coniunctionibus ad angulos
10 de *FGHKL*. Ducantur itaque linee *EA* (*! OA*) et *OB* atque *OP* et *ZQ* (*! OQ*)
equales vel (*! ut*) que debuerant esse minores. Ducantur itaque linee *E'V*,
FV, *G* (*! GV*), *DL* (*! VL*), *VR*, *VT*. Sit *MR* et *EL* (*!*, *del.?*) et *NR* (*! NT*)
equalis *AB*. Quoniam autem proportio *LMF* (*! LVM*), *VXG* (*! NVG*) [trian-
gulorum ad triangulos *RVM*, *NVT* est ut ad triangulos *AOZ*, *ZOB*, et ergo
15 triangulorum *LVR*, *TVG*] ut ad triangulos [*RVM*, *NVT* est ut ad *AOZ*, *ZOB*,
et *FVM*, *FVN* ad *RVM*, *NVT* est ut *POZ* ad *AOZ* et *FVY* equalis] *ACP*
(*! AOP*) [vel] *BCQ* (*! BOQ*), est maior proportio triangulorum suorum qui
sunt ad centrum ad (*! quam*) angulorum illorum, et hoc quoniam [est maior]
singulorum ad singulos, igitur tres superficies, cum sint duple triangulis *HVM*
20 (*! LVM*), *FVM*, *GVN*, addunt super tres superficies equilateri que sunt duple
triangulo *ACZ* (*! AOZ*). Quoniam due relique ipsius super reliquas alterius,
alterum ergo maius equilatero. Et sic in omnibus.

50. CIRCA EQUALES CIRCULOS FIGURAS EQUILATERAS
QUARUM QUE PLURIUM LATERUM FUERIT MAIOR EXISTAT EST
DESCRIBI POSSIBILE.

    Equilaterum et equiangulum pauciorum laterum sumi potest preter trian-
5 gulum et tunc aliud sumendum quod dupplicat (*!*) latera inferioris (*! interioris*)
11v figure; ut si sumatur / quadratus, sumenda est alia exagonus qui dupplicat
(*!*) latera trianguli: quod si sumatur pentagonus, sumatur exagonus vel ortogonus (*! octogonus*).

      3 circonscribantur *Br*
      4 minus *E*, (*?*)*Br*
      6 [*Z*] *addidi*
      7 [et . . . AB] *addidi*
   7–8 ME . . . MGM: in EM, LM, GM et GN (*?*) *E*
      8 et[1] *bis Br* / AZ et: A et EC *Br*
    10 et OB: IOB *Br*
    12 VT: ut (*?*) *E*
 13–15 [triangulorum . . . TVG] *addidi*
    15 ut: VT (*?*) *E*
 15–16 [RVM . . . equalis] *addidi*
    17 [vel] *addidi*
    18 [est maior] *addidi*
    19 superficiei *Br* / sint: sunt *E* / triangulo *Br*
    20 que: qui *Br*
    21 ACZ: AC et *Br*
Prop. 50
     1 50 *mg. sin. E om. Br* l[a] *mg. dex. E*
     7 sumatur[1]: mutatur (*?*) *Br* / sumatur[2]: sumetur *E* / vel: et *Br*

Verbi gratia, sit quadratus in circulo circumscriptus *A* [Fig. P.50]. Item
10 exagonus [equilaterus] et equiangulus *BCDEFG*, et tribus lateribus hinc inde
protractis donec conveniant fiat triangulus equilaterus qui sit *KLMN* (*! KLM*)
et contactus ipsius *N, O, P*. Sit *Q* tertia pars illius quo superhabundat triangulus
super quadratum, figureturque triangulus *NOP*. Abscindantur item trianguli
NKR et *OLS* et *PMT* equales vel minores *Q*, et ab *R, S, T* ducantur con-
15 tingentes circulum donec conveniant cum lateribus exagonii que sunt *RH,*
FX (*! SX*), *ZY* (*! TY*). Habebimus exagonum *RNFXTY* (*! HRXSYT*) equilaterum quoniam *KY* (*! KR*) et *LS* et *MT* sunt equales, atque [ab] angulis
ad contactus linee equales, et ipse est in circulo circumscriptus sed non
equiangulus atque maior quam [quadrato quoniam] triangulo (*! trianguli*)
20 quibus triangulus *KLM* superat eum minus super quadruplum (*! triplum*)
Q, quod est differentia trianguli ad quadratum, et erat demonstrandum.

51. SUPER DATUM LATUS DATI TRIANGULI CUI ET INSISTEN-
TIUM ANGULORUM UTERQUE SIT VEL RECTUS VEL RECTO MI-
NOR QUADRATUM CUIUS RELIQUI ANGULI RELIQUIS LATERIBUS
TRIANGULI INSISTANT DESIGNARE.

5 Sit datus triangulus *ABC* [Fig. P.51] et latus datum *AB*, sitque uterque
angulorum super ipsum consistentium aut rectus aut recto minor, alioquin
linea super ipsam ubicumque ortogonaliter erecta latus reliquum deinceps
non contingunt (*!*); dimittatur igitur perpendicularis *CD* super *AB*, atque
sicut tota *AB, CD* ad *CD* ita sit *AB* ad *E*, linea cui equalis sit *FGH* equidistanter
10 posita ad *AB* in triangulo. Perpendicularibus dimissis *FM* et *HL* super *AB*,
dico ergo *FHLM* esse quadratum. Quia *AB, CD* ad *CD* sicut *AB* ad *CD*
(*! E*) [sic *AB* ad *CD*] ita *AM* et *LB* ad *LM*. Sed *AM* et *LB* ad *FM* sive *HL*
sicut *AB* ad *CD*. Quare *FM* equalis *ML*. Cum ergo sit *FHLM* equilaterum
et rectangulum, patet esse quadratum.

9 in *Br om. E*
11 *ante* equilaterus *scr. E* e
12 Q *correxi ex* quod *in E et* itaque *in Br*
14 NKR et: KRN *Br*
15 exagonii *correxi ex* exagonum / RH *correxi ex* RV *in E et* RB *in Br*
16 -N- *Br* -V- *E*
17 [ab] *addidi*
19 [quadrato quoniam] *addidi*
20 triangulus: triangulis *Br*
21 Q *om. Br*

Prop. 51

1 51 *mg. sin. E om. Br* li*ᵃ* *mg. sin. E* / datum latus *tr. Br*
3 quadratorum (*?*) *Br*
5 datum: dat*ūs* (*!*) *Br*
6 *post* aut¹ *scr. et del. Br* rs / aut²: erit (*?*) *Br*
7 reliqum *E*
9 ad CD: ABCD *Br* / sit¹: fit (*?*) *E*
11 CD² *correxi ex* ED
12 [sic *AB* ad *CD*] *addidi* / LM: HN *Br*

52. IN OMNI ORTOGONIO QUADRATUM SUPER YPOTESIM (! YPOTHENUSAM) CONSTITUTUM MINUS EST QUADRATO QUOD SUPER RELIQUA LATERA DESCRIBITUR.

Sit ortogonius *ABC* [Fig. P.52], ypothenusa *AB*, super quam fit [quadratum]
5　*DEFG*, sitque in triangulo equali et simili quadratum descriptum super utrumque laterum habens angulum communem cum triangulo, quod [quadratum]
sit *H*. Dico ergo *H* esse maius quam *DEFG*. Protrahatur siquidem latus *EF*
donec conveniat cum *AC* in *M* et fiet triangulus [triangulo] *ABC* similis et
triangulo *H*. Sed et triangulus fuit similis triangulo *FEB*. Quia *FG* est maior
10　quam *FC*, maior ergo triangulus *EFB* triangulo *FCM*. Unde triangulus *ABC*,
12r　atque triangulus *H*, maior triangulo *AEM*. Quadratum ergo / *H* maius quadrato *DEFG*, quod fuit ostendendum.

53. IN OMNI OXOGONIO (! OXYGONIO) QUOD SUPER MAIUS LATUS DESCRIBITUR QUADRATUM MINUS EST.

Sit triangulus *ABC* [Fig. P.53], quadratum super *AB* descriptum, sitque
DEFG, atque in alio triangulo equali et simili super *AC*, quod est terminus
5　(! minus) *AB*, statuatur quadratum *H*. Transeat ergo linea *LFM*, applicata
sibi *AC* in *L*, ut sit triangulus *CLF* similis triangulo *FMB*, caditque *L* extra
C. Protrahatur item *FN* perpendicularis ad *AL*, cadetque ut [inter] *FC*, *AE*
(! *FG*), eritque triangulus *FNC* similis triangulo *FEM*. Et quia *FG* est maior
FEN (! *FN*) et ideo *FE* maior *FN*, erit et *FM* maior *FC*. Et sic triangulus
10　*FMB* maior triangulo *FCL*; totus igitur triangulus *ABC* maior triangulo
ALM, quare et triangulus *H*. Maius ergo quadratum *H* quadrato *D[E]FG*
ut proponebatur.

Prop. 52

　　　1 52 (?) *mg. sin. E om. Br* lii^a *mg. sin. E* / orthogonio *E* / ypothesim *Br*
　　　4 ypothenusa *correxi ex* ypoth'a *in E et* ypotēia *in Br* / [quadratum] *addidi*
　　　5 triangulo *correxi ex* trianguli / descriptu *E*
　　　6 comunem *E* / [quadratum] *addidi*
　　　7 H^1 *E*, (?)*Br* / EF: FE *Br*
　　　8 [triangulo] *addidi*
　　　9 et *om. Br*
　　10 FC: FT *E* / EFB: EFK *Br*
　　12 ostensum *Br*

Prop. 53

　　　1 53 *mg. sin. E om. Br* liii^a *mg. dex. E*
　　　3 sitque: sit quia *Br*
　　　4 AC: hac (*sive* HAC) *Br*
　　　5 quadratum H: quadratus B *Br*
　　　7 AL cadetque: .altadp. que *Br* / ut *Br* nt (?) *E* / [inter] *addidi* / FC *correxi ex* FE
　　　8 eritque triangulus *correxi ex* erit quia triangulum *in Br et* erit quadrangulum *in E*
　　　　(*et forte corr. E* quadrangulum *in* qui triangulum)
　　　9 FN erit: fuerit *Br* / FC *om. Br* / sic: sit (?) *E*
　　11 -[E]- *addidi*

54. RECTANGULUM SUPER QUODCUMQUE LATUS TRIANGULI CONSTITUTUM APPLICANS ANGULOS IN MEDIO RELIQUORUM LATERUM EST MEDIETAS TRIANGULI. IDEMQUE MAXIMUM EST OMNIUM RECTANGULORUM IN EODEM DESCRIPTORUM.

5   Sit triangulus *ABC* [Fig. P.54], et super *AB* consistat rectangulum *DEFG* ut apud *F* et *G* secentur *BC* [et *AC*] et ita per equa. Dico ergo hoc rectangulum esse dimidium trianguli. Quia enim *FG* est medietas *AB*, et *DE* erit ut *AD* et *EB*, quare rectangulum *DEFG* duplum triangulis *ADG* et *EBF*. Et quia triangulus *ABC* est quadruplus triangulo *FCG*, erit quadrangulum *ABFG*
10   tres. Quare totius trianguli rectangulum ergo medietas.

Reliquum sic. Statuatur aliud rectangulum super *AB* infra triangulum et sit *HLMN* ita ut *M* et *N* sunt infra *F* et *G* si placet. Et protrahantur *HN* et *LM* donec conveniant cum *FG* ut fiat rectangulum totum *HLTZ*, [et *HLTZ* ad] *D*[*E*]*FG* sicut *HL* ad *DE*, hoc est *MN* ad *FG*, quare sicut *MC* ad *FC*.
15   Itaque *LHTZ* (*! HLTZ*) ad *HLMN* sicut *TL*, hoc [est] *FE*, ad *ML*, sed et *FB* ad *MB*. Et quia *FM* ad *FC* minus quam *FM* ad *MB*, erit *FC* ad *MC* minus quam *FB* ad *MB*. Minus ergo erit *HLTZ* ad *DEFG* quam ad *HLMN*. Maius itaque *DEFG* quam *HLMN*. Sed et si *M* et *N* cadant supra *F* et *G*, eadem erit ratio.

55. DIVISIS LATERIBUS CUIUSLIBET QUADRILATERI PER MEDIUM LINEE PER CONTERMINALIUM LATERUM SECTIONES DEDUCTE SUPERFICIEM PARALLELOGRAMMAM CONSTITUUNT.

Esto quadrangulum *ABCD* [Fig. P.55], divida[n]turque quadrilaterum
12v   (*! quatuor latera*) per medium / apud *E*, *F*, *G*, *H*, et pertranseant linee. Dico
6   quadrilaterum *EFGH* esse parallelogrammum. Producantur linee ab *A* ad *C* et a *B* ad *D*. Erit igitur *EF* equidistans *AC* in triangulo *ABC*, sed etiam *GH*

Prop. 54

    1 54 *mg. sin. E om. Br* liiii^a *mg. dex. E*
    6 [et AC] *addidi*
    9 quadruplum *Br* / FCG *correxi ex* FEG / *post* erit *scr. et del. Br* triangulus
    10 Quare: quarte *Br*
    11 Reliqum *Br*
    12 sunt: sint *Br*
    13 HLTZ¹: HLT et *Br*
 13–14 [et HLTZ ad] *addidi*
    14 -[E]- *addidi* / hoc est: h. *Br*
    15 LHTZ: LHT *Br* / [est] *addidi* / FE (?)E FC *Br* / ad² *bis Br* / et *om. Br*
    16 minus: minis (*sive* nimis) *Br*
    18 DEFG *correxi ex* DCFG / HLMN *correxi ex* LMN
    19 ratio *E* inde (?) *Br*

Prop. 55

    1 55 *om. EBr* lv^a *mg. dex. E*
    3 parallelogrammam *corr. ex* peralellagramam *in E et* parallellagramam *in Br* (*et post hoc lectiones huiusmodi in EBr non laudabo et scribam* parallelogrammam *et similes formas*)
    4 -[n]- *addidi*
    6 EFGH *Br* CFGH *E* / C: E *Br*

eidem equidistat in triangulo *ADC*, quoniam latera triangulorum secta sunt proportionaliter quia per medium. Itaque tam *FE* quam *GH* est medietas
10 *AC*. Equales ergo *EF* et *GH*. Eadem ratione *FG* et *EGH* (*! EH*) equidistabunt *BD* et eius dimidia extra et ob hoc equales. Quia igitur quadrangulum *EFGH* habet opposita latera equalia, habebit equidistantiam.

56. INFRA (*!* INTRA) PARALLELOGRAMMUM ALIUD STATUATUR, APPLICANS ANGULOS IN MEDIO LATERUM ALTERIUS, SI ET ALIUD QUOQUE IN IPSO DESCRIBATUR, ILLUD EXTERIORI SIMILE ESSE NECESSE EST.

5 Si ergo parallelogrammum *ABCD* [Fig. P.56], infra (*!* intra) quod consistat quadrangulum *EFGH*, applicans angulos in medio laterum alterius, atque in illo statuatur quod sit *LMNR*, ergo istud est simile primo. Transeant *EG*, *FH*. Palam ergo quod *LM* et *NR* dimidia sunt *FH*, et *MN* et *LR* dimidia sunt *EG*. Quare *LM* dimidietas *AB*, et *LR* dimidietas *AC*. Item quia angulus
10 *MLR* et angulus *BAC* uterque equalis est angulo [*B*]*EG*, posito quod in communi sectione erunt, et ipsi equales et latera proportionalia, similia erunt parallelogramma.

57. INFRA (*!* INTRA) DATUM PARALLELOGRAMMUM RECTANGULUM ALIUD EQUILATERUM COLLOCARE QUOD IN PUNCTO DATO CUIUSLIBET BREVIORUM LATERUM CIRCUMSCRIPTUM QUADRILATERUM CONTINGAT.

5 Sit datum parallelogrammum [rectangulum] *ABCD* [Fig. P.57], latera breviora *AB*, *CD*, atque in *AB* figatur ubicumque punctus *X*, sitque *AX* maior *XB*. Sitque item *AX* potentior *XB* quadrato linee *YT*. Sit etiam linea Z in quam ducta *BC* faciat equalem quadrato *YT*. Dividatur *BC* in *BT* et *TC*, addatque *BT* super *TC* quantum est. Et palam igitur quod id quod fit ex
10 *BC* in *BT* addit super id quod fit ex *BC* in *TC* quantum est quod fit ex *BC* in Z, et hoc est quadratum *AC* (*!* *YT*). Sed quantum addit quod fit ex hoc in *BT* super id quod fit ex *BC* in *CT*, tantum addit quadratum *BT* super quadratum *CT*. Quadratum ergo *BT* superat quadratum *CT* quadrato *YT*.

10 AC *correxi ex* AE
10, 11 equales: equalis *Br*
Prop. 56
   1 56 (?) *mg. dex.* E *om. Br* lvi^a *mg. sin.* E
   2 angulos: alios *Br* / si: sed *Br*
  10 [B]- *addidi* / [B]EG: EZG (?) *Br*
Prop. 57
   1 57 (?) *mg. dex.* E *om. Br* lvii^a *mg. sin.* E
   3 circonscriptum *Br*
   5 [rectangulum] *addidi*
   6 figatur *Br* figura *in* E / sitque: sit *Br*
   7 Sitque item: sit idem *Br* / YT: XT *Br* / Z: et *Br*
   8 quam: qua *Br* / YT: XT *Br* / BT: BC *Br*
 10–11 BC in Z: BCM et *Br*
  12 BT^1: BC *Br* / CT: TC *Br* / *post* tantum *add. Br* est
  13 CT^1: TC *Br* / BT: BC *Br* / CT^2: TC *Br*

Sit item *AM* equalis *TC* et *CN* equalis *AX* et fiat quadrilaterum *XTNM*.
15 Constat autem quod *XM* equalis *TN* et *XT* equalis est *MN*. Est igitur equidistantium laterum. Quia item quadratum *BT* addit super quadratum *AM*
quantum et quadratum *AX* super quadratum *XB*, erunt quadrata *XM* (*! AX*)
et *AM*, que sunt ut quadratum *XM*, quantum quadratum *BX* et quadratum
BT, que sunt ut quadrata (*! quadratum*) *XT*. Est igitur *XT* equalis *XM*.
20 Equilaterum ergo est quadrangulum *XMNT*, secundum quod exigebatur.

58. INTRA DATUM PENTAGONUM EQUILATERUM ET EQUIAN-
GULUM QUADRATUM DESCRIBERE.

Sit pentagonus *ABCDE* [Fig. P.58], et continuetur linea *EB*, et transea[n]t
perpendiculariter ad *EB* linee *CFG*, *DHB* (*! DHL*), que maiores erunt quam
5 *BC* et *DE*. Sed *FH* equalis erit *CD*. Adiungantur hinc inde ab *C*, *G* due linee
equales *BF* et *HE* ut sit recta *MCFGN*, que erit minor (*! maior*) quam *BE*.
Seceat (*!*) igitur *BE* secundum quod illa [*MN*] secta est apud *B* (*! G*) et *C*,
et hoc fiat in *O* et *P*, eritque *BP* minor *BN* (*! GN*) et ideo minor *BF*, et *EO*
minor *EH*; *ABC* (*! ab O*) itaque et *P* pertranseant perpendiculares *RTX*
10 (*! RPX*), *TOY*, et subtendantur per terminos eorum (*! earum*) linee *RT* et
XY. Dico ergo quadratum esse *RXTY* (*! RXYT*). Item (?) *NEG* (*! NG*) ad
YX ita *FB* ad *PB* (*! PO*) et *FB* ad *PB* ita *CG* ad *RX*, quoniam *GN* equatur
FB. Ergo *OB* (*! OP*) equalis *RX*. Sed *XY* et *RT* equales sunt *PO*. Sic ergo
constat equilaterum esse. Et quod anguli recti iam non est dubium, et ita
15 quadratum.

13r / 59. INFRA (*! INTRA*) ASSIGNATUM EXAGONUM EQUILA-
TERUM ET EQUIANGULUM QUADRATUM DESCRIBERE.

14 TC: DC *Br* / CN *correxi ex* EN
15 XM equalis: X inequalis *Br*
16 BT: BC *Br*
17 et: est *Br*
19 BT: BC *Br*
20 secundum: X *Br* / exigebatur *Br* exhigebatur *E*
Prop. 58
1 58 *mg. sin. E om. Br* [1]viiiᵃ *mg. sin. E.*
3 linea: littera (?) *Br* / -[n]- *addidi*
4 perpendiculariter: principaliter *Br* / erunt *correxi ex* extra
5 Sed: similiter *Br* / erit *om. Br* / ab: AH *Br*
6 recta *correxi ex* rata (?) *in EBr* / BE: BEC *Br*
7 [MN] *addidi*
8 et²: est (?) *E* / BP minor *tr. Br*
9 et P: per *Br*
11 ergo *om. Br* / RXTY: CXTY *Br* / Item NEG: NCG *Br*
12 YX *correxi ex* RX *in E et* XX *in Br* / et: ēst (*!*) *Br* / FB²: FC FB *E* / RX *correxi ex*
PO / equatur *bis EBr*
13 OB: A̧B / RX: YX *Br* / sunt: sūp *E*
  (E above A̧B)
14 recti: rom (*!*) *Br*
Prop. 59
1 59 *mg. sin. E om. Br* lixᵃ *mg. dex. E* / assignant *Br*

Circa eundem exagonum describatur circulus, sectisque per medium arcubus quibus singula latera subtenduntur, productis lineis per sectiones fiat
5 alter exagonus secans alium, et sint note sectionum *A, B, C, D, E, F, G, H,*
K, L, M, N [Fig. P.59]. Ab *A* ergo in *D* ducatur linea, et ab *A* ad *L* [et ad
G], et ab *D* et *L* ad *G*, [et ab *L* ad *D*,] fiatque quadrilaterum et equilaterum
et rectangulum. Probabit[ur] per triangulos exagonorum lateribus insistentes,
probato quod equaliter singula latera sunt divisa, et hoc per cordas dimidiorum
10 arcuum.

60. INTRA QUADRATUM SIVE PENTAGONUM EQUILATERUM
ET EQUIANGULUM QUADRATUM (*!* TRIANGULUM EQUILA-
TERUM) COLLOCARE.

Duobus modis inequalibus [in] figura equilatera et equiangula constituetur
5 triangulus equiangulus vel quod ab angulo vel ab medio lateris procedat.
Verbi gratia: si ab angulo eidem pentagono circulus circumscribatur, et infra
(*!* intra) circulum triangulus equilaterus qui ab angulo pentagoni exeat, et
ubi latera eius duo a communi angulo exeuntia latera secuerint pentagoni
transiet linea que concludet triangulum equilaterum propter triangulorum
10 similitudinem. Si a medio lateris eidem pentagono inscribatur circulus et
circulo triangulus cui duo latera producantur ab uno contactuum donec
lateribus pentagoni obvient, et per puncta convenientium dirigatur linea que
simili modo triangulum equilaterum concedet [Fig. P.60].

61. SI TRIANGULUS EQUILATERUS ET QUILIBET ALIUS
EQUALIS FUERINT CONSCRIPTIONIS, EQUILATERUS MAIOR ERIT.

Sit triangulus equilaterus *A* et alius sit *BCD* [Fig. P.61], cuius aliquod latus
erit maius quolibet alterius,* quod sit *BC*, quod etiam rescindatur ad equali-
5 tatem aliorum ut fiat *EC*, atque sicut *BC* ad *EC* ita sit *FE* ad *DE*, et continuetur
F equidistans *BC*, eritque triangulus *FCE* equalis alii, lateraque pariter accepta

3 eumdem *E*
5 secans: sequens *Br*
6 A ergo: angulo *Br* / in D: MD *Br*
6–7 [et . . . G] *addidi*
7 [et . . . D] *addidi* / et⁴ *om. Br*
8 -[ur] *addidi*
Prop. 60
1 60 *mg. sin E om. Br* lxᵃ *mg. dex. E*
4 [in] *addidi*
5 vel¹: illis (?) *EBr* / ab²: a *Br*
7–8 exeat . . . pentagoni *om. Br*
9 *ante* propter *add. Br* et
11 cuius *Br*
12 obvient: ebment (*!*) *Br*
Prop. 61
1 61 *mg. sin. E om. Br* lxiᵃ *mg. dex. E*
2 fuerint *Br* fuerit *E*
4 * *hab. E supra* maius *et transposui; cf. var. lin. 15* / rescidatur *E*
5 sit *om. Br* / FE ad DE *correxi ex* FC ad DC
6 BC: BT (?) *Br* / eritque: erit et *Br* / FCE: FEC *E*

minora, posito quod *DC* esset minus *EC*, quod vel ipsum vel *BD* superet.
Item fiat triangulus *EGC* equalis triangulo *ECF*. Sed latera *EG* et *CG* inter
se equa. Ipsa ergo minora quam *EF* et *FC*, quare minora quam duo latera

10   *A*. Super linea igitur *EC* triangulus equilaterus *EHC* sistatur qui erit equalis
A qui excedet triangulum *EGC*, alioquin vel ipse esset vel in eo includetur,
quod est impossible cum duo latera eius duobus lateribus alterius sint minora.
Cum ergo excedet, palam est en (*!* eam) esse maiorem. Maior ergo et quolibet
reliquorum.

15   [*triangulus (*!* trianguli) equilateri, et si aliquis contradiceret suppositioni,
scilicet quod etiam non esset forte maius *DC* vel equale, ergo erit maius
aliquo latere *BDS* (*!* *BDC* sive *BD* scilicet?) cum tria latera ista *BD*, *EC*
(*!DC*), *CB* sint equalia tribus lateribus trianguli *A* et *EC* sit equale uni illorum
trianguli *A*, et tunc adde *BD* linee aliam et in eadem proportione quam

20   supposuimus *BC* ad *EC* et intellige figuram reversam.]

62. OMNE QUADRATUM MAIUS EST QUOLIBET ALIO QUAD-
RATO (*!* QUADRILATERO) QUOD IN SCRIPTIONE EI FUERIT
EQUALE.

Sit quadratum *A* et tetragonus *BCDE* [Fig. P.62], cuius protendatur linea

5   diametrus *BD*, atque super eam statuantur hinc inde duo trianguli *BFD*,
BGD equales triangulis *BCD* et *BED*, sintque *BF* et *FD* atque *BG* et *GD*
equales. Quare et ipse minores esse quam *BC*, *CD*, *BE*, *ED*. Transeat igitur
dyameter *FG*, eritque triangulus *FDG* equilaterus et equiangulus triangulo
FBG. Figuretur super *FG* triangulus *FHG* equalis triangulo *FDG*, / sintque

10   *FH* et *HQF* (*!* *HG*) equalis (*!* equales) fiat (*!* del.?). Item *FM* equidistans *HQF*
(*!* *HG*), et *MG* equidistans *FH*, eritque *FM* equalis *MG*, atque triangulus
FMG equalis triangulo *FHG*, sed et triangulo *FDG* et *FBG*. Erit igitur *FGHM*
(*!* *FHGM*) parallelogrammum equilaterum et equale quadrilatero *BCDE*,
latera vero minora lateribus quadrati (*!* quadrilateri). Si ergo fuerit rectan-

15   gulum* erit et quadratum, scilicet [minus] *A*, maius quidem alio *CFGHM*

8   EGC: EGT (?) *Br*
9   et FC *del.* (?) *Br*
10 Super: Sed *Br*
11 EGC: EGT (?) *Br*
13 et *om. Br*
15 *Cum signum * est supra* maius (*in lin. 4*) *in E, ergo add. Br lineas 15–20 post* maius
     in lin. 4
17 EC: et *Br*
18 trianguli: trium (?) *Br*
19 trianguli: triangulorum *Br* / adde: ad DE *Br* / proportionem *Br*
20 intelligite *Br*

Prop. 62

1   62 (?) *mg. sin. E om. Br* lxii^a *mg. dex. E*
5   diametrus *correxi ex* diametris *in E et* dyametris *in Br* / hinc: hinc et *Br*
6   -que¹ *om. Br*
7   esse *correxi ex* extra
12 triangulo²: triangulus *Br*
13 quadrilatero BCDE *correxi ex* quadrato A *in E et* quadrato et *in Br*
15 * *vide inferius var. lin. 19–27* / scilicet [minus] A: SA *Br* / [minus] *addidi*

(*! scilicet FHGM*). Si non equiangulum eo quod minus erit. Palam ergo quidem (*!* quod) est quadratum (*!* quadrilaterum) *BCDE* minus erit quadrato *A*, et hoc est [propositum].

20 [* per quartam primi libri resecando et applicando sive supponendo latera minora lateribus maioribus et angulos equales angulis equalibus, quod constabit facile cogitando, si non rectangulum, ergo *H* aut maior recto aut minor. Si minor, ergo eadem ratione per quartam (*?*) primi [applicetur] geometrice ad quadratum [quod] maius est *BFBG* (*! FHGM*) quadrilatero. Sed si *A* (*! H*) maior recto, ergo parallelogrammum *ANFG* (*! FHGM*) non valeat *FR*

25 (*! F* semi) rectum versus *H*, *M*, *FG* versus (*!* ducta a) *MGF* (*! G* in *F*). Totus minor recto. Et *G* similiter minor recto. Deinde ut prius per quartam [primi] ducta *GMFH* (*! FHGM*)].

63. SI DUE FIGURE EQUILATERE ET EQUIANGULE EODEM AMBITU TERMINENTUR, QUE PLURIUM FUERIT LATERUM MAIOR ERIT.

Exempli gratia: sit quadratus *A* [Fig. P.63] et pentagonus [*B*] eiusdem
5 circumscriptionis. Dico pentagonum maiorem esse. Inscribatur enim circulus *A* et ipsi circulo circumscribatur pentagonus. Habemus autem quod quadratum *A* ad pentagonum *A* sicut omnia latera ipsius ad omnia latera illius. Sed pentagonus *B* ad pentagonum *A* tanquam laterum ipsius ad latera [illius] proportio dupplicata (*!*). Maior ergo proportio pentagoni *B* ad alium [quam]
10 quadrati ad ipsum. Maior ergo pentagonus *B* quadrato. Sed et (*!* quod) quadratus inter pentagonos proportionaliter esse constitutum est manifestum est.

Explicit liber philotegni Iordani 1xiiii (*!*) propositiones continens. Deo gratias.

16 equiangulum: equalium *Br*
17 *post* quidem *add. Br* minus / quadratum: quadri (*!*) *Br*
18 *post* est *add. Br* quod et est / [propositum] *addidi*
19–27 *per. . . . GMFH *mg. infer. add. E et injuste add. Br ad finem prop. 63*
21 H aut: habeat *Br*
22 per quartam: per am (*!*) *Br*
22, 23 [applicetur] *et* [quod] *addidi*
24 parallelogrammum: partialis *Br* / valent *E*
25 H, M: HN *E* H.NZ (*?*) *Br* / MFG: NZ.GF (*?*) *Br*
26 [primi] *addidi*
Prop. 63
1 63 *mg. sin. E om. Br* lxiii*ᵃ mg. sin. E*
4 sit *om. Br* / [B] *addidi*
5 pentagoni (*?*) *E* / enim: a *Br*
6 circōscribatur *Br*
6–7 quadratus *Br*
8 B ad: BAD *Br* / latera: laterum *Br* / [illius] *addidi*
9 B ad: BAD *Br* / [quam] *addidi*
10 et *om. Br*
11 est[1]: est et *Br*
12 phylotegni *Br* / propositiones *correxi ex* proportiones
12–13 Deo gratias *E om. Br*

[Here] Begins The Book of the Philotechnist of Jordanus de Nemore

Containing 64 (! 63) Propositions

[1] CONTINUITY IS THE INDETERMINATION OF LIMIT WITH THE POTENTIALITY OF LIMITATION.[1]

[2] A POINT IS A FIXATION OF SIMPLE CONTINUITY.

[3] SIMPLE [CONTINUITY] OCCURS IN A LINE, DOUBLE [CONTINUITY] IN A SURFACE, AND TRIPLE [CONTINUITY] IN A BODY.

[4] ONE CONTINUITY IS STRAIGHT, ANOTHER CURVED.

[5] THAT IS STRAIGHT WHICH HAS A SIMPLE [I.E. ONE-DIMENSIONAL] MEDIUM.

[6] BUT AN ANGLE IS THE DISCONTINUITY OF CONTINUA THAT COME TOGETHER IN A LIMIT.[2]

[7] NOW A FIGURE IS A FORM ARISING OUT OF THE QUALITY OF [ITS] LIMITS AND [OUT OF] THE METHOD OF APPLYING [THEM].

Then a figure of a surface occurs "out of the quality of [its] limits" because one is contained by curved [limits, i.e. lines], another by curved and straight [limits], and [still] another by straight limits alone. And indeed [of those contained] by curved lines some are contained by one [such line] and others by several. Now [some figures are contained] by straight lines and two or more curved lines, while [others are contained] by three or more straight lines. [Figures arise] "out of the method of applying [limits]" since from it [i.e., the method of application] arises a diversity of angles. For certain ones are made equal by straight lines, and certain are made smaller and certain greater.

[Propositions]

1. (=*VL* I.1) IN EVERY TRIANGLE, IF THE STRAIGHT LINE DRAWN FROM AN OPPOSITE ANGLE TO THE MIDDLE OF THE BASE IS EQUAL TO HALF OF THAT BASE, THAT ANGLE WILL BE A RIGHT ANGLE. BUT IF IT IS GREATER [THAN HALF THE BASE], [THE ANGLE] IS ACUTE; WHILE IF IT IS LESS, [THE ANGLE] IS OBTUSE.

Introduction

[1] See my brief discussion of these definitions in Chapter 2 of Part II above.

[2] Curtze in his edition of the longer version altered the text of this definition by reading *in continuitatis* instead of *incontinuitas*, as all manuscripts of both versions of the tract give. Only *incontinuitas* makes sense, as my translation here reveals.

Let there be triangle *ABC* and let line *BD* be drawn from angle *B* to the middle of *AC*. Therefore, if *BD* = *DC* [see Fig. P.1a], then [one] partial angle at *B* = angle *C*. By the same reason the [other] partial angle at *B* = angle *A*, and so the two angles upon the base, namely *A* and *C*, will be equal to the remaining angle, i.e., the whole angle at *B*, so that the latter will be a right angle. Now if *BD* will be greater [than *DC*] [see Fig. P.1b], the angles on the base will be greater than the remaining angle; therefore it is acute. Contrariwise, if less [see Fig. P.1c], then the latter will be greater than the other two, and it follows thence that it [i.e., the whole angle at *B*] is obtuse.[1]

2. (=*VL* I.2) A LINE DRAWN FROM AN ANGLE TO THE BASE INSIDE A TRIANGLE WHOSE TWO SIDES ARE EQUAL WILL BE LESS THAN EITHER OF THEM, WHILE [IF DRAWN] OUTSIDE IT WILL BE GREATER [THAN EITHER].

Let there be two equal sides *BA* and *BC* in triangle *ABC* [see Fig. P.2a], and inside of the triangle let line *BD* be drawn from angle *B* to the base. Therefore because angle *D* > angle *C* (since it is intrinsic [to it]), angle *D* will be greater than angle *A* because it [namely *A*] is equal to angle *C*. And so *AB* > *BD*. Then let *BD* fall outside of the triangle and be applied to the base which has been extended to *D* [see Fig. P.2b]. And because intrinsic angle *A* > angle *D*, so also angle *C* will be greater than the same [angle]. And so *BD* > *BC*, which we intend.

3. (=*VL* I.3) IF A TRIANGLE HAS TWO UNEQUAL SIDES AND A LINE IS DRAWN INSIDE THE TRIANGLE FROM THE ANGLE WHICH THE SIDES CONTAIN TO THE BASE, IT [I.E. THE DESCENDING LINE] WILL [ALWAYS] BE SHORTER THAN THE LONGER SIDE; BUT IT HAPPENS THAT IT [I.E. THE DESCENDING LINE] CAN BE EITHER EQUAL TO, OR GREATER THAN OR LESS THAN THE SHORTER SIDE.

Let there be triangle *ABC*, whose side *AB* is greater than *BC* [see Fig. P.3]. And, as before, let line *BD* be drawn to the base and inside the triangle, *BD* evidently being less than *AB* since then extrinsic angle *D* > angle *C*. Hence angle *D* is also greater than angle *A*. Now it happens that *BD* is equal to *CB* if angle *C* is acute (when then the remaining angles, namely total angle *B* and angle *A*, will be greater than it) and angle *ABD* is equal to the excess of angle *C* over angle *A*. And so intrinsic angle *D* = angle *C*, and thus the sides [*CB* and *BD*] are equal; and every line drawn [from *B*] within [*BD*] is less than it and every line [drawn] outside [of *BD*] is greater than it.[1]

Prop. 1

[1] MS *Fa* adds a comment (see the text above, var. lin. 11), which I translate as follows: "This proof is evident if a circle is circumscribed, for the angle in the first method will stand in a semicircle, in the second method in a segment greater than a semicircle, and in the third method in a segment less than a semicircle."

Prop. 3

[1] It is evident that, if the angle at *C* happened to be a right angle, then any line *BD* drawn inside of this triangle must be greater than line *BC*. Jordanus does not mention this case, but

4. (=*VL* I.4) IN EVERY TRIANGLE WHOSE TWO SIDES ARE UN-
EQUAL, A LINE DRAWN FROM THE ANGLE CONTAINED BY THESE
[SIDES] TO THE MIDDLE OF THE BASE WILL CONTAIN WITH THE
LONGER SIDE THE SMALLER ANGLE.

Let there be triangle ABC and let $AB > BC$ [see Fig. P.4]. And let BD be
drawn to bisect the base. I say that the [partial] angle at B toward A < the
remaining [partial] angle at B. For let line DE be drawn parallel to CB.
Therefore, because line DE = ½ line BC, [so] also DE < ½ line AB (and ½
line AB = line EB). Therefore angle BDE > angle ABD. Therefore angle
DBC > angle ABD, because angle DBC = angle EDB,[1] and this is what has
been proposed.

5. (=*VL* I.5) IF IN A RIGHT [TRIANGLE] A LINE IS DRAWN FROM
ONE OF THE REMAINING ANGLES TO THE BASE, THE RATIO OF
THE ANGLE FARTHER FROM THE RIGHT ANGLE TO THE ANGLE
CLOSER TO THE RIGHT ANGLE IS LESS THAN THE RATIO OF ITS
BASE TO THE BASE OF THE OTHER.

Now the proof of this is that to be sought in the *Book of Isoperimeters*.[1]
For if the right triangle is proposed and a circle is described according to the

---

that he was aware of it is obvious since he specifies in the proof that angle C is to be acute. He
goes on to say that if angle ABD = angle BDC − angle A, then angle C = angle BDC and so
$BD = BC$. Then from Proposition 2 it is evident that any line BD' drawn inside of BD is less
than BC and any line BD'' drawn outside of BD is greater than BC. Incidentally it will be obvious
that constructing angle ABD equal to angle $C − A$ produces the equality of BD and BC. For if
we construct at A an angle $B'AC$ equal to the angle at C and then from point B we draw line
BD parallel to line $B'A$, then angle $B'AB$ = angle $C − A$. Consequently, because of the parallelity
of $B'A$ and BD, angle BDC = angle $B'AC$ = angle C. Hence $BD = BC$.
Prop. 4

[1] Since BD cuts parallel lines BC and ED.
Prop. 5

[1] I have given the appropriate passage from the *Liber de ysoperimetris* and other pertinent
treatments of this proposition in Appendix III.A below, while I have translated and discussed
some of the passages in Chapter 2 of Part II above. However, I have not yet discussed the proof
substituted in MS *Bu* (see the variant reading to lines 5–11 in the text above). It may be
summarized as follows (referring to Fig. P.5*var. Bu*): (1) Bisect AE successively until $DE < EC$.
(2) Cut off $EF = ED$. (3) Ang. FBE < ang. EBD, because it is on an equal line farther from
the right angle. (4) Then construct ang. GBD = ang. EBD − ang. FBE. (5) Now bisect angle
EBD successively until ang. EBH < ang. EBG. Similarly bisect line ED successively the same
number of times, arriving finally at ER. (6) Thus we have assumed ang. EBD / ang. EBH
= ED / ER. But later the author states and uses an incompatible assumption, namely ang. ABE
/ ang. EBH = AE / ER. I say "incompatible" because there is no way that the angle EBH that
is a submultiple of ang. EBD can also be the ang. EBH that is a submultiple of ang. ABE. (7)
ang. EBF / ang. EBH < ang. EBD / ang. EBH (ang. EBF being less than ang. EBD since it
stands on an equal line farther from the right angle). (8) From (6) and (7) together ED / ER
> ang. EBF / ang. EBH, or, since $ED = EF$, so EF / ER > ang. EBF / ang. EBH. (9) FL /
ER > ang. LBF / ang. EBH, since $FL = ER$, and ang. LBF is on an equal line farther from
the right angle. (10) Now, according to the author, $LC = ER$ or $LC < ER$. If $LC = ER$, so LC
/ ER > ang. CBL / ang. EBR, as in step (9). Therefore, LC / ER > ang. CBL / ang. EBH, since
ang. EBH > ang. EBR. But if $LC < ER$ and $LC = EL'$, then EL' / $L'R$ > EBL' / $L'BR$ (not
proved by the author, but it follows from the extension of this very Prop. 5 to obtuse-angled

length of a line which is subtended by the right angle, the center [of the circle] having been fixed in the terminus of [one of] the line[s] containing the right angle, then [if] the [subtended] line is drawn from the same central angle to the remaining side that contains the right angle the ratio of [one base] segment to the [other base] segment is greater than that of one central angle to the other central angle [the angles being opposite these segments].

6. (=*VL* I.6) IN A TRIANGLE WHOSE TWO SIDES ARE UNEQUAL, IF FROM THE ANGLE [INCLUDED BY THESE SIDES] A PERPENDICULAR IS DRAWN, THE RATIO OF THE SEGMENT OF THE BASE CUT OFF BETWEEN THE PERPENDICULAR AND THE LONGER SIDE TO THE REMAINING [SEGMENT OF THE BASE] WILL BE GREATER THAN THAT OF ANGLE TO ANGLE.

Let there be triangle ABC [see Fig. P.6], with longer side AB and perpendicular BD. And $AD > DC$, for CD is not equal to DA (since if it were, then $CB = BA$ [which is against the datum]) and neither is $CD > DA$ (since, if so, let a line DG equal to DA be cut; thence with BG drawn it follows that $CB > AB$ because $BC > BG$). Therefore, because $AD > DC$, let there be DE equal to DC, and let line BE be drawn. Therefore, since AE / ED > angle ABE / angle EBD by the preceding [proposition], and because $ED = CD$ and angle EBD = angle CBD, so by conjunction AD / CD > angle ABD / angle CBD.

7. (=*VL* I.7) IF TWO TRIANGLES ARE SET ON THE SAME BASE BETWEEN PARALLEL LINES, THE SUPERIOR ANGLE OF THAT ONE WHOSE SIDE OF THE MUTUALLY INTERSECTING SIDES IS GREATER WILL BE SMALLER.

Let there be parallel lines AB and CD, between which triangles EGF and EHF stand on the same base EF, and their sides EG and EF mutually intersect at K [see Fig. P.7]. Therefore, if FH is posited greater than EG, so angle EGF > angle FHE by the following argument. For, since triangle FKG = triangle EKH, [so] FK / EK = KH / KG, by the sixth [book] of Euclid. Therefore, the whole / the whole = FK / KE.[1] Therefore $FK > EK$. Therefore, [let L be marked so that] FK / KE = EK / KL, KL being less than KF. Therefore, with line GL drawn, it follows that angle LGK = angle EHK, for

triangles. Hence there is a circularity at this point). EL / ER > ang. EBL' / ang. EBR, ER being greater than $L'R$. So LC / ER > ang. CBL / ang. EBR, ang. CBL being smaller than ang. EBL and EL' being equal to LC. So finally LC / ER > ang. CBL / ang. EBH, ang. EBH being greater than ang. EBR. (11) Now, by summing (8), (9), and (10), we have EC / ER = ($ED + FL + CL$) / ER > (ang. EBF + ang. LBF + ang. CBL) / ang. EBH = EBC / EBH. (12) So from the second assumption in (6) EC / AE > ang. EBC / ang. ABE. Q.E.D. Thus the author has used the first assumption of step (6) in step (8) and the second, incompatible assumption of step (6) in step (12); and hence the proof will not stand. Also unsatisfactory is the circularity noted in step (10).

Prop. 7

[1] The first part of the argument proceeds as follows: (1) FK / KH = EK / KG. Hence (2) FK / ($FK + KH$) = EK / ($EK + KG$) Therefore (3) FH / EG = FK / EK.

those triangles are similar, and thus the whole angle *FGE* will be greater than angle *EHF*, and this is what is proposed.[2]

8. (=*VL* I.8) IF TRIANGLES STAND ON THE SAME BASE BETWEEN PARALLEL LINES, THAT ONE WHOSE SUPERIOR ANGLE IS THE MAXIMUM WILL BE THE ONE WHOSE REMAINING SIDES ARE EQUAL, AND BY THE AMOUNT THAT THEY [I.E. THE SUPERIOR ANGLES] ARE CLOSER TO IT [I.E. THE MAXIMUM SUPERIOR ANGLE] BY SUCH AMOUNT ARE THEY GREATER THAN THOSE MORE REMOTE [FROM IT].

Let the triangle whose sides [other than the base] are equal be *ABC* and the other *ADC* [see Fig. P.8]. Therefore angle *CBD* is obtuse. For sides *AB* and *BC* are equal, and so angle *C* is acute; but angle *C* and the total angle at *B* [together] are equal to two right angles; and so the total angle at *B* is obtuse. Therefore *CD* > *AB* because *CD* > *BC* and *AB* = *BC*. Therefore, by the preceding [proposition], angle *B* > angle *D*. Also let triangle *AEC* whose angle *E* falls between *B* and *D* be constructed, and *CE* < *CD* by the third [proposition] of this [work]. But *CE* > *AE*, which is evident because angle *EAC* > the partial angle at *C* since it is greater than the whole angle at *C* (for angle *C* is equal to the partial angle at *A*). And so *DC* > *AE*. Then you can argue as before.[1]

9. (=*VL* I.9) IF TWO TRIANGLES HAVING A PAIR OF EQUAL AN-GLES ARE EQUAL, THEN THE PERIMETER OF THE [TRIANGLE] IN WHICH ONE OF THE [FOUR] SIDES INCLUDING THE TWO EQUAL ANGLES IS THE MAXIMUM [OF THESE FOUR SIDES] WILL BE GREATER [THAN THE PERIMETER OF THE OTHER TRIANGLE].

Let the equal triangles be *ABC* and *DEF*, and angles *B* and *E* are equal [see Fig. P. 9], and let line *AB* be greater than [each of] *DE* and *EF*, and accordingly *BC* is less than either of these for the sides are reciprocally pro-portional.[1] Therefore let *DE* be extended to *G* so that the whole *EDG* is

---

[2] The remainder of the argument whose first steps are given in the preceding footnote follows. Since *FH* > *EG* (given), hence (4) *FK* > *EK* (from the third step in the preceding note). So let there be a point *L* such that (5) *FK* / *KE* = *EK* / *KL*. Then (6) *KH* / *KG* = *KE* / *KL*, from steps (1) and (5). Then by VI.6 of Euclid, (7) triangles *EKH* and *LKG* are similar. Thus (8) ang. *KGL* = ang. *EHK*. And so (9) ang. *FGE* > ang. *EHF*. Q.E.D.

Prop. 8

[1] That is, you can argue by Proposition 7 that the vertical angle at *D* is less than the vertical angle at *E*, which angle at *D* is less than the vertical angle at *B* by the first part. The same reasoning would hold for any other angle to the left of *D*, and so the second part of the proposition also holds.

Prop. 9

[1] For "reciprocally proportional" the text has *mutekefia*. This is employed in the Adelard II Version of the *Elements,* Props. VI.13 and VI.14 (=Gr. VI.14 and VI.15), as given in MS Bodleian Library, Auct. F.5.28, xiv r–v. In these same propositions in the Hermann of Carinthia version we also find the same term used, but in the first proposition it reads "mutekefia id est mutue relaciones" (see H. L. Busard, *The Translation of the Elements of Euclid from the Arabic into Latin by Hermann of Carinthia (?)* (Leiden, 1968), p. 122, Prop. VI.13; see also p. 123, Prop. VI.14.

equal to *AB*. And from *FE* let *EH* be cut equal to *CB*, and let line *GH* be subtended, which line will be equal to *AC*, and triangle *ABC* = [triangle] *GHE*. I say, therefore, that line *GH* > *DF*. For let *L* be their [point of] intersection; and because triangles *FED* and *HEG* are equal, [so] *FHL* = *LGD*. But [one] angle is equal to [one] angle. Therefore, *GL* / *LF* = *LH* / *LD*, and the whole *GH* / *DF* = *LH* / *LD*.[2] Therefore, if *LH* > *LD*, the whole [*GH*] > the whole [*DF*]. But if it is said that it is equal (i.e. that *LH* = *LD*), then with line *DH* drawn angle *LDH* = angle *LHD*. And because angle *HDE* < angle *DHE* since angles *C* and *GHE* are equal and *C* > *FDE* (for if it were equal, [triangle] *ABC* would be similar to *FDE*; if it were less, a similar inconsistency will remain; namely, angle *FDG* > angle *GHF*). And so if angle *LDT* is made equal to angle *LHF*, then, since the triangles are similar, *TL* will be equal to *LF* and therefore *GL* > *LF*, and so the whole *GH* > *FD*. And similarly *AC* > *FD*, and (*AB* + *BC*) > (*DE* + *EF*), by the last [proposition] of the fifth [book] of Euclid.[3] Therefore the three [sides of the one triangle] are greater than the three [sides of the other].

Moreover, if *HL* < *LD*, make the following refutation. These triangles *HDG* and *FHD* are equal and are on the same base; therefore they are between parallel lines, and *FD* > *GH*, as the adversary posits. Therefore angle *F* < angle *G* by the antepenultimate [proposition, i.e. the seventh]. But *C* > *G*; therefore *C* > *F*, which is false, and then proceed as before.[4]

10. (=*VL* I.10) IF TRIANGLES ARE SET UPON THE SAME BASE BETWEEN PARALLEL LINES, THE SUM OF THE [TWO] SIDES OF THE ONE WHOSE REMAINING SIDES ARE EQUAL WILL BE LESS [THAN THE SUM OF THE TWO SIDES OF ANY OTHER SUCH TRIANGLE], AND BY THE AMOUNT THAT THE SIDES [OF THAT SECOND TRIANGLE] ARE CLOSER TO THEM, BY THAT MUCH LESS [IS THEIR SUM] THAN [THE SUM OF THE] MORE REMOTE SIDES [OF STILL ANOTHER SUCH TRIANGLE].

Let two triangles *ABC* and *ADC* be between two parallel lines [see Fig. P.10a], and let *AB* = *BC*; from *B* let a line be extended until equal to *BC* and let the whole line be *ABG*. But also let *AD*, which can be the longer side, be extended until equal to *CD* at point *H*, and let *G* be connected with *H* and with *D*. And because angle *CBD* = angle *DBG* on account of the parallel lines (for the extrinsic angle *B* = angle *A* and [angles] *A* and *C* are equal on account of the equality of *AB* and *BC* and the fact that *C* and *B* are equal alternate angles of *BD* and *AC*) and [because] line *BG* = line *BC* and line *BD* is common, [so] base *GD* = *DC* = *DH*. Therefore, since angle

---

[2] This is derived as follows: (1) tri. *LDG* = tri. *FLH*, and the angles at *L* are equal. Hence, by VI.14 (=Gr. VI.15) of Euclid, (2) *GL* / *LF* = *LH* / *LD*, or *GL* / *LH* = *LF* / *LD*. (3) (*GL* + *LH*) / *LH* = (*LF* + *LD*) / *LD*. Therefore (4) *GH* / *DF* = *LH* / *LD*.

[3] This is Proposition V.25.

[4] See the expanded treatment of the last part of the proof given in MS *Fa* (cf. the text above, Prop. 9, var. lin. 22–26).

DGH = angle DHG, total angle AGH > angle AHG, and therefore line AH > line AG. From this is clear what has been proposed.

Let the same figure serve for the second part [but cf. Fig. P.10b], and let $BA > BC$. And because angle CAB < angle ACB, [so] angle DBG < angle CBD by reason of parallelity. And because $BG = BC$, base $DG < DC$, and therefore $DG < DH$. Therefore, since angle GHD < angle DGH, [so] it [i.e. angle GHD] will be less than the whole angle AGH, and thus line AG < line AH, according to what the proposition demands.

11. (=VL I.11) IN THE CASE OF ANY TWO TRIANGLES WHOSE BASES ARE EQUAL, THE RATIO OF ONE TO THE OTHER WILL BE AS THAT OF THE ALTITUDE OF THE ONE TO THE ALTITUDE OF THE OTHER.

Let there be triangles ABC and DEF whose bases AC and DF are equal [see Fig. P.11], and let perpendiculars be erected from the termini of the aforesaid bases; and with parallels to the bases drawn through B and E, [so] rectangles $ACGH$ and $DFLM$ are formed. Therefore, because rectangle / rectangle = perpendicular / perpendicular; and because the triangles are halves of the rectangles, and also because the perpendiculars determine the altititudes of the triangles, triangle / triangle = altitude / altitude.

12. (=VL I.12) IN THE CASE OF ANY TWO TRIANGLES IN WHICH THE TWO EQUAL SIDES OF THE ONE ARE EQUAL TO THE TWO EQUAL SIDES OF THE OTHER, THE RATIO OF THAT [TRIANGLE] WHOSE BASE IS THE GREATER TO THE OTHER [TRIANGLE] WILL BE LESS THAN THAT OF ITS BASE TO THE BASE OF THE OTHER.

And so let triangles ABC and DEG be designated [see Fig. P.12], and AC > DG, and sides AB and BC are equal [to each other] and are equal to the equal [sides] DE and EG. And so, with the bases bisected, let perpendiculars BF and EH be drawn, and accordingly perpendicular BF will be less than EH. For $DH^2 + EH^2 = AF^2 + FB^2$; but $AF^2 > DH^2$ since the [whole] base is greater than the [whole] base; therefore $EH^2 > BF^2$; therefore $EH > BF$. And so let line KLM be drawn in triangle ABC parallel to AC and equal to DG, and let AC / $KLM = KLM$ / PT. Therefore, because BL / $BF = KM$ / AC, [so] PT / $KM = BL$ / BF. Therefore PT / $KM > BL$ / EH. But BL / EH = tri. KBM / tri. DEG, by the preceding [proposition]. Therefore PT / $KM > KBM$ / DEG. But AC / PT = tri. ABC / tri. KBM because they are similar. Therefore, AC / $KM >$ tri. ABC / tri. DEG or AC / $DG >$ tri. ABC / tri. DEG.

13. (=VL I.13) IF THERE ARE TWO EQUAL TRIANGLES, THEIR BASES ARE RECIPROCALLY PROPORTIONAL[1] TO THEIR AL-TITUDES.

Let triangles ABC and DEG be constructed as usual [see Fig. P.13], and perpendiculars determine the altitudes, and let the perpendiculars be drawn

---

Prop. 13

[1] Both *mutue* and *mutekefia* may be rendered as "reciprocally proportional." See above, Prop. 9, n. 1.

from the termini of the bases, and let lines parallel to the bases proceed through B and E until rectangles $ACFH$ and $DGKL$ are formed; and because the triangles are equal so too are the rectangles, for the latter are double the triangles. Therefore, $AC / DG = KG / CF$, for they are reciprocally proportional, and this is what is proposed.

14. ($=VL$ II.1) WITH [TWO] LINES GIVEN, TO DIVIDE EITHER OF THEM SO THAT ONE OF THE SEGMENTS IS TO THE REMAINING [SEGMENT] AS THAT SAME REMAINING [SEGMENT] IS TO THE OTHER OF THE PROPOSED [LINES].

Let the two lines AB and BC be given and conjoined [see Fig. P.14], and on the conjoined line let us designate semicircle ADC and erect perpendicular BD. With the latter posited as a diameter let us draw circle BDF about center G and extend line $AFGE$, and from B we connect line BE and draw FH parallel to BE. Therefore because [by Prop. III.36 of Euclid] $AE \cdot AF = AB^2$, AB being a tangent, [so] $AE / AB = AB / AF$. Also, on account of the parallel lines, $EF / FA = BH / HA$, and permutatively $AF / AH = EF / BH$. Hence the whole $AE / AB = FA / AH$. And because $EA / AB = AB / AF$, [so] $AB / AF = AF / AH$. Therefore, $AB / FA = FE / BH$. And so permutatively $FE / BA = BH / FA$, and $BD = EF$, and $BC / BD = BD / AB$, and finally $BC / EF = BH / AF$. But $EF / BH = AF / AH$. Therefore, $CB / BH = BH / AH$, and [inverting the proportion and] taking it conversely, $AH / HB = HB / BC$, which was proposed.[1]

15. ($=VL$ II.2) WITH TWO LINES PROPOSED, TO DIVIDE ONE OF THEM SO THAT THE SUM OF THE OTHER LINE AND THE GREATER SEGMENT OF THE DIVIDED LINE IS TO THE SAME GREATER [SEGMENT] AS THE GREATER SEGMENT IS TO THE LESSER [SEGMENT OF THE DIVIDED LINE].

As before let the given lines be AB and BC [see Fig. P.15]. After they are joined let semicircle ADC be constructed on the whole line. Then upon the terminus of line AB in common point B let an angle equal to half a right angle be constructed, the line BD having been drawn. And from D let perpendicular DE be dropped to ABC. Therefore, because angle BED is a right angle, [so] angle BDE will be half a right angle. Therefore line $DE = BE$. And so, since line DE is a mean proportional between lines CE and EA, [so] $(CB + BE) / BE = BE / EA$.

Prop. 14

[1] We may summarize the proof as follows: (1) $AE / AB = AB / AF$, since $AE \cdot AF = AB^2$. (2) $EF / FA = BH / HA$, by similar triangles. Rewrite as $AF / AH = EF / BH$. (3) $AE / AB = FA / AH$, by the composition of ratios followed by the permutation of the new ratios and the substitution of equal magnitudes, i.e. $(EF + FA) / FA = (BH + HA) / HA$, followed by the permutation of these ratios and the substitution of AE and FA for $EF + FA$ and $BH + HA$. (4) $AB / AF = AF / AH$, taking (1) and (3) together. (5) $AB / AF = FE / BH$, taking (2) and (4) together. Rewrite as $FE / AB = BH / AF$. (6) $BD = EF$, both being diameters of the smaller circle. (7) $BC / BD = BD / AB$, by the well known property of the circle. (8) $BC / EF = BH / AF$, by (7), (6), and (5) together. Rewrite as $BC / BH = EF / AF$. (9) But $EF / BH = AF / AH$, by similar triangles. Rewrite as $EF / AF = BH / AH$. (10) $BC / BH = BH / AH$, by (8) and (9) together. By inversion and conversion, this may be rewritten as $AH / BH = BH / BC$. Q.E.D.

16. (=*VL* II.3) TO CUT A GIVEN LINE SO THAT THE RATIO OF ONE OF [ITS] SEGMENTS TO THE OTHER IS THAT OF THE SUM OF THE OTHER SEGMENT AND ANY OTHER GIVEN LINE TO THE SAME [GIVEN LINE].

As before let the lines be *AB* and *BC* [see Fig. P.16] and let the [second] given line be *BC*, and semicircle *ADC* upon these lines, and perpendicular line *BD*, and let line *CD* be connected, and with the center posited in *C* circular segment *ED* will be drawn. Therefore, because $AC / DC = DC / BC$,[1] and because $DC = EC$, [so] $AC / EC = EC / BC$. Therefore, by disjunction $AE / EC = EB / BC$. Therefore permutatively $AE / EB = EC / BC$, and this is what is proposed.

17. (=*VL* II.4) WITH TWO LINES GIVEN, TO CUT ONE SO THAT THE OTHER [GIVEN LINE] IS TO ONE SEGMENT OF THE DIVIDED LINE AS THE SUM OF THE SAME [GIVEN LINE] AND THE REMAINING SEGMENT OF THE DIVIDED LINE IS TO THAT SAME [SEGMENT].

Let the two lines be *AB* and *BC* [see Fig. P.17] and let them be continued [in a straight line], and also let us apply to them directly [i.e. in a straight line] a [line] equal to *BC*, which [line] let be *EC*, and upon line *AE* let circle *ADEG* be described. Let us draw line *DG*, which is equal to *AC*, and let it be inserted in the circle so that diameter *AE* cuts [it] in *F* in such a way that $FD = AB$ and $GF = BC$. Therefore, because [by Prop. III.34 (=Gr. III.35) of Euclid] $EF / DF = FG / FA$, [so] $FE / AB = BC / AF$. Hence, permutatively, $FE / BC = AB / AF$. And since $BC = CE$, therefore disjunctively $FC / CB = FB / FA$. So permutatively $FC / FB = BC / AF$, which has been proposed.

18. (=*VL* II.5) WITH TWO LINES PROPOSED OF WHICH ONE IS LESS THAN ONE FOURTH OF THE OTHER, TO ADD TO THE SHORTER LINE [A LINE] SUCH THAT THE RATIO OF THE ADDED LINE TO THE LINE COMPOSED [OF THE SHORTER LINE AND THE ADDED LINE] IS THAT OF THE COMPOSITE LINE TO THE OTHER PROPOSED LINE.[1]

Let the given lines be *AB* and *BC*, and let them contain a right angle, with rectangle *ABCD* completed [see Fig. P.18a]. Then upon line *AB* let us construct a rectangle equal to rectangle *ABCD* and deficient by a square that would complete [the rectangle] on the whole of line [*AB*], by [the 27th (=Gr. 28th) proposition of] the sixth book of Euclid. And let that [applied rectangle] be *AEFG*, and line $EF = EB$. The adversary [says that] $AE = EB$. Dissolution:[2]

Prop. 16

[1] This follows, for, by the property of the circle, $(AC - BC) / DB = DB / BC$, or $AC \cdot BC - BC^2 = DB^2$. And $DB^2 + BC^2 = DC^2$ by the Pythagorean theorem. Hence $AC \cdot BC = DC^2$, and so $AC / DC = DC / BC$.

Prop. 18

[1] See the discussion of this proposition and Jordanus' use of the technique of application of areas given above in Chapter 2 of Part II.

[2] For the term *dissolutio*, see my *Archimedes in the Middle Ages*, Vol. 1, pp. 169n and 444. It indicates a proof *per impossibile*.

Rectangle AF = [rectangle] DB and [one] angle is equal to [one] angle. Therefore, $AB / AE = EF / BC = EB / BC$, and so $BC = \frac{1}{4} AB$, which is against the hypothesis. Nor is AE less than $\frac{1}{2} AB$. For, according to this, $AB / AE < AB / BC$; and so $EB < \frac{1}{2} AB$. Proceed. [Rectangle] AF = [rectangle] DB. Therefore, $AB / AE = EB / BC$, and so $BC < AE$, and also $BC < EB$; and from EB let there be taken a line equal to it [i.e. to BC], and let that line be HB. And so $AB / EA = BE / HB$. Therefore permutatively $AB / EB = AE / HB$. Therefore, $AB / BE = BE / EH$, according to that [19th] proposition of the fifth [book] of Euclid: if line / line = part / part, therefore [that ratio is also] that of the residual [part] to the residual [part].[3] Therefore, transposing and inverting the ratios $EH / EB = EB / AB$, and this is what has been proposed [as is clear] to any one contemplating [it] diligently.

Another proof. Let there be a line [composed] out of AB and BC [see Fig. P.18b], on which semicircle ADC is described, and let perpendicular DB be drawn, which will be less than $\frac{1}{2} AB$, for BD is the mean proportional between AB and BC. And then, as above, let AB be bisected at E; and with semicircle AGB drawn let EG be erected, which, since it is greater than BD, is also greater than EL equal to the same [BD]; and with line DL drawn, let there be a common section of DL and circumference [AGB] at T. From T let a perpendicular TM be dropped to AB, and $TM = DB$. But $DB^2 = AB \cdot BC$ and $TM^2 = AM \cdot MB$. Therefore $AB \cdot BC = AM \cdot MB$, and thence one is to proceed as above.

19. (=VL II.6) WHEN THE RATIO OF THE LINE ADDED TO THE SHORTER LINE TO THE LINE COMPOSED [OF THE ADDED LINE AND THE SHORTER LINE] IS GREATER THAN THAT OF THE COMPOSITE LINE TO THE LONGER [LINE], IT IS NECESSARY THAT THE SHORTER [LINE] IS LESS THAN ONE FOURTH OF THE LONGER [LINE].

If $EH / EB > EB / AB$, [then] $BH < \frac{1}{4} AB$ [see Fig. P.19]. For, because of the assumption $AB / EB > EB / EH$.[1] Therefore, $AB \cdot EH > EB^2$. For, if $AB / EB = EB / EH$, [then] $AB \cdot EH = EB^2$. Therefore, if the ratio is greater the rectangle is greater. Therefore let a square $EBGD$ be constructed on EB and a rectangle on AB whose other side BL is equal to EH, and let line HKM be drawn. [Therefore] EHK and KLG are squares because they are similar to the whole square [$EBDG$]. But the supplements [i.e. rectangles] HL and DK are [each] proportional means between those [squares]. Therefore the supplements are either equal to the squares or are less than them, by the last [proposition] of the fifth [book] of Euclid. But the supplements equal each other. Therefore supplement HL is either $\frac{1}{4}$ square EG or less than $\frac{1}{4}$. But rectangle AL > square EG. Therefore $HL < \frac{1}{4} AL$. Therefore $AB \cdot HK > 4 HB \cdot KH$. Therefore $HB < \frac{1}{4} AB$, and this is what has been proposed.

---

[3] The statement of the substance of the nineteenth proposition of Book V of the *Elements* does not come *verbatim* from any of the known medieval translations of the *Elements*.
Prop. 19
[1] This is clear since $(AB / EB) \cdot (EB / EH) > (EB / AB) \cdot (EB / EH)$. The next step is clear, for $(AB / EB) \cdot (EB \cdot EH) > (EB / EH) \cdot (EB \cdot EH)$, which reduces to $AB \cdot EH > EB^2$.

20. (=*VL* II.7) IF THE SHORTER [OF TWO PROPOSED LINES] IS PROPORTIONAL BETWEEN THE SEGMENTS [PRODUCED BY THE DIVISION] OF THE LONGER [OF THE PROPOSED LINES], AND IF THE RATIO OF A LINE ADDED TO THE SHORTER TO A LINE COMPOSED [OF THE SHORTER AND THE ADDED LINE] IS GREATER THAN THAT OF THE COMPOSITE LINE TO THE LONGER [OF THE PROPOSED LINES], THEN NECESSARILY THE SAME COMPOSITE LINE IS GREATER THAN ONE OF THE SEGMENTS OF THE LONGER [OF THE PROPOSED LINES].

Let the composite line be *BCD* and let rectangle *AEF*[1] be equal to rectangle *ABC* [*AB* and *BC* being the two proposed lines with *AB* the greater; see Fig. P.20], [with the rectangle *AF*] being deficient from the whole [rectangle on *AB* by] the squared surface *FB*. And let *AB* be divided at *E*, and from *AB* let [line] *BM* be cut equal to [line] *BCD*. And so *BM* is equal to *EB* or is greater or is less. If it is greater, then I have the proposition [immediately]. For then the composite line, since it is equal to *BM*, is greater than one of the segments of *AB*. Now if it [i.e. *BM*] is equal to *EB*, it cannot be that *AE* = *EB*. For, if this is so, since *BC* is a mean proportional between *AE* and *EB* by hypothesis, then $BC^2 = MB^2$ or $BC^2 = BD^2$, and so *BC* = *BD*, the part to the whole, which is impossible. Also it cannot be that *BD* [or its equal *BM*] is equal to *EB* and also that *AE* > *EB* or *AE* > *MB*. For, since *BC* is the mean between *AE* and *EB*, $BC^2 = AE \cdot EB$ and thus BC^2 is equal to the product of a greater and a greater, which is impossible, for each of *AE* and *EB* is greater than *BC*. Therefore, let *BM* fall this side of *E* and let it be less than *EB*. And so let there be made on *AB* rectangle *BNQPA* with the latitude *MB*. And with line *MR* erected, since line *BM* < line *EB* and line *EF* > [line] *BN*, therefore [lines] *GF* and *BN* [produced] meet at *T*. With line *MR* produced to *Z*, so rectangle *AMR* > [rectangle] *AEF*. Proof: *CD* / *BD* > *BD* / *AB* [by hypothesis]. Therefore by [inverting and] converting [the expression], *AB* / *DB* > *BD* / *CD*. Therefore $AB \cdot CD > BD^2$, i.e., $AB \cdot CD > MB^2$. But $AB \cdot CD$ = [rectangle] *CD'*.[2] But the surface [*AN*] is completed and the square of *MB* is *MN*. Therefore [rectangle] *CD'* > *MN*. But surface *ABCD* [i.e. $AB \cdot BD$] is equal to rectangle *AN*; therefore [rectangle] *AR* > [rectangle] *AC*. Therefore [rectangle] *AF*, equal [to rectangle *AC*], is less than the same [rectangle *AR*]. Therefore with the common [area *AQ*] subtracted, [rectangle] *ER* > [rectangle] *PF*. Therefore [rectangle] *RT*, the supplement equal [to *ER*], is greater than [rectangle] *PF*. Therefore line *RN* > [line] *PQ*. Therefore [line] *BM* is also

Prop. 20

[1] See the discussion of this proposition in Chap. 2 of Part II, above. Notice that here the author represents rectangles by three letters, as here by *AEF* and later in the proof by *AMR*. This is essentially the naming of rectangles by their determining sides. In one case he uses four letters *ABCD*. He also uses the method of representing a rectangle by the letters at opposite angles of the rectangle, e.g. *AN*, *PF*, *ER*, *RT*, etc.

[2] The older text of MSS *E*, *Br*, and *M* is corrupt here, where it assumes the supplementary rectangle is *BD*. I have changed it to *CD'* and added that supplementary rectangle to rectangle *ABC*.

greater then [line] *AE*; and so, if it is less than one of the segments, it is greater than the remaining [segment]. [Q.E.D.].

21. (=*VL* II.8). WITH A POINT MARKED IN ANY ONE OF THE SIDES OF A TRIANGLE, TO PRODUCE A LINE FROM IT WHICH BISECTS THE TRIANGLE.

Let the triangle be *ABC* [see Fig. P.21] and the given point be *D* in side *AB*, to whose midpoint let line *CE* be drawn from angle *C*, and also let line *CD* be connected. Then from *E* let *EG* be drawn parallel to line *DC*, and let *G* be connected to *D*, letting [the line so drawn] cut *EC* at *T*. Therefore, because tri. *CDE* = tri. *DGC*, with the common [area] subtracted tri. *ETD* = tri. *GTC*. Therefore, with equals added, surface [*ADGC*], which line *DTG* cuts off, will be equal to triangle *EAC*, which [latter] is one half of the whole triangle, for *EC* bisects the triangle, and this is what has been proposed.

22. (=*VL* II.13) WITH A TRIANGLE GIVEN AND A POINT MARKED OUTSIDE [OF THE TRIANGLE], TO DRAW A LINE PROCEEDING THROUGH THE POINT WHICH BISECTS THE TRIANGLE.[1]

Let the triangle be *ABC* [see Fig. P.22], and let the point *D* be taken outside of the triangle between lines *AEF* and *HBL*, which lines bisect [two] sides of the triangle and the triangle itself, and [let that point be] as far outside as you like. For if the point were to fall on one of those [lines], the conclusion would be given by inspection. Therefore, with the point placed between those [lines], let us draw from this [point] a line parallel to line *AC* until it meets with *CB*, however far that line need be extended, and let the point of juncture be *G*. And let line *DC* produce a triangle which is related to triangle *AEC* (which is one half of the given triangle) as line *CG* is related to some [line], and let that [line] be *MN*. Also let *GC* be divided, by the argument of the 14th [proposition of this work], into *GK* and *KC* so that *GK* / *KC* = *KC* / *MN*, and let line *DK* be extended to meet line *AC* in *P*. And triangles *DGK* and *KPC* will be similar. And tri. *DGK* / tri. *KPC* = (*GK* / *KC*)², i.e., *DGK* / *KPC* = *GK* / *MN*. Also *GK* / *KC* = *DK* / *KP* because the triangles are similar, and *GK* / *KC* = *KC* / *MN* [for *MN* was so taken to satisfy the proportion]. Therefore, *DK* / *KP* = *KC* / *MN*. But *DK* / *KP* = tri. *DCK* / tri. *CKP*. Therefore, *KC* / *MN* = tri. *CKD* / tri. *CKP*. But it has been proved earlier that *GK* / *MN* = tri. *DGK* / tri. *CKP*. Therefore, whole line *CG* / *MN* = tri. *DCG* / tri. *CKP*. But, by hypothesis, [tri.] *DGC* / [tri.] *CEA* = *CG* / *MN*, and *CEA* is one half the given triangle. Therefore *CKP* is one half the given triangle. And this is what is proposed.

23. (=*VL* II.17) WITH A POINT GIVEN INSIDE A PROPOSED TRIANGLE, TO DRAW A LINE THROUGH THIS [POINT] WHICH BISECTS THE TRIANGLE.

Let a triangle be constructed that is described by the points *A*, *B*, and *C* [see Fig. P.23], and let the point included in it be *D*, [located] in the direction

Prop. 22
[1] See the discussion of this proposition in Chap. 2 of Part II.

of B between lines AG and BE that bisect the opposite sides and the triangle as well. And let line FDH be drawn through D parallel to line AC, and let line DB be connected. And let line BF / some line MN = tri. BDF / tri. BCE, and BCE is one half the given triangle. Also let BF / line TY = tri. BFH / tri. BCE. But FBH / $CBE > FBD$ / CBE. Therefore, BF / $TY > BF$ / MN. Therefore $MN > TY$. But BF / $BC = BC$ / TY because triangle BFH is similar to triangle BEC.[1] Therefore, BF / $BC > BC$ / MN. Therefore, by the 19th [proposition] of this [work], $FC < \frac{1}{4} MN$. And let line FZ be added to line FC so that ZF / $ZC = ZC$ / MN, by the 18th [proposition] of this [work], and $ZC < BC$ if one recalls to mind subtly what has been conceded before and also the proof given above in the 18th [proposition] of this [work]. And let line ZDK proceed through Z and D. Therefore, because tri. BDF / tri. $ZDF = BF$ / ZF,[2] and also tri. ZFD / tri. $ZCK = ZF$ / MN (since the triangles are similar),[3] therefore BF / MN = tri. BFD / tri. ZKC. But BF / MN = tri. [BFD] / [tri. BCE, and BCE] is one half the given triangle. Therefore triangle ZKC is also one half the same [given triangle], with the line proceeding through D bisecting [the given triangle], and this is what has been proposed.

24. (=VL II.18) TO DRAW FROM ONE POINT WITHIN A GIVEN TRIANGLE TO THE THREE ANGLES THREE [LINES] WHICH TRISECT THE TRIANGLE.[1]

Let the triangle be ABC [see Fig. P.24], and from one of the sides, BC, let a third part be cut off, namely CD. And let line DE be drawn parallel to AC. Let G be placed in the middle of DE, and let lines AD, AG, and CG be drawn. And because tri. AGC = tri. ADC, and triangle ADC is a third part of the given triangle (since its base is a third part of the [base of the] whole [triangle]), [so triangle] AGC will be a third part of the same [given triangle]. And so with line GB drawn a triangle GEB is produced which will be equal to triangle GBD since the bases are equal. And also triangles GEA and GDC

Prop. 23

[1] By similar triangles, $(BF$ / $BC)^2$ = tri. BFH / tri. BEC. But TY was assumed so that tri. BFH / tri. $BEC = BF$ / TY. Therefore BF / $TY = (BF$ / $BC)^2$ and hence BF / $BC = BC$ / TY.

[2] Tri. $BDF = \frac{1}{2} h_1 \cdot DF$ and tri. $ZDF = \frac{1}{2} h_2 \cdot DF$, with h_1 and h_2 the altitudes of the triangles. Therefore tri. BDF / tri. $ZDF = h_1$ / h_2. But h_1 / $h_2 = BF$ / ZF, and so tri. BDF / tri. ZDF = BF / ZF.

[3] Tri. ZDF / tri. $ZCK = (ZF$ / $ZC)^2 = (ZC$ / $MN) \cdot (ZF$ / $ZC) = ZF$ / MN.

Prop. 24

[1] The proof is evident, but we should note that the first part of it is concerned with finding the point from which the three lines are drawn to the angles. This point is the center of gravity of the triangle, but Jordanus makes no mention of this. Hence Archibald is somewhat loose in the first part of his statement when he says that "Proposition 18 of Jordanus [i.e. II.18 of the longer version and P.24 of the *Liber philotegni*] is devoted to finding the centre of gravity of a triangle and it is stated in the form of a problem on divisions." See R. C. Archibald, *Euclid's Book on Divisions of Figures* (Cambridge, 1915), p. 23. I mention this because I do not want the reader to expect any Archimedean mechanical implications in Jordanus's treatment of the divisions of triangles such as are found in the propositions of Book I of *On the Equilibrium of Planes*. See my *Archimedes in the Middle Ages*, Vol. 2, pp. 116–24.

are equal because they are between parallel lines [and have equal bases]. Therefore tri. *AGB* = tri. *CGB*, and accordingly any one of these [three triangles] is one third of the whole [given triangle], and so from *G* three lines proceed to the angles and trisect the triangle, and this is what has been proposed.

25. (=*VL* II.19) FROM AN ANGLE OF AN ASSIGNED QUADRAN-GLE TO DRAW A LINE WHICH BISECTS ITS WHOLE SURFACE.[1]

Let the proposed quadrangle be designated by points *A*, *B*, *C*, and *D* [see Fig. P.25], and let lines *AGC* and *BGD* proceed through the opposite angles. Therefore, if *AG* = *GC*, tri. *BCD* = tri. *BDA* since *AG* / *GC* = tri. *ADB* / tri. *BCD*, which could be established by means of the partial triangles. But if it is posited that *GC* is greater than *AG*, let line *CE* equal to *AG* be cut off from *GC*. And so let *EL* be drawn parallel to *BG*, *L* having been fixed in line *DC*, and let *B* be connected to *L*. And because tri. *DBC* / tri. *LBC* = *DC* / *LC*, and *DC* / *LC* = *GC* / *CE* = *CE* / *AG*, and *GC* / *AG* = *CBD* / *ADB* by means of the partial triangles, [so] tri. *DBC* / tri. *LBC* = tri. *DBC* / tri. *ADB*. Therefore tri. *ADB* = tri. *LBC*. Therefore, with line *LD* bisected at *T* and with line *BT* drawn, since tri. *DBT* = tri. *TBL*, [so] also tri. *TBC* = surface *TDAB*, and so when *BT* is drawn it will bisect the quadrangle, and this is what has been proposed.

26. (=*VL* III.1) IF THREE PARALLEL LINES IN A CIRCLE INTER-CEPT ARCS THAT ARE EQUAL TO EACH OTHER THE [PERPEN-DICULAR] DISTANCE BETWEEN THE LONGEST [LINE] AND THE MIDDLE [LINE] WILL BE GREATER [THAN THE PERPENDICULAR DISTANCE BETWEEN THE MIDDLE LINE AND THE SHORTEST LINE], AND IT [I.E. THE LONGEST LINE] WILL INCLUDE WITH THAT [MIDDLE LINE] A GREATER SEGMENT OF THE CIRCLE.

Let lines *AB*, *CD*, and *EF* in the circle be parallel [see Fig. P.26], and let *AB* be longer than *EF*, and let *CD* be the middle line such that arc *AC* = arc *CE*. And therefore, because the alternate angles are equal, if lines are imagined as drawn from *A* to *D* and from *D* to *E*, the arcs in which those angles [*DAB* and *ADC*, and *CDE* and *DEF*] fall are equal, and so [arcs] *BD* and *DF* are equal to one another and are equal to the other [arcs *AC* and *CE*]. Therefore let lines *AC*, *CE*, and *AE* be connected. And because [line] *AC* = line *CE* (by reason of the arcs), and angle *ACD* > angle *DCE* (since the same [angle *ACD*] is in a greater arc), [so] *AG* > *GE*, *G* having been placed at the section of *CD* and *AE*. Therefore, with a perpendicular drawn from the center until it meets with *EF* in *H* and touches line *AB* in *L*, *LA* will be greater than *EH*, since they are halves of the wholes [*AB* and *EF*] and *AB* > *EF* by hypothesis. Because angle *A* and *E* [i.e. angles *CAG* and *CEG*] are equal and [angle] *ACG* > [angle] *GCE*, therefore [angle] *CGE* is obtuse. Therefore a perpendicular [from *E*] will fall between *A* and *L*. Moreover, with perpen-

Prop. 25
    [1] See the account of this proposition in Chap. 2 of Part II, above.

dicular EZT drawn, $ZT > EZ$, for AG / GE = TZ / ZE, by reason of parallelity. And so the first part is manifest. But the remaining [part] is [also] manifest after a perpendicular is drawn through EF with respect to the remaining sides.[1] And this is what has been proposed.

27. (=VL III.2) IF THE SAME ARC UNDERGOES SEVERAL [DIFFERENT] DIVISIONS, THE SUM OF THE CHORDS SUBTENDED BY THE EQUAL SEGMENTS [PRODUCED BY THE EQUAL DIVISION] OF THE ARC IS GREATER [THAN THE SUM OF THE TWO CHORDS SUBTENDING THE SEGMENTS PRODUCED BY ANY DIVISION OTHER THAN THE EQUAL DIVISION], AND THE CLOSER [THE TWO LATTER CHORDS] ARE TO THEM [I.E. TO THE EQUAL CHORDS] SO MUCH LONGER [IN SUM] ARE THEY THAN [ANY PAIR OF] MORE REMOTE [CHORDS IN SUM].[1]

Let the arc be AB and its equal division be at C, and let there be two other [divisions] the closer one at D and the farther one at E [see Fig. P.27], and let there be subtended chords AC, AGD, AHE, BGC, BHD, and BE. Because triangles AGC and BGD are similar and line AC > line BD, [so] will $AC + GC > BD + DG$. Therefore, since $(AC + CG)$ / GA = $(BD + DG)$ / BG, [so] $AC + CG + GB > BD + DG + GA$, by the last [proposition] of the fifth [book] of Euclid.[2] Whence the first part [of the proposition] is manifest. By similar reasoning you argue that $AD + BD > AHE + BE$, according to what is proposed.

28. (=VL III.3) IF EQUAL LINES CUT OFF ARCS IN UNEQUAL CIRCLES, THEY WILL CUT OFF LESS FROM THE LARGER [CIRCLE] AND MORE FROM THE SMALLER [CIRCLE.]

Let the designated circles be A the larger and B the smaller [see Fig. P.28], with A and B placed in the centers of these [circles]. And in circle A let the line be designated CD and the line equal to it in [circle] B be EF. From the centers let also lines AGT and BHK be drawn perpendicular to lines [CD and EF]. And with lines BE and AC drawn, since $EH = CG$, [so] $BH < AG$, for $AG^2 + GC^2 > BH^2 + HE^2$, by reason of AC^2 and BE^2 being equal to these sums respectively. And so let $GL = BH$; and, with LC drawn, it will also be equal to BE. But, with DL also drawn, it will be equal to LC. And

Prop. 26

[1] See the account of this proposition in Chap. 2, Part II, above. Notice that the proof of the second part of the proposition was omitted in the original version, no doubt because it is obvious. But MS Fa adds a proof (see the text above, var. lin. 18–19); "With lines FK, KD, and ET drawn, segment $ABDC$ will be greater than segment $DFEC$. Proof: TZ / ZE = rect. $TKPZ$ / rect. $ZPFE$. But $TZ > EZ$. Therefore the one rectangle is greater than the other rectangle. Then TZ / ZE = tri. TZC / tri. ZCE. Therefore tri. TZC > tri. ZCE. Even greater then is $TACZ$ than that triangle ZCE. Therefore, with equals added, namely segments AC and CE, the quadrangle plus the segment to which it is added is greater than the triangle plus the added segment. By a similar method for the other part of the figure that quadrangle $KBDP$ + seg. BD > tri. PDF + seg. FD. This leads [immediately] to what has been proposed."

Prop. 27

[1] See the account of this proposition in Chap. 2 of Part II, above.

[2] See footnote 3 to Prop. 9 above.

each of these is greater than LT, according to that [i.e. the seventh proposition] of Euclid in the third [book]: if from a point assigned in a diameter outside of the center, etc.[1] And so with a circle described about center L according to radius LC and with LT extended up to M according to the quantity of that [radius], then a circle equal to circle B will pass through [points] C, M, and D, and arc CMD = arc EKF, and arc CMD > arc CTD since it includes it, and [so] also [arc] EKF > arc CTD, and this is what has been proposed.

29. (=VL III.4) IF UNEQUAL LINES CUT OFF ARCS IN THE SAME CIRCLE, THE RATIO OF THE ARCS WILL BE GREATER THAN THAT OF THE CHORDS, WHILE THE RATIO OF THE SEGMENTS OF THE CIRCLES [CUT OFF BY THESE CHORDS] WILL BE GREATER THAN THE SQUARE OF THE RATIO OF THE CHORDS.

In circle of center A let there be drawn lines: BC the longer and DE the shorter, and let the diameter of it be GAH [see Fig. P.29]. Therefore let GAH / KL = BC / DE, and let its [i.e. KL's] circle be $KMNL$, with arc MN posited as similar to arc BC, and let chord MN be subtended. Proceed: GAH / KL = circumference / circumference, as is in the *Book on Curved Surfaces;*[1] and the ratio of circumference to circumference is that of [their] similar arcs and also of their chords, as is had in the *Book on Similar Arcs.*[2] Therefore GH / KL = BC / MN. Therefore permutatively GH / BC = KL / MN. But by hypothesis GH / BC = KL / DE. Therefore DE = MN. And because arc MN > arc DE from the preceding [proposition] and because line BC / MN = arc $[BC]$ / arc $[MN]$, [so] BC / DE < arc BDC / arc DE, for arc BDC / arc DE > arc BDC / arc MN, and so the first part [of the proposition] is manifest.

Also, because the ratio of similar [circular] segments is that of [their] circles, and the ratio of the circles is the square of the ratio of their diameters and therefore is the square of the ratio of the chords, [so] seg. BDC / seg. MN = $(BC / MN)^2$ = $(BC / DE)^2$. And because segment MN > segment DE, [so] seg. BCD / seg. DE > $(BC / DE)^2$, and this is what has been proposed.[3]

Prop. 28

[1] This is the beginning of the paraphrase of Proposition III.7 of the *Elements*. It is not exactly like the reading of any of the known versions of the *Elements* but seems most like the reading of the common text of the Adelard II and Hermann of Carinthia Versions (cf. MS Oxford, Bodleian, Auct. F. 28, viii r and Busard's *The Translation of the Elements of Euclid from the Arabic into Latin by Hermann of Carinthia (?)*, p. 58): "Si in diametro circuli punctus preter centrum signetur. . . ." Proposition III.7 in the Adelard I Version (MS Oxford, Trinity College 47, 167r) reads: "Si supra diametrum circuli punctus alius a centro assignatus fuerit. . . ." Furthermore the same proposition in the Gerard of Cremona Version (MS Paris, BN lat. 7216, 14v) reads: "Si super dyametrum circuli punctum signetur quod sit extra centrum . . ." and in the anonymous version from the Greek (MS Paris, BN lat. 7373, 20v) reads: "Si in circuli diametro sumatur punctus aliquis qui non sit centrum circuli. . . ."

Prop. 29

[1] See Chap. 2 of Part II, n. 10.

[2] *Ibid.*, n. 11 and n. 12.

[3] Notice that the segment cut off by chord BC is designated as BCD, that is the segment in the direction of D. In the longer version it is simply called the segment BC.

30. (=*VL* III.5) IF A DIAMETER ORTHOGONALLY CUTS TWO PARALLEL LINES IN THE SAME SEMICIRCLE, THE RATIO OF THE SEGMENTS WHICH THEY [I.E. THE PARALLEL LINES] CUT OFF FROM THE DIAMETER WILL BE GREATER THAN THAT OF THE ARCS WHICH ARE SUBTENDED BY THEM [I.E. THE PARALLEL LINES].

Let the diameter of a circle be *ABGD* [see Fig. P.30], while the parallel lines are *CBE* and *HGL*, which lines the diameter bisects and cuts orthogonally. I say, therefore, that *BGD* / *GD* > arc *CDE* / arc *HDL*. For let lines *EKD* and *EL* be drawn. Then [angle] *EDL* is obtuse because it falls in an arc greater than a semicircle. Therefore just as the fifth [proposition] of this [work] has been proved as in the *On Isoperimeters*,[1] so it can be proved here by sectors of a circle described according to line *LK* that line *EKD* / *KD* > angle *ELD* / angle *KLD*. Also angle *ELD* / angle *KLD* = arc *ED* / arc *HD*. Therefore *ED* / *KD* > arc / arc. But line *ED* / *KD* = *BD* / *GD*, by reason of parallelity. Therefore *BD* / *GD* > arc *ED* / arc *HD*; therefore *BD* / *GD* > arc *CDE* / arc *HDL*, the latter arcs being double the former arcs, and this is what has been proposed.

31. (=*VL* III.6) WITH TWO LINES [DRAWN] TANGENT TO A CIRCLE FROM THE SAME POINT, IF [TWO LINES] SHORTER THAN THOSE [TANGENTS] ARE TANGENT TO THE SAME CIRCLE, THE RATIO OF THE LINES OR OF THE SURFACES CONTAINED BY THESE [LINES] AND ARCS WILL BE GREATER THAN THAT OF THE ARCS.[1]

Let the center of the circle be *A* [see Fig. P.31] and let the longer lines tangent to the circle be *BC* and *BD* and the shorter [lines] be *HE* and *HF*. Then let lines *AC*, *AD*, *AE*, and *AF* be drawn to the points of contact, and also [let be drawn lines] *AB* and *AH*. Let [lines] *GC* and *LD*, equal to *HE* and *HF*, be cut off from *BC* and *BD*. With lines *AG* and *AL* drawn, and because *BC* / *GC* > angle *BAC* / angle *GAC* by the fifth [proposition] of this [work], and angle / angle = arc / arc, [so] tri. *BAC* / tri. *GAC* > arc / arc. Also, since tri. *AGC* = tri. *LAD*, and each [triangle] is one half of quadrangle *AFHE* and arc = arc, [so] quadrangle *ACBD* / quadrangle *AEHF* > arc *CD* / arc *EF*. But sector *ADC* / sector *AEF* = arc [*CD*] / arc [*EF*]. Therefore, similarly, residual surface *CBD* / residual surface *EHF* > [arc / arc], and this is what has been proposed.

Prop. 30

[1] See the account of this proposition in Chap. 2 of Part II above, where I mention that Jordanus holds that Prop. 5 can be proved for an obtuse-angled triangle as well as for a right triangle. Indeed in the *Liber de triangulis Iordani* the enunciation of Proposition 5 is modified to include an obtuse-angled triangle (see Prop. I.5 in the text of the *Liber de triangulis Iordani* in Part III below).

Prop. 31

[1] See the account of this proposition in Chap. 2 of Part II above.

32. (=*VL* III.7) IF TWO LINES [DRAWN] FROM THE SAME POINT ARE TANGENT TO A CIRCLE AND LINES EQUAL TO THEM ARE [DRAWN] TANGENT TO A LARGER CIRCLE, THEN [IN THE LATTER CASE] THEY INCLUDE A LONGER ARC OF THIS [CIRCLE].

Let the center of the larger [circle] be A and that of the smaller [circle] be T [see Fig. P.32], and let the lines tangent to the smaller [circle] be BC and BD and those equal to them tangent to the larger circle be HE and HG. Now let diam. of smaller circ. / diam. of larger [circ.] = CB / EL, EH having been extended to L. And from L let a tangent line LM be drawn. Also, from the centers let lines CT, TD, AE, AG, and AM be drawn. Then LE / HE = quadr. $AELM$ / quadr. $AEHG$, which can be had from a part of the preceding proof. But since quadrangles $AELM$ and $TCBD$ are similar by hypothesis, [so] $AELM$ / $TCBD$ = $(LE$ / $BC)^2$ = $(LE$ / $HE)^2$, HE being equal to BC. Therefore quadrangle $AEHG$ is a mean proportional between quadrangle[s] $AELM$ and $TCBD$. Also arc CD is similar to arc EM, for $AELM$ is similar to $TCBD$ and angle T = whole angle A [i.e. angle CTD = angle EAM]. And so TC or TD is less than AE or AM. [Then] TD and AM are as the cutting arcs CD and EM, and arc CD will be as if included by EM. Therefore, by the *Book on Similar Arcs*, EM and CD are similar arcs.[1] Therefore arc EM / arc CD = radius / radius = LE / BC = LE / HE. But LE / HE = $AEHG$ / $TCBD$. Therefore arc EM / arc CD = $AEHG$ / $TCBD$. But, as is had in the preceding [proposition], arc EM / [arc] EG < line EL / [line] EH, or arc EM / arc EG < $AEHG$ / $TCBD$.[2] Therefore EM / EG < EM / CD. Therefore EG > CD, and this is what is proposed.

33. (=*VL* III.8) WITH TWO CIRCLES TANGENT TO EACH OTHER, IF FROM THE POINT OF CONTACT A LINE IS DRAWN THROUGH BOTH OF THEM, IT WILL CUT OFF SIMILAR SEGMENTS FROM THOSE [CIRCLES].

Let the tangent circles be ABG and ACF [see Fig. P.33], and let line ABC be drawn to cut them, and let line AGF be drawn to proceed through their centers. And because angle GAC exists in both of them, [so] arc BG will be similar to arc CF. Therefore what remains of the semicircles, namely AB and AC, will be similar, and accordingly the segments of the circle will be similar, with lines BG and CF having been drawn. For if lines BG and CF are drawn, angle B and similarly angle C will be a right angle and thus lines BG and CF will be parallel. Therefore angle G = angle F. Therefore the arcs in which they fall will be similar, for the arcs beyond which they fall will be similar by reason of the parallels BG and CF. And this is what is proposed.

Prop. 32

[1] H. L. L. Busard and P. S. van Konigsveld, "Der *Liber de arcubus similibus* des Ahmed ibn Jusuf," *Annals of Science,* Vol. 30 (1973), p. 389: "[1] Ex eo quidem est quod accidit in arcubus similibus. Omnes namque geometre diffiniunt eos esse [similes] arcus qui angulos recipiunt equales," and so on.

[2] See my account of Proposition 32 in Chap. 2 of Part II above, where again I stress the importance of Proposition 5 to Jordanus' exposition of his geometric trigonometry.

34. (=*VL* III.9) IF A CIRCLE IS TANGENT TO ANOTHER [CIRCLE]
INSIDE AND FROM THE [POINT OF] CONTACT A LINE PROCEEDS
THROUGH THEIR CENTERS, THEN ANY LINE STANDING PER-
PENDICULAR TO IT [I.E. THE FIRST LINE] ON BOTH SIDES AND
PASSING THROUGH BOTH CIRCLES [PRODUCES THE FOLLOWING
CASES OF ARCAL INTERCEPTIONS]. [1] IF IT IS DRAWN INSIDE[1]
OF THE CENTER OF THE LARGER [CIRCLE]—WHETHER IT CUTS
THE OTHER [I.E. SMALLER CIRCLE] OR IS TANGENT TO IT—IT
WILL INTERCEPT FROM THE SMALLER [CIRCLE] TOWARD THE
[POINT OF] CONTACT LESS [ARCAL LENGTH THAN IT DOES FROM
THE LARGER CIRCLE]. [2] BUT IF IT [PROCEEDS] THROUGH THE
CENTER OF THE LARGER [CIRCLE] AND IS TANGENT TO THE
SMALLER [CIRCLE], IT WILL INTERCEPT THE SAME [ARCAL
LENGTH] FROM EACH [CIRCLE] [3] BUT CONTRARIWISE IF IT
[PROCEEDS] OUTSIDE [OF THE CENTER OF THE LARGER CIRCLE
AND IS TANGENT TO THE SMALLER CIRCLE[2] IT WILL INTERCEPT]

Prop. 34

[1] I have remarked in Chap. 3 of Part II above that Jordanus appears to have understood the word *infra* as "inside" in this treatise. In my text I have added in parentheses the word *intra*, implying that perhaps Jordanus originally used *intra* instead of *infra*, but I think (in view of the use of the latter in all of the manuscripts) it is more likely that Jordanus simply used *infra* everywhere when he meant *intra*. At any rate, that the meaning is surely that of *intra* is evident here from its contrast with *extra*.

[2] I have explained the significance of the phrases I have added to the third part of the enunciation in my account of this proposition in Chap. 2 of Part II above. As I suggested there such additions have to be supposed if the third case is taken as true. This reasoning is strengthened by the fact that after the proof of the third case (described in the proof with just the conditions I have added to the text of the enunciation) Jordanus has added the phrase with which proofs are customarily ended, "et hoc est quod proponitur" (see line 44). The fourth case that follows in lines 45–51 is not included in the enunciation. This may mean that Jordanus had found the enunciation elsewhere and then thought of this fourth as an additional case that ought be considered. Or it may mean that Jordanus himself discovered the theorem and that someone else added the fourth (and indeed fifth) case shortly after the time of the proposition's original composition. The fourth case holds that if the secant perpendicular proceeds through the center of the larger circle (as indicated by *EG* in Fig. P.34e) it will cut more arcal length from the larger circle than from the smaller. The proof is sound and need not be pursued further. We should note however that in this fourth case the secant perpendicular has been directed through the center of the larger circle as in the second case but that it here cuts the smaller circle rather than being tangent to it as it was in the second case. A fifth case is briefly given (see lines 52–53). There the secant perpendicular is directed below the center of the larger circle as in the third case but allowed to cut the smaller circle rather than being tangent to the smaller circle as it was in the third case. The author does not tell us the relative arcal interceptions from the two circles in this fifth case. And it is just as well that he did not, for the relative intercepts change as we move *E′G′* down between points *M* and *C*. It is obvious that when *E′G′* is at *M* in the beginning we have the fourth case and thus it intercepts more arcal length from the larger than the smaller circle. It is also obvious that at the end of its motion when *E′G′* passes through *C* we have the third case and thus it intercepts more arcal length from the smaller than the larger circle. And so it is evident that as *E′G′* moves between the limits of *M* and *C* it passes through some point before which it intercepts more from the larger circumference and after which it intercepts more from the smaller circumference.

ALWAYS GREATER [ARCAL LENGTH FROM THE SMALLER CIR-
CLE THAN FROM THE LARGER].

Let the tangent circles be *ABCD* and *AEFG* [see Fig. P.34a], and let *ACF*
be drawn by proceeding through their centers *M* and *N*, and let line *EBDG*,
cutting the smaller circle, proceed perpendicularly [to *ACF*] between *M*, the
center of the larger circle, and *A*, and let line *KLT* parallel [to *EBDG*] be
drawn so that if a line were extended from *E* to *A* it would proceed through
K and *KLT* would be in the smaller circle and cut off arc *KAT*. And so arc
EAG / arc *KAT* = line *ZA* / [line] *LA* which is manifest by [Proposition]
VI.2 of Euclid and by the preceding [proposition] of this [work]. But *ZA* /
LA > arc *BAD* / arc *KAT*, by the proposition that is the fourth from this
one [i.e. by Proposition 30 of this work]. Therefore arc *EAG* / arc *KAT* > arc
BAD / arc *KAT*. Therefore arc *EAG* is greater [in length] than [arc] *BAD*.

Also let the perpendicular be one that proceeds between *M* and *A* and is
tangent to the smaller circle [see Fig. P.34b]. Therefore *EAG* will be less than
a semicircle. Moreover let a similar arc be assumed from the smaller circle
and thus that [arc] will be less than a semicircle [i.e. semicircumference].
Moreover let that arc be called *KAT*, and let the center of the smaller circle,
as before, be *N*. And so *NA* / *LA* > semicircum. [of smaller circ.] / arc *KAT*.
Therefore 2*NA* / *LA* > whole circum. [of small. circ.] / arc *KAT*. Or *CA* /
LA > circum. [smaller circ.] / arc *KAT*. But *CA* / *LA* = arc *EAG* / arc *KAT*.
And so arc *EAG* > whole circum. [of circ. *AC*].

Further, let *EMG* be one that proceeds through the center of the larger
[circle] and is tangent to the smaller one [see Fig. P.34c]. Therefore the
semicircle [i.e. semicircumference] of the larger [circle] will equal the [cir-
cumference of the] smaller one. For diam. *AF* / diam. *AM* = circum. /
circum. But the [one] diameter is double the [other] diameter. Therefore the
[one] circumference is double the [other] circumference. Therefore the half
[of the circumference of the larger circle] is equal to the circumference of
the smaller [circle], and [so] arc *EAG* is equal to the circumference *ACMD*.

Again, let *ECG* be outside [of the center *M*] while cutting the larger [circle]
and being tangent to the inside circle [see Fig. P.34d]. I say that [the circumference of] the interior circle is greater than the arc toward the point of
contact whose chord is *ECG*. Therefore let line *BMD* be drawn through the
center *M* and cut both circles. Then *MF* / *CF* > semicircum. [of circ. *AF*]
/ arc *EFG*. Therefore *CF* / *AF* < arc *EFG* / whole circum. [of circ. *AF*].
Therefore disjunctively *CF* / *CA* < arc *EFG* / arc *EAG*. Therefore conjunctively *FA* / *CA* < whole circum. [of circ. *FA*] / arc *EAG*. But *FA* / *CA*
= circum. of larger [circle] / [circum. of] smaller [circle]. Therefore [circum.
of] larger [circle] / [circum. of] smaller [circle] < circum. of larger circle /
arc *EAG*. Therefore the circum. of the smaller [circle] > arc *EAG*, and this
is what is proposed.

Thereafter let *BMD* be one that proceeds through the center of the larger
[circle] and cuts the smaller one [see Fig. 34e]. The arc of the smaller [circle]
will be less [in length] than the semicircle [i.e. semicircumference] of the

larger one. But this is manifest if a [third] circle is described according to [a diameter that is] half of diameter *AF*, namely *AM*. For then that circle [i.e. circumference] will be equal to the semicircle [i.e. semicircumference] of the larger [circle], as has been proved in the third part of this proposition. But arc *BAD* would be less [in length] than that [circumference of circle *AM*], as has been proved in the preceding part of this proposition. Therefore arc *BAD* is less than the semicircle [i.e. semicircumference] *EAG* of the larger [circle].

Finally, call *M* the center of the larger [circle] and let it [i.e. the perpendicular] proceed under *M*, i.e. outside [of *M*], and cut circle *AC* [see the line *E'G'* in Fig. 34e], and prove [it] by the aforesaid method.

35. (=*VL* III.10) WITH [ONE] CIRCLE TANGENT TO ANOTHER ON THE INSIDE, (1) A LINE DRAWN FROM THE CENTER OF THE LARGER [CIRCLE] THAT TRAVERSES BOTH [CIRCLES] AND [THUS PROCEEDS] BEYOND THE [POINT OF] CONTACT WILL INTERCEPT, IN THE DIRECTION OF THE [POINT OF] CONTACT, AN ARC SHORTER [IN LENGTH] FROM THE INTERIOR [CIRCLE THAN FROM THE LARGER CIRCLE] IF IT [I.E. THE INTERIOR CIRCLE] IS DRAWN [TO CUT THE DIAMETER OF THE LARGER CIRCLE] OUTSIDE THE CENTER [OF THE LARGER CIRCLE]. (2) [IT WILL INTERCEPT] AN EQUAL [ARCAL SEGMENT FROM BOTH CIRCLES] IF [THE INTERIOR CIRCLE IS DRAWN TO CUT THE DIAMETER] AT THE CENTER [OF THE LARGER CIRCLE]. (3) BUT IF [THE INTERIOR CIRCLE CROSSES THE DIAMETER] INSIDE [THAT CENTER, THE SECANT INTERCEPTS] MORE [ARCAL LENGTH FROM THE INTERIOR CIRCLE THAN FROM THE LARGER ONE].[1]

Let the circles *ABC* and *ADE* be tangent as before, and let *AFEC* be the diameter and *F* the center of the larger [circle]. And let line *FDB* proceed [as indicated in Fig. P.35]. Let *A* be connected to *D* and the line extended to *G*, *G* having been placed in the circumference of the larger circle, and let line *FG* be drawn. Therefore if [as in Fig. P.35a] the interior circle is drawn outside of *F*, [then] $AD > GD$. Therefore let the perpendicular *FZT* fall upon *AG*. And since the ratio of the angles is the same as that of the arcs, line *ZDG* / [line] $DG <$ arc *TG* / arc *BG*, and therefore whole line *ADG* / [line] $DG <$ arc *AG* / [arc] *BG*, and by [successive disjunction,] inversion, [and conjunction,] line *AG* / [line] $DA >$ arc *AG* / [arc] *BA*.[2] But arc *ABG* / arc $AD =$ line *AG* / line *AD*, since they are similar. Therefore arc $AB >$ arc *AD*.

If the interior [circle] proceeds through center *F* [see Fig. 35b], then [arc] *AF* will be a semicircle [i.e. semicircumference] and *D* will be a right angle

---

Prop. 35

[1] See the account of this proposition in Chap. 2 of Part II above.

[2] The argument is as follows: (1) line *AG* / line *DG* < arc *AG* / arc *BG*. (2) line *DA* / line *DG* < arc *AB* / arc *BG*, by disjunction of the ratios. (3) line *DG* / line *DA* > arc *BG* / arc *AB*, by inverting the ratios. (4) line *AG* / line *DA* > arc *AG* / arc *AB*, by conjunction of the ratios.

and $AD = DG$, and [arc] ABG / [arc] ACD = [line] AG / [line] AD. Therefore [arcs] AB and ACD are equal [in length].

But if it [i.e. the interior circle proceeds] within the center [F], [then] DG > DA, [see Fig. P.35c], and the perpendicular FZT will fall between D and G, and arc TBA / [arc] BA > [line] ZDA / [line] DA, and similarly whole arc GBA / [arc] BA > line GDA / [line] DA. But arc GBA / arc DA = line GA / [line] DA. And so arc GA / [arc] BA > [arc] GA / [arc] DA. And so [arc] BA is less [in length] than [arc] DA, according to what we intend.

36. (=*VL* III.11) IF [ONE] CIRCLE IS TANGENT TO [ANOTHER] CIRCLE ON THE INSIDE, THE LINE DRAWN FROM THE CENTER OF THE SMALLER [CIRCLE] THAT CUTS BOTH [CIRCLES] WILL, IN THE DIRECTION OF THE [POINT OF] CONTACT, CUT OFF AN ARC GREATER [IN LENGTH] FROM THE LARGER OF THEM.

Let the tangent circles be AB and AD [see Fig. P.36] and let line ACB proceed [as indicated] with [point] C placed in the circumference of the smaller circle, and let the center of the same be E, and let lines EA, EDB, and EZT be drawn, the last line being perpendicular to ACB, and EB > EA. [Then] BZ / ZA > angle BEZ / angle AEZ, by the sixth [proposition] of this [work],[1] and therefore BZ / ZA > [arc] DT / [arc] TA. So also whole line BZA / [line] ZA > arc DTA / arc TA. And because arc AB is similar to arc AC, [arc] AB / [arc] AC = chord ACB / chord AZC, by the *Book on Similar Arcs*.[2] Therefore, if you remember what has gone on before, arc AB / [arc] ATC > [arc] AD / [arc] AC. Therefore arc AB > arc ATD, and this is what we have proposed.

37. (=*VL* III.12) GREATER IS THE DIFFERENCE BETWEEN THE SURFACES WHICH ARE CONTAINED BETWEEN ARCS THAT EQUALLY EXCEED ONE ANOTHER AND LINES TANGENT [TO THESE ARCS] [I.E., THE DIFFERENCE BETWEEN THE FIRST AND THE SECOND SURFACE IS GREATER THAN THAT BETWEEN THE SECOND AND THE THIRD SURFACE, AND SO ON], JUST AS INDEED GREATER IS THE DIFFERENCE [OR DISTANCE] OF THE TANGENT LINES.[1]

In the first place let the greatest arc be AB [see Fig. P.37] with tangent lines AC and CB, and let the middle [arc] be DB with one tangent DE [and

---

Prop. 36

[1] See the account of this proposition in Chap. 2 of Part II above. Notice once more the importance of Proposition 5, from which Proposition 6 flows. It is Proposition 6 that is used in this proof.

[2] Busard and van Koningsveld, "Der *Liber de arcubus similibus*," p. 399, Prop. 5. Prop. 5 tells us that the ratio of the chords of similar arcs is as the ratio of the diameters of the circles including the similar arcs. But the ratio of the diameters is as the ratio of the circumferences, and the ratio of the similar arcs is as the ratio of the circumferences. Hence the ratio of the chords is as the ratio of the similar arcs.

Prop. 37

[1] See the account of this proposition in Chap. 2 of Part II above.

the other *BE*], and let the smallest arc be *BF* with one tangent *FG* [and the other *BG*], and from the angles at the center let lines *CHZ*, *ELZ*, and *GMZ* proceed, which lines will bisect the given arcs [*AB*, *DB*, and *FB*]. And therefore, because arcs *AD* and *DF* are equal and because line *EZ* > [line] *GZ*, [so] line *CE* > *EG*, since angle *CZG* is bisected. Therefore the first part [of the proposition] is manifest, namely that the difference or distance from *AC* to *DE* is greater than the distance from *DE* to *FG*, for *CE* > *EG*, which lines he (the philotechnist?) here calls the distances of the tangents.[2]

The second part is manifest by supposition, for it is supposed, with *AD* and *DF* equal, that *DE* is beyond [i.e. is inside of] *AC* and *FG* is beyond [or inside of] *DE*; and since the angles of contingence are equal, [so] *ADEC* > *DEFG*.

38. (=*VL* IV.1) WITH [ONE] CIRCLE DESCRIBED ABOUT A FIGURE OF UNEQUAL SIDES AND ANOTHER CONSTRUCTED INSIDE, IT IS IMPOSSIBLE FOR THEM TO HAVE THE SAME CENTER.

Let the non-equilateral [figure] *ABG* be inscribed in circle *A* [see Fig. P.38] and circumscribed about circle *C*, and let [point] *C* be where line *AB* is tangent to the interior circle, and let the center of the interior circle be *D*. Therefore, with lines *DA*, *DC*, and *DB* drawn, if *D* is posited as [also] the center of the exterior [circle], then since [in this circumstance] *DA* = *DB*, [so also] *BC* = *CA*. Therefore, with lines drawn to the remaining points of contact and to the angles, you will argue that all the sides bisected at the points of contact are equal, and also that their halves are equal since all the lines to the points are equal, and thus all the sides will be equal,[1] which is against the hypothesis.

39. (=*VL* IV.2) OF TRIANGLES DESCRIBED IN CIRCLES ON THE SAME BASE, THE ONE WHOSE REMAINING SIDES ARE EQUAL IS THE MAXIMUM, AND [THE ONES WHOSE REMAINING SIDES] ARE BY A CERTAIN AMOUNT CLOSER [I.E. WHOSE APEXES ARE CLOSER TO THE APEX OF THE ISOSCELES TRIANGLE] ARE BY THAT AMOUNT GREATER THAN THOSE [WHOSE APEXES] ARE FARTHER [FROM THE APEX OF THE ISOSCELES TRIANGLE].

Let triangle *ABC* whose remaining sides are equal be on the base *AB* within a circle [see Fig. P.39], and [on the same base] let there be triangle *ABD* whose sides are unequal, with *D* placed [on the circumference] between *A* and *C* and with line *AC* cutting *BD* at *H*. And so it is evident that triangle

---

[2] The subject of *dicit* in this clause is a puzzle. I have suggested in parentheses "the philotechnist" by which I mean "the lover of geometrical art," that is, the expert in geometry. But it perhaps refers rather to the author of some fragment translated from the Arabic which Jordanus used as his source for this proposition and in which the term *distantia* was used in this rather unusual sense. At any rate, when Jordanus uses *hic* ("here") in this clause the reference is no doubt to its earlier use in line 11 of this proposition (see the Latin text above).

Prop. 38

[1] See the account of this proposition in Chap. 2 of Part II above.

AHD and triangle *BCH* are similar.[1] And because *BC* > *AD*, [each of] these being [one of] the remaining sides [of the triangles], [so] triangle *BCH* > triangle *AHD*. Then with the common [triangle *AHB*] added [to each of the triangles] triangle *ACB* > triangle *ADB*. The second part [of the proposition] will also be evident by the same reasoning.

40. (=*VL* IV.3) OF THE TRIANGLES WHICH EXIST IN A CIRCLE ON ITS CENTER, THE MAXIMUM IS THE RIGHT [TRIANGLE]. MOREOVER IN THE CASE OF OBTUSE-ANGLED [TRIANGLES] BY THE AMOUNT THAT THE OBTUSE ANGLE IS GREATER, AND IN THE CASE OF ACUTE-ANGLED [TRIANGLES] BY THE AMOUNT THAT THE ACUTE ANGLE IS LESS, SO IN SUCH AN AMOUNT WILL THIS TRIANGLE BE LESS BY THIS REASON: EVERY OBTUSE-ANGLED [TRIANGLE] AND ACUTE-ANGLED [TRIANGLE] WHOSE ANGLES ARE AT THE CENTER OF THE CIRCLE AND IN WHICH THE PERPENDICULAR DRAWN FROM THE CENTER TO THE BASE OF THE ONE WILL BE EQUAL TO HALF THE BASE OF THE OTHER— THESE TRIANGLES, I SAY, ARE EQUAL.[1]

Let the center of the circle be *A* [see Fig. P.40], and the right triangle *ABC* and the other [triangle] *ABD* with line *AB* drawn from the center common to both triangles. Then let perpendiculars be drawn to the bases [of the triangles], *AE* on *BC* and *AH* on *BD*. Therefore, with a center also placed in the middle of *AB* [at *Z*], let a circle be drawn through *E*, which (since it is a right angle) will fall in the semicircle [i.e. lie on the semicircumference]. This circle will also go through *A*, *H*, and *B*. By the first of the first of this [work],[2] it is manifest that *AE* and *EB* are equal, the right angle [at *A*] having been bisected [by *AE*]. Therefore, by the preceding [proposition] triangle *AEB* > triangle *AHB*. Wherefore the double [namely triangle *ABC*] > the double [namely triangle *ABD*], according to what we intend.[3]

41. (=*VL* IV.5) ANY TWO OPPOSITE SIDES OF ANY QUADRILATERAL CIRCUMSCRIBED ABOUT A CIRCLE ARE [TOGETHER] EQUAL TO THE REMAINING [SIDES] TAKEN TOGETHER.

Let the quadrilateral be *ABDC* tangent to a circle in points *E*, *F*, *G*, and *H* [see Fig. P.41] so that *E* is in line *AB*, and *EB* = *BF* and *FD* = *DG*. Therefore *EB* + *DG* = *BD*. Similarly *AE* + *GC* = *AC*. Therefore *AC* + *BD* = *AB* + *DC*, according to what is proposed.

Prop. 39

[1] The triangles are similar because of the equality of the angles *H* in each triangle and the equality of the angles at *D* and *C*, those angles being subtended by equal arcs.

Prop. 40

[1] See the account of this proposition in Chap. 2 of Part II above.

[2] I have discussed in Chap. 3 of Part II above the significance of this single case of a passage in MS *E* that might reflect a division of the *Liber philotegni* into books.

[3] For additional proof in MS *Fa*, see the text above, var. lin. 14–17.

42. (=*VL* IV.6) ANY PARALLELOGRAM CONSTRUCTED ABOUT A CIRCLE IS EQUILATERAL.

Let the parallelogram be *ABCD* [see Fig. P.42], and *AB* + *CD* = *BC* + *AD* [by the preceding proposition]. But *AB* = ½ (*AB* + *CD*) because *AB* = *CD* [from the fact that *ABCD* is a parallelogram]. But also *BC* = ½ (*BC* + *DA*). Since the totals are equal and the halves are equal, therefore *AB* = *BC*. Therefore the individual sides are equal to the individual sides,[1] and this is the intention of the demonstration.

43. (=*VL* IV.7) WITH A TRIANGLE CONSTRUCTED IN A CIRCLE, TO DESCRIBE A RECTANGLE EQUAL TO IT IN THE SAME CIRCLE.[1]

Let the triangle constructed in the circle be *ABC* [see Fig. P.43a], and let its side *AB* be bisected at point *E*, and let line *DEC* go through [it] perpendicularly, and let *D* be connected to *A*, and let *EF* be drawn parallel to *AD*, and let line *FD* be drawn. Therefore triangle *EFD* = triangle *EFA*. Therefore triangle *DCF* = triangle *ECA*, which latter is half the given triangle. Also let line *FZ*, parallel to *CED*, proceed from *F* to the circumference, and let lines *CZ* and *DZ* be drawn. And this triangle, namely *CDZ*, will be equal to half the given triangle because *CFD* is equal to each of these triangles. But its angle *CZD* is a right angle since *DEC* is a diameter. Therefore if a right triangle *CGD* similar [and equal] to it is constructed in the other direction so that *GD* is parallel to *CZ*, [then] *CZDG* will be a rectangular parallelogram equal to triangle *ABC*.

But if *CE* is not perpendicular to *AB* [see Fig. P.43b] but diameter *DZ* is perpendicular to *AB*, let perpendicular *CH* descend from *C* on diameter *DEZ*, and *CH* will be parallel to *AB*, and let line *HA* be drawn, and triangle *AEH* = triangle *AEC*. Also with line *ZA* drawn and line *HL* parallel to it and line *ZL* drawn, triangle *ZLE* will be equal to the same [triangle *AEH* and thus to the latter's equal, *AEC*], for *ALH* and *ZHL* are equal, being on the same base between parallel lines. Then, as above, let *DL* be drawn, and *EM* parallel [to *DL*], *M* having been placed on line *ZL*; and, with *D* connected to *M*, triangle *DMZ* will be equal to the same [triangle *ZLE* and thus to its equal, *AEC*]. Then with *MN* parallel to the diameter *ZED* and with *DN* [and *ZN*] protracted, a right triangle *ZDN* will be formed and it is equal to half the given triangle. Therefore, with parallelogram *ZNDY* completed as before, that which has been proposed is manifest.

44. (=*VL* IV.8) BETWEEN ANY TWO SIMILAR REGULAR POLY-GONS ONE OF WHICH IS INSCRIBED IN A CIRCLE AND THE OTHER CIRCUMSCRIBED [ABOUT THE CIRCLE], THERE EXISTS AS A PRO-PORTIONAL MEAN A [REGULAR] POLYGON INSCRIBED IN THE SAME CIRCLE THAT HAS TWICE AS MANY SIDES.[1]

Prop. 42
    [1] That is, *AB* = *BC* = *CD* = *DA*.
Prop. 43
    [1] See the account of this proposition in Chap. 2 of Part II above.
Prop. 44
    [1] See the account of this proposition in Chap. 2 of Part II above.

Let [equilateral] triangle *ABC* be circumscribed about a circle with center *C* [see Fig. P.44] and let [equilateral] triangle *DEF* be inscribed [in it], applying the angles of the latter to the points of contact of the former. Therefore, with lines *ZD* and *ZHGA* drawn, let line *DF* be bisected at *H* and arc [*DF*] similarly at *G*. Triangle *ZDH* will be similar to triangle *ZDA*. And so let *D* be connected to *G* and a triangle *ZDG* will thus be formed. Therefore, because *ZA* / *ZD* = *ZD* / *ZH*, [so] *ZA* / *ZG* = *ZG* / *ZH* [*ZG* being equal to *ZD*]. Therefore triangle *ZAD* / triangle *ZDG* = triangle *ZDG* / triangle *ZDH*. With lines also drawn from *Z* to *B*, *Z* to *C*, *Z* to *E*, and *Z* to *F*, since the lines which are drawn to the exterior angles [i.e. the angles of *ABC*] bisect the arcs, [then] with chords extended in the individual half-arcs a hexagon may be formed which has twice as many sides [as the given triangles] and whose partial triangles existing on the individual sides you will argue by the aforesaid reasoning [concerning triangles *ZAD*, *ZDG*, and *ZDH*] are mean proportionals between the partial triangles of the given triangles. And so the whole hexagon will be the mean proportional between the triangles; and it is thus for other [regular] figures.

45. (=*VL* IV.9) IF REGULAR POLYGONS ARE INSCRIBED IN EQUAL CIRCLES, THAT WHICH HAS THE MORE SIDES WILL BE THE GREATER, AND THE RATIO OF IT [I.E. THE GREATER POLYGON] TO THE OTHER IS GREATER THAN THE RATIO OF ITS PERIMETER TO THE PERIMETER OF THE OTHER.

Let square *ABCD* be described within a circle [see Fig. P.45a], and let equilateral triangle *EFG* be described in another circle equal to the first circle [see Fig. P.45b]. Now let four lines be drawn from the angles of the square to the center of its circle, which let be *O*, and let three lines be drawn from the angles of triangle *GEF* to the center of its circle, which let be *T*. And the square will [thus] be divided into four equal triangles and the triangle into three. And because the individual sides of the triangle are greater than the individual sides of the square, so the ratio of three angles of the triangle to three angles of the square will be greater than that of three sides of the triangle to three sides of the square.[1] Therefore the ratio of three angles of the triangle to four angles of the square will be greater than three sides of the triangle to four sides of the square. Then since the ratio of one side of the triangle to one side of the square is less than that of an arc of the former to an arc of the latter, so also the ratio of the perimeter of the triangle to the perimeter of the square is less than that of the three arcs [of the former] to the four [arcs of the latter]. [Therefore perimeter / perimeter < circumference / circumference, and *a fortiori*] therefore triangle / square < circumference / circumference. But the one [circumference] is equal to the other. And so the triangle is less than the square, as we intend.

46. (=*VL* IV.11) IF [TWO] REGULAR POLYGONS ARE CIRCUMSCRIBED ABOUT EQUAL CIRCLES, THAT WHICH HAS THE FEWER

Prop. 45

[1] The argument is somewhat incoherently presented here, but the reader will be able to follow it in my account of this proposition in Chap. 2 of Part II above.

SIDES WILL BE THE GREATER, AND THE RATIO OF IT TO THE OTHER IS AS THAT OF ITS PERIMETER TO THE PERIMETER OF THE OTHER.

Let there be circumscribed about equal circles the equilateral triangle *ABC* [see Fig. P.46a] and the square *DEFG* [see Fig. P.46b], and from the centers of the circles, *H* and *L*, let lines be protracted to the angles and to the points of contact. With the triangle divided into three triangles and the square into four, all [of the partial triangles] will be of the same altitude since the lines to the points of contact are equal. But the bases of the partial triangles of the triangle [considered singly] are greater than the bases [of the partial triangles] of the square [considered singly] since the angles [of the partial triangles of the triangle] at the center [when considered singly] are greater [than the angles at the center of the partial triangles of the square when considered singly]. Therefore, since all [three triangles] of triangle / three triangles of square = all [three] sides of triangle / three sides of square, so [whole] triangle / square = perimeter of triangle / perimeter of square. But, since side of triangle / side of square > angle of side of triangle at center / angle of side of square at center,[1] and accordingly side of triangle / side of square > arc of side of triangle / arc of side of square, [so] three sides of triangle / three sides of square > three arcs [of sides of triangle] / three arcs [of sides of square]. Therefore all sides [of triangle] / all [sides of square] > all arcs [of triangle] / all [arcs of square]. [Therefore since perimeter of triangle / perimeter of square > all arcs / all arcs, and since area of triangle / area of square = perimeter of triangle / perimeter of square], therefore triangle / square > arcs / arcs. But the arcs [of the triangle] equal the arcs [of the square, the circles being equal]. Therefore the triangle is greater than the square, according to what is proposed.

[46+1.] (=*VL* IV.4) EVERY PARALLELOGRAM DESCRIBED IN A CIRCLE IS A RECTANGLE.

Let the parallelogram described in the circle be *ABCD* [see Fig. P.46+1]. Since its opposite sides are equal so also are their arcs. Therefore arc *AC* = [arc] *CA*. Therefore, when line *AC* has been drawn, it will be a diameter, and accordingly angles *B* and *D* will be right angles, and so also the remaining [angles *A* and *D* will be right angles]. Another proof. Angles *A* + *C* = [angles]

Prop. 46

[1] This results from Proposition 5, with the ratios altered conjunctively. The proof given in MS *Fa* (see the text above, var. lin. 19–20) follows: "That the ratio of the sides is greater than that of the angles at the center is proved. *BC* > *DE*; therefore ½ *BC* > ½ *DE*. Therefore let *BK* be cut so that *KS* = ½ *DE*, and *KP* is the other half. And from the center *Q* let lines proceed to *S* and *P*. Therefore because *BS* / *KS* > angle *BQS* / angle *SQK* [by Proposition 5 of this work], so *BK* / *KS* > *BQK* / *SQK* by conjunction. Therefore, it will also be so for the doubles [of *BK* and *KS* and their central angles], namely *BC* / *SP* > angle *BQC* / angle *SQP*. But angle *SQP* is a right angle [as is the central angle of *DE* at *L*] because *S*[*K* and] *KQ* are equal and accordingly each angle upon the base is half a right angle since *K* is a right angle, and by the same reasoning *KQP* is half a right angle. [Accordingly triangle *SQP*, as it lies, is completely equivalent to triangle *DLE*.] Hence that which was intended is evident."

$B + D$ since together they are equal to two right angles. But $A = C$ and $B = D$. Therefore any one of them is a right angle.

47. IF IN EQUAL CIRCLES ON EQUAL BASES TWO POLYGONS ARE CONSTRUCTED WHOSE SIDES ARE EQUAL IN NUMBER, THAT ONE WHICH HAS ALL OF ITS REMAINING SIDES EQUAL WILL BE THE GREATER.

Now we first propose that if two polygonal figures are inscribed in equal circles and the sides of one are equal to the sides of the other in whatever way the sides are arranged, then these [polygons] will also be equal.[1] With this assumed let there be described in equal circles quadrilaterals on equal bases AB and HL [see Fig. P.47], the quadrilateral whose remaining sides are equal being $ABCD$ and the other one $HLMN$. Therefore one of the sides of the latter will be greater than any one of the equal sides of the other. And since [on account of the initial proposal] the equality of the figure would not be changed thereby, let the greater side be LM, for if it were another side, that which ought to be joined to the base [for the purpose of the proof] would not be joined to the base. Therefore, with line HM drawn, let there be constructed on it a triangle to the circumference and let it be HMO, which will be greater than another [triangle HMN] and its sides [HO and OM] together with the side [LM] that is greater than the individual sides of $ABCD$ are greater [than the sum of sides HN, ON, and LM]. Then let lines EG and ZT [equal respectively to OH and OM] be drawn parallel to [lines] AD and DC in their circle, and let $HO = MO$. Also let PR be equal to AD and parallel to LM in its circle. Also let XY proceed parallel to each [of PR and LM] and bisect arcs LP and MR, and the individual half-arcs will be equal to arcs DG and DZ and [to the arcs] opposite them [namely to arcs AE and CT]. Therefore surface $LPRM >$ surface $ADGE +$ surface $DCTZ$. Therefore it is manifest that [circular] segments $LM + MO + OH >$ [circular segments] $AD + DC + CB$. Therefore quadrangle $ABCD >$ [quadrangle] $HLMO$. And so $ABCD > HLMN$, and it will be thus in all [such polygons].

48. IF TWO POLYGONS [HAVING THE SAME NUMBER OF SIDES] ARE DESCRIBED IN EQUAL CIRCLES, THE ONE EQUILATERAL AND THE OTHER NOT EQUILATERAL, THE EQUILATERAL [POLYGON] WILL BE THE GREATER.

Let the equilateral polygon $ABCDE$ be constructed in its circle [see Fig. P.48] and another [non-equilateral polygon] $FGHKL$ [in its circle]. And so some side of the latter will be greater than any side of the former, and let it [i.e. the greater side] be GH, and upon it let there be constructed a third polygon with just as many sides [as those of the other polygons] but whose

---

Prop. 47

[1] This preliminary proposal that two polygonal figures described in equal circles which have the same number of equal sides are equal regardless of the arrangement of the sides is introduced so that Jordanus may assume that side LM, which is longer than AD, can be placed so that it adjoins the base HL, as his argument requires. The proposition is discussed in Chap. 2 of Part II above.

remaining sides are equal [to one another] and this [third polygon] will be greater than prior [polygon *FGHKL*].¹ And let this third polygon be *GHMNO*. And so to four sides of *ABCDE* let there be subtended parallel lines that are also equal to the four equal sides of that [polygon] *GHMNO*, i.e. to [sides] *HM*, *MN*, *NO*, and *OG*. And to *GH* let there be subtended a line equal to *AB*. As in the preceding [proposition] we shall have exterior [circular] segments, i.e. of circle *GHMNO*, that are greater [in sum] than the [exterior] segments of circle *ABCDE*. Therefore polygon *ABCDE* > another polygon *GHMNO*. Therefore it [i.e. polygon *ABCDE*] > polygon *FGHKL*, and this was to be demonstrated. And it will be also demonstrated in a similar way in regard to other [polygons].

49. IF TWO POLYGONS WITH AN EQUAL NUMBER OF SIDES ARE CIRCUMSCRIBED ABOUT EQUAL CIRCLES AND ONE OF THEM IS A REGULAR POLYGON AND THE OTHER IS NOT, THE ONE WHICH IS REGULAR WILL BE THE LESS.¹

Let equilateral pentagon *ABCDE* be circumscribed [see Fig. P.49] and let its center be *O* and one of its points of contact [with its circle] be *Z*. And let another [circumscribed] pentagon be *FGHKL* which is not equilateral, and let its center be *V* and let two [of the latter's] points of contact [with its circle] be *M* and *N* [and let side *KH* be equal to side *AB*], and let *LE'*, *ML*, *GS*, and *GN* [each] be greater than *AZ* and any of the remaining [half-sides of *ABCDE*], while the remaining lines [*FM* and *FN* drawn from the] conjunctions [i.e. points of contact] to the angles of *FGHKL* are [each] less than them [i.e. the half-sides equal to *AZ*]. And so let lines *OA* and *OB* be drawn and also equal lines *OP* and *OQ* so that those lines which need to be less than [the half-sides of the regular polygon will be cut off]. And so let lines *E'V*, *FV*, *GV*, *VL*, *VR*, and *VT* be drawn. Let *MR* + *NT* = *AB*. Now since tri. *LVM* / tri. *RVM* = tri. *LVM* / tri. *AOZ* and tri. *NVG* / tri. *NVT* = tri. *NVG* / tri. *ZOB*, therefore tri. *LVR* / tri. *VRM* = tri. *LVR* / tri. *AOZ*, and tri. *TVG* / tri. *NVT* = tri. *TVG* / tri. *ZOB*, and tri. *FVM* / tri. *RVM* = tri. *FVN* / tri. *NVT* = tri. *POZ* / tri. *AOZ*, and *FVY* = *AOP* = *BOQ*, the ratio of the triangles at the center [in sum] is greater than the ratio of the angles of those [triangles] because the ratio of the individual triangles to the individual triangles [each] is greater [than the ratio of the angles of the individual triangles to the angles of the individual triangles, considered singly]. Therefore the three surfaces [*LE'VM*, *FMVN*, and *GNVS*] are [in sum] greater than [the sum of] three surfaces of the regular polygon each [equal to *BZOH'* and thus] double triangle *AOZ*, since the former [three surfaces] are double the triangles *LVM*, *FVM*, and *GVN*. Since the two remaining surfaces of the

Prop. 48
¹ This follows from Proposition 47. The argument of the whole proposition is given in Chap. 2 of Part II above.
Prop. 49
¹ I have discussed and expanded the proof of this proposition in Chap. 2 of Part II above. It represents a culmination of Jordanus' geometric trigonometry.

latter are upon [i.e. are equal to] the [two] remaining surfaces of the former, therefore the one [i.e. irregular polygon] is greater than the equilateral [polygon]. And it is thus in regard to all [such polygons].

50. IT IS POSSIBLE TO DESCRIBE ABOUT EQUAL CIRCLES EQUILATERAL FIGURES OF WHICH ONE OF MANY SIDES IS GREATER [THAN OR EQUAL TO (?) ONE OF FEWER SIDES].[1]

Except for a triangle [which cannot have more sides than another regular polygon] there can be assumed a regular polygon of fewer sides and then another polygon which has twice as many sides as an interior polygon. So that if a square is taken [as the first polygon], then the other polygon to be taken is a hexagon which has twice as many sides as a triangle. But if a pentagon is [first] taken, then either a hexagon or an octagon may be taken [as the second polygon].

For example, let square A be circumscribed about a circle [see Fig. P.50]. Also [let] a [regular] hexagon $BCDEFG$ [be circumscribed about an equal circle], and, with three sides protracted in both directions until they meet, a triangle may be formed which is KLM and the points of contact of it [with the circle will be] N, O, and P. Let Q be a third part of that by which the triangle exceeds the square, and let the [interior] triangle NOP be drawn. And let triangles NKR, OLS, and PMT be cut off, which triangles are equal to or (*del.* equal to or ?) less than Q. And from R, S, and T let tangents to the circle be drawn so that they meet with the sides of the hexagon, which lines are RH, SX, and TY. So we shall now have an equilateral hexagon $HRXSYT$, since $KR = LS = MT$, and the lines from the angles to the points of contact are equal. And it [i.e. the new hexagon] is circumscribed about the circle but is not equiangular and it is greater than [or equal to ?] the square since the triangles by which the triangle KLM exceeds it [i.e. hexagon $HRXYS$] are less than [or equal to ?] triple Q, which is the difference between the triangle and the square. Q.E.D.

51. TO CONSTRUCT ON A GIVEN SIDE OF A GIVEN TRIANGLE, EACH ANGLE OF WHICH GIVEN SIDE IS A RIGHT ANGLE OR LESS THAN A RIGHT ANGLE,[1] A SQUARE WHOSE REMAINING ANGLES ARE ON THE REMAINING SIDES OF THE TRIANGLE.

Let the given triangle be ABC [see Fig. P.51] and the given side AB, and let each of the angles on it [i.e. AB] be either a right angle or less than a right angle [but without both being right angles], for otherwise a line wherever erected on it perpendicularly does not touch a remaining side of the triangle. Therefore let perpendicular CD be erected on AB, and let $(AB + CD) / CD = AB /$ line E. Let line FGH, equal to E, be placed in the triangle parallel to AB. With the perpendiculars FM and HL dropped to AB, I say that $FHLM$

Prop. 50

  [1] See the account of this proposition in Chap. 2 of Part II above.

Prop. 51

  [1] That is, one of the base angles is a right angle and the other is acute, or both base angles are acute.

is a square. Since $(AB + CD) / CD = AB / E$, so $AB / CD = (AM + LB) / LM$. But $(AM + LB) / FM = (AM + LB) / HL = AB / CD$. Therefore $FM = ML$.[2] Therefore, since $FHLM$ is equilateral and rectangular, it is evident that it is a square.

52. IN EVERY RIGHT TRIANGLE THE SQUARE CONSTRUCTED ON THE HYPOTENUSE [AND TOUCHING THE REMAINING SIDES OF THE TRIANGLE] IS LESS THAN THE SQUARE WHICH IS DESCRIBED ON THE REMAINING SIDES [AND TOUCHES THE HYPOTENUSE].[1]

Let the right triangle be ABC [see Fig. 52] and the hypotenuse be AB, and on the latter square $DEFG$ is formed. And let there be described in a similar and equal triangle a square on both sides having an angle common with the triangle, which square let be H. I say, therefore, that $H > DEFG$. If in fact side EF is extended until it meets with side AC [extended] in M a triangle similar to triangle ABC and to triangle H will be formed. But also [formed] was a triangle [FCM] similar to triangle FEB. Because side $FG > FC$ [and $FG = FE$ and $FB > FE$, therefore $FB > FC$, and] therefore triangle EFB > triangle FCM. Consequently triangle ABC, as well as triangle H, is greater than triangle AEM. Therefore the square H [inserted into triangle H in similar fashion as square $DEFG$ is inserted into the smaller triangle AEM] will be greater than square $DEFG$. Q.E.D.

53. IN EVERY ACUTE-ANGLED TRIANGLE THE SQUARE WHICH IS DESCRIBED ON THE LARGEST SIDE [AND TOUCHES THE OTHER SIDES] IS LESS [THAN THAT ON EITHER OF THE SHORTER SIDES].

Let the [acute-angled] triangle be ABC [see Fig. P.53] and let square $DEFG$ be described on side AB, and in another equal and similar triangle let square H be constructed on AC, which is less than AB. Therefore let LFM proceed, with AC extended to L, so that triangle CLF is similar to triangle FMB and L falls beyond C. Also let FN be drawn perpendicular to AL, and it will fall between FC and FG, and triangle FNC will be similar to triangle FEM. And because $FG > FN$ and hence $FE > FN$, so also will $FM > FC$. And so triangle FMB > triangle FCL. Therefore the whole triangle ABC > triangle ALM. Hence also triangle H > triangle ALM. Therefore the square H [inserted in triangle H in the same way that square $DEFG$ is inserted in the smaller triangle ALM] will be greater than the square $DEFG$, as was proposed.[1]

54. THE RECTANGLE CONSTRUCTED ON THE SIDE OF A TRIANGLE BY APPLYING ITS [I.E. THE RECTANGLE'S] ANGLES TO THE MIDPOINTS OF THE REMAINING SIDES [OF THE TRIANGLE]

---

[2] See the account of this proposition in Chap. 2 of Part II above.

Prop. 52

[1] See the account of this proposition in Chap. 2 of Part II above.

Prop. 53

[1] This proof is similar to that of Prop. 52, and, needless to say, precisely the same kind of argument would be given if square H were constructed on the other short side BC. See the account of this proposition in Chap. 2 of part II above.

IS HALF THE TRIANGLE, AND THIS SAME [RECTANGLE] IS THE MAXIMUM OF ALL RECTANGLES DESCRIBED [ON THE SAME SIDE] IN THE SAME [TRIANGLE].[1]

Let the triangle be *ABC* [see Fig. P.54] and on *AB* let rectangle *DEFG* stand so that *BC* and *AC* are bisected at *F* and *G*. I say, therefore, that this rectangle is half the triangle. For, since $FG = \frac{1}{2} AB$ and $DE = AD + EB$, hence rectangle $DEFG = 2$ (tri. *ADG* + tri. *BEF*). And since tri. *ABC* = 4 tri. *FCG*, quadrangle *ABFG* = 3 tri. *FCG*. Therefore the rectangle is half of the whole triangle [for *ABC* / *ABFG* = 4/3 and *DEFG* / *ABFG* = 2/3, and hence *ABC* / *DEFG* = 2/1].

The rest [of the proposition] is as follows. Let another rectangle be constructed on *AB* below the triangle [*GCF*] and let it be *HLMN* so that *M* and *N* are below *F* and *G*, if one pleases. And let *HN* and *LM* be extended until they meet with *FG* [extended in both directions] so that the total rectangle *HLTZ* may be formed. And *HLTZ* / *DEFG* = *HL* / *DE* = *MN* / *FG*; therefore *HLTZ* / *DEFG* = *MC* / *FC*. And so *HLTZ* / *HLMN* = *TL* / *ML* = *FE* / *ML*. But *FB* / *MB* = *FE* / *ML*. And because *FM* / *FC* < *FM* / *MB*, [so] will *FC* / *MC* < *FB* / *MB*. Therefore *HLTZ* / *DEFG* < *HLTZ* / *HLMN*. And so *DEFG* > *HLMN*. But also if *M* and *N* fall above *F* and *G*, the argument will be the same.

55. WHEN THE SIDES OF ANY QUADRILATERAL HAVE BEEN BISECTED, THE LINES DRAWN THROUGH THE SECTIONS [I.E. MIDPOINTS] OF COTERMINAL SIDES FORM A PARALLELOGRAMMATIC SURFACE.

Let the quadrangle be *ABCD* [see Fig. P.55] and let the four sides be bisected at *E*, *F*, *G*, and *H*, and let the lines proceed [from these points as described]. I say that quadrilateral *EFGH* is a parallelogram. Let lines be drawn from *A* to *C* and from *B* to *D*. Therefore *EF* will be parallel to *AC* in triangle *ABC*, and also *GH* is parallel to the same [*AC*] in triangle *ADC*, since the sides of the triangles have been cut proportionally because they have been bisected. And so *FE* as well as *GH* is ½ *AC*. Therefore *EF* = *GH*. By the same reasoning *FG* and *EH* are parallel to *BD*, and the latter's halves are outside, and so they [i.e. *EH* and *FG*] are equal. Therefore, because the quadrangle *EFGH* has equal opposite sides, it will be a parallelogram.

56. IF WITHIN A PARALLELOGRAM ANOTHER IS CONSTRUCTED BY APPLYING ITS ANGLES TO THE MIDPOINTS OF THE SIDES OF THE OTHER, AND IF ANOTHER [I.E. A THIRD PARALLELOGRAM] IS DESCRIBED IN IT [I.E. THE SECOND PARALLELOGRAM], IT IS NECESSARY THAT THAT [THIRD PARALLELOGRAM] IS SIMILAR TO THE OUTSIDE [PARALLELOGRAM].

Therefore, if there is a parallelogram *ABCD* [see Fig. P.56] within which quadrangle *EFGH* is described by applying [its] angles to the midpoints of

Prop. 54
[1] See the account of this proposition in Chap. 2 of Part II.

the sides of the other [i.e. *ABCD*], and if in the latter [i.e. *EFGH*] a [parallelogram] *LMNR* is constructed [also by applying its angles to the midpoints of the sides of *EFGH*], therefore that last [parallelogram *LMNR*] is similar to the first [parallelogram *ABCD*]. Let *EG* and *FH* proceed. Therefore it is clear that $LM = NR = \frac{1}{2} FH$ and that $MN = LR = \frac{1}{2} EG$. Therefore $LM = \frac{1}{2} AB$ and $LR = \frac{1}{2} AC$. Also, because angle *MLR* and angle *BAC* each are equal to angle *BEG*, it having been posited that they will be in a common section and these are equal and the sides are proportional, [so] the parallelograms will be similar.[1]

57. TO PLACE WITHIN A GIVEN RECTANGULAR PARALLELO-GRAM AN EQUILATERAL [POLYGON] WHICH TOUCHES THE CIR-CUMSCRIBED QUADRILATERAL IN A GIVEN POINT OF EITHER OF ITS SHORTER SIDES.[1]

Let the rectangular parallelogram be *ABCD* [see Fig. P.57] with shorter sides *AB* and *CD*, and in *AB* let point *X* be fixed anywhere, and let $AX > XB$. Further let $AX^2 - XB^2 = YT^2$. Also let $BC \cdot Z = YT^2$. Let *BC* be cut into *BT* and *TC*, with $BT > TC$. And it is clear, therefore, that $BC \cdot BT > BC \cdot TC$ and that $BC \cdot BT - BC \cdot TC = BC \cdot Z = YT^2$. But $BC \cdot BT - BC \cdot CT = BT^2 - CT^2$. Therefore $BT^2 - CT^2 = YT^2$. Also let $AM = TC$ and $CN = AX$, and let quadrilateral *XTNM* be formed. But it is clear that $XM = TN$ and $XT = MN$. Therefore it [i.e. *XTNM*] is of parallel sides. Further, since $BT^2 - AM^2 = AX^2 - XB^2$ and $AX^2 + AM^2 = XM^2$ and $AX^2 + AM^2 = BX^2 + BT^2 = XT^2$, [hence $XM^2 = XT^2$, and] therefore $XT = XM$. Therefore quadrangle *XMNT* is equilateral, according as that which was required.

58. TO DESCRIBE A SQUARE WITHIN A REGULAR PENTAGON.

Let the pentagon be *ABCDE* [see Fig. P.58], and let line *EB* be drawn, and let lines *CFG* and *DHL* proceed perpendicularly to *EB*, which lines will be greater than *BC* and *DE*. But $FH = CD$. From *C* and *G* let there be added in opposite directions lines equal to *BF* and *HE* so that a straight line *MCFGN* results, which line is greater than *BE*. Therefore let *BE* be cut at *O* and *P* in the same proportion that line *MN* is cut at *G* and *C*, and *BP* will be less than *GN*, and therefore $BP < BF$ and $EO < EH$. And so from *O* and *P* let perpendiculars *RPX* and *TOY* proceed, and lines *RT* and *XY* are subtended by their termini. I say, therefore, that *RXYT* is a square. For [$GN / GC = BP / PO$ and] $NG / YX = FB / PO$ and $FB / PB = CG / RX$ since $GN = FB$ and by similar triangles. Therefore $OP = RX$. But $XY = RT = PO$. So, therefore, it is clear that it [i.e. *RXYT*] is equilateral. And there is no doubt that [its] angles are right angles and thus that it is a square.[1]

Prop. 56
  [1] See the different proof of a similar proposition by Witelo in his *Perspectiva,* Bk. I, Prop. 41 (S. Unguru, *Witelonis Perspectivae liber primus* [Wrocław etc., 1977], pp. 74, 238).
Prop. 57
  [1] See the account of this proposition in Chap. 2 of Part II above.
Prop. 58
  [1] See the account of this proposition in Chap. 2 of Part II above.

59. TO DESCRIBE A SQUARE WITHIN A REGULAR HEXAGON.

Around the same hexagon let a circle be described. And after the arcs by which the individual sides are subtended have been bisected and lines produced through the sections have been drawn, another hexagon cutting the first one may be produced. And let the points of the sections be *A, B, C, D, E, F, G, H, K, L, M,* and *N* [see Fig. P. 59]. Therefore let a line be drawn from *A* to *D*, and from *A* to *L*, and from *A* to *G*, and from *D* and *L* to *G*, and from *L* to *D*, and [so] a regular quadrilateral is formed. This will be proved by the triangles that stand on the sides of the hexagons, it having been proved that the individual sides are equally divided, and this [is proved] by means of the chords of half the arcs.[1]

60. TO PLACE AN EQUILATERAL TRIANGLE WITHIN A SQUARE OR A REGULAR PENTAGON.

An equilateral triangle will be constructed in a regular polygon in two different ways, for it may proceed from an angle [of the polygon] or from the middle of a side. For example [see Fig. P.60], if [it is to be constructed] from an angle, let a circle be circumscribed about the same pentagon, and within the circle let there be an equilateral triangle which goes out from an angle of the pentagon, and where its two sides that go out from the common angle cut the sides of the pentagon a line will pass that [also] encloses an equilateral triangle on account of the similarity of the triangles.[1] If [it is to be constructed] from the middle of a side, let a circle be inscribed in the same pentagon and an [equilateral] triangle in the circle. Then let two sides of it be produced from one of the points of contact until they cross through to the sides of the pentagon, and through the points of juncture let a line be directed, which line in a similar way yields an equilateral triangle.

61. IF AN EQUILATERAL TRIANGLE AND ANY OTHER TRIANGLE ARE OF EQUAL PERIMETER, THE EQUILATERAL TRIANGLE WILL BE THE GREATER.[1]

Let the equilateral triangle be *A* and the other triangle *BCD* [see Fig. P.61], and some one side of the latter is greater than any side of the other* [triangle], which greater side let be *BC*. Also let it [i.e. the greater side] be cut down to equality with any side of the other [equilateral triangle], so that it may become *EC*. And let [*DE* be extended to *F* so that] *BC / EC = FE / DE*, and let a line parallel to *BC* be drawn through *F*, and triangle *FCE* will be equal to the other triangle [*BCD*], and its [i.e. *FCE*'s] perimeter is less [than *BCD*'s perimeter], it having been posited that *DC* would be less than *EC* because it [i.e. *EC*] would exceed either it [i.e. *CD*] or *BD* [and the

---

Prop. 59
  [1] See the account of this proposition in Chap. 2 of Part II above.
Prop. 60
  [1] The proposition is given specificity by the diagram Fig. P.60, which I have added, and by the account that I give of this proposition in Chap. 2 of Part II above.
Prop. 61
  [1] See my elaboration of the proof in Chap. 2 of Part II above.

same argument would apply with either supposition]. Then let [point G be selected on the parallel through F so that] triangle EGC be made equal to triangle ECF [while side EG = CG]. But [since] sides EG and CG are equal to each other, therefore EG + CG < EF + FC. Therefore EG + CG is less than two sides of [triangle] A. Therefore let equilateral triangle EHC be placed on line EC, which triangle will be equal to A and will exceed triangle EGC (for otherwise it would either be equal to it or included in it, [either of] which is impossible since the two sides of that [triangle EGC] are less than two sides of the other [triangle EHC]). Therefore since it [i.e. EHC] will exceed that [CGE], it is clear that it is greater. Therefore it [i.e. EHC or its equivalent A] is greater than any of the remaining [equal triangles, and thus greater than triangle CBD, which has a perimeter equal to it].

*[Comment on alterius:][2] "[i.e.] the equilateral triangle." And if someone would contradict the supposition, evidently [by saying that] perhaps it might not also be greater than DC or equal [to it], then it therefore will be greater than another side, namely BD, since these sides BD, DC, and CB [together] equal the three sides of triangle A, and EC is equal to one of those [sides] of triangle A, and then add to line BD another [segment] so that it [i.e. the whole line extended] will be in the same ratio [to BD] that we have supposed BC is to EC, and understand the figure as being reversed.

62. EVERY SQUARE IS GREATER THAN ANY OTHER QUADRI-LATERAL HAVING A PERIMETER EQUAL TO ITS [PERIMETER].[1]

Let the square be A and the quadrilateral BCDE [see Fig. P.62], and let the latter's diagonal BD be drawn, and upon it let there be erected in the opposite directions two triangles BFD and BGD equal [respectively] to triangles BCD and BED, and let BF = FD and BG = GD. Therefore BF + FD < BC + CD and BG + GD < BE + ED [by Proposition 10]. Then let diagonal FG be drawn, and triangle FDG will be both equilateral and equiangular with triangle FBG. Let triangle FHG equal to triangle FDG be constructed on FG, with FH made equal to HG. Also FM is parallel to HG and MG is parallel to FH, and FM = MG, tri. FMG = tri. FHG, and tri. FDG = tri. FBG. Therefore parallelogram FHGM will be equilateral, and it will be equal to quadrilateral BCDE, while its [i.e. FHGM's] perimeter is less than the perimeter of the quadrilateral [BCDE]. Therefore if it [i.e. FHGM] is rect-angular*, it will also be a square, evidently [one] less than A, [and] indeed it is greater than another [i.e. any other] FHGM. [For] if it is not equiangular so it [i.e. FHGM] will be less than it [i.e., less than what it was when it was rectangular]. Therefore it is clear that the quadrilateral BCDE [equal to FHGM] will be less than square A, and this is what has been proposed.

---

[2] This comment was surely added by Jordanus or someone else after the completion of the original proposition since it was added in MS E on the inferior margin. In the later MS Br the comment was added to the text after maius in lin. 4, producing an awkward break in the proof. In the Latin text I have bracketed the whole comment of lines 15–20.

Prop. 62
[1] See my account of this proposition in Chap. 2 of Part II above.

*[Comment on "Therefore . . . rectangular" *et seq.*]²—by the fourth of the first book,³ and "by cutting and applying," i.e. by superimposing smaller sides on larger sides and [one of] the equal angles on [one of] the equal angles, which will be easily clear after cogitation [see Fig. P.62a, top figure]. If it is not rectangular, then [angle] *H* is greater than a right angle or less. If less, therefore, by the same argument with [Proposition] I.4, [it may be applied] geometrically to square [*FHG'M'*, in the second figure of Fig. P.62a], which square is greater than the quadrilateral *FHGM* [and thus *a fortiori* square *A* is greater than *FHGM*]. But if *H* is greater than a right angle, therefore the parallelogram *FHGM* cannot have at *F* a semi-right angle toward either *H* or *M*, with *FG* having been drawn from *G* to *F*. Therefore the whole angle [at *F*] is less than a right angle. And similarly *G* is less than a right angle. Then [proceed] as before with [Proposition] I.4, *FHGM* having been drawn [i.e. applied].

63. IF TWO REGULAR POLYGONS ARE BOUNDED BY THE SAME PERIMETER, THAT WHICH HAS MORE SIDES WILL BE GREATER.

For example, let *A* be a square and *B* a [regular] polygon having the same perimeter [see Fig P.63]. I say that the pentagon is the greater [in area]. For let circle *A* be inscribed [in the square] and let a [regular] pentagon [*A*] be circumscribed about this circle. Now we have it that square *A* / pentagon *A* = perimeter of sq. *A* / perim. of pent. *A* [by the second part of Proposition 46]. But pent. *B* / pent. *A* = (perim. of pent. *B* / perim. of pent. *A*)² [by VI.18 (=Gr. VI.20) of Euclid]. Therefore pent. *B* / pent. *A* > sq. *A* / pent. *A*. Therefore pentagon *B* is greater than square *A*.

But it is manifest that the square is proportionally constituted between the pentagons.¹

[Here] ends the Book of the Philotechnist by Jordanus, containing 64 (*!*) propositions. Thanks to God.

---

² The remark I have given in note 2 to Prop. 61 above applies equally to Prop. 62, except that in MS *Br* the comment is unjustly added to the end of Prop. 63. One can see how this could happen if the scribe of MS *Br* was copying from an exemplar like MS *E*, for with Propositions 62 and 63 on the same page, and with Prop. 63 the last proposition, the appearance of the comment to Prop. 62 below Prop. 63 may have beguiled the scribe into adding the comment to Prop. 63. Again note that in the Latin text I have bracketed the whole comment of lines 19–27.

³ I do not see why the author of the comment should bother to cite Prop. I.4 of Euclid, which establishes the congruence of triangles. One could say, I suppose, that if all four angles of the rhombus are right angles, then all four triangles into which the rhombus may be resolved would be congruent right triangles, and hence all four sides (which are the hypotenuses of these right triangles) would be equal.

Prop. 63

¹ See my account of this proposition in Chap. 2 of Part II above.

PART III

The *Liber de triangulis Iordani*

CHAPTER 1

The *Liber de triangulis Iordani:*
Its Origin and Contents

In the preceding part of my volume I have always distinguished the *Liber philotegni,* which I believe to have been the original tract of Jordanus on triangles and other polygons, from the so-called longer version, which I have referred to as the *Liber de triangulis Iordani* and which I have said was in all likelihood composed by a later author who recast many of the proofs of the original work, omitted many others, and added still others. We must now examine the reasons for this conclusion. Before doing so I note (using the *sigla* of the manuscripts adopted below in the next chapter) that the title I have given for the longer version is that found in MSS *Fb* and *G.*[1] It is also present in the upper margin of MS *H,* but without the word *Liber.* MSS *Pb* and *Es* have similar titles: *Jordanus de triangulis* and *Jordani de triangulis.* Also similar is the title found in the margin of MS *D: Geometria Iordani vel Iordani de triangulis* and the title in the colophon of MS *Pb: Liber Iordani de triangulis.*

The first and most important indication that the *Liber de triangulis Iordani* was put together, revised, and supplemented by an author other than Jordanus is the omission in the longer work of Propositions 47–63 of the *Liber philotegni,* for these are some of Jordanus' best propositions and ones that seem to represent the principal objectives of the *Liber philotegni.*[2] Now if Jordanus composed those propositions, and I do not doubt that he did compose them since they are included in the only two manuscripts to specify the original title of *Liber philotegni* and to join that specification with the assertion that the treatise contains sixty-four (*!* sixty-three) propositions,[3] then it is inconceivable that Jordanus should drop these important and essential propositions in order to replace them by Propositions IV.10 and IV.12–IV.28 of the *Liber*

---

[1] See the variant readings to the title in the text below for all of the references to the title given here; also see the variant reading to the colophon for the reference given here to the colophon in MS *Pb.*

[2] See Part II, Chap. 2, the text after footnote 1.

[3] *Ibid.,* text above n. 13.

297

de triangulis Iordani, which, though often interesting, had little bearing on the treatise and which were almost all fragments or parts of works translated from the Arabic with little change from the original forms of enunciations and proofs, as I shall observe below. This is a particularly significant point, for one of the virtues and characteristics of Jordanus as a mathematician was his skill in taking earlier enunciations and devising new proofs of his own (as, for example, in the case of the propositions which he apparently took from the *Liber divisionum* of Euclid and fashioned proofs that seem to be his own).[4] As a matter of fact, the addition to the *Liber de triangulis Iordani* of Propositions IV.10 and IV.12–IV.28 represents a move by the author toward making the work a more general geometric tract instead of one having the specific objective of establishing certain relationships between regular and irregular polygons as had the *Liber philotegni.* This rather general character of the *Liber de triangulis Iordani* produced by the omission of the final propositions of the *Liber philotegni* and the addition of Propositions IV.10 and IV.12–IV.28 was obviously recognized by the scribe of MS *D* who prefaced the ordinary title of the work with an alternate and more general one: *Geometria Iordani,* as I have already indicated above.

There are several other indications that the author of the *Liber de triangulis Iordani* was not Jordanus. (1) In the first of six citations to Jordanus' *Arithmetica* found in the *Liber de triangulis Iordani* (see Propositions I.12, II.6 twice, II.15, II.16 and III.9), Jordanus' name appears with the title, which would be unlikely if Jordanus himself were the author.[5] Furthermore none of these citations to the *Arithmetica* is couched in first-person terms like that found in Jordanus' citation of his *Liber philotegni* in the *Elementa de ponderibus.*[6] (2) We also see in the *Liber de triangulus Iordani* a move away from the lean and spare citation of Euclid's *Elements* found in the *Liber philotegni* to a copious citation of the *Elements;* furthermore the frequent citations of the *Elements* in the *Liber de triangulis Iordani* are always by specific book and proposition numbers instead of by book number alone as they occasionally are in the *Liber philotegni.*[7] This point becomes particularly significant when we realize that the other genuine works of Jordanus, though

---

[4] For the propositions that seem to have originated in the *Liber divisionum* of Euclid, see Appendix III.A below, and for a discussion of Jordanus' treatment of these propositions, see Part II, Chap. 2.

[5] It is significant, I believe, that Jordanus is specified as the author of the *Arithmetica* in the first of the references to it in the *Liber de triangulis Iordani.* One would suspect that had Jordanus himself written that first reference he would have used some first-person term to identify himself as the author of that work. I know that it is often said that authors in the Middle Ages cited themselves in the third person. But there is no evidence of this practice in the works of Jordanus. In fact, as we have already seen in Part II, Chap. 1, n. 12, Jordanus cited his *Liber philotegni* in his *Elementa de ponderibus* in the first person. In the same work Jordanus also cited his still undiscovered *Preexercitamina* in the first person (*ibid.,* n. 8). In no other work which can be established as Jordanus' composition did he cite himself in any fashion.

[6] See Part II, Chap. 1, n. 12.

[7] *Ibid.,* the text over footnote 15.

dependent to some extent on the *Elements,* scarcely ever cite it.[8] Hence the ubiquitous citation of the *Elements* bespeaks a style of proof at variance with the known style of Jordanus. (3) In Proposition IV.3 of the *Liber de triangulis Iordani* (=Prop. 40 of the *Liber philotegni*), the use of the third-person *dicit* when the author speaks of the *ratio* that appears at the end of the enunciation seems to separate the author of the proof from the author of the enunciation. Indeed Jordanus in Proposition 40 simply ignored the *ratio,* no doubt believing its role in the second part of the proof to be obvious. Compare Proposition III.10, line 12, where a reference to the enunciation in the proof appears to be *dicit* rather than *dico,* which again seems to separate the author of the proof from the author of the enunciation, and see a similar reference in

---

[8] The extreme cases of Jordanus' works where no specific reference is made to Euclid's *Elements* despite some dependence on the contents of that work are the following: (1) the *Elementa de ponderibus,* (2) the *Arithmetica* (3) Version 1 of the *Liber de plana spera* (the version that in all likelihood is Jordanus's original version), and (4) *De datis numeris.* For (1) see the text in E. A. Moody and M. Clagett, *The Medieval Science of Weights* (Madison, Wisc. 1952, 2nd pr. 1960), pp. 127–42. Though the reader might not be surprised by the lack of references to Euclid in the *Elementa de ponderibus,* he should realize that later versions often added references to Euclid's *Elements.* For example, see the text of the version known as the *Aliud commentum,* which has a great many citations to Campanus' version of the *Elementa* of Euclid, in J. E. Brown, "The *Scientia de ponderibus* in the Later Middle Ages," thesis, University of Wisconsin, 1967, pp. 173–343, *passim,* and particularly pp. 723–24, where the Euclidian citations are listed; and also see other texts presented by Brown in his Appendixes I–III, pp. 570–711. For (2) I have used one copy of the *Arithmetica* appearing in MS Paris, BN lat. 16644, 2r–93v, a manuscript of the thirteenth century. That copy has no reference to Euclid, though it should be remembered that Campanus so felt the pertinence of the *Arithmetica* to Euclid's *Elements* that he added a large number of the definitions, postulates, and propositions found in the *Arithmetica* to Books VII, VIII, and IX (and perhaps to Book V) of the *Elements.* See H. L. L. Busard, "The Translation of the *Elements* of Euclid from the Arabic into Latin by Hermann of Carinthia (?), Books VII, VIII and IX," *Janus,* Vol 59 (1972), pp. 132–39, whole article pp. 125–87, and also the later text of Busard's: *The Translation of the Elements of Euclid from the Arabic into Latin by Hermann of Carinthia (?) Books VII–XII* (Amsterdam, 1977), pp. 9, 17–20. For (3) I have used the edition of R. B. Thomson, *Jordanus de Nemore and the Mathematics of Astrolabes: De plana spera* (Toronto, 1978), pp. 86–134. I note Thomson's judgment on the three versions of the *De plana spera* (p. 74): "The text of the *De plana spera* is found in three different versions; the first seems to be the closest to the treatise written by Jordanus, while Versions 2 and 3 are different expansions of this basic text . . ." The reader should realize that the author of Version 2 makes the same kind of move regarding the quoting of Euclid's *Elements* as does the author of the *Liber de triangulis Iordani:* he adds a great number of citations though there were no citations in Version 1. Finally I should note that for the fourth work I have used the edition of B. B. Hughes, O.F.M., ed., *Jordanus de Nemore: De numeris datis* (Berkeley, Los Angeles, London, 1981). Notice that Hughes indicates that three of Jordanus' propositions in the *De numeris datis* (Props. IV.7, IV.8, and IV.29) may be traced to the *Elements,* though Jordanus does not specify these sources (see pp. 100 and 109 for the text of these propositions, and also pp. 185, nn. 114, 117; 186, n. 136). I did not have at hand any manuscript of the "Communis et consuetus" (with its *Tractatus minutiarum*) but I did consult the *Demonstratio de algorismo* (with its *de minutiis*) in the thirteenth-century copy, Naples, Bibl. Naz. Latin MS VIII.C.22, 51r–53r. I found six references to Euclid (five on folio 51r and one on 53r), four of which were to the proper book of the *Elements* alone and two of which were to the book and proposition numbers. The mixture of the two kinds of citation is like that occasionally found in the *Liber philotegni* of Jordanus.

Proposition III.5, line 6. (4) The author of the *Liber de triangulis Iordani* four times uses the word *commentum* to refer to the proofs of propositions (see Propositions III.9, lin. 32; III.10, lin. 23, twice; IV.11, lin. 9), while Jordanus never uses this term in his *Liber philotegni*. (5) Not only did the author of the *Liber de triangulis Iordani* seem to depart from Jordanus' practice of adding his own proofs to enunciations he took over from earlier authors (as I have noted above), but at least once he added a proposition (i.e. Prop. IV.13) that was partially erroneous in both enunciation and proof. Whether the errors were of his own commission or were those of some author he had copied the proposition from, they represent a lack of mathematical competence foreign to Jordanus. Furthermore, the author of the *Liber de triangulis Iordani* occasionally added a word or phrase to Jordanus' enunciations that produced an ambiguity or added a further case of the proposition that was not sufficiently demonstrated or clarified in the proof. An example of the first kind of addition occurred in Proposition II.18 where the author of the longer treatise added to the enunciation of Proposition 24 of the *Liber philotegni* the word *signato* causing the enunciation to be understood as follows: "To draw from a *designated* point within a given triangle to the three angles three [lines] which trisect the triangle." Ordinarily in geometrical parlance the use of *signato* would indicate that the point was a *given* point.[9] But in fact here in this proposition it is the point which must first be found before the lines may be drawn. Now it is true that the author of the new version of the proposition did not alter Jordanus' correct proof substantially, and perhaps he merely meant that we must first mark that point or rather fix it before we draw the lines. Still I believe the change to represent an infelicity that a mathematician of Jordanus' competence would not be capable of. An example of the second kind of addition occurs in Proposition I.5 where the author of the longer version has correctly added to the enunciation of Proposition 5 of the *Liber philotegni* the phrase *vel ambligonio,* thus extending the proposition to an obtuse-angled triangle. But, after making this addition, the author does not indicate in the proof that the same line of proof that allowed for the demonstration of the proposition in a right triangle would also be satisfactory for the proof of the proposition's applicability to an obtuse-angled triangle (see my comments on this proposition below). (6) Finally it should be noted that all of the manuscripts that give the complete text of the *Liber de triangulis Iordani* date from the fourteenth century or later (see the manuscripts listed under the rubric *Sigla* in the next chapter below) and even those manuscripts of the *Liber philotegni* that show

[9] If the reader will examine the references to *signo* in the indexes to Volumes 3 and 4 in my *Archimedes in the Middle Ages,* he will see that *signatum* is often used in the sense of *datum,* though occasionally it merely means "marked" or "designated" without any sense of *datum.* But *signato* clearly means *dato* in the enunciations of Propositions II.8 and II.13 of the *Liber de triangulis Iordani* (cf. II.17 where *dato* is used in precisely the same context). These usages the author takes over from the equivalent enunciations of Propositions 21, 22, and 23 of the *Liber philotegni.*

some influence of the longer version (see Chap. 3 of Part II above) are dated no earlier than the late thirteenth century (e.g. MSS *Fa* and *Br*).[10] One further observation may have some bearing on the question of when in the thirteenth century the author of the *Liber de triangulis Iordani* fashioned it. The author does not cite and apparently did not know the version of the *Elements* of Euclid compiled by Campanus in or before 1259.[11] For in Propositions I.9 and III.2, he cites the last proposition of Book V of the *Elements,* by which he clearly means Prop. V.25, and Campanus in his version of the *Elements* added a series of propositions (V.26–V.34). One could dismiss these cases by saying that the author was merely reproducing the similar citations of the "last of the fifth" found in the equivalent Propositions 9 and 27 in the *Liber philotegni.* However in several other propositions when the author of the *Liber de triangulis Iordani* found it necessary to give authority for the procedures guaranteeing the manipulations of ratios in expressions where the relationships of the ratios are ones of "greater than" or "less than" he does not cite the relevant additions of Campanus to the fifth book but rather cites the equivalent propositions of the *Arithmetica* of Jordanus.[12] This could mean either that the *Liber de triangulis Iordani* was written before Campanus' version of Euclid, or simply that the author composed his version later than Campanus' text but did not have access to that text. There is no conclusive way to decide between these alternatives.

When discussing the *Liber philotegni* in Part II, Chapters 2 and 3, I concluded that the propositions in that work were numbered consecutively,

---

[10] The reader should also realize that some of the manuscripts that contain parts of the section of propositions added to Book IV are from the thirteenth century, as I have indicated in the description of the manuscripts under the rubric *Sigla* in the next chapter. This can be easily accounted for if we note that all such manuscripts have no author or title that connects these propositions to the *Liber de triangulis Iordani* and hence their source was surely some copy or copies of the original translations or of Latin propositions made from them that go back to the twelfth or early thirteenth century. The most interesting of such manuscripts is MS *Ve,* which contains Propositions IV.14–IV.28 in a form that closely resembles the final form that the compositor of the *Liber de triangulis Iordani* gave them. In all likelihood this manuscript represented the source used by the compositor.

[11] See J. Murdoch, "The Medieval Character of the Medieval Euclid, etc.," *Revue de synthèse,* 3rd Ser., Vol. 89 (1968), p. 73, n. 18, for a Florentine MS of Campanus' version dated May 10, 1259. Cf. D. E. Smith, *Rara arithmetica* (Boston and London, 1908), pp. 433–34, for another manuscript apparently datable between 1255 and 1261 (or if the reference after the colophon to Jacques Pentaléon as Patriarch of Jerusalem implies a dedication of the *Elementa* to him before he became Pope Urban IV, then the composition of Campanus' version of the *Elementa* would have to be placed between 1255 and 1259, in view of Murdoch's discovery of the Florentine manuscript of 1259).

[12] For the citations of the *Arithmetica* of Jordanus in the *Liber de triangulis Iordani,* see the text above note 5; and for the Latin texts of these propositions of the *Arithmetica,* see Part II, Chap. 2, n. 4. This point is particularly interesting, for the relevant citations of the *Arithmetica* were propositions fashioned for numbers and not for continuous magnitudes, and hence the author of the *Liber de triangulis Iordani* apparently felt compelled to add "in continuis" (i.e., "in regard to continua") to his citations of the *Arithmetica* in Propositions II.6, lines 5–6; II.15, line 5; II.16, line 19; and III.9, lines 44–45.

whether or not that work was divided into books. But in the case of the *Liber de triangulis Iordani* there is no doubt of its division into books, each of which had its own proposition numbers (that is, the propositions of the whole work were not numbered consecutively throughout the work). In confirmation of this I note citations of propositions by book and proposition number in the proofs of the following propositions, pointing out to the reader that these citations as given are for the most part in all of the manuscripts of the *Liber de triangulis Iordani* (and even in the very few cases where the citations are omitted from one or more manuscripts, the citations are in the majority of manuscripts): Proposition II.13, line 13, citing Prop. II.1; Proposition II.16, line 12, citing Prop. II.5, and lines 15–16, citing Prop. II.6; Proposition II.17, line 7, citing Prop. II.12, and line 16, citing Prop. II.6, and line 17, citing Prop. II.5; Proposition III.4, line 7, citing Prop. II.14; Proposition III.5, line 11, citing Prop. I.5; Proposition III.6, line 11, citing Prop. I.5; Proposition III.7, line 39, citing Prop. II.14; Proposition III.9, line 29, citing Prop. III.5; Proposition III.10, line 22, citing Prop. I.5, Proposition IV.9, line 13, citing Prop. I.12, and line 15, citing Prop. III.4; Proposition IV.11, line 9, citing Prop. III.6, and line 28, citing Prop. I.5; Proposition IV.12, line 8, citing Prop. I.5; and Proposition IV.13, lines 9–10, citing Prop. IV.8.

In addition to the above noted references to the proposition numbers by books in the proofs of the *Liber de triangulis Iordani,* there are at the beginnings of the book divisions (usually in the margins) references to one or more of the books in MSS *DHFbFcEs*. But there are no such references in MSS *SG* or in any of the manuscripts (other than *Fc*) which contain only fragments of the work. These conclusions can be confirmed by examining the variant readings for the beginning of the work and for the first propositions of each of Books II, III, and IV. Now in regard to proposition numbers added at the beginning of each enunciation, the scribes (when giving any numbers at all) were generally inconsistent. The only manuscript to have a number for every proposition is MS *S*, where the propositions are numbered consecutively throughout the treatise. Hence, since Proposition I.5+ is numbered 6 in MS *S*, we find the propositions consecutively numbered from 1–73, this despite the fact that MS *S* includes all but one of the ordinal references by book that I have noted above. MS *H* comes closest to the author's intent regarding the numbering of the propositions. With Proposition I.5+ numbered as 6,[13] we find that MS *H* numbers the propositions of Book I from 1–14, those of Book II from 1–19, and those of Book III from 1–12. Then, mysteriously, the scribe of *H* stopped numbering the propositions so that the propositions of Book IV are without numbers (perhaps because he was not entirely certain where Book IV began; see below, Prop. IV.1, var. line 1). MSS *Pb* and *Es* (like MS *S*) number the propositions consecutively, but MS

---

[13] The original author apparently did not intend to have a number for Proposition I.5+, since later in Proposition IV.9 he cited Proposition I.12 by that number rather than by Proposition I.13, which would have been the proper number if Proposition I.5+ had been numbered as I.6.

Pb (not having numbered Proposition I.5+) correctly numbers the propositions through Proposition 42 (=Prop. III.10) but after this makes numerous errors of commission and omission (see the variant readings for the remaining proposition numbers). But MS *Es*, in the same tradition as *Pb*, numbers all but the last proposition. In doing this, the scribe numbers the propositions through IV.23 correctly from 1–67 (as in MS *Pb*, Proposition I.5+ has no number in MS *Es*). Then the scribe of *Es* numbers Propositions IV.24–IV.27 with numbers 58–61, the last proposition being without a number, as I have said. All other manuscripts, either of the whole text or of its fragments, fail to number the propositions at all. An explanation for this confusion of proposition numbers which I have described may be that the author of the *Liber de triangulis Iordani,* while perfectly clear in his mind that each proposition has an ordinal number that gives its position in one of the four books, nevertheless neglected to mark the proposition numbers in the margins before the enunciations. But what is surprising is that no other scribe but that of MS *H* read the work carefully enough to realize that he would confuse the reader or at least slow him up unless he numbered the propositions ordinally for each book. Indeed, as we have noted, even the scribe of *H* abandoned his correct numeration after the end of Book III, failing to number the propositions of Book IV.

Before examining in detail the changes of and additions to the *Liber philotegni* made by the author of the *Liber de triangulis Iordani,* it will be useful first to sketch them in a more general way. Book I contains all of the first thirteen propositions of the *Liber philotegni* and in addition a supplementary proposition which I have designated here as Proposition I.5+. Book II contains Propositions 14–25 of the *Liber philotegni* and seven additional propositions (Propositions II.9–II.12 and II.14–II.16) which (save for II.14) the author felt necessary for the proof of the various conclusions concerning the division of surfaces. Book III contains Propositions 26–37 of the *Liber philotegni* and no further propositions. Finally, as we have noted earlier, Book IV, while omitting Propositions 47–63 of the *Liber philotegni,* contains Propositions 38–46 of that work, to which it adds Proposition IV.4, a proposition which was perhaps an early addition to the *Liber philotegni,* Propositions IV.10, and IV.12–IV.13, propositions that were probably developed by the author of the *Liber de triangulis Iordani* because of the incompleteness of the version of the *Liber philotegni* which was his point of departure, and finally Propositions IV.14–IV.28, which were propositions apparently translated from a miscellany of Arabic works and which had been collected together in some fashion before the author of the *Liber de triangulis Iordani* added them to his work. I have one general remark to add to this outline of the *Liber de triangulis Iordani.* Though the author starts from the *Liber philotegni* and takes over the many propositions that I have just mentioned, he sometimes changes the enunciations slightly and almost always alters the language (and at times the argument) of the proofs of those propositions he has taken over, as we shall see below. On the other hand, he makes little change in the Arabic propositions he has added to the fourth book, as I have said earlier. For example, he even fails to revise the text of added Proposition IV.19 enough to indicate that it is essentially equivalent to Proposition IV.3 which he took over from Proposition 40 of the *Liber philotegni*.

Though the primary dependency of the author of the *Liber de triangulis Iordani* was upon the *Liber philotegni* of Jordanus, since his main objective was to produce a new version of the *Liber philotegni*, he did cite other works. As I have said above, his work has a large number of citations to specific theorems of the *Elements* of Euclid. Indeed he has cited the *Elements* in almost all of the proofs of the propositions he drew from the *Liber philotegni*, and in some of the propositions he added to Books I, II, and IV. All but the following propositions contain at least one and sometimes many citations to the *Elements:* Propositions II.7, II.11, II.12, II.15, III.11, IV.5, IV.12, IV.14, and IV.18–28. From this list of propositions where there is no citation of Euclid it is evident that it is precisely in the so-called Arabic propositions (IV.14–IV.28) that there are either one or two citations alone (IV.15–IV.17) or no citations at all (IV.14, IV.18–IV.28). This is another indication of the truth of what has been said earlier about the practice of the author of the *Liber de triangulis Iordani* of not making any significant changes in the Arabic propositions. I have already said that the version of the *Elements* of Euclid known to our author was not that prepared by Campanus. From the numbering of the Euclidian propositions, it appears that the version being cited was one of the versions associated with Adelard of Bath (or possibly that associated with Hermann of Carinthia), but certainly was not the translation of Gerard of Cremona from the Arabic or the anonymous translation from the Greek. Other works cited by the author of the *Liber de triangulis Iordani* are the *Liber de curvis superficiebus* of Johannes of Tinemue and the *Liber de similibus arcubus* of Aḥmad ibn Yūsūf. Both are cited in Proposition III.4 and were evidently taken from the citations given by Jordanus in the equivalent Proposition 29 of the *Liber philotegni*. But our author also cites the *Liber de similibus arcubus* in Proposition III.9 though there is no citation of this work in the equivalent Proposition 34 of the *Liber philotegni*. We should also note that our author does not follow Jordanus in citing the *Liber de ysoperimetris* (cited in Propositions 5 and 30 in the *Liber philotegni* but not in the equivalent Propositions I.5 and III.5 of the *Liber de triangulis Iordani*). One entirely new work mentioned by the later author is Jordanus' *Arithmetica*, the citation of which I mentioned above (see n. 5 and the text over that note). The only other work specifically cited in the *Liber de triangulis Iordani* is the *Perspectiva* of Alhazen, given as an authority in Proposition IV.20, the proposition which was probably fashioned from the *Verba filiorum* of the Banū Mūsā by some Latin author other than the author of the *Liber de triangulis Iordani* (see the discussion of this proposition below in this chapter and also in Appendix III.B).

Now we may proceed to the individual propositions of the *Liber de triangulis Iordani* and their relations to the propositions of the *Liber philotegni*. When the propositions and their proofs found in the *Liber de triangulis Iordani* are essentially the same as the equivalent propositions of the *Liber philotegni,* the reader can usually find some reconstruction and commentary on the proofs of these equivalent propositions in Part II, Chap. 2 above, and the reader is urged to consult that chapter as well as the relevant footnotes to the English translations of the propositions in both works. The prefatory definitions that precede Proposition I.1 were taken without change from the *Liber philotegni* and so need no comment here (but see the remarks concerning these definitions made above in Part II, Chap. 2). The proofs found in the first four propositions of the two works are essentially the same. However, there is considerable difference in their language and form. Recall that the proofs in the *Liber philotegni* were given in terms of magnitudes specified by given letters, that is they were proofs of the normal sort found in the *Elements* of Euclid. But the proofs in the *Liber de triangulis Iordani* for these propositions were more directions for or outlines of proofs than the proofs themselves and the magnitudes are dealt with in a general way rather than as specific ones with designated letters. But what gives them the semblance of proof is that each step that is outlined is ordinarily supported by a reference to Euclid's *Elements.* This proof in the form of an outline resembles that found in a great many propositions in the Adelard II Version of the *Elements.*[14] Hence I suppose that this outline form may have been suggested to the author of the *Liber de triangulis Iordani* by his acquaintance with the Adelard II Version, which was the most popular of the early versions of the *Elements.*[15] Concerning the nature of the proofs themselves in these first four propositions, we need only remark that in Proposition I.3 the author has added a case not given in Proposition 3 of the *Liber philotegni,* namely the case in which the short side of the triangle meets the base at a right or obtuse angle. In this case the line descending to the base inside the triangle is always greater than the shorter side (cf. the English translation of the *Liber philotegni,* Prop. 3, n. 1).

In Proposition I. 5 the proof intended is obviously that given in the *Liber de ysoperimetris.* But, as I noted above, instead of contenting himself with a reference to the *Liber de ysoperimetris,* as Jordanus had done, the author of Proposition I.5 omits that authority and sketches the proof briefly (again with no specific magnitudes having designated letters). As I have observed above, the author of Proposition I.5 adds to the enunciation the case in which the triangle is obtuse-angled, though there is no mention of this in the proof, and indeed manuscripts *D* and *Fb* have the following marginal remark regarding this addition: "Note that *ambligonium* (obtuse-angled) is not in the text but it (the proof or the proposition) is the same for an obtuse-

---

[14] M. Clagett, "The Medieval Latin Translations from the Arabic of the *Elements* of Euclid, with Special Emphasis on the Versions of Adelard of Bath," *Isis,* Vol. 44 (1953), p. 22, full article, pp. 16–42.

[15] *Ibid.,* p. 21.

angled triangle as for a right triangle." Furthermore, MS *H* tries to rectify the omission of the proof by adding *vel ambligonium* in line 5 (see the variant readings for that line) and in fact the scholar who prepared manuscript *H* also made the triangle in his diagram for Proposition I.5 an obtuse-angled triangle (see Fig. I.5*var.H*). I believe that the author of the *Liber de triangulis Iordani* was led to his addition to the enunciation by the following observation made by Jordanus in Proposition 30 of the *Liber philotegni:* "Therefore just as the fifth [proposition] of this [work] has been proved as in the *On Isoperimeters,* so it can be proved here by sectors of a circle described according to line *LK* that line *EKD / KD* > angle *ELD /* angle *KLD*" where triangle *EDL* is an obtuse-angled triangle (see the English translation of the *Liber philotegni,* Prop. 30, n. 1).

In all manuscripts of the *Liber de triangulis Iordani* we find in some form the proposition which I have called Proposition I.5+. It was, I believe, a marginal addition made either by the author of the *Liber de triangulis Iordani* or by an early commentator (because of its presence in all of the completed manuscripts). Whether it was meant to be an additional, separate proposition or merely an addition to Proposition I.5 as its second half, I am convinced that it was not a part of the text as originally conceived by the author of the *Liber de triangulis Iordani.* That it was not conceived as a separate proposition seems guaranteed by the fact mentioned above (see note 13), namely that all of the manuscripts have a passage later that cites Proposition I.12 by the number "12" instead of by the number "13" which it would have to be if Proposition I.5+ had been intended as a separate proposition with its own number "6." That the proposition seems to have been a marginal addition is supported by the state of confusion that exists concerning the position and separation of its enunciation and proof. Let me explain. The enunciation of Proposition I.5+ (lines 1–5) appears to be joined to the text of the enunciation of Proposition I.5 in MSS *GPbFbFcEs* (as well as in the margin of MS *D*) while the proof (lines 6–19) was added to the end of Proposition I.4 in MSS *GPbEs* (as well as in the margin of MS *D*) but to the end of the proof of Proposition I.5 in MSS *FbFc* (that is, essentially in MS *Fb* since *Fc* is merely a fragment copied from *Fb*). Two manuscripts, *S* and *H*, add the whole proposition to the text after Proposition I.5 and number it as Proposition "6." This confusion can most easily be explained by the existence of an early manuscript like *D* in which the proof of the marginal proposition was placed in the margin opposite the proof of Proposition I.4 while the enunciation was placed in the margin below the enunciation, thus following the style of presentation occasionally found in manuscripts of the *Elements* of Euclid in which each proof is placed before its enunciation instead of after it.[16] Presumably this did not confuse the scribes of *S* and *H* who decided merely to add the proposition to the text in the more normal fashion of enunciation followed by proof. The fact that it was an addition however was betrayed by

[16] *Ibid.,* p. 22.

the fact that the two manuscripts kept the later citation of Proposition I.12 intact. Now obviously the scribes of MSS *GPbEs* (which throughout represent the same tradition) followed the stupid mistakes of the originator of the tradition in (1) separating proof and enunciation, and in (2) placing the proof with the proof of Proposition I.4 and the enunciation with the enunciation of Proposition I.5. But the scribe of *Fb* saw that such a separation and positioning was not correct and so he simply added the enunciation of Proposition I.5+ to the end of the enunciation of I.5 and the proof to the end of the proof of I.5. One could, I suppose, say that this is what the original author or commentator intended when he placed the proposition in the margin. However the fact that it was done in only one manuscript of the complete text throws doubt on this possibility.

Whatever the origin of Proposition I.5+ might have been, we should observe that it played no seminal role in the treatise as did Proposition I.5. If we refer to Fig. I.5+ we can easily follow the intent and proof of the proposition. As in Proposition I.5 we start with a right (or obtuse-angled) triangle QCD, and we cut side QC at O, QC being the so-called "cut side," and we draw a line OH (parallel to side QD). Then we are to prove that angle HOC / angle $HQC < QC$ / OC. We now connect Q and H. With QH as a radius and Q as a center, we draw an arc BHA (i.e., one cutting QD at B and QC extended at A). Then by a proof similar to that described in Proposition I.5 we can show that DH / $HC >$ angle HQD / angle HQC. Therefore by the conjunction of ratios $(DH + HC)$ / $HC >$ (angle HQD + angle HQC) / angle HQC, i.e. DC / $HC >$ angle DQC / angle HQC. But QC / $OC = DC$ / HC since OH was drawn parallel to QD. Therefore QC / $OC >$ angle DQC / angle HQC. But angle $DQC =$ angle HOC. Therefore QC / $OC >$ angle HOC / angle HQC, and so by converting the ratios we have proved what was sought.

In Proposition I.6 the author of the *Liber de triangulis Iordani* again presents a proof in outline form that is essentially the proof of Proposition 6 of the *Liber philotegni*, with, however, one erroneous or at least superfluous instruction at the end of the proof, namely to proceed by means of the preceding proposition first to treat the ratios disjunctively before treating them conjunctively (see the English translation below, Proposition I.6, n. 1). I should also note that our author does make the enunciation somewhat clearer by stressing that the angle from which the perpendicular is dropped to the base is that contained by the unequal sides. But this is hardly necessary to stress in Proposition 6 of the *Liber philotegni*, since it is clear from the proof and diagram that the perpendicular BE is drawn from the angle contained by BC and BA.

Proposition I.7 takes essentially the same form as Proposition 7 of the *Liber philotegni* and the proof needs no explication here. We should note, however, that the proof of Proposition I.7 is not given in mere outline as was the case of the proofs of Propositions I.1–I.6, but it is of the normal Euclidian type with the magnitudes specifically designated. And indeed, from this point on, the proofs of the *Liber de triangulis Iordani* are quite often of this type, as they are in the *Liber philotegni*. But I must again stress that though the form and line of proof are essentially the same in many of the equivalent propositions in the two versions, the language of the *Liber de triangulis Iordani* continues to differ from that of the *Liber philotegni*.

Comparing Proposition I.8 with its equivalent Proposition 8 of the *Liber philotegni*, we note some minor changes: (1) In the enunciation of Proposition I.8 the author stresses that we are dealing with any number of triangles (on the same base and inserted between parallel lines) by adding the term *quotlibet* before *trianguli* (though to be sure the use of *trianguli* alone in the enunciation of Proposition 8 implies the same universality). (2) Proposition I.8 adds a trivial corollary missing in Proposition 8, namely that those triangles whose superior angles are equidistant from the superior angle of the isosceles triangle are equal to each other.

A comparison of Proposition I.9 with Proposition 9 reveals once more that we have essentially the same proof. Indeed the proof in Proposition I.9 starts off as if the author were going to make a close copy of the proof of Proposition 9 but then begins to diverge and continues to do so until the end of the proof. Also Proposition I.10 is essentially like Proposition 10, except that in Proposition I.10 we find that three specific triangles are immediately constructed (see Fig. I.10) so that a figure with two diagrams does not have to do double duty as does Fig. P.10 in the *Liber philotegni*.

The proofs given for Propositions I.11, I.12, and I.13 are as clear as the proofs of their equivalent Propositions 11–13. But a few comments are necessary. I note that in Proposition I.11 the author adds the definition of the altitude of a triangle which Jordanus had not deigned to do. Indeed the outline for proof in Proposition I.11 is much fuller and hence more elementary than the equivalent proof in Proposition 11. I also note in passing that Propositions I.11 and I.13 retain the outline form of the proofs, while Proposition I.12 is a normal proof with specifically designated magnitudes. Further, I observe that the author of Proposition I.12 remarks at the end of the proof that it rests on the following rule: "If the ratio of the first to the second is that of the third to the fourth, and that of the second to the fifth is greater than that of the fourth to the sixth, [so] the ratio of the first to the fifth will be greater than that of the third to the sixth." This rule had not been mentioned by Jordanus in the *Liber philotegni*. The author notes that it can be demonstrated by Euclid V.16 and by II.12 of the *Arithmetic* of Jordanus. As I have said, this is the first citation of the *Arithmetic* by the author of the *Liber de triangulis Iordani*. I have also remarked earlier on the possible significance of its third-person form for the question of the authorship of the *Liber de triangulis Iordani*. Finally I remind the reader once more of the significance of the citations of the *Arithmetic* in giving authority to the manipulations of ratios in "greater-than" and "less-than" relationships, manipulations that Euclid had already demonstrated for proportions (see Part II, Chap. 2, n. 4, above).

Now let us turn to Book II of the *Liber de triangulis Iordani*. The auxiliary Propositions II.1–II.7 are for the most part proved in a manner similar to those found in Propositions 14–20 of the *Liber philotegni*. Slight and insignificant variations are found in the enunciations. Proposition II.5 contains the same two proofs which Jordanus has given in Proposition 18 of the *Liber philotegni*, but its author has interchanged the two proofs, placing Jordanus' second proof as his first one. Note that at the beginning of the second proof the author tells us that his proof is valid for $BC = \frac{1}{4} AB$ and for $BC < \frac{1}{4} AB$ (see above, Part II, Chap. 2, n. 5). Indeed the author had accordingly altered Jordanus' enunciation to read that the shorter line "is less than or equal to" one quarter of the longer line instead of repeating Jordanus' assertion of Proposition 18 that it was "less than" that quantity. Note that the author's second proof is entirely a direct proof and so it abandons the disproof of a case proposed by the adversary in Jordanus' proof, namely that $AE = EB$. Further note that the author of the *Liber de triangulis Iordani* completes both proofs, while Jordanus produced his second proof to the point where he had shown that $AB \cdot BC = AM \cdot MB$ (see Fig. P.18b), $AM \cdot MB$ being equal to rectangle $AEFG$ in Jordanus' first proof (see Fig. P.18a). Jordanus then instructs the reader to proceed as in the first proof (see above, my summary of Jordanus' Proposition 18 in Part II, Chap. 2).

The proof in Proposition II.6 is somewhat longer than that found in Proposition 19 of the *Liber philotegni*. Still it needs no further commentary. The proof of Proposition II.7, on the other hand, is considerably shorter than Jordanus' Proposition 20, and is quite different in form and content. Referring to Fig. II.7, we note that AB and BC are the proposed lines, with BC the shorter, and that AB is divided at E so that $BE / BC = BC / AE$. By hypothesis, add line CD such that $CD / DB > DB / AB$. Hence by Proposition II.6 of this work, $BC < \frac{1}{4} AB$. But since AB is divided into AE and EB, one of the segments must be greater than $\frac{1}{4} AB$. Let it be EB. Therefore $EB > BC$ and so $BC > AE$. But $DB > BC$, the whole being greater than its part. Therefore $DB > AE$, and this is what had to be proved. The author does not concern himself with application of areas in this proposition as had Jordanus.

In Proposition II.8 the author adds the obvious case where the point is the midpoint of a side of the triangle (point E in line AB of Fig. II.8). Then line EC is drawn and the triangle is bisected, by Prop. I.38 of Euclid. Jordanus had not bothered with this case as a separate part of the proof, though he mentioned it as part of the more general proof of the proposition. We should note, however, that the trivial first part was included as an initial case by both Savasorda and Leonardo Fibonacci in their proofs of the same proposition (see Appendix III.A for the texts of their proofs), and so perhaps our author was following one of them in his revised proof. It could be argued that it was Leonardo Fibonacci whom he was following, for the proof of the more general case in the *Liber de triangulis Iordani* is more like the proof in Leonardo's work than that in Savasorda's work. But this is not conclusive, since the general proof added by the author of the *Liber de triangulis Iordani* is even more like that of Jordanus', and so one could say that he could easily have taken the first part from Savasorda and the second part from the work he was revising, namely the *Liber philotegni* of Jordanus.

To Propositions II.1–II.8, all of which were taken from the *Liber philotegni,* the author of the *Liber de triangulis Iordani* now adds four Propositions (II.9–II.12) which were not in the *Liber philotegni.* The first three are necessary for the proof of Proposition II.12, and Proposition II.12 is the crucial auxiliary proposition for Proposition II.13, as we shall see. Proposition II.9 is an exceedingly elementary proposition. By Proposition I.44 of Euclid parallelograms equal respectively to the two given triangles are constructed on line *AB* (see Fig. II.9). Then the rectangles are to each other as their second sides, and hence the triangles equal to those rectangles are also to each other as those second sides.

In Proposition II.10 unequal triangles *ABC* and *DEF* are proposed (see Fig. II.10). The proposition requires that we cut from the larger triangle a triangle of the same altitude as the larger triangle but of area equal to that of the smaller triangle, and also that we construct on the base of the smaller triangle extended a triangle equal in altitude to that of the smaller triangle but equal in area to the larger triangle. By Proposition I.44 of the *Elements* of Euclid we first construct on line *BC* a parallelogram having an angle equal to *C* and an area equal to triangle *DEF*. Let the diagonal *BG* be drawn. Then if *H* is marked so that *CH* = 2 *CG*, and, if *HB* is drawn, then obviously we have constructed triangle *HBC* of the same altitude as that of triangle *ABC* and of the same area as that of triangle *DEF*, as the first part of the proposition required. In the second part, we again construct by Proposition I.44 of Euclid a parallelogram having an angle equal to *D* and an area equal to triangle *ABC*. Then we double *DK* to produce line *DN*. With line *EN* drawn we have produced a triangle *DEN* equal in altitude to triangle *DEF* and in area to triangle *ABC*, and thus the whole proposition has now been completed.

In Proposition II.11 we are required to construct on a given line a triangle equal to a given triangle. The technique is that already used in the previous proposition. The given triangle is *A* (half of the double triangle in Fig. II.11) and the given line is *BC*. We first double the given triangle. Then by I.44 of Euclid we construct on line *BC* a parallelogram equal to double the triangle. Finally we draw a diagonal to *C* in the parallelogram and the triangle thus formed on *BC* is half the parallelogram and thus equal to given triangle *A*.

The author now presents in Proposition II.12 the principal auxiliary proposition to the proof of Proposition II.13. Proposition II.12 requires the solution of the following problem: "With a straight line given, to find another straight line to which the prior [straight line] is related as is any given triangle to another given triangle." In his solution the author uses all of the preceding auxiliary propositions which he had added. With triangles *A* and *B* and line *DC* all given (see Fig. II.12), we first determine (by Proposition II.9) whether the triangles are equal. If they are equal, the line that is sought is equal to *DC*. If they are not equal (and *A* is the larger), then (by Proposition II.11) we place on *DC* a triangle *DGC* equal to triangle *A*. Then (by Proposition II.10) we construct on line *DC* a triangle with an altitude equal to that of triangle *DGC* and an area equal to triangle *B*, and the base of that triangle will have been determined as *DE*. Hence *DE* is the line sought, for (by Proposition II.9) *DC* / *DE* = tri. *A* / tri. *B*. Note that in his solution the author remarks that we could in our original step just as well have constructed on *DC* the smaller triangle, and then by a similar series of steps we could have found a line longer than *DC* on which a triangle of equal altitude as that of the triangle on *DC* (which latter triangle is equal to triangle *B*) and whose area is equal to triangle *A*. It simply depends on which triangle we wish to be the antecedent in their ratio. The fact that our author felt compelled to add Proposition II.12 (and its antecedent propositions) before presenting the proof of Proposition II.13 is a striking example of the difference between his approach and that of Jordanus. Clearly Jordanus expected more of his reader than did our author. At any rate Jordanus in his equivalent Proposition 22 simply instructs the reader to find a line like that constructed in Proposition II.12 but without telling him how to do it.

The author of the *Liber de triangulis Iordani* in Proposition II.13 substantially repeats the treatment and solution presented by Jordanus in Proposition 22 of the *Liber philotegni*. Worth noting is the statement at the end of the proof: "And by this same procedure you will lead the adversary [i.e. the falsigraph] to an impossibility, namely that the whole is equal to [its] part, if he posits point *K* to be elsewhere than between *E* and *B* or point *P* to be elsewhere than between *H* and *A*, and triangle *AEC* will always be greater than the whole [*CK'P'*] or a part [of *CKP*, see Fig. II.13b]." The refutation is not given but the figure appearing in the MSS *H* and *Fb* shows the veracity of the author's statement, for if *K'* were below *E*, and thus *P'* were to the left of *H*, it is clear that triangle *CK'P'*, which the argument says should equal *AEC*, is at the same time a part of *AEC*. Or if *K* is above *B* and consequently *P* were to the right of *A*, then triangle *AEC* is both equal to *CKP* (as the argument holds) and a part of *CKP* [see the English translation of Prop. II.13, n. 1]. But our author's statement is hardly useful since the argument of the proof clearly shows that *K* must be between *E* and *B* and accordingly *P* between *H* and *A*. Again our author seems to be anticipating the needs of an unsophisticated reader.

Following Proposition II.13 the author of the *Liber de triangulis Iordani* adds three more auxiliary propositions, Propositions II.14–II.16, II.14 being for use later in the course of the proofs of Propositions III.4 and III.7, Proposition II.15 being for use in the proof of Proposition II.16, and Proposition II.16 being necessary for the proof of Proposition II.17. Returning to Proposition II.14 we see that it is exceedingly simple (see Fig. II.14). If straight lines *A*, *B*, and *C* are given, we are to find a fourth line *D* such that *A* / *B* = *C* / *D*. Our author proposes a line *E* such that *A* / *E* = *E* / *B*, by VI.9 (=Gr. VI.13) of Euclid. Then he constructs on *A* and *E* similar triangles such that tri. *A* / tri. *E* = line *A* / line *B* (by the corollary to VI.17 [=Gr. VI.19] of Euclid). Now by Proposition II.12 of his own work, the author draws line D such that tri. A / tri. E = line C / line D. Therefore line A / line B = line C / line D, and so D is the required line.

Proposition II.15 is given without specifically designated magnitudes, but we can neatly describe it in specific terms as follows. Let a be the whole, b a part of it, and c a part of b. Now if a / b > b / c, then $(a - b)$ / $(b - c)$ > a / b. But if a / b < b / c, then $(a - b)$ / $(b - c)$ < a / b. As the author says, these conclusions follow directly from Propositions II.13 and II.14 of the *Arithmetic* of Jordanus (see above, Part II, Chap. 2, n. 4).

Proposition II.16 is, as I have said, the last of the auxiliary propositions in Book II. It was advanced by the author of the *Liber de triangulis Iordani* undoubtedly because he felt it to be necessary for the proof of the next proposition. Its enunciation is long and clumsy but becomes clear if we express it in terms of the specific magnitudes of Fig. II.16, which is essentially like Fig. II.5a, i.e. AB is the longer line, BC the shorter, and MH is one line added to BC, or its equal HB, and KH is a second line added to HB. The first part of the proposition holds that if BC < ¼ AB and if KH / KB > KB / AB, and if MH / MB = MB / AB, then KH > MH. But the second part declares that if KH / KB < KB / AB, then MH > KH. And the third and fourth parts are converse to the first and second. The only condition that the author places on the proposition is that the initial longer line AB is longer than any assumed added line KH. Only the first part is proved. As in the proof of Proposition II.6 of this work, AB / KB > KB / KH. Therefore, by the first part of the preceding proposition, i.e., Proposition II.15 of this work, AK / HB > AB / KB. By Proposition II.27 of the *Arithmetic* of Jordanus (see above, Part II, Chap. 2, n. 4), $AK \cdot KB$ > $AB \cdot HB$ (or BC). Therefore by VI.8 and VI.16 (=Gr. VI.17) of Euclid, the perpendicular erected at K and extending to the lower circumference is greater than BD (and also than its equal TM). Hence K is closer to the center E (and farther from point B) in diameter AB than is point M. Therefore KB > MB. And if we subtract HB from each magnitude, then KH > MH, or MH < KH, which is what was sought. Though the author does not give a proof for the second part, it would be just like the proof given for the first part. That is, we would simply convert the greater-than signs to less-than signs. By assumption, KH / KB < KB / AB. Inverting and converting the ratios AB / KB < KB / KH. Then by the second part of the preceding proposition, i.e. Proposition II.15, AK / HB < AB / KB. Hence $AK \cdot KB$ < $AB \cdot HB$. Therefore the perpendicular erected on K to the lower circumference is less than BD and hence less than its equal TM. Hence K is farther from E (and closer to B) than is M. Therefore KB < MB. If we subtract HB from each magnitude, KH < MH, or MH > KH, as the second part asserts. We need not present proofs of the third and fourth parts (which, as I have said, are converse to the first and the second). We can merely state them: (3) if KH > MH, then KH / KB > KB / AB, and (4) if KH < MH, then KH / KB < KB / AB.

Now the author of the *Liber de triangulis Iordani* is fully prepared to present the proof of Proposition II.17, which he has taken from Proposition 23 of the *Liber philotegni*. Thus he uses his auxiliary Proposition II.12 for drawing line *MN* such that *BF* / *MN* = tri. *BDF* / tri. *BEC* and line *TY* such that *BF* / *TY* = tri. *BFH* / tri. *BEC* (see Fig. II.17). Jordanus had simply assumed that the reader knew how to find such lines. Similarly the author of the *Liber de triangulis Iordani* used the first part of the preceding proposition (Proposition II.16) to declare that *FZ* < *FB* (after, by Proposition II.5, he had marked off line *FZ* such that *FC* / *ZC* = *ZC* / *MN*). Presumably he now felt that he had put Jordanus' proof on a sounder footing.

The proofs of the final propositions of Book II, namely Propositions II.18 and II.19, are like the proofs of their equivalent Propositions 24 and 25 of the *Liber philotegni* and need no further comment. However, I have mentioned earlier the possible significance of the addition of the word *signato* to the enunciation of Proposition II.18, the addition perhaps implying that the point from which the three lines to the angles are to be drawn to trisect the triangle was a given point when in fact it was a point to be determined.

The general remarks I have already given concerning Propositions 26–37 of the *Liber philotegni* in Part II, Chap. 2, above apply equally to the propositions of Book III of the *Liber de triangulis Iordani* and I refrain from repeating them here. Concerning Proposition III.1 (equivalent to Proposition 26) I note that, while Jordanus had merely said that the second part of the proof is manifest (without proving it), the author of Proposition III.1 briefly outlines the proof as follows (see Fig. III.1): "You will easily conclude the second part [of the proposition], namely that surface *ACDB* > surface *CEFD*, from the fact that *TZ* > *ZE* and *KY* > *YF* and from VI.1 [of Euclid] taken with respect to the partial parallelograms and partial triangles abutted to them on each side." That is, because *TZ* > *ZE* and *KY* > *YF*, par. *ZK* > par. *EY*, tri. *TCZ* > tri. *ECZ*. Further, circ. seg. *AC* = circ. seg. *CE*, and circ. seg. *BD* = circ. seg. *DF*, and tri. *TCA* and tri. *KBD* are included in surface *ACDB* without any matching triangles in *CEFD*. Consequently *TZYK* + *TCZ* + *TAC* + *KDY* + *KBD* + circ. seg. *AC* + circ. seg. *BD* > *ZEFY* + *ZCE* + *DYF* + circ. seg. *CE* + circ. seg. *DF*. Q.E.D.

There are no differences (other than in language) between the proofs of Proposition III.2–III.4 and those of Propositions 27–29. I note, however, that the author of Proposition III.4 cites his own auxiliary Proposition II.14. In Proposition III.5 the author changes the enunciation somewhat without changing the meaning. He says that the parallel lines cut the diameter orthogonally instead of saying with Jordanus that the diameter cuts the parallel lines orthogonally. In the proof the author of Proposition III.5 says that angle *D* (i.e. angle *CDL*) is either right or obtuse, while Jordanus correctly says that it is an obtuse angle since it falls in an arc greater than a semicircle. Our author once more merely encapsulates the remainder of the proof by citing the authorities: "Argue, therefore, by I.5 of this [work], by the last [proposition] of [Book] VI of Euclid, by VI.2 [of Euclid], and by conjunct ratio that line *BD* / line *GD* > arc *GD* / arc *HD*, and therefore line *BD* /

line *GD* > arc *CDE* / arc *HDL* since these [latter arcs] are double the prior [arcs], and this is what has been proposed." The author, as I have said, drops Jordanus' reference to the *Liber de ysoperimetris*. Furthermore, this encapsulation somewhat obscures the steps of the proof (for which see my account of Proposition 30 of the *Liber philotegni* in Part II, Chap. 2, above). The proofs of Proposition III.6 and its equivalent Proposition 31 are essentially the same except that again in Proposition III.6 the proof is encapsulated by the citation of authorities instead of given in specific detail as it was in Jordanus' proof. Furthermore our author adds an obvious and elementary statement after the completion of the proof that Jordanus did not bother with: "And in this figure you will demonstrate that the longer lines [i.e. tangents] include a greater arc and that from the angle which they contain they dispatch a longer line to the center, and contrariwise, if one of those [conditions] pertains in regard to [a pair of] tangents [that is, if they include a greater arc or if the line to the center from their angle is longer], then those [tangents] are longer." Once more we see that our author has demanded less geometrical knowledge from his reader than had Jordanus.

After the completion of the proof of Proposition III.7, which the author has substantially taken from Proposition 32 of the *Liber philotegni,* he adds three short additional corollaries or problems: (1) that *EM* and *CD* are similar arcs (see Fig. III.7); (2) if two sets of coterminal lines are tangent to two circles so that they include similar arcs, the ratios of the lines, of the diameters, and of the arcs will be the same; and (3) with two unequal circles proposed to one of which two lines from the same point are tangent, to assign a point outside of the other circle from which may be drawn two tangents to that other circle that are equal to the prior tangents. The proofs or solutions of these corollaries are simple and need no commentary here. They are, I might add, corollaries not needed for succeeding propositions, and hence it is not surprising that they were not present in the *Liber philotegni*. They constitute further evidence that the author of the *Liber de triangulis Iordani* was making some attempt to produce a treatise of a more general character.

In Proposition III.8 the author makes the enunciation more general than that found in its equivalent Proposition 33 of the *Liber philotegni* by adding the words *vel intra vel extra* to make the proposition apply to circles that are tangent to each other both on the outside and the inside. Jordanus had omitted any such words and had confined his proof to circles tangent on the inside. He did this because the succeeding propositions concerned themselves with circles tangent on the inside, and our proposition was cited in Propositions III.9 and III.10 (in III.11 it is not specifically cited but is understood). Hence I presume that the author's addition is one more attempt to produce a more general geometric tract from Jordanus' rather more specifically oriented work. The proof of Proposition III.8, like those of earlier propositions, is cast in an outline form without specifically designated magnitudes. In this respect it differs from the proof of Proposition 33 of the *Liber philotegni.*

While it is evident that Proposition III.9 depends closely on Proposition

34 of the *Liber philotegni,* there are some interesting changes. In the first place the author of Proposition III.9 adds to the enunciation of the second case the word *sola,* which gives the following meaning to that case: "(2) But if it [proceeds] through the center of the larger [circle] and is tangent [to the smaller circle], it will intercept in this case alone the same [arcal length from each circle]." Further in the third case the author adds the expression *et contingat* giving the following meaning to that case: "(3) But if it [proceeds] outside [of the center of the larger circle] and is tangent [to the smaller circle], in this case it will intercept greater [arcal length] from the smaller [circle than from the larger]." I have already explained in my account of Proposition 34 in Part II, Chap. 2, that this addition made by the author of the *Liber de triangulis Iordani* apparently represented the intent of the enunciation given in Proposition 34 of the *Liber philotegni* (whether framed by Jordanus or taken by Jordanus from some other work). It will be recalled that Jordanus had used the usual terminal phrase after the proof of the three cases as here understood in Proposition III.9, and so he evidently was acting as if the phrase *et contingat* was understood as a part of the third case (see the English translation to the *Liber philotegni,* Proposition 34, n. 2). The additional cases which were added in Proposition 34 after the terminal phrase (whether added by Jordanus or some early commentator) were then outside of the intent of the enunciation and so the author of the *Liber de triangulis Iordani* simply omitted these extra cases. The omission of these further cases, i.e. his exclusive consideration of the cases specified in his modified enunciation, gave him the authority to make the addition of *sola* in the enunciation of the second case. For if only these cases are considered, then it is true that in this case alone of the three cases are equal arcal lengths intercepted from the larger and the smaller circles (but see the discussion of the fifth case of Proposition 34 given in the translation of the *Liber philotegni,* Prop. 34, n. 2). Notice finally that the author of Proposition III.9 has economized in his diagrams, giving two diagrams (see Fig. III.9a–b) that do the service of four of the diagrams in the *Liber philotegni* (see Fig. P.34a–d, Fig. P.34e being used for the fourth and the fifth cases not considered by the author of the *Liber de triangulis Iordani*).

While Proposition III.10 does not differ greatly from its equivalent Proposition 35, the reader might find useful a brief summary of it (see Fig. III.10). The so-called larger circle with the center at D has within it three other circles all tangent to it at A; the first cuts the diameter below D, the second cuts it at D, and the third cuts it above D. Now if we draw from center D a line $DECOG$ that intersects all three interior circles and proceeds to the circumference of the larger circle, the points of intersection are at O, C, and E, and the point at the circumference is G. The proposition declares (actually the author says *dicit* in reference to the enunciation, apparently thereby distinguishing himself from Jordanus) that (1) arc $AG >$ arc AO, (2) arc $AG =$ arc AC, and (3) arc $AG <$ arc AE. Let us draw straight lines AOK, ACZ, and AEB. We produce thereby angles AOD, ACD, and AED, AOD being acute,

ACD being right, and *AED* being obtuse. Then draw line *DR* through the midpoint *N* of *AK*, and line *DK* through the midpoint *T* of line *AB*. Hence *DR* and *DK* are perpendicular to lines *AK* and *AB* respectively. Thus the angles *N*, *C*, and *T* (all opposite *AD*) are right angles. Then all parts of the proposition may be proved by Proposition I.5 of this work together with the last proposition of Book VI of Euclid, the two rules given respectively in the comments to Propositions I.12 and III.9 of this work, by Proposition III.8 of this work, and by the equal proportionality of similar arcs and their chords. Hence we see that the author has reduced the heart of the proof to his quite common outline form in which he lists the authorities for the steps without specifying the steps as had Jordanus in Proposition 35 of the *Liber philotegni*. Again the author of the *Liber de triangulis Iordani* has economized on the diagrams for this proposition, producing a single diagram (see Fig. III.10) instead of the three diagrams given by Jordanus (see Fig. P.35).

No special comment need be made concerning Proposition III.11. After specifying the magnitudes in precisely the same fashion as they were in Proposition 36 of the *Liber philotegni*, the author gives no proof but merely says: "With [all of] this completed, argue what has been proposed as in that which has been put forth before." The last proposition of Book III, namely III.12, has a proof for the first part that is simple and needs no comment for anyone who has considered the proof of Proposition 37 of the *Liber philotegni*. The proof of the second part is based on that found in Proposition 37 but is a bit more detailed and I note its line of direction here. We are to prove that surface *AKGS* > surface *SGRD* (see Fig. III.12). Line *AT* (equal to *SG*) is cut from *AK* and *SL* (equal to *DR*) is cut from *SG*. Draw line *TL*. Then since the angles of contingence at *A* and *S* are equal and the sides in the extracircular surfaces *ASLT* and *SDRG* are equal by superposition, and since *ASLT* is a part of *AKGS*, therefore *AKGS* is greater than the equal of *ASLT* and so is greater than *SGRD*, as the proposition requires.

Let us turn now to the fourth and last book of the *Liber de triangulis Iordani*. This is of course the book that suffered the greatest change when its author took over the propositions of the *Liber philotegni*. Propositions IV.1–IV.3, IV.5–IV.9, and IV.11 are equivalent to Propositions 38–46 of the *Liber philotegni*. Proposition IV.4 (equivalent to Proposition 46+1) appears to have been taken from an addition made to the original text of the *Liber philotegni*, as I shall explain later. Propositions IV.10 and IV.12–IV.13 seem to have been composed by the author of the *Liber de triangulis Iordani* since they can all be tied to earlier propositions of the work. Finally we note that Propositions IV.14–IV.28 were all (or almost all) added to the text by its author from a collection of Arabic geometric propositions that had been translated from the Arabic by Gerard of Cremona either as parts of a longer work (like the *Verba filiorum* of the Banū Mūsā) or as scattered fragments (see my discussion of these propositions below in this chapter and in Appendix III.B).

The proof of Proposition IV.1 has been transformed from its specific form in Proposition 38 of the *Liber philotegni* into the outline form so often adopted by the author of the *Liber de triangulis Iordani*. At the end of the proof of Proposition IV.1 the author says that "by this same method you will demonstrate the proposition for any rectilinear figure of unequal sides," thus meaning that the proof given for a triangle of unequal sides is valid in its substance for other rectilinear figures. Again Jordanus had not indicated that this is so. But that he intended such an understanding is clear from his calling the figure *non equilaterus* without *triangulus* appended (though he has given in his diagram a triangle). Now our author of Proposition IV.1 called the figure "triangle *ABG* of unequal sides" and then felt obliged to note that the method used for the triangle is equally applicable for other rectilinear figures.

The enunciation of Proposition IV.2 differs from that of its equivalent Proposition 39 by the addition of the phrase *ex eadem parte,* which simply means that the triangles being compared to the isosceles triangle and to each other are all to the same side of the isosceles triangle. The proofs of the two propositions are the same. However the author of Proposition IV.2, after the completion of the proof, shifts to a case where the triangles to be compared to the isosceles triangle are not on the same side of the isosceles triangle when he says that "the triangles [whose apexes are] equally distant from it [i.e., the apex of the isosceles triangle] are equal."

I have already discussed Proposition IV.3's equivalent Proposition 40 of the *Liber philotegni* in Part II, Chap. 2. I remarked there that Jordanus did not specifically cite the *ratio* given in his enunciation, though he certainly understood its necessity for the proof of the second part of the proposition, which he apparently thought to be too obvious to give. But the author of Proposition IV.3 not only mentioned the role to be played by the *ratio* in proving the second part of the proposition (and in doing so he used the verb *dicit* which appears to distinguish him from Jordanus, as I have said), but he also decided that the *ratio* itself should be proved. His proof (see Fig. IV.3b) follows. "Now let the acute-angled triangle on center A be ABC. Let the perpendicular dropped to its base be AE. And let the obtuse-angled triangle be ABD with AH the perpendicular dropped to its base. And let circle $AHEB$ be described as before. The perpendiculars will also bisect the whole triangles. If, therefore, line AH = line EB, so the arc will be equal to the arc. Therefore, with common arc HE added to each, you will argue by III.26 (=Gr. III.27) [of Euclid], by hypothesis, and by I.4 of Euclid that the halves of the triangles are equal and consequently the wholes. But if line AE is posited as equal to HB, you will similarly argue [what was proposed] after the common arc HE has been subtracted from both [arcs]." So once again our author has thought it useful to prove an elementary geometric statement that Jordanus had left without proof.

Proposition IV.4 was taken, I believe, from some version of the *Liber philotegni* where it had been added after Proposition 46. The author of the *Liber de triangulis Iordani,* in adding this proposition, presents an outline form of the proof (reduced to a single sentence) that distinguishes it from the specific proof given to it when it was added to the *Liber philotegni*.

Furthermore our author thought that it would more appropriately appear at this point of the tract than after his Proposition IV.11 (equivalent to Proposition 46). The proofs of Propositions IV.5 and IV.6 are also reduced from their equivalent but specific forms in Propositions 41 and 42 of the *Liber philotegni* to outline forms of one sentence each. Proposition IV.7 and its proof were taken from Proposition 43 of the *Liber philotegni* and need no commentary here (but see my account of Proposition 43 above in Part II, Chap. 2). The same is true for Proposition IV.8, whose enunciation and proof were obviously drawn from Proposition 44 of the *Liber philotegni* (though as usual the proof is differently expressed).

The source of Proposition IV.9 was Proposition 45 of the *Liber philotegni,* but its proof was tied to the comparison of a square with a regular pentagon rather than to the comparison of an equilateral triangle with a square as had been the proof of Proposition 45. Hence let me describe the proof of Proposition IV.9 briefly (see Fig. IV.9). We are to prove that if regular polygons are described in equal circles: (1) that which has more sides is greater, and (2) the ratio of the areas of the two polygons is greater than the ratio of their perimeters. Divide the polygons into triangles by drawing lines from the centers of the circles in which they are inscribed to the angles of the polygons. Let one of the four equal triangles of the square be ABC and one of the five equal triangles of the pentagon be EDO. Line BC > line DO, for a fourth part is always greater than a fifth. Hence by Proposition I.12 of this work, tri. ABC / tri. EDO < line BC / line DO. Hence tri. ABC / tri. EDO < arc BC / arc DO. Then if we take 4/5 of each ratio, square / pentagon < 4 arc BC / 5 arc DO. But 4 arc BC and 5 arc DO each comprise the same circumference. Therefore square / pentagon < 1, and hence the pentagon is greater than the square. Thus the first part of the proposition is proved. Now, since tri. ABC / tri. EDO < line BC / line DO, as we noted above, then, by inverting the ratios, tri. EDO / tri. ABC > line DO / line BC. Taking 5/4 of each ratio (the author says: "and so by proceeding through the single [terms]"), pentagon / square > perimeter of pentagon / perimeter of square, as the second part of the proposition required.

Proposition IV.10 is one added by the author of the *Liber de triangulis Iordani,* it not having been present in the *Liber philotegni.* As I note below in Appendix III.B, I have not located the source of this proposition in any of the translations from the Arabic in which I found the sources of most of the succeeding propositions. Hence it was probably composed by the author of the *Liber de triangulis Iordani* or (less probably) by some other Latin geometer. I say "less probably" because the proposition begins with a sentence almost identical to the sentence with which Proposition IV.9 began and the latter was written by the author of the *Liber de triangulis Iordani.* The proposition holds that if any side of a regular polygon circumscribed about a circle is bisected at its point of tangency with the circle, and if the successive points of tangency are connected by straight lines, a regular polygon similar to the given polygon is formed. It holds further that every arc between proximate points of tangency is the same numbered part of the circumference as the number of sides of the polygon. The proof of this trivial proposition is obvious and needs no explication here.

Proposition IV.11 is the last proposition taken from the *Liber philotegni* and its proof and that of Proposition 46 of the latter work are almost exactly the same (except for the usual differences of language). In the case of both proofs, the second part of the enunciation is demonstrated before the first. In the course of proving the first part of the enunciation, the author of Proposition IV.11 tells us that "the ratio of sides to sides is greater than that of the three angles at Q to the four angles at L (as we shall demonstrate later)" (see Fig. IV.11). Then upon the completion of the proof the author of Proposition IV.11 does indeed add a demonstration of this statement. Let line SP (with midpoint K and equal to side DE of the square with midpoint Z) be imposed on side BC of the triangle so that K is the midpoint of both SP and BC. And because $BC > DE$ (and so greater than SP) the half of the one line is greater than the half of the other. Let lines SQ and PQ be drawn. Therefore tri. KPQ = tri. ZLE, and tri. SQP = tri. DLE. "Argue [the conclusion], therefore, from I.5 of this [work] twice, and by conjunction and by doubling, for perpendicular QK bisects the bases and the angles (because the sides are equal)."

In Appendix III.B below I suggest that Propositions IV.12 and IV.13 were probably composed by the author of the *Liber de triangulis Iordani*. I reason this way because (1) no sources of them have been found among the manuscripts including the translations from the Arabic by Gerard of Cremona, manuscripts which provided the sources for most of the remaining propositions added to Book IV, and because (2) these two propositions have references to earlier propositions of the *Liber de triangulis Iordani* while none of the succeeding propositions added to Book IV have such references. Proposition IV.12 bears resemblance to Propositions I.5, I.5+, and I.6, and it is surprising that the author did not add it to Book I. Perhaps the reason for its earlier omission is that it was not used in any of the propositions prior to IV.12. The proposition holds that if a straight line is drawn from an angle included by the equal sides of an isosceles triangle to the base so that it divides that angle and the triangle into unequal parts, the ratio of the greater part of the angle to the lesser is greater than the ratio of the greater part of the base to the lesser. The proof is brief (see Fig. IV.12). Let ABC be the isosceles triangle and let BE be the line drawn to the base that divides the triangle into unequal parts. Also drop the perpendicular BF to the base, which perpendicular will bisect the angle at B and the base AC. Then "argue [the proposition] by I.5 of this [work], by disjunction, by conjunction, and by the proportioning of the double." We may expand these steps, noting a somewhat different order of them from that given by the author. (1) Angle CBE / angle EBF < line CE / line EF, by I.5 of this work. (2) Angle EBF / angle CBE > line EF / line CE, by inverting the expression in (1). (3) Angle CBF / angle CBE > line CF / line CE, by conjunction. (4) Angle CBA / angle CBE > line AC / line

CE, by doubling the ratios in (3) and with angle *CBA* = 2 angle *CBF* and line *AC* = 2 line *CF*. (5) Therefore, angle *EBA* / angle *CBE* > line *EA* / line *CE*, by disjunction. Q.E.D.

As I have already pointed out, Proposition IV.13 was partially erroneous in both enunciation and proof. The correct first part tells us (1) that the line protracted from the center of the circle to any angle of an equilateral triangle circumscribed about the circle is bisected by the circumference. This part of the proposition is correctly and economically proved by referring to the method followed in Proposition IV.8 of this work and by the corollary to Proposition XIV.1 of Euclid. Expanding this abbreviated outline form of the proof, we can easily construct a specific proof (see Fig. IV.13). By the argument in IV.8 of this work, *KB* / *FB* = *FB* / *EB*. Then, by the corollary to XIV.1 of Euclid, *FB* = 2 *EB*. Therefore *KB* = 2 *FB*. Q.E.D. The second and the third parts of the proposition (which I have double-bracketed in the English translation) tell us (2) that a line protracted from the center of a circle to any angle of the square circumscribed about the circle is cut at the circumference "according to a ratio having a mean and two extremes" and (3) that the segment of the line beyond the circumference is equal to the side of a regular decagon [inscribed in the circle]. No diagram is given, but one is not needed. If $r + d$ is the length of the line drawn from the center to an angle and r is the radius of the circle, then the second part of the proposition holds that $(r + d) / r = r / d$ [or, by VI.16 (=Gr. VI.17) of Euclid, $(r + d) \cdot d = r^2$]. But in fact, by Proposition III.35 (=Gr. III.36), in the case of the line from the center to an angle of the square, $(2r + d) \cdot d = r^2$, and so the second part is false. And if the second part is false, so is the third, for from Proposition III.9 we know that, if d is a side of the inscribed regular decagon, then $(r + d) \cdot d = r^2$, as in the second part. But since the second part is false, so too is the third part which depends on the second. Two of the scribes realized that there were errors here. The scribe of MS *H* tells us in a marginal note (see the text below, Prop. IV.13, var. lines 3–7): "The text as well as the commentary [i.e. proof] is false." Similarly MS *D* has a marginal note: "The second part seems to contradict the penultimate [proposition] of the third of Euclid with the help of the sixteenth of the sixth of Euclid" (*ibid.,* var. to lines 8–12). I should reiterate here that the inclusion of these erroneous parts of Proposition IV.13 by the author of the *Liber de triangulis Iordani* is very telling evidence that that author was not Jordanus, who was surely too accomplished a geometer to commit or accept such elementary errors.

I have given reasons below in Appendix III.B for suspecting that Propositions IV.14–IV.16 constitute a small tract on quadrature which was translated from the Arabic and was added to the *Liber de triangulis Iordani* by its author without much change. Proposition IV.14 holds that any mean proportionals between the same extremes are equal, a proposition that is an auxiliary proposition to Proposition IV.16. Its proof is simple (see Fig. IV.14): (1) Let $A / B = B / D$, and $A / C = C / D$. (2) If it is supposed by falsigraph that *B* is not equal to *C*, let $B > C$, and let *A* be the larger extreme. (3) Then

$A / C > A / B$. (4) Hence $C / D > B / D$, by (1) and (3). Therefore (5) $C > B$, which contradicts falsigraph's supposition in (2). The same argument would hold if we let $B < C$. Q.E.D.

Proposition IV.15 is a special case of Proposition IV.8, as the scribe of MS *H* tells us in a marginal note (see the text below, Prop. IV.15, var. to lines 1–3). Hence one would have supposed that the author of the *Liber de triangulis Iordani* would not have bothered to have added this proposition. The fact that it was included appears to give support to my conclusion that the author of the *Liber de triangulis Iordani* added the three propositions (IV.14–IV.16) much as they existed in the form of their translation from the Arabic. In fact there is no real mathematical reason for Proposition IV.15 to be given in connection with the quadrature problem. It holds that an octagon inscribed in a circle is the mean proportional between an inscribed and a circumscribed square. The proof concentrates on the third and the fourth parts of the figure (see Fig. IV.15) "because the geometer will easily and with zeal infer the whole from the third and fourth [parts]." Line *OE* bisects *AB* at *I* and is perpendicular thereto. Now angle *O* is common to triangles *OEB* and *OIB*, while angle *I* (in tri. *OIB*) and angle *B* (in tri. *OEB*) are right angles. Therefore the two triangles are similar. Therefore their sides are proportional, i.e. $OE / OB = OB / OI$. Then $OB = OK$ (since they are equal radii). Therefore $OE / OK = OK / OI$. Since triangles *OEB*, *OKB*, and *OIB* have equal altitudes, tri. *OEB* / tri. *OKB* = tri. *OKB* / tri. *OIB*. Therefore equal multiples of these triangles are also proportionals, and the circumscribed square, the inscribed octagon, and the inscribed square are equal multiples of the triangles *OEB*, *OKB*, and *OIB* respectively. Therefore the proposition follows.

The question still remains as to why the original author added the proposition. I suspect that he wished to set aside the view held in some quarters that the circle was the mean proportional between the circumscribed and the inscribed squares, a view perhaps arrived at by a misunderstanding of Bryson's quadrature (see my Volume 1, pp. 426–27). This interpretation may have been the object of the comment added in MS *Pe* to the beginning of the proposition's curious corollary (see my English translation of Proposition IV.15, n. 3, for a discussion of the corollary).

The last of the trio of propositions under discussion is the quadrature proposition itself: "To construct a square equal to a proposed circle." Let the circle be *A* (see Fig. IV.16). Let there be another circle *B*. Let squares *DE* and *FG* be circumscribed about the circles. By Proposition XII.2 of Euclid circle *A* / circle *B* = sq. *DE* / sq. *FG*. Hence, permutatively, sq. *DE* / cir. *A* = sq. *FG* / cir. *B*. Now let *C* stand as a third proportional after *DE* and *A*, *C* being either a circle or some other kind of surface, as say a rectilinear figure. In the first instance let *C* be a circle, about which a square *HK* is circumscribed. Hence $DE / A = A / C$. But also, by XII.2 of Euclid, $DE / A = HK / C$. Therefore *HK* as well as *A* is a mean proportional between *DE* and *C*. Hence [by Prop. IV.14 of this work] circle *A* and *HK* are equal.

Q.E.D. A proof is also given if C is not a circle but is a rectilinear figure. Let that figure be transformed into square *RSYX* by Proposition II.14 of Euclid. Now square *DE* is the larger of the extremes and hence the side of *DE* is greater than the side of *RY*. Whence let *MT*, equal to side *RX*, be cut off from side *MD* [and draw *TN* parallel to *ME*]. Hence, *MN* is a rectangle contained by *ME* and *MT*. Therefore *MN* is a mean proportional between squares *DE* and *RY*. But circle *A* was also a mean proportional between square *DE* and surface *C* (or its equal square *RY*). Therefore [by IV.14 of this work] circle *A* and rectangle *MN* are equal. Then if we convert *MN* to a square by Proposition II.14 of Euclid, we shall have the required square equal to a circle.

As I have already said in an earlier discussion of this proposition in Volume 1 (see pp. 567–68), the intent of the author is to find a figure which is a third proportional term after the circumscribed square and the given circle:

> In the first part of the proof that figure is posited as being a circle, while in the second it is a rectilinear figure. In both cases it is shown that the desired square equal to the proposed circle is, like the original circle, a mean proportional between the circumscribed square and the third proportional term. But it is evident that we are not told how to construct the third proportional surface, whether it is a circle or a rectilinear figure, but only that there exists such a third proportional term. We are accordingly at a loss to construct the desired square equal to the proposed circle.

Proposition IV.17 is an isolated proposition extraneous to the main theorems of either the *Liber philotegni* or of the *Liber de triangulis Iordani*. In Appendix III.B below I argue that its source was some translation from the Arabic by Gerard of Cremona. The proposition is a problem which requires that, if we have two given squares, we circumscribe one as a gnomon about the other. The solution is quite simple (see Fig. IV.17). Let the two squares be *AD* and *EG*. We prolong side *AB* by the magnitude *BN* equal to side *HG*. Then we draw line *DN*. By the Pythagorean theorem $DN^2 = BN^2 + BD^2$. But BN^2 and BD^2 are equal to the two given squares. Therefore lay off *AM* on line *AN* such that $AM = DN$. On *AM* construct the square *AK*, which is obviously equal to the sum of the given squares. Then, since square *AD* is within square *AK*, the gnomonic remainder is obviously equal to the other square *EG*, as the proposition requires.

Proposition IV.18 is another isolated proposition which I believe to have had its source in a translation from the Arabic by Gerard of Cremona (see Appendix III.B below). Putting it in its positive form, we see that the proposition tells us that two [adjacent] sides of a parallelogram include the largest area when they meet perpendicularly, i.e., the rectangle so formed has the largest area of all parallelograms that have the same adjacent sides. Again we have a very simple proof (see Fig. IV.18). Let *AE* be a parallelogram with sides *AB* and *AC* meeting at an acute angle. Erect from *B* a perpendicular to line *CE*, which meets it at *G*. Angle *G* is right and hence is the maximum angle in triangle *BEG*, and so $BE > BG$. Let *BG* be extended to *F* so that

BF = *BE*. Construct the rectangle *AF* and extend *CE* to meet *AD* in *H*. Parallelograms *AHGB* and *ACEB* are equal because they are on the same base and have the same altitude. Hence rectangle *AF* equally exceeds its part *AHGB* and the latter's equal *ACEB*. The same proof would obtain if sides *AB* and *AC* meet at any other acute or any obtuse angle.

Proposition IV.19 (whose source is unidentified) is another independent proposition that is not without interest. It holds that of those triangles in which two sides of the one are equal to two sides of the other the one whose two sides include a right angle is the greatest of all such triangles. Let us examine the proof (see Fig. IV.19). First take triangle *ABC* whose sides *AC* and *AB* form a right angle. Then take any line *AE* which is equal to *AB* and which forms an acute angle with *AC*. Complete the triangle *AEC*. Also complete triangle *AEB*. Since *AE* = *AB*, the base angles at *B* and *E* of triangle *AEB* are equal, and hence each is less than a right angle. So from *B* draw a line *BF* parallel to *AC* which meets *AE* extended at *F*, and *F* is beyond *E* because angle *ABC* is a right angle and *ABE* is acute. Connect *F* and *C*. Hence triangles *ABC* and *AFC* are equal since they are on the same base and are between parallel lines. But triangle *AFC* is greater than *AEC* because angle *ABF* is a right angle while *ABE* is an acute angle so that *AEC* becomes a part of triangle *AFC*. Hence the triangle whose two sides include a right angle is greater than any triangle whose two sides include an acute angle.

The same argument may be used when the two sides include an obtuse angle. Take any line *AH* equal to line *AB* and meeting line *AC* at an obtuse angle. Draw line *HC* to complete the triangle. Also complete triangle *AHB*. Since *AH* = *AB*, the base angles of this last triangle are equal and each is less than a right angle. Then draw line *BG* parallel to *AC* and meeting *AH* extended at *G*. And *G* is beyond *H* because angle *ABG* is a right angle and *ABH* is acute. Draw line *GC* forming triangle *AGC*. It is clear then that triangles *AGC* and *ABC* are equal since they are on the same base between parallel lines. But triangle *AHC* is a part of triangle *AGC* and so is less than it and also is less than its equal, triangle *ABC*. And so we have proved the proposition for both acute angles and obtuse angles. The author then poses an incomprehensible impossibility, namely a case in which *AE* would fall inside of *CH*. But he holds that even then, if *E* is joined with *C*, the triangle will still be less than *AGC* and so less than *ABC*. It will occur to the reader that this proposition is equivalent to Proposition IV.3, as I indicated earlier. But the compositor of the *Liber de triangulis Iordani* neglects to comment on this equivalence.

Proposition IV.20 concerns the classical problem of trisecting an angle. It gives three treatments. The first (lines 3–24) consists of a paraphrase of Proposition XVIII of the *Verba filiorum* of the Banū Mūsā translated by Gerard of Cremona. The second (lines 25–28) is a minor modification of part of the solution of the Banū Mūsā, while the third (lines 29–43) is a proof that gives formal geometric authority for the *neusis* that lies at the heart of the preceding proof. That authority is a proposition from the *Perspectiva* [of

Alhazen] whose proof is based on the use of conic sections.[17] I have treated Proposition IV.20 in Volume 1 (pp. 344–48, 366–67, 666–77) and need not discuss it at further length here, except to remark that in my earlier discussion (before I had realized that the *Liber de triangulis Iordani* was composed by some one other than Jordanus) I presumed that Jordanus had suggested the third treatment. I say now that there is no evidence to connect Jordanus with that treatment or indeed with putting the three treatments together. However, as I point out below in Appendix III.B, it seems probable that the person who produced the paraphrase of Proposition XVIII of the *Verba filiorum* also composed the second and third treatments, for the author links the second solution (or modification) to the first (see lines 25–28) and he links the third to what has gone before (lines 29–31). But regardless of the identity of the clever geometer who produced this whole proposition (and had the wit to say that he found "nothing certain" in the mechanical solution embraced by the first and second parts), it is evident that the complete proposition was a part of that collection of Arabic-based propositions that the author of the *Liber de triangulis Iordani* added to his tract almost intact.

Proposition IV.21 is a proposition slightly modified from a fragment translated by Gerard of Cremona from the Arabic (see Appendix III.B). The problem is to find a point within a triangle from which lines to the angles will divide the triangle into three parts each of which has a given ratio to the whole. Proposition II.18 is the special case of this proposition when all the parts are equal so that each part is ⅓ of the whole triangle. Let the triangle be *ABG* (see Fig. IV.21). Then the ratio that each part has to the whole is indicated by dividing line *AG* into three segments at *D* and *E* that have the ratios to the whole line which the parts of the triangle are to have to the whole triangle. Thus we seek point *T* such that tri. *BTG* / tri. *ABG* = *DG* / *AG*, tri. *ATB* / tri. *ABG* = *AE* / *AG*, and tri. *ATG* / tri. *ABG* = *ED* / *AG*. The solution is simple. We draw line *DZ* parallel to side *GB* and line *EH* parallel to side *AB*. These lines intersect in point *T*, which is the required point from which we draw lines *AT*, *TG*, and *TB*. This is proved as follows. [Tri. *BDG* / tri. *ABG* = *DG* / *AG* since their altitudes are equal.] But tri. *BDG* = tri. *BTG* since they are on the same base between parallel lines. Thus tri. *BTG* / tri. *ABG* = *DG* / *AG*. [Similarly tri. *AEB* / tri. *ABG* = *AE* / *AG*.] Therefore, since tri. *AEB* = tri. *ATB* (again because they are on the same base between parallel lines) so tri. *ATB* / tri. *ABG* = *AE* / *AG*. And since the ratios of the first two parts of the triangle to the whole triangle are the same as the ratios of two parts of the line to the whole line, hence the ratio of the third part of the triangle to the whole triangle will be as the

---

[17] The proposition is cited in the *Liber de triangulis Iordani* merely as "per figuram 19. quinti perspective." I have shown in Volume 4 of my *Archimedes in the Middle Ages*, pp. 19–20, n. 41, that this reflects a numbering system associated with manuscripts of the *Perspectiva* which I call the "Royal College tradition." This is the proposition which Risner labels as V.34. I have translated and discussed it in Vol. 4, pp. 25–26, 28–29.

ratio of the third part of the line to the whole line, i.e., tri. ATG / tri. ABG = ED / AG.

Proposition IV.22 seeks to find between two unequal quantities two other quantities such that the four quantities are in continued proportion. As I observe below in Appendix III.B, the first proof of this proposition (lines 4–42) was taken directly from Proposition XVI of the *Verba filiorum* of the Banū Mūsā (see Vol. 1, pp. 334–41). The source of the second proof is a fragment translated by Gerard of Cremona from the Arabic, which is edited below in Appendix III.B and which was added in substantially the same form to the *Practica geometrie* of Leonardo Fibonacci (*ibid.*, p. 664). My previous comments on these two proofs (*ibid.*, p. 365–66 and 658–61) make further discussion of them unnecessary.

Proposition IV.23's source was a long fragment translated by Gerard of Cremona from the Arabic and edited below in Appendix III.B. It seeks to inscribe a regular heptagon in a circle. Before examining the solutions given in Proposition IV.23, we should look at a beautiful *neusis*-based solution appearing in an Arabic work entitled *On the Division of the Circle into Seven Parts* and attributed to Archimedes. No such work is extant in the Greek. The pertinent part consists of the following two propositions:[18]

Proposition 16

Let us construct square $ABCD$ [Fig. IV.23*Arch. 1*] and extend side AB directly toward H. Then we draw the diagonal BC. We lay one end of a rule on point D. Its other end we make meet extension AH at a point Z such that tri. AZE = tri. CTD. Further, we draw the straight line KTL through T and parallel to AC. And now I say that $AB \cdot KB = AZ^2$ and $ZK \cdot AK = KB^2$ and, in addition, each of the two lines AZ and $KB > AK$.

Proof:

(1) $CD \cdot TL = AZ \cdot AE$ [given]. Hence (2) $[CD(=AB)]$ / $AZ = AE$ / TL. Since tri. ZAE is similar to tri. ZKT and to tri. TLD, hence (3) AE / $TL = AZ$ / $[LD(=KB)]$, AB / $AZ = AZ$ / KB, and $[TL(=AK)]$ / $[KT(=KB)]$ = $[LD(=KB)]$ / ZK. Therefore (4) $AB \cdot KB = AZ^2$ and $ZK \cdot AK = KB^2$, and each of the lines AZ and $KB > AK$. Q.E.D.

Proposition 17

We now wish to divide the circle into seven equal parts (Fig. IV.23*Arch. 2*). We draw the line segment AB, which we set out as known. We mark on it two points C and D, such that $AD \cdot CD = DB^2$ and $CB \cdot BD = AC^2$ and in addition

---

[18] This translation-paraphrase is given in my article "Archimedes," *Dictionary of Scientific Biography*, Vol. 1 (New York, 1970), pp. 224–25, whole article, pp. 213–31. It was made from the German translation of C. Schoy, *Die trigonometrischen Lehren des persischen Astronomen Abû 'l-Raihân Muḥ ibn Aḥmad al-Bîrûnî* (Hannover, 1927), pp. 82–84. See J. Tropfke, "Die Siebeneckabhandlung des Archimedes," *Osiris*, Vol. 1 (1936), pp. 636–51, and Tropfke's *Geschichte der Elementar-Mathematik*, 3rd. ed., Vol. 3 (Berlin and Leipzig, 1937), pp. 127–28. The earlier article of Schoy, "Graeco-Arabische Studien," *Isis*, Vol. 8 (1926), pp. 21–40, is still useful.

each of the two segments AC and $DB > CD$, following the preceding discussion [i.e., Prop. 16]. Out of segments AC, CD and BD we construct tri. CHD. Accordingly $CH = AC$, $DH = DB$ and $CD = CD$. Then we circumscribe about tri. AHB the circle $AHBEZ$ and we extend lines HC and HD directly up to the circumference of the circle. On their intersections with the circumference lie the points Z and E. We join B with Z. Lines BZ and HE intersect in T. We also draw CT. Since $AC = CH$, hence angle HAC = angle AHC, and arc AZ = arc HB. And indeed, $AD \cdot CD = DB^2 = DH^2$ and [by Euclid VI.5] tri. AHD is similar to tri. CHD; consequently angle DAH = angle CHD, or arc ZE = arc BH. Hence BH, AZ and ZE are three equal arcs. Further, ZB is parallel to AH, angle CAH = angle CHD = angle TBD; $HD = DB$, $CD = DT$, $CH = BT$. Hence, [since the products of the parts of these diagonals are equal], the 4 points B, H, C and T lie in the circumference of one and the same circle. From the similarity of triangles HBC and HBT, it follows that $CB \cdot DB = HC^2 = AC^2$ [or HT / HC = HC / HD] and from the similarity of tri. THC and tri. CHD, it follows that $TH \cdot HD = HC^2$. And further $CB = TH$ [these being equal diagonals in the quadrilateral] and angle DCH = angle HTC = 2 angle CAH. [The equality of the first two angles arises from the similarity of triangles THC and CHD. Their equality with 2 angle CAH arises as follows: (1) AHD = 2 angle CAH, for angle CAH = angle CHD = angle CHA and angle AHD = angle CHA + angle CHD; (2) angle AHD = angle BTH, for parallel lines cut by a third line produce equal alternate angles; (3) angle BTH = angle DCH, from similar triangles; (4) hence angle DCH = 2 angle CAH. And since angle HBA = angle DCH, hence angle HBA = 2 angle CAH]. Consequently, arc AH = 2 arc HB. Since angle DHB = angle DBH, consequently arc EB = 2 arc HB. Hence, each of arcs AH and EB equals 2 arc HB, and accordingly the circle $AHBEZ$ is divided into seven equal parts. Q.E.D. And praise be to the one God, etc.

The key to the whole procedure is, of course, the *neusis* presented in Proposition 16 that would allow us in a similar fashion to find the points C and D in Proposition 17. In Proposition 16 the *neusis* consisted in drawing a line from D to intersect the extension of AB in point Z such that tri. AZE = tri. CTD. The way in which the *neusis* was solved by Archimedes (or whoever was the author of this tract) is not known. Ibn al-Haytham, in a later treatment of the heptagon, mentions the Archimedean *neusis* but then goes on to show that one does not need the Archimedean square of Proposition 16. Rather he shows that points C and D in Proposition 17 can be found by the intersection of a parabola and a hyperbola.[19]

The popularity of this problem among the Arabs is well known,[20] and

---

[19] Schoy, *Die trigonometrischen Lehren,* pp. 85–91. This is superseded by the excellent study of R. Rashed, "La construction de l'heptagone régulier par Ibn al-Haytham," *Journal for the History of Arabic Science,* Vol. 3 (1979), pp. 309–386. Rashed not only gives an analysis and an edition of the Arabic text of the first of Ibn al-Haytham's two works on the heptagon (*Tract on the Lemma for the side of the Heptagon*), a work already translated into German by Schoy in the reference indicated above, but Rashed also edits, translates, and analyzes the second, longer tract of Ibn al-Haytham (*Tract on the Construction of the Heptagon*).

[20] A. Anbouba "Construction of the Regular Heptagon by Middle Eastern Geometers of the Fourth (Hijra) Century," *Journal for the History of Arabic Science,* Vol. 1 (1977), pp. 319 (summary), 384 *et prec.* for Arabic article (see Arabic pp. 73–105). See also the partial French translation in *Ibid.* Vol. 2 (1978), pp. 264–269.

hence it is not surprising that Gerard of Cremona should have found the miscellaneous treatments embraced by the fragment he translated. Let us examine the three parts of the proposition. The first is a mechanical solution (lines 3–49). By it we are to insert in a circle of center G the side $D'B$ of a regular heptagon (see Fig. IV.23). Bisect radius AG at H. Erect perpendiculars HQ and GD. Join A to D and extend that line indefinitely in the direction of D. It will intersect HQ at E. Connect E with G and extend EG in both directions until it intersects the circumference at M and L. Connect D and L. Bisect DG at T and from T protract an indefinitely long perpendicular TZ. Now we shall set the lines in motion as follows. Line AD (with its indefinite extension) is moved about A as a center so that it takes enough of the indefinite extension to keep D on the circumference. As a consequence of this motion, line ML moves about center G as its intersection E with QH (which line remains fixed) slides along QH toward H. Thus M is moving along the circumference toward A and L is moving on the circumference toward B. As a consequence of the motions of AD and ML, line DL is always becoming smaller and radius DG is rotating about center G. As DG moves, TZ (the fixed perpendicular at T) also moves and always intersects the shrinking DL at K. Now these interlocking motions continue until point K falls upon diameter AB at K'. The motion is then stopped and the various lines are at the positions indicated by the prime signs: AD at AD', ML at $M'E'L'$, DG at $D'G$, and TKZ at $T'K'Z'$. The result is that the chord of arc $D'B$ is the side of a regular heptagon inscribed in circle G. That this is so, we can see as follows. Angle $D'GK'$ is double angle $D'AG$ since it is extrinsic to triangle $D'AG$, which is isosceles since its sides are radii. Now angle $D'AG$ is equal to angle AGE' because $AH = HG$ and HE' is perpendicular to AG. Therefore angle $D'GK'$ is double angle AGE'. Furthermore, angle $E'GD'$, extrinsic to triangle $D'GL'$, which is isosceles because its sides are radii, is equal to double angle $GD'L'$. But angle $GD'L' =$ angle $D'GK'$ because $GT' = T'D'$ and $T'K'$ is perpendicular to $D'G$ (thus making triangles $GT'K'$ and $D'T'K'$ congruent). Therefore $E'GD'$ is double angle $D'GK'$. Therefore the semicircumference $BD'A$ equals $3\frac{1}{2}$ times arc $D'B$, and hence the circumference is 7 times arc $D'B$. Therefore its chord is the side of a regular heptagon.

Now let us turn to the second treatment of the problem (lines 50–56). This brief statement indicates in a general way what we may make specific by consulting Fig. IV.23*var. Ve.* When a line AB is divided into three segments AD, DC, and CB such that $BC / AD = AD / DB$ (DB being the sum $DC + CB$) and that $DC / CB = CB / AC$ (AC being the sum $DC + AD$) and we form a triangle with the three segments as its sides (i.e. triangle AED), then its greatest angle AED is double its middle angle EAD and that angle EAD is double the smallest angle ADE. Then if we circumscribe a circle about this triangle, the smallest side AE is the side of a regular heptagon inscribed in that circle. Now it should be immediately evident that triangle AED is precisely the triangle CHD in Archimedes' proof (see Fig. IV.23*Arch. 2*), where line AB is divided into the segments having the same relationships as those of line AB here in Proposition IV.23, and where angle $HDC = 2$ angle DCH, and angle $DCH = 2$ angle CHD. Furthermore it is obvious in Archimedes' proof that triangle *AHB*, which was constructed by finding *H* as the intersection of one arc of radius *DB* with a second arc of radius *AC*, is similar to triangle *CHD* (since angle *BHA* = 2 angle *HBA* and angle *HBA* = 2 angle *BAH*). Archimedes showed that arc *HB* is a seventh part of the circumference, or that side *HB* is the side of a regular heptagon inscribed in a circle circumscribed about triangle *AHB*. But since triangle *CHD* is similar to *AHB*, it is equally evident that if we circumscribe a circle about triangle *CHD*, then its smallest side *DC* would be the side of a regular heptagon inscribed in that circle, and this in fact is what has been asserted in this second part of Proposition IV.23. Incidentally MS *Ve* has added a proof that if line *AB* is divided in the manner indicated, the angles of triangle *AED* will have the stated relationships (see the English translation of Proposition IV.23 below, n. 6, where I have provided an English translation of *Ve*'s proof).

The final treatment found in Proposition IV.23 (lines 57–71) expounds an Indian rule, much of which "depends on belief alone without demonstration, but the difference between it and the truth is not a sensible quantity," as the author says. The rule is one that may be used to find approximately the side of any regular polygon inscribed in a circle. This rule we may summarize in more modern fashion as follows: $s^2 = (r \cdot 2r \cdot 9) / \{[n \cdot (n-1)/2] + 3\}$, where s is the side and r is the radius. Though the rule is given with an indication that we could find the side of the heptagon from it, this is not actually done here. If we followed the rule, we should find for a heptagon that $s = \frac{1}{2}\sqrt{3}\ r$. The author further notes that the Indians also pose that the side of a regular heptagon is half of the side of an equilateral triangle inscribed in the same circle.

Propositions IV.24 and IV.25 concern the excesses of the sides of triangles with unequal sides. IV.24 restricts itself to a right triangle of unequal sides in which the longest side exceeds the middle side by the same quantity that the middle exceeds the shortest. We may express the proposition in terms of the specific triangle *ABG* in Fig. IV.24. The sides of the triangle are *AG* the shortest, *AB* the middle, and *BG* the longest. It is given that $AB - AG = BG - AB$. Let us mark off *BE* equal to *AB* and *BD* equal to *AG*. Hence $DE = EG$, and let us call the equal excess throughout the proof *EG*. Hence in Proposition IV.24 we have to prove (1) that $AB = 4\ EG$, $AG = 3\ EG$, and $BG = 5\ EG$, and (2) that $AG = \frac{1}{4}$ perimeter of tri. *ABG*, while $AB = \frac{1}{3}$ same perim. and $BG = \frac{5}{12}$ same perim. [Since $BG = 2\ AB - AG$ (given), $BG^2 = 4\ AB^2 - 4\ AB \cdot AG + AG^2 =] 4\ BE \cdot EG + BD^2$. By the Pythagorean theorem, $BG^2 = BE^2 + BD^2$. Hence $BE^2 + BD^2 = 4\ BE \cdot EG + BD^2$. Therefore $BE = AB = 4\ EG$, and so $BD = AG = 3\ EG$ and $BG = 5\ EG$ (by subtracting *DE* from *BE* and adding *EG* to *BE*), as the first part of the proposition holds. Now the perimeter of triangle $ABG = 4\ EG + 3\ EG + 5\ EG = 12\ EG$. Hence $AB = \frac{1}{3}$ perim., $AG = \frac{1}{4}$ perim., and $BG = \frac{5}{12}$ perim., and the second part of the proposition follows.

In Proposition IV.25 the concern is with any triangle of unequal sides, and we are told that the ratio of the excess of the longer side over the shorter to the excess of the larger segment of the base cut off by the so-called case perpendicular over the shorter segment cut off by the same perpendicular will be equal to the ratio of the base to the sum of the other two sides. In terms of the specific magnitudes of Fig. IV.25 we are to prove that if we have a triangle ABG with AB the shorter side, AG the longer side, BG the base and AD the perpendicular to the base, then $(AG - AB) / (DG - DB) = BG / (AB + AG)$. With A as the center draw a circle of radius AB cutting the longer side at V and the base at E. Extend GA to Z on the circumference. Then $VG = AG - AB$ (AB being equal to AV) and $EG = DG - DB$ (DB being equal to DE). [By the Pythagorean theorem $AG^2 = AD^2 + DG^2$ and $AB^2 = AD^2 + DB^2$. Then subtracting the second equation from the first, $AG^2 - AB^2 = DG^2 - DB^2$ or $(AG + AB) \cdot (AG - AB) = (DG + DB) \cdot (DG - DB)$. Now if we substitute the equal quantities given above], therefore $BG \cdot EG = ZG \cdot GV$. Therefore, $BG / ZG = GV / EG$. But $ZG = AG + AB$. Therefore $BG / (AG + AB) = (AG - AB) / (DG - BD)$. And so the proposition is proved.

The last three propositions (IV.26–IV.28) have their source in another fragment translated by Gerard of Cremona from the Arabic, that is all but lines 19–29 of Proposition IV.28 (see Appendix III.B for the text of this fragment). It is not without interest that in MS *Ve* the three propositions bear the title *Propositiones de proportionibus* (see text below, Proposition IV.26, var. to line 1). The overall objective of Propositions IV.26 and IV.27 is to show, in the case of three continually proportional lines, that the ratio of the first to the third is equal to the square of the ratio of the first to the second. Proposition IV.28 follows this with a similar conclusion for four continually proportional lines, namely that the ratio of the first to the fourth is equal to the cube of the first to the second. In proving these propositions concerning continually proportional lines, the author uses and develops theorems like the first three found in the *Liber de proportionibus*, a work anonymous in most manuscripts but attributed to Jordanus in one manuscript and to Thābit ibn Qurra in another, and similarly the first three present in the *Tractatus Campani de proportione et proportionalitate*. We may summarize these three theorems as follows: (1) If $H = A / B$, then $H \cdot B = A$, (2) If A, B, and C are any three like quantities, then $A / C = (A / B) \cdot (B / C)$, and (3) If A, B, C, and D are any four like quantities, $A / D = (A / B) \cdot (B / C) \cdot (C / D)$.[21]

In the specific proof of Proposition IV.26 the author proves that with three lines disposed in any fashion the ratio of the first to the third is equal to the ratio of the product of the first and the second to the product of the second to the third. This is easily shown (see Fig. IV.26). Let AB, GD, and ET be the three lines. After drawing an indefinitely long straight line, we lay off on

---

[21] See Clagett, *Archimedes in the Middle Ages*, Vol. 2, pp. 13–24. Above all see H. L. L. Busard, "Die Traktate *De proportionibus* von Jordanus Nemorarius und Campanus," *Centaurus*, Vol. 15 (1971), pp. 193–227.

it segment HT' equal to AB. At T' we erect a perpendicular $T'L$ equal to GD. Finally from point T' we mark off on the indefinite line a segment $T'K$ equal to ET. A line parallel to HK is drawn through point L and the rectangles HL and LK are completed. Their altitudes are the same. Therefore $HL / LK = HT' / T'K$. But $HT' = AB$, and $T'K = ET$. Therefore $AB / ET = (AB \cdot GD) / (GD \cdot ET)$, the latter products being equal to the rectangles HL and LK.

Now in Proposition IV.27 the author sets out to prove first that $AB / ET = (AB / GD) \cdot (GD / ET)$, which by modern procedures is immediately obvious. However in the medieval geometrical theory of ratios and proportions and their manipulations, a separate proof is required, or at least so the author feels. Let me summarize the proof briefly (see Fig. IV.27). From the preceding proposition we have (1) $AB / ET = (AB \cdot GD) / (GD \cdot ET)$. (2) Let $H = AB / GD$; hence $H \cdot GD = AB$ ("since ratio is division").[22] (3) Let $T' = GD / ET$; hence $T' \cdot ET = GD$. (4) Let $L = AB / ET$; hence $L \cdot ET = AB$. Now we are to prove that $L = H \cdot T'$. Let us assume (5) that there is some K such that $H \cdot T' = K$, and thus we are to prove that $K = L$. (6) Lines H, T', and ET are three lines, and hence from Prop. IV.26, we know that $H / ET = (H \cdot T') / (T' \cdot ET)$, (7) $H / ET = K / DG$, from (6), (5), and (3). (8) Therefore $H \cdot GD = K \cdot ET$, permutatively from (7). (9) So $AB = K \cdot ET$, from (8) and (2). (10) $L \cdot ET = K \cdot ET$, from (9) and (4). (11) Hence $K = L$, and so we have proved that $L = H \cdot T'$ and hence that $AB / ET = (AB / GD) \cdot (GD / ET)$. Now we are prepared to prove the main object of the two propositions, namely that $AB / ET = (AB / GD)^2$ when AB, GD, and ET are continuously proportional lines, that is when $AB / GD = GD / ET$. This is exceedingly simple, for we merely have to substitute AB / GD for its equal GD / ET in equation (11), and the result is what we desire: $AB / ET = (AB / ET) \cdot (AB / ET)$.

As I have already said, Proposition IV.28 considers four continuously proportional lines. In terms of the magnitudes of Fig. IV.28 it concludes that with A, B, G, and D the continuously proportional lines, $A / D = (A / B)^3$. First take three lines A, G, and D. By the main part of Prop. IV.27, $A / D = (A / G) \cdot (G / D)$. Then take the three continually proportional lines A, B, and G. By the final conclusion of IV.27, $A / G = (A / B)^2$. Therefore putting the two equations together, $A / D = (A / B)^2 \cdot (G / D)$. But $G / D = A / B$ because the four lines are continually proportional. Therefore A / D

---

[22] This fits in with the concept of the "denomination" of a ratio given in the two treatises on ratios and proportions mentioned above and in the preceding footnote and the citations in that note will lead the reader to the specific passages which are pertinent. Needless to say, it is the concept of ratio as a division that is behind the popular view among the Arabic authors which we may summarize as follows: one pair of magnitudes has the same ratio to a second pair of magnitudes if the series of quotients (arising from continuous division) of the first pair is equal term by term to the series of quotients of the second pair, whether the two series are finite or infinite. For a general treatment of this subject see E. B. Plooij, *Euclid's Conception of Ratio and his Definition of Proportional Magnitudes as Criticized by Arabian Commentators* (Rotterdam [1950]).

$= (A / B)^3$, which is what the proposition held. A second demonstration was added to this proposition, but it was not a part of Gerard of Cremona's fragment, and I presume was added by the author of the *Liber de triangulis Iordani* or some other Latin author. I have reconstructed and translated that additional proof in my translation of Proposition IV.28, n. 1, below.

Thus ends the rather diverse collection of propositions added to the *Liber de triangulis Iordani*. I have suggested that it was less coherent and indeed less satisfying as an original work than Jordanus' *Liber philotegni* from whence it departed. However, in adding the sundry propositions from the Arabic at the end of the work, its author did a service in preserving vestiges of the Arabic solutions of some of the classical problems of Greek geometry with which Archimedes and others of the best Greek geometers concerned themselves: problems like the trisection of an angle, the finding of two means between the two given magnitudes so that the four magnitudes are in continued proportion, and the inscription of a regular heptagon in a circle.

Chapter 2

The Text of the
Liber de triangulis Iordani

The critical text of the *Liber de triangulis Iordani* presented below is based on all of the extant manuscripts listed with *sigla* at the end of the chapter (though the late manuscript *Es* has been collated only through Proposition I.8). I undertook a new edition of the work since the edition published by Curtze in 1887 (see the bibliographical reference under the description of MS *D* in the *Sigla* below) was based on MS *D* alone (with occasional references to MS *Bu*). Hence many of the preferred readings of the other manuscripts were not available to Curtze. Furthermore Curtze's text included a substantial number of misreadings of the text in MS *D* or other changes made by Curtze (often silently) as the result of his misunderstanding of the text.[1] I mention

---

[1] I note the following instances (the references are to variants with the proposition and line numbers noted, the references almost always being followed by *injuste Dc*): the change of *termini* to *terminorum* (Intro. var. lin. 2), of *incontinuitas* to *in continuitatis* (Intro. var. lin. 9), of *sit* to *si* (I.3 var. lin. 6), *aut* to *vel* (I.3 var. lin. 11), of *sigillatim* to *singillatim* (II.9 var. lin. 4), of *habeat* to *habet* (II.14 var. lin. 7), of *linea* to *linee* (II.16 var. lin. 2), *minor* to *maior* (II.16 var. lin. 3), *omni* to *omnium* (II.16 var. lins. 3 and 6), after *linea* the unjust addition of [*MA*] (II.16 var. lin. 14), the change of *similis* to *minor* (II.17 var. lin. 13), of *CGB* to *DGB* and *DGA* to *CGA* (III.2 var. lin. 20), of *circumferentiam* to *circumferentiarum* (III.10 var. lin. 11), *Age* to *Argue* (IV.7 var. lin. 10), of *HA* to *AH* (IV.7 var. lin. 25), of *trigoni* to *trianguli* (IV.7 var. lin. 25), of *erit triangulus ZLH* to *triangulus ZHL erit* (IV.7 var. lins. 26–27), of *constitues* to *constituens* (IV.7 var. lin. 35), of *medietate* to *medietati* (IV.11 var. lin. 25), the omission of *argues* (IV.13 var. lin. 10), the change of *extremitatum* to *medietatum* (IV.14 var. lins. 1–2), of *illorum* to *eorum* (IV.15 var. lins. 14 and 16), of *proportionalia* to *proportionales* (IV.15 var. lin. 17), the silent omission of the corollary (IV.15 var. lins. 18–19), the change of *dulk* to *diametrum* (IV.17 var. lin. 6), of *perinde* to *permutatim* (IV.17 var. lin. 10), of *ac-* to *AD* (IV.17 var. lin. 10), of *contingant* to *contingunt* (IV.18 var. lin. 2), the omission of *est* (IV.19 var. lin. 12), the change of *sive* to *cum* (IV.19 var. lin. 26), of *etiam* to *erit* (IV.19 var. lin. 28), of *caderet* to *cadet* (IV.19 var. lin. 28), of *Age* to *Argue* (IV.20 var. lin 14), of *equedistanter* to *equedistans* (IV.20 var. lin. 35), of *erectam* to *erecti* (IV.22 var. lin. 18), of *determinavimus* to *declaravimus* (IV.23 var. lins. 11 and 30), of *AD predicte* to *ad precedens* (IV.23 var. lin. 18), of *sicut est* to *super* (IV.23 var. lin 20), of *et erit puncti* to *cadit punctus* (IV.23 var. lin. 31), of *Age* to *Argue* (IV.25 var. lin. 7), of *HT'[1]* to *HL* (IV.26 var. lin. 17).

---

the consequences of some of the more serious of Curtze's errors in the English translation below (Intro., n. 1; Prop. II.16, nn. 1–2; Prop. II.17, n. 2; Prop. III.2, n. 2: Prop. IV.14, n. 1; Prop. IV.15, n. 3; Prop. IV.17, n. 4; and Prop. IV.23, n. 3) and so I need not elaborate on them at this point, except to lament the complex of errors in Curtze's text of Prop. II.16 which indicates that Curtze did not have the faintest notion of the meaning of the enunciation. Further I should briefly remark that Curtze gave no indication of the actual forms of the diagrams, silently changing them to fit the enunciations and proofs as necessary.[2] Finally I note that Curtze included no translation and only a skimpy and not always correct analysis of the propositions, and that he had no knowledge of the distinctiveness of the *Liber de triangulis Iordani* as compared to the original *Liber philotegni* composed by Jordanus. For him there was only one work, namely the *Liber de triangulis Iordani,* and this was the work of Jordanus. Nor did Curtze have any precise information about the fragments of Arabic texts which Gerard of Cremona had translated and which the author of the *Liber de triangulis Iordani* employed for many of his added propositions in Book IV, though of course Curtze knew of the material drawn from the *Verba filiorum* of the Banū Mūsā since he was the first editor of that work.

In the preceding chapter I discussed the title which I have adopted for the longer version: *Liber de triangulis Iordani,* and I mentioned the variant forms of this title that appear in all of the manuscripts. I also discussed there the division of the work into books and the different schemes of numbering the propositions that are found in the various manuscripts, concluding that the author surely had numbered the propositions separately for each of the four books despite the wide variety of those schemes. Now let us look at the manuscripts of the text and their mutual relationships. In general, all of the complete manuscripts (*DSHGPbFbEs*) together with the fragments listed below represent essentially the same text. However there are some rather distinctive relationships existing between certain of the manuscripts which need to be described. MS *D* contains a great many marginal notes, all of which I give in the variant readings below (occasionally depending on the readings of those notes given by Curtze—with *siglum Dc*—where the notes are no longer legible or have been washed away by the water damage which

---

[2] A number of the diagrams are made to conform to the generality of the enunciations by Curtze: e.g. in Figs. I.2–I.3, I.11, I.13, II.18, etc. where Curtze draws scalene triangles though all of the manuscripts have isosceles triangles. This is certainly permissible but Curtze should indicate the status of the drawings in his manuscript. A few of Curtze's diagrams do not include all of the letters and lines. For example, see Fig. IV.7b, where Curtze has omitted lines *ME* and *MD*. Curtze gives the reconstructed diagram of IV.22a but does not give us the diagram that appears in the manuscripts. Letter [*K*] is mismarked in Curtze's Fig. IV.23. Curtze omits line *K* in Fig. IV.27 and omits Fig. IV.28 entirely. Since Curtze used only one manuscript for the most part, he cannot give the reader the sense of the great and complicated variety that exists in the diagrams in the manuscripts, which I have attempted to communicate in the long legends I have added to the diagrams.

MS *D* suffered during World War II).[3] The notes appear also in MS *Fb* for the most part and sometimes they are added directly to the text in MS *Fb*. Further, some of the notes are present in the fragmentary copies *Fc* and *Ve* (where they are in a later hand of the fourteenth century). Hence it is clear that there is a fairly strong tradition of such notes. Furthermore there are substantial additions and changes in the text in MS *H*, which is the most original and diverse of the various manuscripts, and, I might say, is also often the most intelligent of the copies.[4] Intelligent though its readings may be, I am convinced that they are not the readings of the original author since the longer readings of *H* are idiosyncratic and do not appear in any other manuscript. But often these additions or changes in *H* do divine the intention of the author which is not so clearly represented in the text (I have already commented on the fact that the scribe of *H* saw the necessity of renumbering the propositions in each book in order to make sense of the many internal references to book and proposition number given by the author in the proofs of the propositions). Note further that the compositor of *H* not only correctly asserted the falseness of [parts of] the enunciation and proof of Proposition IV.13 (see Prop. IV.13 var lins. 3–7), as was also implied in a marginal note of MS *D* (see IV.13 var. lins 8–12), but he went so far as to omit the false parts of the enunciation though he included the brief and false proof of the omitted parts of the enunciation. Incidentally the fact that the false parts of the enunciation are present in all but three manuscripts (*SHFb*) and that the whole proof is in all of the manuscripts is another clear indication, I believe, that MS *H* cannot have been the original text of the author of the *Liber de triangulis Iordani*. I should also remark on the evident honesty of the commentator in *H* when he declares that he does not understand the first method of finding two mean proportionals between two given quantities in Proposition IV.22 (i.e. Archytas's method) nor its proof (see Prop. IV.22 var. lin. 1). He is the only scribe to admit this, though I am sure that he was not alone in this ignorance since the geometry of the method is very subtle (see Volume 1, pp. 365–66) and beyond the understanding of most medieval geometers (including the author of the *Liber de triangulis Iordani*, I should think) and furthermore the diagram given for this complicated method was probably inadequate in the Latin manuscript of the *Verba filiorum* from

---

[3] For examples of some of the longer notes that appear in *D* and *Fb* (and sometimes in *Fc* and *Ve*) see the variant readings to the following propositions and line numbers: I.1, 5–6, 6–9; I.4, 8; I.7, 16; I.9, 28; II.1, 25; II.2, 1–4; II.7, 6; II.16, 23–27; III.5, 5, 10–14; III.6, 17; III.9, 30–32, 39–49; III.12, 18–20, 21–26; IV.9, 6–24; IV.11, 7; IV.13, 8–12; IV.14, 3–7; IV.16, 17–19; IV.18, 3–10.

[4] For the longer emendations and additions given in MS *H* see the variant readings to the following propositions and line numbers: I.4, 5–8; I.5+, 18–19; I.9, 25–28; I.10, 10–12; I.12, 28–29; II.1, 5–7, 9–13; II.5, 14, 18–19; II.6, 5; II.8, 4–9; II.12, 9; II.13, 18–19; II.14, 5–6; II.18, 8; II.19, 14–15; III.1, 17; III.2, 20; III.4, 21–24; III.5, 10; III.9. 30–32, 45; III.12, 7–8, 14–20; IV.3, 29–30; IV.9, 17–19; IV.11, 28–30; IV.12, 8–9, IV.13, 3–7; IV.15, 9–19; IV.17, 3–5, 9; IV.18, 6–10; IV.19, 8–11, 13–17, 24–27; IV.21, 9–12; IV.22, 1; IV.26, 13–14, 18–19.

which this method was drawn as it is in the manuscripts of the *Liber de triangulis Iordani* itself (see the legend to Fig. IV.22a).

One more special relationship needs to be mentioned, namely that which exists among the texts in the complete MSS *GPbEs* (and among the partial copies in MSS *Bu* and *Pc*). MSS *G* and *Pb* have almost identical readings throughout the text, as a careful perusal of the variant readings given below will confirm. Though the fact that *Pb* has diagrams and proposition numbers while *G* does not tempts us to conclude that *Pb* is the source of *G*, there are indications that *G* may be the source, or perhaps the principal source, of *Pb*. One such indication is that in several instances the ambiguity of letter forms in *G* produces apparent errors in the designations of magnitudes, and these errors seem to be carried over into *Pb* where there is no ambiguity in letter formation. A principal example of this is MS *G*'s form of the letter *b* which often looks like the letter *l* and in such cases appears in MS *Pb* as the letter *l* (e.g., see the variant readings to the following propositions and line numbers: I.9, 5; II.3, 8; II.4, 5, 10; II.5, 7, 8, 15 [twice], 18, 20, 21), and there are similar ambiguities in *G* where *h* looks like *l* and *q* like *a* and MS *Pb* has *l* and *a* (see I.5+, 6, 16). Another instance in which MS *G* appears to be the source of an erroneous reading in MS *Pb* occurs in Prop. I.12, lin. 7, where *G* has written *llll*^{or} (for *quatuor*) in such a way that it looks like *minor,* and indeed *Pb* has unambiguously written *minor* (i.e. *mīor*). A more general observation supporting the priority of MS *G* is that, though the two MSS are extremely close in their readings, on a number of occasions MS *Pb* has a different reading where *G*'s reading is the common reading of the other manuscripts.[5] If the scribe of *G* were copying *Pb* (instead of the other way around, as I believe) we should not expect the scribe of *G* to correct *Pb* in so many cases and always to arrive at the reading found in the text. On the one hand it is easy to conceive of the scribe of *Pb* making simple copying errors as he copied *G* and his attention wandered. Now if I am right and the scribe of *Pb* used *G* as a source for the text, it appears that he also had access to some other manuscript which had a full complement of diagrams, for it would have been exceedingly difficult (almost impossible) for him to reconstruct the diagrams in a way that conformed so closely in so many instances to the general tradition of the diagrams found in the other manuscripts. The third manuscript in the tradition of *G* and *Pb* is MS *Es*. As I have said earlier, it adopts a system of numbering the propositions which is like that of *Pb*. I note that the scribe of *Es* occasionally found his medieval exemplar difficult

---

[5] Some of the many cases of *Pb*'s diversion from *G* and all other manuscripts are noted in the variant readings to the following propositions and lines: I.1, 2 ("basi"); I.3, 6 ("et 19"); I.6, 14; I.7, 14 ("angulo B"); I.9, 28; I.10, 6 ("AC usque"); I.12, 16 ("KM¹"), 25 ("sit¹"); I.13, 4 ("que"); II.1, 16 ("ea est"), 20 ("HB"), and so on. Also note that the scribe of *Pb* almost invariably expands *G*'s abbreviations for *ille* and *illarum* (i.e., *i*^{e} and *i*^{arum}) to *iste* and *istarum* (e.g., see I.9, 19 and I.10, 13), a practice so common that it would appear that he is dependent on the abbreviations in *G* and not on the readings in some other manuscript where the words are written out in the form he uses.

to read, for he gives the abbreviated readings above his expanded readings or in the margin (e.g. see Intr. var. lin. 10; I.4 var. lin. 5; I.5 var. lins. 8, 10; I. 7 var. lin. 13; I.8 var. lins. 14, 16). As I have noted above, I give no variant reading from *Es* after I.8 (except in the case of the numbers used for the propositions). The parts of the text found in MSS *Bu* and *Pc*, which are also in the tradition of complete texts *G* and *Pb*, will be discussed below.

The manuscripts containing parts of the text of the *Liber de triangulis Iordani* are separately listed below in the *Sigla*. These manuscripts may be classified in regard to their relationship to the text in four categories. (1) The first are the manuscripts that also include Propositions 1–46 of the *Liber philotegni* of Jordanus, namely MSS *Fa* and *Bu*. In MS *Fa* the propositions from the *Liber philotegni* are given first and then follow Propositions IV.12–IV.13 and IV.10 from the *Liber de triangulis Iordani* (note that MS *Fa* also includes Proposition 46+1 in the form found with the *Liber philotegni* rather than in the form of Proposition IV.4 of the *Liber de triangulis Iordani*). The inclusion in this manuscript of only Propositions IV.10 and IV.12–13 from the *Liber de triangulis Iordani* may indicate that these propositions were composed by the author of the *Liber de triangulis Iordani* before he added the whole collection of Propositions IV.14–IV.28 (see my account of these three propositions in Appendix III.B below). On the other hand we should perhaps not make too much of the fact that in MS *Fa* there is no more of Book IV than the above-noted propositions, for there is considerable evidence that the scribe of *Fa* made use of the notes found in MSS *D* and *Fb* of the *Liber de triangulis Iordani,* which, it will be recalled, are manuscripts containing the whole text, and so perhaps he took them from some early copy of the whole text of the *Liber de triangulis Iordani*. In this connection the reader should compare the variants to Prop. 1, lines 9 and 11, of the *Liber philotegni* with the variants to Prop. I.1, lines 5–6 and 6–9, of the *Liber de triangulis Iordani;* those of Prop. 37, lines 10–12 and 14–15, with those of Prop. III.12, lines 18–20 and 21–26; that of Prop. 45, lines 18–19, with that of Prop. IV.9, lines 6–24. Also we can see the dependence of *Fa* on the longer version in the addition made to the enunciation of Proposition 5 of the *Liber philotegni* (see the variant to line 3), for that addition is the enunciation of Proposition I.5+ of the *Liber de triangulis Iordani* (see the enunciation of Prop. I.5+ and the comments on that enunciation in the variant to lines 1–19). As for MS *Bu*, it includes the shortened version of the *Liber philotegni,* i.e. Propositions 1–46 and 46+1), together with Propositions IV.10 and IV.12–IV.28. It also includes in the margins the additional propositions added by the author of the *Liber de triangulis Iordani* to Book II (see the description of MS *Bu* under the *Sigla* below). As I indicated above, the parts of the *Liber de triangulis Iordani* found in MS *Bu* were taken from some manuscript in the tradition of *G* and *Pb*. (2) The second category of manuscripts containing fragments includes those which were presumably copied from some manuscript containing a complete text. In this category I mention MSS *Fc* and *Pc*. MS *Fc*, containing Propositions I.1–II.13, was copied directly from *Fb*.

It contains some of the notes that are in *Fb* and *D*. But I link it with *Fb* rather than with *D* since on one occasion it adds the note to the body of the text as does *Fb* rather than leaving it in the margin as does *D* (see Prop. I.7, var. lin. 16). MS *Pc* includes all of the propositions added to the fourth book of the *Liber de triangulis Iordani* except for Propositions IV.4 and IV.10. It thus has Propositions IV.12–IV.28. My guess is that the scribe had a copy of the *Liber philotegni* already at hand so that he believed that he need copy only Propositions IV.12–IV.28 from his exemplar of the *Liber de triangulis Iordani*. Whatever were the circumstances provoking the copying of this part of the *Liber de triangulis Iordani* in MS *Pc*, it is clear that the exemplar from which the scribe copied was primarily in the tradition of MSS *GPbBu*, as the variant readings clearly show. (3) The third group of fragmentary copies appear to be those related to some collection of Propositions IV.14–IV.28 that was made prior to the adding of the collection to Book IV of the *Liber de triangulis Iordani*. This category included above all MS *Ve*, which was done in the thirteenth century (though its marginal notes, some of which are like those found in MSS *D* and *Fb*, are in a fourteenth-century hand). Perhaps the fragments in MS *Pe* (including Propositions IV.14–IV.18), which appears to have been written prior to 1250, and MS *Gu* (written in 1480), were taken from a copy of the collection represented by MS *Ve*. At any rate, I believe the collection in *Ve* was put together from the various fragments of Arabic translations made by Gerard of Cremona which I have edited below in Appendix III.B, and the reader should see the additional manuscripts described under the *Sigla* of Appendix III.B. Since the form of the propositions given in *Ve* is much closer to the form found in the complete copies of the *Liber de triangulis Iordani* than to the form given in the original sources appearing in the manuscripts of Gerard's translation, I suppose that *Ve*'s collection represents a penultimate version of this collection, the last version being that found in the *Liber de triangulis Iordani* itself. If this order of composition of the manuscripts of the collection is correct, we would then have to conclude that the interior titles employed in manuscript *Ve*, like *De quadratura circuli* for Propositions IV.14–IV.16 and *Propositiones de proportionibus* for Propositions IV.26–IV.28 (see the description of MS *Ve* below under the *Sigla*), were eliminated when the author of the *Liber de triangulis Iordani* added this collection to Book IV. (4) A final group of manuscripts containing fragments includes those which have only one or two individual propositions and which may have been taken from a more complete text of the added propositions, though in somewhat paraphrased form. This group comprises MSS *Od*, *R*, and *Oc*. At any rate all of the manuscripts which I have categorized in these four groups have been collated for my text below.

I shall make no effort to review here the wide variety of spellings found in the many manuscripts I have used. In general my decision on behalf of a given spelling is based on its being the most common spelling in the manuscripts. For example, I have decided for *diameter* instead of *dyameter*, *ypotesis* instead of *ypothesis*, *orthogonius* instead of *ortogonius* (and similarly for other words with the stem *orthogon-*), *secare* instead of *seccare, sicut* instead of *sicud, commentum* instead of *comentum, equedistans* instead of *equidistans* (unlike the manuscripts of the *Liber philotegni* those of the *Liber de triangulis Iordani* most frequently use the former spelling rather than the latter), *parallelogrammum* instead of *parallelogramum, parallellogramum,* or *paralellogramum* (here the variety of spelling was so wide and the reading preferred by the author so uncertain that I thought it best to adopt the transliterated Greek spelling found in MS *Es*), *corollarium* instead of *corrolarium, corelarium, correlarium* or *correllarium* (again I was so uncertain as to the author's spelling that I adopted the spelling found in MS *Es*), *aggregatum* instead of *agregatum, arismetica* instead of *arsmetica* or *arsmetrica, circumscribo* instead of *circonscribo* (and similarly for other words beginning with *circum-*), *duplico* instead of *dupplico,* and so on (the reader may peruse the variant readings and the Latin index for other examples). As in the other texts in this volume I have followed my common practice of writing *-ti-* before a vowel in place of *-ci-*, though the author may have written *-ci-*. Surely nothing would have been gained by attempting to decide in all cases whether the scribe in each manuscript has written one or the other, particularly since a case may be made that even when the *-ci-* form is used the scribe sometimes intended *-ti-*.

My use of capitalization for the enunciations has been explained in my comments on the texts of the first two parts of the volume. Indeed all of the editorial practices I have described in the preceding parts are followed once more and so need no additional comment here. But a few words concerning the diagrams may be in order. As usual I have added detailed *legenda* to the diagrams which indicate the great variety existing among diagrams in the various manuscripts. These *legenda* give ample support to the following observations. The diagrams of MS *D* have suffered greatly from the water damage to the manuscript which I mentioned earlier. Hence the diagrams are very often indistinct or even not visible at all. Except for the first few diagrams added by John Dee to MS *G* that MS is without diagrams. There are also no diagrams in the long fragment of MS *Fc*. The diagrams in *Pb* are unusually complete and MS *Es* tends to follow the diagrams in *Pb*. The diagrams in *S* and *H* are usually quite good (and indeed in terms of draftsmanship the diagrams in *S* are the best of all). The diagrams in MS *Fb* are often crude and inaccurate and the reader should place no confidence in them. One interesting point is that often the scribes (and thus perhaps the original author) used an isosceles triangle in the diagrams when the proposition in fact referred to any triangle and thus a scalene triangle might have been better.

The marginal folio numbers of my text are drawn from MS *D* and indeed they were also used in Curtze's text. This will allow for ready comparison of the two texts. No special remarks concerning the English translation need be made since the observations which I have made concerning the translations of the texts in the first two parts of the volume equally apply to my translation of this text. I note however that I have added to the proposition numbers in my translation the numbers of the corresponding propositions in the *Liber philotegni*. Finally I conclude this chapter with a general description of each manuscript of the *Liber de triangulis Iordani*.

Sigla

Complete Copies

D = Dresden, Sächische Landesbibliothek, MS Db 86, 50r–61v, early 14c. *D* contains propositions equivalent to Props. 1–46 of the shorter version. To these propositions are added Prop. I.5+, Props. II.9–II.12, II.14–II.16, IV.4 (with a proof that differs from that in Prop. 46+1 of the shorter version), IV.10, IV.12–IV.28. M. Curtze based his text of the longer version on this manuscript: *Jordani Nemorarii Geometria vel de Triangulis Libri IV, zum ersten Male nach der Lesart der Handschrift Db. 86 der Königl. Oeffentlichen Bibliothek zu Dresden herausgegeben, Mitteilungen des Coppernicus-Verein für Wissenschaft und Kunst,* 6. Heft (Thorn, 1887). This text has been designated as *Dc* in my critical apparatus. The codex was described by M. Curtze, "Ueber eine Handschrift der. Königl. Oeffentl. Bibliothek zu Dresden," *Zeitschrift für Mathematik und Physik,* Vol. 28 (1883), *Historisch-literarische Abtheilung,* pp. 1–13. Cf. A. A. Björnbo and S. Vogl, "Alkindi, Tideus, und Pseudo-Euklid," *Abhandlungen zur Geschichte der mathematischen Wissenschaften,* 26₃. Heft (1912), pp. 130–31. It contains a great many mathematical works but was badly damaged by water during World War II, particularly as regards the marginal notes and diagrams. However, I was able to read a large proportion of the text.

S = London, British Library, Sloane MS 285, 80r–92v, 14c. It is inadequately described in E. J. L. Scott, *Index to the Sloane Manuscripts in the British Museum* (London, 1904), p. 30. This codex has two notes on folio 1v: "Geometrie thome abbatis xiiii⁰ loco" and "Euclidis Geometria, Liber de visu. Randulphe breretanii . . . ." The following works are included therein: folios 24r–65v, Euclid's *Elements* in the Adelard II Version, with some slight differences in Books I–IV.5; 66r–74v, Euclid's *De visu* (i.e. his *Optica*) in what Lindberg has called Version 1 (D. C. Lindberg, *A Catalogue of Medieval and Renaissance Optical Manuscripts,* Toronto, 1975, p. 51); 74v–79v, Euclid's *De speculis* (i.e., his *Catoptrica*), as noted by Lindberg (*ibid.,* p. 49); 80r–92v, the *De triangulis Iordani,* as indicated above; 93r–96r, some miscellaneous notes in a later hand; 96v, blank; 97r, "randulphe breretanii"; 97v, blank.

H = London, British Library, MS. Harley 625, 123r–130r, 14c. This fragment is part of an Oxford manuscript that was probably bequeathed to Merton College by Simon Bredon in 1372. See the excellent description and reconstruction of the contents of the original manuscript by A. G. Watson, "A Merton College Manuscript Reconstructed: Harley 625; Digby 178, fols.

1–14, 88–115; Cotton Tiberius B. IX, fols. 1–4, 225–35," *Bodleian Library Record,* Vol. 9 (1973–1978), No. 4, pp. 207–17. As Watson shows (pp. 208–209) the manuscript was in John Dee's possession. It is clear from a comparison of the variant readings present in MS *H* and the texts of the fragments translated by Gerard of Cremona which served as the sources of many of the propositions added to Book IV of the longer version (see App. III.B) that the scribe of MS *H* consulted those fragments and altered the text of the *De triangulis Iordani* accordingly.

G = Norwich, Norfolk Record Office, on deposit from the Gunton estate, no number, 11r–26r, middle 14c. Note that folios 1–9, once from a different manuscript, are from the early 14c. This codex was called to my attention by N. R. Ker, who sent me a preliminary description of it. Later I examined the manuscript and through the courtesy of Miss Jean Kennedy, the County Archivist, a microfilm copy of the manuscript was provided to me. As the result of my examination and Ker's notes, I give the following description of the contents of the manuscript. Folios 1r–5r, [a *Theorica planetarum*], inc., Circulus [. . .] vel egresse. . . ; 6r–9v, inc., "Quia tam in ista operatione . . . mensurande. Incipit tractatus astrolabii . . . Cum volueris scire gradum . . ." (Apparently Messahala, *On the Astrolabe,* see L. Thorndike and P. Kibre, *A Catalogue of Incipits of Mediaeval Scientific Writings in Latin,* 2nd ed. [Cambridge, Mass., 1963], c. 356); 11r–26r, *Liber de triangulis Iordani,* as noted above; 26r–36r, [Euclid, *De visu,*], inc. "Ponatur ab oculo rectas lineas . . ." (cf. Lindberg, *Catalogue,* p. 50); 36r–42v [Euclid, *De Speculis*] inc., "Rectum visum esse cuius medium . . ." (cf. Lindberg, *Catalogue,* p. 42); 42v–45r, [Abhomadi Malfegeyr, *De crepusculis,*] often attributed to Al-hazen, as here in MS *G* where we read on 42v (probably in John Dee's hand): "Incipit liber Allacen de crepusculis corruptissime scriptus," inc. "Attendere (*!* Ostendere) quid sit crepusculum . . ." (cf. Lindberg, *Catalogue,* pp. 15–16); 45r–47r, [*Liber Iordani de ponderibus,* Version P; see E. A. Moody and M. Clagett, *Medieval Science of Weights* (Madison, Wisc., 1952), pp. 150–65,] inc., "Incipit tractatus iordani de ponderibus. Cum sciencia de ponderibus . . ."; 47v–53r, [*De ratione ponderis,* see Moody and Clagett, pp. 174–227,] inc. "Omnis ponderosi motum esse. . . ." (note that folio 47v terminates with the enunciation of Prop. R1.02 and folio 48r begins with R2.03 and then the content of folios 47v and 48r are repeated on 48v and 49r; from there the text continues to the end of the work; thus the proof of Prop. R1.02 and all of Props. R1.03–R2.02 are missing; my guess is that one or more leaves are missing; on folio 53r we find the colophon "Explicit liber iordani de ratione ponderis"); 53r, a fragment on the crown problem published in *Archimedes in the Middle Ages,* Vol. 3, p. 1292, inc., "Si fuerit aliquod corpus ex duobus mixtum corporibus . . ."; 53r–54v, [*De canonio;* see Moody and Clagett, pp. 64–75], inc., "Si fuerit cononium (*!* canonium) simetrum. . . ."; 54v, a stray proposition on the addition of weights, inc. "Omne pondus cum quotlibet ponderibus. . . ."; 54v–55v, Version 1 of Hero's theorem on the area of a triangle in terms of its sides, inc. "Si trianguli tria latera . . ." (this is a copy of the text published in *Archimedes in the Middle Ages,* Vol. 1, pp. 642–47); and 55v–57v [Alhazen, *De speculis comburentibus,*] inc., "De sublimiori quod geometrie . . ." (see the edition by J. L. Heiberg and E. Wiedemann, "Ibn al Haiṯams Schrift über parabolische Hohlspiegel," *Bibliotheca mathematica,* 3. Folge, Vol. 10 [1909–10], pp. 201–37); the text in MS *G* ends in the middle of Prop. 5, with the catch words "qualiter protram (*!*)" for the next quire, which quire is now missing (i.e. the text in MS *G* ends in the Heiberg-Wiedemann text, p. 228, line 10). This manuscript was once in the possession of John Dee. On folio 10v (otherwise blank) Dee has written: "Joannes Deeus 4 Aprilis 1550" and then added a brief table of contents:

	triangulis ubi de quadratura circuli est
"Jordani de	perspectiva
	speculis
	crepusculis
	ponderibus ____(?) 2°
Mukefi	Speculis comburentibus. de Sectione mukefi"

He also has added marginal notes concerning statements in the Introduction to the *De triangulis* and to Prop. I.1 (see the Variant Readings below). Dee also added the figures for Props. I.1 and I.2, the only figures for the *De triangulis* given in MS *G.* The codex is without binding.

Pb = Paris, Bibliothèque Nationale, MS lat. 7378A, 29r–36r, 14c. Very closely tied to the text in MS *G,* this codex is described in the *Catalogus codicum manuscriptorum Bibliothecae Regiae,* Vol. 4 (Paris, 1744), pp. 349–50. Cf. L. Thorndike, *A History of Magic and Experimental Science,* Vol. 3 (New York, 1934), p. 304; Clagett, *Archimedes in the Middle Ages,* Vol. 1, p. xxvi; E. Grant, *Nicole Oresme: "De proportionibus proportionum" and "Ad pauca respicientes"* (Madison, Wisc., 1966), pp. 379–80. This codex contains a wide variety of mathematical, astronomical, and physical works of the thirteenth and fourteenth centuries, including several works of Jordanus and related treatises (cf. Lindberg, *Catalogue,* pp. 15, 34, 41, 49, 51, 70; Thomson, "Jordanus de Nemore: Opera," p. 135).

Fb = Florence, Biblioteca Nazionale, MS Conv. soppr. J.V.18 (=Codex S. Marci Fiorent. 216), 17r–29v, 14c. This copy has most of the marginal notes found in MS *D* and some additional ones (peruse the variant readings below), and its text often resembles that of *D.* The codex was described by A. A. Björnbo, "Die mathematischen S. Marcohandschriften," *Bibliotheca mathematica,* 3. Folge, Vol. 12 (1911–12), pp. 218–22 (cf. the new edition of Björnbo's articles on this collection, Pisa, 1976, pp. 88–92). The codex contains primarily mathematical works (cf. Thomson, "Jordanus de Nemore: Opera," p. 137, for the Jordanus items).

Es = Escorial Library, MS N. II.26, 1r–15v, 16c. This copy is in the tradition of MSS *GPb.* The scribe had difficulty in reading the exemplar from which he was copying and some of the marginal notes bear upon this difficulty.

The codex is very inadequately described by G. Antolín, *Catálogo de los códices latinos de la Real Biblioteca del Escorial,* Vol. 3 (Madrid, 1913), p. 146. In fact the content of this codex in folios 1r–46r is identical with that of MS *G* (folios 11r–57v) and I note it briefly as follows: folios 1r–15v, *Liber de triangulis Iordani,* as noted above; 16r–24v, Euclid, *De visu;* 25r–30r, Euclid, *De speculis;* 30r–32v, Abhomadi Malfegeyr, *De crepusculis;* 33r–35r, *Liber Jordani de ponderibus* (Version P); 35v–40v, *Liber Jordani de ratione ponderis* (note that the block of propositions missing from the copy in MS *G* is included in MS *Es*); 41r, the fragment on the crown problem noted in my description of MS *G;* 41r–42r, *De canonio;* 42v, the stray proposition on the addition of weights noted in my description of MS *G;* 42v–43r, Version 1 of Hero's treatment of the area of a triangle in terms of its sides; 43v–46v, Alhazen, *De speculis comburentibus* (including the end of the treatise missing from MS *G*); 47r, blank except for two lines of notes (each four words in length); and 47v, blank. There are three more leaves (missing from my film of this manuscript). Antolín indicates laconically "(fol. 48) Theorica planetarum." For the *Liber de triangulis* I have included variant readings from MS *Es* only through Prop. I.8 (though I have reported on the proposition numbers throughout the text).

Manuscripts Containing Parts of the Text

Fa = Florence, Biblioteca Nazionale, MS. Conv. soppr. J.I.32 (=Codex S. Marci Fiorent. 206), 124r–135v, end of 13c. In addition to the *Liber philotegni,* this copy contains from the longer version of the *De triangulis* Prop. IV.4 (with a different proof, on 133v), Props. IV.12–IV.13, and IV.10 (in that order, on folios 135r–v). This copy of the last three propositions has been collated in my text below. For a description of the manuscript, see the *Sigla* to the *Liber philotegni* above.

Fc = Florence, Biblioteca Nazionale, MS Conv. soppr. J.X.40 (=Codex S. Marci Fiorent. 201), 57r–66r, 15c. This MS contains the text through Prop. II.13 without title, proposition numbers, and diagrams. This fragment was copied from MS *Fb* and has some of the additional notes of MS *Fb,* but no diagrams. The codex is described by A. A. Björnbo, "Die mathematischen S. Marcohandschriften in Florenz," *Bibliotheca mathematica,* 3. Folge, Vol. 12 (1911–12), pp. 201–202 (cf. the new edition of Björnbo's articles on this collection, Pisa, 1976, pp. 69–70). Björnbo erroneously indicates folio 47r as the beginning of the *De triangulis.* The codex contains Version III of Jordanus' *Demonstratio de plana spera* (see Thomson, "Jordanus de Nemore: Opera," p. 122).

Ve = Venice, Biblioteca Nazionale Marciana, MS Lat. Zanetti (fondo antico) 332 (=No. 1647), 289v–293v, 13c. *Ve* contains Props. IV.14–IV.28 without proposition numbers. It also contains some marginal notes in a fourteenth-century hand that are like those in MSS *D* and *Fb.* Neither Jordanus' name nor the title *De triangulis* appears on this copy, but it gives as titles *De quadratura circuli* and *Propositiones de proportionibus* (see the variant readings for Prop. IV.14, line 1, and Prop. IV.26, line 1). The codex is described by J. Valentinelli, *Bibliotheca manuscripta ad S. Marci Venetiarum,* Vol. 4 (Venice, 1871) pp. 218–20. The section including the *De triangulis* is not properly identified by Valentinelli as being a fragment of that work. This rich manuscript contains many mathematical works, including, on folios 86r–233r, a combined text of the *Elements* of Euclid in the versions known as Adelard I and Adelard II (see M. Clagett, "King Alfred and the Elements of Euclid," *Isis,* Vol. 45 [1945], pp. 269–77). For the works of Jordanus included in the codex, see Thomson, "Jordanus de Nemore: Opera," p. 138, and for its optical items, see Lindberg, *Catalogue,* p. 137.

Pc = Paris, Bibliothèque Nationale, MS lat. 7434, 84v–87v, 14c. *Pc* contains Props. IV.12–IV.28, without title and proposition numbers. The text here resembles that of MSS *GPbBu* but is occasionally independent of it (peruse the variant readings for the text below). The codex is described in the *Catalogus codicum manuscriptorum Bibliothecae Regiae,* Vol. 4, p. 358. It contains astronomical, mathematical and optical works. For the optical works, see Lindberg, *Catalogue,* p. 135.

Bu = Basel, Oeffentliche Bibliothek der Universität, MS F.II.33, 146r–150v, 14c. In addition to containing the *Liber philotegni* (Props. 1–46, on folios 146r–148v) it has the following propositions from the longer version of the *De triangulis:* Props. II.9–II.12 and II.14–II.16 on the margins of 147r–v, Prop. IV.4 (148v, with the different proof of Prop. 46+1 of the *Liber philotegni*), Prop. IV.10 (148r–v), and Props. IV.12–IV.28 (149r–150v). For additional, related propositions on triangles given on the upper and lower margins of folio 149r, see Part II, Chap. 3, n. 2. All of the propositions of the longer version in this copy have been collated with the text below. For a description of the codex, see the *Sigla* to the *Liber philotegni* above.

Pe = Paris, Bibliothèque Nationale, MS lat. 16648, 58v–59r, 13c. *Pe* contains Props. IV.14–IV.18, without title, proposition numbers and diagrams. It is noteworthy that these propositions follow directly after the *Elementa* of Euclid, Book X–XV, in the version I have called Adelard III (see Clagett, "Medieval Latin Translations of Euclid," p. 25). The principal colophon of that work reads (folio 58r): "Explicit edit[i]o alardi bathoniensis in geometriam euclidis per eundem a. bathoniensem translatam." Thus the juxtaposition of the above-noted propositions and Alard's (i.e. Adelard's) commentary and the spelling of Adelard's name as Alardus encourages us to suppose that it was from a manuscript like this that the scribe of MS *Gu* copied Props. IV.14–IV.18, IV.21 and IV.25 under the designation of the *Greater Commentary* of Alardus (see the description of MS *Gu* below in the *Sigla*). I say "a manuscript like this" because MS *Pe* itself could not have been the exemplar from which the scribe of MS *Gu* copied his propositions since MS *Gu* includes Props. IV.21 and IV.25 (as well as some other propositions) which are not in MS *Pe*. For a description of this codex, see the posthumous work of A. Birkenmajer, *Études d'histoire des sciences et de la philosophie du moyen âge* (Wrocław, etc., 1970), p. 163, where, following Delisle, he identifies the first part of MS *Pe* (that is, at least through folio 91v, and perhaps through 93v) with MS Sorb. LVI 8, which Birkenmajer further identifies with item No. 40 of Richard de Fournival's catalogue. The rest of the codex is identified by Birkenmajer (p. 172) with MS Sorb. LVI 21, and then with item No. 58 of the Fournival catalogue (though I doubt this last identification).

Od = Oxford, Bodleian Library, MS Digby 174, 136v, this proposition 13c. It contains a variant version of Prop. IV.15 only, without title and proposition number. It is followed by the two quadrature proofs published in my *Archimedes in the Middle Ages,* Vol. 1, pp. 578–80 (see the comments on this codex therein, p. xx). Note that the two quadrature proofs are of the nature of Prop. IV.16. For a description of the codex, see W. D. Macray, *Catalogi codicum manuscriptorum Bibliothecae Bodleianae. Pars nona, codices a . . . Kenelm Digby . . . donatos, complectens* (Oxford, 1883), cc. 184–86.

R = Florence, Biblioteca Riccardiana, MS 885, 199bis r, 14c. Contains Props. IV.15 and IV.22 only, Prop. IV.15 being in the version of MS *Od.* No title or proposition numbers. The codex is listed in the *Inventario e stima della Libreria Riccardi* (Florence, 1810), p. 21.

Oc = Oxford, Corpus Christi College, MS. 251, 84v, 13c. *Oc* contains Prop. IV.16 only, without title or proposition number. For a description of the codex, see H. O. Coxe, *Catalogus codicum manuscriptorum qui in collegiis aulisque Oxoniensibus hodie adservantur,* Vol. 2 (Oxford, 1852), p. 104. Cf. Clagett, *Archimedes in the Middle Ages,* Vol. 1, p. xxi.

Gu = Glasgow, Glasgow University Library, MS Gen. 1115 (formerly Be 8.y.18), 210r–211v, dated 1480 (fol. 172v). *Gu* contains Props. IV.14–IV.18, IV.21, and IV.25. Props. IV.14–IV.16 are under the rubric "Incipit quadratura circuli secundum alardum" (see the text below, Prop. IV.14, variant to line 1) and have a colophon: "Explicit quadratura circuli secundum magistrum alardum in maiori comento (*!*)" (*ibid.,* Prop. IV.16, variant to line 22). Props. IV.17–IV.18, IV.21, and IV.25 (and some additional nonpertinent propositions) are under the rubric: "sequuntur quedam extracta a comento (*!*) eiusdem" (*ibid.,* Prop. IV.17, variant to line 1). See the excellent description in N. R. Ker, *Medieval Manuscripts in British Libraries,* Vol. 2 (Oxford, 1977), pp. 919–22. Cf. the detailed description of folios 202r–214v in Clagett, *Archimedes in the Middle Ages,* Vol. 3, pp. 157–59. I have discussed in Appendix III.B the attribution of the propositions from the *De triangulis* in this manuscript to "Alardus."

* * * * *

For manuscripts of those passages from translations by Gerard of Cremona which were the sources of many of the propositions of Book IV of the *De triangulis,* see Appendix III.B (*Sigla*).

THE BOOK ON TRIANGLES OF JORDANUS (THE LONGER VERSION OF THE BOOK ON TRIANGLES) THE LATIN TEXT AND ENGLISH TRANSLATION

50r / Liber de triangulis Iordani

[1.] CONTINUITAS EST INDISCRETIO TERMINI CUM TERMINANDI POTENTIA.

[2.] PUNCTUS EST FIXIO SIMPLICIS CONTINUITATIS.

5 [3.] SIMPLEX AUTEM CONTINUITAS IN LINEA EST, DUPLEX QUOQUE IN SUPERFICIE, TRIPLEX IN CORPORE.

[4.] CONTINUITAS ALIA RECTA, ALIA CURVA.

[5.] RECTUM QUOD NON OMITTIT SIMPLEX MEDIUM.

[6.] ANGULUS AUTEM EST CONTINUORUM INCONTINUITAS
10 TERMINO CONVENIENTIUM.

[7.] FIGURA VERO EST EX TERMINORUM QUALITATE ET APPLICANDI MODO FORMA PROVENIENS.

Superficiei igitur figura accidit ex terminorum qualitate, quia alia curvis, alia curvis et rectis, alia tantum rectis terminis continetur. Et curvis quidem

Title and Introduction

1 Liber de triangulis Iordani *Fb om. Fc* Incipit liber de triangulis Iordani *G (et supra scr. m. rec. G* Jordani de triangulis) Liber primus de triangulis *D in m. Taw secundum Dc* Geometria Iordani vel Iordani (?) de triangulis *mg. D* DE TRIANGULIS IORDANI *S* I IORDANI *mg. sup. H* Incipit Jordanus de triangulis *Pb* Incipit Jordani de triangulis *Es*

2 indiscretio *DGPbFbFcEs* discretio *SH /* termini: *injuste et tacite corr. Dc in* terminorum

4 de Punctus . . . continuitatis *scr. Joh. Dee mg. G* Non semper: cum enim sint duo puncta extremitatibus linee, non semper nec omnino in terminis est sectio; nec hanc facit puncti definitionem sed proprietatem quandam eius dum linea secatur / fixio *DFbFc* fictio *SG* ficcio *HPb* sectio *Es /* continuitatis: conterminatis *Fc*

5 Simplex: Implex (!) *Fb /* continuitas *tr. FbFc post* linea / est *tr. H ante* in

6 quoque *supra scr. Es /* ante triplex *add. H* et / triplex *mg. Es, om. GPb*

8 de Rectum quod *scr. Joh. Dee mg. G* Rectum quid / non omittit: in (?) omittit *D /* obmittit *FbFc*

9 incontinuitas: in continuitatis *injuste corr. Dc*

10 convenientium *corr. mg. Es ex* complentum comburentium con'ventum

11–12 de Figura . . . proveniens *scr. Joh. Dee mg. G* Figurae definitio bipartita

13–16 de Superficiei . . . amplioribus *scr. Joh. Dee mg. G* Explicat primam partem

14 alia curvis *DGPbFcEs om. SH* alia curvi *Fb / post* rectis² *add. H* aut tantum curvis / terminis continetur *tr. S*

346

15 uno vel pluribus, rectis autem et curvis duobus vel pluribus, rectis vero tribus vel amplioribus. Ex applicandi modo, quoniam ex eo provenit diversitas angulorum. Quidam enim rectis equales, et quidam minores, et quidam maiores efficiuntur.

1. IN OMNI TRIANGULO, SI AB OPPOSITO ANGULO AD MEDIUM BASIS DUCTA LINEA DIMIDIO EIUSDEM EQUALIS FUERIT, ERIT ILLE ANGULUS RECTUS; QUOD SI MAIOR, ACUTUS; SI VERO MINOR, OBTUSUS.

5 Si enim fuerit linea dimidio basis equalis, erunt duo anguli ad basim coniunctim sumpti tertio equales per quintam primi Euclidis bis; ergo et ille tertius necessario rectus est per 32. eiusdem [Fig. I.1]. Si autem fuerit maior, erunt et illi tertio maiores per 18., erit igitur acutus; si autem minor, et reliqui tertio minores, erit igitur obtusus per 32. primi.

15 pluribus¹ . . . pluribus² *om. Pb* / rectis¹ . . . pluribus² *om. GEs*
16 *supra* amplioribus *scr. Es et Joh. Dee in G* pluribus
16–18 *de* Ex. . . . efficiuntur *scr. Joh. Dee mg. G* Explicat secundam partem definitionis figurae
16 aplicandi *Fc* / *post* applicandi *scr. et del. S* i *et Fb* n
17 rectis equales *om. FbFc*
Prop. I.1
1 1 *mg. sin. extrema H mg. sin. Pb* (?), *Es, om. DGFbFc* 1ᵃ *mg. dex. S*
1–9 *de* In. . . . primi *scr. Joh. Dee mg. G* Possit clare demonstrari ex 9 tertii Euclidis et 3ⁱ conversa quoniam constabit basim bifariam sectam diametro circuli circumscripti
1 In omni: Nommi (*!*) *Fc* / omni (?) *Fb*
2 basis: basi *Pb* basim *Es* / *post* eiusdem *add. H* basis
2–3 erit ille *tr. FbFc*
2 erit *om. GPb et tr. H ante* rectus *et tr. Es post* obtusus *in lin. 4*
3 *ante* angulus *scr. et del. S* tri- / vero *om. GPbEs*
4 optusus *FbFc* / *post* obtusus *add. Es et Joh. Dee in G* erit
5 *mg. hab. Es* quatuor lineas quas non legere possum
5–6 *de* Si . . . equales *scr. mg. DFb* vel quoniam anguli super basim equipollent angulo extrinseco ad B
5 fuerit . . . equalis: linea descendens fuerit equalis dimidio basis et per 5. primi Euclidis *H* / *supra* linea *scr. Joh. Dee in G* ducta ab angulo / admidio (*!*) *Fc*
5–6 erunt . . . quintam *mg. D et text. in aliis MSS*
5 erunt: sunt *H et tr. H post* tertio *in lin. 6*
6 coniunctum *GPb* / equalis *GPb* / per . . . bis *om. H hic* / *supra* bis ergo *hab. Es*
────── (?) probabis / et *om. H*
6–9 *de* ergo. . . . primi *scr. mg. D*(secundum *Dc*)*Fb* Hec probatio manifestior (*D,* maior *Fb*) est si circulus circumscribatur quia angulus B primo modo consistet (*D, ?Fb*) in semicirculo, secundo in maiori portione, tertio modo in portione minori (*bis Fb*) semicirculo
7 tertius: tertio *S* / per . . . eiusdem *tr. H ante* ille *in lin. 6* / 32: 31 *GPb, ?Fc* / eiusdem: Euclidis *Fc*
8 erunt et: erit *Fc* / et¹ *om. H* / illi: illi duo anguli *H* / 18: 16 *S* 18 primi quare ut prius tertius *H* / *post* 18 *supra scr. Es* eiusdem / igitur *om. H* / *post* igitur *scr. et del. S* obtusus per 32. / minor . . . reliqui: linea descendens sit minor dimidio basis etc. anguli supra basim *H* / reliqui: *aliquid quod non legere possum in Es*
9 *post* tertio *add. H* agent (?) / minores: minoris *G* / per . . . primi *om. H* / 32: 31 *GPb* 1 (?) *Fc* / *post* primi *add Es* duas lineas interlineares et duas lineas mg. quas non legere possum

2. INFRA (! INTRA) TRIANGULUM CUIUS DUO LATERA SUNT EQUALIA LINEA AB ANGULO AD BASIM DUCTA QUOLIBET LA-TERUM MINOR ERIT, EXTRA VERO MAIOR.

Ductis duabus lineis, una quidem extra donec concurrat cum basi, alia
5 vero intra triangulum ad quemcumque punctum basis, patet per 5. et 16. primi Euclidis quod que infra triangulum ducta est minori angulo opponitur quam unum laterum trianguli, qui autem extra, maiori; per 19. igitur argue [Fig. I.2].

3. SI TRIANGULUS DUO HABUERIT LATERA INEQUALIA, ET AB ANGULO QUEM CONTINENT INFRA (! INTRA) TRIANGULUM LI-NEA FUERIT AD BASIM DUCTA, LONGIORE BREVIOR ERIT, BRE-VIORI VERO EQUALEM, SIVE MAIOREM, SIVE MINOREM ESSE
5 CONTINGIT.

Quod sit longiore brevior per 18. et 19. primi facile probabis; reliquum autem cito ostendes posse contingere, si latus brevius contineat cum basi angulum acutum, quia tunc poterit linea descendens continere cum basi ex eadem parte angulum illi equalem, et tunc erit equalis breviori lateri; vel
10 maiorem, ut si ducta sit propius, et fiet minor per premissam; vel minorem,

Prop. I.2

    1 2 *mg. sin. extrema H mg. sin. Es, Pb* (?), *om. DGFbFc* 2ª *mg. dex. S* / Infra: Nam (?) *Fb et post* Infra *scr. et del. Fb* z
    2 *ante* ab *scr. et del. Fc* ad basi (!) / *ab bis Es et del. Es secundum* / *ante* angulo *scr. et del. Fc* t'
    4–6 Ductis . . . que: Ex 5ª enim et 16ª primi argue quod quelibet linea *H*
      4 Ductiis (!) *Fc* / concurat *Fc* / cum: in *GPbEs* con *Fb,* (?) *Fc* / basim *FbEs* / alio (?) *Fb*
      5 quodcunque *Es* / patet: pateat *GPbEs*
    5–6 *supra* per . . . primi *hab. Es aliquid quod non legere possum*
      6 que *om. GPb* / *post* est *scr. et del. H* minor eo quod
      7 *ante* trianguli *scr. FbFc* patet *et del. Fb* / qui: quod (?) *S* que *PbFb* / autem: et *S* / igitur *GPbEs* igitur *sive* 8ⁱ *DSFbFcH*

Prop. I.3

    1 3 *mg. sin. HEs,* (?)*Pb, om. DGFbFc* 3ª *mg. dex. S*
    2 quem: quam (?) *S* / *ante* infra *add. H* illa latera / infra: intra *Es*
    4 equalem (?) *S*
    6 sit longiore: suª (!) cugiʳᵉ (?) *GPb* / sit: si *injuste hab. Dc* / *supra* per . . . facile *scr. Es* quia maius latus. quare maiori angulo est / 18: 16 *SH* / et 19 *om. Pb* / facile probabis: argue *H* / probabis: probatur (?) *Fb* probasis (!) *S* / reliqū *S*
    7 *mg. hab. Es* potest cuius linea intra _____ (?) _____ (?) cum basi vel maiorem vel equalem vel minorem collaterali (?) super eadem basi angulo (?) _____ (?) _____ (?) / ostendes: ostenderis *S* ostendens *Fc* / latus: eius latus *H* / brevius: huius (?) *S* / basim *G*
    8 *ante* acutum *scr. et del.* (?) *Fb* con *sive* com/ aҫcutum (?) *Fc* / quia: quod *S om. H* / poterit (?) *Pb* potest *H* / descendens (!) *G* / continere (?) *Es* / *post* continere *scr. et del. Pb* contra (?) / cum basi: collaterali (?) *Es* / cum: con *sive* com *Fc* / basi (?) *Pb* rasi (!) *G*
    8–9 ex . . . parte *om. H*
    9 tunc: sic *H* / brevior (?) *Fc*
    10 ducta sit *tr. H* / *supra* propius *scr. Es* quam (?) sit / per premissam *om. GPb, lac. Es*

50v ut si ducta / sit remotius, et fiet maior; si autem rectum aut obtusum, semper erit maior [Fig. I.3].

4. IN OMNI TRIANGULO CUIUS DUO LATERA SUNT IN-EQUALIA, LINEA AB ANGULO AB IPSIS CONTENTO AD MEDIUM BASIS DUCTA CUM MAIORE IPSORUM MINOREM ANGULUM CONTINEBIT.

5 A medio basis ducatur linea recta equedistans priori lateri in latus longius [cf. Figs. I.4] cadetque in eius medium per 2. sexti, eritque eadem medietas brevioris per 4. sexti, quare et minor medietate longioris; argue igitur per 18. et 29. primi.

5. SI IN ORTHOGONIO VEL AMBLIGONIO AB UNO RELIQUO-RUM ANGULORUM AD BASIM LINEA DUCATUR, ERIT REMO-TIORIS ANGULI AD PROPINQUIOREM RECTO MINOR PROPORTIO QUAM BASIS SUE AD BASIM ALTERIUS.

11 si ducta *om. G* / ducta sit *om. Pb tr. H* / sit: fit (?) *G* / autem *SHFbFc* aut *DGPbEs* / aut: vel *injuste hab. Dc* / semper: continebit angulum qui (?) *H*

12 *post* maior *add. Es* breviori et (?) minor maiori

Prop. I.4

1 4 *mg. sin. HEs,* (?)*Pb, om. DGFbFC* 4ª *mg. dex. S* / In omni: Nonni (*!*) *Fc*

1–2 inequa *Pb*

2 *ante* ab² *scr. et del. D* sub

4 *post* continebit *add. H* quam cum minore

5–8 A . . . primi: In triangulo ABC cuius longius latus sit BC [Fig. I.4*var. H*] ducatur linea a B angulo ad medium basis que sit linea BD et a D puncto ad latus longius ducatur linea DE equedistanter lateri breviori que eadem in medium lateris longioris per 2. 6ᵗⁱ, eritque eadem DE medietas brevioris per 4. 6ᵗⁱ; quare erit minor EB medietate longioris igitur per 18. primi angulus EBD erit minor angulo ADB. Sed angulus EDB et angulus ABD sunt equales per 29. primi; igitur angulus EBD minor est angulo ABD, quod fuit probandum *H*

5 *post* medio *add. FbFc* autem / recta: recte *S* / priori: preter (?) *GPb* primiter (?) *Es*
                                         i
   (*et supra scr. Es* pter)

6 *de* cadetque . . . medium *mg. scr. Es* quia parelela (*!*) secat latera (?) secat (?) proportionaliter / 2: 5 (*sive* 2) *Pb* 2 (?) *Fc* / eritque: erit quia *Fc* / supra eadem *scr. Es* eadem _____ (?)

7 *supra* brevioris *scr. Es* lateris

8 *post* et *add. FbFc* per / 29: 19 *S* / *ante* primi *add. GPbEs* adinvicem 34. eiusdem / *post* primi *add. D* (*secundum Dc*) *Fb* potest etiam alio modo demonstrari (*Dc,* probari *Fb*) si designetur linea DE equedistans (*Dc, om. Fb*) maiori linee [Fig. I.4*var. DcFb*], quia linea DE est dimidium linee (*Fb, om. Dc*), quod patet per secundam sexti (quod . . . sexti ?*Fb*) erit (*Dc,* ?*Fb*) et DE maior dimidio AB, quod est EB. Igitur angulus (*Dc, om. Fb*) EBD (*Dc,* BD *Fb*) est maior BDE (*Dc,* EBDE *Fb*); igitur *EBD* est maior (*Dc,* om. *Fb*) DBC (*om. Fb et correxi ex* DBE *in Dc*) quia anguli coalterni sunt equales et hoc est propositum / *post* primi *hab. GPbEs* probationem Prop. I.5+ (*q.v.*)

Prop. I.5

1 5 *mg. sin. HPbEs om. DGFbFc* 5ª *mg. dex. S* / in *om. H* / ortogonio *SFc* (*et post hoc lectiones huiusmodi non laudabo*) / vel *supra scr. D* / ambligonio *GPbEs* ambligonii (?) *H* ambligonium *DSFbFc et de* ambligonium *mg. hab. D* (*secundum Dc*)*Fb* nota quod ambligonium non est de textu sed item est de illo sicut de recto

2 angulorum *om. FbFc* / erit: est *Fb* et (?) *Fc*

3 *post* recto *add. H* seu obliquo (*!*)

4 *post* alterius *add. GPbFbFcEs et mg. D* enunciationem Prop. 5+ (*et vid. var. ibi*)

5   Ad quantitatem linee inter (*! intra*) orthogonium ducte describatur circulus
cuius circumferentia latus angulo recto oppositum secabit, latus vero perpendiculare absque contactu includet per antepremissam; quod si ad circumferentiam protrahatur directe, fient duo sectores alternatim maiores et
minores partialibus triangulis; igitur per octavam quinti et primam et ultimam
10   sexti argumentare (*?*) [Fig. I.5].

[5+] [In all MSS; compare variant readings for differing locations] ET
ANGULI RECTO PROPINQUIORIS SUPER LATUS SECTUM CON-
STITUTI AD ANGULUM REMOTIOREM MINOR EST PROPORTIO
QUAM LATERIS SECTI AD EIUS PARTEM RECTO ANGULO PRO-
5   PINQUIOREM.

Ad huius ostensionem linea *HO* infra (*! intra*) triangulum *QHC* [cf. Fig.
IV.5+] protracta, cuius angulus *C* sit rectus vel obtusus; protrahatur a puncto
Q linea equedistans linee *HO* donec concurrat cum linea *CH*, sitque in
puncto *D*. Posito ergo pede circini in *Q* describatur circulus secundum quan-
10   titatem *HQ*, quem necesse est secare lineam *QD* et lineam *QC* includere per
19. et 16. primi Euclidis. Secet igitur lineam *QD* in puncto *B*, et protrahatur

5 quantitate *GPb* / inter: intra *Es* / orthogonium *corr. Fb ex* orthogonale / *post* orthogonium *add. H* vel ambligonium / circulis (*?*) *G* / *post* cir- *scr. et del. Es* circulus
6 circonferentia *Fb* / *post* recto *add. H* vel obtuso / secabit *tr. H ante* latus¹ / seccabit
GPb
6–7 latus . . . perpendiculare: et reliqu[u]m latus *H* / perpendicularis *Pb*
7 includit *S* / si *om. Es*
7–8 circonferentiam *FbFc*
8 directe fient: ducatur (*?*) et fierent *Es* (*et mg. scr. Es* dirᵗ et fie't) / *ante* sectores *scr.
et del. Pb* sectiones / maiores et: maiorem *Fc*
9 igitur per: sibi *FbFc* / octavam: 9 *Pb*, *?G* / *post* et¹ *add. Dc* per *sed om. omnes MSS*
10 argumentare: argentare (*!*) *D* argumentam *S* argumentum elice *H* arguerentur *Fc et
ex corr.* (*?*) *Fb* / *post* argumentare *add. G* per ute_ (*?*) et qᵗⁱ *et Pb* per utramque (*?*)
8. 5ᵗⁱ *et Es* per ute'rᵉ (*?*) et 5ⁱ (*et ante* 5ⁱ *scr. et del. Es* aliquid quod non legere possum)
/ *post* arguerentur *add. FbFc* probationem Prop. I.5+ (*q.v.*) *et post* argentare *mg. add.
Dc* istam eandem probationem

Prop. I.5+
1 5+ *addidi* 6 *mg. sin. H* 6ᵃ *mg. dex. S*
1–19 Et. . . . proposito *hab. SH hic, sed enunciatio (lin. 1–5) est post* alterius (*lin. 4,
Prop. 5) in MSS GPbFbFcEs et mg. D (secundum Dc) et probatio (lin. 6–19) est post
primi (lin. 8, Prop. 4) in MSS GPbEs et in fine (lin. 10) Prop. 5 in MSS FbFc et mg.
D (secundum Dc)*
2 recto *om. FbFc* / *post* recto *add. H* seu ambligonio
6 huiusmodi *FbFc* / HO: QO *G* AD *Pb* AQ *Es* / QHC: QLT *G* QLC *?Pb, Es*
7 *post* obtusus *add. H* vel rectus
8 equedistans *DSH* equedistanter *GPbFbEs* equedistantem *Fc* / HO: HQ *Es* / concurrat
HGPbFbEs concurat (*?*) *Fc* concurrit *Dc* contrabat (*?*) *S* / cum: circa (*?*) *Fb* / CH
(*sive* OH) *Fc* / *post* CH *add. H* ulterius protracta
9 D: i.e. D *GPb, ?Es* / in *om. S*
9–11 circulus . . . protrahatur *om. GPbEs*
10 quem *FbFc* quam *SHDc* / et *om. Fc*
11 19: 19 et 19 *S* / et¹: et per *Fc* / lineam QD *tr. H*

QC usque ad *A*. Cum ergo ex ultima sexti Euclidis et hac regula: que est proportio arcus ad arcum ea est sectoris ad sectorem, cuius probatio est eadem probationi ultime sexti, et ex utraque parte octave quinti et prima
15 sexti maior sit proportio anguli *HQC* ad angulum *HQD* quam linee *HC* ad lineam *HD*, erit econtrario maior proportio *DH* ad *HC* quam anguli *HQD* ad angulum *HQC*; ergo coniunctim proportio *DC* ad lineam *HC* maior est quam anguli *DQC* sive *HOC* ad angulum *HQC*. Deinde ex 4. sexti Euclidis argue propositum.

6. IN OMNI TRIANGULO CUIUS DUO LATERA INEQUALIA SUNT, SI AB ANGULO QUEM CONTINENT AD BASIM PERPENDICULARIS DUCATUR, PORTIONIS BASIS QUE INTER IPSAM ET MAIUS LATUS DEPREHENDITUR MAIOR ERIT AD RELIQUAM PROPORTIO QUAM
5 ANGULI AD ANGULUM.

Ad hoc primum ostende quod inter perpendicularem et terminum longioris lateris maior portio basis intercipitur quam inter perpendicularem et terminum minoris lateris [Fig. I.6]. Non enim equalis per 4. primi, necque minor, quia si hoc, re[s]cindatur ergo ficta maior ad equalitatem ficte minoris, et a puncto

12 Cum: tum *GPbEs* / ergo: igitur *HEs* (*et post hoc lectiones huiusmodi non laudabo*)
12–16 ex . . . econtrario: per premissam sit *H*
  12 ultima: ult. (?) *Es* / sexti *om. S* sesti *Fc* (*hic et saepe; post hoc lectiones huiusmodi non laudabo*) / Euclidis *om. FbFc* / hac: hanc *Es*
  13 ea: eadem *Fc* / *ante* probatio *scr. et del.* (?) *Fc* prop / probatio: propositio *Es*
  14 eidem *Fb* / probationi: propositioni *Es* / ex *om. Fb*
  15 anguli: anguliṣ *Fc* / HQC: HQD *S* / HQD: HAD (*sive* HQD) *Es*
15–16 ad lineam: aliam *G*
  16 econtrario: necessario *FbFc* / anguli HQD: DQH anguli *H* / HQD: HAD *PbEs*
  17 angulum HQC *tr. H* / HQC: HAC *GPbEs* / coniunctim: coniunctum (?) *G* coniūtim *Fc* / *post* coniunctim *add. H* per 18. 5ᵗⁱ Euclidis / lineam *om. H*
  18 DQC: DAC *PbEs* / sive HOC *om. H* / HOC: hoc *S* HQC *Es* / angulum: gulum (!) *G* / HQC: HAC *Pb*
18–19 Deinde . . . propositum: quare per 4. 6ᵗⁱ Euclidis proportio QC ad OC maior erit quam anguli DQC ad angulum HQC: quare per 29. primi proportio QC ad OC maior erit quam anguli HOC ad angulum HQC; igitur econtra minor *H*
  18 4 *corr. Es ex* eiusdem
Prop. I.6
  1 6 *mg. sin. Pb, ?Es, om.* DGFbFc 7 *mg. sin. H* 7ᵃ *mg. dex. S* / omni: oni *Fc* / sunt *om. H*
  2 angulọm *Fb* / basem *DSGFc*
  4 deprenditur *Fc* / proportio: portionem *GPb, ?Es*
  5 ad *supra scr. G* / *post* angulum *add. Es* proportio
  7 portio: proportio *S* / intercipitur: aⁿcipitur *G, ?Pb* intercipiatur *Es* / perpendiculare *G*
  8 enim: vero *Es* / equalis: equaliter *GPb* / *ante* per *scr. et del. Es* sunt / 4: 8 *Fb* / neque *DSFbFc* Euclidis nec etiam *H* nec etiam *GEs, ?Pb*
  9 si hoc: sive (*sive* sit) hec *G* / si: sit *Pb* sic *Es* / hoc re[s]cindatur ergo: recisa *H* / re[s]cindatur: recindatur *DS et ex corr. Es, ?Fb* recidatur *GPb* rectiⁿndatur (!) *Fc* / ficta: secta *Es* / equalitatem: qualitatem *DS* / ficte: secte *Es*
9–10 et . . . et: per lineam ductam ab angulo supremo *H*

10 sectionis ducatur linea ad angulum supremum, et sequetur oppositum ypotesis
per secundam presentis. Quia ergo est necessario maior, rescindatur et ipsa
ad equalitatem minoris et a puncto sectionis ducatur linea usque ad angulum
supremum, sicut diximus de priori. Et hoc facto per premissam primo disiunctim, postea coniunctim proportionando propositum convinces.

7. SI SUPER EANDEM BASIM INTER LINEAS EQUEDISTANTES
DUO TRIANGULI STATUANTUR, CUIUS LATUS LATERUM
SESE SECANTIUM MAIUS FUERIT, EIUS ANGULUS SUPERIOR
MINOR ERIT.

5   Constitutis triangulis sint latera sese secantia maius *AB* et minus *CD* [Fig.
I.7]; punctus quoque sectionis vocetur *E*; cumque sint trianguli equales per
37. primi, dempto communi relinquentur duo equales trianguli habentes
duos angulos, scilicet ad punctum *E*, equales; ergo per 14. sexti proportio
linee *AE* ad lineam *EC* est sicut proportio *EB* ad *ED*, quare et sicut totius
10   *AB* ad totam *CD* per 13. quinti, et sic maior est *AE* quam *EC*. Sit autem
sicut *AE* ad *EC* ita *EC* ad lineam *EF* resectam ex linea *AE*, ducaturque linea
recta ab *F* ad *D*. Convinces ergo per 6. et 4. sexti adiuvante 22. quinti et per
diffinitionem similium superficierum, quod pars anguli *D* quam continent

10 supremum *S* supremum *DGPbFbFc* supremo *H* (*cf. var. lin. 9–10*) suprapositum
Es / ypotesis *GPb* ypothesis *S* ypotese *H* ipotesis *D* ipothesis *FbFc* hypothesis *Es*
11 presentis: presetis (*!*) *Fc* huius *H* / est *om. Fc* / necessario (*?*) *G* / rescindatur *DSEs*
recindatur *HGPbFbFc*
12–13 et . . . priori: per lineam ductam ab angulo supremo *H*
12 *post* sectionis *scr. et del. Fb* s / ducatur *om. Pb* / ad² *om. DS*
13 supremum *S om. FbFc* suppremum *DPb* supremo *H* (*cf. var. lin. 12–13*) suprapositum
Es suppom̄ (*?*) *G* / diximus *omnes MSS sed forte corr. D ex* duximus / *post* per *supra*
scr. H hanc (*?*)
13–14 disiuctim *G*
14 coniunctim: disiunctim *GPbES* / postea: et postea *H* / convinceris (*!*) *Pb*
Prop. I.7
1   7 *mg. sin. PbEs om. DGFbFc* 8 *mg. sin. H* 8ᵃ *mg. dex. S* / equidistantes *DFbFc* (*et*
post hoc lectiones huiusmodi non laudabo)
5   sint: sic (*sive* sit) *FbFc*
6   punctus . . . E: et sit E punctus sectionis *H* / E *om. FbFc* / equalis (*?*) *G*
7   37: 38 *H*, *?Fc* / relinquentur *DHFbFcEs* relinquantur *SGPb* / *mg. scr. et del. Es*
lineas tres
8   angulos *DH et ex corr. Es* triangulos *SGPbFbFc* / scilicet . . . E: ad E punctum *H*/
scilicet: sibi *Es* (*et postea scr. et del. Es* oppositos) / E *om. S* / 14: 18 *FbFc* / sexti:
16 (*?*) *Es*
9   EC: CE *Fb* ED *S* / totiud (*!*) *FbFc*
10   AB *om. FbFc* / CD: DC *H* ED *Fb*, *?Es* / 13 *DHFbFc*, *?Es* 13 (*sive* 12) *S* 12 *Pb*,
?G / est: erit (*?*) *H* / EC: ED *H* EI *FbFc* / Sit *bis Fb* sit sic *Fc*
11   EC¹,²: ED *H* / lineam *om. H* / EF: IF *Fb* / *ante* ex *scr. et del. Pb* et (*?*) / linea¹ *corr.*
Fb ex lineam
12   D *om. FbFc* / Convinces: convertes *Es* / 6 (*?*) *Fb* 8 *Fc*
12–14 adiuvante . . . DF: angulus EDF *H*
12   adiuvante . . . quinti *om. text. D sed hab. Dc* / adiuvante *ex corr. Fc* / *ante* 22 *scr.*
et del. Pb aliquid quod non legere possum / 22: 21 *Es* / *ante* quinti *add. Fb* et
13   *ante* superficierum *scr. et del. Fb* spēri (*?*) / superficierum *bis Fc*, *?G* / *supra* superficierum (*?*) (*quod del. Es*) *scr. Es* sr' orum *et mg. add. Es* superiorum / quod: et *S*

linee *DE* et *DF* equalis est angulo *B*; quare et totus *D* maior quam *B*, et hoc
15 est propositum. Et sequitur per 4. primi, quod, si latera sese secantia sint
equalia, anguli superiores sunt equales, et per 8., si anguli, et latera.

8. SI TRIANGULI QUOTLIBET INTER LINEAS EQUEDISTANTES
SUPER EANDEM BASIM CONSISTANT, EIUS SUPERIOR ANGULUS
MAXIMUS ERIT CUIUS RELIQUA LATERA SUNT EQUALIA,
ET QUANTO EI PROPINQUIORES, TANTO REMOTIORIBUS
5 AMPLIORES.

Sit basis *AB* [Fig. I.8], super quam constituantur trianguli, unus scilicet
51r equalia habens reliqua latera cuius superior / angulus sit ad punctum *C*, et
alius ponens conum in *D*, et tertius remotius ad hoc, scilicet in *E*. Quia ergo
cuius latera sunt equalia eius anguli ad basim sunt equales, necesse est eosdem
10 acutos esse, quare et sui coalterni acuti et sui cointrinseci (*!* coextrinseci)
obtusi. Et quia obtusus maximus est in triangulo, maximum latus ei opponitur,
et ideo linea *BD* maior est linea *BC*, ergo maior sua equali *AC*, ergo per
premissam angulus *D* minor est angulo *C*. Et quia linea *DB* maior est quam

14 DE et DF *omnes MSS et ex corr.* Es / est *om.* H / angulo B *tr.* Pb / B[1]: ABC H /
   D: D angulus H / maior: maior est H / et hoc: quod H / et[3] *om.* S
15 sint: sunt H
16 *post* equalia *add. MSS* quod *sed delendum est* / sunt: sint Pb / 8 . . . latera: quia
   per hanc omnium duorum triangulorum equalium quorum omnes (*DcFb,* communes
   Fc) anguli unius sunt equales angulis alterius latera equos angulos respicientia vel
   continentia equalia esse (*DcFc,* ostendentur *Fb*), necesse est huius demonstratio patet
   per suppositionem *FbFc et mg.* D (*partim secundum Dc*) *post* latera / *mg. add.* D
   (*secundum Dc*) *FbFc* patet (*DcFb, ?Fc*) etiam alio modo demonstrari per 14. et 4.
   sexti (sesti *Fc*) et (*om. Fc*) per 11 (*! DcFc,* 41 *? Fb*) et 13 quinti (*Dc, om. FbFc*) et
   per hanc regulam: si fuerit proportio primi ad secundum (*DcFc, om. Fb*) sicut secundi
   ad primum (*DcFc,* pri *Fb*) erunt (*DcFc,* sunt *Fb*) ipsa equa (*Dc,* equalia *Fc,* equ *Fb*)

Prop. I.8

1 8 *mg. sin.* PbEs *om.* DGFbFc 9 *mg. sin.* H 9[a] *mg. dex.* S / trianguli quotlibet *tr.*
   H / inter *om.* S / *post* inter *add.* H duas
2 eamdem *FbFc* / basem S / consistant: constituerint (?) H
5 ampliores: ampliciores DG, *?Pb* / *post* ampliores *et lac. add.* Es maiores
6 Sit . . . quam: Super basim AB H
7 equalia *tr.* H *post* latera / cuius: cuiusvis (!) *Fb* / superior . . . punctum: angulus
   superior sit H / superior *om.* S / C (?) S
8 ponens *lac.* Es (*et mg. hab.* Es scilicet _____ ?) / ponens . . . in[1]: cuius angulus sit
   H / ponens conum: *lac. et* continens (?) GPb / et *om.* GPb, *lac.* Es (*et mg. hab.* Es
   scilicet, et) / remotius . . . in: cuius angulus sit H / huc S / *post* E *add.* H inter
   lineas equedistantes / Quia *corr.* H *ex* quare
9 ad: super H / eosdem: eos H consequentes Es (*et supra scr.* Es aliquid quod non
   legere possum)
10 acutos esse *tr.* H / sui[1] (?) *Fc* / *post* coalterni *add.* H equales erunt
11 optusus *FbFc* / obtusus . . . triangulo: obtuso angulo trianguli H / maximus: maxime
   FbFc / est *om.* GPb / ei *om.* H
12 et *om.* H / est *om.* GPbEs / BC *DSHFbFc* (*et corr.* Es *ex* BE?) BE GPb / ergo[2]: ergo
   et H
13 pre- *supra scr.* G / C: E GPb / *post* C *add.* H quod est p[m] (probatum) / Et: sunt (?)
   H / DB (?) D / est[2] *om.* Pb

AD, quia maiori angulo opponitur, que cum minor est quam linea *BE* per
15   3. presentis, erit ergo *BE* maior quam *AD*. Ergo per premissam angulus *E*
minor est angulo *D*, et sic patet quod angulus *C* maximus est, et si infiniti
essent, et semper remotiores ab eo propinquioribus minores; nec non ab eo
equedistantes sibi invicem equales erunt per 29. et 4. primi.

9. SI DUO TRIANGULI QUORUM DUO ANGULI EQUALES SUNT
FUERINT EQUALES CUIUS LATUS LATERUM DUO EQUOS AN-
GULOS AMBIENTIUM MAXIMUM FUERIT, EIUS OMNIA LATERA
PARITER ACCEPTA MAIORA ERUNT.

5   Sint trianguli equales *ABC* et *DEF* [Fig. I.9], quorum anguli *B* et *E* equales,
sitque linea *AB* maior quam *DE* et maior etiam quam *EF*. Dico quod latera
trianguli *ABC* pariter accepta maiora sunt lateribus trianguli *DEF* pariter
acceptis. Quia ergo linea *AB* maior est quam *DE* aut *EF*, per 14. sexti linea
BC minor est utraque earum. Ergo per ultimam quinti linee *AB* et *BC* pariter
10   accepte maiores sunt lineis *EF* et *ED* pariter acceptis. Restat ergo ostendere
quod linea *AC* sit minime minor linea *FD*. Ostendam autem quod nec minor,
nec equalis, immo maior. Protrahatur ergo linea *DE* a puncto *D* donec sit
equalis linee *AB*, et sit hoc ad punctum *G*, et a linea *EF* resecetur linea
equalis linee *CB*, sitque *HE*, et ducatur linea a puncto *H* ad punctum *G*
15   secans lineam *FD* in puncto *L*, fietque triangulus *HEG* equalis triangulo

14 AD: A̧BD *G* ABD *Es* (*et mg. hab. Es* scilicet BC *?*) / *post* AD *scr. et del.* D BE
(*?*) / quia: eo quod *H* / apponitur *G* (*sed non Pb*) / cum: tum (*?*) *G*
15 presentis (*?*) *Pb* huius *H* / ergo: et *H* / BE (*?*) *Fb* / AD *lac. Es et supra scr. Pb* BD
mg. m. diff. G
16 est[1]: est quam *H* / patet . . . et: igitur *H* / C maximus *ex. corr. G* / C (*?*) *Fb, om.
Es* (*sed mg. hab. Es* scilicet, C)
17 ab[1] eo: a C sunt *H* / propinquioribus minores *tr. H* / nec non: vero non *Es* (*sed del.
Es et supra scr.* non vero *et mg. add.* scilicet, non nec) / nec (*?*) *G*
18 sibi: simul (*?*) *Es* / invice (*!*) *Fb* / equales erunt *tr. H* / 29. et 4.: 19. et 24. *Fb* 19. et
14. (*sive* 15.) *Fc* / et 4: 24 *SH* / *postea numeris propositionum exceptis lectiones MS
Es non laudabo*

Prop. I.9
1 9 *mg. sin. PbEs om. DGFbFc* 10 *mg. sin. H* 10ᵃ *mg. dex. S*
1–2 equales . . . equales: sunt equales equales fuerint *H*
2 duo *correxi ex* duorum *in H et ex* dico *in DSGFbFc et ex* dico (*sive* duo) *in Pb*
5 ABC: ALT (*sive* ABC) *GPb* / et[1] *del.* (*?*) *Fb* / E *om. GPb* / *post* E *add. H* sint
6 DE: linea DE *H* / et: vel (*?*) *G* / maior etiam *tr. H* / etiam: est *GPb* / EF:
DEF *FbFc* / quod: quo *Fb* / *supra* quod *scr. Fc* ergo
7 ABC: ALC (*sive* ABC) *GPb* / trianguli[2]: anguli (*?*) *Fb* / DEFF (*!*) *Fc*
8 linea[1] *om. FbFc* / DE: linea DE *H* / *ante* per *hab. H* erit
9 BC[1]: BȨC *G* / est *om. H* / *ante* linee *scr. et del. Pb* linea (*?*) / BC[2]: BR̩ᶜ *G* HC (*?*)
Fb
10 EF et ED: DE et EF *H*
11 sit minime: non sit *H* / minime minor: maior *GPb* / *post* minime *scr. et del. Fb*
AC / FD: DF *H*
12 immo *DSH* ymmo (*?*) *G* ymo *Pb* imo *FbFc* / Protrahatur ergo *tr. GPb* / DE *supra
scr. Fb* ED *H* / D: B̩D *G* DE *FbFc*
13 a *om. GPb* / EF: QF *GPb*
14 equalis linee *bis G* / CB: EB *Fb* CH *Fc* / a: Q *Pb*
15 *post* FD *add. FbFc* et linea BD (*sive* HD *Fc*) / fietque: sitque *GPb* / HEG: HEF *S*

ABC per 4. primi, quare et equalis triangulo *FED*, et linea *HG* equalis linee *AC*. Dempto igitur communi, scilicet quadrangulo *EHLD*, remanent duo trianguli equales habentes duos angulos equales, scilicet ad punctum *L*, et ideo si ab *H* ad *D* ducatur linea recta, alia vero ab *F* ad *G*, erunt ille due
20 equedistantes per 39. primi vel per secundam sexti. Quia ergo supra lineam *HD* maior est angulus ad *H* quam ad *D*, nam linea *DE* maior est linea *HE*, ideo supra lineam *FG* maior est totalis angulus *F* quam totalis *G*. Et ex hoc sequitur indirecte quod linea *HG*, que est equalis linee *AC*, nec minor, nec equalis est linee *FD*. Relinquitur itaque quod maior, et hoc est propositum.
25 Et argues quod non minor, ex antepremissa et 14. sexti et 13. quinti et 19. primi, et quod non equalis, ex eo quod sequitur per antepremissam, scilicet quod si latera sese secantia sunt equalia, anguli superiores sunt equales, et ex 14. sexti et 13. quinti.

10. SI SUPER EANDEM BASIM INTER LINEAS EQUEDISTANTES TRIANGULI STATUANTUR, CUIUS RELIQUA LATERA EQUALIA

16 per: propter (*sive* per *bis*) *G*
17 communiter *G*
18 equales . . . L: ad L equales *H* / scilicet: et *Pb*
19 si (?) *Pb* / ab H: aḍ BH *GPb* / linea recta: due linee iᵗ rē (recte) *GPb* / ille: iᵉ *G* iste *Pb* / due: duo (!) linee *H*
20 *ante* equedistantes *add. Pb* (*sed non G*) linee / vel: et *Fb*, ?*Fc*
21 maior¹ (?) *D* / maior est¹ *bis GPb*
21-22 ad¹ . . . angulus: totalis *GPb*
21 nam *SFbFc* eo quod *H* itā (!) *D*
22 super *H* / *ante* FG *scr. et del. S* HD / est: est et *FbFc*
23 indirecte *omnes MSS et ex corr. G* / nec¹ *om. GPb*
24 Relinquitur: reli (!) *Fb* reli' *Fc* / itaque: igitur *H* / quod: ea (?) *Fc* / maior: sit maior *H*
25-28 Et. . . . quinti: Quod autem non sunt equales sequitur ex antepremissa eo quod anguli superiores essent equales et si sic linea FH et GD essent equales, quod est contra 2ᵃᵐ 6ⁱ, vel sequitur aliter quod GL et FL essent equales per 14. 6ⁱ. Quare per 5. primi anguli LFG et LGF essent equales et HFD et HGD similiter essent equales per antepremissam. Ergo totus F esset equalis toti G, quod est contra ypotesim. Quod autem FD non sit maior HG probatur quia, si sic, tunc (?) per 14. 6ⁱ et 13. 5ᵗⁱ FL esset maior LG, quare angulus FGL per 19. primi esset maior angulo LFG et totus angulus G erit minor toto angulo F, igitur angulus LGD minor est quam angulo LFH, cum tum (*sive* tamen) per antepremissam et per hoc assumptum quod DF est maior HG sequitur angulum HFD esse minorem angulo HGD; patet igitur primum propositum *H*
25 sexti *om. FbFc* / quinti: hᵗⁱ (!) *GPb*
26 et: vel (?) *G* (*sed et in Pb*) / quod² *om. FbFc* / per antepremissam: premissa *S*
28 ex *om. Pb* (*sed non G*) / quinti: prima (!) quinti *GPb* / *post hanc probationem mg. add. D* (*secundum Dc*) *Fb* quod linea HG sit maior linea FD sic potest ostendi. Si enim LH est maior LD, et tota maior tota. Si autem equalis vel minor, erit angulus LDB (!*LDH?*) equalis vel minor angulo LHD, et quia angulus HDE est minor angulo DHE, remanebit angulus FDG maior angulo GHF. Si itaque fiat angulus LDE equalis angulo LHF, quoniam trianguli sunt similes, erit EL maior LF, et ideo GL maior eidem, et sic tota GH (*Dc,* ḤGH *Fb*) maior FD, resumpta 14. 6ᵗⁱ et 13. quinti
Prop. I.10
1 10 *mg. sin. PbEs om. DGFbFc* 11 *mg. sin. H* 11ᵃ *mg. dex. S* / eandem: eamdem *FbFc* enadem (!) *G*
2 *ante* trianguli *add. H* quotquot / *ante* cuius *scr. Fb* cu

FUERINT EADEM PARITER ACCEPTA MINORA ERUNT, ET
QUANTO EIS PROPINQUIORA, TANTO REMOTIORIBUS BREVIORA.

5   Statuantur super basim AB tres trianguli omnino sicut in antepremissa
[Fig. I.10], et protrahatur linea AC usque ad punctum F ita quod linea CF
sit tanquam linea CB; et protrahatur linea AD in punctum G ita quod linea
DG sit tanquam DB; et protrahatur linea AE ad punctum H ita quod linea
EH sit tanquam linea EB. Deinde ducatur linea recta inter F et D, et alia
10   inter G et E. Et ex 5. et 29. bis et 4, et iterum ex 5. et 19. primi ostendes
lineam AG maiorem esse linea AF; et ex 29. primi bis et 24. et 18. ostendes
lineam AH maiorem esse quam linea AG, et sic de infinitis. Semper minima
erit AF, et propinquiores breviores, et, quia singule illarum linearum sunt
sicut singula duo latera pariter accepta, patet propositum. Ostendes etiam
15   quod singuli trianguli quorum coni equedistant a puncto C habent reliqua
latera pariter accepta equalia, nam sese secantia sunt equalia, quia anguli

4 propinquiorum *GPb* / bereviora *Fb*
5 Statuatur *Fc* / omnino *om. H*
6 *post* linea¹ *scr. et del. S* AD in punctum G / AC usque *om. Pb (sed non G̀)* / ad: in
    S / CF *DHGPb* EF *SFbFc*
7 tanquam linea: equalis linee *HFc* / tanquam: tamquam *Pb (hic et saepe)* equalis
    Fb / CB: ȨB *G* / et *om. GPb* / linea² *om. FbFc* / AD: a D *(sive* AD) *Fc* / AD in: ad
    GPb AD usque ad *H* / G *om. GPb*
8 tanquam: tamquam *FbFc (hic et saepe)* equalis linee *H* / DB: V̧DB *G* / linea¹ *om.*
    FbFc / ad *supra scr.* G
9 tanquam linea: equalis linee *H* / EB: HȨB *Fb* / Deinde: tenr̄ G ceiñ *Pb* / inter F et
    D: ab F ad D *H* / inter: super *GPb* / et² *om.* (?) *Fb*
10 inter G et E: a G ad E *H* / E: CE *GPb*
10–12 Et. . . . AG: cum igitur in triangulo ABC anguli super basim sunt equales per 5.
    primi et angulus FCD equalis est angulo CAB per 29. primi et etiam angulus DCB
    equalis angulo CBA per eandem, sequitur quod angulus FCD et angulus BCD sunt
    equales. Sed et [cum] duo latera BC et CD sunt equalia duobus lateribus FC et CD,
    sequitur (?) per 4. primi [quod] DF linea est equalis DB linee et angulus CDF equalis
    angulo CDB. Sed DB et DG sunt equales ex ypotesi. Igitur DF et DG sunt equales;
    cum igitur per 20. primi AD, DF simul sumpte maiores sunt quam AF, sequitur
    quod ADG maior est quam AF. Item cum anguli FDC et BDC sunt equales per
    prius arguta, erunt FDE et BDE equales per 13. primi. Igitur angulus GDE est minor
    angulo BDE; cum igitur duo latera GD, DE erunt equalia duobus lateribus BD, DE
    et angulus BDE maior angulo GDE, sequitur ex 24. primi quod linea BE sit maior
    linea EG. Sed EB et EH sunt equales *(et scr. et del.* sunt equales) ex ypotesi. Igitur
    EH est maior EG. Igitur linea AH est maior 2 lineis AE et EG. Sed AE et EG sunt
    maiora AG per 20. primi. Igitur AH erit maior AG *H*
10 5.¹: quinto *(!) FbFc* / 29.: 19ª *FbFc* / 4: 14 *FbFc* 15. (?) primi et 4 *G* 15 primi 4
    Pb / 5²: 4 *Fc* / 19: 11 (?) *Fc* / ostendens *Fb*
11 lineam: literam (?) *GPb* / esse: eº (?) *GPb* / linea AF: lineam *Fc* linea *Fb* / 29: 19
    FbFc / 24: 4 *FbFc* 2e *(sive* 24) *G* / 18: ig (?) *GPb* 16 *S* / ostens *(!) FbFc*
12 infiniti *FbFc*
13 propinquiorus *(!) GPb* / *post* breviores *add. H* remotioribus / illarum: istarum *Pb*
14 singula *om. H* linea *S* / ostendens *FbFc* / etiam: est *Fc*
15 coni: puncti superiores *GPb* / equedistanter *Fc*
16 nam *GPb* etenim (?) *DFb* si aut *S* omnia *Fc*, *?H*

superiores equales et reliqua duo sunt sibi invicem equalia per hoc et per 29. et 4. primi et 8.

11. OMNIUM DUORUM TRIANGULORUM QUORUM BASES EQUALES ERIT PROPORTIO UNIUS AD ALTERUM TANQUAM ALTITUDINIS IPSIUS AD ALTITUDINEM ALTERIUS.

Altitudo trianguli est linea perpendiculariter ducta a cono trianguli ad
5 basim eiusdem intra vel extra, cui quidem equalis est omnis linea que est perpendicularis super lineas equedistantes inter quas consistit triangulus. Fiant ergo duo trianguli super equales bases [cf. Fig. I.11], et erectis perpendicularibus
51v lateribus basium compleantur parallelogramma / equealta triangulis et eisdem dupla per 41. primi. Quia ergo bases sunt equales, erunt parallelogramma
10 ex illa parte eiusdem altitudinis; ergo per primam sexti proportio unius ad alterum est sicut proportio laterum perpendicularium supra bases; quare et eadem est proportio triangulorum inter se quia multiplicium et submultiplicium eadem est proportio.

12. OMNIUM DUORUM TRIANGULORUM QUORUM UNIUS DUO LATERA EQUALIA DUOBUS EQUALIBUS ALTERIUS LATERIBUS EQUA FUERINT, CUIUS BASIS MAIOR FUERIT, IPSIUS AD ALTERUM MINOR ERIT PROPORTIO QUAM BASIS EIUS AD BASIM
5 ALTERIUS.

17 per¹: et per *GPb*
18 et¹ . . . 8.: 24. primi *S* / 4: 24 *H* / et 8. *om. GPbH*

Prop. I.11

1 11 *mg. sin. PbEs om. DGFbFc* 12 *mg. sin. H* 12ª *mg. dex. S* / quorum: duorum quorum *Fb* / *post* bases *add. H* sunt
2 alterum: alteram *GPb* / tamquam *PbFbFc* (*et post hoc lectiones huiusmodi non laudabo*)
4 est *om. GPb*
5 *post* quidem *add. GPb* per 29. primi
7 erectis: rectis *FbFc*
8 lateribus *correxi ex* lateris *in D* (*secundum Dc*) *SFbFc et ex* a sumis *in H et ex* a terminis *in Pb, ?G* / basium: basiis (!) *G* basis *Pb* / compleatur *FbFc* / parallelogramma *correxi ex* parallma *in H et ex* paralellograma *in SFb et D* (*secundum Dc*) *et ex* parallellograma *in G, ?Pb et ex* paraleligograma (!) *FbFc* (*et post hoc lectiones huiusmodi non laudabo*) / equealta: eque alta *FbFc* equialta *D* equealtera *S* / trianguli *G* (*sed non Pb*) / eisdem: eiusdem *FbFc* ad eos *H* (*et tr. H post* dupla)
9 *ante* 41 *scr. et del. S* 14 / 41 (?) *D* ei (*sive* 41) *G* / primi *om. S*
10 illa: ista *Pb* / primam: xi. primi *Fc* / proportio *om. FbFc*
11 alteram *Pb* / est *om. GPb* / *ante* laterum *scr. et del. S* ad / laterum: latera *Fc* lateru (!) *S*
11–12 quare . . . quia: cum igitur *H*
11 et: et ex *GPb*
12 est *om. FbFc*
13 *post* proportio *add. H* patet propositum

Prop. I.12

1 12 *mg. sin. PbEs om. DGFbFc* 13 *mg. sin. H* 13ª *mg. dex. S* / duorum triangulorum *tr. Fb* / quorum *om. GPb*
2 equalibus *om. FbFc* / alterius lateribus *tr. FbFc* / lateribus: equalibus *GPb*
4 basis: basim *S* / basim: basis (?) *S*
5 alterius *om. FbFc*

Sint due bases inequales maior *AC* et minor *DG* [Fig. I.12], super quas constituantur duo trianguli quorum quatuor reliqua latera sunt sibi invicem equalia, et a mediis punctis basium ducantur linee in conos triangulorum, scilicet a medio *AC* linea *FB*, et a medio *DG* linea *HE*. Erunt ergo linee *FB*
10 et *HE* perpendiculares per 8. primi et altitudines triangulorum, eritque linea *FB* minor quam linea *HE* per penultimam primi, cum sit linea *FC* maior quam linea *HG*. Et sumpta industria ex tertia et 31. primi Euclidis collocetur infra triangulum *ABC* quedam linea equedistans *AC* basi et equalis linee *DG*, que est minor basis, voceturque *KM* et secet perpendicularem *FB* in
15 puncto *L*. Sit autem que proportio est *AC* ad *KM* ea *KM* ad lineam *PT* per 9. sexti; erit igitur econverso *PT* ad *KM* sicut *KM* ad *AC*; sed *KM* ad *AC* sicut *BL* ad *BF* per 4. sexti et 15. quinti; et quia *BF* minor est quam *EH*, ideo maior est proportio *BL* ad *BF* quam *BL* ad *EH* per 8. quinti, et ideo maior quam trianguli *KBM* ad triangulum *DEG* per premissam; igitur et
20 proportio *PT* ad *KM* maior est eadem. Sed que est proportio *AC* ad *PT* ea est trianguli *ABC* ad triangulum *KBM* per corollarium 17. sexti. Conclude ergo quod maior est proportio linee *AC* ad lineam *KM*, que est equalis linee *DG*, quam trianguli *ABC* ad triangulum *DEG*, et hoc est propositum.

Concludes, inquam, ex hac regula: si que est proportio primi ad secundum

6 Sint: Sĩt (*!*) *Pb* Sunt *Fb* / *ante* maior *add. Fb* AC (*sed etiam hab. Fb* AC *post* maior)

7 quatuor: 1111ᵒʳ *G* minor *Pb* / sunt: sint *GD* / sibi invicem: se (?) invi'cē *Fb*

8 conos: conis *GPb*

9 *post* AC *add. H* ducatur / HE: LE (*sive* HE) *G* / Erunt ergo *tr. S* / linee: linea *G*

10 HE: LE (*sive* HE) *G* / *ante* primi *add. Fc* aliquid quod non legere possum / *post* et² *add. H* erunt

11 HE: LE (*sive* HE) *G* / FC: et *S* AF *H*

12 HG: DH *H* / supta *Fc* / et 31: et ita *Fc* / 31 (?) *Fb* / Euclidis *om. HFc*

13 triangulum ABC *tr. FbFc* / quedam: quidem (?) *Pb*

14 basis (?) *Fb* / -que *om. GPb* / *post* KM *scr. et del. S* ad lineam PT per 9ᵃᵐ sexti (*habet enim S* va- *supra* ad *et* -cat *supra* sexti) / secet: secceᵗ *G* seccet *Pb*

15 que: quod que *H* / proportio est *tr. H* / ea: ea sit *H*

16 KM¹: lineam KM *Pb* / sed . . . AC *om. GPb* et *H*

17 BL *ex corr. Fc* DL *S* / BF¹ (?) *D* / *post* BF¹ *add. Fc* et forte *Fb* quam BL ad EH / 4: 8 *Fc* 8 (*sive* 4) *Fb* / 15. quinti: 3ᵃᵐ 6ᵗⁱ *H* / EH: CH (?) *D*

18 maior: minor *S* / *ante* BL² *scr. et del. Pb* BF / BL² *om. H* / EH: C̃H (?) *G* H̃ (*!*) *Pb* / 8: 6 *S*

19 *post* maior *add. Fb*, ?*Fc* est / KBM: KM *GPb* / et: est *FbFc*

20 ea: eadem *H*

21 ABC: ALC (*sive* ABC) *G* / KBM: HBM *G* / corollarium *correxi ex* correllarium *in S et ex* correlarium *in H et ex* corre'um *in D et ex* corrll' *in G et ex* correᵐ *in Pb et ex* correll' *in FbFc* (*N.B. Sed credo quod forte scripsit auctor* correllarium *sive* correlarium; *post hoc lectiones huiusmodi non laudabo*) / 17 *HGPb om.* DFbFc FA (?) *S* / concludo *GPb*

22 ergo *om. Pb* (*sed non G*) / AC *om. S* / lineam *om. FbFc*

23 *post* ABC *add. FbFc* quam / *post* triangulum *add. FbFc* ad / et hoc: quod *H* / et (?) *Fc*

24 Concludes inquam: hoc autem concludes *H* / hac regula: ista *H*

25 ea sit tertii ad quartum, et secundi ad quintum maior sit quam quarti ad
sextum, erit primi ad quintum maior quam tertii ad sextum. Cuius demonstratio ex 16. quinti et 12. secundi arismetice Iordani habetur. Sic ergo primum
AC, secundum *PT*, et tertium triangulus *ABC*, et quartum triangulus *KBM*,
quintum linea *KM*, et sextum triangulus *DEG*.

13. SI FUERINT DUO TRIANGULI EQUALES, ERUNT EORUM
BASES EORUNDEM ALTITUDINIBUS MUTUE.

Super bases propositorum triangulorum constituantur parallelogramma
rectangula equealta triangulis [cf. Fig. I.13], que quidem, quoniam sunt trian-
5 gulorum equalium dupla per 42. (*!* 41.) primi, necessario sunt equalia; argue
igitur per 13. sexti.

Incipit liber secundus

1. DUABUS LINEIS DATIS QUAMBILET ILLARUM ITA DIVIDERE
UT SICUT UNUM DIVIDENTIUM AD RELIQUUM ITA IDEM RELI-
QUUM AD ALTERAM PROPOSITARUM.

25 ea: eadem *H* / sit¹: sicut *Pb*
25–26 et. . . . Cuius *om. GPb*
    25 et secundi: secundi vero *H* / et *om. S* / sit² *om. H* / *post* sit² *scr. et del. Fb* 5 / quam
        bis Fb / quarti *om. S* quartum *Fb* quantum *Fc*
    27 quinti . . . Iordani: et 12. quinti *H* / 12. secundi: 2 12. *G* 21 *Pb* / arismetice *SFbFc*
        arsmetice *D* arismetrice *GPb* / Iordani habetur: ordini vel habentur *Fc* / *post* Iordani
        add. Fb aliquid quod non legere possum / primum *om. GPb*
    28 *ante* AC *scr. et del. Pb* HC / AC: AE (?) *D* / *ante* secundum *add. GPb* et / et¹
        om. H
28–29 *est signum* ♀ *in mg. H hic et hab. H mg. infer.* conclude igitur quod maior est
        proportio etc.—in 13. huius ad illud (?) *signum* ♀; ratio illius conclusionis postea in
        eodem commento subdicitur
    28 KBM: HBM (?) *G*
    29 sextum: sestum (?) *Fc*
Prop. I.13
    1 13 *mg. sin. PbEs om. DGFbFc* 14 *mg. sin. H* 14ᵃ *mg. dex. S* / fuerunt (?) *Pb* / duo
        om. SH / *ante* eorum *scr. et del. S* duorum
    2 eorundem: eorumdem *Pb* eorum *FbFc* / altitudines *FbFc*
    4 rectam gulam (*!*) *Fb* / eque alta *PbFbFc* / que: qua *Pb* / quoniam *om. GPb*
    5 dupla *tr. FbFc post* primi / per . . . primi *mg. D om. SHGPb*
5–6 argue . . . sexti: per 13. igitur 6ᵗⁱ patet propositum *H*
Title and Prop. II.1
    1 Incipit liber secundus *Fc om. SG* Liber secundus de triangulis *hab. D in m. Taw ante*
        Prop. II.5 Secundus liber *H?Pb* Liber secundus *Fb* Hic incipit secundus liber quantum
        (?) colligitur ex coniunctione (?) 20 (?) propositionibus (?) *Es*
    2 1 *om. DGFbFc* 1ᵃ *mg. sin. H* 14 *mg. sin. PbEs* 15ᵃ *mg. dex. S*
3–4 unum . . . reliquum: una pars divise ad reliquam eius partem ita illa reliqua
        pars *H*
    3 reliquum: reliqū *S* (*et post hoc lectiones huiusmodi non laudabo eo quod assumo*
        reliqū *stare pro* reliquum
3–4 reliquum: reliquam *GPb* reliquum *FbFc* / *post* reliquum *add. S* ad reliqū ita idem
        reliqū
    4 alteram *omnes alii MSS et ex corr. Fc* / pro- *supra scr. Fb*

5   Coniungantur date linee, sitque tota composita *AC* [Fig. II.1], et punctus
coniunctionis sit *B*, et super totam *AC* designemus semicirculum, et a puncto
B extrahatur perpendicularis usque ad circumferentiam, cadatque in punctum
D. Et describamus circulum parvum cuius diameter sit linea *BD*, et a puncto
A ducatur linea recta *AFE* secans circulum parvum super centrum eius.
10   Deinde ducatur linea recta inter *E* et *B*, et a puncto *F* ducatur alia equedistans
illi donec secet lineam *AB*, et punctus sectionis sit *H*. Dico ergo ita sectam
esse lineam *AB* in puncto *H* quod que est proportio *AH* ad *HB* ea est *HB*
ad *BC*, et hoc est propositum. Ad hoc autem sic ratiocinabis. Cum linea *AB*
contingat circulum parvum per 15. tertii et linea *AE* secet eundem, ergo per
15   penultimam eiusdem quod fit ex *AE* in *AF* equum est quadrato linee *AB*.
Ergo per 16. sexti que est proportio *AE* ad *AB* ea est *AB* ad *AF*. Sed per
secundam sexti que est proportio linee *EF* ad *AF* ea est *BH* ad *HA*; ergo
permutatim *EF* ad *BH* sicut *AF* ad *AH*, quare et sicut totius ad totum per
13. quinti; sed hoc est sicut *AB* ad *AF*, ut ostendimus nuper; ergo a primo
20   per 11. quinti sicut *EF* ad *HB* ita *BA* ad *AF*. Ergo permutatim *EF* ad *BA*

5–7 Coniungantur . . . circumferentiam: Sint linee date AB, BC que coniungantur se-
     cundum rectum et super totam AC designetur circulus ad cuius circumferentiam
     extrahatur perpendicularis a puncto B *H*

6 coniunctionis: disiunctionis *GPb* / et¹ *om. Fc*

7 cadatque: cadat quod (?) *G*

8 D *om. FbFc* / describamus . . . parvum: describatur circulus parvus *H* / parvum:
   partium *FbFc* / cuius *corr.* (?) *Fb ex* eius / dyameter *GPb* (*et post hoc lectiones
   huiusmodi non laudabo*) / linea BD: DB *H* / BD: LD (*sive* BD) *G*

9 A ducatur: adducatur *FbFc*

9–13 ducatur. . . . ratiocinabis: qui est in extremo linee dividende protrahatur linea per
     centrum illius parvi circuli usque ad eius circumferentiam que sit linea AFE et protracta
     linea BE ducatur ab F ad AB lineam linea FH equedistanter linee BE. Dico igitur
     AB sic esse sectam ut sicud AH ad HB ita HB ad BC et hoc est propositum. Sic
     igitur ratiocinas *H*

9–10 AFE. . . . recta *om. FbFc*

9 AFE: ABE *Pb* (*sed non G*) / seccans *GPb* (*et post hoc lectiones huiusmodi non laudabo*)

9–10 parvum . . . puncto: per *S*

10 E: EB *G*

11 donec secet *tr. D* (*secundum Dc*) / sectam: sectio *Fc*

12 *post* HB² *add. Fb* ad HB

13 sic: ergo *S* / ratiocinabis *DS,?G* ratiocinabitur (?) *Pb* (*et ante hoc scr. et del. Pb*
   ratiocinabilis et linea) rationabitis (?) *Fb* rationabiliter (?) *Fc* / Cum : et *GPb*

14 contingit *Fc* / circulum *bis Pb* / et *om. DS* / linea: lineam *Fc* / *post* eundem *add. H*
   circulum

15 eiusdem: tertii *H* / fit: sit *D* (*secundum Dc*) / *ante* AE *scr. et del. Pb* ea

16 Ergo *om. GPb* / *ante* sexti *scr. et del. D* ergo (?) que (?) est / *post* sexti *add. Fb*
   ergo / AE: AC *G* / ea est: eadem est *H* eadem *Pb* / AB ad EF: EF ad BA *D* (*secundum
   Dc*)

17 proportio linee *tr. D* / linee *om. H* / ea: eadem *H* / HA: AH *Pb* / *ante* ergo *add.
   Fb* et

18 *ante* EF *add. H* sicud / sicut¹: ita *H* / *post* totius *add. H* AE / *post* totum *add. H*
   AB

19 sicut: sic *D* sit *G* / ut . . . nuper: prout nuper ostendimus *H*

20 per: patet *Fc* / sicut: sive *FbFc* / HB: BH *Pb* (*sed non G*) / AF *om. FbFc* AD *S* FD
   (?) *G* FA *Pb*

sicut *HB* ad *AF*. Sed *EF* est equalis linee *BD*, ad quam se habet *CB* sicut ipsa *BD* ad *BA* ex 30. tertii et 8. sexti. Ergo *CB* ad *EF* sicut *EF* ad *BA*, quare et sicut *HB* ad *AF*. Argues ergo per equam proportionalitatem sicut *CB* ad *EF* sic *HB* ad *AF*; sed sicut *EF* ad *HB* sic *AF* ad *HA*, ergo sicut *CB* ad *HB*
25 ita *BH* ad *HA*; transeverte ergo, et habebis propositum.

2. DUABUS LINEIS PROPOSITIS ALTERAM EARUM ITA DIVIDERE QUOD SICUT RELIQUA CUM MAIORE DIVIDENTIUM SE HA-
52r BET AD EANDEM MAIOREM ITA EADEM MAIOR SE / HABEAT AD MINOREM.

5 Coniungantur, ut prius, date linee ad punctum *B* [Fig. II.2], et super totam *AC* describamus semicirculum. Deinde super diametrum ad punctum *B* erigatur linea continens cum ea angulum semirectum, que protracta ad circumferentiam cadat in punctum *D*, a quo dimittatur perpendicularis super diametrum cadens in punctum *E*. Dico ergo quod in *E* fit sectio quam queris.
10 Nam, quia uterque angulorum supra *BD* semirectus est per 32. primi, erit per 6. eiusdem linea *DE* equalis linee *BE*. Quare, cum sit *DE* medio loco proportionalis inter *CE* et *EA*, erit et *BE* similiter. Ergo que est proportio

21 EF (?) *Fc* / BD: LD (*sive* BD) *G* / quam: quem *H*
22 8: 6 *S*
23 HB: BH *Fb*
23–24 Argues . . . AF¹ *om. S hic sed post* sicut² *in lin. 24 hab. S* CB ad EF sicut HB ad AF / Argues . . . HA *om. H*
23 proportionem (?) *Pb* / CB: DB *Fc*
23–24 CB . . . sicut² *om. Pb*
24 sed: et *FbFc* / HA: BA *Fc* rça *G* / *post* ergo *add. H* permutatim / CB: et (?) B *Fc* / HB³: BH *H*
25 BH . . . propositum *non bene legere possum in Pb* / transeverte ?D transeunte (*sive* transeverte) *SGPb* transverte *FbDc* transrçe (!) verte *Fc* / transeverte ergo: ergo econtrario sicud AH ad HB ita HB ad BC (*sive* BE) *H* / et habebis: quod est *H* / et *om. G* / *post* propositum *mg. hab.* DFbFc *argumentum* (DFc, ?Fb, *et non aliter* sicut in Dc) *hoc ultimum probatur per regulam supra positam* (hab. Dc *injuste* propositam) in (Fc, ?D, *om.* Fb) *proportione equalitatis*

Prop. II.2
1 2 *om.* DGFbFc 2ᵃ *mg. sin. H* 15 *mg. sin.* PbEs 16ᵃ *mg. dex. S*
1–4 *mg. hab.* DFbFc *Intentio propositionis est hec: quod composita* (DFc, ?Fb) *ex indivisa et maiore portione alterius linee divise se* (*om.* Fc) *habet* (habeat Fc) *ad maiorem portionem sicut maior portio ad minorem*
2 cum: con (!) *Fb*
3 eamdem *FbFc* (*et post hoc lectiones huiusmodi non laudabo*) / habet *FbFc*
5 Comiungatur (!) *Fc* / et *om. S*
6 AC *om.* GPb / describatur semicirculus *H* / *ante* Deinde *scr.* Fb de / B *om. S* (*et corr.* (?) Pb *ex* D) Dᵃ *G*
7 ea: diametro *H* / semirectum: semicirculum *FbFc* / *ante* cir- *scr. et del. S* semicirculum
7–8 circonferentiam *Fb* (*et post hoc lectiones huiusmodi non laudabo*)
8 cadatque *FbFc* / dimittatur (?) *G*
9 E¹: D *FbFc* / ergo *om. Fc*
10 BD: LD (?) *Pb* / semirectus est *tr. H* / 32: 31 (?) *Fc* / erit *om. S et G*
11 6: 8 (?) *FbFc* / DE¹ *om.* GPb / Quare *primo add.* D *post* sit *et postea indicat transpositionem ante* cum / DE² *tr.* FbFc *ante* cum
12 CE: C *D* (*sed non* Dc) / *post* EA *add. H* ex 30ᵃ 3ⁱⁱ et 8a 6ⁱ / *ante* Ergo *add. H* medio loco proportionalis et cetera easdem

CE ad *BE* eadem est *BE*, que est maior portio, ad *EA*, que est minor, et hoc est propositum.

3. DATAM LINEAM SIC SECARE UT QUE UNIUS PORTIONIS AD RELIQUAM EA SIT ILLIUS RELIQUE CUM QUALIBET DATA LINEA AD EANDEM DATAM PROPORTIO.

Sit linea dividenda *AB*, et alia data sit *BC*, coniunganturque in puncto *B*,
5 et super totam *AC* fiat semicirculus, et erigatur perpendicularis *BD* sicut superius, ducaturque linea inter *C* et *D*, et ad eius quantitatem, posito centro in *C*, circinetur portio circuli secans lineam *AB* in puncto *E*, eritque in *E* sectio quam queris. Nam que est proportio *AC* ad *EC* ea est *EC* ad *BC* per ultimam partem 8. sexti, eo quod linea *EC* est sicut linea *DC*; ergo per 19.
10 quinti que est *AE* ad *EB* eadem est *EC* ad *BC*, et hoc est propositum [Fig. II.3].

4. DATIS DUABUS LINEIS ALTERAM EARUM SIC SECARE UT SICUT SE HABET RELIQUA AD UNUM DIVIDENTIUM ITA COMPOSITA EX EADEM RELIQUA ET RELIQUO DIVIDENTIUM SE HABEAT AD IDEM RELIQUUM.

5 Sint date linee *AB* et *BC* [Fig. II.4], et coniungantur in puncto *B*, atque toti composite addatur quedam linea equalis linee *BC*, sitque *CE*. Deinde describatur circulus cuius omnis diameter sit equalis linee *AE*, in quo quidem circulo collocetur linea equalis linee *AC* per primam quarti Euclidis, sitque

13 maior: minor *FbFc* / portio: proportio *S* / minor *omnes alii MSS, et corr. D ex* maior

Prop. II.3

1 3 *om. DGFbFc* 3ᵃ *mg. sin. H* 16 *mg. sin. PbEs* 17ᵃ *mg. dex. S*
2 ea: eadem *H* / cum: com *Fb*
3 datam: data *G* dạntam *Fb* / *post* datam *tacite add. Dc* lineam / proportio: proportionem *GPb* portio *FbFc*
4 AB *supra scr. Fb* / BC: DC *GPb* / -que *om. Fb*
5 AC: AB *GPb* / s- *in* semicirculus *supra scr. D* / BD: LD (*sive* BD) *G*
5–6 sicut superius *om. H*
6 ducaturque: et perducatur *H* / et² *om. PbFc* / posita *GPb*
7 C: O *GPb*
8 querit (*?*) *Fc* / est¹ *om. D* / portio *FbFc* / ad EC: CE *GPb* / ea: eadem *H* / BC: LT (*sive* BC) *G* LC (*?*) *Pb*
9 8: 4 *S* / sicut linea: equalis linee *H* / DC: DḄC *Fc*
10 EB (*?*) *H* EC *omnes alii MSS; vide n. 1 meae translationis* / EC: CE *GPb* / BC: CB *H*

Prop. II.4

1 4 *om. DGFbFc* 4ᵃ *mg. sin. H* 17 *mg. sin. PbEs* 18ᵃ *mg. dex. S* / earum *bis Fb*
2 sicut: sic (*?*) *D* / reliqua: reli_(*?*) *Fb* reli *Fc* / ad unum *tr. FbFc post* dividentium
3 *supra* reliqua *scr. D* indivisa
4 reliqum *SFbFc* (*et post hoc lectiones huiusmodi non laudabo*)
5 date: dat. *D* / et¹ *om. HPb* (*sed non G*) / BC: LC (*sive* BC) *GPb* (*et post hoc lectiones huiusmodi non laudabo*) / coniugatur *G*
6 toti *om. GPb* / additur *Fb* / *post* addatur *add. GPb* atque composito addatur / *post* linea *scr. et del. Fc* que / sitque: que sit *H* / CE: C *Fb*
7 omnis *om. H*
8 quarti: quinti *FbFc*

GD; a qua resecetur quedam portio equalis *AB*, sitque *DF*, eritque residua
10 portio, scilicet *FG*, equalis linee *BC*. Deinde ducatur quedam diameter in
circulo transiens per punctum *F*, que, quoniam est equalis *AE*, vocetur eodem
nomine, et signentur in ea sectiones *B* et *C*. Dico ergo quod in puncto *F* fit
sectio quam requiris. Nam per 34. tertii et 15. sexti que est proportio *EF* ad
DF ea est *GF* ad *AF*; ergo propter equalitatem que est *EF* ad *AB* ea est *BC*
15 ad *AF*; ergo permutatim que est *EF* ad *BC* ea est *AB* ad *AF*; ergo disiunctim,
quoniam *BC* equatur *CE*, que est *CF* ad *BC* ea est *BF* ad *AF*, et permutatim
que est *CF* ad *BF* ea est *BC* ad *AF*. Converte ergo et dic quod que est *BC*
ad *AF* ea est *CF* ad *BF*, et hoc est propositum.

5. DUABUS LINEIS PROPOSITIS QUARUM UNA SIT MINOR
QUARTA ALTERIUS VEL EQUALIS, MINORI TALEM LINEAM AD-
IUNGERE UT QUE ADIECTE AD COMPOSITAM EADEM SIT COM-
POSITE AD RELIQUAM PROPOSITARUM PROPORTIO.

5   Sint date linee maior *AB* et minor *BC* [Fig. II.5a], et coniungantur ut
solet in puncto *B*, et describatur semicirculus super totam *AC*, et erigatur
perpendicularis *BD*. Si ergo est linea *BC* minor quarta parte linee *AB*, erit
et *BD*, cum sit proportionalis inter ipsas, minor medietate *AB*. Dividatur
ergo *AB* per equalia ad punctum *E*, et circinetur super eam semicirculus,
10 erigaturque perpendicularis *EG*, a qua resecetur quedam linea equalis *DB*,

9 equalis: equales *Fc* / sitque: que sit *H* / DF: DEF *Fb* / eritque: erit *FbFc*
10 scilicet: sitque *H* / *ante* BC (*sive* LC) *scr. et del. Pb* BE
11 que (?) *Fc*
12 *ante* B *scr. et del. Pb* B *et injuste del.* -s *in* sectiones / fit: sit *GPb*
13 34: 38 *FbFc* / portio *FbFc*
14 ea^{1,2}: eadem *H* / EF: proportio EF *H*
15 ea: eadem *H* / disiunctum *GPb*
16 quoniam . . . CE *FbFc, mg. D, om. SHGPb* / equat *Fc* / BC^2: CB *H* EF *GPb* / ea:
    eadem *H* / AF: FA *GPb* / et: igitur *H* ergo *Fb*
17 CF: EF *GPbFb* / ea: eadem *H* / est^2 *om. S* / BC^1: proportio BC *H* / Converte: coniuncte
    (?) *S* / BC^2: BE *G* LE (*sive* BE) *Pb*
18 BF: HF (*sive* BF) *GPb*
Prop. II.5
    1 5 *om. DGFbFc* 5^a *mg. sin. H* 18 *mg. sin. PbEs* 19^a *mg. dex. S* / *mg. hic hab. D in*
    m. Taw liber secundus de triangulis / sit: est *SH*
    2 minorem *FbFc*
    3 copositam *Fb*
  3-4 cōmposite *Fb*
    4 portio *S*
    5 date: due *Fb* / et^1 *om. GPb* / cōniungantur *Fb*
  5-6 ut solet *bis G*
    6 B: V (?) *GPb*
    7 BD: LD *Pb* / BC: LC (?) *Pb* / line (!) *Fb*
  7-8 erit et BD *bis G*
    8 BD: LD (?) *Pb* / AB: ADB *G*
    9 E *om. FbFc*
   10 -que *om. Fc* / perpendicularis *omnes alii MSS et ex corr. Fc* / reseccetur *GPb* (*et
    post hoc lectiones huiusmodi non laudabo*) / linea: lineam *Fc*

sitque *LE*, ducaturque linea recta inter *L* et *D*, et punctus in quo secat circumferentiam minorem sit *T*, a quo dimittatur perpendicularis *TM*, que erit equalis linee *DB* per 34. primi et proportionalis inter *AM* et *MB* per 8. sexti. Ergo per 16. et secundam partem 15. eiusdem sicut se habet *AB* ad

15 *AM* ita *MB* ad *BC*; et si hoc, ergo *BM* maior est quam *BC*. Resecetur ergo ab ipsa quedam linea equalis linee *BC*, sitque *HB*. Dico ergo quod linea *HM*, que superest, est linea quam querimus. Quia enim *AB* se habet ad *AM* sicut *MB* ad *HB*, que est sicut *BC*, erit per 19. quinti *MB* ad *HM* sicut *AB* ad *MB*. Converte ergo et dic quod *HM* ad *MB* sicut *MB* ad *AB*, et hoc est

20 propositum cum sit *HB* sicut *BC* que est minor propositarum.

Est autem alio modo facere istud idem, tam et si *BC* sit equalis quarte parti linee *AB*, quam et si sit minor; sed si sit maior frustra laborabis hac arte. Utrum ergo sit minor quarta aut equalis, coniungantur *AB* et *BC* ita quod contineant angulum rectum ad punctum *B* [Fig. II.5b], compleaturque

25 parallelogrammum rectangulum sub ipsis contentum *ABCD*, cui fiat equalis trigonus *BDN* super *BN*, que est dupla ad *BC*, et mediante eo trigono fiat

11 sitque: sit quia *S* / recta *om. H*
12 T *om. GPb* / dimittatur: divitatur (?) mittatur *Fc*
13 erit: est *H* / DB: BD *FbFc*
14 Ergo . . . eiusdem: cum igitur per 16. 6^{ti} quadratum BD et per consequens quadratum TM linee valet quadrangulum quod fit ex AB in BC et idem quadratum valet illud quod fit ex AM in MB per eandem. Igitur illud quod fit ex AB in BC valet illud quod fit ex AM in MB; quare per secundam partem 15. 6^{ti} *H* / *ante* 16 *scr. et del.* (?) *FbFc* 18^{vem} (!) / *post* 16 *add. Pb* aliquid quod non legere possum (*sed forte* 5^{am}) / se habet *om. H*
15 ad: ald *Fb* / BC^1: BE (?) *G* LE *Pb* / hoc: sic *H* / BM: MB *H* / BC^2: LC *Pb* / ergo^2 *om. FbFc*
16 ipsa . . . linea: ea linea MB que sit *H* / sitque HB *om. H*
17 superest: super *FbFc* / lineam *FbFc* / Quia: quod *S* / *ante* enim *scr. et del. Pb* igitur / AB: LAB *Fb*
18 ad^1: d *Fc* / HB: BH *H* / sicut: equalis *H* / BC: BCA *G* LC (?) *Pb* / *post* BC *add. mg.* D prius permutatim argumentando AB ad MB sicut AM ad BH *et hab. GPb* erit 10 (?*G, om. Pb*) quinti (*om. Pb*) prius permutatim arguendo ab AD in B sicut AM ad BH
18–19 erit . . . HM: prius permutatim argumentando AB *FbFc* / *de* erit . . . MB^1 *scr. H mg. infer.* "erit per 19. quinti MB ad HM etc.": videtur melius ad propositum si sic dicatur "erit per divisam (*sive* diversam) proportionalitatem etc. ut prius"
19 dicit (?) *Pb* / sicut MB *om. S* / sicut: ita *H* / MB^3 (?) *Fb* AM *Fc* / ad^3: et *GPb* / AB: BA *H* BH *FbFc*
20 sit *om. FbFc* / BC: BE (?) *G* LC (?) *Pb*
21 tam *om. FbFc* / et *om. H* / *ante* si *scr. et del. Pb* fa / BC: LC *Pb* / quarti *FbFc*
22 parti *omnes alii MSS et ex corr. Fc* / et *om. H* / si^1: sij *Fb* / *post* sit^1 *add. Fc* B (?) / sed: et *FbFc* / sit maior *tr. FbFc*
22–23 hac arte *om. H*
23 arte: parte *FbFc* / Utrum: sive *H*
24 compleaturque: et compleatur *H*
25 contenttum (!) *Fc* / *ante* ABCD *add. H* quod sit
26 trigonius *G* / BDN: BND *H* BDM.BDN *Pb* LDN (?) *Fc* / super BN *om. GPb* / est: sit *H* / ad: a *Pb*
26–27 et . . . cui: cui fiat equale pall'm (parallelogrammum) super basim AB ita quod *H*
26 eo: ea (?) *G* a *Pb*

super lineam *AB* parallelogrammum, cui desit ad complendam superficiem
iuxta totam lineam superficies quadrata per 27. sexti; eritque / rectangulum
et contineatur sub lineis *AE* et *EF*, eritque *EF* equalis *EB*. Et quia per 13.
sexti que est proportio *AB* ad *AE* ea est *EF* ad *BC*, ideo *EF*, et per consequens
EB, maior est quam *BC*. Rescindatur ergo ab ea quedam linea equalis *BC*,
sitque *BH*: dico ergo quod que superest, scilicet *EH*, est linea quam querimus.
Quia enim que est *AB* ad *AE* ea est *EB* ad *HB*, erit per 19. quinti que *AB*
ad *EB* ea *EB* ad *HE*. Converte ergo, et habebis quod optasti.

6. CUM SIT LINEE BREVIORI ADIECTE MAIOR PROPORTIO AD
COMPOSITAM QUAM COMPOSITE AD LONGIOREM, BREVIOREM
QUARTA LONGIORIS MINOREM ESSE NECESSE EST.

Ut si *EH* ad *EB* sit maior proportio quam *EB* ad *AB* [Fig. II.6], dico quod
erit *HB* minor quam quarta pars *AB*. Erit per 11. secundi arismetice in
continuis maior proportio *AB* ad *EB* quam *EB* ad *EH*, vel per 10. quinti
Euclidis. Nam per illam patet quod id ad quod se habet *EB* sicut se habet
EH ad ipsum minus est quam *AB*, sitque illud *ZB*. Et cum *AB* sit maior
quam *ZB*, maiorem habet proportionem ad *EB*, et ideo maiorem quam *EB*
ad *EH*; et si hoc, ergo rectangulum quod continetur sub *AB* et *EH* maius
est quadrato linee *EB* per 27. secundi arismetice, vel quia rectangulum quod

27 compl'endam *S*
28 *ante* per *add. H* illud autem facias / 27: 17 *Fc*, ?*Fb*
28–29 eritque . . . EF¹ *om. S* et sit EFGA *H*
28 eritque: erit *G*
29 lineis: linea *GPbFbFc* / eritque EF *om. GPbFbFc* / eritque: erit igitur *H* / EF²:
    F *S* / Et: LT (?) *Fc*
30 ea est: eadem erit *H* / ideo EF *om. H* / et *HDc om. DSGPbFbFc*
31 EB: CB *Fc* / *post* EB *add. H* ad BC quare EB / est *SH* et *supra scr. D, om. GPbFbFc*
    / Rescindatur *S*, ?*H* recidatur (?) *G* recidatur *DPbFbFc* / quedam linea: BH *H* et
    om. H sitque BH *in lin.* 32
32 BH: HB *GPb* / que . . . EH: EH que superest *H* / que: nec illud quod *GPb* / que
    tr. D post superest / EH: CH *Fc*
33 *ante* Quia *scr. et del. Fc* quam / est¹: est proportio *H* / AE: DE *FbFc* / ea: eadem
    H / EB: AB *FbFc* / HB: BH *H* / eritque *FbFc* / que²: que est *H*
34 ea EB *om. FbFc* / ea: eadem est *H* / HE: LE (?) *G* (*sed* HE *in Pb*) / Converte ergo:
    igitur conversim que est HE ad EB eadem est EB ad AB *H* / et . . . optasti: quod
    est propositum *H* / habebis: lēb' (?) *G*

Prop. II.6

1 6 *om. DGFbFc* 6ª *mg. sin. H* 19 *mg. sin. PbEs* 20ª *mg. dex. S* / adrecte (!) *GPb*
4 EH: ᴱH *Fb*
5 Erit: eritque *FbFc* / *post* Erit *add. H* enim / de per . . . arismetice *mg. scr. H* nota
    quod allegat conclusiones acceptas arismetrice / arismetice (=arithmetice): arisᶜᵉ *G*
    arismetrice (?) *Pb* arsmetice *DSFc* arsmetrice *H*, ?*Fb*
6 maio (!) *Fc* / EB²: EH *Fc* / EH: EB *Fc* / 10: ideo *S*
7 illam: istam *Pb* iᵃᵐ *G* / id: illud *HGPb*, ?*Fb* / ad *om. H* hic / *post* habet¹ *habet H*
    ad / se habet²: EB ad H
8 ipsum *SDc om. H* ipsam *DGPbFbFc* / *post* est *scr. et del. Fb* ad ipsam
9 habebit *Fb* / habet proportionem *tr. SH*
10 hoc: sic *H* / rectangulum: quadrangulum *H*
11 EB: CB *G* / per 27: 37 *Fc*, ?*Fb* / arismetice *G* arsmetice *DS* arismetrice *HPbFc*
    arsmetrice (?) *Fb*

continetur sub *ZB* (quod est minus quam *AB*) et sub *EB* est equale quadrato *EB*. Quadretur ergo linea *EB* et distinguatur in quadrato eius gnomo circa quadratum linee *EH*, cuius uno latere educto compleatur rectangulum con-
15 tentum sub *AB* et *BL*, que est equalis linee *EH*. Quoniam autem in omni quadrato utrumque supplementum proportionale est inter duo quadrata circa diametrum consistentia, ut patet per primam sexti bis, item et supplementa sunt equalia per 43. primi, ergo non erunt supplementa pariter accepta maiora quadratis pariter acceptis per ultimam quinti; ergo nec erunt maius medietate
20 totius quadrati. Et ideo unum illorum, scilicet *HBL*, non erit maius quarta parte totius quadrati. Et quia rectangulum *ABL* maius est quadrato totali, erit supplementum *HBL* necessario minus quarta parte rectanguli *ABL*; ergo linea *HB* est minor quam quarta *AB* per primam sexti.

7. SI MINOR FUERIT PROPORTIONALIS INTER DIVIDENTIA MAIORIS, ATQUE ADIECTE AD MINOREM LINEAM SIT MAIOR PROPORTIO AD COMPOSITAM QUAM COMPOSITE AD MAIOREM, EANDEM COMPOSITAM ALTERO DIVIDENTIUM MAIOREM ESSE
5 NECESSE EST.

Sit maior linea *AB* divisa in *AE* et *EB* [Fig. II.7], inter quas sit *BC* minor linea proportionalis ita quod que est *EB* ad *BC* ea sit *BC* ad *AE*; sit quoque linea adiecta *DC* linee *BC*. Et quia ex ypotesi maior est proportio *DC* ad

12 *ante* ZB *hab. H* EH et (*sed om.* et sub EB) / minus: maius *GPb* / quam *om. H* / EB: AB.EB *Pb*
13 EB^2: a EB *FbFc* / distinguatur (!) *FbFc* / gnomo (?) *D* gomo (!) *FbFc*
14 EH: EB (?) *Fc* / educto *om. FbFc* / *ante* contentum *scr. et del. G* educto compleatur
14–15 contenttum (!) *Fc*
15 *post* et *scr. et del. Pb* EH maius est quadrato linee EH et / Quoniam: cum *H* / autem: aut *Fc*
16 suplementum *DSH* (*post hoc lectiones huiusmodi non laudabo*) / proportionale est *tr. H* / est *om. FbFc* / inter duo: düo inter *S* / inter (?) *D*
17 consistentia: consistentiam *S* constituta *H* / bis *om. FbFc* / *post* bis *add. H* sumptam
19 *ante* pariter *scr. et del. Pb* ma / *ante* quinti *scr. et del. Pb* 6^{ti} / ergo . . . erunt: erunt igitur illa (*sive* nec ?) *Pb*
20 illorum: istorum *Pb*
21 totius *om. H* / *post* quadrati *supra scr. Pb* C / *post* totali *add. H* eo quod sit ex AB in HE
22 necessari (?) *S* / parte: partąe *Fb*
22–23 ergo . . . HB *bis G*
23 *post* sexti *add. Pb* secundum quod (?) proponitur (?)

Prop. II.7
1 7 *om. DGFbFc* 7^a *mg. sin. H* 20 *mg. sin. PbEs* 21^a *mg. dex. S*
2 ad *supra scr. Fb*
6 *mg. hab. DFb* potest autem ista probatio (? *Fb*) ostendi sine (? *Fb*) hac (? *Fb*) ypotesi quod adiecte ad minorem (*D, om. Fb*) ad compositam sit maior proportio quam composite ad maiorem. Sit (*D, om. Fb*) illa enim minor linea medio loco proportionalis, aut est equalis uni dividentium, aut maior, aut minor, eodem quoque autem dato necesse est, compositam altero dividentium esse (*Dc, ?Fb*) maiorem
7 EB: proportio EB *H* / ea . . . BC^2: ea BC *supra scr. Pb* / ea: eadem *H* / sit^1 . . . AE *om. G sed supra scr.* ad / AE: EA *Pb* / sit quoque: sitque *GPb*
8 adiecta: adrecta (?) *Pb* / BC: BE *Pb, ?G* / ypotesi *HGPb* ypothesi *SFbFc, ?D* / DC^2: DE *D*

DB quam *DB* ad *AB*, erit per premissam *BC* minor quam quarta pars linee
10   *AB*. Sed cum linea *AB* dividatur in *AE* et *EB*, necesse est quod altera earum
sit maior sua quarta, sitque, si placet, *EB*. Ergo *EB* erit maior quam *BC*. Et
si hoc, ergo *BC* erit maior quam *AE*, cum sit proportionalis inter dividentia.
Sed *DB* maior est quam *BC*, cum sit omne totum maius sua parte; ergo *DB*
maior quam *AE*, et sic maior quam alterum dividentium, et hoc est pro-
15   positum.

8. IN QUOLIBET LATERUM TRIANGULI PUNCTO SIGNATO AB
EO LINEAM EXTRAHERE QUE TRIANGULUM PER EQUALIA PAR-
TIATUR.

Sit triangulus *ABC* [Fig. II.8]. Si ergo signetur punctus in medio alicuius
5   lateris, ut in *E*, qui sit medius punctus lateris *AB*, et ducatur linea ad oppositum
angulum, ut ad *C*, patet per 38. primi quod divisus erit triangulus *ABC* per
equalia.

Si autem signetur non in medio, sed alibi, ut in puncto *D*, ducatur linea
DC et alia illi equedistans *EG*, ducaturque linea inter *G* et *D* secans lineam
10   *EC* in puncto *T*. Dico quod ipsa dividit triangulum *ABC* per equalia. Nam
trianguli *DEC* et *DGC* sunt equales per 37. primi. Dempto ergo communi

9   eritque *FbFc* / lineas (?) *Fc*
10   AB^2: A *S* / AE: A *S* / *ante* quod *scr. et del.* (?) *Pb aliquid quod non legere possum*
        (*sed forte* quam *sive* pro ?)
11   sit maior *tr. FbFc*
11–12   BC . . . quam *om. GPb* / Et . . . BC: cum sit omne totum maius sua parte *FbFc*
12   hoc: sic *H*
13   est *om. Pb* / quam *bis Pb*
14   maior^1: maior erit *H* maior est *GPb* / sic: sit *G* / maior^2 . . . dividentium: DB altero
        dividentium extat *H* / *post* alterum *scr.* G n (?) a / et hoc: quod *H*
Prop. II.8
1   8 *om. DGFbFc* 8^a *mg. sin. H* 21 *mg. sin. PbEs* 22^a *mg. dex. S* / punto (!) *Fc*
2   extraherere (!) *S*
4   punctum *H*
4–9   alicuius. . . . ducaturque: protracta linea ab eo ad angulum oppositum, divisus erit
        triangulus per equalia per 38. primi et eodem modo econtrario si signetur in angulo
        protrahatur ad medium basis opposti. Si autem alibi signetur ut in puncto D ducatur
        linea DC et ab angulo C ad basis medium ducatur CE. Deinde ab E puncto ducatur
        EG equedistans DC. Deinde ducatur *H*
4–6   alicuius . . . ut *om. GPb* a *S* / alicuius . . . angulum *mg. D*
5   lateris *om. FbFc*
5–6   *mg. hab. Fb aliquid quod non legere possum*
6   38: 3.g *GPb*
8   *ante* Si *scr. et del. S* nam trianguli DC et alia illi equidistans (*habet enim S* va- *supra*
        nam *et* -cat *supra* equidistans) / non . . . sed *om. Fc* / ducitur D (*secundum Dc*)
9   DC: DE *G*, ?*Pb* / illi *om. GPb* / *ante* D *scr. et del. Fc* Z
10   T: D *GPb* / Dico: di^t (?) *Pb* / dividit (?) *Pb* / per: in duo *Pb* (*sed non G*)
11   trianguli: triangulum *GPb* / DEC: DC *Fb* / DGC: D̥E̥G̥E̥ *G* DGE *Pb* / equales:
        equalea (!) *G*, ?*Pb* / ergo *om. S* / *post* communi *add. H* DTC *et hab. Fb* triangulo
        et Fc triangulo DTC *et mg. infer. scr. Fb* Si (*sive* Sed) non (*sive* nota) superficies (?)
        plana a ——— (?) ——— (?) scindet (?) ducens que (?) triangulum (?) per equalia
        partiatur

erunt trianguli *DTE* et *CTG* equales. Addito eodem ergo erit superficies *ADGC* equalis triangulo *AEC*, qui medietas totius.

9. PROPOSITIS DUOBUS TRIANGULIS, AN SINT EQUALES, AN QUIS EORUM MAIOR FUERIT, PERPENDERE.

Super rectam lineam que sit *AB* [Fig. II.9] constituantur ex eadem parte duo parallelogramma rectangula ipsis triangulis singillatim / equalia per 44. primi, eritque inter ipsa rectangula eadem que est inter sua secunda latera proportio per primam sexti, quare et eadem inter triangulos.

10. PROPOSITIS DUOBUS TRIANGULIS INEQUALIBUS EX MA-IORE TRIANGULUM SIBI EQUEALTUM ET MINORI EQUALEM RESCINDERE, ET SUPER BASEM MINORIS QUANTUMLIBET PRO-TRACTAM TRIANGULUM MINORI EQUEALTUM ET MAIORI EQUALEM CONSTITUERE.

Sint propositi trianguli, maior *ABC* et minor *DEF* [Fig. II.10]. Age ergo ad partem primam sic. Super lineam *BC* fiat parallelogrammum equale triangulo *DEF*, cui sit angulus sicut *C* per 44. primi, et ducatur in eo diameter ab angulo *B* in oppositum eius angulum, qui sit *G*. Dupletur ergo linea *CG* opposita linea *GH*, et ducatur linea inter *H* et *B*. Dico ergo quod triangulus *HBC* est sicut *DEF* per 41. primi.

53r

5

5

10

12 DTE *SD* (*secundum Dc*) DET *HFbFc* DEC *GPb* / CTG: CGT *H* ECG *G* ECG (*sive* CTG) *Pb* / ergo: igitur scilicet DACT *H* / erit *om.* *D*

13 ADGC: ADGE (?) *GPb* / AEC: ACE *Fc* ADE *GPb* / *post* qui *add.* *Fc* et / *post* totius *add.* *H* igitur et cetera

Prop. II.9

1–6 *mg. Bu*

1 9 *om.* *DGFbFcBu* 9ᵃ *mg. sin.* *H* 22 *mg. sin.* *PbEs* 23ᵃ *mg. dex.* *S* / sint: sunt *D* (*secundum Dc*) / an² *GPbD* (*secundum Dc*) *Bu* aut *SHFbFc*

2 quis: qui sunt *S* / eorum: illorum *H*

3 rectam (?) *Bu* coᵘnr *G* (*sed rectam? in Pb*) / que . . . AB *om. H*

4 singillatim *H, tacite Dc* sigillatim *DSGFbFcBu* signatim (?) *Pb* / 44: 48 *Fb, ?Fc*

5 inter¹: in *Pb* (*sed non G*) / ipsam *Bu* / rectangula: rectangulam *FbFc* triangula *S* / est *om. H* / *post* est *scr. et del. G* sunt / secunda: erecta *H*

6 inter *om. GPbBu*

Prop. II.10

1–15 *mg. Bu*

1 10 *om.* *DGFbFcBu* 10ᵃ *mg. sin.* *H* 23 *mg. sin.* *PbEs* 24ᵃ *mg. dex.* *S* / tri- *supra scr.* *Pb*

2 equealtum: eque alterum *FC, ?Fb* / minori *HGPbBu* minorem *DSFbFc* / equalen (!) *D*

3 rescidere *Bu* / quantumlibet: quamcumque *G*

3–4 pertractam *Fc*

4 maiori: mąinori *Fc*

6 propositi trianguli *tr. H* / maior *om. GPbBu* / et *om. Fc*

7 partem primam *tr. H* / supra *GPb* / fiat: erige *H*

7–8 equale triangulo *tr. S*

7 equale *tr. H post* DEF

8 C: ĘC *G* / 44: 48 (*sive* 44) *Fb* 38 *Fc*

9 oppositum . . . G: angulum G oppositum *H* / anguli *Fb*

10 opposita . . . et²: ex parte linea GA et ducta linea ab H termino eius ad *H* / apposita *Pb, ?G* / GH: GA *S* / duca *S* / ergo *om. H*

11 DEF: EF *D* / 41: 8ᵃᵐ *Fc* / *post* primi *add.* SFb sexti *et Fc* sesti *et GPbBu* et primam 6ᵗⁱ

Ad partem secundam sic age. Fiat super lineam *DE* parallelogrammum equale triangulo *ABC*, cui sit angulus sicut *D*, et ducatur in eo diameter ab angulo *E* ad oppositum angulum, qui sit *K*, eritque triangulus *DEK*, qui

15 duplatus modo priori reddit *DEN*, qui est sicut *ABC*.

11. SUPER DATAM LINEAM TRIANGULUM TRIANGULO PROPOSITO EQUALEM COLLOCARE.

Sit datus triangulus *A*, et linea data *BC* [Fig. II.11]. Dupletur ergo datus triangulus, et super lineam datam, sicut solet fieri, fiat parallelogrammum

5 equale totali triangulo duplo, quo diviso per diametrum sit quod intentum est.

12. DATA RECTA LINEA ALIAM RECTAM LINEAM INVENIRE AD QUAM SE HABEAT PRIOR SICUT QUILIBET DATUS TRIANGULUS AD QUEMLIBET DATUM TRIANGULUM.

Sint dati trianguli *A* et *B*, et data linea sit *DC* [Fig. II.12]. Considera ergo

5 an trianguli sint equales: nam tunc erit linea quam queris equalis *DC*. Sin autem sit maior *A* et minor *B*, collocabis ergo super lineam *DC* triangulum equalem illi eorum quem volueris in proportione antecedere, sitque *DGC*, quem vel minuendo ut si fuerit sicut maior vel augendo ut si fuerit sicut minor, equalis reliquo per premissam ducta linea *GE*, eritque linea *DE* quam

12 DE: DEF *S*
13 ABC cui: age sicut *GPb* AEGC (?) sicud *Bu*
14 E: C *Fc* / oppositum angulum *tr. H*
14–15 qui² . . . ABC: medietas parallelogrammi; sumpta igitur KN equali KD et protracta linea EN erit triangulus DEN qualis queritur *H*
15 ABC: habet se *Bu*

Prop. II.11

1–6 *mg. Bu*
1 11 *om.* DGFbFcBu 11ᵃ *mg. sin. H* 24 *mg. sin.* PbEs 25ᵃ *mg. dex. S* / triangulum *om.* Pb triangulo *GBu* / *post* triangulo *add.* Fc et
1–2 proposit (!) *D*
2 equale *GBu*
3 linea data *tr. H* / BC: BE *GPbBu* / duplicetur *HS*
3–4 datus triangulus *tr. Bu*
4 et *om.* DGPbBu / *ante* super *scr. et del.* D sicut solet / sicut: sic *GPbBu* / fiat *om.* FbFc / parallelogrammum *om.* GPbBu
5 sit: fit *H*
5–6 intentum: inventum *GPbBu*

Prop. II.12

1–11 *mg. Bu*
1 12 *om.* DGFbFcBu 12ᵃ *mg. sin. H* 25 *mg. sin.* PbEs 26ᵃ *mg. dex. S* / rectam *bis* Fb / lineam *om. Bu*
2 quilibet: quibus *GPb*
4 dati: lati (!) *Fb* / et² *om.* GPbBu / DC: CD *Bu*
5 *post* equales *add. H* per 23. huius / erit: est *H* / DC: DE DC *Bu*
6 A *infra scr.* G / et *om.* GPbBu / B: ḎB *G*
7 *ante* in *scr. et del.* S illi eorum / portione *FbFc* / antecedere: añdc'e (?) *Bu* / DGC: DGE (?) *G*
8 vel (?) *Fc* / ut si¹ *bis* Fb / fuerit¹ *mut. S in* fuit / si²: siṭ *Fb* / fuerit²: fuit *S* / sicut² *om.* DSFbFc
9 *ante* equalis *add. H* fiat alius triangulus / equalis: equa *injuste Dc* / per premissam: secundum modum datum in antepremissa *H* / *ante* DE *scr. et del.* Fb ED

10   queris, vel maior vel minor quam *DC* secundum quod in proportione maiorem
vel minorem triangulum posueris antecedere.

13. TRIANGULO DATO ET PUNCTO EXTRA IPSUM SIGNATO LI-
NEAM PER PUNCTUM TRANSEUNTEM DESIGNARE QUE TRIAN-
GULUM PER EQUALIA PARTIATUR.

Sit triangulus *ABC* et punctus *D* extra triangulum exceptus inter lineas
5   *AEF* et *HBL* que dividant latera trianguli atque ipsum triangulum per equalia
et sint extra quamtumlibet protracte [Fig. II.13a]. Si enim in aliqua talium
poneretur punctus *D*, finem mox sumeret intentio. Ipso ergo posito extra
omnem talem ducamus ab eo lineam equedistantem linee *AC* donec concurrat
cum latere *CB* quantumlibet protracto, punctusque concursus sit *G*. Du-
10   caturque linea *CD*, et compleatur triangulus *CDG*, qui sicut se habet ad
triangulum *AEC*, qui est dimidium dati trianguli, ita se habeat linea *CG* ad
lineam *MN* per premissam. Dividatur ergo linea *CG* secundum rationem
prime huius secundi in puncto *K* ita quidem quod sicut *GK* ad *KC* ita sit
KC ad *MN*, et continuetur linea *DK*, que et protrahatur donec offendat
15   lineam *AC* in puncto qui sit *P*. Dico ergo quod linea *DP* dividit triangulum
ABC per equalia. Nam quia triangulus *CKP* similis est triangulo *KDG* per
4. sexti et equedistantiam linearum et 15. primi et diffinitionem similium
superficierum, ideo erit proportio eius ad ipsum sicut linee *MN* ad lineam

10 *ante* DC *scr. et del. Fb* CD / DC: DE *GBu* CD ˙/. DC *Fc* / in *om. GPbBu*
10–11 maiorem . . . minorem: maiore vel minore *GPbBu*
11 antecedentem *injuste Dc* / *post* antecedere *add. Fc* (?) cetera (?)
Prop. II.13
1 13 *om. DGFbFc* 13ᵃ *mg. sin. H* 26 *mg. sin. PbEs* 27ᵃ *mg. dex. S*
2 que: qui *GPb*
3 partiatur *om. S* dividet *H*
4 exceptus: acceptus *H*
5 AEF: DEF *S* DEF (*sive* AEF) *Fc* / que dividant: dividentes *H*
6 sint: sicut *FbFc* / quantalibet *FbFc* / *ante* talium *scr. et del. S* alium
7 ponetur *S* / D *om. H*
8 lineam *tr. FbFc post* ducamus *in. lin. 8* / AC: AEC *G* / concurat *Fc*
9 protracte *GPb* / *ante* punctusque *add. FbFc* punctus
10 et: ut *H*
11 AEC: ACE *GPbFc* / *sub linea* 11ᵃ *mg. inf. add. Fb* quatuor lineas quas non legere
possum / habeat: habet *Pb* (*sed non G*)
12 CG: CD *S*
13 secundi *om. Fc* / quidem *om. H* / quod *om. FbFc* / GK *alii MSS et ex corr.*
FbFc / KC: KE *G* / sit *om. Pb*
14 continuetur: continetur (?) *GPb* (*et scr. Pb bis* continetur (?) . . . DK *et del. primum*)
/ que et: et ulterius *H* quare (?) *GPb*
14–15 offendat lineam: concurrat cum linea *H*
15 qui sit *om. H* / ad P *desinit textus Fc* / ergo *om. SGPbFb* / dividit (?) *Fb*
16 per: in duo *Pb* (*sed non G*) / CKP: EKP *S*
17 4. sexti: propter *H* / sexte (?) *Fb* / diffinitione *D* (*secundum Dc*) , ?*Pb* (*sed non G*)
17–18 similium superficierum *tr. H*
17 *post* similium *scr. et del. Fb* est triangulo
18 superficiei *Fb*
18–19 erit . . . sexti: per 17. 6ⁱ erit proportio CKP trianguli ad KDG triangulum sicud linee
MN ad lineam KG *H*
18 sicut *om. Fb*

KG per corollarium 17. sexti. Sed triangulus *KDG* ad triangulum *CDG* se
20 habet sicut linea *KG* ad lineam *CG*. Ergo a primo per equam proportionalitatem triangulus *CKP* se habet ad triangulum *CDG* sicut linea *MN* ad
lineam *CG*; sed ad eundem eodem modo se habuit triangulus *AEC*, qui est
medietas dati trianguli; ergo triangulus *CKP* est sicut triangulus *AEC* medietas
dati trianguli *ABC* per 9. quinti, et hoc est propositum. Et per istum eundem
25 processum deduces adversarium ad impossibile, videlicet, quod totum sit
equale parti, si ipse ponat punctum *K* alibi esse quam inter *E* et *B*, vel
punctum *P* alibi esse quam inter *H* et *A*; et erit semper vel totum vel pars
triangulus *AEC* [Fig. II.13b].

53v
14. PROPOSITIS TRIBUS RECTIS LINEIS QUARTAM SUBIUNGERE
AD QUAM SE HABEAT / TERTIA PROPOSITARUM SICUT PRIMA
AD SECUNDAM.

Sint tres linee: prima *A*, secunda *B*, tertia *C* [Fig. II.14], sitque sicut *A* ad
5 *E* ita *E* ad *B* per 9. sexti, atque super *A* et *E* fiant trianguli similes, eritque
proportio trianguli *A* ad triangulum *E* sicut linee *A* ad lineam *B* per corollarium
17. sexti. Inveniatur ergo per antepremissam linea ad quam se habeat linea
C sicut triangulus *A* ad triangulum *E*, sitque *D*, et ipsa est quam queris.

15. SI FUERIT PROPORTIO TOTIUS AD PARTEM MAIOR QUAM
PARTIS EIUSDEM AD SUAM PARTEM, ERIT RESIDUI TOTIUS AD

19 per: ad *Fb* / 17.: iac *S* / sexte (?) *Fb*
20 sicut: sive *S* sine (?) *Fb* / *post* CG *add.* H per primam 6^i
21 CDG *GPbFb* EDG *S* GDG *H* CGD *D* (*secundum Dc*)
23 trianguli: anguli *GPb*
23–24 ergo . . . quinti *FbD* (*secundum Dc*) ABC; quare per 9^{am} 5^{ti} CKP et AEC sunt equales
et per consequens CKP est medietas ABC trianguli dati *H* / ergo . . . trianguli *om.*
SGPb
24 et hoc: quod *H*
25 inpossibile *Pb*
26 alibi (?) *Fb* al̨libi *Pb* / inter: intra *GPb* / *post* vel *scr. et del. Pb* parvam (?)
27 et^2: quia *H*

Prop. II.14
1–8 *mg. Bu*
1 14 *om.* DGFbBu 14 *mg. sin.* H 27 *mg. sin.* PbEs 28^a *mg. dex.* S / quartam: quaḍṛatam
Fb / subiugere *Pb*
3 ad: a *S*
4 prima . . . C: A, B, C *Bu* / B: E *S* / sitque: sintque *S*
4–5 sitque . . . B: et fiat E proportionalis inter A et B *H*
5 ita E *om. Fb* / E^2: CE *G* EC *Pb* ^{E}C *Bu* / atque: deinde *H* / *ante* similes *scr. et del.*
Fb ABCD
5–6 similes . . . trianguli *om. S* / eritque . . . A^1: per 19. 6^{ti} ex qua sequitur quod
triangulus A se habet *H*
5 -que *om. Fb*
6 A^1: ad *Fb* / linee: linea *H* / A^2 *om. Fb*
7 17. *om. Bu* 1917. *G* / habeat *omnes MSS habet* injuste *Dc*
8 C: E *Pb* (*sed non G*) / et . . . est: est igitur D *H*
Prop. II.15
1–8 *mg. Bu*
1 15 *om.* DGFbBu 15 *mg. sin.* H 28 *mg. sin.* PbEs 29^a *mg. dex.* S

RESIDUUM PARTIS MAIOR PROPORTIO QUAM TOTIUS AD PAR-
TEM; ET SI MINOR, MINOR.

5   Nam per 13. et 14. secundi arismetice demonstras in continuis, si fuerit
proportio totius ad totum maior quam detracti ad detractum, erit residui ad
residuum maior quam totius ad totum, et si minor, minor [cf. Fig. II.15].
Ex hoc igitur facile propositum consequeris.

16. CUM FUERIT LINEA BREVIOR MINOR QUARTA PARTE LON-
GIORIS, LINEA EI ADIECTA CUIUS PROPORTIO AD COMPOSITAM
EST SICUT COMPOSITE AD LONGIOREM MINOR EST OMNI
ADIECTA EIDEM BREVIORI CUIUS AD COMPOSITAM [PROPORTIO]
5   FUERIT MAIOR QUAM COMPOSITE AD LONGIOREM: ET MAIOR
OMNI CUIUS FUERIT PROPORTIO MINOR. ET CONVERTITUR
QUOD OMNIS EA MAIOR MAIOREM ET MINOR MINOREM OPTI-
NET PROPORTIONEM AD COMPOSITAM QUAM COMPOSITA AD
LONGIOREM, HOC OBSERVATO, QUOD LONGIOR PRIMA SIT SEM-
10   PER LONGIOR OMNI ASSUMPTA.

Fiat hic omnino eadem dispositio qualis est prior earum que facte sunt
super quintam huius secundi, illa scilicet que fit per circuitum et cum eisdem
notis. Sit autem linea KH [Fig. II.16], que adiecta linee HB, que est sicut
BC, minor linea maiorem optineat proportionem ad KB quam KB ad AB.
15   Dico ergo quod KH maior est quam MH. Erit enim, sicut patuit super sextam
huius, maior proportio AB ad KB quam KB ad KH, et ideo per primam

3–4 parten (!) D
    4 si corr. Pb ex sit
    5 Nam: Iam (?) Bu / arismetice G aris^{ce} Pb arisme^{ce} Bu arsmetice DSFb arsmetrice H
       (et hab. mg. H nota de arsmetrica) / demonstras: demostrantis H demostratum (?)
       Bu
    8 post Ex textus Bu absecatur / facile mg. GPb
Prop. II.16
   1–27 mg. Bu
    1 16 om. DGFbBu 16 mg. sin. H 29 mg. sin. PbEs 30^a mg. dex. S / linea: line (!)
       D / minor om. Pb
    2 linea: linee injuste Dc / ei: eis S / adiecta HGPbBu adiecte SFbDc adiect D / compositam
       (?) Bu
    3 minor: maior injuste corr. Dc ex minor in D / omni: omnium injuste Dc
    4 ante eidem scr. et del. S i / eidem: idem Fb / [proportio] add. Dc, sed. hab. H
       proportio post maior
    5 maior: minor FbD (secundum Dc)
    6 omni: omnium injuste Dc / post omni add. H adiecta
    7 maior om. Bu
   12 quinta GPb, ?Fb / post huius scr. et del. Pb sexti / illa (?) Bu / scilicet: videlicet
       GPbBu / circuitum: circinum Fb, ?D
   13 KH: HK SH KL Fb / que adiecta tr. D / que^1: que est GPbBu / adiecta: addita H
       adiacta Fb
   14 post linea injuste add. Dc [MA] / maiore GPb, ?Bu / quam: quod Fb
   15 erint (?) Pb
   16 maior proportio mg. H / maior: minor GPbBu / AB corr. (?) Pb ex ad / ante quam
       scr. et del. Pb ad / et om. Bu

partem premisse maior est proportio *AK* ad *HB* quam *AB* ad *KB*. Et si hoc, ergo rectangulum contentum sub *AK* et *KB* maius est eo quod continetur sub *AB* et *HB* sive *BC* per 27. secundi arismetice in continuis. Ergo per-
20 pendicularis erecta a puncto *K* ad circumferentiam minorem maior est per-pendiculari *BD* per 8. et 16. sexti Euclidis, quare et maior perpendiculari *MT*. Et si maior, ergo semidiametro *EG* propinquior per 14. tertii Euclidis et 13. Ergo et punctus *K* necessario magis approximabitur ad punctum *E* et elongabitur a puncto *B* in diametro *AB* quam punctus *M*. Ergo linea *KB*
25 maior est quam *MB*, quare et *KH* quam *MH*, dempta communi *HB*. Ceteras quoque partes propositionis ex eadem industria facile demonstrabis, si minime perspicacis ingenii diceris.

17. PUNCTO INFRA (! INTRA) PROPOSITUM TRIGONUM DATO LINEAM PER IPSUM DEDUCERE QUE TRIANGULUM SECET PER EQUALIA.

Sit triangulus *ABC* [Fig. II.17], et punctus infra (! intra) ipsum datus sit
5 *D* comprehensus ex parte *B* inter lineas *AG* et *BE* dividentes opposita latera, nec non et triangulum, per equalia, ducaturque linea per *D* equedistans linee

17 est *om. SH* / si: sic *GBu* sit (?) *Pb*
18 *ante* contentum *add. GPb* m *et Bu* n *sive* in / eo *om. Fb* quam id *GPbBu*
19 arismetice *correxi ex* arisme^ce *in Bu et* arismetrice *in GPb et* arsmetice *in DS et* arsmetrice *in HFb*
20 a: et *Fb*
21 *ante* 8 *scr. et del. Fb* 2 (?) / quare: quia *Pb* (*sed non G*)
22 MT: MC *GPb* M *Bu* / Et *om. GPb* / *post* ergo *scr. et del.* G C / semidiametro: semidiamentro (!) *Fb* semi mediametro (!) *Bu* / propinquier (!) *G* (*et forte Pb*)
23 et 13 *om. Bu*
23–27 *de* Ergo. . . . diceris *mg. scr. Fb et D* (*secundum Dc*) Sed nota quod si K cadat (*Fb,* cadet *Dc*) in E sive inter E et H, de facile patet propositum, quia tunc perpendicularis ad (*Fb,* a *Dc*) punctum (?*Fb,* puncto *Dc*) K erecta erit maior vel minor linea (?*Fb,* NL ? sive *Dc*) BD. Sin autem, secundum (*Dc, lac. Fb*) quod si (*Dc,* hoc *Fb*) composita (*Fb,* comperta *Dc*), scilicet KB, sit equalis MA, erit eadem proportio adiecte ad compositam (*Dc, om. Fb*) que (*Dc, om. Fb*) composite ad maiorem propositarum ex 9. secundi et 13. Euclidis et ex 8. et secunda (*Dc, om. Fb*) parte 15. (*Dc, om. Fb*) sexti et 19. quinti. Si autem KB (*Dc, om. Fb*) sit minor MA, maior erit proportio adiecte etc.; et (*Fb, om. Dc*) si vero maior, erit minor proportio etc. et eisdem pro-positionibus (*Dc,* proportionibus *Fb*) utendum est quibus et prius, sed illis in (*Dc,* ?*Fb*) maiori (*Dc,* maior *Fb*) vel in minori proportione sumptis
23 et²: ad *Bu* / magis: maius *Bu* / approximabitur *DFbBu* aproximabitur *GPb* appro-pinquabitur *S,* ?*H* / *post* et³ *add.* H E plus
24 elongabitur: e. longabitur *SFb* / in: i *S* / AB: ad *S* / KB: KH *Fb*
25 KH *H,* ?*S* KB *GPbFbEsBuDc* / MH: MK *GPbBu* / communi: communiter *GBu* comuni *Fb*
26 propositas (?) *H* / demonstrabis (?) *H*
26–27 si . . . diceris *om. Bu*
Prop. II.17
1 17 *om. DGFb* 17ª *mg. sin.* H 30 *mg. sin.* PbEs 31ª *mg. dex.* S / infra: intra *Pb* (*sed non G*) / positum *GPb*
5 B: H (?) *Fb* / opposita latera: latera opposita *Pb* latera apposita *G*
6 -que *om. Fb*

AC, que sit *FDH*, et continuetur linea *DB*. Inveniatur ergo per 12. huius quedam linea, sitque *MN*, ad quam se habeat linea *BF* sicut triangulus *BDF* ad triangulum *BEC*, qui est medietas dati trianguli. Inveniatur et alia, sitque
10 *TY*, ad quam se habeat *BF* sicut triangulus *BFH* ad triangulum *BEC*. Et quia triangulus *BFH* maior est triangulo *BDF*, erit *MN* maior quam *TY* per
54r 8. et 10. quinti. Est autem *BF* ad *BC* sicut *BC* / ad *TY* per corollarium 17. sexti, eo quod triangulus *BFH* similis est triangulo *BEC* propter equedistantiam linearum. Sed *BC* ad *TY* maior est proportio quam ad *MN* per
15 secundam partem 8. quinti. Ergo maior est proportio *BF* ad *BC* quam *BC* ad *MN*; quare et *FC* minor est quarta parte linee *MN* per sextam huius. Addatur ergo linee *FC* ex parte *F* quedam linea per quintam huius, sitque *FZ*, cuius ad compositam *ZC* sit proportio sicut *ZC* ad *MN*; eritque *FZ* minor quam *FB* per primam partem premisse. Continuetur ergo linea *ZD*,
20 que et protrahatur donec offendat lineam *AC* in puncto *K*. Dico ergo quod linea *ZDK* dividit triangulum *ABC* per equalia. Nam triangulus *BDF* ad triangulum *ZDF* sicut linea *BF* ad lineam *ZF* per primam sexti; sed triangulus *ZDF* ad triangulum *ZKC* se habet sicut linea *ZF* ad lineam *MN* per corollarium 17. sexti et similitudinem triangulorum; ergo a primo per equam
25 proportionalitatem triangulus *BDF* ad triangulum *ZKC* se habet sicut linea *BF* ad lineam *MN*. Sed eodem modo se habuit ille idem ad triangulum *BEC*. Ergo per secundam partem 9. quinti triangulus *ZKC* est equalis triangulo *BEC*, qui est medietas *ABC*.

18. INFRA (! INTRA) DATUM TRIANGULUM A PUNCTO UNO SIGNATO TRES LINEAS AD ANGULOS TRES QUE TRIANGULUM PER TRIA EQUALIA DIVIDANT PROTRAHERE.

7 continuetur: continetur *GPbFb* / DB: AB *Fb* / 12 (?) *Pb* / post huius *add. H* secundi
8 quedam linea *tr. Pb* (*sed non G*) / sitque: que sit *H* atque *Pb*, *?G* / habeant (?) *Fb* / linea[2]: ita *GPb* (*et post* ita *scr. et del. G* habeat) / BF: FB *H*
9 *post* triangulum *add. GPb* m / BEC: HEC *S* / qui: quidam *D* (*secundum Dc*) / *post* Inveniatur *scr. et del. S* ergo per 12. / et: etiam *H* / sitque: linea *H*
12 8. et *om. H* / 10: x (?) *G* / autem: quare *GPb* / BC[1]: BE Ḅ *G* / 17.: 16ᵉ *Pb* 16. *G*
13 *ante* similis *scr. et del. G* similis IS (?) / similis (?) *D* (*sed injuste hab. Dc* minor)
15 8.: 4ᵛᵉ (!) *S*
16 *post* huius *add. H* secundi (?)
17 Addatur ergo *tr. GPb* / FC: FC (*sive* et) *D* / sitque: que sit *H*
18 FZ[1]: HZ *S* FE *GPb* / ZC[2]: ZI (?) *S*
19 quam *om. S* / Continuetur: continetur *G*, *?Pb* / ZD: DZ *G* DZ ZD DZ *Pb*
20 que *om. H* / offendat *alii MSS et forte DFb*
21 ZDK *H et ex corr. mg. D* ZD ZHC (?) *S* ZD hⁿc *GPb* ZDB *Fb* / *post* Nam *scr. et del. Fb* ADF
22 *ante* sicut *add. H* est / per *om. GPb*
23 triangulum: angulum *Fb* / ZKC *DGPb* ZBC *SFb* ZCK *H* / *post* habet *scr. et del. S* habet
26 BF: habet *S* / se *om. GPb* / ille: iste *Pb*
27 9: 19 *Fb* / quinti: vⁿᵗⁱ (?) *D* et quinti *GPb* / ZKC: ZEKC (*sive* et EKC) *Fb* ZBC (*sive* ZKC) *S*

Prop. II.18
1 18 *mg. sin. H om. DGFb* 31 *mg. sin. PbEs* 32ᵃ *mg. dex. S* / Intra *H*

Sit datus triangulus *ABC* et ab uno laterum, ut ex latere *BC* [Fig. II.18],
5 abscindatur tertia pars per 11. sexti, sitque *DC*, et protrahatur linea *DE*
equedistans linee *AC*, cuius medius punctus *G*, a quo ducantur linee recte
ad *A* et ad *C* puncta et ad *B* punctum. Dico quod iste tres linee dividunt
triangulum per tria equalia. Et hoc ex 38. primi et prima sexti ducta linea
recta inter *A* et *D* demonstrabis. Erit enim *ADC* triangulus, qui est equalis
10 *AGC*, tertia totius per primam sexti, et duo reliqui equales.

19. AB ANGULO QUADRANGULI ASSIGNATI LINEAM RECTAM
EDUCERE QUE TOTAM QUADRANGULI SUPERFICIEM PER DUO
EQUALIA PARTIATUR.

Ab oppositis angulis assignati quadranguli ducantur in eo due diametri,
5 que sint *AC* et *BD* [Fig. II.19], sese intersecantes in puncto *G*. Dico ergo
quod, si qua earum reliquam per equalia dividat, ipsa totum quadrangulum
per equalia distinguit, et hoc per 38. primi bis et communem scientiam: si
equalibus equalia addas, tota fient equalia, convinces. Si vero neutra earum
reliquam per equalia dividat, non tamen perit ars. Ponamus ergo quod *GC*
10 sit maior quam *GA*; resecemus ab ipsa ei equalem, que sit *EC*, ducaturque
ab *E* puncto linea *EL* equedistans linee *GD*, fixo *L* in latere *DC*, et continuetur
linea *BL*. Age ergo: proportio trianguli *DBC* ad triangulum *LBC* est sicut

4 Sit: Si *S* / ab: aḅ ex *Fb* / ut ex: scilicet a *H* / ut *om. S*
5 pertrahatur (?) *Fb*
6 *post* punctus *add. H* sit
7 ad A: ab AC̣ *G* ab AC *Pb* / C: ẹ^C *G* e^t *Pb* / puncta . . . punctum: et ad B puncta *H*
/ ad²: ab *S* / iste tres *tr. S* / dividuntur *S*
8 per tria equalia: in 3 partes equales *H et add. mg. dex. H* et sic ad talem figuram *et*
add. mg. infer. H quod triangulus AGB sit equalis BGC probatur, nam partes eorum
terminate ad B sint equales per 38. primi et EGA et DGC sunt equales per 38. primi;
igitur totus triangulus toto triangulo equalis / ex (?) *Fb* / 38 (?) *Pb* 34 (?) *S* / prima:
primam *Fb*
9 inter (?) *GPb* / demonstratio *Fb*
10 AGC: AGE *Pb*, ?G / equale *D*

Prop. II.19
1 19 *om. DGFb* 19ª *mg. sin. H* 32 *mg. sin. PbEs* 33ª *mg. dex. S* / *post* angulo *scr. et*
del. S trianguli
2 superficie *GPb*
3 partiantur *GPb*
4 duo *Fb*
5 sint: sunt *GPb* / AC et: ACA *S* / et *om. H* / ergo *om. GPb*
6 qua (?) *Pb* Ḳ 4ª (?) *G*
7 distinguit: distingunt (?) *D* distinguint (?) *SGPb* / et hoc. *om. H* / 38: 34 *S* / bis: bis
sumptam *H*
8 equalibus equalia *tr. Fb* / totam *D* / tota . . . convinces: et cetera *H* / fient: fierent
S fiant *Fb* / convn̄ices (?) *S*
9 non . . . ars *om. H* / ergo *om. H*
10 resecemus (?) *Fb* / resecemus . . . ei: a qua resecemus sibi *H* / ei *om. GPb* / EC: Ẹ^C
G e^t *Pb* / ducanturque *Pb* / -que *om. Fb*
11 E: eo *Fb* / GD: GB (?) *Fb* / fixo *bis Fb* fixa *GPb* / et *om. Pb*
12 Age . . . proportio: proportio igitur *H* / LBC *HGPb* ABC *DSFb* / *post* sicut *add. Fb*
est

proportio linee *DC* ad lineam *LC* per primam sexti, quare et sicut linee *GC* ad *EC*; sed hoc est sicut *GC* ad *GA*. Sed sicut *GC* ad *GA* ita triangulus *DBC*
15 ad triangulum *DAB* per partiales triangulos et primam sexti et 13. quinti. Ergo a primo *DBC* triangulus se habet ad *DAB* sicut et ad *LBC*, quare et illi equales per 9. quinti. Divisa ergo linea *DL* per equalia ad punctum *T* ducatur linea inter *T* et *B*, et dico quod ipsa dividit quadrangulum per equalia, quod ex predictis et 38. primi et communi scientia argues.

Incipit tertius liber de triangulis

1. SI TRES LINEE IN CIRCULO EQUEDISTANTES EQUALES INTER SE ARCUS COMPREHENDANT, MAXIME AD MEDIAM MAIOR ERIT DISTANTIA ET MAIOREM CUM EA CIRCULI PARTEM COMPRE-
5 HENDET.

Sint in circulo tres linee equedistantes, prima *AB*, media *CD* priori minor vel saltem equalis, tertia et minima sit *EF* [Fig. III.1], sitque arcus *AC* equalis arcui *CE*, et corda corde equalis erit. Et ductis ex transverso lineis *DA* et *DE* patet quod, quia anguli coalterni sunt equales et in equos arcus cadunt
10 per 25. tertii, erunt *BD* et *DF* arcus et corde et sibi invicem et reliquis equales. Continuetur ergo linea *AE* subtensa angulo *C* secans lineam *CD* in puncto

13 DC: DĘC *G* CDC *Fb et postea scr. et del. Fb* et continuetur / quare (?) *Fb* / sicut linee *tr. D* / sicut *om. Fb* / linee GC *tr. Fb*
14 *ante* ad¹ *add. Fb* sicut / Sed . . . GA² *D* (*secundum Dc*) *om. SGPbFb*
14–15 Sed . . . quinti: et ita triangulus GBC ad triangulum GBA et triangulus GDC ad triangulum GDA; ergo eodem modo se habet DBC totalis ad totalem DBA *H*
14 DBC: ABC (?) *Fb*
15 DAB: DBAB *G* / et¹: et per *GPb*
16 et¹ *om. H* DBC *G* DHC (*sive* DBC) *Pb* / LBC: ABC *Fb*
17 equales: sunt equales *H* / ad punctum: in puncto *H* / T: D *GPbFb*
18 inter . . . ipsa: TB que *H* / quod: quid *Fb*
19 ex: est *Fb* / 38 (?) *Pb* / et² . . . argues: satis patet *H* / *post* et² *scr. et del. G* primi / communi: *lac. S*
Title and Prop. III.1
1 Incipit . . . triangulis *mg. D* (*secundum Dc*) *om. SGPbEs* Liber tertius de triangulis *Dc* 3ᵘˢ liber *H* Liber tertius (?) *mg. sin. Fb*
2 1 *om. DGFb* 1ᵃ *mg. sin. H* 33 *mg. sin. PbEs* 34ᵃ *mg. dex. S* / circulo: sc'ulo *G* / equadistantes (!) *Fb*
3 conprehendant *G*
4 maiorem: maior est *S* / circuli: sc'uli *G* st'uli *Pb*
4–5 conprehendet *G*
6 AB: AD *GPb* / CD: CB *GPb* / priore *GPb*
7 saltem equalis: si (*sive* sive) *Fb* / saltim *SGPb* / tertium *GPb* / *ante* EF *scr. et del. Fb* prima AB, media CD / EF: ES *GPb*
8 arcui: *lac. Fb* / CE: EC *Fb* / ex: a *Fb* / DA: a DA *Pb*
8–9 et DE: BC et DE, CF *H*
9 quod *om. GPb* / in: ita *Fb*
10 25: 15 (*sive* 25) *Fb* / invicecem (!) *Pb*
11 continuetur (?) *GPb* / linea: li. *Fb* / secans (?) *Fb*

G, atque a duobus punctis *E* et *F* dimittantur perpendiculares super *AB*—
quas quidem intra circulum cadere necesse est, cum linea *EF* inferior (*!*
interior?*) sit *AB* et eidem equedistans—, que sint *ET* et *FK* secantes lineam
15 *CD* in punctis *Z, Y,* et continuentur *TC* et *KD.* Habes ergo unde ages ad
54v utramque partem pro/positionis. Nam, quia per 27. tertii arcus *AB* maior
est arcu *EF,* ideo *CAD* arcus maior est arcu *CED* per communem scientiam,
et ideo maior est angulus ad punctum *C,* cui subtenditur linea *AG,* quam
reliquus, cui subtenditur linea *GE.* Quare et *AG* maior est quam *GE* per 24.
20 primi Euclidis. Et si hoc, ergo linea *TZ* maior est quam linea *ZE* per secundam
sexti, et hoc est prior pars propositionis, nam distantia linearum dicitur linea
que est perpendicularis super utramque. Secundam partem, scilicet quod
superficies *ACDB* sit maior superficie *CEFD,* facile concludes ex hoc, quod
TZ est maior quam *ZE* et *KY* maior quam *YF,* et ex prima sexti habito
25 respectu ad partialia parallelogramma et partiales triangulos eisdem utrinque
subnixos.

2. SI IDEM ARCUS IN PLURES DIVISIONES SEPARETUR, QUE
EQUALIBUS IPSIUS PORTIONIBUS SUBTENDUNTUR CORDE CON-
IUNCTE MAIORES ERUNT, ET QUANTO EIS PROPINQUIORES,
TANTO REMOTIORIBUS LONGIORES.

5 Esto arcus *AB* [Fig. III.2], cuius divisio in portiones equales sit apud *C,*
et alie due divisiones, sint propinquior apud *D* et remotior apud *E,* atque ad
hec tria puncta protrahantur sex corde ita quod due ad quodlibet, una quidem

---

12 duobus: duo *GPb* / perpendiculares . . . AB *om. Fb hic sed add. post* equedistans
    in lin. 14
13–14 quas *(Dc,* per quas *Fb)* . . . equedistans *add. mg. D* et *Fb (sed non in aliis MSS)*
13 EF *corr. Fb ex* est
14 et[1]: et in *Fb* / sint: sunt *GPbFb* / FK: KP *Pb*
15 continuetur *Fb* / TC: CT *H* / Habes ergo *om. Fb*
16 quia *om. GPb* / *ante* per *add. H* linee AB et EF sunt inequales ideo *H*
17 *post* est[1] *add. GPb* m *(sive* in) / ideo . . . scientiam: et per consequens arcus ABD
    maior est arcu EFD per communem scientiam eo quod equale additur utrique *H* /
    CAD: CD.AD *GPb* / comunem *Fb*
18 maior: minor *Fb* / est *om. GPb*
19 reliqus *SG* / cui *om. Fb* / GE[1]: CGE *GPb* / 24: 17 *(?) Fb*
20 hoc ergo *tr. Fb* / hoc: sic *H* / TZ: EZ *S* / ZE: ṬZE *G* TZE *Pb*
21 est *om. GPb* / nam *(?) G* / dicitur: erit *H* / *ante* linea *hab. Pb* illa *(sed non G)*
23 CEFD: ZCFD *Fb* / *ante* facile *add. H* sic / ex *bis Fb* / quod *(?) D*
24 TZ: TCZ *(?) H* / habita *H*
25 respectu *om. H* / et: et ad *H* / triangulos: triangulus *Pb* angulos *S* / utrumque *GPb*
    utriusque *Fb*
26 subnexos *SH*

Prop. III.2

1 2 *mg. sin. H om. DGFb* 34 *mg. sin. PbEs* 35[a] *mg. dex. S*
2 proportionibus *GPb*
5 portiones: partes *GPb* / equales *om. Pb (sed non G)*
6 *post* ad *add. GPb* atque
7 tria: tres *(?) D* / sex: sed *(?) Fb*

ab *A* et alia ab *B*. Et cum sint in universo sex, quatuor intermedie tantum
sese intersecabunt in punctis tribus, qui sint *H*, *G*, *K*, eruntque singuli duo
10 trianguli ad quemlibet illorum punctorum coniuncti sibi invicem similes, eo
quod equianguli, nam anguli in eisdem coniuncti sunt equales, et similiter
anguli *C*, *D*, *E* ad circumferentiam sunt equales, eo quod cadunt in equos
arcus. Age ergo, cum sint trianguli *ACG* et *BGD* similes, que est proportio
AC ad *BD* ea est *CG* ad *DG*, et totius coniuncti ad totum coniunctum. Sed
15 *AC* maior est quam *BD*, quia maiori arcui subtenditur, per 27. tertii; ergo
coniunctum ex *AC* et *CG* maius est coniuncto ex *BD* et *DG*; sed et hoc
adhuc maius est quam linea *GB* per 20. quinti (*!*, *del.*) primi. Et quia coniunctum ad coniunctum est sicut linea *AG* ad *BG* propter similitudinem
triangulorum et 13. quinti, argue ex ultima quinti quod linea coniuncta ex
20 *AC* et *CGB* maior est quam linea coniuncta ex *BD* et *DGA*, et reliqua convinces
eodem modo.

3. SI LINEE EQUALES IN CIRCULIS INEQUALIBUS ARCUS RE-
SECENT, DE MAIORI MINOREM ET DE MINORI MAIOREM RESE-
CABUNT.

Sint duo circuli inequales: maior *A* et minor *B* [Fig. III.3], positis *A* et *B*
5 in centris, colloceturque in *A* linea *DC*, et alia ei equalis in *B*, que sit *FE*,
et continuentur linee *AC* et *BE*, ducaturque perpendicularis super *DC* et

8 ab^2: a *H* / in universo: unumquoque *Pb* unumquod *G* / *post* sex (*i.e.* vi) *scr. et del.*
Fb corde ita quod
9 sese intersecabunt: se secabunt *H* / sint: sunt *HGPb*
10 quamlibet (*?*) *Pb* / sibi: igitur *Fb*
12 ad *bis Fb* / eo quod *om. Fb*
12–13 cadunt . . . arcus: sunt super eundem arcum *H*
13 sint: sit *Fb* / BGD: LGD *GPb*
14 ad^1: at (*sive* AC) *S* / BD: LD (*sive* BD) *GPb* / DG: GD *H* / *post* DG *scr. et del. H*
et AG ad GB / *post* et *add. H* per consequens
15 maior: minor *Fb* / quam *om. SH* / per: et per *GPb*
16 coniunctim *S* / *ante* ex^1 *scr. et del. Pb* vel *sive* per / est *om. GPb* / coniunctō (*!*)
S / et^2 *om. GPb*
16–17 et^3 . . . adhuc: coniunctum ex BD et DG *H*
17 linea *om. H* / GB: GH *S* / 20: 27 *GPb* / quinti *om. H* / quia *om. H*
18 BG: lineam LG *Pb* LG *G*
19 et . . . quod: igitur per ultimam quinti *H* / et 13: *lac. Fb* / 13.: 23^{am} *S* / coniuncta:
conincta (*!*) *G*, *?Pb*
20 CGB: GB *D* DGB *injuste Dc* / DGA: CGA *injuste Dc* / et^3: eo quod BG est minimum
inter illa proportionata et coniunctum ex AC, CG est maximum *H*
20–21 convinces eodem modo: vero eodem modo convinces *H*
21 *post* modo *add. G* et 37. (*sive* 27.) tertii indirecte *et hab. Pb* et 37. 3^{ii} indirecte
Prop. III.3
1 3 *om. DGFb* 3^a *mg. sin. H* 35 *mg. sin. PbEs* 36^a *mg. dex. S* / arcus *om. Fb*
1–2 resecent *D* (*et non* resecant *sicut in Dc*) rescecent (*!*) *Fb*
2 maiore *SH* / de^2 *om. GPb* / minori *G*, *?Pb* minore *DSHFb*
2–3 rescecabunt (*!*) *Fb et add. Fb* portionem
6 *ante* linee *scr. et del. S* ec / linee *corr. G ex* linea

protrahatur ad circumferentiam in punctum *T*; similiter et *BH* sit perpendicularis super *FE*, que et protrahatur in circumferentiam ad punctum *K*. Et erunt *GC* et *HE* equales, quia sunt medietates *DC* et *FE* linearum equalium per 3. tertii Euclidis. Et cum sit linea *AC* maior quam linea *BE*, eo quod maioris circuli semidiameter est, erit linea *AG* maior quam linea *BH* per penultimam primi Euclidis. Sit ergo *GL* sicut *BH* et ducantur linee *LC* et *LD*, quarum utraque erit sicut *BE* per 4. primi Euclidis, atque maior quam *LT* per septimam tertii. Protrahatur ergo *LT* usque ad punctum *M* ita quod *LM* sit equalis uni earum; et posito centro in *L* describatur circulus *DMC*, qui erit sicut circulus *B*. Erit arcus *DMC*, cum sit equalis arcui *FKE* per 27. tertii, maior arcu *DTC*, eo quod ipsum circumdat, et hoc est propositum, nam arcus arcum circumdans maior est circumdato.

4. SI LINEE INEQUALES IN EODEM CIRCULO ARCUS RESECENT, ERIT ARCUUM PROPORTIO MAIOR QUAM CORDARUM, PORTIONUM VERO CIRCULORUM MAIOR QUAM CORDARUM DUPLICATA.

In circulo cuius centrum sit *A* [Fig. III.4], collocentur linee, maior *BC* et minor *DE*, et diameter eius sit *GAH*, que se habeat ad lineam *KL* sicut *BC* ad *DE* per 14. secundi huius, et fiat circulus cuius diameter sit *KL*, in quo per lineam *MN* resecetur portio similis portioni quam resecat linea *BC* in circulo *A*. Et quia diametri ad diametrum est proportio ut circumferentie ad

7 in: ad *GPb*

7–8 similiter . . . perpendicularis: et alia perpendicularis protrahatur (*bis Pb*) a B *GPb*

8 super: fiunt (?) *Fb* / que *om. GPb* / et: etiam *H* / in *om. S* ad *GPb*

9 Et *om. GPb* / HE: BE *G* / DC: ӶDC *GPb*

10 BE: BC *GPb*

11 semidyameter *Pb* / est *om. H*

12 GL: GI (*sive* GL) *Fb* / et² *om. H*

13 BE: BC *G* / atque: et *H*

14 *post* tertii *add. H* Euclidis / LT²: LC (?) *Fb*

15 earum: itaque (?) *Fb* / L: LM *GPb*

16 qui . . . DMC *om. Pb* (*sed non G*) / *post* erit *add. G* ex primo principio tertii Euclidis / circulus *om. SH* / Erit: et est (*sive* erit) *H* / FKE: KFE *Fb*

17 arcu: accu (!) *G* / DTC: D et C *GPb* ATC (*sive* DTC) *Fb* / circondat *G*

18 maior: minor *Fb*

Prop. III.4

1 4 *om. DGFb* 4ᵃ *mg. sin. H* 36 *mg. sin. PbEs* 37ᵃ *mg. dex. S* / eodem: eo *Fb* / rescecent (!) *Fb* (*et post hoc lectiones huiusmodi non laudabo*)

2–3 portionum: proportio *GPb*

3 circulorum: circuli proportio *H* / maior: maiorum *S* / *post* cordarum *add. H* proportio

3–4 duplicata *alii MSS et ex corr. S*

5 A: si (?) *G* si' (?) *Pb*

6 DE: E.DG *Fb* / habeat *HDc* habet *DSGFb*, ?*Pb*

6–7 sicut . . . KL *om. Pb* (*sed non G*)

7 DE: DC *Fb* / secundi huius *tr. H* / secundi *om. S* ii (?) *Fb* / sit *om. H* / qua *H*

8 quam: quilibet (?) *Pb*

10   circumferentiam, ut ostensum est in libro de curvis superficiebus, et que
     circumferentie ad circumferentiam ea est arcuum similium et etiam suarum
     cordarum, ut habetur in libro de similibus arcubus: ergo sicut *GH* ad *KL*,
55r / que est sicut *BC* ad *DE*, ea est *BC* ad *MN*; ergo *DE* et *MN* sunt equales
     per nonam quinti. Ergo et arcus *DE* minor est arcu *MN* per premissam, cum
15   sit circulus *A* maior reliquo. Sed proportio arcus *BC* ad arcum *MN* est sicut
     linee *BC* ad lineam *MN* sive *DE*, cum sint arcus similes. Ergo ipsius ad
     arcum *DE* maior est proportio quam linee *BC* ad lineam *DE*, et sic patet
     prior pars propositionis. Item quia similium portionum est proportio que et
     circulorum, atque circulorum que diametrorum duplicata, quod patet per
20   secundam duodecimi Euclidis, et diametrorum duplicata sicut cordarum
     similium portionum duplicata, erit portionis *BDC* ad portionem *MN* [pro-
     portio] sicut linee *BC* ad lineam *MN*, sive *DE*, duplicata. Ergo per nonam
     quinti ad portionem *DE* erit eius proportio maior, cum sit portio *DE* minor
     portione *MN*, cum sit arcus minor arcu et corda equalis corde.

     5. SI DUE LINEE IN EODEM CIRCULO EQUEDISTANTES DIA-
     METRUM ORTHOGONALITER SECUERINT, PORTIONUM QUAS DE

10–11 ut . . . est: et etiam *H* / ut . . . circumferentiam *om. S*
   10 ut: et *Fb* / in libro: linee (?) *Fb*
   11 ea: eam *S* / etiam *hic om. H*
11–12 suarum cordarum *tr. Fb*
   12 ut *om. GPb* / in libro: linea *Fb* / de libro . . . arcubus *scr. mg. H* Nota librum de
      similibus arcubus
   13 ea est: ita *H* / *mg. hab. D* duas lineas quas non legere possum et quibus non refert
      Dc / DE et *tr. Fb* / equale *Fb*
   14 et *om. H* / minor est *tr. Fb*
   15 sit: sicut *Pb* / A *tr. H ante* sit / portio *Fb* / est *om. GPb*
   16 MN sive *om. GPb* / *post* sive *add. H* ad lineam / DE *om. Fb* / cum . . . similes:
      arcus BC ad arcum MN maior est proportio quam BC (quam BC *bis G*) arcus ad
      DE arcum ex 8. 5^i (5^{ti} *Pb*), ergo ipsius scilicet arcus BC (*sive* BE) hinc *GPb* / ipsius:
      proportio arcus BC *H*
   17 proportio *hic om. H* / DE^2: T^{D}E *G* / et *supra scr. D* / sic: sicque (*sive* sicut?) *Pb*
   18 *post* pars *add. G* prior / propositionis: proportionis *Fb* / portionum: proportionum
      GPb / *post* proportio *add. H* eadem
   19 atque . . . quod: sed et circulorum proportio duplicata diametrorum ut *H* / que:
      que est *Pb* / *ante* duplicata *scr. et del. G* dy- / dupplicata *D*
   20 duodecimi: 11. (*sive* 12.) *Pb* 13^{mi} (?) *Fb* / et: et proportio *H* / dupplicata *D* / *post*
      duplicata *supra scr. H* est
   21 portionum: proportio *H* proportionum *GPb* / dupplicata *D*
21–24 erit. . . . arcus: igitur per 9^{am} 5^{ti} portionis BC ad portionem DE maior erit proportio
      quam duplicata proportio linee BC ad lineam DE cum sit DE portio minor MN
      portione eo quod arcus erit *H*
   21 portionis: proportionis *GPb* / BDC: BÇDC *G*
21–22 [proportio] *add. Dc*
   22 dupplicata *D*
22–23 nonam quinti *scr. et del. Pb sed add.* et 19. 5^{ti} *et hab. G* 915^{ti} (!)
   23 portio: proportio *DSFb*
Prop. III.5
    1 5 *om. DGFb* 5^a *mg. sin. H* 37 *mg. sin. PbEs* 38^a *mg. dex. S*
    2 orthogonaliter *HGPb* ortogonaliter *DSFb* (*et post hoc lectiones huiusmodi non laud-
      abo*) / de *om. GPb*

DIAMETRO RESECANT MAIORIS AD MINOREM MAIOR ERIT PRO-
PORTIO QUAM ARCUUM QUI AB EIS SUBTENDUNTUR.

5   Circuli diameter sit *ABGD* [Fig. III.5], linee vero equedistantes quas ipsa
orthogonaliter et per medium secat sint *CBE* et *HGL*. Dicit ergo quod proportio *BD* ad *GD* maior est quam arcus *CDE* ad arcum *HDL*. Fiat enim
triangulus *CDL*, cuius lateris quod est *CD* et linee *HG* communis sectio sit
K. Quia ergo maximum latus illius trianguli est linea *CL*, erit et angulus *D*
10   maximus suorum angulorum; quare aut rectus aut obtusus. Argue ergo, per
quintam primi huius et ultimam sexti Euclidis et secundam eiusdem et con-
iunctam proportionem, quod maior est proportio linee *BD* ad lineam *GD*
quam arcus *CD* ad arcum *HD*, et ideo maior quam arcus *CDE* ad arcum
HDL, cum sint isti dupli priorum, et hoc est propositum.

6. DUABUS LINEIS AB EODEM PUNCTO CIRCULUM CONTIN-
GENTIBUS SI MINORES ILLIS EUNDEM CIRCULUM CONTINGANT,
MAIOR ERIT LINEARUM, SIVE AB IPSIS ET ARCUBUS CONTEN-
TARUM SUPERFICIERUM, PROPORTIO QUAM ARCUUM.

3 resecant: resecuerint (*?*) *Pb* recuerint (*!*) *G*
5 *mg. hab. D et Fb* Ita intellige quod oportet centrum circuli esse (*D, om. Fb*) in linea
EL (*sive* EB, *sed juste* EC) vel in portione CAL / ABDGD *G* / vero: q̄ō *S* / quas
DcH quos *injuste DSGPbFb*
6 et[2] *om. H* / Dicit *DSGPbFb* dico *HDc*
7 BD ad GD: GD ad LD (*sive* BD) *GPb*
8 quod: quo *G* / est CD: OCD *GPb* / et *om. GPb*
9 Quia: cum *H* / ergo *om. Fb* / *post* ergo *add. GPb* maiori portioni (*?G*, parte minori
?Pb) subtenditur / latus *bis Pb* / est: sit *H* / linea *om. GPb* / erit: et maximum habet
(*?*) *GPb* / et angulus: triangulus *S* / et *om. H*
10 aut[1]: angulus (*sive* auitem *?*) *Fb* / *post* obtusus *add. H* eo quod CL vel transit per
centrum vel inter centrum et D, aliter enim foret esse propinquior alteri extremo
diametri AD quam foret HL et de CE minus resecaret de diametro quam HL sumendo
portionem minoris resectionis totaliter extra centrum quia sic intelligitur propositio
10–14 *de* Argue.... propositum *mg. scr. DFb* Si CAE semicirculus in proportione (*Dc*,
proportio *Fb, ?D*) sit communis, sic arguatur (*DFb*, argumentandum *injuste Dc*). Que
est proportio DA linee ad BD sic (*DFb*, ea est *injuste Dc*) totius circumferentie (*D*,
lac. Fb) ad arcum CDE; sed maior est proportio BD ad GD quam arcus CDE ad
arcum HDL ex iam habita conclusione. Ergo maior est proportio DA ad GA (*D*,
om. Fb) quam totius circumferentie ad arcum HDL; ergo maior est proportio GA
ad DA quam arcus HDL (*?D*, HAL *?Fb*) ad totam circumferentiam. Sed que est
proportio DA (*Fb*, ad *D*) ad (*Fb*, DA *D*) BA ea est totius circumferentie ad arcum
CAE. Ergo maior est proportio GA ad BA (*DFb*, AB *Dc*) quam arcus DAL (*Fb*, HDL
?D) ad arcum CAE, et hoc est propositum. Si vero portio semicirculo minor fuerit
communis et portio semicirculo maior antecedens (*D*, dens *Fb*), ex istis duobus iam
conclusis per equam proportionalitatem concludetur propositum
11–12 coniuctam *S*
12 quod: et *Fb*
13 CDE: DEC *H*
14 sint isti *tr. HGPb* / et *tr. D post* est

Prop. III.6
1 6 *om. DGFb* 6[a] *mg. sin. H* 38 *mg. sin. PbEs* 39[a] *mg. dex. S*
2 minoris *S*
3 maior erit *Fb* (*et cf. vers. brev.*) erit maior *SH* erit *DGPb* (*sed. cf. lect. lin. 4*)
3–4 contententarum (*!*) *Fb*
4 superficierum: sn̄ srerum (*?*) *GPb* / *ante* proportio *hab. GPb* maior

5   Circulum cuius centrum sit *A* contingant due linee *BC* et *BD* [Fig. III.6],
et alie due minores *HF* et *HE*, et a centro ducantur quatuor perpendiculares
super singulas quatuor contingentes, scilicet ad quatuor punctos contactuum
per 17. tertii, fientque duo quandrangula divisibilia in triangulos equales per
lineas ductas *AH* et *AB*. Resecentur autem ex contingentibus maioribus due
10   linee equales contingentibus minoribus, que sint *CG* et *DL*, fientque trianguli
minoribus equales ductis lineis *AG* et *AL*. Igitur ex 5. primi huius et ultima
et prima sexti et coniuncta proportione concludes quod maiorum linearum
ad minores, sive superficiei triangule *CBD* ad superficiem triangulam *FHE*,
maior est proportio quam arcus *CD* ad arcum *FE*, et hoc est propositum.
15   Et in hoc scemate demonstrabis quod maiores linee maiorem arcum comprehendunt, et ab angulo quem continent maiorem lineam ad centrum mit-
tunt, et e contrario, quibus unum istorum accidit, ille maiores sunt.

7. SI DUE LINEE AB EODEM PUNCTO CIRCULUM CONTINGANT,
SI EISDEM EQUALES MAIOREM CIRCULUM CONTINGANT,
MAIOREM DE IPSO ARCUM COMPREHENDENT.

       5 et BD *om. GPb*
       7 supra *GPb* / scilicet *om. H* / puncta *H* / contactū *Fb*
       8 triangulos: angulos *Fb*
       9 et *DSHFb* ad *GPb*
     10 fiantque *S*
     11 et[1] *om. Fb*
     12 coniuncta proportione *H* coniunctam proportionem *injuste DSGPbFb* / concludes
        om. H
     13 superficiei: ei (!) ficiei (*sive* siciei) *GPb* / triangule *om. GPb* triangulorum *H* /
        triangulam: triangulorum *SH* quadrangulam *GPb* / FHE (?) *G*
     14 hoc est *tr. GPb*
     15 in: nr' *G* ñr *Pb* ex *H* / scemate (=schemate) *SFb*, ?HGPb* stemate (?) *D*
     16 *ante* maiorem *scr. et del. Pb* linee
     17 *post* sunt *add. Dc* et *Fb* hic et iterum in *mg. infer* [*cf. Fig. III.6b*] Demonstratio huius
        consequentie: AK, KP contingentes sunt equales DE, EB contingentibus. Ergo arcus
        AP equalis arcui DB. Protrahantur linee (*Dc, tex. Fb,* KC *mg. Fb*) AZ, KMZ, PZ,
        BZ, ENZ, DZ (*mg. Fb, Dc,* DE *tex. Fb*). Igitur quoniam AZ, KZ sunt equales KZ,
        ZP (*tex. Fb, Dc,* PZ *mg. Fb*) et basis basi, erit angulus KZA equalis angulo KZP et
        arcus AM equalis arcui MP. Eadem (eas *mg. Fb*) ratione arcus NB equalis (*mg. Fb,*
        Dc, equales *tex. Fb*) erit (*Dc, om. tex. Fb mg. Fb*) arcui ND; item KP, PZ sunt equales
        EB, BZ, et angulus angulo. Ergo angulus KZP (*mg. Fb, tex. Fb,* KZB *Dc*) est equalis
        angulo EZB; quare arcus MP et NB equales (*Dc,* equalis *mg. Fb tex. Fb*) erunt, et
        etiam arcus AP, DB quoniam sunt dupli NB et MP, ut ostensum est. Item sunt (*Dc,*
        sint *mg. Fb tex. Fb*) arcus AP, DB equales ex suppositione (*mg. Fb, Dc,* sumptione
        tex. Fb); erunt ergo contingentes (*om. mg. Fb*) contingentibus equales. Erit enim
        angulus AZP equalis angulo DZB, quare medietas medietati, scilicet PZM (*tex. Fb,*
        Dc, PMZ *mg. Fb*), BZN. Sed et angulus P rectus angulo B recto, et linea ZP (*mg.*
        Fb, tex. Fb, ZB *Dc*) linee ZB (*mg. Fb,* ZCB *tex. Fb,* ZP *Dc*); equalis ergo per 26.
        (*mg. Fb, tex. Fb,* 16. *Dc*) primi Euclidis erit KP equalis EB; quare habemus propositum
    Prop. III.7
     1 7 *om. DGFb* 7ᵃ *mg. sin. H* 39 *mg. sin PbEs* 40ᵃ *mg. dex. S* / circulum (?) *Fb* /
        continguant (!) *Fb*
     2 continguant (!) *Fb*
     3 comprehendent *corr. Pb ex* comprehendunt

Sint due linee *BC* et *BD* contingentes circulum minorem [Fig. III.7], qui
5   sit *T*, et alie due istis equales sint *HE* et *HG* contingentes circulum maiorem,
qui sit *A*. Positis *A* et *T* in centris, et ductis ab eis perpendicularibus ad
punctus contactuum compleantur duo quadrangula. Dico ergo quod arcus
EG est maior arcu *CD*. Sicut ergo diameter minoris se habet ad diametrum
maioris, sive semidiameter ad semidiametrum, ita se habeat linea *EH*, que
10   est sicut *CB*, ad lineam maiorem, que sit *EHL*. Et a puncto *L* dimittatur
altera contingens, que sit *LM*, atque ducta linea *AM* compleatur quadran-
55v   gulum *ELMA*, quod quidem simile erit quadrangulo *CBDT*, nam / latera
sunt proportionalia, nec non et anguli equales, quod patet per sextam sexti,
protractis lineis *AKL* et *TZB*, que dividunt illa in equos triangulos. Et si
15   similiter dividatur quadrangulum *EHGA* protracta linea *AH*, patebit per 15.
quinti et primam sexti et 17. eiusdem et hac regula quinti: cum fuerint tres
quantitates proportionales etc., quod ipsum est proportionale inter reliqua
duo quadrangula, nec non et in ea proportione in qua est linea *LE* ad lineam
HE, que quidem proportio maior est per premissam quam proportio arcus
20   *EM* ad arcum *EG*. Sed quia proportio arcuum similium est sicut proportio
circumferentiarum, et hec sicut diametrorum vel semidiametrorum, ideo erit
proportio arcus *EM* ad arcum *CD* sicut *EA* ad *CT*, et ideo sicut *LE* ad *HE*,
cum sint *EM* et *CD* arcus similes. Ergo maior est proportio arcus *EM* ad
arcum *CD* quam eiusdem ad arcum *EG*. Ergo per 8. quinti arcus *EG* maior
25   est arcu *CD*, et hoc est propositum. Quod autem *EM* et *CD* sint arcus similes
patet, constitutis intra circulos quadrangulis *EKMS* et *CZDR*. Nam quia
angulus *A* est equalis angulo *T*, ut preostensum est, erit angulus *S* equalis

5 et² *supra scr. Pb*
7 punctus (*4ª declinatio*): puncta *H* / compleatur *Fb*
7–8 arcus EG *tr. SH*
8 Sicut: ut *GPb*
9 linea *om. Fb*
10 CB: BC *Fb* / *post* maiorem *add. DS* se / que: sequi *GPb* seque *Fb* / EHL: Ḥ EHL
    S / Et: sit *GPb*
14 TZB: CZB *Fb* / illa: ista *Pb* / equos: equales (?) *D*
15 15: ih (?) *Fb*
16 sexti *tr. H post* 17. *et del. H* eiusdem
16–17 et² . . . etc. *om. H*
16 hac: hanc *G* / fuerat (!) *GPb*
17 etc.: et tamen (?) *GPb* / *post* est *add. H* medium
18 ad lineam *bis H et del. primum* / ad *om. GPb*
19 HE: LE *Pb* LE (*sive* HE) *G* / quidam *H*
20 EM: EN *G*, ?*Pb* / similium *om. GPb*
22 arcus *om. SH* / *ante* CD *scr. et del. Fb* et CD arcus similes / sicut²: sive (?) *Fb*
24 arcum¹ *corr. S ex* arcus / *ante* arcum² *scr. et del. G* n (?) / 8: 8 (*sive* 4) *S* 4 (*sive* 8)
    Fb
25 est¹ *om. GPb*
26 constitutis: cum s̄i̅tis (!) *G* cum si'tis (!) *Pb* / intra: infra *SH*
26–28 EKMS. . . . angulus *om. Pb*
26 CZDR: ÇḌCZDN *G* CZDA *Fb* / quia *supra scr. D om. GFb*
27 ut *om. G*

angulo *R*, cum sint eorum subdupli per 19. tertii, et ideo angulus *K* equalis angulo *Z* per 21. eiusdem, et ideo arcus similes. Et retento hoc eodem scemate

30 demonstrabis quod si duos circulos singule due linee conterminales contingant ita quod similes arcus comprehendant, erit linearum et diametrorum et arcuum eadem proportio.

Preterea scies propositis duobus circulis inequalibus, quorum alterum due linee ab eodem puncto contingant, punctum extra reliquum assignare, a quo

35 ducte ad eundem contingentes prioribus sint equales. Scis enim ex quocumque circulo cuilibet arcui similem arcum subtensa corda resecare et a termino corde contingentem educere que se habeat ad alteram earum que contingunt alium circulum sicut diameter ad diametrum sive corda ad cordam, quod idem est per 14. secundi presentis libri.

8. DUOBUS CIRCULIS SESE VEL INTRA VEL EXTRA TANGEN-TIBUS SI A CONTACTU UTRUMQUE CIRCULUM PERTRANSIENS LINEA RECTA DUCATUR, SIMILES DE ILLIS PORTIONES AB-SCINDET.

5 Quocumque modo fuerit circulorum contactus ducatur linea per eorum centra [Fig. III.8], que quidem contactui applicetur per 11. tertii et circumferentie utrique ex opposita parte, distinguetque utrumque circulum in semicirculos. Ducatur igitur quecumque alia linea pertransiens utrumque circulum et applicata ista in puncto contactus et factis quadrangulis, quorum partes

10 sunt trianguli rectanguli in semicirculis consistentes per 30. et 21. tertii, et

29 Z: ZT (?) *Fb et add. Fb aliquid quod non legere possum* / 21: 11 (?) *GPb* / eiusdem: 3ⁱ *H* / *ante* arcus *scr. et del.* (?) *Pb* LE / *ante* retento *scr. et del. Pb* recto / scemate *DSGPbFb* scemate (*sive* stemate) *H* stemmate *injuste Dc*
30 *ante* singule *scr. et del. Pb* figure
31 similes arcus *tr. H et supra scr. H* arcus / arcus *om. S* / *post* erit *scr. et del. Pb* linee (?) inequalibus quorum alterum due linee
32 eadem proportio *tr. H* / eadem: earum *Fb*
33 Propterea *Fb*
34 asignare *D*
35 sint: sunt *H*
36 cuilibet *H* cuivis (?) *Fb* cuius *DSGPb* cuiusvis *Dc* / resecare (?) *Fb* / et *om. S*
37 corde (?) *PbFb* cordo (?) *G* / contingentem: contingente *GPb* / habeant *Fb* / alteram: lineam (*sive* alteram) *Fb* / contingunt *DSGHFb* contingent *Dc,* ?*Pb*
38 ad diametrum *bis H et del.* secundum / sive: vel *H* / quod: et (?) *Fb*
39 14.: 10. quartam *GPb* / presentis libri: huius *H*
Prop. III.8
1 8 *om. DGFb* 8ᵃ *mg. sin. H* 40 *mg. sin. PbEs* 41ᵃ *mg. dex. S* / vel extra *om. Pb*
5 *ante* contactus *scr. et del. S* contactus
5–6 per . . . tertii *om. Fb*
6 que (?) *Pb* / quidem *om. H* / applicatur *H*
7–9 distinguetque . . . contactus: distinguentur circuli per aliam lineam transeuntem per contactum *H*
7 distinguetque: distinguet quod *S*
7–8 in . . . . circulum *om. S*
9 ista: isti *SGPbFb* / contacto *Pb,* ?*G* / factis: fiñs *Pb,* ?*G* / quadrangulus *GPb*
10 sunt: sint *DH* sicut *G* sicut (*sive* sint) *Pb* / *ante* in *scr. et del. Pb* et vel i' semicirculis et / 30.: 20. (?) *S* 20. 3ⁱⁱ *H* / et¹: deinde per *H*
10–12 tertii . . . fuerit *om. Fb*
10 et² *om. GPb*

descriptione similium arcuum et 32. primi argue et per idemptitatem angulorum si fuerit contactus intra, et per angulos contra se positos si fuerit
contactus extra, vel utrinque ex 31. tertii ducta contingente.

9. SI CIRCULUS ALIUM INFRA (! INTRA) CONTINGAT ET A CON-
TACTU LINEA PER CENTRA EORUM TRANSEAT, QUECUMQUE
LINEA EI PERPENDICULARITER INSISTIT HINC INDE PER UT-
RUMQUE CIRCULORUM TRANSIENS, SI INFRA (! INTRA) CEN-
TRUM MAIORIS DUCATUR, SIVE ALIUM SECET SIVE CONTINGAT,
DE MINORI VERSUS CONTACTUM MINUS CONCLUDET; QUE AU-
TEM SUPRA CENTRUM MAIORIS ET CONTINGIT, HEC SOLA TAN-
TUMDEM, QUE VERO EXTRA ET CONTINGIT, HEC DE MINORI
CONCLUDIT MAIUS.

Disponamus tres circulos infra (! intra) se contingentes ad punctum *A* [Fig.
III.9a], sitque centrum minimi *O*, et medii *N*, et maximi *M*, et continuetur
linea *MA*, transibitque per *O* et *N* per 11. tertii, sitque diameter minimi
minor semidiametro maximi, et sit *ZA*, et diameter medii maior. Sit ergo
linea *EG* ducta per maximum circulum secans lineam *MA* apud punctum
Z, qui est inter *M* et *A*, orthogonaliter secabit igitur tam maximum circulum
quam medium et continget minimum. Dico ergo quod arcus *EAG* quem
ipsa resecat a maximo maior est arcu quem ipsa resecat a medio ex eadem
parte, qui sit *PAQ*, nec non et maior tota circumferentia minimi / circuli,
et hoc est quod dicitur, si infra (! intra) centrum maioris ducatur, sive secet
sive contingat, de minori versus contactum minus concludet. Ducatur ergo
linea recta inter *E* et *A* et secet circulum medium apud *K* et minimum apud

11 et¹ *om. S* / ydemptitatem *S*
11–12 angulorum: anguli *DSH*
12 intra: infra *HGPb*
13 utrumque *S* / contingente: contingenti *SH*
Prop. III.9
1 9 *om. DGFb* 9ᵃ *mg. sin. H* 41 *mg. sin. PbEs* 42ᵃ *mg. dex. S* / alium: circulum *H*
3 insistit *alii MSS et ?D (sed* insistens *secundum Dc)*
5 continguat (!) *Fb*
6 minori *omnes alii MSS* minore *D (secundum Dc)*
7 et *om. Fb* / contingit: contendit *S (et scr. et del. H* contendit *et postea supra scr. H*
transiens maiorem contingit)
7–8 tantundem *Fb*
8 et *om. HGPb (et supra scr. H* centrum) / hec *om. H*
9 concludit *omnes MSS* concludet *Dc*
10 infra se *tr. H*
11 minimi *HGPb om. Fb* minimum *DS* / et² *om. GPb* / M *om. S*
12 linea MA *DGPb* MA linea *Fb (et tr. Fb ante* per) MN linea *S (et tr. S ante* per) M
cum N *H* / transibitque: que transibit *H* / et N: usque ad contactum *H* / *post* N
add. Fb et / diameter *om. Fb*
13 maior: sit maior *H*
15 Z: ẹt (?) Z *Fb* / qui: que *H* / secabit *bis S*
16 quam: tam *GPb* / et continget *om. Fb* / EAG: EDG *Fb* / quem: quam *HGPb*
17 ipsa¹: ipso *S* / est: erit (?) *H* / quem: quam *H* / ante ex *scr. et del. Pb* ex e
18 sit: fit *Fb*
19 est: erit (?) *H* / infra: intra *H*
20 minori *omnes MSS* minore *Dc* / minus: unius (?) *GPb*
21 et² *om. D*

B, et alia linea inter *G* et *A* secans medium circulum apud *T* et minimum apud *C*, et continuentur linee *BDC* et *KLT*, que quidem erunt sibi invicem et linee *EG* equedistantes—nam tres portiones trium circulorum in quibus super arcum cadit angulus *A* sunt similes, et eorum medietates similes per premissam, et ideo anguli *B, K, E* equales et anguli *C, T, G* similiter. Quod ergo arcus *EAG* sit maior arcu *PAQ* argue ex hac regula, quod eadem est proportio similium arcuum et suarum cordarum, que quidem habetur ex libro de similibus arcubus, et ex 2. sexti et ex quinta huius tertii et 10. et 15. quinti. Quod autem sit maior quam circumferentia minimi, ex eisdem argues protracta orthogonaliter in minimo diametro *ROS,* et ex regula posita in fine commenti super 12. presentis, si deus voluerit.

Modo disponamus aliter [Fig. III.9b], scilicet, ut diameter circuli minimi

25

30

22–23 et³ . . . *C om. Fb*

22 et³ *om. SPb*

23 continuentur: protrahantur *H* continentur *GPb* / *ante* BDC *scr. et del. Pb* B / KLT: KLC (*?*) *S*

25 sunt: inter *GPb*

26 equales *tr. H post* G / similiter *om. HGPb* / Quod *omnes alii MSS* quod (*sive* quia) *D* quia *Dc*

27 maior *omnes alii MSS, ?D* minor *Dc* / est *om. S*

28 ex: de *S* in *H*

29 10: 14 *GPb*

30–32 Quod . . . voluerit: nam per rectam EA arcus ad KA arcum sicud EA linea ad BA sicud per 2ᵃᵐ 6ᵗⁱ sicud ZA ad BZ (*?*). Sed ex 5ᵃ 6ⁱ (*?*) tertii maior est (*sive* erit) proportio ZA ad BA (*sive* LA) quam PA arcus ad KA arcum. Igitur maior est proportio EA arcus ad BA arcum quam sit PA arcus ad eundem BA arcum. Igitur per 10. 5ᵗⁱ EA arcus erit maior quam PA arcus. Igitur per 15. 5ᵗⁱ EAG arcus est maior arcu PAQ. Quod autem EAG sit maior quam circumferentia minimi circuli et ex eisdem argues protracta orthogonaliter in minori diametro ROS et ex regula posita in fine commenti 13ᵉ propositionis primi huius. Sit enim AZ primum et AO secundum et ZRA (*?,* ZBA) arcus 3ᵐ et RA arcus 4ᵐ et DA linea 5ᵐ et BA arcus 6ᵐ et sicud ZA primum ad OA 2ᵐ ita ZBA 3ᵐ ad RA 4ᵐ. Sed maior est proportio OA secundi ad DO (*!*) 5ᵐ quam RA 4ᵗⁱ ad BA 6ᵐ per 5ᵃᵐ huius 3ⁱⁱ. Igitur per regulam in fine commenti maior est proportio ZA primi ad DA 5ᵐ et per consequens EA ad BA per 2ᵃᵐ 6ⁱ quam ZBA 3ⁱⁱ ad BA 6ᵐ. Sed igitur EA linea ad BA lineam ita EA arcus ad BA arcum. Igitur maior est proportio EA arcus ad BA arcum quam ZBA arcus ad eundem BA arcum. Quare per 10ᵃᵐ 5ᵗⁱ EA arcus est maior ZBA arcu et per consequens ex 15. 5ᵗⁱ EAG est maior tota circumferentia minimi circuli, quod fuit propositum *H* / de Quod . . . presentis *mg. hab. D* (*secundum Dc*) *et Fb* Vel sic argues. Maior est proportio OA ad AD quam semicirculi ad arcum BAC per quartam ab ista. Ergo dupli OA, que est ZA, maior est proportio ad DE (*! Dc, sed* DA *sicut forte in Fb*) quam totius circumferentie ad arcum BAC. Sic itaque maior est arcus EAG totali circumferentie, quoniam ZA ad DA sicut EAG ad BAC

30 sit: si *GPb* / ex: et *GPb*

31 pertracta *Fb* / ROS: RES *GPb*

32 in fine commenti *bis GPb* / comenti *D* / super: supra *GPb* / 12. *Dc et correxi ex* xiᵐⁱ *in DS et* xi. *in Fb et* ei (*sive* 41.) *in GPb*

33 disponamus: supponamus *H* / scilicet ut (*?*) *Pb* / scilicet: aliter (*?*) scilicet (*?*) *G* videlicet *Fb* / ut: quod *H*

sit linea *MA*, que est semidiameter maximi, et sequitur ex hoc quod circum-
35 ferentia eius sit equalis medietati circumferentie illius, et ideo patet quod si
ducatur linea *EG* per centrum maximi et contingens minorem (*!* minimum),
tandumdem de maximo quantum et de minimo concludet. Sed cum ipsa
sic ducta secet circulum medium apud puncta *K, T*, sit ita. Dico quod arcus
KAT minor est arcu *EAG*. Ostendam enim quod est minor circumferentia
40 *MA*, que est illi equalis, eodem modo quo usus fui prius quando duxi diametrum *ROS*, ducta nunc diametro medii circuli *BNC*, et hic utar eisdem
quibus usus fui ibi, una cum hac regula: si fuerit proportio primi totius ad
suum detractum maior quam secundi ad suum, erit primi totius ad suum
residuum minor quam secundi ad suum, que ex 12. et 11. et 13. secundi
45 arismetice in continuis fidem habet. Et hoc modo patet quod, si ducatur

34 *ante* que *add. D* que est diameter / que: qi (*?*) *D* / *ante* semidiameter *scr. et del. S*
  e (*?*) diameter a (*?*) / *ante* ex *add. Fb* etiam
35 medietati circumferentie *Dc* semicircumferentie *H* circumferentie *DSGPbFb* / illius:
  alterius *H*
36 EG: GE *Fb* / et *om. H*
37 tantumdem (*?*) *G* / et *om. H* / concludet *omnes MSS* abscindet *Dc*
38 ducta: dicta *SHPFb*, *?G* / medium (*?*) *Fb* / T: D *GPb* / sit ita *om. H* / ita: et ita
  Fb / quod: ergo *Fb*
39 *post* minor *add. GPb* m (*sive* in)
39–49 *de* Ostendam. . . . indirecte *scr. mg. sin. D et mg. infer. Fb* Nam que est proportio
  diametri ad diametrum ea est circumferentie ad circumferentiam, ut ostensum est
  in libro de curvis superficiebus. Sed diameter ad diametrum est dupla; ergo circumferentia ad circumferentiam est dupla; ergo medietas est equalis circumferentie (est
  . . . circumferentie *Dc, sed om. Fb*) minoris. Vel sic argue (*Dc*, argumentate *?Fb*).
  Maior est proportio AD ad MD (*Dc*, MA *Fb*) quam circumferentie (*Dc*, semicirculi
  Fb) circuli (*om. Fb*) ad arcum KDT (*Fb*, KDC *Dc*). Quare econtrario ergo minor est
  (*Fb*, erit *Dc*) MD ad DA quam arcus KDT (*Fb*, KD *Dc*) ad circumferentiam totam;
  ergo divisim minor est proportio MD ad MA quam arcus KDT (*Fb*, KDC *Dc*) ad
  arcum KAT (*Fb*, KAC *Dc*). Ergo coniunctim (*Dc*, coniunctum *Fb*) minor est proportio
  DA ad MA quam (*FbD, sed om. Dc*) totius circumferentie ad arcum KAT (*correxi
  ex* KAC *in Dc et* KT *in Fb*). Sed que est proportio DA ad MA ea est proportio
  circumferentie maioris ad minorem. Ergo minor est proportio circumferentie maioris
  ad minorem quam eiusdem ad arcum KDT (*Fb*, KDC *Dc*). Ergo circumferentia
  minor maior est arcu KAT (*Fb*, KAC *Dc*)
40 illi *HFb* illa *DSG* ista *Pb* illo *Dc* / fui: fuit *S* / duxi: dixi *GPb*
40–41 dyametrum ROS *bis Pb*
41 ducta: dicta *D* / *ante* nunc *scr. et del. Fb* tunc / nunc *om. H* / circuli: *lac. G, om.*
  Pb / eidem *GPb*
42 ibi: prius *H* / totius *bis S*
43 detractam (*?*) *G* / erit primi: primo erit *Fb*
44 residuum (*?*) *Pb* res.duum *G* / ad suum *bis Fb* / 12: k (*sive* 12) *G* 13 (*?*) *Fb*
45 arismetice *G* arsmetice *DS* arsmetrice *H* arismetrice *Pb* armetice (*!*) *Fb* / Et hoc:
  arguatur igitur sic: proportio AD primi ad NO 2^m est sicud ABD 3^{ii} ad BD 4^m. Sed
  ND 2^i ad MD 5^m maior est proportio quam BD 4^i ad KD 6^m per 5^{am} huius 3^{ii}. Igitur
  maior est proportio AD primi ad MD 5^m quam ABD 3^{ii} ad KD 6^m. Igitur per regulam
  assumptam iam minor erit (*sive* est) proportio AD ad AM quam ABD ad AK. Sed
  sicud AD ad ACH (*?*) ita AKD (*?*) semicircumferentia ad AM semicircumferentiam.

extra centrum *M* linea *PDQ* contingens circulum medium, erit arcus *PAQ* minor circumferentia *DA*, et ostendet subtilis quod nulla perpendicularis equum de utroque concludit nisi que per centrum maioris transiens minorem contingit ex 17. primi Euclidis indirecte.

10. CIRCULO ALIUM INFRA (*!* INTRA) CONTINGENTE LINEA A CENTRO MAIORIS DUCTA UTRUMQUE PERTRANSIENS ET PRETER CONTACTUM DE INTERIORE, SI IPSE INTERIOR EXTRA CENTRUM MAIORIS ROTETUR, ARCUM MINOREM VERSUS CONTACTUM CONCLUDET; SI SUPRA CENTRUM, EQUALEM; SI VERO INFRA (*!* INTRA), MAIOREM.

5

Circulum maximum, cuius centrum sit *D* [Fig. III.10], contingant tres circuli infra (*!* intra) ad punctum *A*, quorum unus sit magnus ut ambiat et intra se includat punctum *D*, secundus minor ut contingat *D*, tertius minimus ut non attingat *D*. Ducatur autem linea recta a puncto *D* preter contactum secans circumferentiam uniuscuiusque maximi apud *G*, magni apud *O*, minoris apud *C*, minimi apud *E*. Dicit ergo quod arcus *AG* maior est arcu *AO*, et equalis arcui *AC*, et minor arcu *AE*. Ducantur igitur tres linee ab *A* per tria puncta, que sunt *O*, *C*, *E*, in circumferentiam maximi circuli ad puncta *K*, *Z*, *B*, atque ad eadem puncta ducantur tres linee a puncto *D*. Opponitur ergo linea *AD* tribus angulis collocatis super lineam *DG* ex parte *A*, quorum unus, scilicet apud *C*, rectus est per 30. tertii Euclidis, et alius apud *O* acutus, et tertius apud *E* obtusus. Ducatur ergo a puncto *D* linea perpendicularis

10

15

Igitur minor est proportio AKD semicircumferentie ad AM semicircumferentiam quam ad AK. Igitur AM semicircumferentia maior est quam arcus AK per 8. 5^{ti}. Liquet igitur propositum. Hoc igitur *H* / quod: quia *Fb*

46 circulum medium *tr. Fb*
47 subtilis *HFb* subtiles *DSG, ?Pb* / perpendicularis: preparando (?) *S*
48 nisi que *om. GPb*
49 ex: et ex *GPb* / indirecte: in directione *SH* in directe *G*

Prop. III.10

1 10 *mg. sin. H om. DGFb* 42 *mg. sin. PbEs* 43^a *mg. dex. S* / Sirculo (*!*) *Fb, sed mg. hab. Pb* C-
2 et *om. H*
3 contractum (*sive* conttactum) *Fb*
7 contingunt *Fb*
8 A *supra scr. Pb, om. Fb* / magnus: ita magnus *H*
9 ut: et *H*
10 attingat: atingat *D* contingat *Pb* detingat *Fb* / linea: una linea *H* / recta: erecta *Fb* / *post* preter *add. Fb* non
11 circumferentiam *omnes MSS* circumferentiarum *injuste Dc* / maximi *om. GPb* / O: D *Fb*
12 Dicit *omnes alii MSS* dico *HDc* / AO: AD *SFb*
13 arcui: arcui (*sive* arcus) *Fb* / arcu: arcui *G* / AE: AC (?) *H*
14 in *om. GPb*
15 Z: et (?) *Pb* / *ante* eadem *scr. et del. Fb* tres linee / a: et *Fb*
16 collocans *GPb*
17 *ante* C *scr. et del. Pb* E / C: T *Fb* / rectus: tractus (?) *Fb*
18 optusus *G*

super *AK* et ad medium eius, cadetque inter *O* et *A* ad punctum *N*, que et
20 educatur in *R*; et alia perpendicularis ducta ad medium *AB* cadet inter *E* et
B ad punctum *T*, que et educatur in *K*, sit ita. Hiis ergo sic dispositis, quoniam
anguli *N*, *C*, *T* recti sunt, ex quinta primi huius et ultima sexti Euclidis et
duabus regulis, quarum una ponitur in commento 12. et alia in commento
premisse, et ex antepremissa et proportionalitate similium arcuum et suarum
25 cordarum totum propositum demonstrabis, si deus ingenium tuum dirigat.

11. SI CIRCULUS CIRCULUM INFRA (*!* INTRA) CONTINGAT, LI-
NEA A CENTRO MINORIS DUCTA PER UTRUMQUE DE MAIORE
EORUM VERSUS CONTACTUM MAIOREM ARCUM RESECABIT.

Sit contactus circulorum apud *A* [Fig. III.11], et centrum minoris sit *E*,
5 continueturque linea *AE*, atque ab *E* ducatur linea secans utriusque circum-
56v ferentiam, minoris apud *D* et maioris / apud *B*. Dico ergo quod arcus *AB*
est maior arcu *AD*. Ducatur ergo linea inter *A* et *B* secans minorem circumferentiam apud *C*, et continuetur linea *EC*, et ab *E* ducatur perpendicularis
ad medium *AC*, ubi sit *Z*, que et educatur in *T* et *G*; et hoc completo argue
10 propositum sicut in premissa. Vale.

12. SUPERFICIERUM QUE INTER ARCUS EQUALITER SESE EX-
CEDENTES ET LINEAS CONTINGENTES CONTINUANTUR (*!* CON-

19 super AK: sunt AB *Fb*
19-20 et[1] . . . R: que transiens per medium AK in puncto N educatur in R transibitque
inter O et A *H*
19 eius cadatque: eiusque *S* / N *om. G*
20 in R: MR (?) *SG* / et[1]: ducatur etiam *H* / ducta *om. H* / medium: metium (?) *Fb* /
cadet: que cadet *H* / inter: inter medium *GPb*
21 et: etiam *H* / in K sit *bis Pb* / in K: MK (?) *S* / K sit ita: v (?) *H* / *ante* sit *scr. et
del. Fb et alia*
21-25 *de* Hiis. . . . dirigat *scr. mg. H* argue (?) probationem
21 sic: ita *Pb*
22 recti sunt *tr. H*
23 comento *Fb* / 12.: 13. primi huius *H* k[e] (*sive* 12[e]) *GPb* 13. (*sive* 12.) *Fb* / *mg. hab.*
D (*secundum Dc*) et ex proportione econtrario facta et propositione sumpta iuxta
decimam octavam quinti
25 si: sed *H* si (?) deus (?) *Pb* / dirigeat (?) *GPb*
Prop. III.11
1 11 *mg. sin. H om. DGFb* 42 (*!*) *mg. sin. Pb* 43 *mg. sin. Es* 44[a] *mg. dex. S*
4 contractus *Fb*
5 ducatur *non legere possum in Pb* educatur *H* / utrusque (*!*) *Fb*
5-6 circumferentia *Fb*
6 B: D *Fb* / ergo *om. HFb*
7 ergo: enim *H* / et *supra scr. Fb*
8 continuetur: continetur *GPb*
9 et[1] *om. Fb* / et[2]: et in *H* / hoc completo *om. H*
10 propositum *om. H*
Prop. III.12
1 12 *mg. sin. H om. DGFb* 43 (*!*) *Pb* 44 *mg. sin. Es* 45[a] *mg. dex. S*
1-2 excedentis *Fb* / *mg. hic injuste hab. D in m. Taw* (*secundum Dc*) Liber quartus de
triangulis
2 continuantur: cominatur (*!*) *Fb*

TINENTUR) SICUT ET IPSARUM CONTINGENTIUM ERIT
MAIORUM DIFFERENTIA MAIOR.

5   Super circulum, cuius centrum sit Z [Fig. III.12], signentur arcus sese
excedentes equaliter, quorum maximus sit AB, quem contingant linee AK
et KB, et medius sit SB, cuius una contingens sit SG, et minimus sit DB,
cuius una contingens sit DR, atque a tribus punctis, que sunt K, G, R,
ducantur linee ad Z que dividunt predictos arcus per equalia, offendant quoque
10   circumferentiam apud puncta E, O, C. Intendo ergo duo, scilicet, quod linea
KG sit maior quam GR, et etiam quod superficies $AKGS$ sit maior superficie
$SGRD$. Cum enim ex suppositione sint arcus AS et SD equales, erunt arcus
EO et OC equales, eo quod sunt differentie medietatum predictorum arcuum,
quorum sunt AS et SD differentie totorum. Est enim regula quod differentia
15   medietatum est medietas differentie totorum, nam sicut se habet totum ad
totum ita differentia totorum ad differentiam similium partium, quod patet
ex 19. quinti Euclidis. Et quia EO et OC sunt medietates equalium, ideo
sunt equales, quare et anguli ad centrum equales. Ergo per tertiam sexti

3 contingentium *om. GPb*
4 maior *omnes MSS* (*sed Dc in n. leg.* minor)
5 sit: est *Fb*
6 excendentes (*!*) *Fb* / excedentes equaliter *tr. H*
7 et KB *om. GPb* / medius: eius medietas *H* / SB: EB *SH*
7–8 cuius . . . atque: quam contingant DR et RB sit etiam S medius punctus inter A et
        D ita quod arcus AB per tantum excedat arcum SB sicud arcus SB excedit arcum
        DB et contingant arcum SB due linee SG et GB. Deinde *H*
7 cuius . . . DB *om. S* / SG: AG *GPb*
7–8 et³ . . . sit *om. Fb*
7 minimus: minus *GPb*
8 R: E *GPb*
9 ducanturque *Fb* / offendant quoque: offendantque *H*
10 puncta *om. Fb*
11 sit¹: at (*?*) *Fb* / GR: GFR *Fb* GK (*sive* GR) *S* (*et forte hab.* S K *pro* R *saepe*) / quod
        bis (*?*) *Pb* / AKSG *Fb* / sit²: sitque *Pb*
12 *post* SGRD *scr. Fb* OGRD (*sive* SGRD) / ex *supra scr.* D *om. SGPbFb* / suppositione:
        ypotesi *H* / sint: sicut *G* sint (*sive* sicut) *Pb* / AS: AT *G* AC (*sive* AT) *Pb* / SD: ST
        S CD *GPb*
13 *post* equales *supra scr. H per* 19. 5ᵗⁱ / sunt: inter *G* / arcuum: arcū *GPb*
14 *post* SD *scr. et del. Pb* due
14–20 Est. . . . primum: quare et anguli ad centrum sunt equales; igitur per 3ᵃᵐ 6ⁱ Euclidis
        KG maior est quam GR cum sit KZ maior quam ZR eo quod angulus R sit maior
        angulo K per 16. primi Euclidis. Sic igitur patet primum *H*
14 differentia: differentie *Fb*
15–16 ad totum *om. GPb*
18 equales *om. GPb*
18–20 *de* Ergo . . . Euclidis *scr. mg. Fb et* D (*secundum Dc*) Aliter est (*Fb*, idem *Dc*) idem
        (*Fb*, ostenditur *Dc*) etiam sic (*!* si) angulus ZRK ambligonius, quoniam idem etiam
        (*Dc, ?Fb*) potest (*Dc*, est *Fb*) ostendi (*Dc, om. Fb*) de ambligonio quod ostenditur in
        5. primi (*Dc*, huius *Fb*) huius (*Dc*, primi *Fb*) de triangulo ortogonio. Quare maior
        est proportio KG ad GR quam anguli KZG ad angulum GZR. Sed (*Fb*, scilicet *Dc*)
        anguli ad angulum sicut erit GR ad GR. Ergo maior est KG ad GR quam erit GR
        ad GR. Ergo per primam partem 8ᵛᵉ quinti (*Dc, om. Fb*) erit (*Dc, om. Fb*) KG maior
        quam GR
18 *ante* tertiam *scr. et del. S* sextam tertii

Euclidis *KG* maior est quam *GR*, cum sit *KZ* maior quam *ZR*, eo quod
20 angulus *R* sit maior angulo *K* per 16. primi Euclidis; patet ergo primum.
Secundum patebit, si linea *AK* rescindatur ad equalitatem *SG*, sitque *AT*, et
linea *SG* ad equalitatem *DR*, sitque *SL*, et continuetur linea *TL*. Ostendes
ergo quod superficies *ATLS*, cum sit pars superficiei *AKGS* est equalis superficiei *SGRD* per suppositionem, sicut ostenditur quarta primi Euclidis,

20 primi *om. S*
21–26 *de* Secundum. . . . equalia *mg. scr. Fb et D (secundum Dc)* Secunda pars aliter
constat per suppositionem sic [Fig. III.12*var. DcFb*]. Superponatur (*Dc,* supponatur
Fb) enim DE super AC (*Fb,* AE *Dc*), et sit AK (*Fb,* DK *Dc*), et a K procedat contingens
ad circulum, que continget (*Fb,* contingat *Dc*) circulum super punctum inter F et B,
quoniam neque super F, neque super B, quia tunc accidat (*Dc,* accidet *Fb*) lineam
econtrario (*Dc, om. Fb*) esse (*Dc, om. Fb*) ductam stare super duas intersecantes se
ortogonaliter, quod est inconveniens; quod (*Fb,* qui *Dc*) et (*Fb,* etiam *Dc*) non contingat
citra (*Fb,* infra *Dc*) F (*et add. Fb* vel ultra) vel ultra B, quoniam si (*Fb,* nec *Dc*) citra
(*Fb,* extra *Dc*) F ante contingentiam pertransiret FG et post contingentiam iterum
productis utrumque contingentibus et sic accidat (*Dc,* accidet *Fb*) duas rectas lineas
includere (*Dc,* includes *?Fb*) superficiem. Si ultra B, idem (*Dc,* vel *Fb*) accidet (*Fb,*
accidit *Dc*) inconveniens quoniam (*Fb,* quia *Dc*) ante contingentiam bis pertransiret
CB. Sit ergo contingens KSP (*Dc,* KN *?Fb*). Dico quod superficies ADSK equalis est
superficiei DFGE. Et usque iam suppono istud argumentum: Extremitates sunt equales
extremitatibus, ergo superficies superficiei. Probatio per (*Dc, om. Fb*) premissam (*hic
add. et del. Fb aliquid*) AK equalis est DE ex ypotesi (*Fb,* ipotesi *Dc*), et arcus AD
arcui DF similiter (*et postea scr. et del. Fb* PB equalis AD quare sunt *?* equales *?*)
ex ypothesi (*Fb,* ipotesi *Dc*). Item DS (*Dc,* DF *?Fb*) linea equalis GF. Probatio. AK,
KP contingentes sunt equales DE, EB (*Fb,* AB *Dc*) contingentibus. Ergo arcus AP
est equalis arcui DB. Quare dempto communi, scilicet DP, erit PB equalis AD (*Fb,*
TB *Dc*), quare et (*Dc, om. Fb*) suo equali DF. Ergo communi addito, scilicet FP, erit
arcus *DP* equalis arcui FB. Igitur DS, SP contingentes equales sunt FG, GB contin-
gentibus. Quare DS et FG sunt equales. Item, quoniam AK, KP sunt equales, quod
(*Fb,* qui *Dc*) patet (*Fb,* pro- *Dc*) ductis lineis a contactu (*Dc,* centro *Fb*) ad contactum
(*?Fb,* contactus *Dc*) et concursum per dulkar[n]on (*Fb,* dupiernon *Dc*) et AK equalis
ED, et DE, EB (*Dc,* OB *Fb*), erit KP equalis *EB* (*Dc, om. Fb*). Sed SP equalis GB.
Igitur residuum SK (*Dc, ?Fb*) equale residuo EG. Ergo (*Fb,* superficies *Dc*) superficies
(*Fb,* ergo *Dc*) ADSK equalis superficiei DFGE. Sed superficies ADEC maior est
superficie (*Dc, om. Fb*) ADSK (*?D,* ADK *Dc, om. Fb*). Ergo (*Dc, om. Fb*) maior est
(*Dc, om. Fb*) superficie DFGE, et hoc est quod voluimus ex principali intentione
ostendere (*Dc,* demonstrare *Fb*). Nunc volumus etiam (*Dc, lac. Fb*) figere (*Dc, om.
Fb*) secundum (*Dc,* per *Fb*) suppositam suppositionem. Ducantur igitur (*D, bis Fb,*
etiam *Dc*) AD (*Dc,* AE *Fb*) DF arcuum corde et DK, FE (*D . . . E Dc,* DF *Fb*) linee.
Probatio huius (*Dc,* ac' *?Fb*): quia (*Dc, om. Fb*) superficies ADSK, DFGE (*Dc,* DFG
Fb) habent equales extremitates, ergo sunt equales. Triangulus ADK equalis est triangulo DFE per 8. primi Euclidis. Ergo demptis portionibus equalibus (*Dc, lac. Fb*)
erit (*Dc, ?Fb*) residuum residuo (*DFb,* residui *Dc; et scr. et del. antea Fb* residui equale
FGC) equale. Item DSK (*Dc,* BSK *?Fb*) triangulus equalis (*Dc* equale *Fb*) est (*Dc,
om. Fb*) FGE triangulo similiter per 8.; quare superficies ADSK equalis est superficiei
DFGE
21 *post* Secundum *add. H* sic / recindatur *HGPb* / equalitatem: equalem *Fb*
21–22 sitque . . . linea[1]: ita quod AC sit equalis *SG* et recindatur *H*
22 *ante* ad *scr. S sed non del.* ad e^a (equa-) / SL: sibi equalis SL *H* SI (?) *GPbFb* (*et
saepe hab. GPb* I *pro* L) / TL: TI *Fb*
23 ATLS: ATIS *Fb* / cum sit: que est *H* / AKGS *DSH* AKSG *GPbFb*
24 superpositionem *H*

25   cum sint anguli contingentie *A* et *S* equales et latera hinc lateribus inde
      equalia.

Liber quartus de triangulis

1. CIRCA FIGURAM INEQUALIUM LATERUM DESCRIPTO CIR-
CULO ALIOQUE INFRA (! INTRA) CONSTITUTO EORUM IDEM ESSE
CENTRUM EST INPOSSIBILE.

5   Sit exemplum de triangulo *ABG* inequalium laterum [Fig. IV.1], cui in-
      scribatur circulus, et alius circumscribatur. Posito ergo eodem centro illorum
      circulorum, qui sit *C*, ductis ab eo lineis tam ad angulos trianguli quam ad
      punctus contactuum ex 17. tertii Euclidis et tertia eiusdem et ex hac regula,
      quod omnes due linee ab eodem puncto eundem circulum contingentes sunt
10   equales, que probatur per penultimam tertii Euclidis, convinces triangulum
      illum equilaterum fore, quod est contra ypotesim. Et eodem modo demon-
      strabis proposita quacumque figura rectilinea inequalium laterum.

2. TRIANGULORUM SUPER EANDEM BASEM IN CIRCULO DE-
SCRIPTORUM EX EADEM PARTE MAXIMUS EST CUIUS LATERA
RELIQUA SUNT EQUALIA, ET QUANTO EI PROPINQUIORES TANTO
REMOTIORIBUS MAIORES.

5   Sit super basim *AB* in circulo triangulus *ACB* [Fig. IV.2], cuius reliqua
      latera sint equalia, et triangulus *ADB*, cuius latera inequalia, et minus *AD*,
      et tertius *AGB* posito *G* inter *A* et *D*. Et puncta sectionum sint *H*, *E*, *K*;
      eruntque singuli duo trianguli ad quodlibet illorum coniuncti similes, eo

25 latera: altera *GPb* / hinc *tr. H ante* inde
Title and Prop. IV.1
      1 Liber . . . triangulis *hab. D in m. Taw ante Prop. III.12, om. SGPbEs* Quartus liber,
        ut credo (?) *H* Liber 4ᵘˢ (?) *mg. Fb*
      2 1 *om. DHGFb* 44 (?) *mg. sin. Pb* 45 *mg. sin. Es* 46ᵃ *mg. dex. S* / Sirca (!) *Fb, sed*
        hab. Fb C- *in mg.*
      3 alioque: alio *GPb*
      4 inpossibile *DSGPb* impossibile *Fb* īpossibile *H*
      5 ABG: ABCD *S*
      6 *post* circumscribatur *add. Fb* circulus / Posito *omnes alii MSS, ?D* preposito *Dc* /
        eodem *om. S* / illorum: illorum 2 *H* iᵒʳᵘᵐ *G* istorum *Pb*
      7 qui: que *Fb* / ad¹ *om. GPbFb*
      8 punctus (*4ᵃ declinatio*): puncta *H* / et¹: et ex *H*
  8–10 et² . . . Euclidis *juste tr. Dc hic, sed hab. omnes MSS post* ypotesim *in lin. 11*
     11 equilaterum fore *tr. H*
     12 lateris *Fb*
Prop. IV.2
      1 2 *om. DHGFb* 45 (?) *mg. sin. Pb* 46 *mg. sin. Es* 47ᵃ *mg. dex. S* / basim *H*
      2 ex: et ex *GPb* / eadem: eandem *Fb* / cuius: eius *S*
    2–3 latera reliqua *tr. H*
      5 AB: AD *S*
      6 equalia *om. GPb* / latera² (?) *Fb* / minus: minimus (?) *Pb* minᵘˢ (*forte* minimus) *Fb*
      7 posito. . . . Et *om. H* / *ante* G *scr. et del. Pb* gᵒ (=ergo) / G: gᵒ (=ergo) *S* / D: CD
        (?) *S* B *Fb* / *post* puncta *add. H* igitur / H, E, K: K, H, E *H* / E: O *G*
      8 *ante* duo *scr. et del. Pb* d' / quodlibet: quemlibet *Fb* / illorum: eorum *SH* iᵒʳᵘᵐ *G*
        istorum *Pb* / coniucti *GPb*

quod equianguli. Posito ergo quod sectio linearum *DB* et *AC* sit apud *E*,
10 dico quod triangulus *BEC* est maior triangulo *AED* per corollarium 17. sexti,
eo quod linea *CB* est maior linea *AD*, quia maiorem arcum resecat. Quare
et addito communi, scilicet triangulo *AEB*, utrobique patet quod triangulus
ACB maior est triangulo *ADB*. Et similis est ratio de reliquis. Patet autem
facile quod ab eo eque distantes sunt equales.

3. TRIANGULORUM QUI IN CIRCULO SUPER CENTRUM CON-
SISTUNT MAXIMUS EST ORTHOGONIUS. AMBLIGONIORUM AU-
57r TEM QUANTO OBTUSUS AN/GULUS MAIOR, ET OXIGONIORUM
QUANTO ACUTUS ANGULUS MINOR FUERIT, TANTO ET IPSE
5 TRIANGULUS MINOR ERIT HAC RATIONE: OMNIS AMBLIGONIUS
ET OXIGONIUS, QUORUM ET ANGULI SUPRA CENTRUM EIUSDEM
CIRCULI CONSISTUNT, ET QUORUM ALTERIUS BASI INSISTENS
PERPENDICULARIS A CENTRO FUERIT EQUALIS DIMIDIO BASIS
ALTERIUS, ILLI, INQUAM, SUNT EQUALES.

10 Sit centrum circuli *A*, et triangulus orthogonius *ABC* [Fig. IV.3a], et ambligonius *ABD*, facta *AB* linea communi omnium, et tertius *ABE*, cuius
angulus ad *A* sit maior priori angulo obtuso. Et ex alia parte sit triangulus
orthogonius *ABT*, similiter et oxigonius *ABF*, et tertius, cuius angulus ad *A*
sit minor priori acuto angulo, sit *ABG*, et a puncto *A* dimissis perpendicularibus
15 singulorum super bases dividentur singuli per equalia. Posito ergo centro in
medio linee *AB* circinetur circa illam circulus. Transibit per terminos omnium
perpendicularium, quia omnis angulus rectus constitutus supra aliquam lineam cadit in circumferentiam semicirculi constituti supra eandem. Vocetur
autem perpendicularis in orthogonio *AO*, eritque equalis *OB*, nam quia anguli

9 secto *GPb*
11 eo quod *tr. Fb* / est: cum *Fb* / quia: propter hoc quod *H*
11–13 maiorem. . . . ACB *om. GPb*
12 triangulo *corr. S ex* triangulos
13 ACB: AEB *S*
13–14 Patet . . . equales: liquet igitur propositum *H*
14 eque distantes: *lac. GPb* eque *S* eq̄d' *Fb*

Prop. IV.3
1 3 *om. DHGFb* 46 *mg. sin. Pb* 47 *mg. sin. Es* 48ᵃ *mg. dex. S*
3 maior: est maior *H* / oxigoniorum: orthogoniorum *GPb*
6 super *H*
7 consistunt *tr. H ante* eiusdem *in lin.* 6 / et quorum *tr. DGPb*
8 a: et a *Fb*
11 comuni *Fb* / ABE: ABC *G*
12 ad: CD (?) *GPb* ab (*sive* ad) *Fb* / sit¹: ut *Fb*
13 ABT *GPb* AB *D* ABC *SFb,* ?*H* / similiter *om. H* / oxigonius: exigonius (?) *G* ortigonius
(!) *Fb*
15 super *supra scr. D et om. GPb*
16 *post* circulus *add. H* qui / transit *G,* ?*Pb* / *ante* terminos *scr. et del. S* circulos /
omnium (?) *G, om. S*
17 constituatur *S* / super *H*
18 cadet *H* / semicirculi: circuli *H* / super *H* / Vocetur: nocetur (?) *G* vacetur *Fb*
19 AO (?) *D* / OB: AB *Fb* / nam quia: namque *GPb* / nam *om. H* / quia: et *Fb* / anguli
om. SH

20   C et B sunt semirecti, et ideo anguli ad O recti, erunt et partiales anguli ad
A semirecti, et ideo anguli A, B equales, quare et latera AO et OB equalia.
Argue ergo per premissam primo de medietatibus, postea de totis. Quia autem
dicit: hac ratione etc. sic patebit.

Sit modo super centrum A triangulus oxigonius ABC [Fig. IV.3b], super
25   cuius basem dimissa perpendicularis sit AE; et triangulus ambligonius sit
ABD, super cuius basem dimissa perpendicularis sit AH, et circumducatur
circulus $AHEB$ sicut et prius. Divident quoque perpendiculares totales triangulos per equalia. Si ergo sit linea AH equalis linee EB, erit et arcus arcui.
Addito ergo utrique communi arcu HE ex 26. tertii et ypotesi et quarta primi
30   Euclidis argues medietates triangulorum equales esse, et totos per consequens.
Similiter autem argues, si ponatur linea AE equalis linee HB, sublato ab
utroque arcu communi HE.

4. OMNE PARALLELOGRAMMUM IN CIRCULO DESCRIPTUM
EST RECTANGULUM.

Distincto parallelogrammo per diametrum ductam ad eius oppositos angulos argue ex 29. primi et 21. tertii [cf. Fig. IV.4].

5. OMNIS QUADRILATERI CIRCA CIRCULUM DESCRIPTI DUO

20   sunt *omnes MSS* sint *Dc* / ideo *om. H* / recti: sunt recti *H* / erunt *om. H* / anguli[2]
om. H

21   quare *om. Fb* / AO et: EO (?) *G* et *Pb* / eaqualia (!) *D*

22   *ante* postea *add. H* et / Quia: Quod *Fb*

23   *mg. infer. add. Fb (cf. var. Fa in vers. brev. lin. 14–17)* _____ (?) quanto obtusus
angulus maior e[t] acutus minor tanto perpendicularis a centro remotius cadet ab A
(! E) (*et lac.*) semper propinquius D et ampligonius (?) semper propinquius B, hoc
noto quod _____ (?) _____ (?) perpendicularis super aliquam lineam semper est
inter angulos acutos super eandem / hac: hic (?) *Fb*

24   oxigonius: oxeogonius (?) *G* ortogonius *PbFb* / super: sunt *Fb*

25   basim *HFb* / dimissa: dīssa *Pb* (*et scr. et del. Pb* dimūsa ?) / perpendit *Fb* perpend'
S

25–26   AE. . . . sit *om. S*

25   triangulus *om. H* / ambligonius sit: sit ambligonium *H* / sit[2]: sic *Fb* sicut *G* sicud
Pb

26   perpendit *Fb*

27   AHEB: AHED *S*

28   et *om. H* / *post* arcus *add. H* equalis

29   utrilibet *H* / arcu: arcui *GPb* / *ante* ex *scr. et del. Pb* aliquid quod non legere possum

29–30   ex . . . consequens: erit arcus HB equalis arcui AE; quare linee HB et AE sunt
equales et ex ypotesi *AH* et *EB;* et anguli ad H et E recti; igitur per 4. primi medietates
triangulorum sunt equales et per consequens totales trianguli *H*

29   ex *om. S* / 26: 36 (*sive 26*) *Fb* / ypotesi: ypothesi *S* ipotesi *D*

30   argues: arcues (!) *S* / *ante* triangulorum *add. Fb* angulorum / totas *GPb*

31   autem *om. H* / AE: AC *Fb*

32   arcu: arcui *G* arcui *Pb* / *ad finem huius propositionis mg. dex. add. D* quinque lineas
quas non legere possum

Prop. IV.4

1   4 *om. DHGFb* 47 *mg. sin. Pb* 48 *mg. sin. Es* 49[a] *mg. dex. S*

QUELIBET LATERA OPPOSITA SUNT EQUALIA RELIQUIS PARITER
ACCEPTIS.

Argue ex hac regula, quod omnes due linee ab eodem puncto eundem
5 circulum contingentes sunt equales [cf. Fig. IV.5].

6. QUODLIBET PARALLELOGRAMMUM CIRCA CIRCULUM
CONSTITUTUM EST EQUILATERUM.

Ex premissa et 34. primi Euclidis hoc demonstrabis [cf. Fig. IV.6].

7. TRIANGULO IN CIRCULO CONSTITUTO EQUUM EI IN EODEM
CIRCULO PARALLELOGRAMMUM RECTANGULUM DESIGNARE.

Sit triangulus in circulo constitutus *ABC*. Considera igitur aut sit duum
equalium laterum aut omnium inequalium. Ponamus ergo primo quod latera
5 *AC* et *BC* sint equalia [Fig. IV.7a]; dimissa igitur linea ab angulo *C* ad
medium lateris *AB* perpendiculariter ei insistet per 8. primi, atque super
centrum transibit per corollarium prime tertii, sitque *CE*. Et continuetur in
D, ducaturque linea *DA* et alia ei equedistans, que sit *EF*, posito *F* in *AC*,
et ducatur linea *FZ* equedistans linee *CED*, et continuentur linee *CZ* et *DF*.
10 Age ergo: trianguli *EFD* et *EFA* sunt equales per 39. primi, quare et trianguli
CFD et *CEA*, qui est medietas dati trigoni, sunt equales communi apposito
[tri]angulo *CFE*. Sed *CFD* et *CZD* sunt equales; ergo *CZD*, cum sit ortho-

2 rectangulum: triangulum *GPb*
3–4 eius . . . angulos: angulos oppositos *H*
3 oppositos: appositos *Fb*
3–4 angulos *om. SGPb*
4 argue . . . tertii: tertii ex 29. primi propositum argues *H* / 29 (?) *Fb*
Prop. IV.5
1 5 *om. DHGFb* 48 (?) *mg. sin. Pb* 49 *mg. sin. Es* 50ª *mg. dex. S* / quadralateri (!) *Fb*
2 *ante* reliquis *add. H* duobus
Prop. IV.6
1 6 *om. DHGFb* 48 (!) *mg. sup. Pb* 50 *mg. sin. Es* 51ª *mg. dex. S*
3 demonstras *Fb*
Prop. IV.7
1 7 *om. DHGFb* 49 (?) *mg. sin. Pb* 51 *mg. sin. Es* 52ª *mg. dex. S* / equm (!) *Fb*
3 *ante* sit² *scr. et del. G* D / sit²: sint *S* / duum: dicum (!) *Fb*
6 ei: er (?) *G* ex (*sive* er) *Pb* / 8: 4 (*sive* 8) *S* 4 *H* (*et scr. mg. m. rec. H* per 4. primi
Euclidis videtur magis per 8. primi Euclidis) / primi: primi Euclidis *H*
7 per *om. GPb* / prime: primi *S*
7–8 in D: MD *S*
8 F in: FM *S*
9 continentur *GPb* / et³ *om. Pb* (*sed non G*)
10 Age *omnes MSS* Argue *injuste Dc*
10–12 per. . . . equales *om. S*
10 per . . . quare *om. H* / trianguli (?) *Pb*
11–12 CEA. . . . et *om. H*
11 apposito *correxi ex* opposito
12 [tri]- *addidi* / *ante* CFE *scr. et del. G* sed *et scr. et del. Pb* quod / sunt: sunt etiam
H
12–13 ergo . . . semicirculi: per 37. primi Euclidis igitur triangulus CZD *H*
12 sit: sint (?) *Pb*

gonius, eo quod angulus Z consistit super arcum semicirculi, est equalis
triangulo CEA. Fiat ergo cum linea CT angulus super lineam CED ex altera
15   parte equalis angulo quem continet linea DZ cum linea CED, et ducta linea
DT habebis parallelogrammum rectangulum $TCZD$ equale triangulo ABC,
57v   quia medietas medietati. Nam anguli T et Z recti sunt, / quia in semicirculo
constant, et linee CT et DZ equales et equedistantes per 25. et 24. tertii et
27. primi Euclidis.
20   Modo si sit omnium inequalium laterum triangulus ABC [Fig. IV.7b],
ergo linea DE, que dividit latus AB orthogonaliter et per equalia, pertracta
super centrum ad circumferentiam non ibit ad angulum C sed alibi, sitque
ad punctum Z. Descendat ergo linea CH perpendiculariter super lineam
DEZ, eritque equedistans linee AE per 28. primi. Ductis igitur lineis CE et
25   HA erit triangulus HAE equalis triangulo EAC, qui est medietas dati trigoni.
Item ducta linea ZA et ei equedistante HL, et continuata ZL erit triangulus
ZLH equalis triangulo HAL, et ideo triangulus ZLE equalis triangulo HAE
communi apposito triangulo HLE, quare et equalis dimidio [dati] trigoni.
Ducatur ergo linea DL et ei equedistans EM, posito M in linea ZL, continu-
30   eturque linea DM; erit igitur triangulus EMD equalis triangulo EML, et ideo
triangulus ZMD equalis triangulo ZLE communi apposito ZME, qui fuit
sicut EAC, medietas dati trigoni. Ducatur ergo linea MN ad circumferentiam equedistans linee DEZ. Et ductis lineis ZN et DN erit triangulus

13 super: sicud Pb (*sed non G*) sunt Fb / arcu GPb / est: et GPb
14 CEA: CAE H / CT $SHFb$ ET (*sive* CT) D ET (?) GPb
15 CED: DEC H
16 DT: DC Fb / TCZD: TCDZ H
17 medietas: medietates G, ?Pb
18 et² *om.* GPb / equedistantes: eq̄d' D equed' S equidem GPb / 24: 28 H 4 Fb
19 27: 17 (?) Fb
21 pertracta $DSGPbFb$ (*et scr. et del. Pb antea* protr)
22 ibit $HGPb$ ibi $DSFb$ (*et quia hab. D ibi add. Dc* transibit *post* alibi) / sitque (?) D
    per super (?) G super (?) Pb
23 ad (*sive lac.*) G / descedat Pb / CH: CB GPb
24 *post* eritque *scr. et del. Pb* ea / AE: AC Fb / 28: 24 H, ?S (*et mg. scr. m. rec. H* 28.
    primi)
25 HA *omnes MSS* (*et corr. Fb ex* DA) AH Dc / trigoni *omnes MSS* trianguli *injuste*
    Dc
26 HL: HB GPb
26–27 erit triangulus ZLH *omnes alii MSS* triangulus erit triangulus erit ZLH GPb triangulus
    ZHL erit *injuste Dc*
27 HAE: HE S
28 communi . . . triangulo: propter communem triangulum H / communi *om.* GPb /
    apposito *correxi ex* opposito / [dati] *addidi*
29 DL . . . ZL: A Fb
29–30 continueturque: et continuetur H contineturque GPb
30 triangulus: triganus (!) Pb triangule Fb
31 ZLE: ZLC (*sive* ZLT) D / communi apposito S apposito communi H communi
    opposito $DGPbFb$ / ZME H, *om. tex. in omnibus MSS* scilicet ZME *mg. dex. D*
31–32 qui . . . EAC: est (*sive* erit) igitur ZMD sicud H
31 fuit (?) D sunt GPb
32 sicut *om.* Fb / trigoni: trianguli H
33 equedistantis GPb equedistantes Fb / *post* DEZ *scr. et del. Fb* que est diameter / ZN:
    NZ H

orthogonius *ZDN* super lineam *ZD*, que est diameter, equalis medietati dati
35 trigoni, cui equalem super diametrum ex alia parte constitues sumpta su-
pradicta industria, qui sit *ZDY*, et habebis parallelogrammum rectangulum
ZNDY equale triangulo *ABC*, sicut exigebatur.

8. INTER QUASLIBET DUAS FIGURAS POLIGONIAS EQUILA-
TERAS ET SIMILES, ET QUARUM UNA IN CIRCULO INSCRIPTA,
ALIA CIRCUMSCRIPTA FUERIT, PROPORTIONALIS CONSISTIT,
QUE DUPLO PLURIUM LATERUM EXISTENS INFRA (*!* INTRA)
5 EUNDEM CIRCULUM DESCRIBITUR.

Sit exemplum de triangulis. Sit ergo triangulus *ABC* circumscriptus circulo,
cuius centrum sit *Z*, et triangulus infrascriptus sit *DEF*, applicans angulos
suos ad contactus alterius [Fig. IV.8]. Ducantur ergo linee a *Z* ad angulos
utriusque trianguli; que ergo ducantur ad angulos *A*, *B*, *C* secant latera trianguli
10 inscripti orthogonaliter et per equalia tam latera quam arcus, sicut patet ex
17. tertii et 4. primi et ultima sexti. Punctus ergo in quo linea *ZA* secat
lineam *DF* sit *H*, et punctus in quo secat arcum sit *G*. Ergo per corollarium
8. sexti linea *GZ*, cum sit equalis linee *DZ*, proportionalis est inter totam
AZ et partem eius *HZ*. Ducta ergo linea *GD* erit per primam sexti triangulus
15 *DGZ* proportionalis inter triangulum *ADZ* et partem eius *HDZ*; subtensis
ergo cordis medietatibus singulorum arcuum fiet exagonus, qui est duplo
plurium laterum, qui erit per 13. quinti proportionalis inter triangulos *ABC*
et *DEF*, cum possis hoc modo arguere undique. Et ex eis argues si proposite
fuerint figure poligonie multo plurium laterum.

9. SI FIGURE POLIGONIE ET EQUILATERE CIRCULIS EQUALIBUS
INSCRIBANTUR, QUE PLURIUM LATERUM FUERIT MAIOR ERIT,
ET PROPORTIO IPSIUS AD ALIAM MAIOR QUAM OMNIUM

---

35 cui equalem: cuius angulo Z equale angulum *H* / equalem: equales *GPb* / constitues:
constituens *injuste Dc*

36 sit: sunt *Pb* / habebis (*?*) *Fb*

37 equale triangulo *bis G*

Prop. IV.8

1 8 *om. DHGFb* 49 (*?*) *mg. sin. Pb* 52 *mg. sin. Es* 53ᵃ *mg. dex. S* / qualibet (*!*) *Fb* /
duas *bis G*

2 et¹ *supra scr. D* / et² *om. H*

3 alia: et alia *H* / consistit *corr. G ex* constit

6 Sit ergo: et sit *H*

8 linee *om. GPb* / a Z: AZ (*?*) *GPb* / Z: centro Z *H* / ad² *supra scr. G*

9 ergo: autem *Fb* / *ante* latera *scr. et del. S* angulos

10 inscripta *GPb* / ex: per *H*

11 4: 8 *GPb* / et *om. GPb* / ultimam *H*

13 sit equalis *tr. Fb* / equalis: reliquis *GPb* / est: erit *H* / inter: sunt *Pb, ?G*

14 AZ: AE *GPb* / Ducta . . . GD: Ductis igitur lineis GD, EF *H* / sexti: 16ⁱ *Pb, ?G*

15 DGZ (*?*) *D* GDZ *SH* / *post* DGZ *add. Fb* et / partem eius *tr. GPb*

18 eis: eisdem *H*

19 polligonie *DS*

Prop. IV.9

1 9 *om. DHGFb* 50 (*?*) *mg. sin. Pb* 53 *mg. sin. Es* 54ᵃ *mg. dex. S* / polligonie *DS* (*et
post hoc lectiones huiusmodi in istis MSS non laudabo*)

SUORUM LATERUM AD OMNIA LATERA ALTERIUS PARITER AC-
5   CEPTA.
Demonstrationem, que ad omnia poligonia communis est, de quadrato
et pentagono constitutis in circulis equalibus exercebimus. In utroque ergo
circulo ductis lineis rectis a centro ad angulos singulos poligonii erit utrumque

6–24 *de* Demonstrationem. . . . prius *hab. mg. D* (*secundum Dc*) *et mg. infer. Fb* Demonstratio huius argumenti: minor est proportio 4 triangulorum quadrati ad 4 triangulos pentagoni quam 4 laterum quadrati ad quatuor latera pentagoni, igitur (*?Fb*,
ergo *Dc*) minor est proportio 4 triangulorum quadrati ad quinque triangulos pentagoni
quam 4 laterum quadrati ad 5 (*et add. Fb* ad) latera pentagoni. Sit linea AB divisa
super puncta T et S et X sicut 4 partiales trianguli totius quadrati [Fig. IV.9*var*
DcFb(a)] linea vero KD divisa super puncta C, L, N, I sit sicut 5 trianguli pentagoni.
Item sit linea EF divisa super puncta M, R, Z sicut 4 latera quadrati, linea vero PH
divisa super puncta (*Dc,* A *Fb*) G, O, V (*Dc,* VN *Fb*), Y sit sicut 5 latera pentagoni.
Quoniam ergo minor est proportio AB ad CD quam EF ad GH, erit (*Dc, ?Fb*) AB
ad minorem CD sicut EF (*Dc,* CF *? Fb*) ad GH (*Dc,* QH *? Fb*), quia ad maiorem
CD (*Dc,* ẽ D *Fb*) semper minor esset, quod patet. Sit ergo AB ad GD (*Dc,* quod *Fb,*
QD?) sicut EF ad GH (*Dc,* HG *Fb*). Quoniam autem minor est AT (*Dc,* AD̦ *Fb*) ad
KC quam EM ad PG, sit AT (*Dc,* AC *Fb*) ad KZ (*!* KQ) sicut EM ad PG; quare et
quadrupli (*Dc,* quadranguli *Fb*) AT (*Dc,* AC *Fb*), scilicet AB, ad KZ (*!* KQ) sicut
quadrupli EM, scilicet EF, ad PG per penultimam 5^{ti} Euclidis et tertiam (*Dc, ? Fb*).
Per eandem, quia AB ad QD sicut EF ad HG, erit AB ad aggregatum ex KZ (*!* KQ)
et QD sicut EF ad PH. Sed AB ad KCD minor est proportio quam eiusdem ad
aggregatum ex KZ (*!* KQ) et QD per secundam (*Dc,* eiusdem *Fb*) partem 8. (*Dc, ?*
Fb) quinti. Ergo minor (*Dc,* maior *Fb*) est proportio AB ad KD (*Dc,* K *Fb*) quam
EF ad PH, et hoc est propositum. Aliter potest (*Dc, om. Fb*) idem (*Dc, ?Fb*) demonstrari
sic: minor est proportio AB ad CD quam EF ad GH. Ergo econtrario maior est
proportio CD ad AB quam GH ad EF. Sed que est KD ad CD (*Dc,* EF̦ CD *Fb*)
eadem est PH ad GH. Ergo per regulam positam in fine (*Dc,* finem *Fb*) commenti
(*Dc,* comenti *Fb*) super 12^{am} presentis maior est proportio KD ad AB (*Dc,* AD *? Fb*)
quam PH ad EF. Ergo minor est proportio AB ad KD quam EF ad PH, et hoc (*?*
Fb, hec *Dc*) est propositum.
    Probatio quod minor est proportio lateris trianguli ad latus quadrati quam arcus
ad arcum [Fig. IV.9*var. DcFb*(b)] Quoniam arcus EF ad arcum BC sexquitertia (*Fb*
sequitertia *Dc*) est proportio, quia eadem est que (*Dc,* que est *Fb*) anguli ad angulum,
scilicet ETF ad BAC. Sed BAC (*Dc,* BAT *Fb*) rectus est, et (*Dc, om. Fb*) ETF (*Dc,*
om. Fb) continet rectum et tertiam recti quia duplus est ad angulum EFG (*Dc,* EGD
Fb) per 19. tertii Euclidis. Item proportio linee EF ad lineam CB est subsexqualtera.
Probatio: Proportio laterum duplicata est proportio quadratorum per 18. sexti; sed
quadratorum (per . . . quadratorum *Dc, om. Fb*) sexqualtera, quia quadratum EF
triplum est ad (*Dc, om. Fb*) quadratum (*Dc, om. Fb*) semidiametri per 8. (*Dc,* 4. *?*
Fb) 13. libri Euclidis et quadratum BC duplum est ad quadratum eiusdem semidiametri
(*Dc, lac. Fb*). Igitur EF ad BC est proportio subsexqualtera, et arcus ad arcum sexquitertia (*Fb,* sesquitertia *Dc*). Quare minor est proportio (*Fb, om. Dc*) EF ad BC
quam arcus ad arcum

6 polligonia *DFb* (*et post hoc lectiones huiusmodi in istis MSS non laudabo*) / communis
est *tr. H* / de *om. SH*
7 *mg. hab. D* (*sed non Fb*) propositis (*Dc,* propositum *?D*) triangulo et quadrato ex
tertia huius ad primam partem propositionis patet ratiocinatio / exercebimus *om.*
GPb excebimus (*!*) *Fb* / ergo *om. Fb*
8 lineis rectis *alii MSS et ?D* rectis lineis *Dc* / uterque (*?*) *GPb*
8–9 utrumque poligonium *tr. H*

poligonium divisum in triangulos equales totidem quot latera habet. Sit ergo
10 unus quatuor triangulorum quadrati *ABC*, et unus ex quinque triangulis
pentagoni sit *EDO*, positis *A* et *E* in centris [Fig. IV.9]. Age ergo: linea *BC*
maior est quam linea *DO*, quia maiorem arcum resecat, maior enim semper
est quarta quam quinta. Ergo per 12. primi huius minor est proportio trianguli
ABC ad triangulum *EDO* quam linee *BC* ad lineam *DO*, et ideo minor quam
15 arcus *BC* ad arcum *DO* per quartam tertii huius. Ergo per 13. quinti minor
est proportio totius quadrati, quod precise distinguitur in quatuor triangulos,
ad quinque triangulos pentagoni quam totius circumferentie circuli *A* ad
totam circumferentiam circuli *E*, que quidem proportio equalitas est; ergo
totum quadratum *A* minus est quinque triangulis pentagoni *E*; ergo totum
20 pentagonum maius est quadrato et sic patet prima pars. Item, quia minor
58r est proportio trianguli *ABC* ad triangulum *EDO* quam linee / *BC* ad lineam
DO, erit econtrario maior proportio trianguli *EDO* ad triangulum *ABC* quam
linee *DO* ad lineam *BC*, et sic discurrendo per singulos argues secundam
partem ex 13. quinti, sicut fecisti prius.

    10. QUODLIBET LATUS POLIGONII [EQUILATERI] CIRCULO
CIRCUMSCRIPTI APUD CONTACTUM SECTUM EST PER EQUALIA,

      9 totidem *tr. H post* in / quot: e' *G* est *Pb* / latera habet *tr. H* / Sit: Si *S*
  11 BC: BE *SGPb*
  12 semper *om. H*
  13 *post* quinta *add. H* eiusdem
  14 EDO: EDC *GPb*
  15 *ante* ad *scr. et del. G* ar / quartam: 27. *H* / huius *om. H*
  16 quod *SHFb* quam (?) *GPb* qui *Dc* / precise *GPbDc* prescise *SHFb*
17–19 quinque . . . E: triangulum EDO quam totius circumferentie circuli A ad arcum
      DO; igitur per eandem 13. minor est proportio totius quadrati ad ad (!) totum pen-
      tagonum quod est quintuplum ad triangulum EDO quam totius circumferentie circuli
      A ad totam circumferentiam circuli E que est quintupla ad arcum DO. Sed circum-
      ferentie sunt equales *H*
  17 quinque: v *Fb om. SGPb* quatuor *injuste Dc* / triangulos: angulos *Fb* / pentagonii
      (?) *Fb* / A *om. GPb*
  18 totam . . . circuli: circuli circumferentiam totius *Fb*
18–19 ergo . . . E *Dc om. SFb* (*sed injuste hab. Dc* quatuor *pro* quinque)
  19 minus . . . totum: in minus *GPb* / totum *om. H*
  20 *mg. hab. Fb aliquid quod non bene legere possum:* scilicet (?) patet quod non solum
      erit excessus (?) preter (?) bases sed ——— (?) proportio (?) ——— (?) distantiam
      (?) est ——— (?) equidistans ——— (?) ——— (?) / maius est *tr. H*
  21 *ante* trianguli *scr. et del. Pb* est proportio / EDO: ABC EDO *Fb* EBO (?) *S* / quam:
      quod *Fb*
  22 econtrario (?) *Fb*
  23 decurrendo *Fb*
  24 prius (?) *G*
Prop. IV.10
    1 10 *om. DHGFaFbBu* 51 (?) *mg. sin Pb* 54 *mg. sin. Es* 55ª *mg. dex. S* / Quolibus
      (!) *Fa* Quolibet *Fb* / poligonii *HGPbBu*, ?*Fa* poligoni *DSFb* / [equilateri] *om.*
      SGPbBuFaFb sed supra scr. H equilateri sumpti *supra scr. D*
    2 sectum *om. S* divisum *H*

ET SI INTER CONTACTUS CONTINUENTUR LINEE, SIMILE POLI-
GONIUM INCLUDENT. UNDE PATET QUOD OMNIS ARCUS INTER
5 DUOS CONTACTUS PROXIMOS COMPREHENSUS TOTA PARS EST
CIRCULI QUOT SUNT IN POLIGONIO LATERA.

Nunc in triangulis demonstrationem communem ad omnia poligonia exercebimus. Sit ergo centrum circuli G [Fig. IV.10], cui circumscriptus triangulus sit ABC, ductisque lineis a centro ad contactus et etiam ad angulos A,
10 B, C, patet per 4. et 15. primi Euclidis omnes angulos apud G equales esse;
cumque sint anguli apud contactus equales, eo quod recti sunt, patet per 26.
primi Euclidis quod linea BE est equalis linee EC, et sic de reliquis. Item
continuatis lineis inter contactus, quia omnes anguli super centrum sunt
equales, argues ex quarta primi Euclidis triangulum DEF esse equilaterum.
15 Et ex hoc manifestum est quod arcus EF est tertia pars circuli DEF, nam
eque corde equis subtendentur arcubus, et triangulus DEF est quarta pars
trianguli ABC ex 2. et 4. et 17. sexti.

11. SI CIRCA EQUALES CIRCULOS FIGURE EQUALIUM LA-
TERUM DESIGNENTUR, QUE PAUCIORUM LATERUM FUERIT
MAIOR ERIT, EIUSQUE AD ALIAM PROPORTIO TANQUAM LA-
TERUM IPSIUS AD LATERA ALTERIUS PARITER ACCEPTA.
5 Modo sit exemplum de triangulo equilatero ABC circumscripto circulo
Q, et de quadrato DEFG circumscripto circulo L [Fig. IV.11]. Est ergo quodlibet

3 contactus: contactu Fa / continuentur linee tr. Bu / continuentur (?) D / similie Fa
5 post contactus add. Fa propōnis (!) / ante pars scr. et del. Pb partitur
5–6 est circuli tr. Fb
6 quot: quod GBu / poligonia Fa
7 Nunc . . . triangulis: Cum triangulus GPbBu / communem: uēm (?) D / omnia: ō
et lac. S / poligonias Bu
7–8 excebimur GPb excebimus Bu
8 Sit: si GPb
8–9 cui . . . etiam om. S a quo protrahantur linee H
9 sit: ad (?) Fb / et om. Fa
10 post per add. S Euclidis (?) / 4 HGPbBu, ?DSFb 8 Fa / et 15. supra scr. H / 15 (?)
Fa / Euclidis omnes: Euclidem omnis Fa / equalis Bu
11 recti sunt tr. HBu
12 ante est scr. et del. (?) Fb G / post reliquis add. S 3 / Item: cum S argues et patet
primum H
13 contiquatis Fb / ante lineis add. H igitur
14 argue Fa ergo Bu / Euclidem Fa / esse equilaterum om. GPbBu
15 Et om. Fa / ex om. Pb / DEF: DF SH
16 equis: equs (!) D / subtenduntur PbFbBu, ?G / et: Item H etiam Fa / est om. GPbBu
17 ex: et ex GPbBu ex et Fa / 17: 27 Fa / post sexti add. Bu Euclidis patet propositum
Prop. IV.11
1 11 om. DHGFb 52 (?) mg. sin. Pb 55 mg. sin. Es 56ᵃ mg. dex. S
1–2 equalium laterum: equilatere H
2 pauciorum SH paucorum DGPbFb
3 eiusque: eiusdem GPb
4 alterius: ipsius GPb
5 mg. hab. Fb secundum patet (?) quod _____ (?) est loco para _____ (?, sive proportionalis) et erit cum (sive omni) distantia una (?) / sit: fiat H

latus trianguli maius quolibet latere quadrati, quia medietates sunt maiores medietatibus, eo quod maiorem arcum comprehendunt per premissam et per hoc quod dictum est in fine commenti super sextam tertii huius, nam
10 tertia pars alicuius maior est quam quarta eiusdem vel sui equalis. Ductis igitur utrobique perpendicularibus a centris ad contactus, erit triangulus *ABC* divisus in tres triangulos equales et quadratum in quatuor. Et quia perpendiculares sunt undique equales, patet quod omnes septem trianguli sunt eiusdem altitudinis, et ideo per primam sexti sunt proportionales suis basibus.
15 Ergo proportio trium triangulorum trianguli ad quatuor triangulos quadrati, et hoc est totius trianguli ad totum quadratum, est sicut laterum eius ad latera illius, et sic patet secunda pars. Sed quia laterum ad latera maior est proportio quam angulorum trium apud *Q* ad quatuor angulos apud *L*, sicut ostendemus in proxima sequente, et angulorum ad angulos proportio est
20 sicut arcuum trium hinc ad quatuor arcus inde per ultimam sexti, et hec proportio equalitas est, sequitur ergo a primo quod triangulus sit maior quadrato, et sic patet prima. Quod autem sit maior proportio laterum quam angulorum probatio. In medio *BC* apud contactum sit *K*, et in medio *DE* sit *Z*. Quia ergo maior est *BC* quam *DE*, et utraque suarum medietatum
25 maior est utraque medietate illius, sit ergo linea *SKP* sicut *DE* manente *K* in medio, et continuentur linee *SQ* et *PQ*. Erit ergo triangulus *KPQ* sicut triangulus *ZLE* per 4. primi Euclidis, et ideo totus *SPQ* sicut totus *DEL*, et angulus ad *Q* sicut angulus ad *L*. Argue ergo ex quinta primi huius bis et

7 *post* quadrati *mg. hab. D (secundum Dc) et Fb* quoniam anguli super centrum maiores sunt quia hii et illi 4 rectis sunt equales
9 per *om. SH* / tertii huius: huius quarti *H* / tertii: circuli *S*
10 Ductis: demptis *GPb*
11 contractus (?) *Fb* / *post* contactus *add. H* et etiam ductis lineis ad angulos poligonorum
12 triangulos: angulos *GPb*
13 *ante* septem (*i.e.* 7) *scr. et del. Pb* a
14 primam *om. GPb*
16 et hoc est *bis GPb* / est[2] *H om. DSGPbFb*
17 illius: alterius *H*
18 Q: QL *Fb* / sicut: sic *GPb* / *post* sicut *add. H* statim
19 in . . . sequente *om. H*
20 quatuor: iii *GPb*
21 equalitatis *H* / est *om. Fb et tr. H post* hec *in lin.* 20 / sequitur ergo: igitur sequitur *H* / a primo *om. H*
22 *post* prima *add. H* pars
23 et *om. GPb*
24 et: est *H*
25 est *om. H* / medietate: medietati *injuste Dc* / linea *om. GPb*
26 medio: metio (*!*) *Fb* / et[1] *om. GPb* / sicut: sit *Fb*
27 totus[1,2]: totius *Fb*
28–30 Argue . . . sunt: est igitur per 5. primi huius minor proportio anguli PQC ad angulum KQP quam basis PC ad basim KP. Ergo coniunctim minor est proportio anguli KQC ad angulum KQP quam basis KC ad basim KP. Ergo duplando minor est proportio anguli BQC ad angulum SQP, et per consequens ad angulum DLE, quam basis BC ad basim SP, et per consequens quam ad basim DE. Igitur maior est proportio lateris

coniunctim et duple, nam perpendicularis *QK* et bases et angulos dividit per
30   equalia, eo quod latera equalia sunt.

12. SI IN TRIANGULO CUIUS DUO LATERA EQUALIA FUERINT
AB ANGULO QUEM CONTINENT AD BASEM LINEA RECTA DU-
CATUR QUE TAM ANGULUM QUAM BASEM PER INEQUALIA DIVI-
DAT, ERIT MAIORIS AD MINOREM DE PARTIBUS ANGULI MAIOR
58v   PROPORTIO QUAM MAIORIS AD MINOREM / DE PARTIBUS BASIS.

6   Sit triangulus *ABC* [Fig. IV.12], et linea ducta ad basem sit *BE*, atque a
medio basis erigatur linea *FB*, que quidem super basem orthogonalis erit et
angulum *B* per equalia dividet. Argue ergo per 5. primi huius et disiunctim
et coniunctim et duple proportionando.

13. LINEA PROTRACTA A CENTRO CIRCULI AD ALIQUEM AN-
GULUM TRIANGULI EIDEM CIRCUMSCRIPTI EQUILATERI APUD
CIRCUMFERENTIAM SECTA EST PER EQUALIA, ET PROTRACTA

ad latus quam anguli ad angulum *H* / *de* Argue . . . sunt *mg. scr. D (sed om. Fb)*
Angulus autem SQP rectus (?) est quoniam SK et KQ sunt equales, et ob hoc uterque
(*D*, utique *Dc*) angulus super basim semirectus cum sit K rectus et eadem ratione
KQP semirectus est; quare patet intentum

29 *ante* bases *scr. et del. G* sabes (!)

Prop. IV.12

1   12 *om. DHGFaFbPcBu* 53 *mg. sin. Pb* 56 *mg. sin. Es* 57ᵃ *mg. dex. S* / in *om. GPbBu*
/ latera equalia *tr. Pc*

2   basem *DSGPbFb* basim *HFaPcBu* (*et post hoc lectiones huiusmodi non laudabo*)

3–4   dividit *GPbBu*

5   proportio: portio *GPbBu*

6   triangulus: in angulo *Pc* / et *om. Fa* / BE: E *GPbBu*

7   medio: metᵒ *Fb* / erigatur: ereatur (!) *Bu* / quidem: qued' *Bu* / orthogonalis: ortogona
S / erit *om. Fa*

8–9   Argue . . . proportionando: igitur per 5. primi huius minor est proportio CBE anguli
ad EBF angulum quam CE basis ad EF basim. Ergo econtrario maior est proportio
FBE anguli ad EBC angulum quam FE basis ad EC basim. Igitur coniunctim maior
est proportio FBC anguli ad EBC angulum quam FC basis ad EC basim. Igitur
duplando maior est proportio totius ABC anguli ad EBC angulum quam totius AC
ad EC. Igitur disiunctim maior est proportio ABE anguli ad ABC angulum quam
AE ad EC, et hoc est quod intendimus *H*

8   Argue *om. Bu* / primi huius *tr. Bu* / et disiunctim *om. GPbPcBu sed hab. Fb et mg.
dex. D* (*et cf. var. H in lin. 8–9 superius*)

8–9   disiunctim et coniunctim: coniunctim *Fa*

8   disiunctim: econtrario *S*

9   coniunctim: coniunctum *DS* / et² *om. PbPcBu* / proportionando: proportionanto (!)
G (*et non legere possum in Pb*) proportio (?) *Fa* proportionante *Bu, et add. Bu* patet
propositum

Prop. IV.13

1   13 *om. DHGFaFbPcBu* 54 *mg. sin. Pb* 57 *mg. sin. Es* 58ᵃ *mg. dex. S* / Linea: Si
linea *PbBu,* ?*G* / aliquem: adliquam (!) *G* aliquam *PbBu*

2   *post* eidem *add. H* circulo / equilateri *tr. H post* trianguli *in lin. 2* / equelateri *Bu*

3–7   Et . . . decagoni *DGPbPcFaBu om. SHFb* (*et add. mg. H forte de textu om.* tam
textus quam commentum est falsum)

AD ANGULUM QUADRATI CIRCUMSCRIPTI SECTA EST APUD
5 CIRCUMFERENTIAM SECUNDUM PROPORTIONEM HABENTEM
MEDIUM ET DUO EXTREMA, ESTQUE PORTIO EXTRA DEPRE-
HENSA LATUS DECAGONI.

Recepta dispositione antepremissa et ducta linea inter contactus trianguli
[Fig. IV.13], argues primam partem modo arguendi super octavam huius
10 quarti et ex corollario prime decimi quarti Euclidis. Secundam partem argues
ex penultima primi Euclidis et 4. secundi eiusdem bis et 16. sexti et 24.
duodecimi.

14. QUELIBET MEDIA PROPORTIONALIA EARUNDEM EX-
TREMITATUM SUNT EQUALIA.

Esto exemplum *B* et *C* media proportionalia inter *A* et *D* [Fig. IV.14],
que nisi sint equalia, sit *B* maior quam *C* et *A* maior extremitas; ergo *A* plus

---

4 circumscripti . . . apud *Fa om. DGPbPcBu*
5 circonferentiam *GPb* / *post* circumferentiam *add. D* secat
6 portio *correxi ex* proportio *in DGPbPcFaBu*
8–12 de Recepta. . . . duodecimi *scr. mg. D et mg. infer. Fb* vel sic primam partem
argumentare, ducta (*Fb,* Ducatur *Dc*) AC linea a contactu usque ad sectionem, que
erit latus exagoni. Quare triangulus ABC erit equilaterus cuius quilibet angulus duas
(*Dc, ?Fb*) tertias unius recti continebit. Ergo per 32. primi Euclidis CAD et ADE (*Dc,*
ADT *?Fb*) anguli (*Dc,* angulo *Fb*) sunt due tertie unius recti. Quoniam ergo ABD
(*Fb,* AD *D*) et BDA anguli sunt equales uni recto, et ABD (*Dc,* ABE *Fb*) angulus
est bisse unius recti, erit CDA angulus tertia pars recti. Similiter (*Dc,* in *Fb*) CAD
angulus tertia pars recti. Quare illi (*Dc,* illis *Fb*) equales erunt. Ergo per 6. primi
Euclidis AC sive BC et CD latera sunt equalia, et hoc est propositum (*Dc,* proportio
Fb). Secunda pars videtur contradicere penultimam (*correxi ex* penultime *in Dc*)
tertii Euclidis adiuvante 16. sexti Euclidis (videtur . . . Euclidis *Dc, om. Fb*)
8 Recepta: Retenta *Fa* / antepremisse *Fb* / trianguli: anguli *GPbPcBu*
9 argues: arguam (*sive* argues) *Bu* / super: sunt *Fb*
10 quarti *om. Fa* / correlariis (?) *Pb* / prime decimi quarti: 15. 4^{ti} *H* / decimi quarti:
14 (?) *Fa* / argues *injuste om. Dc*
11 Euclidis: Euclidem *Fa* / et 4: 14 (*sive* et 4) *Fa* / 16 *om. Pc*
11–12 et³ . . . duodecimi *om. Bu*
11 24: 18 *Fb*

Prop. IV.14

1 *mg. super. fol. 289v hab. Ve* DE QUADRATURA *et fol. 290r* CIRCULI *et similiter
in fol. 290v et 291r* / *supra lineam hab. Gu titulum* Incipit quadratura circuli secundum
Alardum / 14 *om. DHGPbPcPeFbBuVeGu* 58 *mg. sin. Es* 59^{a} *mg. dex. S* / earundem:
earum *S* duarum *H* eorundem *Fb*
1–2 extremitatum: quantitatum *Gu* medietatum *injuste Dc*
3–7 de Esto. . . . propositum *scr. mg. D* (secundum *Dc*) *Fb et Ve* Vel sic: Proportio A
ad D est proportio A ad B duplicata; similiter proportio A ad D est proportio A ad
C duplicata. Ergo proportio A ad B duplicata est proportio A ad C (*DcVe, om. Fb*)
duplicata (*DcVe, om. Fb*). Ergo que est A ad B simpla eadem est A ad C (*bis Fb*)
simpla. Ergo B est equale C
3 Esto exemplum: Sint *H* / B *om. GBu et inser. Pb* / C *corr. Bu ex* se / *ante* media
add. Pb medium / *ante* inter *scr. et del. Pe* earundem extremitatum / A et D: AD
Pe
4 nisi: non *Gu* / *post* sit *add. Gu* ergo

5   superat *C* quam *B*; sed *B, C* proportionaliter superant *D* et superantur ab
A; ergo *C* plus excedet *D* quam *B* excedat eundem *D*; ergo *C* maior est quam
B, contra falsigraphum. Patet ergo propositum.

15. OCTOGONUS CIRCULO INSCRIPTUS INTER QUADRATUM
EIDEM INSCRIPTUM ET QUADRATUM CIRCUMSCRIPTUM PRO-
PORTIONALIS.

Dispositione itaque proposite figure sic pariter applicentur, ut proposita
5   figura ostendit [Fig. IV.15], quod geometer industrius facile colliget ex tertio
et quarto lineis ductis a centro tam ad angulos exterioris quam interioris

5 superat: separat *S* / sed: si *GPbPc* sit *Bu* / B^2 *om. GPbPcBu* / *post* proportionaliter
scr. et del. Gu D / superant D: superante (*!*) *Bu* / superantur *H* superatur
DSGPbPcPeFbBuGuVe

6 *post* plus *scr. et del. S* separati C quam B sed BC / excedet: excedit (*?*) *H* / excedat:
excedat (*sive* excedit) *HFb*

7 B *om. Fb* / *ante* contra *add. H* quod est / contra falsigraphum: quod est falsum
Gu / falsigraphum *GHBu* phellsigraphearum (*sive* phellsigrahi quod) *DFb* phelsigraphi
S falsigraphat (*?*) *Pb* phalsigraphi *Ve* falsigraphicum *Pc* / *ante* Patet *add. SGPbPcVe*
quod (*?*) / Patet . . . propositum *om. Bu*

Prop. IV.15

1 15 *om. DHGFbPcPeBuROdVeGu* 55 (*!*) *mg. sin. Pb* 59 *mg. sin. Es* 60ᵃ *mg. dex. S*

1–19 Octogonus. . . . [habetur]: Si circulo inscribatur quadratum et eidem circulo circumscribatur aliud quadratum, octogonum inscriptum eidem circulo erit inter illa
duo quadrata medio loco proportionale. Sit (*R, Exemplum* _____ *?Od*) quadratum
EN circumscriptum circulo O et MF (*Od, et corr. R ex* quod F) quadratum inscriptum
O et CGF octogonum inscriptum O (*Od, om. R*) circulo [Fig. IV.15*var. ROd*]. Dico
quia CGF est medio loco proportionalis (*!R, ?Od*) inter EN, MF quadrata. Dispositio:
ducatur EN, (*R,* $\overset{\text{E}}{\text{LN}}$ *Od*) diameter ab E in N et (*R, om. Od?*) necessario transibit
per O centrum et per C et T angulos octogoni, quod quia probare facile est lectoris
relinquo industrie vel si placet priusquam inscribatur O circulo octogonum CGF
ducatur EN diametraliter (*R, diametrum Od*) transiens per O et dividet tam GM
cordam tam GM arcum in duo equa, et a C in G et M ducantur due corde CG, CM
et erunt latera octogoni equilateri (*R et ex corr. Od*) circulo inscriptibili (*R, inscripto
Od*). Ratio age: tam G quam M est rectus et O communis. Ergo (*R, ?Od*) EGO,
OGM (*ante* OGM *scr. et del. Od* OAGM *?* trianguli, ad GCO eadem *?* primi que)
trianguli sunt similes. Ergo proportio EO ad OG ea est (*Od, om. R*) OG (*?*) ad OM.
Ergo que est EG ad OC ea est OC ad OM. Ergo per primam sexti que est proportio
EGO trianguli ad CGO eadem est CGO (*R, om. Od*) ad M'GO. Ergo CGO triangulus
est medio loco proportionalis inter EGO et M'GO; similiter undique examinatis (*?*)
partibus invenies triangulos octogoni (octogoñ *ROd*) constitutentes (*R, insistentes
?Od*) esse inter triangulos EN, MG quadrata constitutentes medio loco proportionalis
(*?*). Ergo octogonum inter duo quadrata est medio loco proportionalis (*?*) quod pro-
posuimus (*R,* ppoᵘˢ *Od*) *ROd*

1 Octogonus: Ottogonus (*!*) *G* Ortogonius *Gu*

1–3 *mg. scr. H* illud probatur in suo universali in 8ᵃ huius

2 eidem . . . circumscriptum: circumscriptum eidem et inscriptum eidem est *Gu* /
eidem: eiusdem *H* / et *supra scr. Pc* / circumscriptum *DSFb* circumscriptum est
HPcPeVe circumscriptum erit *Bu* circonscriptum erit *GPb*

4 Dispositione . . . figure: Dispone itaque sic figuram ut latera ipsius *Gu* / Dispositione:
Dispositio *Pe* Dispone *Ve* dispositiones *H* / itaque proposite *tr. Pe* / posite *Bu* / figure:
signate *Pc*

5 ostendat *Gu* / industrius: industria *Gu* industrias *Ve* / colligat *Gu*

6 *ante* lineis *scr. Pe* li / tam *mg. Gu* / exteriorẹs $\overset{\text{i}}{\text{Pb}}$ / quam: tam *Pe* / interiorẹs $\overset{\text{i}}{\text{Pb}}$

tetragoni. Itaque *OE* dividit *AB* equaliter in *I*, quod colligitur ex 8. primi inspectis *AOE*, *OEB* triangulis, et per 4. eiusdem, inspectis *AIE*, *EIB* triangulis, sicque perpendicularis est ad *AB* secundum 3. tertii. Istorum itaque trian-
10 gulorum *OEB*, *OIB*, *O* angulus est communis, et item *I* et *B* sunt equales, ut recti; ergo *B* et *E* reliqui sunt equales; ergo trianguli sunt equianguli; ergo proportionalium laterum eadem est proportio, scilicet *OE*, *OB* et *OB*, *OI*; ergo, mediante *OB*, eadem est quoque *OE*, *OK*, *OI*. Sed, cum sint in eadem altitudine, *OEB*, *OKB*, *OIB* trianguli sunt proportionales, ergo et illorum
15 equemultiplicia. Sed tres date figure constant triangulis sic se habentibus numero equalibus ipsis figuris; ergo sunt quasi illorum equemultiplicia, ergo ipsa quoque sunt proportionalia quod proposuimus.

Corollarium huius: si autem circulus et octogonus sibi inscriptus sunt proportionales, quod est impossibile, [propositum habetur].

16. PROPOSITO CIRCULO EQUALE QUADRATUM CONSTI-TUERE.

7 *ante* OE *scr. et del. Gu* OD / OE: AE (*?*) *Bu* eo *Pc* / in I *om. H* ini (*?*) *Pc* / colligatur
   S / 8: viii (*?*) *GPb*
8 inspectis[1] *DBu* inscriptis *SHGPbPcPeVeGu* intractis (*?*) *Fb* / OEB *om. Fb* AEB
   Gu / et *om. Pc* / inspectis[2] *DFbBu* inscriptis *SHGPbPcPeVeGu* / EIB triangulis *tr.*
   Pe / EIB: IEB *H*
9 -que: quod *SHVe*, ?*DBu* / *post* est *add. Dc* OE (*sed non in MSS*) / AB: ABC *Bu* /
   secundum: per *H* / 3.: vii *Pe*
9–19 Istorum. . . . [habetur]: igitur AZ et per consequens ZI est medium proportionale
   inter EZ et ZO; quare et trianguli cum sint eiusdem altitudinis, et patet propositum
   multiplicando *H*
10 O angulus *tr. Dc* (*sed non in MSS*) / angulus *om. Pe* / item: idem *S* iterum *Gu* / et[2]
   om. GPbPcBu
11 B et E: BE *Pe* / equales *om. Pe* / eque anguli *Bu*
12 *ante* laterum *add. Fb* partium / *ante* eadem *hab. Dc* ergo (*sed non in MSS*) / scilicet
   tr. Pe ante eadem / OE: AE(*?*) *Pe* / et OB *om. Fb* / OB, OI: DB, OR (*?*) *Bu* / OB[2]:
   EB *GPb* / OI: OR *S*
13 OB: AB *Pe* / est quoque *tr. Pe* / OK: OB *Fb* / *post* OI *scr. et del. Fb* ergo mediante
   OB / Sed: ergo *Pe* / *ante* sint *add. Fb* sic / sint *om. Pe*
14 proportionaliter *Gu* / illorum: istorum *PbBu* eorum *injuste Dc*
15 eque-: equa *Fb* / tres: tria *Bu* / date: dicte *VeGu* / constat *Bu*
16 numero (*?*) *GPb* uno *Pc* ymmo *Bu* / ipsis figuris *om. Pe* / quasi: quam (*?*) *S* quoque
   GPbPc / illorum: istorum *Bu* eorum *injuste Dc*
17 ipsa *om. Pe* / quoque *om. PcGu* quam *Pb* que quoque *Ve* / proportionalia: proportionales *injuste Dc*
18–19 Corollarium . . . [habetur] *om. Gu, et tacite om. Dc* (*quamquam hab. D*)
18 Corollarium: correlarium *BuVe* corell' *DGPbPe* correllario *SFb* corelario *Pc* / huius
   Pe, (*?*) *BuVe*, *om. FbPc* 13° (*?*) (*sive* 12°) *GPb* 23 (*?*) *S* / *ante* si *add. Pe* ergo circulus
   est medii (*!* medium) proportionale inter quadratum inscriptum et circum (*!* circumscriptum) / si *om. Bu*
19 quod: quid *FbPc* / *post* quod *scr. et del. D* enim (*?*) / inpossibile *SVe* / [propositum
   habetur] *addidi* ergo et cetera *Bu*

Prop. IV.16
1 16 *om. DHGFbPcPeBuVeOcGu* 56 *mg. sin. Pb* 60 *mg. sin. Es* 61ᵃ *mg. dex. S* /
   equalem *Pc*
1–2 constituere: constituunt *Bu* describere *Oc* / *mg. hab. Pc* Hic putat actor (*i.e.* auctor)
   demonstrare circuli quadraturam (*et add. mg. infer. Pc:*) tenet ergo e (*?*) iste locus a
   proportione transum^{eri} (*sive* transum^{oi}) in illa que sunt diversarum specierum sicut

Esto exemplum *A* circulus [Fig. IV.16]. Dispositio. Adiciatur et alius circulus *B*, quorum utrique circumscribatur quadratum et diameter, eritque quadratum
5   circumscriptum quasi quadratum diametri ipsius circuli; ergo secundum 2. duodecimi eadem est proportio *A*, *B* circulorum et *DE*, *FG* quadratorum; ergo permutatim eadem est *DE*, *A* et *FG*, *B*. Statuatur itaque *C* quasi tertia superficies proportionalis post *DE* et *A*. Erit autem *C* vel circulus vel aliusmodi ut rectilinea superficies. Sit primo circulus *HK* quadrato circumscripto. Itaque
10   eadem est proportio *DE*, *A* et *A*, *C*. Sed tunc secundum 2. duodecimi eadem est *DE*, *A* et *HK*, *C*; ergo tam *A* quam *HK* est medium proportionale inter *DE* et *C*. Ergo *A* circulus et *HK* quadratum sunt equalia, quod proposuimus.

circulus et quadratum non est per se necesse neque ex per se notis manifestum. Item hic est petitio principii quoniam supponit actor proportionem esse quadrati ad circulum et hoc est demonstrandum. Item cum dicit ergo eadem est proportio DE ad A et FG ad B verum est quia nulla (?) dicit adversarius et patet instantia sicut bene (? bū) est proportio quadra[ti] dyametri ad quadratum coste et cum (?) u$^{ll'n}$ (? *irrationalis* ?) est dyametri ad costam, nam sunt incomensurabiles erit (?) (*et inferius est linea excisa quam non legere possum, et supra* ver _____ (?) est hec proportio esse nota

3 *mg. hab. Pb* peccat quia non potest dari tertia (?) proportionalis post quadratum et circulum quoniam ratio quadrati ad circulum supponit (?) quae quaeruntur / Esto. . . . Dispositio: Sit circulus A *Gu* / Esto exemplum: sit *H* / exemplum: ex° *Oc* / Dispositio *om. GPbPcBu* propositus cui *H* / *post* Dispositio *add. Oc* et / *et om. H* / circulus: qui sit *H*

4 circonscribatur *GPb* (*et post hoc lectiones huiusmodi non laudabo*) / *post* et *add. H* protrahatur / quadratum²: quadratis *Bu* q̄ *Pe* (*et post hoc lectiones huiusmodi non laudabo*)

5 quasi: q *S* quarta *Pb*, *?G* quod *Bu* / quadratum *om. Oc* / dyametri *scr. Gu post* circuli *sed add. Gu signum transpositionis post* quadratum / ipsius circuli *om. H* / ipsius: illius *VeGu* ipsi *Bu* / secundum: per *Gu* / 2: primam *Pe*

6 supra duodecimi (*i.e.* 12.) *scr. Pc* Euclidis / *post* duodecimi *add. H* Euclidis / est *om. SPe* / A, B *tr. VeGu post* circulorum / A, B: ab *SBu* / circulo *SBu*

7 *post* ergo *add. H* et / permutatim *HVeOcGuDc*, *?Fb* mutatim *SGPbPcBu* / DE, A: A, DE *Oc* / DE: DE ad *HPc* / FG: GF ad *H* / B: ad B *Pc* / C: E *GPc*, *?Pb* / quasi: a *Oc*

8 de superficies *add. mg. Pc* ut loquit (?) falsigrafia / proportioni *Ve* / *de* proportionalis *mg. add. Oc* _____ (?) D quomodo (?) / post: p° *Pc* / DE: D *Bu* / A: I *Bu* / Erit autem: aut erit *Oc* / C *HFbPeBuGu* E *SGPcVe*, *?Pb* / aliusmodi: alius huiusmodi *Bu* alteriusmodi *Gu*

9 ut *om. Fb* / primus *Bu* / quadrato: quarto *Fb*

9–10 *de* Itaque . . . C *mg. scr. Pc* per ypotesim

9 *post* Itaque *add. Bu* quod

10 supra DE *scr. Pc* quadratum / A¹: ad A *HGPbPcBu* (*et supra scr. Pc* circulum) / supra A² *scr. Pc* circuli / C: ad C *HGPb* ad E *PcBu* (*et supra scr. Pc* circulum) / Sed . . . secundum: et per *H* / Sed *bis Gu et del. Gu* primum / tunc *om. Oc* cum (?) scilicet *Pb* ita *Fb* iterum (?) *Pe* / *ante* secundum *scr. et del. Gu* sunt / 2. duodecimi: 1^{am}xii (?) *Pe*

11 A¹: ad A *HGPbPcBu* / C: ad C *HGPb* ad E *PcBu* (*et supra scr. Pc* nescio) / *post* C *scr. et del. Fb* aliquid quod non legere possum) / ergo *om. Pe* / supra A² *scr. Pc* circulum / A²: H *PeBu* HA *GPb* / HK²: HB *Fb* / supra HK² *scr. Pc* quadratum / medium proportionale *tr. VeGu* / proportionaliter (?) *Oc*

12 DE: D^E *Bu* / C: E *Pc* / A *om. Fb* / proposuimus: proponitur *H* proportionalis *Fb*

Amplius sit *C* alia figura quam circulus. Ea itaque redigatur in quadratum secundum ultimam secundi, angulis signatis per *R, S, Y, X*. Itaque, cum *DE*

15 sit maior extremitas, maior est quam *RY*, ergo et latus latere maius. Resecetur ergo [de] *MD, MT* ad equalitatem *RX* et exibit *MN* parallelogrammum ex *ME, MT* descriptum. Ergo *MN* est medium proportionale inter *DE, RY*, scilicet quadrata suorum laterum cum quilibet tetragonus inter quadrata suorum laterum medio loco est proportionalis. Sed *A* circulus fuit medium

20 proportionale inter eadem. Ergo *A* circulus et *MN* parallelogrammum sunt

59r equalia. / Quadretur ergo *MN* secundum ultimam secundi, et erit eius quadratum equale *A* circulo proposito, quod proposuimus.

13 C: E (*?*) *Pc* / Ea itaque: que *H* / redigatur: reducatur *Pc*

14 *supra* secundi *scr. Pc* Euclidis / angulis . . . per: quod sit *H* / angulis signatis: angulus signatus *Pc* / angulis: anguli *GPb* angulus *?Fb* / R: K (*?*) *Oc* / Y *om. Fb* V *Oc,* (*?*)*Pe* / Itaque cum *tr. H* / Itaque: ita quod *Pb* itaque quod *Bu* / *supra* DE *scr. Pc* quadratum

15 quam: ergo maior est ergo *Fb* / RY (*?*) *Pc* (*et supra scr. Pc* quadratum) RV (*?*) *Pe* KV *Oc* / ergo: quam *Fb* / *et om. PcOc* / latus latere *tr. Fb* / maius: angius (*!*) *G* anglus (*!*) *Pb* angulus *Bu* / Resecetur *HFbOcGu, ?PeVe* Resecentur *DSGPbPc* recensentur *Bu*

16 ergo: itaque *Pe* / [de] *addidi et tacite add. Dc* quamquam *om. omnes MSS* / MD, MT: in D, in T *Oc* / MT: in T *HPe* T *Pc* / RX: RY *Bu* KX *Oc* / exhibit *S* / MN *om. Oc* / parallelogrammum: porell' *Fb*

17 MT *om. Fb* in MT *H* in NT *Gu*

17-19 *de* Ergo. . . . proportionalis *mg. scr. D* (*secundum Dc*) *et mg. Ve et mg. infer. Fb et text. Gu post* proportionalis *in lin. 19* Cuius demonstratio est: proportio DE ad RY est (*et Gu*) MD (in D *Ve*) ad RX (RY *del. Gu et add.* RX, *?Fb*) sive proportio MT (MT proportio *VeGu*) duplicata. Sed que est (*om. Ve*) proportio MD ad MT (*om. Fb*) ea est DE ad MN. Ergo proportio DE ad (*om. Fb*) RY (RX *?Ve*) est proportio DE ad CY (MN *Gu, ?Ve*) duplicata. Quare (cum *VeGu*) MN est medium (*VeGu,* media *FbDc*) proportionale (*VeGu,* proportio *FbDc*)

17 *post* MN *add. H* parallelogrammum / proportionale: proportionaliter *SPc* proportionalis *PbBu, ?G* / DE: DE et *H* / RY: RV *Pe* R *Fb* KY *G, ?Pc* et KY *Bu, ?Pb* KV *Oc* et RY *Gu*

18 *ante* scilicet *add. Pe* seu TS (*?*) / scilicet quadrata: seu TS quadrati *Oc* / scilicet *om. SHGu et Bu* / suarum *GPbBu* / laterum: lñe lat' *Fb* / *post* laterum *add. Gu* etc. (*?*)

18-19 cum . . . proportionalis *om. PeOc*

18 cum quilibet: qui omnis *GPc* qui (*sive* que) omnis *Bu* qui omnis est (*?*) *Pb* quilibet enim *VeGu* / cum *om.* S [nam] *Dc*

18-19 quilibet . . . est *om. Fb*

19 laterum *HGuDc om. DSGPbPcBuVe* / medio . . . est: sit medio *H* / est *tr. Gu ante* medio / *post* proportionalis *add. Gu var. not. in lin. 17-19* / *post* proportionalis *hab.* H ut elici potest ex prima sexti / circulus: circulo *Oc* / fuit: sint *Bu* fuerat *Pe*

20 inter eadem: inter (*?*) eas *S* / inter: in *Bu* / eadem: DE et RY *H* / A *bis Gu et del.* Gu *primum, om. Pc* / et *om. Pc* / *post* parallelogrammum *add. GPbBu* dans oppositum ducatur ad inconveniens, scilicet pars equalis toti, per 9. 5 Euclidis; istud idem probatur in antepremissa / sunt *om. GPbPcBu*

21 equalia: equales *OcGu, et add. Gu* etc. (*?*) / erit *supra scr. Pb*

22 *mg. infer. m. diff. hab. Fb* undecim lineas et primas tres non legere possum sed hic sunt reliquae _____ (*?*) quadratum circumscriptum _____ (*?*) _____ (*?*) _____ (*?*) erit (*?*) quadratum (*?*) in eadem proportione quam ipsum erit (*?*) circulo inscripto (*?*), tunc necessario illud quadratum erit equale circulo inscripto in _____ (*?*) quadrato

17. PROPOSITIS DUOBUS QUADRATIS ALTERUM ILLORUM RE-LIQUO GNOMONICE CIRCUMSCRIBERE.

Esto exemplum *AD* et *EG*. Dispositio [Fig. IV.17]. Protrahatur igitur *AB* ad equalitatem *HG*, sitque *BN* equalis *HG* linea ducta a *D* in *N*. Ratio. Age.
5 Cum *B* angulus de ratione quadrati sit rectus, quadratum *DN* secundum dulk est equale quadrato *AB* et *BN*, et ita *AD*, *EG* quadratis mediante *DN*. Cum enim *DN* sit brevior *AB* et *BN* simul iunctis, rescindatur *AN* ad equa-litatem *DN*, et *MK* perpendicularis ad illam sit ei equalis, similiter *IK*, et habebis quadratum *AK* equale duobus, ergo gnomo (*!*) residuus ab *AD* est

quod ille circulus et quadratum primum (*?*) sunt duorum terminorum proportio (*!* proportionalia) media / *post* proposuimus *add. Pc* et cetera / *post* proposuimus *add. Gu* Si autem inter duas quantitates vis venire (*del. ?*) et (*?*) invenire tertiam propor-tionalem quadra latus (*? lateris ?*) unius quantitatem. Deinde quadra latus alterius ut duo ista quadrata angulis se contingant. Postea ab angulis quadratorum produc lineas quas necesse est concurrere (*?*). Ex prima itaque 6^i Euclidis probabis istam superficiem esse inter duo quadrata medio loco proportionalem. Explicit quadratura circuli secundum magistrum Alardum in maiori comento.

Prop. IV.17

1 *supra lineam hab. Gu titulum:* Sequuntur quedam extracta a comento eiusdem [*i.e.* magistri Alardi] *cf. var. lin.* 22 *in Prop. IV.16* / 17 *om. DHGFbPcPeBuVeGu* 56 (*?*) *mg. sin. Pb* 61 *mg. sin. Es* 62^a *mg. dex. S*

1–2 reliquo: alio *Fb*

2 g̊romonice *Pc* / circumscribere *omnes alii MSS, ?G, et mg. Bu* cir- *et eras. text. Bu*

3 Esto exemplum: Sint quadrata *H* / et EG: OG *G, ?Pb* / et *om. HPcBu* / Dispositio *om. HGu*

3–5 Protrahatur . . . quadrati: et protrahatur AB ultra usque ad N ita quod BN sit equalis HG et protrahatur linea DN. Cum igitur ratione quadrati B angulus *H*

3 igitur *om.* (*?*) *Pb* itaque *Pe*

4 HG: AG *Pe* / sitque *om. GPbBu* atque *Fb* / BN: UN *Pc* VN *Bu* / equalis: *lac. Fb* / *post* HG^2 *add. Gu* et sit / a D: ad *PcBu* / D: B *Fb* / in N: MN *PcBu* / Ratio. Age: cum igitur *Gu* / Ratio *omnes alii MSS, ? mg. Pc, ?Ve, lac. text. Pc* quia (*?*) *D*

5 B angulus *tr. Gu* / sit: sint *Pe*

5–6 secundum dulk *om. Gu*

5 secundum: per *H*

6 dulk: dullk *Fb* dialk *Pc* drarum (*?*) *Ve* diametrum *injuste Dc* / est: erit *H* et *tr. H ante* quadratum *in lin.* 5 / quadrato: 2 quadratis *H* quadratis quadrato *Gu* / AB: DB *HGu* / BN: VN *Bu, ?G*

6–7 et^2 . . . . BN *om. SH*

6 EG: CE *GPbBu* CG *Pc* et EG *Gu*

7–9 Cum . . . duobus *om. Pe*

7 Cum: a *Bu* / brevior: breviori (brevior *PcBu*) per 20. primi Euclidis *GPbPcBu*

7–8 rescindatur . . . equalis: rescisa igitur AN in puncto M ad equalitatem DN et erecta MK perpendiculari et equali ad illam et *H*

7 AN *omnes MSS* AM *injuste Dc*

8 et^1 *om. GPbPcBu* / *post* illam *add. Bu* vel ad istam

9 AK *corr.* (*?*) *H et Dc ex* DEN *in Bu et* DN *in omnibus aliis MSS* / equali *Bu* / *post* duobus *add. H* quadratis GE et AD cuius pars est AD / gnomo residuus: residuus est gnomo *H* / gnomo: gnomon *Gu* gomo (*!*) *Fb* / residuis *Ve* / ab: *om. Pe* AB *Pc* / est *om. GPbBu*

9–11 ab . . . proposuimus *om. H*

10   equalis quadrato *EG*, sicque perinde est acsi *EG* gnomonice circumscriberetur ab *AD*, quod proposuimus.

18. NULLE DUE LINEE TANTUM SPACIUM AMBIUNT QUAM SI PERPENDICULARITER SE CONTINGANT.

Describatur *AE* parallelogrammum ex *AB*, *AC* ad acutum angulum se tangentibus [Fig. IV.18]. Deinde a *B* erigatur *BG* perpendicularis ad *CE*.
5 Age: *G* angulus est rectus; ergo maximus in suo triangulo; ergo *BE* est maximum latus. Protrahatur itaque *BG* desinens in *F* in equalitatem *BE* ita, secundum quod *BF* sit equalis *BE*, et secundum exigentiam *AB*, *BF* describatur *AF* parallelogrammum, *CE* protracta in occursum *AD*. Ratio. Age.

10 EG¹ *om. Gu* / perinde: parium (?) *Bu* idem *Gu* permutatim *injuste Dc* / ac- *omnes MSS* AD *injuste Dc* / EG² . . . circumscriberetur: circumscriberetur EG gnomonice *Gu* / EG² (?) *D* CG *G* / gomonice (!) *FbBu* / circumscribetur *PcBu* circumscr' *Pe*
11 ab *correxi ex* ad *in DSGu,* ?PeFbVe (*et om. GPbPcBu; injuste hab. Dc* AB) / quod proposuimus: et cetera (?) *BuPe*

Prop. IV.18
1 18 *om. DHGFbPcPeBuVeGu* 57 *mg. sin. Pb* 62 *mg. sin. Es* 63ᵃ *mg. dex. S* / Nulle (?) *G* / spacium: spatium *Bu* spatii (!) *Pe* spaciunt (!) *Fb* / quam: quantum *Gu*
2 sese *PeVe* / contingant *omnes MSS* contingunt *injuste Dc*
3–10 de Describatur. . . . ubique *mg. add. D* (*secundum Dc*) *et mg. FbVe* Ex quinta (secunda *Fb*) secundi (quinta ! *Fb*) Euclidis elicitur quod quadratum cuiuslibet linee maius est (est maius *Ve*) paralellogramo (!) rectangulo cuius duo latera rectum angulum continentia simul iuncta sunt dupla ad latus quadrati per quadratum, scilicet excessus maioris lateris rectanguli supra latus quadrati. Quod si quesierit quis (*Ve, quia Dc,* ?*Fb*) artem inveniendi inter duas quantitates (lineas quantitates *Fb*) tertiam proportionalem sic fiet. Quadra latus unius quantitatum; deinde quadra latus alterius, ut (unde *Fb*) ista (duo *Ve*) duo (ista *Ve*) quadrata (*om. Fb*) angulis se contingunt (contingant *Ve*). Postea ab angulis quadratorum produc lineas quas necesse est concurrere (?*Fb*). Ex prima itaque sexti Eulidis probabis (probatur *Fb*) istam superficiem esse inter dicta (duo *Fb*) quadrata medio loco proportionalem
3 *ante* Describatur *add. Pe* dispositio / Describantur GPbBu, ?Pc / AE: AC *G* AO *Pb* / AC: CE *GU* / ad *om. GPbBu* / acutum angulum *tr. Bu*
4 *ante* Deinde *scr. et del. Bu* a B / *ante* BG *add. Gu* perpendicularium (?) / BG: VG (*sive* BG) *GPb* OG *Bu* / ad CE: super AB ad quantitatem AC et fiat parallelogrammum AF *H* / ad: a *Bu* / CE: GE *Pe*
5 *ante* Age *add. Fb* AG / Age G: Age igitur *Ve* igitur *Gu* / angulus est: angulus an est angulus est *Fb* / est¹: e *GPb* / BE: LC (*sive* BC) *GPb* BC *Bu,* ?*Fb* / est²: etiam *Pc*
6–10 Protrahatur. . . . ubique: Igitur BF sibi equale longius est quam BG. Cum igitur BH et AE parallelogramma sunt super eandem basim inter lineas equedistantes, erunt equalia. Igitur quanto AF maius est quam AG tanto maius est quam AE et sic utrobique *H*
6 itaque *om. Fb* / BG: VG *Bu* / in²: ad *PeGu*
6–7 ita . . . BE *om. Pe* / ita secundum: recta (?) scilicet ita *Gu*
6 ita: recta *Ve*
7 secundum: scilicet *S* / BF¹: VF *GPb* OF *Bu* / sit equalis *tr. GPbBu* / BE: BC (?) *Fb* ḄEI *GPbBu* / exigentia (?) *D* / AB: AD *Gu* ad (*sive* AD) *Ve* / BF² *bis Pb* et BF *Pc*
8 AF *om. S* DF *Gu* / occursum: *lac. S* recursum *GPbBu* concursum *Pc* / AD: ADE *Bu* DA *Gu* / Ratio. Age: Tunc sic *Gu* / Ratio *om. Fb*
8–9 Age. Cum: a G *in Bu*

Cum *AG, AE* parallelogramma sint ab eadem basi, ipsa sunt equalia. Ergo
10   *AF* quanto maius est quam *AG* tanto quam *AE*; sic generaliter accidit ubique.

19. QUORUMCUMQUE TRIANGULORUM LATERA DUO SUNT
EQUALIA DUOBUS SESE RESPICIENTIA CUIUS LATERA CONTI-
NENT ANGULUM RECTUM ILLE EST MAXIMUS OMNIUM TRIAN-
GULORUM.

5   Esto exemplum. Sint *AB* et *AC* duo latera continentia angulum rectum
[Fig. IV.19], et ab *A* angulo protrahatur *AE* linea ad equalitatem *AB*, et ab
A angulo exterius protrahatur *HA* linea ad equalitatem *AB*, et postea a *B*
ducatur linea *CB* subtensa *A* angulo recto, et postea a *B* ducatur linea ad
terminum *AE*, scilicet ad *E*, et *AB* et *AE* latera sunt equalia; ergo anguli
10   supra basim, que est *BE*, sunt equales; ergo uterque minor est recto; ergo *B*
est minor recto. A *B* igitur ducatur linea equedistans *AC*, et de necessitate
cadet extra *E*, eo quod *CAB* angulus est rectus, et *B* angulus supra basim,
ut prius dictum est, minor recto; unde *B* totalis est rectus, et ita illa linea
equedistans cadet extra *BE*; transeat igitur per *F*. Et protrahatur *AE* latus

9 Cum: in *G* / AE: et AE *Gu* / post AE *scr. et del. Fb* A / paralellogramum (*!*) *supra
   scr. Gu* / sint: sunt *S* / ab . . . basi: super eandem basim *Gu* (*et supra scr. Gu* AB)
   / eodem *FbPc*
10 *ante* AF *supra scr. Gu* paralellogramum (*!*) / maius: magis *Bu* / *supra* AG *scr. Gu
   aliquid quod non legere possum* / tanto: et *Pe* / *post* tanto *add. Gu* maius est / AE:
   AE quam AE *Pc* / sic: et sic *VeGu* / accidit *om. Pe* / *post* ubique *add. Gu* et sic
   probatur propositum

Prop. IV.19
   1 19 *om. DHGFbPcBuVe* 58 *mg. sin. Pb* 63 *mg. sin. Es* 64ª *mg. dex. S*
   2 respicientibus *H*
   5 Esto exemplum *om. H* / Sint *om. Pc* / et *om. H*
   7 exterius: extremis *Pc* / HA: AH *HVeDc* / linea: etiam *H* / equaliter *Ve*
   7–8 postea . . . CB: protrahatur CB basis *H*
   7 a: ab *Fb* / B: A *Bu*
   8 linea¹ *om. Fb* / CB: ad CB *Bu* / sustensa *Fb*
   8–11 postea . . . est: protrahatur CH, CE, et BE; cum igitur _____ (*?*) AB et AE latera
      sunt equalia, erunt anguli supra basim equales; quare uterque erit *H*
   8 a: ab *Fb*
   8–9 ad . . . AE¹: AC *Fb*
   9 ad E: AC *Bu* / et¹: postea ducatur *Ve*
   10 supra: super *Bu* / minor est *tr. Pc* / est² *supra scr. Bu*
   11 est minor *tr. Ve* / B: BE *Ve* / equedistans: equidem *Pc*
   12 *post* extra *scr. et del. Pc* BE transeat igitur per F et protrahatur / CAB (*?*) *Fb* / est
      omnes MSS, om. Dc
   12–13 B . . . est¹: ABE angulus *H*
   12 supra: super *Bu*
   13 minor *om. GPbBu* / B: V *Bu* / totalis . . . illa: est minimus in ista *Bu* / totalis *om.
      GPb* / rectus: mi's (*!*) *GPb*
   13–17 et. . . . equales: transiat igitur BF quousque concurrat cum AE ulterius protracta
      usque ad F et ducatur linea CF. Age igitur ABC et AFC trianguli sunt equales quia
      super eandem basim inter lineas equedistantes *H*
   13 et ita: in *GPb* / post linea *scr. et del. Ve* est
   14 equedistans: equidem *Pc* / transiat *GPbVe et cf. var. H in lin. 13–17*

15   ad *F* et a contactu cum *F* ducatur linea ad *C*, scilicet *FC*, et alia ab *E* angulo
ad *C*. Respice igitur *ABC* triangulum et *AFC*, qui sunt super eandem basim
inter lineas equedistantes; ergo sunt equales. Sed *AEC* triangulus, cuius angulus
A partialis scilicet est acutus, est minor *AFC*, quia est pars eius, ergo est
minor *ABC*, et ita minor est triangulus cuius latera continent angulum acutum
20   quam ille cuius latera continent angulum rectum. Item de obtuso. Similiter
a *B* ad *H* ducatur *BH* linea; habebis, ut prius, quod anguli supra *BH* basim
sunt equales, quia *AB* et *AH* sunt equalia, et ita uterque illorum angulorum
est minor recto. A *B* ergo ducatur equedistans *AC*, ut prius, et cadet extra
H eadem ratione ut prius; transeat igitur per *G*. Postea protrahatur *AH* usque
25   *G* in continuum et directum, et postea ducatur linea a *G* ad *C* et alia ab *H*
ad *C*. Erunt itaque *AGC* et *ABC* eiusdem altitudinis sive inter lineas equedistantes super eandem basim, et ita sunt equales. Sed *AHC* est pars *AGC*,
et ita minor, et ita etiam minor *ABC*. Si autem *AE* latus caderet intra *CH*,

15 cum F: OF *Bu* / cum (?) *Ve* / F^2 *om. S* / FC (?) *Pb* / E *om. Bu*
16 *post* igitur *add. Fb* ex (?)
16–17 ABC. . . . Sed *om. GPbPcBu*
17 inter: ut *S*
18 A partialis scilicet: ad A *H* / A: AB *DSFbVe* / est minor *tr. Pc* / AFC: AF *Bu* AFE
Ve / quia est: cum sit *H*
19 *post* minor^1 *add. H* quam / *post* ABC *add. Pc* per 37. primi
19–20 et . . . rectum: quod est alterum propositum, videlicet de angulo acuto *H* / acutum
. . . angulum *om. Ve*
19 et ita *bis S* / ita *om. Pb* (*sed non G*) / *ante* triangulus *scr. et del. Pb* aliquid quod
non legere possum
20 quam ille: illo *Pc* / cuius *om. GPbBu* / obtuso *HGPbPc* optuso *DSFbBuVe*
20–23 Similiter . . . recto: cum enim AB et AH sint equales, erunt anguli supra basim
equales, quare et uterque acutus *H*
21 a B ad H: AB et AH *S* / *ante* habebis *hab. SFbVe* et
22 sunt^1: sint *GPbBu* / illorum: i^{orum} *G* istorum *PbBu*
23 ut *bis Bu* / et *om. PbFb*
24 eadem . . . prius *om. H* / transiat *H* / per: usque ad *H* / G: 8^{am} *G*, ?*PbBu*
24–27 Postea. . . . equales: cui concurrat AH ulterius protracta et protrahatur linea GC;
sunt igitur ACG et ABC trianguli equales quia super eandem basim inter lineas
equedistantes *H*
24 AH: AB *Bu*
25 et directum *bis Fb* / directum et: rectum *GPbBu* / postea: tunc *Pc* / ab: ad *GPbBu*
26–27 ad. . . . basim *om. Pc*
26 AGC: AGE *Ve* / eiusdem: eius *Ve* eiusdidem (!) *GBu* / sive: sit *Pb* (*sed non G*) sive
(*sive* sine) *Bu* cum *injuste Dc*
27 super: sunt *S* et super *Ve* / AHC: ABC *PbBu*, ?*G* / AGC: AG *Fb*
28 ita^1: per consequens *H* / *post* ita^1 *scr. et del. G* i / minor^1: minor eo *H* / et . . .
minor^2: igitur est minor quam *H* / etiam: erit *injuste Dc*
28–31 Si . . . minor *om. H*
28 autem: ernt (!) *Bu* / latus: locus *Ve* / caderet *DSGPbVe*, ?*Fb* cadens *Pc* cadunt *Bu*
cadet *injuste Dc* / *post* intra *supra scr. Bu* et (?) / CH: CB (*sive* CH) *G* CB *PbBuVe*,
?*Pc*

quod est impossibile, scilicet quod sic cadat, tunc non oportet nisi ab eius
30 termino lineam ducere ad *E*, et erit tunc triangulus pars alterius, et ita manifeste minor. Et sic patet propositum.

20. QUEMLIBET ANGULUM RECTILINEUM IN TRIA EQUA DI-
VIDERE.

Sit angulus *ABG* acutus in tria dividendus [Fig. IV.20a]. Super *B* sumpto
centro describatur circulus *DZM*, et protrahatur *DB* in *L*, erigaturque *BZ*
5 perpendicularis ad *DL*, protrahamque lineam *ZE* in *H* et [non] ponam linee
ZH finem determinatam, et resecabo de *ZH*, *ZQ* equalem *DB* semidiametro.
Ymaginemur igitur quod linea *ZEH* moveatur versus *L* ita quod *Z* motu
suo non recedat a circumferentia, et linea *ZH* non cesset transire super *E*
sed semper inhereat puncto *E*, et non cesset *Z* moveri quousque *Q* sit super
10 *BZ*, sitque terminus illius motus *T*. Erit ergo et quasi pars linee *ZH*, vel, ut
aliter dicam, *ZH* iacebit super *TE*. Eritque *TS* equalis *ZQ* sive *BD* semidiametro. Dico autem *TL* esse tertiam arcus *DE*. Protrahamus a puncto *B*,
59v *BM* equedistantem *TE* linee et protraham / *BM* in *K*, et coniungantur puncta

29 inpossibile *DSGPbBuVe* / sic: si *Pb* / cadat *SPbPcVe*, ?*Fb* cadet *GBuDc* / tunc: mne
(!) mne (!) *S* nine (?) tunc *G* nive (?) tunc *Pb* mne (?) tunc *Pc* nme (?) tunc *Bu* /
oportet: oportet non oportet *G* / ab eius: a eiusdem *Bu*: ab: a *SGPbPcFb*

30 termino *corr. Dc et forte Ve ex* tertio (*sive* tercio) *in aliis MSS* / ducere: duce *S*
ducere duce *Pb* / ad E: ADC *Pc* / E (?) *Pb* C *SGVe* C (*sive* T) *Bu* / alterius: alius
GPbBu

31 *post* propositum *add. H* de obtuso

Prop. IV.20

1 20 *om. DHGFbPcBuVe* 59 *mg. sin. Pb* 64 *mg. sin. Es* 65ª *mg. dex. S* / rectilineum:
rectilinium *Bu* rectum *Pc*

3 angulus: triangulus *GPbBu*

4 circulus *om. Fb* / *post* DZM *add. H* et / *post* protrahatur *add. Ve* -que

5 ad DL: super BL *H* / DL: DI *Bu* / protrahamque: protrahaturque *GPb Bu* / *post*
protrahamque *add. S* et (*sive* z) / lineam *alii MSS et forte ex corr. Bu* / [non] *juste
add. Dc; cf. Vol. 1, p. 346, lin. 9*

6 determinatum *GPbBu* / equalem: elenūlaem (!) *Bu*

7 Imaginemur *DSFb* / ZEH: ZEB *Bu* / L HFbVe (*et cf. Vol. 1, p. 346, lin. 12*) A
SGPbPcBuDc (*et post* A *scr. et del. S* circi ?)

8 ZH: ZA *S* / *post* E *add. H* quiescens

9 et non: neque *H*

10 BZ: VZ *Bu* / sitque: siṇtque *Pc* sintque *GPb*, ?*Bu* / terminus: tres *GPb*, ?*SFbBu* Z
Pc / illius motus *tr. Ve* / illius *scr. et del. Pc* / motus: medius (?) *G* medio (*sive*
medius) *Pb* / *post* motus *add. Pc* in

10–11 Erit . . . super: ita quod terminus iaceat ZH quasi super lineam *H*

10 et: ET (?) *Pc* / quasi: q *GPb*

11 *mg. hab. Ve* huius demonstrationem concludere (?), et patet ratio in angulo recto
quia tres medietates semidiametri dividunt angulum in tres partes equales ――――
(?) et hec (?) erit medietas semidiametri et hec (?) est tertia anguli dati / Eritque TS:
erit ęTS *Fb* / BD: LD *GPbBu*

12 autem: igitur *H* / TL: TB (?) *Bu* / *post* tertiam *add. H* partem

13 TE linee *tr. GPbBu* / BM²: MB *H* / *ante* in *scr. et del. Pc* et / *post* et² *scr. et del. G*
conti / puncta: puncti *GPbFb* ?*Bu* puncti (*sive* puncta) *Ve*

T, *M*. Age: *TS* equalis est *MB* et equedistans. Ergo *MT*, *BS* sunt equales et
15 equedistantes; et *BZ* est perpendicularis ad *DL*; ergo *MT* secat *DL* ad angulos
rectos; ergo *DL* secat *MT* cordam in duo equa; ergo *ML*, *LT* arcus sunt
equales. Item *ML*, *DK* arcus sunt equales, quia *MK*, *DL* sese intersecantes
in centro *B* faciunt angulos adinvicem equales. Ergo a duplici pari *KE* arcus
ad *DK* est duplus. Ergo angulus *KBE* ad *KBD* est duplus. Diviso ergo *KBE*
20 in duo equa erit angulus propositus *ABG* in tria equalia divisus. Si vero
proponatur angulus maior acuto in tria equalia dividendus, dividatur primo
ille in duas medietates, quarum utraque pars erit angulus acutus. Deinde
dividatur utraque illarum medietatum in tria equa secundum dictum modum.
Constat ergo propositum.
25 Paululum quoque apertius idem probabitur hoc solo variato, quod pro
HZ protrahatur *LEN* [Fig. IV.20b]. Et cum *LBZ* sit rectus, sit *OL* equalis
BL linee. Ymaginemur ergo *NL* sic moveri versus *Z* et *LN* semper pertranseat
super *E*, moveatur *NL* quousque *O* sit in *BZ*, [et] cetera ut prius.
De divisione anguli in tres partes equales michi nequaquam sufficit dicta

14 Age: cum igitur *H* AG *FbBu* Argue *injuste Dc* / equalis est *tr. GPbBuFb* / equedistans:
equidem *Pc* (*et post hoc lectiones huiusmodi non laudabo*) / *mg. hab. Ve* quia sunt
inter equedistantes que sunt sibi equales invicem (?) et ad equalium equedistantium
terminos compl'emus (?)
14–15 BS . . . MT *om. SH*
14 BS: bis *GPbBu* / *post* sunt *add. GPbBu* per 33. primi
15 et: etiam (?) *Bu* / BZ: VZ *Bu* / *supra* ad DL *scr. Ve* puncta (?) / ergo *om. GPbBu* /
secat: faciat *Bu* / *post* DL² *add. GPbBu* per 39. primi / ad² *om. S*
16 *post* rectos *add. H* propter hoc quod BZ ita facit / *post* rectos *add. Pc* per 29. primi
/ secat: seccat *Bu* / *ante* cordam *add. Fb* in / cordam *om. H* / equa: equalia *HPb*
(*sed non G*) / *post* equa *add. Pc* per tertiam tertii et 4. primi et 27. tertii / ergo²:
quare et *H* / *post* ergo² *add. GPbBu* per 3. tertii et 9. primi et 27. (*Bu*, 27. *sive* 37.
GPb) tertii (*om. Bu*) / LT: BT *GPb*, ?*Bu*
17 Item: Sed et *H* / DK: AK *Fb* / quia: eo quod *H*
18 centro: puncto *H* / dupplici *GPb* / KE: KC (*sive* KE) *GPbBu* RC (*sive* KE) *Ve*
19 DK: LDK (?) *Fb* / KBE¹: KB *Fb* / ad² . . . duplus²: duplus ad angulum *H* / KBD:
DBK *H* KLD (*sive* KBD) *GPb* KID *Bu* / *ante* Diviso *scr. et del. G* ergo angulus
20 equa: equalia *Pc*
21 ponatur *H* / equalia: qualia (?) *D*
22 ille *om. Pc* iᵉ *G* iste *Pb* / Deinde: Etenim *S* et tunc *H*
23 utraque: i.tᵃ que *Bu* / illarum: istarum *PbBu* iᵃʳᵘᵐ *G*
25 quoque: quidem *Pc* ergo *Bu* / idem: hoc *Pc* / probabitur *DSFbPcBuVe*, ?*H* probatur
Dc, ?*GPb* / hoc: hic *Bu* / solo: solum *H* sol (*sive* solus) *S* / pro *om. Pb* (*sed non G*)
per *HBu*
26 protrahatur: variatur *PbPcBu* / LEN: LON (?) *H* / LBZ: IBZ *Bu* / OL: OI *Pc* enim
GPbBu
27 line (!) *Fb* / Imaginemur *DS* Imaginemus *Fb* / NL: L (?) *D* / sic: sicut *Pc* / moveri
(?) *Bu* / et *omnes alii MSS* quod *H* ut *Dc* / *post* LN *scr. et del. Fb* et cum LBZ sit
rectus et / pertranseat: transiat *H* pertranseant *Bu*
28 moveatur *omnes alii MSS* et moveatur *H* noveatur (!) *Bu* moveaturque *Dc* / NL:
vel (?) *GPb* / O: E *Fb* / [et] *add. HDc sed om. omnes alii MSS* / ut: sicud *H*
29–31 De. . . . demonstro *om. Pc*
29 divisione anguli: dīo trianguli *GPbBu* / dictam *G*

30 demonstratio, eo quod nichil in ea certum reperio. Ut autem michi me sufficientem faciam, hoc idem sic demonstro. Datus angulus acutus sit *ABG* [Fig. IV.20c]. Igitur in *B* posito pede circini describatur circulus, et protrahatur *AB* ad *L* in periferia, et a centro super *DL* extrahatur perpendicularis *BZ*, et a puncto *E* per *BZ* semidiametrum ducatur linea per figuram 19. quinti

35 perspective ut *TS* sit equalis semidiametro *BL*. Ducatur ergo *BM* equedistanter linee *TSE*, et protrahatur ad *K*. Quia ergo *BM*, *TS* sunt equales et equedistantes, erunt *BS* et *MT* equales et equedistantes. Ergo, cum angulus *LBZ* sit rectus, erit *BFT* rectus. Ergo *MT* secatur per lineam *BF* per equalia. Ergo arcus *TM* est duplus ad arcum *ML*. Sed arcus *MT* est equalis arcui

40 *KE* propter equedistantes. Ergo arcus *KE* est duplus ad arcum *ML*, ergo et ad arcum *DK*. Dividatur ergo *KE* per equalia, et habetur propositum. Si fuerit angulus maior acuto, dividatur in duos acutos et utriusque sumatur pars tertia, et habetur propositum.

21. IN OMNI TRIANGULO NOTO EST PUNCTUM INVENIRE, QUO CONTINUATO CUM ANGULIS TRIANGULI DIVIDETUR TRIAN-GULUS PER TRES PROPORTIONES NOTAS.

30–31 eo. . . . demonstro *om. GPbBu*
   30 eo: ita *S* / in ea: ma (*?*) *D*
   31 Datus angulus *bis Pb* / Datus: datis *GBu* / acutus: actus (*?*) *Fb*
   32 Igitur . . . describatur: posito igitur centro in B circumscribatur *H* / Igitur *om. GPbBu* / circini *DPcVe* circum- (*?*) *SGPbFbBu*
   33 a *HGPbPcBuVe, om. DSFb* e *Dc* / DL: DI *Bu*
   34 ducatur *bis Fb* / *post* figuram *add. GPbBu* per / 19 (*?*) *S*
   35 TS sit: ST est *scr. et del. H et tunc supra scr. H* sit TS / TS: IS *Pc* / *ante* sit equalis *scr. et del. Ve* sit equalis / *supra* BL *scr. Ve* per primam (*?*) / *mg. hic hab. Ve pluria nota quae non bene legere possum et ideo ista omitto*
35–43 Ducatur. . . . propositum *om. H sed scr. et continua* (*?*) *sicud prius*
   35 BM: B *Bu* / equedistanter: equedistantem *Fb* equedistans *injuste Dc*
   36 Quia: Quare *Ve* / BM: VM (*sive* BM) *GPb* VM *Bu* B (*?*) *Fb*
   37 erunt . . . equedistantes *om. Ve*
37–38 equales . . . MT *om. Fb*
   37 equales et *non legere possum in Pb*
   38 *post* rectus *add. Pc* per 29. primi Euclidis / *post* BFT *add. GPbBu* per 29. primi Euclidis / *post* BF *add. Pc* per tertiam tertii Euclidis
   39 TM: MT *Fb* / *post* arcum *add. Fb* ad / *post* ML *add. Pc* per 27. tertii Euclidis
39–40 Sed. . . . ML *om. Ve*
   40 *post* KE² *add. S* per equalia / ML (*?*) *Fb*
   41 ad *om. GPbBu* / et *juste add. Pc et Dc sed om. DSGPbFbBuVe*
41–43 Si . . . propositum *om. Bu*
   42 acuto: a centro *S* / sumantur *Fb*
Prop. IV.21
   1 21 *om. DHGFbPcBuVeGu* 6[0] (*?*) *mg. sin. Pb* 65 *mg. sin. Es* 66ª *mg. dex. S* / noto: nato *GPb* dato noto *Bu* (*et del. Bu* noto)
   2 cum: com *Fb* / angulus *Bu* / trianguli *om. Fb*
   3 per: in *Fb* / proportiones *Ger.* (*cf. Append. III.B) Dc* (*et vide var. lin. 4 inferius*) portiones *omnes alii MSS* partes (*?*) *Bu*

Sit triangulus *ABG* [Fig. IV.21]; ponam ergo proportionem notam in linea
5 *AG*, et dividam eam per ipsam in punctis *D* et *E*. Sit ergo *DZ* equedistans
GB, et fiat *EH* equedistans *AB*, secentque se in puncto *T*. Dico *T* esse punctum
quem querimus. Continuentur enim *E* et *D* cum *B*, et *T* cum *A* et *G* [et *B*];
cum igitur duo trianguli *BTG* [et *DBG* erunt equales, proportio trianguli
BTG] ad totum triangulum *AGB* est sicut *DG* ad *AG*. Ostenditur ergo quod
10 proportio trianguli *ATB* ad *ABG* est sicut *AE* ad *AG*, quia trianguli *ATB*,
AEB sunt equales—sunt enim super basim *AB* et inter lineas equedistantes
AB et *EH*—; ergo residuus triangulus, scilicet *ATG*, est ad totum triangulum
ABG sicut residua *DE* ad *AG* lineam, et hoc est quod voluimus.

22. INTER DUAS QUANTITATES PROPOSITAS DUAS ALIAS IN-
VENIRE UT CONTINUENTUR QUATUOR QUANTITATES SECUN-
DUM PROPORTIONEM UNAM.

Sint due linee: *M* longior, *N* brevior [cf. Fig. IV.22a]. Fiat circulus *ABG*,
5 cuius diameter *AB* sit equalis quantitati *M*, fiatque corda *AG* equalis *N*,

4 proportionem: portionem *FbGu*
5 et[1]: e *Fb* / per ipsam *om. Gu* / D: DE *Fb* / et[2]: z *scr. et del. Pc, et supra scr. Pc* et
6 et *bis Pb* / fiet *Bu* / secetque *Bu* / se *om. Fb* seị *S* se invicem *H* / *ante* esse *scr. et del. Fb* ante
7 queris *GPbPcBu* / *post* enim *add. Fb* in puncto / E: C *G*
7-8 et[2] . . . igitur: G *DSFbPc* / et[2] . . . cum *om. VeGu* / cum[2] . . . igitur: BG *GPb* LG *Bu*
7 [et B] *hab. H sed om. alii MSS*
8 duo *om. H* / trianguli BTG: triangulus DGB sicut *H*
8-9 [et . . . BTG] *add. Dc* quia est equalis GBD per 38. primi *Pc* et BTA sunt *Gu*
9 AGB est: GAB *H* / AGB: AVG *Bu* / est *om. Gu* sunt *Ve* / *supra* sicut . . . AG *scr. Pc* per primam 6[ti] / DG: GD linea *H* / *post* DG *supra scr. Gu* et AC / AG: GA lineam *H, et mg. add. H* per primam 6[i]
9-12 Ostenditur . . . EH: est triangulus GTB qui est equalis GDB per 37. primi ad totum triangulum sicut GD ad GA. Item per easdem triangulus AEB, et per consequens triangulus ATB sibi equalis, est ad totum triangulum sicud AE ad AG *H*
9 ostendetur *Gu*
9-10 ergo . . . trianguli[1] *om. S*
10 ATB[1]: ACB (?) *S* / ATB[2] *bis Gu et del. Gu primum*
11 sunt enim: quia sunt *GPbPcBu* / enim *om. Fb*
12 AB: AG *SFb* ABZ (?) *G* AZ (?) *Pb* ATZ (?) *Bu* / et *om. VeGu* / *post* EH *add. mg. infer. Gu* Similiter ergo proportio trianguli BTG ad ABG est sicut DG ad AG quia trianguli BTG et DBG sunt equales, sunt enim super basim BG et inter lineas equi-distantes BG, DZ (*nota quod ista additio est similis additioni in Dc, var. lin. 8-9*) / scilicet *om. Fb*
13 ABG *om. H* / residua *om. H* residuum *Gu* / lineam *om. H* / quod voluimus: propositum *Pc*

Prop. IV.22
1 22 *om. DHGFbPcBuVeR* 61 *mg. sin. Pb* 66 *mg. sin. Es* 67[a] *mg. dex. S* / Inter: In *G* / alias: lineas SH / *mg. hic scr. H* nescio istam conclusionem iuxta primum modum probare, nec probationem primam intelligere
2 quatuor: ii (?) *Bu*
4-42 Sint. . . . unam *om. R*
5 fiatque: sintque *GPbBu* / AG: DG *GPbPcBu* / N: Q *GPbBu*

erigaturque *BZ* perpendicularis ad *AB*, producaturque *AG* ad concursum *BZ*, et erigam super arcum *AGB* superficiem medietatis columpne ita ut sint linee que protrahuntur in ea secundum rectitudinem ad arcum *AGB* perpendiculares super superficiem circuli *ABGD*, et revolvam quod describam
10 super lineam *AB* semicirculum cuius superficies sit erecta semper super superficiem circuli *ABDG* ad angulos rectos, et sit arcus *AHE*, et figatur punctum *A* arcus *AHE* in loco sicut centrum, et revolvatur arcus *AHE* super punctum *A*, et sit superficies eius in revolutione sua semper stans ad angulos rectos super superficiem circuli *ABDG*, ut arcus *AHE* secet superficiem medietatis
15 columpne erectam super arcum *AGB*. Et figatur linea *AB* sicut meguar et revolvatur triangulus *AZB* super meguar *AB* donec occurrat linea *AZ* sectioni superficiei medietatis columpne, et designat punctum *G*. Tunc linea *AZ* in
60 r revolutione sua describet medietatem / circuli *GQD* erectam ad angulos rectos supra superficiem circuli *ABGD*; et signabo super locum in quo occurrit
20 linea *AZ* sectioni superficiei medietatis columpne punctum *H*, et figatur arcus *AHE* ex revolutione sua apud punctum *H*, et protraham duas lineas *AH*, *AE*, et signabo ubi occurret linea *AH* arcu *GQD* punctum *L*, et protraham ex puncto *L* perpendicularem super superficiem circuli *ABGD* que sit *LK*;

6 *ante* BZ *scr. et del.* (?) *G* eri (?) / BZ: videlicet (?) *Bu* / producaturque: -que *supra scr. Fb* producatur quia *Bu*
7 AGB: AGD *Pc*
8 line (!) *Fb*
9 ABGD D (*secundum Dc*) *et cf. Banū Mūsā* (vol. 1, p. 336, lin. 22) AD.DG *HGPbPcBu*, ?*S, et ex corr. Fb* ADBG *Ve* / et *om. GPbBu* / quod: vel *Ve*
10 *ante* lineam *scr. et del.* (?) *Fb* superficiem / AB: AD *SH* / erecta: recta *Fb* / semper *om. HVe*
11 ABDG *omnes MSS* ABGD *Dc* (*et cf. Banū Mūsā, ibid., lin. 24*) / sit *HBuDc* sint *DSGPcVe*, ?*FbPb* / archus *Bu* / figatur: figuratur *S* figura *Bu*
12 sicut *bis Ve et del. Ve primum* / centrum: cenim (?) *Pc* / puncta *GPbPcBu*
13 *post* A *scr. et del. S* arcus
13–14 sua . . . secet *om. Bu*
13 rectos *om. Fb*
14 super *om. GPb*
14–15 ut . . . AGB *om. SH* / medietatis columpne *tr. Fb*
15 *ante* erectam *add. Fb* et designat / erecta *Bu* / AGB: ABG *Fb* AGL (*sive* AGB) *Bu* / figatur: erigatur *Fb* / mēguar *Fb*
16 AZB: AB D (*secundum Dc*) AZV (*sive* AZB) *G* AZV *PbBu* AXB *Pc* AZR *Ve* / mēguar *Fb* / donec: super donec *SGPbFbBu* semper donec *H* / linee *Pc* / sectioni: super sectionem *H*
16–17 sectioni. . . . AZ *om. Fb*
17 designat punctum: designato puncto *H* / designat *SGPbPcBuVe* designet *Dc* / *post* Tunc *hab.* D (*secundum Dc*) ex *sed om. omnes alii MSS*
18 describet *juste add. Ve sed om. omnes alii MSS* / erectam: erectum *SPbPcBu* erectum (*sive* erectam) *G* erecti *injuste Dc* / ad: a' *Pc*
19 supra: super *Dc* / signato *GPb*, ?*Bu* / locus *Fb* / occurrit: occidit *Pc*
20 AZ *corr. Dc ex* ad Z (*sive* ADZ) in *DSHFbPcVe* et Z in *GPbBu* (*cf. Banū Mūsā, ibid., p. 338, lin. 34*) / sectionem *H* / superficies *GPbPcBu* / *post* columpne *add. Bu* et designat / figatur: signatur *Bu*, ?*G* figuratur *Pb* / arcus *om. Bu*
22 AE: AC *GPbBu* / occurrit *omnes alii MSS* occidit *Pc* occurret *Dc* / AH *correxi ex* AB *in MSS* (*et cf. Banū Mūsā ibid., lin. 36*)
23 ex: extra (?) *S* / ABGD: ABG *Fb*

propter quod est sectio communis superficiei semicirculi *AHE* et superficiei
25 semicirculi *GQD*, et unaqueque earum dictarum superficierum est pererecta
super superficiem circuli *ABGD* ad angulos rectos. Ergo linea *LK* est perpendicularis. Et protraham lineam *LT*. Palam ergo, quia erigatur super lineam
AL ad angulos rectos, propter quod linee multiplicatio *GK* in lineam *KD*
equalis est ei quod fit ex linea *LK* in se sive suum equale. Verum id quod
30 fit ex *GK* in *KD* equum est ei quod fit ex *TK* in *KA*. Ergo quod fit ex *TK*
in *KA* est equum ei quod fit ex *LK* in se sive suum equale. Ergo angulus
ALT est rectus. Et iam ostensum est quod angulus *AHE* trianguli *AHE* est
rectus quoniam ipse cadit in medietatem [circuli] *AHE*, et quod angulus
ATH est rectus quoniam *HT* est perpendicularis super superficiem circuli
35 *ABDG*, et est una linearum que protrahuntur in medietate superficiei columpne secundum rectitudinem ad arcum *AGB* in superficie circuli *ABGD*.
Sed linea *AT* est in superficie circuli *ABGD*. Ergo angulus *ATH* est rectus.
Ergo in unoquoque triangulorum *AHE*, [*ATH*,] *ALT*, *AKL* est angulus rectus,
et angulus *HAE* communis est omnibus. Ergo sunt trianguli similes. Ergo
40 proportio linee *EA* ad *AH* est sicut linea *AH* ad *AT*, et sicut linea *AT* ad *AL*.
Sic, si linea *AE* est equalis *M* et linea *AL* est equalis *N*, ergo inter *M* et *N*
sunt *AH* et *AT*, et continuantur secundam proportionem unam.

24 est: eius *Bu* / sectio . . . semicirculi *juste corr. Dc ex* sectionis semicirculi superficiei
in *MSS* / superficiei[1] *om. Ve*

25 GQD *bis Pb* GQS *Fb* / unaqueque *forte sic in omnibus MSS* (*cf. Banū Mūsā, Vol.
1, p. 338, lin. 40*) utraque *Dc* / dictarum *om. GPbBu* duarum *Dc* / est: etiam *Ve* /
pererecta: recta *Fb*

26 *ante* ad *scr. et del. S* que sit LK / *post* rectos *scr. et del. Fb* propter quod multiplicatio
GB in linea / *post* Ergo *scr. et del. Fb* multiplicatio

27 LT: BT (?) *H* / Palam: param *H* / quia *om. GPbBu* / erigitur *Ve*

28 quod *om. GPbBu* / linee multiplicatio *tr. H* / GK: GL *Fb* / in: que *GPb* / lineam:
linea *D*, ?*GPb* / KD: GK *Bu*

29 in se: et (*sive* ec) *Bu* / sive: sive in *H* / id: illud *GPb*

30 fit[1] *om. Pc* sit (?) *GPb* / equum: equm *DFb*

30–31 Ergo . . . KA *om. Fb*

30 TK[2]: TH (?) *Bu*

31 in se sive: i. e. ī sive (?) *Bu* / sive: sive in *H*

33 cadet *Fb* / [circuli] *add. Dc* / AHE: ḤAHE *Fb*

35 ABDG: ABGD *Bu* / protrahantur *Bu* / medietatem *Ve*

35–36 columpne: çǫn columpno *G*

36 superficiem *Fb* / ABGD: ABDG *GPbFbBu*

37 Sed: g (*i.e.* igitur?) *Bu* / AT: AC (?) *GPb*

38 Ergo: cum *Fb* / unoquoque: uno quorum (?) *Pb* / triangulorum *juste corr. Dc ex*
angulorum *in MSS* (*cf. Banū Mūsā, ibid., p. 338, lin. 55*) / ALT: ATH *Ve et addidi*
[ATH] (*cf. Banū Mūsā, ibid., lin. 56*) / AKL *om. Fb* AKR *Bu*

39 HAE *Ve* AHE *in aliis MSS* (*cf. Banū Mūsā, ibid., lin. 56*) / sunt: sicut *GPcBu*, ?*Pb*

40 proportio *HGPbBuVe* (*cf. Banū Mūsā, ibid., lin. 57*) proportione *DSFbPc* / EA *Ve*
(*et cf. Banū Mūsā, ibid., lin. 57*) E *et lac. DFb* E *SHGPbPc* AD *Bu* AK *Dc* / AH[1]:
HAH *Fb* / AH[2]: AEH *GPbBu* / AT[1] *VeDc* (*cf. Banū Mūsā, ibid., lin. 58*) ALT
DSFbPcBu, ?*H* AHT (?) *GPb* / et *HVeDc* (*cf. Banū Mūsā ibid., lin. 58*) *om.*
DSGPbPcFbBu / AT[2]: AC *GPb* ALT *Fb* / AL: *VeDc* (*cf. Banū Mūsā, ibid., lin. 57*)
ALS *DSGPbPcFb*, ?*H* ALT *Bu*

41 Sic si *DSFbPc sed H* / Sic: Sed sic *Ve* Sed *Banū Mūsā* (*ibid.*) sit *GPbBu* / AL: AB
GPbBu / est[2] *om. Bu* / inter: sunt (?) *Bu*

42 et[2] *om. GPbPcBu* / proportio *G*

Aliter ad idem. Sint due linee *AB, BG* [Fig. IV.22b], et angulus earum sit rectus. Deinde continuabo *AG* et faciam super lineam *AG* trianguli *ABG*
45 circulum *ABGH* fiatque perpendicularis *AD* a puncto *A* super lineam *AB*, et ex puncto *G* fiat perpendicularis *DG* super *BG*, et protraham utramque, hanc in *Z*, illam in *E*. Deinde faciam transire regulam que moveatur super punctum *B*, et non separetur ab eo, et abscindat duas lineas *DZ, DE*, et non cesset moveri donec illa pars regule que est inter *Z* et *B* sit equalis ei parti
50 regule que est inter arcum *BG* et *E*. Sit ergo illud in hoc situ ut sit regula *EHBZ*, et sit *EH* equalis *BZ*. Ergo quod fit ex *ZH* in *ZB* est equum ei quod fit ex *BE* in *HE*. Verum *EB* in *HE* equum est *DE* in *GE* [et *HZ* in *ZB* est equalis *DZ* in *ZA*]. Ergo *DZ* est in *ZA* sicut *DE* in *EG*. Ergo proportio *DE* ad *DZ* est sicut *AZ* ad *GE*. Sed proportio *ED* ad *DZ* est sicut *BA* ad *AZ*.
55 Ergo proportio *BA* ad *AZ* est sicut proportio *AZ* ad *GE*, et est etiam sicut proportio *GE* ad *GB*. Stat ergo propositum.

23. CIRCULO PROPOSITO EPTAGONUM EQUILATERUM ET EQUIANGULUM INSCRIBERE.

Sit circulus *ABG*, centrum *G* [Fig. IV.23]; dividatur *AG* in duo equa super *H*, et erigantur ex *H* et *G* perpendiculares ad *AG*, sintque *HQ, GD*. Iungatur

43 Aliter . . . idem *bis Fb, om. R* / Sint: sunt *GPbPcFbBu* / AB, BG: EG, AB, BG *GPbBu* / et . . . earum: quarum angulus *H*
44 et faciam: factam *R* / *ante* faciam *scr. et del.* (?) *G* super / AG² *juste add. H* (*cf. Leon., Vol. 1, p. 664, lin. 4*) *sed om. omnes alii MSS*
46 DG: DB *Bu* GD *VeR* / super *om. GPbBu* / protraham *omnes alii MSS et ex corr. R*
47 hanc *om. GPbPcBu* / Z: 3ᵃᵐ (?) *Bu* / illam: et illam *H* / Deinde: de n. m. *Bu*
48 non *supra scr. H* / separatur *H* / abscindat: abscindit *S* abscindet *H*
49 que: quod *D* / ei: illi *HR*
50 regule: regne (!) *G*, ?*Pb* / est *SHFbPcVeR, om. DGPbBu* / BG: HG *S* / *post* illud *add. R* ita / situ: *lac. Pc* (*et hab. mg. Pc* snn ?)
51 sit *om. R* / EH: TH *Bu* / *post* BZ *add. R* Ergo ZB est equalis EH / ZH: EH *Fb* / ZB (?) *Fb* / est equum *tr. H*
52 ex *om. Fb* / Verum . . . est: que est equalis ei quod fit ex *H* / Verum . . . HE *om. S* / equum: equalis *Ve* equa (?) *S*
52–53 [et . . . ZA] *addidi* (*cf. Leon., ibid., lin. 13*)
53 ZA²: ZH *Bu* / sicut: est sicut *R* / *ante* DE¹ *scr. et del. Pb* de (?) / EG: GE *Bu* / DE²: D *S* ED *H*
54 GE: ḌGE *Bu* / AZ² *HVeR* (*cf. Leon. ibid., lin. 16*) Z *DSGPcBu*, ?*Pb* ZE (?) *Fb*
55 BA . . . proportio² *bis Fb* / AZ² *HRDc* (*cf. Leon, ibid., lin. 17*) AG *DSGPbPcBu,* ?*Fb* AD (?) *Ve* / GE: AGE *Ve* / est etiam *tr. Pc* / etiam *om. H*
56 Stat . . . propositum *om. Bu* / Stat: constat *HR*

Prop. IV.23
1 23 *om. DHGFbPcBuVe* 62 (!) *mg. sin. Pb* 67 *mg. sin. Es* 68ᵃ *mg. dex. S*
3 ABG: ABD *H* ABC *Pc* / *ante* centrum *add. HBu* cuius / dividaturque *H* / AG *om. S* semidiameter AG *H* / equa: equalia *H*
4 H¹: HẸ *Fb* punctum H *H* / erigantur *HVe* erigatur *DSGPbFbPc* eriatur (!) *Bu* / ex . . . sintque: super AG due perpendiculares *H* / G: GḤ *Fb* E *Pc* / perpendicularis (?) *Bu* / GD: FD *GPbPc*
4–5 Iungatur . . . protrahatur: et protrahatur linea AD et ulterius *H*
4 iungantur *Fb*

5 *A* cum *D* et protrahatur in infinitum extra circulum. Abscindet ergo perpendicularem *HQ* super *E*; continuabo *G* cum *E*, et protraham eam in duas
partes circumferentie usque ad *M* et *L*, et continuabo *D* et *L*, et dividam
DG lineam in duo equa super *T*, et protraham ex *T* perpendicularem *TZ*,
et non ponam eius finem. Et movebo lineas *AD*, *LM*, *GD*, *DL* hoc modo:

10 ponam motum *AD* super *A* et *LM* et *DG* super *G*, et *DL* super *D*; nec
separetur aliquod illorum ab eo quod determinavimus ei in motu suo. Sit
perpendicularis *HQ* fixa super *AG*, et perpendicularis *TZ* super *GD* fixa, et
movebimus *AD* super *A* ad partem *B*. Sit linea *AD* propter istud addita, et
sit additio eius ex parte *D* cum *A* fixum, et sit *D* permutatum cum motu

15 eius, cum ipsum sit punctum super quod secat linea *AD* lineam continentem
circulum, et sit etiam accessio eius versus *B* super circumferentiam cum illo
motu. Et sit *D* duarum linearum *GD*, *DL* ligatum cum puncto *D* linee *AD*
super circumferentiam in motu *AD* predicte inseparabile ab illo, et sit quotiens
ut abscindat linea *AD* per motum suum lineam perpendicularem que est

20 *HQ*, abscindat ipsam cum ea super unum punctum linea *LGM* sicut est

5 protrahatur *om. Fb* / Abscindet: AB. Scindet *Fb* ab cindet *Ve*
6 HQ: H.HQ *GPbPc* (*et forte del. Pb* H) / G cum: igitur super *GPbPc* G super *Bu* /
   G: igitur (*?*) *Fb* / eam: illam *H*
7 circumferentia *Bu* / L¹: B (*sive* L) G L *Pb* / continuabo (*?*) *Pb* / L²: B *Pb* / et³: deinde
   H
8 DG: GD *Fb* / equa: equalia *H* / TZ: CZ (*?*) *Bu*
9 LM: LM (*sive* BN) *G* BN *Pb* / DL: DL (*sive* DH) *G* DL (*?*) *Pb*
10 *ante* motum *scr. et del. Bu* intrum (*?*) / motum *om. Pc* / *post* A *scr. et del. Fb* ad
   partem B sit linea eius AD / DG: GD *Ve* DE *D*
11 superetur (*!*) *GPbPc* / aliquod: ad *Fb* aliquis *Pc* / illorum: iᵒʳᵘᵐ *G* istorum *PbBu* eorum
   H / quod: quam *H* / determinavimus *omnes MSS* (*et cf. Ger. App. III.B*) declaravimus
   injuste Dc / in *om. H* / Sitque *Bu*
12 GD: CG *Fb*
13 AD *om. H* / ad *bis Fb* / B *om. Ve* / Sit: et sit *HVe* / istud: illud *Dc*
14 sit¹: fit *Bu* est (*?*) *Ve* erit *Dc* / eius: EL *D* (*secundum Dc*) / A: autem sit *Ve* A sit
   H / *post* fixum *supra scr. Bu* sit / sit² *om. H* / *post* D² *scr. et del. Fb* permutatum
   com motu eius et sit D additio eius ex parte D cum A fixum et sit D com motu eius
   fixum enim inde (*?*) sit / permutatum: punctatum *Pb* (*sed non G*)
15 cum: com *Fb* (*et post hoc lectiones huiusmodi non laudabo*) / *ante* secat *add. GPb*
   stat *sed ante* secat *scr. et del. Bu* fiat
16 sit *om. Pb* (*sed non G*) / etiam: f (*sive* etiam) *G* f *Pb* / *pro* etiam *scr. et del. Bu* aliquid
   quod non legere possum / circonferentiam *Fb* (*et post hoc lectiones huiusmodi non
   laudabo*)
17 D¹ *scr. et del. Bu, semper H* / DL *HVe* (*et Ger. App. III.B*) DB *DSGPb* DB (*sive*
   DL) *Fb* et BD *Pc* / ligatum *omnes alii MSS* ligatio *H* ligamentum *BuDc* / cum *om.*
   Bu
18 super *om. GPbBu* ad *Pc* / AD predicte: ad precedens *injuste Dc* / predicta (*?*) *Pc* /
   inseparabile *ex corr. Bu* (*cf. Ger. App. III.B*) insensibile *DSGPbFbPcVe* inseparabilis
   H inseparibile *Dc* / illo: isto *Bu* iᵒ *GPb* / sit: sic *S* / quotiens ut *mut. H in* ut quotiens
19 ut *bis G*
19–20 linea . . . abscindat *om. Pc*
19 linea *om. Bu* lineam *SGPbFb* lineam *Ve* / *ante* AD *scr. et del. Fb* DO
20 HQ *HVe et ex corr. Bu* (*cf. Ger. App. III.B*) AQ *DSGPbFb* / unum: eundem *H* /
   LGM: in GM *S* / sicut est: et sit continue illud *H* super *injuste Dc*

punctum *E*, et *TA* (*!* ei) est simile, et est motus *LM* super punctum *G*, sicut diximus. Est autem acceptio puncti *L* linee *LM* per motum suum cum *AD* super punctum perpendicularis *HQ* versus *B*, cum puncti *E* sectionis super perpendicularem *HQ* acceptio per motum suum predictum sit versus *H*. Et
25 sit linea *DL* transiens per motum suum super punctum *L* linee *LM* super circumferentiam inseparabilis ab eo in motu suo. Minuitur ergo linea *LD*, et est eius diminutio a parte *L* eius cum punctum *D* eius non variatur, sicut de transitu eius narravimus, cum puncto *D* linea *DG* et linea *AD*. Cum ergo movebimus lineam *AD* secundum quod narravimus de motu eius, et sequetur
60v   / lineas reliquas secundum quod determinavimus, erit [*TZ*] perpendicularis
31 et abscindet per motum *GD* lineam *DL*, et erit puncti sectionis super ipsam acceptio versus *K'* diametri circuli, et punctum sectionis est *AB* et *DL* permutatum in motu suo. Non ergo cessat perpendicularis *TZ* abscindere lineam donec abscindat punctum sectionis super eam super lineam *AB*, sicut est
35 casus perpendicularis. Cum ergo cadet, firmabimus lineam *AD* in loco suo,

21 et[1] . . . simile *om. H* / et TA *DGPbFbPcBuVe* ita *S* et ei *Ger. (App. III.B, et cf. n. 3 meae transl.)* / simile *omnes MSS* similis *Dc*
21–22 super . . . LM *om. SH*
21 G *correxi ex* L *in MSS (cf. Ger. App. III.B)*
21–22 sicut diximus *om. Bu*
22 autem: a' *Pb* / L: E *GPbBu* / cum: in *GPbPc*, *?Bu*
23 *post* punctum *add. Ve* unum / E *om. GPbBu*
24 motum: medium *S* / predictum *om. Fb* / H *om. GPbBu*
25 DL *correxi ex* EL *in MSS (cf. Ger. App. III.B)* / suum *PbDc et ex corr. H, om. SGFbPcBuVe* / super[1] *SHVe (cf. Ger. App. III.B)*, *om. GPbPcFbBu* per *Dc* / punctum *om. Pb (sed non G)* / linee: linea *Pb (sed non G)*
26 inseparabilis *om. Bu* / eo *om. GPbBu* / LD: DL *Fb*
27 est *om. GPbBu* / diminutio (?) *S*
27–28 eius[2] . . . AD *om. H*
27 eius[3] *om. Bu* / variatur: Ḍ videtur *Fb* videtur *Pc*
28 D: DG *Fb* / et *om. Bu* / Cum *bis Fb*
29 lineam *om. Pc* / narravimus: variamus *Bu*, *?Pc* / *ante* de *scr. et del. Fb* com puncto D / eius *om. Fb* / sequetur: consequenter *H*
30 relinquas (!) *D* / secundum *HGer. (App. III.B)* istud *SGPbPcFbBu* illud *Ve* / determinavimus: declaravimus *Dc*
30–31 erit . . . et[1]: Tunc perpendicularis TZ *Ger. (App. III.B)*
30 erit: TZ *H* / [TZ] *addidi*
31 et[1] *om. H* / GD *Ger. (App. III.B)* DG *ex. corr. supra scr. H* GB *DSGPbPcBuVe* GB (*sive* GD) *Fb* / et erit puncti: cadit punctus *injuste Dc* / et erit *HGer. (App. III.B)* erunt *DSGPbFbPc* et erunt *Ve* cadit (?) *Bu* / puncti: punctum *GPbBu* / ipsam: eam *Fb*
32 acceptio *om. Fb* / K' diametri: AB diametrum *H* / K': *hic et postea signas primas addidi* / dyametrum *Pb* / punctum: punctus *PbDc* / est . . . DL: TZ et AB erit *H* / DL *BuGer. (App. III.B)* DB *DSGPbPcFb* OB *Ve*
32–33 permutatum *HGer. (App. III.B)* in permutatum (*sive* inpermutatum) *omnes alii MSS*
33 cesset *H* / *supra* lineam *scr. H* AB *et post* lineam *add. H* AB
34–35 punctum. . . . cadet: in eodem puncto in quo pro tunc linea DL abscindet AB ut in puncto K; quo peracto *H*
34 eam *om. S* / super[2] *om. SDc*
35 Cum (?) *G* c̄u (!) *Pb* / ergo: non (*sive* item) ergo *Bu* / cadat *GPbPcBu*

et figemus motum reliquarum linearum et punctorum propter hoc, dico quod completum est quod voluimus, et quod corda arcus $D'B$ est latus eptagoni. Age: angulus $D'GK'$ extrinsecus trianguli AGD' duum equalium crurium est duplus anguli $D'AG$. Sed angulus $D'AG$ est equalis angulo AGE' propter quod AH est equalis HG, et perpendicularis HE' est communis duobus triangulis AHE', GHE'. Ergo angulus $D'GK'$ est duplus anguli AGE', et iterum angulus $E'GD'$ extrinsecus trianguli $D'GL'$ duum equalium laterum est duplus anguli $GD'L'$. Verum angulus $GD'L'$ est equalis angulo $D'GK'$, quia GT' est equalis $T'D'$, et perpendicularis $T'K'$ est communis duobus triangulis $D'K'T'$, $GK'T'$; ergo angulus $E'GD'$ est duplus anguli $D'GK'$. Quibus subtenditur medietas circuli sunt triplum et medietas equalis anguli $D'GK'$; ergo arcus $AD'B$, qui est medietas circumferentie, est triplum et medietas equalis arcus $D'B$. Ergo circumferentia est septuplum $D'B$. Ergo corda eius est latus eptagoni equilateri et equianguli, quod est propositum.

Quando dividitur linea in tres sectiones, et proportio sectionis postreme earum ad primam sicut proportio prime ad residuum linee, et est media et postrema, et est proportio medie ad postremam sicut proportio postreme ad residuum, et est media et prima, fit ex hiis tribus sectionibus triangulus cuius

40

45

50

36 motum *alii MSS, ?Pb* noṁ *Pc* in omni *Bu* moveri (?) *G* / propter: in *Fb* / hoc *om.*
   Bu / *post* hoc *add. Fb* quo *et Dc* quod
37 quod² *om. GPbBu* / corda *om. Ve* / eptagoni: epta um (!) *Bu*
38 Age *omnes MSS* Argue *Dc* / trianguli: triangulus *G* triangulo *Pb*
39 duplus *Ger. (App. III.B)* duplum *omnes MSS* / D'AG²: GDAG *Bu* / AGE': EGA
   H / propter: propter ea *PbBu*
40 quod: hoc quod *H*
41 GHE' *omnes MSS* GEH *Dc* / D'GK' *H et ex corr. Bu, et Ger. (App. III.B)* DK *Ve*
   AHK *DGPbPc* AHB (*sive* AHK) S ḶAHE *Fb* / duplus *HFb* duplum *DSGPbPcBuVe*
   / AGE': EGA *H*
42 extrinsecus: angulus extrinsecus *Fb* / D'GL': DLG *Pc* / duplus *HGer. (App. III.B)*
   duplum *DSGPbPcFbBuVe*
43 GD'L'¹: DGL *S* / GD'L'²: GAL *S* / D'GK' *HGFbVe* GDK DGK *Pb* GDK *DSPcBu*
   / GT' est: TG *Fb* / GT' *Ger. (App. III.B)* TG *H* ut *DSGPbBu* NT *Pc*
44 communis: equalis *Fb* / triangulis *tr. Ve post* GK'T' / *post* D'K'T' *add. H* et
45 GK'T' (?) *Fb* / est duplus *tr. H* / anguli D'GK': GDK (?) *Fb* / *ante* Quibus *add. H*
   Igitur omnes anguli (*cf. Ger. App. III.B*) / substenditur *Fb*
46 circuli sunt: circumferentie est *Ve*
46–47 anguli . . . equalis *om. Ve*
46 anguli: arcus anguli *Fb* / D'GK': GDK *Fb*
47 AD'B *HGer. (App. III.B)* ABD *DSPc* ABD (*sive* ABO) *Fb* ALD *PbBu, ?G* / equalis
   arcus *tr. Fb* / *ante* arcus *scr. et del. S* anguli DHK
48 D'B¹: BD *H* / *ante* circumferentia *scr. et del. Bu* medietas / eius: DB *H* / eptagoni:
   epta uni (!) *Bu*
49 equianguli et equilateri *Bu*
50 Quando . . . linea *om. Fb* / Quando: quoniam *GPbPcBu* / dividitur *omnes MSS*
   dividatur *DcGer. (App. III.B)* / et *supra scr. Bu* / postreme *mg. H et tr. H ante*
   sectionis, *om. S*
51 *post* primam *add. H* sit / et¹ . . . media *om. GPbBu* / et¹: quod *H*
51–52 medium et postremum *H*
52 media *Pc*
53 et¹: quod *H* / medium et primum *H* / fit *om. Fb* / triangulis *S*

angulus maior est duplus medii, et medius duplus minori. Cum ergo circulus
55 continet hunc triangulum, est arcus qui subtenditur angulo minori arcus
corde eptagoni cadentis in illum circulum.

Hec est questio Indorum dicens in extrascriptione cuiusvis figurarum
equalium laterum cadentis in circulo. Et plurimum quidem positionis Indorum
non est nisi credulitas sola absque demonstratione, et in eo propinquitas
60 inter quam et veritatem non est quantitas sensibilis. Et hec est operatio quam
nunc dicam. Duc medietatem in diametrum totam semper; deinde quod
aggregatur duc in 9 semper et semper serva aggregatum. Deinde proice ex
numero laterum figure cuius quantitatem vis extrahere unum laterum eius
semel semper, et accipe medietatem eius quod remanet, et duc eam in nu-

54 maior: minor (?) *Fb* / est *bis Pc* / minori: minoris *HPcGer.* (*App. III.B*)
54–55 circulus continet *tr. Ve*
55 continet *bis Pb* continent (?) *Fb* / substenditur *Fb*
56 in *om. Pc* / illum: i^m *G* istum *Pb* / *post* circulum *add. Ve* Huius demonstratio sic
   elicitur. Sit AED triangulus [*vide Fig. IV.23var. Ve*] ex AD et DC et CB prout exiget
   (?) proportio constitutus (?), protrahaturque EF ad equalitatem ED sive TB (*! CB*)
   et linea GA ad equalitatem AE sive DC. Ergo ex 16. sexti et prima secundi Euclidis
   quadratum AD valet quadratum ED et ductum AE in EF; quare quadratum (? linea)
   DH, protracta perpendiculari super AF, erit quadratum AD equale quadratis DH et
   EH et ductui AB (*! AE*) in EF. Ergo ex penultima primi et communi dempto erit
   quadratum AH equale quadrato HE et ductui AE in EF quia AF dividam per equalia
   in puncto H ex conversa v^te secundi Euclidis et sic ex quarta primi linee AD et DF
   sunt equales. Conclude ergo ex 32 (?) et vi^a primi angulum AED duplum esse angulo
   DAE. Omnino (?) eodem modo demonstretur quod angulus DAE est duplus angulo
   ADE protracta EK perpendiculariter super DG, quam necesse est cadere intra triangulum DEA cum uterque angulus super basim sit acutus *et sub Fig. IV.23var. Ve*
   scr. Ve Nota quod angulus AED est est (*!*) maior recto quoniam quadratum AD plus
   p^t (*! valet?*) quam quadratis AE et ED, angulus vero EFD minor recto; quare necesse
   est DH perpendiculariter cadere inter E et F
57 Hec: hic *Fb* / *post* questio *scr. et del. Pb* inodo um° (?) / dicens *om. Bu* decens *H*
   docens *Ve* / in *DSHFbVe, om. GPb* ex *Pc* de *ex corr. Bu, Dc* / extrascriptione
   DSHFbVe extractione lateris *H* (*et supra scr. H* lateris) extractione *Ger.* (*App. III.B*)
   transcriptione *GPbPcBu* / cuiusvis: illiusvis *PbBu* (*sed non G*) / *mg. hab. H* Nota
   regulam indorum mirabilem tamen veram
58 equalium *bis Fb* / cadendis (*!*) *Bu*
59 sola: solas (?) *S* / et: et est *H* / eo: eo est *VeGer.* (*App. III.B*)
60 sensibilis *omnes alii MSS, ?Bu* / Et *mg. H* / hec est *tr. H* / est^2 *om. S*
61 Duc: autem (?) *GPbBuPc* / *post* medietatem *add. HGer.* (*App. III.B*) diametri / in
   om. Fb / totum *Pc* / semper *om. H*
62 aggregatur *SPbPcBu* agregatur *DHVe* ag'gatur *GFb* (*saepe hab. MSS* agre- *pro* aggre-
   sed ubique in istis ultimis propositionibus scribo aggre- *et post hoc lectiones huiusmodi
   non laudabo*) / 9 *HGer.* (*App. III.B*) 18 *DFbVe* 14 *S* ig (*sive* 18) *GPbBu* 11 (*sive* is)
   Pc / semper^{1,2} *om. H* / serva *HPcBuVe, ?GPb* sua *DSFb* / prohice *DFbVe*
63 cuius *om. GPb et forte supra scr. Bu*
63–64 unum . . . semel: unde eius *et lac. S*
63 *post* unum *scr. et del. Fb* e
63–64 laterum . . . semper *om. H*
64 semel: simul *Ve* / semper *om. Fb* / eius: cuius *Pb* / remanet (?) *H*
64–65 numerum: unum *Ve*

65 merum laterum figure et adiunge ad illud quod aggregatum est tria semper,
et per illud quod aggregatur divide illud quod servasti, et quod egreditur est
quadratum lateris. Quando ergo sic operatus fueris super quam exigitur demonstratio, exibit ad hunc numerum. Et scias quod ipsi ponunt latus eptagoni
cadentis in circulo per equalitatem medietatis lateris trianguli cadentis in eo,
70 et non est in manibus eorum super illud demonstratio plus quam inventio:
intelligite ergo et cetera.

24. OMNIS TRIANGULI ORTHOGONII INEQUALIUM LATERUM
SI ILLUD QUOD ADDIT LATUS EIUS MAXIMUM SUPER LATUS
EIUS MEDIUM EST EQUALE EI QUOD ADDIT MEDIUM LATUS SU-
PER MINIMUM, TUNC LATUS EIUS MINIMUM EST TRIPLUM IL-
5 LIUS ADDITIONIS, ET MEDIUM EST QUADRUPLUM ILLIUS AD-
DITIONIS, ET MAXIMUM EST QUINTUPLUM EIUS. ET ITERUM LA-
TUS MINIMUM EST QUARTA OMNIUM LATERUM TRIANGULI, ET
MEDIUM EST TERTIA OMNIUM LATERUM TRIANGULI ET MAIUS
EST RESIDUUM UNIUS, SCILICET DUE SEXTE ET MEDIETAS UNIUS
10 SEXTE OMNIUM LATERUM TRIANGULI.

Sit triangulus *ABG* [Fig. IV.24], *A* rectus, *BG* latus maximum, *AB* medium,
et *AB* sit equale *BE*, et *AG* equale *DB*. Ergo palam est quod *DE* est equale

65 adiunge *HPcBuVe* adiungere *DSGPb* / quod aggregatum: e (?) congregatum *Fb* /
aggregatum: congregatum *S* / est *om. D* / semper *om. H*

66 per: semper (?) *Fb* / illud (?) *Fb* / quod aggregatur: agregatum *H* / quod[1] *om. S* /
divide *DSHVe* deinde *GPbPcFbBu* / *post* quod[3] *add. GPb* et / egreditur *DSFbVeGer.*
(*App. III.B*) egredietur *GPbPcBu* egredetur *H* / *ante* est *add. Bu* etiam

67 *post* sic *scr. et del. D* ut / *post* fueris *mg. add. H* et feceris operationem / quam *omnes
MSS* quod *Dc* / exigitur *HPcVe*, *?D* erigitur (*sive* exigitur) *SGPbBu* exigatur *FbGer.*
(*App. III.B*)

68 exibit *om. Pc* exibis *H*

69 cadentis *bis Fb*

71 intelligite *DSHVe* inteligite *Fb* intellige *PcGer.* (*App. III.B*) intelligere (?) *GPbBu*

Prop. IV.24

1 24 *om. DHGFbPcBuVe* 63 *mg. sin. Pb* 58 (!) *mg. sin. Es* 69[a] *mg. dex. S* / Omnis
corr. Pc ex omnes *et hab. Pb* Omnis (!) / orthogonii in-: ortogonium (?) *Fb* / ortogonii
SBuVe (*et post hoc lectiones huiusmodi in istis MSS non laudabo*)

2 adit *Fb*

4-5 illius: illiuds *Fb*

5 *ante* illius *add. DFb* est

7 laterum trianguli *tr. Fb*

8 tertia: tertium *Pc*

9 unius[1] *om. H* / unius[2]: minus *G sed mut. m. rec. G in* unius / *mg. infer. hab. Fb*
octo lineas quas non legere possum

10 omnium *corr. m. rec. G ex* o'n̄ (?)

11 trianguli *SGBuVe* / ABG: ALG *GPb* / latus maximum *tr. Ve* / *post* medium *scr. et
del.* (?) *Fb* AG minimum (*cf. Ger. App. III.B*); ergo BG ductum in se est equale *et
hab. mg. Fb* sic dividatur (?) ut (?)

12 AB sit *tr. H* / AB *om. Fb* / equale[1] *Ger.* (*App. III.B*) equalis *omnes MSS* / AG: age
GPbBu / *post* AG *add. Fb* sit / equale[2] *SGPbPcFbBuVe* equalis *HD* (*secundum Dc*)
/ *post* Ergo *add. Pc* ex suppositione

EG. Ergo *BG* ductum in se est equale *BE* ducto in *EG* quater et *BD* ducto
in se. At *BG* in se est equale *BE* in se et *BD* in se propter illud quod
61r premisimus. Reiecta ergo multiplicatione *BD* in se / remanet *BE* in se equale
16 ei quod fit ex eodem *BE* in *EG* quater. Ergo *BE* est quadruplum *EG*, et *BD*
est triplum eius, et *BG* est quintuplum eius, et *BE* est equale *AB*, et *BD* est
equale *AG*. Si autem aggregemus istas equalitates, provenient 12 similia et
sunt omnia latera tria. Nam *AG* ex eis est tria, et illud est quarta eorum, et
20 *AB* est quatuor, et illud est tertia eorum, et *BG* est quinque, et illud est due
sexte et medietas sexte. Constat ergo quod voluimus.

25. CUIUSLIBET TRIANGULI DIVERSORUM LATERUM PRO-
PORTIO EIUS QUOD ADDIT LATUS LONGIUS SUPER LATUS BRE-
VIUS AD ILLUD QUOD ADDIT CASUS SUPER BREVIOREM EST
SICUT PROPORTIO BASIS AD DUO LATERA AGGREGATA.

5 Sit enim triangulus *ABG* [Fig. IV.25] et ponam *AG* longius *AB*, et ponam
perpendicularem eius *AD*. Dico quod proportio additionis *AG* super *AB* ad
additionem *DG* super *DB* est sicut *BG* ad *AB* et *AG* aggregata. Age: ponam

13 BG: LG *Pb* BC *Ve* / *mg. hab. Fb* est quadratum DE (?) _____ (?) _____ (?) *et mg.*
  super. hab. Fb _____ (?) _____ (?) *secundam* 10^{am} _____ (?) *et lac. et tunc* quadratum GB est quadrato BD quia (?) est duplum quadrato BE cum quadrato DE
  _____ (?) / quater *HVeGer*. (*App. III.B*) consequenter *Pc* quantum *SGPbFbBuDc*
  / BD: LD (*sive* id) *GPbBu*
14 *post* se[1] *add. H per* 8. *secundi Euclidis* / At: sed *H* fat (?) *Fb* / BG: LG (?) *Bu / mg.*
  hab. Ve ex viii *secundi Euclidis* / BE: LE *GPb* / BD: HD (?) *G* HD *PbBu*
15 premissimus (?) *Fb* / multiplicatio *DSVe* / BD: LD (?) *Bu*
16 quod *om. Bu* / eadem (?) *Ve* / BE *HGPbPcBu* DE *DSVe* BG (?) *Fb* / EG quater:
  DG (?) et (?) quadratum *Fb* et *add. mg. Fb* cum (?) triplo (?) DE / quater *HPb Ger*.
  (*App. III.B*), *om. Ve* quantum *DSGPbPcBu* DB *G / ante* BE[2] *add. H per primam* 6^i
  / BD: LD (?) *Bu*
17 *post* eius[1] *add. H* eo quod DE et EG sunt equales / eius[2] *om. Pb* (*sed non G*) / et[2]
  forte supra scr. Fb sed *H* / BD: LD *Pb* / est[4] *om. H*
18 autem *om. Ve* / 12: 13 (?) *Bu* / et: que *H*
19 quarta: quinque *Dc* / et[2]: est *Ve*
20 est[1] *H, om. DSFbVe* et *GPbBu* / quatuor: quarta *DSVe*, ?*Fb* / BG: LG *GPb* / est[3]
  om. PcVe et *SGPbBu* / quinque: quinta *DSFbVe*
21 et . . . sexte *om. Fb*

Prop. IV.25

1 25 *om. DHGFbPcBuVeGu*, ?*Pb* 59 (!) *mg. sin. Es* 70ᵃ *mg. dex. S* / trianguli: anguli
  Fb / *post* diversorum *scr. et del. Fb* diverso
3 *post* casus *add. H* longior (*cf. Ger. App. III.B*) / *post* casus *scr. Gu et supra scr. lin.*
  3 Ve si perpendicularis a cono ad basim ducta cadat intra triangulum / breviorem
  alii MSS et ex corr. Bu / est *HGPbPcBuVeGu* et DS et (*sive* est) *Fb* erit *Dc*
4 *post* sicut *add. VeGu* est
5 *mg. hab. H* nota quod hec conclusio non _____ (?) basim inter latera / enim *om.*
  Gu
5–6 et[1] . . . AD: cuius AG sit latus longius et ab angulo A descendat perpendicularis AD
  super basim BG *H*
5 *post* longius *add. GuDc* quam / AB et ponam *VeGuDcGer*. (*App. III.B*) i.e. medium
  imponam AB *Pc* inponam (*sive* imponam) AB *DSGFbPbBu* (*et add. Bu* breviorem)
6 AD: scilicet AD *GPbBu* / Dico quod: dicoque (?) *D* / *post* Dico *scr. et del. Gu* p
7 Age *SVe, om. HGu* age (*sive* AG) *D* age ergo *GPbPcBu* AG *Fb* Argue *injuste Dc*

enim punctum *A* centrum et lineabo circulum cum longitudine *AB*, qui sit
circulus *VZBE*, et protraham *AG* in directum usque ad *Z*. Palam est igitur
10   quod *VG* est illud quod addit *AG* super *AB*, et quod *EG* est illud quod addit
DG super *DB* quoniam *DB* est equale *DE*. Ergo quod fit ex *BG* in *EG* est
sicut quod fit ex *ZG* in *GV*; ergo *BG* ad *ZG* est sicut *VG* ad *EG*. Sed *ZG*
est *AB* et *AG* simul sumpte. Ergo basis *BG* ad *AG* et *AB* simul sumpta est
sicut superfluitas *AG* super *AB* ad superfluitatem casus *DG*, et est *DG* (*! GE*),
15   super *BD*. Constat ergo quod voluimus.

26. VOLO OSTENDERE QUOD OMNIUM TRIUM LINEARUM
PROPORTIONALIUM PROPORTIO PRIME AD SECUNDAM DUPLI-
CATA EST PROPORTIO PRIME AD TERTIAM. QUANDO ERGO VOLU-
MUS OSTENDERE ILLUD, OSTENDEMUS QUOD OMNIUM TRIUM
5   LINEARUM, QUOCUMQUE MODO SINT, PROPORTIO PRIME AD
TERTIAM EST SICUT PROPORTIO AGGREGATI EX MULTIPLICA-
TIONE PRIME IN SECUNDAM AD AGGREGATUM EX MULTIPLI-
CATIONE SECUNDE IN TERTIAM.

8 enim *om. S / ante* A *scr. et del. Ve* E / A *om. Gu /* lineabo: liniabo *DSVe* describam
Gu / cum . . . AB: ad longitudinem B *Bu* in longius B (*sive* V) *GPb /* cum longitudine:
secundum longitudinem *H /* cum: in *PcBu /* AB H *et ex corr. Bu* V D B *SFbPcVeGer.*
(*App. III.B*)

9 VZBE: V.BE *D* VTBE *Fb* NZBE (?) *Bu* UZBE *Pc* (*et semper hab. Pc* U *pro* V) /
AG: AB *S* GA *H /* in directum: inductum *Bu / ante* est *add. Fb* autem / est: etiam
(?) *Ve*

10 VG: NG *Pc, ?Bu*

11 *ante* quoniam *scr. et del. Gu* qm̄ (?) / quoniam DB *om. S /* quoniam: cum *H /* est[1]:
sit *H /* DE: D (?) *D / post* DE *add. Pc* hoc patet per penultimam tertii Euclidis /
Ergo: cum igitur ex 35. 3[i] *H / ante* fit *scr. et del. Gu* sit

12 GV: GB (*sive* GV) *Fb / post* GV *add.* H per 15. 6[i] */ ergo om. H /* BG: VG *Pc / post*
EG *add.* GPbPcBu per 15. 6[i] Euclidis (*et mg. add. Bu aliquid quod non legere possum*)
/ Set *Ve*

13 AB (?) *D* sicud AB *H /* sumpte: sumpta *Gu /* ad: et *SVe* (*et supra scr. Ve* ad) / supra
AG[2] *scr. D* et / sumpta est *tr. DSFb*

14 super . . . ad *om. GPb /* super AB *om. Bu /* ad *supra scr. Bu /* DG[1]: AG *Fb /* et est
DG *DSFbVeGu, om.* HGPbPcBu et est GE *Ger.* (*App. III.B*)

15 BD: D *D* DB *G /* quod *om. Bu / post* voluimus *add. Gu* demonstrare

Prop. IV.26

1 *mg. super. f. 292v hab. Ve* PROPOSITIONES *et f. 293r* DE PROPORTIONIBUS *et
insimul illa faciunt titulum pro Props. IV.26–IV.28 /* 26 *om.* DHGPbPcFbBuVe 60
(*!*) *mg. sin. Es* 71[a] *mg. dex. S /* Volo . . . quod *om. Bu*

2 prime *DcGer.* (*App. III.B*) primi *DSGFbPcBuVe, ?PbH /* secundam *HGPbPcBu* secundum *DSFbVe*

3 proportio *alii MSS, ?D /* quando: quia *ex corr. Pc*

3–4 volumus: voluimus *VePb* (*sed non G*)

5 quecumque *H /* modo *om. SHFb*

6 est: et *Fb / post* proportio *scr. et del. Pc* prime / aggregati *H et Ger.* (*App. III.B*)
                                         i
aggregata̧ *Pc* prime agregata (*sive* aggregata) *DSGPbFbBuVe*

6–7 multiplicatio *Fb*

7 secundam: secunda *S /* ad aggregatum: ad ag'gatum *H* et ag'gato *DGFb* et agregata
                                i
S et agg'to *Pb* et agg'gato̧ *Pc* et ag°gatio *Bu* et ag'gata *Ve*

Cuius exemplum est, ut sint tres linee *AB* et *GD* et *ET* [Fig. IV.26]. Dico
10 ergo quod proportio *AB* ad *ET* est sicut proportio multiplicationis *AB* in
GD ⟨ex⟩ multiplicatione *GD* in *ET*, cuius hec est demonstratio. Ponam lineam
longam et abscindam de ea quod sit equale *AB*, quod sit *HT'*, et protraham
ex puncto *T'* perpendicularem super *HT'*, et abscindam ab ea quod sit equale
GD, sitque *T'L*. Et iterum abscindam quod sit equale *ET*, quod sit *T'K*, et
15 faciam transire super punctum *L* lineam equedistantem *HK*, et complebo
duas superficies *HL, LK*. Ergo altitudo utraque una. Ergo proportio superficiei
de superficie est sicut proportio *HT'* ad *T'K*. Sed *HT'* est equalis *AB*, et *T'K*
est equalis *ET*. [Ergo proportio *AB* ad *ET*] est sicut multiplicatio *AB* in *GD*
ad *GD* in *ET* et illud est quod demonstrare voluimus.

27. ET QUIA IAM OSTENDI HANC PROPOSITIONEM, TUNC OS-
TENDAM ITERUM QUOD OMNIUM TRIUM LINEARUM, QUO-
CUMQUE MODO SINT, PROPORTIO PRIME AD TERTIAM EST SICUT
PROPORTIO PRIME AD SECUNDAM MULTIPLICATA IN PROPOR-
5 TIONEM SECUNDE AD TERTIAM.

9 et[1] *om. H* / GD: DG *GPbBu* / ET *om. Bu* EZ *hic et ubique in Ger.* (*App. III.B*)
10 ergo *om. Fb* / ET: et *SGPbBu*
11 GD[1]: DG *Bu* / ex multiplicatione: e̱x̱ multiplicationem *Pc* / ex: et *Bu* / ET: et
Bu / hec *tr. Fb post* demonstratio
12 ea *HGPbPcBu* (*et supra scr. Ve*) eo *DSFb* / AB: CB.AB *G* EB (*sive* CB), AB *Pb*
EB.AB *Bu* (*et del. Bu* EB) / HT': HĈ *G* HE *Ve*
13 T' *corr. GBu ex* et T (*N.B. hic et ubique in ista propositione signum primum addidi*)
13–14 et. . . . T'K: que sit equalis GD et sit illa TL; deinde ex prima linea capta reseco
lineam TK, que sit equalis linee ET *H*
13 ab ea *om. S*
14 GD. . . . equale *om. S* / ET: et *SPbVe* e[t] *G, ?Bu* / sit[2] *supra scr. Pb*
16 *ante* superficies *scr. et del. Fb* lineas / HL: HK *Pc* / Ergo[1]: quare *H* / utraque: est
H / *post* una *add. Ve* est / superficiei: superficies *Fb*
17 de superficie: ad superficiem *GPbPcBu* HL ad superficiem LK *H* superficiei HL ad
superficiem LK *Ve* / superficie: superficiei *Fb* / HT'[1] *omnes MSS* HL *injuste Dc* /
T'K[1]: TLK *Fb* / *post* AB *add. H* et TL equalis GD
18 est[1] *om. HFb* / ET[1]: et *S* / [Ergo . . . ET] *juste add. Dc et cf. Ger.* (*App. III.B*) /
est[2]: et est *GPbPc*
18–19 est[2] . . . voluimus: et HL superficies resultat ex (*supra scr.*) multiplicatione (*supra
scr.*) HT in TL et LK superficies ex multiplicatione TL in TK; igitur et cetera *H*
18 sicut *supra scr. Ve*
19 ad GD *correxi ex Ger.* (*App. III.B*) *et* et GD *in mg. Bu et* ad multiplicationem GD
et in multiplicationem *Ve* (*sed om. DSGPbFbPc*) / *ante* voluimus *scr. Fb* vol (?) /
volumus *Pc*

Prop. IV.27
1 27 *om. DHGPbFbPcBuVe* 61 (!) *mg. sin. Es* 72[a] *mg. dex. S*
1–2 Et . . . quod *om. Bu*
1 Et: Set *Fb* / quia *om. GPb* / propositionem *HFb* proportionem *GPbGer.* (*App. III.B*)
propōm *DSPcVe*
1–2 ostendam: ostend'a *S* ostenda *Fb*
2 *ante* trium *scr. et del. Fb* triangulorum
2–3 quodcumque *D*
4 multiplicata *in corr. Fb ex* multiplicatam (*et add. Fb* in) / multiplicatam *SBu* / in
supra scr. G
4–5 proportionem: proportione *GPbBu*
5 *ante* secunde *scr. et del. Bu, ?G* prime *et add. Pb* prime

Ponam tres lineas *AB, DG, ET* [Fig. IV.27]; et ponam proportionem que est *AB* ad *DG* lineam *H*. Ergo linea *H* quando multiplicatur in lineam *GD* est linea *AB*, quoniam proportio est divisio. Et ponam proportionem que est *GD* ad *ET* lineam *T'*. Ergo linea *T'* quando multiplicatur in *ET* est *GD*;
10 et ponam proportionem que est *AB* ad *ET* lineam *L*; ergo linea *L* quando multiplicatur in *ET* est *AB*. Dico ergo quod multiplicatio linee *H* in lineam *T'* est linea *L*, quod sic demonstratur. Multiplicabo *H* in *T'*; ergo erit *K*. Dico ergo quod linea *K* est equalis linee *L*, quod sic probatur. Linea *H* et linea *T'* et linea *ET* sunt tres linee, quarum prima est linea *H* et earum
15 postrema est linea *ET*. Ergo proportio prime, que est *H*, ad postremam, que
61v est *ET*, erit sicut proportio aggregati ex multiplicatione / linee *H* in lineam *T'* de aggregato ex multiplicatione linee *T'* in lineam *ET*. Sed aggregatum ex multiplicatione linee *H* in lineam *T'* est linea *K*, et aggregatum ex multiplicatione *T'* in lineam *ET* est linea *DG*. Ergo proportio linee *H* ad lineam
20 *ET* est sicut proportio linee *K* de linea *GD*. Ergo multiplicatio *H* in *GD* est sicut multiplicatio *K* in *ET*. Sed multiplicatio *H* in *GD* est *AB*. Ergo multiplicatio *K* in *ET* est *AB*, et iam fuit multiplicatio *L* in *ET*, *AB*. Ergo linea *L* est equalis linee *K*. Iam ergo ostensum est quod proportio linee *AB* de *ET* est sicut proportio linee *AB* de *GD* multiplicata in proportionem *GD* de *ET*.

6 ET: EZ *hic et ubique in ista propositione in Ger.* (*App. III.B*) / ponam: primam *Fb*
7 ad *om. Fb* / DG: GD *Ve* G.DG *Pb* / Ergo . . . H *GPbPcBuGer.* (*App. III.B*), *om. DSFbVe* que *H*
8 est¹ *HGPbPcBu* et *FbVe* erit *Dc* / linea: lineam *FbVe* / divisio: denominatio *H* / ponam proportionem *tr. Ve* / ponam *om. Fb* / *post* ponam *add. Bu* et
9 GD¹: AB *Pc* / ET¹: et *GPbBu* / T'¹: *hic et ubique signum primum addidi* / T'² *tr. Pc ante* linea / *ante* ET² *hab.* H lineam / ET²: $\underset{E}{\mathrm{A}}$T *Fb* AT *Bu*
10 ponam *om. Fb* / L¹,²: B (*sive* L) *Bu*
11 ET: E *S* lineam ET *H* / quod: quoniam *GPbPcBu* quo *Fb*
11–12 linee . . . T'¹ *mg. H*
12 ergo erit: et fiat *H* / K: linea K *Bu*
13 Dico *om. Bu* / est *om. Ve*
14–15 earum postrema *tr. Fb*
15 prime . . . est² *om. H* / prime *Ger.* (*App. III.B*), *om. DSGPbPcFbBuVe*
15–16 postremam . . . est *om. H*
16 erit *om. Ve* est *SGPbPcBu* / aggregati: aggregata *Pc* agᵉ gata *GPbBu* / linee *om. H* / H: CH *D* EH *SFb*
17 T'¹: G *Fb* / de aggregato: ad ag'gatum *H* ad ag'gatam *GPc* ad aggᵉtam *Pb* ad agᵉgatam *Bu* / *ante* Sed *injuste add. GPbBu* (*et del. Bu*) sed aggregatum (*sive* agregatum) ex multiplicatione linee (*bis Bu*) T (et *Bu*) in lineam ET
18 *ante* linea *add. Bu* sicud
19 *post* T' *add. Ve* linee
19–20 Ergo . . . GD *om. S*
19 linee *om. H* / H *alii MSS et ex corr. Bu* K (?) *D* EH *GPb* / lineam² *om. H*
20 *post* ET *add. Pc* per 17. 7ⁱ / est¹ *om. DVe* / proportio *om. H* / linee . . . linea: K ad *H* / K: ad *Fb* / de linea: ad lineam *GPbPcBu* / *post* GD¹ *add. H* per 15. 6ⁱ aut per 21. 7ⁱ *sed add. Pc* ex 19. 7ⁱ / Ergo *om. H* / H (?) *Fb* / in: et *DSVe*, ?*Fb*
21 K: H *G*, ?*PbBu*
21–22 K. . . . multiplicatio *om. Ve*
21 AB: AD *Fb*, ?*D*
23 de: ad lineam *H* ad *GPbPcBu* / ET: et *S*
24 *ante* linee *add. Fb* H / de¹: ad *HGPbPcBu* / de²: ad lineam *H*

25 Et quia iam ostendi hanc proportionem, tunc manifestum est quod omnium linearum proportionalium proportio prime ad tertiam est sicut proportio prime ad secundam duplicata.

28. ET VOLO ITERUM, CUM OSTENSUM SIT QUOD OMNIUM TRIUM LINEARUM PROPORTIONALIUM PROPORTIO PRIME AD TERTIAM EST SICUT PROPORTIO EIUS AD SECUNDAM DUPLI- CATA, OSTENDERE QUOD OMNIUM QUATUOR LINEARUM CON-
5 SEQUENTIUM SECUNDUM PROPORTIONEM UNAM PROPORTIO PRIME AD QUARTAM EST SICUT PROPORTIO PRIME AD SECUN- DAM TRIPLICATA.

Cuius exemplum est, ut sint quatuor [linee] A, et B et G [et] D consequentes secundum proportionem unam [Fig. IV.28a]. Dico igitur quod proportio A
10 ad D est sicut proportio A ad B triplicata, quod sic demonstratur. Tres linee sunt A et G et D. Ergo proportio A ad D est sicut proportio A ad G multiplicata in proportionem G ad D. Et A, B, G sunt tres linee proportionales. Ergo proportio A ad G est sicut proportio A ad B duplicata; ergo proportio A ad D est sicut proportio A ad B duplicata multiplicata in proportionem G ad
15 D. Sed proportio G ad D est sicut proportio A ad B; ergo proportio A ad D est sicut proportio A ad B duplicata multiplicata in proportionem A ad B, et est sicut A ad B triplicata; ergo proportio A ad D est sicut proportio A ad B triplicata, et illud est quod voluimus.

25 quia om. GPbBu / ostendenda S / proportionem PbFbGer. (App. III.B) propom̄ DSHGPcVe propōnē Bu propositionem Dc
27 dupplicata D

Prop. IV.28

1 28 om. DHGPbPcFbBuVeEs 73ª mg. dex. S / Et . . . quod om. Bu
2 prime om. H
4 quatuor linearum tr. Pc
4–5 consequentium alii MSS, ?Pb cosequentium (!) Fb
5 proportio alii MSS, ?D
6 sicut bis Pb
8 [linee] addidi ex Ger. (App. III.B), sed om. omnes MSS / et¹ . . . et³: B, G H / et² om. Bu / G et D: D et G Fb / [et³] addidi ex Fb et Ger. (App. III.B), sed om. alii MSS
10 sicut: autem S / ad² om. Pb / post ad² scr. et del. G G multiplicata in proportio (?) G ad D / post demonstratur scr. Pb -atur forte quia in G scriptum est demr̄ atur / ante Tres add. Bu que
11 et¹ om. PbBu / A³: AC (?) Pb (sed non G)
12 proportionem: proportione DSFbPcVe proportio (?) GPbBu
13 A²: AD Fb / dupplicata D
13–14 ergo . . . B bis Fb / A ad D: ad prima lectio Fb A ad D secunda lectio Fb
14 D: G.H (sive G.B) GPb / A om. GPb / dupplicata D / proportionem: proportione DSFbPcVe proportio GPbBu
15 D¹: V Bu / Sed (?) D / est om. D
15–16 ergo . . . B mg. Bu / proportio² . . . est bis GPb (sed scr. et del. Pb in secunda lectione triplicata ante est)
15 A²: Aḍ Fb
16 dupplicata D / proportionem: proportione Ve
17 est¹ om. GPbPcBu hoc est H
18 B: V Bu / triplicata om. Pb (sed non G) riplicata (!) D / volumus Pc

Et nobis quidem possibile est venire cum demonstratione super veritatem
20 eius quod narravimus per modum alium cum factum sit illud quod premissum
est de narratione eius in hac figura [Fig. IV.28b]. Manifestum et illud est.
Quoniam proportio *ET* ad *TB* est sicut proportio [*TB* ad *BH* et est sicut
proportio] *BH* ad *HT'*, ergo quantitates *ET*, *TB*, *BH*, *HT'* sunt proportionales.
Ergo proportio prime ad quartam est proportio prime ad secundam multi-
25 plicata in proportionem prime ad tertiam propter quod non ponitur quantitas
secunda media inter primam et quartam multiplicatam. Sic proportio prime
ad secundam per proportionem secunde ad quartam existens proportio prime
ad quartam est proportio prime ad tertiam (*!* quartam); ergo *ET* ad *HT'* est
sicut proportio *ET* ad *TB* multiplicata per proportionem *ET* ad *BH*.

19-29 Et. . . . BH *non hab. Ger. (App. III.B)*
   19 nobis quidem: nota quod *H* / nobis: *lac. Ve* / invenire *Ve* / veritatem: veritate *PcDc*
      utate (*!*) *D*
   20 narravimus: variamus (*?*) *GPbBu* variavimus (*!*) *Pc* / alium: qui *Bu*
   21 narratione: nartōe *G* / et . . . est: est illud *Pc*
   22 ET: et *Bu*
22-23 [TB² . . . proportio] *addidi*
   23 BH¹: TH *Fb* / HT'¹: *hic et postea primum signum addidi* / HT'² *om. Ve*
   25 in *HFb, om. DSGPbPcBu* per *VeDc* / *ante* tertiam *scr. et del. Pb* secundam / propter:
      propter ea *GPbBu* / non *om. GPbBu* / interponitur *Fb*
   26 Sic: sit *H*
   27 per *om. SH* / secunde: prime *Fb* / *ante* existens *add. Fb* se
   28 proportio: proportione *GPbBu* / ergo ET: G et *S* / ET: et *FbBu* / HT': VT *Pb* (*forte*
      quia H *in* G *est simile* V) ut *Bu*
   29 multiplicat *Fb* / BH: HB *H* / *post* BH *add. Pb* Explicit liber Iordani de triangulis.
      Deo gratias amen

The Book on Triangles of Jordanus

[1] CONTINUITY IS THE INDETERMINATION OF LIMIT WITH THE POTENTIALITY OF LIMIT.[1]

[2] A POINT IS A FIXATION OF SIMPLE CONTINUITY.

[3] SIMPLE CONTINUITY OCCURS IN A LINE, DOUBLE [CONTINUITY] IN A SURFACE, AND TRIPLE [CONTINUITY] IN A BODY.

[4] ONE CONTINUITY IS STRAIGHT, ANOTHER CURVED.

[5] THAT IS STRAIGHT WHICH HAS A SIMPLE [I.E. ONE-DIMENSIONAL] MEDIUM.

[6] BUT AN ANGLE IS THE DISCONTINUITY OF CONTINUA THAT COME TOGETHER IN A LIMIT.

[7] NOW A FIGURE IS A FORM ARISING OUT OF THE QUALITY OF [ITS] LIMITS AND [OUT OF] THE METHOD OF APPLYING THEM.

Then a figure of a surface occurs "out of the quality of [its] limits" because one is contained by curved [limits, i.e. lines], another by curved and straight [limits], and [still] another by straight limits alone. And indeed [of those contained] by curved lines some are contained by one [such line] and others by several. Now [some figures are contained] by straight lines and two or more curved lines, while [others are contained] by three or more straight lines. [Figures arise] "out of the method of applying" [limits] since from it [i.e. the method of application] arises a diversity of angles. For certain are made equal by straight lines, and certain are made smaller and certain greater.

1. (=P.1) IN EVERY TRIANGLE, IF THE STRAIGHT LINE DRAWN FROM AN OPPOSITE ANGLE TO THE MIDDLE OF THE BASE IS EQUAL TO HALF THE BASE, THAT ANGLE WILL BE A RIGHT ANGLE. BUT IF IT (THE LINE) IS GREATER [THAN HALF THE BASE], IT (THE ANGLE) IS ACUTE; WHILE IF IT IS LESS, [THE ANGLE] IS OBTUSE.

For if the line is equal to half the base, the two angles at the base taken together will equal the third, by [Prop.] I.5 of Euclid applied twice [see Fig. I.1]. Therefore the third angle is necessarily a right angle by I.32 [of Euclid]. But if it (the line) is greater [than half the base], those angles [at the base together] will be greater than the third, by [I.]18 [of Euclid], and therefore it (the third angle) will be acute. But if it (the line) is less [than half the base],

Introduction

[1] For the introductory definitions, see my notes to the English translation of the *Liber philotegni*, and particularly n. 2 where I mention Curtze's misreadings in Definition 6, which certainly would cause the reader to misunderstand that definition completely. The text of these definitions is the same in both versions. May I remind the reader when reading the *Liber de triangulis Iordani* always to consult the discussion of this text in Part III, Chap. 1, and, where the propositions appear in both versions, also to consult the discussion in Part II, Chap. 2.

the remaining [angles] will be less than the third, and therefore it (the third angle) will be obtuse by I.32.

2. (=P.2) A LINE DRAWN FROM AN ANGLE TO THE BASE INSIDE A TRIANGLE WHOSE TWO SIDES ARE EQUAL WILL BE LESS THAN EITHER OF THEM, WHILE [IF DRAWN] OUTSIDE IT WILL BE GREATER [THAN EITHER].

With two lines drawn, one indeed outside until it meets the base and the other inside the triangle to any point of the base, it is evident, by I.5 and I.16 of Euclid, that that which has been drawn inside the triangle is opposite a smaller angle than is one of the sides of the triangle. But that which is outside [is opposite] a greater [angle]. Therefore argue [what has been proposed] by [I.]19 [of Euclid; see Fig. I.2].

3. (=P.3) IF A TRIANGLE HAS TWO UNEQUAL SIDES AND A LINE IS DRAWN INSIDE THE TRIANGLE FROM THE ANGLE WHICH THE SIDES CONTAIN TO THE BASE, IT [I.E. THE DESCENDING LINE] WILL [ALWAYS] BE SHORTER THAN THE LONGER [SIDE]: BUT IT HAPPENS THAT IT [I.E. THE DESCENDING LINE] IS EQUAL TO, OR GREATER THAN, OR LESS THAN THE SHORTER [SIDE].

That it is [always] shorter than the longer side you easily prove by I.18 and I.19 [of Euclid]. Moreover you will quickly show that the rest [of the proposition] follows. [For] if the shorter side contains an acute angle with the base [see Fig. I.3], then a line descending [from the angle to the base] can contain with the base in the same direction (1) an angle equal to that [acute angle], and then it (the descending line) will be equal to the shorter side; or (2) [an angle] greater [than the acute angle], so that if it has been drawn nearer [to the acute angle], it (the descending line) will be less [than the shorter side], by the preceding [proposition]; or (3) [an angle] less [than the acute angle], so that if it (the descending line) has been drawn farther [from the acute angle], then it (the descending line) will become greater [than the shorter side]. Moreover, if [the shorter side makes with the base] a right or an obtuse [angle], it (the descending line) will always be greater [than the shorter side; see Fig. I.3].

4. (=P.4) IN EVERY TRIANGLE WHOSE TWO SIDES ARE UN-EQUAL, A LINE DRAWN FROM THE ANGLE CONTAINED BY THESE [SIDES] TO THE MIDDLE OF THE BASE WILL CONTAIN WITH THE LONGER [SIDE] THE SMALLER ANGLE.

From the middle of the base let a line parallel to the shorter side be drawn to the longer side [cf. Figs. I.4] and it will fall on the latter's midpoint, by VI.2 [of Euclid], and the same line will be one half of the shorter side, by VI.4 [of Euclid], and hence less than half of the longer side. Therefore argue [what has been proposed] by I.18 and I.29 [of Euclid].[1]

Prop. I.4

[1] There are two specific proofs similar to the proof given in Prop. 4 of the *Liber philotegni:* one is in MS *H* (see the text of Prop. I.4 above, variant reading to lines 5–8) and the other is

5. (=P.5) IF IN A RIGHT-ANGLED OR OBTUSE-ANGLED[1] [TRI-ANGLE] A LINE IS DRAWN FROM ONE OF THE REMAINING AN-GLES TO THE BASE, THE RATIO OF THE ANGLE FARTHER FROM THE RIGHT ANGLE TO THE ANGLE CLOSER TO THE RIGHT AN-GLE IS LESS THAN THE RATIO OF ITS BASE TO THE BASE OF THE OTHER.

Let a circle be described whose radius is the length of the line drawn inside the right triangle and whose circumference will cut the side opposite the right angle while it will include without contact the perpendicular side, by the penultimate [proposition]. But, if the latter is projected to the circumference, two sectors will be formed that are respectively more and less than the partial triangles [formed by the line drawn inside the triangle; see Fig. I.5]. Therefore argue [what has been proposed] by V.8, and the first and last [propositions] of [Book] VI [of Euclid].

5+. AND THE RATIO OF THE ANGLE CLOSER TO THE RIGHT ANGLE AND CONSTRUCTED ON A SIDE THAT IS CUT TO THE ANGLE FARTHER [FROM THE RIGHT ANGLE] IS LESS THAN THE RATIO OF THE [WHOLE] CUT SIDE TO THE PART OF THE CUT SIDE CLOSER TO THE RIGHT ANGLE.

For the demonstration of this draw a line HO within the triangle QHC [see Fig. I.5+] whose angle C is either right or obtuse, [and] let there be drawn from point Q a line parallel to line HO until it meets in point D with CH [extended]. Therefore with the [fixed] foot of the compass placed in Q let a circle be described with radius HQ, which [circle] necessarily cuts QD and includes QC, by I.19 and I.16 of Euclid. Therefore, let it cut QD in point B and let QC be extended to A. Therefore, since, by the last [proposition] of [Book] VI of Euclid and this rule: "the ratio of arc to arc is that of sector to sector" (whose proof is the same as the proof of the last [proposition] of [Book] VI) and by each part of V.8 and VI.1, angle HQC / angle HQD > line HC / line HD, [so] inversely DH / HC > angle HQD / angle HQC. Therefore, conjunctively, [line] DC / line HC > angle DQC (or HOC) / angle HQC. Then argue [what has been proposed] from VI.4 of Euclid.[1]

6. (=P.6) IN A TRIANGLE WHOSE TWO SIDES ARE UNEQUAL, IF FROM THE ANGLE WHICH THEY CONTAIN A PERPENDICULAR IS DRAWN TO THE BASE, THE RATIO OF THE SEGMENT OF THE

the marginal proof added by MSS D and Fb (*ibid.,* variant reading to line 8). Notice the considerable variety of diagrams in the various manuscripts, as given below with the designation Fig. I.4 followed by the various *sigla* of the manuscripts.

Prop. I.5

[1] I have discussed the addition of the obtuse-angled triangle to this enunciation above in my account of this proposition in Part III, Chap. 1. See also the various proofs of this proposition discussed in Part II, Chap. 2.

Prop. I.5+

[1] I have explained the various ways in which this enunciation and its proof were added to the manuscripts in Part III, Chap. 1, above. I have also outlined the proof there.

BASE WHICH IS CUT OFF BETWEEN THE PERPENDICULAR AND THE LONGER SIDE TO THE REMAINING [SEGMENT OF THE BASE] WILL BE GREATER THAN THAT OF ANGLE TO ANGLE.

For this, first demonstrate that a greater segment of the base is intercepted between the perpendicular and the terminus of the longer side than between the perpendicular and the terminus of the shorter side [see Fig. I.6]. For it is not equal by I.4 [of Euclid]; nor is the one less [than the other], because if so then let the one imagined to be the greater be cut to equality with the one imagined to be less, and from the point of section let a line be drawn to the superior angle, and then would follow the opposite of the hypothesis, by the second [proposition] of the present [work]. Therefore, because it [i.e. the segment between the perpendicular and the terminus of the longer side] is necessarily the greater, let it be cut to equality with the lesser and from the point of section let a line be drawn to the superior angle, as we have said in the prior [case]. And, with this done, you will by means of the preceding [proposition] clearly demonstrate what has been proposed by first manipulating the ratios disjunctively and then conjunctively.[1]

7. (=P.7) IF TWO TRIANGLES ARE SET ON THE SAME BASE BETWEEN PARALLEL LINES, THE SUPERIOR ANGLE OF THAT ONE WHOSE SIDE OF THE MUTUALLY INTERSECTING SIDES IS GREATER WILL BE SMALLER.

With the triangles constructed [see Fig. I.7], let there be mutually intersecting sides: AB the greater, CD the smaller, and also let the point of intersection be called E. And, since the triangles are equal by I.37 [of Euclid], with the common area subtracted there remain two equal triangles having two equal angles at E. Therefore, by VI.14 (=Gr. VI.15) [of Euclid], line AE / line EC = EB / ED; hence AB / CD = EB / ED by V.13 (=Gr. V.12) [of Euclid], and so $AE > EC$.[1] But let AE / EC = EC / EF, line EF having been cut

---

Prop. I.6

[1] This is made clear in the specific proof of Proposition 6 of the *Liber philotegni* (see Part II, Chap. 2). There only conjunction of ratios is used as follows: (1) DF is cut off equal to BD and thus angle FAD = angle BAD. Then (2) since AD is perpendicular to BC, so FC / DF > ang. CAF / ang. FAD, by Prop. I.5. So (3) by conjunction DC / DF > ang. CAD / ang. FAD. Therefore (4) DC / BD > ang. CAD / ang. BAD, substituting the equal quantities from (1). But the author of the *Liber de triangulis Iordani* says that the proof will be effected by the preceding proposition (i.e. Prop. I.5), first by the manipulating of ratios disjunctively and then conjunctively. The only way to save this statement would be to erect a quite unnecessary argument to precede the very argument I have given above: CD / BD is equal to, less than, or greater than ang. CAD / ang. BAD. Therefore by disjunction of ratios either $(CD - BD)$ / BD is equal to, less than, or greater than (ang. CAD − ang. BAD) / ang. BAD. Thus, by the equalities of (1) CF / FD is equal to, less than, or greater than ang. CAF / ang. FAD. But, by Proposition I.5, CF / FD > ang. CAF / ang. FAD. Hence, reversing the steps, and by the conjunction of ratios, CD / BD > ang. CAD / ang. BAD.

Prop. I.7

[1] We may expand the argument as follows: (1) AE / EC = EB / ED, by VI.14 (=Gr. VI.15) of Euclid. (2) AE / EB = EC / ED, by alternation. (3) $(AE + EB)$ / EB = $(CE + ED)$ / ED,

from line AE [to satisfy the proportion], and let a straight line be drawn from F to D. Therefore you will argue clearly from [Euclidian propositions] VI.6 and VI.4 (with the help of V.22) and from the definition of similar surfaces that the part of angle D which lines DE and DF contain is equal to angle B [i.e. CBE], and hence whole D [i.e. angle CDA] is greater than B, and this is what has been proposed. And it follows by I.4 [of Euclid] that if the sides that cut each other are equal, the superior angles are equal; and by I.8 [of Euclid], if the angles [are equal], [so] also are the sides.

8. (=P.8) IF ANY NUMBER OF TRIANGLES STAND ON THE SAME BASE BETWEEN PARALLEL LINES, THAT ONE WHOSE SUPERIOR ANGLE IS MAXIMUM WILL BE THE ONE WHOSE REMAINING SIDES ARE EQUAL, AND BY THE AMOUNT THEY [I.E. THE SUPERIOR ANGLES] ARE CLOSER TO IT [I.E. THE MAXIMUM SUPERIOR ANGLE] BY SUCH AMOUNT ARE THEY GREATER THAN THOSE MORE REMOTE [FROM IT].

Let the base be AB, and let triangles be constructed on it, one of which has equal remaining sides and its superior angle at point C [see Fig. I.8]. A second [triangle] has its apex at D, and a third its apex at E farther [from C than is D]. Therefore, because the sides of triangle ABC are equal, its angles at the base are equal and, necessarily, acute. Hence their alternate [angles] are acute and their extrinsic [angles] obtuse [i.e., BCF is acute and PBD (and thus its equal BCD) is obtuse].[1] And because an obtuse angle is the maximum [angle] in a triangle, the maximum side is opposite it; and therefore line BD is greater than line BC; therefore $BD > AC$, AC being equal to BC; therefore, by the preceding [proposition] angle D is less than angle C. And because line $DB > AD$ (being opposite a greater angle) and $DB <$ line BE (by the third [proposition] of this work), therefore $BE > AD$. Therefore by the preceding [proposition] angle $E <$ angle D, and thus it is evident that angle C is the maximum. And if there is an infinitude [of superior angles] always farther from it (the superior angle of the isosceles triangle), they will always be less than those closer to it. And those [superior angles] equidistant from it are equal to each other by I.29 and I.4 [of Euclid].[2]

i.e. $AB / CD = EB / ED$, by conjunctive proportionality. (4) $EB > ED$, since $AB > CD$ (the latter being given). (5) Therefore, $AE > EC$, from (4) and (1) together. The text continues the argument to its conclusion as follows: (6) Hence we may cut from AE a line EF such that $AE / EC = EC / EF$. (7) Connecting DF, it is evident that tri. DEF is similar to tri. BCE, since, by (1) and (6), $EB / ED = EC / EF$, and the angle at E in each triangle is the same. (8) Hence ang. $CBE =$ ang. CDF. (9) Thus ang. $CDA >$ ang. CBE. Q.E.D.
Prop. I.8

[1] The word *cointrinseci* in the text seems to be an error, for *extrinseci* is required, as is evident in my bracketed phrase here in the translation. Thus BCF is the alternate angle of angle ABC and is acute, while angle PBC is the extrinsic angle of ABC and is obtuse. Hence, since ang. $PBC =$ ang. BCD, ang. BCD is also obtuse. Accordingly side BD in tri. BCD is longer than side BC and is also longer than the latter's equal AC.

[2] Thus in Fig. I.8 tri. $AFB =$ tri. ADB. This trivial corollary does not appear in the enunciation. Nor is it mentioned in any way in Prop. 8 of the *Liber philotegni*.

9. (=P.9) IF TWO TRIANGLES HAVING A PAIR OF EQUAL ANGLES ARE EQUAL, THEN THE PERIMETER OF THE [TRIANGLE] IN WHICH ONE OF THE [FOUR] SIDES INCLUDING THE TWO EQUAL ANGLES IS THE MAXIMUM [OF THESE FOUR SIDES] IS GREATER [THAN THE PERIMETER OF THE OTHER TRIANGLE].

Let the equal triangles be *ABC* and *DEF* [see Fig. I.9], whose equal angles are *B* and *E*, and let line *AB* > *DE* and also let *AB* > *EF*. I say that the sides of triangle *ABC* taken together are greater than the sides of triangle *DEF* taken together. Therefore because line *AB* > *DE* and *AB* > *EF*, by VI.14 (=Gr. VI.15) [of Euclid] line *BC* is less than each of them [i.e. *BC* < *AB* and *BC* < *EF*].[1] Therefore, by the last [proposition] of [Book] V [of Euclid],[2] *AB* + *BC* > *EF* + *ED*. It remains, therefore, to show that line *AC* is not at all less than line *FD*. Moreover, I shall show that it is neither less nor equal, but rather is more. Therefore let line *DE* be extended from point *D* until it equals line *AB*, and let this be at point *G*; and from line *EF* let a line equal to *CB* be cut, and let it be *HE*. And let a line be drawn from point *H* to point *G*, cutting line *FD* in point *L*. And triangle *HEG* will [thus] become equal to triangle *ABC*, by I.4 [of Euclid]. Hence it will also be equal to triangle *FED*, and line *HG* will equal line *AC*. Therefore, with the common quadrangle *EHLD* subtracted, there will remain two equal triangles, having a pair of equal angles at point *L*. Therefore, if a straight line is drawn from *H* to *D* and another from *F* to *G*, then those two lines will be parallel, by I.39 or VI.2 [of Euclid].[3] Therefore, because angle *H* on line *HD* is greater than angle *D* on that line, for line *DE* > line *HE*, therefore the whole angle *F* on line *FG* is greater than the whole [angle] *G* on that line. And from this it follows indirectly that line *HG*, which is equal to line *AC*, is neither less than nor equal to line *FD*. And so it remains that it is greater, and this is what has been proposed. And you will argue that it is not less by the penultimate [proposition], and by [the Euclidian propositions] VI.14 (=Gr. VI.15), V.13 (=Gr. V.12), and I.19; and that it is not equal from that which follows from the penultimate [proposition], namely that if the sides that cut each

Prop. I.9

[1] This is evident, for, by Prop. VI.14 (=Gr. VI.15) of Euclid, *AB* / *DE* = *EF* / *BC*. Hence, since *AB* > *DE*, so *EF* > *BC*; and *AB* was the maximum of the lines and is thus also greater than *BC*. Hence *BC* is less than each of *AB* and *EF*.

[2] This is Proposition V.25, which shows that the version of the *Elements* being quoted by the author of this tract is not the version of Campanus, for in the latter we have a good many extra propositions (see the text over footnotes 11–12 in Part III, Chap. 1).

[3] This is obvious by using either of the two Euclidian propositions. In the first instance, note that if the equal triangles *DLG* and *HLF* are added to tri. *DHL*, then tri. *DHG* = tri. *DHF*. Then since these triangles are on the same base, they must be between parallel lines, i.e. lines *DH* and *FG*, as we know from Prop. I.39 of Euclid. It may also be proved in the second instance by Prop. VI.2 as follows. Since tri. *EHG* is identical with tri. *BCA* and thus *EG* = *AB* and *EH* = *BC*, and from VI.14 (=Gr. VI.15) of Euclid *AB* / *DE* = *EF* / *BC*, therefore, by substituting the equals, *EG* / *DE* = *EF* / *EH*. And so in triangle *EFG* line *HD* cuts two of its sides proportionally and thus is parallel to the third side *FG* by Prop. VI.2.

other are equal the superior angles are equal, and by VI.14 (=Gr. VI.15) and VI.13 (=Gr. VI.14) [of Euclid].

10. (=P.10) IF TRIANGLES ARE SET UPON THE SAME BASE BE-TWEEN PARALLEL LINES, THE SUM OF THE [TWO] SIDES OF THE TRIANGLE WHOSE REMAINING SIDES ARE EQUAL WILL BE LESS [THAN THE SUM OF THE TWO SIDES OF ANY OTHER SUCH TRI-ANGLE], AND BY THE AMOUNT [THAT THE TWO SIDES OF THAT SECOND TRIANGLE ARE] CLOSER TO THEM, BY THAT MUCH LESS [IS THEIR SUM] THAN [THE SUM OF THE] MORE REMOTE SIDES [OF STILL ANOTHER SUCH TRIANGLE].

Let three triangles be set upon base AB [see Fig. I.10], completely as in the penultimate [proposition], and let line AC be extended to point F so that CF equals CB; and let line AD be extended to point G so that DG equals DB; and let line AE be extended to point H so that line EH equals line EB. Then let a straight line be drawn between F and D and another between G and E. And you will show from I.5, I.29 (twice), I.4, and again I.5 and I.19 [all of Euclid] that line AG > line AF; and from I.29 (twice), [I.]24, and [I.]18 [again, of Euclid] you will show that line AH > line AG, and thus for an infinitude [of such extended lines].[1] [Line] AF will always be the least [of such lines], and those closer [to AF] will be less; and because any of these lines is equal to the two sides [of the relevant triangle], that which has been proposed is evident. You will also show that any [two such] triangles whose apexes are equidistant from point C have remaining sides whose sums are equal, for their sides that intersect each other are equal since their superior angles as well as the remaining two sides are equal to each other by this [argument] and by I.29, I.4, and [I.]8 [of Euclid].

11. (=P.11) IN THE CASE OF ANY TWO TRIANGLES WHOSE BASES ARE EQUAL, THE RATIO OF ONE TO THE OTHER WILL BE AS THAT OF THE ALTITUDE OF THE ONE TO THE ALTITUDE OF THE OTHER.

The altitude of a triangle is a line perpendicularly drawn from the apex of the triangle to its base (either inside or outside [of the triangle]). Indeed any line which is perpendicular to the parallel lines between which the triangle stands is equal to the altitude. Therefore let two triangles be made on equal bases [see Fig. I.11], and, with perpendicular sides erected on the bases, let parallelograms be completed which are [respectively] equally high as the triangles and which are double the triangles by I.41 [of Euclid]. Therefore, because the bases are equal, the parallelograms in that direction will be of the same altitudes [as the triangles]; therefore by VI.1 [of Euclid] the ratio of one to the other is as the ratio of the perpendicular sides on the bases; hence the same is the ratio of the triangles to each other because the ratio of multiples and submultiples is the same.

Prop. I.10

[1] The proof of this sentence has been expanded in MS *H* (see Prop. I.10, variant reading to lines 10–12).

12. (=P.12) IN THE CASE OF ANY TWO TRIANGLES IN WHICH THE TWO EQUAL SIDES OF THE ONE ARE EQUAL TO THE TWO EQUAL SIDES OF THE OTHER, THE RATIO OF THAT [TRIANGLE] WHOSE BASE IS GREATER TO THE OTHER [TRIANGLE] WILL BE LESS THAN THAT OF ITS BASE TO THE BASE OF THE OTHER.

Let there be two unequal bases: the greater *AC* and the lesser *DG* [see Fig. I.12]. Upon these bases let two triangles be constructed whose four remaining sides are equal to one another, and from the middle points of the bases let lines be drawn to the apexes of the triangles, namely line *FB* from the middle of *AC* and line *HE* from the middle of *DG*. Therefore lines *FB* and *HE* will be perpendiculars by I.8 [of Euclid] and are altitudes of the triangles, and line *FB* < *HE* by the penultimate [proposition] of [Book] I [of Euclid], since line *FC* > line *HG*. And with care taken and by means of I.3 and I.31 of Euclid a certain line parallel to base *AC* and equal to line *DG* (which is less than the base) may be located inside of triangle *ABC*, and let the line be called *KM*, and let it cut the perpendicular *FB* in point *L*. Moreover, by VI.9 (=Gr. VI.13) [of Euclid], let *AC* / *KM* = *KM* / line *PT*.[1] Therefore, inverting the proportion, *PT* / *KM* = *KM* / *AC*. But *KM* / *AC* = *BL* / *BF*, by VI.4 and V.15 [of Euclid]. And because *BF* < *EH*, therefore *BL* / *BF* > *BL* / *EH*, by V.8 [of Euclid]. And therefore *BL* / *BF* > triangle *KBM* / triangle *DEG*, by the preceding [proposition]. Therefore, *PT* / *KM* > triangle *KBM* / triangle *DEG*. But *AC* / *PT* = triangle *ABC* / triangle *KBM*, by the corollary to VI.17 (=Gr. VI.19) [of Euclid]. Conclude, therefore, that the ratio of line *AC* to line *KM*, which is equal to line *DG*, is greater than that of triangle *ABC* to triangle *DEG*, and this is what has been proposed.

You will draw this conclusion, I say, from this rule: If the ratio of the first to the second is that of the third to the fourth, and that of the second to the fifth is greater than that of the fourth to the sixth, [so] the ratio of the first to the fifth will be greater than that of the third to the sixth. The demonstration of this is had by V.16 [of Euclid] and by II.12 of the *Arithmetic* of Jordanus.[2] Therefore [in the proposition at hand the terms are] as follows: the first, *AC*; the second, *PT*; the third, triangle *ABC*; the fourth, triangle *KBM*; the fifth, line *KM*; and the sixth, triangle *DEG*.[3]

13. (=P.13) IF THERE ARE TWO EQUAL TRIANGLES, THEIR BASES ARE RECIPROCALLY PROPORTIONAL TO THEIR ALTITUDES.

Prop. I.12

[1] That is, let *PT* be of such magnitude that the proportion is satisfied.

[2] Using a modern expression, we may illustrate the rule as follows: Assume that *a* / *b* = *c* / *d* and that *b* / *e* > *d* / *f*. Then if we multiply the ratios of the last expression by the equal ratios of the first, the result is that $(a / b) \cdot (b / e) > (c / d) \cdot (d / f)$. Hence *a* / *e* > *c* / *f*, as the rule states. For the relevant proposition of Jordanus' *Arithmetica* (namely II.12), see Part II, Chap. 2, n. 4.

[3] Hence, by the rule stated here: *AC* / *KM* > tri. *ABC* / tri. *DEG*, and, since *KM* = *DG*, *AC* / *DG* > tri. *ABC* / tri. *DEG*, which may be rewritten in the form of the enunciation: tri. *ABC* / tri. *DEG* < *AC* / *DG*.

Upon the bases of the proposed triangles let rectangles be constructed that are as equally high as the triangles [see Fig. I.13]. These rectangles will necessarily be equal since, by I.41 [of Euclid], they are double the equal triangles. Therefore argue [that which has been proposed] by VI.13 (=Gr. VI.14) [of Euclid].

Here Begins the Second Book.

1. (=P.14) WITH TWO LINES GIVEN, TO DIVIDE EITHER OF THEM SO THAT ONE OF THE SEGMENTS IS TO THE REMAINING [SEGMENT] AS THAT SAME REMAINING [SEGMENT] IS TO THE OTHER OF THE PROPOSED [LINES].

Let the given lines be joined, and let the whole composite line be AC [see Fig. II.1] and let the point of juncture be B, and upon the whole AC let us draw a semicircle, and from point B let a perpendicular be drawn to the circumference, and let it fall on point D. And let us describe a small circle whose diameter is line BD, and from point A let straight line AFE be drawn, cutting the small circle [and passing] through its center. Then let a straight line be drawn between E and B, and from point F let another [line] parallel to EB be drawn until it cuts line AB, and let the point of section be H. I say, therefore, that line AB is so cut in point H that $AH / HB = HB / BC$, and this is what has been proposed. For this, you will reason as follows.

Since line AB is tangent to the small circle by III.15 (=Gr. III.16) [of Euclid] and line AE cuts the same [circle], then by the penultimate [proposition] of the same [Book III] that [rectangle] which arises from AE and AF is equal to the square of the line AB. Therefore, by VI.16 (=Gr. VI.17) [of Euclid],[1] $AE / AB = AB / AF$. But, by VI.2 [of Euclid], $EF / AF = BH / HA$. Therefore permutatively $EF / BH = AF / AH$, and hence the whole $[AE] /$ whole $[AB] = AF / AH$ by V.13 (=Gr. V.12) [of Euclid]; but $AE / AB = AB / AF$, as we just demonstrated. Therefore, immediately, by V.11 [of Euclid] $EF / HB = BA / AF$. Therefore permutatively $EF / BA = HB / AF$. But $EF = $ line BD and $CB / BD = BD / BA$ by III.30 (=Gr. III.31) and VI.8 [of Euclid]. Therefore $CB / EF = EF / BA$ and $EF / BA = HB / AF$. Therefore you will argue by equal proportionality that $CB / EF = HB / AF$. But $EF / HB = AF / HA$; therefore $CB / HB = BH / HA$. Then invert and convert [the ratios] and you will have that which has been proposed.

Prop. II.1
[1] That is, by the second part of VI.16 (=Gr. VI.17) of Euclid. The argument from this point runs as follows: (1) $AE \cdot AF = AB^2$ (by the penultimate of Book III of Euclid). (2) $AE / AB = AB / AF$ (by alternation). (3) $EF / AF = BH / HA$ (by VI.2 of Euclid), or, rewriting the proportion, $AF / AH = EF / BH$. (4) $EF / BH = AF / AH = AE / AB$, by the similarity of triangles. (5) Then, from (2) and (4), $AB / AF = AF / AH$. (6) From (3) and (5), $AB / AF = EF / BH$. (7) Then, permutatively, $EF / AB = BH / AF$. (8) Now $BD = EF$ and $BC / BD = BD / AB$. (9) Therefore $BC / EF = EF / AB$. (10) Therefore, from (7), (8), and (9), $BC / EF = BH / AF$, or $BC / BH = EF / AF$. (11) But, from (3) and (9), $BC / BH = BH / AH$, and, inverting the proportion and transposing the ratios, $AH / BH = BH / BC$. Q.E.D.

2. (=P.15) WITH TWO LINES PROPOSED, TO DIVIDE ONE OF THEM SO THAT THE SUM OF THE OTHER LINE AND THE GREATER SEGMENT OF THE DIVIDED LINE IS TO THE SAME GREATER [SEGMENT] AS THE GREATER SEGMENT IS TO THE LESSER [SEGMENT OF THE DIVIDED LINE].

As before, let the given lines be joined at point B [see Fig. II.2], and upon the whole AC let us describe a semicircle. Then upon the diameter at point B let a line be erected that contains with AC half a right angle. That line protracted to the circumference let fall on point D, from which let a perpendicular be dropped to the diameter, falling on point E. I say, therefore, that that section which you seek is made at E. For, because each of the angles on BD is half a right angle by I.32 [of Euclid], line DE = line BE by I.6 [of Euclid]. Therefore, since DE is a mean proportional between CE and EA, so also in the same way will BE be [a mean proportional between those lines]. Therefore $CE / BE = BE / EA$, BE being the greater segment and EA the lesser; and this is what has been proposed.

3. (=P.16) TO CUT A GIVEN LINE SO THAT THE RATIO OF ONE OF [ITS] SEGMENTS TO THE OTHER IS AS THAT OF THE SUM OF THE OTHER SEGMENT AND ANY [OTHER] GIVEN LINE TO THE SAME GIVEN [LINE].

Let AB be the line that is to be divided, and let another given [line] be BC, and let them be joined in point B, and upon the whole AC let a semicircle be made, and let perpendicular BD be erected as above, and let a line be drawn between C and D. With that line as a radius and with a center placed in C, let a segment [i.e. arc] of a circle be drawn that cuts line AB in point E, and the section you seek will be in E. For $AC / EC = EC / BC$ by the last part of VI.8 [of Euclid][1] since line $EC = DC$. Therefore by V.19 [of Euclid] $AE / EB = EC / BC$, and this is what has been proposed [see Fig. II.3].

4. (=P.17) WITH TWO LINES GIVEN, TO CUT ONE SO THAT THE OTHER [GIVEN LINE] IS TO ONE SEGMENT OF THE DIVIDED LINE AS THE SUM OF THE SAME GIVEN LINE AND THE REMAINING SEGMENT OF THE DIVIDED LINE IS TO THAT SAME [SEGMENT].

Let the given lines be AB and BC [see Fig. II.4], and let them be joined in point B, and let there be added to the whole composite line [AC] a certain line equal to BC, and let it be CE. Then let a circle be described whose whole diameter is equal to line AE, in which circle let a line equal to line AC be

---

Prop. II.3

[1] See the English translation of the *Liber philotegni,* Prop. 16, n. 1, where it is shown that $AC / DC = DC / BC$, and hence, since $EC = DC$, we may conclude that $AC / EC = EC / BC$. Then, by the disjunction of the ratios, $AE / EC = EB / BC$, and, finally, by alternation, $AE / EB = EC / BC$. Incidentally, the text here is silent concerning the step involving disjunction. It may be that the author intended to write before *que* in the last line: "que AE ad EC eadem est EB ad BC; ergo permutatim". The translation of the text with the addition would then be: "Therefore by V.19 [of Euclid] $AE / EC = EB / BC$, and hence permutatively $AE / EB = EC / BC$, and this is what has been proposed."

placed by IV.1 of Euclid, and let it be GD. From this line let there be cut a certain segment equal to AB, and let it be DF; and the remaining segment, evidently FG, will be equal to line BC. Then let a certain diameter be drawn in the circle, passing through point F, which diameter, since it is equal to AE, let be called by that same name [AE], and let the [points of] section in it be designated B and C. I say, therefore, that the section which you require takes place in point F. For, by III.34 (=Gr. III.35) and VI.15 (=Gr. VI.16) [of Euclid], $EF / DF = GF / AF$; therefore, by equality, $EF / AB = BC / AF$; therefore, permutatively, $EF / BC = AB / AF$. Therefore, since $BC = CE$, disjunctively $CF / BC = BF / AF$; and, permutatively, $CF / BF = BC / AF$. Therefore transpose the ratios and say that $BC / AF = CF / BF$, and this is what has been proposed.

5. (=P.18) WITH TWO LINES PROPOSED OF WHICH ONE IS LESS THAN OR EQUAL TO ONE FOURTH OF THE OTHER, TO ADD TO THE SHORTER LINE [A LINE] SUCH THAT THE RATIO OF THE ADDED LINE TO THE LINE COMPOSED [OF THE SHORTER LINE AND THE ADDED LINE] IS THAT OF THE COMPOSITE LINE TO THE OTHER PROPOSED LINE.

Let the given lines be a greater line AB and a lesser line BC [see Fig. II.5a], and let them be joined in the customary way in point B, and let a semicircle be described on the whole AC, and let a perpendicular BD be erected. Therefore, if line $BC < ¼$ line AB, so BD (since it is the mean proportional between them) will be less than $½AB$. Therefore let AB be bisected at point E, and let a semicircle be described on it, and let perpendicular EG be erected. From EG let a certain line equal to DB be cut, and let it be LE, and let a straight line be drawn between L and D, and let T be the point in which this line cuts the lesser circumference. From T let perpendicular TM be dropped, which perpendicular will equal line DB by I.34 [of Euclid] and will be the [mean] proportional between AM and MB by [the corollary to] VI.8 [of Euclid]. Therefore by VI.16 (=Gr. VI.17) and the second part of VI.15 (=Gr. VI.16) [of Euclid] $AB / AM = MB / BC$.[1] And if this [is so], then line $BM > BC$. Therefore let there be cut from BM a certain line equal to line BC, and let it be HB. I say, therefore, that line HM, [by] which [BM] exceeds [BH], is the line which we seek. For, since $AB / AM = MB / HB$, HB being equal to BC, [so] by V.19 [of Euclid] $MB / HM = AB / MB$.[2] Invert this

---

Prop. II.5

[1] The argument is constructed as follows: (1) $TM = BD$ (by I.34 of Euclid). (2) $AB / BD = BD / BC$ (by the corollary to VI.8 of Euclid). (3) $AB / TM = TM / BC$, by (1) and (2) together. (4) $AM / TM = TM / MB$ (also by the corollary to VI.8). (5) $AB \cdot BC = AM \cdot MB$, by the second part of VI.15 (=Gr. VI.16) of Euclid. (6) Therefore $AB / AM = MB / BC$.

[2] This is obvious by the following argument: (1) $AB / AM = MB / HB$. (2) $(AB - AM) / (MB - HB) = AM / HB$, or $MB / HM = AM / HB$. (3) By the alternation of (1), $AM / HB = AB / MB$. (5) Therefore, by (2) and (3) together, $MB / HM = AB / MB$, and inverting this proportion we have what was proposed, namely $HM / MB = MB / AB$.

proportion and say that $HM / MB = MB / AB$, and this is what has been proposed since $HB = BC$ and BC is the lesser of the proposed lines.

But there is another way to do this same thing, as well if $BC = \frac{1}{4}AB$ as if $BC < \frac{1}{4}AB$. But if $BC > \frac{1}{4}AB$, you will labor in vain by this art. Whether $BC < \frac{1}{4}AB$ or $BC = \frac{1}{4}AB$, let AB and BC be joined so that they contain a right angle at point B [see Fig. II.5b], and let a rectangle $ABCD$ contained under these [lines] be completed. Let triangle BDN equal to it (rectangle $ABCD$) be constructed on BN, where $BN = 2 \, BC$, and by means of that triangle let there be constructed on line AB by VI.27 (=Gr. VI.28) a parallelogram [equal to rectangle $ABCD$] and deficient by a square surface from a [rectangular] surface to be completed on the whole line [AB, i.e. the rectangle contained by AB and FE][3] and it (the parallelogram) will be a rectangle contained under lines AE and EF, and $EF = EB$. And because, by VI.13 (=Gr. VI.14) [of Euclid], $AB / AE = EF / BC$, therefore EF (and consequently EB) $> BC$. Therefore let there be cut from EB a certain line BH equal to BC. I say that the line EH, [by which [EB] exceeds [BH]], is the line which we seek. For, since $AB / AE = EB / HB$, [so] by V.19 [of Euclid] $AB / EB = EB / HE$. Therefore invert and transpose and you will have what you desired.

6. (=P.19) WHEN THE RATIO OF A LINE ADDED TO THE SHORTER LINE TO THE LINE COMPOSED [OF THE ADDED LINE AND THE SHORTER LINE] IS GREATER THAN THAT OF THE COMPOSITE LINE TO THE LONGER [LINE], IT IS NECESSARY THAT THE SHORTER LINE IS LESS THAN ONE FOURTH OF THE LONGER [LINE].

So that if $EH / EB > EB / AB$, I say that $HB < \frac{1}{4}AB$ [see Fig. II.6]. By II.11 of the *Arithmetic* [of Jordanus][1] in regard to continua, or by V.10 of Euclid, $AB / EB > EB / EH$. For by that [expression] it is evident that the line to which EB is related as EH is to EB is less than AB, and let that line be ZB. And since $AB > ZB$, it (AB) has a greater ratio to EB, and therefore $AB / EB > EB / EH$. And if this is so, the rectangle contained under AB and EH is greater than the square of line EB, by II.27 of the *Arithmetic* [of Jordanus][2] or because the rectangle which is contained under ZB (less than AB) and EB is equal to the square of EB. Therefore let line EB be squared and let there be distinguished in the square its gnomon about the square of line EH; with one of whose sides drawn, let there be completed the rectangle contained under AB and BL (BL being equal to line EH). But since in every square each supplement [i.e. supplementary rectangle] is the [mean] pro-

---

[3] This is the technique of application of areas. See my discussion of this proposition in Part III, Chap. 1 above.

Prop. II.6

[1] See Part II, Chap. 2, n. 4 for the text of Jordanus, *Arithmetica*, Prop. II.11.

[2] *Ibid.*, for the text of Prop. II.27.

portional between the two squares standing about the diagonal,[3] as is evident by VI.1 [of Euclid] twice, and also the supplements are equal by I.43 [of Euclid], therefore the supplements taken together will not [ever] be greater than the squares taken together by the last [proposition] of [Book] V; therefore they will not [ever] be greater than half the whole square [*EG*, which since it includes the two smaller squares and the two rectangles must be greater than the two squares]. And therefore one of those [rectangles], namely *HBL*, will not [ever] be greater than one fourth of the whole square [*EG*].[4] And because rectangle *ABL* > the whole square [as was proved in the beginning of the proof], so, necessarily, supplementary rectangle *HBL* < ¼ rectangle *ABL*. Therefore line *HB* < ¼*AB* by VI.1 [of Euclid].

7. (=P.20) IF THE SHORTER [OF TWO PROPOSED LINES] IS PRO-PORTIONAL BETWEEN THE SEGMENTS [PRODUCED BY THE DI-VISION] OF THE LONGER [OF THE PROPOSED LINES], AND IF THE RATIO OF A LINE ADDED TO THE SHORTER TO A LINE COMPOSED [OF THE SHORTER AND THE ADDED LINE] IS GREATER THAN THAT OF THE COMPOSITE LINE TO THE LONGER [OF THE PRO-POSED LINES], THEN NECESSARILY THE SAME COMPOSITE LINE IS GREATER THAN ONE OF THE SEGMENTS [OF THE LONGER OF THE PROPOSED LINES].

Let the greater line *AB* be divided into *AE* and *EB* [see Fig. II.7] and let the lesser line be proportional between *AE* and *EB* so that *EB* / *BC* = *BC* / *AE*. Also let line *DC* be added to line *BC*. And because, by hypothesis, *DC* / *DB* > *DB* / *AB*, so by the preceding [proposition] *BC* < ¼ line *AB*. But since line *AB* is divided into *AE* and *EB*, it is necessary that one of the segments is greater than ¼*AB*, and, if one wishes, let [that] segment be *EB*. Therefore *EB* > *BC*. And if this is [so], therefore *BC* > *AE* since it (*BC*) is proportional between the segments. But *DB* > *BC*, since every whole is greater than its part. Therefore *DB* > *AE*, and so *DB* is greater than one of the segments [of *AB*], and this is what has been proposed.

8. (=P.21) WITH A POINT MARKED IN ANY ONE OF THE SIDES OF A TRIANGLE, TO PRODUCE A LINE FROM IT WHICH BISECTS THE TRIANGLE.

Let there be triangle *ABC* [see Fig. II.8]. Then if a point is marked in the middle of one side, as in *E*, the middle point of side *AB*, and if a line is

---

[3] Since the altitudes of square *KE* and rectangle *KB* are the same, so area of sq. *KE* / area of rect. *KB* = *EH* / *KL*, by VI.1 of Euclid. Similarly, rect. *KB* / area of sq. *KG* = *EH* / *KL*. Hence, area sq. *KE* / area rect. *KB* = area of rect. *KB* / area of sq. *KG*. Similarly, area of sq. *KE* / area of rect. *DK* = area of rect. *DK* / area of sq. *KG*. Therefore each of the rectangular supplements is the proportional mean between the squares *KE* and *KG*.

[4] This is evident, for if *a* = sq. *KE*, *b* = rect. *DK*, *c* = sq. *KG*, then, as we noted before, *a* / *b* = *b* / *c*. Then by V.25 of Euclid, *a* + *c* > 2 *b*. Hence the sum of the rectangles (=2*b*) is always less than the sum of the squares (*a* + *c*). Furthermore, since *b* = ½ (2*b*) and *b* < ½ (*a* + *c*) and 2*b* < ½ (2*b* + *a* + *c*) or 2*b* < ½ sq. *EG*, hence *b* < ¼ sq. *EG*, i.e., rect. *HBL* < ¼ sq. *EG*.

drawn to the opposite angle, as to C, it is evident by I.38 [of Euclid] that triangle ABC will have been bisected.

But if the point is not marked in the middle [of a side] but elsewhere, as in point D, [then] let line DC be drawn and another [line] EG parallel to it, and let a line be drawn between G and D cutting line EC in point T. I say that the last line bisects triangle ABC. For triangles DEC and DGC are equal by I.37 [of Euclid]. With common [area DTC] subtracted, triangles DTE and CTG will be equal. Therefore, with the same [area $ADTC$] added, surface $ADGC$ will equal triangle AEC, which triangle is half the whole [triangle ABC].

9. WITH TWO TRIANGLES PROPOSED, TO JUDGE WHETHER THEY ARE EQUAL OR ONE OF THEM IS LARGER.[1]

Let there be constructed on straight line AB [see Fig. II.9] in the same direction two rectangles respectively equal to these triangles, by I.44 [of Euclid], and the ratio between these rectangles will be that between their second sides by VI.1 [of Euclid]. Hence it (the latter ratio) is also the same as that between the triangles.

10. WITH TWO UNEQUAL TRIANGLES PROPOSED, TO CUT FROM THE LARGER A TRIANGLE EQUALLY HIGH AS IT AND EQUAL TO THE SMALLER, AND TO CONSTRUCT ON THE BASE OF THE SMALLER PROTRACTED AS FAR AS WE LIKE A TRIANGLE EQUALLY HIGH AS THE SMALLER AND EQUAL TO THE LARGER.

Let the proposed triangles be ABC, the larger, and DEF, the smaller [see Fig. II.10]. Proceed therefore to the first part [of the proposition] as follows. On line BC, by I.44 [of Euclid], let a parallelogram be constructed equal to triangle DEF, which parallelogram we let have an angle equal to C; and let a diagonal be drawn in it from angle B to its opposite angle G. Then let line CG be doubled in the opposite direction [toward A] by line GH, and let a line be drawn between H and B. I say, therefore, that triangle HBC = triangle DEF by I.41 [of Euclid].

Proceed to the second part as follows. On line DE let a parallelogram be constructed equal to triangle ABC, which parallelogram we let have an angle equal to D, and let a diagonal be drawn in it from E to [its] opposite angle K, and so the result will be a triangle DEK, which if doubled in the prior way produces DEN, [and so DEN] which is equal to [the parallelogram is also equal to] ABC.

11. TO PLACE ON A GIVEN LINE A TRIANGLE EQUAL TO A PROPOSED TRIANGLE.

Let the given triangle be A and the given line BC [see Fig. II.11]. Then let the given triangle be doubled. And let a parallelogram be constructed on

---

Prop. II.9

[1] The next four propositions were added by the author of the *Liber de triangulis Iordani,* and their proofs and objectives have been discussed above in the account of these propositions in Part III, Chap. 1.

the given line in the customary way equal to the whole double triangle. When this parallelogram has been divided by a diagonal, that which has been intended will result.

12. WITH A STRAIGHT LINE GIVEN, TO FIND ANOTHER STRAIGHT LINE TO WHICH THE PRIOR [STRAIGHT LINE] IS RE-LATED AS IS ANY GIVEN TRIANGLE TO ANOTHER GIVEN TRIANGLE.

Let the given triangles be *A* and *B* and the given line *DC* [see Fig. II.12]. Then consider whether the triangles are equal, for [in case they are equal] then the line which you seek will be equal to *DC*. But if they are not equal, let *A* be the larger and *B* the smaller. And you will place on line *DC* a triangle equal to that one which you wish to be the antecedent [term] in the ratio, and let it be *DGC*. Then by diminishing it if it is equal to the larger [triangle] or by augmenting it if it is equal to the smaller [triangle], there will result after line *GE* has been drawn a triangle equal to the remaining triangle, by the preceding [proposition], and there will also result the line *DE* which you seek, which line is either greater or less than *DC* according to whether you posit the larger or smaller triangle as the antecedent.

13. (=P.22) WITH A TRIANGLE GIVEN AND A POINT MARKED OUTSIDE OF IT, TO DRAW A LINE PROCEEDING THROUGH THE POINT WHICH BISECTS THE TRIANGLE.

Let the triangle be *ABC* [see Fig. II.13a] and let the point *D* be outside of the triangle but between lines *AEF* and *HBL* which bisect sides of the triangle and also the triangle itself, and let these lines be protracted as far as one likes. For if point *D* were placed on one of such [bisecting lines], the intention would soon assume the end [i.e., the construction would immediately give the solution]. Therefore, with the point placed outside of any such [bisector], let us draw from it a line parallel to line *AC* until it meets with side *CB* protracted as far as one wishes, and let the point of juncture be *G*. And let line *CD* be drawn and triangle *CDG* completed. So by the preceding [proposition] let there be a line *MN* such that triangle *CDG* / triangle *AEC* = line *CG* / line *MN*, triangle *AEC* being one half the given triangle. Then, following the argument of II.1 of this [present work], let line *CG* be divided in point *K* so that *GK* / *KC* = *KC* / *MN*, and let the line *DK* be drawn and then be protracted until it meets line *AC* in point *P*. I say, therefore, that line *DP* bisects triangle *ABC*. For, since triangle *CKP* is similar to triangle *KDG* (by VI.4 [of Euclid], the parallelity of lines, I.15 [of Euclid], and the definition of similar surfaces), therefore *CKP* / *KDG* = line *MN* / line *KG* by the corollary to VI.17 (=Gr. VI.19) [of Euclid]. But triangle *KDG* / triangle *CDG* = line *KG* / line *CG*. Therefore immediately, by equal proportionality, triangle *CKP* / triangle *CDG* = line *MN* / line *CG*. But by the same method triangle *AEC* / triangle *CDG* = line *MN* / line *CG*, triangle *AEC* being half the given triangle. Therefore by V.9 [of Euclid] triangle *CKP* = triangle *AEC*, which latter triangle is half the given triangle *ABC*, and this is what has been proposed. And by this same procedure you will lead the adversary [i.e. the falsigraph] to an impossibility, namely that the whole is equal to [its] part, if he posits point *K* to be elsewhere than between *E* and *B* or point *P* to be elsewhere than between *H* and *A*, and triangle *AEC* will always be [greater than the] whole [*CK'P'*] or a part [of *CKP*, see Fig. II.13b].[1]

14. WITH THREE STRAIGHT LINES GIVEN, TO SUBJOIN A FOURTH TO WHICH THE THIRD OF THE PROPOSED [LINES] IS RELATED AS THE FIRST IS TO THE SECOND.[1]

Let there be three lines: the first, *A*; the second, *B*; and the third, *C* [see Fig. II.14]. And let $A / E = E / B$ by VI.9 (=Gr. VI.13) [of Euclid], and let similar triangles be constructed on *A* and *E*; and [so] triangle *A* / triangle *E* = line *A* / line *B* by the corollary to VI.17 (=Gr. VI.19) [of Euclid]. Therefore by the penultimate [proposition] let there be found the line to which line *C* is related as triangle *A* is to triangle *E*, and let it be *D*, and this [line] is the one you seek.

15. IF THE RATIO OF THE WHOLE TO A PART IS GREATER THAN THAT OF THE SAME PART TO A PART OF IT, [THEN] THE RATIO OF THE REST OF THE WHOLE TO THE REST OF THE PART IS GREATER THAN THAT OF THE WHOLE TO THE PART: AND IF LESS, [THEN] LESS.

For you may demonstrate, by II.13 and II.14 of the *Arithmetic* [of Jordanus][1] in regard to continua, that if the ratio of a whole to a whole is greater than of a subtracted part [of the one] to a subtracted part [of the other], so the ratio of the remaining [part of the one] to the remaining [part of the other] is greater than that of whole to whole, and if less, less. From this, therefore, you easily deduce that which has been proposed [see Fig. II.15].

16. WHEN THE SHORTER LINE [OF TWO GIVEN LINES] IS LESS THAN ONE FOURTH OF THE LONGER, THE LINE ADDED TO IT WHICH HAS A RATIO TO THE [LINE] COMPOSED [OF THE ADDED LINE AND THE SHORTER LINE] EQUAL TO THAT OF THE COM-

Prop. II.13
[1] This last sentence represents an addition by the author of the *Liber de triangulis Iordani*. Fig. II.13b illustrates it, for it is obvious therefrom that if *K* is above *B* so that *P* is to the right of *A*, then triangle *CKP* would simultaneously be equal to triangle *AEC* (by the proof) and greater than twice *AEC*. Similarly, if *K'* were below *E* so that *P'* were to the left of *H*, then triangle *CK'P'* would simultaneously be equal to triangle *AEC* and less than triangle *AEC*. Hence in the first instance *AEC* is equal to a part of *CKP* and to the whole of *CKP* and in the second instance *CK'P'* is equal to the whole of *AEC* and is also a part of *AEC*. Hence the contradiction in both cases is the same. The reader should consult the account of this proposition in Part III, Chap. 1, and also that of the equivalent Proposition 22 of the *Liber philotegni* in Part II, Chap. 2. See also the treatment of this proposition by Leonardo Fibonacci in his *Practica geometrie*, the text of which I have given below in Appendix III.A.
Prop. II.14
[1] The next three propositions were added by the author of the *Liber de triangulis Iordani*, and their proofs and objectives have been discussed above in the accounts of these propositions in Part III, Chap. 1.
Prop. II.15
[1] See Part II, Chap. 2, n. 4, for the text of Jordanus' *Arithmetica*, Props. II.13 and II.14.

POSITE [LINE] TO THE LONGER [LINE] IS LESS[1] THAN ANY LINE ADDED TO THE SAME SHORTER [LINE] WHICH HAS A RATIO TO THE COMPOSITE LINE GREATER THAN THAT OF THE COMPOSITE [LINE] TO THE LONGER [LINE]. AND IT IS GREATER[1] THAN ANY [ADDED LINE WHICH HAS A RATIO TO THE COMPOSITE LINE] LESS [THAN THAT OF THE RATIO OF THE COMPOSITE LINE TO THE LONGER LINE]. AND CONVERSELY ANY LINE MORE THAN IT [HAS A] GREATER [RATIO] AND [EVERY LINE] LESS [THAN IT] HAS A LESSER [RATIO] TO THE COMPOSITE [LINE] THAN THAT OF THE COMPOSITE [LINE] TO THE LONGER [LINE], WITH THIS RESERVATION, THAT THE INITIAL LONGER LINE IS ALWAYS LONGER THAN ANY ASSUMED [ADDED LINE].

Let the disposition be completely of the same sort as the first of those which have been fashioned for II.5 of this [work, see Fig. II.5a], namely that which is done by means of the circle, keeping the same things noted [there]. Moreover, let there be line KH [see Fig. II.16] added to line HB (equal to BC, the lesser line) such that $KH / KB > KB / AB$.[2] I say, therefore, that $KH > MH$. For, as was evident in the proof to [II.] 6 of this [work], $AB / KB > KB / KH$, and therefore, by the first part of the preceding [proposition], $AK / HB > AB / KB$. And if this [is so], therefore the rectangle contained under AK and KB is greater than the rectangle contained under AB and HB (or BC) by II.27 of the *Arithmetic* [of Jordanus][3] in regard to continua. Therefore the perpendicular erected from point K to the lesser circumference is greater than perpendicular BD by VI.8 and VI.16 (=Gr. VI.17) of Euclid, and therefore it (the perpendicular from K to the lesser circumference) is greater than perpendicular MT. And if it is greater [than MT], it is closer to the radius EG by III.14 (=Gr. III.15) and III.13 (=Gr. III.14) of Euclid. Therefore point K is necessarily closer to point E and farther from point B in diameter AB than point M. Therefore line $KB > MB$, and thus $KH > MH$, the common line HB having been subtracted. You will easily demonstrate as well the other parts of the proposition by the same procedure, if you should speak with [even] the least of perspicacious ingenuity.

17. (=P.23) WITH A POINT GIVEN INSIDE A PROPOSED TRIANGLE, TO DRAW A LINE THROUGH THIS [POINT] WHICH BISECTS THE TRIANGLE.[1]

Prop. II.16

[1] As I pointed out earlier in Part III, Chap. 2, n. 1, Curtze in his text of this enunciation in line 3 changed the correct reading of *minor* to *maior* (see the variant reading to line 3), and also in line 5 he incorrectly has *minor* instead of *maior* (see the variant reading to line 5). These two errors along with the false readings of *omnium* for *omni* in lines 3 and 6 clearly show that Curtze did not understand the enunciation.

[2] Curtze's understanding of the proof was also deficient, for there is no reason for his having added *ma* [i.e. *MA*] after *linea* in line 14 (see the variant reading to line 14). For a brief account of the objectives and proof of this proposition, see my account of it in Part III, Chap. 1.

[3] See Part II, Chap. 2, n. 4, for the text of Jordanus, *Arithmetica,* Prop. II.27.

Prop. II.17

[1] Consult not only the account of this proposition in Part III, Chap. 1, and that of its equivalent Proposition 23 from the *Liber philotegni* in Part II, Chap. 2, but also the text of its proof from Leonardo Fibonacci's *Practica geometrie* given below in Appendix III.A.

Let there be a triangle *ABC* [see Fig. II.17], and let the point inside of it be *D*, included in the direction of *B* between lines *AG* and *BE*, which bisect the opposite sides and also the triangle, and let a line be drawn through *D* parallel to line *AC*, which line let be *FDH*, and let line *DB* be drawn. Therefore, by [II].12 of this [work] let a certain line *MN* be found such that *BF* / *MN* = triangle *BDF* / *BEC*, *BEC* being half the given triangle. Also let another line *TY* be found such that *BF* / *TY* = triangle *BFH* / triangle *BEC*. And because triangle *BFH* > triangle *BDF*, so also *MN* > *TY* by V.8 and V.10 [of Euclid]. But *BF* / *BC* = *BC* / *TY* by the corollary to VI.17 (=Gr. VI.19) [of Euclid], because triangle *BFH* is similar[2] to triangle *BEC* on account of the parallelity of the lines [*FH* and *CA*]. Further, *BC* / *TY* > *BC* / *MN* by the second part of V.8 [of Euclid]. Therefore *BF* / *BC* > *BC* / *MN*, and so *FC* < ¼*MN* by II.6 of this [work]. Therefore by II.5 of this [work] let there be added in the direction of *F* a certain line *FZ* such that line *FC* / [composite line] *ZC* = *ZC* / *MN*. And [so] *FZ* < *FB* by the first part of the preceding [proposition]. Therefore let line *ZD* be drawn and [then] protracted until it meets line *AC* in point *K*. I say, therefore, that line *ZDK* bisects triangle *ABC*. For triangle *BDF* / triangle *ZDF* = line *BF* / *ZF* by VI.1 [of Euclid]; but triangle *ZDF* / triangle *ZKC* = *ZF* / *MN* by the corollary to VI.17 (=Gr. VI.19) [of Euclid] and by the similitude of triangles. Therefore immediately, by equal proportionality, triangle *BDF* / triangle *ZKC* = line *BF* / line *MN*. But, by the same method, triangle *BDF* / triangle *BEC* = line *BF* / line *MN*. Therefore by the second part of V.9 [of Euclid] triangle *ZKC* = triangle *BEC*, which latter triangle is half of *ABC*.

18. (=P.24) TO DRAW FROM A DESIGNATED[1] POINT WITHIN A GIVEN TRIANGLE TO THE THREE ANGLES THREE [LINES] WHICH TRISECT THE TRIANGLE.

Let the given triangle be *ABC* [see Fig. II.18], and let a third part of one of [its] sides, say side *BC*, be cut off by VI.11 (=Gr. VI.9) [of Euclid], and let it (that third part) be *DC*, and let line *DE* be drawn parallel to *AC* and let its middle point be *G*. From *G* let straight lines be drawn to points *A*, *C*, and *B*. I say that these three lines trisect the triangle. And you will demonstrate this by I.38 and VI.1 [of Euclid], having drawn a straight line between *A* and *D*. For triangle *ADC*, which equals [triangle] *AGC*, will be one third of the whole [triangle] by VI.1, and the two remaining [triangles *AGB* and *CGB*] are equal.[2]

---

[2] Curtze erroneously reads *minor* instead of *similis,* though MS *D* apparently had *similis* (see the variant reading to line 13).

Prop. II.18

[1] For the possible implication of the addition of the term *signato* here, see Part III, Chap. 1, n. 9, and the text above that note.

[2] This is immediately evident because tri. *BGE* = tri. *BDG* since *G* is the midpoint of *ED*, and tri. *AGE* = tri. *CGD* since they have equal bases and are between parallel lines. If we add the two sets of equal triangles, we can conclude that triangles *AGB* and *CGB* are equal, and thus each of them is one-third of the whole triangle, since together they are two-thirds of triangle *ABC*, it having been proved that triangle *AGC* is one-third of triangle *ABC*. This line of reasoning was specifically given in Proposition 24 of the *Liber philotegni.*

19. (=P.25) FROM AN ANGLE OF AN ASSIGNED QUADRANGLE TO DRAW A STRAIGHT LINE WHICH BISECTS THE WHOLE SURFACE OF THE QUADRANGLE.

From the opposite angles of the assigned quadrangle let there be drawn two diagonals in it, which diagonals let be AC and BD, intersecting each other in point G [see Fig. II.19]. I say, therefore, that, if each of them (the diagonals) bisects the other, it bisects the whole quadrangle, and you will prove this by I.38 [of Euclid] twice and by the axiom: if you add equals to equals, the wholes become equals. But if neither of them (the diagonals) bisects the other, the [geometric] art is still not at loss. Then let us posit that $GC > GA$, and let us cut from GC a [segment] EC equal to GA, and let there be drawn from point E a line EL parallel to line GD, L having been fixed in side DC, and let BL be drawn. Proceed therefore: triangle DBC / triangle LBC = line DC / line LC by VI.1 [of Euclid], and hence DBC / LBC = GC / EC. But GC / EC = GC / GA, and further GC / GA = triangle DBC / triangle DAB by means of the partial triangles, VI.1, and V.13 (=Gr. V.12) [of Euclid]. Therefore immediately triangle DBC / triangle DAB = DBC / LBC; hence these [triangles DAB and LBC] are equal by V.9 [of Euclid]. Therefore, with line DL bisected at point T, let a line be drawn between T and B, and I say that it will bisect the quadrangle, which you will argue from the aforesaid I.38 [of Euclid] and the axiom [equals added to equals yield equals].

Here Begins the Third Book on Triangles

1. (=P.26) IF THREE PARALLEL LINES IN A CIRCLE INTERCEPT ARCS THAT ARE EQUAL TO EACH OTHER, THE [PERPENDICULAR] DISTANCE BETWEEN THE LONGEST [LINE] AND THE MIDDLE [LINE] WILL BE GREATER [THAN THE PERPENDICULAR DISTANCE BETWEEN THE MIDDLE LINE AND THE SHORTEST LINE], AND IT [I.E. THE LONGEST LINE] WILL INCLUDE WITH THAT [MIDDLE LINE] A GREATER SEGMENT OF THE CIRCLE.

Let there be three parallel lines in a circle: the first, AB; the middle, CD, less than or at least equal to the first; and the third and shortest, EF; and let arc AC = arc CE, and [so] the chord will equal the chord [see Fig. III.1]. And with transversals DA and DE drawn, it is evident that, since the alternate angles are equal and they fall in equal arcs by III.25 (=Gr. III.26) [of Euclid], arcs (and chords) BD and DF will be equal to each other and to the remaining [arcs and chords AC and CE]. Therefore let line AE be drawn, subtending angle C and cutting line CD in point G, and from the two points E and F let perpendiculars be dropped on AB, perpendiculars which necessarily fall inside the circle (since line EF is interior to [perpendiculars drawn from the termini of] AB and is parallel to that same [line AB]). The perpendiculars from E and F let be ET and FK. They cut CD in points Z and Y, and let TC and KD be drawn. Therefore you have what is required to proceed to each part of the proposition. For, since by III.27 (=Gr. III.28) [of Euclid] arc AB > arc EF, therefore arc CAD > arc CED by the [fifth] axiom [of Book I of Euclid], and therefore the angle at C to which the line AG is subtended is greater than the remaining angle [at C] to which GE is subtended. Hence AG > GE by I.24 of Euclid. And if this [is so], then line TZ > line ZE by VI.2 [of Euclid], and this is the prior part of the proposition, for the line which is perpendicular on each [of two parallel lines in the circle] is called the "distance between the lines." You will easily conclude the second part [of the proposition], namely that surface $ACDB$ > surface $CEFD$, from the fact that TZ > ZE and KY > YF and from VI.1 [of Euclid] taken with respect to the partial parallelograms and partial triangles abutted to them on each side.[1]

2. (=P.27) IF THE SAME ARC UNDERGOES SEVERAL [DIFFERENT] DIVISIONS, THE SUM OF THE CHORDS SUBTENDED BY THE EQUAL SEGMENTS [PRODUCED BY THE EQUAL DIVISION] OF THE ARC IS GREATER [THAN THE SUM OF THE TWO CHORDS SUB-TENDING THE SEGMENTS PRODUCED BY ANY DIVISION OTHER THAN THE EQUAL DIVISION], AND THE CLOSER [THE LATTER TWO CHORDS] ARE TO THEM [I.E. TO THE EQUAL CHORDS] SO MUCH LONGER [IN SUM] ARE THEY THAN [ANY PAIR OF] MORE REMOTE [CHORDS IN SUM].

Let the arc be AB [see Fig. III.2]. Let its division into equal segments be at C, and let there be two other [divisions]: the closer one at D and the more remote one at E, and to these three points [of division] let there be protracted six chords so that there are two chords at each point: one indeed from A and another from B. And since these [chords] are in all six, the four inter-mediary ones will intersect each other in three points: H, G, and K, and a pair of triangles will be conjoined at each of the points [of intersection] and the two individual triangles [in each pair] are similar to one another because they are equiangular (since the angles in which they are conjoined are equal, and similarly, the angles at C, D, and E are equal because they fall in equal arcs). Proceed, therefore. Since triangles ACG and BGD are similar, AC / BD = CG / DG and conjunctively $(AC + CG)$ / $(BD + DG)$ = AC / BD. But AC > BD because it is subtended to a greater arc by III.27 (=Gr. III.28) [of Euclid]. Therefore $AC + CG$ > $BD + DG$. But $AC + CG$ is still greater than line GB by I.20 [of Euclid]. And because $(AC + CG)$ / $(BD + DG)$ = AG / BG by the similitude of triangles and by V.13 (=Gr. V.12) [of Euclid], argue by the last [proposition] of [Book] V^1 (=V.25) [of Euclid] that $AC + CGB$ > $BD + DGA$,[2] and you will prove what remains in the same way.

Prop. III.1

[1] Compare the proof of the second part here to that given in MS *Fa* of the *Liber philotegni* and translated in note 1 of the English translation of Prop. 26 of the *Liber philotegni*.

Prop. III.2

[1] See note 2 to Prop. I.9 above.

[2] Notice that Curtze erroneously changed *CGB* and *DGA* into *DGB* and *CGA* (see the variant reading to line 20).

3. (=P.28) IF EQUAL LINES CUT OFF ARCS IN UNEQUAL CIRCLES, THEY WILL CUT OFF LESS FROM THE LARGER [CIRCLE] AND MORE FROM THE SMALLER [CIRCLE].

Let there be two unequal circles: the larger A and the smaller B [see Fig. III.3], with A and B placed in the centers, and let line DC be located in A and another [line] equal to it in B, which latter line let be FE, and let lines AC and BE be drawn, and let a perpendicular on DC be drawn and [then] protracted to the circumference in point T; similarly let BH be a perpendicular on FE and [then] protracted to the circumference at point K. And $GC = HE$ because they are [respectively] halves of equal lines DC and FE by III.3 of Euclid. And since line $AC >$ line BE because it is the radius of a larger circle, line $AG >$ line BH by the penultimate [proposition] of [Book] I of Euclid. Therefore let $GL = BH$; and let lines LC and LD be drawn, each of which will equal BE by I.4 of Euclid and be greater than LT by III.7 [of Euclid]. Therefore let LT be protracted to point M so that LM is equal to one of them [i.e. lines LC and LD], and with the center placed at L let circle DMC be described, which circle will equal B. [So] arc DMC, since it is equal to arc FKE by III.27 (=Gr. III.28) [of Euclid], will be greater than arc DTC because it will include it, and this is what has been proposed, for an arc including an arc is greater than the included.

4. (=P.29) IF UNEQUAL LINES CUT OFF ARCS IN THE SAME CIR-CLE, THE RATIO OF THE ARCS WILL BE GREATER THAN THAT OF THE CHORDS, WHILE THE RATIO OF THE SEGMENTS OF THE CIRCLES [CUT OFF BY THESE CHORDS] WILL BE GREATER THAN THE SQUARE OF THE RATIO OF THE CHORDS.

In the circle whose center is A [see Fig. III.4] let the lines be located: the longer BC and the shorter DE, and let its diameter be GAH, which let be related to line KL as BC is to DE by II.14 of this [work],[1] and let a circle be constructed whose diameter is KL. In this circle let a segment be cut off by line MN which is similar to the segment which BC cuts off in circle A. And because diameter / diameter = circumference / circumference, as has been demonstrated in the *Book on Curved Surfaces*,[2] and [because] circum-ference / circumference = arc / similar arc = chord / chord, as is had in the *Book on Similar Arcs*,[3] therefore $GH / KL = BC / DE = BC / MN$. Therefore $DE = MN$ by V.9 [of Euclid]. Therefore arc $DE <$ arc MN by the preceding [proposition] since circle A is larger than the other [circle]. But arc BC / arc $MN =$ line BC / line MN (or DE) since arc BC is similar to arc MN. Therefore

Prop. III.4

[1] Notice that Prop. II.14 here cited is one of the author's auxiliary propositions that were not in the *Liber philotegni*. In this sentence I have adopted the reading *habeat* from MS H though the rest of the manuscripts have *habet*. I have done so because the author here intends a suppositive expression.

[2] See my *Archimedes in the Middle Ages*, Vol. 1, p. 462–467.

[3] See Part II, Chap. 2, nn. 11 and 12, above.

arc *BC* / arc *DE* > line *BC* / line *DE*, and thus is evident the prior part of the proposition.

Also, since the ratio of similar segments [of circles] is the same as that of the circles, and [since] the ratio of circles is the square of that of [their] diameters (which is evident by II.12 of Euclid), and [since] the square of the ratio of diameters is equal to the square of the ratio of the chords of similar segments, so the segment *BDC* / segment *MN* = (line *BC* / line *MN*)^2 = (*BC* / *DE*)^2. Therefore by V.9 [of Euclid] segment *BC* / segment *DE* > (*BC* / *DE*)^2 since segment *DE* < segment *MN* because the arc is less than the arc and the chord is equal to the chord.

5. (=P.30) IF TWO PARALLEL LINES IN THE SAME CIRCLE CUT THE DIAMETER ORTHOGONALLY, THE RATIO OF THE GREATER TO LESSER OF THE SEGMENTS WHICH THEY [I.E. THE PARALLEL LINES] CUT OFF FROM THE DIAMETER WILL BE GREATER THAN THAT OF THE ARCS WHICH ARE SUBTENDED BY THEM [I.E. THE PARALLEL LINES].

Let the diameter of the circle be *ABGD* [see Fig. III.5], while the parallel lines which it cuts orthogonally and bisects let be *CBE* and *HGL*. He says, therefore, that *BD* / *GD* > arc *CDE* / arc *HDL*. For let the triangle *CDL* be formed and let the common section of its side *CD* and line *HG* be point *K*. Therefore, because line *CL* is the longest side of that triangle, the angle *D* will be the greatest of its angles. Hence it is either right or obtuse. Argue, therefore, by I.5 of this [work], by the last [proposition] of [Book] VI of Euclid, by VI.2 [of Euclid], and by conjunct ratio, that line *BD* / line *GD* > arc *CD* / arc *HD*, and therefore line *BD* / line *GD* > arc *CDE* / arc *HDL* since these [latter arcs] are double the prior [arcs], and this is what has been proposed.

6. (=P.31) WITH TWO LINES [DRAWN] TANGENT TO A CIRCLE FROM THE SAME POINT, IF [TWO LINES] SHORTER THAN THOSE [TANGENTS] ARE TANGENT TO THE SAME CIRCLE, THE RATIO OF THE LINES OR OF THE SURFACES CONTAINED BY THESE [LINES] AND ARCS WILL BE GREATER THAN THAT OF THE ARCS.

Let two lines *BC* and *BD* be tangent to a circle whose center let be *A* [see Fig. III.6], and let two other shorter [tangents] be *HF* and *HE*, and from the center let four perpendiculars be drawn respectively to the four tangents at the four points of tangency by III.17 (=Gr. III.18) [of Euclid] and there will be formed two quadrangles divisible into equal triangles by lines *AH* and *AB*, when they have been drawn. Moreover let there be cut off from the longer tangents two lines *CG* and *DL* equal to the shorter tangents, and with lines *AG* and *AL* drawn there will be formed triangles equal to the smaller [triangles]. Therefore from I.5 of this [work], from the last and the first [propositions] of [Book] VI [of Euclid], and from conjunctive ratio you will conclude that the ratio of the longer lines to the shorter or of the triangular surface *CBD* to the triangular surface *FHE* is greater than the ratio of arc *CD* to arc *FE*, and this is what has been proposed.

And in this figure you will demonstrate that the longer lines include a greater arc and that from the angle which they contain they dispatch a longer line to the center, and contrariwise, if one of those [conditions] pertains in regard to [a pair of] tangents [that is, if they include a greater arc or if the line to the center from their angle is longer], then those [tangents] are longer.[1]

7. (=P.32) IF TWO LINES [DRAWN] FROM THE SAME POINT ARE TANGENT TO A CIRCLE AND IF LINES EQUAL TO THEM ARE [DRAWN] TANGENT TO A LARGER CIRCLE, THEN [IN THE LATTER CASE] THEY INCLUDE A LARGER ARC OF THIS [CIRCLE].

Let the two lines tangent to a smaller circle T be BC and BD [see Fig. III.7] and let two other lines equal to them and tangent to a larger circle A be HE and HG. With A and T placed in the centers and with perpendiculars drawn from A and T to the points of tangency, let two quadrangles [$CBDT$ and $EHGA$] be completed. I say, therefore, that arc $EG > CD$. Therefore let the diameter of the smaller circle be related to the diameter of the larger, or the radius to the radius, as line EH (or its equal CB) is related to a longer line, which let be EHL. And from point L let there be drawn another tangent LM, and with line AM drawn let the quadrangle $ELMA$ be completed. This quadrangle will indeed be similar to quadrangle $CBDT$, for the sides are proportional and the angles are equal, which is evident by VI.6 [of Euclid], lines AKL and TZB which divide those quadrangles into equal triangles having been drawn. And similarly if quadrangle $EHGA$ is divided when line AH has been drawn, it will be evident by [Euclidian propositions] V.15, VI.1, VI.17 (=Gr. VI.19), and by this rule of the fifth [book, i.e. Def. 10 (=Gr. Def. 9)]: "When there are three proportionals etc." that quadrangle $EHGA$ is proportional between the other two quadrangles.[1] Further $EHGA$ / $CBDT$ = line LE / line HE. By the preceding [proposition] line LE / line HE > arc EM / arc EG. But because the ratio of similar arcs is equal to the ratio of circumferences and also to the ratio of diameters or radii, therefore arc EM / arc CD = line EA / line CT = LE / HE (since EM and CD are similar arcs). Therefore arc EM / arc CD > arc EM / arc EG. Therefore by V.8 [of Euclid] arc EG > arc CD, and this is what has been proposed.

Moreover that EM and CD are similar arcs is evident if quadrangles $EKMS$ and $CZDR$ have been inscribed in the circles. For since angle A = angle T (as has been demonstrated before), so angle S = angle R since angles S and R are halves of angles A and T by III.19 (=Gr. III.20) [of Euclid]. Therefore

---

Prop. III.6

[1] Concerning this added paragraph, see my account of the proposition in Part III, Chap. 1 above. Note the trivial proof added in *DcFb* of the proposition that if two sets of tangents are equal, they include equal arcs (see the variant reading to line 17).

Prop. III.7

[1] This is evident, for with $EH = CB$ and EL drawn so that CT / $EA = EH$ / EL, then tri. TCB / tri. $EAH = CT$ / EA and tri. EAH / tri. $EAL = EH$ / EL. And so tri. TCB / tri. EAH = tri. EAH / tri. EAL. But these triangles are halves of the quadrangles. Therefore quadrangle $AEHG$ is the mean proportional between quadrangles $CBDT$ and $ELMA$.

angle K = angle Z by III.21 (=Gr. III.22) [of Euclid], and therefore the arcs are similar.

And with this same figure[2] retained, you will demonstrate that if two sets of coterminal lines are tangent to two circles so that they include similar arcs, the ratios of the lines, of the diameters, and of the arcs will be the same.

In addition, you will know how, with two unequal circles proposed to one of which two lines from the same point are tangent, to assign a point outside of the other [circle] from which may be drawn to that same [other circle] tangents that are equal to the prior [tangents]. For you know how to cut off from any circle an arc similar to an arc of any other [circle] by means of a subtended chord and [you know how] to draw a tangent from the terminus of a chord which is related to one of the tangents to another circle as the diameter is related to the diameter or the chord to the chord, which is the same as II.14 of the present [work].[3]

8. (=P.33) WITH TWO CIRCLES TANGENT TO EACH OTHER EITHER ON THE INSIDE OR ON THE OUTSIDE, IF FROM THE [POINT OF] CONTACT A STRAIGHT LINE IS DRAWN PASSING THROUGH BOTH OF THEM, IT WILL CUT OFF SIMILAR SEGMENTS FROM THESE [CIRCLES].[1]

In whatever way the contact of the circles is made [i.e. whether inside or outside] let a line be drawn through their centers [see Fig. III.8], which indeed by III.11 [of Euclid] let be applied to the [point of] contact and to each circumference in the opposite direction, and it will divide each circle into semicircles. Then let any other line that passes through both circles be drawn after it has been applied to the point of contact. And with quadrangles[2] formed whose parts are right triangles standing in semicircles by III.30 (=Gr. III.31) and III.21 (=Gr. III.22) [of Euclid]; and by the description of similar arcs and by I.32 [of Euclid] argue [the proposition]—and by the identity of the angles if the contact is inside and by vertical angles if the contact is outside, or in both cases by III.31 (=Gr III.32) [of Euclid] if a tangent [through the point of contact] has been drawn.

9. (=P.34) IF A CIRCLE IS TANGENT TO ANOTHER [CIRCLE] INSIDE AND FROM THE [POINT OF] CONTACT A LINE PROCEEDS

---

[2] Curtze here adopts the reading *stemmate* (which makes no sense) instead of the obviously correct *scemate* (=*schemate*). See the variant reading to line 29.

[3] See note 1 to Prop. III.4 above. This is the same as finding the fourth proportional when three are given, and this knowledge was assumed when line *EHL* was proposed in the foregoing proof. Incidentally, the three additional corollaries or problems presented by the author of the *Liber de triangulis Iordani* were not mentioned by Jordanus in his presentation of the equivalent Proposition 32 in the *Liber philotegni*.

Prop. III.8

[1] The author of the *Liber de triangulis Iordani* has added to Jordanus' enunciation the expression *vel intra vel extra* in line 1 and the word *recta* in line 3. For the significance of the first addition, see my account of this proposition in Part III, Chap. 1, above.

[2] There are no such rectangular quadrangles specified in the diagrams of Fig. III.8 in the manuscripts. I have added broken lines to complete the rectangles here mentioned.

THROUGH THEIR CENTERS, THEN ANY LINE STANDING PER-
PENDICULAR TO IT [I.E. THE FIRST LINE] ON BOTH SIDES AND
PASSING THROUGH BOTH CIRCLES [PRODUCES THE FOLLOWING
CASES OF ARCAL INTERCEPTION]. (1) IF IT IS DRAWN INSIDE OF
THE CENTER OF THE LARGER [CIRCLE] WHETHER IT CUTS THE
OTHER [I.E. SMALLER CIRCLE] OR IS TANGENT TO IT—IT WILL
INTERCEPT FROM THE SMALLER [CIRCLE] TOWARD THE [POINT
OF] CONTACT LESS [ARCAL LENGTH THAN IT DOES FROM THE
LARGER CIRCLE]. (2) BUT IF IT [PROCEEDS] THROUGH THE CEN-
TER OF THE LARGER [CIRCLE] AND IS TANGENT [TO THE
SMALLER CIRCLE], IT WILL INTERCEPT IN THIS CASE ALONE THE
SAME [ARCAL LENGTH FROM EACH CIRCLE]. (3) BUT IF IT [PRO-
CEEDS] OUTSIDE [OF THE CENTER OF THE LARGER CIRCLE] AND
IS TANGENT [TO THE SMALLER CIRCLE], IN THIS CASE IT WILL
INTERCEPT GREATER [ARCAL LENGTH] FROM THE SMALLER
[CIRCLE THAN FROM THE LARGER].[1]

Let us set out three circles that touch each other inside at point A [see
Fig. III.9a], and let the center of the smallest be O, of the middle N, of the
largest M, and let line MA be drawn and pass through O and N by III.11
[of Euclid], and let the diameter ZA of the smallest [circle] be less than the
radius of the largest and the diameter of the middle [circle] greater [than
ZA]. Therefore let line EG be drawn through the largest circle and cut MA
orthogonally at point Z, which is between M and A. Therefore it will cut
the largest as well as the middle circle and will be tangent to the smallest. I
say, therefore, that arc EAG, which EG intercepts from the largest [circle],
is greater than arc PAQ, which it cuts from the middle [circle] in the same
direction, and also that it (arc EAG) is greater than the whole circumference
of the smallest circle, and this is what is said, namely, if it is drawn inside
the center of the larger [circle]—whether it cuts or is tangent [to the smaller],—
it will intercept less from the smaller toward the [point of] contact.[2] Therefore
let a straight line be drawn between E and A and let it cut the middle circle
at K and the smallest [circle] at B, and let another line [be drawn] between
G and A, cutting the middle circle at T and the smallest [circle] at C, and
let lines BDC and KLT be drawn, which lines will be parallel to each other
and to line EG, for the three segments of the three circles in which angle A
falls in an arc are similar and their halves are equal by the preceding [prop-
osition], and therefore angles B, K, and E are equal and similarly angles C,
T and G. Therefore argue that arc $EAG >$ arc PAQ from this rule: the ratio

Prop. III.9

[1] The expression of the third part of this enunciation is here more restrictive than in the
equivalent Proposition 34 of the *Liber philotegni,* since the secant is said here not only to proceed
outside of the center of the larger circle but also to be tangent to the smaller circle. I have
discussed the significance of this restriction for the understanding of the third part of the proposition
in my discussion of Proposition 34 in Part II, Chap. 2, above.

[2] This is the first interception indicated in the enunciation by (1).

of similar arcs is the same as that of their chords, which indeed is had from the *Book on Similar Arcs*,[3] and from VI.2 [of Euclid], III.5 of this [work], and V.10 and V.15 [of Euclid]. Moreover that it (arc *EAG*) is greater than the circumference of the smallest circle you will argue from the same things after the diameter *ROS* has been drawn orthogonally, and from the rule placed at the end of the comment to [I.]12 of the present [work], if God wills [it].

Now let us set out [the data] in another way [see Fig. III.9b] so that the diameter of the smallest circle be line *MA*, which is [also] the radius of the largest, and it follows from this that the circumference of it (the smallest circle) is equal to the semicircumference of that (the largest). And therefore it is evident that if line *EG* is drawn through the center of the largest [circle] and is tangent to the smallest, it intercepts just as much from the largest as from the smallest. But since this [line *EG*] so drawn will cut the middle circle at points *K* and *T*, let it be thus. I say that arc *KAT* < arc *EAG*. For I shall show that arc *KAT* is less than circumference *MA*, which is equal to that [arc *EAG*], by the same method that I used before when I drew diameter *ROS*, [after] I have now drawn diameter *BNC* of the middle circle, and I use the same things here that I used there, and in addition this rule: if the ratio of the first whole to its subtracted part is greater than that of the second [whole] to its [subtracted part], so the ratio of the first whole to its remaining part will be less than that of the second [whole] to its [remaining part], which has validity from II.12, II.11 and II.13 of the *Arithmetic* [of Jordanus][4] in regard to continua. And by this method it is evident that if line *PDQ* is drawn outside of center *M* and tangent to the middle circle, arc *PAQ* < circumference *DA*, and one who is subtle will show indirectly by I.17 of Euclid that no perpendicular [secant] intercepts an equal amount from each [circle] except that which passes through the center of the larger [circle] and is tangent to the smaller one.[5]

10. (=P.35) WITH [ONE] CIRCLE TANGENT TO ANOTHER ON THE INSIDE, (1) A LINE DRAWN FROM THE CENTER OF THE LARGER [CIRCLE] THAT TRAVERSES BOTH [CIRCLES] AND [THUS PROCEEDS] BEYOND THE [POINT] OF CONTACT WILL INTERCEPT, IN THE DIRECTION OF THE [POINT OF] CONTACT, AN ARC SHORTER [IN LENGTH] FROM THE INTERIOR [CIRCLE THAN FROM THE LARGER CIRCLE] IF THAT INTERIOR [CIRCLE] IS DESCRIBED [TO CUT THE DIAMETER OF THE LARGER CIRCLE] OUTSIDE THE CENTER [OF THE LARGER CIRCLE]. (2) [IT WILL INTERCEPT] AN EQUAL [ARCAL SEGMENT FROM BOTH CIRCLES] IF THE [INTERIOR CIRCLE IS DRAWN TO CUT THE DIAMETER] AT THE CENTER

---

[3] This is evident from Propositions 4 and 5 of the *Liber de similibus arcubus* (see Part II, Chap. 2, notes 11 and 12) together with Proposition III of the *Liber de curvis superficiebus*.

[4] For the text of Prop. II.13 of the *Arithmetica*, see Part II, Chap. 2, n. 4.

[5] See the English translation of the *Liber philotegni*, Prop. 34, n. 2.

[OF THE LARGER CIRCLE]. (3) BUT IF [THE INTERIOR CIRCLE CROSSES THE DIAMETER] INSIDE [THAT CENTER, THE SECANT INTERCEPTS] MORE [ARCAL LENGTH FROM THE INTERIOR CIRCLE THAN FROM THE LARGER ONE].

Let three circles be tangent on the inside at point A to the largest circle whose center let be D [see Fig. III.10]. Let one of these be large so that it encircles and includes point D, let the second one be smaller so that it is tangent to D, and let the third be the smallest so that it does not reach D. Now let a straight line be drawn from point D [to a point] beyond [the point of] contact and let it cut the circumference of each [circle], the largest one at G, the [less] large one at O, the [next] smaller one at C, and the smallest one at E. He says,[1] therefore, that (1) arc AG > arc AO, that (2) arc AG = arc AC, and (3) that arc AG < arc AE. Therefore let three lines be drawn from A through the three points O, C and E to the circumference of the largest circle at points K, Z, and B, and to these latter points let there be drawn three lines from point D. Therefore line AD lies opposite to the three angles located on line DG in the direction of A. One of these, evidently the one at C, is a right angle by III.30 (=Gr. III.31) of Euclid, the second at O is acute, and the third at E is obtuse. Therefore let a line be drawn from point D perpendicular to AK at its middle, and it will fall between O and A at point N, and let it (the perpendicular) be extended to R. Another perpendicular drawn to the middle of AB will fall between E and B at point T, and let it be extended to K. Let it be thus. Therefore, with these [lines] so set out, since N, C and T are right angles, you will demonstrate every thing which has been proposed by means of I.5 of this [work][2], by the last [proposition] of [Book] VI of Euclid, and by two rules, one of which is placed in the comment to [Proposition I.]12 [of this work][3] and the other in the comment to the preceding [proposition of this work, namely III.9], and also by means of the next preceding [proposition of this work, namely III.8] and by the equal proportionality of similar arcs and their chords, if God directs your ingenuity.

11. (=P.36) IF [ONE] CIRCLE IS TANGENT TO [ANOTHER] CIRCLE ON THE INSIDE, THE LINE DRAWN FROM THE CENTER OF THE SMALLER [CIRCLE] THROUGH BOTH [CIRCLES] WILL, IN THE DIRECTION OF THE [POINT OF] CONTACT, CUT OFF AN ARC GREATER [IN LENGTH] FROM THE LARGER OF THEM.

Prop. III.10

[1] I have already commented on the possible significance of the use of the third-person form *dicit* to my argument that the author of the *Liber de triangulis Iordani* was not Jordanus but a later author. (see Part III, Chap. 1).

[2] The reader will again note the importance of Proposition I.5 to the establishment of this proposition, as it has been to so many others.

[3] There is some difficulty in the manuscripts concerning the number of the proposition here quoted (see variant to line 23). But, as in the preceding proposition, it is clear that it ought to be Proposition I.12 that is being cited, so long as Proposition I.5+ is not numbered as Proposition 6.

Let the contact of the circles be at A, and let the center of the small [circle] be at E [see Fig. III.11], and let line AE be drawn, and from E let there be a line drawn cutting the circumference of each [circle], the smaller at D and the larger at B. I say, therefore, that arc $AB >$ arc AD. Therefore let there be drawn between A and B a line that cuts the smaller circumference at C, and let line EC be drawn, from E let a perpendicular be drawn to the middle of AC at Z, which perpendicular let be extended to T and G. With [all of] this completed, argue what has been proposed as in that which has been put forth before. Farewell![1]

12. (=P.37) GREATER IS THE DIFFERENCE BETWEEN THE SUR-FACES WHICH ARE CONTAINED BETWEEN ARCS THAT EQUALLY EXCEED ONE ANOTHER AND LINES TANGENT [TO THESE ARCS] [I.E., THE DIFFERENCE BETWEEN THE FIRST AND SECOND SUR-FACE IS GREATER THAN THAT BETWEEN THE SECOND AND THE THIRD, AND SO ON], JUST AS GREATER IS THE DIFFERENCE [OR DISTANCE] OF THE TANGENT LINES.

On the circle whose center let be Z [see Fig. III.12] let there be designated arcs that equally exceed one another. Let the longest arc be AB, to which lines AK and KB are tangent; and let the middle [arc] be SB and its one tangent be SG; and let the shortest arc be DB and its one tangent be DR. And from the three points K, G, and R let there be drawn lines to Z, which lines bisect the aforesaid arcs, and let those lines fall on the circumference at points E, O, and C. I intend, therefore, two things: (1) that line $KG > GR$, and (2) that surface $AKGS >$ surface $SGRD$. For, since from the supposition arcs AS and SD are equal, the arcs EO and OC will be equal because the latter arcs are the differences between the halves of the aforesaid arcs, the differences of the wholes being AS and SD. For the rule is that the difference of the halves is half the difference of the wholes, for the whole to the whole is related as the difference of the wholes to the difference of [their] similar parts, which is evident from V.19 of Euclid. And because EO and OC are halves of equals, they [themselves] are equals; hence the angles at the center are equal. Therefore by VI.3 of Euclid $KG > GR$ since $KZ > ZR$ because angle $R >$ angle K by I.16 of Euclid. Therefore the first [part of what has been intended] is evident. The second will be evident if line AK is cut off so that $AT = SG$ and SG is cut off so that $SL = DR$, and let line TL be drawn. Therefore you will show that surface $ATLS$ (since it is part of surface $AKGS$) is equal to surface $SGRD$ by superposition, [and it will be shown] just as I.4 of Euclid is shown,[1] since the angles of contingence at A and S are equal

---

Prop. III.11

[1] Apparently at first the author thought that he would complete the third book here. But apparently he then decided to include Proposition III.12 in this book as well. Taw apparently adopted the author's first idea because he added in the margin of MS D before Prop. III.12 the phrase: *Liber quartus de triangulis* (see the variant reading to line 1 of Prop. III.12).

Prop. III.12

[1] The citation of Prop. I.4 of Euclid is not appropriate since the triangles understood in that proposition are rectilinear triangles, while the surfaces under consideration here in Prop. III.12

and the sides in the one surface are [respectively] equal to the sides of the other.

The Fourth Book on Triangles

1. (=P.38) WITH [ONE] CIRCLE DESCRIBED ABOUT A FIGURE OF UNEQUAL SIDES AND ANOTHER CONSTRUCTED INSIDE, IT IS IMPOSSIBLE FOR THEM TO HAVE THE SAME CENTER.

Let the exemplum be of a triangle ABG of unequal sides [see Fig. IV.1]. Let one circle be inscribed in it and another circumscribed [about it]. Therefore, with the same center C proposed for those circles, and with lines drawn to the angles of the triangle as well as to the points of contact, you will prove by III.17 (=Gr. III.18) and III.3 of Euclid, and by this rule: any two lines tangent to a circle from the same point are equal (which is proved by the penultimate [proposition] of [Book] III [i.e. III.35 (=Gr. III.36)] of Euclid), that that triangle [ABG] would be equilateral, which is against the hypothesis. And by this same method you will demonstrate the proposition for any rectilinear figure of unequal sides.

2. (=P.39) OF TRIANGLES DESCRIBED IN A CIRCLE ON THE SAME BASE IN THE SAME DIRECTION, THE ONE WHOSE REMAINING SIDES ARE EQUAL IS THE MAXIMUM, AND [THE ONES WHOSE REMAINING SIDES] ARE CLOSER BY SOME AMOUNT TO IT [I.E. WHOSE APEXES ARE CLOSER TO THE APEX OF THE ISOSCELES TRIANGLE] ARE BY THAT AMOUNT GREATER THAN THOSE [WHOSE APEXES] ARE FARTHER [FROM THE APEX OF THE ISOS-CELES TRIANGLE].

Let there be a triangle ACB in a circle on base AB, a triangle whose remaining sides are equal [see Fig. IV.2], and also a triangle ADB whose sides are unequal with AD the shorter [side], and a third triangle AGB with G placed between A and D. And let the points of the sections [of the sides] be H, E, and K; and any pair of triangles conjoined at any of those points are similar because they are equiangular. After it has been posited that the section of lines DB and AC is at E, I say that triangle BEC > triangle AED by the corollary to VI.17 (=Gr. VI.19) [of Euclid] because line CB > AD (since it cuts off a greater arc). Therefore, with the common triangle AEB added to both sides, it is evident that triangle ACB > triangle ADB. And the argument regarding the remaining [triangles] is the same. Moreover it is easily evident that the triangles [whose apexes are] equally distant from it [i.e. the apex of the isosceles triangle] are equal.

3. (=P.40) OF THE TRIANGLES WHICH EXIST IN A CIRCLE ON ITS CENTER, THE MAXIMUM IS THE RIGHT [TRIANGLE]. MORE-OVER IN THE CASE OF OBTUSE-ANGLED [TRIANGLES] BY THE

contain a curved side. What the author seems to be asserting is that, with the equality of the angles of contingence at A and S, and with the equality of the sides (whether straight or curved), one figure can be superimposed exactly on the other, and hence the figures are equal.

AMOUNT THAT THE OBTUSE ANGLE IS GREATER, AND IN THE CASE OF ACUTE-ANGLED [TRIANGLES] BY THE AMOUNT THAT THE ACUTE ANGLE IS LESS, SO IN SUCH AN AMOUNT WILL THIS TRIANGLE BE LESS BY THIS REASON: EVERY OBTUSE-ANGLED [TRIANGLE] AND [SOME] ACUTE-ANGLED [TRIANGLE] WHOSE ANGLES ARE AT THE CENTER OF THE SAME CIRCLE AND IN WHICH THE PERPENDICULAR FROM THE CENTER TO THE BASE OF THE ONE WILL BE EQUAL TO HALF THE BASE OF THE OTHER— THOSE TRIANGLES, I SAY, ARE EQUAL.

Let the center of a circle be A [see Fig. IV.3a], and a right triangle ABC, and an obtuse-angled [triangle] ABD, and a third [triangle] ABE whose angle at A is greater than the prior obtuse angle, with AB made the common line of all [the triangles]. And in the other direction let the right triangle be ABT, and similarly the acute-angled [triangle] ABF, and a third [triangle] ABG whose angle at A is less than the prior acute angle. And with perpendiculars dropped from point A to the bases of the individual [triangles], the individual [triangles] will be bisected. Therefore, with the center placed in the middle of line AB let a circle be described about it. It will pass through the termini of all the perpendiculars because every right angle constructed on some line falls in the circumference of the semicircle constructed on the same [line]. Moreover let the perpendicular in the right [triangle] be called AO, and it will be equal to OB, for, since C and B are halves of a right angle, therefore the angles at O will be right angles and the partial angles at A will be halves of a right angle; therefore angles A and B are equal and accordingly sides AO and OB are equal. Therefore argue by the preceding [proposition] first concerning the halves and afterwards concerning the wholes. And because he says "by this reason etc." it will be thus evident.

Now let the acute-angled triangle on center A be ABC [see Fig. IV.3b]. Let the perpendicular dropped to its base be AE. And let the obtuse-angled triangle be ABD with AH the perpendicular dropped to its base. And let circle $AHEB$ be described as before. The perpendiculars will also bisect the whole triangles. If, therefore, line $AH = $ line EB, so the arc will be equal to the arc. Therefore, with common arc HE added to each, you will argue by III.26 (=Gr. III.27) [of Euclid], by hypothesis, and by I.4 of Euclid that the halves of the triangles are equal and consequently the wholes. But if line AE is posited as equal to HB, you will similarly argue [what was proposed] after the common arc HE has been subtracted from both [arcs].[1]

4. (=P.46+1) EVERY PARALLELOGRAM DESCRIBED IN A CIRCLE IS A RECTANGLE.

With a parallelogram divided by a diagonal drawn to its opposite angles [see Fig. IV.4], argue [the proposition] by I.29 and III.21 (=Gr. III.22) [of Euclid].

Prop. IV.3
[1] This last paragraph is a proof of the *ratio* mentioned in the enunciation. See my account of this proposition in Part III, Chap. 1, for a discussion of the *ratio* and this proof.

5. (=P.41) ANY TWO OPPOSITE SIDES OF ANY QUADRILATERAL DESCRIBED ABOUT A CIRCLE ARE [TOGETHER] EQUAL TO THE REMAINING [SIDES] TAKEN TOGETHER.

Argue from this rule: any two lines tangent to the same circle from the same point are equal [see Fig. IV.5].

6. (=P.42) ANY PARALLELOGRAM CONSTRUCTED ABOUT A CIRCLE IS EQUILATERAL.

From the preceding [proposition] and I.34 of Euclid you will demonstrate this [see Fig. IV.6].

7. (=P.43) WITH A TRIANGLE CONSTRUCTED IN A CIRCLE, TO DESCRIBE A RECTANGLE EQUAL TO IT IN THE SAME CIRCLE.

Let the triangle constructed in a circle be ABC [see Figs. IV.7]. Then consider whether it is of two equal sides or of all unequal sides. Let us posit first that sides AB and BC are equal [see Fig. IV.7a]. Therefore, with a line dropped from angle C to the middle of side AB, it will stand perpendicular to it by I.8 [of Euclid], and it will pass through the center by the corollary to III.1 [of Euclid], and let it be CE. Let CE be extended to D, and let line DA be drawn and another line EF parallel to it, F having been placed in AC, and let line FZ be drawn parallel to line CED and let lines CZ and DF be drawn. Proceed therefore: triangles EFD and EFA are equal by I.39 [of Euclid]; hence also triangles CFD and CEA are equal, the common triangle[1] CFE having been added [to each of the equal triangles EFD and EFA], and CEA is half the given triangle. But CFD and CZD are equal; therefore CZD, since it is a right triangle (because angle Z is in an arc of a semicircle),[2] is equal to triangle CEA. Then let there be made on line CED with line CT in the opposite direction an angle equal to the angle which line DZ contains with line CED, and with line DT drawn you will have a rectangle $TCZD$ equal to triangle ABC because the half [of the one is equal] to the half [of the other], for angles T and Z are right [angles] (because they stand in a semicircle) and lines CT and DZ are equal and parallel by III.25 (=Gr. III.26), III.24 (=Gr. III.25), and I.27 of Euclid.

Now, if there is a triangle ABC all of whose sides are unequal [see Fig. IV.7b], therefore line DE, which is perpendicular to and [thus] bisects side AB, when drawn upon the center to the circumference will not proceed to angle C but elsewhere to point Z. Therefore let line CH descend perpendicularly to line DEZ, and CH will be parallel to line AE by I.28 [of Euclid]. Therefore, with lines CE and HA drawn, triangle HAE = triangle EAC, EAC being half the given triangle. Also, with line ZA drawn, and with line HL [drawn] parallel to ZA, and [further] with ZL drawn, triangle ZLH = triangle HAL, and therefore triangle ZLE = triangle HAE, the common triangle

---

Prop. IV.7

[1] All the manuscripts have *angulo,* but the sense of the argument demands *triangulo,* and so I have emended the text to read [*tri*]*angulo.*

[2] This causal clause is not needed. We merely note that tri. CFD = tri. CEA and that tri. CFD = tri. CZD. Hence it is immediately evident that tri. CZD = tri. CEA.

HLE having been added [to each of the equal triangles *ZLH* and *HAL*], and hence *ZLE* is equal to half the [given] triangle. Therefore let line *DL* be drawn, and [also] line *EM* parallel to *DL*, with *M* having been placed in line *ZL*. And let line *DM* be drawn. Therefore triangle *EMD* = triangle *EML*; and therefore triangle *ZMD* = triangle *ZLE*, the common [triangle] *ZME* having been added [to each of the equal triangles *EMD* and *EML*], and *ZML* was equal to *EAC*, half the given triangle. Then let line *MN* be drawn to the circumference and be parallel to line *DEZ*. And, with lines *ZN* and *DN* drawn, there will result a right triangle *ZDN* on line *ZD*, which is the diameter, and *ZDN* is equal to half the given triangle. [Then,] with the zeal mentioned above, you will construct a triangle equal to *ZDN* in the opposite direction, and let it be *ZDY*, and [so] you will have rectangle *ZNDY* equal to triangle *ABC*, as was demanded.

8. (=P.44) BETWEEN ANY TWO SIMILAR REGULAR POLYGONS ONE OF WHICH IS INSCRIBED IN A CIRCLE AND THE OTHER CIRCUMSCRIBED [ABOUT THE CIRCLE], THERE EXISTS AS A PROPORTIONAL MEAN A REGULAR POLYGON INSCRIBED IN THE SAME CIRCLE THAT HAS TWICE AS MANY SIDES.

Let the exemplum be of triangles. Therefore let there be a triangle *ABC* circumscribed about a circle whose center let be *Z* [see Fig. IV.8], and let triangle *DEF* be inscribed, applying [its] angles to the [points of] contact of the other [triangle with the circle]. Then let lines be drawn from *Z* to the angles of each triangle. Therefore those lines which are drawn to angles *A*, *B*, and *C* cut the sides of the inscribed triangle orthogonally and [thus] bisect the sides as well as [their] arcs, as is evident by III.17 (=Gr. III.18), I.4, and the last [proposition] of [Book] VI [of Euclid]. Therefore let the point in which line *ZA* cuts line *DF* be *H*, and let *G* be the point in which it cuts the arc. Therefore, by the corollary to VI.8 [of Euclid] line *GZ*, since it is equal to line *DZ*, is the proportional mean between the whole *AZ* and its part *HZ*. Therefore, with line *GD* drawn, triangle *DGZ* will be a proportional mean between triangle *ADZ* and its part *HDZ* by VI.1. Therefore, with the chords of the halves of the individual arcs subtended, a hexagon is formed which has twice as many sides [as the triangles]. Hence by V.13 (=Gr. V.12) the hexagon [so formed] is a proportional mean between triangles *ABC* and *DEF* since you could argue by this method in every direction [i.e., for all of the other triangles making up the circumscribed and inscribed triangles and the inscribed hexagon]. And from these [same reasons] you may argue [the proposition] if the [regular] polygonal figures proposed are of many more sides.

9. (=P.45) IF REGULAR POLYGONS ARE INSCRIBED IN EQUAL CIRCLES, THAT WHICH HAS THE MORE SIDES WILL BE THE GREATER, AND THE RATIO OF IT [I.E. THE GREATER POLYGON] TO THE OTHER IS GREATER THAN THE RATIO OF ITS PERIMETER TO THE PERIMETER OF THE OTHER.

We shall give the demonstration, which is common to all [regular] polygons, [only] for the square and the [regular] pentagon inscribed in equal circles.

Therefore, if straight lines are drawn in each circle from the center to the individual angles of the polygon, each polygon will be divided into as many equal triangles as the polygon has sides. Therefore let one of the four triangles of the square be *ABC* [see Fig. IV.9] and one of the five triangles of the pentagon be *EDO*, *A* and *E* having been placed in the centers. Proceed therefore. Line *BC* > line *DO* because it cuts off a greater arc, for a fourth [part] is always greater than a fifth. Therefore by I.12 of this [work] triangle *ABC* / triangle *EDO* < line *BC* / line *DO*, and therefore triangle *ABC* / triangle *EDO* < arc *BC* / arc *DO* by III.4 of this [work]. Therefore by V.13 (=Gr. V.12) [of Euclid] less is the ratio of the whole square (which is precisely divided into four triangles) to the five triangles of the pentagon than is the ratio of the whole circumference of circle *A* [i.e. 4 arc *BC*] to the whole circumference of circle *E* [i.e. 5 arc *DO*], which latter ratio is one of equality. Therefore the whole square in *A* is less than the five triangles of the pentagon in *E*; therefore the whole pentagon is greater than the square, and thus the first part is evident. Also, since triangle *ABC* / triangle *EDO* < line *BC* / line *DO*, therefore, inverting the expression, triangle *EDO* / triangle *ABC* > line *DO* / line *BC*; and so by proceeding through the single [terms] you argue the second part by V.13 (=Gr. V.12) [of Euclid] as you have done before.

10. ANY SIDE OF A REGULAR POLYGON CIRCUMSCRIBED ABOUT A CIRCLE IS BISECTED AT THE [POINT OF] CONTACT: AND IF BETWEEN THE [POINTS OF] CONTACT LINES ARE DRAWN, THEY WILL INCLUDE A SIMILAR POLYGON. WHENCE IT IS EVIDENT THAT EVERY ARC COMPREHENDED BETWEEN TWO PROXIMATE [POINTS OF] CONTACT IS THE SAME NUMERICAL PART OF THE [CIRCUMFERENCE OF THE] CIRCLE AS THE NUMBER OF SIDES IN THE POLYGON.

Now we shall give the demonstration, which is common to all [regular] polygons, [only] for triangles. Let the center of the circle be *G* [see Fig. IV.10]. Let [equilateral] triangle *ABC* be circumscribed about the circle, and with lines drawn from the center to the [points of] contact and also to the angles *A*, *B*, and *C*, it is evident by I.4 and I.15 of Euclid that all the angles at *G* are equal; and since the angles at the [points of] contact are equal (because they are right angles), it is evident by I.26 of Euclid that line *BE* = line *EC*, and thus for those that remain. Also, with lines drawn between the [points of] contact, since all the angles at the center are equal, you will argue from I.4 [of Euclid] that triangle *DEF* is equilateral. And from this it is manifest that arc *EF* is a third part of the [circumference of] circle *DEF*, for equal chords are subtended by equal arcs, and that triangle *DEF* is a quarter part of triangle *ABC* by VI.2, VI.4, and VI.17 (=Gr. VI.19) [of Euclid].[1]

Prop. IV.10

[1] Regarding the composition of this proposition, see my remarks in the account of it in Part III, Chap. 1.

11. (=P.46) IF [TWO] REGULAR POLYGONS ARE CIRCUM-
SCRIBED ABOUT EQUAL CIRCLES, THAT WHICH HAS FEWER SIDES
WILL BE THE GREATER, AND THE RATIO OF IT TO THE OTHER
IS AS THAT OF ITS PERIMETER TO THE PERIMETER OF
THE OTHER.

Now let the exemplum be of an equilateral triangle ABC circumscribed
about circle Q and of a square $DEFG$ circumscribed about circle L [see Fig.
IV.11]. Therefore any side of the triangle is greater than any side of the
square because the halves [of the one] are greater than the halves [of the
other] (because they comprehend a greater arc by the preceding [proposition])
and by that which was said in the end of the comment on III.6 of this [work],
for a third part of something is greater than a fourth part of the same thing
or of its equal. Therefore, with perpendiculars drawn on both sides [i.e. in
both figures] from the center to the [points of] contact, triangle ABC will be
divided into three equal triangles and the square into four. And because the
perpendiculars are everywhere equal, it is evident that all seven triangles are
of the same altitude, and therefore by VI.1 [of Euclid] they are proportional
to their bases. Therefore the ratio of the three triangles of the triangle to the
four triangles of the square, i.e. of the whole triangle to the whole square, is
as that of the sides of the one to the sides of the other, and thus the second
part is evident. But because the ratio of sides to sides is greater than that of
the three angles at Q to the four angles at L (as we shall demonstrate in what
follows) and the ratio of angles to the angles is that of the three arcs of the
one to the four arcs of the other by the last [proposition] of [Book] VI of
Euclid, and the latter ratio is one of equality, therefore it immediately follows
that the triangle is greater than the square, and so is evident the first part.

Moreover [here is] the proof that the ratio of the sides is greater than the
ratio of the angles. In the middle of BC let K be at the contact, and in the
middle of DE let it be Z. Therefore, because $BC > DE$ and each of the halves
of the one is greater than each half of the other, therefore line $SKP =$ [line]
DE with K remaining in the middle, and let lines SQ and PQ be drawn.
Therefore triangle $KPQ =$ triangle ZLE by I.4 of Euclid, and therefore the
whole $SPQ =$ the whole DEL. Argue, therefore, from I.5 of this [work] twice
and by conjunction and by doubling, for perpendicular QK bisects the bases
and the angles (because the sides are equal).

12. IF IN A TRIANGLE WHOSE TWO SIDES ARE EQUAL A
STRAIGHT LINE IS DRAWN FROM THE ANGLE WHICH THEY
CONTAIN TO THE BASE AND IF IT DIVIDES THE ANGLE AS WELL
AS THE BASE INTO UNEQUALS, THE RATIO OF THE GREATER
PART OF THE ANGLE TO THE LESSER IS GREATER THAN THE
RATIO OF THE GREATER PART OF THE BASE TO THE LESSER.

Let the triangle be ABC and the line drawn to the base be BE [see Fig.
IV.12], and from the middle of the base let line FB be erected, which indeed
will be perpendicular to the base and will bisect angle B. Argue [the prop-

osition] by I.5 of this [work], by disjunction, by conjunction, and by the proportioning of the double.[1]

13. THE LINE PROTRACTED FROM THE CENTER OF A CIRCLE TO SOME ANGLE OF AN EQUILATERAL TRIANGLE CIRCUM-SCRIBED ABOUT THE SAME [CIRCLE] IS BISECTED AT THE CIR-CUMFERENCE [[AND ONE PROTRACTED TO THE ANGLE OF A CIRCUMSCRIBED SQUARE IS CUT AT THE CIRCUMFERENCE AC-CORDING TO A RATIO HAVING A MEAN AND TWO EXTREMES (I.E. ACCORDING TO A MEAN AND EXTREME RATIO) AND THE SEGMENT TAKEN OUTSIDE [THE CIRCUMFERENCE] IS THE SIDE OF A DECAGON]].[1]

With the disposition of the penultimate [proposition, i.e. IV.11] accepted and with a line drawn between the [points of] contact [see Fig. IV.13], you will argue the first part by the method of arguing followed in IV.8 of this [work] and by the corollary to XIV.1 of Euclid.[2] You will argue the second part by the penultimate [proposition] of [Book] I of Euclid [i.e. I.46 (=Gr. I.47)], by II.4 twice, by VI.16 (=Gr. VI.17), and by XII.24 (! XIII.4) [of Euclid].[3]

14. ANY MEAN PROPORTIONALS OF THE SAME EXTREMES[1] ARE EQUAL.

For example, let B and C be mean proportionals between A and D [see Fig. IV.14]. Now if they are not equal, let B > C, and let A be the larger extreme. Therefore A exceeds C more than it exceeds B. But [each of] B and C exceed D in the [given] proportion and they are [each] exceeded by A. Therefore C exceeds D more than B exceeds D, and therefore C is greater than B, which is against the falsigraph.[2] Therefore what has been proposed is evident.

Prop. IV.12

[1] As I have noted in my account of this proposition in Part III, Chap. 1, the expanded steps of the proof involve a different order of manipulating the ratios from that stated here in the proof.

Prop. IV.13

[1] I have added the double brackets about the false part of the enunciation, though I believe that it was a part of the proposition when added by the author of the *Liber de triangulis Iordani*. See my discussion of this proposition in Part III, Chap. 1.

[2] *Ibid.*, I have included a brief proof of the correct part of the enunciation.

[3] *Ibid.*, I have discussed the proof of the incorrect parts of the enunciation. In fact, the falsity of the second and third parts of the enunciation can be argued by the very propositions of Euclid cited here in supposed affirmation of those parts of the enunciation. By Prop. I.46 (=Gr. I.47) and Prop. VI.16 (=VI.17) of Euclid, we would see that $(2r + d) \cdot d = r^2$. On the other hand, if, as the enunciation wishes, $r + d$ is divided in the mean and extreme ratio, then by Prop. XIII.4 of Euclid we would conclude that $(2r + d) \cdot d = 2r^2$, which is contradictory to the preceding determination.

Prop. IV.14

[1] Curtze has falsely substituted *medietatum* for the correct *extremitatum* as given in the manu-scripts. Though this is no doubt a slip, it constitutes a horrendous error.

[2] See the account of this proposition and its use for the proof of Prop. IV.16 in Part III, Chap. 1.

15. AN OCTAGON INSCRIBED IN A CIRCLE IS PROPORTIONAL BETWEEN A SQUARE INSCRIBED IN THE SAME CIRCLE AND A SQUARE CIRCUMSCRIBED [ABOUT IT].[1]

And so let the proposed figure be applied in the way that the proposed diagram shows [see Fig. IV.15], because the geometer will easily and with zeal infer the whole from the third and fourth [parts of the figure, i.e. those of triangles AOE and BOE] after the lines have been drawn from the center to the angles of the interior as well as exterior square. And so OE bisects AB at I, which is inferred from I.8 [of Euclid] after triangles AOE and OEB have been examined[2] and from I.4 of Euclid after triangles AIE and EIB have been examined, and so OE is perpendicular to AB by III.3 [of Euclid]. And so angle O is common to triangles OEB and OIB, and also angles I and B are equal (being right angles); therefore the remaining [angles] B and E are equal. Therefore the triangles [OEB and OIB] are equiangular; therefore the ratio of their proportional sides is the same, that is, $OE / OB = OB / OI$. Therefore by the mediacy of OB ($=OK$), $OE / OK = OK / OI$. But since they have the same altitude, the triangles OEB, OKB and OIB are proportionals [i.e., $OEB / OKB = OKB / OIB$]. Therefore equal multiples of those triangles are also proportionals. But the three given figures [namely the outside square, the octagon, and the inside square] consist of equal multiples of the triangles [OEB, OKB, and OIB respectively]. Therefore these [given figures] are proportionals, which [is what] we proposed.

Corollary of this: Even if the circle and the octagon inscribed in it are [equal mean] proportionals, which is impossible, [the proposition still holds].[3]

16. TO CONSTRUCT A SQUARE EQUAL TO A PROPOSED CIRCLE.[1]

Let the exemplum be circle A [see Fig. IV.16]. Disposition.[2] Let another circle B with [its] diameter be added; let a square be circumscribed about

Prop. IV.15

[1] See my discussion in Part III, Chap. 1, as to why this proposition appeared with Props. IV.14 and IV.16.

[2] I have chosen *inspectis* rather than *inscriptis* here, though most manuscripts have the latter reading. See the variant reading to line 8.

[3] This is a confusing corollary, which Curtze silently omitted even though it exists in MS D (and indeed in all but one manuscript, as the variant reading to lines 18–19 reveals). Perhaps the reading in MS Pe is the correct one, except for its omission of *non*. Adding the *non*, we would then translate "Corollary of this [proposition]: Therefore the circle is not the mean proportional between the square inscribed in it and the square circumscribed about it. But even if the circle and the octagon were [equal, mean] proportionals, which is impossible, [the proposition still holds]." For texts which one might interpret as holding that the circle is the mean proportional between the two squares, see my *Archimedes in the Middle Ages,* Vol. 1, pp. 426–27.

Prop. IV.16

[1] See my account of this proposition in Part III, Chap. 1, and my earlier text of it in Vol. 1, pp. 567–75. In the course of a marginal note (see the variant reading to lines 1–2) the scribe of MS Pc says that "here there is a *petitio principii* since the author supposes that the ratio of the square to the circle exists, but this is what has to be proved." Similarly a marginal note in MS Pb tells us (variant reading to line 3) that "he errs because the third proportional after the square and the circle cannot be given, since the ratio of the square to the circle supposes the [very] things which are sought."

[2] The use of the terms *exemplum* and *dispositio* as parts of the proof of the proposition is like that found in one copy of the Adelard III Version of the *Elements* of Euclid (M. Clagett, "The

each of these circles. And the circumscribed square [in each case] will be equal to the square of the diameter of the circle. Therefore by XII.2 [of Euclid] circle A / circle B = square DE / square FG. Therefore permutatively DE / A = FG / B. And so let C stand as a third proportional surface after DE and A. Now C will either be a circle or a surface of another kind, as [for example] a rectilinear surface. In the first place let it be a circle which is circumscribed by square HK. And so DE / A = A / C. But then by XII.2 [of Euclid] DE / A = HK / C. Therefore HK as well as A is a mean proportional between DE and C. Therefore circle A and square HK are equal, which [is what] we proposed.

Further, let C be a figure other than a circle. And so let it be converted into a square by the last [proposition] of [Book] II [of Euclid], with [its] angles at R, S, Y, and X. And also since DE is the larger extreme [among the three proportional terms], DE is greater than RY, and therefore a side [of DE] is greater than a side [of RY]. Therefore let MT, equal to RX, be cut off from MD, and there will result a parallelogram MN contained by ME and MT. Therefore MN is a mean proportional between DE and RY, i.e. between the squares of their sides, since any rectangle is a mean proportional between the squares of its sides.[3] But circle A was a mean proportional between them [i.e. between square DE and C (or square RY)]. Therefore circle A and parallelogram MN are equal [by IV.14 of this work]. Therefore let MN be converted to a square by the last [proposition] of [Book] II [of Euclid], and this square will be equal to the proposed circle, which [is what] we proposed.

17. WITH TWO SQUARES PROPOSED, TO CIRCUMSCRIBE ONE OF THEM GNOMONICALLY ABOUT THE OTHER.[1]

For example, let there be [squares] AD and EG. Disposition [see Fig. IV.17].[2] Let AB be extended by an amount equal to HG, and let the extension equal to HG be BN, the line having been drawn from D to N. Proof.[3] Proceed. Since B is a right angle by the nature of a square, the square of DN is equal to the square of AB plus [the square] of BN by "dulk" [i.e. "possessor of two horns," namely the Pythagorean theorem],[4] and so the squares AB (AD)

Medieval Latin Translations from the Arabic of the *Elements* of Euclid, with Special Emphasis on the Versions of Adelard of Bath," *Isis,* Vol. 44 [1953], p. 34). These same terms for the division of a proposition are also widely used in the *Liber de curvis superficiebus* (see the text in Vol. 1, pp. 470, 478, 496, etc.).

[3] For the demonstration of this, see the variant reading to lines 17–19 (and compare Vol. 1, p. 575n).

Prop. IV.17

[1] See the account of this proposition in Part III, Chap. 1, and my discussion of the sources of Props. IV.17 and IV.18 in Appendix III.B below.

[2] For the use of *exemplum* and *dipositio,* see above, Prop. IV.16, n. 2.

[3] The expression *Ratio. Age* was used in many of the propositions in the *Liber de curvis superficiebus* (see the text in Vol. 1, pp. 468, 470, 476, 478, etc.).

[4] Curtze was unfamiliar with the term "dulk" (=*dulkarnan,* the possessor of two horns, i.e. the Pythagorean theorem, see Vol. I, p. 97n), for he converted the term to *diametrum* (see the variant reading to line 6).

and *EG* [have been converted to a single square] by the mediacy of *BN*. For, since *DN* < *AB* + *BN*, let *AN* be cut [at *M*] equal to *DN*, and let *MK*, perpendicular to *AM*, be equal to it, and similarly *IK* [equal to it], and [so] you will have a square *AK* equal to the two [proposed squares.] Therefore the gnomon that remains after *AD* is equal to square *EG*, and so[5] it is just as if *EG* were circumscribed gnomonically about *AD*, which [is what] we proposed.

18. NO TWO LINES ENCLOSE [I.E. DETERMINE IN PARAL-LELOGRAMS] AS MUCH SPACE AS WHEN THEY MEET PERPEN-DICULARLY.[1]

Let *AE* be a parallelogram described by *AB* and *AC*, which lines meet at an acute angle [see Fig. IV.18]. Then from *B* let *BG* be erected as a perpendicular to *CE*. Proceed. *G* is a right angle and therefore *G* is the maximum [angle] in its triangle. Therefore *BE* is the maximum side. And so let *BG* be extended, ending in *F* so that *BF* = *BE*. And, according to what is needed, let parallelogram *AF* be described by *AB* and *BF*, with *CE* extended to meet *AD*. Proof. Proceed. Since *AG* [i.e. *AHGB*] and *AE* are parallelograms on the same base, they are equal. Therefore *AF* is as much greater than *AG* as it is greater than *AE*. And thus [the same proof] occurs generally everywhere.

19. IN THE CASE OF TRIANGLES IN WHICH TWO SIDES [OF ONE] ARE RESPECTIVELY EQUAL TO TWO SIDES [OF ANOTHER], THE ONE WHOSE SIDES CONTAIN A RIGHT ANGLE IS THE MAXIMUM OF ALL [SUCH] TRIANGLES.[1]

For example, let *AB* and *AC* be the two sides containing a right angle [see Fig. IV.19], and from angle *A* let line *AE* be protracted so that it equals *AB*, and from angle *A* also let *HA* be protracted outside so that it equals *AB*, and afterwards let line *CB* be drawn from *B* subtending right angle *A*, and afterwards let a line be drawn from *B* to the terminus of *AE*, namely to *E*, and *AE* and *AB* are equal sides. Therefore the angles on base *BE* are equal. Therefore each is less than a right [angle]. Therefore *B* is less than a right angle. Therefore let a line be drawn from *B* that is parallel to *AC*, and of necessity it will fall outside of *E* because *CAB* is a right angle, and angle *B* on base [*BE*], as has been said, is less than a right [angle]. Whence the whole [angle] at *B* is a right [angle], and so that line parallel [to *AC*] will fall outside of *BE*. Therefore let it proceed through *F*. And let side *AE* be extended to *F* and from the contact at *F* let a line be drawn to *C*, namely [line] *FC*, and another [line] from angle *E* to *C*. Therefore consider triangle *ABC* and [triangle] *AFC*, which are on the same base between parallel lines, and therefore

---

[5] Curtze unjustly reads *permutatim* where the manuscripts have *perinde,* and shortly thereafter Curtze incorrectly alters the *ac-* in *acsi* to *ad* [i.e. *AD*] (see variant readings to line 10).

Prop. IV.18

[1] For the proof of this proposition, see my account of it in Part III, Chap. 1, and concerning its source see Appendix III.B.

Prop. IV.19

[1] The Arabic or other source of this proposition is not yet determined. For its proof and its equivalence to Prop. IV.3, see my account of it in Part III, Chap. 1.

will be equal. But triangle *AEC*, whose partial angle *A* is clearly acute, is less than [triangle] *AFC* because the one is a part of the other, and [so *AEC*] is less than [triangle] *ABC*, and so the triangle whose sides contain an acute angle is less than the one whose sides contain a right angle.

Also [the same is true] in regard to the [triangles with an] obtuse [angle]. Similarly, let line *BH* be drawn from *B* to *H* [with *H* so located that *AH* = *AB*]. You will have as before that the angles on base *BH* are equal because *AB* = *AH*, and so each of these angles is less than a right [angle]. Therefore, as before, let a line be drawn from *B* parallel to *AC*, and it will fall outside of *H* by the same reason as before. Therefore let it proceed through *G*. Afterwards let *AH* be extended to *G* continuously in a straight line, and afterwards let a line be drawn from *G* to *C* and another from *H* to *C*. And so triangles *AGC* and *ABC* will be of the same altitude (or they are between parallel lines) and they are on the same base, and so they are equal. But *AHC* is a part of *AGC*, and so is less, and thus is also less than *ABC*. Now if side *AE* would fall inside of *CH*, which is impossible (that is, that it could so fall), then it will be only necessary to draw a line from its terminus to *E*, and then [the one] triangle will be a part of the other, and so is manifestly less.[2] And so what has been proposed is evident.

20. TO DIVIDE ANY RECTILINEAR ANGLE INTO THREE EQUAL PARTS.

Let acute angle *ABG* be the one to be trisected [see Fig. IV.20a]. With *B* assumed as the center, let circle *DZM*[1] be described, [and] let *DB* be extended to *L*, and let *BZ* be erected as a perpendicular to *DL*, and I shall extend *ZE* to *H* and I shall not pose any determined end to line *ZH*. And I shall cut off from *ZH* a [line] *ZQ* equal to radius *DB*. Therefore let us imagine that line *ZEH* is moved toward *L* in such a way that *Z* during its motion is not separated from the circumference, and line *ZH* continues to pass through and adhere to point *E*, and *Z* continues to be moved until *Q* falls on *BZ*, and let the terminus of the motion [of *Z*] be *T*. Therefore it will be as a part of line *ZH*, or in other words *ZH* will lie on *TE*. And *TS* = *ZQ* = radius *BD*. I say, moreover, that [arc] *TL* = ⅓ arc *DE*. From point *B* let us draw *BM* parallel to line *TE*, and I shall extend *BM* to *K*, and let the points *T* and *M* be connected. Proceed. *TS* = *MB* and the two lines are parallel. Therefore *MT* and *BS* are equal and parallel. And *BZ* is perpendicular to *DL*. Therefore *MT* cuts *DL* at right angles. Therefore *DL* bisects chord *MT*. Therefore arcs *ML* and *LT* are equal. Also, arcs *ML* and *DK* are equal because *ML* and *DL*, intersecting each other at center *B*, form mutually equal [vertical] angles. Therefore, by equality twice, arc *KE* = 2 [arc] *DK*. Therefore angle *KBE* = 2 angle *KBD*. Therefore, when *KBE* has been bisected, the proposed angle *ABG* will have been trisected.

---

[2] I simply cannot make any sense out of the impossible case that has been presented in this sentence. I suppose that in some fashion the letters have become scrambled.

Prop. IV.20

[1] Points *Z* and *M* are to be determined later; hence it is poor geometric form to include them in the specification of the circle at this juncture.

Now if the angle to be trisected is greater than an acute angle, let it first be bisected so that each half will be an acute angle. Then let each of those halves be trisected by the said method. Therefore what has been proposed is clear.

The same thing will also be proved a little more clearly with one change made, namely that instead of *HZ* let [line] *LEN* be drawn [see Fig. IV.20b]. And since *LBZ* is a right [angle], let *OL* = line *BL*. Therefore let us imagine that *NL* is so moved toward *Z* and let *LN* always pass through *E*. Let *NL* [continue to] be moved until *O* falls on *BZ*, and so on as before.

The said demonstration concerning the trisection of an angle does not at all suffice for me, for I find nothing certain in it. To make it suffice for me, I demonstrate the same thing as follows. Let the given acute angle be *ABG* [see Fig. IV.20c]. Therefore, with the foot of a compass placed in *B*, let a circle be described, and let *AB* be extended to *L* in the circumference, and from the center let *BZ* be erected as a perpendicular to *DL*. And by Proposition V.19 of the *Perspective* [of Alhazen][2] let a line be drawn from point *E* through radius *BZ* so that *TS* = radius *BL*. Therefore let *BM* be drawn parallel to line *TSE* and be extended to *K*. Therefore because *BM* and *TS* are equal and parallel, *BS* and *MT* will be equal and parallel. Therefore since *LBZ* is a right angle, *BFT* will be a right [angle]. Therefore *MT* is bisected by *BF*. Therefore arc *TM* = 2 arc *ML*. But arc *MT* = arc *KE* because of the parallel [lines]. Therefore arc *KE* = 2 arc *ML*. Therefore arc *KE* = 2 arc *DK*. Therefore if *KE* is bisected, what has been proposed is had. If the angle is greater than an acute [angle], let it be divided into two acute angles and let a third part of each be taken, and [again] what has been proposed is had.[3]

21. TO FIND A POINT IN EVERY KNOWN TRIANGLE BY MEANS OF WHICH WHEN IT IS CONNECTED TO THE ANGLES OF THE TRIANGLE THE TRIANGLE WILL BE DIVIDED ACCORDING TO THREE KNOWN RATIOS.[1]

[2] For a discussion of the numbering of this proposition of Alhazen, see my *Archimedes in the Middle Ages,* Vol. 4, p. 30, n. 55. Needless to say, the assumption there that Jordanus was the author of the *Liber de triangulis Iordani* has to be abandoned in view of my conclusion in this volume that the author of this work was not Jordanus.

[3] In MS *Ve* a brief and rather confused solution of the trisection of a right angle is alluded to (see the variant reading to line 11). Perhaps the author intended a solution somewhat like the following (see Fig. IV.20 n.3). We wish to trisect right angle *ABG*. We draw a circle of radius *BD* so that it cuts the legs of the angle at *D* and *Z*. Then we inscribe half a hexagon in the upper half of the circle, whose sides *ZT*, *TM*, and *MN* are accordingly equal to the radius *BD*. Then we extend *BD* to *L* on the circumference, cutting *TM* at the midpoint *O*. We draw *BQ* perpendicular to *MN*, cutting *MN* at its midpoint *P*. We draw line *MB*, extending it to *K* on the circumference. Also extend *QB* to the circumference at *E*. Hence we have now trisected the right angle, for the central angles *LBM*, *MBQ*, and *QBN* are each equal to one third of a right angle. Therefore their equal vertical angles *DBK*, *KBE*, and *EBZ* each equal one third of a right angle. See my description of the proposition as a whole above in Part III, Chap. 1, and its sources in Appendix III.B below.

Prop. IV.21

[1] Prop. II.18 is a specific case of this proposition, whose proof is described in my account in Part III, Chap. 1. In Appendix III.B see the text of the fragment translated by Gerard of Cremona which provides the source of Prop. IV.21.

Let the triangle be *ABG* [see Fig. IV.21]. Therefore I shall pose the known ratio[s] [i.e. the relationships of the three parts to the whole triangle] in line *AG*, and I shall divide *AG* by means of this ratio [i.e. these relationships] in points *D* and *E*. Therefore let *DZ* be parallel to *GB*, and let *EH* be made parallel to *AB*, and let these [lines *DZ* and *EH*] intersect in point *T*. I say that *T* is the point we seek. For let *E* and *D* be connected with *B*, and *T* with *A*, *G*, and *B*. Therefore, since triangles *BTG* and *BDG* will be equal, [so] triangle *BTG* / whole triangle *AGB* = *DG* / *AG*. Then it is shown that triangle *ATB* / *ABG* = *AE* / *AG* because triangles *ATB* and *AEB* are equal (for they are on the same base *AB* and between parallel lines *AB* and *EH*). Therefore the remaining triangle *ATG* is to the whole triangle *ABG* as the remaining [line segment] *DE* is to line *AG*, and this is what we wished.

22. TO FIND BETWEEN TWO PROPOSED QUANTITIES TWO QUANTITIES SUCH THAT THE FOUR QUANTITIES ARE IN CONTINUED PROPORTION.[1]

Let there be two lines: *M* the longer, *N* the shorter [see Fig. IV.22a]. Let a circle *ABG* be made whose diameter *AB* is equal to quantity *M*, and let a chord *AG* be made equal to *N*, and let *BZ* be erected as a perpendicular to *AB*, and let *AG* be extended until it meets *BZ*, and I shall erect on arc *AGB* the surface of a half cylinder such that the rectilinear elements in it protracted to arc *ABG* are perpendicular to the surface of circle *ABGD*, and I shall describe on line *AB* a semicircle whose surface is always erected on the surface of circle *ABGD* at right angles, and let the arc be *AHE*. And let point *A* of arc *AHE* be fixed in place as a center and let arc *AHE* be rotated about *A*, and let its surface remain, during its rotation, always at right angles to the surface of circle *ABDG* so that arc *AHE* cuts the surface of the half cylinder erected on arc *AGB*. And let line *AB* be fixed as an axis and let triangle *AZB* be rotated about axis *AB* until line *AZ* makes a [common] section with the surface of the half cylinder, and it marks point *G*.[2] Then line *AZ* in its rotation will describe the semicircle *GQD* erected at right angles to the surface of circle *ABGD*. And I shall designate point *H* as the place where line *AZ* intersects the [common] section of the surface of the half cylinder [and arc *AHE*]. And let arc *AHE* stop rotating when it arrives at point *H*. And I shall draw two lines *AH* and *AE*, and I shall designate point *L* as the place where line *AH* meets arc *GQD*, and I shall draw from point *L* a perpendicular to the surface of circle *ABGD*, and this perpendicular is *LK* since *LK* is the common section of the surface of semicircle *AHE* and the surface of semicircle *GQD* and each of the said surfaces is erected at right angles to the surface of circle *ABGD*. Therefore line *LK* is perpendicular. And I shall draw line *LT*. It is clear, therefore, that *LT* is erected at right angles to line *AL*, for

---

Prop. IV.22

[1] For the origins of the two proofs of this proposition in (1) Prop. XVI of the *Verba filiorum* of the Banū Mūsā and (2) a fragment translated from the Arabic by Gerard of Cremona, see my account of this proposition in Part III, Chap. 1 above, and also consult Appendix III.B below.

[2] See my *Archimedes in the Middle Ages*, Vol. 1, p. 339n.

$GK \cdot KD = LK^2$. But $GK \cdot KD = TK \cdot KA$. Therefore $TK \cdot KA = LK^2$. Therefore *ALT* is a right angle. And now it has been shown that angle *AHE* of triangle *AHE* is a right [angle] since it falls in semicircle *AHE*, and that *ATH* is a right angle since *HT* is perpendicular to the surface of circle *ABDG*, and it is one of the rectilinear elements in the surface of the half cylinder protracted to arc *AGB* in the surface of circle *ABGD*. But line *AT* lies in the surface of circle *ABDG*. Therefore *ATH* is a right angle. Therefore in each of the triangles *AHE*, [*ATH*,] *ALT*, and *AKL* there is a right angle and angle *HAE*[3] is common to all [of the triangles]. Therefore the triangles are similar. Therefore *EA* / *AH* = *AH* / *AT* = *AT* / *AL*. Thus, if line *AE* = *M* and *AL* = *N*, therefore *AH* and *AT* are between *M* and *N* in continued proportion.

Another [solution] of the same thing.[4] Let the two lines be *AB* and *BG* [see Fig. IV.22b], joined at a right angle. Then I shall draw *AG* and make circle *ABGH* on line *AG* of triangle *ABG*. And let perpendicular *AD* be erected on line *AB* from point *A* and perpendicular *DG* on line *BG* from point *G*, and I shall extend both of them, the one to *Z* and the other to *E*. Then I shall lay out a rule to be moved about point *B* without ever being separated from it and to cut the two lines *DZ* and *DE* and to continue to be moved until that part of the rule between *Z* and *B* is equal to the part of the rule between arc *BG* and *E*. Therefore in this position let it be as rule *EHBZ* [in the diagram], and let *EH* be equal to *BZ*. Therefore $ZH \cdot ZB = BE \cdot HE$. But $EB \cdot HE = DE \cdot GE$ [and $HZ \cdot ZB = DZ \cdot ZA$].[5] Therefore $DZ \cdot ZA = DE \cdot EG$. Therefore *DE* / *DZ* = *AZ* / *GE*. But *ED* / *DZ* = *BA* / *AZ*. Therefore *BA* / *AZ* = *AZ* / *GE* = *GE* / *GB*. Therefore what has been proposed stands [*AZ* and *GE* being the mean proportionals between *BA* and *GB*].

23. TO INSCRIBE A REGULAR HEPTAGON IN A PROPOSED CIRCLE.[1]

Let the circle be *ABG* with center *G* [see Fig. IV.23]. Let *AG* be bisected at *H*, and let perpendiculars *HQ* and *GD* be erected from *H* and *G*. Let *A* be joined to *D* and [then] indefinitely extended outside of the circle. Therefore it will cut perpendicular *HQ* at *E*; and I shall connect *G* with *E* and extend it in both directions to the circumference at points *M* and *L*, and I shall connect *D* and *L*, and I shall bisect line *DG* at *T* and I shall protract from *T* a perpendicular *TZ* without posing any determined end to it. And I shall move lines *AD*, *LM*, *GD*, and *DL* in this way: I pose the motion of *AD* about

---

[3] All the manuscripts of the complete text of the *Liber de triangulis Iordani* falsely have *AHE*, but in the text of the *Verba filiorum* we find the correct reading *HAE* (see Vol. 1, p. 338, line 56).

[4] This is the second solution, which I first published on the basis of Leonardo Fibonacci's *Practica geometrie* in Vol. 1, pp. 662–66, above. See the purer text based on manuscripts of Gerard of Cremona's translation in Appendix III.B below.

[5] The bracketed clause is necessary and is included in the text of Gerard's translation, but is missing in the manuscripts of the *Liber de triangulis Iordani*.

Prop. IV.23

[1] See the long account of this proposition of Part III, Chap. 1. Compare also Appendix III.B where the pristine version translated by Gerard of Cremona is found.

A, [those of] *LM* and *DG* about *G*, and [that of] *DL* with respect to *D* [and *L*] without any of them being separated during their motions from what we have determined for them.[2] Let perpendicular *HQ* be fixed on *AG* and perpendicular *TZ* fixed on *GD*, and we shall move *AD* about *A* in the direction of *B*. Accordingly let line *AD* be [continually] added to [from its indefinite extension], and let its addition be in the direction of *D* since *A* is fixed, and let *D* be changed as it is moved since it is the point at which line *AD* cuts the circumference of the circle, and also let its approach when moved be toward *B* on the circumference. And let *D* of lines *GD* and *GL*, which is tied to the *D* of line *AD* on the circumference, be inseparable from it in the motion of the aforesaid *AD*, and let it be that wherever line *AD* cuts the perpendicular line *HQ*, line *LGM* cuts it [*HQ*] at one and the same point,[3] namely point *E*. And the motion of *LM* is about *G*, as we said. Moreover the approch of point *L* of line *LM* by [the latter point's] motion with *AD* on point [*E*] of perpendicular *HQ* is toward *B* since the approach of the section point *E* by the aforesaid motion on the perpendicular *HQ* is toward *H*. And let line *DL*, passing by its motion through point *L* of line *LM* on the circumference, be inseparable from *LM* in its motion. Therefore line *LD* is decreased, and its diminution is in the direction of *L* since point *D* is not varied [in respect to line *DG*], as we have already explained concerning its transit, and with point *D* [there is an accompanying motion] of lines *DG* and *AD*. Therefore when we shall move line *AD* in the manner explained regarding its motion and it will follow the remaining lines in the way we have determined, the perpendicular [*TZ*] will [continue to be perpendicular] and will cut line *DL* [continually] by the motion of *GD* [to which it is affixed], and the approach of the point of section [*K* of *TZ* and *DL*] is toward *K'* on the diameter of the circle,[4] and the point of section of line *AB* and *DL* is changed in its motion. Therefore let perpendicular *TZ* continue to cut line [*DL*] until [in its position *T'Z*] it cuts the point of section of that line [*DL*]

---

[2] That is, with the properties assigned to them remaining the same.

[3] The awkward phrase in Gerard's text was "et ei est simile." Apparently the author of the *Liber de triangulis Iordani* or an early scribe changed it to read "et *TA* est simile". If it were the author, we would have expected him also to have changed "simile" (neuter) to "similis" (feminine) to agree with *TA* (i.e. linea *TA*). And indeed Curtze made just such a change in his text. But all of the manuscripts having the phrase retain the reading "simile". I believe it evident that "simile" in Gerard's text agreed with "punctum" and so the expression "et ei est simile" of Gerard's text was merely a circumlocution which, taken with "unum punctum", signified "unum et idem punctum" (i.e. "one and the same point", as I have here rendered it in the translation). It is rather interesting that the intelligent manuscript *H* omits the phrase "et *TA* est simile" and changes "super unum punctum" to "super eundem punctum". Even if we accept Curtze's emendation and read "et *TA* est similis", the phrase is false, since *TA* is not similar in any meaningful way. For *T* is a fixed point on *DG* (which is in motion) and thus *T* does not slide along *DG* in the manner that *E* slides along *QH* (which is fixed in position).

[4] From this point onward I have added prime signs in the translation to the points that have reached their final positions, that is when all motion has stopped.

with line *AB*, where it is the case perpendicular[5] [of triangle *D'GK'*]. Therefore when this coincidence takes place, we shall halt the line *AD* in its position [*AD'*], and we shall accordingly fix the [previously noted] motions of the remaining lines and points, and that which has resulted is what we wished, and the chord of arc *D'B* is the side of a [regular] heptagon [inscribed in the circle]. Proceed [as follows]. Angle *D'GK'*, extrinsic to triangle *AGD'* of two equal legs, is double angle *D'AG*. But angle *D'AG* = angle *AGE'* because *AH* = *HG* and perpendicular *HE'* is common to the two triangles *AHE'* and *GHE'*. Therefore angle *D'GK'* = 2 angle *AGE'*. And again angle *E'GD'*, extrinsic to isosceles triangle *D'GL'*, is double angle *GD'L'*. But angle *GD'L'* = angle *D'GK'* because *GT'* = *T'D'* and *T'K'* is common to the two triangles *D'K'T'* and *GK'T'*. Therefore angle *E'GD'* = 2 angle *D'GK'*. Therefore those angles to which a semicircumference is subtended are 3½ angle *D'GK'*. Therefore arc *AD'B*, which is half the circumference, equals 3½ arc *D'B*. Therefore the circumference is 7 arc *D'B*. Therefore its chord is the side of an equilateral and equiangular heptagon, which is what has been proposed.

When a line is divided into three segments and (1) the ratio of the last of these [segments] to the first is as the ratio of the first to the rest of the line (i.e. [to the sum] of the middle and last [segments]) and (2) the ratio of the middle to the last is as the ratio of the last to the rest [of the line] (i.e. [to the sum of] the middle and first [segments]), there results from these three segments [as sides] a triangle whose greatest angle is double its middle [angle], and its middle [angle] is double its smallest [angle]. When therefore a circle contains this triangle, the arc which is subtended by the smallest angle is the arc of a chord [which is the side] of the [regular] heptagon falling in that circle.[6]

---

[5] That is, the perpendicular that "has fallen" from the angle *K'* to the base *D'G* of triangle *D'GK'*.

[6] This is an interesting paragraph and I have indicated how it ties in with the so-called Archimedean solution in Part III, Chap. 1, above. We can illustrate these instructions by referring to Fig. IV.23*var. Ve*. If we divide the line *AB* into three segments at points *D* and *C* so that *CB* / *AD* = *AD* / (*CB* + *DC*) and *DC* / *CB* = *CB* / (*CD* + *AD*), and if we construct from the three segments *AD*, *DC*, and *CB* a triangle, there will result a triangle *AED* such that ang. *AED* = 2 ang. *EAD* and ang. *EAD* = 2 ang. *ADE*. MS *Ve* includes a proof of this as follows (see the variant reading to line 56): "The demonstration of this is elicited as follows. Let *AED* be the triangle [composed] out of [sides equal to lines] *AD*, *DC*, and *CB*, constituted as the proportion demands, and let *EF* be protracted equal to *ED* (or *EF* = *CB*), and line *GA* = *AE* (or *GA* = *DC*). Therefore, by VI.16 (=Gr. VI.17) and II.1 [both] of Euclid, $AD^2 = ED^2 + AE \cdot EF$. Therefore, with line *DH* drawn perpendicular to *AF*, $AD^2 = DH^2 + EH^2 + AE \cdot EF$. Therefore, by the penultimate [proposition] of [Book] I [of Euclid] and with the common area subtracted, $AH^2 = HE^2 + AE \cdot EF$ because I shall [have] bisect[ed] *AF* in point *H* by the converse of II.5 of Euclid, and thus from I.4 [of Euclid] lines *AD* and *DF* are equal. Conclude therefore by I.32 and I.6 [both of Euclid] that ang. *AED* = 2 ang. *DAE*. In completely the same way it may be demonstrated that ang. *DAE* = 2 ang. *ADE* after *EK* has been protracted perpendicularly to *DG*, *EK* necessarily falling inside of triangle *DEA* since each angle on the base is acute." A note is added under Fig. IV.23*var. Ve*: "Note that angle *AED* is greater than a right angle since

This [following] is an investigation of the Indians that speaks of the description of any polygon of equal sides [and angles] falling in a circle.[7] And indeed much of the position of the Indians depends on belief alone without demonstration, but the difference between it and the truth is not a sensible quantity.[8] And this is the procedure I now describe. Always [i.e. in the case of all such polygons] multiply the half [diameter] by the whole diameter. Then multiply that product by 9 always, and always retain this [further] product.[9] Then always substract one from the number of sides of the figure whose quantity you wish to find [and do so only] one time, and take half of the remainder and multiply it into the number of sides of the figure, and [then] always add 3 to this product. Divide the result into the number which you retained [above], and that which emerges is the square of the side [of the polygon]. Therefore when you operate in this way on that [specific polygon] which requires, demonstration [i.e. solution], it will proceed to this number.[10] And you should know that these Indians pose that the side of a [regular] heptagon falling in the circle is equal to half of the side of an [equilateral] triangle falling in it,[11] but there is no demonstration of that in their hands other than [this] heuristic device.[12] Therefore understand etc.

$AD^2 > AE^2 + ED^2$, while angle EFD is less than a right angle. Hence necessarily perpendicular DH falls between E and F." Note further that if AD' is the diameter of the circle, the triangle AED' would be equivalent to triangle $BD'A$ in Fig. IV.23.

[7] I have modernized the expression of the Indian rule in my account of this proposition in Part III, Chap. 1.

[8] Note that the Latin text literally says that "the proximity between it and the truth is not a sensible quantity."

[9] The author of the *Liber de triangulis Iordani* may have made a mistake in transmitting Gerard's text. For instead of the correct number "9" (which is given in Gerard's text and in MS *H*) all of the remaining manuscripts of the *Liber de triangulis Iordani* write "18" or some other number (see the variant reading to line 62).

[10] As I have indicated in my account of the proposition in Part III, Chap. 1, if we use the Indian rule on a heptagon, it produces an approximation of the side of a regular hexagon equal to $\frac{1}{2}\sqrt{3}\ r$.

[11] This approximation perhaps had its origin in Hero of Alexandria's *Metrica* Bk. I, Chap. 19, lemma (see the edition of E. M. Bruins, *Codex Constantinopolitanus Palatii veteris no. 1,* Part II [Leiden, 1964], pp. 101–02), where not only this approximation of the side as being equal to half the side of an inscribed equilateral triangle is given but also its equivalent, namely the perpendicular drawn from the center of the circle to the side of a regular hexagon inscribed in it. This latter approximation is found in the *Geometria deutsch* of Mathes Roriczer (see *Gothic Design Techniques: The Fifteenth-Century Design Booklets of Mathes Roriczer and Hanns Schmuttermayer,* ed. and tr. by L. R. Shelby [Carbondale and Edwardsville, Ill., 1977], pp. 118–19. For some reasons Shelby seems puzzled that Roriczer first presents a regular hexagon and then passes on to a heptagon. There is no problem here, for all that the author is doing is first to construct a regular hexagon, then to bisect its side by a perpendicular drawn from the center of the circle to that side, and finally to open dividers the distance between the center of the circle and the midpoint of the side of the hexagon. The opening of the dividers is taken as the distance equal to the length of a side of the regular heptagon, and so the sides of that heptagon are laid off in an equal circle. Hence it is obvious that the author considers the passages designated by Shelby Nos. 6 and 7 as comprising a single complete solution.

[12] In Gerard's translation, which was the source of this proposition, Gerard notes on the margin that the word *esse* is an alternate translation for the word which he translated as *inventio* in the

24. IN THE CASE OF EVERY RIGHT TRIANGLE OF UNEQUAL SIDES, IF THE EXCESS OF ITS LONGEST SIDE OVER ITS MIDDLE SIDE IS EQUAL TO THE EXCESS OF THE MIDDLE SIDE OVER THE SHORTEST [SIDE], ITS SHORTEST SIDE IS TRIPLE THAT EXCESS, AND THE MIDDLE [SIDE] IS QUADRUPLE THAT EXCESS, AND THE LONGEST SIDE IS QUINTUPLE THE EXCESS. FURTHER, THE SHORTEST SIDE IS ONE FOURTH OF ALL THE SIDES OF THE TRIANGLE, THE MIDDLE ONE IS ONE THIRD OF ALL THE SIDES OF THE TRIANGLE, AND THE LONGEST [SIDE] IS THE REMAINING PART OF ONE, NAMELY TWO SIXTHS AND HALF OF ONE SIXTH OF ALL THE SIDES OF THE TRIANGLE.

Let the triangle be ABG [see Fig. IV.24], A the right [angle], BG the longest side, AB the middle side [and EG the shortest side]. And let AB be equal to BE and AG equal to DB. Therefore it is clear that $DE = EG$. Therefore $BG^2 = 4 BE \cdot EG + BD^2$.[1] But $BG^2 = BE^2 + BD^2$ according to what we premised. Therefore, with BD^2 subtracted [from the equals], $BE^2 = 4 BE \cdot EG$. Therefore $BE = 4 EG$, and $BD = 3 EG$, and $BG = 5 EG$, and $BE = AB$, and $BD = AG$. But if we add these equalities, the result will be twelve like quantities equal [in sum] to all three sides, for AG is three of them and that is $\frac{1}{4}$ of the whole, and AB is four [of them] and that is $\frac{1}{3}$ of the whole, and BG is five of them and that is $\frac{2}{6}$ plus $\frac{1}{2}$ of $\frac{1}{6}$ [of the whole]. Therefore what we wished is clear.

25. IN THE CASE OF ANY TRIANGLE OF DIVERSE SIDES, THE RATIO OF THE EXCESS OF THE LONGER SIDE OVER THE SHORTER SIDE TO THE EXCESS OF THE "CASE" [I.E. THE LONGER SEGMENT OF THE BASE CUT BY THE CASE PERPENDICULAR][1] OVER THE SHORTER [SEGMENT CUT BY THAT PERPENDICULAR] WILL BE AS THE RATIO OF THE BASE TO THE SUM OF THE TWO SIDES.

For let the triangle be ABG [see Fig. IV.25] and I shall pose AG longer than AB, and I shall pose AD as its perpendicular. I say that $(AG - AB) / (DG - DB) = BG / (AB + AG)$. Proceed. For I shall pose A to be a center and I shall draw a circle with radius AB, which circle let be $VZBE$, and I shall extend AG in a straight line to Z. It is clear, therefore, that $VG = AG - AB$ [since $AV = AB$] and that $EG = DG - DB$ since $DB = DE$. Therefore $BG \cdot EG = ZG \cdot GV$. Therefore $BG / ZG = VG / EG$. But $ZG = AB + AG$. Therefore $BG / (AG + AB) = (AG - AB) / (DG - BD)$, and $DG - BD = GE$. Therefore, what we wished is clear.

---

text (see the text in Appendix III.B, variant reading to line 79). I would suppose that the Arabic word was *maujūd* (or some other form of the verb *wajada*), which could mean either "that which is found" or "that which exists."

Prop. IV.24

[1] Many of the manuscripts appear to have the false reading *quantum* instead of *quater,* thus making no sense out of the argument (see the variant readings to lines 13 and 16). Indeed Curtze accepted this reading without comment, when one would suppose that he would immediately have seen that such a reading was impossible and accordingly corrected the text.

Prop. IV.25

[1] See Prop. IV.23, note 5 to the English translation.

26. I WISH TO SHOW [ULTIMATELY] THAT, IN THE CASE OF ANY THREE [CONTINUALLY] PROPORTIONAL LINES, THE SQUARE OF THE RATIO OF THE FIRST TO THE SECOND IS EQUAL TO THE RATIO OF THE FIRST TO THE THIRD. THEREFORE WHEN WE WISH TO SHOW THIS LET US [FIRST] SHOW THAT, IN THE CASE OF ANY THREE LINES IN WHATEVER WAY DISPOSED, THE RATIO OF THE FIRST TO THE THIRD IS AS THE RATIO OF THE PRODUCT OF THE FIRST AND THE SECOND TO THE PRODUCT OF THE SECOND AND THE THIRD.[1]

As the exemplum of this let there be three lines: AB, GD, and ET [see Fig. IV.26]. I say, therefore, that $AB / ET = (AB \cdot GD) / (GD \cdot ET)$, of which this is the demonstration. I shall pose a long line and I shall cut from it that which is equal to AB, namely HT', and I shall erect a perpendicular from point T' on HT', and I shall cut from it that which is equal to GD, and let it be $T'L$. And further I shall cut that which is equal to ET, which let be $T'K$ and I shall cause to pass through point L a line parallel to HK, and I shall complete the two surfaces HL and LK. Therefore the altitude of each is the same. Therefore the ratio of the surfaces is as the ratio of HT' to $T'K$. But $HT' = AB$, and $T'K = ET$. Therefore $AB / ET = (AB \cdot GD) / (GD \cdot ET)$, and that is what we wished to demonstrate.

27. AND BECAUSE I HAVE ALREADY SHOWN THIS [PRECEDING] PROPOSITION, THEN I SHALL FURTHER SHOW THAT, IN THE CASE OF ANY THREE LINES IN WHATEVER WAY DISPOSED, THE RATIO OF THE FIRST TO THE THIRD IS EQUAL TO THE RATIO OF THE FIRST TO THE SECOND MULTIPLIED BY THE RATIO OF THE SECOND TO THE THIRD.

I pose three lines: AB, DG, and ET,[1] and I shall pose line H as the ratio of line AB to DG [see Fig. IV.27]. Therefore, when line H is multiplied into line GD, the result is line AB, since ratio is division. And I pose line T' as the ratio of GD to ET. Therefore, when T' is multiplied into ET, GD is the result. And I pose line L as the ratio of AB to ET. Therefore, when L is multiplied into ET, AB is the result. I say, therefore, that line $H \cdot$ line T' = line L, which is demonstrated as follows. I shall multiply H into T' and [some line] K is [posed to] be the result. I say, therefore that line K = line L, which is proved as follows. Line H, line T', and line ET are three lines, of which H is the first and line ET is the last of them. Therefore the ratio of the first, which is H, to the last, which is ET, will be as the ratio of the product of line H and line T' to the product of line T' and ET [by the preceding proposition]. But the product of line H and line T' is line K, and

Prop. IV.26

[1] For the last three propositions on proportions, see the account I have given in Part III, Chap. 1.

Prop. IV.27

[1] Note that Gerard of Cremona's fragment from which this proposition was taken had EZ, which the author of the *Liber de triangulis Iordani* everywhere changed to ET in Props. IV.26–IV.27 (see Prop. IV.26, variant reading to line 9, and Prop. IV.27, variant reading to line 6). Consequently in Prop. IV.27 we find the letter T used twice, and for the second TI have written T' (see the variant reading to line 9). Compare also Fig. IV.28b in the next proposition.

the product of [line] T' and line ET is line DG. Therefore line H / line ET = line K / line GD. Therefore $H \cdot GD = K \cdot ET$. But $H \cdot GD = AB$. Therefore $K \cdot ET = AB$, and already $L \cdot ET = AB$. Therefore line L = line K. Now, therefore, it has been shown that AB / $ET = (AB$ / $GD) \cdot (GD$ / $ET)$. And now because I have demonstrated this ratio (! proposition), it will then be manifest that, in the case of any three proportional lines, the ratio of the first to the third is equal to the square of the ratio of the first to the second.

28. FURTHER, SINCE IT HAS BEEN SHOWN THAT, IN THE CASE OF THREE [CONTINUALLY] PROPORTIONAL LINES, THE RATIO OF THE FIRST TO THE THIRD IS EQUAL TO THE SQUARE OF THE RATIO OF THE FIRST TO THE SECOND, I WISH TO SHOW THAT IN THE CASE OF FOUR LINES FOLLOWING ACCORDING TO ONE RATIO [I.E. FOUR LINES THAT ARE CONTINUALLY PROPORTIONAL], THE RATIO OF THE FIRST TO THE FOURTH IS EQUAL TO THE CUBE OF THE RATIO OF THE FIRST TO THE SECOND.

As the exemplum of this let there be four lines A, B, G and D that are continually proportional [see Fig. IV.28a]. I say, therefore, that A / D = $(A$ / $B)^3$, which is demonstrated as follows. A, G, and D are three lines. Therefore A / $D = (A$ / $G) \cdot (G$ / $D)$ [by Proposition IV.27]. And A, B, and G are three proportional lines. Therefore [by the end of the same proposition] A / $G = (A$ / $B)^2$. Therefore A / $D = (A$ / $B)^2 \cdot (G$ / $D)$. But G / $D = A$ / B. Therefore A / $D = (A$ / $B)^2 \cdot (A$ / $B)$, and $(A$ / $B)^2 \cdot (A$ / $B) = (A$ / $B)^3$. Therefore A / $D = (A$ / $B)^3$, and this is what we wished.

And it is possible for us to advance a demonstration of the truth of what we have said by another method when that which has been premised is produced in this figure [Fig. IV.28b].[1] That is manifest. Since ET / TB = TB / $BH = BH$ / HT', therefore quantities ET, TB, BH and HT' are proportionals. Therefore the ratio of the first to the fourth is as the ratio of the first to the second multiplied by the ratio of the first to the third on account of the fact that a second mean is not placed between the first [mean] and the fourth [term when applying the preceding proposition to the three lines ET, TB, and HT']. So the ratio of the first to the fourth is equal to the ratio of the first to the second multiplied by the ratio of the second to the fourth [i.e. EH / $HT' = (ET$ / $TB) \cdot (TB$ / $HT')$]. Therefore [since ET / BH = TB / HT' because the lines are continually proportional], ET / HT' = $(ET$ / $TB) \cdot (ET$ / $BH)$. [And by IV.27 again ET / $BH = (ET$ / $TB) \cdot (TB$ / $BH)$. Therefore ET / $HT' = (ET$ / $TB) \cdot (ET$ / $TB) \cdot (TB$ / $BH) = (ET$ / $TB) \cdot (ET$ / $TB) \cdot (ET$ / $TB)$, and this is what we proposed.][2]

Prop. IV.28

[1] The alternate proof, no doubt added by the author of the *Liber de triangulis Iordani* or some other Latin author, may be outlined and filled in as follows. (1) ET / $TB = TB$ / BH = BH / HT' (given). (2) Therefore ET, TB, BH, and HT' are proportionals and ET / BH = TB / HT'. (3) By Prop. IV.27, ET / HT' = $(ET$ / $TB) \cdot (TB$ / $HT')$. (4) Hence, from (2) and (3), ET / HT' = $(ET$ / $TB) \cdot (ET$ / $BH)$. (5) But also, from IV.27, ET / BH = $(ET$ / $TB) \cdot (TB$ / $BH)$. (6) Therefore ET / HT' = $(ET$ / $TB) \cdot (ET$ / $TB) \cdot (TB$ / $BH)$, or, from (6) and (1), ET / HT' = $(ET$ / $TB) \cdot (ET$ / $TB) \cdot (ET$ / $TB)$. Q.E.D.

[2] The bracketed material, which I have added, was omitted by the author, perhaps because it is obvious.

PART IV

APPENDIXES

APPENDIX I

Corrections and Short Additions to the Earlier Volumes

Note: See the list of corrections and additions in Volume 3, pp. 1249–57.

Volume 1

P. *xx, under 5.Bd*, line 5: For* codium *read* codicum.
P. *xxiii, under 20. Ha, line 4: For* none *read* nona.
P. *xxiv, under 24. Ka, line 4: For* non *read* nona.
P.17: Note that toward the end of the period in which Plato of Tivoli made his translations, the well-known translator from the Arabic, Hermann of Carinthia, completed (in 1143) his *Liber de essentiis,* which has the following reference to Archimedes, notice of which, with the text of the passage (67vA-B), I owe to the kindness of Dr. C.S.F. Burnett, whose new text and translation of the work was recently published (Hermann of Carinthia, *De essentiis* [Leiden, 1982], p. 142): "Cum itaque minus quam duplum .lxiiii. diametron circuli lunaris perficiat, circuli vero solaris diametron duplum .mccx., ex quibus—ut Archimedes describit—ipsi circulorum am/-bitus reperiuntur—lunaris quidem minus quam .cccc., solaris vero fere viidcxxv. . . ." The numbers given here are slightly puzzling, for if we simply divided the respective given circumferences by twice the respective given radii, we would deduce that in the case of the lunar circle the value of π would have been 3.125 and in the case of the solar circle it would have been 3.150. It is more likely that he simply used the value of 22/7 (which was assumed constantly in the handbook traditions and in Proposition II of the *De mensura circuli*) in both calculations. If he did this, then he should in the first case have found a circumference of less than 402.25 (while in fact he reported a circumference of "less than 400," which may have simply been a poor rounding off) and in the second case he should have computed the circumference as about 7605.71 (while in fact, he reported a circumference of 7625, which I suppose could have been an inadvertent error, "2" having been written instead of "0"). Whatever is the truth on the value of π that Hermann used, it must be realized that

if he employed a Latin source for the reference to Archimedes, it would almost have to have been the early translation of the *De mensura circuli* that was perhaps executed by Plato of Tivoli since the more common translation by Gerard of Cremona was certainly made later than the date of the completion of the *Liber de essentiis*. It is of course not impossible that he found the reference to Archimedes in some Arabic source such as the Arabic text of the *De mensura circuli* (or some work in which that text was quoted) or such as Ptolemy's *Almagest* (for the pertinent reference to the Greek text and Gerard of Cremona's later translation from the Arabic see Volume 3 above, p. 378, n. 39) where Archimedes is also mentioned in connection with the determination of the ratio of circumference to diameter. Or Hermann's Arabic source could have been still another work that reflected the Ptolemaic passage. But the interesting point about Hermann's reference, as Dr. Burnett has pointed out, is that he used the Greco-Latin form of *Archimedes* rather than one of the several Arabo-Latin forms which I have mentioned in Volume 1 (pp. 16–17, n. 5). Regardless of where he learned of Archimedes' view of quadrature, he might have taken the Greco-Latin form of his name from one of the many classical Latin references to Archimedes that I have discussed in Appendix III to Volume 3.

P. 224, last paragraph: As I have shown here in Volume Five, the compositor of the longer versions of the *Liber de triangulis Iordani* was undoubtedly not Jordanus but probably someone living toward the middle of the thirteenth century. Hence any reference to that longer work as being by Jordanus must now be corrected.

P. 366. See the preceding comment.

PP. 567–75, 658–77: Again see the penultimate comment. It is pertinent to the texts discussed in these appendixes, all of which come from the parts added to the longer version of the *De triangulis* and not from the *Liber philotegni* of Jordanus. The reader will realize that all of the propositions discussed in these appendixes have been treated again here in Volume 5. See particularly Appendix III.B below.

P. 634, line 11 from the bottom: For Quaestions *read* Quaestiones.

Volume 2

P. 7: A. Paravicini Bagliani, "Nuovi documenti su Guglielmo da Moerbeke OP," *Archivum Fratrum Praedicatorum,* Vol. 52 (1982), pp. 135–43, presents three documents which show that Moerbeke was present in Perugia as a papal legate to absolve Perugia of an interdiction in January of 1284. The author suggests that the documents allow us to suppose "with a certain probability" that Moerbeke died not in Corinth, as is usually supposed, but rather in Italy.

P. 244, 37vN: For TZA *read* TZD. Though the manuscript has TZA, I should point out that —A is a correction in the hand of Andreas Coner.

Volume 3

PP. 158–59: Concerning the paragraphs marked (5) and (6), note once again that the author of the longer version of the *De triangulis* was almost certainly not Jordanus.

P. 159, line 13: For three *read* four *and in line 14: For* 21. *read* 21, 25.

P. 420, n. 20: Professor Roger Herz-Fischler of Carleton University has kindly informed me that the copy of Pacioli's version of Campanus' Euclid in the Bibliothèque Nationale in Paris (Rés. V.104) [*Euclidis . . . opera a Campano . . . tralata* (Venice, 1509)] also has interesting handwritten annotations. He generously provided me with prints of a proof of the first proposition of Archimedes' *De circuli quadratura* that occupies parts of the first two leaves (1 * v–2 * r), the text of which I present here, noting that the author has had access to the Greek text and / or to a translation dependent on the Greek text, and that he paraphrased and expanded the text of Archimedes in the manner of the various medieval versions that bear the title *De quadratura circuli* and which I have published in Volume One. The Latin letters on the diagram (Fig. Ap. I.1) are precisely as in the diagrams present in the translation of Jacobus Cremonensis (see Archimedes, *Opera quae quidem extant omnia* [Basel, 1544], Lat. pag., p. 55). I have changed the punctuation slightly, italicized the letters referring to magnitudes and stripped these letters of the periods that encompass them.

/ De circuli quadratura

1*v

Dicit Archimedes quod area cuiuscunque trianguli orthogonii cuius unum duorum laterum eius ambientium angulum eius rectum est aequale circunferentie propositi circuli, et aliud semidiametro eiusdem circuli, est
5 aequalis areae ipsius circuli proposti; quod ego sic demonstro. Sit propositus circulus *abcd* cuius centrum *n* [Fig. Ap.I.1]. Et sit triangulus *E* qui sic se habeat ad propositum circulum ut proponitur. Dico aream trianguli *e* (*! hic et ubique postea*) esse aequalem areae circuli *abcd* propositi. Et si non: sit per adversarium area propositi circuli *abcd* maior area trianguli *e*. Et
10 inscribatur ipsi circulo *abcd* proposito quadratum secundum doctrinam 6ᵉ quarti: et dividentur arcus quibus subtenduntur latera quadrati vel quorum cordae sunt latera quadrati *abcd* per aequalia, secundum doctrinam 29ᵉ tertii. Et ducantur ab angulis quadrati *abcd* ad puncta media arcuum lineae rectae, et fiant hoc modo figurae rectilineae intra circunferentiam
15 propositi circuli *abcd* donec inciderimus, seu deveniemus ad aliquam figuram rectilineam cuius area sit maior area trianguli *e*. Necesse est enim devenire ad aliquam talem: ex quo per adversarium area circuli *abcd* propositi est maior area trianguli *e*. Et tunc a centro *n* circuli *abcd* propositi ducatur perpendicularis super unum laterum talis figurae, secundum doc-
20 trinam 12ᵉ primi, quae sit *nx*. Erit *nx* minor semidiametro circuli *abcd* propositi, et ex consequenti minor latere trianguli *e* aequali semidiametro

circuli *abcd* propositi. Erit etiam tota linea claudens figuram ipsam maiorem
triangulo *e* ad quam deveniemus minor latere trianguli *e* aequali circunferentiae propositi circuli *abcd* cum sit minor circunferentia propositi circuli.
25 Et ex consequenti propter hoc area dictae figurae erit minor area trianguli
e, quod est contra ypothesin, positum enim fuerat quod esset maior: quod
sic demonstratur. Si enim ex duabus lineis ambientibus angulum rectum
trianguli *e* abscindentur duae equales istis secundum doctrinam 3^e primi:
et angulo recto *e* subtendatur basis, erit triangulus proveniens minor trian-
30 gulo *e* per conversionem ultimae conceptionis primi; quare et figura ipsa,
quod est propositum. Sit modo per adversarium ut area circuli *abcd* propositi sit minor area trianguli *e,* et circumscribatur ei quadratum, secundum
doctrinam 7^e quarti; et arcus circunferentiae circuli *abcd* propositi introclusi
inter puncta costarum huius quadrati contingentia circunferentiam circuli
35 *abcd* propositi dividantur per aequalia, secundum doctrinam 29^e tertii. Et
per puncta media divisionum circumducantur lineae rectae contingentes
2*r circunferentiam circuli, secundum / doctrinam 16^e tertii, et a centro *n*
circuli *abcd* propositi per punctum *a* contactus ducatur linea *nao*. Rectus
enim erit angulus *oar,* per doctrinam 17^e tertii. Quare per comunem scien-
40 tiam, si una quantitas comparetur ad duas aequales et cetera, et per 18^{am}
primi, latus *or* maius est latere *rm,* nam *rm* est aequalis *ra* et *or* est maior
ra per 18^{am} primi. Sumantur itaque portiones similes portioni *pfa* quae
omnes simul iunctae sint minores eo in quo area trianguli *e* excedit aream
circuli *abcd* propositi. Erit enim propter hoc area huius figurae rectilineae
45 circulo circumscriptae minor area trianguli *e,* quod est absurdum, maior
enim esse probatur. Cum enim linea *na* sit aequalis lateri perpendiculari
trianguli *e* per ypothesin et circunferentia dictae figurae sit maior altero
latere trianguli *e* eo quia est maior circunferentia circuli *abcd* propositi,
quae posita fuit aequalis altero lateri trianguli *e,* erit propter hoc area dictae
50 figurae maior area trianguli *e* et non minor, quod est contra ypothesin;
positum enim fuerat quod esset minor, quod sic demonstratur. Prolongetur
latus trianguli *e* aequale circunferentiae circuli *abcd* propositi ad aequali-
tatem circunferentiae dictae figurae et subtendatur basis angulo recto trianguli *e,* erit triangulus procreatus maior triangulo *e* per ultimam concep-
55 tionem primi, quare et figura ipsa, quod est propositum. Quia ergo, ut
demonstratum est, area circuli *abcd* propositi non potest esse maior area
trianguli *e* neque minor, necessario est ei aequalis, quod est illud quod
erat a nobis demonstrandum. Quia ergo area circuli *abcd* propositi est
aequalis areae trianguli *e,* ut demonstratum est, inveniatur secundum doc-
60 trinam 14^e secundi latus tetragonicum eius et quadretur secundum doctrinam 45^e primi. Et arguatur sic. Quia area huius quadrati est aequalis
areae trianguli *e* et area circuli *abcd* propositi est aequalis eidem, ut demonstratum est, erit, per primam conceptionem primi, area huius quadrati
aequalis areae circuli *abcd* propositi, quod restabat a nobis demonstrandum
65 est. Haec Archimedes brevissimis verbis et sub alia verborum serie ad
peritum in geometria loquitur.

P. 1256. To the addition given to *P. 640* I note here four more manuscripts of Version I of Hero's theorem: Paris, BN lat. 16647, 94r–95r, 13c; Florence, Bibl. Naz., Conv. soppr. J.I.32, 18v, 13c; Norwich, Norfolk Record Office, Gunton MS, 54v–55v, 14c (see under *siglum G* in the description of the manuscripts to the longer version above), and Parma, Bibl. Palatina, Fondo Parm. 720, 475v, 13c. In the first two of these manuscripts this fragment is Proposition 3 of the anonymous *Liber de triangulis datis* (see Appendix III.A below).

P. 1565: Add to Anonymous, De isoperimetris *the number* 617n.

Volume 4

P. 3: Another translation of Gerard of Cremona gives us very brief glimpses of conic sections, namely that of Anaritius' *Commentary on the Elements of Euclid.* I was alerted to three of the four passages that follow by the kindness of Dr. P.M.J.E. Tummers, who also gave me the readings of the passages cited from MS Madrid 10010, which I have checked and altered somewhat. I have added here references to the edition of M. Curtze, *Anaritii in decem libros priores Elementorum Euclidis commentarii ex interpretatione Gherardi Cremonensis in codice Cracoviensi 569 servata* (Leipzig, 1899), and to manuscript Vat. reg. lat. 1268. I have punctuated the passages as I saw fit.

[1] Ed., p. 6; Mad., 14r; Vat. 145r: "Species enim (*MSS,* autem *Ed.*) linee sunt multe (*MSS,* tres *Ed.*): scilicet quod earum alie sunt recte, alie circumflexe (*MSS,* circonflexe *Ed.*), alie medie inter rectas et circumflexas (*MSS,* circonflexas *Ed.*) que sunt ac si ex eis forent composite. Harum vero que sunt medie quedam sunt inordinate quam ob rem non indigent eis geometre, sicut sectiones piramidum que sunt formate ad animalium (*MSS,* aliam *Ed.*) similitudinem, et alie infinite; quedam sunt quibus geometre utuntur, sicut sectiones piramidum que sunt alternate et que sunt addite et que sunt diminute. . . ."

[2] Ed., pp. 16–17; Mad., 15r; Vat., 147r: "Inveniuntur tamen multe alie figure que neque sunt circuli et ab una comprehenduntur linea, sicut sector (*!* sectio) piramidis qui vocatur sector (*!* sectio) diminutus et ei similes."

[3] Ed., p. 17; Mad., 15r; Vat., 148r: "Cum residuo quoque (*MSS,* om. *Ed.*) diffinitionis (*Ed., Mad.,* difinitionis Vat.) separavit ipsum a sectore (*!* sectione) piramidis qui vocatur diminutus et ab aliis figuris ei similibus quas una linea sed composita comprehendit, scilicet quod non invenitur in sectore (*!,* sectione; *corr. Vat. ex* sectione) diminuto punctum unum a quo omnes linee recte ad circumferentiam protrahuntur (*Ed.,* protracte sint *MSS*) equales. Invenitur tamen in eo punctum a quo omnes linee recte ad (*Vat.,* ab *Mad.*) circumferentiam protracte sunt equales lineis que ab eodem protracte eis directe coniunguntur (Invenitur . . . coniunguntur *MSS,* om. *Ed.*).

[4] Ed. p. 73; Mad., 20v; Vat., 159v: "Sed quia locutio hec, scilicet (*Ed.*, id est *MSS*), 'cum due linee non fuerint equidistantes, concurrent,' indiguit explicatione (*Ed.*, explanatione *MSS*) et etiam quia sectiones (*Ed.*, sectores *MSS*) piramidum non sunt equidistantes neque concurrunt, ideo (*MSS* linee *Ed.*) Aganis. . . ."

In Passage [1] we obviously have a brief mention of the three conic sections: parabola, hyperbola, and ellipse. The only point worth noticing here is that although Gerard uses the same terms to translate the Arabic terms for the hyperbola and ellipse that he used in the fragment attached to his translation of the *De speculis comburentibus* of Alhazen (see above, Volume 4, p. 8, n. 21), namely *sectio addita* and *sectio diminuta,* he here translates the Arabic term for parabolas by [*sectiones*] *alternate,* surely an erroneous translation, while in the fragment of Apollonius and indeed in the Alhazen tract itself he fails to translate the Arabic but merely ends up with a transliteration, namely *sectio mukefi* (*ibid.,* p. 8, n. 21 and p. 13, n. 33), perhaps an indication that Gerard's translation of the Apollonius and Alhazen pieces was later and that he had seen the error of the earlier translation.

Passage [2] merely notes that the ellipse is an example of a figure contained by a single line that is not a circle and Passage [3] also gives the ellipse as an example of a figure contained by a single line that does not have a center, that is a point from which equal lines may be drawn to the circumference. The additional comment is not clear, but may refer in some way obscured by the translator to the fact that there are two points in the ellipse, namely the foci, the sum of whose distances from any point on the ellipse is a constant. Unfortunately, I am unable to check the reading of the Arabic original, since the published Arabic text of Anaritius's commentary is missing the section that includes Passages [1]–[3] (see R. O. Besthorn and J. L. Heiberg, eds., *Codex Leidensis 399.1 Euclidis Elementa ex interpretatione al-Hadschdschadschii cum commentariis al-Narizii,* Part I, Fasc. 1 [Hauniae, 1893], p. 9, n. 3), and I have seen no Arabic manuscript of this text. Finally Passage [4] is a brief reference to the fact that in the case of a hyperbola [and its asymptote] we have an example of two lines that are not parallel and do not meet. We are told that it is for this reason in part that Aganis (i.e. Geminus) wished to abandon the reading of Euclid's postulate.

I must also thank Dr. Tummers for pointing out two passages in the *Commentary on the Elements* believed to be by Albertus Magnus that refer to conic sections and he generously cited these passages in the reading of MS Vienna, Dominikanerkloster Bibliothek 80/45, which I have checked in the manuscript and altered slightly.

[1] MS, 106v: "Quod autem dicit 'in cuius medio' etc., excludit figuram que vocatur sector (! sectio) pyramidis que quidem est una linea contenta sed in eius medio non est tale punctum [i.e. centrum]. Est tamen punctum in ea a quo omnes linee ad circumferenciam sunt equales 〈eis〉 que sibi

directe coniunguntur, eo quod sector (! sectio) pyramidis est figura ex
transverso secans piramidem et vocatur sector (! sectio) diminutus." This
comment concerns Euclid's definition of a circle and the fact that all the
radii there are equal, though not in the ellipse. As Tummers suggests, the
general source of this is no doubt Anaritius' Passage [3].

[2] MS, 116r: "Hanc vero Euclidis probationem [i.e. Propositionis I.29]
plurimi sapientum calumniati sunt, eo quod innititur petitioni quarte, que
non satis nota est. . . . Videtur enim apparentem habere instantiam quia
si pyramidis basis in infinitum dilatetur et amplietur, et superficies piramidem non recte sed ex transverso secans—que superficies ab Appollonio
(!) vocatur sector (! sectio) muchephy—semper sector (! sectio) basi erit
propinquior et tamen numquam cum basi concurret. Quod ergo accidit
in superficie et corpore, potest aliquis putare eciam in lineis accidere; ergo
petitio non est satis manifesta." As I indicated to Dr. Tummers I cannot
satisfactorily explain either the source or the exact meaning of this passage.
One might think that its principal source was Anaritius' Passage [4] and
that the author meant to adduce the example of the hyperbola and its
asymptote. But it is reasonably clear that he does not say this, for his
example uses the term for a parabola given in Gerard's translations and
not Gerard's term for a hyperbola, and further the argument is couched
in terms of surfaces approaching each other and not lines. One possible
(although very crude) explanation of the passage, which at least has the
virtue of staying close to the text, is the following. If we imagine the size
of the base of a cone constantly increasing as the vertical angle of the cone
is constantly increased, then as this increase is going on the angle which
the plane of the parabola makes with the base of the cone is constantly
diminishing, though it never becomes zero so long as the cone still exists.
Then if the author considered the term *concurret* in its literal meaning of
"will run along with," he might then mean that the plane of the parabola
gets closer and closer "to running along with" the plane of the base without
ever doing so. The last sentence of the passage might well be thought of
as support of my interpretation, for the effect of that sentence is that what
happens in the case of surfaces (that is, the surface of parabola getting
closer to coincidence with the plane of the base) and in the case of bodies,
can also be conceived of as happening to lines, and so the parallel postulate
is not well established. This is of course a preposterous argument but it
may very well be the argument that our commentator intended.

PP. 19–20, n. 41, 30–31, n. 55: Again I remind the reader that I have shown
here in Volume Five that the author of the longer version of the *De
triangulis* was not Jordanus.

P. 101: The *Speculi almukefi compositio* seems to have been known to Nicole
Oresme in the middle of the fourteenth century, or at least its Proposition
11, for he devotes a question to the problem of lines that, extended infinitely,
always come closer to each other but never meet (Nicole Oresme, *Quaestiones super Geometriam Euclidis,* ed. of H. L. L. Busard [Leiden, 1961],

Quest. 4, pp. 9–10): "*Utrum due linee recte possint [semper] protendi in infinitum et semper approximari et nunquam concurrere. Et arguitur quod sic ⟨ex⟩ auctoritate cuiusdam auctoris geometrie, qui demonstrat illam conclusionem esse possibilem in corporibus piramidalibus. . . . Ad conclusionem dico primo quod, si linee sint recte, impossibile est illas [sic] approximari quin concurrant. . . . Secunda conclusio est quod, si iste due linee essent ambe curve vel una recta et alia curva, tunc possibile esset quod protrahentur in infinitum et semper approximarentur et nunquam concurrerent.*" (I have altered the punctuation slightly). It is the wording of the second conclusion that convinces us that Oresme is referring to the *Speculi almukefi compositio* and not to the original *De duabus lineis* (edited in Chapter Two of my Volume Four), for like the author of the former work Oresme adds the example of two curved lines (i.e. two hyperbolas) to the example of one curved line and one straight line (i.e. a hyperbola and its asymptote) which is found by itself in the *De duabus lineis*. Oresme's further discussion has no references to the hyperbola or to conic sections in any form.

P. 248: Though I did not speculate in Volume Four on where Werner might have found a copy of the *De duabus lineis* (which he quite clearly had read), I can note here that there was a copy of a work that appears to have been the *De duabus lineis* in the library of Andreas Stiborius in Vienna about 1500 under the title of *Demonstratio linearum semper approximantium et nunquam concurrentium* (see Clagett, *Archimedes in the Middle Ages*, Vol. 3, p. 347n.).

P. 469, under Unguru: For Ibn al-Haytham *read* Witelo.

P. 565, under Jordanus: For 42 *read* 55.

The *Inventa* of John Dee Concerning the Parabola

When studying the continuing influence of the medieval traditions of conic sections in Volume Four of my work, I was unaware of the content of John Dee's treatment of the parabola that exists only in autograph in British Library MS Cotton Vitellius C. VIII, 280r–306r (old pagination 279r–305r). But subsequent investigation of this work showed me that it belonged among those Renaissance works that made use of the medieval traditions of conic sections. Hence I resolved to edit this text and append it to this volume so that it might be available to readers of my work.

Our initial examination of the manuscript (designated in the variant readings below by the siglum *C*) reveals that folio 280r contains two forms of the title, which I may summarize under three rubrics as follows: "[1] Inventa Joannis Dee Londinensis circa sectionem illam coni recti atque rectanguli quae Parabola veteribus mathematicis appe[11a]batur. 1558. Martii 8. [2] De speculis comburentibus libri 5. [3] In primis duobus: inventa Joannis Dee Londinensis quae (*del.*) circa illam coni recti atque rectanguli sectionem quae ab antiquis Mathematicis Parabola appellabatur." All of the title in [1] is crossed out, but the date is left. And thus the date remains with [2] and [3] as part of the title. Some other nonpertinent material on folio 280r is also crossed out, presumably by Dee. As I reconstruct the circumstances, Dee commenced his work with the title and date given in [1]. He then composed 49 definitions and 48 propositions, and at the end of Proposition 48 he added phrases typical of colophons that praise the Lord and his Son (see text below, mg. folio page 297r, lines 1–4). I believe that Dee later (but still in 1558, since that date was not deleted) decided to compose a complete work *On Burning Mirrors,* extending the medieval treatment of this subject to five books. At this point he must have crossed out the title in [1] and added the titles present in [2] and [3], signaling his intention to compose the larger work on burning mirrors, of which the part he had already composed on the parabola would (with some expansion) constitute the first two books. But apparently his determination flagged and he was able to complete the work only through Proposition 69. At the end of that proposition he wrote the proposition number 70, and then he abruptly terminated the text without adding either the enunciation or proof of the contemplated Proposition 70. In view of his failure to implement his larger intention, I have decided to adopt the subtitle of [3] as the convenient title of reference for the work that is given in the title page of my volume.

It will be noticed by the reader after examining the marginal folio numbers I have included in the text below that the leaves are in some disarray, at least in part as the result of the fire of 1731 that destroyed or damaged this and other Cotton manuscripts.[1] After the title and introductory paragraph on folio 280r, we must advert to 284r for the beginning of the text, which runs to Proposition 67 on 306r (with a table and Propositions 53 and 54 out of place on folios 288r-v). Propositions 68-69 are also out of order, occupying folios 281v-83r. Folios 280v-281r and 306v contain miscellaneous mathematical material not pertinent to Dee's *Inventa,* and 283v is blank.

Not only has this treatise of Dee's on the parabola never been edited, it has seldom been discussed. Exceptions are an article by N. H. Clulee and the thesis of I. R. F. Calder, in which brief references to the treatise are made, Clulee at least putting the tract into the proper tradition of Alhazen and Witelo while Calder's views are less satisfactory.[2] Calder sees the treatise as dependent on Apollonius' *Conics* for its definitions. This is true only for

---

[1] K. Sharpe, *Sir Robert Cotton 1586-1631. History and Politics in Early Modern England* (Oxford, 1979), p. 83. Cf. the description of Cotton MS Tiberius B.IX for another example of a manuscript that was badly burned in this fire in Clagett, *Archimedes in the Middle Ages,* Vol. 4 (Philadelphia, 1980), p. 113.

[2] N. H. Clulee, "Astrology, Magic, and Optics: Facets of John Dee's Early Natural philosophy," *Renaissance Quarterly,* Vol. 30 (1977), pp. 675-76 (whole article, pp. 632-80). Clulee's remarks regarding the medieval treatment of the parabola and burning mirrors are exceedingly sketchy, but in 1977 my long account of this treatment in Volume 4 of my *Archimedes in the Middle Ages* had not yet appeared. To give some idea of the unsatisfactory remarks of Calder, I quote his "John Dee: Studied as an English Neoplatonist," thesis, London University, Dec., 1952. Vol. 1, pp. 461-62: "The surviving fragment [i.e., of Dee's work] consists only of a long series of 'definitions,' drawn from Apollonius, describing the nature and properties of conic sections, particularly the parabola, and of a reflecting surface modelled on this curve (for which only, he stresses, all rays normal to the axis will come to a common focus) followed by a series of some sixty-seven problems arising out of these, as for example [Prop. 2] 'Data combustionis distantia, latus.e. rectonii (!) elicere, quod eidem parabolae quadrat,' some of which give evidence of his considerable geometrical skill and ingenuity." This one passage teems with imprecise and erroneous statements. In the first place, as I say above this note, only the first six definitions are at all closely related to Apollonian definitions. Second, Calder leaves the impression that though the parabola is the chief subject of the tract, other conic sections are mentioned. This is false, for only the parabola is treated. In the third place, Dee does *not* assert that in the parabolic reflecting surface "all rays normal to the axis will come to a common focus," which is a mathematical absurdity. Rather, like his medieval predecessors, he understood that all incident rays parallel (not normal) to the axis reflect to a common focus. Fourth, there are sixty-nine propositions and not sixty-seven. Finally, the transcription that Calder gives of Proposition 2 (the only transcription he gives of any proposition) is wrong, for instead of *latus.e. rectonii* the text in fact correctly has *latus erectum.*

the first six definitions (and even there only indirectly, since there is evidence of some influence on Dee of the various medieval definitions related to the cone, as I shall observe below). Calder further remarks that the work seems to indicate Dee's acquaintance with the lost fifth book of Apollonius' *Conics* (known in Arabic only, but not in the West before the seventeenth century), which remark is certainly not true and has no support from Dee's treatise.[3] My impression from Calder's remarks, then, is that he has not closely studied the text, and it is quite clear that despite Dee's ownership of Memmo's translation of the *Conics,* Dee made little or no use of the translation of Apollonius' work. Since, then, it does not appear to have been Apollonius' work that inspired the tract, it seems quite likely that it was Dee's acquisition of manuscripts in 1550 and 1555 that included Alhazen's *De speculis comburentibus* which caused his interest in the subject and so led him to compose the *Inventa* in 1558.[4] It could be that it was not merely Alhazen's *De speculis comburentibus* which stimulated his interest in the parabola, for it is probable that Dee had access to most of the principal medieval treatments of the parabola. Thus he owned the earliest extant manuscript of the medieval *Speculi almukefi compositio,* the most original treatment of the parabola found in the Middle Ages.[5] Furthermore Dee was well acquainted with Al-

---

[3] *Ibid.,* Vol. 2, p. 216. In the Catalogue of Dee's works, we find listed Apollonius' *Conics* in the Memmo translation of 1537 (see British Library, MS Harley 1879, 21v). This of course had only Books I–IV, all that were extant in Greek (see my *Archimedes in the Middle Ages,* Vol. 4, pp. 311–13). Book V of the *Conics* was not available in Latin translation from the Arabic until the appearance of C. Ravius' *Apollonii Pergaei Conicarum sectionum libri V, VI, et VII* (Kilonii, 1669) and Edmond Halley's edition of the *Conics: Apollonii Pergaei Conicorum libri octo et Sereni Antissensis De sectione cylindri et coni libri duo* (Oxford, 1710), see Clagett *ibid.,* pp. 6 and 319. In fact Dee's text has nothing to do with normals as maxima and minima (the chief subject of Book V of the *Conics*), though in one diagram (Fig. Ap.II.29), there is an incidental designation of the *perpendicularis contingentis* (evidently a normal) that has no pertinence to Proposition 68. (I should note at this point that all of my references to John Dee's Catalogue are to his copy preserved in British Library, MS Harley 1879. But I have also located the various works in the other of his copies, Trinity College MS 0.4.20. Soon we shall have an edition of the Catalogue published by A. G. Watson and R. J. Roberts under the title *John Dee's Library Catalogue* [London, The Bibliographical Society, forthcoming].)

[4] For these two manuscripts, see M. R. James, *Lists of Manuscripts Formerly Owned by Dr. John Dee* (Oxford, 1921), pp. 15 (MS T.2), 21 (MS T.44). The first manuscript I have identified as the Gunton MS kept at the Norfolk Record Office in Norwich (see my description of the manuscript above under *siglum G* in the manuscripts used for the longer version of the *Liber de triangulis Iordani,* where I note Dee's inscription: "Joannes Deeus 4 Aprilis 1550"). Alhazen's *De speculis comburentibus* is on folios 55v–57v (the text is not complete, for an additional quire seems to have become separated from the unbound codex). The second manuscript is, as James notes, Brit. Library Cotton Vesp. A.II. Alhazen's *De speculis comburentibus* is on folios 140r–44r, while Gerard of Cremona's fragmentary translation from Apollonius' *Conics* follows on folios 144v–45v. The manuscript has the following inscription by Dee: "Ioannes Dee 1555." Note that this manuscript was misdesignated by Calder as A.xi (*op. cit.,* Vol. 2, p. 214).

[5] See footnote 1 above for a reference to my description of this manuscript (MS Brit. Library Cotton Tiberius B.IX, 231r–35r), which A. G. Watson showed to be part of a longer manuscript owned by Dee ("A Merton College Manuscript Reconstructed: Harley 625; Digby 178, fols. 1–

hazen's *Perspectiva,* there being three manuscripts of it in his possession in 1556.[6] He also borrowed a copy of Witelo's *Perspectiva* in 1556.[7] These last three works together with Alhazen's *De speculis comburentibus* represented the chief elements in the medieval comprehension of conic sections, as I have shown in Volume Four of this work. It is also probable that Dee was influenced by Johann Werner's *Super vigentiduobus elementis conicis* and Oronce Fine's *De speculo ustorio* which were markedly dependent on medieval sources, and of which he owned copies.[8] To all of these sources available to Dee we must also add Archimedes' *On the Quadrature of the Parabola,* which Dee knew and quoted in his treatise, in the translation of Jacobus Cremonensis as emended by Regiomontanus and published in 1544 (see the discussion of Proposition 43 below and the reference to his copy of the Archimedes in note 17). Hence, as we shall shortly see, Dee's tract is based on a mélange of medieval material and the Archimedean approach of *On the Quadrature of the Parabola,* though it is cast in Dee's original form and contains some original (but not highly significant) discoveries of his own.

The dual source of Dee's treatise is perhaps reflected in the title itself since in it we find specified the parabola as a section of a right-angled right cone. It was just such a generation of the parabola that was followed by most of the medieval authors and also by Archimedes.[9] Indeed there is no whisper in Dee's tract of the more general Apollonian generation of the parabola from any cone. Following the rewritten title (which I have discussed above), Dee added short introductory remarks, stressing that the reader will find that the text is expounded by numbers and elucidated by mathematical demonstration. It is of course not surprising that he should also have asserted the utility of his work, a common enough convention.

Advancing to the tract itself, I remind the reader that it contains forty-nine definitions and sixty-nine propositions, and that Dee seems to imply

14, 88–115; Cotton Tiberius B.IX, fols. 1–4, 225–35," *Bodleian Library Record,* Vol. 9, 1976, pp. 207–16). The first part of the manuscript, i.e. Harley 625, has Dee's inscription: "Joannes Dee 1569 . . . ." If this is the date when Dee acquired the manuscript, it could not have influenced him in his composition of the *Inventa* of 1558. But it seems probable that Dee was already acquainted with Regiomontanus' revision of the text that was published under the title *De sectione conica orthogona, quae parabola dicitur* by A. H. Gogava in 1548 in his edition of Ptolemy's *Quadripartitum* (for full bibliographical entry see the bibliography attached to Volume 4 [p. 468] of my *Archimedes in the Middle Ages*), since he knew Gogava and in fact had visited Louvain the very year in which Gogava's version of the *Quadripartitum* appeared. For Dee's copy of this volume, see MS Harley 1879, 31v. Note that the volume also contained a truncated version of Alhazen's *De speculis comburentibus.* Concerning Dee's acquaintance with Gogava and his stay in Louvain from 1548–50, see Clulee, *op.cit.* in n. 2, pp. 638–39.

[6] See James, *Lists of Manuscripts,* p. 12, items 20–22.

[7] *Ibid.,* p. 12, item 33. Note that Dee's Catalogue indicates that he also owned Witelo's *Perspectiva* in the 1535 edition (as well as the later edition of 1572 which contained both Alhazen and Witelo but was of course printed long after Dee had completed his *Inventa*). For these copies see British Library, MS Harley 1879, 21r, 23v.

[8] See Dee's Catalogue (MS Harley 1879, 29v [Werner], 34v and 77v [two copies of Orontius Fine] for his copies of these works.

[9] Clagett, *Archimedes in the Middle Ages,* Vol. 4, p. 358.

in the titular phrase "In primis duobus" that the definitions and propositions extant in the tract are to be grouped in two books. I cannot be sure precisely where the division of books was to take place, but I have suggested in my text below that the definitions were to be included in Book I and the propositions in Book II. And so I have added such rubrics in brackets at the appropriate places.

Viewing the treatise as a whole and comparing it with the medieval tracts of Volume Four, the reader will realize that however dependent Dee's work is on the works of his medieval predecessors, its overall format is quite distinct from theirs. Not only does Dee have far more definitions than do the medieval works, many of them (e.g. Definitions 24–49) are original with him. Furthermore a very large number of the propositions that follow are *problems* of what we may call the "data-type", where one or more magnitudes related to the variables of the parabola are given and a further magnitude is sought (e.g., Props. 1–34, 39–41, 43, 53–57, 61–69). In addition, a significant number of them call for the mechanical construction of a parabola or of the straight lines upon which a mechanical construction may be effected (e.g. Props. 35–38, 42, 44–45, 59–60), with a sub-class concerning tables of computed lines used in the construction of parabolas (cf. Props. 46–47, the porisms and an attachment or admonition to Props. 45, 51, and 52). However, a few of Dee's propositions (like most of those in the medieval treatises) assert geometrical properties of the parabola and require formal proof (e.g. Props. 48–52, the deleted 58, and 58*bis*). Finally I should note that on a number of occasions Dee has given geometrical constructions to illustrate his rules for finding magnitudes. Though all of this change in form with respect to the earlier works indicates originality on Dee's part, we cannot, I believe, conclude that Dee was as original a mathematician as either Regiomontanus or Werner, though surely more so than Oronce Fine, to compare him only with other mathematicians of the Renaissance who used the medieval treatments of conic sections.

Turning now to the definitions for a somewhat more extended treatment, I note initially that the first six definitions concerning the cone originate ultimately in Apollonius' *Conics* but in a form that derives from a fragment of these definitions translated by Gerard of Cremona.[10] Still not even that derivation seems to be an exclusive one. For it is almost certain, in view of the books he owned, that Dee was familiar with the similar definitions that appear in the medieval and earlier Renaissance texts, and particularly in the treatise of Johann Werner.[11] For example, in the first definition, Dee like Werner and Fine uses the term *conus* instead of the medieval *pyramis rotunda,* though the medieval *curva superficies* is one of the expressions retained by Dee. Furthermore, note that while Dee generally follows the Apollonian definition of the cone in terms of a line drawn from a fixed point outside the plane of a circle and revolved through the circumference of the circle,

[10] *Ibid.,* pp. 4–5.
[11] *Ibid.,* pp. 269–71 (cf. pp. 362–64).

unlike Apollonius he does not draw a double cone, and indeed he defines the cone before defining its conic surface, which latter Apollonius had presented first. The fact that Dee does not give the double cone may merely reflect the Euclidian definition of the cone adopted in the medieval treatises that described only a single cone, a cone produced by the rotation of a right triangle about one of the sides including the right angle. So presumably Dee modified his definition from Gerard's fragment that was included in both of his copies of Alhazen's *De speculis comburentibus* or from the alternate definition found in Werner's work. Definitions 7–13, although written down in Dee's words, all describe terms or concepts that are prevalent in the above-noted medieval works and their Renaissance derivatives. Perhaps the most important of these definitions is his definition of the right-angled right cone, which will, as I have said, serve Dee for the generation of the parabola. That generation is described in Definitions 14 and 15, the first concerned with a parabolic linear section and the second with a parabolic area. Note that here and throughout the tract Dee, like Werner and Fine, abandons the more popular medieval expression *sectio mukefi* for the less popular *parabola*. In connection with both the linear section and the area he uses the adjective *ustorius* to describe the figure's capacity for burning. This word was taken over and used in English in the Renaissance and I have decided to adopt it in my English translation below, even though the Oxford English Dictionary indicates that it is now obsolete. I do so because it is frequently used and the practice saves a circumlocution like "capable for burning". The basic content of Definition 14 goes back to one of the definitions found in Gerard of Cremona's fragment (but translated from the introduction by the Arabic editor rather than from Apollonius' text) or back to one of the other medieval descriptions of that generation known to Dee.[12] Definitions 15–22 comprise various lines of a parabola generated from a right-angled right cone that are all found in the medieval accounts of the parabola: the base of the parabola (which Dee defines as the diameter of the base of the cone from which the parabola is generated that is perpendicular to the base of the conic triangle), the total sagitta of the parabola (the common section of the conic triangle and the cutting plane in which the parabola lies), a line of order (a line parallel to the base of the parabola), the point of combustion (the midpoint of the whole sagitta, in modern terms the "focal point"), the distance of combustion (the segment of the sagitta extending from the vertex of the parabola to the point of combustion,[13] in modern terms "the focal distance from the vertex"), the latus rectum (the line of order through the point of combustion; as in Fine's account always designated by Dee as *latus erectum* and never *latus rectum*, though both terms were used in medieval works like

---

[12] *Ibid.*, pp. 8, 71–72, 116–17, 204–05, 270, 363.

[13] Regiomontanus, unlike Dee later or his medieval predecessors, used the expression *distantia combustionis* as the heading for a column of numbers pertaining to the length of lines of reflection (see Clagett, *Archimedes in the Middle Ages,* Vol. 4, p. 222, last column).

the *Speculi almukefi compositio*).[14] In Definitions 23–24 Dee introduces the concept of "vertical," which evidently has a literal meaning of "toward the vertex," for a vertical line of order (Def. 23) is one that crosses the sagitta between the point of combustion and the vertex, and a vertical part of the sagitta (Def. 24) is a segment of the sagitta one of whose termini is at the vertex and the other between the vertex and the point of combustion. These vertical lines (and the vertical diametral line which we shall mention later) were located within a vertical parabolic segment, that is the parabolic segment whose base is the latus rectum through the point of combustion (see Def. 41). Definitions 25–26 then introduce the concept of "corresponding" that is repeated often in later definitions and propositions. In Definition 25 the vertical line of order "corresponding" to a given vertical part of the sagitta is that line of order drawn through the lower terminus of the vertical part of the sagitta. Contrariwise in Definition 26 the vertical part of the sagitta corresponding to a given vertical line of order is the vertical part of the sagitta cut off by the given line of order. See the graphic representation of these corresponding lines in Fig. Ap. II.5. It is evident that these mutually corresponding lines are the variables in the equation of the parabola; and, with the latus rectum known, if you fix one of these lines you also fix its corresponding line. It is perhaps useful to note that one of the early modern definitions of the word sagitta in English (a defintion now obsolete) is as the abscissa of a curve (see the Oxford English Dictionary). And of course half of the line of order is clearly the ordinate. Thus the corresponding lines here described represent simultaneous abscissas and ordinates of the parabola. Definition 27 characterizes a tangent to a parabola. Definition 28 describes a line of solar incidence while Definition 30 describes a line of solar reflection. Coupled with these are Definitions 29 and 31 that define angles of solar incidence and solar reflection that are formed by the tangent and the lines of incidence and reflection (cf. Fig. Ap. II.6). They are essentially the concepts found in the medieval treatises, though Dee has added to each of the four definitions the adjective *solaris,* to distinguish the incoming rays (which are parallel to the sagitta) and their consequent angles of incidence together with their lines of reflection and their consequent angles of reflection from what Dee later calls lines of *arbitrary* incidence (which are not parallel to the sagitta) and their consequent lines of reflection and angles of incidence and reflection (see below Propositions 67–69). Also a new but obvious addition of Dee's is Definition 32, which defines an angle of solar combustion (an angle formed by a line of solar incidence and its consequential line of solar reflection). Definitions 33–38 define, for each of the above-noted three angles formed at the same point, ones that correspond first to a given vertical part of the sagitta and then to a given vertical line of order (cf. again Fig. Ap. II.6). Definition 39 probably holds that each of the said angles corresponds

---

[14] *Ibid.,* p. 118, lines 49–50, for the use of both terms in the *Speculi almukefi compositio.* For the exclusive use of *latus erectum* for the parameter by Fine, see *ibid.,* pp. 325, 363 (def. 12).

to the same vertical line of order (obviously to the one at whose terminus they are formed) and Definition 40 defines that vertical part of the sagitta to which the three angles correspond as the one whose lower terminus rests on the given line of order. Then, as I remarked earlier, Definition 41 defines a vertical segment of the parabola as the one whose base is the latus rectum through the point of combustion. Finally, Definitions 42–49 all concern diametral lines (cf. Fig. Ap. II.7). Definition 42 tells us that a diametral line is a straight line drawn parallel to the sagitta from some point on the parabola to the base of the parabola or to some other line of order. Diametral lines play no part in the medieval treatment of conic sections and perhaps occurred to Dee when he undertook the study of Archimedes' *On the Quadrature of the Parabola,* as he later seems to intimate when discussing Proposition 43. It is not surprising that Dee in Definition 43 defines a vertical diametral line as a line parallel to the sagitta drawn from the parabola to the latus rectum or to some other vertical line of order. The rest of the definitions describe the mutual correspondence of diametral lines and the various lines and angles previously described and demand no further comment.

Passing now to the second book of Dee's *Inventa,* we are prepared to discuss Dee's sixty-nine propositions. Key to many of them is the equation of a parabola, which we may express as follows: (½ line of order)^2 = (latus rectum)·(part of sagitta), or in more modern form, $x^2 = L \cdot y$ where L is the latus rectum, which equation has its origin ultimately in Apollonius' *Conics* but was no doubt learned by Dee from one of his medieval books, for example from Alhazen's *De speculis comburentibus* or Witelo's *Perspectiva* or the *Speculi almukefi compositio.*[15] I say this because the knowledge of the formula in Dee's work appears in the context of treatments of the distance of combustion and the point of combustion, and so precisely in the context in which it is found in the medieval tracts. Thus Propositions 1 and 2 (to find the latus rectum when the distance of combustion is given, or to find the distance of combustion when the latus rectum is given) are both solved by the assumed relationship: distance of combustion = ¼ latus rectum. The equation of the parabola is clearly indicated in the solutions of Propositions 3 and 4 (given the latus rectum and some vertical part of the sagitta, to find the vertical line of order corresponding to the given part of the sagitta; and given the latus rectum and some vertical line of order, to find the vertical part of the sagitta corresponding to the given line of order) and indeed underlies the solutions of a large number of the remaining propositions, in particular the succeeding short propositions (Props. 5–34), as the reader will readily see without any further guidance.

In Proposition 35 Dee passes on to the first of several propositions that are concerned with the mechanical description of a parabola. In that prop-

[15] *Ibid.,* p. 14, for Alhazen's *De speculis comburentibus:* "Sed quadratum *BZ* est equale multiplicationi *AZ* in *L,* que est linea recta (! latus rectum), sicut ostendit Apollonius bonus in libro de piramidibus." [cf. Fig. I.1 on p. 472]. For the similar proposition in Witelo's *Perspectiva,* see *ibid.,* p. 93, and in the *Speculi almukefi compositio, ibid.,* pp. 120–22, 207–09.

osition a vertical part of a sagitta is given along with the latus rectum of a parabola (or one or another magnitude from which the latus rectum could be determined by means of earlier propositions: the distance of combustion, or the vertical line of order corresponding to the vertical part of the sagitta, or the whole sagitta of the parabola, or the axis of the right-angled right cone from which the parabola is generated, or the base of the parabola). Hence with the vertical part of the sagitta given and with the latus rectum known (or determinable from what is given), the vertical part of the sagitta is divided into any number of parts. Consequently by the basic equation of the parabola we can determine the lengths of all the lines of order that pass through the points of division of the sagitta. Then one may draw through the termini of the determined lines of order a single curved line and the result is the parabola which is sought. Proposition 36 has the same objective but starts with a given line of order and with the latus rectum known (or with one of the magnitudes from which the latus rectum may be determined known). Then using the given line of order and the latus rectum which has been given or determined one can find the vertical part of the sagitta corresponding to the given line of order. After this he may proceed exactly as in Proposition 35 to divide the vertical part of the sagitta into equal parts, to determine the length of the lines of order passing through the points of division, and to draw a single curve through the ends of the determined lines of order. Proposition 37 is merely a special case of Proposition 36, the given line of order being the latus rectum, with the corresponding part of the sagitta obviously being the distance of combustion and hence one-fourth of the latus rectum. With the sagitta thus determined, the procedure of Proposition 35 is followed, and the parabola so constructed.

In Proposition 38 we are instructed how to draw a tangent to a parabola at the end of a given line of order, regardless of which of the many ways we use to determine the corresponding vertical part of the sagitta. Once the latter has been determined, it is doubled beyond the vertex and the superior terminus of the extension is joined to the end of the given line of order to produce the tangent. This depends on the converse of Apollonius' *Conics*, Proposition I.35, but was no doubt drawn from a medieval source such as Proposition 1 of Alhazen's *De speculis comburentibus* or Proposition IV.39 of Witelo's *Perspectiva* or Proposition 7 of the *Speculi almukefi compositio*.[16] Proposition 39 then shows how to calculate the magnitude of the line of tangency from the end of the extended sagitta to either end of the given line of order. This is done by means of the Pythagorean theorem as follows (consult Fig. Ap. II.9). Take half of the given line of order (i.e. the half AC). Square that half. Double the determined corresponding vertical part of the sagitta (i.e. part CD to produce the double CE). Square that double. Take the square root of the sum of these two squares and the result is the magnitude of the line sought (i.e. line AE). Proposition 40 tells us how to calculate the magnitude

---

[16] *Ibid.*, pp. 15, 91–92, 124–27.

of a vertical diametral line whose distance from the sagitta on a given line of order is given, the vertical part of the sagitta corresponding to the given line of order having also been given. The procedure is clear when we consult Fig. Ap. II.10. Since *AC* and *DC* are given, the latus rectum can be determined by the equation of the parabola. Then since the latus rectum is the same for all segments of the same parabola and since *FO* is equal to *EC*, which latter is given, then *DO* can be calculated (again by the use of the equation of the parabola). Therefore with *DC* and *DO* both known, we now know *OC* and hence its equal *FE*, the diametral line whose magnitude is desired. Proposition 41 gives us another solution for the magnitude of a diametral line when we are given a vertical line of order, its corresponding vertical part of the sagitta, and the distance of the diametral line from the sagitta (or the distance from the terminus of the given line of order which would allow us to find the distance from the sagitta). Following Fig. Ap. II.11, we see that lines *AC*, *DC*, and *EC* (or *AE*) are given. With line *OR* (equal to *EC*) drawn as in the preceding proposition, *DR* may be calculated. We let *FR* be double *DR*. Hence by Proposition 39 a line *FO* (continued to meet *CA* at *P*) is tangent at *O*. Now we have two equiangular triangles *FRO* and *PCF*. Thus *FR* / *RO* = *FC* / *CP*. But *FR*, *RO*, and *FC* are known. Hence *CP* is also known. If from *CP* we subtract the given distance *EC*, the remainder *EP* becomes known. Hence in the proportion *PC* / *CF* = *PE* / *EO* the first three terms are known, and hence so will be the fourth, the diametral line that is sought. It is evident that here and everywhere Dee's principal algebraic calculating procedure is the so-called "Rule of Three," which casts the problem in the form a simple proportion in which the first three terms are known and the fourth is sought. The fourth term is then found by the cross-multiplication of the second and third terms and the division of that product by the first term.

In Proposition 42 we are told another way to protract as many vertical lines of order as we wish upon a given vertical part of the sagitta, when the vertical line of order corresponding to the given vertical part of the sagitta is given. Note that in this way we do not have to divide the given vertical part of the sagitta into equal parts. Rather it allows to take any point on a given vertical line of order (e.g. point *E* in Fig. Ap. II.12). Then half of a new line of order *KO* is constructed equal to *EC*. Then any number of such lines may be constructed after taking any number of given points on the given line of order. Then *DO* (or its equivalent for any other points on the given line of order) can be calculated by the equation of the parabola. Or one may wish simply to draw an arbitrary number of such lines of order (or their halves) and then draw the parabola through the end of those lines of order.

Proposition 43 gives us still another way of expressing the magnitude of a vertical diametral line with the ultimate objective of drawing a parabola through the ends of a forest of such diametral lines. This depends on the use of Proposition 5 of Archimedes' *On the Quadrature of the Parabola*, which

Dee quotes almost verbatim from Jacobus Cremonensis' translation as corrected by Regiomontanus and published in 1544.[17] Dee tells us that he discovered this method (and he believes he is the first to have done so) while he was working on the methods discussed in the earlier propositions (i.e. Props. 40 and 41). Consulting Fig. Ap. II.13, drawn from the Archimedean proposition with little change, we note that Dee first quotes as proved by Archimedes: $AK / KC = KH / HL$. In Dee's porism he assumes that this proportion is inverted (he does not specifically tell us this) and then he concludes conjunctively that $AC / AK = KL / KH$. Now line of order AC is given, as is DK (for the distance of the diametral line from the sagitta is given). Hence AK is also known. But KL is also known as is clear by considering equiangular triangles LKC and EDC. From those similar triangles we know that $CD / DE = CK / KL$. Line CD is half the given line of order, DE is double the given vertical part of the sagitta by Proposition 39 since CE is tangent at C, and CK is known from the fact that CD and KD are given. Hence the fourth term KL is now known. Then returning to the original proportion given in the porism, we now know the first three terms and hence the fourth term KH, which is the line sought. Hence since we may conceive of what he calls the Archimedean right triangle CFA drawn about any parabolic segment, then the argument outlined will be satisfactory to determine any diametral line HK. Dee also outlines another procedure based on the following proportion deduced permutatively from the Archimedean conclusion: $AC / KL = AK / KH$. The two ways of using this proportion are rather obvious and need no repetition here.

Proposition 44 gives us still another way of determining a vertical diametral line by using an Archimedean right triangle (see Fig. Ap. II.14). Suppose that we do not yet have the parabola drawn (and all of these propositions are ones to allow us to find a forest of vertical diametral lines through whose termini we may draw a parabola), but the line of order AB is given along with the corresponding vertical part DC of the sagitta, which we double. Then if we draw a line from B through the summit of the double of DC, it will be tangent to the parabola at B (when that parabola is completed). If we erect a perpendicular on point A so that it meets the tangent at F, we have the so-called Archimedean right triangle. Now if we want to find the diametral line at given point H, first we draw line GH parallel to line AF. Then from point H we draw HR parallel to line FB. From point R on line AF we draw line RB. It will cut GH at O, and line OH will be the vertical diametral line sought, for by reference to Proposition 43 Dee demonstrates that O is on the parabola determined by the given lines AB and DC. As Dee notes "this is a beautiful and easy mechanical way, for we need here no

---

[17] Archimedes, *Opera quae quidem extant omnia* (Basel, 1544), Lat. pag., pp. 144–45. For Dee's copy of this work, see his Catalogue (MS Harley 1879, 21v) where Dee has misdated the work as 1554 instead of the correct 1544. In the copy of the Catalogue in MS Trinity College O.4.20, p. 4, Dee first wrote 1554, and then corrected it to 1544.

operation with numbers." Now that we have several ways to find the magnitudes of vertical diametral lines, Dee puts forth the new way to draw a parabola when a vertical line of order and its corresponding vertical part of the sagitta are given. Recall that earlier he divided the vertical part of the sagitta into as many parts as he wished and then computed the lengths of lines of order through the points of division or alternatively he drew mechanically as many lines of order as he wished. Then the parabola was produced by a drawing a single curved line through the ends of the manifold lines of order. Now in Proposition 45 the parabola is to be produced by drawing a curved line through the ends of a forest of diametral lines. He does this by dividing the line of order into as many parts as he wishes and then he calculates the lengths of the vertical diametral lines to erect on those points. In the course of describing this procedure he notes that tables of numbers (including the lengths of diametral lines) may be developed by using Propositions 40, 41, and 43, the tables calculated for a parabola one of whose lines of order is given as is its corresponding vertical part of the sagitta (so long as the latter does not exceed one-fourth of the line of order). I remind the reader that no such tables are given here or later, though later in an admonition following Proposition 52 Dee leaves space for such a table to be produced by Proposition 40. Presumably the table would have been like that prepared by Regiomontanus in his notes to his version of the medieval *Speculi almukefi compositio.*[18] The example of the parabola which is constructed in Proposition 45 has a given line of order of 1½ feet and the corresponding vertical part of the sagitta is ⅓ of one foot. To have more points on the given line of order in order to erect a denser forest of vertical diametral lines you may wish to convert the units of measure to smaller units. Conversion to new units would mean the conversion of the numbers in your tables. But when you convert the numbers you first need to convert your units of the line of order, then the corresponding units of the vertical part of the sagitta, and finally those of the latus rectum. Dee supposes that the foot is converted first to inches and the inches are divided into eight parts. Then the parabola he has suggested would have a line of order of 144 parts and a corresponding vertical part of the sagitta of 32 parts. But one need compute diametral lines for only 72 of the 144 parts of the line of order, since each diametral line erected on each division of the 72 parts on one half of the line of order would be matched by an equal diametral line in the other half of the line of order, located an equal distance from the sagitta. He finally notes that the distance of burning of this parabola is 5½₁₆″. Now at this point Dee presents a table that would help in his unit conversions for this parabola. At first glance this table seems puzzling, but on closer examination its purpose becomes clear. Four columns are given, though six ought to have been prepared to complete the table. The first, third, and fourth columns indicate the numbers of parts into which half the line of order is to be divided, from 1 to 72. The

[18] See Clagett, *Archimedes in the Middle Ages,* Vol. 4, pp. 222–23.

second column gives us a number that allows us to compute first the number of such units in the corresponding part of the sagitta and then the number of those units in the latus rectum, the units of measure adopted for the line of order being indicated in the first column. But unfortunately the entries concerning the numbers of units for the corresponding vertical parts of the sagitta stop at the end of the second column (that is with "53" instead of proceeding further in an additional column opposite the third and still another column opposite the fourth). But now let us see in detail how the table works. If half of the given line of order is divided into nine parts (i.e. into parts 1″ long), we look at the first column under 9 and we read in the second column 60 0. This we subtract from 64 0, and the result, 4 0, i.e. exactly four, is the number of 1″ long parts that are in the sagitta when the line of order has nine parts. Further it is evident that in terms of such 1″ parts the latus rectum is 81/4, using the equation of the parabola. But if half the line of order is divided into eighteen parts (i.e. eighteen ½″ parts), the corresponding part of the sagitta will be exactly eight such parts (i.e. 64 − 56) and the latus rectum will be 81/2 such parts. Further, if Dee had composed a matching column for the entries in the third column, he would have had opposite 27 (i.e. 27 one-third inch units) the number 52 0, and so the number of one-third inch units in the corresponding vertical part of the sagitta would be twelve (i.e. 64 − 52). Hence the latus rectum in terms of such units would be (81 · 3)/4. And opposite 36 would have been 48 0, and the number of units of the corresponding vertical part of the sagitta would be sixteen (i.e. 64 − 48), and the latus rectum in such units would be 81. Finally, the number opposite 72 in the last column would have been 32 0, and so the number of units in the corresponding vertical part of the sagitta would have been 32 (i.e. 64 − 32), and the latus rectum in terms of such units would have been 162. Note that opposite numbers 2–8, 10–17, and 19–24 in the first column, the numbers of the second column do not have zeros after them. The reason is that they should all have some additional fractions, which for some reason Dee did not wish to add. Thus opposite 3, we should have in the second column 63⅔, for this number would give us the proper sagitta of 1⅓ units (i.e. 64 − 62⅔).[19] Such a sagitta would then give us in terms of these units a latus rectum of 27/4. One could similarly work out all of the missing fractions to add to the numbers in the second column that do not have 0 after them.

Proposition 46 surely is a trivial one since Dee appears to be saying there that the numbers in our tables are the same, regardless of whether they count greater or lesser units of measure. Proposition 47 is also clear. It simply means that if you have a table that allows you to determine a large parabolic segment (i.e. that will give you a forest of diametral lines for such a segment), it will also allow you to display smaller frusta, that is small segments, of the

---

[19] No doubt, if Dee had put the values of the fractions in their proper places, he would have used sexagesimal fractions, as did Regiomontanus in his table (see table mentioned in note 13 above). Thus, instead of 2/3, Dee would have probably written 40 (for 40/60).

given parabolic segment. The intent of this proposition will be evident if we turn back to Fig. Ap. II.7. Suppose that we have tables that give us the magnitudes of a series of vertical diametral lines (including BC) on a line of order EO determined from a given corresponding vertical part AD of the sagitta and from a given latus rectum and suppose further that we seek to find the magnitudes of diametral lines on BI, a smaller line of order corresponding to a given smaller vertical part AH of the sagitta of the parabola. First we subtract BH from OD (designated as the maximum number of our lines of order in the given tables). This will give us point C and so our tables will give us the magnitude of BC. Then obviously, if we subtract BC from all the diametral lines between C and D, we would have the magnitudes of a series of diametral lines on BH that correspond in position to the diametral lines on CD. If we draw a single curved line through the superior ends of the computed diametral lines on BH (or rather on the whole line of order BI), we would have described the smaller parabolic segment BAI which we desired and we would have done so by means of our original tables.

Proposition 48 turns away from tables and asserts that if we have two parabolas with the same given line of order, the one which has the greater vertical part of the sagitta corresponding to the common line of order has a smaller distance of combustion and a smaller latus rectum. This would follow from computations made by using Propositions 7 and 8, as I have suggested in my reconstruction in the English translation. I note once again that, at the end of this proposition, Dee appears to have added a colophon, from which I concluded earlier that Dee at first decided to end his treatise here, only to decide later to continue the tract further. Proposition 49 expands and generalizes Proposition 48. It holds that the vertical parts of the sagittas of two parabolic segments on the same vertical line of order are inversely proportional to the distances of combustion of the two parabolas. The demonstration is obvious and needs no explanation here. Proposition 50 now takes two parabolas that have different lines of order corresponding to equal vertical parts of their sagittas and says (1) that the distance of combustion of the parabola is greater whose vertical line of order is greater, and (2) that the ratio of the distances of combustion is that of the squares of the halves of the given lines of order. Hence if we need to know the distance of combustion of a second parabola when we know the distance of combustion of the first and the two lines of order, we merely apply the rule of three. The demonstration is obvious.

Proposition 51 declares that if we have two parabolic segments on the same line of order and the ratio of the corresponding vertical parts of the sagittas of the segments is as 2 to 1, then the ratio of each of all the diametral lines of the parabola with the double sagitta to each of the corresponding diametral lines of the other parabola is also 2 to 1. Consult Fig. Ap. II.18, where we notice that Archimedean right triangles have been constructed about parabolic segments ACB and AEB. The parabolic segments have a common line of order AB and the former's vertical part of the sagitta CD

is twice the latter's vertical part of the sagitta *ED*. Dee proves that any vertical diametral line *RM* is also twice the corresponding vertical line *OM*. By Proposition 43 we know that *AM / MB = MR / RL* and that *AM / MB = MO / OS*. Therefore *MR / RL = MO / OS*. Therefore by inversion *LR / RM = SO / OM*. Conjunctively *LM / RM = SM / OM*. Hence permutatively *LM / SM = RM / OM*. But *LM = 2 SM* from the fact that *XD = 2 CD* (line *BXK* being tangent to parabola *ACB* at *B*) and from the similarity of triangles. Hence *RM = 2 OM*, which is what we wished to prove. Then follow two porisms that are obvious. The first is that on the basis of this theorem our table of diametral lines will allow us to construct parabolas on the same line of order whose sagittas are double, quadruple, octuple and so on, or are subdouble, subquadruple, suboctuple and so on, to the sagitta whose diametral lines are given in our tables by taking the aforementioned multiples or submultiples of the diametral lines given in our tables. The second porism is that from the preceding porism and Propositions 48 and 47 the reader will see how manifold are the uses of our tables, though Dee apologizes for pointing out the obvious. Then Proposition 52 further generalizes Proposition 51 by asserting that if two parabolas are constructed on the same line of order, the ratio of any pair of corresponding diametral lines of the parabolas will be that of the vertical parts of the sagittas of the two parabolas corresponding to the same line of order. The proof is framed for parabolas on the same line of order whose corresponding parts of their sagittas are related as $2\frac{1}{3}$ to 1. The reader will see that the proof is almost identical with that of Proposition 51 and hence needs no elucidation here. At the end of his proof Dee remarks that "you can demonstrate the same thing for [parabolas having] any other ratio [of corresponding vertical parts] and for all the diametral lines which are taken at equal distances from their sagittas." It is not surprising that Dee then adds a porism to the effect that by means of the rule of three our tables of diametral lines could then be used for the construction of any other parabola on the same line of order as that assumed in the tables as long as the ratio of corresponding vertical parts is known, for that ratio would indicate to us which multiple or submultiple of the magnitudes of the diametral lines given in the tables is needed to construct the new parabola. At this point Dee intended to present a detailed table of vertical diametral lines where the maximum line of order was to be 12000 parts (whose half therefore is 6000), with a second column of corresponding diametral lines for the various lines of order leading up to the one of 12000 parts. Unfortunately, Dee did not add the table but only indicated the proposed place for the table (see the text below). However he does leave us an admonition concerning the table, to the effect that the reader might not want (or indeed be able) to have a graduation of the line of order so fine as 12000 units. Hence Dee gives a table he calls a Table of Election in which the last column has entries that go from 2000 to 12000 at steps of 1000 each. The first column includes entries of one half of the entries in the last column, the second column entries that are one third, the third column entries that are one

fourth, and the fourth column entries that are one sixth of the entries of the
last column. It is obvious that he only gives entries that are aliquot parts in
units of 1000. He then concludes that you can transform the number in the
table into the graduation you have decided upon by the rule of three. But
the procedure he alludes to is by no means clear, especially his reference to
a right triangle, unless that reference is simply to his Archimedean method
of finding diametral lines.

Moving now to the finding of angles of solar incidence by means of sine
tables, Dee tells us in Proposition 53 how to find the magnitude of such an
angle when the line of order and vertical part of the sagitta corresponding
to the same angle are given. We should note that in several of the propositions
that follow Dee uses the expression *sinus totus* ("whole sine") by which
he of course means the sine of 90°, i.e. 1. In Fig. Ap. II.20 we let *AB* and
CD be the given lines corresponding to the angle of solar incidence *QAK*.
First we double *CD* to produce *DE*. Then, by Proposition 38 line *AE* will
be the tangent at *A*. The magnitude of *AE* will be given by Proposition 39.
Then angle *AED* is equal to angle *QAK*, since *AK* is parallel to *ED* and line
EAQ cuts both of them. Then the rule for finding the magnitude of angle
AED is as follows. In a proportion, that is the application of a rule of three,
the first number is the magnitude of line *EA*, the second number is the
magnitude of line *DA* (i.e. half the given line of order), the third number is
1 (i.e. the whole sine). Hence the fourth number in a rule of three may now
be found and it will be the sine of angle *DEA*, which sine we shall locate in
a table of sines and find the desired magnitude of angle *DEA*, which is, as
we have said, equal to the angle *QAK*. Proposition 54 instructs how to find
the angle made at the superior terminus of a vertical diametral line by the
line of tangence and that diametral line, the following being given: the vertical
line of order on which the diametral line is erected, the distance of the vertical
line from the sagitta, and the vertical part of the sagitta corresponding to the
given line of order. He gives the rule in general terms but has a figure (Fig.
Ap. II.21) to which we may relate the rule. Subtract the given vertical diametral
line *DE* from the given vertical part of the sagitta *BF*. Double the remainder
BG, and the result is *HG*. Square *HG*. Also square the given distance *DF*
(or rather its equal *EG*). Add the two squares. Take the square root of this
sum and we have the magnitude of the tangent line *HE*. Make *HE* the first
number in a rule of three, the known distance *EG* the second number, and
1 (i.e. the whole sine) the third number. The fourth number may now be
found and is the sine of angle *EHG*. Then look up that sine in a table of
sines and we shall have the angle sought, since that angle is obviously equal
to angle *EHG*. Then Dee adds a note to the effect that he has added (in the
non-existent table, I might add) all of the angles of the vertical diametral
lines which he has given in the table. Dee points out that this proposition
differs little from the preceding one since it is obvious that the diametral line
is seen to be a certain part of a line of [solar] incidence. The admonition
that Dee adds here is not clear though the reading of the text is completely

legible. He seems to be saying that the same angles are made not only with the line of contingence but also with the parabolic linear section itself. But such mixed angles play no role at all in the treatment of parabolas and hence I may be wrong in this interpretation of the admonition.

Following the two propositions on angles Dee presents three propositions that concern diametral lines. Proposition 55 gives a rule for finding the magnitude of a line of order on which a given diametral line stands at a given distance from the sagitta, the vertical part of the sagitta corresponding to the line of order also being given. The solution is straightforward. The given diametral line is subtracted from the given vertical part of the sagitta. Then using the remainder and the given distance of the diametral line from the sagitta, we can find the latus rectum of the parabola by means of the equation of the parabola. Then again by the equation of the parabola and using the given vertical part of the sagitta and the recently determined latus rectum we can find half of the line of order we seek. Hence its double is the desired magnitude. In Proposition 56 the diametral line and the line of order on which it stands are given, as is the vertical part of the sagitta corresponding to the given line of order, and the problem is to seek out the distance of the diametral line from the sagitta. The solution is similar to the one given in the preceding proposition and rests on finding the latus rectum and applying the equation of the parabola to that latus rectum and the difference between the given vertical part of the sagitta and the given diametral line. Proposition 57 gives the distance of a given diametral line from the sagitta on a given line of order. The problem is to find the vertical part of the sagitta that corresponds to the given line of order. The solution is obvious by reference to Fig. Ap. II.22. First note that $BO + OC = BC$ and then that $AC - BC = AB$. Now $AB / BC = BD / DE$ by Proposition 43, line EC being a tangent to the parabola. Thus with AB, BC, and BD now known, we can find DE by the rule of three. Adding DE to DB, we now have BE. By similar triangles $CB / BE = CO / OS$. Now CB, BE, and CO are known. Hence the fourth term OS may be found. But $OS = 2\ RO$ by Propositions 38 and 43, and so we have found the desired vertical part RO of the sagitta. One could fashion similar problems and solutions involving diametral lines and other lines already defined, such as the whole sagitta of the parabola, the base of the parabola, and the axis of the cone from which the parabola is generated.

Dee now returns to propositions involving angles of incidence and reflection. The first of these I have retained as Proposition 58, though it was unquestionably deleted in favor of Proposition 58*bis*. It holds that an angle of solar incidence at any point on a parabola is equal to the angle of reflection at the same point. Parts of two proofs are presented, neither being complete. Both the enunciation and the first proof are clearly deleted by Dee. The first proof starts out very much like the proof of the more general Proposition 1 of Alhazen's *De speculis comburentibus.*[20] Indeed, as we see from the proof

---

[20] Clagett, *Archimedes in the Middle Ages,* Vol. 4, pp. 15–17.

of Proposition 58*bis*, Dee refers to the authors who have written on burning mirrors for the demonstration of the equality of angles of incidence and of reflection, and so he is clearly substituting the authority of the earlier treatises (like that of Alhazen) for his abandoned Proposition 58. The new Proposition 58*bis* asserts that the length of a line of reflection is equal to the sum of the distance of combustion and the extension of the sagitta beyond the vertex cut off by a tangent to the parabola at the point of reflection. This proposition also goes back to the earliest of the treatises on burning mirrors, namely that of Alhazen, where it appears as a part of the proof of Proposition 1.[21] Dee's proof may be followed by referring to Fig. AP. II.25. We need to prove that $AB = BD$. By Proposition 53 we know that angle EAF = angle BDA. Further (Dee says) all the authors on burning mirrors tell us that angle EAF = angle BAD (which was, as I have said, the original but now deleted Proposition 58). Therefore angle BAD = angle BDA, and the proposition immediately follows since then triangle BAD would be an isosceles triangle. With this proposition established, Dee in Proposition 59 shows how to find where a parabolic section whose line of combustion and some vertical part of the sagitta are both known cuts a perpendicular which passes through the lower terminus of the given vertical part of the sagitta. We may follow this by alluding to Fig. Ap. II.26. We let AB be the given line of combustion and AC the given vertical part of the sagitta. Draw an indefinitely long perpendicular DE through point C. Extend AC so that $AO = AC$. Then open a compass to the distance BO. Placing the fixed foot of the compass on the point of combustion B, strike off point Q on indefinite line DE, and Q will be the desired point where the parabola cuts the indefinite perpendicular, by the converse of Proposition 58*bis*.

Proposition 59 leads directly to Proposition 60, which concerns the mechanical construction of a parabolic segment according to a given vertical part of the sagitta when the distance of combustion is given. This is so obvious that it hardly needs all of the attention that Dee gives it. For we may select any number of points C through which we draw indefinite perpendiculars, and, taking the sum of the given distance of combustion and the external extension of the doubled vertical part of the sagitta terminated at any of the points C, we would find where the parabola intersects the new perpendiculars. Accordingly we could establish a large number of such points of intersection of the parabola and the perpendiculars, and hence if we draw a single curved line through these many points, we would, as in earlier propositions, have a mechanically drawn parabola. In Dee's proof he constructs a vertical parabolic segment, that is, the segment whose largest indefinite perpendicular runs through the point of combustion. This means that he doubles the distance of combustion and then opens his compass to that doubled distance and strikes off on the indefinite perpendicular extended through the point of combustion to the point where the parabolic segment cuts the perpendicular.

---

[21] *Ibid.*, p. 15, where he notes the equality of BE and BH in Fig. 1.1. on p. 472.

From that point he then proceeds as I have indicated to find the points of intersection of the parabola with other perpendiculars between the point of combustion and the vertex. He notes that the same procedure holds for any segment of the parabola whose vertical part of the sagitta is less than the distance of combustion.

Proposition 61 returns to the finding of optical angles, this time the finding of the angle of combustion when an angle of incidence is given. Since an angle of incidence equals its angle of reflection and those two angles together with the angle of combustion are equal to 180°, the angle of combustion is found by doubling the angle of incidence and subtracting that double from 180°. Proposition 62 seeks to elicit the magnitude of the angle of incidence formed by a line of incidence drawn parallel to the sagitta from a given point outside of the vertical segment of the parabola but in the plane of that segment. The key to this proposition is to realize that such a given point acts as if it were the center of the sun so that the problem is precisely the same as finding an angle of solar incidence when a line of order and a corresponding vertical part of the sagitta are both given. Dee notes that if the perpendicular distance from the given point to the sagitta extended is equal to half the maximum line of order of your given parabolic segment, Proposition 53 will immediately provide the solution. If it is less than half, then Proposition 40 will find you the diametral line. From this you will know how to proceed, for you will be able to find a half of a new line of order equal to that distance. Then with the diametral line subtracted from the initially given vertical part of the sagitta you will be able to find the vertical part of the sagitta corresponding to the new line of order. Hence you may now apply again the rule of Proposition 53 to find the magnitude of the angle of incidence.

In Proposition 63 Dee gives the angle of incidence and the vertical part of the sagitta corresponding to that angle and then seeks the line of order corresponding to that angle. The solution is given as a verbally expressed rule, which we may illustrate by reference to Fig. Ap. II.20. With CD and angle QAK given, the proposition seeks the line of order AB corresponding to the given angle of incidence QAK. Since angle QAK is given, then so is its equal angle DEA. Subtract that angle from 90° and you will have angle DAE. Since CD is given, then so is its double, DE. Find the sines of both angles DEA and DAE. Then the following proportion is evident: sin DAE / DE = sin DEA / DA. Then since sin DAE, line DE, and sin DEA are all known, therefore DA will be known. But line AB = 2 DA and therefore line AB is known. Proposition 64 is closely similar (again following Fig. Ap. II.20), except that DA and angle QAK are given and the vertical part of the sagitta, CD, is sought. The same proportion as in Proposition 63 may be rewritten as follows: sin DEA / DA = sin DAE / DE. Then since sin DEA, line DA, and sin DAE are all known, so also DE will be known. But DE = 2 CD, and so line CD will be known, and this is what was sought.

Proposition 65 presents the problem of finding the magnitude of an angle of incidence (in the vertical segment of a parabola) which corresponds to a given angle of combustion. The solution is simple. Subtract the given angle of combustion from 180° and take half of the remainder, and the result is the angle sought. Then follows what I believe to be a porism that appears to assert that we can use one vertical segment of a parabola (i.e. a segment whose base is not greater than the latus rectum) for any given angle of combustion so long as the angle sought does not exceed [twice] the angle of incidence, i.e. so long as the angle of combustion is not more than 90°, for if the angle of combustion is more than 90° it is obvious that the point of incidence and reflection would lie on the parabolic line beyond its base (i.e. beyond the latus rectum). I decided that this was a porism to Proposition 65 and not a new Proposition 66, since (although written in a larger hand as enunciations always are) the next proposition is unambiguously numbered 66. The first added comment seems to suggest that Proposition 65 is useful for all natural phenomena or operations that are in the form of propagations like light, that is the propagation of planetary influences, of species, and so on. The second comment is not completely clear to me, but I believe that the following explanation (using Fig. Ap. II.25) is the probable one. If the line of reflection *AB* were made the diameter of a circle, then this circle may be called the circle of combustion. Then, Dee tells us, that if a larger angle of combustion than angle *FAB* is taken in the same parabola, then obviously the point of contact on the parabola would be farther from the point of combustion (i.e. focus). Hence the line of reflection would be greater and so the circle of combustion constructed on that line would be greater. One can also compare such angles of combustion directly for two different parabolas that possess a common given line of order, for then the angles of combustion would possess the same line of incidence but the line of reflection from the parabola whose point of combustion is above that of the other on the common sagitta would lie above the other line of reflection and thus the angle of combustion would be greater. We can conceive of the two angles of combustion being compared either in the circle of combustion of the smaller line of reflection or in the circle of combustion of the longer line of reflection. In either case the angles would be directly comparable. Dee refrains from elaborating this subject, since, he says, it would take too long to lay it bare.

Proposition 66 presents the problem of finding the angle that a given line of order makes with the tangent at its terminus when we know the corresponding vertical part of the sagitta. By Proposition 53 the angle of solar incidence (e.g. angle *KAQ* in Fig. Ap. II.20) may be found. This angle is equal to angle *DEA* because of the parallelity of lines *AK* and *DE*. Hence, if we subtract this angle from 90°, we shall have the magnitude of angle *EAD*, which is what we seek.

Proposition 67 is the first of three propositions that concern angles of arbitrary incidence and reflection, that is angles that are formed at a point of tangency by lines of incidence that are not parallel to the sagitta. In Proposition 67 a vertical line of order and its corresponding vertical part of the sagitta are given. Then, if a straight line is drawn from either end of the given line of order to some given point on the sagitta other than the point of combustion, the problem is to find the magnitude of arbitrary incidence that this line makes with the tangent to the parabola at the end of the line of order. We may illustrate Dee's solution by reference to Fig. Ap. II.28. By Proposition 66 we find the magnitude of angle *EBS* and set that result aside. Then we subtract the given vertical part *EO* of the sagitta from the given distance *OA* (*A* being the given point on the sagitta extended). Conserve that remainder, *EA*, and then square it. Also square *EB*, i.e. half of the given line of order. Add EA^2 and EB^2. Take the square root of that sum and you will have the magnitude of *BA*, our line of arbitrary incidence. Then use the rule of three as follows. Put *AB* as the first number, the whole sine (i.e. 1) as the second number, either *EB* or *EA* as the third number. When the fourth number has been found, it is either the sine of angle *EAB* (if you have taken *EB* as the third number) or the sine of angle *ABE* (if you have used *EA* as the third number). If it is the sine of *EAB*, you find the corresponding angle *EAB* in a table of sines, which, if you subtract it from 90°, will give you the magnitude of angle *ABE*. Then add angle *ABE* to angle *EBS*, which you found at the beginning. Subtract that sum from 180° and you will have the angle of arbitrary incidence that you seek. Now if you took *EA* as the third number and thus found angle *EBA* directly, you would repeat the steps just outlined above and find the angle of arbitrary incidence. Dee has given a corollary to this proposition, of which so little remains that I cannot properly reconstruct it. Still I am sure that it concerns the determination of angle *ABD*, when angle *DBS* is the angle of arbitrary reflection. Thus we are probably told to double the angle of incidence (after its determination) and then subtract the double from 180°.

Proposition 68 is somewhat similar to Proposition 67 but considerably more complicated. We may describe its intent and solution by reference to Fig. Ap. II.29. For parabola *BCA* we are given vertical line of order *BA* and the corresponding vertical part of the sagitta *CM*. We are also given some point *G* in the sagitta which has been extended toward infinity, the extended sagitta being designated *CMX*. Then through *G* a line *IGN* perpendicular to *CMX* is extended in both directions toward infinity. Then a second point is given, this one in line *IGN* such that its distance from the first point *G* is either less than the length *AM* (and in that case the second point is *H*) or more than that length (and in that case the second point is *I*). In the first case we draw lines of arbitrary incidence from point *H* to each end of line *AB* (i.e. lines *HA* and *HB*). Then tangents are drawn to the parabola at points *A* and *B*. Hence we first are to determine in this proposition the magnitudes of angles *HAF* and *HBE*.

Draw line *AN* parallel to *CG*. Extend line *AH* until it meets the extended sagitta at *X*. Triangle *AMX* and *HGX* are similar, and hence *HG* / *GX* = *AM* / *MX*. Now *HG* and *AM* are known. *GX* may be found as follows. Triangles *HAN* and *GHX* are similar. Therefore *HN* / *NA* = *HG* / *GX*. The first three terms are known; therefore *GX* will be known. Add *MG*, which is known, to *GX*, and so *MX* will be known. Then you will proceed as in Proposition 67 and will accordingly find angle *HAF*. Now to find the magnitude of the second angle, *HBE*, first note that triangles *LMB* and *LGH* are similar. Thus *GH* / *GL* = *BM* / *ML*. Permutatively *GH* / *BM* = *GL* / *ML*. So conjunctively (*GH* + *BM*) / *BM* = (*GL* + *ML*) / *ML*. But *GH* and *BM* are known, and similarly *GM*, i.e. *GL* + *ML*, is also known. Hence *ML* can be found. Once that is found, *L* will be as if given, and so once more Proposition 67 will allow you to determine angle *HBE*, the second of the angles of arbitrary incidence that you seek.

Now if instead of assuming *H* as our second point, we assume second point *I* so that *GI* is greater than *MA*, let us draw as before lines of arbitrary incidence from *I* to points *A* and *B*. Hence in this part of the proposition we are to find angles *IAF* and *IBE*. Angle *IAF* may be found by finding point *K* in precisely the same manner as we found point *L* earlier and then applying Proposition 67. Now for finding angle *IBE* we first draw line *GB* and perpendicular *BO*. Proposition 67 teaches us how to find angle *GBE*, which we conserve. Then we subtract angle *GBE* from 180° and the result is angle *GBD*, which we also conserve. From angle *GBD* we subtract angle *MBD*, which latter angle Proposition 66 has taught us to find. The remainder will be angle *GBM*, which we subtract from 90°, and the remainder is angle *BGM*. And angle *BGM* will equal angle *GBO* because of the parallelity of lines *BO* and *MG*. Now all we have to find is angle *OBI*, which we find as follows. We subtract *BM* (given) from *IG* (given), and the result is *IO*. Now *BO* = *MG* (given). Therefore we have two sides of the right triangle *OIB*. Hence we may determine the third side *BI*. So now by the rule of three, the first number is *BI*, the second number is the whole sine (i.e. 1), and the third is *IO*. Therefore we can find the fourth, which is the sine of *OBI*. Looking this up in a table of sines, we shall have the magnitude of angle *OBI*. We join it to angle *GBO* (found earlier). We subtract the sum from angle *GBE* (found earlier) and the remainder is angle *IBE*, which is the second of the angles sought.

The last proposition that Dee gives, Proposition 69, assumes that a vertical part of the sagitta and its corresponding line of order are given. If an arbitrary line of reflection is constructed at one end of the given line of order, this proposition seeks to find the point in the sagitta at whose distance from the vertex of the parabola the line of arbitrary reflection cuts the sagitta. If we look back at Fig. Ap. II.28, we may follow Dee's solution easily. Proposition 66 allows us to find angle *EBS*. Then we subtract it from the given angle of arbitrary reflection. The result is angle *EBD*. If we subtract that angle from 90°, we have angle *EDB*. Then we take the sines of both these angles from a table of sines. Now we are prepared to use the rule of three. The sine of *EBD* is the first term, half of the line of order, *EB*, is the second, and the sine of *DBE* is the third. Since these three terms are known, we can find the fourth, namely *ED*. Add *ED* to the given vertical part of the sagitta, *EO*, and the result wll give you the distance of *D* from the vertex *O*.

With this proposition and the number 70 for a projected next proposition, Dee's treatise ends abruptly, and I have discussed the significance of this ending at the beginning of this introduction. There now remains only to speak briefly about my edition of the text and the English translation which I have provided. The principal difficulty which I incurred in establishing the text arose from the fact that the pages of the manuscript were all burned at the top, and hence one or two lines were lost on almost every page. When both the probable content and the language seemed clear to me (as the result of the preceding and succeeding lines) I attempted to suggest in brackets the probable reading of the Latin text. But when the content but not the exact language was clear to me I left five dots in the Latin text to indicate the burned portion, while attempting to suggest the probable content by adding bracketed phrases in the English translation. When neither content nor language seemed clear to me, I left five dots in both the Latin text and English translation. At any rate, I have always carefully indicated in the variant readings where the burned lines occurred in the text.

I have added marginal references in my text to indicate each page of the manuscript, and I have numbered successively and arbitrarily the lines for each page, with the marginal folio numbers appearing as rubrics for the variant readings at the bottom of the page. Both in the text and on the diagrams I have used capital letters to mark the points and magnitudes, though Dee is not consistent in his practice. So far as the texts of the enunciations are concerned, I have abandoned my usual practice of capitalizing the enunciations because there were so many enunciations with very short proofs or solutions. The result would have been an unsightly mass of capital letters had I stuck to my usual procedure. I have capitalized *Euclides* wherever it occurs, though most of the time Dee did not. However Dee consistently capitalized *Archimedes*. I have punctuated the text as I thought the meaning demanded. For example, I have often eliminated commas between subjects and predicates.

Dee has many times corrected the Latin text in the margin while indicating which part of the text is to be deleted. In almost all cases I have accordingly substituted the marginal readings and reduced the rejected textual reading to the variant readings. There are two exceptions. In Proposition 54 I have kept the deleted textual reading in the text since the corrected marginal reading has been partially destroyed (see 300r, variant reading for lines 2–7). I have also retained in the text the deleted Proposition 58 along with the substituted Proposition 58*bis* because of its interesting relationship with medieval tracts on burning mirrors. The diagrams I have copied directly from Dee's and they appear intact with their legends. These legends I have translated and added to the English translation at the appropriate places.

Finally we should note a few minor characteristics of Dee's manuscript. Dee has added in the margins before many of the propositions a sign that looks like the letter Q, sometimes with one line drawn through the tail and sometimes with two such lines. I do not know its significance. The letters *a* and *e* are everywhere written together when forming the dipthongs *ae*. The letter *e* when written alone often has an apostrophe-like sign added to it. Dee's letters *I* and *J* are indistinguishable from each other and I have always transcribed them as *I* except twice in the readings for the title where I have transcribed the genitive of Dee's first name as *Joannis*. Dee vacillates between *angulus* and *angulum* and between *triangulus* and *triangulum* as the nominative forms of those words. Dee always writes *-cunque* and probably *utrunque*. On several occasions Dee uses the Greek term πόρισμα but only once does he add the accent.

The English translation which I have added is quite literal but not, I hope, excessively turgid. One literal rendering is "part" for *pars* in the expression *pars verticalis sagittae* where we might better use the translation "segment." I have done this because Dee ordinarily uses *portio* or *segmentum* (or *frustum* if it is a small segment) when he wants to emphasize that we are dealing with a segment. The reader will also remember from my discussion above of the definitions that I retain the Latin terms *ustorius* and *sagitta* as English terms, though their English usage is now obsolete or rare. In the case of *ustorius* I have done so to prevent the use of circumlocutions, in that of *sagitta* to distinguish the axis of the parabola from the axis of the cone from which it is generated. Note also that I have always translated *punctum combustionis* by "point of combustion" rather than by "focus." This I have done for two reasons: to keep the medieval context of burning mirrors and to preserve Kepler's priority in the use of the term focus.[22]

---

[22] *Ibid.*, p. 335, n. 37.

Discoveries of John Dee Concerning that Section of a Right-angled Right Cone which was Called a Parabola by Ancient Mathematicians [Being Two Books of a Projected Five on Burning Mirrors]

/ 1558 Martii 8

De speculis comburentibus libri 5. In primis duobus: Inventa Joannis Dee Londinensis circa illam coni recti atque rectanguli sectionem quae ab antiquis Mathematicis Parabola appellabatur.

5   Omnia hic habes tam numerorum praxi exposita tam etiam mathematicae ἀποδείξεως certitudine illustrata.

Quas autem et quam immensas utilitates hic liber habet philosophi, perspectivi, et naturae indagatores celebratissimi haud ignorant experienti magis addsunt (*!*)_____(*?*)

/ [Liber I.]

Definitiones

1. Cum extra superficiem alicuius circuli descripti punctum accipiatur, a quo per circumferentiam ipsius circuli ducatur linea recta, in infinitum ex-
5   currere permissa, eademque linea per totam descripti circuli circumferentiam circumducatur, illam nusquam egrediendo, et illo eius termino qui ad acceptum constituitur punctum, toto interea tempore quiescente: corpus illud quod a duabus superficiebus comprehenditur, circulo scilicet illo primo et curva illa superficie quae inter quiescens punctum et circuli circumferentiam
10   a deducta recta linea describebatur, CONUM vocamus [cf. Fig. Ap.II.1].

2. Vertex coni est punctum illud quiescens.

Fol. 280r
>1 *circa* 1558. . . . 8 *scr. et del.* C Inventa Joannis Dee Londinensis circa sectionem illam coni recti atque rectanguli quae Parabola a veteribus mathematicis appel[la]batur
>3 *ante* circa *scr. et del.* C quae
>5 tam¹ *supra scr.* C / *post* numerorum *scr. et del.* C praxi *sed supra scr.* C examini praxi (*et del.* examini) / *post* exposita *scr. et del.* C et quae horum pulcherrima quasque / tam etiam *supra scr.* C (*et mg. hab.* C et etiam)
>6 ἀποδείξεως *sine spiritu et accentu scr.* C

Fol. 284r
>1 [Liber I.] *addidi* (*cf.* primis duobus *in 280r, lin.* 2)
>9 *post* curva *scr. et del.* C cul-

3. Basis coni est circulus ille per cuius circumferentiam circumducta linea coni curvam descripsit superficiem.

4. Axis coni est recta linea verticem coni cum centro basis coni connectens.

284v / [5. Conus rectus est cuius axis ad suam basim perpendicularis existit.]

6. Conus scalenus est cuius axis ad suam basim perpendicularis non existit [cf. Fig. Ap.II.2].

7. Latus conicum coni recti est recta linea a vertice coni ad circumferentiam
5 basis extensa.

8. Superficies conica coni recti est superficies coni curva ex circumductione lateris conici per circumferentiam basis eius termino qui ad coni verticem existat quiescente descripta.

9. Triangulus conicus coni recti est superficies plana que diametro basis
10 coni et duabus aliis lineis rectis ab eiusdem diametri terminis eductis et ad verticem coni concurrentibus comprehenditur.

10. Basis trianguli conici est eadem que coni basis est diameter [cf. Fig. Ap.II.3].

11. Conus rectus et rectangulus est cuius trianguli conici angulus quem
15 basis eiusdem trianguli conici subtendit rectus est.

12. Conus rectus acutiangulus est quando dictus angulus acutus est.

13. Conus rectus obtusiangulus est quando obtusus fuerit angulus praedictus.

285r / [14. Cum latus conicum coni recti et rectanguli circumdatur per circumferentiam basis coni] superficie[m] efficiens, et sumatur prae[dicto] basi coni diameter quae basim trianguli conici ad rectos secuerit angulos, si iam per illam diametrum planum transire intra conum intelligatur, conumque
5 ipsum in duo segmenta dividere, a toto eius transitus tempore, primo plano iuxta latus conici trianguli applicato, parallelum existens, communem sectionem duarum superficierum, huius scilicet quae aequidistanter primo plano conum pertransierit et curvae ipsius conicae superficiei, PARABOLICAM SECTIONEM LINEAREM USTORIAMQUE deinceps vocabimus [cf. Fig.
10 Ap.II.4].

15. PARABOLA USTORIA est plana superficies a lineari sectione parabolica ustoria comprehensa, et dicta basis coni diametro.

16. Basis parabolae nostrae ustoriae est conicae basis illa diameter quae trianguli conici basim ad rectos secuit angulos.

13 coni *corr. C ex* conies (?)
Fol. 284v
   1 [5. . . . existit] *addidi eo quod hic textus interiit*
   6 coni recti: c. r. *supra scr. C*
   10 rectis: r. *supra scr. C*
                                        b.   a.
   16 Conus rectus acutiangulus: Acutiangulus conus rectus *C*
Fol. 285r
   1–2 [14 . . . coni] *addidi eo quod hic textus interiit*
   2 -[m] *addidi* / -[dicto] *addidi*
   3 *ante* basim *scr. et del. C aliquid quod non legere possum (sed forte* erit)
   5 *post* segmenta *scr. et del. C* varia
   13 conicae *corr. C ex* coni / illa *corr. C ex* ille / quae *correxi ex* qui

15   17. Sagitta tota sive diameter parabolae ustoriae est communis sectio duarum superficierum, trianguli videlicet conici et plani secantis conum ad sectionis parabolicae ustoriae generationem.

    18. Linea ordinis est recta parabolae ipsius basi parallela, in parabolae superficie extensa et utrumque suum terminum in sectionis parabolicae linearis 20 concavitate collacatum habens.

285v   / [19.] . . . . .

    20. Punctum combustionis . . . . . illud quod in sagittae totius medio habetur.

    21. Combustionis distantia est sagittae totius illa pars quae inter verticem 5 parabolae et combustionis punctum continetur.

    22. Latus erectum est illa linea ordinis quae per combustionis punctum sagittam totam secat.

    23. Linea ordinis verticalis est illa quae inter combustionis punctum et verticem parabolae sagittam perstransit.

10   24. Sagittae pars verticalis est illa quae semper unum eius terminum habet ipsum parabolae verticem, alterum vero inter verticem et combustionis punctum collocatum.

    25. Linea ordinis verticalis sagittae parti verticali respondens est illa quae illius sagittae partis terminum inferiorem tangit.

15   26. Sagittae pars verticalis lineae ordinis verticali respondens est illa quae a vertice parabolae ducta ad ipsam lineam ordinis terminatur cui respondere dicitur [cf. Fig. Ap.II.5].

    27. Linea contingens sectionem parabolicam linearem est recta iuxta aliquod punctum in convexitate ipsius linearis sectionis applicata, intra parabolae 20 superficiem nulla sui parte cadens licet utrinque in infinitum excurreret.

286r   / [28. Linea] incidentiae solaris est recta quae (?) . . . . . ipsi sagittae aequidistans ad ipsum . . . . . [contingentiae punctum] extendatur.

       15 *ante* 17 *mg. hab. C* a / sive diameter *supra scr. C*
       18 *ante* 18 *mg. hab. C* e

Fol. 285v
       1 [19.]. . . . . *addidi eo quod hic textus interiit et est in mg. aliquid quod non legere possum* (*sed forte est* 19. Vertex est punctum quod est terminum sagittae in sectione lineari parabolae existens.)
       2 . . . . . *addidi eo quod hic textus interiit*
    2–3 *supra* in . . . habetur *scr. C* hoc definiveris prius, non erit ergo definitio *et est in mg. aliquid quod del. C et quod non legere possum*
  18–19 aliquod . . . in *supra scr. C*
     20 *mg. hab. C* 28 perpendicularis contingentiae. 29 latus contingentiae. 30 hypothenusa contingentiae. 31 Triangulus contingentiae. 32 Angulus ———— (*lac. sed forte* lineae) ordinis est qui a linea ordinis efficitur cum latere (*supra scr.*) contingentiae ———— (*? sectionem?*) ad ———— (*? eiusdem?*) lineae ordinis alterutrum finem.

Fol. 286r
       1 [28. Linea] *addidi eo quod hic textus interiit* / . . . . . *addidi eo quod hic textus interiit*
       2 . . . . . [contingentiae punctum] *addidi eo quod hic textus interiit; et forte hab. C* usque *in fine.* . . . .

29. Angulus incidentiae solaris est qui infra perpendicularem contingentiae efficitur et a linea incidentiae comprehenditur cum illa linea quae parabolicam
5 linearem sectionem tangit ubi linea incidentiae solaris in ipsa sectione finitur.

30. Linea reflexionis solaris sive linea combustionis est recta quae a termino lineae incidentiae illo educitur qui ipsi sectioni inhaeret et per combustionis punctum transit.

31. Angulus reflexionis solaris est ille qui supra perpendicularem contin-
10 gentiae a linea reflexionis cum contingente efficitur.

32. Angulus combustionis est ille angulus quem linea incidentiae solaris cum linea reflexionis solaris constituit.

33. Angulus incidentiae lineae ordinis verticali respondens est ille qui ad alterutrum terminum eiusdem lineae ordinis constituitur.

15 34. Angulus incidentiae sagittae parti verticali respondens est ille qui ad alterutrum finem lineae ordinis verticalis eidem sagittae parti verticali respondentis constituitur.

35. Angulus reflexionis lineae ordinis verticali respondens est ille qui ad eiusdem lineae ordinis alterutrum terminum constituitur.

20 36. Angulus reflexionis sagittae parti verticali respondens est ille qui ad alterutrum finem linee ordinis eidem sagittae parti verticali respondentis constituitur.

286v / [37. Angulus combustionis lineae ordinis verticali respondens est ille qui ad alterutrum terminum] eiusdem lineae ordinis [constituitur].

38. Angulus combustionis sagittae parti verticali respondens est ille qui ad alterutrum finem lineae ordinis eidem sagittae parti verticali respondentis
5 constituitur [cf. Fig. Ap.II.6].

3-4 infra . . . et *mg. scr.* C
5 solaris *supra scr.* C
7-8 et . . . transit *mg. scr.* C; *in textu scr. et del.* C angulumque cum eadem contingente constituit aequalem angulo quem linea incidentiae (*et postea hab.* C *aliquid quod prius del.* C:) a cuius termino educit cum eadem contingente facit, verum [in] partes adversas
9 solaris *supra scr.* C
9-10 supra . . . contingentiae *mg. scr.* C
11, 12 solaris *supra scr.* C
15-17 qui . . . constituitur *supra scr.* C, *sed infra scr. et del.* C a quo si linea ipsi parabolae basi parallela ducatur per ipsius sagittae terminum inferiorem transit
20-22 qui . . . constituitur *mg. scr.* C, *sed in textu scr. et del.* C a quo si vel lateri erecto vel basi parabolae parellela ducatur per ipsius sagittae partis (*supra scr.*) terminum inferiorem transit
Fol. 286v
1-2 [37. . . . terminum] *addidi eo quod hic textus interiit*
2 [constituitur] *addidi*
3 *ante* combustionis *scr. et del.* C incidentiae (?)
3-5 qui . . . constituitur *mg. scr.* C, *sed in textu scr. et del.* C a quo si linea ducatur ipsi lateri erecto vel basi parabolae parallela, per inferiorem terminum ipsius sagittae partis transit

287r / [39] . . . . . dictorum angulorum aliquis . . . . . [respondet?] datae (?) parabolae verticali.

40. Sagittae pars verticalis dictis tribus angulis respondens est illa cuius terminus inferior finitur ad ipsam lineam ordinis quae ipsis tribus angulis
5 respondet.

41. Parabolae partem verticalem illam vocabimus quae a latere erecto et sectionis parabolicae linearis portione ad ipsius lateris erecti fines terminata comprehenditur.

42. Linea diametralis est recta ab aliquo puncto linearis sectionis para-
10 bolicae ad parabolae basim vel aliquam lineam ordinis ducta et ipsi sagittae parallela.

43. Linea diametralis verticalis est illa quae a sectione lineari parabolica ad ipsum latus erectum vel ad aliquam aliam lineam ordinis verticalem ducta ipsi sagittae est parall[ela].

15 44. Linea diametralis verticalis lineae ordinis verticali respondens est quae ab alterutro termino eiusdem lineae ordinis ad ipsum latus erectum ducitur vel [ad] aliam lineam ordinis verticalem.

45. Linea diametralis verticalis sagittae parti verticali respondens est illa a cuius superiori termino linea ordinis ducta sagittae parti verticali respondens,
20 eius autem inferior terminus est vel in ipso latere erecto vel alia linea ordinis verticali.

287v / [46. Linea diametralis verticalis angulo incidentiae solaris, et angulo reflexionis solaris], et angulo combustionis respondens est illa quae a dictorum

---

Fol. 287r

    1 [39.] . . . . . *et.* . . . . . [respondet?] *addidi eo quod hic textus interiit*

    3–5 cuius . . . respondet *mg. scr. C, sed in textu scr. et del. C* cuius terminum inferiorem si agatur recta linea (*supra scr.*) ordinis (*supra scr.*) parallela ipsi lateri erecto puncto contingentiae occurret ad quod dicti tres anguli sint constituti

    6 *ante* 41 *scr. mg. C* f.2 / vocabimus *corr. C ex* vocabamus (?) / *post* quae *scr. et del. C* est

    9–10 *post* parabolicae *scr. et del. C* ducta *et etiam supra scr. et del. C* excepto vertice

    10 vel . . . ducta *supra scr. C*

    13 vel . . . verticalem *supra scr. C*

    14 -[ela] *addidi*

    17 vel . . . verticalem *postea add. C* / [ad] *addidi*

                             b.   a.
    18 *post* Linea *scr. et del. C* ordinis / verticalis diametralis *C*

    19 *post* ordinis *scr. et del. C* ipsi lateri erecto parallela / *post* ducta *scr. et del. C* per ipsum / parti *supra scr. C* / verticali *scr. et del. C sed addidi* / respondens *supra scr. C*

    20–21 eius . . . verticali *mg. scr. C, sed in textu scr. et del. C* terminum inferiorem transit; quare etiam ipsius sagittae partis verticalis complementum vocabimus, ut et sagittae partem verticalem complementum huius, respecto (?) distantiae combustionis vel alterius sagittae partis, ipsa combustionis distantia minoris

Fol. 287v

    1–2 [46. . . . . solaris] *addidi eo quod hic textus interiit*

angulorum loco ad ipsum latus erectum cadit vel [ad] aliam lineam ordinis verticalem.

5   47. Angulus incidentiae solaris, reflexionis solaris, et (! vel) combustionis angulus lineae diametrali verticali respondens est ille qui ad ipsius lineae diametralis superiorem terminum constituitur [cf. Fig. Ap.II.7].

48. Linea ordinis verticalis lineae diametrali verticali respondens est illa cuius unus terminus cum superiori termino ipsius lineae diametralis com-
10   munis est.

49. Sagittae pars verticalis lineae diametrali verticali respondens est per cuius inferiorem terminum si agatur linea ordinis uno eius fine ad superiorem terminum ipsius diametralis terminabitur.

adverte ad
289r

/ [Liber II.]

[Propositiones]

[1. Dato latere erecto parabolae, distantiam] combustionis notam facere quae eidem parabolae est (?).

5   Divide lateris erecti quantitatem per 4, et numerus quotientis distantiam combustionis monstrat.

2. Data combustionis distantia, latus erectum elicere, quod eidem parabolae quadrat.

Multiplica distantiam combustionis per 4 et productum erit latus erectum
10   quod quaeritur.

3. Dato latere erecto, et sagittae aliqua parte verticali, lineam ordinis verticalem datae sagittae parti respondentem eruere.

Multiplica latus erectum per sagittae partem datam, et producti accipe radicem quadratam; illam radicem duplato, et exibit linea ordinis quaesita.

3 [ad] *addidi*
4 verticalem *supra scr. C*
5 *mg. hab. C*

| definitiones 8 | linea_____
Ang. △ reflexionis
. . . . .
. . . . .
. . . . .
. . . . .
hypothenusa contingentiae. . . .
perpendicularis contingentiae
latus contingentiae . . . . . | 4 definitiones

▷ triangulus est
contingentiae |

8 *post* illa *scr. et del. C* recta quae
9 *post* terminus *scr. et del. C* ad / cum *supra scr. C*
12 *post* terminum *scr. et del. C* linea acta ipsi lateri erecto parallela

Fol. 289r

1 [Liber II.] *addidi (cf.* primis duobus *in 280r, lin. 2)*
2 [Propositiones] *addidi (cf.* Definitiones *in 284r, lin. 2)*
3 [1. Dato . . . distantiam] *addidi eo quod hic textus interiit*

15   4. Dato latere erecto, et aliqua linea ordinis verticali, sagittae partem verticalem datae lineae ordinis respondentem invenire.

Dimidium lineae ordinis accipe; illud dimidium quadrabis, illudque quadratum dividas per latus erectum, et in quotiente erit quod cupis.

5. Data combustionis distantia, et sagittae aliqua parte verticali, lineam
20   ordinis verticalem datae sagittae parti respondentem notam efficere.

Per secundam huius invenias latus erectum. Deinde per 3^{am} absolve propositum.

6. Data combustionis distantia, et linea aliqua ordinis verticali, sagittae partem verticalem datae lineae ordinis respondentem exhibere.
25   Per secundam huius elicias latus erectum et per 4^{am} quod reliquum est indagato.

7. Data aliqua linea ordinis verticali, et sagittae parte verticali datae ordinis lineae respondente, latus erectum monstrare.

Datae ordinis lineae dimidium capias, illudque dimidium quadrato, ac
30   quadratum illud dividas per sagittae partem datam, nam quotiens tibi satisfaciet.

289v   / [8. Data aliqua linea ordinis verticali et sagittae parte verticali datae lineae] ordinis respondente, combustionis distantiam exprimere.

Per 7^{am} huius discas latus erectum, et statim te prima docebit quanta sit combustionis distantia.
5   9. Dato latere erecto, sagittam totam inventam ostendere.

Dimidium lateris erecti est nostrae totius sagittae quantitas.

10. Data sagitta tota, latus erectum elicere.

Praemissa te satis instruit.

11. Data sagitta tota, axem coni nostri ex quo sagitta illa parabolica habetur
10 explicare.

Sagittam totam quadrato; illud quadratum duplato; illius dupli radicem quadratam extrahas, nam illa radix est coni nostri axis, sive altitudo.

12. Data sagitta tota, basim nostrae parabolae exponere.

Per undecimam huius explicare quantus sit axis nostri coni, et illam quan-
15 titatem duplato, sic enim habebis basim quaesitam, quam in definitionibus nostris aequalem supponimus diametro basis ipsius coni.

13. Dato latere erecto, axem nostri coni cognitum efficere.

Per 9^{am} exquiras sagittam totam, et per 11^{am} perficias.

14. Dato latere erecto, basim parabolae notam reddere.
20 Per nonam huius elicias sagittam totam, et per 12^{am} procedas ad propositum.

15. Data sagitta tota, combustionis distantiam declarare.

Dimidium sagittae totius est combustionis distantia.

16. Data combustionis distantia, sagittam totam exprimere.

Per praemissam patet.

    20 verticalem *supra scr. C*
Fol. 289v
    1–2 [8. . . . . lineae] *addidi eo quod hic textus interiit*

25   17. Data combustionis distantia, axem nostri coni invenire.

Per praemissam disce sagittam totam, et per 11^{am} efficies quod cupis.

290r   / [18. Data combustionis distantia, basim nostrae parabolae invenire.

Per praemissam disce axem coni; eius] quantitatem duplato, et eris voti compos.

19. Data sagitta tota, et aliqua sagittae parte verticali, lineam ordinis ver-
5 ticalem datae sagittae parti respondentem enodare.

Per decimam habebis latus erectum et deinde per 3^{am} progrediaris.

20. Data sagitta tota, et linea aliqua ordinis verticali, sagittae partem verticalem datae lineae ordinis respondentem cognoscere.

Per decimam huius elicias latus erectum, et per 4^{am} pervenies ad id quod
10 quaeritur.

21. Dato axe sive altitudine nostri coni, sagittam totam nostrae parabolae
una exhibere.

Axem sive altitudinem quadrato; eius quadrati dimidium accipe, illiusque
dimidii radix quadrata est sagitta tota.

15   22. Dato axe nostri coni, combustionis distantiam notam facere in nostra
parabola.

Per 21^{am} investiges sagittae quantitatem, et 15^a huius voto satisfaciet.

23. Dato axe nostri coni, latus erectum nostrae parabolae notum efficere.

Per 21^{am} habebis sagittam totam, et per 10^{am} latus erectum.

20   24. Dato axe nostri coni, et sagittae aliqua parte verticali in nostra parabola,
lineam ordinis verticalem datae sagittae parti respondentem exposcari.

Per 23^{am} discas latus erectum, et 3^a tibi satisfaciet.

25. Dato axe nostri coni, et linea aliqua ordinis verticali, sagittae partem
verticalem datae lineae [ordinis] respondentem exprimere.

25   Vigesima tertia te de latere erecto informabit, et deinde tertia huius sagittae
partem quaesitam dabit.

26. Dato axe nostri coni, basim parabolae elicere.

Duplato axem, et habebis basim nostrae parabolae.

290v   / [27. Data basi nostrae parabolae, sagittam totam elicere.

Dimidium basis parabolae quadrato; et illud quadratum dimidia;] dimidii
radix quadrata [est sagitta tota].

28. Data basi nostrae parabolae, combustionis distantiam elicere.
5   Vigesima septima tibi dabit sagittam totam, et 15^a combustionis distantiam.

29. Data basi nostrae parabolae, latus erectum eruere.

Sagittam eruas per 27^{am} huius, et latus erectum per decimam.

30. Data basi parabolae nostrae, et sagittae aliqua parte verticali, lineam
ordinis verticalem datae sagittae parti respondentem exprimere.

Fol. 290r
    1–2 [18. Data. . . . eius] *addidi eo quod hic textus interiit*
      24 [ordinis] *addidi*
Fol. 290v
    1–2 [27. . . . dimidia] *addidi eo quod hic textus interiit*
      3 [est . . . tota] *addidi eo quod hic textus interiit*

10 Per 29^{am} huius cognosces latus erectum, et deinde per tertiam procedas ad propositum.

31. Data basi parabolae nostrae, et linea aliqua ordinis verticali, sagittae partem verticalem datae lineae ordinis respondentem notam efficere.

Vigesima nona dabit latus erectum, et quarta reliquam rationem operis
15 explicabit.

32. Ubicunque innotescit sagitta tota, combustionis distantia, cum sagittae aliqua parte verticali ibidem, et nota est linea diametralis verticalis sagittae parti verticali notae respondens.

Si enim subtrahas sagittae partem verticalem notam ab ipsa sagitta tota
20 vel combustionis distantia, residuum erit linea diametralis verticalis illi sagittae parti respondens.

33. Quaecunque linea diametralis verticalis respondet sagittae parti verticali, eadem linea respondet lineae ordinis verticali quae eidem sagittae parti verticali respondere dicitur.

25 Quare per praemissam, habita linea diametrali verticali quae sagittae parti respondet verticali, etiam habes lineam diametralem verticalem quae lineae ordinis verticali respondeat modo eadem linea ordinis respondet sagittae parti verticali cuius nostra linea diametralis est complementum.

34. Quaecunque linea diametralis verticalis respondet lineae ordinis ver-
30 ticali, eandem respondere oportet omnibus angulis qui cum linea contingente ad alterutrum finem ipsius lineae ordinis constituentur.

291r / [Linea ordinis verticalis et sagittae] pars verticalis quae dictis angulis respondet cognita fuerit ut per _____ (?45?) et 44 definitionem et 32^{am} et 33^{am} propositionem, et cetera.

35. Data aliqua sagittae parte verticali, et latere erecto, vel combustionis
5 distantia, vel linea ordinis verticali datae sagittae parti responden[te], vel sagitta tota, vel axe coni ex quo nostra desumitur parabola, vel basi ipsius parabolae, sectionis parabolicae linearis portionem quae ad illius lineae ordinis verticalis fines terminatur quae ipsi datae sagittae parti respondet mechanice delineare.

10 Divide sagittae partem datam in quot velis partes aequales, in quibus partibus si detur latus erectum per 3^{am} disces quantitatem lineae ordinis cuiusque quae per dictas partes aequales transit. Si distantia combustionis detur in eisdem partibus, inde per 2^{am} discas latus erectum, et fac ut iam

       13 respontem (!) C
       16 combustionis distantia *mg. scr. C, et postea scr. et del. C* vel
       20 vel . . . distantia *mg. scr. C*
       23 eidem *supra scr. C*
       30 *post* respondere *scr. et del. C* dum
   Fol. 291r
       1 [Linea . . . sagittae] *addidi eo quod hic textus interiit*
       1–2 angulis respondet *mg. scr. C, sed in textu scr. et del. C* diametralis est complementum
       2 *ante* 32^{am} *scr. et del. C* 33
       5 -[te] *addidi*
       7 *post* portionem *scr. et del. C* describere

diximus de lineis ordinis verticalibus per dictas partes sagittae transeuntibus.

15 Si autem detur linea ordinis datae sagittae parti respondens, tunc per 7^{am} habebis latus erectum, et fac ut supra docuimus. Si sagitta tota, tum ex 10^a habebis latus erectum, et tunc reliquum nosti opus. Si axis coni cum sagittae parte detur, tunc per 23^{am} acquires notum lateris erecti. Denique si tibi detur basis cum sagittae parte verticali, tunc 29 explicabit latus erectum, atque

20 inde ut ante docuimus elicies quantitates omnium linearum ordinis quae per partes illas divisionis sagittae verticalis transeunt, per quarum linearum fines si continuaveris (?) unam lineam curvam, videbis prodire quod desideras.

Exempli gratia, si detur sagitta longitudinis 5 unciarum, et sit *AB*, [Fig. Ap. II.8], et cuperem pro latere erecto 100 unciarum portionem parabolae

25 describere quae terminaretur ad fines lineae ordinis quae datae sagittae parti verticali respondet, tunc multiplico 5 per 100 et productum 500, cuius radix est $\sqrt{}500$, vel prope 22$^{16}/_{45}$. Haec duplicata exhibet longitudinem lineae ordinis per *B* transeuntis. Eodem modo si ad finem 4 unciarum, ubi ponatur *C*, vellem ordinis lineam trahere, tunc per 3^{am} multiplico 4 per 100 et fiet 400,

30 cuius radix erit $\sqrt{}400$, id est 20 praecise, et hoc est dimidium lineae ordinis

291v per *C* transeuntis. Ad tertium / . . . . . lineam ver _____ (?) . . . . . propositum absolvet, considera ut quam . . . . . plurimas recte possis partes, hanc sagittae partem distribuas, ita enim absolutissimum opus erit.

36. Data aliqua linea ordinis verticali, et latere erecto, vel combustionis

5 distantia, vel sagittae parte verticali datae lineae ordinis respondente, vel sagitta tota, vel axe coni ex quo nostra rescinditur parabola, vel base ipsius parabolae, sectionis parabolicae linearis portionem quae ad datae lineae ordinis fines terminetur mechanice delineari.

Si cum linea ordinis verticali detur latus erectum, tunc per 4 exquiras

10 sagittae partem verticalem respondentem; et per praecedentem perficies opus. Si combustionis distantia detur, tunc per 6 habebis sagittae partem verticalem respondentem, et praecedens (35 scilicet) aperiet tibi rationem operis. Sin autem una detur sagittae pars respondens, ex praecedente satis disces. Si vero sagitta tota, tunc 20 recte te instruet de sagittae parte verticali respondente;

15 qua habita considera rationem operis in 35. At si detur axis nostri coni, 25 te docebit de sagittae parte respondente quam dividas et tractes ut in praecedente admonuimus. Denique si tibi nota fuerit basis parabolae cum aliqua linea ordinis verticali, tunc ex 31 habebis sagittae partem verticalem datae lineae ordinis respondentem quam cum habueris et diviseris in partes aequales

20 pro arbitrio, auxilio lateris erecti, per singulas partes traduces ad rectos angulos lineas ordinis quarum finibus per lineam curvam apte coniunctis exibit quod exoptas, ut in 35 praecedente patuit.

23 *ante* detur *scr. et del. C aliquid quod non legere possum*
30 *ante* id *scr. et del. C* vel fiet (?)
31 tertium *correxi ex* tertiam
Fol. 291v
 1 . . . . . ^{1,2} *addidi eo quod hic textus interiit*
 2 . . . . . *addidi eo quod hic textus interiit*

37. Dato latere erecto, linearem sectionem parabolicam quae ad dati lateris [erecti] fines terminetur mechanice protrahere.

292r / . . . . . semper supputande quantitatem . . . . . partis verticalis ad tuam propositam divisionem . . . . . per quam lineam ordinis eris (?) traducturus . . . . . (quoniam?) 35 satis aperte monuisse videbatur, si exemus ostendas (?).

5 38. Quotcunque modis, data primum linea ordinis verticali, nosci possit sagittae pars verticalis respondens datae ordinis lineae totidem viis ac modis pervenire possumus ad descriptionem lineae contingentis ipsam sectionem linearem parabolicam ad alterutrum finem datae ordinis lineae.

Producatur enim semper sagittae pars verticalis versus ipsum verticem
10 parabolae ita ut pars extra sit aequalis ipsi sagittae parti verticali; quo facto coniunge alterutrum terminum datae lineae ordinis cum supremo extraductae fine, et linea sic ducta [erit] linea contingens desiderata.

39. Quibuscunque modis per praecedentem 38^{am} dat[a] fuerit linea contingens sectionem linearem parabolicam, lateris contingentis quantitatem
15 explicare quod datis sagittae parti et lineae ordinis respondet.

Accipe dimidium lineae ordinis verticalis ad cuius alterutrum finem linea contingens ipsam sectionem linearem parabolicam tangit; et illud dimidium quadrato. Deinde accipe duplum sagittae partis verticalis ipsi ordinis lineae verticali respondentis; illud duplum quadrato. Adde simul haec duo quadrata,
20 et producti radix quadrata exhibebit quantitatem lineae contingentis ab ipso contactus puncto usque ad concursum cum sagittae parte verticali protracta, ut in proxima praecedente patet [cf. Fig. Ap.II.9].

292v / [40. Cognita linea aliqua ordinis, et sagittae parte verticali cognitae lineae ordinis respondente], si in cognita linea ordinis accipiatur (?) aliquod punc[tum] cuius distantia ab ipso medio lineae ordinis detur, quantitatem lineae diametralis verticalis a dicto puncto erigendae ad ipsam sectionem
5 linearem parabolicam exprimere.

---

24 [erecti] *addidi*

Fol. 292r

1 . . . . .^{1,2} *addidi eo quod hic textus interiit*
2 . . . . . *addidi eo quod hic textus interiit*
3 . . . . . *addidi eo quod hic textus interiit*
9 *post* semper *scr. et del. C* inventa (?)
10 ita *corr. C ex* qui (?) / *ante* parti *scr. et del. C* vertica-
11 *ante* ordinis *scr. et del. C* ad
12 [erit] *addidi*
13 -[a] *addidi*
14–15 lateris . . . respondet *mg. scr. C, sed in textu scr. et del. C* eiusdem contingentis quantitatem [ex]plicare a loco contactus ad concursum cum (*supra scr.*) sagitta duplata
22 *ante* patet *scr. et del. C* descripsimus

Fol. 292v

1–2 [40. . . . respondente] *addidi eo quod hic textus interiit*
3 -[tum] *addidi*

Sit data linea ordinis *AB* [Fig. Ap.II.10] et sagittae pars verticalis respondens datae lineae ordinis *CD*. Si iam in *AB* accipiatur aliquod punctum ut *E*, et ab eodem puncto ad sectionem parabolicam erigatur linea diametralis verticalis *EF*, oportet iam ipsius *EF* quantitatem edocere. Per *F* imaginor lineam
10   parallelam protrahi ipsi *EC* quae erit lineae ordinis dimidium; quod dimidium notum erit quoniam est aequale ipsi *EC*, distantiae scilicet puncti accepti ab ipso medio lineae ordinis datae. Per 4 iam habebis *DO*, scilicet sagittae partem verticalem respondentem *FOR*. Nam unum est tantum latus erectum in una parabola. Quare cum per *AB* et *DC* illud latus notum fiat per 7^{am} non potest
15   fieri quin *DO* prodeat per 4^{am}. Subtrahas ergo *DO*, notam, ab ipsa *DC*, prius cognita, et remanebit *OC*, quae aequalis est *FE* lineae verticali diametrali, quod fecisse oportuit. Summa igitur operis haec est: "Quadrato ipsam distantiam *EC* vel similem quantumcunque, et illud quadratum divide per latus erectum, et numerum quotiens subtrahe ab ipsa *DC* data, et quod remanet
20   erit linea diametralis verticalis quaesita."

41.   Cognita linea aliqua ordinis verticali, et sagittae parte verticali cognitae ordinis lineae respondente, sumaturque ut in proxima praecedente punctum aliquod in linea ordinis dicta, cuius distantia vel ab alterutro fine vel a medio ipsius lineae ordinis cognoscatur, si iam ab ipso sic accepto puncto erigenda
293r   esset linea diametralis verticalis ad sectionem linearem parabolicam, / [quantitatem illius lineae diametralis exprimere].

Linea ordinis *AB* cognita [Fig. Ap.II.11] et sagittae verticalis pars respondens *CD* etiam nota sit; [da]ta etiam sit distantia puncti *E* vel ab *A* vel ab *B* vel
5   ab ipso medio puncto lineae ordinis, scilicet *C* (nam omnes hae distantiae se mutuo manifestas faciunt quacunque earum data cum tota *AB*). Iam per praecedentem eliciatur *DR*, et sit *FR* dupla ipsius *DR*; quare *FR* cognita est. Et *OR* etiam dimidium lineae ordinis respondentis ipsi *DR* notum est, quoniam est aequale ipsi *EC*. Ergo per 39 *FO* linea contingit sectionem para-
10   bolicam linearem ad punctum *O*. Producatur *FO* linea quousque concurrat cum *CA* linea, etiam sufficienter protracta. Ita enim habebimus duos triangulos *FRO* et *FCP* aequiangulos; unde ut *FR* ad *RO* sic *FC* ad *CP*. Sed *FR*, *RO*, et *FC* (?) cognita sunt; quare et *OP* (! *CP*). At *EC* prius erat data; quare et *EP* modo innotescet. Et (?) iam considero duo alios triangulos *OPE* et *FPC*
15   aequiangulos. Quare ut *PC* ad *CF* sic *PE* ad *EO*. Ante novimus *PC*, *CF*, et *PE*; quare nunc habemus *EO* lineam diametralem verticalem quaesitam. Ratio operis haec erit: "Quadrato distantiam puncti dati a medio lineae ordinis; divide illud quadratum per latus erectum, et quotientem duplato. Serva illud duplum pro primo numero. Quotientem dictum adde sagittae
20   parti verticali quae primo cognitae lineae ordinis respondet; erit ille numerus

---

6 *mg. sin. scr. et del. C.* . . . . quadrato (*sive* quadratum) AC et a qu[adrato] AC
    subtrahe quadratum ipsius EC (?) et res- (?) per latus erectum, et prodibit CE (?)
Fol. 293r
   1–2 [quantitatem . . . exprimere] *addidi eo quod hic textus interiit*
    4 [da]- *addidi*
   20 *post* ille *scr. et del. C secundus*

tertius; atque secundus erit distantia illa puncti accepti. Operare iam per regulam trium, et quartum elicito numerum; ab hoc quarto etiam distantiam puncti subtrahe. Residuum illud serva pro tertio numero novae operationis. Primus numerus in secunda operatione sit ille qui quartus eliciebatur in
25   prima operatione, et secundus sit ille qui tertius in prima operatione erat. Iam operare pro novo quarto numero iuxta regulam trium, et fies voti compos."

293v   / [42. Data linea ordinis, et sagittae parte verticali datae lineae ordinis] respondente, super partem sagittae (?) verticalem lineas (quot velis) ordinis protrahere quarum nulla praescribatur maior quam ipsa linea ordinis primo data.

5   Haec persimilis est 35 et 36, tamen aliquo modo differe videbitur propius consideranti. Sit data linea ordinis *AB* [Fig. Ap.II.12] et sagittae pars respondens *CD*. Si iam in *AB* resecetur linea quantacunque libet cuius dimidium semper statuatur in *C* puncto, statim determinabimus locum eius in sagitta ut fiat linea ordinis. Sit *EF* linea cui aequalem lineam ordinis super *CD*
10   statueremus. Sit dimidium ipsius *EF* linea *CE*. Quadrato *CE* et divide illud quadratum per latus erectum, nam quotiens tibi exhibebis sagittae partem verticalem cui data linea *EF* erit linea ordinis verticalis respondens. Similis est etiam haec propositio ipsi 4^{ae}. Tamen hanc, subeuntem manus quodam simplici contextu, nolui pretermittere. Nam ex hac quis possit alias aliis
15   ennunciatas verbis ad nostras eiusdem propositi reducere. Praeterea volupe erit per hanc lineas ordinis collocare quantas cupis et linea non fiat aequalis distributi ipsius sagittae partis verticalis, ut in 35 et 36 constituimus (?).

43. Alio adhuc modo lineae diametralis verticalis quantitatem exprimere quae a dato puncto lineae ordinis datae ad ipsam parabolicam sectionem
20   erigitur: modo una detur sagittae verticalis pars quae datae lineae ordinis respondet, et etiam distantia dati puncti a medio ipsius lineae ordinis, ut in 40 et 41 supposuimus prius.

Hanc viam ego primam et primus omnium (quod sciam) in opus deduxi ut et praecedentes 40^{am} et 41^{am} excogitavi dum (?) ista[s] describerem. Hanc
25   ego pluris facio quod ex ista plures aliae et utiles pendere videbuntur ut ex ipsarum operationibus apparebit. Ex quinta Archimedis de quadratura parabolae:

294r   / "[Esto portio contenta a linea recta et] coni rectanguli sectione *A*[*BC* et] ducatur a puncto *A* linea *AF* aequidistans diametro [Fig. Ap.II.13]. A puncto

Fol. 293v
    1 [42. . . . . ordinis] *addidi eo quod hic textus interiit*
    3 *post* nulla *scr. et del. C* alteri aequalis / maior . . . ipsa *ex corr. C*
    5 et 36 *supra scr. C*
    17 *post* 36 *scr. et del. C* proposuimus
    23 (quod sciam) *supra scr. C*
    24 *post* 41^{am} *scr. et del. C* inveni / -[s] *addidi*
Fol. 294r
    1 [Esto . . . et] *addidi ex Quadr. parab. Archimedis, Prop. 5, in transl. Jacobi Cremonensis, eo quod hic textus interiit; mg. hab. C* [ex quinta Archime]dis de [quadratura] parabolae / -[BC et] *restauravi ex Quad. parab. ut supra*

[*C*] ducatur contingens sectionem coni concurrens cum *AF* in puncto *F*. Si iam ducatur aliqua in triangulo *FAC* quae sit aequidistans ipsi *AF*, ipsa ducta
5 secundum eandem proportionem a sectione rectanguli coni secabitur, et ipsa *AC* ab ipsa producta, similis vero rationis erit pars lineae *AC* versus *A* cum parte lineae ductae quae est versus *AC* lineam."
Erit ergo ut *AK* ad *KC* ita *KH* ad *HL*.

Nostrum πορισμα

10 [1.] Ergo coniunctim ut *AC* ad *AK* ita *KL* ad *KH*.
AC nota supponitur in nostra hac 43, et *DK* etiam datur (*K* enim supponitur esse illud punctum in linea ordinis acceptum); quare et *AK*, ut autem habeas *KL*. Considerato duos triangulos *KLC* et *EDC* aequiangulos. Unde ut *CD* ad *DE* ita *CK* ad *KL*; *CD* autem est dimidia lineae ordinis datae, et *DE*
15 (dupla sagittae partis verticalis, scilicet *DB*, ut in 39 vidisti); quare non plus (?) *KL* latere. Huiusmodi ergo semper concipe triangulum circa quamcunque datam parabolae portionem, et per has regulas invenies *HK* et quamcunque aliam diametralem verticalem ad *AC* ductam:
"Multiplica puncti accepti (ut est *K* in exemplo) distantiam a puncto
20 contactus (scilicet *C*) per duplum sagittae partis verticalis datae, et productum divide per dimidium datae lineae ordinis. Quotiens enim erit tota quaedam linea sagittae parallela et ad acceptum punctum cadens sectionemque linearem
294v parabolicam transiens. Ad eliciendum / . . . . . pendet."
2. Ergo permutatim ut *AC* ad *KL* sic *AK* ad *KH*. Primo modo:
"Subtrahe distantiam puncti accepti ex tota linea ordinis data. Residuum multiplica per quantitatem lineae ex praecedente regula inventae (ut in ex-
5 emplo erat *KL*), et productum divide per totam lineam ordinis datam, et quotiens erit linea diametralis verticalis ad acceptum punctum erigenda quam invenire desiderabamus."
Secundo modo: "Multiplico totam lineam prius inventam per residuum lineae ordinis datae (deducta scilicet distantia puncti accepti ex tota linea

---

3 [*C*] *addidi ex Quadr. parab. ut supra / post* cum *scr. et del.* C puncto
6 similis *C* proportionaliter eiusdem *Quadr. parab. ut supra*
6–7 cum parte *C* cuius pars *Quadr. parab. ut supra*
7 quae est *C, om. Quadr. parab. ut supra*
8 *mg. hab.* C AK   KC   KH   HL *et post* HL *in textu scr. et del.* C Ergo permutatim etiam
9 πορισμα *sine accentu scr.* C
13 ut *mg. scr.* C
15 plus (?) *correxi ex* p̄t̄ (=potest)
16 concipe *supra scr.* C, *sed in textu scr. et del.* C supposita
17 has *corr.* C *ex* hanc
18 *post* ductam *mg. hab.* C 3   12   6, 3   12   4, 3   8   4
Fol. 294v
1 . . . . . *addidi eo quod hic textus interiit*
2 *post* KH *scr. et del.* C vel ex ipsa Archimedis propositione cum nostra hypothesi in propositione hac praemittenda
9 *mg. hab.* C⎯ EB   EH   GH (*sive* KH)

10 ordinis data, ut in primo modo fecisti), et productum divide per lineam
ordinis totam. Nam quotiens exhibebit lineam diametralem quaesitam." Opus
istud pene idem est cum primo nisi quod in primo modo residuum illud ex
tota linea ordinis erat secundus numerus in regula trium et hic est tertius,
ut statim tibi ex ipsorum porismatum verbis apparere potest.

295r / [44. Lineam diametralem verticalem erigendam a puncto dato lineae
ordinis] invenire, proposita quacun[que linea] ordinis verticali et parte
sagi[ttae] verticali cognita in numeris vel non.

Sit proposita linea ordinis *AB* 60 unciarum [Fig. Ap.II.14]. Sit sagittae
5 verticalis pars *CD* 6 unciarum. Iam construatur triangulus rectangulus Archimedis, de qua (!) diximus in praecedente, ex linea scilicet contingente
sectionem linearem parabolicam ad unum finem nostrae datae lineae ordinis,
quae sit hypothenusa; linea ordinis sit unum laterum angulum rectum trianguli
continentium; reliquum ab altero fine lineae ordinis ad rectos erigatur angulos
10 e[t] cum dicta contingente concurrat. Talis statim fiet triangulus si producas
sagittae partem da[tam] quousque sui dupla fiat (ut in 39 explicatum est),
et ab altero fine lineae ordinis per summitatem istius duplae lineae rectam
satis trahas, et postremo ab altero fine lineae ordinis erigas perpendicularem
ad concursum cum illa hypothenusa, ut animadvertere potes in triangulo
15 *ABF*, ut (?) hanc rationem descripsi. A quo iam libet puncto in ipsa *AB*
trahas lineam ad *FB* hypothenusam et parallelam ipsi *AF* et *GH* sit illa; et
ab eodem puncto *H* trahas lineam ad *AF* parallelam ipsi *FB*, et sit *HR*. Si

10 *mg. hab. C* AE GH EH
13 *mg. hab. C* ⏜ B AE EG EH
14 *post* potest *scr. et del. C* Tertius autem modus est iste. Divide distantiam puncti per
residuum lineae ordinis quando ipsa distantia maior est quam dimidium lineae ordinis,
sive ipsum residuum per distantiam quando minor est dimidio lineae ordinis datae.
Quotiens (si fractiones habet annexas) reduc ad minimos terminos *et mg. inferius
hab. C* Triangulus artificii (*!* Archimedis) est (*del., et supra scr.* dicemus triangulum)
rectangulus quem (*del. C*) cuius basis est linea ordinis (*et postea scr. et del. C:* hypothenusa vero latus _____ linea [latus, *supra*] contingens (?) quod respondet ab
altero fine ordinis eiusdem. . . . . [*hic sunt plura verba quae non legere possum*]
versus easdem partes). . . . . (*plura verba quae non legere possum*) erigatur (*del. C,
et supra scr.* extenditur.) perpendicularis . . . altero latere contingente quod respondet
product̄ (*?, del. ?*) in directum producto concurrat. Triangulum artificii _____ (?)
ex (*del.*) ab his tribus continere (?) lineis, ordinis scilicet linea, perpendiculari, et latere
(?) contingente productum (?)

Fol. 295r
1–2 [44. . . . . ordinis] *addidi eo quod hic textus interiit*
2 -[que linea] *addidi*
3 -[ttae] *addidi*
4 *post* Sit² *scr. et del. C* lineae ver-
5 rectangulus *supra. scr. C*
7 *post* ordinis *scr. et del. C* aliquid quod non legere possum
9 *ante* reliquum *scr. et del. C* req-
10 -[t] *addidi*
11 -[tam] *addidi*
15 quo *corr. C ex* quae (?)
16 et² . . . illa *mg. scr. C*
17 *post* FB *scr. et del. C* Si iam / *ante* HR *scr. et del. C* GK (?)

iam ab ipso *R* puncto ad alterum finem lineae ordinis rectam duxeris, haec
secabit *GH* ita quod pars versus *H* erit nostra quaesita linea diametralis
20   verticalis, scilicet *OH*. Et hanc pulcherrimam esse viam mechanicam existimo
et facillimam, nullis enim hic numerorum operationibus egemus.

Demonstratio huius

Sunt duo trianguli aequianguli *ARB* et *HOB*; erit ergo ut *AH* ad *HB*, *RO*
ad *OB*. Sunt alii duo trianguli aequianguli *ROH* et *GOB*. Quare erit ut *RO*
25   ad *OH* sic *OB* ad *OG*; quare permutatim ut *RO* ad *OB* sic *OH* ad *OG*. Sed
RO ad *OB* erat ut *AH* ad *HB*. Ergo *OH* ad *OG* est ut *AH* ad *HB*. Ergo
punctum *O* est in sectione lineari parabolica per ea quae ostendimus in 43.
295v   / [45. Data linea ordinis verticali,] data etiam sagittae parte verticali respondente, sectionem linearem parabolicam ad datae ordinis lineae fines
terminantem describere per lineas diametrales.

Dividas lineam ordinis datam in quam multas apte possis partes aequales.
5   Deinde pro dimidio illarum partium lineas disce diametrales verticales per
quem velis modorum in 40, 41, 43, et 44 explicatorum, et singulas suis locis
statuas, semper duas eiusdem longitudinis collocavi aequali a medio distantia.
Postremo coniunge per lineam curvam omnes fines dictarum linearum et
prodire videbis sectionem parabolicam linearem quam cupis. Potes ergo per
10   40, 41, et 43 tabulas quasdam componere numerales, ubi primo supponatur
longitudo lineae ordinis quantacunque velis et etiam sagittae pars verticalis,
quantam tibi libebit modo ne excedas quartam partem ipsius lineae ordinis.
Nam sufficiet ad naturae operationes contemplandas si ipsum latus erectum
nunquam intra suum speculum recipias. Et si facias magna specula (qualia
15   sola tibi exe[m]plamus), non potes ad latus erectum usque convexitatem
columnare in uno saltem speculo.

Sit exempli gratia linea ordinis sesquipedalis [Fig. Ap.II.15] et sagittae
verticalis pars respondens ⅓ unius pedis. Distribue iam lineam ordinis in
uncias, 18 scilicet, et quamque unciam in 6 vel 8 partes. Similiter et sagittae
20   partem datam distribuas in similes portiones, et compleas rectangulum parallelogrammum, ex linea ordinis et sagittae parte factum lineis parallelis per
singulas partes tum ipsius lineae ordinis tum sagittae ductis, ut in proposita
figura videre potes, ubi qualium partium trium (*!* quatuor) est *CD*, talium
296r   est *AB* 18. Disce iam lineas diametrales verticales ab / . . . . . [d]uplex tibi
conficienda tabula [ubi] ordinis linearum prima erit et secunda diametralium

18 R *corr. C ex* KH
19 *post* quod *scr. et del. C* sectiones ver-
25 *post* Sed *scr. et del. C* p (?)
Fol. 295v
1 [45. . . . . verticali,] *addidi eo quod hic textus interiit*
13 *post* si *scr. et del. C* semper ad
15 -[m]- *addidi*
Fol. 296r
1 . . . . . [d]- *addidi eo quod hic textus interiit*
2 [ubi] *addidi eo quod hic textus interiit*

respon[dentium], quales nos tibi supputavimus duas. Suppone[mus] unciam unamquamque divisam in 8 partes, longitudinem autem lineae ordinis as-
5 sumpsimus 18 unciarum et sagittae partem 3 (*! 4*) unciarum. Unde distributis unciis in suas octavas, longitudo ipsius lineae ordinis totius erit 144 (at nos tantum pro dimidio, scilicet 72, opus habemus tabulas supputare; semper deinde transferemus lineam inventam etiam in alium locum lineae ordinis tantum a sagitta distantem quantum inventa nostra distat ab eadem sagitta),
10 et sagittam ergo habebi[mus] in hac nostra parabola 32 octavarum partium unius unciae. Comburet ergo hoc speculum ad 5 uncias ab ipso vertice parabolae et preterea $\frac{1}{16}$ unius unciae. Ad quot usus hac una tabula inserviet mox per aliquot a nobis inventas propositiones edocebimus.

0	64	0	25	50
1	63		26	51
2	63		27	52
3	62		28	53
4	62		29	54
5	61		30	55
6	61		31	56
7	60		32	57
8	60		33	58
9	60	0	34	59
10	59		35	60
11	59		36	61
12	58		37	62
13	58		38	63
14	57		39	64
15	57		40	65
16	56		41	66
17	56		42	67
18	56	0	43	68
19	55		44	69
20	55		45	70
21	54		46	71
22	54		47	72
23	53		48	0
24	53		49	0

296v / [46.] . . . . . parabolis.

Quas enim nos uncias supposuimus si tu vel palmos vel pedes existimaveris, eadem erit numerorum ratio in talibus partibus quales accipis pro tuo opere. Et contra quae nos uncias si tu grana tociens (?) aequae erunt tibi usui hae
5 nostrae tabulae.

3 -[dentium] *addidi* / -[mus] *addidi*
10 -[mus] *addidi*
Fol. 296v
1 [46.]. . . . . *addidi eo quod hic textus interiit*

47. Eadem tabula etiam quantarumcunque descripseris parabolarum portiones, exhibebit adhuc earundem portionum frusta minora si cupias.

Si enim commutaveris nostras uncias in palmos, et cuperes habere frustum
cuique sagittae partem tantum esse 3 palmorum velles, combustionis dis
10   tantiam et latus erectum nostrarum tabularum a latere ipsarum tabularum
posuimus ut semper ad manus esse paratas possint. Elice lineam ordinis
respondentem tuis tribus palmis per 3[am] huius. Dimidia lineam ordinis inventam et illud dimidium subtrahe [a] alio dimidio lineae ordinis tabularum,
scilicet a maximo numero lineae nostrae ordinis in tabula positae. Et residui
15   quaere lineam diametralem in nostra tabula; illam lineam diametralem pone
seorsim ut eandem subtrahas ab omnibus sequentibus, et prodibunt tibi
novae lineae diametrales in tua nuper inventa linea ordinis collocandae, ubi
collocari debent nisi prorsus hebes sis non potes ignorare. Et si linea subtrahenda non inveniatur in tabulis, nosti tamen quanta interstitio in ipsa
20   linea ordinis ab ista diametrali linea prima linea tuae tabulae quae proposito
inservire potest distet, quod satis est et intellige bene quod dico.

48. Eadem manente linea ordinis, si mutetur sagittae pars verticalis respondens cuius maior fuerit sagittae pars verticalis, eiusdem minor erit com
297r   bustionis distantia, et eius / [latus erectum etiam minus erit] . . . . . Deo
maximus et . . . . . qui mundi huius principatum tenet. Deo . . . . . _____
nimus. At qui missus mundo, id est mundo mortuus; cum Deo regnat cui
honor et gloria.

5   49. Quae erit proportio inter duas diversas sagittae partes verticales quae
uni lineae ordinis respondet (at in duabus diversis parabolis) eadem erit in
combustionum distantiis at reciproco modo relationis [cf. Fig. Ap.II.16].

Si ergo quacunque alia praeter nostram tabularem sagittae partem data,
cuperes noscere si nostra subtenderetur linea ordinis quan[ta] esset com
10   bustionis distantia in illa alterius sagittae terminis (?): "multiplica semper

6 quantarumcunque *ex corr.* C
8 palmos *bis* C *et del.* C *primum*
9 *post* palmorum *scr. et del.* C aeque
15 *post* pone *scr. et del.* C a puncto (?)
16 *post* ut *scr. et del.* C illam
18 *post* linea *scr. et del.* C ordinis
Fol. 297r
1–4 *mg. hab.* C

| 1 | 1 | 1 | 1 |
| 5 | 50 | 8 | 31¼ |

A   D   B   C
reciprocus modus
referendi
1 [latus . . . erit] *et.* . . . . . *addidi eo quod hic textus interiit*
2 . . . . . [1,2] *addidi eo quod hic textus interiit*
9 -[ta] *addidi*

nostram sagittam per suam combustionem; productum divide per sagittam externam _____, quotiens enim dabit combustionem illius alterius parabolae cum illa sagitta sive adferatur maior sagitta quam nostra est sive minor."

Eius rei demonstratio pendet ex hac propositione: Si duo diversi numeri
15 unum dividant, quae est proportio dividentium eadem erit et exeuntium. Duo diversi numeri sunt diversae nostrae sagittae, idem numerus est quadratum dimidii lineae ordinis, exeuntes sunt ipsa latera erecta quae erunt in proportione ea quae diximus. At obiiciet quis: De combustione hic fit sermo et non de lateribus erectis. Verum cum combustionis distantia est quarta sui
20 lateris erecti, apparet quod et combustionum eadem erit proportio quae laterum erectorum. Nam ut totum ad totum ita dimidium ad dimidium et quarta ad quartam alterius. Patet ergo demonstratio. Et haec ultima pars demonstrationis pendet ex vigore huius propositionis: Si unus numerus duos dividat, erit exeuntium ea proportio quae ipsorum dividendorum. Duo diversi
25 numeri sunt duo diversa latera erecta quae dividimus per 4 (ut apparet in _____); erunt ergo exeuntes quartae in eadem proportione cum ipsis lateribus erectis.

297v / [50. Eadem manente sagittae parte, si mutetur linea ordinis] verticalis respond[ens], maior erit combustionis distantia in illa cuius linea ordinis maior, et ea erit proportio inter combustionis distantias quae est inter quadrata quae fiunt ex dimidiis linearum ordinis datarum.

5 Ut habeatur ergo distantia combustionis in quacunque alia linea ordinis praeter nostram tabularem vel inter duas quascunque alias, accipe quadrata dimidiorum linearum ordinis datarum, et propone combustionem tibi notam, et pone ad regulam trium hoc modo [cf. Fig. Ap.II.17].

Demonstratio huius 50^e

10 Quia unus numerus duos dividit, erit exeuntium eadem proportio quae dividendorum. Duo diversi numeri sunt quadrata quae fiunt ex dimidiis linearum ordinis datarum. Unus numerus est eadem sagittae pars verticalis

11 *post* per^2 *scr. et del. C aliquid quod non legere possum*
12 *post* externam *forte hab. C* hae (?)
13 *post* illa *scr. et del. C* externa / *post* sagitta *scr. et del. C* quam nostra tabularis est
15 *mg. hab. C* Demonstratio
19 *post* erectis *scr. et del. C* quare / *post* cum *hab. C* per *sed delendum est*
21–22 Nam . . . alterius *forte del. C*
23 *post* vigore *scr. et del. C* primi
25–26 *post* in *lac. hab. C*
Fol. 297v
1 [50. . . . ordinis] *addidi eo quod hic textus interiit* / verticalis *correxi ex* verticales
2 -[ens] *addidi*
7 *post* notam *scr. et del. C* multiplica quadratum combustionis

quae utrisque respondet; quare clarum est quod latera erecta sunt in proportione quadratorum dictorum si latera erecta et combustionis distantiae
15   ut in praecedente docuimus.

51. Si, eadem manente linea ordinis, sagitta alia dupla prioris assumatur,
erit omnium linearum diametralium in parabola duplae sagittae proportio
dupla ad diametrales alterius, illas quidem quae aequali cum prioribus distantia
298r   / [a sagitta sunt].

. . . . . sagitta . . . . . quod quaecunque linea diametralis ca[det a] sectione lineari parabolica *ACB* [Fig. Ap.II.18] ad lineam ordinis *AB* dupla erit
lineae ordinis (*!* diametralis) qu[ae] ad idem punctum lineae ordinis *AB* cadet
5   a sectione lineari parabolica *AEB*. Describatur nobis triangulus Archimedis,
et sit in illo triangulo una linea ipsi *AK* aequidistanter ducta ab ipsa contingente
ad lineam ordinis, et sit *LM* secans *ACB* in *R* puncto et *AEB* in *O* puncto.
Dico *RM* ad *OM* esse duplam. Per 43 nostram apparet esse ut *AM* ad *MB*
sic *MR* ad *RL* pro parabolae portione *ACB*, et similiter *MO* ad *OS* pro
10   parabolica portione *AEB*; ut ergo *MR* ad *RL* sic *MO* ad *OS*, et vicissim
igitur ut *LR* ad *RM* sic *SO* ad *OM*. Ergo coniunctim ut *LM* ad *RM* sic *SM*
ad *OM*. Ergo permutatim ut *LM* ad *SM* sic *RM* ad *OM*. At *LM* dupla est
ipsius *SM*, nam ipsa *XD* est dupla ipsius *CD* (*KXB* enim est contingens *ACB*
ad *B* punctum). Sunt duo trianguli aequianguli *XCB* et *LSB*. Sunt etiam
15   duo alii *CDB* et *SMB*; quare ut *BX* ad *XC* sic *BL* ad *LS*. Ergo ut *BX* ad *BL*
sic *XC* ad *LS*; eadem ratione erit ut *BC* ad *CD* sic *BS* ad *SM*. Ergo permutatim
ut *BC* ad *BS* sic *CD* ad *SM*. Sed *BC* ad *CS* (*!* *BS*) est ut *BX* ad *BL*, nam
sunt ut *BD* ad *BM*; ergo ut *XC* ad *LS* sic *CD* ad *SM*. Ergo permutatim ut
XC ad *CD* sic *LS* ad *SM*. Verum *XC* facta erat aequalis ipsi *CD*. Ergo *LS*
20   est aequalis ipsi *SM*; quare tota *LM* dupla est ipsius *SM*, quod est propositum.

16 *post* prioris *scr. et del. C* sagitta respondens

Fol. 298r

1 [a . . . sunt] *addidi eo quod hic textus interiit*
2 . . . . .^1,2 *addidi eo quod hic textus interiit* / -[det a] *addidi*
2-20 *de istis lineis mg. scr. C* Demonstratio
4 -[ae] *addidi*
8 *post* OM *scr. et del. C* este (*?*)
8-10 *mg. hab. C*   AM   MB   MR   RL
                                MO   OS
                      MR   RL   MO   OS (*sed cf. var. lin. 10*)
10 vicissim *corr. C ex* permutatim
11 ut^1 *bis C et del. C primum*
12 *mg. hab. C* lemma
13 *post* contingens *scr. et del. C* aliquid quod non legere possum / *mg. hab. C*
    CD   SM   BX   BL
    XC   LS
16 *post* ratione *scr. et del. C* ut
17-18 nam . . . BM *mg. scr. C*
20 quare . . . SM *mg. scr. C*

πορισμα

Tabularum nostrarum hinc alius patet usus ad varias conficiendas parabo[las] / . . . . . subduplae . . . . . ____ tuplae et ceterae sagitta ad nostram tabularem sagittam, modo eadem asservetur linea ordinis.

Si ergo pro linea ordinis nostrae aequali vel[les] cum dupla sagitta parabolae portionem linearem describere, dupla singulos nostros numeros in tabula diametralium linearum positos et tibi usui erunt ex tuo voto; sic per 4 si cum quadrupla sagitta, et cetera. Similiter, si, cum alia sagitta cuius nostra dupla est, velles cum nostra linea ordinis parabolicam portionem protrahere, divide singulos nostros numeros per 2 et habebis quod cupis. Similiter per 4 dividas si nostram illius externae et novae sagittae facias quadruplam.

πορισμα

Per porisma ergo praecedens et $48^{am}(?)$ et 47^{am} propositionem quam multiplex (?) erit nostrarum tabularum usus.

Hoc volui in tuam memoriam redigere, non diffidens ingenio tuo quo vel ipse hoc consectarum (! consecturum) quam primum intellexisses.

52. "Si super eandem lineam ordinis vel super duas aequales duae parabolicae portiones constituantur inaequalium sagittarum, quaecunque erit illarum inaequalium sagittarum proportio eadem erit et similiter collocatarum linearum diametralium inter se in duabus istis parabolicis portionibus."

Cum hanc inveneram propositionem et demonstraveram, magno pertusus eram gaudio: eoque / . . . . . praecede[nte] [de]monstratione, excepto quod maior [sa]gitta sit exempli gratia ad minorem dupla sesquitertia. Procedamus ergo et hic videbis eandem demonstrationem quam in praecedente; non potest ergo esse difficilis.

Sit *CD* dupla sesquitertia ad *ED* [Fig. Ap.II.19]. Reliqua constructio patet ex antecedentibus. Dico quod *RM* ad *OM* habet proportionem duplam sesquitertiam. Primum apparet *XD* ad *GD* habere proportionem duplam sesquitertiam, nam *XD* dupla est ipsius *CD*, et *GD* dupla supponitur ipsius *ED*. Sed *CD* ad *ED* est dupla sesquitertia; ergo earundem dupla sunt in eadem

---

21 πορισμα *sine accentu scr.* C

23 -[las] *addidi*

Fol. 298v

1 . . . . . .^{1,2} *addidi eo quod hic textus interiit*

10 πορισμα *sine accentu scr.* C

14 *ante* quam *scr. et del.* C *aliquid quod non legere possum*

Fol. 299r

1 . . . . . *addidi eo quod hic textus interiit* / -[nte] *et* [de]- *addidi* / *post* quod *scr. et del.* C sunt

2 [sa]- *addidi*

3 *mg. scr.* C Demonstratio

10   proportione. Sed ut *XD* ad *GD* sic *LM* ad *SM*, nam ut *BX* ad *XD* sic *BL*
ad *LM*. Ergo permutatim ut *BX* ad *BL* sic *XD* ad *LM*. Sed ut *BX* ad *BL* sic
BD ad *BM*, et ut *BD* ad *BM* sic *GD* ad *SM* (in duobus triangulis *DGB* et
SMB aequiangulis). Ergo ut *BX* ad *BL* sic *GD* ad *SM*, ergo et ut *XD* ad *LM*.
Cum ergo sit ut *XD* ad *LM* sic *GD* ad *SM*, ergo permutatim ut *XD* ad *GD*
15   sic *LM* ad *SM*, quod probasse oportuit. Dico denique *RM* ad *OM* esse ut
LM ad *SM*. Hoc sepius supra ostendimus. Verum denuo aperiamus veritatem.
Ut *MB* ad *MA* sic *LR* ad *RM* et ut eadem *MB* ad *MA* sic *SO* ad *OM*, ut
patuit in 43. Ergo ut *LR* ad *RM* sic *SO* ad *OM*. Ergo coniunctim ut *LM* ad
RM sic *SM* ad *OM*. Ergo permutatim ut *LM* ad *SM* sic *RM* ad *OM*, quod
20   demonstrasse praecipue oportuit. *LM* ad *SM* erat ut *XD* ad *GD*, et *XD* ad
299v   / . . . . . Idem de quacunque alia proportione demonstrare potes et de lineis
diametralibus atque (?) omnibus modo accipiantur in aequalibus distantiis
a suis sagittis.

πόρισμα

5   Per regulam ergo trium possis nostram tabulam ad quamcunque aliam
sagittae partem verticalem applicare, servata semper nostra linea ordinis datae
sagittae respondente.
Dic ergo: nostra sagitta praebet istam externam sagittam quam lineam
diametralem dabit haec nostra, et videbis quam quaeris lineae longitudinem.

10   Admonitio de alia praxi cum tabula nostra.

Si forte nolis tuam lineam ordinis distribuere in tot partes quot nos in hac
apposita tabula designavimus ut maximis inserviet negociis, vel non possis
si velles tot sensibiles partes imprimere tuae propositae lineae hoc utaris
consilio. Vide columnam a latere quam insignavimus titulo hoc COLUMNA
15   ELECTIONIS ubi statim in principio proponitur numerus partium dimidiae
lineae ordinis, cuius longitudinem si distribuas in 6000 accipe singulos or-
dinatim in ipsa tabula. Sic in _____ accipe pro tua prima et brevissima
reverte   lineam tabulae dum descendis in tua columna e regione tuae columnae, et
ad   hic pro secunda tua / . . . . . ad sagittam tabulae vel ad tuam . . . . . si
288r   [tabu]la nostra formaveris proportionaliter scilicet (?) si tua linea ordinis

        13 ut¹ *ex corr. C*
        17 *post* OM *scr. et del. C* Ergo
Fol. 299v
           1 . . . . . *addidi eo quod hic textus interiit*
           4 πόρισμα *hic solum cum accentu scr. C*
           9 quaeris *corr. C ex* quaerite (?)
          17 tabula *ex corr. C / post* in *lac. hab. C*
Fol. 288r
           1 . . . . . ¹,² *addidi eo quod hic textus interiit*
           2 [tabu]- *addidi /* si *bis C et del. primum*

fuerit ad sagittam tuam duodecupla vel si dimidia lineae ordinis tuae sit ad tuam [sagittam] sextupla, quod idem est.

5   Tabula linearum diametralium ubi linea ordinis verticalis supponitur 12000, dimidia autem 6000, et sagittae pars verticalis 1000.

Columna Electionis

				0	0	
						1
1					2	
	1				3	
2		1			4	
					5	
3	2		1		6	
					7	
4		2			8	
	3				9	
5					10	
					11	
6	4	3	2	12	000	
6	4	3	2			

Exempli gratia (left margin label)

per 40^{am} fa[cta] → per 40^{am} fa[cta]

TABUL[A]E

LOCUS

Deinde per regulam trium transforma tabulae numerum ad tuam distributionem, data enim est linea in nova denominatione. Ergo per modum trianguli rectanguli _____ (*?*) numerum et cetera.

10   53. Quantitatem anguli incidentiae solaris per tabulas sinuum elicere; modo dentur linea ordinis et sagittae pars verticalis respondentes eidem angulo.

---

    4 [sagittam] *addidi*

10–11 Quantitatem . . . angulo *mg. scr. C post* brevius sic; *sed in textu scr. et del. C:* Si ad finem cuiuscunque cognitae lineae ordinis (cognita etiam sagittae parte verticali, cognitae seu datae lineae ordinis respondente) linea incidentiae solaris cadat, eius anguli quantitatem quem linea contingens sectionem parabolicam ad idem punctum, ad quod lineae incidentiae cadit cum eadem (*scr. et del. prius C*) ipsa linea incidentiae facit per tabulas sinuum notam efficere

288v   /. . . . . Deinde . . . . . pri _____ tum (?) lineam nostram contingentiae
constituas primum. Secundum autem ipsum dimidium datae lineae ordinis.
Tertium denique sinum totum illarum tabularum quibus in hoc negocio
uteris, et cum multiplicaveris tertium per secundum productumque diviseris
5   per primum, exeuntem quotientis numerum quaere in eisdem tabulis ex
quibus tuum sinum totum desumpsit, nam ex regione illius sinus recti invenies
angulum quaesitum. Hoc autem sic demonstrabimus.

Sit data linea ordinis *AB* [Fig. Ap.II.20] et sagitta data *CD*. Dupla autem
CD, sit *DE*, et contingens erit (per 38) *AE*, cuius quantitatem per 39[am]
10   elicuisti et opus nostrum exhibuit angulum *AED*, quem, aio, aequalem esse
angulo quaesito. Nam sit linea incidentiae solaris *KA* et producatur *EA* linea
contingens ultra *A* ad *Q* vel ulterius, quaestio erat de ipso *KAQ* angulo
incidentiae, et dixi *AED* aequalem esse huic angulo quaesito, quod patet
quoniam linea incidentiae solaris et sagitta duplata sunt parallelae (!) per
15   definitionem lineae incidentiae solaris et in illas incidit recta, scilicet linea
QAE. Ergo angulus *QAK* aequalis est angulo *AED*, quod demonstrasse
adverte   oportuit.
ad
300r   54. Si ad superiorem terminum alicuius lineae diametralis verticalis datae
ducatur linea ipsam sectionem parabolicam contingens, quantitatem / [anguli
qui illa linea contingentiae cum linea diametrali data facit] exquaerere per
sinuum tabulam; modo etiam cognoscantur prius haec tua linea ordinis a
qua illa diametralis erigitur ad ipsam sectionem parabolicam et eiusdem
5   diametralis distantia a sagittae parte verticali quae illi cognitae lineae ordinis
respondet, ac tertio in loco ipsa sagittae pars verticalis respondens dictae
ordinis lineae etiam sciatur.

Subtrahe datam lineam diametralem a sagittae parte verticali quae illi
lineae ordinis respondet super quam ipsa diametralis erigitur [cf. Fig. Ap.II.21].
10   Residuum duplato; duplum illud quadrato. Deinde quadrato distantiam datae
diametralis ab sagitta. Haec duo quadrata coniunge. Eius producti radicem
quadratam extrahe. Hanc radicem constituas primum numerum in regula
trium; secundum autem facies ipsam distantiam a sagitta; tertium denique

---

Fol. 288v

1 . . . . .[1,2] *addidi eo quod hic textus interiit* / pri——tum: primentum (?) C
6 *post* nam *scr. et del.* C e
10 *post* AED *scr. et del.* C At m
12 *ante* ultra *scr. et del.* C versus / *post* A *scr. et del.* C de angulis (?)
18–19 54. . . . quantitatem *scr. et del.* C; *hic retineo in textu* (*cf. var. infra*, 300r, *lin.* 2–7)
18 datae *supra scr.* C

Fol. 300r

1–2 [anguli . . . facit] *addidi eo quod hic textus interiit*
2–7 exquaerere . . . sciatur *scr. et del. in textu; hic retineo in textu eo quod textus correctus*
in mg. est incompletus. . . . . diametralis verticalis [et] cognita distantia ab ipsa sagitta
verticali data removeatur et anguli incidentiae solaris datae lineae diametrali respondentis invenire
3 etiam *supra scr.* C / haec tua *supra scr.* C
10 *post* illud *scr. et del.* C servas

sinum totum tabularum quibus uti volueris, nam si quartum inventum nu-
15 merum in eisdem tabulis debite inquiras, invenies illi respondere angulum
numero quaesitum. Nos autem ut liberaremus alios molestis magnis, supputavimus angulos omnesquae singulis nostrarum tabularum lineis diametralibus verticalibus respondente. Haec parum a praecedente differt eo quod
linea diametralis videtur esse quaedam pars lineae incidentiae; ita demonstratio
20 huius ex praemissa patet.

Admonitio de istis angulis.

Licet de linea contingente hic mentionem facimus, et angulo qui cum ea et
aliis lineis memoramus, eosdem tamen angulos cum ipsa lineari sectione
parabolica fieri est indicandum quantum ad ipsam praxim attinet et cetera.
300v   / [55. Si ducantur aliqua linea dia]metralis verticalis [et aliqua] sagittae
pars verticalis lineae ordinis super quam consistit respondens, denturque
linea diametralis, sagittae pars verticalis, et distantia diametralis a sagitta
quantitatem lineae ordinis super quam hae duae lineae datae consistunt
5 explicare.

Subtrahe lineam diametralem a sagittae parte verticali data. Residuum
serva. Quadrato iam distantiam datam et quadratum illud dividas per illud
servatum residuum, nam quotiens erit latus erectum. Iam habito latere erecto,
et sagittae parte verticali, per 3^{am} huius habebis lineam ordinis desideratam.
10   56. Data linea aliqua diametrali verticali quae super lineam ordinis datam
consistit, data etiam sagittae parte verticali datae lineae ordinis respondente,
distantiam quae data diametralis ab ipsa sagittae parte verticali data removetur
notam facere.

Subtrahe diametralem lineam datam a sagittae parte data. Residuum serva.
15 Deinde per 7^{am} elice latus erectum (hic enim linea ordinis et sagittae pars
respondens dantur). Multiplica iam latus erectum per residuum illud prius
servatum, huius enim radix quadrata erit distantia quaesita.
301r   / [57. Data alicuius datae] diametralis [distan]tia ab ipsa sagittae parte
verticali quae datae lineae ordinis respondet, eius sagittae partis verticalis
quantitatem eruere quae datae lineae ordinis respondet.

16–18 *de* Nos . . . respondente *mg. scr. C* angulorum tabula
   16 *post* alios *scr. et del. C* tali
17–18 diametralibus *supra scr. C*
18–19 Haec . . . ita *mg. scr. C*
   19 *ante* incidentiae *scr. et del. C* ind-
   20 *post* huius *scr. et del. C* per (?)
   23 *post* lineis *scr. et del. C* fuit
Fol. 300v
   1 [55. . . . dia]- *addidi eo quod his textus interiit* / [et aliqua] *addidi*
   7 *ante* et *scr. et del. C* per
   15 *post* enim *scr. et del.* (?) *C* sagit[tae]
Fol. 301r
   1 [57. Data . . . datae] *addidi eo quod hic textus interiit* / *ante* diametralis *forte hab.*
   C pars / [distan]- *addidi*

Adde ipsam distantiam lineae diametralis a sagitta dimidio lineae ordinis
5   datae; collectum illud aufer a tota linea ordinis; residuum illud serva; nam
collectum, residuum, et lineam diametralem datam collocabis in regula trium
hoc modo ut residuum sit primus numerus, collectum secundus, et linea
diametralis tertius. Quartum nunc elicite, addesque ipsi lineae diametrali
datae eundem quartum. Productum inde numerum, collectum illud prius
10   e[lectum], dimidium lineae ordinis datae constit[uunt] in regula trium ita
ut collectum sit primus numerus, et ex quarto ille et diametrali data sit
secundus, et tertius sit dimidium lineae ordinis datae. Quartum hinc inventum
numerum dimidia, nam illud dimidium erit sagittae pars quaesita. Huius
demonstratio manifesta est ex 43^a nostra.
15   Nam est ut *AB* ad *BC* sic *BD* ad *DE* [Fig. Ap.II.22], et illa *DE* est noster
quartus numerus quem addimus ipsi *DB*, lineae scilicet diametrali datae.
Unde habemus *BE*. *CB* autem erat nostrum collectum, ut vocabamus hic
supra. Ut autem *CB* ad *BE* ita *CO*, dimidium scilicet lineae ordinis datae,
ad *OS*; *OS* autem est duplum sagittae partis verticalis quaesitae per 38 et
20   43^{am}. Ergo dimidium non latebit quod demonstrasse oportuit. Si bene (?)
301v   iam / . . . . . sagittae . . . . . parabolae, et axae (!) coni in prioribus pro-
positionibus fecimus, utiliter (?) permiscendo ut (?) ad omnes casus parata
esset operantis manus, et hanc propositionem admonitionis loco adiecimus.
Licet per se etiam, nobis utilis erit.
5   58. Angulum reflexionis solaris ex omni puncto portionis verticalis nostrae
parabolae aequalem esse angulo incidentiae solaris ad idem punctum effecto.
Sit angulus incidentiae *ABE* et reflexionis *CBD* [Fig. Ap.II.23]. Dico *CBD*
esse aequalis *ABE* angulo. Considera triangulum *CBD* et eius tres angulos
CBD, *BCD*, et *BDC*, deinde angulum (!) *ABE*, *ABC*, et *CBD*, quae (!) super
10   *EBD* constant aequales duobus rectis. Ut et tres illi anguli trianguli *CBD*
sunt etiam duobus rectis aequales, ergo hii tres illis tribus sunt aequales. Sed
ABE aequalis est *BDC* quoniam *AB* et *CD* sunt lineae parallelae et in eas

---

4 *mg. hab. C* Brevius (?) hic aufer distantiam (*et postea scr. et del. C* lineae datae) a
     linea
8–9 addesque . . . quartum *mg. scr. C, et del hic in textu* Quartum hunc; *sed supra scr.*
     C Productum inde
10 -[lectum] *addidi* / -[uunt] *addidi*
11 ex *supra scr. C* / et diametrali data *corr. C ex* inventus numerus
15–17 *mg. scr. C* petitio principii hic committebatur
17 *post* nostrum *scr. et del. C* quod u-
18–19 *mg. hab. C*   AB BC BD [DE]
                        BC BE CO OS
19 38 *corr. C ex* 43
Fol. 301v
    1 . . . . .^{1,2} *addidi eo quod hic textus interiit*
    5 *post* puncto *scr. et del. C* nostrae parabolae verticali
    7–17 Sit. . . . aequalis *scr. et del. C* sed retineo (*vide intro.*)
      12 *post* ABE *scr. et del. C* pars (?) / *post* est *scr. et del. C* aequalis / *post* BDC *scr. et*
      del. C per

incidit *EBD*. Quare per [29^{am}] primi Euclidis *ABE* et *BDC* sunt aequales et
per eandem rationem *BCD* est aequalis *ABC* angulo quoniam in dictas paral-
15 lelas incidit *BC*. Omnia haec clara sunt ex proprietate linearum parallelarum
et linea illas transeunte. Nam *ABE* est aequalis *BDC* et *ACP* est aequalis
302r *BDC*; ergo *ABE* est aequalis *ACP* et *ACP* aequalis / . . . . .
   Considera iam duos triangulos *ABC* et *BLM* [Fig. Ap.II.24], quorum duo
latera unius sunt aequalia duobus lateribus alterius et anguli hiis aequis
lateribus contenti sunt aequales (quoniam *BM* et *AC* sunt parallela). Ergo
5 et bases, *BC* scilicet et *LM*, erunt etiam aequales, et reliqui anguli reliquis
angulis aequales erunt, alter alteri sub quibus aequalia latera subtenduntur
per 4^{am} primi Euclidis; ergo angulus *BLM* angulo *ABC* et *BML* angulo *ACB*.
Sed etiam dico quod *ABC* est aequalis angulo *LBM*. Sin neget adversarius,
ergo et inaequales, ergo vel maior vel minor erit ipso *LBM*. Si dicat maior,
10 resecetur aequalis ipsi *LBM* et sit *ABN* [et] iam sunt duo trianguli *ABN* et
BLM quoniam duo anguli unius [*hic desinit propositio*]
302v   / 58[*bis*]. Linea reflexionis a quolibet puncto parabolicae nostrae sectionis
est aequalis combustionis distantiae et illi parti sagittae extraductae a cuius
superiori termino extra parabolam existente ad ipsum punctum a quo venit
illa reflexionis linea linea contingens sectionem linearem parabolicam
5 ducitu[r].
   Sit reflexionis linea *AB* [Fig. Ap.II.2.5], et combustionis distantia cum
parte externa a cuius fine descendit linea contingens sectionem parabolicam
linearem ad *A* punctum sit *BD*. Dico *AB* et *BD* esse aequales. Patet per 53^{am}
EAF et *BDA* aequales esse. Sed omnes auctores speculorum parabolicorum
10 comburentium demonstrant angulum incidentiae et [angulum] reflexionis
esse aequales. Ergo *EAF* angulus incidentiae et *BAD* angulus reflexionis sunt
aequales. Sed *EAF* ostendebatur esse aequalis *BDA*. Ergo *BDA* et *BAD* sunt
aequales. Quare isosceles triangulus erit *BAD* per 16^{am} primi Euclidis, et *AB*
et *BD* erunt aequales, quod est propositum.
303r   / [59. Combustionis distantia data, et sagittae parte verticali, lineae] ordinis
verticalis quae sagittae parti verticali datae respondet terminum alterutrum
praefinire ubi cadat.

        13 [29^{am}] *in lac. in C addidi*
Fol. 302r
        1 . . . . . *addidi eo quod forte hic textus interiit*
        6 *post* erunt *scr. et del. C* isti (?) *scilicet*
        10 [et] *addidi*
Fol. 302v
        1 [*bis*] *addidi* / *post* puncto *scr. et del. C* partis verticalis / parabolicae *corr. C ex*
            parabolae (?) / sectionis *supra scr. C*
        4 sectionem linearem *supra scr. C*
        5 -[r] *addidi*
        10 [angulum] *addidi*
        13 *post* Quare *scr. C* per *sed delevi* / *post* BAD *scr. et del. C* et anguli ⸺ (?)
Fol. 303r
        1 [59. . . . lineae] *addidi eo quod hic textus interiit*

Propone tibi combustionis distantiam ex qua resecato tuam sagittae partem
5 verticalem datam; postea producas combustionis distantiam ad longitudinem
aequalem datae sagittae parti. Deinde ad illud punctum in quo a combustionis
distantia resecuisti partem aequalem sagittae parti datae perpendicularem
lineam traduc ab eo puncto utrinque in infinitum; postea a puncto combustionis ad ipsam lineam perpendicularem extendas lineam aequalem com-
10 bustionis distantiae et sagittae parti simul iunctis, et ubi illa linea sic extensa
cadet ad ipsam perpendicularem ibidem est punctum quod quaeris.

Exempli gratia. Sit *AB* [Fig. Ap.II.26] distantia combustionis data et *AC*
sagittae pars verticalis data. Produco *BA* versus partes (!) ipsius puncti *A* ita
ut *AO* constituam aequalem ipsi *AC*. Deinde ad punctum *C* traduco lineam
15 infinitam utrinque ad rectos angulos cum ipsa *AB*, et sit *DE*. Postea a puncto
combustionis (scilicet *B*) extendo versus *DE* lineam aequalem ipsi *BO*, et
ubi eius terminus cadet super lineam *DE* notetur punctum *Q*. Dico quod
punctum *Q* est punctum quaesitum. Huius demonstratio ex praecedenti
pendet et patet.

20 60. Combustionis distantia data, ipsam parabolae partem verticalem vel
ad quantamcum libet sagittae partem parabolicae sectionis linearis portionem
mechanice describere.

Combustionis distantiae datae aliam adiungas rectam lineam in directum
ipsi combustionis distantiae aequalem. Deinde ab ipso vertice parabolae
303v / . . . . . distribuere. Deinde . . . . . prorsus partes et eodem modo ab ipso
vertice procedendo in illam aliam adiunctam lineam transferas. Postea per
puncta singula divisionum ipsius combustionis distantiae lineas traducas valde
longas vel ad minus tam longas quam est latus erectum respondens. Quo
5 facto, ad quam cupis lineam punctum statuere per modum praecedentis
propositionis perpende, et vide eius distantiam a vertice; distantiam extra
verticem in illa alia linea aequalem accipias ab ipso vertice incipiendo; et
ubi illa distantia terminatur nota, nam ab illo termino ad combustionis
punctum longitudinem circino metire, et tunc immoto uno pede circini
10 alium pedem traducas ad lineam tuam electam ita ut exacte in ipsa linea
cadat. Nam eius pedis locus est punctum talem qualem in praecedenti docuimus invenire, sicque ad singulas lineas tuas facis, et postremo omnia illa
puncta continua per lineam unam curvam et et eris compos voti. Qua ratione
unum punctum statuis ex una parte sagittae eadem ut ex altera statuas vel
15 hic vel in superioribus monere non esse opus iudico. Ex se enim res tam

6 a *supra scr.* C
8 *post* lineam *scr. et del.* C super ipsam combustionis distantiam / ab eo puncto *supra
scr.* C / puncto[2] *mg. scr.* C
13 *ante* Produco *scr. et del.* C extendo
15 et . . . DE *mg. scr.* C
16 *ante* versus *scr. et del.* C lineam *et post* versus *scr. et del.* C illam infinitam per
Fol. 303v
1 . . . . .[1,2] *addidi eo quod hic textus interiit*
6 *post* vertice *scr. et del.* C similem

tales patent. Et quod propositio de data quantacunque sagittae parte recitabit, hoc ita est intelligendum ut hac eadem arte portionem describas cuius sagitta minor sit quam ipsa combustionis distantia, destribuendo ipsam sagittae partem ut ipsam combustionis distantiam fecisti, reliqua non mutanda.

20   Sit distantia combustionis data *AB* [Fig. Ap.II.27], aliam ei adiungo lineam in directum ipsi *AB* aequalem, et sit *AC*. Divido *AB* in decem partes aequales, incipiendo ab *A* et pergendo versus *B*. Similiter et *AC* divido in decem, incipiendo ab *A* versus *C* pergendo. Nunc per singula puncta divisionis ipsius

304r   *AB* duco lineas ad angulos rectos cum ipsa *AB* et / . . . . . ab *A* punctis et ad tantam distantiam ab eodem puncto *A* extra parabolam in *AC* unum pedem circini pono et alium ad ipsum combustionis punctum applico. Deinde illum pedem in combustionis puncto positum immotum relinquo et alium

5   pedem (non mutata circini apertura) transfero ad ipsam primam lineam ex utraque parte ipsius sagittae punctum parabolicum statuens. Eodem modo cum aliis secuntur ut videre potes in apposita figura, ubi etiam singula puncta per unam lineam curvam continuo ad designationem propositam perficiendam.

10   Quod 59ᵃ propositio potest aliis verbis proponi ex hiis apparet, istis videlicet vel similibus:

Data combustionis distantia, si ab eadem resecetur sagittae pars verticalis quantacunque, lineam ordinis verticalem resectae sagittae parti verticali respondentem mechanice praescribere.

15   Ad idem res redit, si ipsum problema istis fuisset propositum verbis. Ex isto problemate multa relinquo ingeniosi mathematici sive mechanici contemplationi et praxi.

61. Dato angulo incidentiae angulum combustionis respondentem invenire.

Duplato angulum incidentiae, et illud duplum subtrahas a nonaginta

20   (! 180) gradibus, et residuum monstrabit anguli combustionis quantitatem, sicque in tabula angulorum incidentiae adinventae sunt quantitates angulorum combustionis respondentium.

62. Si extra parabolae nostrae partem verticalem accipiatur aliquod punc-

304v   tum, et in eodem plano cum nostra parabolae por/[tione] . . . . . versus partes ipsius (?) puncti protractam (?), et ab eodem puncto ad concavitatem

17 *post* describas *scr. et del. C* p-

18 quam *supra scr. C*

21 *ante* decem *scr. et del. C* 10

Fol. 304r

1 . . . . . *addidi eo quod hic textus interiit*

2 ab *bis C et del. primum*

8 *post* puncta *lac. hab. C*

10 Quod 59ᵃ *corr. C ex* Quae eadem / *post* proponi *scr. et del. C* hoc modo

19 *post* a *scr. et del. C* 90

20–22 *mg. scr. C* Tabula angulorum combustionis

23 parabolae *corr. C ex* parabolam

Fol. 304v

1 -[tione]. . . . . *addidi eo quod hic textus interiit*

nostrae portionis parabolicae ducatur recta linea ipsi sagittae parallela, anguli
incidentiae quantitatem elicere quem illa linea a puncto accepto protracta
5 facit cum linea parabolicam sectionem contingente ad punctum idem ad
quod ipsa protracta linea in ipsam concavitatem nostrae sectionis incidit;
modo detur etiam linea ordinis, et sagittae pars verticalis eidem lineae ordinis
respondens in proposita parabolae parte verticali.

Si superiorum fueris memor, hoc problema et alia quampluria quae ipsa
10 philosophica praxis ingeret facillime dissolvere potes et perficere. Non quidem
aliud est punctum acceptum quam instar centrum solis in combustionis
opere cui (?) ipsa linea protracta ab eodem puncto an non instar lineae
incidentiae solaris. Si ergo distantia puncti accepti seu propositi (alterius dico
a solis centro) ab ipsa sagitta sufficienter protracta (saltem animi fictione si
15 non re ipsa protracta) sit aequalis dimidio lineae ordinis maximae tuae portionis parabolicae, hinc 53 huius tibi statim satisfaciet. Si vero sit minor ipso
dimidio lineae ordinis dictae, tunc per 40^{am} invenias lineam diametralem
305r utendo distantiam puncti hic accepti, at si in / . . . . . voti compos.

63. Dato angulo incidentiae, et sagittae parte verticali dato angulo respondente, lineam ordinis respondentem invenire.

Subtrahe angulum datum ex nonaginta gradibus; residuum adnotato. In
5 quibus velis tabulis sinuum quaeras tam tui dati anguli tam residui illius
sinus rectos. Pone primum numerum sinum rectum residui illius; secundum
autem statuas duplum sagittae partis verticalis datae, tertium vero sinum
rectum tui dati anguli. Procede iam iuxta regulam trium, et in quotiente
habebis dimidium lineae ordinis quaesitae. Eius ergo duplum est illud quod
10 quaeritur.

64. Dato angulo incidentiae, et linea ordinis eidem angulo respondente,
sagittae partem verticalem eisdem respondentem elicere.

Subtrahe angulum datum ex nonaginta gradibus; residuum serva. Lineam
ordinis datam dimidiato. Iam ad tabulas sinuum te confer et anguli dati et
15 illius complementi seu residui sinus rectos exscribere. Primum numerum
ponas sinum rectum anguli dati, secundum vero ipsum dimidium lineae
ordinis datae, ac tertium facias ipsum sinum rectum residui. Numerus ille
qui quartus ex hoc opere elici debet erit duplum sagittae partis verticalis
quaesitae. Eius proinde dimidium est id quod cupis.

20 65. Dato angulo combustionis in parte parabolae verticali, angulum incidentiae notum facere qui dato angulo respondet.

Subtrahe angulum datum [ex] centum et octoginta gradibus; re[si]dui dimidium capias, nam erit anguli in proposito quaesita quantitas.

9 quampluriam (?) C
14 *ante* ab *scr. et del.* C sit aequalis
15 *post* ordinis *scr. et del.* C hic (?)
Fol. 305r
1 . . . . . *addidi eo quod hic textus interiit*
22 [ex] *addidi* / -[si]- *addidi*

305v   / [Porisma (?) . . . . . prae]cedentibus possis . . . . elicere, qua,
_____(?) una parabolae parte verticali quolibet angulo combustionis uti
queas, modo dati anguli quantitas non excedat nostri anguli quantitatem.

Hoc non solum utile erit ad combustionis opus sed ad aliorum planetarum
5   et aliorum agentium operationes et species dirigendum ad definita loca et
cetera. Utile etiam erit ad diversitatem virtutis combustive in diversis angulis
operantis eliciendam. Et licet in una parabola quo maior est angulus eo maior
est combustionis circulus sub eodem angulo, tamen tu potes in alia parabola
ab aequali circulo quemcunque placet angulum cum priori tuo comparare,
10   fiet enim si ad lineam ordinis aequalem illum alterum angulum statuas. Potes
etiam sub aequalibus angulis varios circulos deducere ad eandem compa-
rationem si non possis comparere, ad quos usus nimis esset longum hic
aperire clare et cetera.

66. Data aliqua linea ordinis verticali, et sagittae parte verticali respondente,
15   quantitatem anguli ad alterutrum terminum datae lineae ordinis constituti.

Per 53^{am} discas angulum incidentiae solaris ad terminum tuae lineae ordinis
datae factum; hunc subtrahe a 90 gradibus et habes quod quaeris.

67. Data aliqua linea ordinis verticali, et sagittae parte verticali eidem
respondente etiam data, si ab alterutro fine datae lineae ordinis ad aliquod
20   aliud punctum sagittae praeter combustionis punctum recta ducatur, eius
306r   anguli quantitatem explicare quem ista recta cum linea / [contingente ibidem
fit] et iam partiamur sagittam in infinitum abire ab ipso vertice ultra basim
si opus fuerit; modo propositi in sagitta puncti distantia ab ipso vertice nostrae
parabolae detur hic semper.

Fol. 305v

    1 [Porisma (?). . . . . prae]- *et* . . . . .^{2} *addidi eo quod hic textus interiit*
    3 dati *ex corr.* C / nostri *corr.* C *ex* nostrae (?)
    6 ad *supra scr.* C / *post* diversitatem *scr. et del.* C comburentium (?)
    7 *post* una *scr. et del.* C circula (!)
   10 *ante* fiet *lac. hab.* C
14–17 66 . . . quaeris *mg. scr.* C
   15 *post* quantitatem *scr. et del.* C eius / *post* anguli *scr. et del.* C quem linea (?) (*et
       postea add.* C ordinis *quod delevi*) / *post* alterutrum *scr. et del.* C suum / *post*
       terminum *scr. et del.* C cum contingente facit (?) invenire *sed forte* invenire *scribendum
       post* constituti *in lin. 15; cf. transl.*
   16 ad *bis* C
   19 *post* lineae *scr. et del.* C od-
   20 sagittae *mg. scr.* C

Fol. 306r

   1–2 [contingente ibidem fit] *addidi eo quod hic textus interiit*
   2–4 et . . . semper *scr. et forte del.* C; *et mg. scr.* C:. . . . . basis partes, sagittam in
       infinitum abire concipiamus ab (?) aliquo in eadem sagitta puncto, linea [incidenti]ae
       arbitrariae ad terminum alicuius [lineae] ordinis datae cadat, et detur distantia (?)
       eius (*del.* C) illius puncti in sagitta accepti [ab ipso] vertice nostrae parabolae, ac
       etiam sagittae verticalis pars quae datae lineae ordinis verticali respondet quantitatem
       _____ (? *del.*) anguli _____ (? propositi?) explicare
   2 *post* abire *scr. et del.* C versus basim

5   Per 67^{am} (! 66^{am}) discas quantitatem anguli qui ad alterutrum terminum
lineae ordinis verticalis datae cum linea contingente ibidem fit, et illum
angulum caute serva seorsim. Deinde subtrahe sagittae partem datam ab ipsa
distantia puncti accepti in nostra illa infinita sagitta. Residuum serva. Residuum illud quadrato. Quadrato etiam dimidium lineae ordinis datae. Haec
10   duo quadrata coniunge. Illius producti radicem quadratam elice, nam illa
erit longitudo lineae nostrae incidentiae arbitrariae. Tunc ingedere (!) tabulas
sinuum rectorum hoc modo, quaeras sinum totum; primus numerus esse
linea ipsa arbitrariae incidentiae. Secundus sinus totus. Tertius vero vel dimidium lineae ordinis datae vel illa residua distantia puncti accepti. Quartus
15   numerus si quaeratur et inveniatur in tabulis sinuum dabit tibi angulum
quemdam (si accepisti dimidium lineae ordinis) qui cum illa linea arbitrariae
incidentiae et sagitta protracta ad punctum acceptum efficitur. Sin vero accepisti illam residuam distantiam, angulus ille erit qui cum linea incidentiae
arbitrariae et linea ordinis efficitur ad punctum contingentiae. Si prior horum
20   fuerit, demas illum angulum ex nonaginta [gradibus] et residuum coniunge
cum illo seorsim servato angulo, et aggregatum illud demas ex 180 gradibus,
nam istud ultimum residuum erit angulus incidentiae arbitrariae. Sin vero
postea erat, coniunge illum angulum ex tabulis sinuum depromptum cum
illo residuo angulo seorsim servato, et illud productum ex 180 [gradibus]
25   auferas et remanebit angulus quaesitus. Demonstratio huius ex ipsa adiuncta
figura ([Fig. Ap.II.28] clare [et] statim apparebit. Sit *A* punctum acceptum
in sagitta protracta.

Corollarium

reverte
ad
281v

Manifestum est ex *BD* versus (?) *D* . . . . . prodices quod angulus
DBA . . . . .
/ 68. Detur linea ordinis verticalis et sagittae pars verticalis datae lineae
ordinis respondens. Deinde a vertice ipso ultra lineam ordinis in infinitum

---

5 67^{am} *corr. C ex* 53^{am} / *post* anguli *scr. et del. C* incidentiae sectori / *post* qui *scr. et*
del. C cadit
6 cum . . . fit *corr. C ex* Deinde angulum incidentiae subtrahas a nonaginta gradibus
7 *post* angulum *scr. et del. C* residuum
20 [gradibus] *addidi*
20–27 coniunge. . . . protracta *mg. scr. C*
24 [gradibus] *addidi*
26 [et] *addidi*
29 . . . . . *addidi eo quod hic textus interiit* / *ante* quod *scr. et del. C lineam textus*
quam non legere possum
30 . . . . . *addidi eo quod hic textus interiit*
Fol. 281v
1 *ante* 68 *mg.* 306r *hab. et del. C* 68. Data linea ordinis verticali et sagittae parte
respondente, si producatur sagitta (*et postea del. C aliquid; forte* in infininitum) et
deinde acipiatur (!) punctus cuius distantia a vertice detur. Deinde. . . . . (*hic textus*
interiit) transeat linea ad. . . . . (*hic textus interiit*) accipiatur punctum secundum
tantae (!) a primo dista s quanta (!). . . . (*et postea in fol. 281v superius scr. et del.*

abire partiamur sagittam ipsam. Si iam in ipsa sagitta accipiatur aliquod punctum cuius distantia ab ipso vertice detur, et per idem acceptum punctum
5   lineam ad angulos rectos cum ipsa sagitta utrinque in infinitum abire concipiamus, accipiaturque in illa transversa perpendiculari punctum secundum cuius distantia a primo accepto puncto vel maior vel minor distat quam dimidium lineae ordinis datae, et ab eodem secundo puncto ad utrunque terminum lineae ordinis datae ducantur duae lineae incidentiae arbitrariae,
10   quantitates angulorum qui cum lineis incidentiae arbitrariae et lineis sectionem parabolicam contingentibus ad utrunque terminum lineae ordinis datae fiunt
282r explicare, modo etiam primi et secundi punctorum / . . . . .

Detur linea ordinis *AB* [Fig. Ap.II.29] et sagittae pars verticalis [respondens *CM*], et producatur *CM* ultra in infinitum, et sit *CMX*; accipiatur punctum quodcunque, et sit *G*. Per *G* ducatur ad rectos ipsi *CMX* linea *IGN* et ita ab
5   utraque parte ipsius *G* in infinitum. In ipsa *IGN* accipiatur secundum punctum (quod ita appellamus quoniam unum prius accepimus), et sit secundum punctum *H*; et sit primo istorum punctorum distantia, scilicet *GH*, minor quam *AM*, dimidium scilicet lineae ordinis datae; ab ipso *H* duco ad *A* et *B* duas lineas incidentiae arbitrariae, scilicet *HA* et *HB*; per puncta *A* et *B*
10   ducantur lineae sectionem contingentes, et sint *DAF* et *DBE*. Quaeruntur iam quantitates angulorum *HAF* et *HBE*. A puncto ergo *A* ad lineam *IGN* duco lineam ipsi *CG* parallelam, et sit *AN*. Iam concipe *CMG* concurrere cum *AH* protracta, et sit punctum concursus *X*. Considero iam duos triangulos *AMX* et *GHX* aequiangulos, ita ut sit sicut *HG* ad *GX* ita *AM* ad *MX*; *GH*
15   nota est, distantia scilicet punctorum data, et *AM* nota est, dimidium scilicet lineae ordinis. Ad habendum ergo *GX* considero triangulum *HAN* aequiangulum ipsi *GHX*. Ergo ut *HN* ad *NA* ita *HG* ad *GX*; *HN* nota est, si *GH* subtrahatur ex *MA*, et *NA* aequalis est ipsi *GM*, et *GH* est distantia punctorum

C: . . . . . (*hic textus interiit*) et extra eandem sagittam accipiatur aliquod punctum quod vel minus vel magis distet ab ipsa sagitta quam est dimidium lineae ordinis datae (*supra scr.*) et (*supra scr.*) ad utrum (*correxi* ex cuius eiusdem utrumque alterutrum *et ex sequente in mg. quod del. C.* Et ad eiusdem datae lineae ordinis utrumque) terminum ab accepto puncto cadant duae (*supra scr.*) lineae incidentiae arbitrariae, quantitatem angulorum incidentiae arbitrariae, quos hae lineae incidentiae arbitrariae cum lineis contingentibus sectionem parabolicam ad utrunque terminum datae lineae ordinis faciunt, exprimere

   7 maior vel minor distat *ex corr. C*
  11 parabolicam *ex corr. C*
Fol. 282r
   1 . . . . . *addidi eo quod hic textus interiit*
   2 *mg. hab. C* 1. proponatur de mi[nore], 2. post de maiore distantia
 2–3 [respondens CM] *addidi*
   3 *ante* accipiatur *scr. et del. C* X
 6–7 et . . . H *mg. scr. C*
   7 scilicet GH *supra scr. C*
   9 et B *mg. scr. C*
  10 et DBE *mg. scr. C*
16–20 considero. . . . 67 *mg. scr. C*

data; ergo *GX* non latebit. Hinc addas *MG* et habebis *MX* . . . . . procedas

282v . . . . . 67 / . . . . . *GH* ad *GL* ita *BM* ad *ML*. Ergo permutatim ut *GH* ad *BM* ita *GL* ad *ML*. Ergo coniunctim ut *GH* et *BM* ad *BM* ita *GL* et *ML* ad *ML*. Sed *GH* et *BM* nota[e] sunt, similiter et *MG*. Ergo *LM* non latebit, et tunc perinde erit ac si nobis fuisse *L* datum, et propositum punctum *L*,

5 et tunc ex 67 disces quod faciendum. Si autem distantia punctorum datorum sit maior dimidio lineae ordinis datae, sit tota (?) *GI*. Sit aut[em] *G* primum punctum et *I* secundum ut supra. Et tunc ad habendum angulum *IAD*, considera duos triangulos *IKG* et *AMK* aequiangulos, et quoad in triangulis *HLG* et *BLM* fecimus, eodem modo efficies *K* punctum datum in ipsa sagitta;

10 iuxta rationem 67 propositionis ita voti fies compos. Postremo pro angulo *IBE* habendo ducas lineam *GB* et ab ipso *B* ad *IG* lineam demittas perpendicularem, et sit *BO*. Per 67^am iam elice angulum *GBE* et illum serva; eundem servatum subtrahe a duobus rectis, scilicet a 180 [gradibus]; et residuum angulum serva. Ab isto residuo aufer angulum quem linea contingens cum

15 linea ordinis facit (per 66). Et residuum illum angulum vocate secundum residuum, quem deme a 90 [gradibus]. Et residuum angulum vocate residuum tertium, qui respondebit ipsi *BGM*, ergo et *GBO*. Restat iam *OBI* (?) angulus adhuc eliciendus, quem hoc modo habebis. Subtrahe *BM* ex *IG* et remanebit *IO*; *BO* autem est aequalis ipsi *MG*. Ergo duo latera trianguli rectanguli *OIB*

20 sunt nota, quare et *BI* hypothenusa. Ergo ex tabulis sinuum hoc modo disces *OBI* angulum. Fac primum numerum hypothenusam *BI*, secundum ipsum sinum totum, tertium autem ipsum latus *IO*. Quartum hinc inventum numerum si quaeras in tabulis sinuum, dabit tibi angulum *OBI*. Eundem ingedere (! iunge) angulo *GBO* prius invento, et productum illud aufer ex *GBE*

25 antea invento, et remanebit tibi angulus quaesitus, scilicet *IBE*.

283r / [69.] . . . . . figurae, si angulus reflexionis arbitrariae constituatur, in

19, 20 . . . . . *addidi eo quod hic textus interiit*
Fol. 282v
    1 . . . . . *addidi eo quod hic textus interiit* / GH ad *correxi ex* GH, GL *ergo permissa*
       in C (et del. C GH *et* ergo permissa)
    3 -[e] *addidi*
    6 *post* sit^1 *scr. et del. C* maius (?) / -[em] *addidi*
    8 *post* AMK *scr. et del. C* et / quoad *ex corr. C* / *post* in *scr. et del. C* similibusque
       similiter
    9 *post* fecimus *scr. et del. C* aliquid quod non legere possum / *post* ipsa *scr. et del. C*
       propos[ita] (?)
   13 [gradibus] *addidi*
   16 *ante* a *scr. et del. C* 180 *et post* a *scr. et del. C* 180 / [gradibus] *addidi*
   21 *post* numerum *scr. et del. C* sinum totum se ipsam (*sive* ipsum)
  23–25 si. . . . . IBE *mg. scr. C*
   24 *ante* GBE *scr. et del. C* GBI
Fol. 283r
    1 [69.]. . . . . *addidi eo quod hic textus interiit*
  1–3 figurae . . . *explicare forte del. C, et mg. scr. et del. C:* hypothenusam contingentiae
    incidentiae (?) et cetera
    1 *post* arbitrariae *del. C* p-

qua _____ distantia ab ipso vertice parabolae linea reflexionis arbitrariae sagittam secabit, explicare.

Disce angulum qui fit ex linea contingente et linea ordinis data per 66, et
5   deinde aufer [eum] ex angulo incidentiae arbitrariae sive reflexionis arbitrariae (nam hii duo sunt aequales). Residuum notas, et deducas eundem residuum ex nonaginta [gradibus], et illud secundum residuum etiam notum [est]. In tabulis sinuum rectorum horum utrorumque residuorum quaeras sinus rectos, et numeros ibidem inventos exscribas. Secundi residui sinum rectum facias
10 primum numerum, et dimidium lineae ordinis secundum; tertium autem facies sinum rectum primi residui anguli, nam si quarto invento numero addas sagittae partem verticalem habebis quod quaeris.

70. [*Hic desinit textus*]

---

    4 Disce *corr. C ex* Subtrahe / *post* angulum *scr. et del. C* incid-
    4–5 per . . . aufer *supra scr. C*
    5–6 *de* deinde . . . aequales *mg. scr. C* iam habes triangulum rectangulum cuius unum latus datum, et omnes anguli noti sunt; nam
    5 [eum] *addidi*
    6 *post* Residuum *scr. et del. C* serva
    7 [gradibus] *addidi* / etiam notum *corr. C ex* quaeras (?) / [est] *addidi*
    8 horum . . . rectos *mg. scr. C*
    9 *ante* Secundi *scr. et del. C* Deinde secundi (?) primum (?)
    13 [Hic . . . textus] *addidi*

March 8, 1558

On Burning Mirrors, Five Books

In the First Two: Discoveries of John Dee of London concerning that section of a right-angled right cone which was called a parabola by the ancient mathematicians.

All things you have here expounded by means of numbers and elucidated by the certitude of mathematical apodeixis.

This book has here things of great utility which distinguished philosophers, perspectivists, and investigators of nature scarcely know, but are at hand for the more experienced [investigator].

[Book I.]

Definitions

1. When a point is assumed outside of the surface of some described circle, and from this point a straight line is drawn through the circumference of this circle and permitted to project to infinity, and that same line is revolved through the whole circumference of the described circle, never departing from it, with its terminus which is placed at the assumed point remaining at rest during the whole time, that solid included by two surfaces, that is by the initial circle and by that curved surface described by the straight line drawn through the point at rest and revolved through the circumference of the circle, we call a CONE. [See Fig. Ap.II.1, where A is the assumed point that remains at rest, BC the circle initially described, ABE the line drawn from the assumed point outside of the circle and imagined as going off to infinity, but always with some point of it touching or cutting the circumference of circle BC.]

2. The vertex of the cone is that point remaining at rest.

3. The base of the cone is that circle through whose circumference the line revolved and described the curved surface of the cone.

4. The axis of the cone is the straight line connecting the vertex of the cone with the center of the base of the cone.

[5. A right cone is one the axis of which is perpendicular to the base of the cone.]

548

6. A scalene cone is one the axis of which is not perpendicular to its base. [See Fig. Ap.II.2, where *ABC* is a right cone, *DEF* a scalene cone, *AB* the conic side, *AG* the axis of the former, and *DH* the axis of the latter.]

7. The conic side of a right cone is a straight line extended from the vertex of the cone to the circumference of the base.

8. The conic surface of a right cone is the curved surface of the cone described by the revolution of a conical side through the circumference of the base, with the terminus of the conical side which is at the vertex of the cone at rest.

9. The conic triangle of a right cone is the plane surface which is contained by the diameter of the base of the cone and two other straight lines drawn from the termini of the same diameter and meeting at the vertex of the cone.

10. The base of the conic triangle is the same as a diameter of the base of the cone. [See Fig. Ap.II.3, where *ABC* is the conic triangle of a right cone and *BC* is the base of the conic triangle.]

11. A right-angled right cone is one in which the angle of its conic triangle subtended by the base of the same triangle is a right angle.

12. An acute-angled right cone exists when the said angle is acute.

13. An obtuse-angled right cone exists when the aforesaid angle is obtuse.

[14. When the conic side of a right-angled right cone is revolved through the circumference of its base] to produce a surface and a diameter of the base of the aforesaid cone is taken, which diameter cuts the base of a conic triangle at right angles, then through that diameter a plane is conceived to pass inside that cone and divide the cone into two parts during the whole course of its transit, the plane having first been applied to a side of the conic triangle and having been made parallel [to the other side of the conic triangle], we shall then call the common section of the two surfaces (i.e., the one surface applied to the side of the conic triangle and being parallel [in the manner described] and the other surface being the curved surface of the cone) A USTORIUS PARABOLIC LINEAR SECTION. [See Fig. Ap.II.4, where *OQERP* is the ustorius parabolic linear section, *ODPREQO* the ustorius parabola, *ODP* the base of the parabola, *ED* the whole sagitta (i.e. axis) of the parabola, *QR* the latus rectum, *E* the vertex of the parabola, *ES* the distance of combustion, and *S* the point of combustion.]

15. The USTORIUS PARABOLA is a plane surface contained by a ustorius parabolic linear section and by the said diameter of the base of the cone.

16. The base of our ustorius parabola is that diameter of the base of the cone which has cut the base of the conic triangle at right angles.

17. The whole sagitta or diameter of the ustorius parabola is the common section of two surfaces, namely that of the conic triangle and that of the plane cutting the cone to produce the ustorius parabolic section.

18. A line of order is a straight line parallel to the base of the parabola and extended in the surface of the parabola, each of its termini being located in the concavity of the parabolic linear section.

19. (*destroyed*)

20. The point of combustion [of a ustorius parabola] is that point which lies in the middle of the whole sagitta [i.e. parabolic axis].

21. The distance of combustion is that part of the whole sagitta which is contained between the vertex of the parabola and the point of combustion.

22. The latus rectum is that line of order which cuts the whole sagitta at the point of combustion.

23. A vertical line of order is one which crosses the sagitta between the point of combustion and the vertex of the parabola.

24. A vertical part of the sagitta is one which always has one of its termini at the vertex of the parabola, while the other is located between the vertex and the point of combustion.

25. The vertical line of order that corresponds to a [given] vertical part of the sagitta is that one which touches [i.e. passes through] the lower terminus of that [given] part of the sagitta.

26. The vertical part of the sagitta that corresponds to a [given] vertical line of order is that one which having been drawn from the vertex of the parabola is terminated at the line of order to which it is said to correspond. [See Fig. Ap.II.5, where *RS* is a vertical line of order, *EK* a vertical part of the sagitta so that *RS* corresponds to *EK* and *EK* corresponds to *RS*, and *OP* is the latus rectum.]

27. A line tangent to a parabolic linear section is a straight line applied to some point in the convexity of the linear section, no part of which line falls within the surface of the parabola even if it would run off to infinity in both directions.

[28. A line] of solar incidence is a straight line parallel to the sagitta that may be extended to the point of contingence [i.e. tangency].

29. An angle of solar incidence is one which is formed beneath the perpendicular of contingence and is included by the line of incidence and that line which is tangent to the parabolic linear section where the line of solar incidence ends in this section.

30. A line of solar reflection or line of combustion is a straight line which is drawn from the terminus of the line of incidence that lies in this section and which crosses through the point of combustion.

31. An angle of solar reflection is the one which is above the perpendicular of contingence and is formed by a line of reflection and the tangent.

32. An angle of combustion is the one which a line of solar incidence forms with a line of solar reflection.

33. The angle of incidence corresponding to a [given] vertical line of order is the one which is constructed at either terminus of the same line of order.

34. The angle of incidence corresponding to a [given] vertical part of the sagitta is the one which is constructed at either end of the vertical line of order corresponding to the same vertical part of the sagitta.

35. The angle of reflection corresponding to a [given] vertical line of order is the one which is constructed at either terminus of the same line of order.

36. The angle of reflection corresponding to a [given] vertical part of the sagitta is the one which is constructed at either end of the line of order corresponding to the same vertical part of the sagitta.

[37. The angle of combustion corresponding to a (given) vertical line of order is the one which is constructed at either terminus] of the same line of order.

38. The angle of combustion corresponding to a [given] vertical part of the sagitta is the one which is constructed at either end of the line of order corresponding to the same vertical part of the sagitta. [See Fig. Ap.II.6, where *AIHDB* is a parabolic linear section, *AGB* its latus rectum, *HKG* its distance of combustion, *IKD* a (vertical) line of order, *EDF* a line tangent to the parabolic linear section, *LD* a line of solar incidence, *LDF* an angle of solar incidence, *GD* a line of solar reflection or combustion, *GDE* an angle of reflection, *GDL* an angle of combustion; *LDF* is the angle of incidence corresponding to vertical line of order *IKD* and to the vertical part *HK* of the sagitta, *GDE* the angle of reflection corresponding to the vertical line of order *IKD* and to the vertical part *HK* of the sagitta, and *GDL* the angle of combustion corresponding to the vertical line of order *IKD* and to the vertical part *HK* of the sagitta, *IKD* the vertical line of order corresponding to the angle of incidence *LDF*, to the angle of reflection *GDE*, and to the angle of combustion *GDL*; and *HK* is the vertical part of the sagitta corresponding to the same three angles.]

[39]. Any one of the said angles [corresponds to] the [same] given vertical [line of order of the sagitta] of the parabola.

40. The vertical part of the sagitta corresponding to the said three angles is the one whose lower terminus ends at the line of order which corresponds to these three angles.

41. We shall call a vertical segment of a parabola that which is bounded by the latus rectum and by the segment of the parabolic linear section terminated at the ends of the latus rectum.

42. A diametral line is a straight line drawn parallel to the sagitta from some point of the parabolic linear section to the base of the parabola or to some [other] line of order.

43. A vertical diametral line is one that is drawn parallel to the sagitta from the parabolic linear section to the latus rectum itself or to some other vertical line of order.

44. The vertical diametral line corresponding to a [given] vertical line of order is the one which is drawn from either terminus of the same line of order to the latus rectum or to another vertical line of order.

45. The vertical diametral line corresponding to a [given] vertical part of the sagitta is the one from whose upper terminus is drawn the line of order corresponding to the [given] vertical part of the sagitta but whose lower terminus lies either in the latus rectum or in another vertical line of order.

[46. The vertical diametral line corresponding to a given angle of solar incidence, or to the (corresponding) angle of solar reflection] or to the [corresponding] angle of combustion is the one which falls from the place of the said angles to the latus rectum itself or to another vertical line of order.

47. The angle of solar incidence or of solar reflection or of combustion corresponding to a [given] vertical diametral line is that which is constructed at the upper terminus of this diametral line. [See Fig. Ap.II.7, where BC and QR are vertical diametral lines, OCDE is the latus rectum, BC the vertical diametral line corresponding to the vertical line of order BHI and to the vertical part AH of the sagitta, and BC corresponds to angles FBC, CBD, and GBD, and those angles will be said to correspond to BC.]

48. The vertical line of order corresponding to a [given] vertical diametral line is the one whose terminus is common with the upper terminus of the diametral line.

49. The vertical part of the sagitta corresponding to a [given] vertical diametral line is the one such that if a line of order is drawn through its lower terminus the line of order will be terminated at one of its ends in the upper terminus of this diametral line.

Book II.

[Propositions]

1. With the latus rectum of a parabola given, to make known the distance of combustion of the same parabola.

Divide the magnitude of the latus rectum by 4, and the number of the quotient shows the distance of combustion.

2. With the distance of combustion given, to elicit the latus rectum which produces a square for the same parabola.

Multiply the distance of combustion by 4 and the product will be the latus rectum which is sought.

3. With the latus rectum and some vertical part of the sagitta given, to root out the vertical line of order corresponding to the given part of the sagitta.

Multiply the latus rectum by the given part of the sagitta and take the square root of the product. Double that root and the line of order sought will result.

4. With the latus rectum and some vertical line of order given, to find the vertical part of the sagitta corresponding to the given line of order.

Take half of the [given] line of order; you will square that half and divide that square by the latus rectum, and in the quotient will be what you wish.

5. With the distance of combustion and some vertical part of the sagitta given, to make known the vertical line of order corresponding to the given part of the sagitta.

By the second [proposition] of this [work] you may find the latus rectum. Then by the third [proposition] complete that which has been proposed.

6. With the distance of combustion and some vertical line of order given, to produce the vertical part of the sagitta corresponding to the given line of order.

By the second [proposition] of this [work] you may elicit the latus rectum and by the fourth seek out what is left [to find].

7. With some vertical line of order and the vertical part of the sagitta corresponding to the given line of order given, to make known the latus rectum.

You may take half of the given line of order and square that half. You may divide that square by the given part of the sagitta, for the quotient will satisfy you [in finding the latus rectum].

[8. Given some vertical line of order and the vertical part of the sagitta] corresponding [to the given line] of order, to find the distance of combustion.

By the seventh [proposition] of this [work] you may learn the latus rectum. Then the first [proposition] will immediately teach you the magnitude of the distance of combustion.

9. With the latus rectum given, to reveal as found the whole sagitta.

Half of the latus rectum is the magnitude of the whole sagitta.

10. With the whole sagitta given, to elicit the latus rectum.

The preceding [proposition] instructs you sufficiently [in this matter].

11. With the whole sagitta given, to find the axis of our cone from which the parabolic sagitta is had.

Square the whole sagitta. Double that square. Take the square root of that double, for that root is the axis or altitude of our cone.

12. With the whole sagitta given, to reveal the base of our parabola.

By the eleventh [proposition] of this [work] find the axis of our cone. Then double that quantity, for thus you will have the desired base, which in our definitions we suppose to be equal to the diameter of the base of this cone.

13. With the latus rectum given, to make known the axis of our cone.

By the ninth [proposition] you seek out the whole sagitta. Then you make complete [this operation] by the eleventh [proposition].

14. With the latus rectum given, to render known the base of the parabola.

By the ninth [proposition] of this [work] you may elicit the whole sagitta. Then by the twelfth you may proceed to that which has been proposed.

15. With the whole sagitta given, to disclose the distance of combustion.

Half of the whole sagitta is the distance of combustion.

16. With the distance of combustion given, to express the whole sagitta.

This is evident by the preceding [proposition].

17. With the distance of combustion given, to find the axis of our cone.

By the preceding [proposition] learn the whole sagitta. Then by the eleventh [proposition] you will produce what you wish.

[18. With the distance of combustion given, to find the base of our parabola.

By the preceding proposition learn the axis of the cone.] Double [its] quantity and you will be master of your desire.

19. With the whole sagitta and some vertical part of the sagitta given, to

make clear the vertical line of order corresponding to the given part of the sagitta.

By the tenth [proposition] you will have the latus rectum, and then you will proceed by the third [proposition].

20. With the whole sagitta and some vertical line of order given, to know the vertical part of the sagitta corresponding to the given line of order.

By the tenth [proposition] you may elicit the latus rectum. Then by the fourth you will arrive at that which is sought.

21. With the axis or altitude of our cone given, to exhibit along with it the total sagitta of our parabola.

Square the axis or altitude; take half of its square, and the square root of that half is the whole sagitta.

22. With the axis of our cone given, to make known the distance of combustion in our parabola.

By the twenty-first [proposition] investigate the magnitude of the sagitta. Then the fifteenth [proposition] of this [work] will satisfy your desire.

23. With the axis of our cone given, to make known the latus rectum of our parabola.

By the twenty-first [proposition] you will have the whole sagitta, and by the tenth the latus rectum.

24. Given the axis of our cone and some vertical part of the sagitta in our parabola, to demand the vertical line of order corresponding to the given part of the sagitta.

By the twenty-third [proposition] you may learn the latus rectum, and the third [proposition] will satisfy you [in your quest].

25. With the axis of our cone and some vertical line of order given, to express the vertical part of the sagitta corresponding to the given line [of order].

The twenty-third [proposition] will inform you concerning the latus rectum, and then the third [proposition] of this [work] will give the part of the sagitta that is sought.

26. With the axis of our cone given, to elicit the base of the parabola.

Double the axis and you will have the base of our parabola.

[27. With the base of our parabola given, to elicit the whole sagitta.

Square half of the base of the parabola. Take half of that square.] The square root of that half [is the whole sagitta].

28. With the base of our parabola given, to elicit the distance of combustion.

The twenty-seventh [proposition] will give you the whole sagitta, and the fifteenth the distance of combustion.

29. With the base of our parabola given, to root out the latus rectum.

You may root out the sagitta by the twenty-seventh [proposition] of this [work] and the latus rectum by the tenth.

30. With the base of our parabola and some vertical part of the sagitta given, to express the vertical line of order corresponding to the given part of the sagitta.

By the twenty-ninth [proposition] of this [work] you will know the latus rectum, and then by the third you may proceed to that which has been proposed.

31. With the base of our parabola and some vertical line of order given, to make known the vertical part of the sagitta corresponding to the given line of order.

The twenty-ninth [proposition] will give the latus rectum, and the fourth will make clear the remaining argument of this operation.

32. Wherever the whole sagitta or distance of combustion becomes known along with some vertical part of the sagitta in the same place, a vertical diametral line corresponding to the known vertical part of the sagitta is also known.

For if you subtract the known vertical part of the sagitta from the whole sagitta or distance of combustion, the remainder will be a vertical diametral line corresponding to that part of the sagitta.

33. Whichever vertical diametral line corresponds to a vertical part of the sagitta, the same line will also correspond to the vertical line of order which is said to correspond to the same vertical part of the sagitta.

Therefore by the preceding [proposition], when the vertical diametral line which corresponds to the vertical part of the sagitta is had, you also have the vertical diametral line which would correspond to the vertical line of order, for the same line of order corresponds to the vertical part of the sagitta of which our diametral line is the complement.

34. Whichever vertical diametral line corresponds to a vertical line of order, the same line will necessarily correspond to all the angles which are constructed with the tangent line at either end of the line of order.

[The vertical line of order or] the vertical part [of the sagitta] which corresponds to the said angles is known, so that by definitions 45 (?) and 44 and propositions 32 and 33, etc. [that is, the proposition will follow].

35. Given some vertical part of the sagitta and [one of the following:] the latus rectum, or the distance of combustion, or the vertical line of order corresponding to the given part of the sagitta, or the whole sagitta, or the axis of the cone from which our parabola is taken, or the base of this parabola, to draw mechanically the segment of a parabolic linear section which is terminated at the ends of that vertical line of order corresponding to the given [vertical] part of the sagitta.

Divide the given part of the sagitta into as many equal parts as you wish. Then if the latus rectum is given in these parts, you will learn by the third [proposition] the magnitude of any line of order which passes through [one of] the said equal parts. If the distance of combustion is given in these same parts, then you may learn by the second [proposition] the latus rectum and [then] proceed, as we have said before concerning the vertical lines of order passing through the said parts of the sagitta. Moreover if the line of order corresponding to the given part of the sagitta is given, then by the seventh [proposition] you will have the latus rectum, and proceed as we have taught above. If the whole sagitta [is given], then from the tenth [proposition] you will have the latus rectum, and then the remaining operation is known. If the axis of the cone is given along with a part of the sagitta, then by the twenty-third [proposition] you will obtain as known the latus rectum. Finally if the base [of the parabola] is given to you along with a vertical part of the sagitta, then the twenty-ninth [proposition] will make clear the latus rectum, and thence, as we have taught before, you will elicit the magnitudes of all the lines of order which pass through those points of division of the vertical [part of the] sagitta. Then if you continue a curved line through the ends of these lines [of order], you will see emerge what you desire.

For example, if a sagitta of 5 inches in length is given, and let it be AB [see Fig. Ap.II.8], and I would wish to describe, for a latus rectum of 100 inches, a parabolic segment which would be terminated at the ends of the line of order corresponding to the given vertical part of the sagitta, then I multiply 5 by 100, and the product is 500, whose square root, $\sqrt{500}$, is nearly $22^{16}/_{45}$. This, when doubled, will display the length of the line of order passing through B. In the same way, if at the end of 4 inches, where let C be placed, I would like to draw a line of order, then by the third [proposition] I multiply 4 by 100 and the result will be 400, whose square root, $\sqrt{400}$, is exactly 20, and this is half the line of order passing through C. For the third [point of division the same procedure will produce the magnitude of the third] ver[tical] line [of order]. Realize that you could [in the same way] correctly [find] as many lines as are the parts into which you have divided the part of the sagitta, for such will be an absolute necessity.

36. Given some vertical line of order and [one of the following:] the latus rectum, or the distance of combustion, or the vertical part of the sagitta corresponding to the given line of order, or the whole sagitta, or the axis of the cone from which our parabola is cut, or the base of this parabola, to draw mechanically the segment of a parabolic linear section which is terminated at the ends of the given line of order.

If the latus rectum is given along with a vertical line of order, then by the fourth [proposition] you may seek out the corresponding vertical part of the sagitta, and [then] by the preceding [proposition] you will complete the operation. If the distance of combustion is given, then by the sixth [proposition] you will have the corresponding vertical part of the sagitta, and the preceding (that is thirty-fifth) [proposition] will open up to you the nature of the operation. But if, moreover, the corresponding part of the sagitta is given at once, you will learn enough from the preceding [proposition]. Now if the whole sagitta [is given], then the twentieth [proposition] will correctly teach you concerning the corresponding vertical part of the sagitta. After the latter has been obtained, consider the nature of the operation in the thirty-fifth [proposition]. But if the axis of our cone is given, the twenty-fifth [proposition] will teach you concerning the corresponding part of the sagitta, which you may divide and treat as we have advised in the preceding [proposition]. Finally if the base of the parabola is known to you along with some vertical line of order, then from the thirty-first [proposition] you will have the vertical part of the sagitta corresponding to the given line of order. Now when you have the vertical part of the sagitta [in any one of the methods noted above] and you divide it arbitrarily into equal parts, with the help of the latus rectum you will draw at right angles [to the sagitta] through the individual parts [of the sagitta] the lines of order, by means of whose ends joined together aptly by a curved line what you desire results, as was evident in the preceding, thirty-fifth [proposition].

37. With the latus rectum given, to draw mechanically the parabolic linear section which is terminated at the ends of the given latus rectum.

[*The Latin text of the solution of this problem is too deficient for an adequate translation, but it is evident that this problem is a special case of Proposition 36, and indeed the techniques of Propositions 35 and 36 make the solution of this problem obvious.*]

38. With a vertical line of order given first, we can arrive at the description of a line tangent to the parabolic linear section at either end of the given line of order in just as many ways as the vertical part of the sagitta corresponding to the given line of order can be known.

For always the vertical part of the sagitta may be extended beyond the vertex of the parabola until the part beyond the vertex is equal to the vertical part of the sagitta. When this has been done conjoin either terminus of the given line of order with the upper end of the outside extension of the sagitta, and the line so drawn [between these termini] will be the desired tangent line.

39. To make clear the magnitude of the side of contingence (i.e. the tangent line) which corresponds to the given part of the sagitta and to the given line of order regardless of how many ways the line of contingence is given by the preceding thirty-eighth [proposition].

Take half of the vertical line of order at either end of which the tangent line touches the parabolic linear section, and square that half. Then double the vertical part of the sagitta corresponding to the vertical line of order. Square that double. Add together the two squares. And the square root of this sum will display the magnitude of the line of contingence protracted from the point of tangency to [its] juncture with the vertical part of the sagitta after it has been extended, as is evident in the immediately preceding [proposition; cf. Fig. Ap.II.9].

[40. With some line of order known along with the vertical part of the sagitta corresponding to the known line of order,] and if some point is taken in the known line of order whose distance from the middle of the line of order is given, to express the magnitude of the vertical diametral line to be erected from the said point to the parabolic linear section.

Let *AB* be the given line of order and *CD* the vertical part of the sagitta corresponding to the given line of order [see Fig. Ap.II.10]. Now if some point such as *E* is taken in *AB* and from this same point a vertical diametral line *EF* is erected to the parabolic section, it is now necessary to teach well the magnitude of *EF*. Through *F* I imagine a line protracted parallel to *EC*, which protracted line will be equal to half a line of order. This half will be known since it is equal to *EC*, namely to the distance of the accepted point *E* from the middle of the given line of order. Now by the fourth [proposition] you will have *DO*, namely the vertical part of the sagitta corresponding to *FOR*, for there is only one latus rectum in a single parabola. Therefore since that latus [rectum] may become known through *AB* and *DC* by the seventh [proposition], it cannot but happen that *DO* comes forth by the fourth [proposition]. Therefore you may subtract *DO*, known, from *DC*, known earlier, and *OC* will remain, *OC* being equal to the vertical diametral line *FE*, and this is what had to be done. The summary of the operation follows: "Square the distance *EC*, or any other similar magnitude and divide that square by the latus rectum. Then subtract the numerical quotient from *DC* (which was given), and that which remains will be the vertical diametral line that is sought."

41. When some vertical line of order is known along with a vertical part of the sagitta corresponding to the known line of order, and if, as in the immediately preceding [proposition], some point is taken in the said line of order whose distance from either end of, or from the middle of, the line of order is known, [and] if now a vertical diametral line would be erected from the accepted point to the parabolic linear section, [to express the magnitude of this diametral line].

Let the line of order *AB* be known as well as *CD*, the corresponding vertical part of the sagitta [see Fig. Ap.II.11]. Also let there be given the distance of point *E* either from *A* or *B* or from the middle point of the line of order, namely *C*, for all these distances become mutually manifest whichever of them is given along with the whole of *AB*. Now by the preceding [proposition] let *DR* be elicited, and let *FR* be double *DR*. Hence *FR* is known. And *OR*, which is half of the line of order corresponding to *DR*, is also known, since it is equal to *EC*. Therefore by the thirty-ninth [proposition] line *FO* is tangent to the parabolic linear section at point *O*. Let line *FO* be produced until it meets with line *CA*, which is also sufficiently protracted. For thus we shall have two equiangular triangles *FRO* and *FCP*. Hence *FR* / *RO* = *FC* / *CP*. But *FR*, *RO*, and *FC* are known. Hence *CP* is also known. But *EC* was given earlier. Therefore *EP* now becomes known. And now I shall consider two other equiangular triangles *OPE* and *FPC*. Hence *PC* / *CF* = *PE* / *EO*. But we knew *PC*, *CF*, and *PE*. Therefore we now have *EO*, the vertical diametral line that is sought. The nature of this operation is as follows: "Square the distance of the given point from the middle of the line of order; divide that square by the latus rectum, and double the quotient. Conserve that double as a first number. Add the said quotient to the vertical part of the sagitta which corresponds to the vertical line of order known at first. This will be the third number, and the second will be the distance of the accepted point. Now operate by the rule of three, and elicit a fourth number. From this fourth number subtract the distance of the point. Conserve that remainder for the third number of the new operation. Let the first number in the second operation be that which was sought as the fourth in the first operation, and let the second be that which was the third in the first operation. Now work for a new fourth number by the rule of three and you will become the master of your desire."

[42. Given a line of order and the vertical part of the sagitta] corresponding [to the given line of order], to protract upon the vertical part of the sagitta as many lines of order as you wish, no one of them being prescribed as greater than the line of order given at first.

This is very similar to the thirty-fifth and thirty-sixth [propositions]. Still, it will be seen to differ in some way to one who considers the matter closely. Let *AB* be the given line of order and *CD* the corresponding part of the sagitta [see Fig. Ap.II.12]. Now if in *AB* any line as large as you wish is cut out, its half being always situated in point *C*, we shall immediately determine its place in the sagitta where it becomes the line of order. Let *EF* be the line to which we would construct an equal line of order. Let *CE* be half of *EF*. Square *CE* and divide that square by the latus rectum, for the quotient will show you the vertical part of the sagitta to which the given line *EF* will be the corresponding vertical line of order. This proposition is also similar to the fourth [proposition]. I did not wish, however, to omit having this in hand in a certain simple context, for from this anyone could reduce other things enunciated in other words to our expression of the same proposition. Moreover it will be satisfactory for locating as many lines of order as you wish and [each such] line need not be graduated equally with the vertical part of the sagitta, as we have established in the thirty-fifth and thirty-sixth [propositions].

43. To express in still another way the magnitude of the vertical diametral line which is erected from a point given in the given line of order to the parabolic section itself, there being given initially a vertical part of the sagitta which corresponds to the given line of order and also [given] the distance of the given point from the middle of this line of order, as we supposed earlier in the fortieth and forty-first [propositions].

I first worked out this way, and I was the first of all [to do so] (as far as I know), when I was thinking out the preceding fortieth and forty-first [propositions] and I was describing them. I do this in several [ways] because several other useful things seem to depend on it, as will appear from their operations. From the fifth [proposition] of Archimedes' *On the Quadrature of the Parabola* [note the following:]

"Let *ABC* be a segment bounded by a straight line and the section of a right-angled cone [i.e., a parabola]; and from point *A* let there be drawn line *AF* parallel to the diameter [see Fig. Ap.II.13]. From point *C* let there be drawn a tangent to the section of the cone that meets with *AF* in point *F*. Now if some line is drawn in triangle *FAC* which is parallel to *AF*, the line drawn will be cut by the section of the right-angled cone in the same ratio

that *AC* [is cut] by the line drawn, while the segment of line *AC* toward *A* will correspond to the segment of the line drawn which is toward line *AC*."
  Therefore *AK / KC = KH /HL*.

Our Porism.

[1.] Therefore conjunctively *AC / AK = KL / KH*.

AC is supposed as known in our forty-third [proposition], and *DK* is also given (for *K* is supposed to be that point accepted in the line of order). Hence *AK* is also [known], so that you may also have *KL*. Consider two equiangular triangles *KLC* and *EDC*. Hence *CD / DE = CK / KL*. But *CD* is half the given line of order and *DE* (double the [given] vertical part of the sagitta, namely *DB*, as you have seen in the thirty-ninth [proposition]) [is known, as is *CK*]; therefore there is nothing more [left to know] but side *KL*. Therefore always conceive of a triangle of this sort around any given segment of a parabola, and by these rules you will find *HK*, and any other vertical diametral line drawn to *AC*:

"Multiply the distance of the accepted point (as *K* is in the example) from the point of contact (namely *C*) by twice the given vertical part of the sagitta. And divide the product by half of the given line of order, for the quotient will be the certain whole line parallel to the sagitta, falling on the accepted point, and crossing the parabolic linear section." [And this line will be useful] for eliciting [its part, the vertical diametral line, as we shall see below].

[2.] Therefore permutatively *AC / KL = AK / KH*.

In the first method [proceed as follows]: "Subtract the distance of the accepted point from the whole given line of order. Multiply the remainder by the magnitude of the line found from the preceding rule (which was *KL* in the example). And divide the product by the whole given line of order, and the quotient will be the vertical diametral line to be erected at the accepted point, the line which you were desirous of finding. [And this is *KH* in our example.]

In the second way [proceed as follows]: "I multiply the whole line previously found by the rest of the given line of order (i.e., after the distance of the accepted point has been subtracted from the whole given line of order, as you have done in the first method), and divide the product by the whole line of order, for the quotient will display the diametral line that is sought." This operation is almost the same as the first except that in the first method the remainder from the whole line of order was the second number in the rule of three and here it is the third, as can appear to you immediately from the words of these porisms.

[44. To find a vertical diametral line to be erected from a given point of a line of order,] with any vertical line of order proposed and a vertical part of the sagitta known (whether in numbers or not).

Let the proposed line of order be *AB* of 60 inches [see Fig. Ap.II.14]. Let the [corresponding] vertical part of the sagitta be *CD* of 6 inches. Now let a right triangle of Archimedes of the sort we described in the preceding [proposition] be constructed out of [the following lines:] (1) a line tangent to the parabolic linear section at one end of a given line of order, this being the hypotenuse, (2) the line of order, this being one of the sides containing the right angle, and (3) the remaining side, being the line erected at the other end of the line of order at right angles to it and meeting the said tangent. Such a triangle will be produced immediately if you extend the given part of the sagitta until it becomes double itself (as has been explained in the thirty-ninth [proposition]), and from the one end of the line of order you draw a straight line sufficiently far through the summit of this double line, and afterward from the other end of the line of order you may erect a perpendicular to meet with that hypotenuse, as you can observe in triangle *ABF* [and] as I described this argument. Now from any point in *AB* you may draw a line to hypotenuse *FB* that is parallel to *AF*, and let it be *GH*; and from the same point *H* you may draw a line to *AF* that is parallel to *FB*, and let it be *HR*. Now if from point *R* you draw a straight line to the other end of the line of order, this line will cut *GH* so that the part toward *H* will be the vertical diametral line that is sought, namely *OH*. And I think this is a beautiful and easy mechanical way, for we need here no operations with numbers.

The Demonstration of This.

There are two equiangular triangles *ARB* and *HOB*. Hence *AH / HB* = *RO / OB*. There are two other equiangular triangles *ROH* and *GOB*. Therefore *RO / OH = OB / OG*. Therefore permutatively *RO / OB = OH / OG*. But [since] *RO / OB = AH / HB*, therefore *OH / OG = AH / HB*. Therefore point *O* is in the parabolic linear section, by those things we have demonstrated in the forty-third [proposition].

[45. Given a vertical line of order, and] given also the corresponding vertical part of the sagitta, to describe by means of diametral lines a parabolic linear section terminating at the ends of the given line of order.

You may divide the given line of order in as many equal parts as you fittingly can. Then for half of those parts you may determine the vertical diametral lines of order by any of the methods you wish of those explained in [Propositions] 40, 41, 43, and 44, and you may stand each of these in its place (I have always located [at one and the same time] the two of the same length which are at equal distances from the middle [of the line of order]). Afterward conjoin all the ends of the said lines by means of a curved line and you will see emerge the parabolic linear section you wish. Therefore you can by [Propositions] 40, 41, and 43 compose certain tables of numbers where at first the length of the line of order of any size you wish is supposed and also a vertical part of a sagitta of any size so long as it does not exceed a fourth part of this line of order. For it will suffice for the operations of nature to be contemplated if you never take the latus rectum inside its mirror. And if you make large mirrors (this kind alone we shall exemplify for you) you cannot columnate [i.e. provide diametral lines] to the convexity with respect to the latus rectum in only a single mirror.

For example, let the line of order be 1½ feet [see Fig. Ap.II.15] and the corresponding vertical part of the sagitta ⅓ of one foot. Now graduate the line of order in inches, evidently 18, and each inch in 6 or 8 parts. Similarly you may also graduate the given part of the sagitta into similar parts, and you may complete a rectangular parallelogram of the line of order and the part of the sagitta by drawing parallel lines through the individual parts of the line of order as well as through those of the sagitta, as you can see in the proposed figure where *OD* is four of such parts and *AB* is 18. Also determine the vertical diametral lines from . . . . A duplex table has to be made where the first [column] will be of lines of order and the second of corresponding diametral lines, two of which sort we have calculated for you. Let us suppose that any inch is divided into 8 parts, and moreover we have assumed the length of the line of order to be 18 inches and the part of the sagitta to be 4 inches. Hence with the inches graduated in their eighths, the length of the whole line of order will be 144 (but we have need to calculate tables for only half [of the parts], namely 72; then we would always transfer [any] intended [vertical] line to another place in the line of order that is just as distant from the sagitta as our intended [line] is distant from the said sagitta), and therefore we shall have in this parabola of ours a sagitta of 32 eighth-parts of one inch. Therefore this mirror will burn at $5\frac{1}{16}$ inches from the vertex of the parabola. For how many uses this one table will serve we shall soon teach well by means of several propositions discovered by us.

0	64	0	25	50
1	63		26	51
2	63		27	52
3	62		28	53
4	62		29	54
5	61		30	55
6	61		31	56
7	60		32	57
8	60		33	58
9	60	0	34	59
10	59		35	60
11	59		36	61
12	58		37	62
13	58		38	63
14	57		39	64
15	57		40	65
16	56		41	66
17	56		42	67
18	56	0	43	68
19	55		44	69
20	55		45	70
21	54		46	71
22	54		47	72
23	53		48	0
24	53		49	0

[46. . . . . .] [*The enunciation occupied lines destroyed by fire and I omit any effort to reconstruct it, but the substance of it surely must be that the numerical tables are valid regardless of which units of measure the numbers represent.*]

For if you consider what we have supposed as inches to be palms or feet, the same will be the nature of the numbers in parts of the sort that you take for your work. Contrariwise, if you have as many grains as we have inches, these tables of ours will equally be of use to you.

47. However large are the parabolas whose segments you describe, the same table will still display smaller frusta [i.e. segments] of those segments if you wish.

For if you change our inches into palms, and you would wish to have a frustum whose part of the sagitta you would like to be only three palms, we have placed beside these tables the distance of combustion and the latus rectum of our tables so that they could always be ready at hand. Elicit the line of order corresponding to your three palms by the third [proposition] of this [work]. Take half of the line of order found and subtract that half from another half of a line of order in the tables, namely from the maximum number of our line of order placed in the table. And seek the diametral line of the remainder in our table. Put that diametral line aside so that you may subtract it from all the following [lines], and there will emerge for you new diametral lines to be located in your recently discovered line of order (you cannot be ignorant of where they ought to be placed unless you are completely stupid). And if the line to be subtracted is not found in the tables, still you know how great an interval in the line of order from the diametral line is the first line of your table which can serve for the proposition, which [knowledge] is sufficient, and [so] understand well what I say.

48. Keeping the same line of order, if the corresponding vertical part of the sagitta is changed to one that is greater, the distance of combustion of the same [latter parabola] will be smaller, and its [latus rectum will also be smaller].

[This is evident by the methods explained in Propositions 7 and 8]. Maximum [praise] to God and [and to his son] who holds the lordship of this world. . . . But who was sent to this world, i.e. to die for the world. May he reign with God, to whom Honor and Glory.

49. The ratio between two different vertical parts of a sagitta which correspond to one line of order (but in two different parabolas) is the same, but in reciprocal relationship, as that between the distances of combustion [of the two parabolas; cf. Fig. Ap.II.16].

Given another part of a sagitta in addition to our tabular part of a sagitta, both having the same corresponding line of order, if you should wish to know the magnitude of the distance of combustion terminated in the other sagitta, "multiply our sagitta by its [distance of] combustion; [then] divide the product by the other sagitta, for the quotient will give the [distance of] combustion of the other parabola with that sagitta, whether a larger or smaller sagitta than ours is introduced."

The demonstration of this matter depends on this proposition: If two diverse numbers divide one number, then the ratio of the divisors is [inversely] as that of the quotients. The two diverse numbers are our sagittas; the same number is the square of half of the line of order, [and] the quotients are the latera recta themselves which are in the ratio we have mentioned. But someone will object: "The statement here is made concerning combustion and not concerning latera recta." But since the distance of combustion is one fourth its latus rectum, it is clear that the ratio of the combustions is that of the latera recta, for a whole is to a whole as a half is to a half and as a fourth of one is to a fourth of the other. Therefore the demonstration is evident. And this last part of the demonstration depends on the force of this proposition: If one number divides two, the ratio of the quotients is that of the ratio of the dividends. The two diverse numbers are the two diverse latera recta which we divide by [the one number] 4 (as is clear in [Proposition 1]); therefore the fourths that result [i.e. the distances of combustion] are in the same ratio as the latera recta.

[50. Keeping the same part of a sagitta, if] the corresponding vertical [line of order is changed], the distance of combustion in that one whose line of order is greater will be greater, and the ratio between the distances of combustion is that between the squares of the halves of the given lines of order.

Therefore, in order that the distance of combustion may be had in any other line of order in addition to our tabular [line] or between any two other [lines of order], take the squares of the halves of the given lines of order and put forward the [distance of] combustion known to you, and then arrange them for the rule of three in the following way [see Fig. Ap.II.17]:

□	□	──
A	B	C
□	□	───

| The square of half the line of order whose combustion is known, whether one is to add more or less. | The square of half the line of order whose combustion is sought. | The known combustion. |

The Demonstration of this Fiftieth [Proposition]

Because one number divides two, the ratio of the quotients will be that of the dividends. The two diverse numbers are the squares arising from the halves of the given lines of order. The one number is the same vertical part of the sagitta which corresponds to both [the given lines of order]. Therefore it is clear that the latera recta are in the ratio of the said squares if the latera recta and the distances of combustion are as we have taught in the preceding [proposition].

51. Keeping the same line of order, if another sagitta double the prior is assumed, the ratio of [each of] all the diametral lines in the parabola having the double sagitta is double that of [each of all the] diametral lines of the other [parabola] that are at a distance [from the sagitta] equal to that of the former [diametral lines].

[Given two parabolas *ACB* and *AEB* (see Fig. Ap.II.18) in which] the sagitta [of one is double the sagitta of the other and both sagittas correspond to the same line of order, we are to prove] that any diametral line which falls from the parabolic linear section *ACB* to the line of order *AB* will be double the diametral line which falls from the parabolic linear section *AEB* to the same point of the line of order *AB*. Let a triangle of Archimedes be described for us and let there be in that triangle a line parallel to *AK* and drawn from the tangent [*BK*] to the line of order, and let it be *LM*, cutting *ACB* in point *R* and *AEB* in point *O*. I say that *RM* = 2 *OM*. By our forty-third [proposition] it is apparent that *AM* / *MB* = *MR* / *RL* for parabolic segment *ACB*, and similarly *AM* / *MB* = *MO* / *OS* for parabolic segment *AEB*. Therefore *MR* / *RL* = *MO* / *OS*, and therefore, by inversion, *LR* / *RM* = *SO* / *OM*. Therefore conjunctively *LM* / *RM* = *SM* / *OM*. Therefore permutatively *LM* / *SM* = *RM* / *OM*. But *LM* = 2 *SM*, for *XD* = 2 *CD* (*KXB* being tangent to *ACB* at point *B*). The two triangles *XCB* and *LSB* are equiangular as also are two others, *CDB* and *SMB*. Therefore *BX* / *XC* = *BL* / *LS*. Therefore *BX* / *XL* = *XC* / *LS*. By the same argument *BC* / *CD* = *BS* / *SM*. Therefore permutatively *BC* / *BS* = *CD* / *SM*. But *BC* / *BS* = *BX* / *BL*, for these ratios are equal to *BD* / *BM*. Therefore *XC* / *LS* = *CD* / *SM*. Therefore permutatively *XC* / *CD* = *LS* / *SM*. But *XC* was made equal to *CD*. Therefore *LS* = *SM*. Therefore the whole *LM* = 2 *SM*, which has been proposed.

Porism

Hence another use of our tables is evident for the construction of various parabolas [namely those whose sagitta is double, quadruple, octuple etc., or sub]-double, [subquadruple, suboc]tuple etc. to our tabular sagitta, with the same line of order conserved.

If therefore you wish to describe a linear segment of a parabola with a double sagitta for a line of order equal to ours, double our individual numbers placed in the table of diametral lines, and they will be useful to you for your desired end. So [multiply these numbers] by 4 if [you wish a parabola] with a quadruple sagitta, and so on. Similarly if you wish to draw a parabolic segment that has our line of order but has another sagitta of which ours is double, divide our individual numbers by 2 and you will have what you wish. Similarly you may divide [the numbers] by 4, if you make our extension of that [sagitta] quadruple the new sagitta.

Porism

By the preceding porism and the forty-eighth and forty-seventh propositions [you will see] how manifold will be the use of our tables.

I have wished to remind you of this, not having [however] any doubt of your ingenuity by which you yourself would immediately have understood that this would follow.

52. "If two parabolic segments of unequal sagittas are placed on the same line of order or upon two equal [lines of order], the ratio of their unequal sagittas will be the same as that of similarly located diametral lines in these two parabolic segments."

When I had discovered and demonstrated this proposition I was pierced with great joy, and here [the proposition may be proved by a demonstration like] the preceding demonstration, except that the greater sagitta we let, for example, be 2⅓ the smaller one. Therefore let us proceed and here you will see the same demonstration as in the preceding [proposition]. Therefore it cannot be difficult.

Let CD be 2⅓ ED [see Fig. Ap.II.19]. The rest of the construction is evident from the antecedent [constructions]. I say that $RM = $ 2⅓ OM. It is immediately apparent that $XD = $ 2⅓ GD, for $XD = 2\ CD$ and GD is posited as $2\ ED$. But $CD = $ 2⅓ ED, for doubles of the same things are in the same ratio [as the things themselves]. But $XD\ /\ GD = LM\ /\ SM$ for $BX\ /\ XD = BL\ /\ LM$. Therefore permutatively $BX\ /\ BL = XD\ /\ LM$. But $BX\ /\ BL = BD\ /\ BM$ and $BD\ /\ BM = GD\ /\ SM$ (in the two equiangular triangles DGB and SMB). Therefore $BX\ /\ BL = GD\ /\ SM = XD\ /\ LM$. Since, therefore, $XD\ /\ LM = GD\ /\ SM$, so permutatively $XD\ /\ GD = LM\ /\ SM$, which we needed to have proved. I say finally that $RM\ /\ OM = LM\ /\ SM$. This we have often demonstrated above. But let us reveal its truth anew. $MB\ /\ MA = LR\ /\ RM$, and $MB\ /\ MA = SO\ /\ OM$, as was evident in the forty-third [proposition]. Therefore $LR\ /\ RM = SO\ /\ OM$. Therefore conjunctively $LM\ /\ RM = SM\ /\ OM$. Therefore permutatively $LM\ /\ SM = RM\ /\ OM$, which was especially necessary to have demonstrated. $LM\ /\ SM = XD\ /\ GD$. And XD [$= $ 2⅓ GD. Hence $LM = $ 2⅓ SM, and so $RM = $ 2⅓ OM, which was to be demonstrated]. You can demonstrate the same thing for any other ratio and for all the diametral lines which are taken at equal distances from their sagittas.

Porism

Therefore, by means of the rule of three you could apply our table to any other vertical part of the sagitta, our line of order having always been conserved as the one corresponding to the given sagitta.

Say therefore that our sagitta shows the further sagitta, which latter will give a diametral line, and you will see the length of the line you seek.

An Admonition Concerning Another Practice with our Table

If perhaps you do not wish to graduate your line of order into as many parts as we have designated in the here-attached table so that it will serve a maximum number of matters, or [if] you could not, [even] if you wished to, impress as many sensible parts in your proposed line, you will avail yourself of the following advice. Look at the column to the side which we have designated by this title: THE COLUMN OF ELECTION, where immediately in the beginning is proposed the number of parts of half the line of order, whose length, if you graduate it into 6000 parts, you take in order in this table. So in [the beginning] take for your first and shortest the [first] line of the table, while you descend in your column opposite to your column, and here for your second . . . . . to your sagitta of the table or to your . . . . . if you have formed our table proportionally, namely if your line of order is twelve times your sagitta or if half of your line of order is six times [your sagitta], which is the same thing.

The Table of the Diametral Lines where the Vertical Line of Order is Supposed to be 12000, its half 6000, and the Vertical Part of the Sagitta 1000.

COLUMN OF ELECTION

				0	0	
						1
	1				2	
		1			3	
	2		1		4	
					5	
	3	2		1	6	
					7	
	4		2		8	
		3			9	
	5				10	
					11	
	6	4	3	2	12	000
	6	4	3	2		

(left vertical label: Exemplification)

Made by means of the 40th

Place of the Table

[*But Dee does not add the table*]

Then by the rule of three transform the number in the table into your graduation, for the line is given in the new denomination. Therefore, by the method of the right triangle [of Archimedes, find] the number, and so on.

53. To elicit the magnitude of the angle of solar incidence by means of tables of sines when the line of order and the vertical part of the sagitta corresponding to that same angle are given.

. . . . . Then you may constitute as the first [term] our line of tangency; as the second, half of the given line of order; finally as the third, the whole sine [i.e. the sine of 90° or 1] of those tables which you use in this matter. And when you multiply the third by the second and divide the product by the first, the number of the quotient you seek out in the same tables from which you took the whole sine, for opposite to that right sine you will find the angle that is sought. Further, we shall demonstrate this as follows.

Let AB be the given line of order and CD the given sagitta [see Fig. Ap.II.20]. Let $DE = 2CD$, and (by the thirty-eighth [proposition]) AE will be a tangent [to the parabola] and its magnitude you have elicited by the thirty-ninth [proposition]. And our operation has displayed angle AED, which, I say, is equal to the angle that is sought. For let the line of solar incidence be KA, and let the tangent line EA be extended beyond A to Q, or farther, [since] the question concerned this angle of incidence KAQ, and I have said that AED is equal to this angle that is sought, which is evident because the line of solar incidence and the doubled sagitta are parallel by the definition of the line of solar incidence, and a straight line cuts [both of] them, namely line QAE. Therefore angle QAK = angle AED, which needed demonstration.

54. If at the superior terminus of some given vertical diametral line a line is drawn tangent to the parabolic section, to seek out by means of a table of sines the magnitude [of the angle which that line of contingence makes with the given diametral line], there being known before both your line of order from which that diametral line is erected to the parabolic section and the distance of that same diametral [line] from the vertical part of the sagitta which corresponds to that known line of order; and in the third place let the vertical part of the sagitta corresponding to the said line of order also be known.

Subtract the given diametral line from the vertical part of the sagitta which corresponds to that line of order on which the diametral [line] is erected [cf. Fig. Ap.II.21]. Double the remainder; square that double. Then square the distance of the given diametral line from the sagitta. Add these two squares. Extract the square of their sum. You may constitute this root the first number in a rule of three; further you may make the distance from the sagitta the second [number], and finally [you may put] the whole sine [i.e. 1] of the tables you wish to use as the third [number]. For if you duly seek the fourth number that has been found [by the rule of three] in these tables [of sines], you will find that the angle which is sought corresponds to that number. But so that we may free others from great annoyances, we have calculated all the angles corresponding to the individual vertical diametral lines of our tables. This differs little from the preceding [proposition] because the diametral line is seen to be a certain part of the line of incidence. Hence the demonstration of this is evident from the previous [proposition].

An Admonition Concerning These Angles

Although we make mention here of the line of contingence, and of the angle which we mention with it [i.e. the line of contingence] and with other lines, still it ought to be indicated that the same angles are made with that parabolic linear section in so far as it pertains to this operation, etc.

[55. If there are drawn some] vertical diametral [line and some] vertical part of the sagitta corresponding to the line of order on which it stands, and if the diametral line, the vertical part of the sagitta, and the distance of the diametral [line] from the sagitta are given, to set forth the magnitude of the line of order on which the two given lines stand.

Subtract the diametral line from the given vertical part of the sagitta. Conserve the remainder. Now square the given distance [of the diametral line from the sagitta], and you may divide that square by the remainder that was conserved, for the quotient will be the latus rectum. Now with both the latus rectum and the vertical part of the sagitta had, by the third [proposition] of this [work] you will have the line of order that is desired.

56. Given some vertical diametral line which stands upon a given line of order and given also the vertical part of the sagitta corresponding to the given line of order, to make known the distance by which the [given] diametral line is removed from the given vertical part of the sagitta.

Subtract the given diametral line from the given part of the sagitta. Conserve the remainder. Then by the seventh [proposition] elicit the latus rectum (for here the line of order and the corresponding part of the sagitta are given). Now multiply the latus rectum by that remainder previously conserved, for the square root of this will be the distance that is sought.

[57. Given the distance of some given] diametral [line] from the vertical part of the sagitta which corresponds to the given line of order, to root out the magnitude of the vertical part of the sagitta which corresponds to the given line of order.

Add the distance of the diametral line from the sagitta to half the given line of order. Subtract that sum from the whole line of order. Conserve that remainder. For you will arrange the sum, the remainder, and the given diametral line in a rule of three as follows: let the remainder be the first number, the sum the second, and the diametral line the third. Elicit now the fourth, and add that same fourth to the given diametral line. Hence the number [so] produced, the sum previously found, and half the given line of order stand in a rule of three so that the [first] sum is the first number, that [second sum] of the fourth and the given diametral [line] is the second [number], and the third is half of the given line of order. Hence take half of the fourth number [so] found, for that half will be the part of the sagitta that is sought. The demonstration of this is manifest from our forty-third [proposition].

For $AB / BC = BD / DE$ [see Fig. Ap.II.22], and DE is our fourth number which we add to DB, namely to the given diametral line. Hence we have BE. But CB was our [first] sum, as we have designated it above. Further CB

/ *BE* = *CO* (half of the given line of order) / *OS*. But by the thirty-eighth and forty-third [propositions] *OS* is double the part of the sagitta that is sought. Therefore [its] half will not be hidden, which [is what] we needed to demonstrate.

If now [you understand] well [what] we have done in prior propositions for the sagitta, ... of the parabola, and the axis of the cone, by usefully mixing [them] together so that the hand of the operator would be prepared for all cases, and we have added this proposition in place of an admonition. Though it is also known per se, it will be useful to us.

58. The angle of solar reflection from every point of a vertical segment of our parabola is equal to the angle of solar incidence produced at the same point.

Let the angle of incidence be *ABE* and the angle of reflection *CBD* [see Fig. Ap.II.23]. I say that *CBD* is equal to angle *ABE*. Consider triangle *CBD* and its three angles *CBD*, *BCD*, and *BDC*, and then [consider] the angles *ABE*, *ABC*, and *CBD* that stand on *EBD* equal to two right angles. As those three angles of triangle *CBD* are also equal to two right angles, therefore these three [angles] are equal to those three [angles]. But *ABE* is equal to *BDC* since *AB* and *CD* are parallel lines and *EBD* cuts them. Therefore by [the twenty-ninth proposition] of the first [book] of Euclid *ABE* and *BDC* are equal, and by the same argument *BCD* is equal to angle *ABC* since *BC* cuts the said parallels. All of these things are clear from the property of parallel lines cut by a line. For *ABE* is equal to *BDC*, and *ACP* is equal to *BDC*. Therefore *ABE* is equal to *ACP*, and *ACP* is equal . . . [*the first proof ends abruptly*]

Now consider the two triangles *ABC* and *BLM* [see Fig. Ap.II.24], in which two sides of the one are equal to two sides of the other and the angles contained by the equal sides are equal (since *BM* and *AC* are parallel). Therefore the bases, namely *BC* and *LM*, will also be equal, and the remaining angles will be equal to the remaining angles, the one to the other, those angles being subtended under equal sides, by the fourth [proposition] of the first [book] of Euclid. Therefore angle *BLM* = angle *ABC*, and [angle] *BML* = angle *ACB*. But I also say that [angle] *ABC* = angle *LBM*. But if the adversary denies [this], and [says] therefore they are unequal, then [angle *ABC*] will be either more or less than *LBM*. If he says more, let there be cut out an [angle] equal to *LBM*, and let it be *ABN*, [and] now there are two triangles *ABN* and *BLM* since two angles of one [*here the second proof abruptly ends, no doubt because the whole proposition is being abandoned*]

58bis. A line of reflection from any point of our parabolic section is equal to the distance of combustion plus that part of the sagitta extended outside [of the vertex] from whose superior terminus that exists outside of the parabola a line tangent to the parabolic linear section is drawn to the same point from which the line of reflection proceeds.

Let the line of reflection be *AB* [see Fig. Ap.II.25], and let *BD* be the line of combustion plus the external part from whose end a line tangent to the parabolic linear section descends to point *A*. I say that *AB* and *BD* are equal. It is evident by the fifty-third [proposition] that *EAF* and *BDA* are equal.

But all the authors of [tracts on] parabolic burning mirrors demonstrate that the angle of incidence and [angle] of reflection are equal. Therefore angle of incidence *EAF* and angle of reflection *BAD* are equal. But *EAF* was demonstrated to be equal to *BDA*. Therefore *BDA* = *BAD*. Therefore *BAD* will be an isosceles triangle by the sixteenth [proposition] of the first [book] of Euclid, and [hence] *AB* and *BD* will be equal, which has been proposed.

[59. Given the distance of combustion and a vertical part of the sagitta], to determine where either terminus of the [line] of order corresponding to the given vertical part of the sagitta falls.

Propose for yourself a distance of combustion, from which cut your given vertical part of the sagitta. Afterward you may produce the distance of combustion by a length equal to the given part of the sagitta. Then at the point in the distance of combustion from which you have cut a part equal to the given part of the sagitta draw a perpendicular line in each direction to infinity. Afterward from the point of combustion to the perpendicular line you may extend a line equal to the sum of the distance of combustion and the [given] part of the sagitta, and where that line so extended falls on the perpendicular, there is the point which you seek.

For example, let *AB* be the given distance of combustion and *AC* the given vertical part of the sagitta [see Fig. Ap.II.26]. I produce *BA* in the direction of point *A* until *AO* equals *AC*. Then at point *C* I draw an infinite line in both directions and at right angles to *AB*, and let it be *DE*. Afterward from the point of combustion (namely *B*) I extend toward *DE* a line equal to *BO*, and where its terminus falls on line *DE* let point *Q* be marked. I say that point *Q* is the point that is sought. The demonstration of this depends on the preceding [proposition] and is evident.

60. Given the distance of combustion, to describe mechanically a vertical part of the parabola or a segment of a parabolic linear section according to any part of the sagitta.

You may add in a straight line to the given distance of combustion another straight line equal to the distance of combustion. Then [proceeding] from the vertex of the parabola [you can] graduate [the line of combustion into a certain number of equal parts]. You may transfer the very [same] parts to that other adjunct line by proceeding in the same way from the vertex. Afterward you may draw through the individual points of the divisions of the distance of combustion very long lines or at least lines as long as is the corresponding latus rectum. Having done this, consider by the method of the preceding proposition how to fix the point of any line which you wish, and see its distance from the vertex. You may [then] take an equal distance outside of the vertex in that other line, beginning from the vertex itself. And where that distance is terminated, mark it, for from that terminus to the point of combustion you measure the length by a compass, and then [with compass opening fixed by that measure and] with one foot of the compass at rest [in the point of combustion] you may transfer the other foot to the [perpendicular] line you have chosen so that it falls exactly on that line, for the place of this foot [of the compass] is a point of the sort that we have taught you to find in the preceding [proposition]. And so you do this for each of your individual [perpendicular lines], and afterward connect all of those points by a single curved line, and you will be master of your desire. I do not judge it to be necessary here or in those things above to advise you as to why you locate one point [on one line drawn] out of one part of the sagitta in the same way as you locate [such a point on another line drawn] out of another [part of the sagitta]. For such matters are evident in themselves. And because the proposition refers to any given part of a sagitta, this is to be so understood that by this same art you may describe a segment whose sagitta is less than the distance of combustion, by graduating that part of the sagitta just as you did for the distance of combustion itself, without changing the rest [of the argument].

Let the given distance of combustion be *AB* [see Fig. Ap.II.27]. And I add to it in a straight line another line equal to *AB*, and let it be *AC*. I divide *AB* into ten equal parts, beginning from *A* and proceeding to *B*. Similarly I also divide *AC* into ten [parts], beginning from *A* and proceeding toward *C*. Now through the individual points of division of *AB* I draw lines at right angles with *AB* . . . . . from *A* points and at such a distance from the same point *A* outside the parabola in *AC* I place one foot of a compass and the other I apply to the point of combustion itself. Then I leave that foot which was placed in the point of combustion unmoved and I transfer the other foot (without the opening of the compass changed) to the very first line in each direction from the sagitta, [thus] locating the parabolic point. They (i.e. points) follow in the same way with the other lines, as you can see in the attached figure, where I also connect the individual points by means of a single curved line for completing the proposed construction.

That the fifty-ninth proposition can be proposed in other words is apparent from these things [described here], namely in the following or similar words:

Given the distance of combustion, if from the same line any vertical part of the sagitta is cut out, to prescribe mechanically the vertical line of order corresponding to the vertical part of the sagitta that has been cut out [from the distance of combustion].

The matter would amount to the same thing if the problem had been proposed in these words. I leave many things [that come] out of this problem to the contemplation and practice of the ingenious mathematician or mechanician.

61. Given the angle of incidence, to find the corresponding angle of combustion.

Double the angle of incidence, and you may subtract that double from 180° and the remainder will show you the magnitude of the angle of combustion, and so in a table of angles of incidence are also found the magnitudes of the corresponding angles of combustion.

62. If some point is accepted outside of the vertical segment of our parabola but in the same plane as our parabolic segment [and if the sagitta of the parabola is] protracted in the direction of this point, and from that same point a straight line parallel to the sagitta is drawn to the concavity of our

parabolic segment, to elicit the magnitude of the angle of incidence which that line protracted from the accepted point makes with the line tangent to the parabolic section at this same point in which the line protracted to the concavity of our parabola cuts [it], there now being given also the line of order and the vertical part of the sagitta corresponding to the same line of order in the proposed vertical part of the parabola.

If you are mindful of the things [said] above, you can easily solve and complete this problem and several others which philosophical practice would throw forth. For indeed the accepted point is nothing more than a likeness to the center of the sun in the operation of combustion, for which the line protracted from the same point would be one equivalent to the line of solar incidence. Therefore if the distance of the accepted or proposed point (other, I say, than the center of the sun) sufficiently protracted from the sagitta (at least by a fiction of the mind if not actually protracted) is equal to half of the maximum line of order of your parabolic segment, hence [Proposition] 53 will immediately give you satisfaction. But if it is less than half of the said line of order, then by the fortieth [proposition] you may find the diametral line by using the point accepted here as if [it were in the line of order, and then you will be master] of your desire.

63. Given the angle of incidence and the vertical part of the sagitta corresponding to the given angle, to find the corresponding line of order.

Subtract the given angle from 90°. Make note of the remainder, and you may seek out in whatever tables of sines you wish the right sines of both your given angle and that remainder. Put the right sine of that remainder as the first number; further you may establish the double of the given vertical part of the sagitta as the second, while [you put] the right sine of your given angle as the third. Now proceed according to the rule of three, and in the quotient you will have half of the line of order that is sought. Therefore its double is that which is sought.

64. Given the angle of incidence and the line of order corresponding to the same angle, to elicit the vertical part of the sagitta corresponding to the same [given magnitudes].

Subtract the given angle from 90°; conserve the remainder. Take half the given line of order. Now betake yourself to tables of sines and write down the right sines of the given angle and its complement or remainder. You may place the right sine of the given angle as the first number, half the given line of order as the second, and the right sine of the remainder as the third. That fourth number which ought to be elicited from the operation will be double the vertical part of the sagitta that is sought. Consequently its half is that which you wish.

65. Given the angle of combustion in the vertical part of a parabola, to make known the angle of incidence which corresponds to the given angle.

Subtract the given angle from 180°. You may take one half of the remainder, for it will be the magnitude of the angle sought in the proposition.

[Porism (?) . . . . .] preceding propositions you can elicit [. . . . .] you may seek to use one vertical part of a parabola for any angle of combustion so long as the magnitude of the given angle does not exceed [double] the magnitude of our angle [of incidence].

This will be useful not only for the operation of combustion but also for the operations of other planets and other agents and for directing species to definite places etc. It will also be useful for the diversity of combustive power to be elicited from the diverse angles of the operator. And although in a single parabola by the amount the angle is the greater by that same amount is the circle of combustion under the same angle greater, still you can in another parabola compare by an equal circle any angle you like with your prior angle, for it will be done if you set that other angle to an equal line of order. You can also draw under equal angles various circles for the same comparison if you could not compare [them otherwise]. It would be too long here to lay bare such uses clearly etc.

66. Given some vertical line of order and a corresponding vertical part of the sagitta, to [find] the magnitude of the angle formed at either end of the given line of order.

By the fifty-third [proposition] you may learn the angle of solar incidence produced at the terminus of your line of order. Subtract this from 90° and you have what you seek.

67. Given some vertical line of order and given also the vertical part of the sagitta corresponding to it, if a straight line is drawn from either end of the given line of order to some other point of the sagitta besides the point of combustion, to set forth the magnitude of the angle which this straight line makes with the line [tangent at the same point] and we already directed the sagitta to proceed toward infinity from the vertex, even beyond the base [of the parabola] if it is necessary, the distance of the proposed point in the sagitta from the vertex of our parabola being always given here.

By the sixty-sixth [proposition] you may learn the magnitude of the angle which is formed at either terminus of the given vertical line of order with the tangent line in the same place, and carefully keep that angle to the side. Then subtract the given part of the sagitta from the distance of the accepted point in our infinite sagitta. Conserve the remainder. Square that remainder. Also square half of the given line of order. Join the two squares. Elicit the square root of that sum, for it will be the length of our line of arbitrary incidence. Employ tables of sines in this way. You may seek the whole sine [and it is 1]. The first number [in the rule of three will] be the line of arbitrary incidence, the second the whole sine [i.e. 1], the third either half of the given line of order or the remaining distance of the accepted point [after the vertical part of the sagitta has been subtracted]. The fourth number when sought and found in the table of sines will give you a certain angle (if you have taken half the line of order) which is formed by that line of arbitrary incidence and the sagitta projected to the accepted point. But if you have taken the residual distance, then the angle [found is that] which is formed at the point of tangency by the line of arbitrary incidence and the line of order. If it is the former of them, you may subtract the angle from 90° and add the remainder to that angle which was set aside [before] and subtract that sum from 180°, for this last remainder will be the angle of arbitrary incidence. But if it is the latter [line, i.e. the remaining distance in the sagitta], add that angle taken from tables of sines to the remaining angle set aside [earlier], and you may subtract that sum from 180° and the angle that is sought will remain. The demonstration of this will appear clearly and immediately from the figure added [see Fig. Ap.II.28]. Let A be the point accepted in the protracted sagitta.

Corollary

It is manifest that from BD toward D . . . . . you will predict that angle DBA . . . . .

68. Let a vertical line of order be given and [also] the vertical part of the sagitta corresponding to the given line of order. Then from the vertex let us direct the sagitta to proceed beyond the line of order toward infinity. Now if in the sagitta some point is taken whose distance from the vertex is given, and through that same accepted point we conceive a line drawn off to infinity at right angles to this sagitta in both directions, and [if] in that transverse perpendicular a second point is taken whose distance from the first accepted point is either more or less than half the given line of order, and from the same second point two lines of arbitrary incidence are drawn to both termini of the given line of order, to put forth the magnitudes of the angles which are formed by the lines of arbitrary incidence and the lines tangent to the parabolic section at both termini of the given line of order, the first and second points [being given and the second point being initially less distant from the sagitta than the length of half the given line of order and then afterward more than half that length].

Let AB be the given line of order [see Fig. Ap.II.29] and let the [corresponding] vertical part of the sagitta [be CM], and let CM be produced further toward infinity, and let it be CMX. Let any point [in it] be taken, and let that point be G. Let line IGN be drawn through G at right angles to CMX on both sides of G toward infinity. In this IGN let a second point be taken (called a "second" point since we have already assumed one before), and let the second point be H. And let the distance between those points first be GH, which is less than AM, namely half the given line of order. From H I draw to A and B two lines of arbitrary incidence, namely HA and HB. Through points A and B let there be drawn lines tangent to the [parabolic] section, and let them be DAF and DBE. Now the magnitudes of angles HAF and HBE are sought. Therefore I draw from point A to line IGN a line parallel to CG, and let it be AN. Now conceive of CMG meeting line AH protracted, and let the point of juncture be X. Now I consider equiangular triangles AMX and GHX, so that $HG / GX = AM / MX$. GH is known, being the given distance between the points, and AM is known, being half the line of order. Therefore, to find GX, I consider triangle HAN equiangular to GHX. Therefore $HN / NA = HG / GX$. HN is known, if GH is subtracted from MA, and NA is equal to GM and GH is the given distance between the points. Therefore GX will not be hidden. Hence you may add MG and you will have MX . . . . . you may proceed [as in Proposition] 67. [I shall consider equiangular triangles *LMB* and *LGH* and so] $GH / GL = BM / ML$. Therefore permutatively $GH / BM = GL / ML$. Therefore conjunctively $(GH + BM) / BM = (GL + ML) / ML$. But *GH* and *BM* are known, and similarly also is *MG* [known]. Therefore *LM* will not be hidden. And so then it will be as if point *L* had been given to us, or as if point *L* was proposed. And then from [Proposition] 67 you will learn what has to be done.

But if the distance between the given points is greater than half of the given line of order, let the whole [distance] be *GI*. Moreover let *G* be the first point and *I* the second point, as above. And then, to find angle *IAD*, consider the two equiangular triangles *IKG* and *AMK*, and just as we proceeded in triangles *HLG* and *BLM* [before], [so now] in the same way you will make *K* a point given in the sagitta. [So] according to the argument of Proposition 67 you will become master of your desire. Afterward, in order to find angle *IBE*, you may draw line *GB* and drop a perpendicular from *B* to line *IG*, and let it be *BO*. By the sixty-seventh [proposition] elicit now the angle *GBE*, and conserve it. Subtract that same conserved angle from two right angles, that is from 180°, and conserve the angle that remains. From that remainder subtract the angle which the tangent line makes with the line of order (by [Proposition] 66). That angular remainder call the second remainder, which you subtract from 90°. And that [last] angular remainder you call the third remainder, which will correspond to *BGM*, and therefore to *GBO*. Now there remains still to be found only angle *OBI*, which you will have in this way. Subtract *BM* from *IG* and *IO* will remain. But *BO* = *MG*. Therefore the two sides of right triangle *OIB* are known. Therefore the hypotenuse *BI* also [is known]. Therefore from tables of sines you will learn angle *OBI* in this way. Make hypotenuse *BI* the first number [in a rule of three], the whole sine [i.e. 1] the second, and side *IO* the third. Hence if you seek out the fourth number, after it has been found, in tables of sines, it will give to you the angle *OBI*. Join it to angle *GBO* found earlier, and subtract the sum from *GBE* found before, and the angle that is sought will remain to you, namely *IBE*.

[69. If the vertical part of the sagitta and its corresponding line of order of our] figure [are given, and] if an angle of arbitrary reflection is constructed [at one terminus of the line of order], to put forth [the point in the sagitta] at whose distance from the vertex of the parabola the line of arbitrary reflection will cut the sagitta.

Learn the angle which is formed by the tangent line and the given line of order by [Proposition] 66. And then subtract it from the angle of arbitrary incidence or arbitrary reflection (for these two are equal). You note the remainder, and you may subtract it from 90°, and that second remainder is also noted. In tables of right sines you may seek out the right sines of both of these remainders and write down the numbers found there. [Then] you may make the right sine of the second remainder the first number [in a rule of three], and half the line of order the second. Moreover you will make the right sine of the first angular remainder the third [number]. For if you add to the fourth number, after it has been found, the [given] vertical part of the sagitta, you will have what you seek.

70. [*Here the text breaks off.*]

Sources Related to Some Propositions in Jordanus' *Liber philotegni* and in the *Liber de triangulis Iordani*

A.

Sources Related to Propositions 5, 6, 14, 18–23, and 25 of the
Liber philotegni and the Corresponding Propositions of the
Liber de triangulis Iordani

For the texts below I have used the proposition numbers of my texts as rubrics, prefixing the letter P to the proposition numbers of the *Liber philotegni* and omitting the title *Liber de triangulis Iordani* from the proposition numbers of that work.

P.5 (=I.5), P.6 (=I.6), I.5+

For proof of Proposition 5, Jordanus in the *Liber philotegni* cites the anonymous *Liber ysoperimetrorum*. The relevant proof occurs in the course of Proposition 1 (see the edition of H. L. L. Busard, "Der Traktat *De iso-perimetris* der unmittelbar aus dem Griechischen ins Lateinische übersetzt worden ist," *Mediaeval Studies,* Vol. 42 [1980], p. 71 [whole article, pp. 61–88]). However I have based my text below on MS *O* (Bodleian Library MS Auct. F.5.28, 105r) primarily because of the additional marginal note and a few readings that differ slightly from those in Busard's text. I have also punctuated the text in a different way. Notice that the objective of the proof quoted here is the conjunctive proportion that plays a role in Propositions I.5+, P.6, and I.6, with the simple proportion given in Propositions P.5 and I.5 being the penultimate step of the proof.

> Quoniam [=quod] vero *gt* recta ad *tk* maiorem proportionem habet quam angulus *gzt* ad angulum *kzt* demonstratum autem est Theoni in commemoratione

2 (demonstratum *ed*

synolis

parvi astronomii nihilominus vero et nunc demonstrabitur [Fig. Ap.III.A.1].
Centro enim *z* et spatio *zk* circuli periferia describatur *mkn* et educatur *zt* in *n*.
5   Quoniam ergo est sicut *gk* ad *kt* ita *gkz* trigonus ad *kzt* trigonum, sed recta *gk*
ad *kt* maiorem proportionem habet quam *mkz* sector ad *zkn* sectorem et com-
ponenti, sed sicut sector ad sectorem ita angulus ad angulum, maiorem ergo
proportionem habet *gt* ad *tk* quam *gzt* angulus ad *kzt* angulum.

An expanded version of this proof exists in a copy that is in Regiomontanus'
hand and bears the title *Iordani de ysoperimetris* (MS Vienna, Nat.bibl. 5203,
142r–v), a version I have mentioned above (see Part II, Chap. 1, n. 9):

Quod vero maior sit proportio *ac* ad *fc* quam anguli / *aec* ad angulum *fec*
sic patet [Fig. Ap.III.A.2]. Nam facto super *e* centro circulo secundum quantitatem
semidiametri *ef* circulus secabit *ae*; sit in *o*. Et secabit *ec* continuatam; sit in *p*.
Tunc sic unus sector, scilicet *oef*, est pars trianguli *aef*; maior est igitur proportio
5   trianguli *aef* ad triangulum *fec* quam sit sectoris *oef* ad triangulum *fec* per
primam partem 8^{ve} 5^{ti}. Proportio autem sectoris *oef* ad triangulum *fec* maior
est quam sit proportio eiusdem sectoris ad sectorem *fep* per secundam partem
8^{ve} 5^{ti}. Igitur a fortiori maior est proportio trianguli *aef* ad triangulum *fec* quam
sectoris *oef* ad sectorem *fep*. Ergo coniunctim per 28^{vam} 5^{ti} maior est proportio
10   trianguli *aec* ad triangulum *fec* quam sit sectoris *oep* ad sectorem *fep*. Sed sector
oep ad sectorem *fep* sicut angulus *aec* ad angulum *fec*. Maior est igitur proportio
trianguli *aec* ad triangulum *fec* quam sit anguli *aec* ad anguium *fec*. Trianguli
autem *aec* ad triangulum *fec* est sicut proportio *ac* ad *fc* per primam sexti et
coniunctim. Igitur proportio *ac* ad *fc* est maior quam anguli *aec* ad angulum
15   *fec*, quod erat ultimo probandum.

Although Jordanus mentions only the *Liber ysoperimetrorum* in connection
with Proposition 5 of his *Liber philotegni*, he might have also seen one or
more versions of the Latin translation of Proposition 9 (=Gr. 8) of Euclid's
Optics. The most popular of the versions from the Greek was done in the
second half of the twelfth century under the title *Liber de visu*, and so I give
here Proposition 9 in that version from the edition prepared by W. R. Theisen,
O.S.B., "The Mediaeval Tradition of Euclid's Optics," thesis, University of
Wisconsin, 1972, pp. 70–71. It will be noticed that the proof of Jordanus'
Proposition 5 is at the heart of Euclid's proof, and that Euclid proceeds to
the conjunctive proportion that plays a part in the proofs of Propositions

---

3 astronomi) *ed*
5 trigonus: trigonum *ed* / trigonum *om. ed* / sed recta: Recta *ed*
6 sector *ed* sectio *O* / sectorem *mg. corr. O ex* sectionem *et post* sectorem *mg. hab. O*
   Hoc est quoniam gzk triangulus maior est sectione (*!* sectore) mzk et kzt trigonus
   minor kzn sectore (*?*); vide viii quinti
7 ergo *om. ed*
8 *post* tk *scr. et del. O* ans
Pseudo-Jordanian Version of Liber ysoperimetrorum
   2–4 facto. . . . sic *mg. super. scr. MS; et in textu scr. et del. MS* sicut ac ad fc ita triangulus
       aec ad triangulum fec. Et que est sectoris oep ad sectorem fep ea est angulus aec ad
       angulum fec. Sed
   10 *post* fec *scr. et del. MS* et sicut sit angulus aec a (*?*)

I.5+, P.6, and I.6. I have not given Theisen's line numbers since no variant readings will be given.

> [Propositio] 9. Equales et equidistantes magnitudines inequaliter distantes ab oculo non proportionaliter spaciis videntur.
>
> Sint due magnitudines *AB* et *GD* inequaliter distantes ab oculo *E* [Fig. Ap.III.A.3]. Dico quod non est sicut apparet, habens *GD* ad *AB* ita *BE* ad *ED*. Accidant enim duo radii *AE*, *EG* et centro quidem *E*, spacio vero *EZ*, describatur periferia *IZT*. Quoniam ergo *EZG* trigonus *EZI* sectore maior est, *EZD* vero trigonus *EZT* sectore minor est, trigonus ergo *EZG* ad *EZI* sectorem maiorem proportionem habet quam *EZD* trigonus ad *EZT* sectorem et permutatim *EZG* trigonus ad *EZD* trigonum maiorem proportionem habet quam *EZI* sector ad *EZT* sectorem et componenti *EGD* trigonus ad *EZD* trigonum maiorem proportionem habet quam *EIT* sector ad *EZT* sectorem. Sed sicut *EGD* trigonus ad *EZD* trigonum, ita recta *GD* ad rectam *ZD*. At vero *GD* recte *AB* est equalis et sicut *AB* ad *ZD* ita *BE* ad *DE* et *BE* ergo ad *ED* maiorem proportionem habet quam *EIT* sector ad *EZT* sectorem. Sicut autem sector ad sectorem ita *IET* angulus ad *ZET* angulum. Recta ergo *BE* ad *ED* rectam maior proportio quam *IET* angulus ad *ZET* angulum, et ex angulo quidem *IET*, *GD* videtur, ex angulo vero *ZET* recta *AB*. Non ergo distantiis proportionaliter videntur magnitudines equales.

The reader may also consult Proposition 9 of the version of the *Optics* translated by Gerard of Cremona under the title *Liber de aspectibus* (see Theisen, *op. cit.*, pp. 341–42), for perhaps that translation was available to Jordanus.

A further possible but not likely source for the demonstrations of Propositions 5 and 6 in the *Liber philotegni* and Propositions I.5, I.5+, and I.6 in the *Liber de triangulis Iordani* occurs in Gerard of Cremona's translation of the *Almagest* (*Almagestum Cl. Ptolemei*, [Venice, 1515], 6v). The pertinent passage is a part of the proof of this proposition:

> Si descripte sunt in circulo due chorde, erit proportio chorde longioris ad chordam breviorem minor proportione arcus chorde longioris ad arcum chorde brevioris.
>
> . . . Producam autem a *d* ad lineam *aeg* [continuatam] perpendicularem *dr* [Fig. Ap.III.A.4]. Et quia linea *ad* est longior linea *ed* et linea *ed* est longior *dr*, erit circulus descriptus supra centrum *d* cum longitudine *de* secans *ad* et pertransiens *dr* [continuatam]. Igitur signabo circulum supra quem sint *b*, *e*, *t*, et producam *dr* ad *t*. Et quia sector *det* est maior triangulo *der* et triangulus *dea* est maior sectore *deb*, erit proportio trianguli *der* ad triangulum *dea* minor proportione sectoris *det* ad sectorem *deb*. Proportio autem trianguli *der* ad triangulum *dea* est sicut proportio linee *er* ad lineam *ea* et proportio sectoris *der* ad sectorem *deb* est sicut proportio anguli *rde* ad angulum *ade*. Ergo proportio linee *re* ad lineam *ea* est minor proportione anguli *rde* ad angulum *eda*. Cum ergo composuerimus, erit proportio linee *ra* ad lineam *ea* minor proportione anguli *rda* ad angulum *ade*. . . .

I said that Ptolemy's account was a "less likely source" for Jordanus' propositions because in fact Ptolemy first proves the inverse of Proposition 5, namely, *re* / *ea* < angle *rde* / angle *eda*. From this he conjunctively concludes that *ra* / *ea* < angle *rda* / angle *eda*. However, the form of proof is precisely like that found in the *Liber de ysoperimetris*.

Finally we should note in connection with Proposition 5 of the *Liber philotegni* that Witelo in Book I of his *Perspectiva* gives Jordanus' enunciation in verbatim fashion and then adds a full proof in the manner of one or another of the sources I have quoted above. I cite the text (without the editor's line numbers and variant readings) from S. Unguru, ed., *Witelonis Perspectivae liber primus: Book I of Witelo's Perpsectiva* (Wrocław, etc. 1977), pp. 232–33:

> [Propositio] 35. In trigono orthogonio ab uno reliquorum angulorum producta linea ad basim, erit remotioris anguli ad propinquiorem recto minor proportio quam partis basis remotioris ad propinquiorem.
>
> Sit trigonum orthogonium *ABC* cius (*!* cuius) angulus *BAC* sit rectus, et a puncto *B* ducatur ad latus *AC*, quod est basis anguli *ABC*, linea recta, que sit *BD* [Fig. Ap.III.A.5].
>
> Dico quod minor est proportio anguli *CBD*, remotioris ab angulo recto, ad angulum *DBA*, propinquiorem ipsi recto, quam partis basis remotioris ab angulo / recto, que est *CD* ad latus *DA* propinquius ipsi angulo recto. Quoniam enim angulus *BAC* est rectus, patet quia angulus *BDA* est acutus, per 32^{am}I^i. Ergo, per 13^{am}I^i, angulus *BDC* est obtusus. Ergo, per 19^{am}I^i, latus *BD* est maius latere *AB* et minus latere *BC*. A centro itaque *B* secundum quantitatem semidyametri *BD* describatur arcus circuli secans lineam *BC* in puncto *E*, et ad ipsum producatur linea *BA* in punctum *F*. Factique erunt duo sectores *BDE* minor trigono *BDC*, et *BDF* maior trigono *BDA*. Et quoniam est proportio sectoris ad sectorem sicut arcus *FD* ad arcum *DE*, ut patet per modum demonstrationis prime VI^i (quoniam omnes sectores eiusdem circuli sunt eiusdem altitudinis, et equimultiplicia arcuum faciunt equimultiplicia ipsorum sectorum). Proportio vero arcus *DF* ad arcum *DE* est sicut anguli *DBF* ad angulum *DBE*, per ultimam sexti. Cum itaque trigonum *CDB* sit maius quam sector *EDB*, et sector *FDB* sit maior trigono *ADB*, erit, per 9^{am} huius, trigoni *CDB* primi ad trigonum *DBA* secundum maior proportio quam sectoris *EBD* tertii ad sectorem *DBF* quartum. Est autem, per 1^{am}VI^i, trigoni *CBD* ad trigonum *DBA* sicut basis *CD* ad basim *DA*. Sectoris vero *EBD* ad sectorem *DBF*, ut patet ex premissis, est proportio sicut anguli *EBD* ad angulum *DBF*. Patet ergo quod maior est proportio linee *CD* ad lineam *DA* quam anguli *CBD* ad angulum *DBA*. Ergo minor est proportio anguli *CBD* ad angulum *DBA* quam lateris *CD* ad latus *DA*, quod est propositum.

Propositions P.14, P.18–P.20 (=II.1, II.5–II.7)

These propositions are reflected in the *Liber de triangulis datis*, whose first two propositions I have edited below under the next rubric. As I note there, it is probable that the *Liber de triangulis datis* was constructed, so far as its first two propositions are concerned, from the *Liber philotegni*. Still it is not impossible that the anonymous *Liber de triangulis datis* represents a fragmentary work translated from the Arabic. If this is the case, then it could have been the source from which Jordanus prepared Propositions 14, 18–20, and 22–23 of the *Liber philotegni.*

P.21 (=II.8), P.22 (=II.13), P.23 (=II.17), P.24 (=II.18), P.25 (=II.19)

The sources of Propositions 21–23 and 25 of the *Liber philotegni* of Jordanus were probably Propositions 3, 26, 19, and 14 of Euclid's *Book of Divisions,* perhaps in the form of Gerard of Cremona's translation of that work.[1] While the translation of Gerard of Cremona is missing, it seems probable that Leonardo Fibonacci Pisano reproduced in his *Liber practice geometrie* much of the content of that translation though he often employed in his section on the division of figures the propositions on that subject included in Savasorda's *Liber embadorum* translated by Plato of Tivoli, as I shall note below in passages [1], [4], and [5], and hence I include in this appendix the geometrical proofs of the four above-noted propositions in the edition by B. Boncompagni, *Scritti di Leonardo Pisano,* Vol. 2 (Rome, 1862).[2] I also include (out of order) in passage [5] the proof given by Leonardo for a proposition equivalent to Jordanus' Proposition 24, though that proposition was not given as part of the Arabic text of Euclid's *Book of Divisions.* In the Leonardo passages quoted below, I have changed the punctuation somewhat, removed acute accents everywhere from the preposition *a*, removed periods from before and after the letters marking points, lines and other magnitudes, and changed consonantal "u" to "v". I note finally that Leonardo has given

---

[1] See the reconstruction of Euclid's *Book of Divisions* produced by R. C. Archibald, *Euclid's Book on Divisions of Figures* (Cambridge, 1915). For the enunciations of the propositions he follows F. Woepcke, "Notice sur des traductions arabes de deux ouvrages perdus d'Euclide," *Journal Asiatique,* 4ᵉ Série, Vol. 18 (1851), pp. 233–44 (full article pp. 217–47). The proofs are generally translated from Leonardo Fibonacci's *Practica geometrie.* Perhaps at least parts of the proofs given by Leonardo were found in the lost translation of Euclid's work executed by Gerard of Cremona (see E. Grant, ed., *A Source Book in Medieval Science* [Cambridge, Mass., 1974], p. 36, item [19]: "Book of Divisions (*Liber divisionum*).") That Leonardo's material came in part from Gerard's translation seems probable when we see the form of the Latin texts given by Leonardo, a form that betrays Gerard's style. For example the constant use of the term *multiplicatio* to render the products that determine surfaces is very much like the practice followed by Gerard of Cremona in translations from the Arabic, as the reader will readily see from Gerard's translations of the *Verba filiorum* of the Banū Mūsā in Volume One and the pieces given below in Appendix III.B. Hence if we must explain why Jordanus (whose *Liber philotegni* seems independent of Leonardo's *Practica geometrie*) contains at least four propositions from Euclid's *Book of Divisions* with proofs, which, though dissimilar in terminology to those same propositions given by Leonardo, are nevertheless somewhat similar in content to those in Leonardo's work, we may reasonably conclude that Jordanus and Leonardo shared at least one common source, and I suspect that common source was Gerard's translation of Euclid's work. I should add however that if that common source was Gerard's translation, the Arabic text from which Gerard translated must have been very much more complete than the text found by Woepcke in Bibliothèque Nationale, MS Arabe suppl. 952.2, for in the text of that latter manuscript most of the proofs were missing and indeed the translator says that he has omitted the demonstrations (with four exceptions) because they are "easy."

[2] See the preceding footnote.

multiple cases for proof in most of these four propositions, but I have limited myself to presenting the proofs that comprise the same objectives as those given by Jordanus and by the author of the *De triangulis Iordani*.

[1] Leonardo, pp. 111–12 (=P.21, II.8, and Euclid 3):

> Et si in aliquo laterum sit punctus datus, a quo lineam rectam protrahere vis dividentem triangulum in duo equa, ut in trigono *bgd*, in quo datus sit punctus *a* super latus *gd*; et sit primus / punctus *a* super dimidium *gd* [Fig. Ap.III.A.6]; copulabo siquidem *a* cum *b*, et erit trigonum *bgd* in duo trigona equalia divisum a linea *ba*, que sunt *bga* et *bad* super equas bases, et sub altitudine una; vel quia factum ex *bd* in *dg* duplum est facti ex *bd* in *da*, duplus est triangulus *bgd* triangulo *bad*, cum habeant unum angulum commune. Sed non sit datus punctus super dimidium alicuius laterum, ut in hoc alio trigono *abg*, in quo datus sit punctus *d* [Fig. Ap.III.A.7], qui sit propius puncto *b*. Dividam latus *bg* in duo equa super *e*, et copulabo rectas *ad* et *ae*; et per punctum *e* protraham lineam *ez* equidistantem lineae *ad*, et copulabo rectam *dz*. Dico quidem, trigonum *abg* in duo equa divisum esse a linea *dz*; quod sic probatur: in (*!* inter) equidistantes quidem *ad* et *ez* et super basem *ad* sunt trigona *ade* et *adz* sibi invicem equalia: comuniter addatur ei trigonum *abd*, erunt duo trigona *abd* et *adz*, hoc est quadrilaterum *abdz*, equalia duobus trigonis *abd* et *ade*, hoc est trigono *abe*. Sed trigonum *abe* dimidium est trigoni *abg*; quare et quadrilaterum *abdz* dimidium est trigoni *abg*; reliquum vero, scilicet trigonum *zdg*, est alia medietas trigoni *abg*: divisum est ergo trigonum *abg* a puncto *d* per lineam *dz* in duas partes equales, ut oportebat facere.

I note incidentally that a quite different proof with an apparently false solution was added as an eighth proposition to the *Liber de similibus arcubus* of Ametus filius Iosephi in two manuscripts of that work.[3] I can not explain why this proof was attached to that work nor how it became so garbled. I suppose that it might well have been a fragment translated from the Arabic. In any case, it has no connection that I can see with the proof given by Jordanus and the similar proof found in Leonardo's work.

I should also note that whatever the main source of Leonardo's proof of this proposition, whether it was Gerard of Cremona's translation of Euclid's *Book of Divisions* or some other fragment bearing the Euclidian proof, Leonardo also had before him the proof found in Savasorda's *Liber embadorum*

---

[3] The proposition is transcribed by Busard from MSS Florence, Bibl. Naz., Conv. soppr. J.V.30, 54v–55r and Paris, BN lat. 11247, 77r, in H. L. L. Busard and P. S. van Koningsveld, "Der *Liber de arcubus similibus* des Ahmed ibn Jusuf," *Annals of Science*, Vol. 30 (1973), p. 405, n. 6:

"(8) A dato puncto in quolibet laterum assignati trigoni lineam in oppositum latus ducere que assignatum trigonum in duo equa secet.

Verbi gratia: Esto trigonus assignatus *bef*, punctusque datus *a*, fiat autem *gn* quadratum equale trigono dato et linea *km* dividat ipsum in duo equa. Super lineam itaque incipientem a dato puncto *a* terminatamque in capite trigoni quod est *b* formetur triangulus *abc* equalis parallellogrammo *gm* cui circumscribatur circulus *bc*. Necesse ⟨est⟩ igitur quod circulus ille secet latus oppositum dato puncto signeturque punctus sectionis *d*. Tracta linea a puncto *a* ad signum *d* dico trigonum propositum divisum esse in duo equa, sunt namque *bac* et *acd* equales trianguli."

No diagram is included with this transcription.

translated by Plato of Tivoli. Savasorda's proof is given below, where it will be noted that it is tied to a previous numerical calculation and it does not simply and surely tell us (as do the proofs of Jordanus and Leonardo) that from the bisecting point [*f*] (see the bracketed letters given on Fig. Ap.III.A.7) we must draw a line [*fe*] parallel to side [*ac*] in order to determine point [*e*], to which the bisector [*de*] that we seek is to be drawn. Savasorda had given in his numerical example the procedure of finding [*e*] by taking [*ce*] the same fraction of side [*cb*] that [*df*] is of [*db*], which of course could and should have been generalized in the geometric proof by drawing [*de*] parallel to [*dc*]. The text quoted is that of M. Curtze, "Urkunden zur Geschichte der Mathematik im Mittelalter und der Renaissance. I. Der 'Liber embadorum' des Savasorda in der Übersetzung des Plato von Tivoli," *Abhandlungen zur Geschichte der mathematischen Wissenschaften mit Einschluss ihrer Anwendungen,* 12. Heft (1902), pp. 132, 134, 136. I have abandoned Curtze's lines, line numbers, and variant readings:

> 4. Item si terminus alterius duorum divisorum in aliqua parte cuiuslibet lateris trigoni fuerit, et suam portionem in directo sui termini quaesierit.
>
> Veluti si in triangulo vel trigono *abc* [Fig. Ap.III.A.7] supra latus *ab* circa punctum *d* terminus divisoris exstiterit, et suam portionem ab ipso *d* puncto postulaverit, utrum in eiusdem lateris dimidio punctus *d* fuerit, observa. Qui si in dimidio lateris inventus exstiterit, nil tibi faciendum supererit, praeter quod ab anguli summitate usque ad praedictum *d* punctum rectam lineam protrahens triangulum in duo secabis aequalia.
>
> / At si punctus *d* non in dimidio praefati lateris inventus fuerit, aliter triangulum dividamus oportet. Exempli namque causa praedictum trigoni latus *ab* 12, secundum vero latus *bc* 10, tertium quoque latus *ac* 15 ulnas continere ponamus, punctumque *d*, qui pro divisoris termino ponitur, prius a puncto *b* per spatium duarum ulnarum elongemus. Linea igitur *ad* 10 ulnas continebit, positoque puncto *f* supra lateris *ab* dimidium lineam *af* 6 ulnas continere non dubitabimus: latus etenim *ab* 12 ulnas habere posuimus. Linea igitur *af* cum sit totius *ab* lineae dimidium in 4 ulnis, quae sunt duae quintae totius *ad* lineae, *ab* eadem *ad* linea superabitur. Quapropter ex latere *ac*, quod est lateri *ad* contiguum, duas quintas a parte *c*, quae est trianguli summitas, accipe, et quod fuerit, puncto impresso *e* signabis. Erit igitur linea *ec* 6 ulnarum: totum namque latus *ac* 15 ulnas continere supra posuimus. Quo facto a puncto *d* usque ad punctum *e* rectam lineam protrahens totus triangulus in duo dividetur aequalia, quorum altera pars erit trigonus *ade*, alteram vero partem superficies *debc* almuncharif sibi perfecte vindicabit.
>
> Quod si praenominatus terminus *d* a puncto *a* per duarum ⟨ulnarum⟩ spatium elongatus fuerit, divisionis lineam non ad latus *ac*, ut prius, sed ad latus *bc* dirigas. Duas namque quintas ex latere *bc*, quod 10 existit ulnarum, a puncto *c* sumens *e* puncto signabis. Erit itaque linea *ce* 4 ulnarum. Divisionis ergo lineam a puncto *d* ad punctum *e* sicut in hac figura cernitur, produces. In hac etenim similitudine divisionis linea semper ad latus maiori portioni contiguum transmittatur, quare, si linea *bd* maior portio fuerit, divisionis lineam ad latus *bc* producas; si vero non ⟨haec⟩, sed *ad* linea portio maior exstiterit, ad latus *ac* producta linea dirigatur.

Istud etiam nullatenus oblivioni traderetur, quod illae duae quintae semper a puncto *c*, quae est trianguli summitas, sunt assumendae, quoniam ad hunc idem punctum divisionis linea producetur, cum terminus, qui est punctus *d*, supra dimidium *ab* lineae ceciderit. Quapropter secundum illam quantitatem, in qua terminus a dimidio lineae elongabitur, erit *e* punctus a puncto *c*, qui est trigoni summitas, elongandus. Hoc autem, et si nullo monstratur exemplo, satis tamen esset apertum. Quod autem exemplo monstravimus, ideo fecimus, ut auditoribus levius et apertius innotesceret.

/ Huius quidem demonstrationem addisces, si a puncto *f*, qui lineae *ab* dimidium sibi vindicat, duas lineas, alteram scilicet ad punctum *c* alteram vero ad punctum *e*, et si a puncto etiam *d* ad punctum *c* aliam rectam lineam produxeris, quemadmodum in hac figura depingitur [Fig. Ap.III.A.7]. His lineis hac in subscripta figura productis, linea *fe* lineae *cd* aequidistans invenietur, eo quod proportio lineae *ce* ad lineam *ea* est ut proportio lineae *df* ad lineam *fa*. Nam linea *ce* duas quintas totius lineae *ca*, linea quoque *df* duas itidem totius *ad* lineae quintas amplectitur. Omnesque duo trianguli, qui super eandem basim ad easdem partes in eisdem alternis lineis conformantur sunt aequales ad invicem. Triangulus igitur *cdf* in hac figura aequus est triangulo *cde*: sunt enim inter duas subalternas lineas *fe*, *dc* et super eandem basim *cd*. Triangulo igitur *cda* communiter assumpto erit totus triangulus *caf* toti superficie *cade* almuncharif aequalis. Triangulus autem *caf* trianguli *abc* dimidium continet, eo quod punctus *f* in dimidio lateris *ab* collocatur, superficies itaque *ceda* almuncharif, quam ei aequalem fore monstravimus, dimidium trianguli *abc*, ut supra diximus, continet.

[2.] Leonardo pp. 116–17 (=P.22, II.13, Euclid 26):

DEMONSTRATIO QUOMODO DIVIDITUR TRIGONUM IN DUO EQUA PER LINEAM EGREDIENTEM A PUNCTO DATO EXTRA IPSUM. Si trigonum *abg* per lineam egredientem a puncto dato *d* extra ipsum in duas equas partes dividere vis [Fig. Ap.III.A.8], lineam *ad* secans latus *bg* super *e* protrahe; siquidem si recta *be* equalis est recte *eg*, factum utique erit propositum; quia *abe* et *aeg* super equas bases sunt, et sub eadem altitudine; unde trigonum *abe* trigono *aeg* iacet equale. Sed non sit *be* equalis recte *eg*, erit utique una earum maior; sitque recta *be* maior; a puncto quidem *d* recta protrahatur *zd* equidistans recte *be*; et / perducatur recta *ab* in *z*. Et quia recta *be* maior est medietate lateris *bg*, rectiangula superficies *ab* in *be* est plus medietate rectiangule superficiei *ab* in *bg*; multo plus superficies *ab* in *zd* est plus medietate superficiei *ab* in *bg*, cum maior sit *zd* quam *be*. Adiaceat siquidem superficies *ib* in *zd* equalis dimidio superficiei que fit ex *ab* in *bg*; et quoniam maior est superficies *ab* in *be* superficie (*correxi ex* superficiei *hic et alibi*) *ib* in *zd*, erit proportio *zd* ad *be* minor proportione *ba* ad *bi*. Sed proportio *zd* ad *be* equalis est proportioni *za* ad *ab*. Disiunctim quidem erit proportio *zb* ad *ba* minor proportione *ai* ad *ib*; quare superficies *zb* in *bi* minor est superficie *ba* in *ai*: adiungatur quidem recte *bi* paralilogramum (*!*) superhabundans figura tetragona equale superficiei *zb* in *bi*; hoc est quod recte *bi* adiungatur quedam linea, que multiplicata in se et in *bi* faciat equale multiplicationi *zb* in *bi*; quod paralilogramum (*!*) sit superficies que sit *ti*; et copuletur recta *tkd*; et quia superficies *zb* in *bi* equa est superficiei *bt* in *ti*, proportionaliter erit ut *zb* ad *bt* ita *ti* ad *ib*; coniunctim ergo sicut *zt* ad *bt* ita *bt* ad *bi*. Sed sicut *zt* ad *bt* ita *zd* ad *bk*; ergo sicut *zd* ad *bk* ita *bt* ad *bi*; quare superficies *kb* in *bt* equa est superficiei *zd* in *bi*. Sed superficies *zd* in *bi* equalis est dimidio superficiei *ab* in *bg*; quare trigonum *tbk* dimidium est trigoni *abg*. Divisum est ergo trigonum *abg* a linea egrediente a puncto *d*, que est recta *dkt* in duas medietates, quarum una est trigonum *tbk*, et alia est quadrilaterum *tkga*; quod oportebat facere.

[3] Leonardo p. 115 (=P.23, II.17, Euclid 19):

Et si fuerit punctus aliquis datus infra trigonum, qui non sit in lineis descendentibus ab angulis super dimidium laterum ipsius; et volueris ipsum dividere in duo equa cum linea transeunte per ipsum punctum; studebis per ea que dicta sunt invenire angulum contentum ab inequalibus sectionibus; quia circa ipsum que sequentur operanda erunt. Verbi gratia: Esto trigonum *abg* [Fig. Ap. III.A.9], in quo datus sit punctus *d*, qui non sit in aliqua rectarum descendentium ab angulis super dimidias bases ipsius; et volumus dividere triangulum *abg* in duas medietates cum linea transeunte per punctum *d*. Deprehendantur primum ad oculum super latera casus linearum descendentium ab angulis per punctum *d*, ut habeatur notitia anguli contenti (*correxi ex* contencti) ab inequalibus sectionibus, qui sit angulus qui ad *g*, et uni laterum contentium ipsum super reliquum latus a puncto *d* equidistans trahatur, que sit recta *de*; et applicetur ei superficies equalis medietati superficiei *bg* in *ag*, que sit superficies *de* in *gz*, hoc est dimidium multiplicationis *bg* in *ag*, dividatur per *de*, et proveniet *gz*. Deinde linee *gz* applicabis paralilogramum (*!*) deficiens figura tetragona, quod sit equale superficiei *ge* in *gz*; et hoc est quod dividatur *gz* in duas partes, quarum una multiplicata per aliam faciat equale multiplicationi *ge* in *gz*: quod aliter fieri non poterit nisi quadratum medietatis lineae *gz* superhabundet superficiem *ge* in *gz* vel sit equale eius: fiat siquidem *zi* in *ig* sicut *ge* in *gz*; et copuletur recta *id*, et emictatur (*!* emittatur) in punctum *t*. Dico quidem trigonum *abg* in duo equa divisum esse a linea *it*, transeunte per punctum *d*; quod sic probatur: quoniam multiplicatio *zg* in *eg* equalis est multiplicationi *zi* in *ig*, erunt sicut *zg* ad *zi* ita *ig* ad *eg*; quare erit sicut *zg* ad aliam partem sui, scilicet ad *ig*, ita *ig* erit ad aliam partem sui, scilicet ad *ie*: sed sicut *gi* ad *ie* ita *gt* ad *de*; ergo est sicut *zg* ad *ig* ita *gt* ad *de*: quare multiplicatio *ig* in *gt* equalis est multiplicationi *zg* in *de*; sed multiplicatio *zg* in *de* est medietas multiplicationis *ag* in *gb*; ergo et *ig* in *gt* est medietas multiplicationis *ag* in *bg*; quare trigonum *itg* dimidium est trigoni *abg*, ut prediximus.

At this point I interrupt the inclusion of the text from Leonardo's *Practica* in order to mention a work entitled *Liber de triangulis datis* that exists in at least two manuscripts of the thirteenth century (*Pf* = Paris, BN lat. 16647, 92v–95r and *Fa* = Florence, Bibl. Naz. Conv. soppr. J.I.32, 18r–v). As I note above in my description of the latter manuscript in the list of *sigla* before the *Liber philotegni*, the first two of the tract's three propositions appear to have been constructed from the *Liber philotegni*. The principal enunciation of the first proposition is equivalent to Proposition 22 of the *Liber philotegni;* but the proof includes the statement and proof of a proposition equivalent to Proposition 14 of the *Liber philotegni* as a subsidiary proposition that the author presents before the proof of the main proposition. Similarly in the case of the second main proposition of the *Liber de triangulis datis,* we note that the main proposition is equivalent to Proposition 23 of the *Liber philotegni* and that three subsidiary propositions equivalent to Propositions 18, 19, and 20 of the *Liber philotegni* are presented and proved before the proof of the main proposition. As I also indicated earlier, Proposition 3 of this anonymous tract is simply Version 1 of Hero's theorem for the area of a triangle in terms of its sides which I published in Appendix IV of Volume 1 of *Archimedes in the Middle Ages*. I give here the texts of the first two propositions (along with their subsidiary propositions) so that the reader may compare them with the relevant propositions of the *Liber philotegni*. I do so here in this appendix because of the bare possibility that these first two propositions are not paraphrases from the *Liber philotegni* but are independent fragments translated from the Arabic as is the case with Proposition 3. I hasten to add, however, that I am much more inclined to believe that they derive from the *Liber philotegni* rather than vice versa. My text is based on manuscripts *Pf* and *Fa*.

Liber de triangulis datis

92v   / Prima propositio. Triangulo dato et puncto extra signato lineam per punctum transeuntem designare que triangulum in duo equa distinguat [=Prop. P.22].

Ad huius demonstrationis facilitatem primo proponimus ostendere quo modo
5   duabus lineis datis unam earum in duas partes separemus quarum una ad aliam sicut alia ad reliquam assignatarum [=P.14].

Sint igitur date linee et coniuncte *ab*, *bc* [Fig. P.14], et supra compositam explicemus semicirculum *adc*, erigentes perpendicularem *bd*, qua posita diametro circumducamus circulum *bedf* circa centrum *g*; producamusque lineam *afge*,
10   et continuantes *e* cum *b* linea *be*, equidistantem ducamus *fh*. Quia igitur quod ex *ae* in *af* equatur quadrato contingentis, scilicet *ab*, erit *ae* ad *ab* sicut *ab* ad *af*. Itemque propter lineas equidistantes erit *ef* ad *fa* sicut *bh* ad *ha*, et permutatim *af* ad *ah* sicut *ef* ad *bh*. Quare coniunctim *ae* ad *ab* sicut *fa* ad *ah*. Et quia ut supra *ea* ad *ab* sicut *ab* ad *af*, erit *ab* ad *fa* sicut *fa* ad *ha*. Erit ergo *ab* ad *fa*
15   sicut *ef* ad *bh*. Itaque permutatim *ef* ad *ba* sicut *bh* ad *af*. Et quia *ef* equatur *db* atque *cb* ad *bd* velud *bd* ad *ba*, erit *cb* ad *ef* sicut *bh* ad *af*. Sed *ef* ad *bh* sicut *af* ad *ah*. In equalitate ergo proportionis *cb* ad *bh* sicut *bh* ad *ha*, quod propositum fuit efficere quia convertitur ut sit *ah* ad *hb* sicut *hb* ad *bc*.

Hoc facto principale exsequemur propositum. Sit igitur triangulus *abc* [Fig.
20   P.22] et punctus *d* extra triangulum exceptum inter lineas *aef* et *gbl* (! *hbl*) que

Prop. I

1 Liber . . . datis *mg. Fa om. Pf*
2 Prima propositio *Pf om. Fa*
3 distinguat *Fa* distungat *Pf*
7 Sint: Sunt *FaPf*
10 fh *Pf* f (*et ras.*) h *Fa*
12 af *Fa* ef *Pf*
13 ah[1]: ḅah *Pf* / ah[2]: ḅah *Pf*
15 bh[2]: ba *Fa*
16 bh[2] *correxi ex* ah *in PfFa*
17 ah: ḅah *Pf* / ergo *Fa om. Pf*
18 hb[1]: ab *Fa*
19 exsequemur *Fa* exequemur *Pf*

dividunt latera trianguli per equalia atque ipsum triangulum et extra quantumlibet
protractas. Si enim in / aliqua earum incideret finem sumeret intentio. Puncto
igitur intra illas posito ab ipso ducamus equidistantem *ac* donec cum *cb* concurrat
quantum necessarium fuerit protracta signumque concursus sit *g* et concludat
triangulum linea *dc* qui sicut se habet ad triangulum *aec*, qui est dimidium dati
trianguli, ita se habeat linea *cg* ad aliquam, que sit *mn*. Dividatur tunc *gc* secundum
premissam demonstrationem in *gk* et *kc* quod sicut se habet *gk* ad *kc* ita *kc* ad
mn, et continuetur linea *dk* in puncto *p* lineam *ac* offendens, eruntque trianguli
dgk et *kpc* similes; *dgk* ad triangulum *kpc* sicut linea *gk* ad lineam *mn*, et quia
triangulus *cdg* ad triangulum [*kdg*] sicut basis *cg* ad basim *kg*, erit in proportionalitate equalitatis triangulus *cdg* ad triangulum *kpc* sicut linea *cg* ad lineam
mn. Sed erat linea *cg* ad lineam *mn* sicut triangulus *cdg* ad dimidium trianguli
abc. Constat itaque triangulum *kpc* esse dimidium dati trianguli, linea *dkp* que
a dato progreditur puncto eum dividente ut proponebatur.

Secunda propositio. Proposito trigono et puncto infra notato, lineam per ipsum
transeuntem que triangulum per equa partiatur designare [=P.23].

Ad huius rei explanationem duabus lineis propositis quarum altera si minor
quarta alterius, maiorem ita dividendam proponimus ut que adiecte ad totam
proportio ea sit composite ad maiorem propositarum [=P.18].

Sint ergo linee date *ab*, *bc* rectum continentes angulum, concluso rectangulo
abcd [Fig. P.18a]. Deinde supra lineam *ab* statuamus rectangulum rectangulo
abcd equale cui desit ad completionem totius linee quadratum, sitque illud *aefg*,
lineaque *ef* equalis linee *eb*. Erit igitur *ab* ad *ae* sicut *ef* sive *eb* ad *bc*. Utraque
igitur tam *ae* quam *eb* erit maior *cb*. De qualibet ergo earum dematur *bc* et si
placet de *bc* cui equalis sit *bh*. / Quia itaque *ab* ad *be* sicut *ae* ad *bh*, erit *ab* ad
be sicut *be* ad *eh*, sicque habebimus propositum quoniam addita est *eh* ad *bc*
que ita se habet ad totam, i.e. *be*, sicut illa ad *ab*.

Amplius. Si adiecte ad compositam fuerit maior proportio quam composite
ad alteram priorem cui secunda est adiectio minorem esse quarta alterius con-
veniet [=Prop. P.19].

Ut si *eh* ad *eb* maior sit proportio quam *eb* ad *ab*, *bh* minor erit quarta linee
ab [Fig. P.19]. Erit enim ob hoc *ab* ad *eb* maior proportio quam *eb* ad *eh*. Et
ideo quod continetur sub *ab* et *eh* rectangulum maius erit quadrato *eb*. Signetur
ergo quadratum super *eb*, quod sit *ebdg*, et rectangulum super *ab* cuius alterum

23 intra: infra *Pf*
24 concludit *Fa*
25 se *Pf* de *Fa*
28 continuetur *Fa* continetur *Pf* / p *Fa* b *Pf*
30 [*kdg*] *addidi*

Prop. 2
   1 Secunda propositio *Pf om. Fa*
   2 designare *Pf* desingnare *Fa*
   4 ita *Pf* illa *Fa*
   8 quadratum *bis Fa. et del. Fb primum*
   9 bc *Pf et ex corr. Fa*
  11 ae: abe *Pf*
  12 *ante* eh[1] *scr. et del. Fa* bh / habebimus *Pf* habemus *Fa*
  17 eh: ch (?) *Pf*
  18 enim *Pf mg. Fa* igitur *text. Fa* / *post* ob *scr. et del. Fa* ab (?) / eh: ch *Pf*
  19 sub *bis Fa et del. Fa primum*

latus *bl* equale est *eh*, producaturque linea *hkm*, sicque inter quadrata *ehk* atque *kld* erit supplementum *hbl* proportionale. Quare duplum eius non erit illis maius cumque sit ipsum alteri (?) supplemento equale non erit ipsum maius quarta quadrati, non ergo erit quarta rectanguli *abl*. Sed proportio rectanguli huius ad
25 idem supplementum sicut *ab* ad *bh*, sicque *bh* minus erit quarta *ab*.

Amplius. Si fuerit adiecte ad *bc* ad compositam maior proportio quam composite ad *ab*, erit eadem composita maior altera duarum [=Prop. P.20], scilicet *ae* vel *eb* cum sit ut supra rectangulum *aefg* equale rectangulo *abc*.

Sit enim illa composita *bcd*, cui equalis resecetur ab *ab* [Fig. P.20] que sit *bm*,
30 fiatque super *ab* rectangulum ad latitudinem *bm*, quod sit *bnpq* (! *bnpa*), erecta linea *mr*. Si igitur *bm* minor fuerit utraque, fit ut *eb* minor sit illarum atque ipsa minor constituatur, sicque *ef* maior *bn*. Concurrant itaque *qf* (! *gf*) et *bn* super *t*, producta *mr* usque *z*, et quia rectangulum *amr* est maius rectangulo *aef* quoniam, cum sit proportio *ab* ad *bm* maior proportione *bm* ad *mh*, erit proportio
35 *am* ad *hb* maior proportione *ae* ad *bm*, quod ergo continetur sub *am* et *mb*, quod est rectangulum *amr*, erit maius eo quod continetur sub *ab*, *bc*, scilicet ei est equale rectangulum *aefg*, et ob hoc ipsum minus est rectangulo *amr* et cetera. Hoc sic communi dempto erit supplementum *er* maius residuo alterius quod sit *gfp*. Quare et supplementum *rt* eodem erit maius, sicque *rn* maior erit *py* (! *pq*),
40 et ideo maior *ae*. Patet igitur quod posito *bm* esse minorem altera sequitur eam maiorem reliqua.

94r
/ Sic igitur principale propositum aggrediamur. Statuatur igitur trigonus descriptus notis *a*, *b*, *g* [Fig. P.23], punctusque *d* intra ipsum comprehensum ex parte *b* inter lineas *ag* et *be* dividentes opposita latera per equa sed et triangulum.
45 Ducaturque linea per *d* equidistans linee *ac*, que sit *fdh*, continueturque linea *db*. Sitque linea *fb* ad aliquam, que sit *mn*, sicut triangulus *bdf* ad triangulum *bec*, qui est dimidium dati trigoni. Sitque tunc *bf* ad *ty* lineam sicut *bfh* triangulus ad *bec*. Et quia triangulus *bfh* est maior triangulo *bfd*, erit *mn* maior *ty*. Est autem *bf* ad *bc* sicut *bc* ad *ty*, quia triangulus *bfh* est similis triangulo *bec*. Quare
50 proportio *bf* ad *bc* est maior proportione *bc* ad *mn*. Minor igitur est *fc* quarta *mn*. Addatur igitur linee *fc* que sit *fz* ita quod *zf* ad *zc* sit sicut *zc* ad *mn* ita tamen (?) ut *zf* (! *zc*) minor sit *bc* ratione premissorum, et transeat linea per *z* et *d*, que sit *zdk*, quia igitur triangulus *bfd* ad triangulum *zfd* sicut linea *bf* ad lineam *zf*, itemque triangulus *zfd* ad triangulum *fck* (! *zck*) sicut *zf* ad *mn*

21 est *Fa om. Pf*
22 suplementum *Fa hic et ubique*
23 non: inde (?) *Fa*
24 ergo erit *Pf* erit igitur *Fa*
27 ad ab: atlab (?) *Fa*
28 ut supra *Fa, lac.* + super *Pf*
31 fuerit *om. Fa*
33 *ante* est *add. Fa* et
38 sic communi *Fa* sicque (?) *Pf* / er: erit *Fa*
43 intra: ita *Fa*
45 continueturque *Pf* continuaturque *Fa*
48 *post* triangulo *scr. Pf et delevi* dec quare proportio
51 linee *correxi ex* linea *in PfFa* / -z: -x *hic et aliquando alibi in Fa* / zf: ex f *Fa*
53 sicut: sint *Pf* / linea: lineam *Fa*
54 *ante* fck *forte scr. et del. Fa* zck

55 quoniam trianguli similes sunt, et *zf* ad *zc* erat sicut *zc* ad *mn*. In equa igitur proportione sicut *bf* ad *mn* ita triangulus *bfd* ad triangulum *zck*. Fuit autem linea *bf* ad *mn* sicut idem triangulus ad dimidium dati trigoni. Quare et triangulus *zck* eiusdem dimidium, linea eum dec'nente (! dividente) transeunte per *d*, sicque executi propositum consequenter figuras ponimus.

[4] I now return to the last Euclidian text from Leonardo, p. 138 (=P.25, II.19, and Euclid 14):

> Primum quidem demonstrare volo quo modo dividatur quadrilaterum diversilaterum in duo equa ab angulo dato. Esto quadrilaterum *abcd*, quod dividere volo in duo equa ab *a* angulo dato: protraham primum dyametrum *bd* subtendentem angulum *bad*: et secabo ipsum a dyametro *ac* super punctum *e*; recte quidem *be* et *ed* aut sunt equales, aut non. Sint primum equales [Fig. Ap.III.A.10]: et quoniam equalis est recta *be* recte *ed*, equale erit trigonum *abe* trigono *ade*, non et trigonum *ebc* trigono *ecd* est equale; quare totum trigonum *abc* toti trigono *acd* iacet equale. Divisum est ergo quadrilaterum *abcd* in duo equa a dyametro *ac* egrediente ab angulo dato; quod oportebat facere. Sed non sit recta *be* equalis recte *ed*. Sed iaceat *bz* equalis recte *zd* [Fig. Ap.III.A.11] et protraham rectam *zi* equidistantem dyametro *ac*, ut in hac secunda figura cernitur; et copulabo rectam *ai*. Dico iterum quadrilaterum *abcd* divisum esse in duas equas portiones a linea *ai* egrediente ab angulo *a* dato, que sunt trigonum *abi* et quadrilaterum *aicd*; quod sic probatur: copulabo rectas *az* et *cz*, et erunt trigona *azd* et *dzc* equalia trigonis *abz* et *bzc*; quare quadrilaterum *azcd* dimidium est quadrilateri *abcd*: et quia trigona *aci* et *acz* sunt super basim *ae* et inter equidistantes *ac* et *zi*, sibi invicem sunt equalia; comuniter si addatur trigonum *acd*, erit quadrilaterum *aicd* equale quadrilatero *azcd*. Sed quadrilaterum *azcd* dimidium est quadrilateri *abcd*; ergo et quadrilaterum *aicd* dimidium est quadrilateri *abcd*, ut oportet.

While there is a substantial section on the division of quadrilaterals in Savasorda's *Liber embadorum,* the part of it that embraces this proposition (ed. of Curtze, p. 146: "15. Ad hunc itaque modum omnia quadrilatera, quorum neutrum duorum diametrorum alterum per aequalia partitur, in duo aequa secabis, cum a quolibet eorum angulorum divisiones facere volueris") does not have a proof that is sufficiently close to either Jordanus' proof or that of Leonardo, which we have just quoted, to warrant its inclusion here.

[5] As I have indicated above, Jordanus' Proposition 24, while not given in the Arabic text of Euclid's *Book of Divisions,* was obviously known in a somewhat different form to Savasorda and later to Leonardo Fibonacci. Hence I give the two texts here:

Leonardo, p. 120:

> Adiaceat iterum trigonum *abg* [Fig. Ap.III.A.12], quod oporteat inter tres consortes dividere; quorum unus quisque velit in sua portione habere unum ex

55 *zf Pf* fz *Fa*
57 sicut: sint *Pf*
58 eiusdem *Pf* idem *Fa*

lateribus trianguli *abg*. Latus quidem *bg* dividam in duo equa super punctum *d*; et copulabo rectam *ad*, et componam *de* (! *dc*) tertiam partem linee *ad*; et copulabo rectas *bc* et *cg*. Dico quidem trigonum *abg* divisum esse in tres equas partes, quarum unaqueque est super unum ex lateribus trianguli *abg*, que partes sunt trigona *abc* et *acg* et *bcg*; quod sic probatur. Quia recta *dc* est tertia pars recte *da*, erit *ac* dupla ex *cd*; quare trigonum *abc* est duplum trigoni *bcd*; propter eadem ergo et trigonum *acg* duplum est trigoni *gcd*. Rursus quia equalis est recta *bd* recte *dg*, equalia sunt trigona *cbd* et *cdg* sibi invicem; quare totum *cbg* trigonum duplum est uniuscuiusque trigonorum *cbd* et *cdg*; et que eidem sunt dupla sibi invicem sunt equalia; quare trigona *acb* et *acg* et *bcg* sibi invicem sunt equalia. Divisum est ergo trigonum *abg* etc.

Savasorda, pp. 136, 138:

5. Item si triangularis campus, ut triangulus *abc*, tribus divisoribus dividendus proponatur, quorum unus supra unum, alius vero supra aliud, tertius quoque supra tertium trianguli latus suam portionem habere voluerit, quodlibet trianguli latus, ut exempli causa latus *ab* supra punctum *d*, in duo partiaris aequalia. Dehinc a puncto *d* usque ad punctum *c* rectam lineam protrahens triangulum in duo aequa secabis. Quo diviso per medium, ex linea *cd* tertiam sui partem a puncto *d* sumens puncto *e* impresso signabis. Post hoc a puncto *e* duas lineas, alteram scilicet ad punctum *a*, alteram vero ad punctum *b* producens in tres aequales partes, quae sunt *cea*, *ceb*, *aeb*, triangulus *abc* dividetur, ut haec figura repraesentat [Fig. Ap. III.A.12].

Istius nempe demonstratio est, quod, quia linea *bd* aequalis est lineae *da*, erit trigonus *cda* trigono *cdb* aequalis, et quia linea *de* tertiam totius lineae *dc* partem continet, trigonus *aed* totius trigoni *acd* tertiam partem continebit. Triangulus *acd* est dimidium trianguli *abc*, triangulus igitur *aec* tertia pars trianguli *abc* remanebit. Simili quoque ⟨modo⟩ tri/angulum *ceb* tertiam trianguli *abc* partem continere probabitur. Hac itaque ratione cognosces, quod triangulus *abc* in tres aequales partes super eius tria latera dividatur.

B.

Sources for Propositions IV.10, IV.12–IV.28
of the *Liber de triangulis Iordani*

As I have indicated above in my discussion of the composition of the *Liber de triangulis Iordani,* the compositor of that longer version added the following propositions in Book IV beyond those found in Jordanus' original *Liber philotegni:* Prop. IV.10, IV.12–IV.28. In this appendix I shall examine the sources of these propositions, using the proposition numbers as rubrics. It is evident from my treatment that the sources may be categorized in three ways. (1) In some cases an independent source for the proposition is not known (and indeed this may merely mean that the compositor of the longer version has himself constructed the proposition *de novo*). (2) In other cases the sources are known and have been previously published (for example in Volume One of my *Archimedes in the Middle Ages*) and in those cases I content myself with indicating where they are available. (3) In still other cases the sources are known as fragments for the most part (if not exclusively) translated by Gerard of Cremona, but their texts have not been published. Accordingly I have edited here the texts of those sources, basing these texts on the following manuscripts.

Sigla

Note: the proposition numbers following the folio numbers refer to the texts under those proposition numbers below.

Pd = Paris, Bibliothèque Nationale, MS lat. 9335, 54v–55r (Props. IV.26–IV.28), 63v–64r (Prop. IV.23), 64r (Prop. IV.21), 64r c.2 (Prop. IV.25), 14c (so usually dated, but could be 13c). The best description is still that of A. A. Björnbo, "Ueber zwei mathematische Handschriften aus dem vierzehnten Jahrhundert," *Bibliotheca mathematica,* 3. Folge, Vol. 3 (1902), pp. 63–75. This should be supplemented by Björnbo, "Studien über Menelaos' Sphärik," *Abhandlungen zur Geschichte der mathematischen Wissenschaften,* 14. Heft (1902), pp. 137–38, by Björnbo and S. Vogl, "Alkindi, Tideus und Pseudo-Euklid," *ibid.,* 26₃. Heft (1912), pp. 138, 171, and by Clagett, *Archimedes in the Middle Ages,* Vol. 1, p. xxvi; Vol. 3, p. 173. This is the best extant manuscript of many of Gerard of Cremona's translations (Cf. Clagett, *Archimedes,* Vol. 1, pp. 227–28, n. 1).

Br = Bruges, Bibliothèque Publique, MS 530, 1r–v (Prop. IV.23), 13c. See the description of this codex in the *Sigla* to the *Liber philotegni* above.

Oe = Oxford, Bodleian Library, MS Digby 168, 122r (old pag. 121r) (Prop. IV.22, second proof), 13c or 14c. See W. D. Macray, *Catalogi codicum manuscriptorum Bibliothecae Bodleianae. Pars nona, codices a . . . Kenelm Digby donatos, complectens* (Oxford, 1883) cc. 172–77. Cf. Clagett, *Archimedes*

591

in the Middle Ages, Vol. 1, pp. xxvi–xxvii, where I suggested 14c for this part of the manuscript.

A = Paris, Bibliothèque de l'Arsenal, MS 1035, 104r–v (Props. IV.26–IV.28), 14c. For a description of this codex, see H. Martin, *Catalogue des manuscrits de la Bibliothèque de l'Arsenal,* Vol. 2 (Paris, 1886), pp. 246–47.

Vr = Rome, Vatican Library, MS Vat. reg. lat. 1268, 238r–v (Prop. IV.26–IV.28), 14c. This codex is described by Björnbo, "Studien über Menelaos' Sphärik," pp. 138–42.

Ma = Madrid, Biblioteca Nacional, MS 10010, 83r–v (Prop. IV.23), 83v (Props. IV.21 and IV.25), 83v–84r (2nd proof of Prop. IV.22), 84r (Prop. IV.24), 14c. The codex is described by J. M. Millás Vallicrosa, *Las traducciones orientales en los manuscritos de la Biblioteca Catedral de Toledo* (Madrid, 1942), pp. 210–11. Cf. Clagett, *Archimedes in the Middle Ages,* Vol. 1, p. xxix.

Proposition IV.10

This proposition was in all likelihood devised by the compositor of the longer version of the *De triangulis Iordani* since it circulated only in manuscripts that contain the whole text of the *Liber de triangulis Iordani* or in manuscripts that contain the text of the *Liber philotegni* in a form influenced by the longer versions (see MSS *FaBu*).

Propositions IV.12 and IV.13

These propositions were probably also composed by the compositor of the longer version. For they too are principally confined either to manuscripts of the longer version or to manuscripts of the *Liber philotegni* that were influenced by the longer version. The only exception is their presence in MS *Pc*, but in that manuscript all of the propositions added to Book IV are in a form almost identical with that found in the tradition of the longer version represented by MSS *GPbBu*. Hence their independent circulation in MS *Pc* is not significant. The composition of these propositions by the author of the longer version also seems to be supported by the inclusion in their proofs of references to earlier propositions of the *Liber de triangulis Iordani,* a practice not evident in those propositions of Book IV which had their sources in translations from the Arabic by Gerard of Cremona.

Propositions IV.14–IV.16

These propositions belong together. They constitute an existence proof of the quadrature of a circle in the manner of an Arabic proof that was attached to the end of a tract on quadrature written by Alhazen (see Clagett, *Archimedes in the Middle Ages,* Vol. 3, p. 1255, entry for P. 569). Hence I suspect that these propositions were translated from the Arabic. They are included under the title *De quadratura circuli* in MS *Ve* (see the text of Prop. IV.14, variant to line 1) but without any indication of the author. In MS *Gu* these propositions appear under the title *Quadratura circuli secundum alardum* and are said in the colophon to be from his *Greater Commentary* (see MS *Gu* in the *Sigla* to the longer version). Of course the Alardus referred to here is simply an abbreviatory form of the celebrated Adelard of Bath. I would suppose that the references in MS *Gu* reflect some manuscript like *Pe*, where these and other propositions follow Adelard of Bath's Version III of the *Elements* of Euclid (see MS *Pe* under the *Sigla* of the longer version). The fact that these propositions follow the text of one of Adelard's versions of the *Elements* does not allow us to conclude that it was Adelard of Bath who rendered them from Arabic. Our doubts about the origin of these propositions in a work or translation of Adelard of Bath are reinforced by the fact that, in addition to Props. IV.14–IV.18, MS *Gu* also includes Props. IV.21 and IV.25 among its extracts from Adelard's *Greater Commentary,* and it is virtually certain that Props. IV.21 and IV.25 were drawn directly from fragments translated by Gerard of Cremona (see below under the headings Proposition IV.21 and Proposition IV.25). Hence, since Gerard's translating activity was later than that of Adelard's, Gerard's translations of at least those two propositions could not have been appended by Adelard to his version of the *Elements.* We should further note that the independently circulating version of Prop. IV.15 in MSS *OdR* is quite different from the normal text of that proposition (see the text of Prop. IV.15, variant to lines 1–19). If I am correct in my suggestion in *Archimedes in the Middle Ages,* Vol. 1, pp. 576–77 that the quadrature proofs which follow *Od's* version of Prop. IV.15 (and which are equivalent to Prop. IV.16 and have the title *De circulo quadrando* in a later hand) were composed later than the text of Prop. IV.16 appearing in the *De triangulis Iordani,* then probably the variant version of Prop. IV.15 in MSS *OdR* was also composed later than the text of Prop. IV.15 appearing in the *De triangulis Iordani.* Hence it seems likely that the text of Props. IV.14–IV.16 that appears with little change in both the complete copies of the *De triangulis Iordani* and in the fragmentary copies where the propositions are not assigned to the *De triangulis Iordani* (MSS *PcVeGu*) is quite close to the original version of those propositions. We should conclude, then, that the compositor of the longer version of the *De triangulis Iordani* simply added them (more or less intact) to his work.

Propositions IV.17 and IV.18

From the argument just recited for Propositions IV.14–IV.16 that centers on the apparent fact that Props. IV.21 and IV.25 were drawn directly from translations by Gerard of Cremona, I propose a similar conclusion for Props. IV.17 and IV.18, namely that they too were translated from the Arabic by Gerard of Cremona. Furthermore, I suggest that the original text of these propositions was simply added to the *De triangulis Iordani* with little change, for it will be noticed that there is no great discrepancy between the text of Props. IV.17 and IV.18 found in the complete manuscripts of the *De triangulis*

Iordani and that found in the fragmentary copies where the propositions are not designated as being from the *De triangulis Iordani.*

Proposition IV.19

I have not found any evidence concerning the source of this proposition. However, from a perusal of the variant readings we may at least conclude that the compositor made little change in the text of this proposition when he added it to the *De triangulis Iordani.* Because it is equivalent to Proposition IV.3, which the author of the *Liber de triangulis Iordani* took from Proposition 40 of the *Liber philotegni,* one might suspect that the source of the proposition was the earlier proposition. However this does not seem to be so, for the whole context of the enunciation and proof differs from that of the earlier proposition which is tied intimately to triangles whose principal angle is at the center of the circle and whose equal sides are radii, and the proof was based on Proposition IV.1 concerning triangles in the circle. In Proposition IV.19 there is not a word about the use of circles. As I stated in Part III, Chap. 1, it is surprising that the compositor of the *Liber de triangulis Iordani* made no reference to the equivalence of Proposition IV.19 and Proposition IV.3. It suggests once more than the compositor took over the added propositions from the Arabic with little or no change.

Proposition IV.20

As I have already noted in my description of the contents of the *De triangulis Iordani,* Proposition IV.20 presents three treatments of the problem of trisecting an angle: (1) in lines 3–24, (2) in lines 25–28, and (3) in lines 29–43. The first treatment was surely paraphrased from Prop. XVIII of Gerard of Cremona's translation of the *Verba filiorum* of the Banū Mūsā (cf. Clagett, *Archimedes in the Middle Ages,* Vol. 1, pp. 344–49, 668). Although the texts do not agree in verbatim fashion, the complete identity of the diagram in most manuscripts of this text (see Fig. IV.20a) with the diagram in the *Verba filiorum (ibid.,* p. 345, Fig. 53) is surely a guarantee of the interdependence of the two texts.

No independent sources have been discovered for the second and third treatments of the trisection of an angle in Prop. IV.20. However, it is clear that the whole proposition in the form in which it appears in the *De triangulis Iordani* (both in the complete manuscripts and in the fragmentary copies) is the product of a single author, for that author has given statements that relate the second to the first treatment (see Prop. IV.20, lines 25–28) and the third to the preceding demonstration (*ibid.,* lines 29–31). It is also probable that the author of the proposition was a Latin author since in the third treatment (lines 34–35) he cites a proposition from the *Perspective* of Alhazen by the number V.19 and that number seems to have originated in one of the Latin traditions of the work of Alhazen (see Clagett, *Archimedes in the Middle Ages,* Vol. 4, pp. 19 n. 41, 30–31 n. 55).

Proposition IV.21

The source of this proposition is a fragment translated from the Arabic by Gerard of Cremona. I have edited it from MS *Pd*, 64r, and MS *Ma*, 83v. The text follows the first of these manuscripts closely (and the marginal folio numbers are taken from that manuscript), since that manuscript is the best of the manuscripts containing collected translations of Gerard of Cremona. In all of my texts from Gerard's translations I have capitalized the letters marking points and lines. Furthermore in all of these texts I have written *-ti-* before vowels even when the manuscripts have *-ci-*, I have not recorded the variant of *igitur* for *ergo*, and I have always rendered *ag'gatur* by *aggregatur* though *agregatur* might have been intended.

64r,C.1	/ Volo ostendere quomodo inveniam in triangulo noto punctum quod cum continuavero cum angulis trianguli dividatur triangulus per tres proportiones notas.
	Sit ergo triangulus, triangulus *ABG* [cf. Fig. IV.21], in quo volo invenire
5	punctum quod cum continuavero cum angulis trianguli dividatur triangulus per proportionem notam. Cum ergo illud voluero, ponam proportionem notam in linea *AG*, et dividam eam per ipsam. Sit ergo proportio *GD* proportio quedam, proportio *DE* proportio quedam alia, proportio *AE* que remanet ex triangulo. Et protraham super punctum, super punctum *D*, lineam equidistantem linee
10	*BG* que sit *DZ* et super punctum *E* lineam equidistantem linee *AB* que sit linea *EH*. Et sit abscisio utrarumque super punctum *T*. Dico ergo quod quando continuabo ipsum cum *A* et *B* et *G* tunc proportio trianguli *BTG* ad triangulum
C.2	*ABG* erit sicut proportio *GD* ex *AG*, / et quod proportio trianguli *ATG* ex triangulo toto est sicut proportio *ED* ex *AG* et quod proportio trianguli *ATB* ex
15	triangulo toto est sicut proportio *AE* ex *AG*, quod sic demonstratur. Ego continuabo *E* et *D* cum *B*. Ergo duo trianguli *BTG*, *BDG* sunt equales. Sed proportio trianguli *BDG* ex triangulo *ABG* est sicut proportio linee *GD* ex linea *GA*. Ergo proportio trianguli *BTG* ex triangulo *ABG* est sicut proportio *GD* ex *AG*. Et similiter ostenditur quod proportio trianguli *ATB* ex triangulo *ABG* est sicut
20	proportio linee *AE* ex linea *AG* aut triangulus *ATB* est equalis triangulo *AEB* propterea quod ipsi utrique super basim *AB* et inter duas equidistantes lineas *AB* et *EH*. Remanet ergo proportio trianguli *ATG* ex triangulo *ABG* sicut proportio *ED* ex *AG*. Et illud est quod voluimus.

Prop. IV.21

  6 proportionem notam[1]: pro[p]ortiones notas *Ma* / *ante* illud *scr. et del. Pd* volueris /
      illud voluero *tr. Ma*
  8 *ante* proportio[1,3] *add. Ma* et (?)
  9 super punctum[2] *om. Ma* / linee: linō Pd
 11 abscisio *Ma* abscissio *Pd*
 17 GD: D̪GD *Pd*
 20 aut *Pd* quia *Ma*
 22 EH: EẒH *Ma*
 23 *ante* ex *scr. et del. Ma* a

Proposition IV.22

The first proof of this proposition (lines 4–42) was drawn directly from Proposition XVI of the *Verba filiorum* of the Banū Mūsā in the translation of Gerard of Cremona (see *Archimedes in the Middle Ages,* Vol. 1, pp. 334–41). The second proof was taken from a fragment translated by Gerard of Cremona. My text of that fragment is based on MS *Ma*, 83v–84r, and MS *Oe*, 122r (old pag. 121r), and the marginal folio numbers are from MS *Ma*. Note that Gerard's text was incorporated with very little change into the *Practica geometrie* of Leonardo Fibonacci Pisano (see *Archimedes in the Middle Ages,* Vol. 1, p. 664).

83v / Volo ostendere qualiter inveniam inter duas lineas duas lineas ita ut continuentur omnes secundum proportionem unam.

Ponam ergo duas lineas *AB, BG* [cf. Fig. IV.22b], et angulus earum sit rectus. Deinde continuabo *AG* et faciam super lineam trianguli *ABG* circulum super

5 quem sit *ABGH*. Deinde protraham ex puncto *A* perpendicularem *AD* super

84r lineam *AB*, et ex puncto *G* / super *BG* perpendicularem *GD*, et protraham utramque secundum rectitudinem usque ad *Z* et *E*. Deinde faciam transire regulam, que moveatur super punctum *B*, et non separetur ab eo, et sic abscidens duas lineas *DZ, ED*, et non cesset moveri donec sit illud quod cadit ex eis inter

10 *Z, B* equale ei quod cadit inter arcum *BH* et *E*. Sit ergo illud ita. Ergo linea *ZB* est equalis linee *EH*. Ergo multiplicatio *ZH* in *ZB* est equalis multiplicationi *BE* in *HE*. Verum *EB* in *HE* est equalis *DE* in *GE*; et *HZ* in *ZB* est equalis *DZ* in *ZA*. Ergo multiplicatio *DZ* in *ZA* est sicut multiplicatio *DE* in *EG*. Ergo proportio *DE* ex *DZ* est sicut proportio *AZ* ex *GE*. Sed proportio *ED* ex *DZ*

15 est sicut proportio *BA* ex *AZ*; et proportio *BA* ex *AZ* est sicut proportio *AZ* ex *GE* et est etiam sicut proportio *GE* ex *GB*. Et illud est quod demonstrare voluimus.

Proposition IV.23

The source of Prop. IV.23 is a fragment translated by Gerard of Cremona from the Arabic. My text of this fragment below is based on the following MSS: *Pd*, 63v–64r; *Ma*, 83r–v; *Br*, 1r–v; *Oe*, 124v (old pag. 123v). The last two copies are incomplete, *Br* containing lines 1–57 and *Oe* lines 58–79. The marginal folio numbers refer to MS *Pd*.

63v,C.1 / Iste modus est sufficiens in arte eptagoni cadentis in circulo.

Prop. IV.22
5 quem *supra scr. Ma*
8 *post* que *scr. et del. Oe* mo² (*i.e.* movetur) / abscindens *Oe*
9 cadit (?) *Ma*
10 *ante* linea *scr. et del. Oe* multiplicatio
12 Verum: sed *Oe*
14 ex¹ *correxi ex* ad *in MaOe* (*et scr. Ma* DE *ad* DZ *in ras.*) / ex²,³ *Ma* ad *Oe*
15 ex¹,²,³ *Ma* ad *Oe* / et *Ma* igitur *Oe*
16 ex *Ma* ad *Oe* / illud *Ma* hoc *Oe* / demonstrare *om. Oe*
Prop. IV.23
1–57 Iste. . . . voluimus *om. Oe*
1 Iste . . . circulo *om. Ma*

Sit ergo circulus *ABD* is circuitu centri *G* [cf. Fig. IV.23]. Quando ergo voluerimus facere in eo eptagonum equalium laterum et angulorum, dividemus lineam
AG in duo media super punctum *H*. Et protrahemus ex duobus punctis *H* et *G*

5   duas perpendiculares super *AD* que sint *HQ, GD*. Et continuabo *A* cum *D* et
protraham ipsam secundum rectitudinem a circulo absque fine. Abscidet ergo
perpendicularem *HQ* super punctum *E*, et continuabo *G* cum *E* et protraham
eam in duas partes usque ad *M* et *L* circumferentie. Et continuabo *D* cum *L*.
Et dividam lineam *GD* in duo media super punctum *T*, et protraham ex eo

10   perpendicularem *TZ*, et non ponam finem eius terminatum. Et movebo lineas
AD, LM, GD, DL sicut narrabo. Ponam motum *AD* super punctum *A*, et *LM*
et *GD* super punctum *G*, et *DL* super punctum *D*. Non separetur aliquod eorum
ab eo quod determinavimus ei in motu suo dicto post hoc. Sitque perpendicularis
HQ fixa super lineam *AG*, et perpendicularis *TZ* fixa super lineam *GD*. Et

15   movebimus lineam *AD* super punctum *A* sicut narravimus ad partem *B*. Et sit
linea *AD* propter illud addita, et sit additio eius ex parte *D* eius, cum punctum
eius *A* sit fixum. Et sit punctum eius *D* permutatum cum motu eius, cum sit
punctum super quod secat linea *AD* lineam continentem. Et sit etiam acceptio
eius versus *B* super circumferentiam cum illo motu. Et sit punctum *D* duarum

20   linearum *GD* et *DL* ordinatum cum puncto *D* linee *AD* super circumferentiam
in motu *AD* predicte inseparabile ab eo. Et sit ut quotiens abscidit linea *AD* per
motum suum perpendicularem *HQ*, abscidat ipsam cum ea super punctum
unum linea *LGM* sicut est punctum *E* et ei simile. Et est motus *LM* super

C.2   punctum *G* sicut diximus ante. Est ergo acceptio puncti *L* / linee *LM* per motum
25   suum cum *AD* super punctum unum perpendicularis *HQ* versus *B*, cum puncti
E sectionis super perpendicularem *HQ* acceptio per motum suum predictum sit
versus *H*. Et sit linea *DL* transiens per motum suum super punctum *L* linee
LM super circumferentiam inseparabilis ab eo in motu suo. Minuitur ergo linea
LD, et est eius diminutio a parte *L* eius, cum punctum *D* eius non mutetur sicut

30   narravimus de transitu eius cum puncto *D* linee *GD* et linee *AD*. Cum ergo
movebimus lineam *AD* secundum quod narravimus de motu eius, et sequetur

2 circulus *bis Ma*
4 punctis *om. Br*
5 AD: AB *Br*
6 finem (?) *Ma* / Abscindet *Br hic et ubique*
8 circonferentie *Br*
9 GD: DG *Ma* / eo *om. Br*
10 TZ *PdBr et corr. Ma ex* TX (?)
11 DL (?) *Ma* / punctum *bis Ma*
14 perpendiculare *Br* / TZ (?) *Ma*
16 additio (?) *Ma*
19 B super: super (?) B (?) *Ma*
20 et *om. Br* / *de* ordinatum *mg. scr. Pd* (*et supra* ordinatum *scr. Ma*) vel ligatum /
    ante cum *scr. et del. Ma* pro / puncto: punctum *Br*
21 sint *Br*
23 E: T (?) *Ma*
26 perpendicularem HQ *non bene legere in Ma possum*
27 H: L (?) *Ma* / DL: DH *Br*
28 Minuitur (?) *Br*
30 GD: DGB *Ma*
31 *post* de *scr. et del. Pd* i

reliquas lineas illud quod determinavimus ei, tunc perpendicularis *TZ* abscidet per motum *GD* lineam *DL*, et erit puncti sectionis super ipsam acceptio versus *K* diametri circuli, et est punctum sectionis *AB* et *DL* et est etiam permutatum

35 in motu suo. Non ergo cessat perpendicularis, scilicet perpendicularis *TZ*, abscidere lineam *DL* donec abscidit punctum sectionis super eam super lineam *AB*, sicut est casus perpendicularis *TK*. Cum ergo cadet, firmabimus lineam *AD* in loco suo, et figemus motum reliquarum linearum et punctorum propter illud. Dico ergo quod iam completum est illud quod voluimus, et quod corda arcus *DB* est

40 latus eptagoni, quod sic demonstratur. Angulus qui est ex *DGK* extrinsecus trianguli *AGD* duorum equalium crurium est duplus anguli eius qui est ex *DAG*. Sed angulus qui est ex *DAG* est equalis ei qui est ex *AGE* propterea quod *AH* est equalis *HG*, et perpendicularis *HE* est communis duobus triangulis *AHEG* [i.e. *AHE* et *HEG*]. Ergo angulus *DGK* est duplus eius qui ex *AGE*. Et iterum

45 angulus *EGD* extrinsecus trianguli *DGL* duorum equalium crurium est duplus anguli eius qui est ex *GDL*. Verum ille qui est ex *GDL* est equalis ei qui est ex *DGK* propterea quod *GT* est equalis *TD*, et perpendicularis *TK* est communis duobus triangulis *DTKG* [i.e. *DTK* et *TKG*]. Ergo angulus *EGD* est duplus anguli *DGK*. Et iam fuit ostensum quod angulus *DGK* est duplus anguli *AGE*. Ergo

50 angulus *DGE* est quadruplus eius qui est ex *AGE*. Ergo omnes anguli tres: *AGE*, *EGD*, *DGK*, quibus subtenditur medietas circuli, sunt triplum et medietas anguli *DGK*. Et propter illud arcus *ADB*, et est medietas circuli, est triplum et medietas arcus *DB*. Ergo tota circumferentia circuli est septuplum arcus *DB*. Ergo arcus

64r,C.1 *DB* est septima circumferentie, et corda eius est latus eptagoni caden/tis in circulo
55 *ABD*. Dividatur ergo circulus per arcus qui sint sicut arcus *DB* et protrahamus cordas eorum. Ergo tunc iam fecimus in circulo eptagonum equalium laterum et angulorum. Et illud est quod demonstrare voluimus.

32 determinavimus: declaravimus *Br*
34 dyametri *Br* / etiam *om. Br*
35 TZ: TX *Pd*
36 abscidit *Pd* abscidet (?) *Br* abscidat *Ma*
37 *de* firmabimus *mg. scr. Pd* (*et supra* firmabimus *scr. Ma*) vel figemus
38 *de* propter illud *mg. scr. Pd* (*et supra* propter illud *scr. Ma*) vel similiter
38–39 Dico ergo *om. Br*
39 DB: BD *Br*
40 DGK: DGB *Br*
41 duplus: duplum *Ma* / anguli *MaBr* angulus *Pd*
42 qui est[1] *mg. Pd*
44 *ante* ex *add. Br* est
46 anguli *Ma* trianguli *PdBr* / GDL[1]: DGL *Br*
47 propterea: propter *Br* / GT . . . TD: DC est equalis GT *Br*
49 AGE: ḌAGE *Ma*
50 est quadruplus *tr. Br*
51, 53 *post* anguli *in lin. 51 et post* arcus[1] *in lin. 53 hab. Ma* equalis equalis (*et secundum supra scr. Ma*)
52 triplum: tripl' *Br*
53 septupl' *Br*
54 septima *MaBr* septuplum *Pd*
55 ABD: ADB *Br* / protraham *Br*
56 corda *Ma*
57 demonstrare voluimus *tr. Br*

Quando dividatur linea in tres sectiones, et est proportio sectionis postreme earum ad primam sicut proportio prime ad residuum linee, et est media et
60 postrema, et est proportio medie ad postremam sicut proportio postreme ad residuum linee, et est media et prima, fit ex istis tribus sectionibus triangulus cuius angulus maior est duplus medii, et medius duplus minoris. Cum ergo continet circulus hunc triangulum, est arcus qui subtenditur angulo minori arcus corde eptagoni cadentis in illo circulo.

65 Hec est questio decens Indorum in extractione cuiuscumque figurarum vis equalium laterum cadentis in circulis. Et plurimum quidem positionis Indorum non est nisi credulitas absque demonstratione. Et in eo est propinquitas inter quam et inter veritatem non est quantitas sensibilis. Et est hec operatio quam nunc dicturus sum. Quod est quia tu multiplicas medietatem diametri circuli
70 in diametrum totam semper, deinde quod aggregatur in novem, et servas aggregatum. Deinde prohicis ex numero laterum figure cuius quantitatem vis extrahere unum laterum eius semel semper, et accipis medietatem eius quod remanet et multiplicas ipsam in numerum laterum figure et adiungis ad illud quod aggregatum est tria semper, et super illud quod aggregatur divide illud quod servasti,
75 et quod egreditur est quadratum lateris. Quando ergo operatus fueris hanc operationem, feceris operationem super quam exigatur demonstratio; exibis ad hunc numerum. Et scias quod ipsi ponunt latus eptagoni cadentis in circulo per equalitatem medietatis lateris trianguli cadentis in eo, et non est in manibus eorum super illud demonstratio plusquam inventio. Intellige ergo.

Proposition IV.24

The source of Prop. IV.24 is a fragment translated by Gerard of Cremona from the Arabic. My text of this fragment below is based on MS *Ma*, 84r, and MS *Oe*, 122r (old pag. 121r). The marginal folio number refers to MS *Ma*.

58–79 Quando. . . . ergo *om. Br*
58 dividitur *Oe* / *post* postreme *scr. et del. Ma* ad residuum linee
59 eorum *Pd*
61 istis *om. Oe*
65 cuiuscumque: eiusque *Ma*
67 est[2] *tr. Oe ante* in
68 inter *om. Oe* / est hec *tr. Ma*
69 dyametri *Oe*
70 dyametrum *Oe*
73 illud: id(?) *Oe*
74 tria *Ma* (*et post* tria *scr. et del. Ma* ipsius) tertia ipsius *Pd* tertium ipsius *Oe* / illud[2]: id (?) *Oe*
75 egredietur *Oe*
76 *ante* feceris *add. PdOe* et / feceris operationem *mg. sin. Ma* / exigitur *Oe*
78 lateris *mg. Oe*
79 *de* inventio *mg. scr. PdOe* (*et supra* inventio *scr. Ma*) vel esse / Intellige ergo *om. Oe*

84r

/ Omnis trianguli orthogonii si illud quod addit latus maius quod subtenditur angulo eius recto super latus eius medium et est unum duorum laterum eius reliquorum est equale ei quod addit latus eius medium super latus ipsius minus, tunc latus eius minus est triplum illius additionis, et medium est quadruplum

5

eius, et maius est quintuplum eius. Et iterum latus eius minus est quarta omnium laterum trianguli, et medium est tertia omnium laterum trianguli, et maius est residuum unius, et est due sexte et medietas sexte omnium laterum trianguli.

Cuius exemplum sit triangulus ABG [cf. Fig. IV.24]. Sitque latus eius longius BG et medium AB et minus AG et angulus eius rectus angulus A et AB sit equale

10

BE et AG equale BD. Ergo manifestum est quod ED est equale EG. Ergo multiplicatio BG in se est equalis multiplicationi BE in EG quater et BD in se. Verum BG in se est equale BE in se et BD in se propter illud quod premisimus. Reiecta ergo multiplicatione BD in se remanet BE in se equale multiplicationi eius in EG quater. Ergo BE est quadruplum EG, et BD est triplum eius, et BG

15

est quintuplum eius, et BE est equale AB, et BD est equale AG. Iam ergo manifestum est quod diximus in similibus. Et iterum quando nos aggregamus similitudines proveniunt duodecim similia, et sunt omnia latera tria. Nam AG ex eis est tria, et illud est quarta eorum, et AB quattuor, et illud est tertia eorum, et BG est quinque, et illud est due sexte et medietas sexte. Iam ergo ostensum

20

est quod ostendere voluimus.

Proposition IV.25

The source of this proposition is a fragment translated by Gerard of Cremona from the Arabic. I have based my text of this fragment on the following MSS: *Pd*, 64r; *Ma*, 83v; and *Oe*, 124v–125r (old pag. 123v–124r). The marginal folio number refers to MS *Pd*.

64r, c.2

/ Omnis trianguli diversorum laterum proportio eius quod addit latus longius super latus brevius ad illud quod addit casus longior super casum breviorem est sicut proportio basis ex duobus lateribus aggregatis.

Prop. IV.24
  1 si *supra scr. Oe*
  2 medium *corr. Ma ex* motuum (?)
  2–3 et . . . reliquorum *om. Oe*
  4 illius *om. Br*
  5 eius² *Oe* ipsius *Ma*
  8 Cuius exemplum *Ma* Verbi gratia *Oe*
  10 ED: DE *Oe*
  12 Verum *Ma* Sed *Oe* / equalis *Oe*
  13 Reiecta *Ma* Eiecta *Oe*
  15 eius *Oe* ipsius *Ma*
  16 similibus *Oe*, ?*Ma* (et *supra scr. MaOe* aliquotiens equalibus)
  16–17 *supra* similitudines *scr. Ma* (et *mg. Oe*) equalitates aliquotiens
  17 latera tria *tr. Oe*
  19 Iam ergo *om. Oe*
  20 ostendere *om. Oe*
Prop. IV.25
  3 ex: ad *ex corr. Ma* / duobus . . . aggregatis: duo latera aggregata *Ma*

Cuius exemplum est triangulus *ABG* [cf. Fig. IV.25]. Et ponam *AG* longius
5   *AB*. Et ponam perpendicularem eius *AD*. Dico ergo quod proportio additionis
AG super *AB* ad additionem *DG* super *DB* est sicut proportio *BG* ad *AB* et *AG*
aggregata. Cuius demonstratio est quod ego ponam punctum *A* centrum *A* et
lineabo circulum cum longitudine *B* (! *AB*), qui sit circulus *UZBE*. Et protraham
AG secundum rectitudinem usque ad *Z*. Manifestum est igitur quod *UG* est
10   illud quod addit *AG* super *AB* et quod *EG* est illud quod addit *DG* super *DB*,
quoniam quando nos continuamus *E* cum *A* est triangulus *AEB* duorum equalium
crurium. Perpendicularis ergo eius cadit super medietatem basis ipsius *BE*. Ergo
multiplicatio *BG* in *EG* est sicut multiplicatio *ZG* in *UG*. Ergo proportio *BG*
ad *ZG* est sicut proportio *UG* ad *EG*. Sed *ZG* est *AB* et *AG* coniuncte quoniam
15   *AB* est equalis *AZ*. Ergo proportio basis *BG* ex *AB* et *AG* aggregatis est sicut
proportio superfluitatis *AG* super *AB* ad superfluitatem casus *DG*, et est *GE*,
super casum *BD*. Et illud est quod demonstrare voluimus.

Propositions IV.26–IV.28

The source of these three propositions is a fragment translated by Gerard
of Cremona from the Arabic. My text of this fragment is based on the following
manuscripts: *Pd*, 54v–55r; *A*, 104r–v; *Vr*, 238r–v. The marginal folio numbers
refer to MS *Pd*. Note that none of these manuscripts contains anything like
lines 19–29 of Prop. IV.28, and thus these lines appear to be an addition of
the compositor of the *De triangulis Iordani*.

54v, c.2   / Volo ostendere quod omnium trium linearum proportionalium proportio
prime ad secundam duplicata est proportio prime ad tertiam. Quando ergo
voluerimus ostendere illud, ostendemus quod omnium trium linearum, quocumque modo sint, proportio prime ad tertiam est sicut proportio aggregati ex
5   multiplicatione prime in secundam de aggregato ex multiplicatione secunde in
tertiam.

     Cuius exemplum est ut sint tres linee: *AB* et *GD* et *EZ* [cf. Fig. IV.26]. Dico
ergo quod proportio *AB* ad *EZ* est sicut proportio multiplicationis *AB* in *GD*
de multiplicatione *GD* in *EZ*. Cuius hec est demonstratio. Ponam lineam longam
10   et abscidam de ea quod sit equale *AB*, quod sit *HT*, et protraham ex puncto *T*
perpendicularem super *HT*, et abscidam in (! de) ea quod sit equale *GD*, sitque
TL. Et abscidam iterum quod sit equale *EZ*, quod sit *TK*. Et faciam transire
super punctum *L* lineam equidistantem *HK*, et complebo duas superficies *HL*,
LK. Ergo est altitudo utrarumque una. Ergo proportio superficiei de superficie
15   est sicut proportio *HT* de *TK*. Sed *HT* est equalis *AB*, et *TK* est equalis *EZ*.

7 ego *om. Oe* / A² *Pd, om. MaOe*
8 UZBE: UZDE *Oe*
12 cadit (*sive* cadet) *Pd* / ipsius: eius *Oe*
13 *de* sicut *scr. mg. Pd* (*et scr. et del. Ma ante* sicut) equalis / ZG *bis Pd et del. Pd
primum*
15 ex *Pd* ad *MaOe* / aggregatis *Pd* aggregatas *MaOe*
17 demonstrare *om. Oe* / *post* voluimus *add. Oe* Explicit
Props. IV.26–IV.28
11 in *corr.* A *ex* de
14–15 *de* Ergo² . . . TK¹ *mg. scr.* A per primam 6ᵗⁱ

Ergo proportio *AB* de *EZ* est sicut proportio superficiei de superficie. Sed superficies prima est multiplicatio *AB* in *GD*, et superficies secunda / est multiplicatio *GD* in *EZ*. Ergo proportio *AB* de *EZ* est sicut multiplicatio *AB* in *GD* de multiplicatione *GD* in *EZ*. Et illud est quod ostendere voluimus. Et hec est forma eius.

Et quia iam ostendi hanc proportionem, tunc ostendam iterum quod omnium trium linearum, quocumque modo sint, proportio prime ad tertiam est sicut proportio prime ad secundam multiplicata in proportionem secunde ad tertiam.

Cuius exemplum est quod ponam tres lineas: *AB* et *GD* et *EZ* [cf. Fig. IV.27]. Et ponam proportionem que est *AB* de *GD* lineam *H*. Ergo linea *H* quando multiplicatur in lineam *GD* est linea *AB*, quoniam proportio est sectio. Et ponam proportionem que est *GD* de *EZ* lineam *T*. Ergo linea *T* quando multiplicatur in *EZ* est *GD*. Et ponam proportionem que est *AB* de *EZ* lineam *L*. Ergo linea *L* quando multiplicatur in *EZ* est *AB*. Dico ergo quod multiplicatio linee *H* in lineam *T* est linea *L*, quod sic demonstratur. Multiplicabo *H* in *T*; ergo erit *K*. Dico ergo quod linea *K* est equalis linee *L*, quod sic probatur. Linea *H* et linea *T* et linea *EZ* sunt tres linee, quarum prima est linea *H* et earum postrema est linea *EZ*. Ergo proportio prime, et est *H*, de postrema, que est *EZ*, est sicut proportio aggregati ex multiplicatione linee *H* in lineam *T* de aggregato ex multiplicatione linee *T* in lineam *EZ*. Sed aggregatum ex multiplicatione linee *H* in lineam *T* est linea *K*. Et aggregatum ex multiplicatione linee *T* in lineam *EZ* est linea *GD*. Ergo proportio linee *H* de linea *EZ* est sicut proportio linee *K* de linea *GD*. Ergo multiplicatio *H* in *GD* est sicut multiplicatio *K* in *EZ*. Sed multiplicatio *H* in *GD* est *AB*. Ergo multiplicatio *K* in *EZ* est *AB*. Et iam fuit multiplicatio *L* in *EZ*, *AB*. Ergo linea *L* est equalis linee *K*. Iam ergo ostensum est quod proportio linee *AB* de *EZ* est sicut proportio linee *AB* de *GD* multiplicata in proportionem *GD* de *EZ*. Et quia iam ostendi hanc proportionem, tunc manifestum est quod omnium trium linearum proportionalium proportio prime ad tertiam est sicut proportio prime ad secundam duplicata. Et hec est forma proportionis.

Et volo iterum, cum ostensum sit quod omnium trium linearum proportionalium proportio prime ad tertiam est sicut proportio eius ad secundam duplicata, ostendere quod omnium quattuor linearum consequentium secundum propor-

17-18 et. . . . GD² *mg. infer. Vr*

   18 EZ¹: EC *Vr* / EZ²: ẸEZ *Pd* EC *Vr*

   19 ostendere voluimus: demō. vo. *Vr* / est² *om. Vr*

   21 ostendidi (*!*) *Vr* / hac *A*

   23 multiplicatam *Pd*

25-26 Et. . . . sectio *om. Vr* (*sed add. m. rec. lin. 6–8* ["et. . . . divisio"] *ex Prop. IV.2[?]
     libri de triangulis Iordani, sed illae lineae partim absecantur*)

28-29 Ergo linea L *mg. Pd*

   30 H *bis Vr et del. Vr secundum.*

   33 *ante* prime *scr. et del. A* linee

34, 35 lineam: linea *H*

   37 linee¹ *corr. A ex* linea

   39 *ante* GD *scr. et del. Pd* AB

   40 EZ: EC *Vr*

   42 ostendidi *Vr* / *ante* hanc *scr. et del. A* hnc

   48 quattuor *Pd* quatuor *AVr*

50 tionem unam proportio prime ad quartam est sicut proportio prime ad secundam triplicata.

Cuius exemplum est ut sint quattuor linee: *A* et *B* et *G* et *D* [cf. Fig. IV.28], consequentes secundum proportionem unam. Dico ergo quod proportio *A* ad *D* est sicut proportio *A* ad *B* triplicata, quod sic demonstratur. Tres linee sunt

55r, c.2 *A* et *G* et *D*. Ergo / proportio *A* ad *D* est sicut proportio *A* ad *G* multiplicata in

55 proportionem *G* ad *D*. Et *A* et *B* et *G* sunt tres linee proportionales. Ergo proportio *A* ad *G* est sicut proportio *A* ad *B* duplicata. Ergo proportio *A* ad *D* est sicut proportio *A* ad *B* duplicata multiplicata in proportionem *G* ad *D*. Sed proportio *G* ad *D* est sicut proportio *A* ad *B*. Ergo proportio *A* ad *D* est sicut proportio *A* ad *B* duplicata multiplicata in proportionem *A* ad *B*, et est sicut proportio *A* ad

60 *B* triplicata. Ergo proportio *A* ad *D* est sicut proportio *A* ad *B* triplicata. Et illud est cuius voluimus declarationem.

49 prime²: pprime *A*
51 quattuor *Pd* quatuor *AVr*
52 *ante* consequentes *add.* *Vr* et
53 B: ḌB *Vr*
55, 57 proportionem: proportione *Vr*